THE MEDIA IN AMERICA

A History

Eighth Edition

THE MEDIA IN AMERICA
A History

Eighth Edition

EDITOR

Wm. David Sloan
University of Alabama

VISION PRESS

THE MEDIA IN AMERICA
A History
Eighth Edition

Vision Press
4195 Waldort Drive
P.O. Box 1106
Northport, AL 35476

Library of Congress Cataloging-in-Publication Data

The Media in America: a history / Wm. David Sloan, editor
      p.   cm.
ISBN   978-1-885219-40-4
       1. Mass media–United States–History. I. Sloan, W. David (William David), 1947-

P92.U5M425 2011
302.23'0973–dc20   CIP

Printed in the United States of America

Editor

WM. DAVID SLOAN is the founder of the American Journalism Historians Association and served a five-year term as editor of its research journal, *American Journalism.* The AJHA recognizes him with its annual "Sloan Outstanding Faculty Research Paper" award. He has published more than thirty other books, among them *Historical Methods in Mass Communication; The Significance of the Media in American History; American Journalism: History, Principles, Practices; American Journalism History: An Annotated Bibliography; Perspectives on Mass Communication History; The Early American Press, 1690-1783; Media and Religion in American History; Great Editorials;* and *Masterpieces of Reporting.* He is co-editor of the seven-volume series "History of American Journalism." He has written more than eighty articles, book chapters, and papers on history and journalistic writing and has been recognized with several research awards for his work in media history. In 1998 he received the AJHA's Kobre Award for lifetime achievement and in 2010 its National Award for Teaching Excellence. He has served as national president of both the AJHA and Kappa Tau Alpha, the mass communication honor society. On its ninetieth anniversary, KTA selected him as one of the five most important members in its history. A professor of journalism at the University of Alabama, he received the Ph.D. in mass communication and United States history from the University of Texas.

Authors

Chapter 1
ORIGINS OF MASS COMMUNICATION

Berrin Beasley is a communication professor at the University of North Florida, where she teaches media history and journalism ethics. Among her research areas is World War II psychological warfare. Before going into teaching, she worked as a newspaper reporter and editor. She received her Ph.D. in communication from the University of Southern Mississippi.

Paul Alfred (Alf) Pratte retired in 2003 from a long career as a professor of communication at Brigham Young University. A former president of the American Journalism Historians Association, he is the author of *Gods Within the Machines: A History of the American Society of Newspaper Editors, 1923-1993.* His articles have appeared in *Journalism Quarterly, Newspaper Research Journal, American Journalism,* and other scholarly and professional journals.

Chapter 2
PRINTING IN AMERICA, 1600-1690

Julie Hedgepeth Williams is the author of *The Significance of the Printed Word in Early America* and co-author of the award-winning *The Early American Press, 1690-1783* and *The Great Reporters: An Anthology of News Writing at Its Best.* She is also the author of *Wings of Opportunity: The Wright Brothers in Montgomery, Alabama, 1910.* She has published chapters on colonial journalism, media and religion, and women in the media in other books. Her dissertation on the history of early American printing received the American Journalism Historians Association's inaugural award in 1997 for the nation's outstanding dissertation in mass communication history. She has served as the president of the AJHA and has served on its Board of Directors. She received her Ph.D. in mass communication history from the University of Alabama and teaches journalism at Samford University.

Chapter 3
THE COLONIAL PRESS, 1690-1765

David A. Copeland has published twelve books, including *The Active Voice: The Media's Role in Defining the Nation; The Idea of a Free Press: The Enlightenment and Its Unruly Legacy; Debating the Issues in Colonial Newspapers;* and *Colonial Newspapers: Character and Content.* He is editor of the eight-volume *Greenwood Library of American War Reporting* and chief editor of the Thomson Gale *19th Century Digital Newspapers Archive.* He is a past president of the American Journalism Historians Association and in 2010 received its Kobre Award for lifetime achievement. He received his Ph.D. in mass communication research from the University of North Carolina and is the A. J. Fletcher Professor in the School of Communications at Elon University.

Chapter 4
THE REVOLUTIONARY PRESS, 1765-1783

Carol Sue Humphrey is the author of the books *"This Popular Engine": The Role of New England Newspapers During the American Revolution; The Press of the Young Republic, 1783-1833; Debating Historical Issues in the Media of the Time: The Revolutionary Era;* and *The Greenwood Library of American War Reporting: The Revolutionary War.* She also has written a variety of articles and book chapters on journalism of the Revolutionary era. She received her Ph.D. in history from the University of North Carolina and teaches history at Oklahoma Baptist University.

Chapter 5
THE PARTY PRESS, 1783-1833

Wm. David Sloan has published a number of articles and book chapters focusing on the political role of the press in America's first party system. His work is largely responsible for today's historical assessment of the press during that period.

Chapter 6
FREEDOM OF THE PRESS, 1690-1804

Butler Cain is a communication professor at West Texas A&M University, where he teaches journalism and advises the student newspaper and radio station. Before joining the faculty, he spent a decade as news director of Alabama Public Radio. He received his Ph.D. in mass communication history from the University of Alabama. In 2007 the American Journalism Historians Association selected his dissertation on press freedom in the nineteenth century as a runner-up for its award for the nation's outstanding dissertation.

Chapter 7
THE PENNY PRESS, 1833-1861

Susan Thompson has written a number of book chapters on media history and is the author of *The Penny Press: The Origins of the Modern News Media, 1833-1861.* She is co-author of *Fundamentals of Media Effects* (an English text that has also been translated into Russian and Chinese) and *Introduction to Media Communication.* She received her Ph.D. in mass communication history from the University of Alabama, where her dissertation on the penny press won the University's outstanding dissertation award. She teaches communication at the University of Montevallo.

Chapter 8
THE ANTEBELLUM PRESS, 1820-1861

Bernell Elizabeth Tripp, a former president of the American Journalism Historians Association, is the author of *The Origins of the Black Press* and has published a variety of articles and book chapters on African-American journalists of the nineteenth century. A journalism professor at the University of Florida, she received her Ph.D. in mass communication history from the University of Alabama.

Chapter 9
THE PRESS AND THE CIVIL WAR, 1861-1865

Kathleen Endres has published a variety of articles on Civil War journalism and on other history topics. She is a former member of the Board of Directors of the American Journalism Historians Association and is a recognized authority on magazine history and women in journalism. She received her Ph.D. in history from Kent State University and teaches journalism at the University of Akron.

Chapter 10
THE FRONTIER PRESS, 1800-1900

William E. Huntzicker has published numerous articles and reviews on the American West and nineteenth-century journalism. He is the author of *The Popular Press, 1833-1865.* It won an Editor's Choice Award from the American Library Association. He received his Ph.D. in American studies from the University of Minnesota. A former member of the Board of Directors of the American Journalism Historians Association, he teaches journalism at St. Cloud (Minn.) State University.

Chapter 11
THE PRESS AND INDUSTRIAL AMERICA, 1865-1883

Paulette D. Kilmer, a communication professor at the University of Toledo, is the author of *The Fear of Sinking: The American Success Formula in the Gilded Age.* She has also published articles and book chapters on various topics in communication history. She is a former member of the Board of Directors of the American Journalism Historians Association. She received her Ph.D. in media studies from the University of Illinois.

Chapter 12
THE AGE OF NEW JOURNALISM, 1883-1900

George Everett specializes in the history of technological influences on the media and has published a number of articles on the 1880s and 1890s. A professor emeritus of journalism at the University of Tennessee, he received his Ph.D. in mass communication from the University of Iowa and has served on the Editorial Board of *Journalism and Mass Communication Quarterly.* He is a former national president of Kappa Tau Alpha, the mass communication honor society.

W. Joseph Campbell is the author of five books, including *Yellow Journalism: Puncturing the Myths, Defining the Legacies* and *The Year That Defined American Journalism: 1897 and the Clash of Paradigms.* He also has had articles published in a number of journals. A journalism professor at American University, he has received a number of awards and has lectured at the Library of Congress, the National Press Club, and the Freedom Forum. Before going into teaching, he was a newspaper and wire service reporter for more than twenty years and covered assignments in North America, Europe, Asia, and West Africa. He received his Ph.D. in mass communication from the University of North Carolina.

Chapter 13
AMERICAN MAGAZINES, 1740-1900

Sam G. Riley is editor of the *Dictionary of Literary Biography's* multi-volume series on *American Magazine Journalists.* He authored *Magazines of the American South,* edited *Corporate Magazines of the United States* and *Consumer Magazines of the British Isles,* co-edited *Regional Interest Magazines of the United States,* and compiled *Index to Southern Periodicals, Index to City and Regional Magazines of the United States,* and two volumes on African Americans in the news media. He has published books on newspaper columnists and celebrity culture and has written on media history for a variety of scholarly publications. A professor of communication at Virginia Tech, he received his Ph.D. in mass communication from the University of North Carolina.

Chapter 14
THE DEVELOPMENT OF ADVERTISING, 1700-1900

Edd Applegate is the author of *The Ad Men and Women: A Biographical Dictionary of Advertising; Personality and Products: A Historical Perspective on Advertising in America;* two volumes in the Dictionary of Literary Biography series; and numerous book chapters. He has also written and co-edited several texts on advertising, and his articles and reviews have appeared in a variety of journals. He has received grants and fellowships from the Freedom Forum Media Studies Center, Gannett Foundation, American Association of Advertising Agencies, American Press Institute, and other organizations. He received his doctorate in mass communications and higher education from Oklahoma State University. He taught advertising and mass communications for more than thirty years before retiring from Middle Tennessee State University in 2010.

Chapter 15
THE EMERGENCE OF MODERN MEDIA, 1900-1945

Dianne Bragg teaches mass communication at the University of Alabama. She specializes in American newspapers in the early twentieth century and during the Civil War era and has presented a number of research papers on both topics. While a student, she served as chair of the Graduate Students Committee of the American Journalism Historians Association. She received her Ph.D. from the University of Alabama with a specialization in media history.

Chapter 16
THE MEDIA AND REFORM, 1900-1917

James Aucoin, a journalism professor at the University of South Alabama, specializes in the history of investigative journalism and is the author of *The Evolution of American Investigative Journalism.* He has also written journal articles and book chapters on journalism history and has served as editor of *The Intelligencer,* the newsletter of the American Journalism Historians Association. He received his Ph.D. from the University of Missouri.

Chapter 17
THE MEDIA AND NATIONAL CRISES, 1917-1945

Debra Reddin van Tuyll is a communication professor at Augusta State University, where she teaches journalism and public relations. She is author of *The Southern Press in the Civil War* and co-editor of *The Civil War and the Press* and *Knights of the Quill: Reassessing Confederate Correspondents and Their Civil War Reporting.* She has served as head of the History Division of the Association for Education in Journalism and Mass Communication and is a former member of the Board of Directors of the American Journalism Historians Association. Before going into teaching, she worked as a newspaper reporter, public relations professional, magazine editor, and medical journal editor. She received her Ph.D. from the University of South Carolina.

Chapter 18
RADIO COMES OF AGE, 1900-1945

Louise Benjamin has published numerous articles and book chapters on the history and regulation of electronic media, especially early broadcast radio. Her book *Freedom of the Air and the Public Interest: First Amendment Rights in Broadcasting to 1935* won the 2002 Franklyn Haiman Award for Freedom of Expression from the National Communication Association. Before receiving her Ph.D. from the University of Iowa, she worked in television as a writer, producer, and director. She teaches at Kansas State University, where she holds the Ross Beach Chair in Electronic Media.

Chapter 19
THE ENTERTAINMENT MEDIA, 1900-present

Jana L. Hyde has published book chapters and book reviews on mass media history, primarily in broadcasting. She teaches business creativity at the University of Colorado at Colorado Springs. She received her Ph.D. in mass communication history from the University of Alabama.

Chapter 20
THE AGE OF MASS MAGAZINES, 1900-present

Therese L. Lueck is professor of communication at the University of Akron and has served as a Fulbright Scholar in China. She is co-editor of the two-volume *Women's Periodicals in the United States* and has published a number of articles and book chapters, many of them about women and journalism. She has served on the Board of Directors of the American Journalism Historians Association. She received her Ph.D. in American culture from Bowling Green State University.

Chapter 21
MODERN ADVERTISING, 1900-present

Vanessa Murphree is the author of *The Selling of Civil Rights: The Student Nonviolent Coordinating Committee and the use of Public Relations*. She has also written about the birth control movement, crisis communication, and historical perspectives on public relations. The American Journalism Historians Association awarded her with a 2003 honorable mention for her dissertation and a 2005 award for "best *American Journalism* article." She received her Ph.D. in mass communication from the University of Southern Mississippi. She teaches at the University of South Alabama.

Chapter 22
PUBLIC RELATIONS, 1900-present

Karen Miller Russell specializes in public relations history and has published numerous articles on that and other topics in media history. Her book *The Voice of Business* is a history of the Hill and Knowlton public relations firm. She won the AEJMC's award for best dissertation in 1995 and the Institute for Public Relations' Pathfinder Award for best research program in 2001. She serves as editor of the *Journal of Public Relations Research*. She received her Ph.D. from the University of Wisconsin-Madison and teaches at the University of Georgia.

Chapter 23
THE MEDIA IN TRANSITION, 1945-1974

David R. Davies is professor of journalism and dean of the Honors College at the University of Southern Mississippi. A former reporter for the *Arkansas Gazette*, he specializes in the history of American newspapers since World War II and media coverage of the civil rights movement. He has written two books, *The Press and Race: Mississippi Journalists Confront the Movement* and *The Postwar Decline of American Newspapers, 1945-1965*. He received his Ph.D. in mass communication history from the University of Alabama.

Chapter 24
THE NEWS MEDIA, 1974-2000

Michael D. Murray is the University of Missouri Board of Curators' Distinguished Professor at the St. Louis campus. He was instrumental in founding media programs at Virginia Tech, the University of Louisville, and the University of Nevada-Las Vegas, where he served as the founding director of the Greenspun School of Journalism and Media Studies. He has published many articles and books on the history of broadcast news, including *The Political Performers*, for which he received a Goldsmith Research Award from Harvard. He is a fellow of the Universities of London and Cambridge and former president of the American Journalism Historians Association. He received the AJHA's 2003 Kobre Award for lifetime achievement. He received his Ph.D. from the University of Missouri.

Chapter 25
THE CONTEMPORARY MEDIA, 2000-present

James Brian McPherson is a communication studies professor at Whitworth University. In addition to journal articles and book chapters, he has authored two books, *Journalism at the End of the American Century, 1965-Present* and *The Conservative Resurgence and the Press*. He has served on the Board of Directors of the American Journalism Historians Association and as editor of *The Intelligencer*, the AJHA newsletter. He was a newspaper reporter and editor for several years and worked in nonprofit and corporate public relations before earning his Ph.D. from Washington State University.

CONTENTS

CONTENTS: FEATURE PAGES

INTRODUCTION

Why Study Media History?

"What's the value of studying history?"

That's a question that both students and professionals in mass communication often ask.

They could find the answer by doing something as simple as visiting a class in a local city school, where some seventh graders might be asking the same question. Many of those youths eventually will recognize, however, the importance of history. Why is it, then, that among educated individuals in communication the question of the value of the study of history so often comes up? Is there something unique about mass communication that makes it difficult for people in this field to recognize what civilized people generally have recognized for centuries?

In answer to the question about the value of history, we can give a variety of reasons. We can say that the study of media history is important for the same reasons that the study of any kind of history is. History has been a major form of study for more than 2,000 years, ever since Herodotus wrote his *History of the Greek and Persian War*. In explaining his purpose, he used the Greek word for "research" that came to be used as our designation of history. "This," he wrote, "is an account of the researches [*historia*] of Herodotus of Halicarnassus, which he publishes, in the hope of preserving from decay the remembrance of what men have done...." Furthermore, among the various disciplines for the study of mass communication, none has the long tradition that belongs to history. Isaiah Thomas wrote *The History of Printing in America* (1810) a century before schools for education in journalism were established, and ever since the beginning of those schools the study of history has been an integral part of the curriculum.

Media history, as one branch of historical study, offers the range of benefits common to all areas of history. Very broadly and most fundamentally, we can state that the past has intrinsic value in itself and a strong appeal to a large proportion of human beings living today. Historical study provides the opportunity to inform later generations about the nature of humankind and historical truth; it offers an explanation for the complexity of past thinking and behavior; it contributes to the authentic record of human experience. The primary goal of historians, therefore, is to explain the past truthfully. In doing so, they seek to capture the thought and feeling of a time past. Historical study would need no further justification than that. Like humankind's interest in art or music or literature and its continuing search for knowledge, history has an innate value.

Still, it is possible to state other, more concrete values of the study of history. First, it has a *civic* value. It provides information important for identity and background. It helps us to know ourselves both individually and collectively. In that sense, we can think of its civic value as being, in part, *professional*, as it helps us to connect with the members of the field of mass communication who have gone before us. Furthermore, the study of history provides knowledge valuable in helping us to understand people and the world around us. Although we may assume that particular events that occurred in the past will never recur in exactly the same way, we also know that an understanding of them will help us to deal with similar events in the future. Whether we are considering wars or social movements or our civilization or our professional field or any other major topic, we can be certain that a knowledge of their history and the answers to the questions they raised serve a purpose for anyone who hopes to be an informed and responsible person today.

A second value of the study of history is *intellectual*. It is a particularly effective means of stimulating and satisfying the human need to think. Because historical understanding requires the full range of rigor, critical thinking, mature judgment, analytical ability, and imagination, it is unsurpassed among scholarly disciplines in exercising the mind.

A third value one gains from studying history is a *moral* one. Theology and ethics used to provide education in moral values; but, as subjects for academic study, those disciplines have fallen by the wayside – particularly in *public* universities. History remains as the primary academic discipline to help us to understand people. It helps us to appreciate those who have different ideas from ours and to value them as human beings, and it provides models for standards of behavior. "If honestly taught," writes Walter Mc-Dougall, a Pulitzer-Prize winning historian, "history is the only academic subject that inspires humility.... It is, for all practical purposes, the religion in the modern curriculum. History helps us to understand the fullness of the human condition as no other academic study can do. A course in history ought to teach wisdom or at least understanding – and if it doesn't, then it is failing to do what it is obligated to do."

Even though the study of media history is recognized as valuable from these fundamental reasons, the distinctive nature of mass communication as a field of study and professional practice also offers reasons for studying its history. In such a field, imbued as it is with vocationalism, practicality, and present-mindedness, questions about the usefulness of history are bound to arise. Many people in mass communication are so interested in professional practices today that they think they have little need to know about history. In such a field, a knowledge of history becomes particularly important. It provides a broader perspective than one gets from studying simply the tools of the trade. For that reason alone, it merits serious study.

Among the panoply of other values that one might recite specifically related to professional aspects of mass communication, here are examples:

*History helps us to understand the present through knowledge of how the present came to be.

*It provides comparisons that help us to assess and evaluate the present.

*It provides, for the craft-oriented, insight into how professional practices can be done well.

*It sharpens critical thinking about the operation of media today.

Indeed, the value that history can bring to the study of mass communication should not be underestimated. Just as one seeks to understand a person or people by knowledge of their background, so it is natural to seek understanding of a contemporary institution by knowledge of its origins, ethical foundations, development, and interaction with the wider culture in which it exists. Both the personal and impersonal influences that affected the course of the development of the media, or of a particular mass medium, need to be assessed. The perspective gained from such inquiry may or may not have a direct effect on the work of today or tomorrow, but it can enlarge one's imagination, view, and judgment about matters relating to that work. Most important, the study of past achievement, even greatness, and of past failure associated with a human institution is surely a guide to comprehending the present and envisioning the future.

If, however, one is to gain the full value of studying history, it must be studied properly. Let's take a brief look at how good historians go about doing their job – and at how you as a student are affected by how well they do it.

Imagine that you wish to come to the best understanding possible of how, for example, journalists in a former time approached their profession. What would be the best way to gain such an understanding? Here, let's draw an analogy.

Imagine that, rather than wanting to understand the past, you wanted to come to a full knowledge of a place you have never been, a far country. The best way to do that would be to go there and spend as much time as you needed getting to know the country and its people. If you were unable to travel there, the next best thing would be to talk by phone to the people, read letters from them, watch television programs they have produced about themselves, read their magazines and newspapers and blogs, and examine any other material or records that they have created. Such items are known, in historical terminology, as *primary sources.*

If you wanted to understand the past in its truest sense, you would do the same thing. Obviously, you could not physically travel to the past – but you could examine the records that people have left. You could attempt to find all that is possible to know about life at a specific time and place in the past. You could try to become so thoroughly familiar with them that you might have the sense that you had actually lived then and there. If you did that, you would be a historian.

Let's take one more look at the study of history but from a different perspective. Assume that for the next few months the demands of the classes you are taking will absorb all your time and you will not be able to do the work of a career historian – yet in those circumstances you still wish to gain a true understanding of the past and, more specifically, of mass communication in the past. If you cannot do the work of the historian, the next best thing is to have a good historian doing the work and then sharing it with you.

You would expect the historian to perform according to certain fundamental principles. You would want your historian to be free of ideological and other bias. You would expect that he or she have a true appreciation of the people of the past and be interested in them on their own terms. You would not want the historian, for example, evaluating journalists of 1800 according to rules of journalistic conduct that only developed later – rules that may be appropriate for today but that did not exist 200 years ago. (That error frequently shows up among historians and is known as *present-mindedness.*) You also would want your historian to be judicious in dealing with material and fair-minded in dealing with people. If you could get a historian who would do all those things and would be rigorous and thorough besides, you probably would have confidence in what he or she told you, for good history must reflect the fundamental fairness of the historian who created it.

That being the case, we can still ask, what processes do historians undertake when producing an account of some part of the past?

In its simplest form, the question can be answered in four words: (1) understanding, (2) sources, (3) extrapolation, and (4) explanation.

First, a historian must gain a basic understanding of the subject at hand from what others have said about it or from materials available about it. In most cases, this learning stage involves a consideration of *historiography* (the study of historical writing).

Second, all pertinent sources relating to the subject must be located, collected, and evaluated. This phase of the historical process involves gaining an appreciation of and an ability to analyze the various types of sources that are applicable to the inquiry.

Third, meaning must be extrapolated from those sources. Extrapolation might involve probes into contextual matters or an unraveling of details of content. There are, moreover, various tools of analyses (e.g., content analysis, comparison of documents, and psychoanalysis, to name a few) to use when appropriate. Historians might also use a variety of theories to see if, without bending the facts, their own study can be illuminated by them.

Finally, historians must explain the material they have collected and examined. They perform this task by addressing certain propositions – causation, generalization, interpretation, and the establishing of significance. In this matter, history is an ongoing process. In studying history, it is well to bear in mind the words of the renowned historian Frederick Jackson Turner, who once explained: "Each age writes the history of the past anew with reference to the conditions uppermost in its own time.... History ... is ever *becoming* – never completed." It is a continuing interpretative effort to understand self and society.

The authors of this book hope that is the type of history you will get in the pages that follow. Each chapter author has been selected for expertise on the topic and for talent in doing historical research, and each is an accomplished writer who can present narrative and explanations clearly. You will note that the bulk of the sources that the authors use is made up of records and other materials left by the people who were involved in the episodes. When the authors have used *secondary sources* – that is, books and articles written by historians – they have been selective, relying only on works written by specialists and authorities on the particular subject under study.

Even so, the student should not assume that any historical narrative or explanation is necessarily and completely accurate. Despite the best intentions, the most rigorous research, and scrupulous editing, there may be other episodes that one might choose for inclusion, some details left out, or different explanations offered. History should be an honest search for answers to important questions. In seeking those answers, you should approach each chapter in this book inquisitively. You will find that the capacity that history has to interact with you as the reader is another of its many values.

THE MEDIA IN AMERICA

A History

Eighth Edition

1

Origins of Mass Communication

Notwithstanding the modern fascination with the here and now of computers, satellites, cyberspace, and the information highway supposedly guiding us into the future, serious students of mass media must look back to their earliest roots. Only then can they truly understand the fields of study linked to journalism, advertising, public relations, the broadcasting trades, and many others. Such study not only provides an idea of the diversity of our technological and philosophical bloodlines rooted in many nations of the world, but it contributes a sense of the primacy of print and writing as the foundation for communication. Thus, by understanding the genesis of mass communication, each of us not only is able to gain a better understanding of the many ancestors and the genealogy of our American media but also is able to relate more fully to the family of humankind.

One of the issues that have confronted historians is whether writing developed slowly over long periods of time, or whether it appeared suddenly. Rather than evolving over thousands of years and being utilized primarily for the mercenary hurly-burly of business, writing may have sprung full-blown from the minds of ancient men and women in the mid-East, Asia, and the Americas as an instrument divinely inspired. A number of scholars point to yawning gaps of evidence and the fact that ancients unanimously called attention to cosmic forces contributing to communication.[1] This chapter, though, like much of the study of the history of early communication, takes a mainly evolutionary point of view.

According to the Bible, everything began with the "Word." The word, in human terms, enabled people to speak coherently. That ability placed them above the animals and allowed them to share thoughts and feelings. Before the dawn of civilization, however, human utterances were confined by space and time. Speakers could not be sure that their words and thoughts would be faithfully transmitted beyond their environment or after their death. Thoughts could be distorted by the passage of time, and personal achievements would rapidly vanish into the past. Ancient tongues spoken by clans thousands of years ago have disappeared.

We do know something about our primitive predecessors, thanks to their practice of keeping records. Although these records lack the clarity of written documents, they reveal much about early humans. Archaeologists have unearthed bones with man-made scratchings that may be 400,000 years old. A younger but particularly interesting bone found in France is engraved with parallel lines, arcs, and other symbols. The signs of this ox rib apparently served to keep track of the seasons, rainfall, river flooding, and other natural phenomena. Radioactive carbon-14 methods indicate the rib is 135,000 years old.[2] No matter how elaborate the carvings of early record keepers, their images and symbols fell far short of expressing ideas, feelings, and abstractions. Perhaps the records also lost their meaning when the original artists were not present to explain them.

To share fully in the thinking of others, *homo sapiens* ("thinking human beings" or literally "wise men") needed some means of carrying their words across space and time. That means was writing. It is among the most revolutionary inventions in the cultural history of humankind.

THE DAWN OF WRITING

Our ancestors had such an appreciation of the importance of writing that many of their legends suggested it had a divine origin. There was a saying among some ancient Indians: "Blessed be he who invented writing."[3] Literary archaeology, a young science,

---

[1]This is the claim of such historians as Hugh Nibley and Curtis Wright. See the works by these historians listed in the "Recommended Readings" at the end of this chapter. Often overlooked, for example, in the traditional evolutionary approach to the origins of writing have been the contributions of Native Americans. Writing in 1973, K. H. Basso and Ned Anderson reported on an "authentic, ingenious, original and highly efficient" writing system that the western Apaches used. Apache shaman Silas John claimed that the entire primitive system came to him suddenly in 1904 as a dream from the Great Spirit for the express purpose of recording ritual prayers and ordinances to be disseminated among his tribe. Basso and Anderson emphasize that, although Silas John knew a little about alphabetic writing, his script and underlying principles departed radically from the English alphabet. Like the Cherokee syllabary that Sequoyah invented around 1820, Silas John's writing system represented the creation of a unique cultural form. As such, Basso and Anderson rank it "among the significant intellectual achievements of an American Indian in the 20th century." K. H. Basso and Ned Anderson, "A Western Apache Writing System: The Symbols of Silas John," *Science* (June 1973): 1013-22.

[2]James Norman, *Ancestral Voices* (New York, 1957), 7.
[3]Quoted in Ernst Doblhofer, *Voices in Stone* (New York, 1961), 13.

Petroglyph

This engraving — called a *petroglyph*, since it was carved in rock — shows six ostriches in what the hunter probably thought of as his magic circle. A petroglyph is a type of *pictogram*, which means "picture sign" and resembles the thing it represents.

has been concerned with the origins of ancient writing. Literary archaeologists have examined that era when humans began composing purposeful messages. They conjecture that writing originated thousands of years ago when humans learned to convey thoughts and feelings through visible signs. These signs were forms of communication and also of art rather than forms of writing as one normally defines the term. At first people may have been interested only in marking a location, such as piling up stones over a gravesite. Hunters may have stuck small branches or sticks in the ground at angles corresponding to the direction of travel of animal herds.

Early record-keepers may have used various objects to help them remember. Among these *mnemonic* (memory-aiding) devices were sticks or bones with carved notches, pebbles in a sack, and knots tied in string. In such a manner, they kept accounts of cattle and agricultural commodities. Mnemonic signs were limited to numerical applications and were probably not used to keep a chronicle of events.[4]

Perhaps the cumbersome nature of these materials provoked the ancients to seek more convenient forms of communicating. Eventually they reduced the size of various constructions like rock piles by simply making representations of them. They took the realities of their world and made pictorial scratchings of them on bones, wood, or stone. In later times, they drew objects on cave walls. Exactly why humans made pictures is the subject of some conjecture, but there seems always to have been an urge to communicate — to leave for others something of oneself. When man began drawing pictures, he demonstrated that he had made con-

siderable progress in his development. Indeed, by making pictures he had reached the first of three successive milestones on the road to writing. The stages were the following:

1. *Pictographic.* A pictogram ("picture sign") was a drawing of a natural object or event. It was often simple, such as a circle with rays emanating from it to suggest the sun. It could also be complex, such as a drawing of an animal with a spear next to it, to convey the notion of hunting. Pictures carved in rocks are called *petroglyphs*, while those painted on rocks are *petrograms*. While it was possible for a grouping of several pictograms to tell a simple story, the meaning was restricted to the content of the pictures.

2. *Ideographic.* The ideogram provided a more sophisticated technique that remedied a major deficiency in the pictogram. The pictogram by itself was unable to convey ideas or abstract concepts such as love, cold, danger, or happiness. To communicate the intangibles of life, clan members had to convert pictures to ideograms by agreeing among themselves that additional meanings belonged to certain pictures. A primitive society might have agreed, for example, that a drawing of the sun's disk and rays meant heat or warmth, not simply the sun. This stage required more intelligence on the part of the clan and a considerable degree of social organization. The ideogram was a significant advance toward writing because pictures now suggested ideas or names of objects or events and thus became symbols.

3. *Phonetic.* This stage saw the linking of the spoken language to the written. Phonetic writing was born when a picture became a single sign that suggested a single sound. The spoken language could now be depicted by combinations of signs. As a result, writing became much easier, and meanings became more precise. This achievement came slowly, and many societies failed to reach this stage on the road to writing. The syllabic writing that developed in the phonetic stage was complicated, and readers were unable to comprehend many of the signs easily. Ultimately, simpler languages appeared that used the alphabet. The latest refinement in the evolution of writing, the alphabet employs a letter sign instead of a syllable for each sound.

WRITING AND THE FIRST CIVILIZATION

Record-keeping and the birth of writing were clearly linked. Before the first civilization appeared in the ancient Near East, some peoples began keeping records with a novel system that resembled modern messages in envelopes. This archaic system used *bullae*, or hollow clay balls, which contained tokens representing livestock. The balls were either round or egg-shaped, about the size of a baseball. The small tokens inside were of many shapes, including spheres, discs, cones, cylinders, and triangles. Tokens have been found throughout the Middle East, distributed widely along the Fertile Crescent, that rich area that arches around the top of the Arabian desert from present day Israel to the Persian Gulf and in which the first civilizations appeared.

Historians usually recognize the area of the lower Tigris and Euphrates Rivers as the home of the first civilizations. A people

---

[4]I.J. Gelb, *A Study of Writing* (Chicago, 1963), 4.

Valley of Civilization
The Tigris-Euphrates river valley in the 25th century B.C. formed one of the earliest centers of civilization and gave humans some of the first forms of writing. It is the site of present-day Saudi Arabia, Iraq, Kuwait, and Iran.

known as the Sumerians produced an urban society there around 3,800 B.C. Although the exact origins of these people remain a mystery, it is clear that they entered the river valley from neighboring hills. The Neolithic (New Stone Age) Garden Cultures located in the hilly terrain in present-day Iraq and adjacent parts of Turkey, Syria, and Iran may have been their original home. The river valley settlements eventually grew into cities in which life became more complex and more sophisticated in terms of social, political, and economic organization. "Civilization" is the term historians use to describe collective life produced by those conditions. The complexities of city life included the need to keep records of commodities and the need to identify private property. It was in this environment that writing may have first appeared.

It was the Sumerians who developed the art of writing. These stocky, round-headed people needed some means of keeping track of their personal property. Their priests required some way to keep accounts of the temple wealth. The priests exacted tribute from the farmers as payment to their gods for use of irrigation water and to ensure divine blessings on future crops. They kept records first by scratching marks on pieces of clay. Later, perhaps around 3500 B.C., they used a more efficient stamp seal, an engraved piece of stone or metal, often shaped like a small cone or bell. The small stones were engraved with a small number of symbols.

A significant advance over the stamp seal was the invention of the cylinder seal. The Sumerians used it to inscribe a continuous record of ownership by rolling an engraved cylinder over a wet clay surface. Historians have noted similarities between the large

cylinders of the modern printing press and the rolling printing of the cylinder seal.[5]

It would be difficult to overestimate the importance of the cylinder seal as a step forward for civilization. It promoted cultural diffusion throughout the Near East by transporting abroad pictures of everyday life in Sumer and spreading its literature. One of the earliest and most influential works of literature was the Sumerian *Epic of Gilgamesh* about the legendary ruler of Uruk. The story contains, among other things, an account of a great deluge that killed every living thing except those aboard an ark.

Cylinder printing also contained the first known examples of sensationalism. When the Sumerians were under the domination of the Akkadians and others from about 2340 to 2125 B.C., the themes of cylinder printing exaggerated muscular features of warriors and portrayed an increasing amount of violence.

The Sumerians achieved the last stage in the development of writing — the phonetic — that linked the spoken with the written language. By 3100 B.C. or earlier they had a full writing system in use, the first civilization to accomplish this. But they, like other river valley civilizations, stopped short of achieving an alphabet. The alphabet represents the simplification of syllable writing to single-sound letters. Another alluvial river, the Nile, nourished a civilization that did simplify much of its language to single-sound script. But even the Egyptian civilization failed to reach a completely phonetic writing through an alphabet.

WRITING IN ANCIENT EGYPT

The origins and early development of Egyptian writing are less certain than of Sumerian writing. Egyptian script appears not to have been a gradual development through the three stages as in Sumer. An element of mystery exists about the rather startling progress the Egyptians made very early toward a phonetic script. At first, in prehistoric times, Egyptians painted pictures on pottery. Their drawings in the pictographic and ideographic stages were skillfully done representations of birds, animals, and deities. Soon after 3000 B.C., however, Egyptian writing abruptly began to use phonetic signs. It became a system of phonetic script written with pictures. Why this happened so suddenly has been a matter of considerable dispute among literary archaeologists.

The early maturity of Egyptian writing probably resulted from Sumerian influence. At the time of greatest cultural diffusion from Mesopotamia, Egypt's writing showed some striking resemblances to Sumerian script. Egypt readily borrowed a number of Sumerian innovations, such as cylinder seal printing, brick architecture, and the potter's wheel. The forms of Egyptian writing were adapted to fit available materials and requirements of Egyptian life. Three kinds of Egyptian writing developed:

1. *Hieroglyphic.* Hieroglyphic, a word with Greek origins, literally means "sacred carved letters." Hieroglyphic writing was used mainly for religious display, for inscriptions on monuments, temple walls, and tombs, and for painted inscriptions on pottery. It

[5]Karlen Mooradian, "The Dawn of Printing," *Journalism Monographs* 23 (1972): 9 and 35.

has also been found on written documents on papyrus. Hieroglyphic apparently had some secular applications, but it remained largely a sacred, somewhat secret writing used mainly by Egyptian priests. Hieroglyphic characters were a mix of ideograms, phonograms, and other phonetic elements.

2. *Hieratic.* For everyday use in business, letters, medical texts, and literary works, Egyptians employed a cursive script brushed onto papyrus. Although it lacked the pictorial quality of hieroglyphic, it was a faithful transcription of hieroglyphic. The main differences were the linkage together of the hieratic characters by the sweep of the brush pen and some minor changes in the signs. Although its name derives from the Greek *hieratikos* ("sacred"), Egyptians used it for both secular and religious writing.

3. *Demotic.* The demotic script (from the Greek *demos,* meaning "people") replaced hieratic as the script used in mundane business. Hieratic had, by the seventh century B.C., acquired so many cursive peculiarities and abbreviations that it was difficult to master by any but the priestly class. It then became an almost exclusively sacred script, and demotic came into popular use. Its hieroglyphic beginnings were barely discernible. It combined whole groups of hieroglyphs into a single sign and used a mixture of picture and sound signs.[6]

Clay tablets unearthed in Egypt in 1999 contain the earliest quasi-alphabetic writing ever found. Although Egyptian writing contained twenty-four single-consonant characters, it was not truly alphabetic. The achievement of a alphabet eluded the Egyptians for religious and social reasons. Their script depended on scribes who kept hieroglyphic secret, and Egypt's social structure discouraged simplification of hieroglyphic so that all levels of society could use it.[7] The cursive scripts, hieratic and demotic, remained faithful to their hieroglyphic origins and never developed further toward an alphabet.

THE FIRST ALPHABET

The invention of the alphabet was one of the most significant events in human history. A system of signs expressing single sounds of speech, the alphabet had its origins in the ancient Middle East. Our own alphabet is a descendant of the Phoenician alphabetic script, following modification of it by the Greeks. The Greek alphabet originated among the Semitic peoples of Egypt, Palestine, and Syria.

There is conjecture as to whether the Phoenicians originated a true alphabet independently or simply adopted it from others and exported it to Greece and elsewhere. In 1999 researchers discovered Semitic inscriptions in limestone in Egypt dating from between 1900 and 1800 B.C., providing evidence of the earliest experiments with an alphabet. That time coincides roughly with the Hebrew captivity in Egypt recorded in the Old Testament.[8] The

Phoenician Alphabet
The Western alphabet that is in use today originated with the Phoenicians around 1600 B.C. The twenty-two letters from the alphabet above are from about 1500 B.C. Some letters of today's English alphabet retain some of the same character designs.

twenty-four monosyllabic symbols in Egyptian hieroglyphics provide evidence of a strong Egyptian influence on the development of the alphabet. Strong arguments also exist for a Sumerian picture-script connection. It is virtually certain, however, that the Greeks adopted Phoenician script. The evidence is found chiefly in the nearly identical form of the letters in both alphabets, the order of the letters, and their names. For example, the Semitic *aleph, beth, gimel* correspond to the Greek *alpha, beta, gamma.*

Phoenician traders used their alphabet as an important part of a mercantile system that spanned the entire Mediterranean and lasted more than a thousand years. In that manner the Semitic alphabet was exported and borrowed. From their homeland on the Eastern Mediterranean coast, what is now Lebanon and Israel, Phoenician merchants sailed to the Greek islands and mainland. Soon they established colonies in Greece, leaving abundant evidence of their presence in alphabetic inscriptions on monuments. The Greek alphabet of classical civilization, built on the letter forms of the Phoenicians, provided the foundation of the Graeco-Roman alphabet. The Graeco-Roman then became the alphabet of Western civilization.

In America the oldest of what appears to be writing dates from about 850 B.C. It is a set of symbols carved across a 26-pound stone from the Olmec civilization in what is now Mexico and Central America.

CHINESE WRITING AND PRINTING

Chinese writing ranks alongside other great systems of ancient

[6]Hans Jensen, *Sign, Symbol and Script,* translated from the German by George Unwin (New York, 1969), 71.

[7]David Diringer, *Writing* (New York, 1962), 48-50.

[8]John Noble Wilford, ["Egyptian inscriptions set earlier date for alphabet"], N. Y. Times News Service, 14 November 1999; and Salah Nasrawi, ["Alphabet debate will not be easy"], Associated Press, 13 December 1999.

writing that originated independently. Although writing in the Middle East originated around 5,000 years ago, Chinese writing has the distinction of being the oldest script that is still in use. It has undergone relatively minor changes in its 4,000-year life. Like other writing systems, Chinese script began from a pure picture form of writing, with phonetic elements added gradually. The oldest evidence of Chinese writing consists of inscriptions on bronze vessels, dating from the Hsia dynasty in 2205 B.C. Bones and tortoise shells were inscribed in the twelfth century B.C. with sacred messages. These "oracle bones" contained divine pronouncements spoken through priests.

Until the third century B.C. the Chinese wrote mostly on bone, stone, wood, metal, and bamboo. In the next three centuries, however, a number of discoveries revolutionized their techniques. They developed a bristle brush for applying ink made from pine soot or black earth. They used it with another invention, a writing surface that was cheap, convenient, and portable — paper. The superintendent of a weapons factory, Tsai-Lun, created paper in 105 A.D. He cooked a mush made of cut-up plant fibers, bark, hemp, rags, and water, and then poured the pulp onto screens made of bamboo strips. When drained and dried, thin sheets of paper were left. The knowledge of paper-making was exported to Korea and Japan about 600 A.D. and passed to the Arabs in 751. Shortly, paper mills sprang up at several locations in the Middle East — in Baghdad, Damascus, and Egypt. Paper entered Europe through Spain in the eleventh and twelfth centuries. Paper manufacturing began in Europe in the thirteenth century, and it was associated with the emergence of the Commercial Revolution.

Within a few centuries of their discovery of paper, the Chinese found a way to reproduce writing by carving designs on wooden blocks, inking the designs, and pressing them on paper. This technique marked the birth of the modern process of printing with a press, paper, and ink. Printers carved the necessarily large number of different Chinese characters from wood blocks and began to produce printed books in the middle of the ninth century. Pi-Sheng, a metalworker, invented a press employing movable letters made of metal, clay, and wood in 1045. This achievement was later eclipsed in Europe, where the letter press met with great success because printers did not have to cope with the 40,000 possible characters in the Chinese written language.[9]

The ancient Chinese developed a system for gathering news from across the large Chinese land mass. They used it, however, only to provide information for the imperial court and not the masses of people. Beginning in 206 B.C. the imperial court of the Han dynasty set up a postal network to obtain news of events throughout the empire. In the T'ang dynasty (618-907 A.D.), a handwritten official news paper, *ti pao*, was published. It circulated news to government officials that had been gathered through the postal network. During the Sung dynasty (960-1278), the *ti pao* was disseminated among intellectuals, and in the Ming period (1367-1644) an even wider circle of readers received it.

[9]Oscar Ogg, *The 26 Letters* (New York, 1961), 188.

Pioneer Printers
The Chinese were pioneers in both writing and printing. They used presses that employed movable type 400 years before the Gutenberg Bible was printed in Europe.

CRETE: PARENT OF WESTERN CIVILIZATION

Writing seems to have sprung up independently in various cultures and civilizations in the centuries immediately following its appearance in southern Mesopotamia about 3100 B.C. The Cretan civilization, centered on the Mediterranean island of Crete, was one of them. Also known as the Minoan civilization, it was one of the parents of the classical civilization of the Greeks and Romans. Crete is particularly interesting because it was the site of one of the great mysteries in the development of printing.

About 2300 B.C. Cretan civilization expanded commercially, culturally, and artistically. These maritime people began writing in a pictorial script that was replaced by two kinds of linear script after 1700 B.C., about the time of Crete's peak as a civilization. Their writing, like ours, read from left to right.

A clay disk with strange markings was found in 1908 at the site of what was once the palace at Phaistos in Crete. It was produced from individual pieces of type that had been pressed onto the clay. This earliest known example of movable-type printing, produced between 1700 and 1600 B.C., predates by more than 3,000 years Gutenberg's invention of movable type. Its picture-signs are unlike the rest of Cretan picture-script. The ancient Minoan would

Scrolls
Scrolls, such as this one of the Pentateuch, were one of the earliest means found to keep large manuscripts together. As books grew larger, however, scrolls became inconvenient, and they gave way to codices that resembled today's books.

have had to rotate the disk to read it. The forty-five different signs used repeatedly on the disk are identical in shape and size. That fact gives rise to the tantalizing speculation that the ancients who imprinted the disk intended to reach a large audience by producing reusable pieces of type.

Classical Civilization

The Greek-speaking peoples of the Mediterranean and the Latin-speaking Romans constituted Classical Civilization (950 B.C. to A.D. 550). Greek culture was heavily influenced by its roots in the Cretan civilization, but Rome simply adopted the same culture from the Greeks about 200 B.C. Generally speaking, classical culture was not the culture of the masses of people. It was the culture of the literate, slave-owning, upper classes who were a small minority of city dwellers. It had no system of general education, and the majority remained illiterate.

The Greeks modified the Phoenician alphabet by changing some unused consonants into much needed vowels. They eventually developed a standard alphabet of twenty-four characters without the *C* and *V* of our alphabet. To accommodate the space and shape of writing surfaces, Greek scribes wrote both left to right and right to left. About the sixth century B.C. they settled on a left-to-right script.

The Greeks used a variety of writing tools and surfaces, includ-

ing papyrus imported from Egypt, brush, reed pen, waxed tablet, and stylus. An improvement over papyrus, parchment came into use after 200 B.C. Both remained as writing surfaces throughout most of the Graeco-Roman period. Around the end of that period, parchment became the basic medium for writing and remained so throughout the early Middle Ages, until paper replaced it in the thirteenth century. Parchment was made by bleaching goat or sheep skin and rubbing the surface smooth. It had many advantages: it was long-lasting, it held ink without smearing, it could be used on both sides, and it could be rolled up or bound into a book.

The Greeks made a remarkable contribution to the technology of communication by developing an optical telegraph for use in warfare. The word "telegraph" means "writing at a distance." Although they lacked electricity, a necessity for modern telegraphy, the Greeks were able to communicate over distances perhaps as early as the fourth century B.C. through the use of signal fires to convey military information.[10]

Ancient Greece provided one of the earliest examples of large-scale censorship. A cleavage in Greek social and political life resulted in the virtual disappearance of certain literary and philosophical works. Between 450 and 350 B.C. the Oligarchs, a group that favored the nobility, state authority, and the Spartan approach to life, challenged the adherents of Athenian democracy, who favored commerce and social equality. The Oligarchs eventually triumphed over the democratic forces. Because the Oligarchs were unwilling to pay for making copies of works that did not favor their position, most of the writings of supporters of Athenian democracy have been lost to history. Thus, the works of Plato, Xenophon, and other allies of the nobility have survived while those of the Sophists and Ionian scientists did not.[11]

It seems ironic that the Classical Age of Greece, whose legacy included the works of eminent philosophers, scientists, poets, and playwrights, had no system for producing and distributing books. Even in the period of greatest literary accomplishment, few hand-copied books were available. Later, however, during the Hellenistic Age (323 to 30 B.C.), the Greek domination of Egypt led to the emergence of Alexandria as the foremost — and only — center for book production for several centuries before the Augustan age in Rome. Alexandria was the largest city in the ancient world, with as many as a million residents. Its magnificent library held about 750,000 papyrus volumes. The Ptolemaic kings of Egypt developed in Alexandria a systematic approach to book production and marketing. Works considered classics were collected by librarians and served as sources for copyists employed by publishers. Alexandrian book dealers thus sold the wisdom of the ancient world to the wealthy leisure classes in Rome, Athens, and elsewhere.

Rome and Mass Communication

In the Roman Empire mass communication reached a level of

[10]Jackson P. Hershbell, "The Ancient Telegraph: War and Literacy," in *Communication Arts in the Ancient World*, Eric Havelock, et al., eds. (New York, 1978), 82-7.
[11]Carroll Quigley, *The Evolution of Civilizations* (New York, 1961), 196-8.

HIGHLIGHTS IN THE HISTORY OF WRITING AND PRINTING

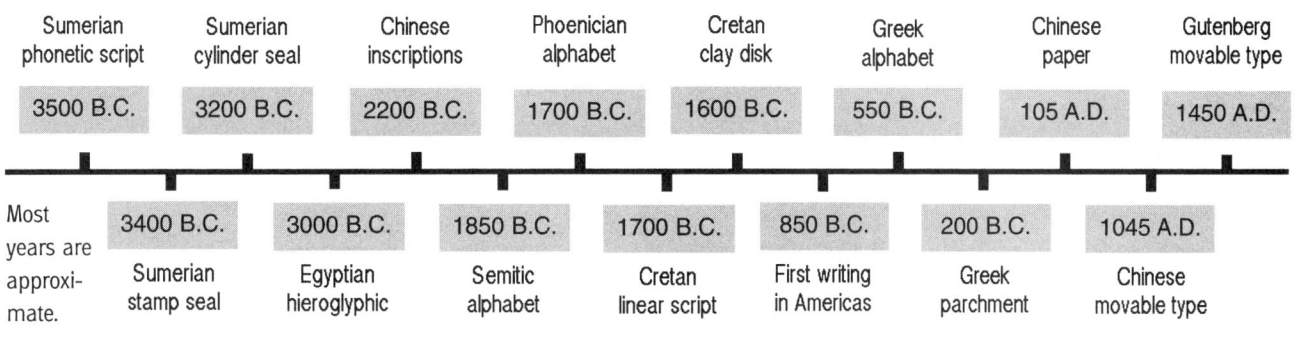

Sumerian phonetic script	Sumerian cylinder seal	Chinese inscriptions	Phoenician alphabet	Cretan clay disk	Greek alphabet	Chinese paper	Gutenberg movable type
3500 B.C.	3200 B.C.	2200 B.C.	1700 B.C.	1600 B.C.	550 B.C.	105 A.D.	1450 A.D.

Most years are approximate.

3400 B.C.	3000 B.C.	1850 B.C.	1700 B.C.	850 B.C.	200 B.C.	1045 A.D.
Sumerian stamp seal	Egyptian hieroglyphic	Semitic alphabet	Cretan linear script	First writing in Americas	Greek parchment	Chinese movable type

sophistication not previously attained. Greeks and other peoples who had fully developed writing systems produced literature, coinage, trade marks, and other forms of communication intended for a wide audience. But in Rome the task of governing a vast empire and supporting far-flung military and commercial ventures required new applications of existing forms of communication. Similarities to these ancient forms can be seen today in the public relations business and in such journalistic forms as business and government reporting, gossip columns, sensationalism, and even zoned editions of newspapers.

The Latin alphabet became the script of the western Roman Empire (and eventually most of Europe and America). It appeared after 600 B.C., having been derived from a local script of the Italian peninsula. At first the alphabet was written entirely in capital letters. Later, cursive forms were employed for everyday use and gave birth to the small letters of our alphabet. In Rome's later days cursives became so popular that the use of capital letters declined. By the Middle Ages, long after the fall of Rome, Roman capitals became so rare that they might have been lost had they not been chiseled into stone. Fortunately, after movable type was invented, medieval type cutters used the beautiful and graceful Roman letters sculpted on monuments as their inspiration.

Rome's upper classes possessed a high degree of literacy. Many who had the leisure to read were vitally interested in public affairs and had a need for information about government, the markets, and events throughout the empire. Ultimately their thirst for news was quenched by a remarkable chronicle, the *Acta Diurna Populi Romani* (daily acts — or occurrences — of the Roman people). The *Acta Diurna* survived for at least two centuries and was a forerunner of the modern newspaper. The words "journal" and "journalism" derive from *diurna*. The *Acta Diurna* developed from three predecessors:

1. The *Acta Senatus*. The deliberations of the Roman Senate were kept in these official records. Similar in content to our *Congressional Record*, they contained mostly speeches and opinions of senators and were kept in an archives where senators could read them. Early forms of the *Acta Senatus* date from 449 B.C.

2. The *album*. This was a white tablet set up outside the home of the Pontifex Maximus at the east end of the Roman Forum. The *album* contained accounts of ceremonies in which the ruling consuls and other officials participated. Updated daily, it also included information about festivals, eclipses, and dedications. The tablets were taken down at the end of the year and stored. Fortunately for historians, the *alba* were kept for centuries, providing an authentic, official chronicle of Roman history.

3. Newsletters. Scribes were paid to compile a summary of news on a regular basis. Some of Rome's wealthy purchased the service for their news-hungry friends outside Rome. The scribes who collected and copied current information were among history's first professional reporters. The quality of their work was occasionally unsatisfactory, provoking complaints from readers, including Cicero. He employed the learned Coelius to produce a regular, perhaps even daily, newsletter of events in Rome. Coelius hired several literate men as reporters to furnish him with general news of all kinds. Acting as editor, Coelius assembled the news into a collection of articles that he sent to Cicero while the latter was a governor in Asia Minor. Cicero apparently wanted primarily political interpretation in the mix of news and cared little for such trivial matters as gladiatorial contests.

These three traditions culminated in the *Acta Diurna* itself, begun by Julius Caesar in 59 B.C. The *Acta* was an official daily publication at first, covering governmental business such as decrees, proclamations, and senate resolutions. It also contained general information about goings-on in Rome and elsewhere, news of famous persons, executions, fires, and weather. It was posted each day in popular places, such as the baths, where illiterates often listened while someone read the news aloud. Many of the wealthy sent literate slaves to make copies of the *Acta* for savoring at a dinner party or for mailing to friends abroad. The *Acta* entertained as well as informed. It departed from its official traditions by the end of the first century A.D. and began reporting court decisions, crime, divorce, marriage, gossip, and bizarre happenings such as the claimed sighting of a phoenix.[12] Because the *Acta* was written on perishable papyrus, no copies have survived.

The Roman emperor Augustus put into operation a worldwide system for the dissemination of information and propaganda. Some historians have called him a genius of government. Reign-

[12]C.A. Giffard, "Ancient Rome's Daily Gazette," *Journalism History* 2 (1975-76): 107.

Roman Coins
One of Roman emperor Augustus' successful uses of propaganda was through the printing on coins, with his likeness on one side and information on the other. The coin in this illustration was created to represent the comet that appeared during his reign, which was claimed to be an epiphany of Julius Caesar, his predecessor.

ing from 29 B.C. to A.D. 14, he seemed to understand that an efficient communication apparatus — controlled by him — was essential to the consolidation of political power. He put the postal system on a regular basis to hasten the delivery of official dispatches to and from governors in the provinces. By this effort he also aided the lively and prosperous book trade in Rome that used the post to send books to locations throughout the expansive empire.

Among Augustus' most innovative contributions to communication was use of the monetary system to disseminate messages. The messages were of great social, political, and economic consequence. They were engraved on coins and thus carried across the continents of Europe, Asia, and Africa by Roman armies, government officials, and merchants. The coins were, in addition to the *Acta Diurna*, another kind of "newspaper" that provided current information. The portrait side remained relatively unchanged while officials frequently revised the flip side to carry a variety of messages reflecting current events. Augustus used coins to inform the public of his military triumphs, public works, governing policies, important anniversaries, happenings within the imperial family, and other current matters.

His engravers and mint supervisors carefully matched the message to the audience, as evidenced by the geographic selectivity exercised in issuing certain coins. Augustus controlled every element of Roman coinage, providing him with a powerful tool in his efforts to manipulate public opinion. Historians of coins acknowledge that he was among history's most successful propagandists.[13]

MEDIEVAL EUROPE: COPYING TO PRINTING

The death of Classical Civilization, a fact even before the end of the Western Roman Empire in 476 A.D., led to cultural disintegration throughout the Mediterranean basin and Europe. For several centuries, literacy declined and communications remained inadequate. Among the casualties of the Roman Empire's demise were the well maintained and secure roads and the markets for literature. With the barbarian invasions, these virtually disappeared, and the literary activities of Rome effectively ceased. The Christian clergy in Europe possessed what little literacy there was.

The oral tradition in communication, as old as humanity itself, remained strong. Towns employed criers to read aloud handwritten bulletins. Ballad singers, who lived by their wits, collected news as they wandered from one community to another. The balladeer gathered a crowd at the village crossroads and sang or recited his story in doggerel. He ceased singing after completing a part of the ballad, continuing only if the listeners paid.

The book had already changed physical form by the early Middle Ages. Roman book publishers, between the first and fifth centuries, had begun to abandon the roll and to make books by binding flat leaves into a volume (a codex). Vellum (calf or lamb skin) was the preferred writing surface until the introduction of paper into Europe after 1100. The use of animal skins contributed to the high cost of books and their scarcity.

In the ten centuries between the end of Rome and the advent of the printing press, manuscript production was the responsibility of the Christian monasteries and, later, medieval universities. It was the Irish, once they were Christianized in the fifth century, who founded the monastic movement, copying the books that Germanic invaders were destroying elsewhere. Monks were the only civilizing influence in much of Western Europe. They were skilled farmers, sharing their knowledge of agriculture with the local folk. Some became expert in glass making, weaving, wood carving, metal working, and brewing. The monasteries were also centers for nurturing the arts, science, and invention.

The prolific period of monastic copying of manuscripts began with the founding of the monastery of Monte Cassino in Italy by St. Benedict in 529. He had an exceptional interest in literature. The *Rule of St. Benedict*, regulations governing the Benedictine order of monks, specifically instructed the monks to occupy themselves with manual labor and holy reading. The reading requirement was intensified during the Church's holiest season:

> On the days of Lent, from morning until the end of the third hour let them apply themselves to their reading…. And in these days of Lent they shall each receive a book from the library, which they shall read straight through from the beginning.[14]

Since the rule could not be implemented if books were in short supply, monastic superiors interpreted the rule as requiring the

[13]Frank J. Krompak, "The World News According to Augustus," a paper presented to the annual convention of the American Journalism Historians Association, Tallahassee, Florida, 1984.

[14]*The Rule of St. Benedict*, Chapter 48, translated by the Order of Saint Benedict, http://www.osb.org/rb/index.html#English.

Scriptorium

Before the invention of printing with movable type, individual copies of books had to be done by hand. Monks did most of the work. Under Charlemagne, emperor of the Holy Roman Empire, every abbot, bishop, and count was ordered to employ a copyist; and every monastery was required also to maintain a scriptorium, outfitted with desks and writing material. Book copying became a life-long occupation for many people. Flaccus Alcuin, Charlemagne's adviser who oversaw the policy on copyist requirements, wrote that "it is a most meritorious work, more beneficial to the health than working in the fields, which profits only a man's body, while the labor of the copyist profits the soul."

production of books by the monks themselves. The call for daily manual labor, then, meant work for some of the more literate monks as copyists in the *scriptorium*, a large, common workroom overseen by the chief scribe, the *librarius*. In some monasteries it was located near a source of heat, to permit work in cold weather. The monks occasionally worked into the night by the light of oil lamps. Copying was gruelling, tedious work. Many monks preferred the manual labor of the farm to the confinement of the copyist's desk. The Benedictines encouraged literacy and penmanship by having the more practiced monastic scribes teach those with lesser skills. The monopoly on literacy by Christian churchmen was fortunate because they preserved not only the philosophical and religious works of the Classical period but works of a secular nature as well.

The monks' achievements as copyists often obscure another important monastic accomplishment in the history of communica-

tion in the Middle Ages — their work as chroniclers or reporters. The monks served not only as scribes, but also as historians, teachers, and collectors of information who faithfully kept chronicles of civil, domestic, social, and agricultural life. Most of the accounts of medieval life extant today come from the secular records, called *cartularies*, that monks meticulously collected. *Cartularies* were institutional and personal legal records, and they often contained narratives of events and circumstances needed to explain the subject of the document. They were, therefore, important documents of communication, and they go back at least to the ninth century. Annuals, histories, and biographies were also produced, even in the Early Middle Ages (500-1000 A.D.). Moreover, some of the writers who chronicled history and events in those centuries were among the most important medieval authors. One has to think only of St. Gregory of Tours, who wrote in the sixth century, and of the Venerable Bede, the most influential scholar of the seventh and eighth centuries, to appreciate the importance of such figures. Bede wrote history, sermons, textbooks, and much else. More than anyone else in his time, he spread historical, Biblical, and chronological knowledge as well as literary criticism. In the process he stimulated interest in history, geography, and science. Consequently, although the literary arts languished in the Early Middle Ages, writing had by no means disappeared.

The prolific publishing of the monasteries in the eleventh century allowed Pope Gregory VII to influence public opinion. He encouraged monks to travel throughout the German Empire to circulate writings that argued on behalf of papal prerogatives and against the schismatic activities of certain German princes.[15] Ironically, the published work that so materially aided the Church against her enemies throughout the Middle Ages became a powerful weapon against her during the Protestant Reformation.

The clerical monopoly on publishing lasted until the thirteenth century when medieval universities became centers of copying. The first efforts at university copying involved the reproduction of lectures. Book suppliers, called *stationarii*, assembled lecture notes into texts and distributed them to students at such centers of learning as the University of Bologna and the University of Paris. No two hand-copied texts were identical, unfortunately, and the accuracy of the information they contained suffered from multiple copyings. Since the texts were composed from students' notes and copied from their wax tablets, many inaccuracies crept in. Students, then as now, frequently misunderstood their lecturers, causing some rather embarrassing misstatements in the published versions of the lectures. The lack of uniformity in texts plagued medieval universities until the introduction of printing.

MOVABLE TYPE

The process begun by the ancient Sumerians culminated in the mid-fifteenth century when a printed sheet was pulled from a printing press in Europe. By 1450, all of the essential ingredients

[15]George Haven Putnam, *Books and Their Makers During the Middle Ages* (New York, 1962), 81-2.

Historians don't know full details about Johann Gutenberg or his work. The idealized painting at left shows him inspecting proofs from his press. In the engraving on the right, the earliest portrait of Gutenberg, he is holding a die of twenty-four letters. The portrait, which may have been an imaginary likeness, first appeared in a book in 1584. Blind and impoverished, he had died in 1468, after forfeiting ownership of his printing system to a creditor, Johann Fust, who got rich printing books and for many years claimed credit as the inventor of printing. Although Gutenberg's biography is not fully known, today he is almost universally credited with inventing printing with movable type.

were at hand to permit the mass production of literature: paper already had largely replaced vellum in manuscripts, the codex had long since replaced the roll as the preferred form for books, and experiments in metallographic printing were under way in France, Holland, and Germany. Metallographic printing, a technique begun about 1430, involved casting a lead printing block or plate from a clay mold. The plate was then inked, and uniform copies could be made. The process, however, produced copies that were frequently illegible. The poor results derived from the irregular manner of impressing each letter die into the clay.

We don't know the full story of Johann Gutenberg, an inventor whose name is associated with the achievement of printing with moveable type. Many of the references to him in history are forgeries, and his name appears nowhere in books claimed to have been printed by him. Most of what is known about him was gleaned from fifteenth-century government and legal records that historians analyzed nearly 300 years after his death. He appears to have been born in Mainz, Germany, around 1395 to an aristocratic family, although court documents indicate he experienced financial problems all his life.

He experimented with printing throughout most of his adulthood, entering into at least two business arrangements related to the topic. It was the second arrangement, a 1450 partnership with Mainz lawyer Johann Fust, that provides historians information about the publishing of Gutenberg's 42-line Bible around 1455. Gutenberg borrowed money from Fust to open his shop and begin printing his great work. A legal dispute occurred between the two as work on the Bibles neared completion, and Fust demanded his money back. Gutenberg was unable to repay the loan, and the court awarded Fust the print shop and printing materials. It is

unclear why Fust demanded repayment of the loan, but historians have posed two possible reasons. The first is that Fust's creditors began insisting he settle his loans. The second is that Fust was an astute businessman who realized that, once printing of the Bibles was complete, Gutenberg would dissolve their partnership and take his printing "secret" with him. But if Gutenberg could not repay his loan, then Fust would own everything, leaving Gutenberg penniless and Fust with a monopoly on printing — and that is exactly what happened. Although Gutenberg continued to work with printing the rest of his life, he achieved neither acknowledgment nor compensation for his innovative work. In his later years he relied on a small pension that a local bishop provided.

While Gutenberg may not have been recognized during his lifetime as the great pioneer in printing, his Bibles were a magnificent success. They were much cheaper to produce and purchase than the standard handwritten Bibles of the time. But exactly how Gutenberg printed his famous Bible is a topic of much speculation. It is generally accepted that Gutenberg (or others) corrected the problems associated with metallographic printing by employing individual metal letters (instead of a whole printing plate) that could be reused in different combinations. By casting a large number of type pieces and sorting these into type cases, a printer merely had to rearrange pieces of type to create a new text. The pieces of type were set in lines or sticks of roughly equal length to form columns of text. Thin strips of lead were placed between columns. The columns were locked into a form called a *matrix* that was then inked. Paper was pressed against the matrix by a device that resembled the grape crusher of the wine maker. In this manner the famous Gutenberg Bible was produced in 1455 or 1456. It had a press run of between 70 and 270 copies. From this modest beginning, the size of press runs grew throughout Europe, and a thousand copies became the norm by 1500. As the rate of book production rose, prices fell, and book publishing became a profitable and international enterprise.

In the first decades following the invention of movable type, an Englishman, William Caxton, took up residence in Germany, where he learned printing. He printed an English translation of the *Recuyell of the Historyes of Troye* (or *History of Troy*) and shipped it to England. It is considered to be the first book printed in English. Caxton, who may have smuggled type into Britain, returned there in 1476 and set up a print shop in London. He issued a number of noteworthy books, including Malory's *Morte d'Arthur* and Chaucer's *Canterbury Tales*. Caxton is important also because his efforts helped to unify England through a common language.

Printing brought with it an end to the monopoly of Church-produced books and made possible the consideration of events and experiences that had previously been ignored. Histories, geographies, biographies, and observations of the physical world replaced the medieval concerns of the spirit. Literacy became widespread in Europe throughout the late Middle Ages. A variety of factors aided reading: the widespread availability of cheaper literature, clear glass windows that allowed the illumination of interior spaces, and the invention of eyeglasses in the seventeenth century. Exposure to new ideas led to a radical transformation in patterns of thought.

Printing also accelerated the Protestant revolt against the authority of the Roman Catholic Church. The Reformation's chief protagonist, Martin Luther, used printing to great advantage, as did his Catholic and Protestant opponents. After he nailed his famous "Ninety Five Theses" denouncing the sale of indulgences on the university church door in Wittenberg in 1517, he had the statement printed and sent to various cities in Germany. His *Address to the Christian Nobility of the German Nation* in 1520 had a circulation of more than 4,000.

The skilled use of movable type — combined with the promulgation of the long-stifled messages of reform in religion, politics, and culture — gives credence to the claim that Luther and his evangelical associates became history's first true mass communicators. The part that women played in the spread of the Reformation also must be noted, as many of them took Luther's doctrine of the priesthood of all believers literally and began to proclaim the Word themselves through devotional works, hymns, and religious poetry. Luther himself believed staunchly in the force of the printed word. Speaking of the power that the spread of the Gospel wielded, he declared in 1522 that "the Word [of God] inflicted greater injury on popery than prince or emperor ever did. I did nothing; the Word did everything." Presaging a "marketplace of ideas" concept that would become popular later in England and America, he observed that "when he [the Devil] sees the Word running and contending alone on the battlefield, then he shudders and shakes for fear. The Word is almighty, and takes captive the hearts."

With Christianity playing a central role in people's lives in the

England's First Printer
William Caxton's *History of Troy* is thought to be the first book printed in English. Caxton learned the printing trade in Germany.

early 1500s, the capacity to print multiple copies of the Bible took on special importance. The cost of individual copies decreased significantly, and reformers could distribute the Scriptures more widely so that access to them was not restricted to the Catholic clergy. With multiple duplication by printing available, reformers began translating the Bible from Hebrew, Greek, and Latin into the common languages of the people. John Wycliffe had translated the New Testament into English by 1382, and Nicholas of Hereford completed the Old Testament translation in 1384. The earliest known printed English version of any part of the Bible was published in 1526 by William Tyndale. The first complete printed version was accomplished by Miles Coverdale in 1535.

For the English-speaking world, of special significance was the translation of the King James Version of the Bible in 1611. Through its prose style, it provided the foundation for a common English language and served as the inspiration for a great part of the body of literature since. Read by millions, it provided the basis not only for religious beliefs but also for nearly every aspect of English and, later, American culture, from ethics and morals to politics and social consciousness.

The division of Europe into Protestant and Catholic areas in the sixteenth century led to attempts by each faction to control the printed word. Protestants and Catholics employed similar methods of censorship. First, they identified certain works as dangerous. Next, the civil government (in both Protestant and Catholic areas of influence) assisted religious authorities in attempts to prevent printing. Lastly, they attempted to control the commerce in books by searches of bookstores and customs inspections of imported books.[16]

Alarmed by the spreading heresy of Protestantism, the Catholic hierarchy was concerned about the possible influence of the printed word. Thus, it attempted to keep the faithful from reading the Bible and the works of Luther and others who challenged Catholic doctrine. In 1564 the papacy issued the *Index of Prohibited Books*. It listed Protestant and heretical religious works, pornography, books on magic and demonology, and certain political works, such as Machiavelli's *The Prince*, which advised authorities to use any means they wanted, rather than accepted standards of moral behavior, to obtain their ends. Catholics were forbidden to read books on the list under threat of severe punishment. The *Index* was updated every fifty years.

FROM LETTERS TO NEWSPAPERS

Europe's ambitious exploration of the world in the fifteenth and sixteenth centuries led to the creation of prosperous mercantile and banking enterprises. One such banking institution, the German house of Fugger, also became known as Europe's foremost newsgathering service. Firms had a need to keep abreast of business news, political intelligence, and other current events. The Fuggers paid correspondents in distant locations to send newsletters back along commercial routes and even across battle lines when necessary. The news was a mix of firsthand observations and rewrites of published material that local correspondents gathered.

The seaport of Venice became an early headquarters for news as a result of its concentration of merchants and bankers. We get our word *gazette* from sixteenth-century Venice. It derives from the Venetian practice of collecting a *gazeta*, a penny or so, from those who wished to hear newsletters read aloud. Printed *gazettes* later replaced the spoken newsletters.

Throughout Europe an insatiable appetite for political news developed after the advent of printing. Balladeers, whose rhymes carried the news before the age of printing, were replaced by broadsides. The broadside was a single news sheet, printed on one side only, with a woodcut illustration on the top half. Below the fold were two columns of text, each begun with large, decorative initials called *swash letters*. Broadsides contained much that is found in the modern newspaper: news, entertainment, and editorials in the form of sermons. Among history's famous broadsides was one in 1493 announcing the results of Columbus' expeditions to the New World. Broadsides were sold by the pile to news hawkers. The hawkers, usually boys, then disposed of them singly by means of loud salesmanship in the streets.

Printed material, however, was too scarce to meet the demand. So Europeans used the most accessible medium — the handwritten newsletter. By the end of the sixteenth century, newsletters had

become a common fixture on the continent. Regular production of newsletters in England, however, had to await the Restoration of the Stuart kings in 1660. The British government itself then became the major publisher. The secretaries of state created their own news service with the aid of a network of diplomatic informants. They collected and disseminated news through postmasters and local officials. In this manner a government monopoly of newsletters prevailed in England until unlicensed newsletters flooded the kingdom in the 1680s.[17]

Another precursor of the newspaper was the news pamphlet, a four-page publication that focused on a single news event. It flourished in Europe and England through the latter part of the sixteenth century. Some pamphlets catered to the public's taste for sensationalism and featured lurid woodcut illustrations designed to entice the prospective purchaser. In 1607 a news pamphlet describing a disastrous flood was printed with the following title:

> A true report of certaine wonderful over-flowings of waters now lately in Summersetshire, Norfolk, and other places in England, destroying many thousands of men, women, and children, overthrowing and bearing downe whole townes and villages, and drowning infinite numbers of sheepe and other cattle.[18]

The pamphlet's dramatic and detailed woodcut showed a cradle with a child in it floating on the water and survivors clinging to trees. Within the narrative of the destruction, the author interspersed pious sayings and scriptural quotations.

The prototype of the modern newspaper was born in Holland in the early seventeenth century. The Dutch tolerated more diversity of expression than other European nations, allowing the development of news media that resembled modern types. By the first decades of the seventeenth century, Amsterdam had become the preeminent news center of the world. The Dutch began publishing *Corantos*, or currents of news, about 1618. These were likely patterned after German and Belgian commercial newsletters, which the Dutch adapted to include a smattering of local news.

The Dutch — not the British — first published an English-language *Coranto*. A news sheet in English, dated December 2, 1620, appeared without a title in Amsterdam. It described a battle near Prague three weeks earlier that led to the start of the Thirty Years War. Printers imitated *Corantos* throughout Europe. In 1621 Thomas Archer published the first *Coranto* in England but was imprisoned for doing so without the government's permission.

In the strict sense, neither the broadside, newsletter, pamphlet, nor *Coranto* could be considered a newspaper. Many were published irregularly, and quite a few failed to survive beyond one issue. A number of them lacked the attribute of timeliness, preferring to deal instead with relatively old matters. Some were simply outright copies of imported newsletters and contained nothing of local interest. Not until 1665 did the English have a news sheet

[16]William Zeisel, ed., *Censorship: 500 Years of Conflict* (New York, 1984), 29-30.

[17]Henry L. Snyder, "Newsletters in England, 1689-1715," in *Newsletters to Newspapers: Eighteenth Century Journalism*, Donovan H. Bond and W. Reynolds McLeod, eds. (Morgantown, W.V., 1977), 4.

[18]Quoted in Mason Jackson, *The Pictorial Press* (London, 1885), 13-4.

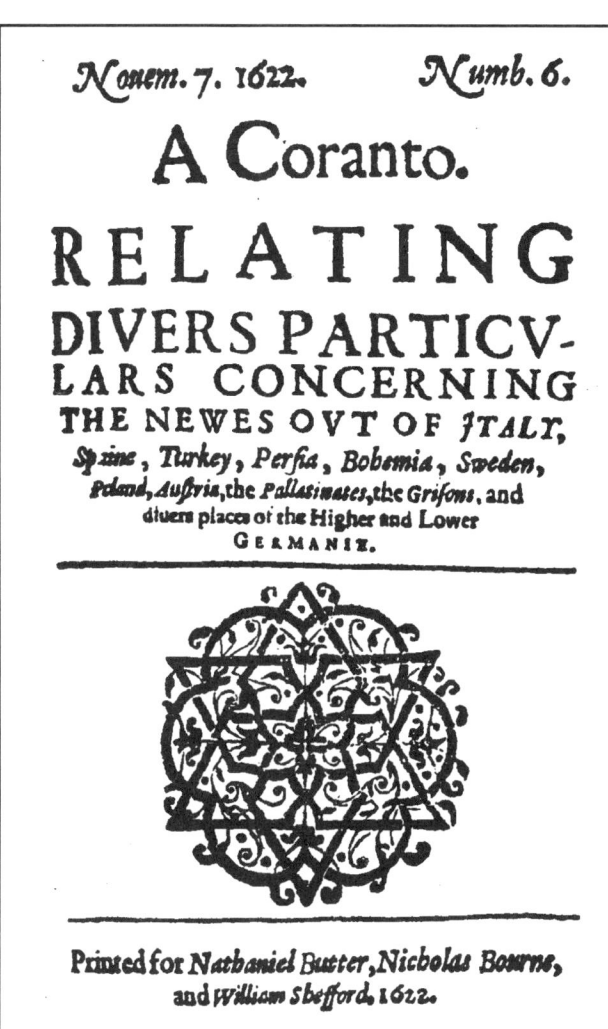

Nonem. 7. 1622.   Numb. 6.

A Coranto.

RELATING

DIVERS PARTICV-
LARS CONCERNING
THE NEWES OVT OF *ITALY*,
Spaine, *Turkey*, *Perfia*, *Bohemia*, *Sweden*,
Poland, *Austria*, the *Pallatinates*, the *Grisons*, and
diuers places of the Higher and Lower
GERMANIE.

Printed for *Nathaniel Butter*, *Nicholas Bourne*,
and *William Sheffard*, 1622.

Corantos
The *Corantos* ("currents of news") of the 1620s were the forerunners of newspapers. Shown above is a typical weekly coranto with serial numbering and dated issues.

that had the characteristics of the modern newspaper.

A semi-weekly newspaper printed on both sides of a single sheet appeared in the university town of Oxford on November 16, 1665. Henry Muddiman was its founder and editor. The Tuesday and Friday paper, the *Oxford Gazette*, was little more than a mouthpiece for the British government. It was published in Oxford only because the plague was ravaging London and much of the government had fled temporarily. In 1666 it became the *London Gazette* when it moved to London and continued publishing government-approved news. The *Gazette*, despite a small circulation and lack of independence, holds the distinction of being England's first newspaper in the modern sense.

The honor of founding England's first daily newspaper, the *Daily Courant*, most likely belongs to a woman. The "E. Mallett" associated with it probably was Elizabeth Mallett. She wrote in the first edition on March 11, 1702: "This Courant (as the title shows) will be publish'd Daily: being design'd to give all the Material News as soon as every Post arrives: and is confin'd to half the

Compass, to save the Public at least half the Impertinences, of ordinary News-Paper."[19] Her association with the paper ceased after two weeks, perhaps because the paper seemed headed for extinction. Samuel Buckley took over and made it a success. The *Courant* was remarkable for its time because it used several techniques practiced by modern journalism: the use of datelines to identify the location and date of news stories, a dedication to objectivity by its avoidance of rumor or gossip, and the clear labeling of opinion and advertising. It lasted thirty-three years.

FROM LICENSING TO LIBERATION

Governmental interference in publishing dates from ancient times when authorities controlled information for purposes of maintaining political or religious orthodoxy. In the English-speaking world, official activities affecting printing and publishing originated under the Tudor monarchs. The first of these sovereigns, Henry VII, who reigned from 1485 to 1509, displayed a shrewd awareness of the power of information. He was among history's early managers of the news, taking extraordinary measures to publish news favorable to himself. He authorized the publication of documents of state and carefully controlled the timing of their publication. That was the case, for example, with his publication of a Papal Bull confirming his own title to the throne. In a sense he became his own publisher of news, frequently circulating information regarding state matters.

His successor, Henry VIII, who ruled from 1509 until his death in 1547, formalized much of the government's interference with the press. After the Church in England was "reformed," the government had considerable authority over it and took over its role as censor. Henry VIII defined heresy, issued censorship rules, and enforced them through the civil authorities. He even issued his own "official" Bible and, along with copies sent to every church in the realm, included instructions that every reader should interpret scripture for himself. Henry VIII inaugurated the system of licensing of the press that lasted until 1695. He created the Court of the Star Chamber, a court that relentlessly prosecuted printers who challenged the authorities. The Crown justified prior censorship by claiming to eliminate heresy and protect local printers from unauthorized competition. A likelier explanation was Henry VIII's desire to maintain control over the printed word for his own political purposes.

Another Tudor, Queen Elizabeth I, who reigned from 1558 to 1603, controlled the press through the Stationers Company. Printers throughout the realm were placed under its jurisdiction a year before she became queen. Government agents censored printed matter, inspected printshops, and kept records on printers' customers, wages, and the number of employees in a printing establishment. The Court of the Star Chamber enforced the laws against unauthorized printing, frequently meting out severe penalties. These included imprisonment, slitting of nostrils, flogging, and even execution in extreme cases.

[19]Quoted in "The London Daily Press," *Westminster Review* 64 (October 1855), 259.

England's First News Periodical

After Parliament in 1641 abolished the Star Chamber, which had restricted the publication of news, *Diurnal Occurences* began publishing the daily proceedings of Parliament. In addition to being the first news periodical produced in England, it also was one of the first periodicals to use illustrations. The woodcut of a session of Parliament, at the top of the page, appeared in several issues.

In the 1600s, though, when news became a feature of English public life, control of the press became more difficult. With its two revolutions and prolonged great struggle between the monarchy and Parliament over the questions of religion and political authority that so charged the age, the seventeenth century stands as the most turbulent one in modern English history. It was also a confusing time for the press. At the beginning of the century, restrictions were so severe that only foreign news along with innocuous news could be printed openly. In 1632 the Court of the Star Chamber, at the request of the Spanish ambassador, prohibited the publication of foreign news. Six years later, however, the publication of foreign news was allowed again, but printers had to wait until 1641 for permission to publish domestic intelligence.

In 1640 the famous Puritan-dominated Long Parliament was summoned. It lasted, in some form, until 1660. On July 5, 1641, the parliamentarians abolished the tyrannical Court of the Star Chamber and the Court of the High Commission, the two main chambers of press control. Five months later *Diurnal Occurences in Parliament* appeared (November 29, 1641). It was a record of daily proceedings intended for weekly publication. It was England's first domestic news periodical.

Other periodical publications soon followed. They were known by various names such as mercuries, passages, intelligences, posts, spies, scouts, etc. Their abundance, along with the variety of pamphlets available in the mid and late seventeenth century, made it an exciting time, if a somewhat unheralded one, in media history.

Notwithstanding some lapses, the government still tried to control the press. Despite the removal of some constraints on printing, the practice of licensing continued. Poet John Milton composed an eloquent denunciation of licensing in 1644 called *Areopagitica* and addressed it to Parliament. His arguments on behalf of free expression did not, however, extend to Roman Catholics or Royalists. After the Cromwellian revolution installed a Puritan government, Milton became a censor for the Puritan regime.

With the restoration of the monarchy in 1660, a period of greater toleration for the press seemed to be close. Indeed, the Licensing Act was allowed to lapse between 1678 and 1682. Nevertheless, the restored Stuart monarch Charles II rejected attempts at toleration after Parliament tried to exclude his brother James from the throne. His confrontation with Parliament, known as the Exclusion Crisis, took place between 1678 and 1681. Although Charles prevailed in the struggle, he took steps afterwards to protect the public from false and misleading information. For that reason successive governments in late seventeenth-century England wished to control the press. They also hoped to gain political advantage by doing so. Licensing, therefore, returned.

All publications, however, were not licensed. Secret, unlicensed publishing of pamphlets and broadsides was common in London. Thomas Babington Macauley, that great British historian of the nineteenth century, described the activities of those who courted disaster by breaking the law:

> There had long lurked in the garrets of London a class of printers who worked steadily at their calling with precautions resembling those employed by coiners and forgers. Women were on the watch to give the alarm by their screams if an officer appeared near the workshop. The press was immediately pushed into a closet behind the bed; the types were flung into the coalhole, and covered with cinders; the compositor disappeared through a trapdoor in the roof, and made off over the tiles of the neighboring houses. In these dens were manufactured treasonable works of all classes and sizes, from half-penny broadsides of doggerel verse up to massy quartos filled with Hebrew quotations.[20]

The Licensing Act also promoted corruption. The Stationers Company, which was legally empowered to send government agents to search houses and printers' shops for unlicensed books, sometimes extorted money from publishers who feared prosecution.

While the Licensing Act was in force, the only newspaper in England was the government's own *London Gazette*. It provided readers only with news filtered through the secretary of state's office. A number of periodicals were published; but lacking current

[20]Thomas Babington Macaulay, *History of England* (1881), Vol. 3: 520.

John Milton and John Locke
The Puritan John Milton (left) wrote *Areopagitica*, that great statement endorsing freedom of discussion, because leaders refused to allow him to circulate a pamphlet on the merits of divorce. *Areopagitica* is one of the most ringing endorsements of free speech ever written, but it is important to note that the core of its argument lay in religious doctrine, not in a political one of free expression. Protestants distinguished themselves from Catholics by claiming broader toleration of dissenting opinion and noted that, for example, it was the Catholic church that had the infamous *Index* of banned books. Milton was Protestant, as was every member of the British House of Commons, for whom he wrote *Areopagitica*. The English philosopher John Locke (right), drawing on his understanding of the individual's right to interpret Scripture, argued that individuals also had the authority to determine the nature of government. That idea served as the basis for the Whig approach to representative government and lay at the heart of the American Declaration of Independence and, indirectly, of American notions on freedom of the press.

news, they were not newspapers in the modern sense. Following the political upheaval known as the Glorious Revolution of 1688-1689, with a newly passed Bill of Rights in force, newspapers began to appear in greater numbers. Finally, licensing and censorship ceased in 1695. That did not mean, however, that the government's desire to influence, and to some extent control, the press vanished. It had not, but other means had to be found to implement that desire. In the eighteenth century a number of devices would be used beginning with the Stamp Tax on newspapers and pamphlets that was passed in 1712.

The liberation of expression came slowly. A number of developments combined to assist in the process: the gradual weakening of medieval notions of absolutism of the power of rulers, the rise of the parliamentary system, the emergence of a middle class in Europe, the rise of Protestantism and of science, and an increasing awareness that the search for truth requires free access to knowledge.

Censorship lost legitimacy during the intellectual revolution called the Enlightenment. Begun in Europe about 1680, the Enlightenment strengthened the notion of individual freedom. Of particular importance to freedom of the press was the work of the Protestant philosopher John Locke. Two of his works, *A Letter Concerning Toleration* (1689) and *Two Treatises on Government* (1690),

stimulated the growth of the spirit of toleration in England and established premises of argument that could be used against press restrictions.

His writings condemned absolutism in any form. His ideas on limited government became a foundation for the liberal political tradition that so influenced English politics in ensuing centuries. They also found favor with some thinkers and leaders across the Atlantic. John Adams, Thomas Jefferson, and other leaders of the American Revolutionary generation, for instance, shared Locke's hatred of tryanny and distrust of government.

The American notion of press freedom derives, in large part, from the link from Locke to America's revolutionary leaders. Although they lived a century and an ocean apart, Locke's work profoundly influenced them. Thus British libertarian ideals concerning the press came to be embodied in our founding documents through the pen of Jefferson and his contemporaries.

RECOMMENDED READINGS

BOOKS

Bjerken, Mildred Prica. *Medieval Paris: The Town of Books*. Metuchen, N.J., 1973. Book production is explained by describing text copying by professional scribes before Gutenberg and publishing by printers afterwards. This book is essential for understanding the role of the medieval university in publishing.

Bond, Donovan H., and McLeod, W. Reynolds, eds. *Newsletters to Newspapers: Eighteenth Century Journalism*. Morgantown, W.V., 1977. This book contains helpful information about newsletters in England in the late seventeenth and early eighteenth centuries.

Brasch, Walter M., and Dana R. Ulloth. *The Press and the State: Sociohistorical and Contemporary Interpretations*. Lanham, Md., 1986. The authors summarize 5,000 years of the tension that exists between the press and government, with political philosophy and freedom of the press being major components.

Cahill, Joseph. *How the Irish Saved Civilization*. New York, 1995. The Christianized Irish founded the monastic movement and then preserved and copied books that Germanic invaders destroyed.

Diringer, David. *Writing*. New York, 1962. Concentrating on ancient peoples and places, this is a complete tracing of the origins and development of writing.

Doblhofer, Ernst. *Voices in Stone*. New York, 1984. This book is a lucid explanation of what writing is. It is valuable for relating the form of writing to the kind of society that produced it.

Eisenstein, Elizabeth L. *The Printing Press as an Agent of Change*. Cambridge, England, 1980. Published in two volumes, this book provides a detailed explanation of the ways in which printing affected European civilization between 1400-1700, focusing on printing's impact on the Renaissance, the Reformation, and the Scientific Revolution.

Febvre, Lucien, and Henri-Jean Martin. *The Coming of the Book: The Impact of Printing, 1450-1800*, 3rd ed. London, England, 2010. This book is a scholarly treatise on the historical and technological development of books and their ramifications for the social and ideological issues that confronted Western Europe.

Gelb, I.J. *A Study of Writing*. Chicago, 1963. This book is especially useful for tracing the evolution of the alphabet and writing.

Havelock, Eric A., and Hershbell, Jackson P., eds. *Communication Arts in the Ancient World*. New York, 1978. The book is an excellent and interesting collection of articles on Greek and Roman innovations and practices in writing, poetry, and propaganda. It includes an article on the ancient telegraph of the Greeks.

Hoe & Co., R. *A Short History of the Printing Press and of the Improvements in Printing Machinery from the Time of Gutenberg up to the Present Day*. New York, 1902. A story of technological improvements, this book is compiled and published by the leading manufacturer of printing presses.

Ingelhart, Louis Edward. *Press Freedoms: A Descriptive Calendar of Concepts, Inter-*

pretations, Events, and Court Actions, from 4000 B.C. to the Present. Westport, Conn., 1987. The author presents an encyclopedia of events and quotations about freedom of the press arranged in chronological order.

Jackson, Mason. *The Pictorial Press: Its Origin and Progress.* London, 1885. (Republished in 1968 by Gale Research Co., Detroit). This book is a valuable classic work on the use of illustrations in early newspapers and broadsides. It contains 150 woodcuts and other engravings from British news publications beginning in the sixteenth century.

Jensen, Hans. *Sign, Symbol and Script.* New York, 1969. This translation from the German attempts to give several sides of scholarly disputes relating to the development of writing. It is lavishly illustrated with line art and photographs.

Kapr, Albert. *Johann Gutenberg: the Man and his Invention*, 3rd ed. Aldershot, England, 1996. This classic biography uses documentary evidence in collaboration with an understanding of cultural and political life in the mid-1400s to evaluate Gutenberg and his impact on printing.

McKitterick, Rosamund. *The Carolingians and the Written Word.* Cambridge, 1989. Literacy and writing were central to the Carolingian culture in the eighth and ninth centuries.

McLuhan, Marshall. *The Gutenberg Galaxy: The Making of Typographic Man.* Toronto, Canada, 1962. The invention of moveable type changed the ways in which people related to each other, including inducing the rise of nationalism, rationalism, and feelings of isolation and alienation.

Morrison, Stanley. *The English Newspaper: Some Account of the Physical Development of Journals Printed in London Between 1622 and the Present Day.* Cambridge, 1932. This is a well researched, illustrated book that historians continue to value.

Nibley, Hugh. *Temple and Cosmos: Beyond This Ignorant Present.* Salt Lake City, 1992. The chapter "Genesis of the Written Word" provides a strong argument for the view that writing originated quickly rather than through a long evolutionary process.

Norman, James. *Ancestral Voices.* New York, 1975. An excellent description of literary archaeology, this book provides a wealth of archaeological information about man's earliest efforts to write.

Oswald, John Clyde. *A History of Printing: Its Development Through Five Hundred Years.* New York, 1928. This is a narrative, encyclopedic account of printing after 1450, with the bulk of attention devoted to Europe.

Putnam, George Haven. *Books and Their Makers during the Middle Ages.* New York, 1962. A reprint of the 1886 edition. This book covers the production and distribution of literature from the fall of Rome to the close of the seventeenth century. It includes detailed descriptions of monks working in scriptoria.

Schramm, Wilbur. *The Story of Human Communication: Cave Painting to Microchip.* New York, New York, 1988. Schramm, a communication theorist, traces the development of communication from the beginning to computers, with the first part of his book exploring the origins of cave paintings, language, and writing.

Wright, Curtis. *The Oral Antecedents of Greek Librarianship.* Provo, Utah, 1977. Writing originated in a creative, inspired process rather than through a long evolutionary period.

Zeisel, William. *Censorship: 500 Years of Conflict.* New York, 1984. This book was published for an exhibition on censorship. It is a richly illustrated series of essays detailing the struggle against authority.

ARTICLES

Basso, K. H., and Ned Anderson. "A Western Apache Writing System: The Symbols of Silas John." *Science* (June 1973): 1013-22. This article provides evidence of the inspired creation of a primitive writing system among American Indians in the early 1900s.

Giffard, C. A. "Ancient Rome's Daily Gazette." *Journalism History* 2 (1975-76): 106-9, 132. This is one of the best sources of information on Rome's lively daily newspaper, the *Acta Diurna*.

Mooradian, Karlen. "The Dawn of Printing." *Journalism Monographs* 23 (1972). The author pulls together archaeological evidence to explain the origins of printing. It concentrates on the stamp seal and cylinder seal of ancient Sumer.

Schmandt-Besserat, Denise. "An Archaic Recording System Prior to Writing." In *5000 Years of Popular Culture*, ed. Fred E. H. Schroeder. Bowling Green, Ohio, 1980. This illustrated article provides evidence that the Sumerians arrived at a system of writing early because their record-keeping was patterned after an already existing system.

West, Louis C. "Imperial Publicity on Coins of the Roman Emperors." *Classical Journal* 45 (October 1949): 19-26. The author details how Roman emperors used the empire's monetary system for propaganda purposes.

2

Printing in America
1600 – 1690

So far as Europeans were concerned, printing appeared in the middle of a long and rich historical timeline. European cultures were well-rooted, steeped in an intellectual history that included a variety of forms of communication such as storytelling, ballad-singing, and the painstaking copying of manuscripts by hand. The printing press interrupted and forever altered the character of European intellectual life, but nevertheless the press came to a Europe that already had an intellectual identity. In its own way, the press had to adapt to serve what already existed. Although well received, it was a modern convenience that had to weave its way into the thick texture of European life.

But that was Europe. America was a different place altogether. Unlike the nations of the Old World, Anglo-America grew up with the printing press. From the very start of European America, the printed word was on hand to persuade, offer opinion, influence, cajole, entertain, inform, enlighten, chastise, guide, and inspire the mass audience. The printing press did not have to work its way into the history of Anglo-America. Instead, Anglo-America worked its way into history by making great use of the press.

That simple fact had a long and indelible effect on the character of the New World and its inhabitants. Without the printed word, European North America would not have begun quite as it did. The printed word coaxed people to the New World, helped guide them here, and gave their presence here a sense of legitimacy and mission. The printed word served as a vital link to Europe in the effort to remake America in the European image. Yet it also helped give Americans an identity different from Europeans by encouraging and spreading concepts that were not the norm in Europe. As transplanted Europeans carved out a new civilization in the wilderness, the printed word helped transform them into Americans.

In the sixteenth and seventeenth centuries, speechmakers and preachers could conceivably reach large audiences, but their words were not readily transportable across time and space to a mass audience. Copyists could write messages in manuscript form, but the human hand can only make so many copies before it must rest. All in all, the cheapest and most convenient way to overcome the constraints of time, space, and human stamina on communication was to use the printed word. The new arrivals in America understood that fact. When they arrived in the New World, they were already accustomed to using the printing press to ease the burdens of communication. They had long enjoyed the printed word for information, enlightenment, and inspiration. They would continue to employ the press to meet those needs, and in so doing they would unconsciously allow the press to help define an America that was different than Europe. Although the first settlers in Anglo-America did not bring a press with them, they had no doubts as to the power and usefulness of the printed word. In fact, many of them had been recruited to America by the printed word.

PRINTING AND COLONIZATION

The earliest American printed literature was not American at all. It came from European presses and had European readers — but nevertheless it was vital to the success and prosperity of the American colonies. During the period of American settlement, promoters and developers flooded Europe with a sea of printed material — pamphlets, books, tracts, flyers, newspaper articles, and anything else they could think of — to reach anyone who might be interested in undertaking or backing American colonization. Through an array of promotional literature, the printing press helped reach a wide variety of readers — wealthy, poor; servant class, merchant class; English, French, Swiss, German; Catholic, Protestant; highly educated, barely educated. Some promoters had a financial stake in the colonization of the region; others had a patriotic interest in seeing their own nation establish colonies or in advancing their religion. For still others, the issue was survival, pure and simple.

The desperate colonial leader of the French community of Charlesfort fell into the "survival" category. In 1562, Commander Jean Ribault and his band of French Huguenots were struggling to establish a home, safe from religious persecution, in Spanish Florida. The community was dying for want of supplies. Starvation

Thomas Hariot

Thomas Hariot was a scientist and explorer in early Virginia who helped issue *A briefe and true report* on the place in 1590. He wrote the text of the book, while his colleague John White drew stunning pictures of American Indians and their towns, as well as of the land's flora and fauna. Hariot wrote in glowing terms of the possibility of converting the Indians to Christianity, a theme that would persist in early American thought. Writers such as Hariot were important in the campaign to persuade Europeans to emigrate to America, but every bit as important were artists such as White, who could depict the strange land in rich detail.

and disease were rampant. In a last-ditch effort to save the distressed colony, Ribault turned to the press. He wrote a book about his adventures in Florida, and in the spring of 1563 he was in England to peddle the work in hopes that it would win financial friends for Charlesfort. The effort was a failure, but the book did have a greater effect. It got Englishmen, who hitherto had been interested only in colonizing Canada, to begin looking at the southern areas around Florida.[1]

Although Ribault failed to raise funds for his colony, his book was one of the first in the mass media of American settlement. The printed word was the lure, the promise, the "official" word about a place so far away that it had been unknown to Europeans a mere seventy years before Charlesfort. Because the mysterious land across the Atlantic could be made thrilling and promising in the pages of books and pamphlets and broadsides, Europeans could begin to discern new opportunities there.

One of the most important promotional writers was the English preacher Richard Hakluyt, who recognized the value of publishing tales that mariners brought back from their voyages. As far as the patriotic Hakluyt was concerned, if England were to build an empire, she had to do it by spreading the gospel of geography. Hakluyt's work featured numerous enthusiastic accounts of far-off lands, such as one from American adventurer Ralph Lane. "[Virginia] is the goodliest and most pleasing Territorie of the world: for the continent is of an huge and unknowen greatnesse...," Lane wrote for Hakluyt. "[I]f Virginia had but horses and kine [cattle] in some reasonable proportion, I dare assure my selfe being inhabited with English, no realme in Christendome were comparable to it." In a lush piece of boosterism, Lane pointed out that the enjoyable, exotic products of other nations — wines, oils, flax, rosins, pitch, frankincense, currants, and sugar — could be cultivated in Virginia.[2]

Hakluyt was not the only author who peddled the romance of Virginia. In 1590, engraver Theodore de Bry teamed up with artist John White and writer Thomas Hariot to issue a sensationally beautiful, eye-catching tract promoting America. The heavily engraved cover featured the book's title, *A briefe and true report*, framed by a beckoning doorway, beautifully drawn Indians, and bountiful American produce. Inside, engravings that de Bry made from John White's expert drawings depicted the natives of Virginia in stunning detail. Hariot, for his part, discussed the commodities of Virginia and the habits of her people. As publisher of the work, de Bry made sure the book reached a huge European audience. He published it in English, French, German, and Latin.

Despite the glowing nature of reports in books such as Hakluyt's and de Bry's, the first colonists found conditions more like those in Charlesfort than the comfortable beauty depicted in de Bry's engravings. By 1611 it was well known that the natives and the colonists of Virginia's Jamestown were not getting along happily. In the face of negative public sentiment, writers of American promotional literature redoubled their efforts to make the place look attractive and safe. The governor of the fledgling Virginia plantation, Lord De-La-Warre, scrambled to counteract ugly rumors by publishing a glowing report of Virginia's fertility and possibilities.[3] Five years later, adventurer John Smith published a detailed book designed to promote America as a satisfying, safe, prosperous alternative to Europe for people from all walks of life. The work, titled *A Description of New England*, spoke to the common man. Smith wrote:

> And here [in New England] are no hard Landlords to racke us with high rents, or extorted fines to consume us, no tedious pleas in law to consume us with their many years disputations

---

[1]Alan Smith, ed., *Virginia 1584-1607: The First English Settlement in North America* (Boston, 1957), xvii-xix. Charlesfort was located at present-day Beaufort, South Carolina.

[2]Richard Hakluyt the younger, *The Principal Navigations, Voiages, Traffiques & Discoveries of the English Nation*, vol. I (originally published between 1589 and 1599; reprint, New York, 1927); also, Ralph Lane to Richard Hakluyt, 3 September 1585, in "An extract of Master Ralph Lanes letter" in Hakluyt, vol. VI, 140.

[3]*The Relation of the Right Honourable the Lord De-La-Warre, Lord Governour and Captaine Generall of the Colonie, planted in Virginea* (London, printed by William Hall for William Welbie, 1611), reprinted in Lyon Gardiner Tyler, ed., *Narratives of Early Virginia, 1606-1625* (New York, 1907), 200-14.

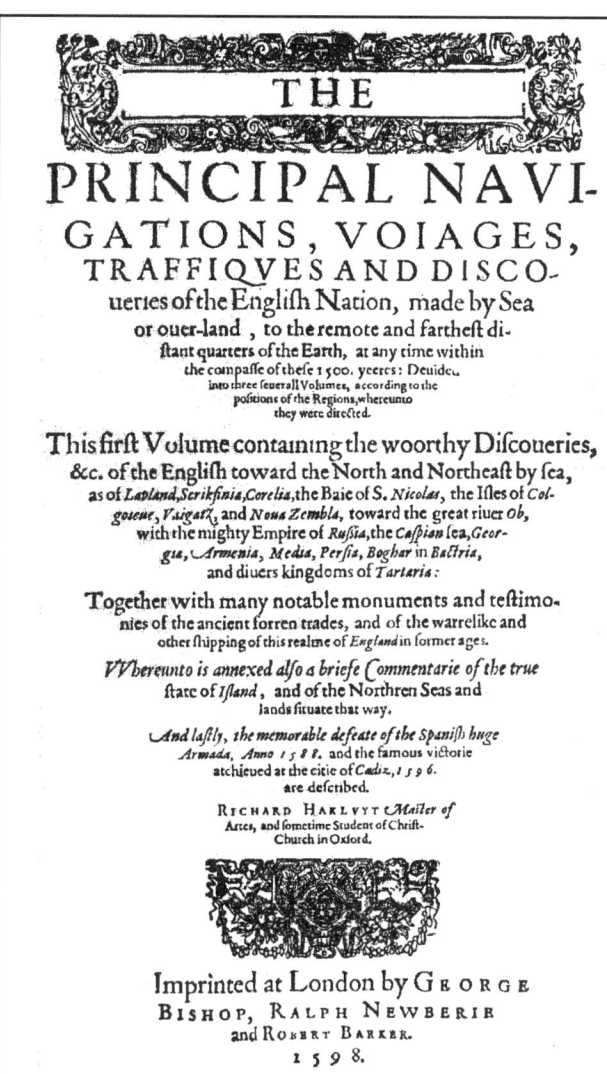

THE

PRINCIPAL NAVI-
GATIONS, VOIAGES,
TRAFFIQVES AND DISCO-
ueries of the Englifh Nation, made by Sea
or ouer-land , to the remote and fartheft di-
ftant quarters of the Earth, at any time within
the compaffe of thefe 1500. yeeres: Deuidc.
into three feuerall Volumes, according to the
pofitions of the Regions, whereunto
they were directed.

Thisfirft Volume containing the woorthy Difcoueries,
&c. of the Englifh toward the North and Northeaft by fea,
as of Lapland, Scrikfinia, Corelia, the Baie of S. Nicolas, the Ifles of Col-
gotene, Vaigatz, and Noua Zembla, toward the great riuer Ob,
with the mighty Empire of Ruffia, the Caffian fea, Georgia, Armenia, Media, Perfia, Boghar in Bactria,
and diuers kingdoms of Tartaria :

Together with many notable monuments and teftimo-
nies of the ancient forren trades, and of the warrelike and
other fhipping of this realme of England in former ages.

VVhereunto is annexed alfo a briefe Commentarie of the true
ftate of Ifland , and of the Northren Seas and
lands fituate that way.

And laftly, the memorable defeate of the Spanifh huge
Armada, Anno 1588. and the famous victorie
atchieued at the citie of Cadiz, 1596.
are defcribed.

RICHARD HAKLVYT Mafter of
Artes, and fometime Student of Chrift-
Church in Oxford.

Imprinted at London by GEORGE
BISHOP, RALPH NEWBERIE
and ROBERT BARKER.
1598.

Promoting Emigration
In promoting British settlement abroad, Richard Hakluyt recognized
the value of publishing tales that mariners brought back to England
from their voyages. His work, like this 1598 edition of one of his
books, featured enthusiastic accounts of far-off lands.

for justice.... [H]ere every [man] may be master and owner of his
own labour and land; or the greatest part in a small time. If hee
have nothing but his hands, he may set up his trade: and by
industrie quickly grow rich....

POPULAR PUBLICITY

The technique of printed publicity proved popular. The founders
of Maryland created a promotional book that offered a starter's kit
for settlement. If a Maryland immigrant were wealthy enough to
support an indentured servant, he need only clip and fill in a pre-
printed blank indenture contract bound into the book. Likewise,
the book included a clip-and-use bill of lading form for shipping
goods across the Atlantic — and it suggested exactly what a settler
needed to include on that bill in the way of food, clothes, bedding,

arms, tools, and household goods.[4]

Other works targeted the lower socio-economic classes, painting America as a Promised Land. John Hammond, in a 1656 work
titled *Leah and Rachel*, spoke to people who might go to the Mary-
land/Virginia area as servants. He contrasted life in Virginia with
life in the poor homes of England. He interviewed a destitute and
pathetic English fagot seller, whose desperate existence made the
hardships of America seem absolutely rosy. Hammond's persuasive intent was obvious: the poor of England were foolish if they
didn't opt for work in America.

Promotional materials sought people of many nationalities and
religious backgrounds. Even more importantly, people from many
of these diverse groups heeded the call to emigrate. That fact produced an interesting population mix in America. A wide variety of
people arrived on the continent and created a basis for the plural-
istic nature of the American populace. That mixture of people
would lay the foundations for democracy. People of lower-class
means in Europe could make a decent living and occasionally a-
mass a fortune in America. The sense that a comfortable life was
available to anyone who was willing to work hard tended to di-
minish the chance that America would build its social structure on
a strict class society, as much of Europe had. The promotional literature of the colonization era helped develop a population tolerant of such an idea.

AMERICAN SETTLERS AS READERS

The earliest American settlers were readers. For good reason, it is
hard to name an exact literacy rate for the settlers who moved
from Europe to America. The new continent was harsh, wild, difficult; and at first no one was able to measure literacy or to set up
institutions centered on literacy. Amenities such as schools were
secondary to more pressing needs such as clearing land for homes
and fields, growing crops for survival, and fending against Native
Americans. Those difficulties, it would seem, would also stymie
intellectual pursuits in the colonies, and no doubt that is partially
true. However, a great many American immigrants of all walks of
life were literate and were involved in reading.

Time and time again in diaries and letters, newcomer Americans mentioned bringing printed material with them across the
ocean. Some brought only the Bible; but others clutched pamphlets, maps, and other printed material. Some brought pamphlets as entertainment for the six- to eight-week voyage across
the Atlantic. Many of them religiously packed supplies necessary
for starting a new life in America by following guidelines listed in
printed tracts. Missionaries came armed with religious texts. Governors came with books necessary to the smooth operation of their
colony.

American immigrants of many social ranks were literate. Literature of the day that described America was not aimed only at so-
called "educated" classes. Tracts, pamphlets, and books about the

[4] *A Relation of Maryland; together with a Map of the Countrey* (London, 1635), reprinted in
Clayton Colman Hall, ed., *Narratives of Early Maryland* (New York, 1925), 76-7, 99-100.

New World were written to entice every level of society, from the servant class to the working class to the merchant class to the extremely rich. They advised readers of the need for individuals as diverse as farmers and haberdashers in America. Authors expected that people from varied occupations and from different socio-economic classes would be both literate and interested in reading the tracts.

Once in America, settlers sent frequent requests to Europe for books, pamphlets, and the latest newspapers. Likewise, it was a time-honored tradition in some families to meet arriving ships to seek the latest printed outpouring of Europe, even though the ships had been weeks in crossing the Atlantic. The Byrd family of Virginia met ships in that manner for generations. A passage from a letter by William Byrd I illustrates how far Americans would go to obtain books from Europe. Byrd had hosted an English traveler at his Virginia plantation in the late 1600s. The two struck a deal: the Englishman would send back much desired books if the Virginian would first send something uniquely American for the traveler's little boy. Byrd sent off his half of the bargain with this reminder, which proved not only that he had a deep desire to read, but also that children have not changed much since 1686, when the letter was written:

> According to your desire I have herewith sent you an Indian habitt for your boy, the best I could procure amongst our neighbor Indians. There is a flap or belly clout 1 pair of stockings & 1 pair mocosins or Indian shoes allso some shells to put about his necke and a cap of wampum.... These things are put up in an Indian baskett, directed as you desired, and there are bow & arrows tyed to itt.... I therefore intreat you to send mee a treatise or two [on] minerall & stones the fittest you find for my purpose either of Mr. Boyles or any other English author, allso Salmons Polygraphice the last edition.[5]

The earliest Americans indeed valued the printed word as a form of connection to Europe, as a pastime, and as a carrier of vital information.

God's Word for Indians

One of the potential conflicts in European colonization of America was, of course, the presence of a Native American population that already had towns, crops, and an established culture of its own in the regions targeted for settlement. The natives were a mystery and a great curiosity to Europeans, who had to learn to negotiate and trade with the Indians in order to establish colonies. Sometimes the relationship with the natives was cordial. In other cases, Indians and Europeans clashed bitterly. As they came into contact with the Native Americans, colonists naturally noticed their cultural habits, which were fascinatingly different from the European way of life. The Indian religion was particularly intriguing. Eu-

John Smith
An adventurer and promoter, John Smith was a swashbuckling figure. Famous for his story of being saved from death by the young Pocahontas, his *Generall Historie of Virginia* discussed many other threats to his life as well as his own heroism that helped subdue the Indians, thus opening Virginia to European settlement. He enthusiastically promoted settlement in both Virginia and New England, shrewdly appealing to a wide variety of Europeans either to finance or to undertake colonization. He assured would-be colonists of the great wealth that America had to offer.

ropeans in general saw it as devil-worship; and that sparked a widespread, passionate fervor to convert the natives to Christianity.

Although the perception of the Indians' spiritual life as a form of demonic worship was misguided, the European settlers' zeal in offering salvation to the Indians was genuine. In pamphlet after pamphlet, the conversion of the "heathen Indians" was put forth as an important goal that would bring an entire race of people to eternal salvation. The desire to convert had some of its roots in Protestants' political need to keep Catholic Spain from bringing the Indians under Spanish rule, and the Spanish had similar aversions to Native Americans becoming a force for Protestantism. Aside from that fact, tracts touting the conversion of natives in America exhibited an honest belief in Christianity as the only way for Indians to find salvation. That evangelistic fervor played into many Europeans' desire to emigrate for their own religious freedom. Truly, America was the land of religious opportunity — Christians of various sects could practice their religion in peace there, and they could at the same time serve God and help the natives by guiding them to true religion.

That idea proved alluring to many settlers. As a pamphlet tout-

[5]William Byrd I to John Clayton, 25 May 1686, in Marion Tinling, ed., *The Correspondence of the Three William Byrds of Westover, Virginia, 1684-1776,* vol. I (Charlottesville, Va., 1977), 61-2.

ing early Carolina explained to readers, the Europeans settling in America might help convert "those poor Indians."[6] That sentiment was typical. A treasury of other tracts sounded the same theme, often in identical words. Convinced by sermon, zeal, and pamphlet, Christian Europeans were ready to show Native Americans how to worship God in order to win spiritual salvation, how to clothe themselves modestly as the Bible required, and how to give up their form of dancing and other heathenish activities.

Therefore, missionaries and ordinary settlers arrived in America with all sorts of religious tracts and books — and, of course, the Bible — to be used in the conversion effort. The printed word was something Native Americans did not have, but they quickly perceived how important it was to the newcomers. A Virginia tribal chief named Wamanto was taken with Englishman John Smith's copy of the Bible. "Hee much wondered at our Bible, but much more to heare it was the Law of our God," Smith recalled in 1624. Smith discussed Genesis with Wamanto, who likened himself to Adam in that he had only one wife at a time. A pleased Smith recorded that the chief seemed ready to learn more about the Bible. To Smith, Indians such as Wamanto proved that the printed word could attract and convert Indians to Christianity.[7]

The Puritans of New England felt a deep commitment to converting the Native American population. As great believers in the printed word and as shrewd employers of the latest technology, they imported their own press in 1638 and set it up for the zealous work of spreading the Gospel among themselves and among the unconverted, both in the European and Native American populations. The press, installed at Harvard College in Cambridge, Massachusetts, had other uses, too. The government issued documents to the public via the press, for example, and education officials used it. Far and away, though, the Puritans used their press most often to produce religious works.

Some of the Puritans' most dramatic evangelistic work featured the energetic John Eliot. He eagerly learned the Indians' language and began the task of converting them to Christianity. Some Indians even formed their own Christian churches and began training for European-style jobs, including printing. Eliot's impressive work, which played a major role in Christianizing American Indians, won much admiration among Englishmen, who read about it in Thomas Shepard's pamphlet, *The Clear Sunshine of the Gospel breaking forth upon the Indians in New England*. That publication and others like it had their intended effect. Amazed after reading about the conversion of Indians, Parliament agreed to incorporate the Company for Propagating the Gospel in New England, an organization dedicated to further evangelizing Indians by producing a Bible for them in their own language. The company underwrote the cost of the Bible, furnishing paper and paying the printers.

John Eliot
John Eliot, a graduate of Cambridge University, migrated to New England in 1631 at the age of twenty-seven. After deciding to become a minister, he began to preach to native Algonquin tribes and learned their language within a year. His translation of the Bible into Algonquin became the first book to be printed in America. He planted fourteen towns for Indian converts with the purpose of helping them keep their own culture, language, and laws. Eventually, the towns' total population grew to several thousand.

THE INDIAN BIBLE: FIRST AMERICAN BOOK

It was only natural that Eliot be appointed to the painstaking task of translating the Bible into the language of the Algonquin Indian tribe. The work was a historic achievement in American printing. It was the first Bible printed in America, with the New Testament published in 1661 and the Old Testament in 1663. In fact, by many people's reckoning, it was the first actual book printed in Anglo-America, although admittedly many pamphlets of the day were loosely called "books."

Such an amazing American achievement was irrepressibly attractive. Word spread quickly to Europe of such a wonder, capturing the imagination of religious-minded Europeans all across the continent. Copies of the Indian Bible found their way to European libraries, and stories of the work remained alive over decades. The Dutch traveler Jasper Danckaerts heard of it in Europe nearly twenty years after its publication, and he was eager to buy the book when he visited America in 1680. He and a friend searched

---

[6]Edward Bland, Abraham Wood, Sackford Brewster, and Elias Pennant, *The Discovery of new Brittaine, Began August 27, Anno Dom., 1650*, reprinted in Alexander S. Salley, Jr., ed., *Narratives of Early Carolina, 1650-1708* (New York, 1911), 6.

[7]Captain John Smith, *The Generall Historie of Virginia, New England & The Summer Isles* (1624), reprinted in Smith, *Virginia 1584-1607*, 347-8, 352..

Indian Bible
John Eliot's translation of the Bible into the language of the Algonquins was the first book printed in America. The New Testament appeared in 1661 and the Old Testament in 1663. Together, they were credited with helping to Christianize 24,000 Indians.

Boston booksellers in vain for a copy and resolved to seek out Reverend Eliot himself, a 45-minute ride away in Roxbury, Massachusetts. Persisting until they located the minister, the Dutch travelers discovered that they could not communicate with him. He did not speak Dutch, and they could only speak broken English. The three managed to find a common ground: they were able to converse in Latin. Eliot told them that he had converted a number of Indians to Christianity but that unconverted Indians despised the Bible and all that it stood for. The words it contained had begun destroying their religion, their worship, their gods. Hating the book, they had carried away all copies of Eliot's Bible in a recent war. Undaunted, Eliot was in the process of printing a second edition so that distribution and conversion could continue. Not wanting to disappoint religious men who had come so far to see the phenomenon of a Bible written in Algonquin, Eliot gave Danckaerts his own copy of the first edition.[8]

European diseases and gunpowder played a big part in reduc-

ing the Native American population, but the role of printed material cannot be overlooked as one factor in subduing Indian culture. Publications pleading with Europeans to convert the Indians not only gave many settlers a mission but also helped plant the idea that God had singled the American continent as a place worthy of His best graces, a place that was blessed for the service of God. That notion would grow in years to come, fueled by many factors — but the idea that European settlers could offer Native Americans eternal salvation was a push in that direction.

PREVENTING FALSE REPORTS

Jasper Danckaerts was pleased by his copy of the Indian Bible, but otherwise he was frequently displeased with his trip to America. Even the map he was using to find his way around was incorrect! It had been printed and bound into a highly respected atlas, but Danckaerts fumed because it was full of inaccuracies. He made careful corrections and sought out the mapmaker when he returned to Holland. He felt that it was imperative that the man make changes before any more incorrect editions of the atlas fell into other travelers' hands.[9]

Danckaerts was not the only American traveler or settler who was surprised by the inaccuracies in literature about America. A large number of colonists left behind diaries, letters, and printed matter complaining that tracts about the New World, particularly promotional ones, were exaggerated or even false. Although some readers did, indeed, find America to be similar to the dazzling descriptions of it, it is a safe guess to say that few found the magical America that promotional tracts had described. Settlement literature, written somewhat like advertisements of today, had a hyperbolic quality that led many eager readers astray. As a trader named Christopher Levett said in a 1628 pamphlet seeking to undo the damage done by exaggerated promotional literature:

And to say something of the Countrey [America]: I will not doe therein as some have done, to my knowledge speak more than is true: I will not tell you that you may smell the corne fields before you see the Land, neither must men thinke that the corne doth grow naturally (or on trees,) nor will the *Deare* come when they are called, or stand still and looke on a man, untill he shute him, not knowing a man from a beast, nor the fish leap into the kettle, nor on the drie Land, neither are they so plentifull, that you may dipp them up in baskets, nor take *Codd* in netts to make a voyage, which is no truer: then that the fowles will present themselves, to you with spitts through them.[10]

Levett had heard false *good* reports that needed correcting, but most writers who hastened to press over false reports wanted to counteract some negative image. When New England settlers

[8]Journal entry of 8 July 1680 by Jasper Danckaerts, in Bartlett Burleigh James and J. Franklin Jameson, eds., *Journal of Jasper Danckaerts, 1679-1680* (New York, 1934; translated from the Dutch edition of 1687 by Henry C. Murphy in 1867), 264. The first edition of the Indian Bible was begun in 1660.

[9]Journal entry of 10 October 1680 by Danckaerts in ibid., 297.
[10]Christopher Levett, *My Discovery of divers Rivers and Harbours* (1628) reprinted in George Parker Winship, ed., *Sailors' Narratives of Voyages along the New England Coast, 1524-1624* (New York, 1968), 282, 286-7.

John Winthrop
Puritan John Winthrop had to wrestle with his conscience before deciding to move to America. Although the radical group of Puritans now known as "Pilgrims" had moved to New England in 1620, Winthrop and conservative Puritans believed that they should stay in England to purify the Anglican church. However, as persecution mounted, it seemed that emigrating was the only answer. Winthrop searched the Bible and found justification for fleeing to New England, where he and fellow Puritans could practice their religion in peace. It was he who originated the idea that Puritan New England should be a shining "city on a hill" to enlighten Christians in Europe as to God's true religion. He later became governor of Massachusetts. In that position, he used printing to attempt to counter rumors and false reports as part of his efforts to assure stability in the colony.

failed in their attempt to raise cattle in North Carolina, they spread the word that the place was unproductive. A group of Carolina-based writers published a pamphlet to answer the rumor. They declared that the land was as good as any they had seen in the entire world, and its timber was superb. The lands in question, they said, would surely accommodate thousands of Englishmen. The pamphlet did not sugar-coat problems with Indians or Spaniards, nor did it gloss over harsh weather conditions of the region, but rather it spelled out the problems in honest detail. The appeal was successful. Many people settled in Carolina as a result of reading the pamphlet.[11]

Rumors plagued all of the colonies. As New England leader John Winthrop noted, "... [I]t was so usual to have false news

brought from all parts, that we were very doubtful of the most probable reports." He found that confused settlers tended to rely on the printed word to clear up misunderstandings. As governor of Massachusetts, he found himself involved in a dispute over lands to the west, which France and England both claimed. Frenchmen believed the Englishmen of Massachusetts were planning a hostile raid into French territories. To prove them wrong, Winthrop and the Council of Massachusetts issued a printed order forbidding Massachusetts residents from making any hostile moves toward the French, unless in self-defense. Winthrop and the council considered the printed order to be an important augmentation of mere verbal diplomacy, as well as an effective educational device. A printed declaration carried a great deal of weight and authoritative proof of English intentions, and it corrected the falsehoods spreading among the French. It also offered clear direction to Massachusetts settlers who might be contemplating an attack.[12]

Despite communication difficulties, Winthrop did live in the Boston area, which was a communication hub with its busy port and its web of well-traveled roads. Settlers in more remote places fared far worse. From the western part of Massachusetts, for example, John Pynchon constantly sent letters back East in hopes of straightening out the numerous rumors that spread through his community of Springfield. He believed he had a duty to quell false reports. The most trustworthy of all the information that bounced around town, he felt, was that which came from the mass media. At one point a Dutchman appeared in Springfield, claiming that French news publications had told of the defeat of the English fleet by the Dutch. Although Pynchon considered such a defeat to be unthinkable, he was inclined to believe it, as it came from a formal news source. He hurried to get a confirmation. The news was, indeed, true.[13]

UNTAINTED BY FALSEHOOD

As Pynchon and so many other colonials agreed, communication with the Mother Country was often distorted by rumor and gossip. At times the printed word seemed to be the only authoritative way to kill those rumors and quash that gossip. The desire to keep overseas communication untainted by falsehood led to the publication of a document that had the appearance of a newspaper. Its author, however, never intended to publish it again, and thus it was not a periodical at all. Printed in 1689, the broadside was titled *The Present State of the New-English Affairs*. It sprang from the pen of Massachusetts leader Increase Mather, who had gone to England to plead for a new Massachusetts charter to replace the one the crown had canceled. Rumors swirled around his trip —

[11]William Hilton, Anthony Long, and Peter Fabian, *A Relation of a Discovery lately made on the Coast of Florida* (London, printed by J.C. for Simon Miller, 1664), reprinted in Salley, *Narratives of Early Carolina*, 37-61.

[12]Journal entry of 23 May 1644 by John Winthrop in James Kendall Hosmer, ed., *Winthrop's Journal, "History of New England," 1630-1649*, vol. II (New York, 1908), 182-3.

[13]John Pynchon to John Winthrop, Jr., 2 March 1664/65, in Carl Bridenbaugh, ed., *The Pynchon Papers, Vol. I: Letters of John Pynchon, 1654-1700* (Boston, 1982), 53-5. Also, John Pynchon to John Winthrop, Jr., 24 January 1666/67, postscript mistakenly dated 1 January 1666, in ibid., 72. The Dutch had won a naval victory over the English at St. Christopher in the Caribbean on 14 June 1666.

The Mathers

Richard Mather (1596-1669)

Increase Mather (1639-1723)

Cotton Mather (1663-1728)

Father, Son, Grandson Gain Fame as America's First Family of Authors

The lives of Richard, Increase, and Cotton Mather were interwoven with the story of the Massachusetts Bay Colony, and their interests involved them intimately in the early stages of printing in Boston.

Richard Mather arrived in 1635 to settle with his family in Dorchester as the Puritans were carving out new lives in the wilderness. In addition to serving the needs of his parish and growing family, he was active in the colony's religious life. He took part in the synods, the religious meetings that guided life in the Puritan commonwealth; and he was one of the authors of the *Bay Book of Psalms*.

The most prominent of Richard's sons was Increase. Educated at Harvard and groomed for the ministry at Trinity College, Dublin, he became a minister at the new North Church in Boston in 1662. In an age when sermons were read for both information and entertainment, he was a patron of the city's first printer. He was famous at home and abroad for his sermons as well as his efforts at biography and history.

Increase was invited several times to

serve as president of Harvard, but in 1688 he instead traveled to England to negotiate for restoration of the colony's charter. An account of these efforts was published in 1689 in broadside form as *The Present State of the New-English Affairs*.

Increase's son Cotton shared his father's Boston pulpit and actively tried to

emulate his scholarship, becoming the most prolific American author of his generation. In addition to producing sermons and histories, he studied natural history and was the first colonial member of the British Royal Society. Well acquainted with Boston's printers, he provided some of the information published in the short-lived *Publick Occurrences*. And in 1721 he was at the center of the inoculation controversy that gave rise to James Franklin's *New-England Courant*.

Present State of the New-English Affairs
All three Mathers were prolific authors and contributed to the public discussions and debates about current affairs. The middle one, Increase, however, also produced what some historians have considered America's first newspaper. On a mission to England to negotiate a new governing charter for the colony of Massachusetts, he published a document in 1689 that had the appearance of a newspaper – *The Present State of the New-English Affairs*. Mather, however, never intended to publish it again, and thus it did not fit the definition of a periodical. It did indicate, however, the concern that he and other colonists had that there be timely accounts of important events. Later, his son, Cotton, provided news for the colonies' first real attempt at a newspaper in 1690 and was at the heart of a controversy that gave rise to their most intemperate paper.

wild rumors, many with no basis in fact. Mather saw the mock newspaper as the surest way to inform the people back home of exactly how their complaints were playing in London. He issued *The Present State of the New-English Affairs* with the dramatic announcement: "This is published to prevent false reports."

It is interesting that Mather chose the format of a newspaper to clear up false reports. Even though no newspaper yet existed in America, colonists read European newspapers, which seemed to carry a solemn weight of authority. Readers saw them as purveyors of truth, the definitive word in a world where communication was easily garbled and distorted during the vast numbers of weeks it took for words to travel across the Atlantic. The newspaper was already a trusted form before it finally made its American debut in 1690. Before newspapers ever took hold in English America, the notion of journalism already involved the concept that the newspaper should be true, honest, clear, and trustworthy.

The foundation of the American newspaper industry was built of stones from the colonial era, when highly intelligent people such as Increase Mather recognized that newspapers — even those from faraway England — were the objects of much faith. People believed them and publications like them, no matter how far away they were printed. News told by word of mouth seemed to operate like the game children play by whispering a phrase in each other's ear. The more the message passed from mouth to ear, the less it resembled the original. Newspapers or pamphlets, however, were printed and therefore were not twisted by repeated telling. They carried a sense of truth. Modern readers of colonial newspapers often complain that the information in them was not timely, especially after six or eight weeks of ocean travel; but that did not really matter so much to colonial Americans. The important thing was that the news in the newspaper or pamphlet had not changed from the original printing. It thus seemed to be the embodiment of truth over rumor.

The idea that the printing press could prevent or cure false reports was significant in people's developing expectations of what journalistic writing was all about. The truthfulness of journalism evolved over time into a permanent goal in mainstream American journalism. Its ancestry was, at least partially, in the preventing of false reports, a prominent feature of the pre-newspaper press.

Ultimately, it was not surprising in the least that the one and only issue of the first American newspaper, *Publick Occurrences both Forreign and Domestick*, also announced that it was printed to prevent false reports.

THE PRINTING PRESS AND PUBLIC DEBATE

Along with their trust that printed material was credible, colonial readers also recognized a strong persuasive effect of the mass media. American pro-settlement promotional literature, for example, proved the ability of the press to advertise, coax, and lure. Convinced that the printed word was both believable and persuasive, Americans frequently rushed to the printing press when they had disputes among themselves. When someone passionately felt his

cause was the correct one, it was natural for him to try to persuade others that he was right by printing and distributing his ideas for all to read. Frequently parties on the other side of the question would answer in print in a calculated struggle to win public opinion.

The printed word in such cases may or may not have persuaded many readers, but it did frequently spark or perpetuate heavy public discussion. Provocative tracts arguing various points helped build up the democratic notion of a "marketplace of ideas," which would one day be a hallmark of American press philosophy. Furthermore, pamphlets, tracts, and books in various wars of words began helping Americans grapple with the concept of what was right, what was correctly a part of the American experience. The literature of debate thus served as seeds of American thought, helping Americans slowly begin to emerge from their European past.

The technique of using print to force American society to confront an issue started early. In 1643 a Mr. Briscoe in Watertown, Massachusetts, challenged the Puritan church rule that everyone pay taxes to fund ministers' salaries. Briscoe himself was not a member of the church and did not wish to be. He audaciously wrote a pamphlet on the taxation question. "This he published underhand, which occasioned much stir in the town," Puritan leader John Winthrop complained. Furthermore, Briscoe went around Massachusetts promoting the book and making reproachful speeches about the tax. Officials brought him before the General Court of Massachusetts, and there he fully admitted both publishing the tract and making the speeches. Conceding that he had been wrong to challenge the policy so brazenly, he was fined £10, and one of the publishers of the tract was slapped with a 40-shilling fine.[14] Briscoe may or may not have been successful at winning converts to his point of view on the matter, but he was successful in creating public debate over the issue — his theme that church and state should be separate would come up over and over again as a bone of contention in Massachusetts. The concept of a government independent of church would evolve over time to be a rather unEuropean, very American ideal. By the late 1600s, Puritan congregations were supporting their own churches without help from non-members. It was the Anglican church — the state church of England — that believed it was entitled to tax support from colonists.

Complaints by individuals such as Briscoe sprang from personal disappointment or small-group discontent. In a bizarre turn of history, however, many of the American colonies experienced unrest of far greater magnitude in the latter half of the seventeenth century. Starting with Bacon's Rebellion in Virginia in 1676 and running through 1690, five colonies underwent violent political upheaval. Angry citizens in two of them overthrew their colonial governors. Public debate, sparked and augmented by the printed word, fueled the violence in at least three of the colonies. All five of the colonies used written argument to try to convince readers to follow one position or the other.

[14]Journal entry of 5 March 1643 by John Winthrop in Hosmer, *Winthrop's Journal*, 91.

William and Mary
When William and Mary ascended the British throne following the Glorious Revolution of 1688, their coronation was a cause for celebration in the American colonies. Puritans supported the overthrow of Catholic King James II, and they and his other opponents used the printing press in their efforts. It was in the aftermath of his overthrow that Increase Mather printed *The Present State of the New-English Affairs* and that Massachusetts two years later would get its first newspaper. The British print above was published in 1689.

The colonial revolts took place in Virginia, Albemarle (North Carolina), New York, Massachusetts, and Maryland. The Albemarle and Virginia factions, which were battling over local governmental problems, did not have access to a press in their own colonies. However, revolutionaries in both settlements issued inflammatory writings to stir up the people. Virginia's factions in 1676 debated the insurrection in widely circulated poetry; and a year later, the Albemarle revolutionaries deliberately sent "seditious libells" all over the area "to put all in a flame."[15] Some of the items may have been printed, although probably some were hand-copied.

PRINTING AND THE GLORIOUS REVOLUTION

However, residents of New York, Massachusetts, and Maryland carried on their insurrections using the printed word. The uprisings in those colonies were all linked to rumors and then confirmation of the fact that Protestants William and Mary had been installed as joint rulers of England, ousting Catholic King James II in November 1688 in a coup called the "Glorious Revolution." Printed documents were at the heart of the debate and unrest.

New Yorkers began hearing unconfirmed rumors of James'

overthrow, and immediately people became agitated. The colony's council and representative convention made haste to get a printed copy of the supposed proclamation of the accession of William and Mary. They wrote to Boston for a copy. Hearing that gentlemen from Connecticut were coming to New York with the document, the council sent riders two days out in hopes of meeting them. They missed each other. Eventually the Connecticut riders did arrive in New York and delivered the printed proclamation to the acting lieutenant govenor, Jacob Leisler. He issued the proclamation without notifying either the council or convention. The council failed to believe Leisler's proclamation until the governing body obtained its own printed version, which eventually arrived dated February 14, 1688/89.[16] In that publication, the new monarchs confirmed that office-holders were required to be Protestants. The council therefore turned Catholics out of office but did not explain the action to Leisler. He had no knowledge of why the offices suddenly changed hands without any apparent authorization. So, although a Protestant himself, he accused the new Protestant office-holders of treason.

Inflammatory pamphlets began to appear. One of the most provocative was titled *A Modest and Impartial Narrative*, which was neither modest nor impartial. The writer, Nicholas Bayard, accused Leisler of maliciously attempting to kindle mob violence among the common people. According to Bayard, Leisler worked hand-in-hand with "his assistant vain glory, together with [his] God-Mother Ambition...." The pamphlet accused Leisler of being "a faithful servant to that black prince of the air" who would continue to act for the devil as long as "the many-headed beasts" — the common man — would stand by him. New York was already seething over the factions' handling of events, and writings such as Bayard's did not help cool things off. Leisler's enemies executed him for treason a few months later.

NEW ENGLAND IN TURMOIL

Meanwhile, in the united colonies of New England, Governor Sir Edmund Andros had been stirring up hatred for some time. Puritans had been accustomed to governing themselves, as allowed under the original Massachusetts charter, but King James had vacated the charter. He had sent Andros to be the governor of a forced alliance between the various colonies of New England. As an Anglican appointed to rule a largely Puritan population, Andros had always been the subject of public distrust. One of his first actions had been to require the use of a Puritan church for Anglican services, a move that greatly angered Puritans.

They also railed against Andros' heavyhanded leadership, which ran contrary to the freedoms New Englanders had long en-

---

[15][Unidentified manservant of Nathaniel Bacon], "Bacon's Epitaph, made by his Man," quoted by an anonymous writer in a manuscript entitled "The History of Bacon's and Ingram's Rebellion, 1676"; and "Affidavit of Thomas Miller concerning the Rebellion of Carolina," both in Charles M. Andrews, ed., *Narratives of the Insurrections* (New York, 1915), 75-7, 153.

[16]England and her colonies formally adopted the Gregorian calendar in 1752. Before that, they used the Julian calendar, which (in Christian countries only) featured New Year's Day on March 25. However, some people, including those of Dutch background in New York, accepted the Gregorian calendar, which placed New Year's Day on January 1. Thus, February 14, 1688/89, would fall near the end of the Julian year 1688 but near the beginning of the Gregorian year 1689. To avoid confusion, prior to 1752 people were in the habit of writing the two applicable years after all dates between January 1 and March 25.

Edmund Andros
Among the Puritans' many complaints against Edmund Andros, the Anglican governor of New England from 1686 to 1689, was that he placed heavyhanded restrictions on the printing press. They also charged that he changed the laws without bothering to inform the populace with printed copies of the changes.

joyed under their own local governments. They singled out restrictions on the printing press as a major blunder by Andros. Increase Mather complained bitterly in a 1688 pamphlet that "the people are at a great loss to *know what* is *Law and what not,*" for Andros had changed the laws without bothering to update the populace with printed copies of the changes.[17] As far as Mather was concerned, printing and distribution of information such as the law were basic necessities.

Massachusetts residents read, repeated, and reprinted Mather's complaints, causing a stern reaction from Andros. He needed to come down hard on rampant anti-governmental expression. Early in 1689, his administration issued an order against seditious publications. It thundered:

Whereas many papers have beene lately printed and dispersed tending to the disturbance of the peace and subversion of the government of this theire Majesties Colonie....

It is therefore ordered that if any person or persons within this Collony be found guilty of any such like Misdemeanour of printing, publishing or concealing any such like papers or discourses, or not timely discover such things to Authority, ... they

shall be accounted enemies to their Majesties present Government and be proceeded against as such with uttermost severity.[18]

By November of 1688, Andros was out of a job as King James was forced from the throne, but Andros did not yet know it. Bostonians were hearing rumors of the king's overthrow in December, and more rumors came again in March; but it took the printed word — or the purported printed word — to persuade them that the rumors were true. On April 4, John Winslow arrived from Nevis, West Indies, with a piece of writing that he said he had copied from a publication issued by the new King William. It instructed all magistrates who had been turned out by James to return to their jobs. Immediately, someone had the paper printed as a broadside, and it spread through Boston. The broadside was enough to turn the tide of public sentiment from restlessness to unrest, despite the tenuous nature of Winslow's claims. The fact that the words had somehow, somewhere supposedly been issued in print as a formal royal publication satisfied many readers.

Powerful Bostonians worked quickly to get rid of Andros. On April 18, Puritan leader Cotton Mather, son of Increase, hired the press to print a declaration, which he read from the balcony of the townhouse in a bid to stir up public sentiment. Among other things, he called Andros and his deputies "Horse-leeches ... [that] have been sucking of us; and what Laws they made it was as impossible for us to know, as dangerous as for us to break; He would neither suffer them to be printed nor fairly published."[19] Bostonians overthrew Andros later that day, without bloodshed. They finally got a formal, printed proclamation of William and Mary as dual rulers in late May, a month and a half after the coup.

The overthrow of Andros did not end the argument over the legalities of such an action. The debate had just begun, and the sides battled in paper and ink. Nathanael Byfield tried to justify the revolution by printing an account of it in both London and Edinburgh, together with Mather's accusations. John Palmer, an Andros supporter, tried to convince readers of the illegalities and nastiness that went on in Puritan New England by defending Andros in *An Account of the State of New England*, a pamphlet printed in London because, Palmer said, the Puritan majority would not allow such a thing to be printed in Boston on the Puritans' presses. In an attempt to counter Palmer's pamphlet and others like it, a number of men on the colonial governing council wrote a pamphlet decrying Andros as arbitrary and illegally installed. Still other writers gathered and published affidavits by people who had been involved in the coup, supporting the revolutionaries.[20]

---

[17]Increase Mather, *A Narrative of the Miseries of New-England, by Reason of an Arbitrary Government Erected there, Under Sir Edmond Andros* (Boston, printed by Richard Pierce, 1688). This was actually a reprint; the first edition appeared in London, according to *The Andros Tracts*, vol. I (New York, 1868), 5.

[18]*Order against seditious publications* (1689), in *Andros Tracts*, vol. III, 107.

[19]Cotton Mather, *Declaration of the Gentlemen, Merchants, and Inhabitants of Boston* (1689), quoted in Nathanael Byfield, *An Account of The Late Revolution in New-England* (London: Printed by Richard Chitwell, 1689), reprinted in Andrews, *Narratives of the Insurrections*, 176-8. The sentence "He would neither suffer them to be printed nor fairly published" was added in Mather's text as a marginal note, marked with an asterisk to be read after the preceding sentence.

[20]Byfield, ibid., 170-82. Also, John Palmer, *An Account of the State of New England* (London, 1690). Also, William Stoughton, Thomas Hinckley, Wait Winthrop, Bartholomew Gedney, and Samuel Shrimpton, *A Narrative of the Proceedings of Sir Edmond Androsse and his Complices* (1691), reprinted in Andrews, *Narratives of the Insurrections*, 239-49.

THE

DECLARATION

OF THE

REASONS and MOTIVES

For the PRESENT

Appearing in Arms

OF

THEIR MAJESTIES

𝔓𝔯𝔬𝔱𝔢𝔰𝔱𝔞𝔫𝔱 𝔖𝔲𝔟𝔧𝔢𝔠𝔱𝔰

In the PROVINCE of

MARYLAND

Licens'd, *November* 28*th* 1689.   J. F.

Although the Nature and State of Affairs relating to the Government of this Province, is so well and notoriously known to all Persons any way concerned in the same, as to the People and Inhabitants here, who are more immediately interested, as might excuse any *Declaration* or *Apology* for this present inevitable *Appearance* : Yet forasmuch as (by the *Plots, Contrivances, Insinuations, Remonstrances,* and *Subscriptions,* carried on, suggested, extorted, and obtained by the Lord *Baltemore,* his Deputies
A   ties

Maryland Rebellion
Following the change in the English monarchy with the Glorious Revolution, Protestants in Maryland took up arms against their Catholic governors. William Nuthead inaugurated the new Maryland press in 1689 by printing this controversial tract defending their actions. The tract complained that Protestant churches had been converted to popery and idolatry.

THE CLASH OF CATHOLICS AND PROTESTANTS

As pamphlets fueled public action and debate on the situation in New England, predominantly Catholic Maryland was undergoing upheaval between Catholics and Protestants. Maryland Protestants had gotten word of the change in the English monarchy, and they accordingly felt justified in taking up arms against their Catholic governors. William Nuthead, a printer newly arrived in the town of St. Mary's from Virginia, inaugurated the new Maryland press by printing a controversial tract defending Protestant actions. The writer of the tract, identified only as J.F., complained that Protestant churches had been converted to popery and idolatry. The Catholic governor had tampered with the popular assembly, nullifying some of the laws it had made and sending home some delegates. In fact, J.F. said, the governor had managed to reconfigure the assembly by disbanding it and then calling it anew with far too few representatives. Furthermore, Protestant orphans were given to Catholics to raise, and Catholic leaders looked the other way when Protestants were murdered. Protestants, J.F. con-

cluded, were in constant fear of losing their life and their property.[21]

It was not a new debate, of course. Protestants and Catholics had clashed in Maryland for many decades. Thirty-four years earlier, Lord Baltimore, the colony's Catholic leader, had tried to counteract public dissatisfaction by issuing a pamphlet titled *The Lord Baltimore's Case*, claiming that he supported both Catholics and Protestants. Protestants responded, charging in print that Baltimore was an enemy to the Anglican church and that he sought a war with Parliament.

The concept that the press should spark and cultivate public debate was not unique to America, but the fact that European-Americans had some sort of access to the press for their entire history made printed public debate an accepted thing. True, there were restrictions on the press, as was common in Europe; but there was also a wide acceptance that debate about various issues was to be public via the mass media. In fact, if factions on one side or another of an American issue found themselves restricted from printing an argumentative document on a nearby press, they would turn to the press of another colony or even of London. They believed that societal disputes simply needed to be made public. It was important to get the word out so that wrongs might be righted or besmirched reputations might be scrubbed clean.

Episodes of printed debate were pivotal in the formation of American thought about the role of media, about the role of dispute, about the public nature of opposing factions, about the necessity of telling all sides. The American character, conceived in the earliest era of the American mass media, accepted it as natural to see debates printed and distributed for anyone to read.

THE OUTPUT OF THE FIRST PRESSES

The earliest printing work for America took place in Europe, but the importation of a press into America opened the doors of debate, religious instruction, rumor-curing, entertainment, and so on — all the functions of the mass media — on Americans' turf. Theoretically, the press became even more accessible than it had been before.

The first press in Anglo-America arrived in Cambridge, Massachusetts, in 1638. As time passed, other printers moved to the Puritan colony. Before the first American newspaper was published in 1690, what exactly were those presses producing? It's easy to say briefly that they issued broadsides, almanacs, and pamphlets, as well as government documents and occasional books. However, the texture of American thought was evident in those early publications. So the output of the earliest presses — as well as people's thought about those presses — is worthy of a closer look.

The press was an accoutrement of civilization that seemed to create both great pride and great fear. Showing one type of

[21]J.F., *The Declaration of Reasons and Motives for the Present Appearing in Arms of Their Majesties Protestant Subjects in the Province of Maryland* (St. Mary's, Maryland, printed by William Nuthead, 1689), reprinted in Andrews, *Narratives of the Insurrections,* 305-14.

A   In Adam's Fall
    we finned all.

B   Thy Life to mend,
    This Book attend.

C   The *Cat* doth play,
    And after flay.

D   A *Dog* will bite
    A Thief at Night.

E   An Eagle's Flight
    is out of Sight.

F   The idle Fool
    is whipt at School.

America's Primer
Americans of the seventeenth century showed a great interest in the education of the young. The *New England Primer*, printed in Boston in 1689, served as the main textbook for fifty years and was used to teach reading for 100 more.

thought on the presence of an American press, William Berkeley, governor of the Anglican colony of Virginia, has become famous for commenting in 1671, "I thank God, *there are no free schools* nor *printing* [in Virginia] and I hope we shall not have these hundred years; for *learning* has brought disobedience, and heresy, and sects into the world, and *printing* has divulged them, and libels against the best government. God keep us from both!" On the other side of the coin, one of the first employees of the Cambridge press was proud that his printshop had a goal of supporting the needs of the government, thus helping a new country to unfold.[22]

The man who imported the first press into Massachusetts, Puritan Reverend Joseph Glover, found plenty of international well-wishers for his venture. He was able to undertake the expense of importing a press by soliciting the help of Puritans in England and in exile in Amsterdam. Like him, they had an interest in seeing a printing press available in the Puritans' model "city on a hill" in America to spread God's word and the enlightened Puritan thought to the corrupt churches of Europe and their deluded fol-

lowers.

Although Glover died en route, his press arrived safely in Massachusetts and inaugurated the era of American printing. Others eventually followed Glover's lead. From 1638 to 1690, American presses churned out documents of varying types, from government decrees to news pamphlets to educational material. The locally produced tracts were not meant strictly for an American audience. Religious writings, especially, found their way back to Europe. Likewise, the Massachusetts press issued 600 copies of the colony's *Book of the General Lauues and Libertyes* with the intention of sending copies to London for distribution to potential settlers. "[T]hey were printed, and now are to be seen of all men, to the end that none may plead ignorance," a Massachusetts settler explained, "and that all who intend to transport themselves hither, may know this is no place of licentious liberty, nor will this people suffer any to trample down this Vineyard of the Lord...."[23] Despite such links with Europe, American printed works were most widely distributed in America.

What types of works were Americans reading from their own presses? Religious publications outnumbered other items because the population was so strongly religious. True, the press came in handy for many other types of documents, but Americans had a keen interest in spiritual writings. Puritans especially believed the press had a powerful ability to reach people and influence them and, perhaps more importantly, to be a tool in the search for ultimate truth. They recognized the wide net that printing could cast, and they used it to better humanity by issuing religious items, including sermons, biographies of godly people, book-length works on religious topics, Bibles, catechisms, religious discussions, and answers and challenges to religious heretics or other sects.

EVANGELICAL WRITINGS

It was natural for Puritans to turn to the printed word in their zeal to establish God's kingdom on earth. After all, their "errand into the wilderness," as they called their move to America, was justified by nothing less than God's word as recorded in the Bible. The Puritans were part of the Protestant movement that shunned the traditional trappings of both the Catholic and Anglican churches, including the priesthood. To devout Puritans, individuals had an obligation to read the Scriptures and reason about them for themselves. That task was not to be left to a priest or a bishop, as it was in the Catholic and Anglican churches. Thus, the tangible, printed Bible was a personal necessity to Puritans, a treasure that opened the Kingdom of Heaven to each individual reader.

As important as the Bible was to the Puritans, the printed word in other forms also carried deep and important religious significance. The Puritan faith encouraged intellectual understanding of the Bible through interpretation, discussion, and argument — which could all be disseminated through printed matter. To the

[22]Berkeley made the remark to his superiors in London, who had asked for an accounting of education in Virginia. See David Freeman Hawke, *Everyday Life in Early America* (New York, 1988), 68-9. The other opinion was shown in a letter from Timothy Green to Isaiah Thomas, 8 August 1792, in the Isaiah Thomas Papers, American Antiquarian Society (Worcester, Mass.), Box 2, Folder 2. In the letter, Green was reminiscing about his great-grandfather, Samuel Green, and indicated that Samuel felt that the shop's output was largely governmental in nature.

[23][Edward Johnson], *A History of New-England From the English planting in the Yeere 1628. [sic] untill the Yeere 1652* (London, Nathaniel Brooke, 1654), reprinted as J. Franklin Jameson, ed., *Johnson's Wonder-Working Providence, 1628-1651* (New York, 1910), 244.

John Foxe

John Foxe, who died in 1587, was the author of *The Book of Martyrs*, one of the most widely read books in the American colonies. Even today it is frequently reprinted. With its accounts of hundreds of heroic Christians who had been put to death for their faith, it provided inspiration to the Puritans who settled New England.

Puritans, existence on Earth meant a relentless search for truth, and the printed word was an awe-inspiring and powerful tool in that search. A surface reading of the Bible was not enough. It took analysis, exposition, convincing, wrangling, restating, and debating to understand God's word fully. Thus it was not surprising that church members spent a lot of energy on a great outpouring of printed messages for the purpose of seeking truth, reaching sinners, and keeping the godly on the straight and narrow.

Of course, Puritans relied on sermon and example to reach the straying and to edify the saintly, but they realized that the printed word could bring those very sermons to hundreds who *hadn't* heard the pastor. The printed word could also preserve the character and feats of the saintly in books or pamphlets, which could circulate long and far. Puritans were sure that such writings had the power to convert or to edify, because they knew that many deep and important decisions in their own history had been inspired by the printed word.

Puritan leader William Bradford was one of many church members who had read and been won over by a variety of books about saintly Christians. One of his favorites was John Foxe's famous *Book of Martyrs*, which "recorded how that besides those worthy martires and confessors which were burned in queen Marys days and otherwise tormented, many ... fled out of the land to the number of 800." Those Protestant refugees from England set up Puri-

tan congregations around Europe.[24] Like the martyrs in Foxe's book, Bradford and his fellow Puritans were the victims of persecution in England. They identified with the martyrs. Inspired by *The Book of Martyrs* and other such writings, they began fleeing England for Holland, where they could practice their religion as they pleased. When Holland proved less than adequate, they fled further to America.

Bradford's earliest "pilgrims," as they came to be known, were considered somewhat radical by their Puritan colleagues who remained in England. However, the more conservative sort, including John Winthrop, were finally persuaded to emigrate by the word of God. It was a monumental struggle to decide whether to emigrate, but over and over again, Winthrop turned to the Bible in an effort to convince both himself and others that emigration to New England was the answer to the ever worsening corruption of the Anglican church.

Since Winthrop was a trusted leader, people looked to him for answers to their fears. Very practical men, for instance, objected to the fact that the area the Puritans intended to settle had no natural fortifications. Winthrop searched the Scriptures and discovered that God intended for His people to learn to trust Him. He argued to the doubters that Paul and his companions in the Bible "were compassed with dangers on every side, and dayley were under the sentence of deathe, that they might learn to trust in the living God." Furthermore, Winthrop pointed out, the book of Deuteronomy confirmed that God had taken the children of Israel into the wilderness, away from "the fleshepottes of Egipt," much like He might be ordering them to leave the fleshpots of a wicked England. That had been a hard lesson for the children of Israel, but Winthrop felt that it had been for the ultimate good.[25] The fact that his answers came from the Bible helped sell the credibility of an American Puritan settlement.

Taking such deep and significant inspiration from the Scriptures and published writings, it was a natural step for Puritans to welcome Joseph Glover's press to their colony in 1638. Printer Stephen Daye had the press up and running in 1638 or 1639 at Harvard College.[26] He first printed the governmental *The Oath of a Freeman*, which all voting males in the colony were required to take. Next, he printed an almanac. However, in short order the Cambridge press began turning out pages and pages of religious discussion, more than any other type of document.

A BLESSING TO RELIGION

The press was a blessing to religion in the colony. By the 1640s, doctrinal differences were developing among congregations of

[24]William T. Davis, ed., *Bradford's History of Plymouth Plantation, 1606-1646* (New York, 1908), 25. The actual title of Foxe's book, although it was commonly called *The Book of Martyrs*, was *Acts and Monuments of the Christian Church*.

[25]John Winthrop, "Objections against this intended Plantation for New E[ngland]: Answered and resolved" (1629), in Stewart Mitchell, ed., *Winthrop Papers*, vol. II, 1623-1630 (Boston, 1931), 114.

[26]The first item from Daye's press was *Oath of a Freeman*. No original copies have survived. However, several people of the era referred to it in their writings. The dates they gave for the *Oath* were ambiguous, but they suggest that it appeared in either March 1638 or March 1639.

```
⁙ THE OATH OF A FREEMAN. ⁙
I·A B· being (by Gods providence) an Inhabitant,
    and Freeman, within the iurisdictiō of this
Common-wealth, doe freely acknowledge my
selfe to bee subject to the governement thereof;
and therefore doe heere sweare, by the great
& dreadfull name of the Everliving-God, that
I will be true & faithfull to the same, & will
accordingly yield affiftance & support therunto,
with my person & estate, as in equity I am bo-
und: and will also truely indeavour to maintaine
and preferve all the libertyes & privilidges there-
of, submitting my selfe to the wholesome lawes,
& ordres made & ftablished by the fame; and fu-
rther, that I will not plot, nor practice any evill
againft it, nor consent to any that shall soe do,
butt will timely discover, & reveall the same to
lawefull authoritee nowe here ftablished, for the
fpeedie preventing thereof. Moreover, I doe
folemnly binde my selfe, in the fight of God,
that when I shalbe called, to give my voyce
touching any such matter of this state, ( in wh-
ich freemen are to deale) I will give my vote
& suffrage as I shall judge in myne owne con-
science may best conduce & tend to the publick
weale of the body, without respect of personn-
es, or favour of any man. Soe help mee God in
the Lord Iesus Christ.
```

The Oath of a Freeman

Although no original copies of *The Oath of a Freeman* exist, the one shown here is a copy based on the original text that had survived in hand-written form. The *Oath* was the first item printed in Anglo-America. It appeared in either 1638 or 1639 from the press of Harvard College in Cambridge, Massachusetts, under the operation of Stephen Daye. All "freemen," or voting members of the colony, took the oath. It promised them that they could speak their mind plainly and according to their own conscience, without pressure from the government.

various New England churches, leading dangerously to false interpretations of God's word. Puritan leaders realized the hazards of such dissent — their colony would no longer function as the model "city on a hill" if it collapsed into disagreement and sects. Calling a synod in 1646, Puritan divines worked out their differences by consulting the New Testament. After agreeing on the direction of the church, they turned to the press to get the word out, to convince erring churches to stay on the right track. True, the rules could and would be preached from the pulpits. But the pastors knew the printed word had authority and clarity beyond mere speaking. They determined that, in print, the rules "might be better scanned and tried of every particular person in the several congregations or churches." Their work, titled *A Platform of Church Discipline,* was published in Cambridge in 1649. Publication meant that all members of the colony might have the opportunity to read about the true church's strivings for godliness.

Puritans enjoyed reading printed debates about religious topics. So long as an idea was not so deviant as to be sinful or heretical, it was fair game. Puritan leaders spelled out their feelings about the importance of printed discussion of religious ideas in a tract titled *Propositions Concerning the Subjects of Baptism and Consocation of Churches.* The governing body of Massachusetts had read over the pamphlet, which detailed the controversial findings of a church synod in 1662. The officials announced that they were perfectly willing to let various factions publish their understanding of religious matters. As long as heresy was not advocated, religious debate was an actual *obligation.* They wrote:

> ... [T]o bear one with another in lesser differences, about matters of a more difficult and controversial nature, and more remote from the Foundation [of church doctrine], and wherein the godly-wise are not like-minded, is a Duty necessary to the peace and welfare of Religion.

Similarly, in 1663 *Another Essay for the Investigation of Truth* called for toleration of printed opinions, even those out of the mainstream. Justifying the publication of views that disagreed violently with certain synodical decisions, the tract's "Apologetical Preface to the Reader" noted calmly that even in the early Christian church, the apostles disagreed with one another. The writer of the preface said:

> Variety of Judgements may stand with Unity of Affections. He that judgeth a Cause before he hath heard both parties speaking, although he should judge rightly, is not a righteous Judge. [Thus] We are willing that the World should see what is here presented.

In fact, the writer announced that it was his moral responsibility to make the dissenters' opinion public so that he would not accidentally withhold the truth from mankind. To the Puritan way of thinking, the press was a tool for learning truth, no matter how much fellow church members disagreed. Contrary to today's popular notions of Puritans, their control of the press was not restrictive. The Puritans allowed — even treasured — the diversified religious discussions available through their press. While they did not tolerate the circulation of "heretical" writings from Anabaptists, Jesuits, and certain other groups, they saw the press as a vital means of uncovering and debating the nature of religious truth.

The only other press in America that had any roots whatsoever by 1690 was operating in Philadelphia. During the four years of its existence, the Philadelphia press had chiefly issued almanacs. However, as the capital of the Quaker colony of Pennsylvania, Philadelphia was the center of Quaker intellectual life. Thus, a number of Philadelphia prints before 1690 were religious in nature, either evangelizing readers into the Quaker religion or carrying on fierce debate with the Puritan press of Massachusetts. The presses of the two religious groups were the bane of each other's existence. No sooner would the Puritan press issue a warning to

Religious Printing
To American colonists in the 1600s, the overriding interest was Christianity, and much of the output of the earliest presses consisted of sermons and other religious material. In fact, this publication of the *Bay Book of Psalms*, printed in 1640 by Stephen Daye, has been called by some the first book printed in Anglo-America. However, it resembled a pamphlet more than a book, as those terms are defined today.

the flock against Quakerism, than the Quaker press would issue a strong response. Likewise, Puritans often felt they were on the defensive against persuasive Quaker books, especially when brought into Massachusetts by Quaker evangelists. The Quaker sect was far more evangelical in nature than the Puritans preferred — and far more so than it is considered today.

Between the Quakers and the Puritans, the only established presses in America before 1690 largely justified their existence by printing religious material. That fact reflected the importance of religion among the earliest American intellectuals and the devo-

tion of early colonists to evangelism via the printed word. Did the arrival of the secular newspaper mark the beginning of the end of religion as the dominant characteristic of American thought? Americans never entirely gave up religion or swapped it for the god of human information, symbolized by journalism. However, before the birth of the newspaper in America, citizens thought of the printed word as a primary tool in the search for the universal truth of God. The press could prevent false doctrines as well as false reports. It could turn a floodlight onto the centers of the soul as colonial Americans searched for their spiritual identity and relationship to the Almighty.

The fact that the earliest Americans felt that their very souls should be made bare, that their search for the very meaning of existence should be public, cements the picture of Americans as inhabitants of the "city on a hill," the phrase the Puritans used to describe how their colony should appear to the corrupt churches left behind in Europe. Jesus had promised that the truth would set mankind free, and it was apparent to the colonists that truth came at least in part through the printed word and could be circulated widely via the mass media. In the modern times of the sixteenth and seventeenth centuries, the truth could fly on the printed page to anyone and everyone, and humanity could be set free.

That ambitious goal became a part of the mystique of America. In the centuries to follow, Americans would think of themselves as specially ordained by God to administer a kingdom agreeable to Him on Earth. The concept was not a very far leap from the Puritans' bold assertions in their own search for truth, expressed in their press for the first half-century of printing in America.

EARLY AMERICANS AS CHILDREN OF THE MEDIA

By the time the first American newspaper started and failed all in one issue in 1690, Anglo-America had grown from a few tenuous outposts dotted about the seacoasts to a solid string of towns and colonies populated by people who were no longer struggling to carve out a meager existence. They had homes, jobs, churches, families. And by that time, too, Americans had already begun formulating an intellectual identity that was intimately linked to their use of the mass media. The printed word had driven them to America, encouraged their Europeanization of the place, taught them to quarrel publicly, and allowed them to search for truth openly. It had entertained and educated them, too.

It may seem funny to consider Americans before 1690 as children of the mass media, but indeed they were. Remote as they were, they had nevertheless grown up in the era of the printing press. They had felt its strength, had personally witnessed its persuasive allure. They believed in and read and used the printed word to communicate with their neighbors, whether those neighbors were across town, in another distant colony, or across the ocean in Europe.

As lifetime consumers of the printed word, the European settlers of America unintentionally began creating a nation that featured the mass media as an integral part of its intellectual identity.

Some Meditations

Concerning our HONOURABLE

Gentlemen and Fellow-Souldiers,

In Pursuit of those

Barbarous NATIVES in the NARRAGANSIT-Country,

and Their Service there.

Committed into Plain Verse for the Benefit of those that Read it.   By an Unfeigned Friend.

[The broadside text is rendered in three columns of small numbered verses, much of it illegible.]

Re-printed at N·London, April 4. 1728

The Land Settled

By the late 1600s, the colonists who had landed on America's shores three-quarters of a century earlier had effectively settled the new land. For the most part, the Native American population on the eastern seaboard had been subdued, with few conflicts with the Indians becoming serious threats to the settlers. Occasional major disturbances did occur — such as King Philip's War in 1675, the subject of the verse in this broadside — but for the most part the settlements along the Atlantic coast were secure. In the process of creating a new country, the colonists had given particular importance to the printing press, and the printed word had contributed to the character that had become distinctively American.

By the time the seventeenth century neared its close, the inhabitants of the New World were prepared for yet unborn American newspapers to fulfill all the roles of the press that Americans had learned and accepted from childhood. Newspapers would be persuaders, factual truth-tellers, correctors of wrongs, entertainers, and vehicles for public debate and education.

The printed word had played those roles throughout the entire history of Anglo-America. Thus America, in a sense, had grown up and would continue to mature under public scrutiny, for it would be forever recorded by the printed word and presented to a large readership. The character of the American populace was

thus deeply linked to the media, and so were such American actions as the subduing of Native Americans, the encouragement of open factional debate, and the acceptance of religious discussion as a basic tenet of American tolerance.

American thought had a basis in the media, for America was never without the presence and influence of a mass medium, not even in the earliest times before Joseph Glover imported a printing press into Massachusetts. There can be no doubt that the American intellectual character, as it developed into something different from the European intellectual character, was propelled and shaped in some part by the mass media. The qualities of printing — openness, debate, appeal to all types of people, and so on — would color the American intellectual landscape from the very start. There were numerous early influences on the development of America as a place distinct from Europe, but the intellectual notions that showed up in the mass media certainly had an impact on the nature of Americans themselves.

RECOMMENDED READINGS

BOOKS

Barbour, Philip L. *The Three Worlds of Captain John Smith*. Boston, 1964. Smith was an adventurer, colonist, and promoter of America. Barbour gives details on how Smith came to publish his *Generall Historie of Virginia* and how it was received.

Berthold, Arthur Benedict. *American Colonial Printing as Determined by Contemporary Cultural Forces, 1639-1763*, reprint edition. New York, 1970 (originally published in 1934). Colonial America exhibited two styles of thought that molded the press: secular-minded Cavalier thought in Virginia and theocratic Puritan thought in New England.

Fernandez-Armesto, Felipe. *Amerigo: The Man Who Gave His Name to America*. New York, 2007. This biography of Amerigo Vespucci includes an extensive and important analysis of early narratives of exploration and how they induced interest in the New World. Of particular interest is the author's commentary on the nature of truth and fiction in these works, as well as the role of editors and printers in spreading (and occasionally correcting) false reports in narratives of exploration.

Gunn, Giles, ed. *Early American Writing*. New York, 1994. This collection covers early American literature from pre-newspaper, post-newspaper, and Native American traditions. Gunn's introduction discusses the importance of European promotional literature, narratives of exploration, and narratives of colonization as tools for populating the American continent.

Hall, David D. *Worlds of Wonder, Days of Judgment: Popular Religious Belief in Early New England*. Cambridge, Mass., 1990. In explaining religious belief in early New England, Hall focuses on colonists' interaction with books. The "well-charted scripts" in published material were key in developing New England's culture.

Hall, David D., and Hugh Amory, eds. *A History of the Book in America: The Colonial Book in the Atlantic World*. Chapel Hill, N.C., 2007. This account, the first in a multi-volume set detailing the history of the book in all its facets, examines reading, writing, and publishing in America from the beginning until 1790. Books helped transfer culture across the Atlantic to America. Essays emphasize the growth of the early American book trade.

Hawke, David Freeman. *Everyday Life in Early America*. New York, 1988. The author looks at all facets of early American life, with references scattered throughout to the intellectual life of the era. Among other things, he addresses the importance of American settlement literature and the significance of printed religious material.

Hulton, Paul. *America 1585: The Complete Drawings of John White*. Chapel Hill, N.C., 1984. A series of introductory chapters offers a biographical sketch of colonial promoter John White and then discusses White's exquisite artistry. The book also examines Theodore de Bry's work as a publisher of White's drawings. The reader is treated to full-color reproductions of White's surviving drawings from 1585 America.

Miller, Perry. *Errand Into the Wilderness*. New York, 1956. Miller explores not only the intellectual climate that fostered the establishment of Puritan New England, but also the often overlooked religious literature of Virginia.

Monaghan, E. Jennifer. *Learning to Read and Write in Colonial America*. Amherst, Mass., 2007. This account examines the process of educating people to read and write,. It examines various types of people who studied to become literate, the type of education they received, and the motives of would-be readers and writers.

Morison, Samuel Eliot. *The Intellectual Life of Colonial New England*. New York, 1956. This book discusses colonial printing, bookselling, and libraries and devotes detailed sections to various types of intellectual output of the American colonies — sermons, histories, political works, and verse.

Murdock, Kenneth B. *Literature and Theology in Colonial New England*. Cambridge, Mass., 1949. Puritans published literature "to keep their supporters strong in the faith, to persuade the doubters, and to arouse the unawakened" and also to protect the colony from slander and criticism.

Parks, George Bruner. *Richard Hakluyt and the English Voyages*, 2nd ed. New York, 1961. This excellent biography of colonial promoter Richard Hakluyt discusses in detail the work he did to publish his famous propagandistic collection of sailors' narratives.

Williams, Julie Hedgepeth. *The Significance of the Printed Word in Early America: Colonists' Thoughts on the Role of the Press*. Westport, Conn., 1999. This book expands on topics mentioned in this chapter, such as settlement literature, evangelistic publications, the press and public debate, and the prevention of false reports.

Wright, Louis B. *The Cultural Life of the American Colonies: 1607-1763*. New York, 1957. Wright discusses books, libraries, literary writings, and the press. The information on press output before 1690 is scanty, but the sections on pre-newspaper reading material are excellent. The work examines why colonists were devoted to reading, and it looks at their enormous outpouring of literature.

---. *Religion and Empire: The Alliance Between Piety and Commerce in English Expansion, 1553-1629*. New York, 1965. "[T]he propaganda and influence of the clergy were powerful factors in creating public sentiment for expansion overseas."

Wright, Thomas Goddard. *Literary Culture in New England, 1620-1730*. New York, 1966 (first published in 1920). Colonial Americans loved to read and amassed well-stocked libraries. Wright discusses Puritan writings and offers analysis on the quality of that literature.

Wroth, Lawrence C. *The Colonial Printer*, reprint edition, Charlottesville, Va., 1964 (original edition, New York, 1931). Wroth explores how society shaped printing and describes the physical needs of the colonial printer, hinting at the intellectual and cultural nature of the colonial era. The press was an outgrowth of colonial life, but it also had some influence on the colonies.

ARTICLES

Dunn, Richard S. "Seventeenth-Century English Historians of America," Chapter IX (pp. 195-225) in James Morton Smith, ed., *Seventeenth Century America: Essays in Colonial History*, New York, 1959. Seventeenth-century writings about America from both sides of the Atlantic "document a most subtle and important phenomenon: the initial development of an American consciousness and a growing sense of distinction between the colonial and his fellow Englishmen at home."

Ford, Edwin H. "Colonial Pamphleteers." *Journalism Quarterly* 13 (1936): 24-36. Colonial pamphlets in pre-newspaper America (a form of editorial expression) set a precedent for the press of times to come by offering intelligent commentary on public affairs. Later newspaper editors would take that notion of editorial writing and make it their own.

McIntyre, Sheila. "Reliable Sources in Early Colonial News," pp. 9-22 in Steven R. Knowlton and Karen L. Freeman, eds., *Fair & Balanced. A History of Journalistic Objectivity*. Northport, Ala., 2005. Early Americans treasured news and had various ways to get it in the absence of newspapers. They tended to favor eyewitness accounts and stories related by friends.

Nord, David Paul. "Teleology and the News: The Religious Roots of American Journalism, 1630-1730." *Journal of American History* 77 (June 1990): 9-38. Puritan writers of news believed that all occurrences took place according to God's plan. The Puritans had a great desire for the entire community to understand God's actions, and thus it was important that news be published.

Pennington, Loren E. "*Hakluytus Posthumus:* Samuel Purchas and the Promotion of English Overseas Expansion." *The Emporia State Research Studies* 14 (March, 1966, no. 3). Although Richard Hakluyt's successor Samuel Purchas is often decried as a pale star in comparison to the brilliant Hakluyt, he was an important philosopher in the process of American colonization. Through promotions of settlement, he provided an important intellectual/philosophical underpinning for colonization.

Shaaber, Matthias A. "Forerunners of the Newspaper in America." *Journalism Quarterly* 11 (1934): 339-47. It was natural for colonial printers in the pre-newspaper era to publish news in broadsides and pamphlets, for news events were always of high public interest. Broadsides and pamphlets in turn helped establish a news tradition that newspapers would adopt in later years.

Williams, Julie Hedgepeth. "Evangelism and the Genesis of Printing in America," 1-16 in Wm. David Sloan, ed., *Media and Religion in American History*. Northport, Ala.: 2000. Colonial Americans were evangelists, and they used printing to spread God's word.

---. "Puritans and the Foundations of Objectivity," pp. 23-35 in Steven R. Knowlton and Karen L. Freeman, eds., *Fair & Balanced: A History of Journalistic Objectivity*. Northport, Ala., 2005. Puritans in early Massachusetts avidly embraced the press, insisting that all factions in debates over church doctrine be allowed to publish their views, even if those views disagreed with church authorities.

3

The Colonial Press
1690 – 1765

The colonial newspaper was not born in isolation but grew out of the milieu in which it was founded. It resulted from a host of interrelated processes: economic, political, religious, cultural, and social. As the newspaper cannot be separated from the environment that nurtured it, neither can colonial life be separated from the larger forces that fueled Western civilization. The roots of the American newspaper are found not in the isolation of the colonies but in the interrelationships of the colonies with each other and with England and Europe.

THE TASTE FOR NEWS

In January 1750, *New-York Gazette* publisher James Parker wrote, "This Taste, we Englishmen, have for News, is a very odd one; yet it must be fed; and tho' it seems to be a Jest to Foreigners, yet it is an Amusement we can't be with out."[1] Parker's comment came nearly fifty years after the first continuously published newspaper in British Colonial America, the *Boston News-Letter*, appeared and after nearly thirty years of growth and refinement of American newspapers. His words were prophetic, too. In the decade following his reflection, newspapers would grow at twice the rate of the population. In fifteen years, they would unite against British taxing policies; and in twenty-five years, many of those same newspapers helped fuel the fires of revolution.

The "Taste for News" that existed in America grew from a number of sources. As colonials conquered the elements and established thriving settlements along the Atlantic seaboard, they wanted to know about the events that affected them. They were interested in economic issues, especially in trade. Benjamin Harris intended for America's first newspaper, *Publick Occurrences Both Forreign and Domestick*, to provide commercial information. His prospectus stated that the newspaper would "assist businesses and [merchants'] Negotiations."[2] The second newspaper in the colonies, the *Boston News-Letter*, was intended as a commercial vehicle, as editor John Campbell stated in the first number:

This News-Letter is to be continued Weekly; and all persons who have any Houses, Lands, Tenements, Farns, Ships, Vessels, Goods, Wares or Merchandise, etc. to be Sold, or Let; or Servants Run-away, or Goods Stole or Lost; may have the same inserted at a Reasonable Rate, from Twelve Pence to Five Shillings, and not to exceed.[3]

Early in the colonial period, trade was essentially one-sided, with America needing imports from England for survival. But as the period progressed, it was England that needed American products. By 1775, for example, England was importing hundreds of thousands of bushels of American grain products. Almost 200,000 bushels entered the port of Bristol in 1774 alone.[4] Trade also explains why thousands of newspaper articles on shipping appeared each year.

Religion also fueled the "Taste for News." Religion had always played a significant role in the lives of colonials. Many of the first settlers to reach America came for religious reasons. The Bible was the one item that almost every settler possessed, and parents insisted that children learn to read so that they could understand the Bible. God provided one of the greatest motivations for Harris to begin a newspaper. He said his principal reason for starting *Publick Occurrences* was so "That Memorable Occurrents of Divine Providence may not be neglected or forgotten, as they too often are."[5] The lives of colonials were intertwined with God. Religious leaders helped establish newspapers, and the religious beliefs of both printers and readers affected the news.

Social issues also played a part in the "Taste for News." Issues such as how to set up and support colleges, the ramifications of disease outbreaks, and Native American-colonial relationships affected all of society. In addition, birth reports and obituaries helped give an overview of the structure of society. America's religious views provided a basis for almost all of this information as it appeared in newspapers.

---

[1]*New-York Gazette Revived in the Weekly Post-Boy*, 22 January 1750, 1.
[2]*Publick Occurrences*, 25 September 1690.
[3]*Boston News-Letter*, 24 April 1704.
[4]*Essex Journal and Merrimack Packet: Or, the Massachusetts and New-Hampshire General Advertiser* (Newburyport), 4 January 1775, 2.
[5]*Publick Occurrences*, 25 September 1690.

POLLARD KEENE, and JOHN KEENE,

just imported from London, and to be
fold wholefale and retail, by
JOHN ELLIOT,

At his Looking-glafs Store, the Sign
of the Bell and Looking glafs, in
Chefnut Street, near the State-houfe,
Philadelphia,

A NEAT Affortment of Looking
Glaffes, in Mahogany and Wal-
nut Frames, curves, gilt and plain, viz. Piers, Sconces, Dref-
fing glaffes and Swingers, Hanging glaffes, Shaving-glaffes, painted and Pocket Glaffes, Mahogany and Book Tea chefts. He
alfo new Quickfilvers and frames old Glaffes, and fupplies People
with new Glafs to their own Frames.   The.

Juft imported in the Ship Friendfhip, Capt. M'Clelland, from
London, and to be fold by
JOHN WHARTON,

In Water-ftreet, near Walnut-ftreet, two Doors below Boyaton
and Wharton's Store,

A LARGE Affortment of EUROPEAN and EAST-
INDIA GOODS.   The.

To be SOLD by
JOHN JENNINGS,

Very cheap by Retail, at his Shop, the North-Eaft Corner of
Front and Arch-ftreets, and where Mr. John Maydwell lately
dwelt,

B LUE and green halfthicks, red flannels, ftriped lincey,
ftriped cotton ditto, ozenbrigs, 3 qr. 7 8ths and yard wide
Irifh linen, 3 qr. 7 8ths yard wide yard 3-8ths and 6-qr. cotton
and linen checks. Irifh fheeting curled Ruffia, brown ...

... in Salifbury Townfhip, Northampton County, on the 15th
Inftant, a bright forrel Horfe, about 14 Hands high, a Star in
his Forehead, and all round, has a fhort bob Tail, is a natural
Pacer, and branded on the off Thigh C H, and is about five Years
old. The Owner is defired to prove his Property, pay the Charges, and take him away. ⊕ LAWRENCE HARTMAN.

C AME to the Plantation of John Beerian, in the Townfhip of Warwick, Bucks County, the Beginning of April,
a bright bay Mare a natural Trotter, about 14 Years old, has
neither Brand nor Ear-mark. The Owner is defired to come and
prove his Property, pay Charges, and take her away.   ⊕

Colonial Advertising
One of the primary motives behind the founding of colonial newspapers was to provide a medium for advertising. The most innovative colonial publisher was Benjamin Franklin, who made advertisements more appealing by adding small woodcut illustrations.

Politics affected the "Taste for News." The great majority of
items in newspapers dealt with the politics of Great Britain or high
matters of state of each colony. As colonials worked out economic,
religious, and social issues, newspapers covered the political dialogue that almost always accompanied them.

The fact that newspapers had become vital in England added to
the "Taste for News" in America because most English printers
who came to America felt that beginning a newspaper was their
obligation. For much of the period, colonials looked eastward for
guidance and leadership. English printers left the Mother Country
and set up shops in America. They had both noble and pragmatic
reasons for beginning newspapers. William Parks started a newspaper in Williamsburg, he told readers, to provide them with "in-
exhaustable Treasures, out of which may be extracted everything

that is necessary for the Support of Virtue, the Suppression of Vice,
the Promotion of Learning, Wit, Ingenuity, &c."[6] In Boston, printer Thomas Fleet gave another reason for printing a newspaper. "I
had a prospect of getting a Penny by it," he said.[7] Both reasons
were valid, and both figure into perhaps the ultimate reason newspapers became so important in England first and then in America.
Newspapers provided information, and information was valuable. As the English philosopher Francis Bacon wrote in a religious
treatise titled *Of Heresies*, "knowledge indeed is power."

Possessing knowledge of ship cargoes before ships arrived
gave merchants and traders economic power. Understanding
scripture and being able to relate that knowledge to people gave
clerics religious power. Knowing what was going on within a
community and being able to control that information provided
social power. Having knowledge of the actions of governments
and being able to influence those decisions produced political
power. This knowledge was originally shared in colonial America
through letters written by influential individuals, usually ministers or political leaders. With the development of newspapers,
though, the dispersal of information became available for everyone because taverns made newspapers available for their patrons'
reading and individual subscribers shared them with people they
knew in their own and in other colonies.

When looked at as a whole, then, newspapers grew from the
society they sought to serve and from the understanding that the
more one knew, the more power one could obtain, whether the
power was political, economic, religious, or social. Newspapers
were a reflection of society and became a vital part of the American landscape. When James Parker noted that colonials could not
be without news, he was affirming the fact that in America people
thrived on information and that this knowledge was power.

COLONIAL FORMS OF COMMUNICATION

Socially, the colonies were changing. At least in the larger towns
social activities grew. Along the coast — where concern was not
focused merely on surviving in the wilderness — people began to
meet, to talk, and to socialize. While social life in Boston, the birthplace of American newspapers, was dull compared to such towns
as Charleston or Williamsburg, even there social activities in the
eighteenth century were strikingly colorful in contrast to the previous century. There — as in other major towns — lived the royal
governor, a wealthy merchant class, and an educated elite. The
taverns of Boston and other towns drew a varied clientele of locals
and strangers passing through; and the talk over ale included gossip, political and religious issues, and business matters. While the
newspaper might not replace the tavern as a social institution, it
could provide snippits of intelligence that could offer grist for a
lively evening's discussion. Over time citizens who frequented
taverns joined together in discussion clubs and eventually wanted
their own newspapers to disseminate their views. The taverns

[6]*Virginia Gazette* (Williamsburg), 10 August 1739.
[7]*Boston Evening-Post*, 27 March 1741.

Taverns
Colonial taverns were, next to the church, the most important public institution and, before the appearance of newspapers, provided the best means for the spread of news. In some colonies, towns were fined if they did not have a tavern, and the taverns were required to set up outside signs announcing their location.

offered a ready market for newspapers.

By the late 1600s all the factors needed to produce a newspaper existed. A growing colonial population, an increasingly wealthy upper-class, a better educated citizenry (brought on to some extent by the desire to read the forerunners of the newspaper), interest in the arts and sciences, and the need to be better informed about government, religion, and commerce all help to explain the establishment of newspapers in colonial America. It was a natural development that evolved from a spoken to a written to a primitive printed form. The need for what has been called "surveillance of the environment" may be found in any historical period. It was this need to know that led in Europe and later in the colonies to means of disseminating information. In the colonies the clergy often passed along tidbits of news from their pulpits; the town crier spoke of events and issues in addition to tolling the hour; and citizens in taverns passed along items of interest to others gathered there.

In colonial America it was primarily the pulpit and the tavern that made possible the surveillance of the environment. Before the newspaper's advent, the clergy performed many of the functions we now associate with newspapers. They disseminated matters of public interest from the pulpit. Many sermons dealt with secular issues, politics, and economics, in addition to matters of the soul. Even advertising was not neglected.[8] The clergy were responsible also for early near-newspapers, broadsides, and pamphlets. These publications were little different from the first newspapers in the colonies, lacking only regularity of publication. Often broadsides and pamphlets were issued to dispel falsehood and rumor. Not surprisingly, combatting false information was often among the chief reasons for the founding of early colonial newspapers.

Despite the efforts of the clergy it was the tavern that made possible the widest dissemination of information. At least at the local level the tavern was often the center of government with town meetings, courts, and town officials convening there. Official documents, jury lists, and public notices were all tacked to the tavern's walls along with news items and advertising notices. Because locals as well as travelers frequented the place, the latest news and gossip were apt to be overheard. Tavern owners subscribed to foreign and, later, domestic newspapers and posted them (along with letters and other publications) for customers to read. Patrons not only brought in news but carried away intelligence to be shared with others.

DIFFICULTIES OF PUBLISHING

Clearly the need existed in colonial America for printed newspapers, which offered a more efficient means of disseminating information than churches or taverns did. There were also, however, severe constraints upon their establishment.

Printing technology changed little in the two and one-half centuries following Johann Gutenberg's perfection of a method for casting and using movable type. By the early eighteenth century the press Gutenberg used, based on the wine press of the fifteenth century, had changed little. Type was still being cast in the same way with the same materials. Paper was still made painstakingly from rags. While inks had not changed, they at least could be made from materials on hand. Combined with the legal constraints of licensing and other forms of press control in Europe, the existing technology made establishing a newspaper, or indeed any kind of printing, a costly and difficult undertaking. Circulation problems compounded the difficulty.

With the exception of ink, nearly all equipment and materials needed to produce a newspaper in the colonies had to be import-

---

[8]Such spoken newspapers reached their zenith in Detroit toward the end of the 18th century when the Reverend Gabriel Richard provided for a crier to announce news and advertising items outside church each Sunday. The announcements evolved into a written newspaper which was posted near the church door. Richard's efforts were rewarded in 1809 with the founding of Detroit's first printed newspaper.

Town Criers

Before the appearance of newspapers, people relied on church sermons, tavern conversation, and town criers for much of their information about public affairs. Preachers, as part of church services, often shared with their congregations information they had received. Taverns served as a popular gathering spot for townspeople, and they frequently posted letters and other sources of information on their walls for customers to read. Once newspapers began publishing, many taverns subscribed to them as a means of attracting customers. This drawing (which first appeared in 1882 in *Harper's Weekly*) shows a town crier reading municipal regulations to a crowd of townspeople.

ed. Although the first press in America arrived in Cambridge, Massachusetts, in 1638, the colonies had only fifty presses at the beginning of the Revolution. In 1750 Christopher Sower, Jr., began building second-rate copies of English presses, but even then the colonies continued to import presses. Until Sower began casting type in 1772, all type was imported. Despite high costs, equipment was available to the colonial printer. Paper was another matter. Having sufficient paper on hand to produce any kind of publication was a constant irritation to printers. Paper was made from rags, and the scarcity of this raw material made domestic paper manufacture chancy at best. It remained necessary to import foreign paper until late in the colonial period. Paper costs resulted in the demand for paper outstripping the supply. Printers, therefore, often resorted to ingenious schemes to get rags to produce newsprint. In a clever poem about a woman's dress, Virginia printer William Parks requested readers give him their used-up cloth to send away to make paper. The poem read:

Nice Delia's Smock, which, neat and whole,
No man durst finger for his Soul;
Turn'd to Gazette, now all the Town,
May take it up, or smooth it down.
Whilst Delia may with it dispense,
And no Affront to Innocence.[9]

Printing equipment and materials might be primitive, hard to get, and expensive; but ultimately the success of a newspaper venture depended on the publisher being able to get his publication to readers. Local distribution of newspapers required only that subscribers pick up their copies at some central location, such as a tavern or the newspaper office, or that printers' servants or apprentices hand-deliver them to subscribers. Beyond the local area, various problems hampered distribution.

Not only did printers need to get their publications into a wide circulation area for advertising purposes, they also needed to receive publications from other colonies to provide editorial materi-

al. Today the mails are taken for granted. During the colonial period the postal service was nearly nonexistent. Only in 1692 did the English crown grant authority for the creation of an intercolonial mail service. The postal service developed slowly and handled letters only. Newspapers were carried only if the printer were a postmaster or could bribe a post rider. Forty years following the granting of the first royal monopoly for a postal service, the mails still were irregular and during winter months might not operate at all. In 1758 fixed postal rates were established for newspapers. By the Revolution, the value of newspapers to government and the public was recognized, and distribution became easier and faster.

Licensing had ended by the early eighteenth century but not legal constraints on printers. A printing press was a weapon, a source of power, for those who could control it. It could be a source of extreme irritation to those who could not. The royal governors attempted to control printing, first through licensing (which gave authorities the power to prohibit newspapers from being printed) and then through the law of seditious libel. If they were unable to stop the establishment of a printing venture, they could attempt to control what the printer issued. For decades following the demise of licensing in England, colonial governments continued the attempt to prevent publication of selected newspapers, sometimes successfully, sometimes not. A series of events over the years eroded colonial authorities' control of printing. The first colonial newspaper was banned. Subsequent attempts at control were less successful. Although James Franklin was jailed in Boston as was John Peter Zenger in New York, both published in defiance of authority. Other printers saved themselves from incarceration by apologizing, using subterfuges, or getting out of the printing business. Despite the constant threats against their newspapers, printers continued to publish. A slow evolutionary process, freedom of the press had to await the nineteenth century to become universal in the United States.

It was against this backdrop that the first abortive attempt to publish a regularly scheduled newspaper in colonial America was made. Not surprisingly, it was made in Boston, the largest, wealthiest, and most culturally advanced town in the colonies.

[9]*Virginia Gazette* (Williamsburg), 26 July 1744.

Colonial Printing
Printers in the 1700s used a system in which (left to right, top pic-ture) individual characters of type were kept in separate compart-ments and then were arranged into words and lines, and the lines were placed in a page form. In the bottom picture, the workers are inking the pages of type and then printing single impressions on individual sheets of paper.

THE FIRST ATTEMPT IN AMERICA

When Benjamin Harris arrived in Boston in 1686, he brought with him not only a knowledge of the newspaper craft but a bold spir-it. He had begun his publishing career thirteen years earlier in London, and his publications were controversial from the begin-ning.[10] An ardent Anabaptist, during his first six years as a print-er he became the leading publicist for the Whig political faction and published a number of religious books, several of which at-tacked Quakers and Catholics. While his early work was no doubt disturbing to the authorities, it was only after the establishment of his London newspaper, *Domestic Intelligences: or News from City and Country*, in 1679, that they began to take notice of his activities. However, it was not the newspaper that led to his undoing. In 1680 he published a pamphlet, *Appeal from the Country to the City*, that was critical of King Charles II. He was convicted of seditious libel and sentenced to prison. Following his release, he continued

to be a royal irritant and published a pamphlet, *English Liberties*, which again led to warrants for his arrest. To escape, he fled first to Holland in 1685 and then sailed with his family to Boston in the fall of 1686.

There he opened a combination bookstore and coffee house. Despite keen competition, he soon had a prosperous business. Be-cause of his capacity for supporting the Protestant cause, he began to exercise a visible public role. First, he returned to publishing almanacs and other literary works. His greatest success came with his publication of the *New England Primer*, a spelling book that was reprinted for decades. It was only a matter of time before Harris, an experienced publisher with wide contacts among his clientele, attempted another newspaper.

In the wake of a Puritan rebellion against the British monarchy, on September 25, 1690, Harris used his experience to publish the first newspaper in the colonies. His goal was to support the new Puritan government. He called the paper *Publick Occurrences Both Forreign and Domestick*. It appeared only once, for four days later the authorities suppressed it. A small publication by today's stan-dards, it was four pages, only three of which contained type. The fourth page was left blank, presumably so that subscribers could add their own news as they passed the newspaper on to friends and relatives. The kind of publication Harris intended was obvi-ous from his prospectus. It would be published monthly, he an-nounced, and carry important colonial as well as foreign news. He was particularly concerned that unfounded rumors not damage the Puritan government that had assumed authority in Mass-achusetts. *Publick Occurrences* contained a variety of news. The sto-ries concerned fire, pestilence, crime, Indians, and French royalty.

Despite Harris' good intentions, the final two items concerned authorities. They interpreted the Indian story to be a criticism of the government and the French story to be in bad taste. The stories recounted atrocities committed by Indian allies of the British against French captives — charging that the government should not be involved with such un-Christian acts — and reported a scandal in which the French king had seduced his daughter-in-law. The governing council banned the publication because it had been issued without a license.

Royal licensing had begun under Henry VIII in 1534 and required printers to obtain the king's permission before establish-ing a publishing venture. Licensing continued in England until the Whigs allowed it to die in 1695. In fact, one of the last victims of the licensing laws in England was Harris. Licensing continued in the colonies until 1730. The authority for colonial licensing was contained in a provision of the royal governors' instructions:

> [F]orasmuch as great inconvenience may arise by the liberty of printing within our said province, you are to provide by all nec-essary orders that no person KEEP any press for printing, NOR that any book, pamphlet, or other matter whatsoever be PRINT-ED without your especial leave and license first obtained.[11]

[10]For an account of Harris and his career, see Wm. David Sloan, "Chaos, Polemics, and America's First Newspaper," *Journalism Quarterly* 70 (1993): 666-81.

[11]Leonard W. Labaree, ed., ["Licensing of Printing Presses and Printing"], *Royal Instructions to British Colonial Governors 1670-1776*, 2 vols. (New York, 1935), 2:495.

Publick Occurrences
Benjamin Harris began publishing *Publick Occurrences*, America's first attempt at a newspaper, to provide information during a period that was marked by much political chaos in Massachusetts. The colony's governing council suppressed it after one issue because Harris had not obtained permission to print it.

AMERICA'S FIRST CONTINUOUS NEWSPAPERS

Royal authorities had no wish to make their own position more precarious by encouraging colonial publication. It comes as no surprise, therefore, to discover that a license was apt to be issued only to a publisher who favored the ruling elite. In fact, it was just such a man who, fourteen years later, started the first continuously published newspaper in the American colonies. The only newspaper that could succeed would have to get the advance approval of colonial authorities. The ideal newspaper published under these conditions would be an official voice of government.

Historically, one government official did fit the mold of a safe printer: the postmaster. There was precedence for a postmaster-

publisher. For decades postmasters in Europe had also served as newspaper publishers. The postmaster occupied an ideal position for obtaining information from newspapers and letters and for mailing copies of his own paper. Being a government-appointed officeholder, he normally also had an inside track for acquiring official information. Neither was it unheard of for a printer-post-master to gain an edge by denying a competing printer use of the mails. As early as 1702 the Boston postmaster, John Campbell, was sending hand-written newsletters to governors, merchants, and others in the colonies. His newsletters were concerned mostly with commercial news — ship arrivals and departures — but they also contained news items about government activities in Boston. Despite having the assistance of his brother, by 1704 Campbell found the burden of writing the newsletter by hand too great. On April 24, 1704, he turned to the printing press to produce the first regularly published newspaper in North America.

The *Boston News-Letter* did not really look like a newspaper by today's standards. It was a single sheet, 8 x 12 3/4 inches, printed on both sides. It was dull in comparison to *Publick Occurrences*, for Campbell was postmaster first, journalist second. He lacked Harris' journalistic skill but succeeded where Harris failed because he recognized that his publication must be "safe" to remain in business. Perhaps the most important line of copy in his paper was the notice "Published by Authority," which appeared in prominent type immediately below the paper's nameplate. The notice indicated that the *News-Letter* had been approved in advance and that the reader should expect only news that supported the royal governor's position. In that regard, Campbell maintained an unblemished record. Like Joseph Dudley, the governor who appointed him postmaster, he was an Anglican. He believed that part of his responsibility was to publish a quasi-official report in the form of a newspaper. He filled it with so much government material that Cotton Mather criticized it as "our paltry news-letter."

The *News-Letter* offered foreign, colonial, and local news. As had *Publick Occurrences*, the first issue of the *News-Letter* contained no advertising, an omission that was corrected in following issues. Advertising in colonial papers played an important role. It not only filled subscribers' desire for commercial information; it also was a source of revenue to help meet the expense of producing the publication. Certainly, Boston, with about 8,000 population, could provide an advertising base to help support a newspaper.

In the first decades of the eighteenth century, printers included what advertising they could but depended upon other material for the bulk of their papers' content. As economic conditions improved, the amount of advertising increased. Many newspapers from the 1750s on printed advertising and news about equally. The most successful printers often included more advertising than news, but this was not true for all printers or papers.

The *News-Letter* also established the early pattern for news content. Foreign news dominated. Campbell may have assumed that local readers knew about local events, thus giving him no reason to run local news. Historians are uncertain of the reason, though, that colonial newspapers initially published little local news. It

The Boston News-Letter.

Publiſhed by Authority.

From **Monday** May 1. to **Monday** May 8. 1704.

[facsimile of early Boston News-Letter newspaper text, largely illegible]

First Successful Newspaper

The *Boston News-Letter*, for which publisher John Campbell had received approval from the royal governor in advance, was not a very exciting newspaper. It did, however, contain information useful for subscribers, and it set the tone for early American journalism. Most of its content was reprinted from foreign sources, and it included little local news.

may simply be that the traditional thinking was that other types of news should be emphasized. No reporters or correspondents worked for the *News-Letter*. So Campbell met incoming ships to pick up foreign newspapers, pieces of gossip, and the mails. These were his sources of information. He began a tradition that lasted well into the nineteenth century: clipping information from other papers. Printers gradually came to count on news that appeared in other papers as more accurate than gossip and letters, and they advertised for correspondents to supply them with local news. Some papers even used news writers (reporters) during the French and Indian War.[12]

With time, printers began to include more local news. Although Campbell depended principally on foreign news, he slowly increased the amount of local news in the *News-Letter*. In 1715, for example, the Congregational minister Cotton Mather, who wrote extensively to people in America and England about the events of the day, found increasingly that his readership consulted Campbell's paper for information. In one letter, he wrote that there was little news to add to "what you have in the public News-Letter."[13] During the French and Indian War and Stamp Act crisis, printers often ran news that was almost entirely related to colonial activities. Whenever crises ended during the colonial period, however, printers often returned to Campbell's formula of news dominated by foreign affairs.

While the *News-Letter* borrowed much of its content and made (according to our modern tastes) dull reading, it managed to survive seventy-two years, the first fifteen as a kind of public enterprise. It probably would have continued as a government mouthpiece had Campbell not been removed as postmaster in 1719. Turning over the office of postmaster was one thing, but relinquishing the *News-Letter* was another. Campbell left office but continued to publish the *News-Letter*, now as an independent enterprise. The new postmaster, William Brooker, perhaps at the behest of government leaders and perhaps recognizing that there was profit to be made in newspaper publishing, contracted with James Franklin, older brother of Benjamin Franklin, to print a second Boston newspaper.

With the first issue of the *Boston Gazette*, December 21, 1719, competition came to newspapers in the colonies. It was a genuine competition. Brooker attempted to keep the *News-Letter* from using the mails while sending his own *Gazette* through the postal system. While the *Gazette* continued Campbell's practice of being the governor's mouthpiece, competition led to at least one innovation, so-called "Prices Current." This feature was of value to shippers, farmers, and merchants because it gave current prices for commodities and imported goods. Campbell for his part converted the *News-Letter* into a voice of the colonial assembly in contrast to Brooker's *Gazette*, which represented the royal governor's position. Whether the governor considered Brooker's support inadequate is unclear. However, within a year he lost the postmastership, and his successor, Phillip Musgrave, took over the *Gazette*. The change in publisher was one of the reasons behind the founding of Boston's third newspaper, the *New-England Courant*, and led indirectly to the beginning of one of the most notable newspaper careers of the colonial period. Shortly after Musgrave acquired the *Gazette*, he replaced James Franklin with Samuel Green as printer. Out of the newspaper business, Franklin was eager to get another printing job.

[12]David Copeland, "'Join or Die': America's Press during the French and Indian War," *Journalism History* 24 (1998): 117.

[13]Quoted in Sheila McIntyre, "'A Weekly Piece of Blockheadism': Exploring Cotton Mather's Hatred of the Boston *News-Letter*," paper presented to the American Journalism Historians Association Annual Convention, London, Ontario, October 1996.

THE NEW-ENGLAND COURANT

At the request of John Checkley and Dr. William Douglass, Franklin in 1721 became the printer for a new kind of newspaper, one that, in addition to printing a little foreign and domestic news, also editorialized. Checkley, Douglass, and other members of Boston's lone Anglican church contributed most of the material that the *Courant* printed. Their goal was to destroy the Puritan clergy's popularity so that Anglicanism could be established as the official church in Massachusetts.[14] Opponents ridiculed them as the "Hell-Fire Club." Despite claiming that the *Courant* would not criticize the Puritan clergy, its first issue opened with a vitriolic attack on the Rev. Cotton Mather for his advocacy of inoculation for smallpox. Most Boston doctors opposed inoculation because they believed it was not scientific, but the primary reason the *Courant* opposed it was because Mather favored it. Its attack on him created a sensation, and battle lines were drawn. Mather supporters published in his defense a broadside, *The Little Compton Scourge, or the Anti-Courant.*

Checkley responded in the *Courant's* third issue with an insulting attack that questioned the morality of Mather's nephew. Checkley's and Franklin's Anglican pastors found the essay so obnoxious that they demanded that Checkley sever his association with the paper, and they persuaded Franklin to offer an apology for the article. But the inoculation affair was only the beginning. The *Courant* then turned its barbs on Governor Samuel Shute.

Commerce was the lifeblood of New England. It affected the livelihood of farmers, shippers, and merchants. Of particular concern to citizens of Massachusetts was the presence off the New England coast of pirate ships and French privateers. Many believed the colonial government was doing little to rid shipping lanes of the menace. In June 1722 the *Courant* printed an item about a pirate vessel marauding near the coast and reported that the government was outfitting a ship to pursue it "sometime this month, wind and weather permitting." Enraged at the insinuation, Governor Shute induced the General Court to order Franklin to jail for three weeks. While in jail, Franklin apologized for his attack and promised to mend his ways. However, he was no sooner out of jail than he printed a column of satirical verse belittling the General Court for jailing him.

By 1723 the *Courant* was attacking the royal government on several fronts. Officials were certain about one thing: Franklin was just too bothersome to ignore. The General Court ordered that he "be strictly forbidden ... to print or publish the *New-England Courant* or any pamphlet or paper of the like Nature, Except it be first Supervised, by the Secretary of this Province."[15] When Franklin ignored the order and printed the next issue of the *Courant*, he was held in contempt. He was able to circumvent the order, though, by simply substituting his younger brother's name for his own as publisher of the *Courant*.

Cotton Mather and the *Courant*
America's leading religious and intellectual figure in the early 1700s, Cotton Mather provided the target for the operators of the *New-England Courant*. When he proposed inoculating against smallpox, a small group of ardent Anglican opponents started the *Courant* as a forum for attacking him.

Benjamin Franklin had been apprenticed to James at the age of twelve in 1718. He learned the printing craft from his brother, but writing he apparently learned in secret. His style came from the English publication the *Spectator*, of Joseph Addison and Richard Steele, which Franklin admitted to imitating. The first public evidence of his writing appeared in the *Courant* in 1722 under the pseudonym "Silence Dogood." These letters ran for six months. They were urbane, witty, and better written than other newspaper articles of the period. James Franklin was unaware of the author's identity. Because of the stormy relationship between the two brothers, it is unlikely he would have printed the letters had he known.[16] When he discovered the authorship, he indeed discontinued the letters, although they were the most popular item in the *Courant*.

Naming Benjamin publisher helped James out of a tight legal tangle, but it also offered the younger Franklin a way out of a disagreeable apprenticeship to his rash, overbearing brother. In order to name Benjamin proprietor of the *Courant*, James was required to release him from the apprenticeship contract. While James released his brother publicly, he drew up secret arrangements that kept Benjamin apprenticed. Less than a year passed before Benjamin sneaked out of Boston. He had little to fear that James would attempt to force him back to his apprenticeship because to do so

[14]See Wm. David Sloan, "The *New-England Courant*: Voice of Anglicanism," *American Journalism* 8 (1991): 108-41, for a detailed account of the newspaper.
[15]*New-England Courant*, 14-21 January 1723.

[16]The brothers appear rarely to have had cordial relations, although, at James' request, Benjamin later accepted James' son as an apprentice in his Philadelphia printing shop.

would have forced James to admit the subterfuge.

The *Courant* limped on for another three years with James back at the helm; but it was a dull image of its former self, and readers and advertising support dwindled. It ceased publication in 1726; and James moved with his family to Rhode Island, where he founded that colony's first newspaper. However, the *Courant* had made a mark. It demonstrated that a newspaper could gain attention with controversy.

The *New-England Weekly Journal*, which Samuel Kneeland founded in 1727, soon filled the void that the *Courant's* demise left. Kneeland started the *Journal* much in the way Franklin had started the *Courant*. He had printed the *Boston Gazette*, but a change of postmaster left him with no newspaper to print. So he started his own. While not a direct descendant of the *Courant*, the *Journal* was influenced by the *Courant's* emphasis on commentary. A major difference between the two newspapers was that the *Journal* allied itself with the Puritan majority and not with the small cabal of Anglicans as had the *Courant*. In its early years the *Journal* printed much original material, but by 1730 it was borrowing heavily from the London newspapers. In 1741 the *Journal* brought about the first newspaper merger in America when it combined with the *Boston Gazette* to become the *Gazette and Journal*.

In 1731 a young Boston lawyer, Jeremy Gridley, founded the *Weekly Rehearsal*. Thomas Fleet, who immigrated to America in 1712 and began a printing business shortly thereafter, bought the paper in 1733. Two years later he changed its name to the *Evening-Post* and eventually transformed it into the most widely read paper in Boston. It was well-written and claimed to be impartial, although Fleet's Anglican sympathies were evident and readers frequently criticized him for bias. His sons continued the newspaper into the Revolution.

A newspaper that was to become a thorn to the Patriots during the Revolution was the *Boston Post-Boy*, founded in 1734. It was another example of a newspaper having been started because a publisher of the *Gazette* did not survive a change in the postmastership. The *Post-Boy*, following a short discontinuance in the 1750s, survived into the Revolution, espousing the Tory cause.

WOMEN AND COLONIAL PRINTING

James Franklin's *Rhode Island Gazette* provided the first recorded opportunity for a woman to be involved in the printing of an American newspaper. The *Gazette* was founded in 1732 and ceased publication the following year.[17] Franklin's wife, Ann, was skilled at setting type and performing the other tasks required of a printer. James spent many of the last years of his life suffering from one illness or another; and Ann, like other colonial women, helped her husband in his printing business. Indeed, it is probable that the *Gazette* was a joint enterprise. In a long letter to the readers of the *Gazette* in 1732, James complained of having been ill. Since Ann

Women in Control

A number of women worked in colonial printing, often alongside their husbands and sons. Often when their husbands died, they assumed control of the family's printing and newspaper operations; and some made their newspapers very successful. Two of the most prominent were Mary Katherine Goddard (left) and Anne Catharine Green (right). The Goddards were one of the most prosperous printing families in the colonies. Mary Katherine managed papers in Rhode Island, Maryland, and Pennsylvania. Green ran the *Maryland Gazette* following the death of her husband in 1767. She then formed a company, Anne Catharine Green & Son, with her son, William. After his death, she continued with the company until her death in 1775, when her two other sons assumed control of the paper.

was clearly able to take over James' printing house when he died in 1735, a reasonable assumption is that she was able to conduct the business, including the newspaper, during his many illnesses.[18] Some twenty-five years later, Ann, with her son, James Jr., started the *Newport Mercury*. She probably had little to do with the day-to-day operation of the newspaper, being sixty-two years old and in failing health. However, when her son died in 1762, Ann became intimately involved with the *Mercury*. She took in a partner, and the two continued the newspaper until her death the following year.[19]

Four other women are known to have been involved with newspapers in the period before 1765. Anna Zenger ran the *New-York Weekly Journal* for her husband while he languished in jail charged with seditious libel for nine months in 1734-1735. She picked up material from her husband and saw that it was set in type and printed.[20] Elizabeth Timothy served as editor of the *South-Carolina Gazette* for seven years following her husband's death in 1738. From the first issue that she published, the newspaper carried the notice that she was editor.[21] Sarah Goddard and her daughter, Mary Katherine, were involved in the publication of the *Providence Gazette and Country Journal*. It belonged legally to Sarah's son William, but the Goddard women appear to have been the force behind the newspaper from its founding in 1762. After

[17]It is unclear whether James was a poor businessman or that Newport was not yet ready for a newspaper. The second attempt, a successful one, was not made for another thirty years. James' widow, Ann, and his son started the second newspaper.

[18]Susan Henry, "Ann Franklin: Rhode Island's Woman Printer," in *Newsletters to Newspapers: Eighteenth Century Journalism*, Donovan H. Bond and W. Reynolds McLeod, eds. (Morgantown, W.V., 1977), 129-43.

[19]Isaiah Thomas, *The History of Printing in America* (Worcester, Mass., 1810; New York, 1970), 325-6.

[20]*New York Weekly Journal*, 18 and 25 November 1734.

[21]*South Carolina Gazette*, 4 January 1739.

George Whitefield

Evangelist Becomes America's First Media Celebrity

When George Whitefield died in 1770, newspapers throughout the colonies treated the event as a tremendous loss. The *Connecticut Journal and New Haven Post-Boy* estimated that at least 15,000 people attended his funeral. The *Boston Evening Post* compared him with the Apostles in greatness and importance.

Over the previous thirty years, Whitefield's preaching had become an intercolonial news event. He was a leading apostle of religious reform in England and the colonies. However, as an evangelist and powerful speaker whose voice Benjamin

Franklin estimated could be heard by 30,000 at one time, he did not always draw acclaim from newspapers. For several years after he arrived in America from England in 1739, the Oxford-educated minister drew mixed reviews from publishers on his preaching style and message. Franklin's *Pennsylvania Gazette* praised him as a follower of Jesus Christ but also accused him of faking attendance figures. Thomas Fleet, publisher of the *Boston Evening Post* and a staunch Anglican who argued vociferously against departures from the church's formality, wrote in 1740 that Whitefield's departure would leave Boston "in a hopeful Way of being restor'd to its former State of Order, Peace and Industry."

Whitefield's impact, however, extended beyond his role in religion as a leading figure in the Great Awakening. By bringing his message to the masses, he challenged the established religious order, and that made for good copy.

The press made him America's first celebrity. He even hired a publicist who promoted his early speaking tours. He gave publishers a story that crossed colonial boundaries. His first American tour rivaled England's declaration of war against Spain as the leading intercolonial news story of 1739-1740.

The evangelistic fervor that his seven preaching tours created helped build a sense of journalistic identity and spiritual strength that would aid America in its war for independence from England soon after Whitefield's death.

The revivalist George Whitefield's preaching to large outdoor crowds gained widespread newspaper attention and made him America's first major trans-colonial news figure.

George Whitefield and the Debate over Newspaper Objectivity

The Great Awakening, that powerful religious movement of the 1740s, brought the argument of newspaper neutrality — what today we would call "objectivity" — to the fore. It was the first episode to become an inter-colonial news event, and it brought out newspaper opinions on conflicting sides. The positions that publisher Thomas Fleet took serve as an example of the argument over press partisanship and neutrality.

Most colonials, who were devout Christians, welcomed the Great Awakening enthusiastically. Fleet did not. He used his *Boston Evening-Post* to support High Church Anglicanism and to criticize the leading evangelist, George Whitefield. He complained that people who did not wish to go to revivals should not be "stigmatiz'd as *atheists*, Profligates, or very irreligious Persons, as they lately have been by many." In one article, he decried Whitefield as a quack.

When readers condemned Fleet for continually publishing criticism, he resorted to the argument that many printers took up in times of trouble. He said simply that he wished "to be look'd upon only as a Printer, and not as a Party." He was, he insisted, nothing more than a press operator who printed what other people — not he — wanted printed. "[A]s I have often declared," he claimed several times, "so do I again declare, that I am of no Party, but act purely as a *Printer*...." Since the public viewed printers simply as businessmen, he also explained that he printed anything he thought he could make a profit on, no matter what his opinion of it was. If anyone were to blame for what newspapers published, he contended, it was the authors who had written the articles.

His unpopular stand lost readers, however, and eventually he felt obligated to recant and apologize.

1765 Mary Katherine managed two other newspapers started by William, the *Pennsylvania Chronicle and Universal Advertiser* and the *Maryland Journal*. Many other women were involved with newspapers after 1765.[22]

PHILADELPHIA NEWSPAPERS

While somewhat smaller in the early eighteenth century, Philadelphia was in many respects similar to Boston. It was a leading seaport with great commercial activity; it was a center of a growing commercial class; it was literate. By 1740 it had become the largest city in America. All the ingredients necessary for the founding of a newspaper were present when on December 22, 1719, the first issue of the *American Weekly Mercury* was pulled from the press. Its founder was a member of one of colonial America's most illustrious printing families.

The patriarch of that family was William Bradford. He began by printing pamphlets and tracts for Quakers; and because he owned the only press in Philadelphia, he also printed government documents. It was the publication of the latter that led to his censure by Quaker authorities in 1693 and his departure for New York, where he printed anti-Quaker tracts and thirty-two years later established that city's first newspaper. When he left Philadephia, he left his printing shop in the hands of an apprentice. The story of Philadelphia newspapers begins with Bradford's son, Andrew.

Andrew Bradford learned the printer's craft in his father's New York shop. In 1712 he returned to Philadelphia to take control of his father's old printing shop. Quaker leadership had mellowed in the intervening years, and Andrew was able to serve both the Friends and the colonial government without the strict oversight his father had endured. In fact he became the official printer and postmaster. These positions placed him in a favorable position to start the Pennsylvania colony's first newspaper. The *American Weekly Mercury* demonstrated a bit more independence than its contemporaries in Boston. It occasionally even criticized the government. However, it did not do so with impunity, for Bradford was arrested for his criticisms of the authorities. He was not prosecuted, however, and the *Mercury* became even more daring. Following Andrew's death in 1742, his widow continued the *Mercury*, but it survived only four years. The newspaper might have continued much longer had it not been for a family dispute.

Some years before his death, Andrew adopted his nephew, William Bradford III, and taught him the printing business. William might have operated the *Mercury* after his uncle's death if not for great animosity between him and his foster mother. On Andrew's death, William founded, as a means of revenge on Mrs. Bradford, a competitor for the *Mercury*, the *Pennsylvania Journal*. If the *Mercury* had been daring, the *Journal* was positively bold. A successful newspaper for fifty years under the editorship of William and his son, Thomas, the *Journal* became a powerful and outspoken champion of the Patriots during the Revolution.

Benjamin Franklin, Printer
Even though Franklin later gained greater fame as a diplomat and inventor, he remained a printer at heart. For his own epitaph, he wrote, "The Body of Benjamin Franklin, Printer, (like the cover of an old Book, its contents worn out, and stript of its lettering and gilding) lies here, food for worms! Yet the work itself shall not be lost, for it will, as he believed, appear once more in a new and more beautiful edition, corrected and amended by its Author."

BENJAMIN FRANKLIN

The newspaper battles in Philadelphia were not only familial; they also involved other newspapers. Bradford's competition arrived in the form of the best known journalist of the colonial period, Benjamin Franklin. Escaped apprentice and world traveler, Franklin entered Philadelphia inauspiciously but by 1728 was already planning to start a newspaper. When another printer, Samuel Keimer, heard of Franklin's plan, he hurried to start his own newspaper. Founded under the clumsy title of *The Universal Instructor in All Arts and Sciences: and Pennsylvania Gazette*, Keimer's paper compared favorably with the *Mercury* and led to Franklin's concern that it might succeed and lock him out of the Philadelphia newspaper business for the forseeable future.

To prevent the *Universal Instructor*'s success, Franklin devised a scheme to destroy the paper.[23] He and several friends wrote a number of essays in the tradition of Joseph Addison, who was ever an inspiration to Franklin, for the *Mercury*, satirizing Keimer. The essays attracted considerable attention to the *Mercury* and ensured Keimer's failure. Whether the "Busy-Body" essays were

[22]Marion Marzolf, *Up From the Footnote* (New York, 1977), 5-6.

[23]*The Autobiography of Benjamin Franklin* (New York, 1939), 77-8.

Franklin's Newspaper

In his autobiography, Benjamin Franklin claimed that he had planned to start a newspaper but that one of his employees confided his plan to the rival printer Samuel Keimer. After Keimer beat him at founding a paper, Franklin then helped Philadelphia's opposing newspaper to ridicule Keimer and the *Pennsylvania Gazette*. As the *Gazette* foundered, Franklin was able to buy it at a low price from Keimer. He then made it one of the most successful newspapers of the colonial period. By the time he was forty-two years old Franklin had secured enough income through his printing business that he was able to retire to follow other pursuits. This painting is the first portrait of Franklin (inset), made in 1748, the year of his retirement.

as influential as Franklin believed is unclear. They did allow him, though, to buy the *Gazette* for a pittance. Soon, Keimer moved to Barbadoes and in 1731 began the *Barbadoes Gazette*. It was the first newspaper published in the Caribbean islands and the first, for many years, published twice a week anywhere in the Americas.

In 1729 Franklin shortened the newspaper's title to the *Pennsylvania Gazette* and turned the paper into a solid one. It carried more news and advertising. By 1750 it printed six pages, up to eight pages on occasion, with heavy advertising. Franklin became Bradford's successor as postmaster, which helped Franklin greatly. The

Gazette and other printing enterprises made him a rich man so that by the age of forty-two he could retire and devote himself to other pursuits. A Franklin protegé from London, David Hall, became sole owner of the *Gazette* in 1766. His family along with several partners continued the newspaper until 1815.

Franklin did not satisfy himself with only the *Gazette* during his long career. He also published the first foreign-language newspaper in the colonies, the *Philadelphia Zeitung*. Along with Louis Timothee, he founded the German-language newspaper in 1732, but it lasted only a few issues. However, its successors, Christopher Sower's *Germantown Zeitung* and Heinrich Miller's *Wöchentliche Philadephische Staatsbote*, were highly successful newspapers. Another Franklin first had to be shared with his competitor, Andrew Bradford. They produced the first magazines in the colonies within three days of each other. Bradford's *American Magazine* and Franklin's *General Magazine* were both released in January 1741. They were short lived, however, both failing within the year.

NEWSPAPERS IN NEW YORK

The third largest city in the colonies was New York, and it was the third city to have a newspaper. William Bradford founded the paper. After abandoning Philadelphia when pressure from Quakers became too great, he moved to New York City at the request of the colonial council to continue his printing business. A cautious man, he waited three decades to begin his own newspaper, after three papers had been founded in Boston, and he had seen his son's success with the *Mercury* in Philadelphia. The *New-York Gazette*, first issued November 8, 1725, was a small, unattractive two-page sheet that was "published by authority." It carried little advertising but managed to survive for nearly two decades.

New York's importance to newspaper development centers on freedom of the press. Its second newspaper was founded because of political developments. As had occurred in Boston, there arose in New York an opposition group to the royal governor. The group wanted its own newspaper; and on November 5, 1733, the *New-York Weekly Journal* was born. A German immigrant, John Peter Zenger, was printer and publisher. He had served his apprenticeship with Bradford and so was a good printer. James Alexander, a lawyer who served virtually as editor-in-chief, stated the newspaper's purpose in a private letter:

> Inclosed is the first of a newspaper designed to be continued Weekly and chiefly to expose [Governor William Cosby] and those ridiculous flatteries with which Mr. Harison [the Recorder and a member of the Council] loads our other Newspaper which our Governor claims and has the privilege of suffering nothing to be in but what he and Mr. Harison approve of.[24]

The *Journal* did as promised. From the beginning it subjected the governor to scathing attacks. His only defense for the next year appeared in Bradford's *Gazette*. Each defense brought a new attack.

[24]Quoted in Livingston Rutherford, *John Peter Zenger* (New York, 1941), 28-9.

New York's First

The *New-York Gazette*, a small unattractive sheet, was that colony's first newspaper. After setting up in the printing business, William Bradford, a cautious man, waited three decades before finally starting the newspaper in 1725.

The controversy between the two factions and the two newspapers revolved around ideological issues. The *Gazette* defended the status quo, the governor, and his council. The *Journal* promoted the opposing faction. The governor decided to crush the *Journal*. On November 17, 1734, after grand juries twice had failed to indict Zenger, Cosby had him arrested and charged with seditious libel, despite the fact Zenger was merely a printer and had not himself written any of the offensive material. He spent nine months in jail but continued to publish the *Journal* from his cell. Finally brought to trial, he was acquitted by a sympathetic jury. While the verdict did not change colonial law, it did help intensify opposition to British authority.

THE FRENCH AND INDIAN WAR

In the 1750s, English and French colonies in America, which hugged the Atlantic seaboard or the St. Lawrence River in Canada, began westward expansion beyond the Appalachian Mountains. Both Britain and France sought to establish settlements in the Ohio Valley, and both claimed the area as their own. The dispute led to a number of skirmishes and the French and Indian War, which lasted from 1754 to 1763. The war, as Boston printer Thomas Fleet noted, became "The Main Subject of the Publick Attention."[25] It captured a large percentage of the news space in America's newspapers until France surrendered Canada in 1760.

The importance of the French and Indian War to colonials and the reason it became the focus of newspapers rest in the fact that it threatened nearly all that was important to colonials. Economically, France disrupted trade at sea and with Native Americans in the backcountry. Religiously, a French victory meant that Catholicism would defeat Protestantism, and American newspapers since *Publick Occurrences* had warned of the dangers that the Roman church posed to America. Socially and culturally, a French victory would have changed the standing order. Politically, the change was obvious and also tied to the religious issue. Britain and France had been at war off and on for years; and Americans in the 1750s, for the most part, still felt as if they were English. Their feelings about the war were eloquently summed up by a writer to the *Virginia Gazette*, calling himself the "Virginia Centinel." He wrote in 1756, "FRIENDS! COUNTRYMEN! ... AWAKE! ARISE! When our Country, and all that is included in that important Word, is in most threatening Danger; when our Enemies are busy and unwearied in planning and executing their Schemes of Encroachments and Barbarity... I need only repeat, YOUR COUNTRY IS IN DANGER."[26]

As newspapers focused on the war, they also turned readers' attention toward Native Americans. Colonial-Indian relations had been a significant part of America's development. From the beginning, newspapers informed readers of Indian activity. Because English settlement forced Indian nations from their homes, the relationship between colonials and Indians was often tenuous at best. Numerous wars took place, and newspapers often referred to Indians during times of unrest as the "Sculking Indian Enemy." But many colonials realized that peaceful co-existence with Indian nations was imperative to survival. During the French and Indian War, Native Americans were viewed as enemies and as sovereign nations capable of forming alliances with individual colonies to fight against the French.

The value of positive relations with Indians helped spur the Albany Congress in June 1754. It was designed to bring colonies together and to bring as many Indian tribes as possible into an alliance with them. Benjamin Franklin pushed strongly for the congress and created the first political cartoon to demonstrate its significance. Printers in other towns quickly copied the "JOIN, or DIE" woodcut that appeared in the *Pennsylvania Gazette* on May 9, 1754. The famous snake, divided into separate pieces, warned colonials that if they did not join together to fight the French they

[25] *Boston Evening-Post*, 15 March 1757.
[26] *Virginia Gazette* (Williamsburg), 30 April 1756.

Founding of Newspapers in the American Colonies 1690-1764

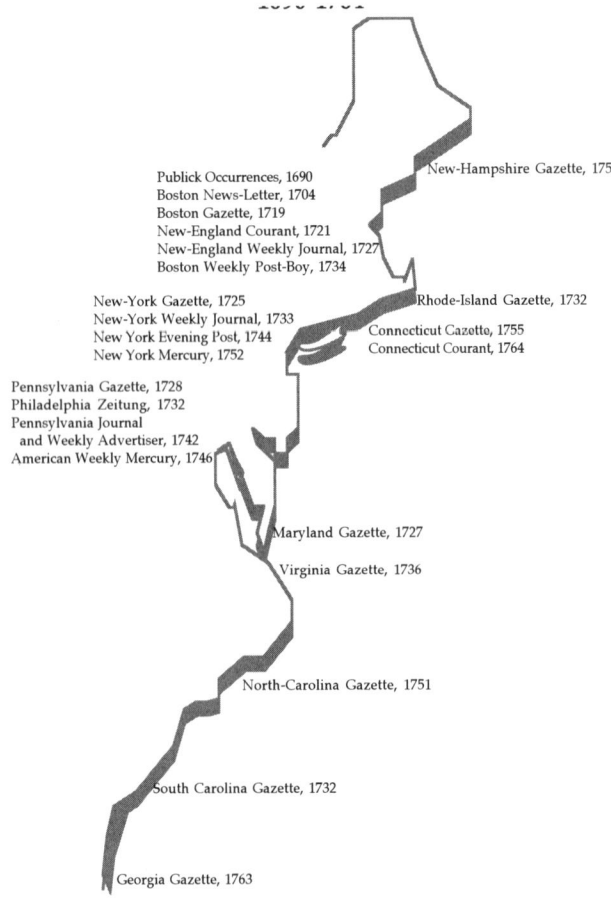

Publick Occurrences, 1690
Boston News-Letter, 1704
Boston Gazette, 1719
New-England Courant, 1721
New-England Weekly Journal, 1727
Boston Weekly Post-Boy, 1734

New-Hampshire Gazette, 1756

New-York Gazette, 1725
New-York Weekly Journal, 1733
New York Evening Post, 1744
New York Mercury, 1752

Rhode-Island Gazette, 1732

Connecticut Gazette, 1755
Connecticut Courant, 1764

Pennsylvania Gazette, 1728
Philadelphia Zeitung, 1732
Pennsylvania Journal
   and Weekly Advertiser, 1742
American Weekly Mercury, 1746

Maryland Gazette, 1727

Virginia Gazette, 1736

North-Carolina Gazette, 1751

South Carolina Gazette, 1732

Georgia Gazette, 1763

The Spread of Newspapers

The founding of newspapers in the colonies was generally based on population growth. The earliest newspapers were located in the larger towns where literacy, a merchant class, and a need by government to present information it considered important provided the impetus. Newspapers did not appear until later in the other colonies, and New Jersey did not have a newspaper until after 1765. In fact, more than two-thirds of colonial newspapers were founded after 1750. Americans everywhere wanted news, but the ability of a locale to support a newspaper financially was another matter. Without a subscription base of at least 300 and sources for ad revenue, a paper could not succeed. By the middle of the 1730s, a dozen newspapers existed. That number remained constant into the 1750s, when an explosion of newspapers occurred. Increased population, commerce, and war stimulated the growth. The French and Indian War (1754-1763) led directly to a number of newspaper starts. By war's end, twenty-three newspapers printed regularly. Listed below are some additional newspapers and their founding dates not shown on the map above. Identifying and distinguishing newspapers can sometimes be difficult because many early papers carried the same nameplate. Sometimes more than one used the same name at the same time. *New York Gazette or Weekly Post Boy*, 1742; *New York Gazette*, 1759; *Maryland Gazette*, 1745; *South-Carolina Weekly Journal*, 1732; *South-Carolina Gazette and Country Journal*, 1765; *Newport* (R.I.) *Mercury*, 1758; *Providence* (R.I.) *Gazette and Country Journal*, 1762; *New-London* (Conn.) *Summary*, 1758; *New-London Gazette*, 1763; *Cape-Fear Gazette* and *Wilmington Advertiser* (North Carolina), 1764; *Portsmouth* (N.H.) *Mercury and Weekly Advertiser*, 1765; and *Wilmington* (Del.) *Courant*, 1762.

would all die separately. The concept was so powerful for Americans that newspapers used it repeatedly during the next thirty years to combat the Stamp Act and as a rallying point before and during the Revolution.

The woodcut, ironically, also became a symbol for what newspapers needed to do. Out of necessity, printers during the war joined together to present news. News was shared as quickly as possible. Timeliness in the eighteenth century was measured in days and weeks, not seconds and minutes. Still, war news from South Carolina, for example, appeared in New Hampshire in less than three weeks after an event, a movement of information that was about as fast as possible. Newspaper printers also began to think of information obtained from other papers as more accurate than word-of-mouth reports; and some papers used "newswriters" to cover the fighting, although the practice was rare and seems to have ended following the defeat of Canada. By joining together to present comprehensive details of the war, newspapers began creating a competent network for information exchange and dissemination that colonials increasingly found they could not do without. Printers continued to use this network during the Stamp Act crisis in 1765.

Great Britain attempted to recoup its costs of fighting the war by levying a number of taxes on the colonies. That action led to another eruption in newspaper starts. Parliament passed the infamous Stamp Act in 1765 to replenish its coffers and as a way to make the colonies pay for their own defense during the war. The colonists considered the act another slight by London. Its timing was poor because the colonies were suffering through a depression following the war. A Stamp Tax on newspapers had existed in Britain since 1712, and similar acts in Massachusetts and New York during the French and Indian War had met little opposition. Colonials, however, vigorously resisted the Stamp Act of 1765. It may ultimately have been that they were no longer prepared to accept orders from London as meekly as in the past.

The Stamp Act hit merchants, lawyers, and printers particularly hard. As the date approached for it to become law, some newspapers ceased publication rather than pay the new tax. Other Americans, however, started newspapers in opposition to the tax. Protests, riots, and problems in getting the taxed paper to America ensured that no newspaper was ever printed with a stamp tax seal. In 1766, Parliament repealed the Stamp Act, but many Americans began to regard Britain's treatment of the colonies as oppressive. Opposition to English polices grew, and newspapers often spearheaded the effort.

RECOMMENDED READINGS

BOOKS

Beasley, Maurine H., and Sheila J. Gibbons. *Taking Their Place: A Documentary History of Women and Journalism.* Lanham, Md., 1994. This overview of the history of women in journalism includes reprints of some of their work.

Brigham, Clarence S. *A History and Bibliography of American Newspapers, 1690-1820.* Worcester, Mass., 1947. This indispensable resource for the colonial journalism historian provides a compilation of names, dates, locations, and existing copies

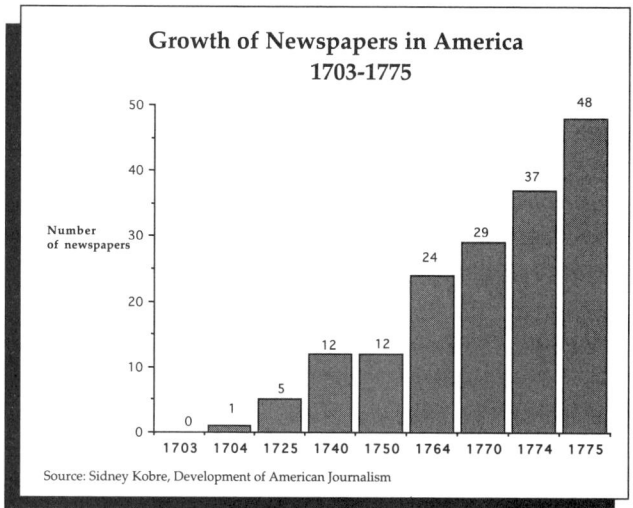

Growth of Newspapers in America 1703-1775

Source: Sidney Kobre, Development of American Journalism

Newspaper Growth

Starting slowly, growth in the number of newspapers in colonial America accelerated after the mid-eighteenth century. As passions increased in the years immediately preceding the American Revolution, newspapers provided a means for Tories and Patriots to present their views.

of virtually all colonial newspapers.

Brown, Richard D. *Knowledge Is Power: The Diffusion of Information in Early America 1700-1865.* New York, 1989. Early Americans were especially interested in having information about a variety of public affairs, and they used a variety of mass and interpersonal means to circulate it and to obtain it.

Clark, Charles E. *The Public Prints.* New York, 1994. Newspapers helped to provide a forum for public discussion.

Cook, Elizabeth C. *Literary Influences in Colonial Newspapers, 1704-1750.* New York, 1912. The colonial newspaper was the most important source in the dissemination of non-sectarian literature in the colonies. It was to a large extent a non-news literary journal.

Copeland, David A. *Colonial American Newspapers: Character and Content.* Newark, Del.: 1997. The author's explanations in this detailed study are essential to understanding colonial newspapers.

---. *Debating the Issues in Colonial Newspapers.* Westport, Conn., 2000. This explanation of the major issues and events of the era provides readings from newspapers to demonstrate how printers and others used the press to influence public opinion.

---. *The French and Indian War, 1754-1763.* Westport, Conn., 2005. The author explains the nature of the war and the press while providing an account of the news coverage of the war.

Frasca, Ralph. *Benjamin Franklin's Printing Network.* Columbia, Mo., 2006. Franklin produced a printing network throughout the colonies to disseminate information, especially his notion of moral truths that would create a better society.

Geitz, Henry. *The German-American Press.* Madison, Wisc., 1992. A series of essays discuss German-American newspapers, magazines, and books.

Kobre, Sidney. *The Development of the Colonial Newspaper.* Pittsburgh, 1944. This "sociological" account examines the development of the colonial newspaper from a social, economic, and political perspective.

Marzolf, Marion. *Up From the Footnote.* New York, 1977. This examination of how women printers and journalists have been treated in the profession contains a useful discussion on women in the colonial period.

Sloan, Wm. David, and Julie Hedgepeth Williams. *The Early American Press, 1690-1783.* Westport, Conn., 1994. This in-depth study, the best general history of the colonial press, looks at newspapers through the end of the Revolution.

Startt, James D., and Wm. David Sloan. *The Significance of the Media in American History.* Northport, Ala., 1994. Sixteen essays profile the various ways media have influenced American life from the colonial period to the present day.

Steele, Ian K. *The English Atlantic 1675-1740.* New York, 1986. Steele's excellent study examines the communication relationships between England and her colonies.

Thomas, Isaiah. *History of Printing in America.* 2 vols. Worcester, Mass., 1810. This standard reference for the colonial period includes biographies of printers and a colony-by-colony description of newspapers.

ARTICLES

Aldridge, A. Owen. "Benjamin Franklin and the Pennsylvania Gazette." *Proceedings of the American Philosophical Society* 106 (1962): 77-81. In colonial newspapers, news was the most important content; and essays, opinions, and literary material were only fillers.

Bradley, Patricia. "Forerunner of the 'Dark Ages': Philadelphia's Tradition of a Partisan Press." *American Journalism* 13 (1996): 126-40. Partisanship was strong in newspapers in colonial Pennsylvania, and it laid a foundation for such practices in later journalism.

Copeland, David A. "'A Receipt Against the Plague': Medical Reporting in Colonial America." *American Journalism* 11 (1994): 204-18. American newspapers kept readers informed of epidemics and potential cures.

—. "In All the Papers: Reporting on Religion in Colonial America." *American Journalism* 13 (1996): 390-415. Religion was the focus of early American life and one of the key subjects appearing in newspapers.

—. "Religion and Colonial Newspapers." 54-67, in Wm. David Sloan, ed., *Media and Religion in American History.* Northport, Ala., 2000. Religion was an integral part of the news and a motivator of events in colonial America.

—. "'Securing the Affections of Those People at this Critical Juncture': Newspapers, Native Americans, and the French and Indian War, 1754-1763." *American Journalism* 19 (Fall 2002): 37-66. Native-American tribes were not just the enemy of Americans; they were viewed as sovereign nations, and the colonies vied to obtain treaties and alliances with them, something newspapers reported consistently during the French and Indian War.

Eberhard, Wallace B. "Press and Post Office in Eighteenth-Century America: Origin of a Public Policy." in Donovan H. Bond and W. Reynolds McLeod, eds., *From Newsletters to Newspapers: Eighteenth-Century Journalism.* Morgantown, W.Va., 1977, 145-54. Except for a supportive postal system, newspapers might have been unable to survive.

Henry, Susan. "Colonial Woman as Prototype: Toward a Model for the Study of Minorities." *Journalism History* 3 (1976): 20-4. Women printers performed a demanding and important service and, as businesswomen, played an important role in the colonial economy.

Hoffman, Ronald. "The Press in Mercantile Maryland: A Question of Utility." *Journalism Quarterly* 46 (1969): 536-44. Newspapers — even though they were helpful, convenient, and useful — were not essential or vital to the prospering of the merchant community or colonial economy.

Kobre, Sidney. "The First American Newspaper: A Product of Environment." *Journalism Quarterly* 17 (1940): 335-45. The economic and social background was the key factor in the origin of the colonial newspaper.

Lambert, Frank. "'Pedlar in Divinity': George Whitefield and the Great Awakening, 1737-1745." *Journal of American History* 77 (1990): 812-37. The popular preacher used the press as a public relations tool.

Marzolf, Marion. "The Woman Journalist: Colonial Printer to City Desk." *Journalism History* 1 (1974-75): 100-7 and 146; and 3 (1976-77): 24-7. These two special issues of *Journalism History* are on the history of women in journalism. A general survey history of women in journalism is provided by Marzolf's two-part series.

Mitchell, Catherine C. "Scholarship on Women Working in Journalism." *American Journalism* 7 (1990): 33-8. This bibliography covers the major works concerning women as journalists.

Nelson, William. "Some New Jersey Printers and Printing in the Eighteenth Century." *Proceedings of the American Antiquarian Society* 21, n.s. (1911): 15-56. Colonial printers were ideological pioneers who, through the power of their trade and the strength of their ideals, helped create the American nation and the profession of journalism.

Nord, David Paul. "Teleology and News: The Religious Roots of American

Journalism, 1630-1730." *Journal of American History* 77:1 (1990): 9-38. "[T]he characteristics of American news, both in its content and reporting, were 'deeply rooted' in the religious culture of New England, and evinced a patterned, recurrent, meaningful, and intelligible approach to news reporting."

Nordin, Kenneth. "The Entertaining Press: Sensationalism in Eighteenth-Century Boston Newspapers." *Communication Research* 6 (1979): 295-320. Sensationalism in American journalism began not with the penny press in the 1830s but with the colonial press.

Oldham, Ellen M. "Early Women Printers in America." *Boston Public Library Quarterly* 10 (1958): 6-26, 78-92, and 141-53. The common characteristic of female printers "was the necessity of supporting themselves, and in most cases their children, upon the death of their husbands." The women had "unusual forcefulness of character."

Sloan, Wm. David. "Chaos, Polemics, and America's First Newspaper." *Journalism Quarterly* 70 (1993): 666-81. Benjamin Harris started *Publick Occurrences* to try to assist the Puritan rebellion in New England.

—. "The Colonial Press, 1690-1765: Mirror of Society or Origin of Journalism?" 28-40, in *Perspectives on Mass Communication History* (Hillsdale, N.J., 1991). This historiographical essay analyzes the approaches that historians have taken.

—. "Neutrality and Colonial Newspapers," chapter 3 in Steven R. Knowlton and Karen L. Freeman, eds. *Fair and Balanced: A History of Journalistic Objectivity.*

Northport, Ala., 2005. "The concept that newspapers should be objective … originated with the concept of the printing press as a mechanical device used simply to produce material for customers."

—. "The *New England Courant*: Voice of Anglicanism." *American Journalism* 8 (1991): 108-41. The purpose of the *Courant*, rather than being to bring about a liberalization of society, as some historians have claimed, was to promote Anglicanism as the official church in Massachusetts.

—. "The Origins of the American Newspaper." 32-53, in Wm. David Sloan, ed., *Media and Religion in American History*. Northport, Ala., 2000. America's first newspapers were started in Boston because it was the leading town in the most Puritan colony in North America.

Spaulding, E. Wilder. "The Connecticut Courant, A Representative Newspaper in the Eighteenth Century." *New England Quarterly* 3 (1930): 443-63. Although colonial newspapers were the "drab, unpretentious by-product of the tiny print shop," they were an integral and important part of American life.

Williams, Julie Hedgepeth. "The Media and the Personification of Society." 45-64 in James D. Startt and Wm. David Sloan, eds., *The Significance of the Media in American History*. Northport, Ala., 1994. Using the *South-Carolina Gazette* as an example, this study describes how newspapers of the colonial era were a reflection of society.

4

The Revolutionary Press
1765 - 1783

The American Revolution may have been the single most important event in the nation's history. During a period of less than two decades of the eighteenth century, Americans developed a political philosophy, declared their sovereignty, fought a war for independence, and transformed a weak inter-colonial alliance into an organization of states.

The Revolution gave the colonial press new functions to fulfill. As the thirteen British colonies slowly dissolved their ties with the mother country, newspapers played an increasingly important role in the growing dispute. Both Patriot and Loyalist writers used pamphlets and the weekly papers to attempt to convince their neutral countrymen to support their side. The most successful were the Patriots, so much so that, by the time the Revolution had begun, pro-British newspapers had disappeared from most colonies.

The American Revolution developed out of many circumstances. The ideas behind the separation from Great Britain derived from dissident Protestantism and Enlightenment rationalism. Of particular importance were the Bible and the works of John Locke and Baron Charles Montesquieu, English and French philosophers, respectively. Basing their thinking on Biblical tenets, dissident Protestants (that is, those opposed to the official Church of England) argued that all men, since they were created by God, inherited certain rights, including liberty and equality. Political philosophers argued that these "natural rights" should be protected by government. Included among these rights were trial by jury and local participation in government. Heavily influenced by the ideas of Locke, a Protestant Enlightenment thinker, Americans came to believe that governments were created by people to bring order to society. Rulers governed not through divine right but through either usurpation or social contract. The contract did not bestow absolute power on rulers but rather entrusted them only with the power needed to protect people's natural rights. When a ruler broke the contract, reasoned Locke, subjects had a right to replace him.[1]

Englishmen and colonials, who considered themselves English-men, believed that the British system of government was the best in the world. Through its balanced system that divided power among King, Lords, and Commons, it gave representation to all sections of society. Maintaining that balance resulted in the preservation of all subjects' rights and interests and thus made tyranni-cal government impossible. Colonials believed that the British constitution protected their rights as British subjects. They thought that their own colonial governments, which were set up under the authority of the British crown and which were modeled after the British structure, helped extend the rights of Englishmen to all parts of the British empire. When colonials discovered, however, that their "rights" could be abrogated whenever they conflicted with the interests of Britons with ties to the government, they began to question their vision of the British constitutional system. It was at times when colonials felt as if the British government were ignoring their right to representation that colonial protest intensified. The eventual result was rebellion.

Two events served as the catalysts for the beginning of the Revolutionary period in media history. One was the end of the Seven Years' War (known as the French and Indian War in North America). The other, even more important in its effect on the press, was the Stamp Act of 1765. When the Treaty of Paris ended the Seven Years' War in 1763 and drove French troops from North America, colonial soldiers and civilians joined their British compatriots in cheers and toasts. The war had been long and bloody. The victory for the first time guaranteed the safety of the entire eastern seaboard from Upper Canada to Florida and opened up the western frontier for development. But it also shifted attention from troubles with the French and their Indian allies and from the common British-colonial interests to differences between England and the colonies. Even during the war, differences had sharpened, especially disagreements over who should raise and support a militia. With the war ended and the common enemies defeated, other problems that had been submerged surfaced. A number of controversies between the colonies and the home government marked the next decade.

After Britain's years of fighting a global war and suffering the

[1]John Locke, *Two Treatises on Government* (1689).

JOIN, or DIE.

JOIN or DIE

Symbol of a Revolution
Benjamin Franklin created the divided-snake cartoon in 1754 (top drawing) to encourage the colonies to unite in opposition to France's military efforts to extend its power in America. With the end of the French and Indian War in 1763, which removed the danger from the American frontier, British and colonial differences began to intensify. Patriot printers revived the cartoon during the opposition to the Stamp Act in 1765 and the "Intolerable Acts" in 1774. The parts of the snake represented the disjointed colonies. It became the most popular visual symbol during the Revolutionary period. The *Constitutional Courant* used the idea as an engraving in the center of its nameplate (bottom drawing), with the slogan "Unite and Conquer" issuing from the serpent's mouth.

sacrifices required, its treasury demanded immediate replenishment. The war had doubled England's national debt, and military and administrative expenses in America had increased several times. Parliament believed that victory benefited all citizens of the Empire and that all citizens therefore should help pay the costs. Americans, however, looked toward the opportunities that victory offered rather than the responsibilities it required. Theirs was a spirit of increasing self-reliance and a chaffing under restraint. The elimination of the French and Indian threat made them feel far less dependent on the mother country. Coupled with that, 3,000 miles of treacherous ocean kept Britain and America apart, isolating the latter and making a shambles of communication. Sailing ships, the primary mode of communication, took about six weeks to cross the Atlantic. The isolation created a pride in what the colonials had created for themselves. While ill-disposed to shoulder the burden for the greatly enlarged British empire, they grew increasingly insistent on their own rights and liberties. They looked with resentment on any attempts by the British government to saddle them with the expenses of war, security, and a mercantile system aimed

primarily at benefiting British industry and business. British officials, concerned about economic problems of the home country, seemed ignorant of American attitudes. The only means that they believed existed for solving their problems was to implement new taxes by the quickest means possible.

In America the tax program covered all manner of goods and services. The Sugar Act of 1764 was the first in a series of laws and was followed by the Stamp Act in 1765. British officials thought it only fair that colonials should help pay the costs of security, but Americans argued that they too had incurred debts during the war and that they already were taxed by local governments to help pay the debts. Colonials looking for more independence in their own affairs were eager to use any opportunity to denounce acts of the British government, and the former cooperative attitude of subjects of the crown turned "into distrust, and foreboding" and then eventually into hatred and repudiation.[2] When Britain enacted the Stamp Act, it enhanced the opportunities for these independent-minded colonials.

It was in the conflict over the Stamp Act that newspapers discovered a new role to play. Printers protested the Act for various reasons. Most feared a loss of income; but, more importantly, they believed it was an infringement on colonial rights because no one had the authority to impose taxes but elected representatives. Since Americans did not vote for members of the British Parliament, they reasoned, Parliament could not impose taxes on the colonies. This concept of the power of taxation, which was developed in the newspaper arguments of 1765, became the basic tenet of colonials in all the disagreements with the mother country until independence was declared in 1776.

LITERACY, NEWSPAPERS, PAMPHLETS, AND REVOLUTIONARY DEMOCRACY

Interpretations of the American Revolution have varied. Throughout most of the nineteenth century, historians described it as a triumph of the forces of liberty and progress over those of tyranny and reaction. Around the turn of the century an imperial school of interpretation gained popularity. Historians of this persuasion placed the Revolution in a broad setting of colonial empire and tried to rid it of patriotic distortion. At the same time another school of historians began to offer yet another interpretation of the Revolution. Known as Progressive historians, they sympathized with the little people, with the farmers and laborers. They believed the Revolution was the result of internal political and social upheavals and of class conflict. It was, in their opinion, as much an internal struggle as it was one against external, or imperial, power. After World War II a number of historians attacked the Progressive interpretation, which had become the most widely used one in American history textbooks. The newer interpretation stressed a consensus view that claimed that both radical and conservative colonial leaders shared a commitment to a common body of aims

[2]James Parker to Benjamin Franklin, 14 June 1765, *Massachusetts Historical Society Proceedings* 16 (1902), 198.

Family Literacy
Family relationships were particularly important in America on the eve of the Revolution, as illustrated in this portrait, "Family Group" (1773) by Charles Wilson Peale. The Puritans who had settled New England in the 1600s had placed a particular emphasis on spiritual growth and the individual's ability to read the Bible. That concern resulted in laws requiring that children be taught reading and other skills. Some colonies considered reading so important that they made it a crime for parents to fail to educate their children. Thus, by the revolutionary era the American populace was highly literate compared with that of other countries.

and ideals.

From the first, the press has been an important source for any historian hoping to discover the nature of the Revolution. It has a significant place in both conflict and consensus interpretations. The former, for instance, contends that the true struggle of Revolutionary printers, writers, and other liberal thinkers was to free the common people from the economic and political domination by the elite. According to this "class struggle" concept, a true democratic process in the colonies was non-existent and a small group of eastern "seacoast aristocrats" controlled the country economically and politically. The bulk of the population was herded together under the thumb of the rich. When they could stand the agony no longer, this ragtag, illiterate mob took up weapons and warred against the landlords, who were in league with the British. The Patriot press, through its propaganda, urged colonials forward, keeping the fire of discontent ablaze and succeeding mightily despite the fact that the revolutionaries could not read.

Such an explanation of the Revolution suffers from a shortage of fact. Better evidence suggests that political democracy had taken root in the colonies and that the Patriot press viewed the Revolution not as a struggle between classes but as a fight for political independence from Great Britain. Even though Americans may have disagreed on isolated issues, their differences took place within a broader realm of agreement on underlying principles, including religious freedom, political self-determination, and individual liberty. The Revolution and the press' role in it were primarily democratic rather than economic or social.

The democratic ideas of American colonials, according to the historian Bernard Bailyn, can be traced through the pamphlets published during the Revolutionary period. Pamphlets served as an important forum for the expression of opinion. They revealed that "the American Revolution was above all else an ideological, constitutional political struggle ... and that intellectual developments in the decade before Independence led to a radical ideal-

ization and conceptualizaton" of American attitudes. The ideas of some of England's more radical political and social thinkers were transmitted directly to the colonials. American leaders feared that a sinister conspiracy had developed in England to deprive citizens of the British empire of their long-established liberties. It was this fear that lay at the base of the views expressed in the pamphlets and newspapers. The ideas in these publications then became the determinants in the history of the Revolution by leading to a change in colonials' beliefs and attitudes. These ideas challenged traditional authority, according to Bailyn, and argued that "a better world than had ever been known could be built where authority was distrusted and held in constant scrutiny; where the status of men flowed from their achievements and from their personal qualities, not from distinctions ascribed to them at birth; and where the use of power over the lives of men was jealously guarded and severely restricted."[3]

The bulk of the evidence on the public's economic opportunity, the extent of political democracy in the colonies, and the colonial literacy rate reveals that the Revolution was not a class struggle. One of the major differences between living in eighteenth-century Europe as opposed to America was the choice among people about how they would grow as a country. The attitude toward literacy typified the differences. The earliest settlements — Plymouth, Boston, and others — were created by religious groups who wished to make a choice for themselves and their offspring about how to worship God. They could not do so in countries with established churches. They were dissidents, many of whom had suffered in numerous ways as the price of personal religious choice. They booked passage to America in the hope of finding freedom in the wilderness. As time passed, more joined them. They tilled the soil, established communities, gave fealty to God, and ultimately became citizens of a truly new social idea. In the

[3]Bernard Bailyn, *Pamphlets of the American Revolution, 1750-1776* (Cambridge, Mass., 1965), "Introduction."

Circulations of Selected Newspapers in the American Colonies

Newspaper	Circulation
Connecticut Courant (1775)	700
Essex Gazette (Salem) (1770)	700
Providence Gazette (1766)	800
Massachusetts Spy (1775)	3500
Constitutional Gazette (1775)	2000
New York Gazetteer (1774)	3600
Pennsylvania Chronicle (1770)	2500
Boston Chronicle (1768)	1500
New-York Journal (1765)	1500
New-York Gazette or Weekly Post-Boy (1766)	550
Boston News-Letter (1719)	300

process, they instructed their young in Scripture — which required the development of literacy for all. From the earliest days of settlement in America, there was an emphasis on the need for education for the young.

That was particularly true in New England, where colonies founded by religious dissidents, especially the Puritans of Massachusetts, passed compulsory education laws in order to assure that everyone could read the Bible. Parents who did not enforce the rules on education ran the risk of having their children removed from the home and given to others. As the religious requirements abated over time, the practice of requiring schooling for all was maintained as a mark of good citizenship. The emphasis was different in the other colonies, but literacy became increasingly important as the mark of a good citizen. By the time of the Revolution, approximately 85% of the adult men in New England could read, while generally one-half to two-thirds of the adult males in the other colonies were literate.

While such experiences did not produce a mass intellectual elite, they did create opportunities for growth and development of citizens as individuals. Few dreamers envisioned a society in which everyone could read and write. Still, the educational system that colonials created, supported by public funds, did allow American youth to grow and to participate — through local newspapers, books, and other media forms readily available to them — in public activities at an early age. That outlook did not develop in any other country at that time. Ambrose Serle, a Tory critic of the New York press, wrote in 1776: "One is astonished to see with what avidity they [the colonial newspapers] are sought after, and how implicitly they are believed, by the great Bulk of the People.... Government may find it expedient in the sum of things, to employ this popular engine."[4]

[4]26 November 1776, *Journals of Hugh Gaine*, Paul L. Ford, ed. (New York, 1902), I: 57.

The popularity of newspapers provides stark testimony to the interest of a large body of the citizenry in the issues leading to the Revolution. Newspapers circulated widely, and the average citizen, not just the aristocrat, read them. Circulation figures reflect a broadly based readership of citizens who were attuned to the events and personalities around them. The Royal Governor of Massachusetts, unnerved over the ranting of the *Boston Gazette*, reported to London: "The misfortune is that seven-eighths of the people read none but this infamous paper."

John Adams testified thus to the reading ability of colonial Americans: "The public institutions in New England for the education of youth, supporting colleges at the public expense, and obliging towns to maintain grammar schools, are not equaled, and never were, in any part of the world."[5] Adams at another point provided further testimony of widespread literacy in America: "A native of America who cannot read and write is as rare an appearance as a Jacobite or a Roman Catholic, that is, as rare as a comet or an earthquake."[6]

Constituting the most literate society in the world at the time, Americans used their knowledge to learn about and further their cause in the conflict with Great Britain. Although Americans often disagreed about the details, they generally came to agree that the colonies would be better off if the British monarchy were replaced with a popular form of government.

THE STAMP ACT OF 1765

The clamor over the Stamp Act indicated that relations between the Crown and its colonies likely would worsen. The taxes imposed by the act were, in the colonials' view, excessive. The situation was charged for collision. The Stamp Act, passed March 22, 1765, to become effective November 1, was aimed at raising revenue to help Britain pay its war debts and the costs of protecting American border areas. Unwisely, the British government selected printers, lawyers, and merchants as the targets. Those individuals, along with clergymen, were the best educated and most publicly involved citizens in the colonies. The act required that all legal documents, official papers, books, and newspapers be printed on stamped paper that carried a special tax. It placed an additional tax on each advertisement.

It portended immediate disaster to printers, requiring that taxes be paid at the rate of a halfpenny per halfsheet, a penny for larger page sizes, and two shillings for each advertisement. The income that printers received from subscribers and advertisers was only slightly greater than the taxes. The tax on job printing was just as high, and printing in languages other than English was taxed at double the standard rate. Printers who violated the rules could be fined from forty shillings to ten pounds. If one published anonymously without stamps, he or she would answer in admiralty courts — which had been established originally to try mar-

[5]Quoted in A.B. Hart, *American History Told by Contemporaries* (New York, 1927), II: 64.
[6]Quoted in Adrienne Koch and William Peden, eds., *Selected Writings of John and John Quincy Adams* (New York, 1946), 18.

Stamp Act Protests
The Stamp Act evoked such violent opposition from both printers and the public. Passed in March 1765, it placed a tax on "every paper, commonly called a pamphlet, and upon every newspaper ... and ... every advertisement to be contained in any gazette, news paper, or other paper, or any pamphlet" published in the colonies. Officials, clergymen, and printers denounced the law. Newspapers responded in various ways, but most claimed that the Stamp Act was a dangerous threat to freedom of the press. By some means or another, all avoided printing on the stamped paper. Opponents in several towns organized demonstrations against the law, hanging effigies of stamp collectors on the community Liberty Tree.

itime cases — without juries, which seemed a violation of the colonies' traditional rights to try cases of local offenses in local courts before juries of local citizens.

Striking as hard as it did at printers, the tax gave them a special reason to use their newspapers to oppose the Stamp Act. Although at first indecisive, they shortly began to stiffen their resolve in the face of what they saw as tyranny. David Ramsay, who lived during the Revolution and wrote its history, observed that printers, "when uninfluenced by government, generally arranged themselves on the side of liberty, nor are they less remarkable for attention to the profits of their profession. A stamp duty, which openly invaded the first, and threatened a great diminution of the last, provoked their united zealous opposition."[7] The press war against the Stamp Act began in Boston. Awakened to the dangers building against them, printers there took to their job cases to argue against the act as a frontal assault on the liberty of the people in general and the freedom of the press in particular.

Perhaps no law in American history evoked such violent opposition as the Stamp Act did. Clergymen denounced it from the pulpit. Colonial legislatures and town meetings passed scathing resolutions against it. The Stamp Act Congress in October denounced it as an unconstitutional invasion of colonial liberties. Merchants organized boycotts against British imports. Groups of Sons of Liberty took actions to prevent its enforcement. On May 30, Patrick Henry of Virginia introduced to the House of Burgesses a resolution proclaiming the colonials' right as Englishmen to possess the sole power of taxation. He described anyone who dissented against such a right as an "Enemy to this his Majesty's Colony." It was an astounding pronouncement, especially disturbing to the British authorities because Virginia was the first and most populous colony. Massachusetts Governor Francis Bernard feared that Henry's resolution "proved an alarm bell to the disaffected."[8]

Meetings called to discuss the Stamp Act sometimes turned in-

to brawls, particularly in Boston and the Middle Colonies; and protest rallies and other strategies were devised to nullify the legislation. Trade with Britain dropped precipitously, and colonials refused to pay their British creditors. On June 3, the *New York Post-Boy* reported that only a fifth as many ships were working the West Indian routes than before the Stamp Act was enacted. Hard cash was increasingly difficult to find. Business experienced "a most prodigious shock." John Hancock lamented that "times are very bad..., the times will be worse here, in short such is the situation of things here that we do not know who is and who is not safe."[9]

Led by the bolder among them, printers gradually came into full opposition to the law. Eventually, newspapers spoke as if with one voice in opposition to the Stamp Act, as though they had become one "mass medium." They carried detailed accounts of public opposition to the act, noting pointedly the names of tax collectors and stories of their being hanged in effigy. No tax collectors thus dared to distribute the stamped paper, leaving printers on November 1 in a dilemma. The law required that they use nothing but stamped paper, but no such paper was available. The absence of paper did not void the penalties for violation of the law. Printers had to determine what path to take. None intended to pay the tax, but deciding how to proceed was not easy. A few newspapers, mainly in the South, temporarily suspended publication; but others challenged the law one way or another.

Some came out defiantly as usual, appearing without the detestable stamp and proclaiming that the Stamp Act was a direct attack on liberty itself. To protect themselves from authorities, some printers claimed that they continued publishing because of threats from Patriots. John Holt ran an "anonymous" letter in his *New York Gazette or Weekly Post-Boy* threatening his business and his body if he did not publish.[10] Others, unfamiliar with the Stamp Act's fine print, attempted to evade the law by changing their newspapers' names and publishing anonymously. Similarly, some tried to side-

[7]David Ramsay, *The History of the American Revolution* (Philadelphia, 1789), I: 61-2.

[8]Letter to Gage, *British Papers Relating to the American Revolution* (Sparks Collection, Harvard College Library, Cambridge, Mass.), I: 43; III: 85.

[9]Quoted in *John Hancock: His Book*, A.E. Brown, ed. (Boston, 1898).

[10]*New York Gazette or Weekly Post-Boy*, 7 November 1765.

Responses to the Stamp Act

Newspaper printers initially reacted to the Stamp Act of 1765 in a variety of ways. A colonial agent to London, Benjamin Franklin at first tried to get two of his friends appointed as agents to supply the stamps. When he recognized how unpopular the act was, he immediately recanted. His printing partner, David Hall, attempted to publish their newspaper, the *Pennsylvania Gazette* (left), safely by noting that publication was continuing without stamps because no stamped paper was available. Their Philadelphia rival, the *Pennsylvania Journal*, took a very different approach. It was among the most defiant. The day before the law was to take effect, its front page was printed in funereal black borders and with a skull of death.

step the letter of the law by removing their serial numbering, thus changing their official status from newspapers to handbills, which were not subject to the act. Even many of those newspapers that suspended temporarily objected vehemently. In late October, the German-language *Philadelphia Staatsbote* outlined its front page in black borders with a skull at the top. On October 31, the day before the act was to take effect, six other papers published with similar make-up. The *Pennsylvania Journal and Weekly Advertiser* assumed the most garish design. It published in the funereal black columns of a tombstone, topped with skull and crossbones, mourning over the death of press liberty.[11] Whatever the course pursued, it is notable that not a single newspaper published on stamped paper.

In March 1766 Parliament, recognizing that the Stamp Act was unenforceable, repealed it. By then, colonial newspapers already had been inspired to oppose British authority. Their continuing opposition helped lead Americans to the Revolution.

POLITICAL PASSION AND REPRESSION

Francis Hopkinson, signer of the Declaration of Independence and member of the Continental Congress, believed the press was vital to Patriot victory in the Revolution, but he argued that newspapers had to play a constructive role in supporting the move for independence. He explained: "[W]hen this privilege is manifestly abused, and the press becomes an engine for sowing the most dan-

gerous dissensions, for spreading false alarms, and undermining the very foundations of government, ought not that government upon the plain principles of self-preservation to silence, by its own authority, such a daring violator of its peace, and tear from its bosom the serpent that would sting it to death?"[12]

Like Hopkinson, Patriots and British officials believed authorities were justified in silencing outrageous speech. Typical of such thinking, a special Patriot commission in Newport, Rhode Island, determined that freedom of the press required "liberal sentiments" but did not allow "wrong sentiments." With a foundation in such thinking, press freedom depended on the issues and circumstances and the degree of clout that Patriots or Tories had. It was permitted for some but not for all.

The Revolutionary period thus created a conflict in terms of modern thinking on freedom of the press. Whereas the modern press is expected to be fair and impartial — a mission, admittedly, it sometimes fails to perform — Patriots and Tories believed that if a newspaper were not wholly for their side, it was against them. As a result, as the Patriots gained strength, the greatest danger to press freedom came not from British authorities but from Patriot mobs and from threats by groups such as the Sons of Liberty. Zealous revolutionaries muffled many voices from New Hampshire to Georgia. The radical Patriots were many and formidable, and they meant business. Personal "rights" that we take for granted today were secondary to the goal of colonial independence.

One of the few proposals put to the First Continental Congress to protect press freedom came from a Tory writing in James Rivington's pro-British *New York Gazetteer*. It read in part: "That whoever, as an instrument of tyranny, or abetter of a mob, shall go about, either by threats, or any other methods to violate the liberty of the press, is an enemy to everything for which a man of sense would think it worth his while to live, or would dare to die."[13]

Such calls for tolerance of dissenting views fell on deaf ears. Patriots suppressed Royalist papers and condemned Patriot papers when they attempted to be impartial. William Goddard, printer of Baltimore's *Maryland Journal*, quarreled with the local Whig Club, a Patriot organization, over a misunderstood irony in a letter recommending that the colonies accept a British peace offer in 1777. Told to leave town within forty-eight hours, he appealed to the Maryland House of Representatives, the Patriot government. It rebuked the Club. Later, when he printed a letter critical of George Washington, he was mobbed, barely escaped hanging, and was forced to print a recantation. He again appealed for state protection, received it, and printed a repeal of the recantation. In New York, just as the Declaration of Independence was about to be unveiled, Samuel Loudon decided to earn some extra income from the Tory side by printing — not writing — for someone else a rejoinder to Thomas Paine's *Common Sense*. Although Loudon's loyalty to the Patriot cause was undoubted, a mob invaded his home during the night, roughed him up, and destroyed the offending pages of type. The following day, he received a warning:

11*Pennsylvania Journal and Weekly Advertiser* (Philadelphia), 31 October 1765.

12*Pennsylvania Evening Post* (Philadelphia), 16 November 1776.
13Unsigned article by a resident of New Jersey, *Gazetteer*, 2 September 1774.

Tarring a Tory
As passions heated up before the Revolution, the Sons of Liberty, the most ardent of the Patriot faction, took a number of actions to intimidate opponents. This cartoon shows members of the group tarring and feathering a Tory collector of the Boston tea tax in 1774. They also forced him to drink scalding tea. The cutline with the cartoon read: "A Method of Macarony Making as Practiced at Boston." Macarony was a plumed hat for gentlemen. The accompanying poem read: "For the Custom House officer landing the tea / They tarred him and feather'd him just as you see / And they Drench'd him so well both behind and before / That he begged for God's sake they would drench him no more."

"Sir, if you print, or suffer to be printed in your press anything against the rights and liberties of America or in favor of our inveterate foes, the King, Ministry, and Parliament of Great Britain, death and destruction, ruin and perdition, shall be your portion. Signed, by order of the Committee of Tarring and Feathering."

AMERICAN TORIES

Because of such conditions the British could not use the press effectively. The power of Patriots and the general anti-British sentiment in the colonies made it difficult for Tory newspapers to serve as useful propaganda organs. Life was hazardous for Tory printers. In the pre-war years, they found themselves increasingly intimidated by Patriots, and during the war they had to depend on the British army. They could publish only in those areas the British occupied; they were attacked everywhere else. In the early years of the Revolutionary period, a few printers were staunch Tories, but most who leaned toward the Crown usually tried to be fair, giving both sides. Patriots attacked the latter, however, and

finally pushed them fully into the Tory camp. John Mein, one of the notable Tory printers, was typical.

Mein was one of many Europeans who chose to leave their homes and spend weeks in the belly of a wooden ship for the opportunity offered in America. A pugnacious Scot, he settled in Boston, where he opened a bookshop, and soon was on the way to success. Within three years after his arrival, though, he had become the target of radical Patriots. At first, he used the printing firm of Benjamin Edes and John Gill, whose families went back four generations in Boston and who would become two of the most fiery Patriot printers. They frequently published advertisements for Mein in their newspaper, the *Boston Gazette*, thus becoming close business associates. In 1767 Mein launched his own paper, the *Boston Chronicle*, intended as a non-partisan journal.[14] But given the city's mood since the Stamp Act, he immediately got into trouble with Patriot committees over his opposition to the non-importation agreements the Patriots made to resist the Townshend Acts, which Parliament had passed in an effort to raise revenue from the colonies after the repeal of the Stamp Act.

By nature a stubborn man, Mein did not hesitate to criticize the Patriots, and the *Chronicle* grew increasingly pro-British. In 1769 it published a reprint from a London journal that spoke badly of William Pitt, a British statesman who was a favorite of American Whigs. The *Gazette*, which held "impartial" papers in contempt anyway, attacked Mein. The following morning he called on Edes and Gill and demanded that they reveal the author's identity. When they refused, the Scot invited them outside one at a time. The two held back. Mein then promised "to cane the first one of them I meet..." and departed. The next afternoon he spied Gill on the street; and "with force of arms, to wit, with a large club," he laid his adversary low with two blows to the head. Then he "beat, wounded, and evil treated" the downed man.[15] Gill won a court judgment of seventy-five pounds. When Mein continued to attack certain Boston "Saints," as he called the radicals, he was hanged in effigy and his home was attacked. When a mob assaulted him on the street, in defending himself he accidentally shot a bystander. To escape prosecution and in fear of his life, he fled to a British ship in Boston harbor and thence to England. The Patriot intimidation of Mein succeeded, noted Tory Peter Oliver, because "the civil power of the country was not sufficient to protect any one who was obnoxious to ye Leaders of the faction,"[16] a statement indicating just how strong the radicals had become. The *Chronicle* ceased publication in 1770.

Of all Tory editors the one with the best imagination and news sense was James "Jemmy" Rivington. The son of a wealthy London publisher, he pursued the family goals of gentility and high style. Something of a rake, he lost in excess of $50,000 playing the horses, one reason he moved to the New World. In Philadelphia he opened a bookstore and then expanded his business to include

[14]John Mein, *Proposals for Printing a New Weekly, called The Boston Chronicle* (22 October 1767).
[15]*Boston Gazette*, 28 August 1769; 15 and 30 January 1770.
[16]Quoted in Douglas Adair and John Shutz, eds., *Peter Oliver's Origin & Progress of the American Rebellion: A Tory View* (San Marino, Calif., 1961), 62.

John Mein and the *Chronicle*
The publisher of the *Boston Chronicle*, Mein provoked the ire of Patriot committees when he differed with them over policies against importing British goods. In the issue of the *Chronicle* for October 9-16, 1769, he listed names of violators of the non-importation agreements. Facing growing threats in Boston, he eventually fled to England.

New York and Boston. Urbane and friendly, he became a popular figure among the upper crust. In 1773 he founded the *New York Gazetteer*. The remainder of the paper's name, *or the Connecticut, Hudson's River, New Jersey, and Quebeck Weekly Advertiser*, indicated something of Rivington's ego and expansive vision. The *Gazetteer* may have been the best printed and most informative newspaper in colonial America. It proved a winner from the outset, with circulation quickly reaching an impressive 3,600 copies, primarily among well-to-do Tories. Included were readers in the West Indies, England, France, and Ireland. But Rivington gained few adherents among Patriots. With his regal bearing and foppish ways, he offered little that they wished to emulate. He thought the Patriot newspapers' claim that they supported truth and justice was ridiculous. As tensions heightened, he vowed that the *Gazetteer*, as it always had done, would continue to offer impartiality equally to the "'sons of freedom' and to those who have differed

in sentiments from them." He emphasized the point by running beneath the paper's nameplate the line "PRINTED at his OPEN and UNINFLUENCED PRESS."

Rivington at first printed both Patriot and Tory contributions. For that, the Sons of Liberty hanged him in effigy and destroyed his shop. He then became openly sympathetic to the British. While most papers removed royal crests from their nameplates in favor of more "democratic" labels, Rivington made a show of his support for the Crown. Finally the inevitable storm broke. In May of 1775 Patriots mobbed the paper's office, and Rivington barely saved his skin thanks to the action of friends. He then was arrested and forced to sign an oath of allegiance to the colonial cause. Once released from jail, though, he continued to print in favor of the British. In November, "King" Isaac Sears, a fugitive from justice and a notorious tough, led a Patriot mob, supported by seventy-five members of the Connecticut Light Horse, against Rivington. They demolished his press and carried off the type. Rivington fled to England, where he gained an appointment as the "King's Printer" in New York. Returning to the colonies, he began publishing the *Royal Gazette* (which Patriots nicknamed "Rivington's Lying Gazette"), issuing deliberately warped accounts of battles and Patriot leaders. At the end of the war, he was forced to suspend publication. Although he apologized for his record, he was beaten once and was thrown into debtor's prison for other people's debts. He died in poverty on Independence Day 1802.

Second only to Rivington in New York Tory printing — and as dedicated — was Hugh Gaine, publisher of the *New York Mercury* (later *Gazette and Weekly Mercury*). An Anglican by faith, he was appointed official printer to the English church and identified with it politically. Most of the paper's coverage dealt with political information copied from Boston papers with pro-British leanings. Although Gaine published first with a non-partisan slant, his basic Tory sentiment earned him respectability among Tory readers. With the onset of the war, he moved to Newark, New Jersey, where for a short time he appeared to support the colonials. Within a month, though, he made amends with the British and returned to New York, which the British army recently had captured. Because of his switching of sides, he gained the Patriot nickname "Hugh Gaine, the Turncoat." At the war's end, he was bold enough to petition the New York legislature to permit him to remain and succeeded in escaping official retribution.

THE PATRIOT PRESS

The Patriot press of the Revolutionary period is best understood as an organ for promoting ideology. Before the war, printers intensified their propaganda efforts against Britain but escaped prosecution because of popular opposition to British authority. Grand juries, made up of colonials, would not indict offending printers; and authorities feared that more high-handed or extra-legal measures would invite violent opposition. Despite such complaints as one by Lord Frederick North, First Lord of the Treasury, that no one could "recollect a period when the press groan'd with such a

Jemmy Rivington, Tory
Challenging the radical Patriots' threat that newspapers had to choose sides, the royalist James Rivington claimed to publish an unbiased newspaper. To goad them, he used the slogan "Printed at his Open and Uninfluenced Press" for his *New York Gazetteer*. For his bold opposition to the Patriot cause, he became a target of numerous threats. When a mob hanged him in effigy, he published an engraving of the scene in his own newspaper. He reported that "some of the lower class of inhabitants" of New Jersey had done the deed "merely for [his] acting consistent with his profession as a free printer."

variety of desperate libels,"[17] the government grew increasingly lax in restricting printers. Having set the precedent during the Stamp Act crisis, authorities discovered they had more and more difficulty reining in insolent printers afterwards. They faced the dilemma of wanting to punish offenders while fearing the result if they attempted to do so.

Isaiah Thomas, proprietor of the *Massachusetts Spy*, was one of many printers who flouted authorities because of their quandary. Summoned before the governor's council for essays critical of Governor Thomas Hutchinson, he snubbed the council's messenger and ignored the order to appear.[18] The council then voted to prosecute him for seditious libel, to which Thomas, joined by a chorus of writers in other papers, responded with trenchant attacks on those officials who would regard freedom of the press so lightly and attempt to punish someone for printing the truth. The council persisted in pursuing the case, presenting charges to a grand jury three months later. The jury refused to indict Thomas. The council believed the jury had been packed but decided to drop the case. "No writer," one essayist in the *Spy* then gibed at Hutchinson, "needs now to stand in fear of you."[19]

Ideologues are most forceful when convinced they are right. Patriot printers were no exception. They believed zealously that they advocated justice and that truth was on their side. Those who opposed them supported injustice and were backed only by error and deceit. Such an outlook made necessary a selective use of material in Patriot newspapers, for publishing material opposed to truth did nothing to advance justice and liberty. "My paper," wrote John Holt of the *New York Journal*, "is sacred to the cause of truth and justice, and I have preferred the pieces, that in my opinion, are the most necessary to the support of that cause" rather than those that were "barefaced attempts to deceive and impose upon the ignorant."[20] To do otherwise, Patriots argued, to print both sides, would give support to those ideas and practices damaging to mankind and liberty. Using such reasoning, printers devoted their papers wholeheartedly to colonial freedom and, eventually, separation from Britain. With the coming of the Revolution itself, they did not stint in encouraging the war effort.

Concerted opposition to the British had begun with the Stamp Act. The newspapers' success in helping to get the act repealed emboldened printers to defy British authorities and showed that the press could be used as an effective propaganda tool. The press therefore came to be regarded as a strong arm of the Patriot movement, and several writers and printers gained widespread recognition.

VOICES OF REVOLT

With the calm that had settled in following repeal of the Stamp Act, colonial unrest might not have gotten out of hand if the British treasury's need for revenue had gone away. The problem remained. To solve it, the new Chancellor of the Exchequer, Charles Townshend, devised a plan to place duties on goods imported into the colonies. In a series of "Letters from a Farmer in Pennsylvania to the Inhabitants of the British Colonies," John Dickinson attacked the taxes on the grounds that they were not for regulation of trade but for raising revenue through "external taxes," which Parliament did not have the power to do. The letters were published first in the *Pennsylvania Chronicle* in 1767 and 1768. They were sound in argument, reasonable in tone, and clear and forceful in style. They did not urge independence from the mother country; and, indeed, Dickinson clearly opposed separation.

[17]Speech reported in the *Massachusetts Gazette and Boston Post-Boy*, 22 April 1771.
[18]*Massachusetts Spy* (Boston), 14 November 1771.
[19]Ibid., 30 July 1772.
[20]*New York Journal*, 5 January 1775.

John Dickinson, "Farmer"
In the essays titled "Letters from a Farmer in Pennsylvania," Dickinson, a Philadelphia lawyer, argued effectively against British tax policies in 1767 and 1768. Although he opposed separation from England, once the colonies declared their independence in 1776, he went on active duty as a colonel in the American army.

The letters were, however, important in the move toward independence because of their influence in prompting the merchant and business class to question British policy.

Boston Patriots were the most industrious in the colonies in promoting independence, and to that end they produced a widely circulated "Journal of Occurrences." Published from late 1768 through the first half of the following year, it detailed Boston's suffering under the Townshend Acts and British military rule. Newspapers throughout the colonies picked up items from it, resulting in the publication of Boston Patriots' views throughout the land.

The most aggressive writer was Sam Adams, a leader of the radical Caucus Club. Its members were committed to independence and, through their writing for the *Boston Gazette* and other activities, exercised a strong leadership in political action in the colonies. It was said that America's course was determined by Massachusetts, that Massachusetts' was determined by Boston, and that Boston's was determined by Adams. It was Adams who, because of his *Gazette* writing and his talent for propaganda, did more than anyone else to promote colonial independence from Britain as a practical, realistic action.

The *Gazette* was the chief radical newspaper in the colonies; and

its owners, Benjamin Edes and John Gill, were the most strident newspaper critics of the British prior to the Revolution. Edes, the more belligerent of the pair, was a man for his time. A mover of political causes, he was intelligent, tough, and dedicated. By 1765 he had served as Boston's Town Constable, Town Scavenger, and Clerk of the Market. He was active in the North End Caucus, a political organization that offered opportunities for debating current issues, airing views, and, in time, hatching intrigues against authority. In 1763, John Adams attended a meeting of that body and attested to its political muscle. Everyone, Adams noted, smoked pipes and drank "Phlip" while selecting "Assessors, Collectors, Wardens, Fire Wards, and representatives" even before they had been selected by the town. Edes also held membership in the "Loyal Nine," that exclusive group of Whigs that would form the nucleus of the Sons of Liberty. Some of its primary functions were to develop strategies to oppose Parliament's authority in the colonies, intimidate Loyalists, and bring moderates into line. Even Sam Adams did not hold membership in that select organization, although he did ally himself with it. Beginning with the Stamp Act crisis, Edes assumed increasing responsibility in the resistance movement.

On the morning of August 14, 1765, residents of Newbury Street stepped from their dwellings to find an effigy of Andrew Oliver, the hated stamp master-designate and secretary of the province, dangling from the Liberty Tree. Alongside hung a huge boot, symbolic of Lord Bute, a power behind the detested tax. Out of the boot peeped a stuffed replica of the devil clutching a copy of the Stamp Act. Oliver's likeness was the creation of Benjamin Edes. The day's activities culminated in the destruction of Oliver's house by the Sons of Liberty, engineered by the Sons' leadership, including Edes. The following week Governor Thomas Hutchinson's mansion fell to the same fate as the Sons destroyed the place and everything in it. Then they pried all the slates from the roof and cut down every tree on the grounds.

When the Tea Act of 1773 brought the issue of British trade monopoly to a boil, Edes was one of a number of Bostonians who guarded the wharves to prevent the opposition from landing the now hated tea. Matters deteriorated rapidly until, on the afternoon of December 16, 1773, a group of radicals joined Edes at his home. There they discussed the tea issue, drank considerably from a china punch bowl, and at dark went to the *Gazette* office nearby. Others who had attended another meeting at Old South Church met them, and all donned Indian disguises. They then proceeded to Boston Harbor, where they boarded three ships and dumped 342 chests of tea overboard.

Frustrated, the hapless Boston Tories railed among themselves. As one of them wrote: "The last Edes and Gill Newspaper is a torrent of envious Calumny, dirtily poured forth from a Sink of Meanness and Defamation." Another complained that "The foul-mouthed Trumpeters of Sedition [Edes and Gill] bellow and rave and drivel like Mad-dogs and clumsy Cur-dogs, under a dying Man's window...."[21] Even though Edes and Gill had provided the

[21]Reprinted in *Boston Gazette*, 5 October and 21 December 1767.

Boston Incendiaries

In Boston, the hotbed of the revolutionary movement, Sam Adams (left) kept the fire stoked with his writing and rabble-rousing. Mobs burned British records and pillaged the home of Governor Thomas Hutchinson. Sam's cousin John Adams, future president of the United States, described the situation, "Our Presses have groaned…. The Crown officers have every where trembled." Sam Adams was connected with the chief radical newspaper in the colonies, Edes and Gill's *Boston Gazette*. It was instrumental in stirring up opposition to the British. When British soldiers fired on a Boston mob, Adams, Edes and Gill, and the Sons of Liberty labeled the incident a "massacre." The *Gazette's* account included woodcuts of caskets representing the Bostonians who were killed. At trial, the commander of the soldiers was defended by John Adams and acquitted.

cutting edge for much of the revolutionary movement, they dissolved their partnership in 1775, on the eve of the Revolution. Each attempted a paper on his own, but neither approached the success of the *Gazette*. Both died in poverty after the war.

The best known writer of the Revolution was Thomas Paine, a professional rebel. His pamphlet *Common Sense* (1776) confronted colonials directly with the idea of independence, paving the way, some historians think, for the Declaration of Independence. His first "American Crisis" paper, beginning with the stirring words "These are the times that try men's souls…," was published in the *Pennsylvania Journal* on December 19, 1776, during the colonies' darkest hours of the war. After the American Revolution ended, Paine went to France to assist in its revolution. He returned to America in 1801 and died in poverty in 1809, ostracized for his attacks on religion. At his death, Thomas Jefferson said of him: "No writer has exceeded Paine in ease and familiarity of style, in perspicuity of expression, happiness of elucidation, and in simple and unassuming language."[22]

Whereas Edes and Gill's *Boston Gazette* was the leading radical newspaper before the Revolution, Isaiah Thomas' *Massachusetts Spy* was the most incendiary publication during the Revolution. Prior to the war, Thomas had been outspoken in his support for independence. He revived the "Join or Die" divided-snake device that Benjamin Franklin had created in 1754, and he never softened his attacks on British trampling of colonial rights and liberties. Accounts such as his reporting of the battle of Lexington in 1775 were designed to stir up the anger of colonials. That account began with this call for action:

Americans! Forever bear in mind the BATTLE OF LEXINGTON! — where British troops, unmolested and unprovoked, wantonly and in a most inhuman manner, fired upon and killed a number of our countrymen, then robbed, ransacked, and burned their houses! nor could the tears of defenseless women, some of whom were in the pains of childbirth, the cries of helpless babes, nor the prayers of age, confined to beds of sickness, appease their thirst for blood! — or divert them from their DESIGN OF MURDER and ROBBERY![23]

After the Revolution, Thomas became manifestly successful as a printer and historian, writing the first history of printing in America and founding the American Antiquarian Society.

More important than any single writer, however, were the Patriots' committees of correspondence. They were created to distribute information and ideas among towns and colonies and to newspapers. Although clergymen and merchants had used similar committees on an *ad hoc* basis in the early 1760s, the impetus for the establishment of standing committees devoted to the Patriot cause came in 1772. In the wake of the attempts by Massachusetts' Governor Hutchinson to insulate the courts from colonial influence, Sam Adams issued a call for standing committees to be set up to resist the action. A Boston town meeting in November appointed a standing committee, and Patriots in other towns and colonies soon followed. They eventually established more than eighty committees. Each circulated letters to other committees and provided propaganda to newspapers. In that way, through informal organization, they succeeded in their goals of keeping the colonies informed of events, issues, and opinions and stirring up antagonism to British efforts to suppress colonial opponents.

[22] Thomas Jefferson to Francis Eppes, January 19, 1821, *The Writings of Thomas Jefferson*, ed. Albert Ellery Bergh (Washington, D.C., 1907), 15: 305.

[23] *Massachusetts Spy* (Worcester), 3 May 1775.

The American Crisis

Thomas Paine Rouses "Scared Rabbits" to Fight

At the end of 1776, America's revolutionary army was in retreat and, it seemed, near defeat. "The rebels," one British officer reported contemptuously, had "fled like scared rabbits." As Christmas approached, the morale of both soldiers and civilians alike seemed at its lowest point. The triumphant British army had moved into comfortable winter quarters at Trenton, New Jersey, apparently unconcerned about the American troops across the Delaware River. Something had to be done to rally the colonials.

During the army's retreat, Thomas Paine – who already had achieved fame with his *Common Sense* essay – may have begun writing the first essay of what he called "The Crisis." Legend has it that he composed the piece on the head of a drum at a fire in the camp of General George Washington's army, with the cold and ragged soldiers gathered around. If there is any truth to the legend, it could be that only the beginning and the end of the essay were completed at that time. On the advice of several officers, he then left the army at Trenton and went to Philadelphia in order to produce a publication that might stir Americans to action.

He found fear spreading and the civilians berating Washington's retreat as disgraceful. He said the situation drove him to write "in what I may call a passion of patriotism," producing the first essay in the "Crisis" series. It appeared first on the front page of the *Pennsylvania Journal* on December 19. It then was reprinted as a pamphlet and soon by printers throughout the colonies.

Washington read the essay, was greatly moved, and ordered it read aloud to his assembled soldiers. According to tradition, Paine's appeal to patriots, especially its sonorous opening lines, had an immediate and heartening effect on the soldiers. The essay began, "These are the times that try men's souls. The summer soldier and the sunshine patriot will, in this crisis, shrink from the service of their country; but he that stands it now, deserves the love and thanks of man and woman."

On Christmas night, Washington led his troops back across the Delaware through a violent snowstorm, attacked the Hessian mercenaries the British had hired, and captured or killed almost a thousand of them. A week later he slipped his army around British General Cornwallis and defeated a small garrison at Princeton. The victories revived American morale and are generally considered turning points in the Revolution.

General George Washington had Thomas Paine's stirring "Crisis" essay read to his dejected troops. On Christmas night, 1776, he maneuvered them across the icy Delaware River, marched to Trenton, N. J., and in a surprise early-morning attack defeated the Hessian mercenaries and captured the town. Frederick the Great of Prussia called the move "the most brilliant" in military history. It was an early turning point in the Revolution. The drawing of the crossing shown above is from the *New York Mirror* in 1842. It was based on Edward Hicks' earlier painting.

THE PRESS AS MORALE BOOSTER

During the years of actual fighting, the press played a vital role as it provided information about the war. More than any other institution, it encouraged the people to support the war effort. Thus, newspapers became the primary morale boosters throughout the Revolutionary era. Printers such as Benjamin Edes and Isaiah Thomas used a variety of means to lift public confidence in the drive for independence. Throughout the war, essays and news stories emphasized the tyranny and corruption of the British and the glory and justness of the American cause.

Patriot newspapers sought to destroy any remaining colonial ties to Great Britain. Describing George III as the "whining King of Great Britain,"[24] the press urged Americans to discard all loyalty to the mother country. Accusations of cruelty and barbarity by the British and their Tory supporters filled newspapers. In 1781, for example, several printers accused Lord Charles Cornwallis of trying to spread smallpox in the South. This plot, a writer declared, "must render him contemptible in the eyes of every civilized nation, it being a practice inconsistent with the law of nations and as repugnant to humanity."[25]

Even more important for morale than attacks on the British were discussions of American successes and future prospects. Printers filled their pages with material on the justness of the American cause and the success of the Continental Army in battle. There was no doubt that the United States would be victorious, for, as one newspaper writer averred, "it is allowed on all hands that the American Army is now equal at least to any in the world for discipline, activity and bravery. There are no soldiers in Europe more exemplary for subordination, regularity of conduct, patience in fatigues and hardships, perseverance in service, and intrepidity in danger."[26] Newspapers worked to increase public resolve by urging all readers to put the war above all other concerns. In 1776, Isaiah Thomas proposed: "Let us not busy ourselves now about our private internal affairs, but with the utmost care and caution, attend to the grand American controversy, and assist her in her earnest struggle in support of her natural rights and freedom."[27] Similar sentiments appeared throughout the war. According to Revolutionary printers, such efforts would produce final victory. Through such discussions, the press sought to help achieve victory by assuring that American morale remained high throughout the armed conflict.

Concern about the content of news stories was commonplace during the Revolution, and the Patriots were aware of the public opinion implications of press freedom. If a free press were designed to create a well-informed citizenry, then the people had to be kept apprised of what was going on in Congress and on the battlefield. This belief was best illustrated as a worried George Washington encouraged the creation of camp newspapers for soldiers

Isaiah Thomas
Thomas produced one of the leading journals favoring the Patriot cause, the *Massachusetts Spy*. After the Revolution, he became the first historian of American journalism.

to read and as he sent old tenting to be made into paper for civilian newspaper use. For its part, the Continental Congress showed its awareness of the importance of information by creating a postal system that permitted the free exchange of newspapers.

Even more apparent was the Patriot awareness of ways to mold public opinion, to create what later leaders would call propaganda designed to enlist allies. Two wartime documents demonstrated the propaganda skills of the Patriots. The Declaration of Independence, although not referring to the press specifically, appealed to international public opinion by noting that "a decent respect to the opinons of mankind requires that they [the Patriots] should declare the causes which impel them to the separation."[28] Despite the fact that the Continental Congress suggested restrictive legislation, its members also wrote the *Address to the Inhabitants of Quebec*, which, in 1774, attempted to convince Canadians to join the thirteen colonies in revolt. The document cited numerous reasons for such a combined effort, listing various rights offered under the new government:

> The last right we shall mention, regards the freedom of the press. The importance of this consists, besides the advancement of truth, science, morality, and arts in general, in its diffusion of

[24]*Boston Gazette*, 19 February 1776.
[25]*Maryland Gazette* (Annapolis), reprinted in *Salem Gazette*, 6 December 1781.
[26]*American Journal* (Providence), 16 December 1779.
[27]*Massachusetts Spy* (Worcester), 28 June 1776.

[28]The Declaration of Independence is reprinted in Bernard Schwartz, *The Bill of Rights: A Documentary History*, 2 vols. (New York, 1971), 1: 252.

Independence

Contemporaries and historians have credited the Patriot press with having a large hand in the decision by the colonies to separate from England. When the Continental Congress adopted the Declaration of Independence in 1776, most colonial newspapers, as the *Pennsylvania Gazette* did, printed on page one the document they had helped to initiate.

> liberal sentiments on the administration of Government, its ready communication of thoughts between subjects, and its consequential promotion of union among them, whereby oppressive officers are shamed or intimidated, into more honourable and just modes of conducting affairs.[29]

During the war, printers filled their newspapers with stories and essays about the fighting. While obviously seeking to keep readers informed, they also hoped to keep them concerned as well. Newspaper efforts to encourage support and involvement and to boost morale went on for years, for the war proved to be a long one. As it came to a close, Benjamin Franklin praised newspapers for their usefulness, for, he explained, "by the press we can

speak to nations.... And we now find, that it is not only right to strike while the iron is hot, but that it may be very practicable to heat it by continually striking."[30] This the Patriot newspapers had clearly done, through both defeat and victory, by their nonstop discussion of the war.

THE INFLUENCE OF THE PATRIOT PRESS

One of the most intriguing questions about the Revolutionary press is what influence it may have had. What role did newspapers, pamphlets, broadsides, and other printed forms have on the initiation and execution of the Revolution? There is no easy answer, for there is no method of determining beyond doubt what the press' influence, if any, was. Today, researchers have enough difficulty determining how persuasive the mass media are, and some argue that the media are only one factor among many that affect people's opinions, with some of the other factors having more importance. If determining causal factors is difficult in contemporary research, it is virtually impossible in historical research. No "scientific" measurements such as opinion polls were taken during the Revolutionary period. In the absence of such measures, the historian is left with relying on what contemporaries said. On that issue, they were in agreement. To a person, they believed that the press exercised a major influence.

Printers, Patriot spokesmen, and government authorities clearly thought the press was important. Otherwise, they would not have placed so much emphasis on it. Washington and other Patriot leaders went to great lengths to aid it, writers and printers used it to express their views to attempt to sway public opinion, and British authorities attempted to suppress it. As early as the mid-1760s the view was widespread that newspapers were playing a central role in affecting popular opinion. A writer in the *Providence Gazette* in 1766, commenting on newspapers' success in opposing the Stamp Act, expressed that view. "The Press," he declared, "hath never done greater Service since its first Invention."[31]

David Ramsay, a Patriot who participated in Revolutionary activities and then wrote the earliest history of the war, concluded that the press was among the most important ingredients in bringing about the Revolution. He wrote: "The exertions of the army would have been insufficient to effect the revolution, unless the great body of the people had been prepared for it, and also kept in a constant disposition to oppose Great Britain.... In establishing American independence, the pen and the press had a merit equal to that of the sword."[32] The number of such comments by contemporaries could be multiplied indefinitely. They make clear the conclusion of people who lived during the period: the press was indispensable in affecting public sentiment leading to the Revolution.

Most historians have reached the same conclusion. Of the lead-

[29]The address is reprinted in ibid., 223.

[30]Benjamin Franklin to Richard Price, 13 June 1782, *Benjamin Franklin: Writings*, ed. J. A. Leo Lemay (New York, 1987), 1049-50.
[31]*Providence Gazette Extraordinary*, 12 March 1766.
[32]Ramsay, *History of the American Revolution*, II, 319.

Cornwallis TAKEN !

B O S T O N, (Friday) October 26, 1781.

This Morning an Exprefs arrived from Providence to HIS EXCELLENCY the GOVERNOR, with the following IMPORTANT INTELLI-GENCE, viz.—

PROVIDENCE, Oct. 25, 1781. Three o'Clock, P. M.

This Moment an Exprefs arrived at his Honor the Deputy-Governor's, from Col. Chriftopher Olney, Commandant on Rhode-Ifland, announcing the important Intelligence of the Surrender of Lord CORNWALLIS and his Army ; an Account of which was Printed this Morning at Newport, and is as follows, viz.—

NEWPORT, October 25, 1781.

YESTERDAY Afternoon arrived in this Harbour Capt. Lovett, of the Schooner Adventure, from York River, in Chefapeak Bay, (which he left the 20th inftant,) and brought us the glorious News of the Surrender of Lord Cornwallis and his Army Prifoners of War to the allied Army, under the Command of our illuftrious General ; and the French Fleet, under the Command of His Excellency the Count de Graffe.

A Ceffation of Arms took Place on Thurfday the 18th Inftant in Confequence of Propofals from Lord CORNWALLIS for a Capitulation.—His Lordfhip propofed a Ceffation of Twenty-four Hours, but Two only were granted by His Excellency General WASHINGTON. The Articles were compleated the fame Day, and the next Day the allied Army took Poffeffion of York Town.

By this glorious Conqueft, NINE-THOUSAND of the Enemy, including Seamen, fell into our Hands, with an immenfe Quantity of Warlike Stores, a Forty-Gun-Ship, a Frigate, an armed Veffel, and about One Hundred Sail of Tranfports.

Printed by B. Edes and Sons, in State Street.

Victory!
When Lord Cornwallis, commander of the British army at Yorktown, Virginia, surrendered, news sped through the states. This broadside records the movement of the news north. Cornwallis' troops had laid down their arms at 2 p.m. on Friday, October 19, 1781. Rhode Island got the news on Thursday, October 25, and Boston the following day.

ing studies on printing and the Revolution, only one has challenged it. In *Broadsides and Bayonets: The Propaganda War of the American Revolution* (1961), a study of the years of actual warfare, Carl Berger argued that propagandists' schemes were less meaningful in affecting opinions and beliefs than were events. Words were less important than facts. By 1777 at the latest, Berger argued, most minds were made up, and propaganda efforts could do little to change them. British and American supporters and officials made a number of attempts to convert, persuade, or intimidate people who seemed vulnerable, but most were futile — because hard facts and people's beliefs about what was really occurring held more weight than what propagandists told people to believe. The greatest impact on public opinion, according to Berger, came

not from the work of propagandists but from news of the war. As a rule, neither persuasive appeal, nor threats, nor tricks could compare in influence with military success or political and economic facts.

Berger was the exception among historians. Arthur M. Schlesinger, the first historian to provide an extensive documentation of press influence, argued that the most important factor in bringing about the Revolution was public opinion and that in changing public opinion the newspaper was the primary agent. When colonials, he said, "began to feel the tightening grip of imperial control after 1763, they naturally resorted to the printing press to disseminate their views and consolidate a favorable public support."[33] Schlesinger's *Prelude to Independence: The Newspaper War on Great Britain, 1764-1776* (1958) studied the role of the press in bringing about what John Adams called the "real American revolution": the "radical change in the principles, opinions, sentiments, and affections of the people" that preceded the Revolution.[34] Unlike most colonials, who saw events from the limited perspective of their own colony, printer-editors often had moved around among several colonies and thus were more continental in their outlook. They therefore held the view that what affected one colony affected all, and they advocated unity among the colonies. The repeal of the Stamp Act was a tremendous victory for the press, Schlesinger argued, and encouraged printers to oppose British authority more intensely. In many events afterward, such as the public uproar against the Tea Act of 1773, it was the newspapers that played a leading role. Eventually, the press' agitation resulted in a declaration of war. While Schlesinger pointed out that a number of factors other than newspapers had helped instigate the war, he argued that the independence movement could not have succeeded "without an alert and dedicated press." Most historians have agreed with Schlesinger.

Although there is disagreement concerning the impact of the Revolutionary newspapers on public opinion, there is little doubt that they fulfilled an important role during the war. They constituted the primary sources of information about the conflict. Although reports were not always accurate, printers hoped they would boost morale by helping to maintain interest in, and support for, the war effort. By publishing accounts from throughout the colonies, the newspapers helped foster a sense of unity and solidarity of purpose that was essential for a successful revolt.

THE WAR'S EFFECT ON THE PRESS

War is not good for the press. Readership may go up and circulation increase because of interest in military events, but war's damages are greater than benefits. Just as that principle has applied to other wars in America's history, it was true of the press during the Revolution. Military operations disrupted publishing, fervor cre-

---

[33]Arthur M. Schlesinger, "The Colonial Newspapers and the Stamp Act," *New England Quarterly* 8 (1935): 63-83.
[34]Letter to Hezekiah Niles, *The Works of John Adams*, C. F. Adams, ed. (Boston, 1850-56), X: 282-3.

ated by the dangers and passions of war restricted freedom of expression, news coverage was made difficult, printing materials were in short supply, and newspaper survival was endangered.

The fortunes of both Patriot and Tory newspapers depended on which army controlled the towns in which they published. Several printers had to flee hurriedly as the opposing army approached. Those who did not move quickly enough had their presses confiscated. Typical was the plight of John Holt of the *New York Journal or General Advertiser*. The British forced him to leave New York City and chased him about Connecticut for several months. Finally he set up a printing shop in Kingston, New York, where he printed a newspaper for less than four months. The British army caught up, burned Kingston, and destroyed part of his materials. He then fled to Poughkeepsie, where he managed to publish a paper with repeated military interruptions until the end of the Revolution. William Bradford III, Patriot printer of Philadelphia's *Pennsylvania Journal*, had similar experiences. Although he was fifty-seven years old at the onset of the Revolution, he served in the army while continuing to publish the *Journal*. He suspended it while fighting with the army in the campaign around Trenton in December 1776-January 1777 and again from September 1777 to June 1778 when the British occupied Philadelphia. When the army left the city, Bradford again resumed publication; but the rigors of his military service left his health and business ruined.

As if military dangers were not enough, Tory printers faced the added threats from Patriot mobs and governing bodies. Although James Johnston of the *Georgia Gazette* was Loyalist in sympathy, even after the shots fired at Lexington in 1775 he was able by his impartiality to continue the paper into the following year. At that time, the Georgia Council of Safety forced it to suspend. When the British army occupied Savannah, Johnston resumed publication and was able to continue for three years. At the end of the war, however, Patriots declared him a traitor and forced him to leave Savannah.

Benjamin Towne provides another typical Tory story. At first, he placed his *Pennsylvania Evening Post* on the Patriot side and succeeded in driving his Tory competitor out of Philadelphia through his constant criticism, and he was the first newspaper publisher to print the Declaration of Independence in 1776. When the British took Philadelphia, although several other printers fled, he stayed and ingratiated himself to British officers by changing his politics. When the British army evacuated the city, the other Tory printers fled, but again Towne stayed, changed his politics, and was allowed to continue his paper, although he was unable to win back his earlier circulation and was ostracized by Patriots.

For all papers, the war added difficulties to a news gathering system that was not sophisticated, to say the least. Neither newspapers nor British or Patriot leaders provided for anything approaching organized coverage of the Revolution. Newspapers relied for their information on the chance arrival of private letters, official messages, and other newspapers. Each paper printed some local information that others picked up, but even that information was paltry; and reports of major events sometimes consisted of no

The Effects of War
The *Georgia Gazette*, founded in 1763 as that southern colony's first newspaper, remained sympathetic to Britain throughout the Revolution. Patriot authorities, however, twice forced it to suspend publication. Most other colonial newspapers also experienced difficulties created by wartime conditions.

more than a paragraph. While such a system during peacetime functioned reasonably well for colonial purposes, it was by later standards crude at best; and war added difficulties. News was tardy. The postal service, which barely had developed beyond its infancy, was hampered by the interference of military campaigns, poor financing, and bad roads that stayed in disrepair. English papers, which had been a prime source of news before the war, were received irregularly. As a result, news of major events sometimes was delayed a month or more, Americans were ill-supplied with information, and rumors and false news abounded.

One of the Patriot press' biggest problems was shortage of supplies, especially newsprint. As a reaction to the Stamp Act and the Townshend Acts, colonials had agreed not to import certain items from Britain, giving Americans the impetus to begin manufacturing presses and type. Paper mills also multiplied in number; but even though sixty or so existed in the colonies at the time of the

Revolution, paper shortages caused the press much trouble. Paper prices went up sharply, mainly because of the scarcity of rags needed in papermaking. The threat that the shortage might mean a cessation or at least a substantial diminution of newspaper publishing worried Patriot leaders. Newspapers carried pleas for saving rags, and Patriot organizations and town meetings gave prizes to women who showed the greatest patriotism by saving the most rags. Even George Washington took time from his military duties to urge women to save the smallest scraps as a patriotic duty.

Although not telling the whole story, the figures on newspaper mortality reveal something of the effect of the Revolution. At the beginning of the war, thirty-seven newspapers were publishing in the colonies. Seventeen of those died during the war, leaving twenty publishing at its end. Thirty-three new papers were started. Of those, eighteen died and fifteen survived. Thus, at the end of the war, thirty-five newspapers were publishing, two fewer than at the beginning. While a difference of two may seem of little importance, it does not indicate the magnitude of the war's effect. At one time or another, seventy papers were being published during the Revolution; only half survived. Such a high death rate during a period of seven years illustrates the hazards war posed for publishing.

The most important impact of the Revolution on the press, however, lay in the change the War of Independence brought to America. Freedom had been gained from the mother country, a new political philosophy took firm root, and the foundation was laid on which would be built a wholly new governmental system. While the American press had been instrumental in helping bring about the Revolutionary War, the war thrust the nation and its newspapers into an independence that soon would result in another revolution in politics and government. For a second time, the press would play a critical role in helping shape the American nation.

RECOMMENDED READINGS

BOOKS

Bailyn, Bernard. *The Ideological Origins of the American Revolution*. Cambridge, Mass., 1967. The ideas found in pamphlets indicate that the American Revolution was primarily an ideological struggle for greater political freedom and equality.

Bailyn, Bernard, and John B. Hench, eds. *The Press and the American Revolution*. Worcester, Mass., 1980. This collection includes incisive essays by various historians.

Berger, Carl. *Broadsides and Bayonets: The Propaganda War of the American Revolution*. Philadelphia, 1961. Events and real conditions during the war were more persuasive than words, rendering both British and American propaganda ineffective.

Bickham, Troy. *Making Headlines: The American Revolution as Seen through the British Press*. DeKalb, Ill., 2009. British newspapers viewed the American Revolution as the latest chapter in the ongoing conflict with France rather than just a colonial rebellion.

Canfield, Cass. *Sam Adams' Revolution 1765-1776*. New York, 1976. "[I]t was primarily Adams who fanned the flame of rebellion.... Without him...American independence could not have been declared in 1776."

Cornebise, Alfred E. *Ranks and Columns: Armed Forces Newspapers in American Wars*. Westport, Conn., 1993. This book covers military journalism from the Revolutionary War through the twentieth century.

Davidson, Philip. *Propaganda in the American Revolution, 1763-1783*. Chapel Hill, N. C., 1941. Without the work of propagandists, independence would not have been declared in 1776.

Foner, Eric. *Tom Paine and Revolutionary America*. New York, 1976. The Revolutionary writer was an important contributor to liberal, democratic philosophy whose main desire was to eliminate inequalities and abuses.

Hixson, Richard F. *Isaac Collins: A Quaker Printer in 18th Century America*. New Brunswick, N.J., 1968. For the publisher of New Jersey's first newspaper, the *Gazette*, most problems during the Revolution were related to business operations, such as obtaining paper and collecting from subscribers.

Humphrey, Carol Sue, ed. *The Revolutionary Era: Primary Documents on Events from 1776 to 1800*. Westport, Conn., 2003. This book provides a collection of newspaper articles from the period.

---. ed. *The Revolutionary War*, Vol. 1 of *The Greenwood Library of American War Reporting*, David A. Copeland, ed. Westport, Conn., 2005. This book provides a collection of newspaper articles about the war.

---. *"This Popular Engine": New England Newspapers during the American Revolution, 1775-1789*. Newark, Del., 1992. During the Revolutionary period, newspapers served as the colonials' most important source of information.

Lorenz, Alfred L. *Hugh Gaine: A Colonial Printer-Editor's Odyssey to Loyalism*. Carbondale, Ill., 1972. Gaine, although insisting on fairness when partisanship was expected, was primarily oriented toward business and did whatever was necessary to prosper.

Miller, John C. *Sam Adams: Pioneer in Propaganda*. Boston, 1936. Adams was the total politician, utilizing considerable emotion and a facile mind to convince others that his way should be their way.

Miner, Ward L. *William Goddard, Newspaperman*. Durham, N.C., 1962. Although a pro-Patriot printer, Goddard insisted on freedom to print material from both sides of the conflict and would not withhold news even though Patriot mobs tried to intimidate him.

Morgan, Edmund S., and Helen M. Morgan. *The Stamp Act Crisis: Prologue to Revolution*. Chapel Hill, N. C., 1953. The authors analyze colonial resistance to the Stamp Act and the emergence of well-defined constitutional principles.

Schlesinger, Arthur M. *Prelude to Independence: The Newspaper War on Great Britain, 1764-1776*. New York, 1958. Newspaper reaction to British authority played a crucial role in the growing tide of revolution.

Shipton, Clifford. *Isaiah Thomas: Printer, Patriot, Philanthropist, 1749-1831*. Rochester, N.Y., 1948. Thomas was the "father of the modern American printing and publishing business."

Sloan, Wm. David, and Julie Hedgepeth Williams. *The Early American Press, 1690-1783*. Westport, Conn., 1994. This in-depth study provides an insightful account of the role of newspapers before and during the Revolution.

Stoll, Ira. *Samuel Adams: A Life*. New York, 2008. Adams loved freedom and became a leading figure in America's successful rebellion against England.

Waldstreicher, David. *In the Midst of Perpetual Fetes: The Making of American Nationalism, 1776-1820*. Chapel Hill, N.C., 1998. Newspaper reporting of public rituals gave them a "national scope" that helped to reinforce the idea of unity and the concept of "one nation."

Walett, Francis G. *Massachusetts Newspapers and the Revolutionary Crisis, 1763-1776*. Boston, 1974. After 1765, the Boston press — through news and propaganda — "played an unusually large part in the movement toward American independence."

ARTICLES

Batchelder, Frank R. "Isaiah Thomas the Patriot Printer." *New England Magazine*, n.s., 25 (November 1901): 284-305. Thomas, a close friend to many Boston radicals, launched his *Massachusetts Spy* with all the flair and bombast of modern tabloids.

Benjamin, S. G. W. "A Group of Pre-Revolutionary Editors. Beginnings of Journalism in America." *Magazine of American History* 17 (January 1887): 1-28. The press exercised great power in influencing public attitudes and events to help bring about the Revolution.

Botein, Stephen. "Printers and the American Revolution," in Bailyn and Hench, *The Press and the American Revolution,* 11-58. Printers were traditionally neutral and impartial, but their attitudes were often determined by political conditions. In periods of political unrest, they found it profitable to be partisan; in quieter times they could afford to open their presses to diverse opinions.

Calkin, Homer L. "Pamphlets and Public Opinion During the American Revolution." *Pennsylvania Magazine of History and Biography* 64 (1940): 22-42. Pamphlets were "of prime importance in forming and shaping the minds of the people," helping to present and form "the ideas and theories of the two sides in the many controversial questions which arose from 1763 to 1783."

Cullen, Maurice R., Jr. "Benjamin Edes: Scourge of Tories." *Journalism Quarterly* 51 (1974): 213-8. Edes was a successful printer who became a leader in the struggle to oppose the Stamp Act.

—. "Middle-Class Democracy and the Press in Colonial America." *Journalism Quarterly* 46 (1969): 531-5. An examination of economic opportunity, the extent of political democracy, and the colonies' literacy rate shows that the Revolution was not a class struggle but a fight for democracy.

Dickerson, O. M. "British Control of American Newspapers on the Eve of the Revolution." *New England Quarterly* 24 (1951): 455-68. Since printing was a business, printers normally ran material that was favorable to authorities who controlled the purse strings.

Frank, Willard C. "Error, Distortion and Bias in the *Virginia Gazette, 1773-74.*" *Journalism Quarterly* 49 (1972): 729-39. The Williamsburg printers tried to produce a powerful journal of opinion. Although they slanted or distorted reports, radicals believed them; and they played a large role in urging Virginians to rebel because the *Gazette* was Virginia's only widely read newspaper.

Frasca, Ralph. "'The Glorious Publick Virtue so Predominant in Our Rising Country': Benjamin Franklin's Printing Network During the Revolutionary Era." *American Journalism* 13 (1996): 21-37. Franklin urged his printing partners to remain impartial. The pressures of the growing conflict, however, pushed most of them firmly into the Patriot camp.

Harlan, Robert. "David Hall and the Stamp Act." *Papers of the Bibliographical Society of America* 61 (1967): 13-37. Realizing that his newspaper was the most important financial aspect of his printing business, Hall allowed the *Pennsylvania Gazette's* editorial policies to conform more and more to those of the Patriot faction.

Henry, Susan. "Margaret Draper: Colonial Printer Who Challenged the Patriots." *Journalism History* 1 (1974): 141-4. As publisher of the *Massachusetts Gazette and Boston News-Letter,* Draper supported the Tory cause. However, in a period during which women were not fully appreciated, "her own considerable contribution to a political cause was quickly subsumed beneath her husband's...."

Humphrey, Carol Sue. "The Media and Wartime Morale: The Press and the American Revolution," 65-77, in *The Significance of the Media in American History,* James D. Startt and Wm. David Sloan, eds., Northport, Ala., 1994. The media have always had an impact on public morale during wartime, and Patriot papers sought constantly to increase support for the war effort through the materials they published.

Moses, James L. "Journalistic Impartiality on the Eve of Revolution: the *Boston Evening Post, 1770-1775.*" *Journalism History* 20 (1994): 125-30. The newspaper's effort to be impartial resulted in its closing. Just prior to the Revolution, "the printer who attempted to remain impartial during the storms of controversy usually found himself in the position of being despised by both sides."

Mott, Frank Luther. "The Newspaper Coverage of Lexington and Concord." *New England Quarterly* 17 (1944): 489-505. Newspaper "coverage was conditioned by the primitive techniques of eighteenth-century news-gathering, by such facilities of communication as existed, and by the stage of development at which the newspaper had arrived." Most newspaper information was not first-hand or timely.

Ours, Robert M. "James Rivington: Another Viewpoint," 219-34 in Donovan H. Bond and W. Reynolds McLeod, eds. *Newsletters to Newspapers: Eighteenth Century Journalism.* Morgantown, W.V., 1977. Rivington, who was the most hated Tory editor during the Revolution because he was accused of distorting and slanting facts, actually acted as he had promised he would: "impartial and neutral."

Parker, Peter J. "The Philadelphia Printer: A Study of an 18th Century Businessman." *Business History Review* 40 (Spring 1966): 24-46. Printing changed between 1758 and 1800. Before the Revolution, the printer was an artisan and merchant. The Revolution accelerated the growth of his business. By 1800, he thought of his business apart from himself.

Parkinson, Robert G. "'An Astonishing Account of Civil War in North Carolina.' Rethinking the Newspaper Response to the Battle of Alamance. "*Journalism History* 32:4 (2007): 223-30. In 1771 "many American printers published a multitude of reports from North Carolina that supported the royal government."

Pomerantz, S. I. "The Patriot Newspaper and the American Revolution." In R. B. Morris, ed., *The Era of the American Revolution* (New York, 1939): 305-31. Printers did commendable jobs in news reporting, avoidance of personal abuse, accuracy of information, moderation of tone, open-mindedness toward the conflicting sides, and adherence to other journalistic principles.

Potter, Janice, and Robert M. Calhoon. "The Character and Coherence of the Loyalist Press," in Bailyn and Hench, 229-72. This analysis of the intellectual and ideological content and character of newspaper essays that supported Britain concludes that the most common themes were disaffection, petulance, ingratitude, and disloyalty.

Randolph, J. Ralph. "The End of Impartiality: *South Carolina Gazette, 1763-75.*" *Journalism Quarterly* 49 (1972): 702-9, 720. Peter Timothy, printer of the *Gazette,* changed to editorial partiality because of the Anglo-American crisis, although as a general rule he believed in press impartiality.

Skaggs, David C. "Editorial Policies of the *Maryland Gazette, 1765-1783.*" *Maryland History Magazine* 59 (1964): 341-9. In Maryland, the *Gazette* was "one of the most significant institutions influencing the change of colonial ideals from dependence to independence, and at the same time leaving such concepts as freedom of religion, speech, and press ingrained in the revolutionary mind."

Sloan, Wm. David. "American Revolutionary Printers, 1765-1783: Powerful Radicals or Ineffective Conservatives?" 41-57, in *Perspectives on Mass Communication History* (Hillsdale, N.J., 1991). This essay analyzes the approaches that historians have taken.

Smith, Jeffery. "War as Monarchial Folly in the Early American Press." *American Journalism* 10 (1993): 83-97. Colonial journalists linked warfare to royalty, thus undermining monarchs' authority. They argued that republican government would eliminate or at least limit military conflict as a solution to international problems.

Spaulding, E. Wilder. "The *Connecticut Courant,* A Representative Newspaper in the Eighteenth Century." *New England Quarterly* 3 (1930): 443-63. "[A]s a medium for agitation the prosaic little American newspaper had as yet no rival in book or magazine printing. Its only rivals, the broadside and the pamphlet, it was to overtake and pass by the end of the Revolution, making of itself the most effective mirror of the life and thought of its community."

Thomas, C.M. "The Publication of Newspapers during the American Revolution." *Journalism Quarterly* 9 (1932): 358-73. "The very nature of the printer's business made neutrality in a civil struggle impossible for him."

Wax, Donald D. "The Image of the Negro in the *Maryland Gazette,* 1745-75." *Journalism Quarterly* 46 (1969): 73-80, 86. The *Gazette* portrayed the Negro as property and in derogatory terms, thus setting a pattern of race prejudice and discrimination deeply rooted in America's past.

Williams, Julie Hedgepeth. "The American Revolution and the Death of Objectivity," chapter 4 in Steven R. Knowlton and Karen L. Freeman, eds., *Fair and Balanced: A History of Journalistic Objectivity.* Northport, Ala., 2005. "As America edged closer to war with Britain, journalistic neutrality got scarcer.... As Patriots saw it, Britain denied Americans their constitutional rights. To restore those liberties, the Patriot press could no longer be open to the British opinion without stabbing the American cause in the back."

Yodelis, Mary Ann. "Who Paid the Piper? Publishing Economics in Boston, 1763-1775." *Journalism Monographs* 38 (1975). Government printing was not necessary for a successful printing business, and government therefore could exercise little financial coercion.

5

The Party Press
1783 - 1833

As the year 1798 came to an end, Federalist politicians looked to the new year with foreboding. They were locked in a battle with their Republican opponents that both sides believed would determine the nature of the new American nation. In the year just closing, the Federalists, in control of the national government, had succeeded in passing the oppressive Sedition Act. Perhaps, they thought, it would work in silencing the opposition.

Still, the Federalists feared for the future. The Republicans yet might find a way to spread their radical views through their newspapers to the general populace. "Give to any set of men the command of the press," Judge Alexander Addison wrote with worry on New Year's Day of 1799, "and you give them the command of the country, for you give them the command of public opinion, which commands everything."[1] Should Republicans succeed at corrupting public opinion, Federalists wondered, what could result but despotism? "Of such force is public opinion," Addison had written earlier during the furor over passage of the Sedition Act, "that, with it on its side, the worst government will support itself, and, against it, the best government will fall."[2]

Federalists by 1799 had come to realize a fact that had been at the essence of American public life almost since the first colonists had stepped ashore in the early 1600s. Public opinion was the basis of public policy, and the printing press provided the forum for it. Because of the democratic nature of the American political system, leaders of the early parties recognized the necessity of appealing to public opinion. Only by doing so could they expect their concepts to be the ones that would be adopted and would shape the nation's political ideals. The primary means through which they hoped to mold public opinion was the press.

As parties began to develop following the adoption of the United States Constitution, on April 15, 1789, John Fenno published the first issue of the *Gazette of the United States*, beginning one of the most politically and journalistically vigorous periods in American history. It would see the American political system take shape and the press play a critical role in determining the direction of that system.

The Federalist-Republican and the Jacksonian periods were passionate political ages marked by intensely bitter partisan opinions. The distinctive characteristic of newspapers from 1783 to 1833 was political partisanship. That characteristic — combined with the fact that partisan fervor frequently gave vent to abusive personal and political attacks — can give the impression that the party press performed poorly. The nature of the press of the time has to be considered, however, in the context of the role it played in America's social and political environment. The contributions editors made to the political system established them as important figures, both journalistically and politically.

The period of the partisan press was a critical one for the nation. From the end of the Revolution, America existed as a confederation until 1788. In that year the Constitution was adopted and transformed the loose grouping of states into a unified nation. During the next forty years, Americans set up an elaborate system of national government, organized their first political parties, and laid the base of their foreign policy for years to come. The Federalist-Republican period of 1789-1816 thus represents one of the most important eras in American history, and many historians have viewed Andrew Jackson's presidency (1829-1837) as the culmination of the early fight for American democracy.

THE PRESS AND THE CONFEDERATION

The 1780s marked a new era in journalism, and many new printers and publishers appeared on the scene. They were optimistic about their young nation's future and the role the press was sure to play. Immediately after the American Revolution ended, however, most of them recognized that the Articles of Confederation were too weak, and they began to support efforts to establish a new form of federal government. Their fears centered on such problems as the difficulty the government had in paying debts incurred during the Revolution, the fact that the individual states were acting in their own selfish interests, and civil unrest as exem-

[1] *Columbian Centinel*, 1 January 1799.
[2] *Russell's Gazette*, 7 June 1798.

"The Federalist"
In the fight for adoption of the Constitution, Virginia and New York, two of the largest states, lagged. In New York, Alexander Hamilton led the battle. He and his co-authors, James Madison and John Jay, produced eighty-five "Federalist" essays with the pseudonym "Publius" and published them in the *New York Independent Journal*. Proponents of the Constitution in Virginia and New York found the series especially useful as a handbook for arguments, and both states voted for adoption. After New York ratified in July 1788, New York City held a huge celebration parade, led by the ship *Hamilton*. Today, the "Federalist" is considered to be one of the most important and incisive works ever produced on the American political system.

plified in "Shays's Rebellion" of rural debtors in Massachusetts and in a mob of disgruntled farmers attacking New Hampshire's state legislature.

Most newspapers supported the call for a Constitutional Convention to work out a more effective national government. When the Convention met for the first time in 1787, its members adopted guidelines for their proceedings that, among other things, closed discussions to the public and the press. Editors agreed that confidentiality was necessary for the convention's frank debate of issues and said little in opposition to the secrecy. Assured of the ability and high character of the men who composed the Convention, they wrote confidently of the expected outcome. The convention was, declared one newspaper, "perhaps the last opportunity which may be presented to us of establishing a permanent system of Continental Government; and, if this opportunity be lost, it is much to be feared that we shall fall into irretrievable confusion."[3]

When the Convention adjourned in September and presented its brief proposed constitution, every newspaper in the country printed a copy, and all immediately opened their columns for a discussion of it. All but twelve papers favored its adoption. Editorial support was so strong that opponents claimed their views did not get a fair hearing in the press. Editors responded that they printed all views and that their reason for publishing few articles opposing adoption of the Constitution was that opponents submitted few. Of the hundreds of articles published in favor of adoption, the most widely republished was the series known as "The Federalist Papers." Written jointly by Alexander Hamilton, James Madison, and John Jay, each signing his contributions "Publius," the essays even today are recognized as perhaps the most insightful pieces ever written on America's constitutional form of government. They appeared in the *New York Independent Journal* from October 1787 to April 1788.

[3]*Freeman's Journal*, 16 May 1787.

By the time the ninth state, the final one needed for adoption, ratified the Constitution in June 1788, the debate had already initiated the appearance of factions in American politics. Supporters of adoption were being called "Federalists." Their opponents, called simply "Anti-Federalists," feared that the new federal government would be too strong, taking power and rights from the states and the people. The animosities between the two factions would quickly intensify as the national government and America's political system began to take shape in the next few years.

THE PRESS AND THE FIRST PARTY SYSTEM

After adoption of the Constitution, Federalists (led by Hamilton) and their opponents (led by Madison and Thomas Jefferson) clashed on several major issues, particularly the federal government's assumption of state debts, the question of whom the United States should support in conflicts between France and Great Britain, and the enactment of the Alien and Sedition Acts in 1798.

The fact that party machinery had not developed to a sophisticated state increased the press' importance. During the first party system, factions at first worked as informal groups rather than as organized political parties, but by 1792 they were exhibiting characteristics of formalized party structure and referring to themselves by the names "Federalists" and "Republicans." Speechmaking and other forms of personal campaigning, however, were not practiced as a part of electioneering. With the 1792 election emphasizing the need for political organization, both parties accelerated their efforts. They tightened party discipline. To promote their cause, Republicans formed numerous "Democratic" societies, with forty or so such clubs existing by 1794. Debate over the Jay Treaty in 1795 and 1796 helped crystallize parties and accelerated advances in party structure, loyalty, and voting.

In preparation for the 1796 election, Republicans held their first congressional caucuses, and small groups of influential leaders selected the candidates of both parties, the Federalists choosing John Adams and the Republicans, Jefferson. The party ticket had appeared. Neither Adams nor Jefferson campaigned, which would have appeared inappropriate; but newspapers waged a vigorous battle.

With Adams' victory, Republicans recognized even more clearly the need of greater efforts at organizing party machinery if they were to win the presidency in 1800. Jefferson, showing a much greater interest in his "campaign" and a determination to win in 1800, early in 1799 wrote out his platform, took every opportunity to express his views in private correspondence, and in other ways generally behaved as a practical politician. Electioneering efforts intensified. Both parties used corresponding committees, circular letters among party adherents, organization committees on the town and county levels, public meetings, party tickets, political addresses, campaign handbills and pamphlets, and newspaper announcements and arguments. Republican efforts, however, were better organized than those of the Federalists; and Jefferson's narrow election may have resulted as much from his electioneering methods and the Republicans' disciplined party organization as from his ideology.

The election brought significant progress in party organization and techniques of appealing to public opinion. Generally, though, party machinery was meager, and formal organization had not developed in some states. After 1800, organization improved for Republicans. They used the press, patronage, local committees, legislative caucuses, state nominating conventions, and other mechanisms with more sophistication and intensity.

Although Federalists were less successful in politics, they also attempted to fashion more sophisticated and effective party machinery. Because of the election defeat, many of the older, hard-line Federalists deserted politics; but more realistic, and generally younger, Federalists adopted the Republicans' techniques in an attempt to recover from the 1800 debacle and convert their party into one that could pursue popular support. They were doomed to failure, however, for their ideas were out of line with majority sentiment among the American public. Following Jefferson's election, the Republicans slowly gained the upper hand; and the 1816 presidential election was the last in which the Federalists ran a candidate. About all that was left of the Federalist party by that time were newspapers still carrying on the old fight.

As the party system emerged, both politicians and editors viewed the press as a major instrument in efforts to influence public opinion and gain political dominance. They attempted in a variety of ways to establish and support friendly newspapers and to silence the opposition. As a result, much newspaper content was political, with opinion and argument emphasized rather than news. Editors thrust themselves into the middle of the political struggles. Their purpose was not to be impartial but to fight however they could for their side. The partisan motives of the press were quite clear, and the sides in the political conflict well drawn.

Since the nature of the political system was based ultimately on the will of the people, appealing to public opinion became crucial. The primary tool was the newspaper. Its intent, unlike that of today's media, was neither to be primarily a news medium nor to be impartial. In the highly partisan environment, the press took on a political function.

"A NATION OF NEWSPAPER READERS"

The press gained its political importance because of the position it occupied as the most important medium for the distribution of news and views. One of the most noticeable features of the period was the growth of newspapers. In 1783, only thirty-five newspapers, all weeklies, served the nation. By 1833, the number had increased to 1,200 and included dailies as well as weeklies.

The early papers published chiefly in the seaports and commercial towns where Federalists were more numerous and most potential advertisers were businessmen with Federalist inclinations. Federalists therefore achieved a decided advantage in numbers of newspapers. In some locales, their papers outnumbered those of the Republicans by margins of five to one. Similarly, the Whig party later was able to maintain superiority in newspaper numbers because more of its members were involved in business than were Democrats.

The primary contributors to newspaper growth were increases in the size of the U.S. population, the appearance of new towns, and the expansion of an ambitious postal system that provided information and inexpensive circulation of newspapers. Much of the increase in the numbers of newspapers occurred with the nation's westward expansion. As population pushed toward the Alleghenies and beyond, papers sprang up with the settlements.

How widely read the newspapers were, however, is difficult to determine. The cost of newspapers and the fact that usually they could be purchased not by individual copies but only by yearly subscription limited circulation. The yearly subscription price for a weekly ranged from $1 to $2. For a daily the price was in the $8 range. During a period in which Americans' average weekly income was less than $5, subscription prices tended to keep papers out of the reach of many people. In cities, subscription lists were confined largely to business and mercantile classes. Editors frequently bartered their newspapers, however, for produce and other goods; and small-town newspapers often had substantial circulations in the surrounding areas.

Still, circulation was relatively small. In 1790, America had ninety-one newspapers, only eight of which were dailies, with a combined circulation totaling perhaps 50,000. By 1800 the number had reached 234, including twenty-four dailies, with a combined circulation of approximately 145,000. The total number of copies produced that year has been estimated at a little more than five million, less than one copy per person. By 1808 the number of papers had reached 329, with a combined circulation of around 215,000. These low figures, however, do not provide an accurate count of the total number of newspaper readers.

Newspapers in the West

One of the notable features of journalism in the party press era was the tremendous increase in the numbers of newspapers. As the United States expanded westward after the Revolution, newspapers followed the settlement. The first newspaper established in the territory west of the Allegheny Mountains was the *Pittsburgh* (Pa.) *Gazette*, founded in 1787. From approximately fifty in 1786, the number of papers soared to 1,200 in 1833. Much of the increase came in the frontier territory of the West and South. The map on the left shows the establishment of the first territory and state newspapers from western Pennsylvania to Texas.

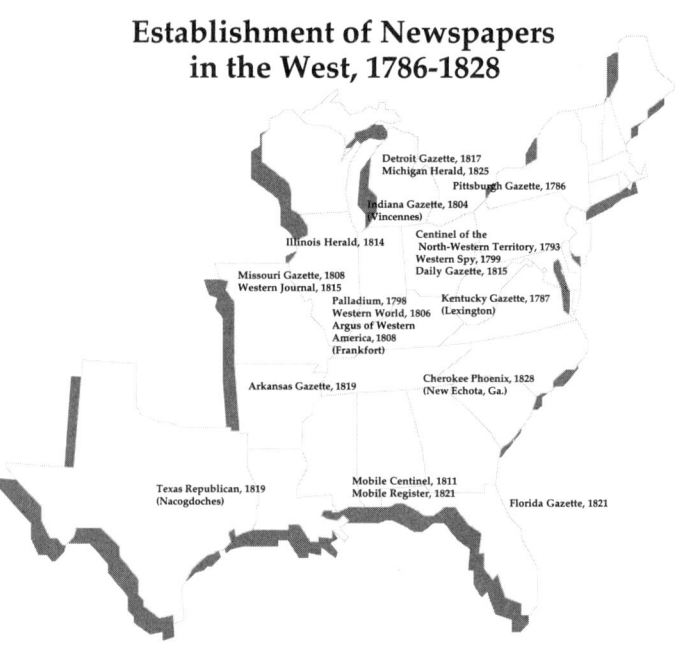

Establishment of Newspapers in the West, 1786-1828

Detroit Gazette, 1817
Michigan Herald, 1825
Pittsburgh Gazette, 1786
Indiana Gazette, 1804 (Vincennes)
Illinois Herald, 1814
Centinel of the North-Western Territory, 1793
Western Spy, 1799
Daily Gazette, 1815
Missouri Gazette, 1808
Western Journal, 1815
Palladium, 1798
Western World, 1806
Argus of Western America, 1808 (Frankfort)
Kentucky Gazette, 1787 (Lexington)
Arkansas Gazette, 1819
Cherokee Phoenix, 1828 (New Echota, Ga.)
Texas Republican, 1819 (Nacogdoches)
Mobile Centinel, 1811
Mobile Register, 1821
Florida Gazette, 1821

There is, in fact, no way of knowing how many people read a single copy of any paper. A writer to the *New York Journal* in 1795 explained that when the *Journal* arrived in western New York, it was "borrowed from one to the other to the distance perhaps of twenty miles."[4] A single subscription sometimes represented an association of several families, and coffee-houses and taverns subscribed to papers for customers to read. In villages with no newspapers, ministers often read the latest news to their congregations. Such interest led contemporaries to remark that America by 1800 had become "a nation of newspaper readers."[5] The editor Noah Webster declared, "Newspapers are the most eagerly sought after, and the most generally diffused. In no other country on earth, not even in Great-Britain, are newspapers so generally circulated among the body of people, as in America." Because of the circulation that resulted from their cheapness and frequency of publication, he added, newspapers had achieved "an eminent rank in the catalogue of useful publications."[6]

By today's standards, these early newspapers were not impressive. The typical newspaper was a small, four-page tabloid (one sheet printed front and back and folded) with a little political, foreign, and national news, and a few columns of advertising, found among letters and essays by local contributors, political arguments clipped from other papers, and editorials by the editor or a contributor. Grayness pervaded each page. The one-column headlines in use since 1690 remained standard, and newspapers carried even major stories under headlines of small type. Although country papers and those in the West stuck to the fairly small, 12" x 16" page sizes, the metropolitan papers tended to enlarge. As if equating page size with quality, some finally were printing pages three

feet wide and five feet deep. By the 1830s the popular, mass-oriented penny papers were jeering at these "blanket" sheets.

THE PRESS AS A POLITICAL INSTRUMENT

The emergence of the newspaper as a spokesman of a political party gave more prestige to the job of editor. Most newspapers continued to function, as they had during the colonial and revolutionary periods, as job-printing operations. Thus most newspaper operators still were printers who also served as writers, typesetters, pressmen, and circulation and advertising managers. Well-developed political argument, however, demanded more intellectual and writing ability from the newspaper operator. Thus emerged the true editor — in the sense of the person who writes opinion and oversees the content operations of the newspaper, in contrast to one who simply prints what others submit — and the standard of ability increased measurably. While many operators of small country papers continued to act more as printers than editors, individuals such as John Fenno of the *Gazette of the United States* and Duff Green of the *United States Telegraph*, Andrew Jackson's spokesman, were primarily editors concerned with editorial and news content.

Close associations between editors and politicians marked the party press period. As political leaders recognized the importance of the press, they worked to encourage newspapers to support their cause. Many new papers started publication. Politicians provided direct support for some of them, while other papers, those founded with the assistance of parties, were able to continue publication because of partisan aid. With the recognition of the newspaper's political significance came a variety of support. Partisan efforts made possible most of the livelihood of some papers. A few editors, enticed by the financial fruits, became little more than sycophants to politicians. Most, though, despite financial condi-

   [4] *New York Journal*, 24 February 1795.
   [5] *Port Folio Magazine*, quoted in Frank Luther Mott, *History of American Magazines* (Cambridge, Mass., 1938-1968), I: 160. Material on readership of newspapers is gathered from *Monthly Magazine*, I (1799): 13-4; and Philadelphia *Aurora*, 11 September 1799.
   [6] *American Minerva*, 9 December 1793.

tions, were sincerely committed to the cause they espoused and continued to publish in support of the party even when they found politicians' support undependable. At a time when advertising and subscriptions brought in little revenue to many newspapers, political support was invaluable. Publishing was not a lucrative business. Advertising often was sparse, and subscription payments were frequently delinquent. Without official favor, many newspapers would have perished. "Subsisting by a country newspaper," the editor of the *Trenton* (N.J.) *True American* wrote in 1802, "is generally little better than starving."[7]

Which party controlled government was critical for newspapers. Office-holders from the presidency down to the town council could bestow patronage on editors in the form of printing contracts and political office. Income from printing of congressional and legislative acts and documents and of items such as letterheads required by government officials could be lucrative. During Jefferson's first term, Samuel Harrison Smith of the *National Intelligencer* received nearly $2,000 per year in printing for the State Department alone. On the state and county levels government printing often was highly profitable. The state printer in North Carolina, to cite one case, received approximately $1,200 a year from 1800 to 1810.[8] Other types of political aid included loans and cash contributions, help in securing subscriptions and distributing papers, legal assistance, and written contributions in the form of essays, letters, and news items.

Whether a newspaper was published through the support of politicians or the independent efforts of journalists, it was recognized as a party spokesman and as a central part of the political system. Frequently, national, state, or local groups or individuals would provide money for starting a paper by outright contributions of cash or a mortgage or loan for printing equipment. Sometimes a group would hire a printer for a new paper and name one of its own members editor. In either situation, the patrons established the papers in the expectation of getting political support. Such papers came to be regarded as organs of these sponsors. Editors of independently established newspapers brought them into the service of a party and also received support from parties, factions, or individual politicians. Yet while financial support from politicians was imperative for the success of newspapers, the instances of editors basing their political loyalties on monetary considerations were rare. Most supported parties because of their agreement with the parties' political beliefs.

In general, the purpose of editors was to present news and views on political action and secondarily to win adherents to the cause. To accomplish these goals, editors and politicians expected the press to perform a number of functions. They may be categorized as the following: (1) promote political ideals, (2) support party principles, (3) defend the party and its politicians, (4) provide a medium for expression of party views, (5) provide "infor-

Seaport Partisans

The earliest partisan newspapers were established mainly in seaports and commercial centers, where business and advertising support were available. Newspapers soon began to proliferate from Maine to the southernmost state of Georgia.

mation" — always presented as "truth" from the party viewpoint, (6) influence public opinion, (7) preach the party line to the party faithful, (8) attack opponents, and (9) provide a method of electioneering.

POLITICAL IMPORTANCE OF THE PRESS

No medium offered such a convenient method for reaching party members and voters as newspapers did. Organizational efforts, mass meetings, and personal correspondence performed to some extent the functions of informing, mobilizing, and persuading party adherents and other voters. The press, however, was able to do these jobs more efficiently and thus became an expeditor of party efforts. Other than pamphlets, newspapers were the only media for general public information. City papers circulated in urban areas containing a significant percentage of the nation's population and frequently had rural subscription lists larger than their city lists. Smaller newspapers throughout the land supplemented

---

[7]*True American*, 26 July 1802.

[8]*Raleigh Star*, 29 November 1810. The fullest treatment of the financial relationship between newspapers and the government is Culver G. Smith, *The Press, Politics, and Patronage: The American Government's Use of Newspapers, 1789-1875* (Athens, Ga., 1977).

Political Passion
The early 1800s marked a period of intense political passion, not only in newspaper columns but in legislative halls. This contemporary cartoon depicts a fight between Matthew Lyon and Roger Griswold. After Griswold insulted him in a debate in the U.S. House of Representatives, Lyon, a Republican Congressman and editor from Vermont, marched across the floor and spat in his face. Griswold responded by attacking Lyon with a cane. Lyon grabbed some fire tongs and retaliated. Other members of the House — at least as the cartoon depicted them — seemed to enjoy the fight. Shortly afterward, Lyon was arrested and convicted under the Sedition Act for writing that President John Adams had an "unbounded thirst for ridiculous pomp, foolish adulation, and selfish avarice."

their city cousins. Although circulations were relatively small, the importance of newspapers was great because the public possessed limited means of obtaining information. People studied newspapers much more thoroughly — reading every word — than they do today because they had so little reading material available. Many papers with strictly partisan purposes charged artificially low subscription rates to increase their readership; and, because all eligible voters did not exercise the franchise, it is possible that most people who did vote were newspaper readers.

Whatever the readership was, the important factor was that politicians, editors, and general citizens believed the press was critical in the political system. All parties had members who believed in the importance of the press and thought newspapers should be used for partisan purposes. On numerous occasions, Jefferson testified to his belief in the value of newspapers. At the height of the XYZ affair in 1798, fearing that two Republican papers might cease publication, he wrote Madison that failure of the papers would be devastating for Republicanism.[9] He assumed that an informed public would make right decisions and that the press could influence views on political issues. "Our citizens," he wrote in 1799, "may be deceived for awhile, and have been deceived; but as long as the presses can be protected, we may trust to them for light."[10] He had in mind Republican presses, for he believed that Federalist newspapers dealt in "lying and scrib-

bling."[11] As the 1800 election approached, he urged Republicans on a daily basis to write articles for publication. "We are sensible," he wrote Madison, "that this summer is the season for systematic energies and sacrifices. The engine is the press."[12] As for writing articles himself, though, he did not like to attract criticism and so rarely contributed to any newspaper.

Party adherents at all levels attributed to the press a major role in influencing public opinion and, like Jefferson, actively encouraged their parties to make use of newspapers. A Republican stated succinctly and explicitly the accepted view of press importance. "If ink and black paint could overpower the enemy," he said, "we should have given him an unmerciful beating."[13]

In such a situation, the editor assumed a major role. Closely involved with politicians and party operations, editors were unusually knowledgeable about political issues and the inner workings of the party. Thus, they occupied ideal positions to serve as party spokesmen and advocates, dispensers of party information, and often political leaders on the local, state, and national levels.

OBJECTIVITY VERSUS PARTISANSHIP

Clearly, editors believed the overriding purpose of the press was to serve a partisan cause. Newspapers were intended to be neither non-partisan nor independent of parties. The contrary was true. Editors frowned on impartiality. The Federalist William Cobbett vowed to readers, as if keeping a trust, that he never would be impartial. Upon beginning *Porcupine's Gazette and Daily Advertiser* he proclaimed, "Professions of impartiality I shall make none." He did not intend to be one of those editors "who look on the conflict with perfect indifference, and whose only anxiety is the strongest side." Any editor who "does not exercise his own judgment, either in admitting or rejecting what is sent to him," he claimed, "is a poor passive fool, and not an editor." He would not allow impartiality to make *Porcupine's Gazette* into "an instrument of destruction to the cause I espouse." His "partiality," he declared, was "for the cause of good government, such as we live under."[14]

Because of their disdain for factionalism, Americans expected at least a facade of impartiality during the early part of the period, but by 1800 many editors made no pretense of impartiality. They proclaimed that to be impartial was to do the country an injustice. At a time when partisan feeling was hot, readers sometimes were annoyed that a paper would not take a partisan stand, and they accorded a neutral editor little merit. Samuel Harrison Smith found that readers and editors alike contemptuously referred to his *National Intelligencer* as "Mr. Silky Smith's National Smoothing Plane" because his partisan zeal was not as evident as they thought it should be.[15] Even to consider impartiality, some editors argued, was dereliction of duty. The editor of *The Port Folio* in

[9]Jefferson to Madison, 26 April 1798, in Paul L. Ford, *The Works of Thomas Jefferson* (New York, 1892-1899), 7: 245.
[10]Jefferson to Archibald Stuart, 14 May 1799, ibid., 378.

[11]Jefferson to John Randolph, 17 September 1792, ibid., 6: 111-2.
[12]Jefferson to Madison, 5 February 1799, ibid., 7: 344.
[13]Samuel Mitchell to Tench Coxe, 3 August 1813, quoted in Jacob Ernest Cooke, *Tench Coxe and the Early Republic* (Chapel Hill, N.C., 1978), 211.
[14]*Porcupine's Gazette*, 5 March 1797.
[15]*Richmond Recorder*, 21 May 1803.

Philadelphia stated adamantly that "he will not publish an impartial paper." Neutral men, he said, "cry amen to every creed, and venture on all sides, without being trusted by any." He did not intend to be like them. "Of such infamous principles," he declared, "the Editor has the deepest abhorrence, and for the silly scheme of Impartiality, he cherishes the most ineffable contempt."[16] Similarly, the editor of the *Baltimore American and Daily Advertiser* announced that he would declare himself openly in support of "the principles of Republicanism" and in opposition to "toryism and royalty." He would have no part of non-partisanship, he proclaimed, for "it is as incongruous for a publication to be alternately breathing the spirit of Republicanism and Aristocracy as for a clergyman to preach to his audience Christianity in the morning, and Paganism in the evening."[17] The reasoning of these editors is clear. They were publishing during a time of political questions that they believed were of critical importance. They would have failed in their devotion to truth and in their duty to serve the best interests of their country had they not stood up for their political convictions. "Objective" news reporting would not have been enough. Advocacy of a cause was imperative.

Despite such denunciations of impartiality, it is evident from them that the idea that newspapers should be impartial did circulate among Americans. If the idea were not current, there would have been no reason for editors to argue against it. Clearly, the concept was one that in earlier times had become expected of newspapers. Thus, the editors' arguments against impartiality suggest that the concept was a strong one that they had to deal with.

Newspapers' continual attacks on politicians and government policies were almost always partisan in nature. They did not result from an adversarial relationship between government and the press as we think of that relationship today. Targets nearly always were members of the opposition party. Republican editors attacked Federalist politicians, and Federalists attacked Republicans. In the second party system, Democrat editors attacked Whigs, and Whigs attacked Democrats. Party and factional loyalties — rather than a belief that the press, per se, should be an adversary of government, per se — accounted for the conflict.

FEDERALIST EDITORS

Hundreds of editors carried the fight for the parties. One of the first was Benjamin Russell. He and William Warden founded the *Columbian Centinel* in Boston in 1784 as a paper for the mercantile classes. After Warden departed as co-owner, Russell, who revered George Washington, transformed it into a political paper devoutly Federalist, favoring adoption of the Constitution and a strong national government. As the battles between Federalists and Republicans intensified in the 1790s, a choice group of political writers aided the *Centinel*. It also received financial aid through state and federal printing, but Russell regarded serving the nation as

[16] Quoted in the *Independent Chronicle*, 7 August 1798.
[17] *Baltimore American and Daily Advertiser*, 16 May 1799.

Gerry-Mander

While Elbridge Gerry was serving as governor of Massachusetts, his party in 1812 drew new political districts for Essex County to assure election of fellow Republicans. Benjamin Russell, editor of the Federalist *Columbian Centinel* in Boston, noticed that the shape of one district resembled that of a salamander. He coined the term "Gerry-Mander," and the *Boston Weekly Messenger* ran a cartoon with head, wings, and claws added. In the accompanying map, the districts along the top and down the left side form the Gerry-Mander's outline. Governor Gerry lost the next election, and "gerrymander" became a part of the American language.

important as getting help from the government. In the early days of the Republic, when the national treasury was small, he declined payment for printing the federal laws.

As a strident opponent of Jefferson, Russell threw his support to Aaron Burr when the presidential election became entangled by the electoral system in 1801. After Jefferson was elected, Russell lamented the nation's fallen condition and predicted the demise of the Federalist party. Still, he stridently continued to advocate its principles. Throughout Jefferson's two administrations, he virulently denounced him. His opposition to Republicanism continued with the election of Madison, and he fought trenchantly against the war with England in 1812. In 1805 he was elected to the Massachusetts House of Representatives and was re-elected each year until 1821. It was Russell who, with the decline of the Federalist opposition after James Monroe's election in 1816, coined the phrase used to describe the few years that followed: "The Era of

Federalist Point Men

In the 1790s the Federalist press was spearheaded by three able journalists. The first party newspaper, the *Gazette of the United States* was founded in the same year as the United States itself, 1789. John Fenno was so devoted to publishing the newspaper that he stayed at his job as a yellow fever epidemic swept Philadelphia in 1793. In a second epidemic in 1798, he again refused to leave the city and contracted the disease. Upon his death, the editorship of the *Gazette* fell to his nineteen-year-old son, John Ward Fenno. As editor of the *American Minerva*, one of the Federalists' leading newspapers in the 1790s, Noah Webster set a comparatively high editorial tone. After leaving journalism, he became famous for compiling the first dictionary of the American language, later editions of which still bear his name. The Federalists' most effective journalist, William Cobbett emphasized the importance of partisanship in newspapers. An editor who did not discriminate in what he published, said Cobbett, was "a poor passive fool." As "Peter Porcupine," he was so effective a writer that he became the target of numerous attacks by Republicans. Reveling in the attention, he wrote his father: "When you used to set me off to work in the morning, dressed in my blue smock-frock and woollen spatter-dashes, ... little did you imagine that I should one day become so great a man as to have my picture stuck in the windows, and have four whole books published about me in the course of one week."

Good Feeling."

Despite the fact that earlier partisan newspapers had existed, the founding of the *Gazette of the United States* in 1789 marked the real beginning of the party press era. American newspapers before Fenno's had practiced partisan politics, but the *Gazette* was the first founded as an organ of one of the factions comprising America's first party system. It foreshadowed the political and journalistic battles that were to take place for the next generation.

Before the appearance of the *Gazette*, New York City — the new nation's capital — had no strong Federalist newspaper. The faction's leaders believed they needed support other than what they got from the mercantile press that was incidentally Federalist. John Fenno, a 38-year-old Boston schoolteacher, proposed an arrangement by which a pro-Federalist newspaper he hoped to start would be given government printing. Federalist leaders, including Alexander Hamilton, satisfied Fenno on the arrangement, and in three months Fenno began publication. Later, with the transfer of the capital to Philadelphia, he moved the *Gazette* there because of the stipulation in his proposal for establishing the paper that it be "published at the seat of government."[18]

Hamilton and other leading Federalists supported and subsidized the *Gazette of the United States*. They intended it to be the

Federalists' mouthpiece in the battle that would determine the nature of the new American government. "To hold up the people's own government, in a favorable point of light," Fenno wrote, "and to impress just ideas of its administration by exhibiting FACTS, comprise the outline of this paper."[19]

From the beginning, Fenno received the support he had requested. Hamilton fed him all the printing of the Treasury Department, he got much of the Senate's printing, and prominent Federalists subsidized him out-of-pocket. It was understood that the *Gazette* would mirror the opinions of its patrons and express the official Federalist positions. Because it was known as the organ of Hamilton, it became the leading paper of the national party leadership, circulating to party leaders and printers in all states. It kept this position throughout the 1790s. Fenno remained as editor until he died of yellow fever in 1798.

His son, John Ward Fenno, then edited the paper for less than two years, after which he became anxious by the loss of political support and sold the *Gazette* to Enos Bronson. Despite the challenge from the newly established *New York Evening Post* — and the weakened position of the *Gazette* — Bronson capably espoused the Federalist cause, and editors throughout the nation continued to rely on the *Gazette* for guidance on political issues. By the final

[18]*Gazette of the United States*, 18 September 1790.

[19]*Gazette of the United States*, 27 April 1791.

years of the Federalist party, however, leadership had shifted to the *Evening Post*.

With the removal of the *Gazette* to Philadelphia, New York City was left without a strong Federalist organ. A group of ten Federalists — including Hamilton, Rufus King, and John Jay — decided to contribute $150 each to begin a paper and induced Noah Webster to move to the city to edit it. The first issue of the *American Minerva* appeared on December 9, 1793. Webster had established a name for himself for his essays in various papers and his political pamphlets. His columns signed "Curtius" and those by Hamilton signed "Camillus" in the *Minerva* became the most widely reprinted on the Jay Treaty. The paper was an ardent supporter of the administration of Washington and of the national Federalist organization. When Washington left office, Webster's support continued for his successor, John Adams. The new president did not gain the favor, however, of Hamilton.

In 1798 Webster, disillusioned with Hamilton's betrayal of Adams, withdrew from the *Minerva* and placed his nephew, Ebenezer Belden, in charge. The rift between Webster and Hamilton had grown so great by the election of 1800 that Webster wrote a pamphlet charging his former patron with being corrupted by jealousy and ambition. Although it remained Federalist in affection, the *Minerva* developed into a commercial paper after Webster left, and its circulation dwindled from about 1,700 to 1,000.

Perhaps the best writer of the period was William Cobbett. Although he lived in America for only six years (1794-1800), he became known as the Federalists' most effective publicist and replaced John Fenno, the official, subsidized party editor, as their leading journalistic advocate. Cobbett began his career as a writer after serving seven years in the British army, mainly in India. Upon leaving the army, he wrote a pamphlet exposing military corruption. That pamphlet inaugurated a career that would make him one of the most famous figures in British journalism history. At this point, however, unable to substantiate the charges he made, he fled to France. Finding France in the throes of revolution and inhospitable for an English émigré, he departed for Philadelphia in 1794. In the United States, he sided with the Federalists and even began to write with an affinity for the British king and for rule by the aristocratic class in his adopted country. This apparent turnaround in philosophy and his condescension toward democracy may be explained by Cobbett's concern that the traditional way of life that he preferred was disappearing.

After making a name for himself with two political pamphlets and a periodical titled *The Political Censor*, in 1797 he launched *Porcupine's Gazette* as a daily newspaper, its name taken from Cobbett's pseudonym, "Peter Porcupine." He was the master of invective. Benjamin Russell described his role harshly but probably accurately. Cobbett, Russell said, "was never encouraged and supported by the Federalists as a solid, judicious writer in their cause; but was kept merely to hunt Jacobinic [i.e., Republican] foxes, skunks, and serpents."[20] Cobbett could be hard on anyone, but he

Federalist Flagship
With support from Alexander Hamilton and other leading Federalists, the *New York Evening Post* was launched with superior offices, supplies, and workmanship. Under the editorship of William Coleman, it quickly took the lead among Federalist newspapers.

especially relished attacking his Republican antagonist Benjamin Bache, editor of the *Aurora* in Philadelphia. He called the *Aurora* "Mother Bache's filthy dishcloth" and described its editor as "the white-livered, black-hearted thing Bache, that public pest and bane of decency." As if that were not enough, he wrote an entire article devoted to Bache, describing him as a mere hireling, an "ill-looking devil ... [whose] eyes never get above your knees."[21]

Cobbett was closely aligned with Hamilton and in 1799, following Hamilton's lead, broke with Adams in the president's re-election attempt. His denunciation of Adams for sending a peace delegation to France and thereby selling out to the "Jacobinical" Republicans was as strong as the criticism Adams received from Republicans for other actions. Adams privately considered using the Alien Law to get Cobbett deported. Instead, Cobbett lost a libel suit to Republican Benjamin Rush and fled to New York. Faced with having to pay a $5,000 judgment, he returned to England in 1800.

---

[20]Quoted in Frederic Hudson, *Journalism in the United States, From 1690 to 1872* (New York, 1873), 154.

[21]*Porcupine's Gazette*, 14 November 1797. For a detailed account of party newspapers' use of such language, see Wm. David Sloan, "Scurrility and the Party Press, 1789-1816," *American Journalism* 5 (1988): 97-112.

Journalism Education

Early Views of Training Influence Pedagogy in Today's Schools

In 1799, a rather curious item appeared in one of America's foremost newspapers, the *Gazette of the United States*. In the March 4 edition, publisher John Ward Fenno wrote that the young nation needed strong journalists to help newspapers keep alive American idealism. In order to develop those kinds of journalists, he argued, "... To well-regulated colleges we naturally look for a source whence such qualifications might in proper form be derived...."

It is not surprising that such a quote, which stands out as one of the earliest known public statements of support for teaching journalism on the college level, would originate with someone like Fenno. He was a graduate of the University of Pennsylvania; and his father, John Fenno, who had founded the newspaper ten years before, was a former teacher who had distinguished himself at Boston's Samuel Holbrook South School of Writing.

But the Fennos were an exception. The chief means by which someone became an editor or publisher until the twentieth century was to serve an apprenticeship in a print shop. There, the prospective journalist concentrated on learning the mechanical operations of the printing trade while working as a "printer's devil." Learning journalism came not from books and classes, but as a function of hands-on learning how to set type and run a press. It was a tradition that was more than 300 years old that could be traced to the German printer Johann Gutenberg.

It was in this environment that the first great American success story took place, the career of Benjamin Franklin. His formal education was limited to two years of grammar school. At age 13 he began as an apprentice to his brother James and later completed his training in the printer's trade in Philadelphia and London by age 20. Over the next twenty-two years he

Early proposals for formal education often got chilly receptions. Some individuals, though, saw the need for education and became strong advocates. Among them were (clockwise from top left) Robert E. Lee, president of what is now Washington and Lee University; Whitelaw Reid, editor of the *New York Tribune*; Joseph Pulitzer, who endowed the school of journalism at Columbia University; and Andrew D. White, president of Cornell University.

earned fame and fortune through his printing business, his publishing of the influential *Pennsylvania Gazette*, and his authorship of a runaway bestseller, *Poor Richard's Almanack*.

In 1869, when the first journalism course in America was offered at Washington College (now Washington & Lee University) in Virginia, there were no textbooks or lectures. Instead, the college added a local printer to its faculty, and the first journalism students fulfilled course requirements by working in the print shop of the local newspaper. In the late 1800s, majors, departments, and diplomas in journalism began to appear; but lessons in typography and press operations were still dominant in journalism education until the mid-1900s.

Today, regardless of whether the

media form is print, broadcast, or online, the old terms so familiar to early American printer-journalists are still prominent: *scoop, slug, sidebar, headline.* Even more so, learning how to contend with the special challenges time and space pose for the media occupies just as much a part of a modern media education as it did for a printer's devil.

Ironically, another quote from Fenno has become recently significant. Newspapers, aided by college-trained journalists, will continue to keep alive the American ideal, Fenno predicted, "till their influence is counteracted." Finding ways to remain relevant among counteracting influences in society and on university campuses is the main concern of the leaders of media corporations and media educators today.

The situation grew bleak for Federalists with the presidential election of that year. Their arch-enemy, Thomas Jefferson, was the victor. To make matters worse for New York Federalists, Republican George Clinton won a landslide victory as governor. He appointed his nephew, DeWitt Clinton, to rid government positions of Federalists. Every day, he ousted members of the opposition. Not only was Hamilton's political condition declining; he was falling into disgrace. Many Federalists blamed his attacks on Adams for the party's loss of the presidency.

Members of the party in New York, beseiged by the Republican editor James Cheetham, felt they needed a strong organ to present their case. In May of 1801, a group of Hamiltonian Federalists gathered in the home of one of New York's wealthiest merchants, determined to start a newspaper. They needed $10,000 seed money. Hamilton and his friends secretly circulated a founders' list among trusted Federalists, asking each to contribute at least $100, and they quickly raised the money. Hamilton put $1,000 into the venture. They selected William Coleman, a lawyer and frequent newspaper writer, to edit the paper. The first issue of the *New York Evening Post* appeared on November 16, with 600 subscribers, most from the inner circle of the state's Federalist party. It was affluent from birth. Intended as the flagship paper of the Federalist fleet, it had a printing shop boasting four complete sets of type at a time when most papers did not have one whole set.

Soon, the *Evening Post* was the recognized spokesman of the leading wing of the Federalist party. Its circulation reached 1,100; and its weekly edition, the *New York Herald*, circulated some 1,600 copies around the country. Much of the circulation resulted from the fact that the papers were known to be Hamilton's voice. Immediately upon its appearance, the *Evening Post* challenged the venerable *Gazette of the United States* for leadership of the Federalist press. Less than a year after its founding, the Republican editor James Callender called Coleman the "Field-Marshal of the Federalist editors." As the mouthpiece of the most earnest Federalists, the *Evening Post* virulently opposed Jefferson's administration even though Coleman was considered more dignified and thoughtful than most editors. He continued as editor through the end of the Federalist party, retaining until the end his position as the party's leading journalistic spokesman.

Federalists made various attempts to establish other papers as national and regional organs, but they met limited success. The most determined attempt was that of Boston Federalists on behalf of the *New-England Palladium*. While Hamilton was working out plans for starting the *Evening Post* in New York, Fisher Ames, Timothy Dwight, and other leading New England Federalists envisioned a national paper in Boston of the stature the *Gazette of the United States* had enjoyed under Fenno. They turned to the *Palladium*. To achieve their goals, however, the paper had to be revitalized. In the spring of 1801, Ames wrote fellow Federalists that the new editor, Warren Dutton, would have to be encouraged, the paper's circulation increased, and party adherents engaged in its publication. Of immediate concern were literary contributions, and Ames asked such politician-writers as Rufus King, George

Cabot, and Oliver Wolcott Jr. to submit material. The necessary support of leading Federalists, however, did not materialize; and the work of keeping the paper supplied with material fell to a few of the more active party faithful. The *Palladium* still became the leading Federalist organ in Massachusetts for a short time. In 1803, however, despite the bright plans Ames had proposed, its editor resigned; and even Ames abandoned the paper and supported the development of another, the *Boston Repertory*.

BACHE, DUANE, AND THE AURORA

Fighting the Federalist newspapers toe-to-toe were several prominent Republican papers. Like Federalists, Republican politicians also helped establish newspapers, but none matched over a long period the leadership that the independently founded *Aurora* in Philadelphia provided. It sustained its leadership without the benefit of inordinate government patronage. Despite the fact that Republicans extended some aid to the paper, its founder, Benjamin Franklin Bache, spent $20,000 of his own to keep it afloat. Started in 1790 when Bache was only twenty-one years old, the paper was consistently strong in opposing the Federalist influence in the national government. Most other Republican editors, who correctly assumed that Bache was on close terms with Jefferson and other national Republican leaders, looked to it for guidance. Grandson of Benjamin Franklin, Bache had spent his early years in France and was kindly disposed to the French cause. When George Washington showed favoritism toward England, Bache turned on him, becoming the first Republican who dared question the president's performance.

Because of Bache's eminence, he became a target of constant Federalist attempts to intimidate and silence him. On one occasion or another, Treasury Secretary Oliver Wolcott threatened to investigate the *Aurora* for treason, Federalist Speaker of the House Jonathan Dayton barred Bache from the House floor, Federalist editors and politicians subjected him to written and verbal attacks, Federalist merchants imposed an advertising boycott on the *Aurora* and barred the paper from their establishments, the government tried Bache for sedition, and individuals and mobs physically attacked him. In the face of such threats, he refused to ease his attacks on Federalist policies. Eventually, as he had expected, a mob assaulted him and his family. On the night of May 7, 1798, during a national crisis over relations between the United States and France, a party of intoxicated Federalist supporters marched on Bache's home. With only the editor, his wife, and their children in the house, the mob banged on the doors and windows and filled the night with insults and catcalls. Soon, however, Bache's friends and neighbors, roused by the commotion, drove off the mob. Two nights later — following a day that President Adams had called to be devoted to prayer and fasting and during which violent denunciations of Republicans had been issued — a mob again marked Bache's home for attack. He assembled and armed friends, who prepared for a defense of the home; and the mob that showed up only broke a few windows.

The *Aurora*

Under Benjamin Franklin Bache, Philadelphia's *General Advertiser* (better known as the "Aurora") took the lead among Republican newspapers because of Bache's inside knowledge of politics and hard-hitting writing style. After Bache died of yellow fever in 1798, his assistant, William Duane (inset), married the widow Bache, took over ownership of the *Aurora*, and enlarged its political influence. Duane was forty years old when he married Mrs. Bache. The portrait above was made when he was in his twenties.

After the failure of the mobs, the United States government proceeded against Bache. Treasury Secretary Wolcott investigated him for treason as a French secret agent after Bache published a secret state paper from the French foreign minister. When the investigation failed, the government then charged him under the Sedition Act for statements he had made in his defense. Before he could be tried, however, yellow fever struck Philadelphia in July of 1798. Residents fled, and by September most newspapers had suspended publication. Like John Fenno, however, Bache remained to carry on his party's fight. On September 6 he contracted the fever and died four days later.

Bache's widow made arrangements to continue the paper. His assistant, William Duane, took over the editorship. Under Duane, who soon married Mrs. Bache and became sole proprietor of the *Aurora*, the paper continued as the Republicans' leading voice. Be-

cause other Republican editors appreciated the prestige Bache had gained for the *Aurora* and admired Duane's own hard-hitting style and exposure of Federalist tactics, they copied much of the material that appeared in the paper, and it became the bible of Republicans not only in Pennsylvania but in other states as well. Federalists, who called the *Aurora* the "great speaking trumpet of the devil,"[22] so feared Duane that he was arrested for seditious libel of President Adams under the common law, arrested twice under the Sedition Act, and nearly indicted under the Alien Act. Despite attempts to silence him, he was undaunted in his loud partisan support of Thomas McKean in his victorious campaign for Pennsylvania governor in 1799 and of Jefferson in his 1800 triumph. Jefferson credited his election in part to Duane's support.

Duane, however, was personally ambitious and eager for government patronage. That led him into bitter factional battles among Republicans for political power in Pennsylvania. He eventually broke with James Madison, and the strife that continued until 1810 finally wore much of the shine from Duane's journalistic stature and political power. Despite his disagreements with the national Republican leadership, his factionalism in state politics, the fact that the national capital moved from Philadelphia to Washington, and the fact that Jefferson shifted much of his support from the *Aurora* in 1801 to the new *National Intelligencer*, the *Aurora* remained the leading national Republican paper. While the *Intelligencer* was a source of news from the capital, the *Aurora*'s editorial comments were reprinted nationwide. "Duane's press," wrote a Madison supporter in 1808, "with all its indecency, is worth for our purposes all others...[because the] circulation of his paper is so universal throughout the United States."[23]

REPUBLICAN EDITORS

Despite the prestige of the *Aurora*, Jefferson and his closest political associates twice turned from it to help establish other official organs: the *National Gazette* in 1791 and the *National Intelligencer* in 1800. Madison was the primary force in getting the *National Gazette* started; and Jefferson, an active participant. Madison proposed the idea for the paper to Philip Freneau, a staunch Republican and Madison's roommate at Princeton. He had gained national fame as the "Poet of the Revolution." Jefferson, then Secretary of State, offered him the job of translator of French. The clerkship, however, was of little value, for the money Freneau had to pay to hire assistants exceeded his salary.

Madison and Jefferson expected Freneau to combat Fenno's *Gazette of the United States* and intended his paper from the start to be a national organ. Because of his intellect and writing ability, Freneau conducted the fight with success. Identified as the personal organ of the national Republican leadership, the *National Gazette* quickly became the leader of the nation's Republican press. It circulated to local Republican officials and editors throughout the

[22]*United States Oracle*, 22 March 1801.
[23]Thomas Truxton to Madison, 17 March 1808, quoted in Noble Cunningham, *The Jeffersonian Republicans in Power* (Chapel Hill, N.C., 1963), 273.

The Burr-Hamilton Duel

Political Attack Ends in Death of Federalists' Leading Light

On the morning of July 11, 1804, the Vice President of the United States, Aaron Burr, shot and killed Alexander Hamilton, the first secretary of the U.S. treasury and one of the nation's most influential citizens. The shooting, a duel, occurred after Burr read in a New York newspaper of an attack on his character by Hamilton.

Hamilton, the leading Federalist, and Burr, a Republican, had long been political enemies. After Jefferson and Burr tied in the presidential election of 1800, Hamilton lobbied for Jefferson in the U.S. House of Representatives. Burr became Vice President; but Jefferson distrusted him, and his national career was stymied. In 1804 he sought to become governor of New York by appealing to a group of disaffected Federalists who believed New York and New England should secede from the Union. In a speech, Hamilton reportedly called Burr "a dangerous man about whom he could detail a still more despicable opinion."

Burr challenged Hamilton to explain or disavow the printed account of his speech. Hamilton's answer failed to satisfy Burr, and so the two men met on a cliff overlooking the Hudson River near Weehawken, New Jersey. It was the same place Hamilton's twenty-year-old son had been killed in a duel three years earlier.

The first eyewitness account of the duel was reported in the *New York Morning Chronicle*, a paper that Burr and other New York Republicans had founded. It reported that both parties took aim and concluded that the conduct of the men involved was perfectly proper, as suited the occasion. In cities such as Philadelphia, Republican papers praised Hamilton as a patriot but were notable for not condemning Burr.

For several weeks, the *New York Evening Post*, a Federalist paper that Hamilton had been instrumental in founding in 1801, ran stories about the duel surrounded by heavy black borders.

A few days before the duel, Hamilton confided to two friends that he did not plan to

return Burr's first fire. "I have resolved, if our interview [duel] is conducted in the usual manner," he had written, "and if it pleases God to give me the opportunity, to reserve and throw away my first fire, and I have thoughts even of reserving my second fire, and thus giving a double opportunity to Col. Burr to pause and reflect." As a result, a dispute arose about whether Hamilton really intended to fire at Burr, and the seconds almost fought another duel.

One of the most notable Americans during the early years of the Republic, Alexander Hamilton was continually involved with newspapers. After co-authoring the "Federalist Papers," he was instrumental in helping to found and support several leading Federalist journals. In 1804, as one of the attorneys in the appeal of the Croswell case, he played a leading role in getting libel law liberalized. Aaron Burr killed him in a duel that resulted in part from the trial. In the illustration above, Hamilton is the figure on the right. It is ironic that he should die for criticizing Burr, a public figure. Hamilton believed the government and officials should not be immune from criticism, and he urged public figures to take an active role in discussing political affairs through newspapers as he often did. A few months earlier, he represented a young Federalist editor, Harry Croswell, in his appeal of a libel conviction in New York. Croswell published *The Wasp* in Hudson as a response to *The Bee*, a local Republican paper, but he stung President Jefferson when he accused him of paying a journalist to attack George Washington and John Adams. Hamilton argued that the press should be "free to publish the truth, from good motives and for justifiable ends, though it reflect on government, on magistrates, or individuals." Croswell's appeal ended in a tie vote in the appeals court, but New York later rewrote its libel laws in light of Hamilton's argument.

Philip Freneau: Poet, Rascal
Philip Freneau had become a national celebrity with his poetry about the American war for independence. He was called "The Poet of the Revolution." With, however, his continual attacks on the federal government through the *National Gazette*, President George Washington condemned him as "that rascal Freneau," and the nickname became better known than his earlier one.

country and provided the model for partisan thinking and writing. Jefferson publicly denied having any connection with it. When opponents found out that he actually was helping subsidize it to criticize the same presidential administration in which he was serving, the revelation caused a major embarrassment for him. In 1793 he resigned as Secretary of State. With his departure went Freneau's clerkship and the printing patronage the *National Gazette* had been getting from the State Department. The paper, which had boasted a circulation of 1,300, ceased publication two weeks later. After the demise of the *National Gazette*, leadership among the Republican press reverted to the *Aurora*.

It was not until seven years later that another national organ was established under the auspices of the party's leaders. It was

Samuel Harrison Smith's *National Intelligencer*. Unlike Freneau's paper, Smith's venture was promoted as much by its editor as by its patrons. Sensing that Jefferson could win the 1800 election, Smith began work during the summer on starting the paper, and in August he solicited aid from Madison. Assured that help would be forthcoming should Jefferson gain the presidency, he began publication even though a major investment of $12,000 to $15,000 would be needed to publish for the first year and extensive patronage was contingent on the election's outcome. Jefferson's victory, however, assured success. In the *Intelligencer's* first year, the Departments of State and the Treasury awarded it the largest share of their printing, and its printing patronage from Congress was substantial. Although Jefferson denied any formal connection with the paper, Smith was one of his close friends and served as the spokesman of the executive branch of the government.

Throughout Jefferson's two terms, Smith remained a faithful, relatively temperate supporter, and the *Intelligencer* not only served as the outlet for official views but also provided extensive accounts of national government operations. It continued as a voice of the Republican cause after Jefferson had left the presidency and even after Smith had left the editorship. In 1810 it was sold to Joseph Gales Jr., who had trained for two years under Smith. During the two administrations of Madison, it served as his official organ. The relationship, though, between the editors and Madison and his Secretary of State, James Monroe, was more distant and formal than the one between Smith and Jefferson. In 1812 William Winston Seaton, Gales' brother-in-law, joined him as co-owner. Gales remained with the paper until his death in 1860; and Seaton, until retirement in 1864.

Among other Republican papers, the most notable were Thomas and Abijah Adams' *Independent Chronicle* in Boston, James Cheetham's *American Citizen* in New York, and Thomas Ritchie's *Richmond Enquirer*. All provided regional press leadership and were involved in party organization. The Adams brothers acquired the *Independent Chronicle* in 1788 and waged a vigorous battle against New England Federalism and Russell's *Columbian Centinel*. In 1799 officials indicted them under both the Sedition Act and Massachusetts libel law. Thomas, the older brother, was too sick to appear at his trial but was found guilty, along with Abijah, who was sentenced to thirty days in jail. The illness and the pending trial forced them to sell the *Chronicle*. Thomas died soon afterward. The *American Citizen* had been established by John Holt in 1766 as the *New York Journal*. In 1800 Cheetham joined the staff as editor and renamed the paper. It was the leading organ of the Clinton faction of the Republican party. The *Enquirer*, founded in 1804, became the organ of Virginia Republicanism and a semi-personal organ of Jefferson.

REGIONAL AND LOCAL PAPERS

While the leading newspapers were found in larger cities, virtually every town in every region of the country had its own partisan papers. In Georgia, Republicans helped establish the *Augusta*

Smith, Gales, Seaton, and the *National Intelligencer*
Under the patronage of the national Republican leadership, the *National Intelligencer* became the official voice of Presidents Jefferson, Madison, and Monroe and something of the official record of government. Partisans who thought Samuel Harrison Smith (inset), its founder, was too mild contemptuously referred to the paper as "Mr. Silky Milky Smith's National Smoothing Plane." After serving as Smith's assistant for two years, Joseph Gales Jr. (top right) bought the paper in 1810. Under his editorship, it was one of Madison's staunchest supporters during the War of 1812. Gales' brother-in-law, William Winston Seaton (bottom right), joined him as a partner in 1812 and served as editor until 1864. The partnership of Gales and Seaton provided an official record of debates in the U. S. Congress until that body finally hired its own reporters. Smith died in 1845, Gales in 1860, and Seaton in 1866.

Chronicle in 1790. When its editor, John E. Smith, died in 1803, Georgia Senator James Jackson hired Dennis Driscol of Baltimore's *American Patriot* to edit it. Jackson then wrote Gov. John Milledge, "I hope he will be properly supported. I have taken the liberty to promise him yours — as well as much of the public [printing] work, as is consistent with your duty. I shall procure him all the subscribers I can."[24] In Buckstown, Maine, William W. Clapp started the Federalist *Gazette of Maine* in 1805 at the encouragement "of a number of respectable men" in the area. When Anthony H. Holland bought the *Gazette* in 1811, he promised that it would continue to "undeviatingly support the politics of Washington."[25] The Newport Republican Association was organized in 1808 to found the *Rhode Island Republican*. It sold shares for $5 each, with the income administered by a board of directors, which oversaw the operation of the newspaper. In Plattsburgh, New York — after the editor of the existing *American Monitor* married and changed the paper's sentiments from Republican to Federalist in accord with the partisan feelings of his wife — local Republican politicians in 1811 formed a joint stock enterprise to begin the *Plattsburgh Republican*. Even in the West, which was just being settled, parties and factions founded newspapers. The *Reporter* was established in Lexington, Kentucky, in 1806 as the home-state organ of Henry Clay. In Louisiana, where many editors served in the army or militia, James Wilkinson, military governor and an associate of Aaron Burr, effectively controlled the newspapers. Editors were told that "the soldier's back should smart for the printer's insolence."[26]

While parties helped establish numerous newspapers, papers entered party ranks in a number of ways. Editors whose political beliefs were in accord with those of a particular party founded most of them as partisan vehicles. Sometimes editors of a different persuasion bought papers and converted them into partisans of the opposition. William Winston Seaton, as one instance, converted the *North Carolina Journal* from Federalist to Republican when he bought it from William Boylan, who had inherited it from his father. On rare occasions, a new editor would be hired who would bring about a conversion.

Even more infrequently, a party might gain a new paper through its editor's changing his ideology and transferring his paper's allegiance from one party to the other. For an editor to change faith, however, was looked on as political treason, and the party faithful usually attributed unclean motives to journalistic Judases. Besides losing respect, wayward papers usually lost financial support and contributing writers. The effect on the *Castine* (Me.) *Journal and Eastern Advertiser* was typical. When it made a gradual swing to the Republican side in 1801, a policy change contrary to prevailing opinion in the area, it suffered a sizable loss of advertising and subscriptions, and the editor decided to remove the *Journal* to Hampden.

The most notorious of the turncoats was James Callender, a former Republican editor who printed a mass of scandalous material about Jefferson, including the story that he had fathered children by one of his slaves. While Callender's biography is infamous, however, it did not exemplify political editors. His desertion of Jefferson in 1801 and subsequent attacks were an anomaly and re-

[24]16 March 1803, quoted in Cunningham, *The Jeffersonian Republicans in Power*, 240.

[25]Quoted in Frederick Fassett Jr., *A History of Newspapers in the District of Maine 1785-1820* (Orono, Me., 1932), 168-9.

[26]In William Bass Hatcher, *Edward Livingston: Jeffersonian Republican and Jacksonian Democrat* (University, La., 1940), 132.

vealed more about Callender's personality than about journalism of the period. A desire for money, for large sales of his works, rather than any desire to aid his party, often motivated his action. He revealed his attitude in a letter to Jefferson in 1799. If only he could sell 1,500 copies of his pamphlets, he wrote, he then would "have some money ... and try to find 50 acres of clear land, and a hearty Virginia female, that knew how to fatten pigs and boil hominy, and hold her tongue; and then adieu to the Rascally society of mankind for whom I feel an indifference which increases per diem."[27] Callender also believed that he had suffered great hardship in his fight for Jefferson's election to the presidency and that Jefferson afterwards had neglected him. He professed his anger at "the ingratitude of the Republicans who after getting into power had left him in the ditch."[28]

THE PRESS AND THE WAR OF 1812

The War of 1812 soundly tested whether the United States would remain a united nation. The war, in which the young nation fought against Great Britain, its former master, resulted from several causes. To Americans, the most important were Britain's support of Indian hostilities along the frontier, interference with American trade, and impressment of American sailors into the British navy.

Republicans and Federalists disagreed, however, over whether those were causes strong enough to require war.[29] With the Republican James Madison serving as the nation's president, Republican editors generally favored the war. They urged unity in support of the war effort. "This is not the time for debating the propriety of war," the National Intelligencer argued. "WAR IS DECLARED, and every patriot must unite in its support."[30] As the war progressed, they emphasized the successes that the American military achieved and downplayed the defeats.

Federalist editors, on the other hand, believed France was America's real enemy and that war with England was not justified no matter what reason Republicans might give. After Congress declared war, however, some stopped all opposition to the war and insisted that their party, along with all other citizens, be loyal to their country. Radical Federalists, though, continued in their resistance. Typifying their fiery stance, the editor of the American Daily Advertiser argued that "THE WAR in which we are engaged is the most hopeless of any ever undertaken by any nation. — It is the fortune of our administration to involve us in a war, in which our success and our defeat would be equally ruinous. If we are defeated, we are overwhelmed with disgrace; if we are victorious, we are victorious over the power which stands between us and the despotism of imperial France."[31]

Maintaining such strident opposition to America's war effort, several of the radical Federalist newspapers became the victims of Republican mobs. The most violent attacks targeted the Federal Republican in Baltimore. On June 22, 1812, four days after Congress declared war and following an editorial in the newspaper that lambasted Republican leaders, a mob destroyed the paper's presses and supplies and burned its building. A month later, the paper resumed publication out of a house stocked with ammunition and defended by supporters, including "Light Horse Harry" Lee, the Revolutionary War general. The July 27 issue carried an inflammatory editorial, written by one of its editors, 27-year-old Alexander Hanson, claiming that high-ranking Republicans had instigated the earlier mob attack. That evening, a mob gathered and began its assault by shattering all the windows in the house. The defenders fired warning shots to get the mob to disperse, but the noise attracted an even larger number of irate people. The mob then forced its way into the house. The defenders killed one member of the mob and wounded several others. Word spread throughout the city, and the size of the mob continued to increase, swelling to more than 1,500. Finally, law and military officials intervened, just as the mob prepared to fire on the house with a cannon. The officials convinced the newspaper's defenders to surrender and to be jailed until an investigation could be made.

The next night, a mob attacked the jail, killing one of the Federalists and inflicting injuries so severe that several others, including Hanson, were maimed for life or had their lives shortened. The only way they escaped death was by feigning to be dead, but the attackers even then stuck them with penknives and dropped hot wax into their eyes to determine if they were faking. Doctors arrived and convinced the rioters that medical science needed the bodies. They tended to the injured and then secretly removed them out of town to safety.

In covering the war itself, newspapers continued to rely on the techniques of newsgathering that they had used since colonial times. They had no reporters and got their news, instead, from official and private letters. Sometimes written by army generals and eyewitnesses to battles, the letters contained many vivid, objective, and accurate accounts. The major newspapers near the scenes of battles, such as the National Intelligencer in Washington and the New York Evening Post, also carried first-hand reports. Other papers reprinted the news items for their local readers. Particularly helpful in providing a chronicle of war action were Hezekiah Niles' thorough though Anglophobic Niles' Weekly Register and a few war journals started specifically for coverage of the conflict.

Despite the differences among newspapers in their attitudes toward the war, virtually all of them, both Federalists as well as Republicans, celebrated when news arrived in February 1815 that the war had ended. "No intelligence," the Federal Republican editorialized, "has occasioned half so much joy."[32] Likewise, all rejoiced at the news of Andrew Jackson's victory at the Battle of

[27]Callender to Jefferson, September 1799, quoted in Noble Cunningham, The Jeffersonian Republicans: The Formation of Party Organization, 1789-1801 (Chapel Hill, N.C., 1957), 171.

[28]James Monroe to James Madison, 23 May 1801, James Monroe Papers, New York Public Library, New York, N.Y.

[29]The best treatment of the general subject of the press and the war can be found in Susan Thompson, "The Press and the War of 1812," unpublished paper presented to the annual convention of the American Journalism Historians Association, 27-30 September 1995, Tulsa, Okla.; and Carol Sue Humphrey, "The War of 1812, 1809-1815," chapter 6 in The Press of the Young Republic, 1783-1833 (Westport, Conn., 1996).

[30]National Intelligencer, 7 June 1812.

[31]American Daily Advertiser, 10 February 1813.

[32]Federal Republican, 14 February 1815.

Major Newspapers and Editors of the Jacksonian Era

Party	National Newspapers	Regional / State Newspapers
National Republican		
Official organs	*National Intelligencer* (Washington) Joseph Gales, 1810-1864 William Winston Seaton, 1812-1864 *National Journal* (Washington) Peter Force, 1823-1841	
Whig		
Official organ		*Evening Journal* (Albany, N.Y.) Thurlow Weed, 1830-1863
Independent		*Republican* (Springfield, Mass.) Samuel Bowles II, 1824-1844 *Courier and Enquirer* (New York City) James Watson Webb, 1826-1861
Jacksonian Democrat		
Official organs	*United States Telegraph* (Washington) Duff Green, 1826-1836 *Globe* (Washington) Francis Blair, 1830-1845	*Enquirer* (Richmond, Va.) Thomas Ritchie, 1804-1845 *New Hampshire Patriot* (Concord) Isaac Hill, 1809-1819 *Argus* (Albany, N.Y.) Edwin Croswell, 1823-1854 *Argus of W. America* (Frankfurt, Ky.) Amos Kendall, 1824-1829

New Orleans a few days after the war had officially ended. "ALMOST INCREDIBLE VICTORY!" the *National Intelligencer* headlined its story.[33]

Victory, however, came at just the wrong time for the Federalist party. Near the end of 1814, a group of New England leaders met at Hartford, Connecticut, to discuss, among other topics, secession from the Union. The Hartford Convention concluded by producing only a list of grievances, but the meeting provoked the intense anger of war supporters. Then, just as the conventioneers were returning to their homes, the news of the end of the war arrived. Republican editorials made fun of Hartford delegates, while labeling all their Federalist supporters traitors to their country, an accusation with which most Americans apparently agreed. The *American Watchman and Delaware Republican* exulted that "the enemies of the country [have] shrunk into their native insignificance before the appalling ranks of republican freemen. They have sunk, never more to rise."[34]

NEWSPAPERS IN THE SECOND PARTY SYSTEM

With the demise of the Federalist party, Republicans were left as America's only party. The one-party system was, however, short-lived. Political turmoil marked the "Era of Good Feeling" of 1816-

1824 as the membership of the Republican party began splitting into factions. By 1824 party unity and discipline had vanished. By the time of the election that year, the split had grown bitter. During the election, John Quincy Adams and William Crawford (Republicans), Henry Clay (Whig), and Andrew Jackson (Democrat) all attracted factional newspapers. No candidate gained a majority of votes in the electoral college. Despite the fact, however, that Jackson had received more votes than any of his opponents, Clay threw his support to Adams. After winning election by the disputed vote, Adams appointed Clay Secretary of State.

By the 1828 election, the factions had divided into two parties, the Whigs (made up of conservative Republicans and old-line Federalists) and Jacksonian Democrats (often associated with the "rise of the common man" in American history). As the Republicans had done earlier, Whigs appealed to the middle classes; but Jacksonian Democrats aimed their appeals more at the masses of Americans as changing state laws enlarged the number of voters eligible to participate in elections. Although this second party system was more sophisticated than the first, its party machinery still was not elaborate in modern terms. Jackson operated through correspondence committees in the states, congressional leaders, a central committee, and newspaper editors. National organization was not extensive, and people still frowned on candidates who campaigned personally.

The parties, however, strengthened and refined their tech-

[33]*National Intelligencer*, 7 February 1815.
[34]*American Watchman and Delaware Republican*, 21 October 1815.

niques and structure. On the national level, factions in Congress realigned. They established and patronized numerous newspapers, began campaign funds, attempted national conventions, and constructed party platforms. On the state and local levels, newspapers sprang up, and factions organized committees to coordinate party operations and held conventions to nominate candidates. All parties and factions were aiming at expanding their popular support and tying the electorate more closely to the party. The parties later became electoral machines, nominating candidates for office and organizing efforts to elect them. Active participation increased among the public. One of the key agents in the new system was the newspaper editor, who helped organize and run party operations, mobilize voters, campaign for candidates during a time when personal campaigning was considered improper, and advocate party views.

JACKSON'S BIG THREE

Like party spirit, newspaper partisanship also intensified during the second party system. When political dealing took the 1824 election from Jackson, he turned to newspapers as one of the primary components of his political organization. Using them more effectively during the 1828 campaign than had any candidate up to that time, he gained widespread popular support. After a campaign surpassing even the one of 1800 in abusiveness, he got the electoral votes of all states except those of the Northeast.

Most important of the Democratic papers were those personally associated with Jackson, first Amos Kendall's *Argus of Western America* in Frankfort, Kentucky, then Duff Green's *United States Telegraph* in Washington, and finally Francis P. Blair's *Washington Globe*. These newspapers promoted Jackson's presidential candidacy and helped him carry out his programs once he gained office.

Kendall was the most important political force to come out of Kentucky since Henry Clay, the Speaker of the U.S. House of Representatives and one of the towering political figures of the era. An early supporter of Jackson and a fellow Westerner, Kendall was instrumental in organizing Jackson's supporters and his 1828 presidential campaign, tasks at which he worked effectively through personal contacts and editorship of the *Argus*, the spokesman of Kentucky Democrats. It was in the *Argus* that Jackson in 1825 first outlined his views on government and his platform for the 1828 presidential campaign. Kendall originated the slogan "The world is governed too much," which was a guiding torch of Jacksonian Democracy, and artfully promoted the image of Jackson as the "farmer soldier" and as a thinker with a "lightning mind" in both military and governmental affairs.

Even more integral to Jackson's success was the *United States Telegraph*, established in 1826 in the aftermath of Jackson's 1824 defeat. Vowing they would not allow the presidency to be stolen from Jackson again in 1828, supporters named as its editor Duff Green, an aggressive and energetic politician-editor who savored political fights. Opponents nicknamed him "Rough" Green for his vigorous and hard-hitting writing. He conceived his role as that of

developing and promoting party organization. Hard-working and imaginative in his political thinking, he relied on correspondence, travel, individual contacts, and his newspaper to play a central role in building the Democratic party machinery. Directing the Washington Central Committee of twenty-four top Democratic politicians from across the nation, he served as national coordinator of efforts to elect Jackson in 1828 and supervised much of the Democrats' national strategy. Despite the service he gave Jackson, however, Green was more devoted to Vice President John Calhoun. Soon after Jackson's election, when it became evident Green was defecting to Calhoun in preparation for the 1832 election, Jackson and his advisers decided they needed to establish another paper as the presidential organ.

The new paper, founded in 1830, was the *Washington Globe*. Its editor, Francis Blair, had followed Amos Kendall as editor of the *Argus of Western America*. He had served as chairman of the Democratic Central Committee in Kentucky during the 1828 campaign and was an ardent Jackson supporter. Perhaps no editor ever was closer to a president than Blair was to Jackson. He, Kendall (who had gone to Washington with Jackson as a personal adviser), and John C. Rives, the *Globe*'s business manager, were among the most important members of President Jackson's "Kitchen Cabinet," which, though informal, exerted greater influence on executive policy than did the official Cabinet of department secretaries. It was Kendall and Blair who took Jackson's ideas of government, often expressed in rambling fashion, and gave them cogent written form. Blair assumed the national role that Green had brought to the position of editor but increased its importance through his close association with Jackson. Not only did he serve as spokesman for the president's views; he also played a hand in shaping executive policy.

THE JACKSONIAN PRESS NETWORK

While the Democrats could not match the Whigs in numbers of papers, their newspapers increased considerably in the late 1820s and were better organized as part of the party's operation. The initiative for establishing Jacksonian papers came from congressmen; but governors, state legislators, county officials, and local politicians aided the efforts. In most states, the Jacksonians succeeded where the Whigs had failed: they were able to tie their leading newspapers closely to the state party organizations. Whig newspapers to a large extent remained independent, whereas the Democrats integrated their leading papers into the party structure and used them as mouthpieces of state parties.

A network of cooperating newspapers stretching across the nation aided party consensus. The *Albany* (N.Y.) *Argus*, edited by Edwin Croswell, played a central role in the power the Albany Regency exerted in New York politics. The Regency, headed by Martin Van Buren, later United States President, probably was the best organized machine in American politics of its day and provided direction for Democrats in several states. When the Regency threw its support to Jackson in 1828, other state party organizations fol-

Leaders of a New Party

Among Jacksonian editors, several had a national influence. Three of the most important were (from left to right), Amos Kendall, Duff Green, and Thomas Ritchie. The first two were Andrew Jackson's national spokesmen, while Ritchie was the leading power in the South. Graduating with honors from Dartmouth College in 1811, Kendall quickly climbed the political ladder. In 1814 he moved to Kentucky to serve as tutor to the children of Sen. Henry Clay. In 1815 he was appointed postmaster at Germantown. The following year he became manager of the *Argus of Western America.* After breaking with Clay, he used the paper to support Andrew Jackson. When Jackson won the presidency, Kendall joined his "Kitchen Cabinet," and Jackson appointed him auditor of the U.S. Treasury. An aggressive politician, Green (nicknamed "Rough" by his opponents) served as editor of the *United States Telegraph.* He was instrumental in building the national Democratic party machinery and in getting Andrew Jackson elected U.S. president in 1828. This photograph of Green was made in his later years, but even then his tough personality was evident. For half a century, Ritchie was one of Virginia's leading political figures and a force on the national scene. Having founded the *Richmond Enquirer* in 1804, he made it the voice of Republicanism in Thomas Jefferson's home state. Through the Richmond Junto, the Virginia political machine, he helped forge Andrew Jackson's followers into the national Democratic Party.

lowed its lead, and it played a critical role in Jackson's election. Croswell, an experienced journalist, was appointed to the post of editor of the *Argus* in 1823 and thereafter rose quickly in the Regency heirarchy, becoming one of the handful of men who directed the organization. Well-educated and tactful, but firmly believing in party politics, he became a leading exponent of Democratic views; and the *Argus* generally was regarded as the most important newspaper in the North.

The Regency's association with Democratic machines in other states increased its influence. The most prominent of the state organizations was the Richmond Junto in Virginia. Thomas Ritchie of the *Richmond Enquirer* headed it. In cooperation with Van Buren and John Calhoun, he shared the credit for structuring Jackson's supporters into the national Democratic party. Through his writings in the *Enquirer*, his leadership in Virginia politics, his ties with leading Democratic politicians in other states, and his politically inspired tours around the country, he helped fashion a tight, nationwide party organization. His national influence in party affairs was demonstrated in 1827 when he effectively chose the individual to be named Speaker of the U.S. House of Representatives. The caucus of Democratic congressmen split between Philip Barbour and Andrew Stevenson, both of Virginia. Someone then suggested that the deadlock be broken by asking the head of the Richmond Junto whom he preferred. Ritchie sent word back that he liked

Stevenson, who then was selected on the first caucus ballot.

Of major importance as other state organs were such papers as the *Charleston Mercury, Nashville Republican, Baltimore Republican,* and *Philadelphia Palladium.* In New Hampshire, Isaac Hill ran the well-oiled state machine; and the paper he edited, the *New Hampshire Patriot,* served as the state's Democratic spokesman. It was generally acknowledged as New England's leading Democratic paper, and Hill later served as New Hampshire governor and United States senator. In Massachusetts in the late 1820s the *Boston Statesman,* edited by the scholarly Nathaniel Greene, played a leading role in the Democratic party. It was succeeded by the *Boston Morning Post,* founded and edited by Charles Greene, brother of Nathaniel. Like the *Statesman,* it served as a mouthpiece of the state party and gained prominence throughout New England.

THE WHIG PRESS

Although Jacksonian Democrats used the press more vigorously, Whigs maintained a majority in newspaper numbers. Sensing a critical need for newspaper support, they spent large amounts of money and devoted tireless effort on the establishment and continuation of papers. Aroused by a surge in the number of new Jacksonian newspapers during John Quincy Adams' presidency (1825-1829), Henry Clay declared, "The course adopted by the Op-

James Watson Webb

The *New York Courier and Enquirer*, Webb's newspaper, had the largest circulation of any newspaper in America in 1830. As a result, Webb and the Albany Regency, the pro-Jackson machine in New York State, wielded wide influence. Jealous, however, that the machine made political decisions without consulting him, in 1832 he broke with the Democratic party and became a leading voice for the opposition, which, upon his advice, began calling themselves "Whigs."

position, in the dissemination of Newspapers and publications against the administration and supporting presses, leaves to its friends no other alternative than that of following their example, so far at least as to circulate information among the people."[35] Along with the eminent National Republican newspapers in Washington — Gales and Seaton's *National Intelligencer* and Peter Force's *National Journal* — a network of newspapers stretching through all the states and into virtually every town of any sizable population supported the party.

The preeminent ones were Samuel Bowles' *Springfield* (Mass.) *Republican*, James Watson Webb's *New York Courier and Enquirer*, and Thurlow Weed's *Albany* (N.Y.) *Evening Journal*. Samuel Bowles II founded the *Springfield Republican* in 1824 as an advocate of the National Republican faction in support of John Quincy Adams. It took up the Whig cause in opposition to Jackson. Known for the quality of its editorials, it was considered the best small-town paper in America for most of the nineteenth century under the editorship of Bowles, his son, and his grandson.

Thurlow Weed got his start in politics in the fervent but short-

[35] Quoted in Robert V. Remini, *The Election of Andrew Jackson* (Philadelphia, 1963), 128.

lived Anti-Mason movement in western New York in the 1820s. Strongly opposed to Jackson, he moved into Whig politics and soon became the party's leading tactical politician. With the *Evening Journal*, founded in 1830, serving as the national spokesman of Whig views, Weed joined with the politician William Seward and Horace Greeley to control New York politics for a number of years and direct national Whig strategy. Greeley would gain great journalistic fame later with the *New York Tribune*.

James Watson Webb founded the *Courier and Enquirer* in 1827 primarily as a newspaper aimed at the mercantile class in New York but also as a supporter of Jackson. By 1830 it had gained a sizeable circulation of around 4,500 and therefore was thought of as influential. The pro-Jackson machine, the Albany Regency, that controlled New York State politics, however, neglected to consult Webb on political matters. Irritated at being left out, in the early 1830s he intensified his attacks on the machine and eventually became estranged from the Jacksonian party because of differences on a number of major issues, especially the rechartering of the Second Bank of the United States. By 1832 he had become a zealous partisan of his new cause. It was Webb who first suggested that the party assume the name "Whig."

NEWSPAPER CONTENT AND STYLE

Believing the proper role of the press was to support political causes and parties, editors devoted a large amount of space to political discussions. Only a few, however, let politics fill their papers. While some newspapers were nothing other than vehicles for political argument, most editors recognized that readers also wanted news. The news they gave readers was to a large extent foreign or national rather than local. Not only did newspapers in the larger seaboard cities emphasize foreign news, but many small-town papers of the West also devoted a large amount of space to it. European news, comprising the bulk of the foreign information, varied from about one month to six months in age. News from America's political centers was fresher and a little better covered. Local papers reported events, and other major papers picked up their accounts often within a week. Outside the metropolitan areas, national news was somewhat stale. It usually was clipped from other papers or taken from letters written by acquaintances in Washington, Philadelphia, Boston, New York, Baltimore, or another eastern city.

Newspapers largely neglected local news. They subordinated even important happenings to national and foreign events. There was no tradition in journalism of emphasizing local events. Editors may have thought they should not take up space with news that local residents already knew, or they may have considered it necessary to emphasize non-local news because newspapers were the only source for such information. That did not mean, though, they ignored local political events. Most partisan papers covered local politics fully. Indeed, politics made up the bulk of local news. In the cities, unlike in small towns, papers frequently published accounts of local non-political happenings. Most were about such

Newspaper Style

Typical of newspapers of the party period, the *Journal* of Kennebec, Maine, emphasized word content rather than graphics. Most of its news was national in nature, taken from newspapers in the nation's major cities and news centers.

occurrences as deaths and marriages of prominent residents, disasters such as fires and storms, murders and suicides, and local improvements (reported with boasting and pride) such as settlement, water systems, education, and transportation facilities.

Newspapers also included such items as essays (with morality and religion being popular topics, along with social and economic ones), accounts of public lectures, advice on agricultural practices, and letters on local matters. Summaries of current affairs and mercantile or shipping information might fill the remainder of the news columns. Anecdotes and reports of oddities enlivened newspapers; and most editors apparently felt compelled to help improve the cultural appreciation of their readers through poetry, a literary section, excerpts from informative books, and book reviews.

Along with newspapers, several hundred magazines provided political, religious, and literary material. Prominent were the *Farmer's Weekly Museum*, founded by Isaiah Thomas and continued under Joseph Dennie, who also was noted for his political

magazine *Port Folio*; the literary and polemical quarterlies *North American Review* and *American Quarterly*; and Hezekiah Niles' news magazine, *Niles' Weekly Register*.

While the writing in some magazines showed real literary style, much in both magazines and newspapers was dry according to later tastes. It was often formal, wordy, flowery, and tedious. At the same time, many editors had broad general educations in the humanities and classics and possessed first-hand knowledge of politics. Thus, such devices as literary allusions dotted their writing, and their political pieces displayed a thorough understanding of issues and arguments.

The most striking characteristics of newspaper writing, however, were personal invective and abusive political attacks. Editors rarely hesitated to call opponents names or accuse them unjustifiably of some evil. Name-calling sometimes approached art, but it often exhibited no quality better than crudeness. Editors referred to opponents as "insane," "incompetent," "cowardly," "worthless," and other epithets. Sometimes, they tried to be a little more imaginative and came up with names such as "prating poppinjay" and "addled cat's paw" and "double-faced weather-cock."

As absurd as some of the name-calling was, accusations were just as bad. Republicans accused George Washington of, among other things, being a blasphemer and John Adams of being subservient to the British. The most repeated and telling charges against Jefferson were that he was an atheist and that he had fathered children by one of his slaves. Although press abusiveness died down somewhat during the presidency of James Monroe (the "Era of Good Feeling"), conditions changed drastically when Andrew Jackson came onto the national scene. Personal deprecation rose again, surpassing even that of the Jeffersonian presidency. Newspapers published such abusive charges during the 1828 election campaign that Jackson and John Quincy Adams refused to speak to one another when Jackson arrived in Washington for his inauguration. Those charges included speculations that Jackson had lived in adultery with his wife before she had received a divorce from her first husband and that Adams had had pre-marital relations with his wife.

THE RELIGIOUS PRESS

A substantial number of papers, approximately 100 in 1830, were purely religious ones. Even though their editors considered a religious press necessary for the support of Christianity, most secular newspapers mirrored the Protestant beliefs and morés of the large majority of Americans and published large amounts of material with an obvious religious tone. Many Christian journalists, however, were concerned about how the press had taken on the extreme partisanship of the times. They believed that American journals needed to be lifted to a higher plane.

The experience of Nathaniel Willis, who started the Christian *Recorder* in Boston in 1816, provided one example. While editing the *Eastern Argus*, a Republican organ in Portland, Maine, he found he could not depend on the party's politicians. First, he re-

Nathaniel Willis
The founder of America's first religious newspaper, the *Boston Recorder* in 1816, Willis also became an important editor in the field of juvenile magazines. In 1827, he founded the *Youth's Companion* in Boston. It had begun as a department of the *Recorder*, and it remained in publication for more than a century, until 1929. In the original proposal for the magazine, Willis wrote, "This is a day of peculiar care for Youth.... Our children are born to higher destinies than their fathers; they will be actors in a far advanced period of the church and the world...." The *Youth's Companion* became one of the most important in the history of juvenile magazines. Willis died in 1870 at the age of ninety.

luctantly published a libelous article one of his backers contributed upon the assurance that the writer would bear all responsibility. Then the writer and party members refused to assist Willis in paying the damages a jury assessed. While helping the Republicans turn the Federalists out of office, "I learned," Willis declared, "that politicians are not only ungrateful, but supremely selfish. They used me as the cat's-paw, but took good care to keep all the chestnuts for their own eating."[36]

After experiencing a religious conversion, Willis began to try to tone down the vitriolic writing in the *Argus*. "I am willing to support the Republican cause," he told his backers, "so long as I can with truth and fairness, but I had done with personalities and misrepresentations." His backers criticized the moderation and threatened to start another party organ. So in 1808 Willis sold the *Argus* to an editor more committed to Republican partisanship. After moving to Boston and opening a print shop, he produced a

variety of religious material and then started the *Recorder* as a means of keeping the public informed of current events and controversies involving religion.

Depending on definitions, the first religious newspaper in the United States may have been the *Herald of Gospel Liberty*, founded by a Baptist minister, Elias Smith, in 1808 in Portsmouth, New Hampshire. Containing mainly the texts of sermons that Smith delivered, however, it resembled a circular more than a newspaper. The first religious publication exhibiting the true characteristics of a newspaper probably was Willis' *Recorder*.

By the 1830s, numerous religious newspapers, almost exclusively Christian, were publishing throughout the country. Most of their editors had been trained for the ministry rather than for printing or the newspaper business. As a general rule, therefore, they served their editorial functions well, but their lack of an intense profit-motive frequently left them in financial straits. When they did make a profit, most used the money to support other Christian work such as missionary activities or training of young men for the ministry.

The impetus for religious periodicals came from a variety of sources. Many publications were polemical and waged elaborate doctrinal battles with other papers both of the same denomination and of different faiths. The main concern, however, was moral and social issues. The Second Great Awakening in the 1820s sparked a spiritual revival nationwide, and numerous individuals established newspapers to encourage greater efforts. They spent much of their energy promoting the spread of the Gospel, but they also labored at the forefront of such efforts as helping orphans, promoting world peace, eliminating alcoholism, and abolishing slavery. Christians, one newspaper editorialized, should "aim at nothing more or less than the greatest good of our country" by "diffusing the light of the gospel" and engaging in benevolent works.[37]

DEVELOPMENTS IN JOURNALISTIC PRACTICES

Although the purpose and practices of the party press were definitely partisan, today's historian searching for the genesis of purely "journalistic" devices can find a number of them in the party period. One was the daily newspaper. The first was Benjamin Towne's *Pennsylvania Evening Post and Daily Advertiser* in Philadelphia. When Towne converted from weekly to daily publication in 1783, he hoped to provide the mercantile class with up-to-date shipping news. The following year, John Dunlap began a second daily, the *Pennsylvania Packet and Daily Advertiser*, by increasing the publication frequency of his weekly. It aimed at the same audience and soon forced Towne to suspend publication.

As interest shifted to political affairs, another innovation occurred: coverage of sessions of Congress. The House of Representatives had opened its doors to the public in 1789, two days after its first session began. Federalists, however, controlled the Senate. They believed they could best conduct the nation's business out of sight of the prying eyes of the public. They barred not only mem-

[36]Nathaniel Willis, *Autobiography of a Journalist* (Boston, 1858).

[37]*New York Religious Chronicle*, 13 May 1826.

The Origins of Daily Newspapers

In 1783, Benjamin Towne started America's first daily newspaper by increasing the publication frequency of his weekly *Pennsylvania Evening Post and Daily Advertiser*. In September of the following year, John Dunlap also converted his competing paper, the *Pennsylvania Packet and Daily Advertiser* (left), into a daily. The purpose of both was to serve the commercial needs of the city. The competition lasted only briefly, for Towne was forced to suspend about a month after Dunlap had moved to daily publication. His paper was crammed with ads, as illustrated by the front page shown here. The first dailies were begun for financial reasons. Rather than trying to provide the most recent news, publishers started the papers because their weekly editions could not accommodate the abundance of advertising they were receiving. That purpose was reflected in the names of many of the papers, including New York City's first daily, the *Advertiser* (right).

bers of the public but even members of the House. Into this situation in 1791 stepped the ardent anti-Federalist Philip Freneau. From the first issue of the *National Gazette* he printed proceedings of the House, and in February 1792 he began an editorial crusade for opening the Senate's doors. Finally, responding to public demand, the Senate approved a measure in February 1794 to open its sessions. The leader in coverage of Congress throughout the period was the *National Intelligencer*. From 1800 until the Civil War, it served as the authoritative source of information about the national government.

One of the major developments that affected newsgathering was the Post Office Act of 1792. Urged on Congress by James Madison, who believed that government should encourage the extension of knowledge and the exchange of ideas, the act provided that newspapers could send exchange issues to other papers free of charge. Editors used exchange papers as a chief newsgathering tool. Newspapers were expected to cover important local events and thus furnish other papers with information about those events. The process worked as an informal news service system. The Post Office Act provided a lifeline to many western papers and enhanced the coverage of news by papers all over the country.

Changes occurred also in the printing of editorial opinion. Previously, newspapers usually had presented opinions in long essays or even as series of essays, as a long pamphlet would be if divided into sections. Contributors wrote most of them. During the party press period, what is considered the true editorial emerged. Conductors of papers became "editors" and not just printers, and the writing talent of America's newspaper operators improved. In the 1790s these editors began to show a preference for brief comments over long essays. Following the lead of Barzillai Hudson and George Goodwin of the *Hartford* (Conn.) *Courant*, Noah Webster of New York's *American Minerva*, James Cheet-

ham of New York's *American Citizen*, and John Fenno, they began printing opinions in articles separate from the news. Some editors reserved a specific column for their editorials. The column often carried a standing title or signed editorials to signify that the opinion was the editor's. By 1810 the editorial form was widespread; and by the end of the period, pamphlet-style opinion virtually had disappeared.

The editorials revealed a variety of qualities that have become commonplace in American journalism. Many were dull and poorly reasoned. Party newspapers, like those of today, sometimes were filled with columns of tedious reading. Little better could be expected when individuals trained as printers rather than writers ran so many papers.

On the other hand, occasional pieces gleamed. Editors of state and national stature were so closely involved with politics that they could comment with knowledge and authority. They were aware of the subtleties of the questions related to the political system, and the editorials of the opposing sides presented thorough and sound debate on the nature of the system. Name-calling and false charges unfortunately stuck out like festering sores, but intermingled with them were many soundly reasoned and well written editorials that both argued the practical political points of immediate importance and provided discussions of essential questions about the American political system.[38]

Partisanship motivated another innovation: the first correspondents assigned to cover the national capital. Until newspapers began using correspondents, they got most of their news from Washington through private letters from acquaintances in

[38]The range and quality of editorial writing are documented in Jerry Knudson, "The Jefferson Years: Response by the Press, 1801-1809" (Ph.D. diss., University of Virginia, 1962); and Wm. David Sloan, "The Party Press: The Newspaper Role in National Politics, 1789-1816" (Ph.D. diss., University of Texas, 1981).

Hoe Cylinder Press

In the 1820s R. Hoe & Co. of New York introduced the first cylinder press ever used in the United States. It was based on a design by Frederick Koenig of Saxony. He had constructed a press that looked much like the handpresses of the day, only including a pulley to move the typeform and a self-inking system. He then modified the machine to include a cylinder to replace the platen; and the first practical, flatbed cylinder press emerged. Paper wrapped around the cylinder and pressed against the inked bed of type, which moved back and forth. Iron frames attached to the cylinder held the sheets of paper in place. Steam was used to power the press, and more than 800 sheets per hour could be printed, with one press man placing the paper and another removing it after it had been printed. The Hoe press refined Koenig's design and speeded up printing capabilities to 2,000 four-page papers per hour.

the city and from stories in the *National Intelligencer* or other papers such as the *Federalist* located in the capital. The *Federalist*'s accounts, though, were inferior to those of the *National Intelligencer*, and Federalist editors did not like having to rely on the Republican *Intelligencer* for explanations of government proceedings. In 1808, therefore, the *United States Gazette* in New York and then the *Freeman's Journal* in Philadelphia employed individuals of Federalist views to write reports from Washington. Their arrangements ceased prior to the War of 1812, but in the 1820s a number of papers took up the practice of hiring Washington correspondents.[39]

Emphasis also changed from foreign to domestic news. Until around 1800 a majority of news content originated in Europe. Americans still considered themselves the offspring of England even after the American Revolution and thought of Europe as the center of important affairs. Furthermore, until the development of a satisfactory system of roads and an efficient postal system in the United States, transportation to and communication with England often were more convenient than among states. With internal improvements, however, communication became easier; and as Americans faced more and more serious domestic issues, newspapers' attention naturally turned inward. Even in the late 1700s, when European news still provided most newspaper content, domestic events such as the 1796 and 1800 presidential elections and the furor over the Alien and Sedition Acts of 1798 created periods of intense interest during which domestic news superseded foreign news.

Throughout the period, the major newspapers devoted their attention primarily to national affairs. Papers of regional stature, such as the *Independent Chronicle* and the *Columbian Centinel* in Boston, divided their attention about equally between national and state or local political questions. However, the papers of national scope, such as the *New York Evening Post* and the *National Intelligencer*, from the beginning devoted most of their space to national politics. In the smaller, local papers, there was a slight

trend as the period progressed of expanding interest from local and state affairs to national ones. This change may have been a result of factors such as the development of national party organization or the increasing direct participation readers had in national elections. By 1810 American newspapers' interest had turned irrevocably to domestic rather than foreign news. The War of 1812, with its military encounters within the boundaries of the American nation, encouraged this trend even more.[40]

Despite improvements in roads and the postal system, the slowness of news plagued editors. Newspapers reported important events in other parts of the country many days and often weeks after they occurred. They got their foreign news, one of the staples of American journalism, from foreign papers brought by ships. Often these ships did not arrive, were late, or did not have the papers expected. When the news did arrive, it was weeks behind the event. The War of 1812 awakened Americans to the inconvenience of tardiness of news. Slowness made the public impatient, especially when some impending word of a battle was expected, and newspapers experimented with methods to increase the speed of news transmission. Some eastern papers hired private pony express riders to carry reports more quickly than the mails could. At first, the express was used only for special events such as James Monroe's inaugural address to Congress in 1816, but by the 1830s the practice had become common. In the meantime, the national government in 1825 instituted a special "express post" between major cities, tripling postage rates for the service but cutting delivery time in half.

The period also witnessed one development that revolutionized printing: the cylinder press. The previously used flatbed press required that individual sheets of printing paper be pressed against a flat page of metal type by means of a screw mechanism above the bed. The new press replaced the screw mechanism with

---

[39]Frederick Marbut, "Early Washington Correspondents: Some Neglected Pioneers," *Journalism Quarterly* 25 (1948): 370-5.

[40]The traditional historical assumption has been that domestic news did not predominate until the War of 1812. Recent scholarship, however, has given evidence that the shift to domestic news occurred earlier. See Donald Avery, "The American Newspaper: Discovering the Home Front," *American Journalism* 1: 2 (1984): 51-66; Sloan, "The Party Press"; and Knudson, "The Jefferson Years."

a rotating cylinder. The bed of type moved under the cylinder, which pressed a sheet of paper against it. In 1825 the first newspaper to install the press was the *New York Daily Advertiser*, giving it the capacity to deliver 2,000 four-page papers per hour. In 1832 Richard Hoe invented the double-cylinder press and doubled the capacity to 4,000 copies per hour.

DECLINE OF THE PARTY PRESS

During Jackson's presidency, the press reached its zenith as a partisan voice, and it remained primarily political for years to come. Even with the advent of the popular penny press in the 1830s, most papers continued to operate as partisan organs. The Missouri Compromise of 1820 over the issue of slavery initiated a gradual shift in newspaper loyalties from parties to sections. Then the partisan system was dealt a blow in 1846 when Congress passed legislation requiring the federal government to let bids on printing contracts. That requirement took away the most effective tool parties and politicians had for financing newspaper supporters. In 1860, the Government Printing Office was established, removing much of public printing from private newspapers and further separating the operations of parties from the press. Still, the ideological relationship between parties and papers remained strong, and perhaps as many as 80% of newspapers continued to identify with and work for partisan political goals. It was not until 1884, many journalists and observers believed, when leading Republican papers bolted James G. Blaine in his campaign for the presidency, that newspapers took on a full degree of partisan independence. Still, newspaper editorial allegiance to parties was vigorous as late as World War II.

Even today, some observers note that the news media seem to be becoming more partisan. For many years, some of the prominent outlets — such as the *New York Times* and CBS — have been accused of favoring Democrats, while the appearance of cable television and radio with 24-hour-news and talk shows — such as those on Fox and MSNBC — has led to a proliferation of programming favoring each party.

Despite the growing autonomy of newspapers from political parties in the late 1800s, the period of the party press had witnessed great vigor, and newspapers had played an important role during some of the most critical years of the American political system. Although the nature of American newspapers would change later, the press perhaps never would be any more vital to the political life of the nation than it had been during the age of the party press.

RECOMMENDED READINGS

BOOKS

Ambler, Charles Henry. *Thomas Ritchie, A Study in Virginia Politics*. Richmond, 1913. Ritchie attempted to run the *Richmond Enquirer* on a high moral plane.

Ames, William E. *A History of the National Intelligencer*. Chapel Hill, N.C., 1972. The *National Intelligencer* was more interested in news reporting than vituperative political opinion. The party press played a valuable role in American politics.

Austin, Aleine. *Mathew Lyon: "New Man" of the Democratic Revolution, 1749-1822*. University Park, Pa., 1981. This Progressive, sympathetic biography places Lyon in the context of the Enlightenment, viewing him as one of the Americans who embraced both the right of property and the right to the pursuit of happiness.

Barker, Hannah, and David Vincent, eds. *Language, Print, and Electoral Politics, 1790-1832: Newcastle-under-Lyme Broadsides*. Rochester, N.Y.: Boydell & Brewer, 2001. This collection reproduces more than 300 broadsides from the period.

Brown, Charles H. *William Cullen Bryant*. New York, 1971. This definitive general biography of Bryant focuses on his journalism and literary work. The *Evening Post* was a responsible, respected newspaper, and Bryant was a champion of liberty.

Brown, Walt. *John Adams and the American Press: Politics and Journalism at the Birth of the Republic*. Jefferson, N.C., 1995. Adams had a confrontational relationship with editors.

Clark, Mary Elizabeth. *Peter Porcupine in America: The Career of William Cobbett, 1792-1800*. Philadelphia, 1939. Although Cobbett attempted to help the Federalist cause, his vituperation actually swayed the nation toward Republicanism.

Crouthamel, James L. *James Watson Webb, A Biography*. Middletown, Conn., 1969. Webb was involved in New York and national politics, as he worked for political reform.

Elliot, Robert Neal, Jr. *The Raleigh Register, 1799-1863*. Chapel Hill, N.C., 1955. Joseph Gales was a progressive leader of southern journalism who played an important role in both Jeffersonian and Whig politics.

Humphrey, Carol Sue. *The Press of the Young Republic, 1783-1833*. Westport, Conn., 1996. The best study of the party press, this book provides an excellent overview of the entire period.

Jackson, George. *Uncommon Scold: The Story of Anne Royall*. Boston, 1937. Royall was the "first woman journalist." This account, with special emphasis on the early portions of her life, deals to a large extent with her personality and character, as well as her writing — comparing her to various landmark individuals.

Kielbowicz, Richard B. *News in the Mail: The Press, Post Office, and Public Information, 1700-1860s*. Westport, Conn., 1989. The postal system played a key role in the distribution of newspapers and the resultant democratization of America.

Knudson, Jerry W. *Jefferson and the Press: Crucible of Liberty*. Columbia, S.C., 2006. Newspapers played a key role in the development of American democracy by printing debates and arguments about political issues, through which citizens learned how democracy worked.

Leary, Lewis. *That Rascal Freneau*. New Brunswick, N.J., 1941. Freneau "tried to adapt himself to an essentially uninterested public, and ... he failed."

Nerone, John. *The Culture of the Press in the Early Republic: Cincinnati, 1793-1848*. New York, 1989. Newspaper publishers held to an ideology of impartiality for most of the early American era.

Nevins, Allan. *The Evening Post: A Century of Journalism*. New York, 1922. One of the best histories of an American newspaper, this account considers the *Evening Post* under Coleman and William Cullen Bryant as a paper that, although partisan, was interested in accurate news on many subjects and in well-reasoned opinion.

Pasley, Jeffrey L. *"The Tyranny of Printers": Newspaper Politics in the Early American Republic*. Charlottesville, Va., 2002. The influence that editors played in the first decades of the 1800s — which many politicians deprecated as the "tyranny of printers" — made them the most important figures in America's early party system.

Phillips, Kim Tousley. *William Duane, Radical Journalist in the Age of Jefferson*. New York, 1989. A vehement Jeffersonian, Duane invoked the hatred of the Federalists when he took over Bache's *Aurora*.

Rosenfeld, Richard N. *American Aurora*. New York, 1997. Bache and Duane's *Aurora* played an integral role in the turmoil of the period.

Smith, Elbert B. *Francis Preston Blair*. New York, 1980. The editor Blair was a politician. Not only did he have close relations with presidents Jackson, Van Buren, Lincoln, and Johnson, he also helped establish a political dynasty.

Smith, Jeffrey A. *Franklin and Bache: Envisioning the Enlightened Republic*. New York, 1990. Tthe ideas of Benjamin Franklin and grandson Benjamin Bache contributed to the optimistic liberal ideology of the Revolution and the new nation.

Stewart, Donald H. *The Opposition Press of the Federalist Period*. Albany, N.Y., 1969.

Stewart provides a voluminous study of the content of Federalist and Republican newspapers.

Tagg, James. *Benjamin Franklin Bache and the Philadelphia Aurora*. Philadelphia, 1991. An outspoken Anti-Federalist, Bache became well-known for his harsh criticisms of political opponents.

ARTICLES

Avery, Donald R. "The Emerging American Newspaper: Discovering the Home Front." *American Journalism* 1, 2 (1984): 51-66. Content analysis reveals that "American newspapers began giving less attention to matters foreign and more attention to domestic news in the years just prior to the War of 1812," not during the war, as historians have suggested.

Baldasty, Gerald. "The Press and Politics in the Age of Jackson." *Journalism Monographs* 89 (1984). Newspapers were central to party politics.

Beasley, Maurine. "The Curious Career of Anne Royall." *Journalism History* 3 (1976): 98-102, 136. Anne Royall, a political journalist, "left a 'profile in courage,' the picture of a woman, paranoid or not, who was willing to pursue a man's career and turn into a town freak rather than shrivel up mentally and physically just because convention called upon her to remain quiet."

Boston, Ray. "The Impact of 'Foreign Liars' on the American Press (1790-1800)." *Journalism Quarterly* 50 (1973): 722-30. The effectiveness of the Republican press depended on a group of foreign-born journalists who came to America with common radical political opinions.

Cole, Jaci, and John Maxwell Hamilton. "Another Test of the News: American Partisan Press Coverage of the French Revolution." *Journalism History* 34:1 (2008): 34-41. Republican editors supported the French Revolution, while Federalists deprecated it.

Ewing, Gretchen Garst. "Duff Green, Independent Editor of a Party Press." *Journalism Quarterly* 54 (1977): 733-9. Green was responsible for the great political success of the *United States Telegraph*.

List, Karen K. "The Role of William Cobbett in Philadelphia's Party Press, 1794-1799." *Journalism Monographs* 82 (1983). Cobbett was a nominal Federalist and was more interested in promoting his native Britain than the Federalist party.

Nord, David Paul. "The Evangelical Origins of Mass Media in America, 1815-1835." 68-93. in Wm. David Sloan, ed., *Media and Religion in American History*. Northport, Ala., 2000. Religious societies laid the foundation for mass media through mass printing and distribution of evangelical tracts.

Prince, Carl E. "The Federalist Party and the Creation of a Court Press, 1789-1801." *Journalism Quarterly* 53 (1976): 238-41. Federalist officials' appointment of editors and printers helped in the party's development of a partisan press.

Scherr, Arthur. "'Sambos' and 'Black Cut-Throats': Peter Porcupine on Slavery and Race in the 1790s." *American Periodicals* 13 (2003): 3-30. Cobbett's attacks against southern Republicans and prophesies of imminent, bloody slave revolt appealed to the silent racist majority in 1790s Philadelphia.

Sloan, Wm. David. "The Early Party Press: The Newspaper Role in American Politics, 1789-1812." *Journalism History* 9 (1982): 18-24. The party press played a central role in the American party system and performed a number of specific functions.

—. "The Media and Public Opinion: The Press and Party Politics, 1789-1816." 78-105, in James D. Startt and Wm. David Sloan, eds., *The Significance of the Media in American History*. Northport, Ala., 1994. Leaders of the Republican and Federalist parties used newspapers as the primary means of trying to influence public opinion.

—. "The Party Press, 1783-1833: Political Sycophant or Party Leader?" 58-73, in *Perspectives on Mass Communication History*. Hillsdale, N.J., 1991. This historiographical essay analyzes the approaches that historians have taken.

—. "'Purse and Pen': Party-Press Relationships, 1789-1816." *American Journalism* 6 (1989): 103-27. Editors received a variety of support from parties, but they were motivated primarily by ideology rather than financial considerations.

Snapp, Elizabeth. "Government Patronage of the Press in St. Louis, Missouri: 1829-1832." *Missouri Historical Review* 24 (1980): 190-216. The *St. Louis Beacon* received patronage from local, state, and national government and played a central role in politics. It "contributed to a more vigorous political debate and enabled a broader segment of the American people to receive a more balanced understanding of the major issues."

Stewart, Robert K. "The Exchange System and the Development of American Politics in the 1820s." *American Journalism* 4 (1987): 30-42. Through the exchange of subscriptions, Jacksonian newspapers and party leaders "nurtured a budding party apparatus that enabled the systematic waging of a war of words and ideas from the largest cities to the most remote outposts of the country."

Touba, Mariam. "Tom Paine's Plan for Revolutionizing America: Diplomacy, Politics, and the Evolution of a Newspaper Rumor." *Journalism History* 20 (1994): 116-30. Origins of a 1798 rumor that France planned to invade America reveal diplomats' use of the press.

Winfield, Betty Houchin. "The Press Response to the Corps of Discovery: The Making of Heroes in an Egalitarian Age." *Journalism & Mass Communication Quarterly* 80:4 (2003): 866-83. As exemplified by press reaction to the success of Lewis and Clark's expedition into the Louisiana Purchase, the nation's print media helped make heroes out of early American explorers.

6

Freedom of the Press

1600 - 1804

Any discussion of the development of freedom of the press in the United States begins with certain inherent difficulties. Today freedom of the press conjures up images of arguments before the United States Supreme Court by newspapers, broadcasting corporations, and other institutions for the right to report the news. The term has become a journalistic talisman invoked to provide protection for an institutional press to cover everything from libel prosecutions to contempt of court citations to invasion of privacy actions.

The term was less precisely understood in early American history. In fact, it did not even exist for many years after the invention of movable type. The development of values included in the American concept of freedom of the printing press was slow in coming. But slowly, early Americans laid the groundwork for the concept of freedom of the press as known today. Even as this foundation emerged, our ancestors discovered many of the concerns about the powers of the press that are expressed today and considered many views about the possible limitations that should be imposed on such a powerful instrument of communication.

BRITISH ROOTS OF PRESS FREEDOM

The search for meaning necessarily begins with freedom of the press in Great Britain, for the British emigrants carried their beliefs in religion, in government, and in freedom of speech with them as they established colonies. From these seeds, the ideals and the fears of the new American nation would grow.

Understanding the English heritage of freedom of the press requires abandoning modern definitions and looking instead at practices in context. For instance, when William Caxton set up his press in England in 1476, he did so as a good businessman who had discovered a new way to make money. He had no crusading notions of spreading the truth about government or religion or anything else. A cloth merchant by trade, he even sought royal patronage to increase his chances of selling the books he published. His press printed only books that would be commercially profitable; and, to ensure profitability, he often doctored manuscripts

to insert contemporary principles of chivalry and Christian morality as well as English folk heroes into the stories. Through his decision to publish under royal patronage, he gave early printing a close tie to government, a connection that was maintained for many generations. The tie grew as the government hired his printing press to make multiple copies of documents, a natural extension of the use of the press as a mechanical tool for replacing handwritten manuscripts.

This role of the printing press as a mechanical device continued as it came to serve religion, which in sixteenth and seventeenth century England was closely identified with the reigning monarch. When King Henry VIII established the Church of England in 1529, he opened the door for the Reformation that was sweeping the Continent to invade Great Britain. As the teachings of Martin Luther, John Calvin, and other reformers became popular, the printing press became more important in the lives of the English people. The Calvinists, who became the Puritans in England, preached the priesthood of all believers and placed a high value on individual reading of the Bible to understand God's will. Thus, concern for their souls made the printing press important to them. The person who controlled the presses was immaterial as long as the Puritans had unrestricted access to the Bible.

Only as the Tudor monarchs tried to control the way in which an individual could believe in God and his access to God's word did the printing press become a point of contention. Initial licensing of printing presses in Great Britain stemmed from efforts to restrict access for dissident (meaning non-Church of England) religious materials. This controversy led to increased demands for freedom to speak, initially, on matters of religious beliefs. In turn, the demands for freedom of speech led dissidents to demand access to printing presses to turn out religious documents. Because church and state were so inextricably intertwined, the demands for religious freedom soon expanded into demands for political freedom.

When the subject was not religious in nature, printers were not terribly concerned about licensing measures imposed by the crown. In fact, that historically dreaded institution, the Stationers

Elizabeth I
During the reign of Elizabeth I, England defeated the Spanish Armada and became the most powerful Protestant nation of Europe. Despite her military triumph, she still faced challenges to her authority from Parliament. Its members insisted on considering topics she had banned from discussion, thus opening the door to freer public debate.

Company, was set up by Queen Mary in 1557 at the request of printers who wanted to limit competition. In return for a royal grant of monopoly, those entrepreneurs promised to aid the crown in suppressing undesirable printing, which they did with vigor. The Stationers Company thus became the first in a list of historic infringements on freedom of the press that journalists down through the ages have cited as tyrannical attempts by government to subvert the press. In time, that list would include the Star Chamber, the prosecution of John Peter Zenger, the odious Stamp Act, and the Alien and Sedition Acts. Partisans would see each instance as an example of government interference with the press' freedom and usually would cite it at a time when contemporary affairs seemed to threaten a similar intrusion by government to destroy an important civil liberty. Some of the list of horrors came about innocently enough, as in the cases of the Stationers Company and the Stamp Act. Others such as the prosecution of Zenger and the Alien and Sedition Acts were products of complicated interactions that led to the determination that quieting of dissent was vital to national survival. In the case of the Stationers Company, its founders' main goal was to secure a comfortable living for themselves and their families. The idea that they would be keeping other printers from achieving the same end did not seem to concern them; nor did they worry much about the ethics of the

issue. The matter was simply financial.

When the subject was religious, however, the arguments were sharp, and punishments for divergence from the accepted line could be severe. The Puritans, who would later settle Massachusetts Bay and bring the first printing press to the American colonies, sought to undermine the established church in Great Britain. One line of attack was against royal prohibitions on the freedom of speech and press. When the Puritans were talking about freedom of the press, though, they were not referring to a newspaper publisher advocating a particular point of view. The term "freedom of the press" in Puritan England meant freedom to hire a press to produce copies of tracts denouncing the established church. The concern for freedom to publish on religious matters spilled over into politics.[1]

Although under severe attack, the British system of press control probably would have survived longer had it not been for the avarice of the Stuart kings. Printers who were in the trade as a business, whose ability to make money was based on the possession of royal monopolies to publish certain books, soon found that the Stuarts had sold their patents to others. With their secure source of income gone, some printers looked for other ways to make money and became more willing to put their printing presses at the service of religious malcontents. As the number of such printers grew, so, too, did attempts to regulate what people said about religion and government. The Stuarts, for example, developed the law of seditious libel, designed to protect government from criticism. That law provided for the imprisonment of the printer until he revealed the writer of the publication. Officials clearly recognized that the person who ran the printing press was usually only a mechanic and not the person who wrote the material. The law covered both authoring and printing false material about the king and other officers of government. This and similar oppressive laws gave the infamous Court of the Star Chamber most of its cases during the reign of Charles I. Because of such laws, England plummeted into a great civil war in the 1640s, which ultimately led to the brief imposition of Puritan rule.

COLONIAL PURITANS AND PRESS FREEDOM

Although the English experience with freedom of speech and press continued, by the 1640s and the start of the civil war, the Great Migration of the English already had occurred. Between 1620 and 1642, close to 80,000 Englishmen (2% of the entire population) left Britain. Of those, 58,000 came to North America or to the Caribbean, bringing with them the collective English experience with freedom of speech, press, and religion. To the Puritans who established the Massachusetts Bay Colony in 1628, their heritage meant a certain form of religious belief, freedom of speech to debate the tenets of that belief, and freedom of the printing press to turn out materials to discuss, debate, and advance the faith.

Although most of the Puritans who settled in the new world

[1]See Harold Hulme, "The Winning of Freedom of Speech by the House of Commons," *American Historical Review* 61 (1956): 825-53.

John Milton
The Puritan John Milton (seated) was a noted writer, theologian, and political thinker. Originally planning a career as a clergyman, he devoted himself instead to government work and the advocacy of political and religious freedom. *Areopagitica*, his argument against prior restraint, published in 1644, did not succeed in changing British law, but it did gain popularity later in the American colonies among those who wanted to publish without government oversight. Although Milton had argued against the licensing of books and pamphlets, colonists adopted his argument as a support for general press freedom. Once the Puritans under Oliver Cromwell overthrew the British monarchy in 1649, Cromwell appointed Milton to his Council of State. In that capacity he served as official censor. This drawing from 1867 depicts Cromwell dictating a letter to Milton intended to stop the persecution of religious dissenters.

had left England by 1644, colonial concepts of freedom of the press would long be influenced by a pamphlet written in that year by an unhappy fellow Puritan, John Milton. He had wanted to publish an essay he had written on divorce, but officials in the Anglican Church refused to allow its publication. In response, he wrote *Areopagitica*, an argument against censorship, in which he set forth a theory of freedom of the press that finds adherents today: "And though all the winds of doctrine were let loose to play upon the earth, so truth be in the field, we do injuriously by licensing and prohibiting to misdoubt her strength. Let her and falsehood grapple; who ever knew truth put to the worse, in a free and open encounter?"[2] With those words, he established the marketplace of ideas concept, the notion that all ideas ought to be put forward and that truth always would win over falsehood. The doctrine was advanced for his generation, and it was at times cited as an ideal. What Milton himself thought about the ideal is questionable. In one of those quirks of history, when the Puritan Commonwealth was established, he became an official censor. Not until the beginning of the nineteenth century did Americans generally accept the notion that ideas could battle for acceptance without society crumbling.

Taming the new land was the colonists' first concern, but by 1638 they had set up the first press at Harvard. The first item off the press was an oath that residents above the age of twenty had to take before becoming citizens. It bound them to be "true & faithfull" to the colony and "also truely indeavour to maintaine and preserve all the libertyes & privilidges thereof." Individuals taking the oath also promised to be true to their own conscience when "called, to give my voyce touching any such matter of this state." The importance that this "Oath of a Freeman" attached to such obligations was emphasized by the fact that each person promised to abide by them "Soe help me God in the Lord Jesus Christ," the

highest vow one could make.

Colonists used the press primarily for reproducing religious materials and publishing important colonial documents. Since Puritans owned the press at Harvard, they placed no restrictions on printing until 1662. Then, Massachusetts, which already had faced the theological challenges of the Baptist Roger Williams and Anne Hutchinson, saw the arrival of an uncontrolled commercial press. The Massachusetts General Court established a system of licensing similar to the one already operating in England, allowing only the publication of approved documents. The Court was frank about the reason for censorship: "For prevention of irregularities & abuse to the authority of this country by the printing press, it is ordered, that henceforth no copie shall be printed but by the allowance first had & obtained under the hands of Capt Daniel Gookin & Mr Jonathan Mitchel, until this Court shall take further order therein."[3]

For their time, Puritans were quite broadminded in their thinking about the publication of differing views, especially on political matters and on theological disputes among themselves. Like dominant groups elsewhere, however, they would not tolerate what they considered heretical religious beliefs. They did not think of extending freedom of the press to, for example, Catholics challenging Calvinist doctrine. Overall, though, their licensing efforts were sporadic, their attempts at limiting what individuals used the press to produce were erratic, and the punishment they meted out was comparatively mild. But this early experience established a very important principle in the colonies: no printer was ever free to use his press to print exactly what he wished. Some form of control always existed. The basic question throughout these years was who would exert that control.

For many years after the settlement of the colonies, the English were too busy with their own internal problems to be concerned

[2]The text of *Areopagitica* may be found in numerous sources. One of the most accessible for students of media history is Calder M. Pickett, *Voices of the Past: Key Documents in the History of American Journalism* (Columbus, Ohio, 1977), 8-11.

[3]*Massachusetts Records*, IV pt. II: 62, quoted in Clyde A. Duniway, *The Development of Freedom of the Press in Massachusetts* (Columbus, Mass., 1906), 41-2.

about what was happening on the other side of the Atlantic. With the calming influence that came with William and Mary's ascension to the throne in 1689, the English were ready to turn their attention to all aspects of colonial life, including the way in which the colonists used their presses. In fact, colonial governors increased their concern with what came off those presses even before the first newspaper was published in 1690. Instructions given to governors between 1686 and 1730 included variations of this statement: "Forasmuch as great inconvenience may arise by liberty of printing within our said territory under your government you are to provide by all necessary orders that no person keep any printing-press for printing, nor that any book, pamphlet or other matter whatsoever be printed without your especial leave and license first obtained."[4] Governors' instructions carried such orders even though in 1695 Parliament refused to renew the king's right to license the press.

In some instances, however, specific language authorizing governors to control the press was not necessary. Some governors were naturally hostile to that mechanical device.[5] Regardless of such attitudes, presses continued to arrive in the colonies. So, too, did the problems accompanying their use. But because there were so many colonies and so many officials involved in dealing with the products of the presses, it is impossible to say that the press was treated alike from one end of the Atlantic seaboard to the other. Early in Massachusetts history, religious groups usually owned the presses. Presses reached the southern colonies last; and when they finally arrived, the governors and their advisers carefully supervised them. In New York, the governor himself sought an official printer for the colony, and for almost forty years that printer worked calmly and quietly.

PRESS FREEDOM AND THE FIRST NEWSPAPERS

Although it is sometimes argued that conflicts over the right to use the press to criticize government or religious leaders did not begin until the 1730s with John Peter Zenger, several encounters between printers and authorities occurred before that time. Each clash contributed to the distinctly American heritage of freedom of the press that would develop in later years.

The dispute over the establishment of the first newspaper in the colonies, *Publick Occurrences Both Forreign and Domestick* in Boston in 1690, provides one such example. An assertive Anabaptist publisher, Benjamin Harris, produced a newspaper intended to provide important information as an antidote to rumors about deteriorating political conditions in Massachusetts, only to have the paper suppressed after one issue. The primary reason for the suppression was that Harris had published without authority, meaning that he had not obtained permission from the governor to print the newspaper. Before granting such permission, the gover-

Suppression of *Publick Occurrences*

Following the overthrow of the Massachusetts royal governor in 1688, conditions in the colony became chaotic. In an attempt to help bring order, Benjamin Harris published one issue of America's first newspaper, *Publick Occurrences Both Forreign and Domestick*. The provisional governing council, which included a faction that resented the cleric Cotton Mather's role in the paper, immediately issued an order prohibiting Harris from continuing publication.

nor or his representative had to approve each item planned for publication, which was prior restraint. No continuous newspaper appeared in the colonies until 1704, when the *Boston News-Letter* was published by authority, meaning its publisher had obtained prior approval of its contents.

Individuals who wanted to publish a newspaper without official permission were not the only printers who encountered problems. In 1692, Pennsylvania authorities charged printer William Bradford with using his press to print tracts for a separatist faction that mainline Quakers thought heretical. His first trial ended with a jury deadlocked nine to three in favor of conviction. After waiting almost a year for a second trial, he was released. He quickly left Pennsylvania and headed for New York, where he became the long-sought-after official printer for that colony and set up a profitable business whose only controversial printing was of tracts attacking the Pennsylvania Quakers.

Another early free-press battle, this one in Boston in 1720-1721, centered on who would control the press, which by then had become a pawn in a larger struggle for political control of the colony. The royal governor and his council were on one side, with the commercial classes of Massachusetts on the other. The colonial representative assembly favored the latter group, and the assembly wanted its views on the controversy printed so that colonists would have both sides of the matter to consider. To prevent the assembly from publishing its views, the governor threatened to use the powers to license the press granted him in his royal commission. These instructions had been altered somewhat from their earlier issuance, however, and now required the assembly to par-

---

[4]Quoted in A. C. Goodell, *Proceedings of the Massachusetts Historical Society* (June 1893), 173.
[5]William Berkeley, the Anglican governor of Virginia, for example, remarked in 1671, "I thank God we have no free schools or printing; and I hope that we shall not have them these hundred years. For learning has brought disobediences and heresy and sects into the world; and printing has divulged them and libels against the government. God keep us from both."

ticipate in the licensing process. It refused. The governor's council, when consulted, pointed out that the king had lost his power to license the press; by extension, so had the governor. The assembly thus could have any information published that it wanted. Refusing to concede, the governor asked for a licensing law. Once more the assembly said no. So the governor dissolved it. The *Boston Gazette*, established in 1719, published the governor's dissolution speech; the *Boston News-Letter* printed the full text of the assembly's response. Out of the controversy, then, perhaps for the first time, came the publication of both sides of an important political debate.

After the encounter, licensing was dead in Massachusetts, although that did not prevent the assembly from trying to exercise the power occasionally. The primary motivation behind such attempts was political, as legislators tried to solidify their positions in relation to that of the governor. Never did anyone think of discontinuing control over the press. The struggle was always over who would have the control.

The next major battle also occurred in Massachusetts. In Boston, a handful of zealous Anglicans founded the *New-England Courant*, with James Franklin as publisher, as a forum for attacking the Puritan clergy. The government let the attacks pass with no response, but in June 1722 it jailed Franklin for a month for charging that authorities had not been aggressive enough in suppressing pirates plundering the New England coast. In January 1723, he was in jail again, this time for publishing an essay on hypocrites that had offended members of the colonial assembly. His difficulties brought forth the earliest support for a press colleague in the colonies when Andrew Bradford, writing in his *American Weekly Mercury* in Philadelphia on February 26, 1723, criticized the Massachusetts authorities for taking away Franklin's means of earning a living without giving him an opportunity to defend himself. Bradford, an Anglican, also criticized the Puritan leaders for their role in the controversy.[6]

Printers encountered problems in Philadelphia as well. William Bradford had been run out of the city in 1693 for using his press to publish allegedly heretical material. In 1722, his son Andrew, publisher of the *American Weekly Mercury*, was in trouble with authorities. Andrew Bradford had published a pamphlet by an anonymous author about the poor credit rating of the colony, which he later reproduced as a news story in his newspaper. The colonial council called him in, demanding to know where he had gotten the article. In a less than glowing advocacy of press freedom, he declared that he did not know where the article had come from and that one of his subordinates must have accepted and printed it without his knowledge or permission, of course. He asked the governor and council to pardon him for the mistake. The council accepted his apology and ordered him not to print anything further about colonial affairs without prior approval. Two points made this trial of special interest. First, among the members of the council who imposed prior censorship on Bradford was Andrew Hamilton, who thirteen years later would be John Peter Zenger's

[6]Anna Janney DeArmond, *Andrew Bradford: Colonial Printer* (New York, 1969), 14-5.

William Bradford and the Quakers

When the Quakers were establishing the colony of Pennsylvania, they engaged William Bradford to do their printing. Most of the work that he produced — like *Kalendarium Pennsilvaniense*, the first work printed in Pennsylvania, in 1685 — was of Quaker material. Only nominally Quaker himself, however, he readily printed several trenchant and scurrilous attacks that the radical reformer George Keith wrote against Quaker dogma. In September 1692 Quaker officials arrested him and confiscated his printing equipment. At his trial, he argued that the jury should be allowed to determine not only the facts but the law also — that is, not simply that the material had been published but that it was indeed illegal. The jury split in its verdict, with the nine Quaker members voting for conviction and the three non-Quakers against. Both Bradford and Keith later converted to Anglicanism.

chief defense counsel. Second, Bradford, apparently feeling great remorse for his behavior before the council, editorialized on the problems facing fellow editor Franklin a few months later.

During these encounters, printers were trying to determine their place in society. Although they did not speak in terms of freedom of the press, their words would be classified under that general heading today. Benjamin Franklin, in his famous "Apology for Printers," written in 1731, noted that "Printers are educated in the Belief, that when Men differ in Opinion, both Sides ought equally to have the Advantage of being heard by the Publick; and that when Truth and Error have fair Play, the former is always an overmatch for the latter: Hence they cheerfully serve all contending Writers that pay them well, without regarding on which side they are of the Question in Dispute."[7] The notion of letting truth and error compete with one another for acceptance harkened back to John Milton; but in the political climate of the colonies, printing both sides of a story was impossible. Notice, though, that Franklin was talking about opening the columns of his newspaper to "contending Writers." That was a far cry from the concept of modern journalism in which media staff members are the ones who present information, but remember that during the colonial period the printer was still primarily a technician. The contents of the publications usually were provided by others, often those who had paid for publication.

THE ZENGER TRIAL

The most famous encounter between the press and colonial authorities occurred in New York in the early 1730s, and it swirled around just such a printer-technician rather than the writer of the material. The cause of the contest was political power, who wielded it, and who controlled the means to tell their views to the people. The British took over the New York colony, initially established by the Dutch as New Netherland, in 1664 — after the culture, heritage, and power structure of the colony had been well established. Throughout its early years, the English and the Dutch competed repeatedly for supremacy in New York. John Peter Zenger, the printer-technician, was part of one such fight in 1733.

It was brought on by the death of an English governor in 1731. The new governor, William Cosby, did not arrive in the colony until fifteen months later. Before his arrival, Rip Van Dam, senior member of the governor's council and a member of a very old and respected Dutch family, served as interim governor. His administration was peaceful and popular. Upon finally arriving in New York, Cosby immediately alienated colonists. He demanded that Van Dam give him the salary that Van Dam had collected as interim governor. Then, when Van Dam refused, Cosby sued. When the chief justice agreed with Van Dam, Cosby replaced him.

Each of Cosby's actions had the practical effect of dividing the colonists into two political groups — a court faction, with Cosby as leader, and an opposition group, which had a large following among the people and within the colonial assembly. The opposition party was a magnet for all who had any grievance against the governor, and it grew rapidly, so rapidly in fact that Cosby feared losing control of the colonial assembly through elections in 1734. He managed to keep control, however, with votes won through questionable tactics. When denied their rightful leadership roles in the assembly, members of the opposition sent former Chief Justice Lewis Morris to London to lobby the king.

With this background of political turmoil, opposition leaders

[7]*Pennsylvania Gazette*, 10 June 1731. For a discussion of colonial ideas about publishing for all sides, see Wm. David Sloan, "Neutrality and Colonial Newspapers," chapter 3 in Steven R. Knowlton and Karen L. Freeman, eds., *Fair and Balanced: A History of Journalistic Objectivity* (Northport, Ala., 2005).

William Cosby

Rip Van Dam

Lewis Morris

James Alexander

Political Undercurrents of the Zenger Case

Almost as soon as Governor William Cosby arrived in New York, he ran into trouble with some of the colony's leading figures. His first dealings with the colonial assembly centered on demands for additional money — a gratuity for his having helped procure the repeal of an obnoxious piece of legislation. In fact, he had not helped in the legislative effort and had been specifically forbidden by the king to accept special gifts from the colonial assembly; but still he succeeded in obtaining £1,000, up from the £750 the assembly had offered initially. Still not satisfied, he demanded half of all the money that Rip Van Dam had taken in while he was interim governor. The wily Dutchman would have none of that, but he made a counter offer — he would share his income of about £2,000 if Cosby would split his income for the same period of about £6,000. Needless to say, Cosby was not interested in the counter offer, nor was he dissuaded from his goal. He persuaded the supreme court of the colony to sit as a special court of the exchequer, a body empowered to deal with financial matters, to force Van Dam to pay. Chief Justice Lewis Morris, however, agreed with Van Dam. Cosby thereupon replaced Morris, another man who commanded much respect within the Dutch community, with a much younger man, James Delancey, a decided royalist and a favorite of the governor. In the meantime, Cosby had used trickery to avoid repaying £1,500 that James Alexander had loaned him. It was Alexander who headed the efforts to found a newspaper, Zenger's *New-York Weekly Journal*, as an organ for opposing Cosby's administration.

began to realize the importance of having a newspaper to circulate their views. They had tried spreading their arguments through pamphlets but then realized they needed the quickness and regularity of a newspaper. They also needed a way to conceal their identities. Consequently, they quietly set up the *New-York Weekly Journal* as a vehicle to inform the people of Cosby's transgressions and to raise enough protest to force his recall.

Zenger was not the founder of the paper. In fact, the Dutch faction had established the newspaper before naming its printer. Zenger, who had come to the colonies from the Palatine, had learned his trade under William Bradford. After his apprenticeship, he set himself up in business. It was his publication of a pamphlet giving deposed Chief Justice Morris' side of his firing that brought Zenger to the attention of the opposition leaders, now known as Morrisites. On November 5, 1733, relying on the promises of literary and other aid from the Morrisites, he put out the first edition of the *Weekly Journal*. Working with Zenger, the printer, was James Alexander, a young lawyer, who served as chief editor, although he carefully concealed his relationship with the paper.

By its seventh edition, in December 1733, the *Weekly Journal* was criticizing the governor for allowing a French warship to enter the New York harbor. Supposedly the ship had entered to obtain supplies, but the newspaper claimed its real purpose was to locate harbor fortifications. The court party quickly answered such commentaries and used the columns of William Bradford's *New York Gazette* to launch a vicious journalistic war.

Cosby made some early, unsuccessful attempts to silence the *Weekly Journal*. In January 1734, Chief Justice James Delancey, the governor's appointee, told the grand jury about alleged seditious libels against the governor. The grand jury, however, returned no indictments. A similar attempt during the grand jury's sitting in October 1734 also failed. While the colony's legal system refused to help Cosby silence the newspaper, the *Weekly Journal* added regularly to his list of reasons for seeking its suppression. In a series of issues in September and October 1734, it criticized him for being too selective in choosing members of his council, implying that only his favorites were eligible for certain jobs. It also published an anonymous letter from New Jersey containing a general attack on Cosby and ridiculing the entire government of New York.

After an attempt to force the assembly to charge Zenger with libel failed, Cosby resorted to his only sure source of support. He had his council issue its own warrant charging Zenger with raising sedition, inflaming the minds of the people, holding the king's government in contempt, and casting aspersions on the king's officials. Cosby had him arrested in November 1734, and the printer was confined for a week, causing his newspaper to skip an issue. In the next week's paper, Zenger apologized for the missed edition, noting that he was being held in jail without bail and without access to pen and ink. Finally, the legend goes, he resumed editing his paper by giving instructions to his wife through a hole in his cell door. His bail was set at £400, but he spent nine months in jail even though his Morrisite backers could have raised the money easily. Zenger's hardships created a great deal of public sympathy, making him far more valuable to the Morrisites in jail than out.

James Alexander, the actual editor of the *Weekly Journal*, planned to serve as Zenger's chief counsel and to use the trial to challenge Cosby's rule. To deprive Zenger of adequate counsel, however, Cosby had Alexander and his partner disbarred shortly before the trial began. Thus, although he had a replacement attor-

The Offending *Journal*
The issue of April 8, 1734, was one of two issues of the *New-York Weekly Journal* on which the indictment against the printer John Peter Zenger was based. Although he did not write the material, he was arrested on the charge that the *Journal* aroused citizens to question the rule of Governor William Cosby.

ney the court named, Zenger faced trial without competent representation because the appointee was an ally of Cosby. To the Morrisites that was worse than having no lawyer at all. They wanted someone who would vigorously defend Zenger and criticize Cosby's activities at the same time. They chose a friend of Alexander's, Andrew Hamilton of Pennsylvania, one of the most famous lawyers in the colonies.

Charges against Zenger were based on several articles in the *Weekly Journal* accusing the government of jeopardizing the liberties and the property of the people. The articles also said Cosby had tampered with numerous civil liberties including trial by jury and the right to vote. Hamilton's first courtroom move caught most observers off-guard. He admitted that Zenger had printed and published the newspaper issues in question. Under existing law, all the jury could determine was whether the accused had published the offending articles. If his attorney admitted that his

Andrew Hamilton and the Zenger Trial
When Governor Cosby ordered Zenger's attorneys disbarred, Andrew Hamilton traveled from Philadelphia to take the case. The portrait (left) was made when he was a young man. At Zenger's trial, at age fifty-nine, he told the jury that he had been willing, even at his advanced years, to make the long trip for the cause of liberty. Because of that statement, many historians have mistakenly assumed that he was around eighty years of age. Known for his strident style of argumentation, he disregarded common legal practice of the day and admitted that Zenger had published the issues of the paper in question. He then called upon jury members to judge the truth of the material for themselves. "It is not," he declared, "the bare printing and publishing of a paper that will make it a libel: the words themselves must be libelous, that is, false, scandalous, and seditious, else my client is not guilty."

client had published the pieces as charged, then Zenger was guilty of libel. The colonial attorney general, after hearing the plea, insisted that the jury immediately convict Zenger. Hamilton, however, took a different view.

He argued that the prosecution had to prove that the words in the articles themselves were libelous, false, scandalous, and seditious before a conviction was justified. If the words were not, then the jury had to find Zenger not guilty, Hamilton said. Chief Justice Delancey would not permit such an argument. So Hamilton changed his tactics, turned to the jury, and delivered one of the most powerful courtroom addresses of American history. He appealed to jury members to be their own judges about the truth of Zenger's statements. He denounced unbridled power as exercised by Cosby and appealed to the individual juror's love of liberty as the only defense against tyrannical rulers. The basis of Zenger's defense thus became the notion that citizens had the right to criticize rulers and that citizens as jurors had the authority to determine whether words were false. In fact, Hamilton argued, free speech was essential in the colonies to prevent governors, who were far removed from the restraining hand of their superiors, from abusing their powers:

Men who injure and oppress the people under their administration provoke them to cry out and complain; and then make that very complaint the foundation for new oppressions and prosecutions. I wish I could say there were no instances of this kind. But to conclude; the question before the Court and you, gentlemen of the jury, is not of small nor private concern, it is not the cause of a poor printer, nor of New York alone.... No! It

may in its consequence affect every freeman that lives under a British government on the main of America. It is the best cause. It is the cause of liberty; and I make no doubt but your upright conduct this day will not only entitle you to the love and esteem of your fellow citizens; but every man who prefers freedom to a life of slaver, will bless and honor you, as men who have baffled the attempt of tyranny; and by an impartial and uncorrupt verdict have laid a noble foundation for securing to ourselves, our posterity, and our neighbors, that to which nature and the laws of our country have given us a right — The Liberty both of exposing and opposing arbitrary power (in these parts of the world, at least) by speaking and writing truth.[8]

The jury returned a "not guilty" verdict, which under the law meant jurors had decided Zenger had not published the material in question.

Although historians argue that the trial established two important precedents in libel law — the admissibility of evidence about the truth of the alleged libel and the right of a jury to decide whether a publication was defamatory or seditious — more than fifty years passed before these two principles were established in American law. Even if the precepts were not codified immediately, the trial did make prosecutions under colonial libel laws less certain, showing that a jury could acquit individuals who government officials thought were libelers.

The arguments in the case were critical to colonial political development, for they established in the popular thinking the indi-

[8]*The Trial of John Peter Zenger, of New-York, Printer, Who was lately Try'd and Acquitted for Printing and Publishing a LIBEL against the Government* (Dublin, Ire., 1738), 64-5.

vidual's right to criticize his government, a right that colonists would employ increasingly as the Revolution approached. Helping this cause along was a pamphlet containing the arguments Hamilton made during the trial that Alexander prepared and had printed. The transcripts, which were highly dramatic, transcended legal principles. As the *Pennsylvania Gazette* commented in 1738, if the results of the Zenger case were not incorporated into the law, then they were obviously "better than Law, ... Ought to be Law, and will always be Law wherever Justice prevails."[9] Alexander's pamphlet discouraged additional prosecutions, for potential jurors had been made aware of their power in libel prosecutions.

Zenger much later became a hero in American journalism history. In his own time, he was less important. After Hamilton's rousing victory in court, the Morrisites went out to celebrate; but because of a legal technicality, Zenger spent the night in jail. In early 1736 Cosby died, and the new governor decided to make friends with the Morrisites. Now part of the power structure, the Morrisites showed themselves just as interested in wielding authority as the Cosby supporters they had condemned a few years earlier. This time, the Morrisites did not forget Zenger; during the final years of his life he was the official public printer of New York and New Jersey — a position given only to those who were on the right side of the people in power.

COLONIAL PHILOSOPHY AND PRACTICE

If a printer did become involved in political controversy, he often surrounded his efforts with essays clipped from English newspapers that proclaimed the importance of press freedom. These essays, produced at the height of partisan journalism in England, were reproduced in the colonies from the 1720s through the Revolutionary period. Editors never seemed to tire of telling readers about the importance of the basic freedoms of expression.[10] Favorite quotations came from "Cato's Letters," which appeared in English papers between 1720 and 1723. Written by John Trenchard and Thomas Gordon, the essays touched on a variety of issues relating to constitutional government, including freedom of expression. In 1720, for instance, Cato told readers, "Without Freedom of Thought, there can be no such Thing as Wisdom; and no such Thing as publick Liberty, without Freedom of Speech." Such freedom, he wrote, "is the Right of every Man, as far as by it he does not hurt or controul the Right of another: and this is the only Check which it ought suffer, and the only Bounds it ought to know." Citizens, Cato continued, "ought to speak well of their Governors ... while their Governors deserve to be well spoken of," but governors who mistreat their subjects should be publicly exposed.[11] This essay on freedom of speech and three others on libel, which defended the right of printers to criticize public officials

and measures, formed the heart of the discussion of freedom of expression in the latter part of the colonial period.

Despite such high-minded arguments, invocations of freedom of the press often seemed self-serving. In New York in the 1740s, another struggle between a royal governor and the provincial assembly led to the insistence that the assembly's point of view on a particular issue be published and to a pious declaration that assembly members were firm in their "Resolution to preserve the Liberty of the Press."[12] What they were firm about was their intention to ensure that the people discover the governor's faults through the newspaper. In Massachusetts, attempts by the royal governor in 1768 to take action against Benjamin Edes and John Gill, printers of the *Boston Gazette* and vitriolic Patriots, were met by a smug colonial assembly affirming that "the Liberty of the Press is a great Bulwark of the Liberty of the People: It is therefore the incumbent Duty of those who are constituted the Guardians of the People's Rights to defend and maintain it."[13]

Although much was said about freedom of the press, what that term actually meant remained much in doubt as the colonial period came to a close. Generally when a printer and a government body collided, the printer escaped severe punishment, but the psychological toll on these individuals must have been great. Even trying to determine what could be printed without encountering the wrath of some official was difficult, as Hugh Gaine, printer of the *New York Mercury*, found out in 1753. His transgression was reproducing without permission the king's instructions to a new governor and the governor's speech to the colonial assembly. Gaine was summoned before the assembly and forced to apologize for his efforts to provide news of government to his readers. Unlike today, in the colonial period, publishing any kind of official document — or any debate before the legislature — was dangerous for printers. Information was a closely controlled commodity, perhaps because of the belief that too much knowledge could lead to unrest among the populace. Colonial officials, both the royal governors and the locally elected assemblies, were acting on principles learned from centuries of English experience. Information needed for governance, this heritage maintained, was best left in the hands of those suited to make decisions. The judgment of the general public could not be trusted, and so most citizens were excluded from the process.

As the colonial period ended, those who soon would be Patriots clearly understood the value of the newspaper as a medium of communication that was as important as and more timely than the highly favored pamphlet. But the newspaper had to be carefully controlled in order to foment and successfully wage a revolution. The Zenger case had won the colonists some protection for their criticisms of royal government, and the newspaper was the ideal place for those criticisms to appear. Never did the colonists think that the newspaper's printer should be free to take any side of political controversy. In fact, the freedom to use the

[9]*Pennsylvania Gazette*, 11 May 1738.

[10]For a discussion of the importance of these English writers in colonial newspapers, see Gary Huxford, "The English Libertarian Tradition in the Colonial Newspaper," *Journalism Quarterly* 45 (1968): 677-86.

[11]John Trenchard and Thomas Gordon, *Cato's Letters*, 1st ed., 4 vols. (London, 1724), 1: 97-8. Also see Leonard W. Levy, ed. (London, 1755; reprint ed., New York, 1971), 1: 96-7.

[12]Quoted in Clark Rivera, "Ideals, Interests and Civil Liberty: The Colonial Press and Freedom, 1735-76," *Journalism Quarterly* 55 (1973): 52.

[13]Quoted in Duniway, *Development of Freedom of the Press in Massachusetts*, 127.

Stamps and Press Freedom
When the British government imposed a requirement that newspapers be printed on paper bearing a stamp (left), its main motive was to raise revenue to help pay debts incurred during the French and Indian War. American editors argued, however, that the Stamp Act was a great assault on freedom of the press. The aroused public protested with marches and threats. They equated the law with an assault on their freedoms. When Parliament soon repealed the law, American patriots viewed the repeal as a great victory over the unjust taxes of the British government and as a triumph for freedom of the press. Newspapers, in leading the opposition to the Stamp Act, gained an important role in the growing opposition to Great Britain. Their importance served as one of the later arguments that Americans would make in support of ensuring and protecting freedom of the press.

press to print all sides or any side of controversies depended on the existence of a political stalemate in the colony. Such a condition rarely existed as the Revolution approached. And where one side had the upper hand, the press was carefully controlled. During the Revolution, in those areas where Patriot forces were supreme, their leaders eagerly suppressed printers who had the audacity to support the king or who tried to present both sides of the controversy.

Before the Revolution actually broke out, however, the British again challenged press freedom in America, or at least so the Patriot leaders thought. The conflict stemmed from the British Parliament's passage of the Stamp Act in 1765. The law, which imposed taxes in the form of revenue stamps on a variety of printed materials including newspapers, almanacs, and pamphlets, was similar to legislation that had been in effect in England for years and was designed to help defer the costs of defending and administering the colonies. To the colonists, it seemed another oppressive law enacted by a government more interested in American money than American well-being. Newspaper publishers joined in denouncing the tyrannical nature of the tax. Among their criticisms was the notion that the act was an attempt to suppress American freedom of the press.

With the act's repeal in 1766, newspapers were in the forefront of those claiming credit for Parliament's action. The episode added to what the press perceived as its power over events. From that feeling of power came an even stronger proprietary interest in a still vaguely defined freedom of the press and a greater willingness to use the term indiscriminately. The phrase had not yet become a slogan, but the time when that would happen was draw-

ing near. As a result of the Stamp Act experience, more printers became active Patriots. Some were even key members of the growing Sons of Liberty. These patriot-printers considered their newspapers and their freedom of the press additional weapons to use against a very dangerous foe: the British.

THE AMERICAN REVOLUTION

As the Revolution began, what individuals meant by using the phrase "freedom of the press" is open to question, but they certainly did not mean freedom to print as one pleased. In Boston in 1770, John Mein, publisher of the pro-British *Chronicle*, so offended Patriots that he was attacked in the streets. He fled to England in fear of his life. In 1775 in New York, two Patriot leaders, Alexander McDougall and Isaac Sears, led a mob in smashing Tory printer James Rivington's press. Rivington was out of business for eighteen months — the time necessary for him to import new equipment from England. In 1776, the New Hampshire provincial assembly summoned Daniel Fowle before it to chastise him for publishing an article questioning the trend toward independence. Rivington bounced back several times from attempts at intimidation during the war and, indeed, was the leading Tory publisher in the colonies. Fowle, however, was so upset by the assembly's rebuke that he suspended publication.

Samuel Loudon, Patriot editor of the *New York Packet* and the *American Advertiser*, who was paid to print a loyalist reply to Thomas Paine's *Common Sense*, also encountered popular disapproval. Besides making the mistake of taking on the job, he erred by advertising the tract in his newspaper. He was rousted from his bed in the middle of the night and forced to lead a Patriot mob to the printing plates used to reproduce the tract. He then watched as the mob smashed the type and burned 1,500 copies plus the original manuscript. The mob considered this a great victory for liberty. The next morning, freedom of the press as known today took a decided trouncing as every printer in New York found on his doorstep an intimidating note: "Sir, if you print, or suffer to be printed in your press anything against the rights and liberties of America, or in favor of our inveterate foes, the King, Ministry, and Parliament of Great Britain, death and destruction, ruin and perdition, shall be your portion. Signed, by order of the Committee of tarring and feathering."[14] That effectively stopped loyalist publications in New York for the moment.

Did the Revolutionary leaders believe in freedom of the press? Yes and no. They certainly believed in their freedom to use the press to advance their own interests but refused to grant equal privileges to their opponents. But since the Patriots were so convinced of the rightness of their cause and the evil of their foes, they could convince themselves that they were, indeed, supporting freedom of the press when they limited the abilities of the Tories to reach the public via the press.[15]

Patriot leaders clearly understood a cardinal principle regarding the use of the press — that the wishes of the community set limits to its freedom. An essay in the *Boston Gazette*, which served as the outlet for Samuel Adams' views, explained this societal impact on the use of the press in 1767 by saying that "political liberty consists in a freedom of speech and action, so far as the laws of a community will permit, and not farther."[16] During the Revolution, the Patriots had little tolerance for pro-British sentiment, as their actions demonstrated repeatedly. Such an attitude found expression in various calls for restrictions on freedom of information.

The Continental Congress understood the need to place limitations on freedom of expression during the Revolution. Following the pattern of contemporary legislative bodies, its meetings were closed to printers. Delegates also adopted a resolution calling for the expulsion of any member who revealed the topics of discussion without permission. Such a person might well know how to use the press to make the problems and disagreements within the Congress public knowledge and thus undermine the effort for independence. Anyone who violated the resolution was to be "deemed an enemy to the liberties of America." The Continental Congress also urged states to pass legislation to prevent people from being "deceived and drawn into erroneous opinion." This, however, was the extent of the Continental Congress' efforts to restrict freedom of expression, for although urged to pass a variety of further limitations, its members steadfastly refused to do so.

The Declaration of Independence
When the signers read the Declaration of Independence on the steps of Independence Hall in Philadelphia, colonials believed that its commitment to "life, liberty and the pursuit of happiness" encompassed press freedom. Newspapers throughout the colonies printed the Declaration, and news of its adoption quickly spread. As the Revolution that followed would show, though, many patriots felt that "freedom of the press" was to be enjoyed only by those newspapers that supported the revolt against England. They believed that newspapers could merit freedom only if they supported the proper principles. When newspapers did not give full-hearted support, ardent patriots often tried to intimidate them.

Part of this reluctance may have been due to the uncertain nature of the Continental Congress' power over the states.

In any event, the states adopted all necessary restrictive measures. By 1778, all states had laws requiring loyalty oaths from all male citizens and legislation to protect military information and to punish individuals who criticized the new government or the war effort.[17] Although George Washington did not ask for any special corrective action, he often expressed concern about the explicit reporting of military matters in Patriot newspapers. In a war in which the front lines were so fluid, the chances of the enemy obtaining copies of those publications were good. If that happened, months of planning could be destroyed.

THE MEANING OF PRESS FREEDOM: THE 1780s

By the early 1780s, printers still were debating just what freedom of the press meant. Once again, they reached back to the familiar strains of *Areopagitica*. Eleazer Oswald wrote in the first issue of his Philadelphia newspaper, "The *Liberty of the Press*, so highly extolled by all Persons, has not been clearly defined by any. Some contend for unbounded Liberty, and that this being equally allowed on all sides, Truth and Justice having fair Play, would nec-

---

[14]Quoted in Thomas Jones, *History of New York During the Revolutionary War* (New York, 1879), I: 65.

[15]For a discussion of how the patriots could view their actions as supportive of freedom of the press, see Richard Buel, Jr., "Freedom of the Press in Revolutionary America: The Evolution of Libertarianism, 1760-1820," in *The Press and the American Revolution*, Bernard Bailyn and John B. Hench, eds. (Boston, 1981), 59-97.

[16]Leonard W. Levy, *Freedom of the Press from Zenger to Jefferson* (Indianapolis, 1966), 95.

[17]*Journals of the Continental Congress, 1774-1789*, 2 January 1776, 4: 18, in Leonard Levy, *Freedom of Speech and Press in Early American History: Legacy of Suppression* (Cambridge, Mass., 1960), 181; and Charles C. Tansil, ed., *Documents Illustrative of the Formation of the Union of the American States* (Washington, 1927), 18.

essarily over-power their Opposition, and finally prevail."[18] But did printers understand the ramifications of such a statement?

Regardless of their level of understanding, newspaper printers around the country claimed the talismanic value of "freedom of the press." In 1785 the *Charleston* (S.C.) *Herald* praised the virtues of freedom of the press, saying that because of it, "Magistrates cannot oppress the poor; bawds cannot seduce young females; Generals cannot act with cowardice; Guardians cannot betray their trust; Paymasters cannot pocket public money; Stockjobbers cannot impose upon the credulity of the nation." Even senators, it contended, could not "betray their trust; convert serious matters into jokes; or transfer mountains into molehills."[19] All of this reliance on a free press occurred in an age in which newspaper content came primarily from local nonjournalists or was clipped from publications from other parts of the country. How could such a watchdog role of the press even be considered under such circumstances? Had the rhetoric outpaced the reality? Or were these printers seeing in their publications something hidden from today's observers?

Aside from the question of whether they practiced what they preached, printer-editors of the post-Revolutionary period showed some understanding that freedom of the press was most valuable as a protection for comments made about government. As Francis Bailey of the *Freeman's Journal* in Philadelphia wrote in 1791, "Pieces relative to public measures, and evidently wrote with a design to infuse the public good and general interests ... whether they touch on men or measures, things or persons, there ought to be no restriction.... [T]he press should be free and open, leaving the offender to the ordinary course of the law, if his writings have libellous import."[20] One of his Philadelphia competitors, Eleazer Oswald, agreed:

Considerable Latitude must be allowed in the Discussion of Public Affairs, or the Liberty of the Press will be of no Benefit to Society. As the Indulgence of Private Malice and Personal Slander should be checked and resisted by every legal Means, so a constant Examination into the Characters of Ministers and Magistrates should be equally promoted and encouraged.[21]

These arguments would be heard again during debates over the ratification of the Constitution and in calls for a Bill of Rights. Clearly, the press had to be free to discuss governmental issues, regardless of the actual scope of the term "freedom of the press." With such general agreement on the need for the press to supervise government, the old notion of seditious libel, a crime that stemmed from the criticism of government, seemed dead.

The Articles of Confederation, the nation's first constitution, provide no clues in the search for the meaning of freedom of the press, for they contained no mention of it. However, the new state constitutions did. Reflecting the recent colonial experience, the Virginia Declaration of Rights, drafted in 1776, said, "The freedom of the Press is one of the greatest bulwarks of liberty, and can never be restrained but by despotick Governments." The Maryland Declaration of Rights, drafted the same year, said that "the liberty of the press ought to be inviolably preserved." The Pennsylvania constitution had the most specific of all the new guarantees: "That the people have a right to freedom of speech, and of writing, and publishing their sentiments: therefore the freedom of the press ought not to be restrained." In all, nine of the original thirteen states had constitutions containing free press or free speech clauses prior to or coincidental with the adoption of the Constitution and ratification of the Bill of Rights.[22]

These early state provisions, however, were all vague. In 1789, debate swirled around the interpretation of the Massachusetts guarantee: "The liberty of the press is essential to the security of freedom in a state: it ought not, therefore, to be restrained in this Commonwealth." William Cushing, the state's chief justice, discussed the possible meaning of the language with its author, John Adams. The main thrust of the guarantee, both agreed, was to grant newspapers freedom to comment about the operation of government and political leaders. Cushing praised newspapers, believing that without them the American Revolution would not have been possible, let alone successful. "This liberty of publishing truth can never effectually injure a good government, or honest administrators," he wrote, "but it may save a state from the necessity of a revolution, as well as bring one about, when it is necessary." The guarantee entailed the imposition of no previous restraint on publication, Cushing said, but "when the press is made the vehicle of falsehood and scandal, let the authors be punished with becoming rigour." Adams fully agreed with that interpretation.[23] So another piece of the puzzle begins to fall into place. Freedom of the press initially referred solely to matters concerning government and political leaders. Its guarantees seemed limited to the absence of prior restraint or prior approval of contents. Punishment was assured for anyone who misused that freedom.

Such understanding was widespread throughout the new states. Nevertheless, the new Constitution, proposed in 1787, included no such guarantee. Charles Pinckney, a South Carolina lawyer, suggested that it include a statement that "the liberty of the Press shall be inviolably preserved." But the delegates to the constitutional convention believed that since the federal government was not empowered to invade such liberties, guarantees were unnecessary. They defeated Pinckney's suggestion by a vote of four states for it — Massachusetts, Maryland, Virginia, and South Carolina — to seven against it — New Hampshire, Connecticut, New Jersey, Pennsylvania, Delaware, North Carolina, and Georgia.[24] The New York delegation was evenly divided and did not vote; the Rhode Island delegation was not present.

[18]*Independent Gazetteer*, 13 April 1782.
[19]*Charleston Herald*, quoted in *South Carolina Gazette and Public Advertiser*, 1 October 1785.
[20]*Freeman's Journal*, 13 June 1781.
[21]*Independent Gazetteer*, 13 April 1782.
[22]Quotes from documents are reprinted in Schwartz, *The Bill of Rights*, 1: 235, 266. See also Margaret A. Blanchard, "Filling in the Void: Speech and Press in the State Courts Prior to *Gitlow*," in *The First Amendment Reconsidered*, Bill F. Chamberlin and Charlene J. Brown, eds. (New York, 1982), 18.
[23]Quoted in Leonard Levy, *Emergence of a Free Press* (New York, 1985), 198-9.
[24]Federal Convention, 1787, quoted in Bernard Schwartz, *The Bill of Rights: A Documentary History*, 2 vols. (1971), 1: 437 and 439.

The Constitutional Convention
Secrecy was the word at the most important political meeting ever held in the United States. Delegates to the "Federal Convention" had been charged only with revising the Articles of Confederation. Most delegates, however, soon decided that an entirely new government structure for the Republic was needed, not just alterations in the existing one. Newspaper printers/editors did not have today's attitude that they had the right to cover governmental meetings — or even that there was a good reason to do so — and thus there was little demand for openness. The delegates adopted a number of procedures to assure that details of their discussions and debates did not get out. That may have been a wise move, since many of the delegates themselves were dissatisfied with various compromises, and a public debate might have derailed the deliberations.

CONSTITUTIONAL DEBATE

The Constitution was sent to the states for ratification with no explicit protection for civil liberties. The lack of such protection stirred great debates in state ratifying conventions and led to powerfully written pamphlets demanding what became the Bill of Rights. Although much of the rhetoric dealt with civil liberties, much of the real concern centered on questions of political power and who would wield it. A Bill of Rights became the focal point of debates. Unfortunately, the debates did not provide a hard and fast understanding of the meaning of freedom of the press. Often, protests against the lack of protection for press freedom combined many guarantees without any differentiation among them, such as this from a pamphlet by Virginian George Mason: "There is no declaration of any kind for preserving the liberty of the press, the trial by jury in civil causes, nor against the danger of standing armies in time of peace." Elbridge Gerry, an Anti-Federalist, or opponent of ratification, from Massachusetts, fearful that the new system at first would seem kindly and beneficent and then would turn oppressive, detailed his feelings with more precision:

There is no security in the profered system, either for the rights of conscience or the liberty of the Press: Despotism usually while it is gaining ground, will suffer men to think, say, or write what they please; but when once established, if it is thought necessary to subserve the purposes, or arbitrary power, the most unjust restrictions may take place in the first instance, and an imprimatur on the Press in the next, may silence the complaints, and forbid the most decent remonstrances of an injured and oppressed people.[25]

The Federalists, or supporters of the Constitution, felt such criticisms were unmerited. They had no ulterior motives, they said,

no plans to subvert the people's civil liberties. In fact, argued Pennsylvanian James Wilson, "The proposed system possesses no influence whatever upon the press." He argued that "it would have been merely nugatory, to have introduced a formal declaration upon the subject; nay, that very declaration might have been construed to imply that some degree of power was given, since we undertook to define its extent."[26] Such a concern is heard today as some purists argue that to take press-related cases into court, asking a judicial body to include a particular right within the list of benefits the First Amendment grants, gives jurists just as great an opportunity to exclude that right from the panoply of rights granted under the First Amendment as to include it.

The greatest of all writings on the Constitution was *The Federalist Papers*; and "Federalist No. 84," by New Yorker Alexander Hamilton, reveals someone with a clear understanding of the societal base necessary for the existence of freedom of the press:

What signifies a declaration that "the liberty of the press shall be inviolably preserved"? What is the liberty of the press? Who can give it any definition which would not leave the utmost latitude for evasion? I hold it to be impracticable; and from this, I infer, that its security, whatever fine declarations may be inserted in any constitution respecting it, must altogether depend on public opinion, and on the general spirit of the people and of the government.[27]

This statement has held true throughout United States history. When Americans believed limitations on the right of certain individuals to speak were appropriate — be they abolitionists in the 1830s and 1840s, Southern sympathizers in the North during the Civil War, or socialists and pacifists during World War I — ways were found to curtail their freedom. Such actions later in

---

[25]Quoted in ibid., 450 and 486.

[26]Ibid., 529.

[27]Alexander Hamilton, James Madison, and John Jay, *The Federalist: A Collection of Essays, written in favour of the new constitution*, 1st ed. (New York, 1788), 349-50

Constitutional Debate on Freedom of the Press

John Adams:
"The liberty of the press is essential to the security of freedom in a state: it ought not, therefore, to be restrained in this Commonwealth."
(Massachusetts Constitution)

William Cushing:
"When the press is made the vehicle of falsehood and scandal, let the authors be punished with becoming rigour."

Elbridge Gerry:
"Despotism usually while it is gaining ground, will suffer men to think, say, or write what they please; but when once established, if it is thought necessary ... an imprimatur on the Press ... may silence the complaints ... of an injured and oppressed people."

James Wilson:
"The proposed [U.S. Constitution] possesses no influence whatever upon the press.... [A free-press clause was dangerous, for] that very declaration might have been construed to imply that some degree of power was given, since we undertook to define its extent."

American history followed the spirit of our Patriot forebears who believed destroying Tory presses was congruent with the liberty they were seeking in the Revolution. The importance of public opinion in the preservation of freedom of the press is often one of the most overlooked and underappreciated elements involved in the protection of that right.

The state ratifying conventions featured much rhetoric about freedom of the press but cast little illumination on its meaning. Pennsylvanians probably gave the best explanation when they suggested an amendment to the Constitution that would read, "That the people have a right to the freedom of speech, of writing and of publishing their sentiments; therefore, the freedom of the press shall not be restrained by any law of the United States."[28] Responding to questions as to the meaning of the amendment, future United States Supreme Court Justice James Wilson said it certainly would not mean absolute freedom for the press: "The idea of the liberty of the press is not carried so far as this in any country — *what is meant by the liberty of the press is that there should be no antecedent restraint upon it.*" He added that "every author is responsible when he attacks the security or welfare of the government, or the safety, character and property of the individual."[29] In this way, Wilson indicated that Americans had accepted the legal precept Sir William Blackstone first expounded in England in 1769, that "the liberty of the press is indeed essential to the nature of a free state; but this consists in laying no *previous* restraints upon publications, and not in freedom from censure for criminal matter when published."[30]

Although absent from the constitutional debates because of his assignment as ambassador to France, Thomas Jefferson, a strong proponent of freedom of the press, also believed an amendment prohibiting the federal government from interfering with the press

[28]Quoted in Schwartz, *The Bill of Rights*, 2: 658.

[29]Quoted in Levy, *Emergence of a Free Press*, 204 (emphasis included).

[30]William Blackstone, *Commentaries on the Laws of England*, 4 vols. *Of Public Wrongs* (Philadelphia, 1772), 4: 151.

would not restrict a state's right to enact libel laws. As he wrote to James Madison, "A declaration that the federal government will never restrain the presses from printing anything they please, will not take away the liability of the printers for false facts printed."[31]

Despite the uncertainty of the meaning of freedom of the press, the people wanted a Bill of Rights added, and their approval of the Constitution was based on promises to that effect. The mandate for protecting press freedom was relatively small, however. Twelve states held ratifying conventions between 1787-1788; only Virginia, New York, and North Carolina suggested a press-freedom guarantee.[32] Thus, although the Constitution was ratified and suggestions for a Bill of Rights offered, support for freedom of the press was not overwhelming. The support that existed favored freedom along with responsibility for abuses.

One thing can be said with certainty, however, about the men who wrote the Constitution: they had few compunctions about keeping their deliberations secret. They closed convention sessions to the public and adopted rules to make sure no information was leaked. They posted guards at the doors and kept no official record of debates.[33] It is easy to understand this shroud of secrecy over Independence Hall that Philadelphia summer. Delegates had convened to revise the Articles of Confederation — not to frame a new government — and the direction that the new government was taking was so dramatically different from that which already existed that the framers decided to wait until the entire document was completed and then to unveil it all at one time. Newspapers accepted the secrecy. It was common for legislative bodies to meet in secret, and printer/editors did not have today's journalistic mindset about open meetings. Most trusted the men who were serving as delegates to the convention.[34] Thus, the document that was placed before the American people for ratification came as a complete surprise to most.

THE FIRST AMENDMENT

During debates over adoption of the Constitution, Madison originally had opposed adding any Bill of Rights because he thought it was unnecessary. Realizing that public sentiment favored such amendments if the Constitution were to be ratified, however, he withdrew his opposition. Shortly after the new federal government was installed, he proposed several amendments in the House of Representatives. They were revisions of the same amendments he had argued against in the ratifying debates in Virginia. He suggested two amendments on freedom of speech and press. One read, "The people shall not be deprived or abridged of their right to speak, to write, or to publish their sentiments; and

Bill of Rights
When the Bill of Rights was sent to the states for ratification in 1789, what we know as the First Amendment today was the third in order of priority. The first two proposed amendments dealt with congressional housekeeping affairs. The states rejected the first two proposals, and amendment three became the First Amendment.

the freedom of the press, as one of the great bulwarks of liberty, shall be inviolable." The other proposed, "No State shall violate the equal rights of conscience, or the freedom of the press, or the trial by jury in criminal cases." Regarding the latter amendment, he said, "If there were any reason to restrain the Government of the United States from infringing upon these essential rights, it was equally necessary that they should be secured against the State Governments."[35] Had Congress adopted the second, constitutional guarantees of press freedom would have applied to the states immediately. As it was, it was not until the 1900s that the U.S. Supreme Court extended the First Amendment to the states.

Neither of Madison's versions emerged from Congress. In fact, the language of the First Amendment was revised several times, with the final version — using language proposed by Fisher Ames of Massachusetts and others — being a compromise between advocates in the Senate and the House. Although the House held open debates, the Senate, which drafted the final language of the Amendment, kept its proceedings secret; and its reasons for making changes are unknown. Even the records that are available provide no insight into the meaning of freedom of the press, for that topic was never discussed in debates. The language that emerged, though, is familiar to all:

Congress shall make no law respecting an establishment of reli-

[31]July 31, 1789, Julian P. Boyd, et. al., eds., *The Papers of Thomas Jefferson* (Princeton, N.J., 1950), 13: 442-3.

[32]For a discussion of the legislative history of the Bill of Rights, see David A. Anderson, "The Origins of the Press Clause," *UCLA Law Review* 130 (1983): 471.

[33]For a study of the role of secrecy in the new nation, see Daniel N. Hoffman, *Government Secrecy and the Founding Fathers: A Study in Constitutional Controls* (Westport, Conn., 1981).

[34]See Carol Sue Humphrey, "'Little Ado About Something': Philadelphia Newspapers and the Constitutional Convention," *American Journalism* 5 (1988): 63-80; and Victor Rosewater, "The Constitutional Convention in the Colonial Press," *Journalism Quarterly* 14 (1937): 364-5.

[35]U.S. Congress, House, *Annals of Congress*, 1st Cong., 1st sess., 1: 434, 435, and 755.

James Madison on Freedom of the Press

On newspapers and liberty: "Whatever facilitates a general intercourse of sentiments, as good roads, domestic commerce, a free press, and particularly a circulation of newspapers through the entire body of the people ... is favorable to liberty."

National Gazette, 1791

On press and religion: "It is to the press mankind are indebted for having dispelled the clouds which long encompassed religion, for disclosing her genuine lustre, and disseminating her salutary doctrines." Speech in Virginia Assembly, 1799

On newspaper fairness: "Could it be so arranged that every newspaper, when printed on one side should be handed over to the press of an adversary, to be printed on the other, thus presenting to every reader both sides of every question, truth would always have a fair chance. But such a remedy is not ideal." To N.P. Trist, 1828

gion, or prohibiting the free exercise thereof; or abridging the freedom of speech, or of the press; or the right of the people peaceably to assemble, and to petition the Government for a redress of grievances.

While Congress was setting up the new federal government, several states, dissatisfied with their initial constitutions, drafted new ones that included clarifications about the role of the press in society. In Pennsylvania, a new constitution drafted in 1790 said:

The printing-presses shall be free to every person who undertakes to examine the proceedings of the legislature, or any branch of government, and no law shall ever be made to restrain the right thereof. The free communication of thoughts and opinions is one of the inviolable rights of man; and every citizen may freely speak, write, and print on any subject, being responsible for the abuse of that liberty.

In that clause was found the trend of the future in state constitutions, for many states modeled their versions on it. The printing press, not the newspaper, was to be free for anyone who investigated government. Citizens had the right to share their views on government with each other; but if they abused that right, they could be held legally responsible. The Pennsylvania constitution added, "In prosecutions for the publication of papers investigating the official conduct of officers or men in a public capacity, or where the matter published is proper for public information, the truth thereof may be given in evidence; and in all indictments for libels the jury shall have the right to determine the law and the facts."[36] In this way, Pennsylvania became the first state to write

into its fundamental law the principles first debated during the Zenger case fifty-five years earlier.

Freedom of the press during the early days of the nation was clearly associated with the proper functioning of government. Leaders believed that an informed populace was necessary for the Republic to work satisfactorily — and the press made an informed citizenry possible. Some debates focused on whether by listing what press freedom included and excluded, constitutional guarantees might limit it. Concern also appeared about how state and federal protections of press freedom would mesh, although debates and correspondence made it clear that the federal Bill of Rights in no way prevented states from punishing abuses. Most participants agreed that freedom of the press meant freedom from prior restraint; no one wanted to revive the colonial licensing system. Almost everyone agreed that those who used the press should be held responsible for transgressions. Substantial agreement also existed that individuals who wanted to use the press to publish their thoughts were the ones protected under state constitutions. Press owners and operators were not specifically protected, although they obviously merited protection while using their presses to disseminate information. Because of the way in which the business of journalism would grow, however, with time they would become the chief claimants to the right of freedom of the press. Most political leaders also realized how important public opinion was in guaranteeing the press its freedom.

THE HISTORICAL DEBATE ABOUT THE MEANING OF THE PRESS CLAUSE

The imprecise language used in the early debates caused problems for subsequent generations of Americans. By the latter part of the twentieth century, just what the framers meant became very important. A battle between liberals and conservatives raged over

[36]Pennsylvania Constitution of 1790, Art. IX, sec. 7, in Francis Newton Thorpe, comp. and ed., *The Federal and State Constitutions, Colonial Charters, and Other Organic Laws of the States, Territories, and Colonies Now and Heretofore Forming the United States of America*, 17 vols. (Washington, D.C., 1909), 5: 3100.

the doctrine of original intent — over whether the First Amendment has been interpreted according to the meaning the framers intended. Conservatives argued that liberal judicial interpretations had stretched the Bill of Rights out of shape, eroded fundamental principles touching core religious and family values, and given protection to communication — for example, pornography — that the framers clearly did not intend. To safeguard the Bill of Rights against judicial activism, they argued that one needs to understand its meaning when written. Then, constitutional interpretation could return to the correct foundation rather than being based on judges' moral and political biases. Liberals, on the other hand, argued that the Constitution and Bill of Rights were living documents that used flexible eighteenth-century language to allow changes as time and circumstance demanded.

Historians have waged their own battle over the original meaning of freedom of the press.[37] At stake is the issue of whether the United States has a libertarian or limited heritage on this important right and, by implication, what sort of freedom the press possesses today. Those believing that the heritage is a limited one find most of their evidence in legislative and court records and argue that certain restrictions on press freedom were expected during the early days of the nation. They reason that the Bill of Rights clearly protected only political speech and that even that protection included the expectation that practitioners would exercise their freedom responsibly. Those who believe the tradition is a libertarian one look more at printers' statements about the wide extent of their freedom in those tumultuous times. They also view institutional journalism as a bulwark of American liberty, without which the nation never could have been founded.

Evidence amassed on both sides is impressive, and often scholars reinterpret their foes' proof to provide support for a different argument. Representatives of the institutional press have long advocated the libertarian version, seeing a long and impressive list of journalistic triumphs over attempts to suppress freedom of the press, victories that underscore the vital role of press freedom. Those who believe the heritage is a limited one are of more recent vintage and find themselves trying to overcome popular legend. Scholars on the two sides have locked horns for more than half a century and continue to grapple over the issue.

The problem, of course, focuses on separating rhetoric from reality. Were the laws reality and the printers' comments rhetoric? Or were the printers' comments reality and the laws rhetoric? Or did the truth lie somewhere in between? Obviously there were many federal and state laws on the books that could have restricted press freedom. Just as obviously, printers carried on in the pages of their newspapers as if those laws did not exist. In some cases, laws were enforced; in others, they were not. Today we can only appreciate that a considerable battle was waged over freedom of expression in our nation's early history and that the freedom that exists today was built on that early experience.

George Washington and Press Freedom
The nation's first president detested partisanship and hoped to avoid factionalism in the new government. Republican editors subjected him and his administration to so many bitter attacks, however, that he became exasperated. His reaction, combined with his distrust of the politics of immigrants, particularly of a French conspiracy, led him to support the Alien and Sedition Acts of 1798 even after he had left office. He considered the latter not a repression of press freedom but a legitimate means for the government to protect itself from serious danger.

FEDERALISTS AND REPUBLICANS

Although laws and constitutions and debates over such documents were important during the early national period, a considerable social fabric about press freedom was developing as well. Much of the activity centered around George Washington. During the partisan age of journalism, he was a target of Republican editors. He complained in private about the way the press treated him, but publicly he maintained his support of a free press to provide the information citizens needed to operate a republic. Several characteristics of today's free press emerged in his administrations (1789-1797) as well, including the freedom to criticize an incumbent president harshly without suffering retribution; the ability to obtain information about governmental activities through a vari-

[37]The foremost scholar arguing the limited tradition is Levy, *Emergence of a Free Press.* Among those arguing for a libertarian tradition are Anderson, "The Origins of the Press Clause"; and Jeffery A. Smith, *Printers and Press Freedom: The Ideology of Early American Journalism* (New York, 1988). For a discussion of the historical debate, see Wm. David Sloan and Thomas A. Schwartz, "Historians and Freedom of the Press, 1690-1801: Libertarian or Limited?" *American Journalism* 5 (1988): 159-77.

Thomas Jefferson on Freedom of the Press

On the newly proposed Constitution: "I will now tell you what I do not like. First, the omission of a Bill of Rights providing clearly ... for freedom of religion, freedom of the press...."
To James Madison, 1787

On the Alien and Sedition Acts: "I am for ... freedom of the press, and against all violations of the Constitution to silence by force and not by reason the complaints or criticisms, just or unjust, of our citizens against the conduct of their agents." *To Elbridge Gerry, 1799*

On criticism by Federalist newspapers: "The firmness with which the people have withstood the late abuses of the press, the discernment they have manifested between truth and falsehood, show that they may safely be trusted to hear everything true and false, and to form a correct judgment between them." *To John Tyler of Caroline, 1804*

On the power of states to punish newspapers for libel: "While we deny Congress has a right to control freedom of the press, we have ever asserted the right of the States and their exclusive right, to do so." *To Abigail Adams, 1804*

On the shortcomings of the press: "It is a melancholy truth, that a suppression of the press could not more completely deprive the nation of its benefits, than is done by its abandoned prostitution to falsehood. Nothing can be believed which is seen in a newspaper. Truth itself becomes suspicious by being put into that polluted vehicle.... I really look with commiseration over the body of my fellow citizens, who, reading newspapers, live and die in the belief, that they have known something of what has been passing in the world in their time." *To John Norvell, 1807*

ety of sources, including leaks from authorities; and the ability of a president to manage the press, as Washington himself leaked a copy of his farewell address to a friendly printer in Philadelphia.[38]

Some editors also discovered the value of news and attempted to attend legislative sessions, which traditionally had been closed in Europe and in the United States. Thus, there were repeated contests with Congress about access to its sessions. The House quickly opened its meetings, but sessions of the Senate remained closed for several years.[39]

Finally, the press' ability to interject itself into foreign affairs became clear. Although problems with the French soon would become of overwhelming importance, the continuing diplomatic crisis during Washington's adminstrations involved the British. During these difficulties and Washington's attempt to secure a treaty to resolve them, an official document was leaked to the press for the first time. A Republican senator gave the text of the Jay Treaty to Benjamin Franklin Bache, who rushed it into print. Although upset by the breach of security, Washington had no recourse against Bache. Congress, which could have been persuaded to launch an investigation, was not in session at the time.[40]

Newspapers during the early days of the Republic were tied closely to political factions, and their publishers and patrons test-

ed the limits of their freedom. The newspaper war between the proponents of the visions of America's future as advocated by Alexander Hamilton and Thomas Jefferson continued unabated as the Adams administration (1797-1801) began. Fears increased about the dangers the French connections of Vice President Jefferson and his supporters posed. The French Revolution of 1789, which Republicans welcomed, had, by 1793, turned bloody. The revolutionaries suspended most of their early democratic reforms and employed the guillotine to eliminate thousands of opponents. Problems with the French extended into North America, where they were trying to re-establish a presence by getting the Spanish to give them Louisiana and the Floridas, and trying both to win Quebec away from the British and to rebuild their relationship with the Indians beyond the Appalachian Mountains.

President Adams tried to win peace by sending a special mission to France in 1797-1798. The attempt proved futile. The French diplomats tried to extort money from the United States. If the American negotiators did not come up with it, the French threatened to unleash the French party in America, the Republicans, on the Federalists. The underlying threat was a bloody revolution similar to the one in France. The sordid situation was publicized widely as the XYZ Affair, named after the anonymous French envoys; and war fever ran high. Suspicion of the Republicans reached a peak, and Federalists tried to make political capital from the affair.

Federalists viewed the Republicans as the country's enemies

[38]James E. Pollard, *The Presidents and the Press* (New York, 1947; reprint, New York, 1973), 1-35.
[39]See pp. 90-1 of this book for an account of efforts to gain access to Congressional sessions.
[40]Everette E. Dennis, "Stolen Peace Treaties and the Press: Two Case Studies," *Journalism History* 2 (1975): 6-14.

and determined to destroy their newspapers and eliminate Republicans as a political force. The newspapers in France had, after all, played an important part in bringing down the monarchy. The newspapers in the colonies had been vital in destroying the relationship with Great Britain. History could repeat itself, and Republican newspapers could help destroy the new Republic. Federalists also wanted to keep individuals whom they viewed as dangerous aliens or immigrant radicals — including a number of Republican editors — from influencing American politics. Thus they decided the solution was to suppress, first, the Republican newspapers and then the Republicans themselves.

Such a solution seems unrealistic today; but in the late eighteenth century, political leaders had not learned that parties could co-exist without their differences leading to revolution. In fact, the only major transition of power from one political faction to an opposing group in American history had been the Revolution. The first peaceful transition of power from one political faction to another would not come until 1800, and its impact was so far-reaching that historians call it the "Second American Revolution."

Federalists were wrong about the intentions of Republicans. The latter were not attempting to subvert the Constitution. If anything, they wanted to preserve it for the anticipated presidential bid of Jefferson in 1800, which perhaps frightened Federalists more than any dangers from the French. Republican newspapers, although vocal, were in the minority and were weaker than their Federalist competitors, which had advantages ranging from use of the mails granted to government-appointed postmasters to incomes from government printing contracts. But the realities of the situation did not stop Federalists from pushing through Congress legislation intended to silence dangerous critics.

THE ALIEN AND SEDITION ACTS

In proposing the Alien and Sedition Acts, Federalists contended that they were acting to meet a serious foreign threat within the United States. The legislative package consisted of four laws: a naturalization law increasing the residency requirement for citizenship from five years to fourteen years, an alien enemies law allowing deportation or imprisonment of aliens during wartime, an alien friends act allowing the president to engage in selective deportation of undesirable aliens, and a sedition act aimed at curtailing criticism of the government. The Sedition Act was all-encompassing:

> That if any person shall write, print, utter or publish, or shall cause or procure to be written, printed, uttered or published, or shall knowingly and willingly assist or aid in writing, printing, uttering or publishing any false, scandalous and malicious writing against the government of the United States, or either house of the Congress of the United States, or the President of the United States, with intent to defame said government, or to bring them, or either of them, into contempt or disrepute; or to excite against them, the hatred of the good people of the United

THE PROVIDENTIAL DETECTION

Partisan Suspicion

As animosity built up in the 1790s, Federalists feared that Republicans sympathized with the radicalism of the French Revolution. They published this cartoon in response to Thomas Jefferson's statement to a French official that the Federalists favored "despotism." Such suspicions provided one reason behind the Federalists' repressive Sedition Act of 1798.

States, or to stir up sedition within the United States, or to excite any unlawful combinations therein, for opposing or resisting any law of the United States, or any act of the President of the United States, done in pursuance of any such law, or of the powers in him vested by the constitution of the United States, or to resist, oppose, or defeat any such law or act, or to aid, encourage, or abet any hostile designs of any foreign nation against the United States, their people or government, then such person, being thereof convicted before any court of the United States having jurisdiction thereof, shall be punished by a fine not exceeding two thousand dollars, and by imprisonment not exceeding two years.[41]

The political motivations of the law were clear. The act's provisions protected the sections of the federal government that the Federalists dominated and pointedly excluded Vice President Jefferson. The law also provided for trial by jury for offenders with truth as a defense and with the jurors allowed to determine both the law and the fact of the matter before them, thus putting into federal legislation the principles of libel law argued in the Zenger case. The provision, however, provided little protection. The journalism of the day liberally mixed news and opinion, and most prosecutions under the law involved opinions. Proving the truthfulness of opinion was impossible.

[41]*Statutes at Large*, 1: 596-7.

Major Prosecutions Under the Alien and Sedition Acts 1798-1800

Anthony Haswell
Vermont Gazette
sentenced to 2 months,
fined $200 plus court costs

Thomas Adams
Boston Independent Chronicle
arrested but not tried because of illness
Abijah Adams (brother)
sentenced to 30 days in jail

Charles Holt
New London Bee
sentenced to 3 months, $200 fine

Thomas Cooper
Northumberland Gazette
sentenced to 6 months, fined $400

Ann Greenleaf
New York Argus
indicted 1799 but charges dropped
after she sold the paper

William Duane
Philadelphia Aurora
indicted & arrested several times
but evaded jail

David Frothingham
New York Argus
sentenced to 4 months, $100 fine

James Callender
Richmond Examiner
sentenced to 9 months, fined $200

Luther Baldwin's Sedition

Twenty-five Republicans were arrested under the Sedition Act. Most were editors. The unfortunate Luther Baldwin was indicted, however, for remarks he made at a parade honoring President John Adams. The Philadelphia *Aurora* reported that an observer, seeing the cannon fire after Adams had passed, told Baldwin, "There goes the President and they are firing at his a- -." Baldwin, a little inebriated, replied "that he did not care if they fired thro' his a- -: Then [a Federalist] exclaims ... that is seditious." Other papers picked up the story, one of which asked, "Can the most enthusiastic Federalists or Tories suppose that those who are opposed to them would feel any gratification in firing at such a disgusting target as the a- - of John Adams?"

Federalists almost unanimously lined up in favor of the Alien and Sedition Acts. Although President Adams later said that he had never recommended the Sedition Act to Congress, he willingly used it to prosecute opponents. Alexander Hamilton, who was out of government at the time, found initial proposals too harsh, arguing to his allies that some of the sections might make martyrs out of Republicans. He approved, however, of the amended act as eventually adopted. George Washington, now in retirement, found within the legislation new hope that the nation would survive the divisiveness brought on by the partisans of France that he so feared.

The only leading Federalist who registered opposition was John Marshall, future chief justice of the Supreme Court and one of the three delegates to France whose involvement in the XYZ Affair sparked the initial calls for anti-sedition legislation. He stated his opposition in a campaign tract issued in an effort to win a Virginia congressional seat. He believed that the legislation was "useless" and would "create unnecessary discontents and jealousies at a time when our very existence, as a nation, may depend on our union." He pledged to oppose renewal of the legislation

should he be elected to Congress.[42]

Congressional debates on the bills brought into sharper focus just how Americans interpreted "freedom of the press." The Federalists saw within the proposals no dangers to freedom of the press. In fact, they argued that the legislation extended freedom because it would purge newspapers of false and malicious comments. As Harrison Gray Otis of Massachusetts pointed out in the House of Representatives, "Every independent Government has a right to preserve and defend itself against injuries and outrages which endanger its existence." Freedom of the press "is nothing more than the liberty of writing, publishing, and speaking one's thoughts, under the condition of being answerable to the injured party, whether it be the Government or an individual, for false, malicious, and seditious expressions, whether spoken or written." The Alien and Sedition Acts, he said, would simply punish "licentiousness and sedition" and would not be a prior restraint on the press, which was forbidden.[43] Such an argument for the right of government to preserve itself would not vanish from American history. It was heard again during debates over the adoption of restrictive measures during World War I and during the enactment of laws limiting the freedom of Communists in the 1950s.

Another Federalist, Representative James Bayard of Delaware, stated that the purpose of the Alien and Sedition Acts was to try to influence public opinion. Neither party appealed to the masses, but Republicans trusted the "middling" classes to make the correct decisions; Federalists believed that only the "right sort" of people were capable of running a government. The only way a republic based on popular sovereignty could survive, they believed, was by guiding public opinion, for, as Bayard said:

> This government ... depends for its existence upon the good will of the people. That good will is maintained by their good opinion. But, how is that good opinion to be preserved, if wicked and unprincipled men, men of inordinate and desperate ambition, are allowed to state facts to the people which are not true, which they know at the time to be false, and which are stated with the criminal intention of bringing the Government into disrepute among the people? This was falsely and deceitfully stealing the public opinion; it was a felony of the worst and most dangerous nature.[44]

The majority of the nation's newspapers, which were Federalist, strongly supported the Alien and Sedition Acts, seeing nothing within their language as a threat to press freedom.

THE REPUBLICAN RESPONSE

Republicans viewed the legislation and the abilities of the people differently than Federalists did. Albert Gallatin, who would become secretary of the treasury under Jefferson, argued that "the

[42]John Marshall campaign tract, 20 September 1798, in *John Marshall: Major Opinions and Other Writings*, John P. Roche, ed. (Indianapolis, 1967), 32.

[43]U.S. Congress, House, *Annals of Congress*, 5th Cong., 2nd sess., 8: 2146, 2148, and 2149.

[44]Ibid., 3rd sess., 9: 2960.

Bacon-Face Samuel Chase
Although possessing a keen and respected legal mind, Justice Samuel Chase became notorious for his high-handedness during trials under the Sedition Act. The Republican editor Benjamin Bache wrote that no one could "mistake ... the bacon face of old Chase for the face of justice." Chase's violent temperament created personal enemies even of those who shared his ideology.

bill was intended to punish solely writings of a political nature" and was aimed at preventing Republicans from putting their views before the American people in an election year. "Laws against writings of this kind had uniformly been one of the most powerful engines used by tyrants to prevent the diffusion of knowledge," he added.[45] John Nicholas, a Republican representative from Virginia, was even more pointed in tying the legislation to the 1800 elections: "The people have no other means of examining their [leaders'] conduct but by means of the press, and an unrestrained investigation through them of the conduct of the Government," he said. "Indeed, the heart and life of a free Government, is a free press." Then he added that to restrict the press would be to destroy the elective principle by taking away the information necessary to election and that there would be no difference between such a deprivation and a total denial of the right of election, but in the degree of usurpation.[46]

Although Federalists were able to obtain indictments and convictions of Republican newspaper editors, their main target, Jefferson, remained out of reach. He had long had a personal policy against writing for newspapers, a practice that protected him dur-

ing the two years in which the Alien and Sedition Acts were in effect. So the Federalists settled for actions against leading Republican editors in an effort to silence opposition commentary.

The Republican press carried on as if the laws had never been enacted, and federal courts so zealously enforced the laws that questions arose about whether defendants received fair trials. Judges broadly interpreted the seditious libel formula established in the law to preclude even ordinary political commentary. In all, there were twenty-five arrests, fourteen indictments, eleven trials, and ten convictions under the Sedition Act, eight of which were related to newspaper publications. The legislation and the results of court cases did nothing to discourage Republican newspapers. If anything, editors went to greater degrees of disrespect and criticism of Federalist office holders. Imprisoned Republican editors had the enforced luxury of additional time for writing, and they used it well. As Zenger before them, they became martyrs to a cause and thus built additional support for themselves and their patron, Jefferson.

Republican leaders were not idle either. They considered themselves locked in a struggle for survival and launched a full-scale attack on the Alien and Sedition Acts, taking their cues from Madison and Jefferson, whose Virginia and Kentucky Resolutions provided the philosophical cornerstone for criticism of the laws. Although the Resolutions were primarily an argument for the right of states to nullify federal legislation with which they disagreed — and later would support John C. Calhoun's nullification theory during sectional conflicts leading to the Civil War — they did mention the importance of communication in a free society. Madison noted that the Alien and Sedition Acts were dangerous because they were "levelled against the right of freely examining public characters and measures, and of free communication among the people thereon, which has ever been justly deemed the only effectual guardian of every other right."[47] Jefferson raised the question of the Alien and Sedition Acts violating the First Amendment, which prohibited the federal government from taking action against the press.[48]

The drafting of the Resolutions did give Madison a chance to think about the meaning of freedom of the press, and from his reflections came a remarkably modern statement about the problems inherent in this complicated right. Everyone, Madison said, agreed that freedom of the press meant freedom from prior restraint. But, he asked, did not laws "inflicting penalties on printed publications ... have a similar effect with a law authorizing a previous restraint on them?" It seemed odd, he said, to allow someone to make a statement and then punish the person for speaking. Madison recognized that abuse of free press was likely at times, but "it is better to leave a few of its noxious branches to their luxuriant growth, than, by pruning them away, to injure the vigour of those yielding the proper fruits." Such a policy was the best one to follow because "to the press alone, chequered as it is with abuses,

---

[45]Ibid., 8: 2162.
[46]Ibid., 8: 2162 and 2144.

[47]"Resolutions of 1798," Gaillard Hunt, ed., *The Writings of James Madison*, 19 vols. (New York), 6 (1790-1802), 328-9.
[48]"Resolutions Relative to the Alien and Sedition Laws," Albert Ellery Bergh, ed., *The Writings of Thomas Jefferson*, 20 vols. (Washington, D.C., 1905), 17: 381-2.

Harry Croswell
Harry Croswell, editor of the *Wasp* in Hudson, New York, brought down the ire of Republican politicians when he reprinted a charge from another Federalist newspaper that Thomas Jefferson had paid a Republican editor to criticize John Adams. Jefferson agreed with some of his supporters that the government should make an example of Croswell by prosecuting him for seditious libel. Although the trial court found Croswell guilty, the trial led to important changes enlarging press freedom. This portrait was made years later, after he had become a priest in the Anglican Church.

the world is indebted for all the triumphs which have been gained by reason and humanity over error and oppression." Counted among those triumphs was the successful revolution from Great Britain, which, Madison said, never would have occurred if a sedition act had been in place. Then, he added a practical political argument. "A number of important elections will take place while the act is in force," he noted, and "will not those in power derive an undue advantage for continuing themselves in it, which, by impairing the right of election, endangers the blessings of the Government founded on it?"[49]

Republicans' fears about the effect of the laws on the election of 1800 were not confirmed. Jefferson became the third president of the United States, although his margin over John Adams was a narrow six electoral votes. The Alien and Sedition Acts expired, and Jefferson pardoned anyone convicted under them and still serving prison terms. The legislation had stirred a public debate on press freedom. Recognition that conflicting voices could exist

without the Republic crumbling became an important milestone in the development of freedom of the press.

Although the constitutionality of the Alien and Sedition laws never was tested, some historians believe the Supreme Court would have upheld them. During the controversy, a number of members of the Court said Congress had the power to enact such legislation.[50] The same decision was reached on the sedition laws enacted during World War I. Foreign dangers long have been seen as endowing Congress with extraordinary powers to act, even to the extent of limiting First Amendment freedoms.

JEFFERSON, HAMILTON, AND PRESS FREEDOM

Concluding a discussion on press liberty with a statement that Jefferson, schooled in the value of a free press, acted differently than his predecessors in dealing with opposition newspapers during his administration (1801-1809) would be ideal. However, he only believed in protecting freedom of the press from federal intervention. As with his contemporaries, he believed strongly in the restriction of the press on the state level and argued in 1803 for restoring the press' credibility by "a few prosecutions of the most prominent offenders" under state law. Partisanship influenced his views on press freedom. Federalist newspapers had so defiled the press, he argued, that "the people have learnt that nothing in a newspaper is to be believed. This is a dangerous state of things, and the press ought to be restored to its credibility if possible." He did not object to the Republican press, which was just as partisan and scurrilous as the Federalist. Just as the Federalists argued that the Alien and Sedition Acts really would not violate freedom of the press, so, too, Jefferson thought that action against Federalist publications would simply serve to punish them properly for their partisanship. He did not want "a general prosecution, for that would look like persecution: but a selected one," thinking such an effort "would have a wholesome effect in restoring the integrity of the presses."[51]

In fact, Jefferson ended the critical early period of development of freedom of the press locked in another conflict with Alexander Hamilton. The cause was a prosecution in 1804 of Harry Croswell, editor of a Federalist newspaper, *The Wasp*, in Hudson, New York. He had made the mistake of reprinting some criticism of Jefferson published initially in the *New York Evening Post*. Jefferson decided that Croswell's republication was an example of the licentiousness of the Federalist press that should be punished, and he supported a state case against Croswell for seditious libel. Hamilton defended Croswell on appeal; and, although he lost the case, he delivered a classic statement of freedom of the press:

> The liberty of the Press consists, in my idea, in publishing the truth, from good motives and for justifiable ends, though it reflect on government, on magistrates, or individuals. If it not be

[49]Report on the Resolutions, Hunt, *The Writings of James Madison*, 6: 386, 389, and 397-8.

[50]Edward G. Hudon, *Freedom of Speech and Press in America* (New York, 1963), 53.
[51]Jefferson to Thomas McKean, 19 February 1803, Andrew A. Lipscomb, editor-in-chief, *The Writings of Thomas Jefferson* (Washington, 1904-1905), 9: 449, 451, and 452.

THE

SPEECHES

AT FULL LENGTH

OF

MR. VAN NESS, MR. CAINES,

THE ATTORNEY-GENERAL, Mr. HARRISON,

AND

GENERAL HAMILTON,

IN THE

GREAT CAUSE

OF THE

PEOPLE,

AGAINST

HARRY CROSWELL,

ON AN INDICTMENT FOR A

LIBEL

ON

THOMAS JEFFERSON,

PRESIDENT OF THE UNITED STATES.

New-York;

PRINTED BY G. & R. WAITE, NO. 64, MAIDEN-LANE.

1804.

[Copy right secured.]

Alexander Hamilton and the Croswell Case
When President Thomas Jefferson encouraged a libel prosecution of editor Harry Croswell, the Federalist Alexander Hamilton agreed to serve as one of Croswell's attorneys. The Federalists' intellectual leader, Hamilton enunciated some of America's most insightful ideas on the nature of constitutional government. He also saw clearly the press' role in a democracy and, in the Croswell trial, argued effectively for the right to criticize government. Although the court found Croswell guilty, Hamilton's contention that truth should be accepted as a defense gained wide approval following publication of the arguments in book form. As a result, state governments began adopting the principle.

allowed, it excludes the privilege of canvassing men, and our rulers. This is impossible without the right of looking to men. To say that measures can be discussed, and that there shall be no bearing on those, who are the authors of those measures cannot be done. The very end and reason of discussion would be destroyed.... In speaking thus for the Freedom of the Press, I do not say there ought to be an unbridled license; or that the characters of men who are good, will naturally tend eternally to support themselves. I do not stand here to say that no shackles are to be laid on this license.... I contend for the liberty of publishing truth, with good motives and for justifiable ends, even though it reflect on government, magistrates, or private persons. I con-

tend for it under the restraint of our tribunal. When this is exceeded, let them interpose and punish.[52]

Hamilton lost the case because New York law did not protect the kind of commentary he was defending. The state legislature, so swayed by his argument, though, changed the state's libel law to allow truth to be admitted as evidence and to authorize the jury to determine both the law and the fact of the matter. Thus, New York, the home of Zenger, finally permitted printers to criticize governmental officials. The ability of those using the press to comment about their leaders had been one of the first uses for the press, whether the leaders were spiritual or temporal, royal or colonial, Federalist or Republican. And this freedom to criticize leaders has remained the heart and soul of the American press system regardless of changes over the years.

By 1804, then, the foundation of freedom of the press was well established. It consisted of freedom of individuals to use a press to print their thoughts. Generally, people were given greater freedom when they were discussing public officials; but, in all cases, they were held responsible for the abuse of the press. Federal authorities, the Alien and Sedition Acts notwithstanding, were forbidden to act against the press. State legislatures, however, could enact laws to ensure that those using the press acted responsibly. The principle that freedom of the press meant the absence of prior restraint on publication also was generally accepted.

As the nineteenth century dawned, Americans were beginning to believe that multiple views could be tolerated on the same topic and that those views should be protected through the principle of freedom of the press. This notion, crucial as it is to a true meaning of freedom of the press, did not really become embedded in American thinking until the abolitionist crisis of the 1830s. Despite America's tradition of freedom, tolerance for dissident views was not one of the strongest pillars of its free-press heritage.

PRESS FREEDOMS SINCE 1804

The impact of the events of 1690 to 1804, especially the adoption of the First Amendment, is virtually incalculable. No one can say how the American media might have developed and performed had the nation not had the constitutional guarantee of freedom of expression, but it is fairly certain that things could have been very different. Even though the courts did not apply the First Amendment to the states until the twentieth century, most states included a similar guarantee of press freedom in their constitutions, and — even though the idea that the press should be completely free of all restraint never gained much support — the commitment to freedom enshrined in the First Amendment established a strong philosophical foundation.

Throughout the nineteenth century, the press used America's developing judicial system to expand its freedoms, strengthen its legal protections, and gain access to public records and trials. The

[52]*The Law Practice of Alexander Hamilton*, Julius Goebel, Jr., ed., 5 vols. (New York, 1964), 1: 809-10.

ability to inspect public documents is a buttress of America's press freedoms, and courts began to define what was – and what was not – considered to be a public document in the 1800s. As a result, state, county, city, and town records began to enter the public domain in vast numbers. Journalists also won greater access to documents as courts began overturning state laws that had allowed access by only those people who had a proven interest in a particular record.

The courts generally recognized the press' access right to trials, but it was not universal. In 1842 a Pennsylvania circuit judge declared that "no person will be allowed to come within the bar of the court for the purpose of reporting, except on condition of suspending all publication till after the trial is concluded."[53] Reporters did not challenge the ruling. However, barring reporters from judicial proceedings was not the prevailing view, and other courts supported a citizen's right to view trials. U.S. Supreme Court Justice Joseph Story commented on the issue in 1833, concluding that the "trial is always public."[54]

Contempt by publication remained a constant legal threat. If a judge believed a newspaper article impugned the integrity of the court, threatened the administration of justice, or disrupted an active trial, he could charge, convict, and sentence the author with a fine, jail, or both. Congress placed strict limits on the federal judiciary's contempt authority in 1831, but the same standards did not apply to state court systems until 1941.

Journalists had little, if any, protection against revealing confidential sources. Courts, Congress, and state legislatures often held them in contempt for refusing to divulge the sources of their articles. However, a breakthrough occurred in Maryland in 1896. John Morris, a reporter for the *Baltimore Sun*, had been issued a grand jury subpoena regarding one of his published reports. He refused to divulge his sources and spent the next five days in jail. That action prompted the *Sun* to lead a statewide campaign seeking legislative protection for reporters. Two months later, the state adopted the country's first shield law for journalists.[55] It stated:

> No person engaged in, connected with, or employed on a newspaper or journal shall be compelled to disclose in any legal proceeding or trial, or before any committee of the Legislature or elsewhere, the source of any news or information procured or obtained by him for or published in the newspaper on and in which he is engaged, connected with, or employed.[56]

Maryland's law codified a reporter's protection against being forced to reveal a source by threat of fine or imprisonment. Until then, that "right" generally had been unrecognized by statute, for

it was considered more of an issue of personal or professional honor.

Throughout the nineteenth century, the First Amendment applied only to the federal government and not to the states.[57] However, after the Fourteenth Amendment was ratified in 1868, courts began to interpret its "Due Process Clause" as a guarantee that states could not infringe upon an individual's constitutionally protected liberties, including those contained in the First Amendment. Still, it was not until 1925, in the case of *Gitlow v. New York*, that the U.S. Supreme Court ruled that the Amendment did, indeed, apply to the states.[58]

RECOMMENDED READINGS

BOOKS

Blagden, Cyprian. *The Stationers Company*. London, 1960. The Stationers Company was responsible for enforcing licensing provisions in early England.

Blanchard, Margaret A. *Revolutionary Sparks: Freedom of Expression in Modern America*. New York, 1992. The author provides a comprehensive history of freedom of speech and press from the 1870s to the Reagan presidency.

Brant, Irving. *The Bill of Rights*. Indianapolis, Ind., 1965. This discussion of all parts of the Bill of Rights emphasizes freedom of speech and freedom of the press.

Cash, Arthur H. *John Wilkes: The Scandalous Father of Civil Liberty*. New Haven, Conn., 2006. John Wilkes promoted expansion of press freedoms and civil liberties during the latter half of the eighteenth century, and he became a folk hero in both England and America.

Chenery, William L. *Freedom of the Press*. New York, 1955 (rev. ed., Westport, Conn., 1977). The tradition in early America was one of freedom of expression, with the people fighting against conservative, repressive government to attain and maintain freedom. Chenery, covering major episodes such as the Zenger trial, Alien and Sedition Acts, Jefferson's writings, etc., uses history to argue for freedom in the 1950s.

Cheslau, Irving G. *John Peter Zenger and "The New-York Weekly Journal"; A Historical Study*. New York, 1952. The trial, although a milestone in American freedom, did not establish a legal precedent and "did not sweep out the rigors of the common law" of libel.

Copeland, David A. *The Idea of a Free Press: The Enlightenment and Its Unruly Legacy*. Evanston, Ill., 2006. During four centuries of British and American ideas on press freedom, early clashes involved the right to publish about religion. Eventually, such clashes spread to include freedom in publishing about political matters.

Cornwell, Nancy C. *Freedom of the Press: Rights and Liberties under the Law*. Santa Barbara, Calif., 2004. The U.S. judicial system has struggled throughout history to balance freedom of the press with a host of competing rights, beginning with the abolitionist press of the antebellum and Civil War era.

Curtis, Michael Kent. *Free Speech, "The People's Darling Privilege": Stuggles for Freedom of Expression in American History*. Durham, N. C., 2000. This account looks at episodes involving freedom of expression from the beginning of the colonies through the adoption of the Fourteenth Amendment after the Civil War.

Duniway, Clyde Augustus. *The Development of Freedom of the Press in Massachusetts*. Cambridge, Mass., 1906. Duniway gives a detailed treatment of the development of the press in this most important part of the American continent through the early nineteenth century.

Eldridge, Larry D. *A Distant Heritage: The Growth of Free Speech in Early America*. New York and London, 1994. Eldridge contests Leonard Levy's theory on repression of free speech, concluding that "colonists experienced a dramatic expansion of their freedom to criticize government and its officials across the seventeenth century."

---

[53]*United States v. Holmes*, 26 Fed. Cases 360 (1842).

[54]Joseph Story, *Commentaries on the Constitution of the United States* 662 (1833), quoted in Robert Anthony, "Constitutional Law: Qualified Right of Access to Criminal Trials Recognized," *University of Florida Law Review* 33:2 (Winter 1981): 274.

[55]Maurice Van Gerpen, *Privileged Communication and the Press: The Citizen's Right to Know Versus the Law's Right to Confidential News Source Privilege* (Westport, Connecticut: Greenwood Press, 1979), 127.

[56]Maryland, Laws 1896, Chap. 249, cited in Fredrick Seaton Siebert, *The Rights and Privileges of the Press* (New York: Appleton-Century-Crofts, 1934), 100.

[57]In *Barron v. City of Baltimore*, 32 U.S. 243, an 1833 case, the U.S. Supreme Court ruled specifically that the First Amendment did not apply to the states.

[58]*Gitlow v. New York*, 268 U.S. 652 (1925).

Epps, Garrett. *Freedom of the Press: The First Amendment: Its Constitutional History and the Contemporary Debate*. Amherst, N.Y., 2008. This general survey covers press freedom from Milton to the present. It reprints selections from court decisions and essays by such people as Jefferson. The American press is the freest in the world.

Gleason, Timothy W. *The Watchdog Concept: The Press and the Courts in Nineteenth-Century America*. Ames, Iowa, 1990. The press should serve as a guardian against governmental abuses of power.

Hudon, Edward G. *Freedom of Speech and Press in America*. Washington, 1963. This study attempts to establish a historical basis for the libertarian belief in the need for freedom of expression in a complex society. It is a well-documented study of "the British law of speech and press as it existed in England and colonial America prior to the revolution."

Humphrey, Carol Sue. *The Press of the Young Republic, 1783-1833*. Westport, Conn., 1996. This book's chapter on the Alien and Sedition Acts is especially good.

Knudson, Jerry W. *Jefferson and the Press: Crucible of Liberty*. Columbia, S.C., 2006. Jefferson was inconsistent in his support of press freedom.

Konkle, Burton A. *The Life of Andrew Hamilton, 1676-1741, "The Day-Star of the American Revolution."* Philadelphia, 1941. Chapters 11-14 focus on the Zenger trial. For his service to press freedom, Gouverneur Morris called Hamilton "the day-star of the American Revolution."

Levy, Leonard W. *Emergence of a Free Press*. New York, 1985. This detailed description of the development of press freedom in America is a revision of Levy's landmark work, *Freedom of Speech and Press in Early American History: Legacy of Suppression*, published in 1960.

—. *Jefferson and Civil Liberties: The Darker Side*. 1963; reprint, New York, 1973. Levy's chapter on Jefferson's relationship with the press indicates his willingness to curtail its freedom in certain circumstances.

Martin, Robert W. T. *The Free and Open Press: The Founding of American Democratic Press Liberty, 1640-1800*. New York, 2001. English thinking on the press served as the underpinning for American concepts of press freedom.

Miller, John C. *Crisis in Freedom: The Alien and Sedition Acts*. Boston, 1951. Miller's book is a brief but readable history of the Alien and Sedition Acts.

Mott, Frank Luther. *Jefferson and the Press*. Baton Rouge, 1943. Mott, the journalism historian, provides an admiring look at Jefferson's record on press freedom.

Rutherford, Livingston. *John Peter Zenger, His Press, His Trial, and a Bibliography of Zenger Imprints*. New York, 1904. This standard biography of Zenger includes a bibliography of works on his trial, issues of the *Journal*, and publications by Zenger.

Rutland, Robert A. *The Birth of the Bill of Rights, 1776-1791*. Chapel Hill, N.C., 1955. Rutland traces the factors leading to the adoption of the Bill of Rights.

Schuyler, Livingston. *The Liberty of the Press in the American Colonies Before the Revolutionary War. With Particular Reference to Conditions in the Royal Colony of New York*. New York, 1905. Schuyler's early account provides a good treatment of the relationship between colonial authorities and those using the press.

Siebert, Frederick S. *Freedom of the Press in England, 1476-1776*. Urbana, Ill., 1952. This account is the most widely accepted discussion of the free-press heritage of Great Britain.

Sloan, Wm. David, and Julie Hedgepeth Williams. *The Early American Press, 1690-1783*. Westport, Conn., 1994. The treatments of Puritan ideas of press freedom and the chapters on the Zenger trial and the Stamp Act crisis are especially valuable.

Smith, James M. *Freedom's Fetters: The Alien and Sedition Laws and Civil Liberties*. Ithaca, N.Y., 1956. Smith provides a detailed account of the Alien and Sedition Act controversy.

Smith, Jeffery A. *Printers and Press Freedom: The Ideology of Early American Journalism*. New York, 1988. Smith examines the development of the free-press heritage in the context of the intellectual and political climate of eighteenth-century America.

---. *War and Press Freedom: The Problem of Prerogative Power*. New York, 1999. The Constitution gave the government no extraordinary authority to control the press during wartime. As a result, officials have claimed a "higher law" of survival to limit the news media when the United States has been at war.

ARTICLES

Allis, Frederick S., Jr. "Boston and the Alien and Sedition Laws." *Boston Society, Proceedings* (1951): 25-51. The reaction of Federalists in Massachusetts to the Kentucky and Virginia resolutions against the Sedition Act showed "little sympathy for this Republican nonsense." They favored strict enforcement.

Anderson, David A. "The Origin of the Press Clause." *UCLA Law Review* 30 (1983): 456-541. The author examines the background of the press clause in the Bill of Rights in an attempt to discover its meaning.

Anderson, Frank M. "The Enforcement of the Alien and Sedition Laws." *Annual Report of the American Historical Association* (1912): 113-26. High Federalist officials were energetic in enforcing the laws. Republican charges of unfairness were numerous. Juries were packed, judges interpreted the acts favorably in accord with Federalist intent, and the deportment of some judges was questionable.

Baldasty, Gerald J. "Toward an Understanding of the First Amendment: Boston Newspapers, 1782-1791." *Journalism History* 3 (1976): 25-30, 32. Newspaper printers defined the right to freedom of the press as the right to criticize public officials rather than as a particular legal right existing at the time.

Berns, Walter. "Freedom of the Press and the Alien and Sedition Laws: A Reappraisal," 109-59 in *Supreme Court Review*. Chicago, 1970. "The men principally responsible for the development of liberal law of free speech and press ... were the Federalists Alexander Hamilton and James Kent who were able to do this because, unlike Jefferson and his colleagues and successors, they were not inhibited by an attachment to the institution of slavery."

Buel, Richard, Jr. "Freedom of the Press in Revolutionary America: The Evolution of Libertarianism, 1760-1820," in Bernard Bailyn and John Hench, eds., *The Press and the American Revolution* (Worcester, Mass., 1980), 59-98. Although there were many obstacles to absolute freedom, early Americans viewed freedom as a good ideology — but they believed that freedom should be used for the public good.

Buranelli, Vincent. "Peter Zenger's Editor." *American Quarterly* 7 (Summer 1955): 174-81. The lawyer James Alexander played a key role in the New York *Weekly Journal* and the Zenger trial. Zenger's fame rightfully "grows with the years." The *Weekly Journal*, directed and edited by Alexander, was "the great spokesman for freedom, attempting to educate its readers into the meaning of the concept, and at the same time giving a practical demonstration of the concept in action."

Carroll, Thomas F. "Freedom of Speech and the Press in the Federalist Period: The Sedition Act." *Michigan Law Review* 18 (1920): 615-51. Federalists believed Congress had the right to prohibit publications that interfered with the government in the exercise of its constitutional duties.

Copeland, David A. "The Zenger Trial." In *Profiles in Journalistic Courage*, edited by Robert Giles, Robert W. Snyder and Lisa DeLisle. New Brunswick, N.J., 2001. Though Zenger published the *Weekly Journal* at considerable personal danger, his trial was more about overthrowing corrupt government officials than about freedom of the press.

Covert, Cathy. "Passion Is Ye Prevailing Motive: The Feud Behind the Zenger Case." *Journalism Quarterly* 50 (1973): 3-10. James Alexander developed his ideas of press freedom because of his feud with Gov. William Cosby. His concepts of press freedom — which became important to the American ideology of press freedom — were developed for their usefulness in political battle.

Fisher, Joshua Francis. "Andrew Hamilton, Esq., of Pennsylvania." *Pennsylvania Magazine of History and Biography* 16 (1892): 1-27. Hamilton was "one of the earliest and boldest asserters of the liberty of Speech and Writing" and was preeminent "in the enunciation of the now universally accepted doctrine of the law of libel."

Grotta, Gerald L. "Philip Freneau's Crusade for Open Sessions of the U.S. Senate." *Journalism Quarterly* 48 (1971): 667-71. Grotta provides a brief review of Freneau's efforts to open the Senate to journalists.

Heming, Thomas J. "A Scandalous, Malicious and Seditious Libel." *American Heritage* 19:1 (December 1967): 22-27, 100-06. Although brief, this is one of the few narratives of the Croswell case.

Humphrey, Carol Sue. "'That Bulwark of Our Liberty': Massachusetts Printers and the Issue of a Free Press, 1783-1788." *Journalism History* 14 (1987): 34-8. In the face of attempts by the state government to limit freedom of the press, Massachusetts printers "praised the benefits of a free press and supported the removal of all restrictions."

Huxford, Gary. "The English Libertarian Tradition in the Colonial Newspaper." *Journalism Quarterly* 45 (1968): 677-86. The author traces the influence of "Cato" (John Trenchard and Thomas Gordon) and other British Libertarian writers, through the first half of the eighteenth century, on American writers.

Jenkins, David. "The Sedition Act of 1798 and the Incorporation of Seditious Libel into First Amendment Jurisprudence." *American Journal of Legal History* 45:2 (2001): 154-213. "Federalist judges adapted the common law crime of seditious libel into the Constitution and 1st Amendment jurisprudence and their theoretical understanding of seditious libel lasted well into the 20th century."

Knowlton, Steven R.. "The Media and Popular Sovereignty: Freedom of the Press and Self-Government." 16-44, in James D. Startt and Wm. David Sloan, eds., *The Significance of the Media in American History.* Northport, Ala., 1994. Freedom of expression has been a key aspect of the American concept of self-government. This study traces the idea from John Milton through the 1960s.

Leder, Lawrence H. "The Role of Newspapers in Early America: 'In Defense of Their Own Liberty.'" *Huntington Library Quarterly* 30 (November 1966): 1-16. During the period from 1690 to 1762, American editors did not speculate on press freedom in the first thirty years. Speculation appeared later only as newspapers tried to break a press monopoly.

Mathewson, Joe. "The Long and Strong Tradition of State Protection of Freedom of the Press." *American Journalism* 26:1 (2009): 81-112. Freedom of the press was first conceived and addressed in the constitutions of most of the original states. These constitutions were enacted before U.S. independence and the existence of the First Amendment.

Montagno, George L. "Federalist Retaliation: The Sedition Trial of Matthew Lyon." *Vermont History* 26 (January 1958): 3-16. The author gives a narrative account of the trial, conviction, imprisonment, and political martyrdom of Lyon.

Morris, Richard. "The Case for the Palatine Printer: Zenger's Fight for Free Press," 69-95 in *Fair Trial.* New York, 1953. "The Zenger case destroyed once and for all the notion that government officials were entitled to unqualified allegiance and support and that they were untouchables immune from criticism."

Nelson, Harold L. "Seditious Libel in Colonial America." *American Journal of Legal History* 3 (April 1959): 160-72. After the Zenger trial, legislatures or governors' councils, rather than courts, disciplined printers. The colonial assembly became the major force in limiting the press and freedom.

Plasterer, Nicholas N. "The Croswell Case: Paradox of History?" *Journalism Quarterly* 44 (1967): 125-9. The Croswell case was an important trial that "apparently had a direct and important causal relationship with our present libel laws."

Price, Warren C. "Reflections on the Trial of John Peter Zenger." *Journalism Quarterly* 32 (1955): 161-8. The background to the Zenger case was political, not that of press freedom. The situation of Zenger gained public support probably because of the unpopularity of the corrupt Gov. Cosby. The case did not set a legal precedent.

Rivera, Clark. "Ideals, Interests and Civil Liberty: The Colonial Press and Freedom, 1735-76." *Journalism Quarterly* 55 (1978): 48-53, 124. This overview attempts to re-examine colonial theory and practice regarding freedom of expression.

Robbins, Jan C. "Jefferson and the Press: The Resolution of an Antimony." *Journalism Quarterly* 48 (1971): 421-30, 465. Jefferson's attitudes toward freedom of expression, sometimes thought contradictory by historians, sprang from the same philosophy. He believed self-preservation to be a right of more ultimate importance than freedom of expression.

Schwarzlose, Richard A. "The Marketplace of Ideas: A Measure of Free Expression." *Journalism Monographs* 118 (1989). This account "examines the concept of the marketplace of ideas in terms of its practical and philosophical parallels and as it was developed by John Milton, John Stuart Mill, and several American intellectuals."

Sloan, Wm. David, and Thomas A. Schwartz. "Historians and Freedom of the Press, 1690-1801: Libertarian or Limited?" *American Journalism* 5 (1988): 159-77. This historiographical essay explains the various interpretations historians have applied to early Americans' views on freedom of the press.

Stevens, John W. "Congressional History of the 1798 Sedition Law." *Journalism Quarterly* 43 (1966): 247-56. "[T]he debate on the sedition law opened a dialogue on the role of free expression within a democracy (particularly at a time of crisis) which has continued to this day."

Terwillings, W. Bird. "William Goddard, Victory for Freedom of the Press." *Maryland History Magazine* 36 (June 1941): 139-49. In 1777 Goddard withstood the vigilante pressures of a local Whig Club and refused to reveal the name of the author of an article in the *Maryland Journal.* He received the support of the Committee of Grievances of the Maryland House of Delegates to whom he referred the case.

Uhm, Kiyul. "The Founders and the Revolutionary Underpinning of the Concept of the Right To Know." *Journalism and Mass Communication Quarterly* 85:2 (2008): 393-416. "During the founding period of the nation, the concept of the people's right to know ... was repeatedly articulated and underscored as one of the most important democratic principles."

Williams, Julie Hedgepeth. "Puritans and Freedom of Expression." 17-31, in Wm. David Sloan, ed., *Media and Religion in American History.* Northport, Ala., 2000. Puritans in colonial America were strong advocates of free expression as a means of expressing their religion. They laid the groundwork for America's broad concepts of press freedom.

Yodelis, Mary A. "Courts, Counting Houses and Streets: Attempts at Press Control, 1763-1775." *Journalism History* 1 (1974): 11-5. In this summary of the "constraints exercised against all the Boston newspapers and publishers: legal, economic, violent, symbolic, and rhetorical," the author concludes that the press "remained relatively free, often in spite of bitter partisanship. In fact, freedom may have developed from such partisanship."

7

The Penny Press
1833 - 1861

A revolution in American journalism occurred in the 1830s when the penny press appeared. Its presence had a great impact both on the press and on society, and some of the most famous figures in American journalism were instrumental in its development. As we shall see, a number of explanations have been advanced to account for the emergence of this new dimension of the press, but at this point it is important to hold some basic ideas in mind. The penny press began as the nation was becoming more industrial and urban. It started in the midst of major advances in transportation and communication. Finally, it is worth noting that with the penny press one can begin to see the growth of many of the features associated with the content, production, and distribution of newspapers that have come to characterize the modern metropolitan press.

BIRTH OF AN IDEA

The idea of publishing a cheap newspaper occurred not to a journalist but to a medical student by the name of Horatio David Sheppard. While attending the Eldridge Street Medical School in New York, he often had passed along Chatham Street, known for its "penny a piece" sales, on his way downtown. He noticed how quickly people bought items for a penny. James Parton, a contemporary writer and biographer who was interested in the beginning of the penny press, once reconstructed Sheppard's thoughts about those penny sales in this manner:

> The difference between a cent, and no money, did not seem to be appreciated by the people. If a person saw something, wanted it, and knew the price to be only a cent, he was almost as certain to buy it as though it were offered him for nothing. Now, thought Sheppard, to make a fortune, one has nothing more to do than to produce a tempting article which can be sold profitably for a cent, place it where everybody can see it, and buy it, without stopping — and lo! the thing is done! If it were only *possible* to produce a small, spicy daily paper for a cent, and get boys to sell it about the streets, *how* it would sell! How many

pennies that now go for cakes and peanuts would be spent for news and paragraphs![1]

Unfortunately for Sheppard and his pocketbook, his attempt to put his plan into action failed, even with the help of Horace Greeley and another printer. Greeley would later found an important penny daily, the *New York Tribune*.

But describing the penny press, as these newspapers came to be called, does not explain why they happened at this particular time in history. Thousands of words have been spent on theories, and historians still disagree on how and why the changes came about.

When Benjamin Day brought out the *New York Sun*, the first successful penny daily, on September 3, 1833, there were about 1,200 newspapers publishing in the United States on a regular basis. Most were political, and most were expensive.

The largest of the afternoon newspapers in New York was the *Evening Post*, which had been founded in 1801 as a Federalist publication and funded by Alexander Hamilton and other party leaders. Editing the paper at the dawn of the penny press era was William Cullen Bryant, who is better known in American literature as a poet than a newspaper editor. He joined the paper in 1826 as the assistant of the first editor, William Coleman. When Coleman died in 1829, Bryant took over, gradually acquiring a half interest in the paper and editing it for the next half-century. He was a Jacksonian and eventually turned the newspaper into a Democratic organ. As he grew more concerned with the Democratic Party's support of slavery, he embraced the Free Soil Party and then the Republican Party when it was founded in 1856. He had a strong reputation as an editorial writer but also supported the news side of the operation by hiring correspondents in other American cities and employing Europeans to submit articles from abroad. Although the *Evening Post* failed to keep up with the burgeoning circulations of the newer, cheaper publications, Bryant built it into a prosperous, prestigious newspaper. He semi-retired in 1870 to translate Homer and continued with the paper until he

---

[1]James Parton, *The Life of Horace Greeley, Editor of the New York Tribune* (1855; reprint, New York, 1970), 140.

William Cullen Bryant
Even though his newspaper, the *New York Evening Post*, never achieved the huge circulations of Horace Greeley's *Tribune* and his sensational rivals, the *Sun* and the *Herald*, William Cullen Bryant was a towering figure in nineteenth-century journalism. He served as editor of the *Evening Post* for fifty years, from 1829 to 1878. While establishing himself as one of America's pre-eminent editorial writers and spokesmen on political issues, he also enlarged his international reputation as a poet and a literary critic.

died in 1878.

Day's new penny newspaper was a sharp contrast to the more expensive papers like Bryant's. "A daily newspaper in those days was a solemn thing," as Parton explained:

People in moderate circumstances seldom saw, never bought one. The price was ten dollars a year.... It was not a thing for the people; it appertained to the counting-house; it was taken by the wholesale dealer; it was cumbrous, heavy, solemn. The idea of making it an article to be cried about the streets, to be sold for a cent, to be bought by workingmen and boys, to come into competition with cakes and apples, must have seemed to the respectable New Yorkers of 1831, unspeakably absurd. When the respectable New Yorker first saw a penny paper, he gazed at it (I saw him) with a feeling similar to that with which an ill-natured man may be supposed to regard General Tom Thumb, a feeling of mingled curiosity and contempt; he put the ridiculous little thing into his waistcoat pocket to carry home for the amusement of his family; and he wondered what nonsense would be perpetrated next.[2]

[2]Ibid., 141-2.

Less than twenty years later, according to Horace Greeley, there were about 2,500 newspapers, 250 of them dailies that issued a million copies a day. Greeley told a parliamentary committee in London in 1851 that each county in the United States usually would have at least a weekly newspaper and that counties of 20,000 population, at least in the free states, often would have two. Someone usually started a daily newspaper when a town's population grew to about 15,000.[3] Many of the new dailies differed from the older papers, which not only were more expensive but were distributed by subscription only. The cheaper papers relied more on advertising and boasted of their political independence from parties. Their emphasis was on news, not views.

THE HISTORICAL DEBATE ABOUT THE ORIGINS OF THE PENNY PRESS

What created the phenomenon of the cheap press? Until the last few decades, most historians assumed that it was part of the natural development of the modern newspaper. Frederic Hudson, a nineteenth century journalist who had the distinction of writing the first comprehensive history of American journalism after the advent of the penny press, claimed that the party newspapers of the 1830s were so dull that a change, a revolution, was needed and that it occurred naturally. Another writer of the period, Augustus Maverick, describing the birth of the *New York Times*, said that readers in the 1850s hungered in the vacuum left by the insufficient and unsatisfactory newspapers of the day and that natural forces were at work to produce the *Times* to satisfy them.[4] Hudson and Maverick were both journalists on penny newspapers who believed that the history of journalism was the story of how newspapers and journalism practices had progressively developed over time to reach the advanced stage existing in their own time. Most journalism historians since then, until recently, have held the same assumption. They have considered the penny press to be the origin of "true" journalism, that is, journalism independent of political parties, emphasizing news rather than opinion, and appealing to a mass audience.

Others credit technology and suggest that changes in printing, transportation, and communications had to occur before the penny press could develop. In the 1820s, newsprint manufacturers figured out how to make cheap paper from wood pulp instead of rags. Printing technology, which some historians have emphasized, seems less important, however, for most of the advances that allowed very fast printing did not appear until after the penny press was firmly established. For example, the introduction of the Hoe type-revolving press allowed newspapers to print more cheaply and faster, but it was not introduced until 1848. The stereotyping process, making solid metal plates from papier-mâché impressions, contributed immensely to printing speed; but the first

[3]Greeley's testimony is reprinted in Parton, ibid., 355-61, and in Frederic Hudson, *Journalism in the United States, from 1690 to 1872* (New York, 1873), 540-2.
[4]Hudson, ibid., 408-9, and Augustus Maverick, *Henry J. Raymond and the New York Press for Thirty Years. Progress of American Journalism from 1840 to 1870* (1870; reprint, New York, 1970), 53.

Newspaper Circulation in the United States 1800-1860

Newspaper Circulation Growth 1833-1860

New York Sun (founded in 1833)

after 4 mos.   Nov. 1835   late 1836

New York Herald (founded in 1835)

1836   1850   1860

Boston Daily Times (founded in 1836)

after 4 mos.   1850   1860

Balitmore Sun (founded in 1837)

1838   1850   1860

New York Tribune (founded in 1841)

after 3 weeks   after 7 weeks   1860

New York Times (founded in 1851)

after 10 weeks   1852   1860

American newspaper to acquire it, the *New York Herald*, did not do so until 1861. Steam-operated web presses used improved ink to print both sides of a continuous roll of paper at the same time and cut it into sheets. However, web presses did not appear until 1863. Advances in the speed of communication came when the postal service set up a pony express run between Philadelphia and New York in 1835; but railroads, steamships, and the telegraph were much faster. Railroads began to crisscross the nation in the late 1830s and early 1840s. By the end of the 1830s new steamships were capable of crossing the Atlantic in less than three weeks. Such speed spurred the creation of a number of newspapers that summarized recent developments on one side of the Atlantic and printed them in time to catch the steamships as they departed for readers on the other side.[5] The telegraph was introduced in 1841, and in 1851 attempts began to lay cable for telegraphic communication across the Atlantic.

Still other historians claim that the nation's growing literacy spurred the development of the penny press. They contend that these papers were forced to stress human interest and local news to attract a new and relatively unsophisticated audience. Between 1833 and 1860, the population increased 233%. The development of public education dropped the illiteracy rate to 9%, calculated on the basis of whites over twenty years of age.

Historians have argued recently, however, against these three theories. The history of the penny press as the development of later or modern journalism can be criticized because it uses current assumptions to analyze newspapers of the past for which the assumptions were not necessarily true, and because it assumes that progress, defined by current standards, is inevitable.[6] Michael Schudson, a sociologist, attributed the rise of the penny press to the growth of what he called a democratic market society. More members of the middle class were immersing themselves in business and politics than ever before. In business, the movement was expressed in the growth of a capitalistic middle class; in politics, it was known as Jacksonian democracy. The penny press, Schudson argued, was a product of this new spirit of individualism in business enterprise and independence in politics. It expanded the market by opening up advertising and making the newspaper something cheap enough to be consumed at home.[7]

But even revisionist historians like Schudson have been criticized in the continuing debate over the origins and significance of the penny press. John Nerone accused most historians, whether developmental or revisionist, of perpetrating a "mythology" of the penny press. He argued that "the gist of the mythology is that a small number of daring innovators, working especially in New York City, revolutionized the content and style of American journalism by creating what was essentially the modern popular com-

[5]Richard Schwarzlose discusses these newspapers in "The Foreign Connection: Transatlantic Newspapers in the 1840s," *Journalism History* 10 (1983): 44-9, 67.

[6]For a discussion of the approaches that various historians have taken to the penny press, see James G. Stovall, "The Penny Press, 1833-1861: Product of Great Men or Natural Forces?" in Wm. David Sloan, *Perspectives on Mass Communication History* (Hillsdale, N.J., 1991), 123-38.

[7]Michael Schudson, *Discovering the News: A Social History of American Newspapers* (New York, 1978), 30-50. Schudson himself has been challenged on several points, including his reliance on questionable sources.

The Rotary Press
The Hoe Company built its first Type Revolving Press in 1846 for the *Philadelphia Ledger*. Smaller cylinders surrounded the large central cylinder. As paper passed between the cylinders, the small ones pressed it against the pages of type on the large cylinder. Although the process that the press used was fast, the centrifugal force of the rotations sometimes flung the thousands of pieces of type from the pages and scattered them around the pressroom. The 10-cylinder press shown here was introduced in 1855. Hoe's name became synonymous with rotary printing machines. The *New York Tribune*, *Philadelphia Times*, and many other newspapers in the United States and Europe used his presses.

mercial newspaper. These penny papers were the first commercial papers, the first popular papers, the first politically independent papers, and the first 'news' papers. They were the ancestors of contemporary U.S. newspapers."[8]

Nerone argued that changes in American journalism were more evolutionary than revolutionary, brought about by changes in society and culture. Instead of focusing on large newspapers operated by well-known journalists in Eastern cities, Nerone says, historians should shift their focus to the "typical" newspapers in smaller American communities. Historians should recognize, he says, that American newspapers and readers in the nineteenth century were not all the same, that there were different classes of newspapers, and that the audience was segmented. Yet, Nerone himself has been criticized because of problems with his research and because of his efforts to make generalizations about the penny press from a study of other types of papers.

The best explanation of the origins of the penny press must — as is true with any historical explanation — be based on the best evidence available. Looking at the full range of evidence, we can come to the following conclusions. The advent of the penny press did create a new movement in civilization, as contemporaries claimed. Hundreds of thousands of readers entered a new age of daily mass communication. With all its innovations, the penny press marked a developmental achievement in the history of American journalism. Social and cultural influences — such as rapid urbanization, advancements in printing and communication technology, and increases in literacy — played a significant role in shaping the nature of the penny press, which was born and thrived in response to a society in need of entertainment and information, and succeeded because it continued to entertain and inform. The resulting explanation of the penny press emphasizes that its birth and success were due to enterprising individuals who took risks and sought to produce marketable products for a mass audience of consumers.[9]

LONDON'S INFLUENCE AND EARLY FAILURES

Like several other aspects of American journalism, the penny press had historical precedents in England. There the radical press, which shared the penny press' sympathy for the common people and a penchant for government reform, was started almost single-handedly by a man whose name was already familiar to American readers — William Cobbett. "Peter Porcupine," the partisan journalist who had returned to England from America in 1800, established the weekly *Political Register* in 1815 to espouse radical principles such as universal suffrage for men and annual elections as part of the movement's natural rights philosophy. At its start, the paper was expensive, and workingmen had to buy it in groups in order to afford it for reading aloud at their local alehouses. But on October 26, 1816, Cobbett announced a new edition that would sell for twopence, and the cheap press movement in England was born. Cobbett published the cheap version in foolscap size — a broadsheet of 13" x 16" that displayed articles in four columns — to get around the Stamp Act. Legislators angry at opposition editors placed a heavy tax on newspapers that were folded, but they had failed to write into the law a tax on unfolded papers. Cobbett's paper was successful and widely imitated.

Another aspect of the penny press, its sensationalism, was foreshadowed by another British development, the Sunday newspaper. One of the first such papers was published in 1779, and by 1812 there were at least eighteen in London. They were controversial for at least two reasons. First, they were considered antireligious because they required the workers who produced them and the citizens who bought them to break the Christian Sabbath. Second, their contents were risqué. Still, they were popular with a certain readership, and other cheap newspapers seized upon their approach and began to flourish in the 1820s. Typical of these was the *Terrific Register: or, Record of Crimes, Judgments, Providences and Calamities*. It regaled readers with horrendous tales of violence, illustrated with gruesome pictures of murder, mutilation, and cannibalism. Along with these papers, a revived version of the radical press was also popular in the 1830s, including a new entry from Cobbett, the *Twopenny Trash*.

---

[8]John C. Nerone, "The Mythology of the Penny Press," *Critical Studies in Mass Communication* 4 (1987), 376.

[9]For a fuller account of the founding of penny journalism in the 1830s, see Susan Thompson, *The Penny Press* (Northport, Ala., 2004), 195.

Early attempts at cheap newspapers in the United States failed. Frederic Hudson, who became the managing editor of the *New York Herald*, wrote that James Gordon Bennett, who in 1835 founded the *Herald*, started the cheap press movement by founding the *New York Globe* on October 29, 1832. Actually, the *Globe* was not cheap. A subscription cost $8 a year — cheap compared to the price of the $10 newspapers but still not inexpensive enough for working people to afford. The newspaper failed, Hudson wrote, when the *Globe* tried to show some political independence and politicians moved to cut off its funds and kill it.[10]

Horace Greeley, who like Bennett played a large role in the development of the penny press, was involved in another false start. It was he and his partner at that time, Francis Story, who printed Dr. Sheppard's ill-fated and short-lived *New York Morning Post*. As we have seen, Dr. Sheppard dreamed of producing a cheap daily paper, and he managed to launch the *Post* on January 1, 1833. His naiveté, however, coupled with the New Year's holiday and an overnight blizzard, seemed to conspire against the two-penny sheet. He had wanted to sell the paper for a penny, but Greeley did not think any newspaper could make a profit if it sold for less than two. Sheppard agreed to go along with the higher price to get Greeley in on the venture. Greeley, who was in his early twenties at the time, remembered years later that Sheppard thought the newspaper would sell because it was cheap and because he failed to advertise that the new journal was coming out. But New Yorkers did not read much of anything on New Year's Day, he added, and the snowstorm blocked the streets. The few papers that were delivered to doorsteps were lost in the snow. Few people wanted to stop in the frosty weather to pay for a copy, and the carriers finally gave up and went home.

The paper struggled for two and a half weeks. The printers had started with $150 between them, and Greeley had persuaded someone to give them some credit. Sheppard, rumor had it, had come to New York with $1,500; but Greeley surmised that most of the money must have disappeared before the *Post* came out. The bills were $200 a week, and Sheppard was unable to pay them after the first week. When the circulation limped along at two or three hundred a week, he reduced the price to a penny. "The public would not buy it even at that," Greeley wrote, "and we printers, already considerably in debt for materials, were utterly unable to go beyond the second or third week after the publisher had stopped paying." The printers lost between $50 and $60, more than a month's wages.[11]

THE NEW YORK SUN

In the 1830s, New York City was a bustling metropolis experiencing a population boom. At the beginning of the decade, the population totaled about 200,000; but by its close, more than 312,000 people called the city home. New York was known for its filth and

Young Horace Greeley
Horace Greeley, a printer in his early twenties, was involved in one of the first, but ill-fated, attempts at a cheap newspaper, the *New York Morning Post*. Launched on January 1, 1833, the morning after a blizzard had blanketed New York City, the newspaper never recovered from the disaster. Despite the failure, Greeley later would become one of America's most important journalists.

squalor amid busy streets lined with buildings as high as five stories. The streets, dusty in dry weather, muddy in rain, and slick when covered with snow and ice, were lined with handcarts on the sidewalks and filled with galloping equestrians and speeding horse-drawn carriages and wagons.

By the early 1830s, journalism had begun to change in New York. A new class of newspapers, the labor papers, had made a brief appearance. They were devoted to the tenets of the Working Men's Party and targeted the growing numbers of middle- and lower-class readers. Their contents were much more interesting than the metropolitan leaders – the mercantile and political newspapers that sold for 6¢ a copy or $10 a year.

About this time, however, circulation increases among the urban giants, such as the *Journal of Commerce*, *New York Evening Post*, and especially the *New York Courier & Enquirer*, indicated that people outside the upper classes had begun to purchase them. The *Courier & Enquirer* had started running livelier articles, thanks mostly to the pen of a Scottish immigrant turned reporter named James Gordon Bennett. More importantly, it had begun printing the antics of lowlifes, prostitutes, and drunks in the city's nightly police court.

---

[10]Hudson, *Journalism in the United States*, 409-11.

[11]Greeley discussed his experiences with the *Morning Post* in his autobiography, *Recollections of a Busy Life* (1868; reprint, New York, 1970), 91-3.

The Moon Hoax

The *New York Sun* Stuns Readers with Discovery of Lunar Life

In August 1835 the *New York Sun* astounded readers with the news that life had been discovered on the moon. In a six-part series titled "Great Astronomical Discoveries," the penny newspaper revealed that an astronomer in South Africa had found that the lush lunar surface was covered with trees looking like firs and palms and that animals resembling bison and zebras roamed over it. Then, in the last few installments, readers discovered that the moon also was home to "rational beings," creatures who looked and acted very much like humans – except they had batlike wings and could fly.

The moon stories, supposedly discovered by the *Sun* in a Scottish scientific journal, caused a sensation. Other newspapers rushed to copy them, and the *Sun* saw its own circulation soar.

The articles had barely concluded, however, before both the *New York Herald* and the *Journal of Commerce* denounced them as a hoax.

The latter paper, in particular, had reasons for its claim, because the writer of the stories, Richard Adams Locke, had confessed to a colleague at the *Journal* that he had made the whole thing up.

The *Sun*, however, never admitted that the articles were a hoax, still claiming in mid-September that their source was a credible scientific journal reporting the activities of a respected astronomer. At the same time, it delighted in the fact that the authenticity of the articles had become a news event in itself. The truthfulness of the articles was not even that important, according to the *Sun*, because even those who doubted the stories' veracity admired the skillful writing and appreciated the amusement they had brought.

As the moon hoax showed, entertainment was as much a part of the function of early penny newspapers as information.

The first big story of the penny press era appeared in the *New York Sun* in 1835. The owner, Benjamin Day (lower left), had recently hired Richard Adams Locke (middle left) as his reporter. Locke in short time produced what came to be known as the "moon hoax." The series of stories gained such international attention that other publications reported the discovery of life on the moon, and some created illustrations (above) to try to depict the lunar landscape and beings as Locke described them.

The idea of selling newspapers for a penny apiece was not original to Benjamin Day, a young man who came to New York from Massachusetts to make his fortune, but he was the first to put the idea into successful practice. His *New York Sun* appeared on September 3, 1833. Its size was about 8 x 11 inches. Its first issues contained a few news items, but mostly tall tales and items clipped from other newspapers (such as the police court column).

Day soon took a partner, 21-year-old George Wisner, who agreed to cover the police court and set type for $4 a week. Soon, Day offered him part ownership in the paper rather than raise his salary. The partnership quickly grew stormy, though, as their political and editorial differences surfaced. Despite the *Sun's* continued claim of political neutrality, the editors' political differences caused an editorial dichotomy in the paper's pages from the time of Wisner's arrival until his departure in the summer of 1835, when Day bought him out for $5,000.[12]

The mixed editorial voices, the inclusion of local news items, and the tall tales intrigued and entertained the public from the start, and the *Sun* enjoyed continued growth and expansion throughout the 1830s. One of the most famous tall tales or fiction presented as fact (or "humbugs," to quote the famous promoter P.T. Barnum) occurred after Wisner's departure – the great moon hoax of 1835 written by Richard Adams Locke. It created such a sensation that the *Sun* boasted enormous circulation totals that exceeded *The Times* of London, then the world's circulation leader.

The wealthy Philip Hone, indicative of the public sentiment, wrote in his diary of the hoax: "In sober truth, if this account is true, it is most enormously wonderful, and if it is a fable, the manner of its relation, with all its scientific details, names of persons employed, and the beauty of its glowing descriptions, will give this ingenious history a place with 'Gulliver's Travels' and 'Robinson Crusoe.'"[13] Another contemporary, Edgar Allan Poe, credited the moon hoax with making the *Sun* an enduring success and in establishing the penny press throughout the nation. "From the epoch of the hoax 'The Sun' shone with unmitigated splendor," he wrote. "The start thus given the paper ensured it a triumph.... Its success firmly established 'the penny system' throughout the country, and consequently, we are indebted to the genius of Mr. Locke for one of the most important steps ever yet taken in the pathway of human progress."[14]

Poe's estimation of the importance of the moon hoax in establishing the success of the *Sun* may seem a bit exaggerated, considering that the *Sun's* popularity had grown phenomenally prior to the publication of the moon stories; but his observations about the success of the *Sun* establishing "the penny system" throughout the nation have much merit. Within two years after publication of the hoax, other penny papers destined for great success would be established in Boston, Philadelphia, New Orleans, and Baltimore.

The success of the *Sun* was due to a number of factors. Day's and Wisner's enterprise helped, as did their successful management of the operation and their ability to attract talented employees such as Locke. The everyday contents of the *Sun* also made it popular, including its engaging, conversational writing style, its avoidance of weighty and boring political diatribes, and its emphasis on sensational crime news, local news, and other items of interest to the masses of people. Above all, the appealing price of the *Sun* put it in the reach of all classes of readers.

The accessibility of the *Sun* and other penny newspapers to a new class contributed to social changes already underway in New York. The penny press encouraged and promoted literacy, and it gave the lower classes a sense of empowerment to know that they were enjoying their own daily newspapers in much the same way as the better classes did. Furthermore, as the comment from Hone suggests, even rich New Yorkers read the *Sun*.

The success of the *Sun* and the new breed of newspapers it generated also brought great changes to journalism. At least one of these changes — in newspaper distribution on the streets by newsboys — may be attributed directly to Day. Additionally, entertainment became one of the major goals of editors because of the *Sun's* example.

It could be argued that the emphasis on sensational crime news and fiction passed off for fact caused setbacks in journalism, with the latter, especially, severely undermining the march toward an ideal of objectivity in factual news reporting. Yet, the reporting of sensational news and the perpetration of inventive hoaxes served to generate more popularity and aid the success of the penny press throughout the nation.

The moon stories had made the *Sun* the most popular newspaper in the world; and while it would remain the circulation leader in New York City for the next two decades, it would not maintain a leading position among the penny press because of its owners' unwillingness to expand and raise its price to 2¢ per copy. One of its one-cent competitors would rise from the ashes of a fire in August 1835 to best the *Sun* and other New York rivals, not only in the coverage of the latest news items and the manufacture of entertaining humbugs, but in its saucy brand of editorial satire that seemed to hold nothing sacred.

THE NEW YORK HERALD

More controversial than either Day or Locke was James Gordon Bennett, the innovative, competitive founder of the *New York Herald*. He once had approached Greeley about putting out a cheap daily; and Greeley, perhaps still smarting from his experience with the *Morning Post*, suggested that Bennett look elsewhere. Bennett followed the suggestion, believing he had a mission — to use the daily press to reform and revitalize American society. Consequently, he pulled together $500 and published the first issue of the *Herald* on May 6, 1835, in competition with seven six-penny morning papers, four six-penny afternoon papers, and four small, cheap papers. In the first issue, Bennett declared that the *Herald*

---

[12] See James Stanford Bradshaw's "George W. Wisner and the New York Sun" and Wm. David Sloan's "George W. Wisner: Michigan Editor and Politician" in *Journalism History 6* (1979-80): 112+ and 113-6, respectively.

[13] Allan Nevins, ed., *The Diary of Philip Hone, 1828-1851* (New York: Dodd, Mead, 1936), 173.

[14] Edgar Allan Poe, "Richard Adams Locke," in *The Complete Works of Edgar Allan Poe*, ed., James A. Harrison (New York: Thomas Y. Crowell, 1902), 135.

THE NEW YORK HERALD.

NEW YORK, THURSDAY MORNING, JULY 15, 1841.

James Gordon Bennett and the *New York Herald*
The editor of the *New York Herald* matched his journalistic energy and imagination with a huge idea of his own importance. "My ambition," he wrote, "is to make the newspaper Press the great organ and pivot of government, society, commerce, finance, religion, and all human civilization. I want to leave behind me no castles, no granite hotels, no monuments of marble, no statues of bronze, no pyramids of brick — simply a name. The name of James Gordon Bennett, as one of the benefactors of the human race, will satisfy every desire and every hope." Despite Bennett's personal eccentricities, he seemed to know intuitively what would interest readers. By emphasizing news and sensationalism, he made the *Herald* one of the most popular and successful newspapers of the nineteenth century.

would be a newspaper for everyone. It would refuse to support the line of any political party, as most of the other newspapers did, and would instead report the facts as briefly and honestly as possible. As Bennett said in the second issue, the *Herald* would try to "give a correct picture of the world — in Wall Street — in the Exchange — in the Police-office — at the Theatre — in the Opera — in short, wherever human nature and real life best display their freaks and vagaries."[15]

Bennett's attempts to carry out his plan shocked New Yorkers. His language was frank. He referred to "shirts" instead of linen, "pantaloons" instead of inexpressibles, and "legs" instead of limbs. Once he wrote of the "branches" of public dancers; and to

[15]*New York Herald*, 7 May 1835.

goad his critics he wrote, "Petticoats — petticoats — petticoats — petticoats — there — you fastidious fools — vent your mawkishness on that!"[16] His detailed coverage of crime and the courts put readers in the middle of the story. He angered some with his critical comments about Wall Street and others with his coverage of politics and organized religion. Typical was this piece:

Religion — true religion — consists not in eating and drinking — not in high salaries — not in hanging around the apron strings of rich old women — not in presuming to judge the opinions of others beyond what their acts will justify. Neither does true religion — nor real Christianity consist in believing the dogmas of any church — or [dogmatic statements] of any man. The Bible is before me. Have I not a right to read that book — to draw out from it religious opinions — and to create a belief and a church of my own? ... I went to the source of true religion, and drank of the pure stream, uncontaminated by priest or prelate, parson or minister; and as long as we have these sacred volumes in full circulation here below, defiance may alike be set to the bigots of Catholicity or of Protestantism. We care for neither. We are independent of all. Like Luther — like Paul, we go on our own hook.[17]

The reaction of competitors to Bennett was immediate and negative. The *Sun* and the *New York Transcript* immediately withdrew their business from the firm that was printing the *Herald*. After five years of Bennett and the *Herald*, his opponents organized what became known as the Moral War of 1840. The war broke out in May, and in the vanguard of the attack were the Wall Street press, a few of the smaller New York newspapers, and a number of out-of-town Whig newspapers, all led by the *New York Courier and Enquirer*. Its editor and proprietor, Col. James Watson Webb, once had physically attacked Bennett in the street. The newspapers attacked Bennett and the *Herald* in their columns and tried to persuade businesses to withdraw their advertising. Hotel owners were implored to ban the *Herald*, and anyone who even looked at it was called impious and immoral. The *Herald*'s managing editor, Frederic Hudson, said the war had more to do with Bennett's independence than his "immorality" and that "the issue and success of this independent paper aroused four powerful interests against its editor: the politicians, the clergy, the stock brokers, and the managers of the old newspapers." It was Bennett's "continued boldness and success in 1838 and '9," he claimed, that "brought on the general war of 1840."[18] Hudson contended that the Moral War had little lasting effect on Bennett; but the *Herald* lost circulation, and Bennett tried to curb some of his excesses to gain it back.

One of Bennett's contemporaries commented that the Moral War was actually the third attempt to beat down Bennett and that it grew out of the envy of his competitors. "It was conducted with

[16]Quoted in Isaac C. Pray, *Memoirs of James Gordon Bennett and His Times* (1855; reprint, New York, 1970), 266.
[17]Quoted in ibid., 276-7.
[18]Hudson, *Journalism in the United States*, 456. Hudson discusses the Moral War on pages 456-61.

vindictive pertinacity, by the strongest alliance of spleen, passion, folly, and intellect ever known in the history of Journalism, for such a purpose," wrote Isaac Pray, Bennett's sympathetic biographer. "Never was there arranged a more determined or extensive machinery to destroy the position and prospects of one man, at least by means of the small musketry of words, and the heavier artillery of opinions and denunciation." The newspapers and editors, Pray said, "were chagrined and maddened to see jocose, quizzing, and lampooning paragraphs maintaining favor in the public mind, while their own carefully written, and sometimes brilliant essays, were wholly neglected. Instead of rebuking public taste, however, they undertook to destroy the oracle of it itself."[19]

Pray thought the effort was doomed from the start, because some of those accusing Bennett of immorality "had outraged taste and the feelings of humanity for years upon years" and the public was quick to recognize the hypocrisy. Nor, in Pray's opinion, did the Moral War have much effect on the changes that Bennett introduced at about the same time. "Mr. Bennett was about to exchange his isolated life for the delights of wedlock," Pray wrote, "and it was his regard for the happiness of others that caused him to modify that style of expression which naturally enough offended cultivated minds." Bennett, he claimed, had accomplished his purpose. He had made the newspaper a necessity for thousands and had cured society of its inability to tolerate frank expression. Thus, Pray said, Bennett could afford to tone down his language.[20]

At times Bennett seemed to pay little attention to all his opposition and at others responded editorially in kind. On June 3, 1840, he listed the circulation of the "Wall Street Holy Allies" and claimed that his circulation was higher than all of theirs combined. He also listed the "horse power" of the "lies, impudence, ignorance, hatred, jealousy, cash, credit and virtue" of his opponents — the last three were zero — and compared it to the "horse power" of his own "energy, sobriety, moral courage, intellect, wit, poetry, virtue and cash."[21]

BENNETT THE INNOVATOR

Regardless of the effect Bennett may have had on the prudery of New York society, he deserves credit for a number of innovations in the newspaper business. He put the *Herald* on a pay-as-you-go basis, requiring subscribers to pay for their newspapers in advance and ending the long-standing complaints of editors about their thieving readers. He added money to the newspaper's cash box by creating the "Personals" column and requiring advertisers to change their ads every day. In the past, advertisers ran ads for up to a year at a time without changing copy. Bennett thought the practice was "silly" and a good way to lose money. He refused to let the same ad appear for more than two weeks, and in 1848 he began to accept only one-day runs.

Bennett's most important contribution, however, was his re-

[19]Pray, *Memoirs of James Gordon Bennett*, 264.
[20]Ibid., 265-6.
[21]*New York Herald*, 3 June 1840.

The Innovative Bennett

With the *Herald*, James Gordon Bennett pioneered many newspaper practices that are still with us. One of his most innovative was this, the first full-page news illustration to appear in an American newspaper, published on the occasion of the death of former President Andrew Jackson. The *Herald* printed the illustration on June 25, 1845, followed by publication in the paper's weekly edition the next day.

definition of the concept of news. In colonial days, editors and printers had treated news as if it were history. Their newspapers came out only once a week, and some were excessively slow about getting information into print. Nor were editors or their readers much concerned about the tardiness of news. If people had not read or heard about some event, they still would be interested in it regardless of how late the news was. With improvements in technology and the needs of business for more timely information, however, newspapers began to rush news into print. But even in the 1840s, some news could be weeks late. Reports of congressional debates often appeared in the Washington press several weeks later, and since other newspapers depended on the Washington press for their reports on Congress, citizens were behind in learning what their elected representatives were doing.

Bennett, on the other hand, wanted the *Herald* to publish the reports promptly and in 1841 hired Robert Sutton to set up a corps of Washington correspondents. Sutton, however, wanted extra

Samuel Morse and Telegraphic News
When Samuel F. B. Morse was granted a patent for his magnetic telegraph in 1844, stations began to spring up throughout the United States. When words could speed from one point to another electrically, there was little remaining use for cruder attempts to hasten the news – the pony express, the railroad, fleets of news boats, and carrier pigeon expresses.

income, prompting him to revise and polish reports of debates to suit congressmen. Because the reports were no longer verbatim, they lost much of their value. From that time on, congressmen used the reports as a way of addressing their constituents rather than as a way of debating the questions with each other.[22]

Similar to Bennett's innovative Washington reporting were his efforts to strengthen foreign news. When the first steamship crossed the Atlantic in April 1838, cutting the time between Europe and the United States from six weeks to less than three, Bennett booked passage on the return voyage and started setting up a system of European correspondents. While in Europe, he covered Queen Victoria's coronation and put stringers in Berlin, Brussels, Glasgow, London, Paris, and Rome. After returning home, he hired stringers in Canada, Mexico, and the Republic of Texas. One stringer was Thomas Oliver Larkin, the U.S. consul in Monterey, California, which was then a part of Mexico. When war broke out between the United States and Mexico in May 1846, Larkin reported on military activity from the West Coast.

The *Herald* also pioneered in such areas as sports, business news, and coverage of women. In 1855 Bennett hired Jane Cunningham Croly ("Jennie June") to write about "society." Her byline soon became famous with articles about fashion, beauty, and social gatherings. After leaving the *Herald*, she became a journalism pioneer. She wrote the first syndicated column intended for women. In 1868 when she discovered that the New York Press Club limited its reception honoring Charles Dickens to men, she

reacted by organizing a club for women. "Sorosis" was one of the earliest women's clubs to endure. In 1889 she founded the Women's Press Club of New York City. Late in life when she was appointed to a chair in journalism and literature at Rutgers Women's College, she became the first woman to teach journalism at the college level.[23]

NEWSPAPER COMPETITION

Augustus Maverick, who was one of Bennett's contemporaries, credited (or blamed) him for introducing the era of newspaper competition. "The ruthless Bennett," he contended, "shocked the staid propriety of his time by introducing the rivalries and the spirit of enterprise which have ever since been distinguishing characteristics of New York newspaper life.... The only cheap papers, in 1840, which pretended, with any show of reason, to publish all the news of the day, were the *Herald*, and Moses Y. Beach's *Sun*; and although the former of these was low and often scurrilous, and the latter silly, they attracted readers among the younger inhabitants of New York, who had begun to "tire" of the "phlegm" in the city's other newspapers.[24]

Until Greeley entered the scene in 1841 with his *New York Tribune*, most of the competition involved the *Herald* and the *Sun*, which Day had sold to Beach in 1838. The two papers spent thousands of dollars in trying to beat the other with the news. They set

[22]Ben Perley Poore, *Perley's Reminiscences of Sixty Years in the National Metropolis*, 2 volumes (Philadelphia, 1886), 1: 260-2.

[23]Madelon Golden Schilpp and Sharon M. Murphy, *Great Women of the Press* (Carbondale, 1983), 90-3.
[24]Maverick, *Henry J. Raymond*, 37-8.

up pony express systems and hired trains and used carrier pigeons. Once begun, competition became keener. New York newspapers, including even some of the more somber commercial ones, financed a news boat to meet incoming ships from Europe so the news could be in New York newspaper offices before the trans-Atlantic ships could dock. A breakdown in the system forced many of the papers to finance their own boats. So New York eventually had a fleet that would race to incoming ships and race back with the news.

Bennett tapped into a "pigeon express" founded by Daniel H. Craig, editor and proprietor of the *Boston Daily Mail*. Craig gathered news from the ships sailing into Boston harbor from Europe and sent reports to Bennett by carrier pigeon. From New York, Bennett sent the reports winging to William Swain of the *Philadelphia Public Ledger* and Arunah Abell of the *Baltimore Sun*. Each paper in the pigeon chain contributed its own news items, and the operation got European news to American newspapers three days faster than before. Bennett's rival in New York, the *Sun*, formed its own group of pigeon-linked newspapers; and the competition turned deadly after Craig got access to ships arriving in Halifax, Nova Scotia, before they docked in Boston. The pigeons were forced to fly through a barrage of bullets from sharpshooters to ensure that the news got into print.

What doomed the pigeon express, however, was not the mostly inaccurate fire of rooftop riflemen, but a development that revolutionized communications. In 1837, Samuel F. B. Morse applied for a patent for his magnetic telegraph, which used electricity to send signals over wires. The patent was granted in 1844, and soon a line connected Washington, D.C., and Baltimore. Operators, who could transcribe twenty-five to thirty words a minute, used code to send messages, including news about that year's national nominating conventions of the Whig and Democratic parties. Columns headed "Telegraphic News" began appearing in newspapers. When the telegraph line went up between New York and Boston in 1847, the days of the pigeon express were over.

Bennett exploited the telegraph and used it as a weapon in the New York circulation wars. Other papers were forced to drop out of the race or join in the potentially ruinous competition to see who could get news the quickest. Salvation for many came in the form of the news agency, a cooperative service that the telegraph made possible and, at the same time, necessary for survival. Five agencies existed in 1853, and all were operating on the general pattern established by Charles-Louis Havas when he set up Agence Havas in 1832. The organization, which employed Dr. Bernhard Wolff and Paul Julius Reuter before they founded their own agencies in Europe, established a sub-agency in New York in 1845. The following year, Moses Beach, owner of the *New York Sun*, set up a pony express to carry news of the Mexican War from Mobile, Ala., to Richmond, Va. He offered an equal interest in the venture to other New York newspapers, and four of them accepted.

The agency that would become today's Associated Press grew out of the pony express cooperative that Beach had started and the old Harbor News Association, which six New York newspapers

set up in 1848 to operate a news boat. In 1850 the papers formed the Telegraphic and General News Association of New York to get telegraphic news from Boston, Washington, and other places. The organization went through two name changes before settling on the New York Associated Press in 1858, the name it would keep until it shortened it to the Associated Press in 1893. The NYAP, which had access to its six original members, representatives in other major American cities, and the Reuters news agency, eventually contracted with other regional news agencies in other parts of the United States.[25]

Sometimes the competition to get the news first went to extremes, and reporters played tricks on each other. Maverick recounted, for instance, an occasion when "a messenger for the *Tribune* quietly gathered up the details of some important news, in a distant part of the country, and then ran away with it to New York on an engine which was waiting, under a full head of steam, for the use of the representative of the *Herald*. Of course, the *Tribune* had the news exclusively; and Bennett, very naturally, uttered blasphemies."[26]

Greeley and Bennett were convinced that their innovations in newsgathering and distribution were sound. The former commented in 1851 that apparently the public had gotten used to the competition and to getting news in a timely fashion. "The fact that certain journals have the earliest news soon becomes notorious," he said, "and almost every one wants his newspaper with his breakfast, delivered between the hours of five and half past seven. They take the morning papers to read with their breakfast."[27] Bennett also placed great value on timely news. He was so tough to work against that sixteen newspapers in Boston, New York, Philadelphia, Baltimore, and Washington banded together to try to get the news out before the *Herald*, or so, at least, Bennett told the story. He also declared to his readers that the *Herald* intended to compete against this "Holy Alliance," noting that it was the *Herald* that had introduced such competition into American journalism. "With our fleet of news clippers, manned by the hardiest men in existence, cruising always outside the Hook [Sandy Hook], at distances varying from fifty to two hundred and fifty miles from land, failure in getting news in the speediest way possible," he stated, "may appear out of the question."[28]

Before the advent of the penny press, newspapers relied on the chance arrival of ships and mail for most of their news. Bennett had experienced his share of problems with the slowness of the mail. He had been the Washington correspondent for the *New York Enquirer* in 1828 when he was thirty, and like other Washington correspondents he had been forced to put his letters in the mail by midnight to make sure they got off to northern cities early the next morning. New York newspapers were unable to publish the reporters' letters until two days after they were written, and Boston

25See Robert W. Desmond, *The Information Process: World News Reporting to the Twentieth Century* (Iowa City, Iowa, 1978). Chapter 7 covers the pigeon express, Chapter 8 the telegraph, and Chapter 9 the news agencies.

26Maverick, *Henry J. Raymond*, 39-40.

27House of Commons, report, London, September 16, 1851.

28*New York Herald*, 1846.

Tippecanoe and Tyler, Too
Before founding the hugely successful *New York Tribune*, Horace Greeley edited several Whig newspapers. One of them, the *Log Cabin*, was published during the 1840 campaign to promote William Henry Harrison for president, with John Tyler as his running mate.

papers usually could not publish them before the fourth day. Had it not been for the *Herald*, Bennett told readers, "the public would be to this day trusting to Uncle Sam's mail-bag for the earliest intelligence, both foreign and domestic."[29]

The competition also led to some of the pressure that made a newspaper job such demanding work. "Only those who have been placed upon the treadmill of a daily newspaper in New York know the severity of the strain it imposes upon the mental and physical powers. There is no cessation," one newsman explained. "A good newspaper never publishes that which is technically denominated 'old news,' — a phrase so significant in journalism as to be invested with untold horrors. All must be daily fresh, daily complete, daily polished and perfect; else the journal falls into disrepute, is distanced by its rivals, and, becoming 'dull,' dies."[30]

THE INFLUENTIAL GREELEY

Greeley knew all about hard work, too. Before starting the third major penny newspaper, the *New York Tribune*, he had been a job printer. He had also edited a literary paper and a couple of politi-

cal papers that supported the Whigs. The first of these was the *New-Yorker*, begun on March 22, 1834, while Greeley was running a job-printing business that he had returned to after the *Morning Post* had failed. The *New-Yorker*, which he founded in partnership with another printer by the name of Jonas Winchester, contained mostly literary material picked up from American and foreign publications, some editorials, and some political news. James Parton, a contemporary biographer of Greeley, claimed that the paper was politically neutral; but Thurlow Weed, one of the Whig leaders in New York, was so impressed with it that he asked Greeley to put out a statewide campaign newspaper for the party in 1838. Campaign papers were a common part of politics; and Weed and the Whigs' state committee chairman, thinking that Greeley favored the Whigs' plans for a strong tariff and other Whig policies, offered Greeley $1,000 to edit the publication. Greeley agreed. Although the paper was supposed to be a weekly costing 50¢ a year, most of its circulation was free; and wealthy party members paid its operating expenses.

Greeley was so willing to take on another job partly because he was desperate for money. Although the *New-Yorker*'s original list of twelve subscribers gradually grew to about 9,000, the newspaper never made much money, in part because Greeley sent copies to subscribers on credit and many never paid. He lost about $100 a week throughout 1837. "It was in vain that I appealed to delinquents to pay up," he recalled years later. "Many of them migrated; some died; others were so considerate as to order the paper stopped, but very few of these paid; and I struggled on against a steadily rising tide of adversity that might have appalled a stouter heart."[31] Greeley felt morally committed to continue the *New-Yorker* because at least 3,000 subscribers had paid in advance.

Thus Greeley took on the Whigs' campaign paper, the *Jeffersonian*, to help make ends meet, and the newspaper's year of existence was an exhausting one. The *New-Yorker* was published in New York, but the *Jeffersonian* operated out of Albany, 150 miles away. Greeley would no sooner get the *New-Yorker* to press and assign part of the copy for the next edition than he had to rush to catch the boat to Albany. The hard work, however, paid off. The *Jeffersonian* distributed about 15,000 copies a week and may have been one reason the Whigs won a decisive victory in New York while suffering defeat in other states. In New York, the party took the governorship and the lieutenant-governorship, won control of the state assembly, and made gains in the state senate.

Whig leaders then asked Greeley to edit a newspaper for General William Henry Harrison's run for the presidency in 1840. The paper was named the *Log Cabin* to foster the legend that Harrison, after returning to Ohio from his military ventures, had lived in a cabin. It was published between May 1 and November 1, 1840, with a subscription costing $5. The first page had campaign material, and the second had editorials and letters. There were reports of party victories on the third page, and the fourth page had campaign songs and miscellaneous articles. One of the early tiffs — there were to be others — between Weed and Greeley centered on

[29]Ibid.
[30]Maverick, *Henry J. Raymond*, 220.
[31]Greeley, *Recollections*, 95.

Greeley and the *Tribune*

Horace Greeley was not impressed with other sensational penny dailies when he founded the *New York Tribune* in 1841. He attempted to keep it on a high moral plane while exposing readers to the latest in liberal philosophy. He attracted to the staff the most talented group of journalists of the era. This early, rare daguerrotype by Matthew Brady shows Greeley (seated, second from right) flanked by his top assistants. They are (standing, left to right) William Henry Fry, Charles Dana, Henry Raymond, (seated, left to right) George M. Snow, Bayard Taylor, Greeley, and George Ripley. Most of them became prominent journalists in their own right.

the campaign music. Greeley wanted to publish the songs with music, but Weed thought the plates took up too much space.

Greeley was the type of man and hard-working journalist who won the respect of many of his contemporaries. Weed represents a case in point. He was a journalist of considerable repute as well as a power in the Whig party and, after that, in the Republican party. Greeley, Weed wrote some years later, was "unselfish, conscientious, public spirited, and patriotic ... [and] had no habits or tastes but for work, steady, indomitable work." Regarding their differences, Weed could also recall: "Our sentiments and opinions of public measures and public men harmonized perfectly; our only difference was, that upon the temperance, slavery, and labor questions he was more ardent and hopeful. In this I gave him credit for fresher and less disciplined feelings."[32]

Another astute observer, Benjamin Perley Poore, also was impressed with Greeley, and wrote of him: "He was a man of intense convictions and wielded an incisive, ready pen, which went straight to the point without circumlocution or needless use of words. Although he was a somewhat erratic champion of Fourierism, vegetarianism, temperance, anti-hanging, and abolition, there was a 'method in his madness,' and his heretical views were evidently the honest convictions of his heart. Often egotistical, dogmatic, and personal, no one could question his uprightness and thorough devotion to the noblest principles of progressive civilization. Inspired by that true philanthropy that loves all mankind equally and every one of his neighbors better than himself, he was often victimized by those whose stories he believed and to

whom he loaned his hard-earned savings. The breath of slander did not sully his reputation, and he never engaged in lobbying at Washington for money, although friendship several times prompted him to advocate appropriations for questionable jobs — the renewal of patents which were monopolies, and the election of public printers who were notoriously corrupt."[33]

THE NEW YORK TRIBUNE

When Greeley put out the first issue of the *Tribune* on April 10, 1841, there were about a hundred periodicals and twelve daily newspapers in New York City. Four Whig papers sold for $10 each a year, and two other political newspapers that sold for the same price supported the Democratic party. There were three cheap, non-aligned dailies, along with Beach's *Sun* and Bennett's *Herald*. For all practical purposes the latter was Democratic. The absence of a cheap, Whig-oriented daily was one reason Greeley brought out the *Tribune* on what he described as a "leaden funereal morning, the most inhospitable of the year." It was the morning of New York's funeral parade and pageant for President Harrison, who had died after serving only a month in office.

But Greeley had ideas other than politics for his newspaper. He did not intend to establish a strictly Whig paper. In fact, as he later recollected, he had as much disdain for "servile partisanship" as he did for "mincing neutrality." What political position, then, did he wish to support? He later answered that he had tried to find the "happy medium" between the extremes of partisanship. The position he wished to defend was that "from which a journalist might

[32]Thurlow Weed, *Autobiography of Thurlow Weed*, edited by his daughter, Harriet A. Weed (Boston, 1883), 467.

[33]Poore, *Perley's Reminiscences*, 1: 238-9.

openly and heartily advocate the principles and commend the measures of that party to which his convictions allied him, yet frankly dissent from its course on a particular question, and even denounce its candidates if they were shown to be deficient in capacity or (far worse) in integrity." He even argued that "a journal thus loyal to its guiding convictions, yet ready to expose and condemn unworthy conduct or incidental error on the part of men attached to its party, must be far more effective, even party-wise, than though it might always be counted on to applaud or reprobate, bless or curse, as the party's prejudices or immediate interest might seem to prescribe."[34]

Other newspapers did not greet Greeley's *Tribune* with joy. The *Sun* tried to destroy it shortly after it came out for fear that the *Sun* would lose business to Greeley. It attempted to bribe Greeley's carriers to give up their routes and threatened that they would not be allowed to sell the *Sun* if they also sold the *Tribune*. It also sent newsboys to beat up Greeley's carriers. Despite the intimidation, Greeley secured 500 potential subscribers from names his political colleagues provided, printed 5,000 copies of the first issue, and almost managed to give away all that he could not sell. During the first three weeks, he acquired 300 new subscribers a day; and by the seventh week, the *Tribune* was printing 11,000 copies, all that its press could handle. The four columns of ads in the first issue ballooned to thirteen in the 100th issue. Such growth and profits forced Greeley to buy new presses that could print 3,500 copies an hour; and at the end of the first year, the *Tribune* had 12,000 subscribers.

Greeley hoped to publish a newspaper in which readers could find everything they needed to keep up with important events by reading only that one paper. Noticing Bennett's success with his stable of correspondents, Greeley moved to establish his own. He sent his city editor, Charles A. Dana (who later was to become one of the nation's outstanding journalists), to Europe during the political upheavals of 1848 and 1849 to cover events in Berlin, London, and Paris. Greeley also had four stringers in Europe, two in Canada, and still more in Mexico, Cuba, and Central America. Bayard Taylor, who was famed for his travel writing and poetry, worked as a roving correspondent from 1844 to 1854. He covered the 1849 California gold rush and Commodore Matthew Perry's attempts to open up Japan to western trade in 1853. He also wrote extensively from Africa, China, Egypt, India, and the Middle East.

In Rome for the Italian revolution of 1848-1849 was Margaret Fuller. Greeley had been publishing her work since 1844 after being impressed with her influential feminist tract, *Woman in the Nineteenth Century*. She brought to her job as literary critic and general reporter a keenly honed mind that was largely self-educated, a wealth of contacts among the Transcendentalists, and experience as co-editor of *The Dial*, the Transcendentalist magazine. In 1846 she left for Europe, following a German Jewish immigrant with whom she had had a secret romantic relationship. Greeley published her articles from London about a number of British literary figures and her later articles from Rome, where she went in

[34]Greeley, *Recollections*, 137.

Margaret Fuller
One of the earliest female foreign correspondents, Fuller began writing for Horace Greeley's *New York Tribune* in 1844. Returning to the United States from Europe in 1850, she died, along with her Italian husband and their son, when their ship struck a sand bar near New York Harbor during a storm.

1847 after getting caught up in the cause of Italy, struggling to free itself under the banner of Giuseppe Garibaldi from French and Austrian domination. She became the secret lover of the Marchese Giovanni Angelo d'Ossoli and bore a son in 1848. She took d'Ossoli's name and continued writing articles about European politics and the Italian revolution. When the revolution collapsed during the French bombardment of Rome in February 1849, the d'Ossolis fled to Florence, where their questionable marital status shocked the English-speaking community and outraged Greeley to the point that he refused to continue printing her correspondence.

While Greeley developed an excellent reputation for covering the news, he offered his readers more. The *Tribune* published lectures, book excerpts, serialized novels, poems, and book reviews. It took such a high moral ground — refusing to publish reports of police courts, sensational murder trials, and the theater — that it became known as the "Great Moral Organ."

The thing that set the *Tribune* apart, however, was its editorial position, which was a reflection of its owner. He neither smoked nor drank and was an ardent prohibitionist. He was against slavery and capital punishment, and he supported labor unions and westward expansion.

Having seen the sufferings of the poor during the terrible winter of 1838, Greeley became a socialist for a number of years. It was, in fact, his interest in socialism of the Brooke Farm variety that produced the first major difference between him and Weed. In 1842, Greeley allowed a group to buy the right to run the articles of Albert Brisbane, a well-known socialist, in one column a day on the front page of the *Tribune*. Weed thought that Brisbane would try to remodel the American social system and replace it with his own brand of socialism. The disagreement, Weed remembered, was friendly; and he noted that Greeley later changed his views on socialism. But the change did not occur before Greeley allowed his managing editor, Charles Dana, to publish many articles between 1851 and 1862 under the byline of Karl Marx, the founder of communism. Dana was impressed by Marx, whom he had met in Cologne in 1848, and a few years later employed him to contribute biweekly articles on European affairs. Friedrich Engels, Marx's loyal collaborator, wrote many of these articles at first; but by 1853 Marx was writing most of them himself. After the Crimean War ended in 1856, American interest in Europe waned; and, as the boom of the early 1850s faded, the *Tribune* had to economize. Consequently, Dana cut back the number of articles he could accept from Marx. In doing so he tried to find other work for Marx in this country with *The American Encyclopedia* and with various magazines. By 1862 when Marx's work for the *Tribune* ended, he had contributed almost 500 articles to the paper.

There is no question of the newspaper's controversial nature. Parton wrote that "men have been heard to talk of their Bible, their Shakespeare, and their *Tribune*, as the three necessities of their spiritual life." But those who did not like the paper, he added, "dislike it excessively, and are wont to protest that they should deem their houses defiled by its presence."[35] A piece appearing in the *Tribune* in the early 1850s demonstrated its position. The writer explained that "in a world so full as this is of wrong and suffering, of oppression and degradation, there must be radical causes for so many and so vast practical evils." Much of the world's progress, he went on to say, resulted from "the fearless thought and speech of those who dare be in advance of their time — who are sneered at and shunned through their days of struggle and of trial as lunatics, dreamers, impracticables and visionaries — men of crotchets, of vagaries, or of 'isms.'"[36]

While the *Tribune* did not always live up to Greeley's professed moral standards, it was an influential newspaper. Farmers treated its weekly edition as gospel, and Greeley's Chautauqua circuit lectures always were well attended. In most of the paramount national issues of the mid-nineteenth century — from abolition to internal improvements, from temperance to westward expansion — Greeley played a pre-eminent role.

THE PENNY PRESS AND THE MEXICAN WAR

Many of the penny press' innovations helped it cover its first big war, the Mexican War of 1846-1848. At issue was much of the territory that is now the southwestern part of the United States but

[35]Parton, *Life of Horace Greeley*, 383.
[36]Ibid., 384.

Go West Greeley

Horace Greeley's impact on American life was great, but nowhere could it be seen more than in the westward migration of America. He repeated the counsel to move west so frequently that by the 1830s he had been tagged with the nickname "Go West Greeley." "Go west, young man" became a national slogan. He continued to urge westward movement after founding the *New York Tribune*. No editor probably ever played a more decisive role in an issue of such national importance.

that then was part of Mexico. Tension had existed between the United States and Mexico ever since the successful Anglo revolution in Texas in 1835-1836, which ended in the creation of the Republic of Texas. When the U.S. Congress approved annexation of Texas in March 1845, the Mexican government cut diplomatic relations with the United States; and both nations posted troops at the Rio Grande. The United States failed in subsequent attempts to buy the California and New Mexico territories. After a border clash near Matamoras in April 1846, the United States declared war the following month.

With his network of stringers, Bennett had positioned himself well to cover the war, but he also had an agreement with the *New Orleans Picayune* to supply him with news. Founded by George W. Kendall and Francis Lumsden in 1837, the *Picayune* was one of twelve English-language dailies that published in New Orleans during the war and was the city's first cheap daily. Kendall, who rode with General Zachary Taylor and saw action at Monterey, Buena Vista, and Vera Cruz, set up an express to speed war news

to the *Herald.* Riders, often forced to evade the fire of Mexican soldiers, carried Kendall's dispatches from the interior of Mexico to
Vera Cruz or Port Isabel on the Gulf of Mexico. Ships ferried the
reports to New Orleans and the *Picayune,* and from there a relay of
sixty riders sped the news to the southern tip of the nation's telegraph system at Richmond, Virginia. This "Great Southern Daily
Express" cut two days off the ten-day period it took mail to get
from New Orleans to New York. Northern readers now waited
only two to five weeks to read news of the fighting in Mexico.

Other northern newspapers made similar arrangements. The
New York Sun, along with the *Charleston Courier* in South Carolina,
was associated with the *New Orleans Crescent;* and Philadelphia's
North American and the *Boston Journal* had an agreement with the
New Orleans Delta. Both New Orleans papers had correspondents
in the field. American papers generally were unable, however, to
post correspondents in Mexican cities. Filling the gap was *La Patria*
of New Orleans, the first Spanish-language daily in the United
States. Many American newspapers reprinted reports from *La
Patria's* correspondents.[37]

The *New York Sun* printed reports from female correspondent
Jane McManus Storm, who had traveled to Mexico with *Sun* owner Moses Yale Beach and his daughter. She left the Beaches to travel alone to the principal American camp, where she took up with
an officer and had access to much information in her reports to the
Sun. She also contributed letters to two other penny newspapers.
Greeley's *Tribune* and the *Philadelphia Public Ledger.*

RAYMOND AND THE NEW YORK TIMES

Working for Greeley during the *Tribune's* first two years was a
young reporter who later would establish the only New York penny newspaper still surviving today, the *New York Times.* In 1843,
the 23-year-old Henry Raymond thought that he was overworked
and underpaid. He had joined Greeley as a staffer on the old *New-
Yorker,* and for his first three weeks he was not even paid. "I added
up election returns, read the exchanges for news, and discovered
a good deal which others had overlooked; made brief notices of
new books, read proof, and made myself generally useful," Raymond recalled.[38] When he got a teaching job and was about to
leave, Greeley rather offhandedly remarked that he could match
the salary the school would pay. So Raymond joined the payroll at
$8 a week.

When Greeley founded the *Tribune,* Raymond became his first
assistant. Although his pay remained the same, his duties increased; and he found himself covering public meetings, writing
editorials and book reviews, clipping material from other papers
to print in the *Tribune,* and making up the newspaper. By 1843, he
had had all he could stand and went to work for the *New York
Courier and Enquirer.* Although he later was to become Greeley's
political rival, Greeley charitably assessed Raymond's years on the

Tribune. In his autobiography, which was published a year before
Raymond's untimely death at the age of forty-nine, Greeley wrote:
"I never found another person, barely of age and just from his
studies, who evinced so signal and such versatile ability in journalism as [Raymond] did. Abler and stronger men I may have met;
a cleverer, readier, more generally efficient journalist, I never
saw."[39]

James Parton also lamented Raymond's departure from the *Tribune,* saying that he could have made the paper into "the great, only, undisputed Metropolitan Journal" sooner than destiny would
allow. Greeley was more of a legislator, a person who could suggest how to solve problems, than he was an editor; and it was as
an editor that Raymond could have been of help. Parton observed
that "Mr. Raymond is not a man of first-rate talent — great talent
would be in his way — he is most interesting when he attacks; and
of the varieties of composition, polished vituperation is not the
most difficult. But he has the right *notion* of editing a daily paper,
and when the *Tribune* lost him, it lost more than it had the slightest idea of — as events have since shown."[40] Whether Parton, writing in 1855 after Raymond founded the *Times,* was right about his
talent, he was certainly right about his newspapering ability.

When the *Times* appeared in 1851, the *Herald* and the *Tribune*
each had its following, but there was a third group of readers who
cared for neither paper. It was to this group of "quiet domestic,
fireside, conservative readers," as Hudson called them, that Raymond and the *Times* appealed.[41] Most people of the mid-nineteenth century took a daily paper to find out what was going on in
the world. "They are averse," Parton noted, "to profligacy and
time-serving [a reference to Bennett's *Herald*], and yet are offended
at the independent avowal of ideas in advance of their own [a reference to Greeley's *Tribune*]."[42]

Before the appearance of the *Times,* the reader was faced with
little choice. As Augustus Maverick, Raymond's contemporary
and biographer, once complained, the alternative was "either the
six-penny journals of Wall street, with meagre supplies of news, or
the cheaper *Tribune* and *Herald,* with all the intelligence of the day
overlaid and almost extinguished by the Socialistic heresies of the
one and the abominable nastiness of the other." What choice was
that? Maverick claimed that "heads of families feared to take the
Tribune to their homes, because its teachings were the apotheosis
of vice. They could get their tidings of the news of the world
through Bennett's *Herald* only at the cost of wading through heaps
of rubbish. The predicament was unpleasant."[43]

Although in appearance the *Times* was much like the others —
four pages of six columns each, with the front page displaying foreign and local news — it would offer a new alternative. Raymond
planned to publish a paper comprehensive in content and
independent in terms of political preference. It would champion
"the public good." Sometimes that would lead it to be conserva-

[37]See Desmond, *The Information Process,* Chapter 10; and Tom Reilly, "'The War Press of New
Orleans': 1846-1848," *Journalism History* 13 (1986): 86-95.
[38]Quoted in Maverick, *Henry J. Raymond,* 29.

[39]Greeley, *Recollections,* 138-9.
[40]Parton, *Life of Horace Greeley,* 205.
[41]Hudson, *Journalism in the United States,* 621.
[42]Parton, *Life of Horace Greeley,* 382.
[43]Maverick, *Henry J. Raymond,* 53.

Henry Raymond and the *New York Times*
In contrast to the approaches of Horace Greeley's *New York Tribune* and James Gordon Bennett's *Herald* — and in a pointed gibe at his rivals — Raymond stated that in starting the *New York Times*, "[w]e do not mean to write as if we were in a passion, — unless that shall really be the case; and we shall make it a point to get into a passion as rarely as possible."

tive; sometimes, radical. "We do not believe," he wrote in the paper's prospectus, "that *everything* in society is either exactly right or exactly wrong; what is good we desire to preserve and improve; what is evil, to exterminate and reform."[44] With time, the paper developed a reputation for fair, careful, accurate reporting with an emphasis on foreign affairs. It was a newspaper designed for the masses but without the sensationalism of the *Sun* and the *Herald* or the sometimes scatterbrained ideas of the *Tribune*.

At first, the *Times* faced uncertainty. Raymond spent six months in Europe recuperating from health problems immediately before the first issue appeared, relying on his employees to get the paper ready to go. Some of the other papers threatened their carriers with loss of routes if they also carried the *Times*, but the *Times* lived long enough to attract some of its rivals' best employees. The circulation climbed to 20,000 in the first ten weeks, partly because Raymond had the paper delivered free for a week to thousands of homes. At the end of his first year, Raymond estimated the *Times* had spent $13,000 on editors, $25,000 on mechanical work, $40,000 on paper, and $50,000 on the press and "general outfit," a total of $128,000 — and all before turning a profit. His own salary was $50 a week, and he was forced to take it because he was having trouble getting some of his back salary from his previous employer. The other investors, however, had to wait until the paper became

profitable before they could begin to get their money back.

Because of his first-year expenses, Raymond raised the price of the *Times* to 2¢ an issue, the same price readers were paying for the *Herald* and the *Tribune*. He used the extra income to double the number of pages, but the price increase lost him a third of his circulation, which he had claimed at the end of the first year to be 25,000. The loss was only temporary, though, and by 1860 the *Times* was not far behind the *Tribune* in circulation. Both trailed the *Herald* and the *Sun*.

THE POLITICAL RAYMOND

Raymond was as much involved in politics as Greeley, although Raymond worked much more successfully with party machinery. In fact, he might have been able to make the *Times* much better had he not spent so much time on politics. He served in the New York legislature and U. S. Congress, participated in national political conventions, and was elected lieutenant governor of New York. In 1852, he decided to be a journalist and stay out of politics, but the pledge lasted only two years before he jumped back into the political arena. Maverick thought that was "the great misfortune of his life" and wrote: "Had Raymond remained a journalist, untouched by the corrupting influences of party chicanery, and unsullied by evil association, the record of his life would have had no deep shadows."[45]

Nevertheless, some of Raymond's political efforts were of consequence in state and national politics. He played a major role in the Whig party in New York during the early 1850s, and he served as a Whig in the New York assembly from 1849-1851. In 1856 he became a supporter of the recently formed Republican party. Thereafter, he remained active in that party and was one of its key figures. He became President Lincoln's steadiest supporter in New York during the Civil War. By 1864, he was considered one of the nation's Republican leaders. While serving as a congressman from New York from 1865 to 1867, he became the administration's leader in the House of Representatives. He was a supporter of President Andrew Johnson's moderate reconstruction policy after the Civil War; but the failure of that policy severely damaged his political influence. In 1866 he was expelled from the Republican national committee when it became clear that his opinions differed from those of the majority of that body. Afterwards, until his death in 1869, he devoted most of his efforts to the *Times*.

Even though the character of newspapers had changed by the 1850s, friends still gave some of them political favors. The superintendent of the federal Bank Department, for example, had been a shareholder in the *Times* and gave it the contract to publish the weekly statements of the metropolitan banks. The *Times* was supposed to pass on the proof-slips so other newspapers could publish the information as news, but it invariably was late in getting them to the *Tribune*. Greeley wrote a nasty letter to the superintendent in 1853, beginning an acrid exchange of letters between the two in which the banking official denied a conflict of interest. In

[44]*New York Times*, 18 September 1851.

[45]Maverick, *Henry J. Raymond*, 142.

one of the letters, Greeley charged:

> I have a most insolent and scoundrelly letter from your favorite, Raymond, offering to send me these returns at his own convenience if I will credit them to the *Times* (not to the Bank Department, of which only have I asked them), and talking of his willingness to *grant favors* to those who prove worthy of them, but not to be *"kicked into benevolence,"* etc. *All this insolence of this little villain is founded on your injustice.*[46]

Raymond was known as the "little villain" for the rest of his life.

The bad feelings between the two had been growing ever since Raymond left the *Tribune* for the *Courier and Enquirer*. Their differences first became public during their debate over socialism, published by both newspapers before Raymond founded the *Times*. The main source of the trouble, however, may have been that both aspired to political office. Raymond achieved it, but Greeley did not (except for filling out an unexpired term in Congress). "These political honors made the *Times* more antagonistic to the *Tribune*," Hudson wrote. "More favors were showered upon Raymond than upon Greeley, and the latter looked upon the fact as one of ingratitude in every way and sense."[47]

In spite of his political work, Raymond made sure that the *Times* was aggressive in covering the news. When a steamer was lost in 1854, for example, *Times* reporters went all over the city checking out rumors that a survivor had turned up, but they were unable to find him. As the city department editor went home in his horse-car at 3 a.m., he overheard a conversation that indicated that the *Herald* had given the survivor a bottle of wine and was keeping him in its offices. The *Herald* paid well for exclusive news. The *Times* man returned to his office and got a pressroom worker to obtain, somehow, a copy of the *Herald*, which was being withheld from street circulation until 9 a.m. Then the *Times* called all its compositors back to work; and the whole story, stolen from the early edition of the *Herald*, was set in an hour. The *Times* was on the streets by 8 a.m., beating the *Herald* on its own story. The city editor got a $5 a week raise, and the sticky-fingered pressman got a $50 bonus.

REFLECTIONS ON THE CHEAP PRESS

The innovations of the cheap newspapers in New York were picked up by papers in other major cities, and contemporary observers thought that the revolution in the daily press would bring about a revolution in American society. Bennett boasted that a free press conducted by genius and talent could be the real government of a civilized people. He even believed that his type of journalism had "defended pure religion from the insults and attacks of its professed friends." He claimed, "We can at least declare that the aim of this journal [the *Herald*] has ever been to show that religion stripped of cant, hypocrisy, and sectarianism, is the only founda-

New York Times, 1851
The building at 113 Nassau Street was not ready when, "on the night of the 17th of September [1851], the first number of *The Times* was made up" amid construction debris, wrote staff member Augustus Maverick. "All was raw and dismal," as staff worked in "open lofts, destitute of windows, gas, speaking tubes, dumb waiters, and general conveniences." He remembered "sitting by the open window at midnight, looking through the dim distance at [Henry] Raymond's first lieutenant, who was diligently writing brevier [editorial copy] at a rickety table at the end of the barren garret; his only light a flaring candle, held upright by three nails in a block of wood; at the city editor and the newsmen and the reporters, all eagerly scratching pens over paper, their countenances half lighted, half shaded, by other fluttering candles; at Raymond, writing rapidly and calmly, as he always wrote, but under similar disadvantages. And all the night the soft summery air blew where it listed, and sometimes blew out the feeble lights, and grim little [printers'] 'devils' came down at intervals from the printing-room, and cried for copy; and … every man in the company, from the chief to the police reporter, gave his whole mind to the preparation of the initial sheet."

tion on which the prosperity and happiness of nations or individuals can repose."[48]

The early biographers of the leaders of the penny press shared their subjects' enthusiasm. Greeley's biographer, James Parton, thought that the penny press would have more effect on the nation than anything that had happened in the first seventy years of its history. He predicted:

> Its results, in this country, have already been wonderful indeed, and it is destined to play a great part in the history of every civ-

---

[46]Greeley to D.B. St. John, 16 August 1853.
[47]Hudson, *Journalism in the United States,* 626.

[48]Quoted in Pray, *Memoirs of James Gordon Bennett,* 278.

ilized nation, and in that of every nation yet to be civilized.... The Cheap Press — its importance cannot be estimated! It puts every mind in direct communication with the greatest minds, which all, in one way or another, speak through its columns. It brings the *Course of Events* to bear on the progress of every individual. It is the great leveller, elevator and democratizer. It makes this huge Commonwealth, else so heterogeneous and disunited, think with one mind, feel with one heart, and talk with one tongue. Dissolve the Union into a hundred petty States, and the Press will still keep us, in heart and soul and habit, One People.[49]

Isaac Pray, Bennett's biographer, thought that the press' increasing ability to disseminate quickly the words of speakers would profoundly affect the nation and its politics. People could be galvanized to get out from under the control of the old-style political parties and their journals. "Thus Journalism and popular eloquence go hand in hand throughout the country," he wrote, "exciting men to thought and action, not in the old beaten track of political dictators, but on the broad ground of justice and the common welfare."[50]

Even a rival of the cheap press could print praise. Less than two months after the appearance of the *Herald* in 1835, the editor of New York's *Journal of Commerce* wrote that the penny papers were conducted with as "much talent" as their more expensive rivals. He even reflected that "in point of moral character we think candidly they are superior to their sixpenny contemporaries.... The number of newspaper readers is probably doubled by their influence, and they circulate as pioneers among those classes who have suffered greatly from want of general intelligence." Believing the cheaper papers were "less partisan in politics than the large papers, and more decidedly American, with one or two exceptions...," he concluded by wishing his "penny associates all success, hoping that they will grow wise, good, and great, until they make every sixpenny paper ashamed that tells a lie, or betrays its country for the sake of party, or does any other base thing."[51]

The penny press, of course, did not live up to all these expectations; but it did bring about important, if gradual, changes to the nation's newspapers. New readers were attracted to the changes in writing style and content — the increased emphasis on sensationalism, human interest, and local news. While there was an abundance of examples of newspaper hoaxes and while even the mass circulation dailies still were tied to political parties, the relatively neutral reporting of facts — what would be called "objectivity" later — gained ground. Specialization in personnel and newswriting increased as newspapers became larger organizations. Bennett introduced his "money articles," and editorials began to become distinct from news stories. Sportswriting appeared, and there was more on-the-scene reporting from the political battlegrounds in Washington, D.C., and the military battlegrounds of the Mexican War and European revolutions. The printing technology that let the penny press reach its mass audience also let it change the appearance of the product. The newspaper became larger, and there was a greater use of headlines in "decks" (one-column headlines followed by subheads).

Just as important as changes in content were the changes in distribution and financing. The London Plan of circulation on the streets — rather than circulation by subscription only — gave publishers a powerful tool to reach readers who could not be reached by mail. New types of advertising — want ads, personals, and display ads — and the decision to force advertisers to change ad copy every day shifted the financial base of the newspaper from subscriptions to advertising.

The one-person shop was a thing of the past. The newspaper now was often an organization of more than a hundred persons, and its voice spoke to thousands more. It was becoming a ubiquitous institution in American society.

RECOMMENDED READINGS

BOOKS

Bryant II, William Cullen. *Power for Sanity: Selected Editorials of William Cullen Bryant, 1829-1861*. New York, 1994. This anthology provides a chronological collection of the editorials of Bryant, one of the greatest opinion writers of all time.

Carlson, Oliver. *The Man Who Made News*. New York, 1942. James Gordon Bennett was instrumental in the development of news as an instrument to sell newspapers.

Cohen, Patricia Cline. *The Murder of Helen Jewett: The Life and Death of a Prostitute in Nineteenth-Century New York*. New York, 1998. The penny press covered one of the most sensational stories of the day.

Copeland, Fayette. *Kendall of the Picayune*. Norman, Okla., 1943. George W. Kendall brought the penny press revolution to New Orleans. He was one of the first American war correspondents.

Crouthamel, James L. *Bennett's New York Herald and the Rise of the Popular Press*. Syracuse, N.Y., 1989. Bennett made major contributions to journalistic practices.

Dell-Orto, Giovanna. *Giving Meanings to the World: The First U.S. Correspondents, 1838–1859*. Westport, Conn., 2002. American newspapers began using more foreign news from the 1830s on.

Huntzicker, William E. *The Popular Press, 1833-1865*. Westport, Conn., 1999. This survey history covers the penny press, along with journalism in general and alternative publications during the period.

Johnson, Gerald W., Frank R. Kent, H.L. Mencken, and Hamilton Owens. *The Sunpapers of Baltimore*. New York, 1937. The *Baltimore Sun* was that city's leading penny newspaper.

Mitchell, Catherine C., ed. *Margaret Fuller's New York Journalism: A Bibliographical Essay and Key Writings*. Knoxville, Tenn., 1995. This collection focuses on Fuller's journalistic writings at the time she was in charge of the *New York Tribune's* literary department under Horace Greeley.

Muller, Gilbert. *William Cullen Bryant: Author of America*. Albany, N.Y., 2008. An advocate of abolition, Bryant wrote editorials in support of Abraham Lincoln.

O'Brien, Frank M. *The Story of the Sun*. New York, 1918. This history of the first successful penny newspaper provides an account from its founding in 1833 into the twentieth century.

Oslin, George P. *The Story of Telecommunications*. Macon, Ga., 1992. This history provides a detailed and anecdotal account of wired communication, from the telegraph to television.

Schwarzlose, Richard A. *The Nation's Newsbrokers: Volume One, The Formative Years: From Pretelegraph to 1865*. Evanston, Ill., 1989; and *The Nation's Newsbrokers: Volume Two, The Rush to Institution: From 1820 to 1920*. Evanston, Ill., 1990. This history of cooperative newsgathering emphasizes the interrelationship among

---

[49]Parton, *Life of Horace Greeley*, 137-9.
[50]Pray, *Memoirs of James Gordon Bennett*, 418.
[51]*New York Journal of Commerce*, 29 June 1835.

newspapers, telegraph companies, and news agencies.

Seitz, Don C. *The James Gordon Bennetts; Father and Son; Proprietors of the New York Herald*. Indianapolis, 1928. The Bennetts, who ran the *Herald* from 1835 to 1918, formed "the longest newspaper dynasty we Americans have known."

Sloan, Wm. David, Cheryl Watts, and Joanne Sloan. *Great Editorials*, 2nd ed. Northport, Ala., 1997. This anthology gives special attention to the best editorial writers that American journalism has produced. It includes works not only from the penny press era but from colonial times to the present.

Solomon, Martha M. *A Voice of Their Own: The Woman Suffrage Press, 1840-1910*. Tuscaloosa, Ala., 1991. Efforts by women's suffrage publications resulted in heightened awareness of women's issues, which were often ignored by the mainstream newspapers.

Stevens, John D. *Sensationalism and the New York Press*. New York, 1991. From the penny-press era to the present, New York City readers have been particularly interested in tabloid journalism.

Stoddard, Henry L. *Horace Greeley: Printer, Editor, Crusader*. New York, 1946. Greeley was brilliant, independent, generous, resolute, and industrious, yet changeable, profane, lonely, and unhappy. He supported various serious reforms but also was inclined to fads.

Thompson, Susan. *The Penny Press*. Northport, Ala., 2004. The penny press provided the origins of many practices that became standard in journalism. This book is the essential work on the history of the penny press.

Tucher, Andie. *Froth and Scum: Truth, Beauty, Goodness, and the Ax Murder in America's First Mass Medium*. Chapel Hill, 1994. In covering crime, the New York penny press used the emerging concept of objectivity for social and cultural purposes.

Van Deusen, Glyndon Garlock. *Horace Greeley: Nineteenth Century Crusader*. Philadelphia, 1953. Greeley was a symbol of his age and the *New York Tribune* as a national institution, mirroring mid-19th century ideas on such issues as nationalism, reform, and party politics.

Williams, Robert Chadwell. *Horace Greeley: Champion of American Freedom*. New York, 2006. Greeley's lifelong quest was for universal freedom. He became a major figure in American politics and reform movements, including slavery, westward expansion, the Civil War, and the demise of the Whig and birth of the Republican parties.

ARTICLES

Bjork, Ulf Jonas. "The Commercial Roots of Foreign Correspondence: The *New York Herald* and Foreign News, 1835-1839." *American Journalism* 11 (1994): 102-15. Bennett built up a staff of foreign correspondents to compete with the commercial press.

—. "Sketches of Life and Society: Horace Greeley's Vision for Foreign Correspondence." *American Journalism* 14 (1997): 359-75. Greeley's concept of foreign correspondence was that of travel letters that went beyond matters of politics to describe the "feelings, hardships, hopes and antipathies" of people abroad.

—. "'Sweet Is the Tale': A Context for the *New York Sun's* Moon Hoax." *American Journalism* 18:4 (2001): 13-27. Editors recognized the story as a hoax but published it for its entertainment value.

Blondheim, Menahem. "The Click: Telegraphic Technology, Journalism, and the Transformation of the New York Associated Press." *American Journalism* 17 (Fall 2000): 27-52. The telegraph and the press mutually influenced each other.

Borchard, Gregory A. "The *New York Tribune* and the 1844 Election: Horace Greeley, Gangs and the Wise Men of Gotham." *Journalism History* 33:1 (2007): 51-59. Greeley "failed to anticipate the effect of certain variables — including gang activities, a third-party movement, and press leaks — on the election results."

Bradshaw, James Stanford. "George W. Wisner and the New York *Sun*." *Journalism History* 6 (1979-1980): 112, 117-21. Wisner was responsible for most of the contents of the *Sun*, including its police-court reports.

Copeland, David A. "A Series of Fortunate Events: Why People Believed Richard Adams Locke's 'Moon Hoax.'" *Journalism History* 33:3 (2007): 140-50. The *New York Sun's* "moon hoax" "was accepted at the time as factual because [it] was a series based on the contemporary wisdom of the age."

Eberhard, Wallace B. "Mr. Bennett Covers a Murder Trial." *Journalism Quarterly* 47

(1970): 457-63. James Gordon Bennett challenged the contempt power of the court trying a murder case in Salem, Mass. His work demonstrated his audacity and his "deep dedication" to the profession of journalism.

Hoffert, Sylvia D. "New York City's Penny Press and the Issue of Woman's Rights, 1848-1860." *Journalism Quarterly* 70 (1993): 656-65. The New York penny press gave wide attention to the woman's rights movement in the antebellum period and provided a voice for movement activists who lacked a newspaper of their own.

Mulcrone, Mick. "The Famine Irish and the Irish-American Press: Strangers in a Hostile Land." *American Journalism* 20:3 (2003): 49-72. When Irishmen emigrated to the United States during the potato famine, Irish-American newspapers defended them against nativist attacks.

Nelson, Anna Kasten. "Secret Agents and Security Leaks: President Polk and the Mexican War." *Journalism Quarterly* 52 (1975): 9-14. Presidents had problems with national security and the press during the penny press period.

Nilsson, Nils Gunnar. "The Origin of the Interview." *Journalism Quarterly* 48 (1971): 707-13. In the 1830s, penny press reporters, led by James Gordon Bennett, began using question-and-answer story forms and placing an emphasis on human interest material. "From there the step to the interview was very short."

Pickett, Calder. "Technology and the New York Press in the 19th Century." *Journalism Quarterly* 37 (1960): 398-407. For newspapers in the mid-nineteenth century to survive, they had to adopt the new communication and printing technology.

Reilly, Tom. "Newspaper Suppression During the Mexican War, 1846-1848." *Journalism Quarterly* 54 (1977): 262-70. This article demonstrates that military-press conflict is not just a modern-day problem.

—. "A Spanish-Language Voice of Dissent in Antebellum New Orleans." *Louisiana History* 23 (1983): 325-39. In opposing American intervention in Cuba in 1851 and the Mexican War, *La Union* stood up against prevailing sentiment among the Anglo-American populace of New Orleans.

Reiss, Benjamin. "P.T. Barnum, Joice Heth and Antebellum Spectacles of Race." *American Quarterly* 51:1 (1999): 78-107. Barnum used the penny press to claim that Heth was a 161-year-old slave who had nursed George Washington.

Risley, Ford. "Newspapers and Timeliness: The Impact of the Telegraph and the Internet." *American Journalism* 17:4 (2000): 97-103. Newspapers took advantage of the telegraph to publish timely news.

—. "The Savannah *Morning News* as a Penny Paper: Independent, but Hardly Neutral." *American Journalism* 16 (Fall 1999): 19-36. New York penny journalism influenced the Georgia newspaper, but the *Morning News* did not adopt all the features of the cheap-press.

Robinson, Elwyn B. "The *Public Ledger*: An Independent Newspaper." *Pennsylvania Magazine of History and Biography* 64 (1940): 43-55. In Philadelphia, the penny newspaper pursued a political course not tied to parties and a "civic-minded editorial policy ... combined ... [with] unusual enterprise in securing news of important events at the earliest possible moment."

Russo, David J. "The Origins of Local News in the U.S. Country Press, 1840s-1870s." *Journalism Monographs* 65 (February 1980). This study examines the news content in smaller newspapers of the penny press era and afterward.

Shaw, Donald Lewis. "At the Crossroads: Change and Continuity in American Press News, 1820-1860." *Journalism History* 8 (1981): 38-50. A study of the content of American newspapers reveals that the influence of the major newspapers was slow to reach the hinterlands.

Sloan, Wm. David. "George W. Wisner: Michigan Editor and Politician." *Journalism History* 6 (1979): 113-16. Wisner, editor of the *New York Sun*, played an important role in politics and partisan journalism in Michigan after leaving the *Sun*.

Smith, Henry Ladd. "The Beauteous Jennie June: Pioneer Woman Journalist." *Journalism Quarterly* 40 (1963): 169-74. As a member of the *New York Herald* staff, Jane Cunningham Croly was a superior journalist and a leader in the feminist movement. She had a number of significant accomplishments and "firsts."

Taylor, Sally. "Marx and Greeley on Slavery and Labor." *Journalism History* 6 (1979-1980): 103-6. Greeley published articles by the co-founder of Communism.

Zboray, Ronald J., and Mary Saracino Zboray. "Political News and Female Readership in Antebellum Boston and its Region." *Journalism History* 22:1 (1996): 2-14. Women in Boston "became increasingly informed on political events by reading newspapers."

8

The Antebellum Press
1820 – 1861

Sectional controversy leading up to the Civil War can be attributed to many factors. Some historians point to the threat of industrialism and the ultimate conflict between farm and factory. Northerners were intrigued by concepts of industry and trade, while southerners were more concerned with land and farming. Other historians view the conflict as a struggle between cultures: one in the South dominated by a pro-slavery philosophy and another in the North shaped by the increasingly influential forces of reform and democracy. However, one issue, slavery, served as the catalyst and rallying cry for the controversy that eventually would culminate in war. The *New York Commercial Advertiser* declared in 1821 that slavery was responsible for "shedding sectional animosity" upon the country.[1] The question of slavery could be argued on several different levels — financial, moral, patriotic, religious. These were all principles for which men and women pledged their lives to support.[2]

The years prior to the Civil War represented a turning point for America's press. Newspapers had become a mass medium, reaching most of society, and editors were forced to choose sides in the intersectional strife over slavery. The issue threatened not only the country, but also the role and development of the American press. The Missouri Compromise of 1820 provided the impetus for the party press to begin realigning into a sectional press. A press dominated by party loyalty began to give way to a group of editors and publishers concerned with the press' broader civic responsibilities. Although the first shots of the Civil War were not fired until April 12, 1861, newspapers had declared a war of words years earlier, with slavery as the core issue.

THE ABOLITIONIST PRESS

Antislavery publications began to appear throughout the country during the early 1800s. Among the earliest antislavery editors were Charles Osborn, Elihu Embree, and William Swain. Osborn established the *Philanthropist* in Mount Pleasant, Ohio, in 1817, followed two years later by Embree's *Manumission Intelligencer* in Jonesboro, Tennessee. In 1820 Embree changed his weekly, probably the first paper devoted exclusively to the abolition of slavery, to a monthly and changed the name to the *Emancipator*. Swain began publication of the *Greensboro* (N.C.) *Patriot* in 1828, publishing his antislavery material despite local opposition.

Perhaps the most influential early abolitionist publication belonged to Benjamin Lundy, a proponent of the antislavery cause since 1815. He is often credited with keeping antislavery sentiments from dissipating as early as the 1820s. Born in New Jersey, the only child of Quaker farmers, he devised a plan for an antislavery organization to be based in Mount Pleasant, Ohio. Named the "Union Humane Society," it operated on the principle that members would use all legal means to end racial prejudice, to attain civil rights for free blacks, and to secure the freedom of those blacks enslaved illegally.[3]

Lundy continued to espouse his ideas about abolition through his paper, the *Genius of Universal Emancipation*, established in 1821 in Mount Pleasant. It was often referred to as "the little paper with the great name." Lundy's dedication to his cause was evidenced in his methods of operating his paper. He spent much of his time traveling, selling subscriptions for his paper, and lecturing. In some instances, although slight of build, he walked to his destination carrying his office equipment in a large pack. When he arrived in a town that had a printing press, he would stop long enough to write, print, and mail an edition of his paper.

In 1822 Lundy decided to move his operation to a place where slavery existed in a more blatant form — Greeneville, Tennessee. He journeyed 800 miles to Tennessee, making one-half of the trip by steamboat and the other half on foot. He hoped that his *Genius* would serve as a replacement for Embree's *Emancipator*. Before his death in 1820, Embree and the *Emancipator* had provoked widespread hostility in its location so close to the enemy, and Lundy's *Genius* would fare no better. Despite opposition, Lundy produced antislavery material that insulted slaveholders throughout the

[1]Quoted in William B. Hesseltine and David L. Smiley, *The South in American History* (Englewood Cliffs, N.J., 1960), 147.

[2]Harriet Martineau, *The Martyr Age of the United States* (Boston, 1839), 3.

[3]Merton L. Dillon, *Benjamin Lundy and the Struggle for Negro Freedom* (Urbana, Ill., 1966), 18.

GENIUS OF UNIVERSAL EMANCIPATION.

EDITED BY BENJAMIN LUNDY.

"We hold these truths to be self-evident, that all men are created equal, and endowed by their Creator with certain unalienable rights, that among these are life, liberty, and the pursuit of happiness."— *Declaration Independence U. S.*

No. 10.   FOURTH MONTH, 1822.   VOL. I.

Genius of Universal Emancipation

The most influential of the early abolitionist papers was Benjamin Lundy's *Genius of Universal Emancipation*, founded in 1821 in Mount Pleasant, Ohio. The only child of Quaker parents, Lundy had been reared with a strong belief in the sanctity of human life. He moved the paper to Greeneville, Tennessee, in 1822 so that he could publish from a place in which slavery was legal. He produced uncompromising material and provoked widespread hostility. He kept alive his "little paper with the great name" by selling subscriptions while he traveled and lectured. When he came to a town with a printing press, he would stop long enough to produce an issue.

country. In one particularly scornful article, he proclaimed slaveholders to be "whoremongers" who dared to oppose emancipation on the grounds of their lust and greed, making a "business of raising bastards and selling them for money."[4]

In hopes of getting support, Lundy later moved his operation to Baltimore, Maryland. Failing to gain adequate allies, however, he was forced during the winter of 1828-1829 to discontinue his efforts because of lack of funds. By late 1829 he was able to scrape together enough money to resume publication of the *Genius*, later

increasing its publication frequency to weekly. At that point he was joined by a young man who would later establish his own newspaper and become the most militant and best-known abolitionist editor. He was William Lloyd Garrison.

Garrison came to Lundy as an experienced journalist. Taking a route typical of early American journalists, he served as a printer's apprentice and later worked as a journeyman printer. At age twenty he became the youngest editor and publisher in the United States when he took control of the *Free Press* in his hometown of Newburyport, Massachusetts. He later became editor of Boston's *National Philanthropist*, a temperance newspaper. Prior to joining Lundy, he had founded and edited the *Journal of the Times* in Bennington, Vermont, a paper established to support John Quincy Adams for the presidency in 1828.

At the *Genius* Garrison was to be the editor-in-residence, while Lundy went about the country holding meetings and selling subscriptions. The partnership should have been ideal. The two shared strong beliefs that slavery was wrong and should be abolished. They did not agree, however, on what should happen to slaves once they were freed. Garrison, a master of fiery rhetoric, issued pronouncements of his personal faith and commitment to the cause. Having once supported gradual emancipation, he later advocated immediate emancipation and enfranchisement. Lundy, having passed through this passionate stage a decade earlier, preferred to examine more practical measures that he hoped would free some slaves immediately and more as time passed. Along with gradual emancipation, Lundy also favored plans for colonization in Africa.

Because of this major difference in philosophies, Lundy offered this solution: "Well, thee may put thy initials to thy articles, and I will put my initials to mine, and each will bear his own burden."[5] The two shook hands, and the *Genius* became a paper with two voices. However, Garrison was the abler journalist of the two, and his voice emerged the louder. Later explaining his unorthodox approach to attacking slavery, Garrison wrote: "I am aware, that many object to the severity of my language; but is there not cause for severity? ... [U]rge me not to use moderation in a cause like the present!"[6]

Garrison's advocacy of immediate emancipation met stiff opposition in Baltimore. Lundy's appeal for gradual emancipation had been tolerated, but Garrison's bold proposal enraged the citizenry. He soon faced libel charges, and the outcome of the case clearly indicated that antislavery sentiments were at a low ebb in the North. Upon learning that a ship belonging to Francis Todd of Newburyport had sailed from Baltimore to New Orleans with a cargo of slaves, Garrison attacked. He was enraged because the ship's owner was from his hometown. After giving the facts of the story, he editorialized in bold print:

It is no worse to fit out piratical cruisers, or to engage in the foreign slave trade, than to pursue a similar trade along our own

[4]*Genius of Universal Emancipation*, June 1823.

[5]Quoted in Oliver Johnson, *W. L. Garrison and His Times* (1880; reprint, Salem, N.H., 1969), 29.
[6]*Liberator*, 1 January 1831.

William Lloyd Garrison
The editor of the *Liberator* wrote harshly and uncompromisingly about the inhumanity of slavery. His views gained tremendous public attention because his writing possessed a shock effect and a power to arouse violent opposition. Garrison was one of the first to argue that slaves were humans equal to whites and to urge immediate emancipation.

coasts; and the men who have the wickedness to participate therein, for the purpose of heaping up wealth, should be SENTENCED TO SOLITARY CONFINEMENT FOR LIFE; *they are the enemies of their own species — highway robbers and murderers*; and their final doom will be, unless they speedily repent, *to occupy the lowest depths of perdition*.[7]

Garrison did not wait for Todd to read his attack in the *Genius*; he sent him a marked copy. Todd sued for $5,000 for defamation. A grand jury also indicted Garrison for having written and published "a gross and malicious libel." Both Garrison and Lundy were initially charged, but the charges against Lundy were dropped after the judge determined that his absence from the city at the time absolved him of all responsibility for the article. However, although a leading lawyer of Baltimore offered his services free of charge and defended Garrison, after less than fifteen minutes' deliberation the jury returned a verdict of guilty. Garrison

was fined $50 and court costs, totaling $100. Unable to pay either, he was jailed for forty-nine days. The only factual error in his account was that eighty-eight slaves were aboard the ship instead of the eighty-five he reported.

THE LIBERATOR

After completing his jail term, Garrison parted company with Lundy. Lundy contended that financial difficulties had forced an end to the weekly paper, and he was thus returning to the monthly format with less expensive production costs.[8] Using his previous format, he continued his efforts to expose the evils of slavery and praise the merits of colonization. It is uncertain whether he and Garrison separated on a sour note or dissolved their partnership on good terms. Since the issue of colonization had been compromised at the beginning of their relationship, it is likely that the latter was the case. Lundy admired much of Garrison's work, once stating that "nothing but this will reach the adamantine hearts of slavites."[9] Garrison's tribute following Lundy's death in 1839 indicated a great deal of admiration, respect, and gratitude: "Now, if I have in any way, however humble, done anything toward calling attention to slavery, or bringing about the glorious prospect of a complete jubilee in our country at no distant day, I feel that I owe everything in this matter, instrumentally and under God, to Benjamin Lundy."[10]

On January 1, 1831, Garrison founded the *Liberator* in Boston. Free of any obligation to Lundy, he exerted all his efforts to gain immediate emancipation and enfranchisement for freed blacks. In the first issue of the *Liberator* he declared that blacks were as entitled to "life, liberty and the pursuit of happiness" as any white man.[11] He also explained why he had chosen Boston to launch his newspaper. In the North, he claimed, he "found contempt more bitter, opposition more active, detraction more relentless, prejudice more stubborn, and apathy more frozen, than among slaveholders themselves." To show his determination, he wrote: "I *will be* as harsh as truth, and as uncompromising as justice. On this subject, I do not wish to think, to speak, or write, with moderation.... I am in earnest — I will not equivocate — I will not excuse — I will not retreat a single inch — AND I WILL BE HEARD."[12]

Garrison and his *Liberator* roused fear among southerners and stiff opposition from northerners. Slave owners feared his appeals would spark more slave rebellions, while northerners believed he would destroy any chance of compromise between the two regions.

Several efforts were made to suppress, or at least limit, distribution of the *Liberator*. The year the paper was founded, the Georgia legislature offered $4,000 for Garrison's arrest. South Carolina offered $1,500 for the arrest of anyone caught distributing the

---

[7]Quoted in Ralph Korngold, *Two Friends of Man* (Boston, 1950), 38.

[8]*Genius of Universal Emancipation and Baltimore Courier*, 5 March 1830.

[9]Ibid., December 1830.

[10]Quoted in Korngold, *Two Friends of Man*, 41.

[11]*Liberator* (Boston) 1 January 1831. Also see Johnson, *W. L. Garrison and His Times*, 50-66, and George M. Fredrickson, *William Lloyd Garrison* (Englewood Cliffs, N.J., 1968), 244-5.

[12]*Liberator*, 1 January 1831.

The Liberator

In a sense, the founding of the *Liberator* represented the birth of abolitionism. William Lloyd Garrison turned his back on the gradualism and moderation of many of his past antislavery allies. Slavery, he believed, was a sin and had to be abolished. Many of the political radicals, including Senator Charles Sumner and Massachusetts Governor John Andrew, read the *Liberator*.

paper. In the North even James Gordon Bennett of the *New York Herald*, who earlier had argued vigorously for freedom of the press, saw nothing wrong with gagging Garrison. In 1833 a mob stormed a building in which Garrison was holding an antislavery meeting but failed to recognize the editor, who prudently had mingled among the crowd. In 1835 a mob in Boston attacked him, and he had to be jailed for protection. On his cell wall, he inscribed the details of his harrowing adventure, concluding that the "respectable and influential" had attempted to destroy him "for preaching the abominable and dangerous doctrine, that 'all men are created equal,' and that all oppression is odious in the sight of God."[13]

Garrison's infamous reputation created a profound effect upon his newspaper's popularity. The *Liberator* was not an instant success, its circulation never surpassing 600. In the long run, however, Garrison did manage to reach those who were apathetic on the issue of slavery and reinforce the views of those who already embraced antislavery sentiments. He even opened his columns to blacks so they might be able to express their views about slavery. His may have been the first effort by any white editor in America to provide such an opportunity to blacks. His creation of the "Ladies' Department" in the *Liberator* probably offered the first widespread opportunity for black women to voice their opinions in a public forum.

Blacks flocked to join the antislavery movement. For the first three years of the *Liberator's* operation, the majority of the subscribers and supporters were black. In April 1834 only one-fourth of the subscribers were white.[14] This support was partially due to Garrison's fervent vow to devote his life to atoning for the wrongs inflicted upon blacks. He was also respected for his tendency to seek out free blacks and ex-slaves in the North to ascertain their opinions on how to improve the condition of the race. His children later wrote that this passion and devotion led many blacks to assume that Garrison was a black man.[15]

It has been said that Garrison was "the most articulate spokesman of militant abolition. For a generation he was one of the most important forces working for the freedom of slaves."[16] Contrary to

the impression created by some of the revolutionary articles that appeared in the *Liberator*, however, Garrison was not an advocate of violence. He was a strong believer in "nonresistance" (or "nonviolence" as it would be called today). He claimed his philosophy "was simply to desist from the sin of slavery under moral suasion so that the oppressor and the oppressed could enter with clean hands into a new reconciliation and brotherhood." In 1837 he declared, "Next to the overthrow of slavery, the cause of PEACE will command our attention."[17] He did have some difficulty in defending the Nat Turner-led slave rebellion in Virginia in 1831 and John Brown's raid in 1859 without compromising his stand on nonresistance. He managed well. In reference to Turner, he contended that the rebellion was an example of the ultimate violence that slavery would produce. Slavery, therefore, should be abolished immediately. In defense of Brown he wrote:

> A word or two in regard to the characteristics of John Brown. He was of the Old Puritan stock — a Cromwellian who "believed in God," and at the same time "in keeping his powder dry." He believed in "the sword of the Lord and of Gideon," and acted accordingly. Herein I differ widely from him. But, certainly, he was no "infidel" — oh no![18]

As if Garrison's stand on slavery were not enough to irritate the majority of whites in the United States, North and South, he also strongly advocated the rights of women. In conjunction with abolition of slavery, Garrison declared: "As our object is universal emancipation — to redeem woman as well as man from a servile to an equal condition — we shall go for the RIGHTS OF WOMEN to their utmost extent."[19]

LOVEJOY, BIRNEY, AND TAPPAN

Several abolitionist papers would rise and fall by the end of the Civil War. The *Liberator*, however, appeared every week for thirty-five years. Followers of Garrison, "Garrisonians" as they were often referred to, accounted for the establishment of several leading antislavery papers. The *National Anti-Slavery Standard* was published in New York from 1840 to 1870. During the 1850s, Garri-

---

[13]*Liberator*, 7 November 1835.

[14]Benjamin Quarles, *Black Abolitionists* (New York, 1969), 20.

[15]W.P. Garrison and F.J. Garrison, *William Lloyd Garrison, 1805-1879; The Story of his Life as told by his Children*, Vol. I (New York, 1885-1889), 258.

[16]An assessment of William Lloyd Garrison by John Hope Franklin, *From Slavery to Freedom* (New York, 1948), 241.

[17]*Liberator*, 15 December 1837.

[18]*Liberator*, 16 December 1859.

[19]*Liberator*, 31 May 1844.

Elijah Lovejoy, Martyr
Facing threats in St. Louis, Elijah Lovejoy moved his print shop across the Mississippi River to Alton, Illinois. Twice, mobs destroyed the office and press. The third time, in 1837, a mob not only demolished his office but killed Lovejoy as well. He became a martyr to the antislavery cause, and today the annual Elijah Lovejoy Award for Courage in Journalism recognizes journalists who do their job in the face of great dangers.

Lewis Tappan
After breaking with William Lloyd Garrison over the latter's aggressive demands for abolition, Tappan founded the *National Era*, which emphasized moderation and gained the largest circulation of any abolition newspaper.

sonian organizations published the *Pennsylvania Freeman* in Philadelphia and the *Anti-Slavery Bugle* in Ohio. One advocate of the abolitionist movement would become a martyr for the cause.

The issue of slavery had been whipped to such a feverish pitch by the 1830s that attempts were made to restrict freedom of expression on the issue in both the North and the South. In 1835 Elijah Lovejoy, a former Presbyterian minister, established the *St. Louis Observer*. It was a reform paper, and Lovejoy angered numerous readers with his anti-Catholic editorials. Denying that he was an abolitionist, Lovejoy, nevertheless, altered the focus of his paper to include attacks on slavery. When he criticized the leniency of a judge in a trial of persons accused of burning a black man alive, the citizens of St. Louis presented him with a resolution informing him that freedom of expression as guaranteed in the Bill of Rights did not extend to editors such as he.

Lovejoy moved his press across the river to Alton, Illinois. There he set up the *Alton Observer* and continued his crusade against slavery and the injustices inflicted on blacks. In 1837, he prophesied: "God has not slumbered nor has his Justice been an indifferent spectator of the scene.... In due time they [the souls of dead slaves] will descend in awful curses upon this land, unless averted by the speedy repentance of us all."[20]

As had happened in Missouri, Lovejoy again became the object of public outrage. Twice mobs destroyed his office and threw his printing press into the river. Determined and with financial help from antislavery organizations, he set up his third shop in Alton. The mob then took the ultimate step. In 1837 it demolished his office and killed Lovejoy. The antislavery movement had gained a martyr. Abolitionists now possessed persuasive evidence that slave power threatened all of humanity. John Quincy Adams declared that Lovejoy's murder sent "a shock as of an earthquake through the continent." The *Haverhill Gazette* announced that the "late attack upon the freedom of the press at Alton, Illinois, which has at length been consummated in blood and murder, should arouse every press and every voice in the country."[21]

James G. Birney was more fortunate than Lovejoy. As the first editor of the *Philanthropist* in Cincinnati, he was considered a "reasonable" abolitionist. Kentucky-born, he took his slaves to Ohio, emancipated them, and took up the antislavery cause. Although he was mild in sentiments, in 1836 a mob destroyed his printing press, and he barely escaped with his life.

As the antislavery movement grew, it became fragmented. For those who preferred a moderate approach, there was Lewis Tappan, who had broken with Garrison and had helped to form the American and Foreign Anti-Slavery Society. In 1847 he founded the *National Era* in Washington, D.C., and named Gamaliel Bailey editor. He started the paper to "help coordinate anti-slavery sentiments and action among governmental officials." Although modest in its demands, the *Era* opposed "discrimination against blacks" and called for "an end to prejudice." In terms of circulation, the *Era* was probably the most successful of all abolitionist papers. In 1853 its circulation reached 25,000, while most papers of its kind failed to exceed 3,000. One factor that may have contributed to its success was its publication in 1852-1853 of installments of Harriet Beecher Stowe's *Uncle Tom's Cabin*, probably the most widely read literature of the time. It might also have been because of Bailey's moderate abolitionist philosophy, in which he envisioned a more effective strategy that occupied a middle course between compromise and impractical or unpopular tactics. Bailey reasoned that "a majority of the antislavery people of the free

[20]*St. Louis Observer*, 16 April 1835.

[21]Reprinted in *Liberator*, 8 December 1837.

Lydia Maria Child
Born in 1802, Lydia Maria Child was strongly anti-slavery from her youth. She thought most people in the North were too mild in their opposition to slavery. Upon reading the early issues of William Lloyd Garrison's *Liberator*, though, she declared that he "got hold of the strings of my conscience, and pulled me into Reforms.... Old dreams vanished, old associates departed, and all things became new." In 1833 she published *An Appeal in Favor of that Class of Americans Called Africans*. Like Garrison, she was deeply religious and pointed out that slavery contradicted Christian teaching. Like him, she also took a trenchant stand. "I am fully aware of the unpopularity of the task I have undertaken," she declared in the introduction to *An Appeal*, "but though I expect ridicule and censure, it is not in my nature to fear them." As a forum in which she could oppose slavery on a continual basis, in 1840 she helped establish the *National Anti-Slavery Standard*, the American Anti-Slavery Society's weekly newspaper, and served as its editor until 1843.

states without abating their zeal, or compromising their principles, clearly see that mere denunciation may inflame but not convince — may terrify the cowardly, but must arouse the indignation and resistance of men of courage and intelligence."[22] Consequently, according to Bailey's reasoning, southerners who realized that slavery could not survive might be willing to listen to discussion that did not require the complete dismantling of their way of life.

Although divided, abolitionist editors had gained some sup-

[22]*National Era*, 7 January 1847.

port for their cause by 1861, the year the Civil War began. In the North the apathetic began to ponder the question of slavery and in many cases sided with the movement. Some ministers began to see slavery as sinful but were horrified that the "war of words" was now producing human casualties.

THE BLACK PRESS

From its founding in 1827 the black press became a strong ally of the abolitionist press. Approximately forty black newspapers were founded in the United States before the Civil War. The first, *Freedom's Journal*, was established in 1827 in New York City. Initially, the Reverend Samuel E. Cornish, a Presbyterian minister born in Delaware, served as editor, while the proprietor was Bowdoin College graduate John B. Russwurm, a half-white Jamaican who was one of the first blacks to graduate from a U.S. college. In addition to taking a strong stand against slavery, the paper launched an attack against plans of the government and some white and black leaders to establish colonies of American blacks in Africa and Cuba. Cornish believed the plan might benefit some blacks — those who reasoned that full citizenship rights would never be achieved inside the borders of the United States and thus would move — but it offered little promise to the majority. It would, he believed, substantially reduce the black population in America and deny enslaved blacks access to their most important spiritual ally, free blacks.[23] This attack on colonization was made almost four years before William Lloyd Garrison founded the *Liberator* and expressed a similar philosophy.

Cornish and Russwurm were not together long before they disagreed on what policy should be adopted for blacks in the United States. Cornish favored emancipation and enfranchisement, while Russwurm leaned toward colonization, preferably in Liberia. After six months Cornish ended his association with the paper, leaving the operation solely in the hands of Russwurm, who became a staunch supporter of the American Colonization Society. He reversed the paper's position on colonization and continued publication for almost a year, but not without arousing the outrage of much of the paper's black readership. In 1829 he closed shop and left the United States for Liberia to participate in the colonization program.[24]

Following the departure of Russwurm, Cornish returned to the *Journal* with hopes of reviving it and making it a powerful voice against slavery and the colonization movement. In an effort to pump new life into it, he changed its name to *Rights of All*. However, in 1830 a lack of financial support forced him to give up his effort. Such a fate was not uncommon for black-owned papers before the war. Financial difficulties would continue to plague the black press throughout the nineteenth century.

After the demise of *Rights of All*, blacks made several efforts to establish a voice of freedom for slaves. The *African Sentinel and Journal of Liberty* appeared in Albany, New York, in 1831. The *Na-*

[23]*Freedom's Journal*, 6 July and 7 September 1827.
[24]*Freedom's Journal*, 28 March 1829.

Uncle Tom's Cabin

Harriet Beecher Stowe Helps Start Civil War

President Abraham Lincoln is said to have credited Harriet Beecher Stowe with writing a novel that served as the catalyst for the Civil War. In fact, reaction to her novel *Uncle Tom's Cabin* was so intense that Stowe credited God with having written it.

When *Uncle Tom's Cabin* was published in 1852, it sold 50,000 copies in eight weeks, 300,000 in one year, and more than one million in America and England by the following year. It also was published in Germany, France, Sweden, Italy, Portugal, Sweden, Finland, and Russia.

In 1851, Stowe wrote to Gamaliel Bailey, editor of the *National Era*, an abolitionist publication in Washington, D. C., and asked if he would publish a piece of fiction attacking slavery. When the newspaper serialization ended in 1852, a two-volume *Uncle Tom's Cabin* was published by Jewell and Co. of Boston.

Primarily because it published *Uncle Tom's Cabin*, the *National Era* became the most widely distributed abolitionist paper.

Its circulation reached 25,000 at a time when similar publications boasted only 3,000.

Although *Uncle Tom's Cabin* was phenomenally popular in its own day and during the century following the Civil War, Stowe's stereotyping of blacks, and her ten-

Harriet Beecher Stowe's *Uncle Tom's Cabin* originally appeared in serialized form in the *National Era* and soon was issued as a book. It was the most widely read literature of the time. It was the single most important writing in increasing the demand that slavery be abolished. This illustration (top) for the book shows a child, having just been sold by her master, being separated from her mother.

dency to limit the influence of women to the home have rendered the novel objectionable to some modern readers. Despite the criticism, the novel remains one of the most important ever published.

While some critics castigate it as sentimental, melodramatic, and didactic, others defend it is a masterpiece of social realism and celebrate it for its description, irony, humor, Gothic images, dialect, symbolism, and local color.

Stowe is remembered for introducing religious principles into political discussion and for championing the rights of the slave. George Sand said of her, "She has genius as humanity feels the need of genius – the genius of goodness, not that of the man of letters, but that of the saint."

Freedom's Journal's Founders

Samuel Cornish (left) and John Russwurm (right) started *Freedom's Journal*, the first African-American newspaper, in 1827 out of a desire to improve the conditions of their race. Cornish, a Presbyterian minister, and Russwurm, one of the first black Americans to get a college degree, particularly emphasized the spiritual, moral, and educational improvement of free blacks. They also wanted to promote racial unity and the progress of blacks in the North. In starting the paper, they explained, "We wish to plead our cause. Too long have others spoken for us ... for though there are many in society who exercise towards us benevolent feelings; still ... there are others who make it their business to enlarge upon the least trifle which tends to the discredit of any person of colour.... We are aware that there are instances of vice among us, but we avow that it is because no one has taught its subjects to be virtuous...."

tional Reformer was established in Philadelphia in 1833, and the *Spirit of the Times* in New York City in 1836. All were short-lived.

In 1837, however, the *Weekly Advocate* appeared in New York City with Philip A. Bell as proprietor and the veteran Samuel Cornish as editor. Due to its longevity, the *Advocate* often is referred to as America's second black publication. It survived for five years, a long life for a black newspaper during this period. Except for a brief period in 1840, it was published until 1842. After two months of publication, the name was changed to the *Colored American*. One of Cornish's first duties as sole editor was to explain the name change to readers. He argued that the new name emphasized that blacks were actually "more exclusively 'American' than our white brethren," and "colored" was considered an inoffensive word that

was a more acceptable term for addressing blacks than other well-known labels and could be used to unify the black community.[25] As did its predecessors, the *Colored American* drew most of its support from antislavery advocates and was established to promote "the emancipation of the enslaved and the elevation of the free colored people." In 1841 the *Colored American* justifiably claimed to be "the only paper in the United States, published and edited by a colored man, and expressly for colored people." The editorship and proprietorship changed hands several times. Following Cornish's retirement in 1839, Dr. James McCune Smith and Bell became co-editors and Charles Bennett Ray proprietor. Despite the division of authority, the paper managed to maintain consistency in its beliefs, efforts, and editorial content. As part of its attacks against colonization, Ray reasoned in an editorial titled "This Country, Our Only Home":

> Now, probably three-fourths of the present colored people are American born, and therefore American citizens. Suppose we should remove to some other country, and claim a foothold there, could we not be rejected on the ground that we were not of them, because not born among them? Even in Africa, identity of complexion would be nothing, neither would it weigh anything because our ancestry were of that country. The fact of our not having been born there would be sufficient ground for any civil power to refuse us citizenship.[26]

Black religious organizations founded and sponsored several newspapers. These religious publications took a strong social stand and added their voices to the abolitionist press in its fight for freedom. One such paper was the *Christian Recorder* founded in 1846, still surviving as the oldest continuously published black newspaper in America. It was not merely by chance that many of the early black editors were ministers — the Revs. Samuel Cornish of *Freedom's Journal*, *Rights of All*, and *Weekly Advocate*; C.B. Ray of the *Colored American*; and Richard Allen of the *Recorder*, to mention a few. In addition to the fact that an education was more readily accessible to potential clergymen than to the general black population, the Christian concept of love of humanity was a key factor. Furthermore, one authority on the black press has explained, "With the church tied to the largest Negro groups, thus assuring a ready readership, and with the clergymen quite often the most learned individuals in a particular community, it was natural for newspapers to be attached to religious groups and for the ministers to be editors."[27]

Of the black newspapers founded in America before 1856, most, if not all, promoted the antislavery philosophy. However, the circumstances leading to the founding of many of these papers did not involve the question of slavery, but the fact that blacks were denied access to the established press to voice their opinions

[25]*Colored American*, 4 March 1837.
[26]Quoted in I. Garland Penn, *The Afro-American Press and its Editors* (1891; reprint, New York, 1969), 44-5.
[27]Armistead S. Pride, "The Negro Newspapers: Yesterday, Today, and Tomorrow," *Journalism Quarterly* 28 (1951): 183-4.

African-American Women and the Abolitionist Movement
In the abolitionist movement, many women figured prominently, and a number of the most visible ones were African Americans. Three of the most notable were Maria W. Stewart, Mary Ann Shadd Cary, and Charlotte Forten Grimké (left to right above). Each helped promote abolition through writing and publishing. Born in 1803 in Hartford, Conn., Stewart first came to public attention in 1831 with her pamphlet *Religion and the Pure Principles of Mortality*. She also gave public lectures, and her friend William Lloyd Garrison published four of them in *The Liberator*. Born in 1823 in Delaware, Cary was the daughter of Harriet and Abraham Shadd, leaders in Wilmington's black community. With passage of the Fugitive Slave Law in 1850, she moved to Windsor, Ontario, Canada. There in 1853 she founded the *Provincial Freeman* newspaper. In its columns she attacked slavery and advocated civil rights, black education and self-reliance, temperance, and moral reform. Grimké was born in 1837 in Philadelphia, where her parents were involved in activities to help escaped slaves. When she was 19 years old, she began writing poetry, much of which had anti-slavery themes, and Garrison's *Liberator* and the *Anglo-African Magazine* published many of her works. During the Civil War, after the Union military occupied the barrier islands off the coast of South Carolina and Georgia, she taught school in the "Sea Islands Mission" and wrote a series of essays about her experiences under the title "Life on the Sea Islands," which *Atlantic Monthly* published.

on slavery, as well as other concerns, such as education, employment, and moral development. *Freedom's Journal* was founded after black leaders in New York were refused an opportunity to respond to anti-black editorials appearing in several papers Mordecai Noah owned. In 1843 Martin R. Delaney was prompted to establish the *Mystery* in Pittsburgh because the papers there refused to publish letters on slavery from blacks.

In 1847 the *New York Sun* urged readers to vote "NO" on a state constitutional amendment that would have repealed a clause that allowed blacks to vote only if they owned $250 worth of real estate while whites were not required to own any land. Willis Hodges, a black businessman, prepared a rebuttal to the *Sun*'s editorials and submitted it to the paper. The rebuttal was actually a lengthy "letter to the editor." It was not published, however, until after Hodges had paid a $15 fee. The *Sun* modified the article and placed it in the classified advertising section. When Hodges complained, the editor informed him that, contrary to the paper's slogan "The Sun Shines For All," the real policy was "The Sun shines for all white men, and not for colored men." Hodges was told if he had something to say, to start his own newspaper. He worked as a "whitewasher" and sold fruits and vegetables for a year to earn enough money to unveil to the citizens of New York the first issue of the *Ram's Horn* on January 1, 1847. It carried the motto: "We are men, and therefore interested in whatever concerns men."

FREDERICK DOUGLASS

The *Ram's Horn* managed to survive for about eighteen months and once listed 2,500 subscribers. Hodges assumed the role of editor, while Thomas Van Rennselaer, an old friend and well-known restaurateur, served as business manager. Among its contributors and supporters appeared the names of John Brown and Frederick Douglass, two major figures in the antislavery movement. Although Douglass was listed as an assistant editor in August 1847, there is no evidence that he contributed to the *Ram's Horn* anything more than the prestige associated with his name.

Douglass was the best-known black man in America. Born in Tuckahoe, Maryland, he was the son of a white father and a black slave mother. Escaping from slavery in 1838, he settled in New Bedford, Massachusetts, and became a popular speaker. From 1845 to 1847 he lectured in Great Britain and Ireland on the evils of slavery. British sympathizers then bought his freedom from the slaveholder who, legally, still owned him. On his return to the United States, he thus was able to travel throughout the North freely proclaiming the message of immediate abolition of slavery.

A few issues before the demise of the *Ram's Horn*, it had carried a prospectus for a new antislavery newspaper to be called the *Northern Star* (shortened to *North Star*) and to be edited by Douglass. The prospectus read in part:

Frederick Douglass
An escaped slave, Douglass wrote eloquently of the plight of members of his race while exhorting them to self-improvement. "The fact that we are limited and circumscribed," he wrote, "ought rather to incite us to a more vigorous and persevering use of the elevating means within our reach, than to dishearten us. The means of education, though not so free and open to us as to white persons, are nevertheless at our command to such an extent as to make education possible."

Frederick Douglass proposes to publish in Rochester, New York, a weekly antislavery paper.... The objective of The North Star will be to attack slavery in all its forms and aspects; advocate universal emancipation; exact the standard of public morality; promote the moral and intellectual improvement of the colored people; and to hasten the day of freedom to our three million enslaved fellow-countrymen.[28]

The *North Star* began publication on November 1, 1847.

Although Douglass had not been known as a journalist, his paper, according to a nineteenth-century historian, was "readily accepted as one of the most formidable enemies to American slavery. Its aims and purposes, as set forth in the prospectus, drew to it good support from those of the whites who favored abolition."[29] Not everyone, though, welcomed Douglass. His house was burned, and several issues of his paper destroyed. The *New York Herald* advocated that he be "exiled to Canada and his presses

thrown into the lake."[30]

The founding of the *North Star* also caused a break between Douglass and some of his supporters. Douglass had received strong support from leading abolitionists, including William Lloyd Garrison, once his chief sponsor. However, the two parted ways over a dispute over dissolution of the Union. Some abolitionists advocated dissolving all ties with slaveholding states. Douglass did not believe a break-up of the nation would solve the problem of blacks still held as slaves. Nor did he believe the U.S. Constitution was pro-slavery, although he argued that government officials often misinterpreted it. Moderate though he was, he did not hesitate to attack when an official took a pro-slavery stand, at one time calling President James Buchanan "the pliant tool of pro-slavery propagandists, the subsidiary of Southern despotism and a consummate hypocrite."[31] Garrison and Douglass also differed on the need for a newspaper devoted solely to the concerns of a black readership. Garrison maintained that the abolitionist press could aptly respond to the needs of blacks without forcing a split in the loyalties of black subscribers who wished to support both types of newspapers. Douglass, by comparison, believed that only someone who had experienced a similar fate could fully understand the plight of blacks in the United States.

Four years after its founding, the *North Star* was merged with the *Liberty Party Paper* in Syracuse, New York, and renamed *Frederick Douglass' Paper*. The *North Star*'s financial difficulties appear to have been the major reason for the merger, but Douglass remained as editor after the merger. John Thomas, former editor of the *Liberty Party Paper*, became assistant editor. The paper remained essentially the same. It continued its attack on slavery until publication was suspended in 1860.

THE BLACK PRESS' DILEMMA

In 1856 the first black paper to be published on the Pacific Coast, the *Mirror of the Times*, appeared in San Francisco. John H. Townsend and Mifflin W. Gibbs served as editors. The *Mirror* grew out of a meeting of delegates attending the First Colored Convention of California in Sacramento in 1855. It was decided that a black voice was needed in the state — a black newspaper. However, publication did not begin immediately. As outlined by the delegates, its primary concern was to be the problems that blacks encountered within the state and not, primarily, the national or international issue of slavery. The delegates outlined their purpose:

Our sole objective is, to present our grievance to the people at large in our way, and through columns of our own press; show them [whites] the disabilities we labor under; ask them, in respectful terms, to remove them, and we have every reason to be-

[28]*Ram's Horn* (New York), 5 November 1847. Also see Carter R. Bryan, "Negro Journalism Before Emancipation," *Journalism Monographs* 25 (1969): 19.

[29]Penn, *The Afro-American Press and its Editors*, 68.

[30]Quoted in Lionel C. Barrow, Jr., "Historic Role of the Black Press in the Liberation Movement," *National Black Monitor* (November/December 1975): 2.

[31]Quoted in Lionel C. Barrow, Jr., "Role of the Black Press in the Liberation Struggle," *Black Press Handbook*, 1977 (Washington, D.C., 1977): 32-4.

Anglo-African Magazine.

VOL. I. **JANUARY, 1859.** NO. 1.

Apology.

(INTRODUCTORY.)

The publisher of this Magazine was ' brought up ' among Newspapers, Magazines, &c. The training of his boyhood and the employment of his manhood have been in the arts and mysteries which pertain to the neighborhood of Spruce and Nassau streets in the city of New York. Of course the top of the strata, the upper-crust of the laminæ in his geologic region is—the Publisher. . . . To become a Publisher, was the dream of his youth (not altogether a dream, for, while yet a boy he published, for several months, the People's Press, a not unnoticed weekly paper,) and the aim of his manhood. He understands the business thoroughly, and intends, if the requisite editorial matter can be furnished, to make this Magazine 'one of the institutions of the country.'

He would seem to be the right man in the right place; for the class of whom he is the representative in Printing House Square, sorely need an independent voice in the ' *fourth estate.*' Frederick Douglass has said

that ' the twelve millions of blacks in the United States and its environs must occupy the notice and the care of the Almighty :' these millions, in order to assert and maintain their rank as men among men, must speak for themselves ; no outside tongue, however gifted with eloquence, can tell their story ; no outside eye, however penetrating, can see their wants ; no outside organization, however benevolently intended, nor however cunningly contrived, can develope the energies and aspirations which make up their mission.

The wealth, the intellect, the Legislation, (State and Federal,) the pulpit, and the science of America, have concentrated on no one point so heartily as in the endeavor to write down the negro as something less than a man : yet at the very moment of the triumph of this effort, there runs through the marrow of those who make it, an unaccountable consciousness, an aching dread, that this *noir fainéant*, this great black sluggard, is somehow endowed with forces which are felt rather than seen, and which may in ' some grim revel,'

' Shake the pillars of the commonweal!'

Thomas Hamilton and the *Anglo-African*

With black readers hungry for material relevant to them, founder Thomas Hamilton filled his *Anglo-African Magazine* with informative essays and articles on issues and events important to the black community. Raised in the newspaper district of New York City, Hamilton became involved with black publications early in his teen years as a carrier for *The Colored American.* He introduced the *Anglo-African Magazine* to New York City in 1859 in hopes of bolstering the intellects of his fellow black men. The first issue contained his statement of purpose. "In addition to the expose of the condition of the blacks," he declared, "this Magazine will have the aim to uphold and encourage the now depressed hopes of thinking black men, in the United States."

lieve they will be stricken from the statute-books.[32]

The statement referred to several restrictive laws against blacks in California, especially the Testimony and Witness Law which barred blacks from giving testimony or appearing as witnesses in court cases involving whites. The *Mirror* fought vigorously against these laws; but when efforts failed to get them repealed, Gibbs became discouraged with the lack of change in San Francisco and moved to Victoria, British Columbia, in 1858. Shortly afterward, Townsend returned to New York, and the *Mirror* was discontinued. Until 1862 the Pacific Coast would be without another black publication. However, the black press had spread from coast to coast. For obvious reasons, though, no effort would be made to publish a black newspaper in the South until after the Civil War.

[32]Accounts of these meetings are documented in Philip Montesano, "Some Aspects of the Free Negro Question in San Francisco, 1849-1870" (MA thesis, University of San Francisco, 1967); and J. William Snorgrass, "The Development of the Black Press in the San Francisco Bay Area, 1865-1900," *California History* 60 (1981/82): 306-17.

From its founding, the black press had to deal with the dilemma of colonization or enfranchisement. Most papers chose the road to enfranchisement. At least one, however, chose to support a colonization scheme. In 1859, Thomas Hamilton and his brother Robert founded the *Weekly Anglo-African* and the *Anglo-African Magazine.* The paper was to be the more aggressive publication as the brothers championed issues ranging from abolition to racial prejudice. In March 1861, however, they sold it to white abolitionist James Redpath, who was the primary agent for the Haytian Bureau of Emigration, a project to encourage blacks to emigrate from North America to Haiti. Under Redpath's direction, with black journalist George Lawrence Jr. as editor, the paper was used primarily to support the emigration movement. By May 1861 Redpath had adopted the motto, "Man must be free; if not through the law, then above the law." Angered by Redpath's activities, the Hamiltons reclaimed the name of the *Weekly Anglo-African* and by August had re-established the paper, while Redpath continued to publish under the new name of the *Pine and Palm.* In 1862 he resigned his position as emigration agent, and the *Pine and Palm* ceased publication. The Hamiltons published the *Anglo-African* throughout the war. When Thomas died of typhoid fever in 1865, Robert suspended publication for a month, later handing over the editorial reigns to his two sons.

Regardless of how harsh their tone, most of these papers advocated non-violence, as did the abolitionist press. All had the same appeal: the elevation of blacks in the United States to first-class citizenship.

THE SOUTHERN PRESS

Unlike the abolitionist and black papers, southern newspapers were not established, primarily, to fight for a specific cause. They were founded on the same basic business/political principles as leading newspapers in the North. However, the slavery issue forced everyone in the United States to choose sides, and agitation from the abolitionist press forced southern newspapers to take a stand. Considering their economic predicament, southern editors could choose only one road — to support slavery.

Economically, southern newspapers faced greater difficulties than their northern counterparts. According to the 1860 census, the South lagged behind the North in industry, wealth, education, and "free" population. Not only did this mean that southern papers had a significantly smaller advertising base, but it also meant fewer subscribers. The South's free population was the real market for political, religious, literary, and miscellaneous periodicals. Fewer readers resulted in far smaller circulation numbers and fewer newspapers in the South than in the North. Despite these drawbacks, the southern antebellum press was strong. There were several profitable triweekly, biweekly, and especially weekly papers. They showcased the spirit and lifestyle of the South, but they still were not ready for open debate on the issue of slavery.

In the early years of the nineteenth century, the South had few restrictions on discussions regarding slavery. A few abolitionist

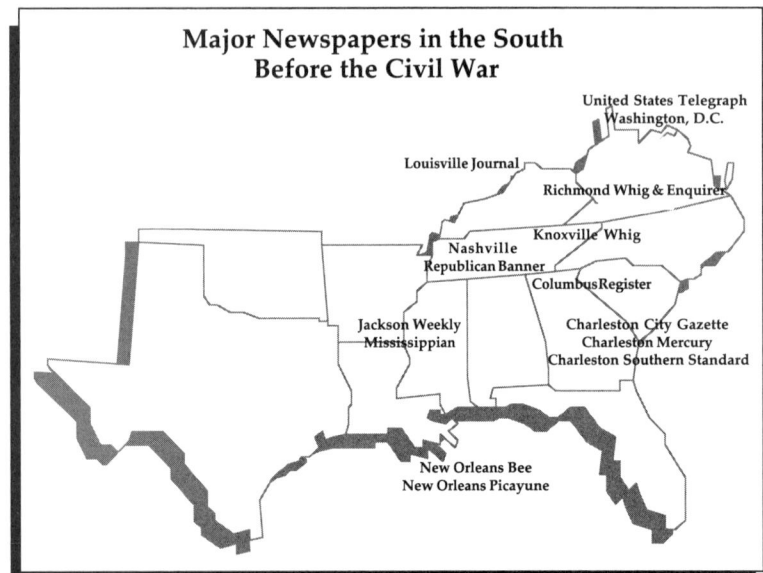

**Major Newspapers in the South
Before the Civil War**

United States Telegraph
Washington, D.C.

Louisville Journal

Richmond Whig & Enquirer

Knoxville Whig

Nashville
Republican Banner

Columbus Register

Jackson Weekly
Mississippian

Charleston City Gazette
Charleston Mercury
Charleston Southern Standard

New Orleans Bee
New Orleans Picayune

North vs. South — in Newspapers
Because the South did not have an industrialized economy and because it had few cities of substantial population, it had fewer newspapers than did the North, and for the most part they were of smaller circulation. The eleven states that would comprise the Confederacy had, in 1860, a total of only 785 publications, compared to 2,768 in the North. Those numbers included daily and weekly newspapers, along with miscellaneous publications such as religious newspapers and literary periodicals. The total for the North did not include 299 publications produced in the border states of Maryland, Kentucky, and Missouri. Although total circulation figures are not available, it is notable that the South had only 105 daily newspapers, compared with 276 in the North.

papers were even published in southern and border states, including Elihu Embree's *Manumission Intelligencer* and the Northern Carolina Manumission Society's *The Patriot*. However, several events began to influence the South's tolerance for open discussions. Two incidents that contributed to this intolerance were the Nat Turner Rebellion of 1831, in which fifty-seven whites were killed in Virginia, and the 1830 publication of *Walker's Appeal* by abolitionist David Walker, whose pamphlet was the first militant assault on slavery and racism. In both instances blacks were encouraged to use all means, including violence, to secure their freedom. To further frustrate efforts for open debate, two gag measures surfaced on the national level in the mid-1830s, reflecting southern attitudes toward abolitionist activities. First, Postmaster General Amos Kendall told postmasters that it would be within their authority to remove incendiary antislavery literature from the mails. Second, Congress passed a law that required antislavery petitions to be tabled without review.

Individual states also began to apply measures to protect themselves from inflammatory antislavery material, including imposing severe restrictions on newspapers and sanctions on individuals who gave any indication of sympathy toward abolition. In 1832 William Gilmore Simms was threatened and forced to sell the *Charleston City Gazette* because of his pro-Union sentiments, and a New York State student working in Tennessee received twenty lashes from the Committee on Vigilance for selling one abolitionist work and carrying another. By 1836 most southern states had laws against literature that had a tendency to "incite to insurrection," and anyone who dared to subscribe to an abolitionist paper did so at the risk of being jailed. Some southern states even considered imposing the death penalty on captured abolitionists.

The South was reacting aggressively to antislavery pressure, and it had its own set of supporters in a group of newspaper editors. They were strong in their devotion to the South and its way of life. The *United States Telegraph* in Washington, *Richmond Whig*

and *Enquirer*, *Columbia* (S.C.) *Register*, the *Bee* and *Picayune* of New Orleans, *Louisville Journal*, *Nashville Republican Banner*, and *Knoxville Whig* were well-established papers and influential sectional spokesmen on issues concerning the South. They occupied the same role in opinion-making in the South as clergymen and politicians. One group of southern editors, known as "Fire-Eaters," supported slavery as strongly as Garrison and Douglass opposed it. Among the best known was Robert Barnwell Rhett, owner of the *Charleston Mercury*.

Rhett, who changed his name from Smith in 1837, was a successful lawyer and real estate operator. He acquired valuable property in Charleston, including the *Mercury*, which he made one of the leading newspapers in the South and which made him one of the most powerful men in the region. He and his followers strongly supported slavery and secession of the South from the Union. In the battle over whether slavery was to exist in Kansas, Rhett urged southerners to support that state's advocates of slavery. He reasoned in the *Mercury*:

Upon the proposition that safety of the institution of slavery in South Carolina is dependent upon its establishment in Kansas, there can be no rational doubt. He, therefore, who does not contribute largely in money now, proves himself criminally indifferent, if not hostile, to the institution upon which the prosperity of the South and this state depends.[33]

Rhett was no less adamant about secession. In 1837 when it was proposed in Congress that slavery be abolished in the District of Columbia, he exploded and declared that "the Constitution had failed to protect the South in the peaceful enjoyment of its rights and that, therefore, it was expedient that the union be dissolved." He also claimed that the North had made tremendous profits from southern products and called the South "the best colony to the

[33]Quoted in Hesseltine and Smiley, *The South in American History*, 242.

The Fire-Eaters

As the antislavery issue took on growing importance, southern newspapers reacted aggressively. With time, the most prominent editors became the "Fire-Eaters." The most vocal was Robert Barnwell Rhett. A native of Beaufort, S.C., he changed his name from Smith in 1837, the same year he was elected a congressman in South Carolina. A states'-rights extremist, he used his *Charleston Mercury* as a mouthpiece of secessionist sentiment. He produced this special "extra" of the *Charleston Mercury* immediately after South Carolina voted to secede.

North any people ever possessed."[34]

By the mid-1800s a younger group of journalists who endorsed the wisdom of the Fire-Eaters emerged to take their place alongside the established leaders. In 1846, James DeBow, at age twenty-six, founded *DeBow's Review* and vigorously defended the South and its institution of slavery. In 1854, 30-year-old Ethelbert Barksdale became editor of the pro-slavery *Weekly Mississippian* in Jackson, and 35-year-old Leonidas W. Spratt became widely known throughout the South as editor of Charleston's *Southern Standard*.

Although all shared a commitment to maintaining the southern way of life, differences other than age did exist among the Fire-Eaters. Rhett and his colleagues had direct contacts with the North and northerners. The DeBows and Barksdales did not. Those who followed Rhett had some hesitation in trying to defend slavery on moral grounds; the DeBows and Barksdales did not. Many of these young men were, according to one historian, "pro-slavery moralists, aggressively avowing their belief in the rightness of slavery." However, one thing bound both groups of editors together in their philosophy: their careers were based on patterns of sectionalism rather than nation-building.[35]

As the words "secession" and "disunion" became more common in the South, the Fire-Eaters began to justify the option of the South going it alone. The *Mercury* declared that the South would

not be hurt economically by separation from the North. In fact, it argued, the region would benefit. It claimed that the South was "in control of her own commerce and destinies" and would "bound forward in a career of prosperity and power, unsurpassed in the history of the world." So strongly did Rhett believe in the South's future that when South Carolina did secede in December 1860, he predicted that "the historians of 2000 A.D. would write glowingly of the Southern Confederacy." He envisioned an empire "extending across the continent to the Pacific, down through Mexico to the other side of the Gulf, and over the Isles of the Sea."[36]

The Jackson *Weekly Mississippian* took a similar approach. It was said of Barksdale and the *Mississippian* that when the paper roared in Mississippi all the little country papers yelped. It was common for the paper to brand any scheme with which it did not agree as "abolitionist" or "traitorous," words that were quick to arouse southern outrage. Thus, it pointed a finger at the North as the primary cause of the South's leaving the Union. It declared:

> It does not seem to occur to the aggressors [the North], that if there is any disunion, in consequence of the aggressors, that they are the disunionists. Disunion, which follows a perverted Union, is the work of the pervertors. He who violates the contract is the author of a dissolution of the contract.[37]

All southern editors were not Fire-Eaters; nor did they agree on the issue of secession. There were some who supported immediate withdrawal from the Union, while others believed that secession should depend on some future event or grievance and not on past ones. Some editors did not believe any type of change would benefit the country, and they advocated continuation of the Union with few changes in conditions. Some were unsure of what road to take. However, following the election of Abraham Lincoln, most southern papers moved toward immediate secession. When the six seceded southern states adopted the provisional constitution for the Confederate States in 1861, Robert Barnwell Rhett's was the first of fifty signatures.

Regardless of their stand, most editors believed that if secession should come, it would take place in a peaceful manner. It is difficult, if not impossible, to determine just how much the papers of Garrison, Douglass, Rhett, DeBow, Barksdale, Spratt, and others had to do with bringing about the Civil War. They must be credited, however, with fanning the flames of hatred that helped turn a war of words into one of weapons.

THE NORTHERN PRESS

By the mid-1800s newspapers had become a strong voice in the affairs of the North. The *Evening Post, Herald, Tribune,* and *Times* of New York, the *Springfield* (Mass.) *Republican,* and *Chicago Tribune* all were established leaders. Although these papers, with the exception of the *Herald,* supported the antislavery movement, it

[34]Ibid., 159 and 204.
[35]Ronald T. Takaki, *Pro-Slavery Crusade* (New York, 1971), 22.

[36]Quoted in Hesseltine and Smiley, *The South in American History,* 606.
[37]Jackson *Weekly Mississippian,* 27 June 1860.

Dred Scott Decision
The fugitive slave who sued in court for his freedom, Dred Scott became the subject of front-page coverage throughout the North. Despite the Supreme Court's decision against him in 1857, his master granted freedom to him, his wife, and two daughters. This story in *Leslie's Illustrated* appeared right after the Court decision and recounted the story of Scott and his family.

would be erroneous to put them in the same category as Garrison's *Liberator* or Lundy's *Genius*, which were founded to attack slavery. The established papers were founded primarily as journalistic ventures that happened to support the abolitionist movement, or at least to oppose the spread of slavery.

From a business point-of-view, northern papers were far more successful than their southern counterparts, and during the antebellum period they experienced enormous growth. For every paper in the South, there were three in the North. It had three times the political papers and almost four times the number of religious, literary, and miscellaneous publications. Dailies flourished in the cities, while towns seemed to be ideal locations for weeklies. By 1860 the *New York Herald* had a circulation of 77,000 daily, while the weekly edition of the *New York Tribune* averaged 200,000. In contrast, the *Richmond Dispatch*, one of the South's most successful papers, had a daily circulation of only 8,000 and 5,500 for its weekly edition. Rhett's *Charleston Mercury* had only 550 paid subscribers. Many of the differences in the number of publi-

cations and subscribers can be attributed to the different economic base in the North. Unlike the southern newspapers, the North's newspapers and magazines benefited from the urban, industrial, and retail strengths of the cities.

The *Evening Post*, the oldest paper in this northern group, had gained a reputation as a fighter for the "common man" and freedom of the press. It aligned itself with the antislavery forces and, under the leadership of William Cullen Bryant, had run the spectrum from Jacksonian Democrat to Free Soil to abolitionist Republican. Bryant argued that abolitionist editors had as much right to freedom of expression as any other editors. The *Evening Post* was also strongly pro-Union. When the southern states seceded, it branded them "traitors."

Of the four leading New York papers, the *Herald* came closest to promoting the views of the South. It supported the compromising attitude of the Kansas-Nebraska Bill of 1854, which called for Kansas to be a slave state and Nebraska a free state. The South took the bill as a positive gesture toward slavery, and the *Herald* enjoyed wide acceptance in the region. James Gordon Bennett, the *Herald's* owner, also represented the Democratic party's and the South's view on states' rights, which reasoned that the federal government had no right to interfere with slavery in states that chose the institution. The *Herald* did not, however, support secession by the southern states.

The *New York Tribune*, under its dominating editor, Horace Greeley, became a strong supporter of the antislavery movement. A teetotaler, Greeley fought for prohibition, opposed capital punishment, and hated slavery. At one point he favored allowing the southern states to withdraw peacefully if they wished. "Whenever a considerable section of our Union shall deliberately resolve to go out, we shall resist all coercive measures to keep it in," declared the *Tribune*. "We hope never to live in a republic whereof one section is pinned to the residue by bayonets."[38] This attitude changed as war came closer. By 1850 the *Tribune* had become the most influential, and one of the most anti-southern, papers in the country. Of the popular daily newspapers, it had become the leader of those opposed to slavery. It was so hated in the South that a southern news agent, who made the mistake of accepting an order for fifty copies of the *Tribune*, was seized and arraigned by a vigilance committee, determined to be an abolitionist, and sentenced to hang.

The *New York Times* maintained a more neutral stance on slavery. In 1851, in the prospectus of its first issue, it declared that it did not believe "that everything in society is either exactly right, or exactly wrong; what is good we desire to preserve and improve; what is evil, to exterminate, or reform."[39] That statement set the tone for the paper. However, this stance by editor Henry Raymond was probably more political than emotional. In 1854 after the Whig party split over the free-soil issue, Raymond, an aspiring politician, joined the new Republican party. Although unalterably antislavery, the party formulated a program that would attract those who were undecided on the issue of slavery, as well as those

[38]Quoted in Donald E. Reynolds, *Editors Make War* (Nashville, Tenn., 1966), 157.
[39]*New York Times*, 18 September 1851.

Revenge Elects Lincoln

The Political Grudge
That Changed History

The story of Abraham Lincoln's presidential bid traditionally details his rise from a humble log cabin to his famous campaign as "The Rail Splitter." Less mythic events based in revenge, though, contributed to his nomination at the 1860 Republican Convention in Chicago.

Lincoln had already developed a network of editorial support in the West, including the help of Joseph Medill at the *Chicago Tribune*, but it was Horace Greeley, editor of the *New York Tribune* and, at the time, a disgruntled office-seeker, who unexpectedly turned the vote of delegates to Lincoln.

Thurlow Weed, a powerful New York lobbyist and editor of the *Albany Evening-Journal*, had discovered Greeley in 1837 and hired him to edit the *Jeffersonian*, a campaign paper that promoted William H. Seward for Governor. Greeley produced the newspaper in Weed's Albany office and subsequently referred to the affiliation, which continued to engineer campaigns throughout the 1840s, as "the firm of Seward, Weed, and Greeley."

In 1848, Lincoln was elected as an Illinois Whig to Congress, subscribing to policies promoted by the firm, including the development of a national bank, homestead legislation, a protective tariff, and a limit on the spread of slavery. Such proposals had contributed directly to the presidencies of William Henry Harrison in 1841 and Zachary Taylor in 1849. In 1852, though, the Whig Party collapsed, leaving members to join the Republican Party.

Seward had since become an outspoken Senator and wanted to be President. Weed, as his financial backer, naturally expected Greeley to support Seward in 1860. However, Weed failed to realize how deeply upset Greeley had become over years of neglect at the hands of his partners, who, Greeley said, had failed to support him in his political aspirations. In a

Abraham Lincoln

Thurlow Weed

William Seward

Horace Greeley

"Et Tu, Greeley?"

final moment of frustration, after Greeley had asked Weed to nominate him for New York Governor in 1854 and Weed declined, Greeley responded by writing a bitter resignation letter addressed to Seward that dissolved the firm.

Before the 1860 convention, Republicans were divided between Seward and Lincoln. Although Western Republicans promoted Lincoln's honesty and self-reliance, Seward, with Weed's support, was virtually assured of victory. Greeley, though, who by then had become an influential national editor, had quietly vowed revenge. As a self-appointed delegate for Oregon, he lobbied on the convention floor against Seward, who he alleged would be easily corrupted by the interests of the Eastern establishment.

It took three ballots, but Greeley helped sway delegates from Pennsylvania to vote

After Horace Greeley opposed William Seward.at the 1860 Republican convention, *Vanity Fair* ran this cartoon comparing the episode to the assassination of Julius Caesar. As Caesar (Seward) lies dying, a strong-willed Brutus (Greeley), who has just stabbed him, walks off. Abraham Lincoln, depicted as a "Black Republican" for his opposition to slavery, stands above the melee. The caption is a play on Shakespeare's line in which Caeser asks, startled that his friend would help kill him: "Et tu, Brutus?"

for Lincoln, thus securing his nomination. When Weed learned of his candidate's defeat, he reportedly broke down in tears, claiming he had been unaware of Greeley's grudge.

The act of revenge went unrequited, as Lincoln passed over Greeley's bid for Postmaster General and, humbling Greeley, appointed Seward Secretary of State.

Joseph Medill
Editor of the leading newspaper in the Midwest, the *Chicago Tribune*, Joseph Medill was antislavery and staunchly pro-Union. He considered secessionists to be traitors. In giving directions for the operation of the paper after his death, he declared: "I desire the Tribune as a party organ never to be the supporter of that party [Democratic] which sought to destroy the American union or that exalts the state above the nation."

opposed to slavery. Raymond and the *Times* had also developed a reputation for "reasonableness" in reporting and, unlike Greeley, used a minimum of invective. Not until war actually began did the *Times* take a strong stand on the slavery issue.

In Springfield, Massachusetts, Samuel Bowles III was proving that a newspaper outside New York could have national influence. After taking over the reigns of the *Springfield Republican*, following the death of his father Samuel Bowles II in 1851, he thrust the weekly paper into the mainstream of political and moral thought. Like Raymond, Bowles was a Whig who later turned to the Republican party. Also, like Raymond's *Times*, the *Republican* was not always a staunch supporter of the antislavery movement. Prior to passage of the Kansas-Nebraska Act, it had approved of the Fugitive Slave Law, and it frequently attacked abolitionists for their views. Bowles did not approve of slavery; but he was strongly pro-Union, and he believed that quarrels between the North and South threatened the Union's existence. Later, after abandoning the Whig party, he denounced the execution of John Brown and became one of the first mainstream editors to endorse the Re-

publican party and Abraham Lincoln.

The newspaper field in the Midwest was led by Joseph Medill's *Chicago Tribune*, a strong pro-Union and antislavery paper. Like Bowles, Medill militantly opposed disunion and considered those who advocated secession as abandoning the true principles on which America was founded. Although it appears most Republican papers had to gradually accept the idea of Abraham Lincoln for president — and some never did — he was the *Tribune*'s choice from the beginning. After Lincoln received the nomination in 1860, a *Tribune* editorial declared: "He will take to the Presidential chair just the qualities which this country now demands to save it from impending destruction — ability that no man can question, firmness that nothing can overbear, honesty that can never be impeached, and patriotism that never despairs."[40]

By 1861, battle lines between the North and South had been drawn. There was no "one" issue that brought them to arms, but a combination of several that were rolled into the emotional issue of slavery. As with the rest of the country, most newspapers had been forced to take a stand. It can also be observed in hindsight that the war about to begin, which would so influence the nation's history, also would change American journalism.

RECOMMENDED READINGS

BOOKS

Adeleke, Tunde. *Without Regard to Race: The Other Martin Robison Delany*. Jackson, Miss., 2003. Delany, a pivotal African-American journalist, thinker, and abolitionist, based his complex strategies for racial integration more on America than on separateness and nationalism.

Bacon, Jacqueline, *Freedom's Journal: The First African-American Newspaper*. Lanham, Md., 2007. Cornish and Ruswurm used their paper to connect freeborn black communities and to shape concepts of activism for both black and white leaders.

Blassingame, John W., Mae G. Henderson, and Jessica M. Dunn, eds. *Antislavery Newspapers and Periodicals*, 5 vols. Boston, 1980-1984. This useful work provides an index to the contents of the publications.

Bullock, Penelope L. *The Afro-American Periodical Press, 1838-1909*. Baton Rouge, 1981. The author provides an overview of the development of black magazines and journals and analyzes their contents.

Cain, William E., ed. *William Lloyd Garrison and the Fight Against Slavery: Selections from the Liberator*. Boston, 1995. This selection of Garrison's editorials from the *Liberator* highlights his political philosophies in relation to such topics as slavery, women's rights, and the nature of reform.

Copeland, David A. *The Antebellum Era: Primary Documents on Events from 1820 to 1860*. Westport, Conn., 2003. This collection reprints newspaper articles from the period.

Curtis, Michael Kent. *Free Speech, "The People's Darling Privilege": Struggles for Freedom of Expression in American History*. Durham, N.C., 2000. Many public contests over free speech erupted during the abolitionist movement and the Civil War.

Daniels, Walter C., ed. *Black Journals of the United States*. Westport, Conn., 1982. Daniels includes historical profiles of more than 100 black periodicals published in the nineteenth and twentieth centuries in America.

Dann, Martin E., ed. *The Black Press, 1827-1890: The Quest for National Identity*. New York, 1971. This collection draws items from black newspapers over a 63-year period and groups them according to prevalent themes. It includes an overview and chapter introductions that explain the ideals and purposes of the black edi-

[40]*Chicago Tribune*, 23 May 1860.

tors and writers.

Dickerson, Donna Lee. *The Course of Tolerance: Freedom of the Press in Nineteenth-Century America*. Westport, Conn., 1990. This readable introduction to the subject includes significant material devoted to the dangers posed to press freedom during the antebellum and Civil War periods.

Dillon, Merton L. *Elijah P. Lovejoy, Abolitionist Editor*. Urbana, Ill., 1961. In advocating emancipation, Lovejoy was motivated by religious zeal.

Dumond, Dwight L., ed. *Southern Editorials on Secession*. New York, 1931. This anthology includes 183 editorials selected from seventy-two newspapers, "showing the variety, conflict, and concurrence of opinion in the southern states during and shortly before the crisis of secession."

Fredrickson, George M., ed. *William Lloyd Garrison*. Englewood Cliffs, N. J., 1968. This collection of documents reveals how Garrison viewed the world and how his contemporaries viewed him.

Gill, John. *Tide without Turning: Elijah P. Lovejoy and Freedom of the Press*. Boston, 1958. Not only was Lovejoy a martyr to the antislavery cause, but he staunchly advocated the First Amendment guarantee of press freedom.

Harrold, Stanley. *Gamaliel Bailey and Antislavery Union*. Kent, Ohio, 1986. Through the *Philanthropist*, the organ of the Ohio Anti-Slavery Society, and the *National Era* in Washington, D.C., Bailey played a central role in the abolitionist movement.

Hodges, Willis Augustus. *Free Man of Color*. Knoxville, Tenn., 1982. This is the autobiography of the editor of the *Ram's Horn*.

Hutton, Frankie. *The Early Black Press in America, 1827-1860*. Westport, Conn., 1993. Black editors emphasized social responsibility, morality, and democratic ideals.

Kessler, Lauren. *The Dissident Press*. Beverly Hills, Calif., 1984. Black newspapers served as a voice for black Americans because the mainstream press overlooked, distorted, and downplayed their concerns and accomplishments.

Korngold, Ralph. *Two Friends of Man*. Boston, 1950. William Lloyd Garrison and Wendell Phillips were friends and knew Abraham Lincoln.

Laurie, Bruce. *Beyond Garrison: Antislavery and Social Reform*. Cambridge and New York, 2005. Lesser-known abolitionists, encouraged by African-American editors and leaders, helped spur antebellum Massachusetts to become one of the few Northern states in which African-American males could vote and personal liberty laws protected fugitive slaves from federal authorities.

Mayer, Henry. *All on Fire: William Lloyd Garrison and the Abolition of Slavery*. New York, 2000. Garrison was a pivotal participant in the abolitionist movement who inspired two generations of activists.

McFeely, William S. *Frederick Douglass*. New York, 1991. This detailed biography chronicles Douglass from his life as a slave to his later life in politics and explains the motives behind his work.

Miner, H. Craig. *Seeding Civil War: Kansas in the National News, 1854-1858*. Lawrence, Kan., 2008. Editors around the nation were obsessed with events in Kansas. Their treatment of the events was determined greatly by their partisan leanings.

Osthaus, Carl R. *Partisans of the Southern Press: Editorial Spokesmen of the Nineteenth Century*. Lexington, Ky., 1994. This account of southern journalism focuses on four dominant papers, the *New Orleans Daily Picayune, Charleston Daily Courier, Charleston Mercury, and Richmond Examiner*, before, during, and after the Civil War.

Perkins, Howard C., ed. *Northern Editorials on Secession*, 2 vols. New York, 1942. This anthology of editorials during the crisis of 1860-1861 has an introduction describing the general characteristics of newspapers.

Pride, Armistead Scott and Clint C. Wilson II. *A History of the Black Press*. Washington, D.C., 1997. This account emphasizes the social and political context surrounding the development of black newspapers from 1827 to the 20th century, stressing the function of the press to serve as a voice for blacks.

Ratner, Lorman A., and Dwight T. Teeter, Jr. *Fanatics and Fire-eaters: Newspapers and the Coming of the Civil War*. Urbana, Ill., 2003. The changing attitudes of Southerners and Northerners toward the other made the Civil War seemingly inevitable.

Reynolds, David S. *John Brown, Abolitionist: the Man Who Killed Slavery, Sparked the Civil War, and Seeded Civil Rights*. New York, 2005. Brown seized the nation's attention through use of the press, creating sudden unity in the North and planting the seeds of the civil rights movement by making a pioneering demand

for complete social and political equality for America's ethnic minorities.

Rhodes, Jane. *Mary Ann Shadd Cary: The Black Press and Protest in the Nineteenth Century*. Bloomington, Ind., 1998. Cary was the first black woman to own and operate a newspaper in North America.

Ripley, C. Peter, ed. *The Black Abolitionist Papers*. Chapel Hill, N.C., 1985. This three-volume collection includes items from black newspapers published in the United States, Canada, and the British Isles from 1830 to 1865.

Risley, Ford. *Abolition and the Press: The Moral Struggle Against Slavery*. Evanston, Ill., 2008. Beginning around 1820, newspapers began focusing intensely on the abolition of slavery. As they were able, most continued publishing until passage of the Thirteenth Amendment. Abolitionist newspapers and other publications were critical in the national debate.

Risley, Ford. *The Civil War: Primary Documents on Events from 1860-1865*. Westport, Conn., 2004. This collection arranges documents chronologically according to topics such as elections, peace movements and significant battles.

Sadlier, Rosemary. *Mary Ann Shadd: Publisher, Editor, Teacher, Lawyer, Suffragette*. Toronto, Ontario, 1995. Shadd, the first black woman editor in North America, played an important role in the development of racial pride and nineteenth-century equal rights.

Simon, Paul. *Lovejoy, Martyr to Freedom*. St. Louis, 1964. Elijah Lovejoy, the antislavery editor killed by a mob in Alton, Ill., in 1837, was a model of moral courage. Following a religious conversion, he slowly became an abolitionist.

Streitmatter, Rodger. *Raising Her Voice: African-American Women Journalists Who Changed History*. Lexington, Ky., 1994. The author presents biographies of eleven influential black women journalists from the 1830s to the present.

Tripp, Bernell. *Origins of the Black Press: New York 1827-1847*. Northport, Ala., 1992. The early black press emphasized self-expression and improvement for blacks, not just abolition.

Vogel, Todd, ed. *The Black Press: New Literary and Historical Essays*. New Brunswick, N.J., 2001. Essays on the black press in the nineteenth and twentieth centuries give particular attention to the political, social, and economic tenor of the time.

White, Laura A. *Robert Barnwell Rhett: Father of Secession*. New York, 1931. This is the definitive biography of the fire-eating editor of the *Charleston (S.C.) Mercury*. He argued for secession as early as 1850 and remained a staunch advocate of slavery and southern extremism throughout the Civil War.

Williamson, Scott C. *The Narrative Life: The Moral and Religious Thought of Frederick Douglass*. Macon, Ga., 2002. Douglass began as an evangelical and religious liberal to become a fiery abolitionist, antislavery speaker, and newspaper editor.

Wolseley, Roland E. *The Black Press, U.S.A*. Ames, Iowa, 2nd ed., 1990. Wolseley provides an historical overview of the black press in America from its founding to the present.

ARTICLES

Barrow, Lionel C., Jr. "'Our Own Cause': *Freedom's Journal* and the Beginnings of the Black Press." *Journalism History* 4 (1977): 118-22. The newspaper "gave blacks a voice of their own and an opportunity not only to answer the attacks printed in the white press but to read articles on black accomplishments, marriages, deaths, that the white press of the day ignored."

Binnington, Ian. "Standing upon a Volcano: Cincinnati's Newspapers Debate Emancipation, 1860-1862." *American Nineteenth Century History* 10 (June 2009): 163-86. Cincinnati editors held a range of opinions with regard to emancipation; few believed in unrestrained black freedom.

Bond, Donovan H. "How the Wheeling Intelligencer Became a Republican Organ." *West Virginia History* 11 (April 1950): 160-84. During 1856-1858 the Virginia paper let "all parties express their views in its columns." Its policy "did not fit well with the practices of its orthodox Southern and Democratic contemporaries."

Borchard, Gregory. "The *New York Tribune* at Harper's Ferry: 'Horace Greeley on Trial.'" *American Journalism* 20:1 (2003): 13-31. Greeley's support of John Brown during his trial caused a backlash.

Brewer, William M. "John B. Russwurm." *Journal of Negro History* 13 (1928): 413-22. Russwurm, the editor of *Freedom's Journal*, America's first black newspaper, advocated the colonization of former slaves.

Bryan, Carter R. "Negro Journalism in America Before Emancipation." *Journalism Monographs* 25 (1969). The author lists black newspapers published prior to the

Civil War and discusses their origins, content, and purpose.

Burks, Mary Fair. "The First Black Literary Magazine in American Letters." *CLA Journal* 19 (March 1976): 318-21. The *Anglo-African Magazine* "succeeded in creating a tradition of *belles lettres* among blacks and in establishing a nascent countermovement ... to assimilationist literature."

Cullen, Maurice R., Jr. "William Gilmore Simms, Southern Journalist." *Journalism Quarterly* (1961): 298-302, 412. The South Carolinian was a leading literary figure and "a dedicated journalist who ... placed his life in jeopardy in order to tell in print what he felt *had* to be told."

Domke, David. "Journalists, Framing, and Discourse About Race Relations." *Journalism & Mass Communication Monographs* 164 (December 1997). The author examines racial values and attitudes of a group of leading editors from the nineteenth century, including Frederick Douglass.

Fanuzzi, Robert A. "The Organ of an Individual: William Lloyd Garrison and the Liberator." *Prospects* 23 (1998): 107. Newspapers were particularly important in the rise of the abolitionist movement, as illustrated by Garrison's political work through the *Liberator*.

Fee Jr., Frank E. "Blackface in Black and White: Race, Ethnicity, and Gender in Frederick Douglass' Hometown Newspapers, 1847." *American Journalism* 20:3 (2003): 73-92. Papers in Rochester, N.Y., lampooned African Americans.

Floan, Howard R. "The New York *Evening Post* and the Ante-bellum South." *American Quarterly* 8 (Fall 1956): 243-53. William Cullen Bryant, *Evening Post* editor, in the 1830s attempted to play down divisive issues. As differences between the North and South worsened, however, he grew stronger in his condemnation of southern attitudes and actions.

Franklin, Cathy Rogers. "James Gillespie Birney, the Revival Spirit, and *The Philanthropist*." *American Journalism* 17 (Spring 2000): 31-51. "Birney's *Philanthropist* was based as much on Biblical principles as his desire to see terrible injustices corrected and press freedom protected."

Holmes, J. Welfred. "Some Antislavery Editors at Work: Lundy, Bailey, and Douglass." *CLA Journal* 7 (1963): 48-55. "These three men of diverse talents and viewpoints, while editing their papers in a highly individual manner, struck telling blows against slavery."

Humphrey, Carol Sue. "Religious Newspapers and Antebellum Reform," 104-118 in Wm. David Sloan, ed., *Media and Religion in American History*. Northport, Ala.: 2000. The religious press was instrumental in the rise of reform movements, particularly anti-slavery.

Hutton, Frankie. "The Impact of the Democratic Ideals of the U.S. Constitution on the Early Black Press in America." *Journal of the Afro-American Historical & Genealogical Society* 11:3 (1990): 111-20. Editors of black newspapers believed "freedom of the press was grounded in a sense of social responsibility."

Johnson, David W. "Freesoilers for God: Kansas Newspaper Editors and the Antislavery Crusade." *Kansas History* 2 (Summer 1979): 74-85. In the 1850s fight for a free Kansas, editorials emphasized slavery as a violation of the Bible and God's principles.

Kovarik, Bill. "'To Avoid the Coming Storm': Hezekiah Niles' *Weekly Register* as a Voice of North-South Moderation, 1811-1836." *American Journalism* 9:3-4 (1992): 20-43. Niles attempted to conciliate North/South relations in order to avoid civil war.

Laughlin, Bonnie E. "'Endangering the Peace of Society': Abolitionist Agitation and Mob Reaction in St. Louis and Alton, 1836-1838." *Missouri Historical Review* 95:1 (2000): 1-22. Fear of abolitionist activity led otherwise decent citizens to participate in mob violence, including the murder of editor Elijah Lovejoy.

Malone, Henry T. "The *Weekly Atlanta Intelligencer* as a Secessionist Journal." *Georgia Historical Quarterly* 37 (December 1953): 278-86. With the secessionist crisis of 1860-1861, the *Intelligencer* "became defiantly pro-Southern.... [It] offers an interesting and representative picture of Atlanta journalism during critical times."

Martin, Asa Earl. "Pioneer Anti-Slavery Press." *Missouri Valley Historical Review* 3 (March 1916): 509-28. Abolitionist journals "kept alive the anti-slavery sentiment, organized it and formulated definite plans of operation....They were the pioneers of the movement, struggling almost single-handed against the numerous difficulties that threatened to overwhelm them."

Nord, David Paul. "Tocqueville, Garrison and the Perfection of Journalism." *Journalism History* 13 (1986): 56-63. Garrison's *Liberator*, rather than the penny newspapers, embodied Tocqueville's concept of a democratic press.

Nordin, Kenneth D. "In Search of Black Unity: An Interpretation of the Content and Function of 'Freedom's Journal.'" *Journalism History* 4 (1977): 123-8. The newspaper "tried to establish a sense of fraternity among blacks and chart the course people of color should take to improve their positions in American society."

Nye, Russel B. "Freedom of the Press and the Antislavery Controversy." *Journalism Quarterly* 22 (1945): 1-11. Southern states abridged freedom with the argument that it did not allow the distribution of obnoxious doctrines. Northern legislatures refused to abridge press freedom, and abolitionists quickly recognized the relationship between their cause and constitutional liberty.

O'Kelly, Charlotte G. "Black Newspapers and the Black Protest Movement: Their Historical Relationship, 1827-1945." *Phylon* 43 (1982): 1-14. The content of black newspapers and the response of the black press to the black protest movement were influenced by interrelationships of changes, events, issues, problems, and ideologies.

Peeples, Matthew. "Creating Political Authority: The Role of the Antebellum Black Press in the Political Mobilization and Empowerment of African Americans." *Journalism History* 34:2 (2008): 76-86. Beginning in the mid-1830s, African-American newspapers "became important as platforms of political agency for those who were denied conventional means of political participation in the government."

Perry, Patsy Brewington. "The Literary Content of *Frederick Douglass' Paper* through 1860." *CLA Journal* 17 (December 1973): 214-29. Douglass was "an arbiter of cultural and literary taste....[He] provided rich literary fare for his readers — ...he was, in fact, a champion of belles lettres." (214)

Potter, David M. "Horace Greeley and Peaceable Secession." *Journal of Southern History* 7 (1941): 145-59. Greeley's argument that the southern states should be allowed to secede peaceably was impractical and illusory. It "obscured the clarity of the true alternatives — compromise and war."

Reed, Barbara Straus. "The Antebellum Jewish Press: Origins, Problems, Functions." *Journalism Monographs* 139 (June 1993). The Jewish press in antebellum America addressed issues facing American Jews and served a religious and cultural purpose for its audience.

Robinson, Elwyn Burns. "The *Pennsylvanian*: Organ of Democracy." *Pennsylvania Magazine of History and Biography* 62 (1938): 350-60. In antebellum Philadelphia, the *Pennsylvanian* received patronage from Democratic politicians and supported Democratic, southern interests in slavery and secession.

Shortell, Timothy. "The Rhetoric of Black Abolitionism." *Social Science History* 28:1 (2004): 75. Newspapers such as Douglass' *North Star* and *Frederick Douglass' Paper* were instrumental in advancing antislavery arguments.

Snorgrass, J. William. "The Black Press in the San Francisco Bay Area 1850-1900." *California History* 60 (Winter 1981-82): 306-17. The newspapers had two objectives: "to provide a platform from which blacks could express their views and combat racial prejudice and discrimination in the United States."

Stewart, James B. "The Aims and Impact of Garrisonian Abolitionism, 1840-1860." *Civil War History* 15 (1969): 197-209. The radical "Garrisonian approach to northern politics was not nearly as unsophisticated and unproductive as historians have assumed."

Tripp, Bernell. "The Media and Community Cohesiveness: The Black Press and the Colonization Issue." Chapter 8. In *The Significance of the Media in American History*. James D. Startt and Wm. David Sloan, eds. Northport, Ala., 1994. Black newspapers in the antebellum period waged a debate over what the future of African Americans should be.

Watts, Liz. "Lydia Maria Child: Editor of the National Anti-Slavery Standard, 1841-43." *Journalism History* 35:1 (2009): 12-22. The editor of the *National Anti-Slavery Standard*, "espoused objectivity, derided sensationalism, and applied her own inclusive formula for building circulation, emphasizing material with broad appeal to both men and women while reducing the emphasis on politics."

Whitby, Gary L. "Horns of a Dilemma: The *Sun*, Abolition, and the 1833-34 New York Riots." *Journalism Quarterly* 67 (1990): 410-19. The penny *Sun* provided a popular forum for advocating abolition — even though its two co-editors disagreed on the speed at which abolition should proceed.

9

The Press and the Civil War
1861 - 1865

The Civil War represented the dawning of a new era in war reporting. The changes that it brought about had a major impact on mass communication afterward. In part, the changes were made possible by the economic condition of newspaper and magazine publishing, particularly in the North. The climbing circulations and increasing advertising revenues of newspapers and magazines in major metropolitan areas meant more money could be spent on reporting — and illustrating — the Civil War. Even in the South, where circulation and advertising revenues could not match northern figures, cooperative news enterprises allowed extensive war reporting at affordable prices.

The Civil War also represented the dawning of this new era for reasons quite apart from economics. Technological innovations made this the most immediate war that the general public had ever witnessed. The Civil War was one of the first in which reporters made widespread use of the telegraph. They could wire their newspapers with the most up-to-date information on the battles, and editors could quickly get that news to the reading public via "extras," or added editions of the newspaper. Those "extras" — with the latest information on a battle — were snatched up by readers with insatiable appetites for war news. The premium was on reporting and speed but not necessarily accuracy. The emphasis on speed sometimes caused shoddy reporting, incomplete dispatches, and unethical practices.

Ever in search of a good story, reporters dodged bullets at battlefronts, endured the endless boredom of camp life, and sometimes invoked the ire of generals because of the stories they wrote. They also shared the risks of war. Some died from disease or wounds sustained in the line of duty. Others found that the rigors of war reporting had permanently damaged their health. War reporting was not done, however, just at the front. Reporters were also covering Richmond and Washington, D.C. — ever on the lookout for a good story.

Speed of reporting was not the only aspect of coverage that made the Civil War stand apart from earlier American wars. The Civil War also marked the beginnings of "visual" war reporting. Artists roamed the front, sketching battle scenes, leaders, and camp life. Their drawings seemed to appear instantaneously in a new type of publication, the illustrated news weekly. The speed of publication was made possible by technical changes in the engraving process. Readers could follow the war in detailed maps that charted battles and troop movements, though not necessarily accurately. These maps were primarily in the newspapers and news weeklies of the North. Such publications, in turn, posed a new set of national security questions, which were never satisfactorily answered during the war.

Photography was an even newer innovation that provided an additional dimension to war coverage. No other American war had been so extensively photographed. Although the photos could be reproduced in newspapers and magazines only as line drawings, the public flocked to studios or to traveling photographers to see and to buy photos of the war and its leaders.

THE TELEGRAPH AND THE CIVIL WAR

The 1860s found the nation strung with telegraph lines. About 50,000 miles of wire crisscrossed the nation in a network that could assure virtually "instantaneous" transmission of news. No longer would the public have to wait weeks for the latest reports of battles. Thanks to the telegraph, the reporter could get his story into the editor's hands within hours of the fighting; and the editor, through the use of the "extra," could get the information quickly to readers. The telegraph used in conjunction with the "extra" meant that war coverage was fast. It could do nothing, however, to improve accuracy.

Using the telegraph was expensive. In the North, the telegraphing of battle reports was one of the largest single expenditures a newspaper faced. The *New York Herald* and the *Chicago Times* incurred especially high bills because they emphasized use of the telegraph. The *Herald* paid $1,000, a substantial amount in the 1860s, for its telegraphed story of the capture of New Orleans. Nonetheless, such costs were prices editors were happy to pay — especially if they got the story first. As one northern reporter complained, editors were ever pushing the reporters to get and trans-

"Bull Run" Russell
William Howard Russell of the *London Times* was a celebrated reporter at the beginning of the Civil War. The engraving on the left, which appeared in *Harper's Weekly* in June 1861, showed him inspecting a cannon at a Confederate-held fort in Georgia. His image changed, however, shortly after the first Battle of Bull Run in July. Despite the fact that he sympathized with the Union, he was disturbed about the conduct of Union soldiers at Bull Run. In writing about the battle, he called their behavior "scandalous" and "a disgrace." He endured much press criticism for the report, such as the engraving (right) that appeared in the *New York Illustrated News.* Critics gave him the nickname "Bull Run." By the next spring, he had returned to England.

mit their stories quickly. "To print first, however incorrect and incomplete intelligence," he declared, "was the height of ambitions."[1]

In the South, the pressure to get the story quickly was just as real; but the problem of telegraph expense was relieved somewhat by a cooperative news venture called the Press Association of the Confederate States of America (PA), which negotiated lower telegraph rates for its reporters. After the Civil War began, southern newspapers lost the services of the New York Associated Press. Out of necessity, the Confederate dailies formed a cooperative news venture. Under agreements worked out by the PA, its reporters had access to military and commercial telegraph lines at reduced rates. Newspapers with correspondents in the field found that telegraph expenses were just another item to be added to the skyrocketing costs of production. Later in the war, southern reporters could not even depend on telegraph transmission, as lines rusted on the poles or were burned before invading armies.

In the North and the South, high telegraph rates as well as the uncertainty of transmission led to a certain amount of streamlining of reporter copy. An inverted-pyramid structure for news stories did not exist; but compared to the writing about earlier wars, some Civil War stories seem concise. Compared to today's dispatches, they appear stilted and wordy. The dispatch reporting the surrender of Fort Sumter at the beginning of the war typified the writing style:

FORT SUMTER HAS SURRENDERED.
The Confederate flag floats over its walls.
None of the garrison or Confederate troops are hurt.
Another correspondent says: —
Major Anderson has drawn down the stripes and stars, and displays

a white flag, which has been answered from the city, and a boat is on the way to Sumter.[2]

The telegraph was not the only means of news transmission. Reporters continued to rely on the mails or special messengers, who rushed the dispatches via train, boat, or horseback to newspaper offices.

The emphasis on speed led, in many cases, to inaccurate, shoddy reporting. It also led to unnecessary national security problems. Reporters transmitted everything they learned; but editors, particularly in the North, seldom deleted the information that could aid the enemy. The concept of press responsibility in wartime had failed to keep up with the speed of the telegraph.

UNION REPORTERS

This emphasis on speed put the spotlight on the reporter. Basking in the light was a group of northern reporters who labeled themselves the "Bohemian Brigade." Although the term originally applied to that one group, it could be — and has been — applied to northern reporters in general. They lived the high-spirited, unsettled lives that the term "Bohemian" implies. Many northern reporters, at one time estimated at 500, often lived on the edge. They were a bit disreputable in the public's mind and reprehensible to many generals. Nonetheless, they went to the front, suffered diseases, braved danger, and faced death to report the war.

The names and numbers of all the "Bohemian Brigade" will probably never be known. Some floated into war reporting as "occasionals," paid at space rates, and then disappeared. Others were soldiers who contributed letters to newspapers or magazines back home. Perhaps only 200 were full-time, professional reporters,

[1]Henry Villard, "Army Correspondence," *Nation*, 27 July 1865, 116.

[2]*New York Herald*, 14 April 1861, 1.

who spent extended periods covering the conflict.

Many were ill prepared in training, temperament, or skill to report this or any other war. Special qualities were needed to cover the conflict. One Union correspondent contended that reporting required the "gifts of omnipresence, omnivision and supernatural capacity of intellectual production." As the war continued, this correspondent found fewer reporters were equal to the task. By midwar, he observed, a new set of men, "an altogether inferior class of persons," had made their way into the ranks of army correspondents:

Men turned up in the army as correspondents more fit to drive cattle than to write for newspapers. With a dull or slow perception, incapable of logical arrangement of facts, innocent of grammatical English, they were altogether out of place in the positions they tried to fill. Many added to these defects a lowness of habits and vulgarity of manners that rendered them unfit for association with the higher ranks of the army, and confined them in their intercourse to like-minded subalterns. They could not and did not gain the respect, and with it the confidence, of those high in command, with whom to be on good terms was a prime condition of professional success. They got to be looked upon, as a distinguished general expressed it, "as intolerable and unavoidable nuisances."[3]

Surprisingly little is known about these reporters. A number of them drifted into the war, covered a campaign or two, and then gave up the trade. Others assumed pseudonyms and thereby eluded identification. What is known about them is pieced together by contemporary accounts or by published biographical data on the best known of the reporters. Most of the northern reporters were young — in their twenties. Most had some journalism experience before the war. Of a group of fifty of the best known reporters, nearly half attended college, when few Americans could afford to do so, and more than half were urban born in a primarily rural country.[4]

The vast majority of them were white males. Few minorities covered the war. One notable exception was Thomas Morris Chester, an African American who returned from Liberia to report for the *Philadelphia Press*. His best known reports came from captured Richmond, where he reported — sometimes from slave jails — on freedman reaction to President Lincoln. The few women covering the war reported primarily from Washington, D.C. Of these, the best known was Jane Grey Swisshelm of the *St. Cloud* (Minn.) *Democrat*, who supplemented her journalistic income with a clerkship in the Quartermaster General's office. Nonetheless, she critically reported on the quality of Union hospitals, carrying on a personal, bitter campaign to improve conditions. Mary Livermore also reported on hospital conditions. As an agent of the Northwestern branch of the Sanitary Commission (Chicago), she traveled to hospitals, ministering to soldiers and writing for her hus-

Thomas Morris Chester, Civil War Reporter
Chester was the first African American to be hired as a fulltime reporter for a daily American newspaper. Born in Pennsylvania in 1834, he emigrated to Liberia, where he worked as an editor and publisher in its capital city of Monrovia. He returned to the United States after a year, and the *Philadelphia Press* hired him in 1864 to report on black Union troops fighting in Virginia. His coverage of the capture of Richmond in April 1865 included some of the most detailed first-hand accounts that exist of the fall of the Confederate capital and its aftermath.

band's paper, the *New Covenant*.

New York papers sent the greatest number of reporters to the front. The *Herald* alone dispatched more than sixty. Its tent and wagon became a familiar sight. The *Tribune* and the *Times* never sent as many, yet their reporters would often beat the *Herald* with battle coverage. Other New York papers sent some reporters to cover the war but lacked the reporting presence of the other three dominant New York papers.

Midwestern papers, particularly, came into their own during the war. The *Cincinnati Gazette* may not have had many reporters in the field; but it had one of the best, Whitelaw Reid, who after the war became editor of the *New York Tribune*. The *Gazette's* competition, the *Cincinnati Commercial*, was one of the most popular papers with the men of the western armies. It came to be known as the "soldier's paper." In Chicago, the *Tribune* and the *Times* jockeyed for predominance in battlefield reporting. At one time, the

[3]Villard, "Army Correspondence," 115-6.
[4]Louis M. Starr, *Bohemian Brigade: Civil War Newspapermen in Action* (New York, 1954), 61.

Tribune fielded twenty-nine special correspondents. In spite of his pro-southern sentiments, *Chicago Times* editor Wilbur F. Storey emphasized telegraphic speed. He was alleged to have instructed a reporter: "Telegraph fully all news you can get, and when there is no news send rumors."[5]

However, no single newspaper, not even the mighty *New York Herald*, could match the number of correspondents the New York Associated Press dispatched. Formed in 1848 as a cooperative venture of New York newspapers, the AP enjoyed a real advantage during the Civil War since it had just negotiated special rates with both Union telegraph companies in 1860. Before the war, it had a network of reporters throughout the country. Their number increased once hostilities started. AP coverage came, however, at a price. Newspapers outside of New York were forced to pay exorbitant rates for AP coverage and even more for "special reports." Western newspaper publishers, incensed with the high charges and the inconsistent quality of the New York AP reporting, organized their own cooperative in November 1862. It became known as the Western AP.

Wire and newspaper reporters found that their jobs meant long hours, stress, danger, and low pay. The typical pay for the reporter was just $15 to $35 a week, less than a typesetter made, plus expenses.

Despite the low pay, editors expected reporters to get the news first and get it any way they could. A circular to reporters from the *New York Herald* explains the pressure these journalists worked under: "In no instance, and under no circumstances, must you be beaten."[6] To this end, reporters were known to use any device, ethical or not. A reporter was not above bribery, fabricating eyewitness accounts, and hoaxes. More than one train engineer was bribed by a reporter heading for a telegraph office after a battle. *Herald* reporter William Shanks found that his bribe of an engineer not to let anyone else on the train did little good. A reporter for a competing newspaper was already aboard. *New York Tribune* reporter Junius Browne missed the Battle of Pea Ridge, Arkansas, but that did not stop him from writing a stirring, albeit fictitious, report. A British newspaper reprinted the story as an example of the finest war reporting.[7]

This is not to say there was no good reporting or ethical reporters. Many journalists risked their lives or their health to cover the war and get their stories back to the newspaper office. *New York Herald* reporter Phineas Homans perished when he fell from the deck of a steamer in South Carolina. Another *Herald* reporter, George Alfred Townsend, nearly died of "Chickahominy Fever" following General McClellan in the Peninsula Campaign of 1862. The opposing armies captured and imprisoned some reporters.[8]

Wherever troops fought, reporters usually followed. Reporter George Smalley followed them to bloody Antietam and tried everything to get his story back to the *New York Tribune*. That included riding through a hail of bullets to cover the battle and then traveling day and night to deliver his story to the *Tribune* offices. That story, considered one of the best of the war, was the first on the battle to hit the streets of New York City, the second morning after the fight.

Henry Villard had a different problem covering the Battle of Fredericksburg: he had to convince the *Tribune* to publish his story. He witnessed the terrible destruction at Fredericksburg, where there were more than 12,000 Union casualties, and rushed to Washington, D.C., to file his story. The government censor refused to clear it. Villard was not about to be stopped. He sent his graphic account by special messenger to New York — but the *Tribune* delayed and eventually published only a watered down version. President Abraham Lincoln, however, wanted to know the full details of the fight and summoned Villard to the White House for his eyewitness account.[9]

The best reporting conveyed not just the bare facts of the war but also a sense of the battle. For example, in the last days of the war, George Alfred Townsend, by then with the *New York World*, shared some quiet moments with General Philip Sheridan's men after the Battle of Five Forks:

> I am sitting by Sheridan's camp-fire, on the spot he has just signalized by the most individual and complete victory of the war. All his veterans are around him, stooping by knots over the

[5]*Chicago Daily Journal*, 22 April 1924.
[6]Albert Richardson to Sydney Gay, 11 April 1863, reprinted in Starr, *Bohemian Brigade*, 233.
[7]Franc B. Wilkie, *Pen and Powder* (Boston, 1888), 126-9.

[8]George Alfred Townsend, *Rustics in Rebellion: A Yankee Reporter on the Road to Richmond 1861-1865* (Chapel Hill, 1950), 121-30. Junius Browne, *Four Years in Secessia: Adventures within and Beyond the Union Lines* (Hartford, 1865), 229-368.
[9]George W. Smalley, *Anglo-American Memories* (New York, 1911), 150-2. Henry Villard, *Memoirs of Henry Villard, Journalist and Financier, 1835-1900*, Vol. I, 1835-1862 (New York, reprint, 1969), 388-90.

Reporters for the Union
Among the hundreds of reporters who covered the Civil War at the front, a small number stood out for their exceptional work. Among the best from the New York City newspapers were (clockwise from top left) Henry Villard, *New York Herald* and *Tribune*; George Alfred Townsend, *New York Herald* and *World*; Charles Anderson Page, *New York Tribune*; and George Smalley, *New York Tribune*. Although many people believed that reporters led glamorous lives, even the best ones worked with difficult conditions and faced daily dangers. Townsend, for example, nearly died of camp fever while covering the Peninsula Campaign of 1862. Page described the reporter's life as one of "constant danger, without the soldier's glory." Villard described many reporters as "more fit to drive cattle than to write for newspapers."

bright faggots, to talk together, or stretching upon the leaves of the forest, asleep, with the stains of powder yet upon their faces. There are dark masses of horses blackened into the grey background, and ambulances are creaking to and fro. I hear the sobs and howls of the weary, and note, afar off, among the pines, moving lights of burying parties, which are tumbling the slain into the trenches. A cowed and shivering silence has succeeded the late burst of drums, trumpets, and cannon; the dead are at rest; the captives are quiet; the good cause has won again, and I shall try to tell you how.[10]

The good writing, the tenacious reporting, and the critical analysis of Townsend, Smalley, and Villard never eradicated the new national security problems that reporters and the military had to

deal with. Northern reporters and editors had much difficulty dealing with the concept of press responsibility as it related to national security. Newspapers throughout the Union carried stories about troop movements, reinforcements, and numerical strength of units. Maps in papers, particularly the *Herald*, even pinpointed troop locations at battle sites. Confederate officers soon saw benefits of such coverage. General Robert E. Lee and other officers regularly read northern papers for military intelligence.

Yet, on the positive side — at least as far as military security was concerned — many of these reports were inaccurate. The emphasis on speed meant little time to check for accuracy. During the course of the Civil War, according to newspaper accounts, Richmond surrendered any number of times, General Lee resigned, and Confederate President Jefferson Davis died. Such news must have brought much joy to the reading public in the North, but it had no basis in fact. Sometimes, however, the reporters were not to blame. Union war officials liked to fiddle with the facts, and censors played with casualty figures in reporters' dispatches. At Harper's Ferry in 1862, more than 10,000 Union troops surrendered. A reporter's dispatch contained the correct figure, but censors lowered it to 6,000.[11]

CONFEDERATE REPORTERS

Confederate reporters had some things in common with their northern brothers, but it was the differences that became the most obvious as the war wore on. Like their northern counterparts, Confederate reporters were just trying to fully cover a bloody, destructive war. For them, however, the war was much more immediate, fought in their cities and near their homes.

The war's proximity meant chronic and serious shortages of almost everything needed in publishing — paper, type, ink. The Confederacy had only negligible paper production facilities and type foundries. Editors could, at least, "make do" with homemade ink. Even shoe blacking did the trick for some newspapers. The paper and type shortage was not as easily solved. By 1862, because of the paper shortage, editors had to reduce the number of pages, dimensions of the sheet, and frequency of publication. By the end of the war, some even tried innovative alternatives — printing on writing paper, brown paper, waste paper, even the backside of wallpaper. Type seldom could be replaced. It was merely used and used until it was barely legible. The devastation that the war brought to the southern press can be gauged from the mortality rate of newspapers. In 1860, the South had 105 daily newspapers and 466 weeklies. At war's end, the numbers had fallen to 58 dailies and 226 weeklies.

Manpower shortages, likewise, plagued newspapers. One editor per paper was specifically exempt from the draft. In addition, the editor could request an exemption for every employee indispensable to the operation of the publication. Editors, apparently, took their responsibilities seriously and used their exemption requests sparingly. Some 75% of Confederate printers saw military

[10]"The Battle of Five Forks," *New York World*, 4 April 1865, 1.

[11]*Boston Daily Journal*, 19 September 1862.

service. That meant that papers were chronically understaffed.

As compared to the North, far fewer reporters — only about 100 — covered the war for newspapers and wire services in the South. Included in that number were many soldiers and officers serving as "volunteer" correspondents. The major dailies of the Confederacy did send reporters to the field. They were joined there by wire service reporters, including the southern AP, which no longer had relations with New York, and, in 1863 and after, the Press Association of the CSA.

Reporters faced serious difficulties communicating with their home offices as telegraph and mail service broke down. Even at the beginning of the war, the Confederacy was not as strongly linked via telegraph as the Union, nor was it as well supplied for repairs. Nonetheless, southern reporters made ample use of existing lines. Readers in the Confederacy, like readers of the Union, sometimes searched futilely for up-to-date news on the war. As the war turned against the Confederacy, particularly in 1864 and after, reporters had to get their stories back via a primitive communication network. The Confederate telegraph system was rotting on the poles. Wires rusted, making transmission of news uncertain at best. The telegraph system often fell victim to Union forces. The mail service did not offer a real alternative. With the destruction of railroads and roads, the mail service was crude and military telegraphic transmissions always had priority. That meant battle reports might take days or weeks to reach newspapers. In one instance, it took almost a month for a report from Richmond to reach Mobile.[12]

Coverage often became a matter of guesswork. Battles expected to be important or generals who were friendly drew the largest number of reporters, while unforeseen battles or hostile generals attracted far fewer. That meant battles and sometimes whole campaigns went, at best, underreported. Few reporters were present to cover the opening of the 1862 campaign in the west or the fall of New Orleans. In spite of actions limiting press access at the first battle of Manassas and other campaigns, General Pierre G.T. Beauregard remained popular with newspapers because of his successful military record and his personality. In contrast, General Braxton Bragg would not abide journalists. As he began the invasion of Kentucky in August and September 1862, he gave orders that no one who was not attached to the army — thus excluding reporters — could accompany him. Those who continued faced the prospect of arrest.

Politicians posed a whole different set of problems. The attitude of the Confederate Congress was perhaps best illustrated when it refused to allow the quartermaster's office to sell food to reporters who were covering the army for the Press Association of the CSA.

The PA had a large contingent of reporters in the field. It had been established in 1863 as a cooperative news enterprise of all the southern dailies east of the Mississippi and a number of tri-weeklies.[13] John S. Thrasher, a newsman from Galveston, Texas, over-

saw a staff of about twenty reporters. Working under a specially negotiated agreement with the military, he ordered reporters to keep their dispatches factual and objective — and ahead of all the special correspondents of the newspapers.

That proved difficult. Southern papers had some outstanding reporters. Peter W. Alexander and Felix Gregory deFontaine were among the best. Alexander illustrates how some southern reporters were able to service more than one master. Although the greatest portion of his work appeared in the *Savannah Republican*, he also contributed to the *Atlanta Confederacy*, *Mobile Advertiser and Register*, *Richmond Dispatch*, and *Times* of London. A master writer, he was a lawyer at the outbreak of the war but left his practice in Georgia to resume writing for the *Republican*, where he had served as editor-in-chief during the 1850s. DeFontaine, son of a French nobleman, was born in Boston. After working for several New York papers, he moved to Charleston just before the war. Both reporters came to be known for their finely crafted and fairly accurate dispatches. While Alexander, "PWA" in many of his dispatches, remained in the field for much of the war, deFontaine, "Personne" to readers of the *Charleston Courier*, left much of his battlefield reporting behind in late 1863.

Like their northern counterparts, southern reporters were underpaid, overworked, and physically endangered. Confederate and Union reporters made about the same. The PA paid $25 to $30 a week plus travel and maintenance allowance, but wartime inflation in the South greatly reduced the buying power of these wages. The physical dangers of war coverage were compounded for the southern reporter. At least three Confederate reporters died during the war — and perhaps more since not all southern correspondents have been identified. Others suffered the diseases that ravaged the Confederate troops.

The work of southern reporters also suffered from many of the same flaws as that of the Union reporters. A number of southern dispatches revealed information that today might be considered national security risks. Troop movements and plans of generals were published, a fact not lost on Union officers who read southern dailies for such intelligence.

Confederate generals were not, however, without their methods of control. Some, including Generals Joseph Johnston, Bragg, Beauregard, and Thomas "Stonewall" Jackson, kept reporters out of their camps during certain campaigns. That step, however, did not always stop journalists. One PA reporter tracked down Bragg — after traveling twenty-six miles on foot to report on his troop movements. Sometimes, generals took extreme actions against reporters. Wallace Screws of the *Montgomery Advertiser* languished in jail ten days after writing a comment on movements of the Army of Mississippi. John Linebaugh of the *Memphis Appeal* was arrested for treason after his anti-Bragg reports and a dispatch that mentioned troop movements. For more than two weeks, he was shuttled from detention center to detention center until finally released. Perhaps the greatest punishment was that he missed covering the battle of Chickamauga.

[12]*The War of the Rebellion, A Compilation of the Official Records of the Union and Confederate Armies*, Series iv, vol. 2 (Washington: Government Printing Office, 1900), 160-2, 731. J. Cutler Andrews, *The South Reports the Civil War* (Princeton, N.J., 1970), 43, 479-80.

[13]An initial meeting was held in 1862 to set up the PA, but it was poorly attended. The PA was finally formally established March 1, 1863, in Augusta, Georgia.

Keeping up with the News of War
This painting, titled "War Spirit at Home" and done by Lilly Martin Spencer in 1866, shows a family of a Union soldier reading a newspaper account of the northern victory at Vicksburg, Mississippi. Along with letters from relatives fighting in the Civil War, civilians got nearly all their information about the war from newspapers. Through their emphasis on battlefield reports and the use of such means as the telegraph, newspapers were able to provide news soon after it happened. Although many reports included errors and rumors, most attempted to give an accurate account of the war that kept civilians well informed about battles and other events. Because of the importance that readers attached to news reports during the war, by the end of the war, news had gained preeminence over editorials, marking a major change in journalism history.

There was more to the southern journalist's job than just reporting the news. He also had to carry on that job in a manner consistent with keeping up public morale.

In this regard, the women "correspondents" in the Confederacy had a role to play. The use of pseudonyms by women — and especially southern women — makes it difficult, however, to identify the women who wrote for publication. Constance Cary, a Richmond resident, identified herself as the author of the exchange between "Secessia" (a southern sympathizer in Baltimore) and "Refugitta" (a loyal Confederate woman in Richmond) that appeared in a southern newspaper. In this exchange, Cary wrote about the extravagance of the Union women compared to the frugality and patriotism of the women of the Confederacy.[14]

Cary's exchange illustrated how correspondents could build up Confederate morale. War dispatches could not always be so uplifting. Just how candid should dispatches be during wartime? Southern reporters did write about the extensive disease in camps, but few reported General John B. Hood's staggering casualties in Georgia in 1864. DeFontaine and others wrote of the terrible destruction at Shiloh. "While I write I am sitting on the floor of one of the corridors, with bodies of the living and the dead ranged on either side, and opposite as far as the eye can reach," he described the field hospital. "Groans fill the air, surgeons are busy at work by candle-light, a few women are ministering to the wants of the suffering, the atmosphere is fetid with the stench of wounds, and the rain is pouring down upon thousands who yet lie upon the bloody ground of Shiloh."[15] Yet not every editor would admit in his newspaper the possibility of defeat. Even the disastrous loss of Atlanta was described by the PA thusly, "Whilst the fall of Atlanta is regretted, the people are not at all discouraged."[16]

In the South as in the North, the war had brought revolutionary changes to the press. News was assuming primary importance. The reporter was gaining stature. Even when communications began to break down in the South, both editors and the public continued to demand speed of transmissions and constant up-to-date information. Readers wanted the freshest information on the war. Too often these demands would go unfilled because of the destruction in the South. Yet, in spite of the breakdown in the telegraph and the mail systems, the contentious generals, the risks of death and disease, reporters did their best to cover the war. They were too often inaccurate and, according to certain generals, unmindful of national security matters — but, given the limits of their time, training, experience, and numbers, the reporters of the South probably did the best that could be expected.

THE ARTISTS

The 1850s witnessed the phenomenal growth of a new type of publication, the illustrated news weekly. By the end of the decade, two weeklies in particular were locked in a battle for dominance, *Frank Leslie's Illustrated Newspaper* and *Harper's Weekly*, both published in New York City. *Leslie's* was the older of the two. Launched in 1855, it became an important part of the Leslie family of magazines. *Harper's* was launched in 1857 as a literary and newsweekly that soon adopted the illustrated look. The Civil War only heated up the competition that already existed between these two.

Both publications — along with the *New York Illustrated News*, another weekly — dispatched artists to the front from the very beginning of the Civil War. *Leslie's* once claimed to have had eighty artists covering the war. It is unclear how many artists *Harper's* or the *Illustrated News* had in the field. Northern soldiers who sometimes doubled as "special artists" complicated estimates. The identifiable artists were young, as a group probably younger than the reporters. Financially, they were no better off. Many were paid by space rates: one amount for a simple illustration, more for a double-page spread, still more for the grandiose four-page illustrations that *Leslie's* sometimes published.

That money never compensated the artist for the life he lived. The artist maintained a nomadic existence — roaming from camp to camp, battle to battle, East to West, and back again. The rigors of the work and the travel took their toll. As Henri Lovie wired

[14]Mrs. Burton Harrison (Constance Cary), *Recollections Grave and Gray* (New York, 1911), 124-5.

[15]Personne, "Our Army Correspondence," *Charleston Daily Courier*, 15 April 1862, 1.
[16]PA report reprinted in Andrews, *The South Reports the Civil War*, 462-3.

Winslow Homer

Noted Artist Started as Civil War Illustrator

Winslow Homer is recognized as one of America's foremost artists, acclaimed for his oils and watercolors of the outdoors. But before he became a painter, he was a magazine illustrator, and among his most memorable subjects was the Civil War.

When the war began, the Massachusetts native was a freelance artist for *Harper's Weekly*, one of the most popular illustrated magazines. His mother was an artist, and he had been drawing professionally since the age of about 19, when he was apprenticed to a Boston lithographic house.

His early illustrations for *Harper's* dealt with life in Boston, including a "foot-ball" game in which several of the players wore top hats. His work was notable for its realism, detail, and sense of energy.

Recognizing his talent, editors soon began giving him more important assignments. He was commissioned to cover Abraham Lincoln's inauguration and produced a two-page drawing of the president giving his address in front of the capitol.

As a "special correspondent" for *Harper's* during the war, Homer made several trips to the front. Two of his best known illustrations, "A Cavalry Charge" and "A Bayonet Charge," took readers into the thick of the fighting and provided a real sense of what it was like. But most of his drawings examined everyday life for the army. His work included a variety of subjects: a bivouac fire, surgeons at work, Thanksgiving in camp, winter quarters, and payday.

He also drew larger works, intended to be more of a patriotic character. Many featured multiple scenes tied together by decorative motifs. In "News from the War," for example, one scene showed a woman reacting to tragic news. She is slumped over a table, her face hidden. Another showed an artist, probably Homer's colleague Alfred Waud, sketching soldiers at attention. Onlookers delight in watching the artist

The two-page spread above from *Harper's*, with each page measuring about the size of a tabloid newspaper today, was drawn by Winslow Homer and titled "News from the War." It shows the work of artists and reporters in providing the news. The panels (clockwise from the lower left) are captioned "Our Special Artist," "For the Fleet," "News for the Staff," "Wounded," "From Richmond," and "The Newspaper Train." The middle illustration, "A Cavalry Charge," reveals how detailed Homer's drawings were. Homer painted the bottom picture, "Prisoners from the Front," in 1866, based on an illustration he had made during the Civil War.

work. As works of propaganda, the pictures were meant to inspire. But for the artist they were a chance to show off his realism and sense of humor.

During the war Homer became a serious painter. He turned some of his wartime subjects, including "A Sharpshooter on Picket Duty" and "Prisoners from the Front," into paintings that critics praised. He continued to work as a magazine illustrator for another twenty years, but oils and watercolors became the focus of his work.

Although Homer was not the most prolific Civil War artist – that title goes to Waud – he is widely considered the most accomplished. The drawings he published in *Harper's* established him as one of the nation's outstanding illustrators. They allowed him to refine his growing skills as an artist and guided the course of his remarkable career.

Leslie, "I am deranged about the stomach, ragged, unkempt and unshorn, and need the co-joined skill and services of the apothecary, the tailor and the barber...." But sheer exhaustion was not the only occupational hazard these artists faced. Lovie found that he was mistaken for an enemy scout as he searched for the best location to sketch. He expected some risks, he said, but not from the Union army. He had "no objection to running reasonable risks from the enemy," he added, "but to be killed by mistake would be damnably unpleasant!"[17] Damnably unpleasant from a financial perspective was the risk of losing sketches at a battle. C.E.H. Bonwill of *Leslie's* lost his entire portfolio of the Red River campaign in Louisiana when General Nathaniel Banks' army was beaten back at Sabine Cross Roads in 1864.

Some artists went on to distinguished careers after the war. Political cartoonist Thomas Nast began his style of allegorical cartooning during the war, in addition to his romanticized drawings of battle scenes. Indeed, his version of Santa Claus as a roly poly, bearded figure debuted during the war — visiting Union troops — in *Harper's Weekly*.[18] Winslow Homer, also of *Harper's*, went on to a career in oils and watercolors. During the war, his specialty was camp life. The fame of other artists never reached the post-war stature of Nast or Homer, but their Civil War illustrations stand as lasting reminders of their talent. Their beautiful illustrations in news weeklies and other magazines provided romanticized representations of the war. Alfred Waud of *Harper's*, for example, was a favorite among the reporters in the field and was considered the consummate war artist. George A. Sala of the *London Daily Telegraph* described him as "blue-eyed, fair-bearded, strapping and stalwart, full of loud cheery laughs and comic songs, armed to the teeth, jack-booted, gauntleted, slouch-hatted."[19] There was another Waud in the field. Younger brother William earned his way at *Leslie's*. He made his debut as a war artist sketching Fort Sumter. At *Leslie's*, he was joined by a battery of other talented artists.

These individuals represented only one part of a three-way artistic partnership that produced the magnificent illustrations of the Civil War. The artists in the field, the artists back in New York, and the engravers worked as a team. The pictures that appeared in the illustrated news weeklies and magazines represented the product of that partnership — with all its strengths and weaknesses. The artist in the field was the illustrator in a hurry. He drew everything from battles to leaders, from camp life to sieges. The pencil sketches, never meant to be published, were designed as reference points to be embellished in the editorial offices. Many battlefield drawings carried notes to allow other artists and engravers in New York to fill in the details. They transformed the rough drawings into single, double, and even four-page illustrations. These were powerful illustrations, many with meticulous details only hinted at in the original sketch.

The illustrations appeared surprisingly soon after the event pic-

Alfred Waud, Artist
Soldiers considered Alfred Waud of *Harper's* the complete artist. Union general George Meade sometimes used his talents as an observer. At his request, Waud once scaled a tree to draw enemy lines. "Rebel sharpshooters," he reported, "kept up a fire at me the whole time." Like other artists, he also faced the hardships of the battlefield and frequently was confined to bed because of illness.

tured. The speed and the detail were possible because of an expensive engraving method Leslie is said to have brought from England. Before the introduction of this method, illustrations were the result of a long, tedious process. Each had to be drawn on a block, then engravers cut away wood from the artist's line, and then and only then could the relief block be used for printing. The process could take days, weeks, even months.

Readers during the Civil War did not have to wait that long. With the engraving process brought over from England, the rough battle drawing was transferred to the wood block. The master engraver would then cut the main outlines and indicate the engraving technique to be used. The block was then separated into different pieces to be engraved by a number of craftsmen. When all the parts were completed, they were bolted back together. A master engraver provided the finishing touches, and the illustration was ready to be printed. A process that formerly had sometimes taken weeks had been reduced to hours.

The speed of production had failed, however, to remedy all the problems associated with these illustrations. They suffered from two of the flaws common to the reporting of the period: inaccuracy and a lack of concern for national security. The inaccuracies stemmed from honest mistakes to deliberate misrepresentation. Because artists traveled the front, they ran the risk of missing an important battle or skirmish. Accordingly, a number of "on-the-

[17]*Frank Leslie's Illustrated Newspaper*, Vol. 14, No. 66 (17 May 1862); *Cincinnati Daily Gazette*, 29 June 1861.
[18]*Harper's Weekly*, 20 September 1862; 18 July 1863; 3 September 1864; 12 November 1864; and 3 January 1863.
[19]Quoted in Starr, *Bohemian Brigade*, 254.

The Black Wagons
The so-called "What-is-it wagon" that Mathew Brady's field photographers used during the Civil War was a combination portable darkroom and storage unit. Soldiers dreaded seeing the black, hooded wagon rumble into camp because it too often meant a battle was imminent. The images the field photographers captured were the most starkly real of the war, often showing bodies of soldiers just killed.

spot" illustrations were actually created by artists many miles away who had never witnessed the action. Other inaccuracies resulted from obstructed views at the battle site, the enthusiasm of the artist in the field or back in New York, or the inability of the artist to understand the complexities of battle.

The illustrations sometimes posed national security problems. The problems arose not from the romantic and highly imaginative battle scenes but from the accurate illustrations of military fortifications, diagrams of troop movements, and maps.[20]

PHOTOGRAPHERS

The Civil War was the first American war extensively captured by photography.[21] Samuel F. B. Morse, inventor of the telegraph, had introduced the daguerreotype to America in 1839. In 1853, America had 10,000 daguerrotypists, and they produced 3 million pictures. The Americans and British tinkered with the invention, eventually perfecting the "wet-plate" process that was used in the mobile darkrooms at battle sites of the Civil War.

An army of photographers shot the war. The most famous was Mathew Brady, a successful antebellum photographer with studios in New York and Washington, D.C. It was he who photographed Bull Run and came up with the idea of putting together a photographic history of the war. For that, however, he needed War Department approval. Secretary of War Edwin Stanton approved the idea; but, aside from offering the services of Allan Pinkerton and the Secret Service for protection, he offered no support for Brady's scheme.

Brady would have to underwrite the project, hire the men, and equip the portable darkrooms, the so-called "what-is-it wagons." This was an expensive venture. Brady invested some $100,000 in salaries, equipment, and miscellaneous expenses of his crew of at least twelve photographers. He was banking on a return for his money. He sold his pictures to the general public. Newspapers

and magazines purchased some of his pictures but could not reproduce them as photographs for technical reasons. They had to be converted to line drawings before printing, and the conversion process did not always do justice to the photographs.

Brady's photographers followed the troops in black wagons that stored the glass plates used in photography and doubled as darkrooms. They traveled to various theaters of war, waiting for battles or just chronicling camp life. Their photographs captured the horrors of the war. They stood in stark contrast to the romanticized illustrations of the period. The photographs showed bloated corpses on the battlefield and the tormented wounded in the hospitals, the heroes and the nameless, the desolation of the countryside and the destruction of once great cities, the living skeletons of a Confederate prison, and the hanging of the assassins of a president. As Oliver Wendell Holmes wrote when he saw some Brady war prints: "It is so nearly like visiting the battlefields to look over these views that all the emotions excited by the actual sight of the stained and sordid scene, strewed with rags and wrecks, came back to us, and we buried them in the recesses of our cabinet as we would have buried the mutilated remains of the dead they too vividly represented."[22]

It is difficult to gauge precisely how many of the photos Brady actually took. His name was attached to all photos taken under his sponsorship. That led to tension among certain "Brady" photographers. Several of his best photographers eventually left his employ. Alexander Gardner and Timothy O'Sullivan continued to photograph the war but under their own names. Brady and his photographers were not the only ones in the battlefield. Brady was soon facing competition from talented former employees, professional photographers who had been competitors before the war, and War Department cameramen.

The Confederacy had its own war photographers. George S. Cook of Charleston was the best known. He had been in charge of Brady's New York studio before he struck out on his own. It was his ambrotype of Fort Sumter commander Major Robert Anderson that became so popular in the North early in the war. Andrew B. Lytle of Baton Rouge photographed the war for three years and through several campaigns from a Confederate perspective. He

[20]As examples, see "War Maps and Diagrams," *New York Herald*, 27 July 1861, 1-4; and "The National Battle Ground," *New York Herald*, 12 September 1861, 1.

[21]It was neither the first war nor the first American war photographed. The Crimean War had been extensively photographed for primarily a European audience, and war scenes of the Mexican War had been taken by unidentified daguerreotypists. James D. Horan, *Mathew Brady, Historian with a Camera* (New York, 1955), 40.

[22]Quoted in Horan, ibid., 33.

The Prayer of Twenty Millions

HORACE GREELEY. "Mr. President, 'do you propose to ignore, disregard, and in effect defy' these twenty millions here present, whom I command?"

Horace Greeley's opponents lampooned him mercilessly when he wrote an open letter to President Lincoln in 1862 urging him to proclaim southern slaves free. This caricature from *Harper's Weekly* ridiculed Greeley for being so presumptuous as to imply that he spoke for the citizens of the North. In his letter to the President, which Greeley titled "The Prayer of Twenty Millions," he had begun,

"To ABRAHAM LINCOLN, president of the United States:

"DEAR SIR: I do not intrude to tell you — for you must know already — that a great proportion of those who triumphed in your election, and of all who desire unqualified suppression of the Rebellion now desolating our country, are sorely disappointed and deeply pained by the policy you seem to be pursuing with regard to the slaves of the Rebels. I write only to set succinctly and unmistakably before you what we require, what we think we have a right to expect, and of what we complain...."

Greeley and Lincoln Spar over Freeing Southern Slaves

By the beginning of the Civil War, Horace Greeley was clearly America's best known newspaper figure. His weekly edition of the *New York Tribune*, some said, was the country's first national newspaper. His was the leading voice on many of the most important issues of the day.

Consistently an outspoken opponent of slavery, Greeley had supported the candidacy of Abraham Lincoln in 1860 but had grown impatient over his seeming reluctance as president to issue an emancipation proclamation.

So on August 20, 1862, with the war not yet going well for the Union, Greeley decided to give Lincoln a personal editorial nudge. He published an open letter to the president headlined "The Prayer of Twenty Millions." Abolitionists cheered him, but critics called him arrogant and intemperate for the assumption that he

spoke for everyone in the North.

"What an immense majority of the loyal millions of your countrymen require of you," Greeley wrote, "is a frank, declared, unqualified, ungrudging execution of the laws of the land." He urged Lincoln to declare slaves who came within Union lines immediately free and to insist that military commanders enforce and obey that law.

Perhaps unwittingly, Greeley provided Lincoln with the very opportunity he needed to explain to the country his exact stand on the issue of slavery.

The president's answer came three days later, not in a private letter to Greeley, but in the pages of the old, respected *National Intelligencer*. It had not supported Lincoln and had been outspoken in favoring a system of slavery for economic reasons. Some suggested Lincoln chose the *Intelligencer* just to needle Greeley.

If Greeley's "Prayer" was his most famous editorial, the response by Lincoln is often touted as one of his most elegant messages. "My paramount object in this struggle is to save the Union, and is not

either to save or to destroy slavery," he wrote. In a concluding statement, he explained, "I have here stated my purposes according to my view of official duty; and I intend no modification of my oft-expressed personal wish that all men everywhere could be free."

The *National Intelligencer*, celebrating its good fortune to have been the recipient of the president's letter, took a swipe at Greeley's presumption for his editorial. Other papers said he needed a lesson in etiquette. Greeley published an apology. "Nothing was farther from my thought," he explained, "than to impeach in any manner the sincerity or the intensity of your devotion to the saving of the Union."

When Lincoln made public his preliminary announcement of the Emancipation Proclamation on September 22, just a month after the "Prayer" appeared in the *Tribune*, Greeley's loyal readers were quick to praise the editor, to credit him with hurrying Lincoln along on the freedom issue. In their eyes, he still had plenty of editorial clout left.

The Changeable Greeley
Horace Greeley's critics lampooned him for the unpredictability of the positions he took toward executing the Civil War. In this cartoon, the panel on the left refers to the *New York Tribune's* aggressive recommendation that the Union army should attack Richmond at the beginning of the war, resulting in the northern defeat at Bull Run. The panel on the right ridicules Greeley's contrasting contention in 1863 that the Union should let the South secede in peace.

JIM CROW JUMPING ABOUT SO.

"On to Richmond! The Rebel Congress must not be allowed to meet there in July."—(*See N. Y. Tribune, May and June*, 1861.)

"Let us bow to our destiny, and make the best allowable peace." (*See N. Y. Tribune, Jan.*, 1863.)

assumed another role — camera spy, perhaps the first in U.S. history — photographing Union troops and armaments and sending his pictures to Confederate headquarters.

Lytle, Cook, and the other southern photographers faced special problems. Lacking an extensive Confederate supply of cameras, equipment, or materials, they had to rely on the same northern photographic house that supplied Brady and other Union photographers. Supply was irregular because materials had to be smuggled through Union lines.

For Americans, photography meant that the Civil War — with all its horror, death, and destruction — became the stark reality that no news story or drawing could ever convey. Even today, the photographs stand as powerful reminders of the destruction of war. Civil War photography pointed to a new direction in wartime reporting. Every future American war would be captured on film. The photographer had won his place in wartime journalism.

CENSORSHIP

Censorship is the official control of editorial comment and news content before they appear in a publication. Typically, in the United States, censorship has been done in wartime and, ideally, only to limit the amount of national security material — especially military information — to the enemy. Conventionally, censorship is interpreted as a duty of the military, with accompanying memos, directives, and guidelines issued to the press. In the Civil War, censorship was not as structured, nor was it merely a function of top military leadership. It was also carried on by communities through "mob censorship" or by invading armies.

Before the war, a number of pro-Union editors in the South were intimidated. A.B. Norton of the *Fort Worth* (Tex.) *Chief* was threatened with hanging. He took the hint, sold his paper, and moved on. Mobs destroyed the offices of the *Galveston* (Tex.)

Union, a name that belied the paper's editorial position.

Once the war commenced, little mob action was required. Most southern editors came to support secession and the war soon after Fort Sumter. The few laggards were kept in line via economic harassment or threats. Economic boycotts drove several Unionist papers in the Confederacy out of business.

Mob intimidation played its role in the North as well. Pro-South editor Wilbur Storey of the *Chicago Times* started to transform his editorial rooms into a mini-armory, with loaded muskets and hand grenades ever available in case readers decided to carry out their threats. He rarely left the office unarmed, the wise thing to do in light of the many threats upon his life. Proper Union sentiment was not even enough to protect newspapers from mobs. During the New York draft riots of 1863, one of the targets of a mob was the *Tribune*, which had been a leading proponent of the war.[23]

Hostile military armies also effectively censored newspapers and newsmen. When Union troops took Confederate cities, they sometimes also took control of the newspapers, as they did, for example, with the *Picayune* after the capture of New Orleans. Union occupation did not always silence a newspaper's voice. When Memphis fell to the Yankees, the *Appeal* joined the growing numbers of the southern "refugee" press, newspapers that moved rather than yield to Union control. At various times, the *Appeal* was published in Mississippi, Georgia (including Atlanta), and Alabama, trying to stay one step ahead of northern forces.

Obviously, with so many cities falling to Union forces, the northern army had more opportunities to exercise censorship than the southern troops. There were times, however, when the Confederate army captured and imprisoned northern newsmen. Typically, captured correspondents were quickly turned over for re-

[23]*New York Times*, 28 October 1884, 5. George Smalley, *Anglo-American Memories* (New York, 1911), 161-3.

turn to the North. That was not the case in the instances of Junius Browne and Albert D. Richardson of the *New York Tribune*. Greeley's *Tribune*, with its longtime abolitionist/reform editorial stances, represented a particularly odious publication in the Confederacy. For twenty months, Browne and Richardson languished in Confederate prisons, including the notorious Libby at Richmond. Not even the efforts of President Lincoln could secure their release. Finally, the reporters escaped and made their way back home. The Confederacy had, however, accomplished its mission. For almost two years, it had prevented them from filing any dispatches.

On a day-to-day basis, it was the military that assumed the mantel of censor. The censorship systems of the Union and the Confederacy were designed to keep military information out of enemy hands. Both armies believed that troop movements, armaments, military plans, strengths, and weaknesses were all legitimate topics to exclude from newspapers. Thus, such information was to be deleted from telegraph dispatches back to the home newspaper office. However, as the Confederate and Union military soon discovered, just because censorship provisions might be in place, they were not necessarily effective. The military on both sides found that reporters could — if they were resourceful enough — evade the most structured censorship system. In the North, particularly, reporters soon excelled in the fine art of foiling the army censor.

The northern army censor found that his best weapon of control was the telegraph. The telegraph office represented one central location for monitoring reporter dispatches. From the very beginning, the War Department attempted to capitalize upon that link. The earliest battles were reported under an agreement between General Winfield Scott, then the Supreme Commander of Union forces, and the press. No reports on army movements, mutinies, or anticipated military activity were to be transmitted. The army censor was to clear reports of battles in progress. Union losses at Bull Run prompted Scott to rethink his policies. He slapped a strict censorship on the telegraph. No word of the defeat went over the wire until long after the battle.

It soon became apparent that some sort of formalized censorship system had to be imposed on reporters. In August 1861, Simon Cameron, Secretary of War, ordered that no information about army movements, "without the authority and sanction of the major general in command," be telegraphed. Violators could be executed. Unfortunately, censorship authority was put in the hands of the State Department, which exercised its power unevenly. Early the next year, the War Department took over and substantially beefed up monitoring and threats. Newspapers that published "unauthorized" military news, news not cleared by the army censor, were warned that they could lose the use of the telegraph.[24]

Even that threat, however, did little to stem the flow of military information. If a censor refused to transmit — or substantially eliminated information before transmission — the reporter could

[24]*The War of the Rebellion*, Series 3, Vol. 1 (Washington: Government Printing Office, 1899), 324, 390, 394, 454-5, 899.

VANITY FAIR.

THE THREE BELDAMS.

Herald — Posters of the Sea and Land We three travel hand in hand ; *Tribune* — Of each secret expedition Letting out the sealed commission ; *Times* — So that nothing private here May vex the rebel privateer. *All* — Double, double — Nay, we treble Aid and comfort for the rebel !

Giving Aid and Comfort to Rebels

Critics accused some northern newspapers, in their competition to provide war news, of providing military information to the South. This cartoon caricatures the *New York Herald*, *Tribune*, and *Times*. The caption reads: "*Herald* — Posters of the Sea and Land, we three travel hand in hand. *Tribune* — Of each secret expedition, letting out the sealed commission. *Times* — So that nothing private here may vex the rebel privateer. *All* — Double, double. Nay, we treble aid and comfort to the rebel!"

simply send his dispatch via special messenger or hand deliver it himself. Then editors sometimes published the reports without considering security issues. However, the reporter in the field sometimes paid a heavy price. Thomas W. Knox of the *New York Herald* sent reports back to New York with the estimated size of General William T. Sherman's army just before Vicksburg, a clear breach of established guidelines. Knox was arrested on three counts: giving intelligence to the enemy, directly or indirectly; being a spy; and disobeying orders. If found guilty, he could have been executed. Sherman did threaten to hang him. Instead, Knox was found guilty of only the last charge and was expelled from the Army of Tennessee and ordered never to return.

Another method of control was suspension. In the North, there was a range of opinion on the war: from the pro-southern (Copperhead) papers to the rabidly pro-Union dailies. It was the Copperhead papers that posed the greatest problems. In a number of instances, Union generals found that the best way to control a

Attack on the *Tribune*
During the Draft Riots of July 1863 in New York City, one of the targets was the *Tribune* offices. A mob shattered windows, but the presses escaped damage. The police countercharge saved the paper from more extensive harm. At least seventy-five people died in the riots.

Copperhead newspaper was with a chain and a lock on the door. General Ambrose Burnside shut down the *Chicago Times* for two days for its continuing "disloyal and incendiary sentiments."[25] No such suppressions were needed in the South. Soon after the war began, community pressure had effectively silenced pro-Union papers; and, thus, military suspensions of newspapers were not required.

Southern reporters, however, had to live with a set of censorship guidelines. The guidelines were enacted almost from the beginning of the Confederate government itself. In May 1861, the Provisional Congress of the CSA passed a bill giving President Jefferson Davis power to set up censorship of the telegraph. He did so quickly. Thus, from almost the first battle of the war, the Confederacy already had a telegraph censorship system in place. The next month, the government set up official restrictions on the mail. Postmasters could open and censor mail, although they seldom monitored reporter dispatches.

By July, Secretary of War Leroy Walker outlined for the press the specific areas that posed national security problems. Reporters, he wrote in an open letter to all Confederate journalists, should avoid providing information that could hurt the southern cause. That included information on armaments, troop movements, fortifications, or weaknesses. This letter set the pace for the voluntary censorship that marked Confederate reporting through much of the war. Reporters sometimes obtained and transmitted information that did not specifically follow the guidelines. However, editors exercised considerable restraint in publishing it. For example, reporters for both the *Richmond Dispatch* and *Richmond Enquirer* had transmitted dispatches that included details on General Jubal Early's plan to invade Maryland in 1864, but neither paper published the information. Only two reporters accompanied Early in his thrust north, and neither could communicate with his paper until the general returned to Virginia.

Another way Confederate generals controlled the press was by excluding reporters from campaigns. Many times southern reporters had to rely on northern newspapers to keep up with the news of what Confederate troops were doing.

This does not mean that the southern press never published anything that was of aid to the enemy. A good deal appeared that could be of use, and northern officers regularly monitored southern papers. In many instances, however, Union officers were misled by what they read, for the Confederate papers published inflated estimates of enemy casualties and underestimated the number of southern dead and wounded.[26]

The Civil War represented one of the first U.S. wars in which large-scale censorship had to be imposed. The generals, the politicians, the editors, and the reporters had no real precedents to follow. In general, censorship was ineffective. In spite of the threats, the trials, and the belligerent generals, reporters could and did avoid the army network of censorship. Northern editors exercised less restraint than the Confederate editors did in publishing what today might be considered information that could give aid to the enemy. This would not be the last system of wartime censorship. Americans have tinkered with their wartime censorship systems ever since. The Civil War was just one experiment.

AFTERMATH

American journalism was never quite the same after the Civil War. It could not be. The war had brought too many changes.

The reporting, in spite of all its limitations, helped establish standards for immediacy in wartime coverage that continue even today. Reporters used every possible technological innovation to get stories back to their editors quickly. Certainly, the immediacy of Civil War journalism never equalled the "immediacy" of television coverage of the Persian Gulf War or of the terrorist attack on the World Trade Center in our time. Yet, by nineteenth-century standards, the Civil War had its own "instantaneous" quality that earlier wars had never captured.

The writing was, likewise, changing. While by today's stan-

---

[25]Ibid., Series 1, Vol. 17, Part 2 (Washington: Government Printing Office, 1887), 889-93; and Vol. 23, Part 2, 381.

[26]See *New York Times*, 28 October 1884, 5.

dards, it appears stilted and flowery, nonetheless it was much improved over the reporting of earlier wars. The Civil War set high standards for powerful news reporting, stories that not only told what happened but captured a sense of the battle, the personality of the generals, and the trauma of the event. Alexander, deFontaine, Chester, Townsend, Villard, Smalley, and many others showed later reporters what war reporting could be. It was not a lesson lost on the generations that followed. The best reporting not only detailed what happened but captured a "sense" of the war.

The Civil War also transformed how the public viewed war. No longer would wartime coverage be a matter of words. Photography, especially, would become an accepted part of wartime journalism. It had won its place on the battlefields of Manassas, Antietam, and Gettysburg.

Finally, as a result of the Civil War, the *expectations* of the reading public had changed. Readers would no longer be satisfied with dispatches printed weeks or even months after a battle. The public had come to demand immediate war information.

The Civil War posed a new set of national security questions that today's reporters, editors, broadcasters, government officials, and military officers still have not definitively answered. The balance between the people's right to know and the protection of military information has never been successfully struck.

RECOMMENDED READINGS

BOOKS

Andrews, J. Cutler. *The North Reports the Civil War*. Pittsburgh, 1955. This is the most thoroughly documented, authoritative history on Civil War reporting of the several books that have been published. Despite various obstacles, reporters performed well.

Andrews, J. Cutler. *The South Reports the Civil War*. Princeton, N.J., 1970. Andrews provides a well documented narrative of southern reporters in their attempts to cover the battles of the war.

Blackett, R.J.M., ed. *Thomas Morris Chester, Black Civil War Correspondent*. Baton Rouge, 1989. Following a short narrative biography, Part II includes 277 pages of Chester's war dispatches chronicling the activities of black troops.

Bulla, David W., and Gregory A. Borchard. New York, 2010, *Journalism in the Civil War Era*. The general account covers such matters as how the press dealt with the war, the effect of the war on the press, how politics affected the press, the constraints placed upon the press, and the influence of technology.

Bulla, David W. *Lincoln's Censor: Milo Hascall and Freedom of the Press in Civil War Indiana*. West Lafayette, Ind., 2008. While serving as commander of the District of Indiana in 1863, General Milo Hascall shut down eleven newspapers. He stirred up so much animosity by his strict control of the press that Lincoln removed him.

Bunker, Gary L. *From Rail-Splitter to Icon: Lincoln's Image in Illustrated Periodicals, 1860-1865*. Kent, Ohio, and London: 2001. Bunker analyzes Lincoln's visual evolution in an array of illustrated publications.

Carlebach, Michael J. *The Origins of Photojournalism in the America*. Washington, D.C., 1992. This account covers photojournalism from the age of daguerreotypes to the digital era.

Clinton, Catherine, and Nina Silber, eds. *Divided Houses: Gender and the Civil War*. New York, 1992. Drew Gilpin Faust's essay, "Altars of Sacrifice: Confederate Women and the Narratives of War," points out the importance of women in sustaining Confederate morale.

Cornebise, Alfred Emile. *Ranks and Columns: Armed Forces Newspapers in American Wars*. Westport, Conn., 1993. Both Union and Confederate troops had newspapers. This account notes the troop and hospital papers in the Civil War as well as subsequent wars.

Coulter, Ellis M. *William G. Brownlow: Fighting Parson of the Southern Highlands*. Chapel Hill, N.C., 1937. Brownlow was a zealous Tennessee editor, preacher, and politician. He lived a fiery life, first as a Methodist attacking Baptists and Presbyterians, then as an ardent abolitionist and anti-secessionist.

Crozier, Emmet. *Yankee Reporters, 1861-1865*. New York, 1956. This is a readable account of the activities of northern reporters.

Dicken Garcia, Hazel, and Giovanna Dell'Orto. *Hated Ideas and the American Civil War Press*. Spokane, Wash., 2007. Most journalists were transparently biased. In covering most major events and issues, newspapers made no attempt to be balanced or detached. Yet, "marginalized ideas" persisted and gained acceptance.

Ellis, B. G. *The Moving Appeal: Mr. McClanahan, Mrs. Dill, and the Civil War's Great Newspaper Run*. Macon, Ga., 2003. America's only female editor of a daily paper, the *Memphis Daily Appeal*, moved from Memphis to Mississippi, to Georgia, to Alabama, and finally back to Georgia to cover the war.

Fahrney, Ralph Ray. *Horace Greeley and the Tribune in the Civil War*. Cedar Rapids, Iowa, 1936. Greeley and the *Tribune* exercised a powerful influence, although the editor was inconsistent, sometimes even enigmatic, in his stands.

Harper, Robert S. *Lincoln and the Press*. New York, 1951. Lincoln was tolerant and patient with the press despite the difficulties and complexities of the Civil War, many of which the press created, with the Copperhead newspapers especially troublesome.

Horan, James D. *Mathew Brady: Historian with a Camera*. New York, 1955. This collection contains 500 photographs by Brady, who believed that photographs should serve as an historical record, thus making him a reporter of first rank.

Horner, Harlan H. *Lincoln and Greeley*. Urbana, Ill., 1953. Lincoln and Greeley played critical roles in America from 1860 to 1865. They had similar backgrounds and attitudes, but Lincoln was more compassionate and Greeley egotistical.

Marszalek, John F. *Sherman's Other War: The General and the Civil War Press*. Memphis, 1981. Despite Sherman's anti-press attitude, he and journalists, with little precedent to follow, developed a relatively open working relationship.

Ratner, Lorman, and Dwight Teeter. *Fanatics and Fire-Eaters: Newspapers and the Coming of the Civil War*. Urbana, Ill., 2003. The press helped craft perception and reality in the years leading up to the war.

Reynolds, Donald E. *Editors Make War*. Nashville, Tenn., 1966. Southern newspapers played an important role in bringing on the Civil War.

Sachsman, David B., S. Kittrell Rushing, and Debra van Tuyll, eds. *The Civil War and the Press*. New Brunswick, N.J., 2000. This excellent collection of research covers everything from the organization of the news story to images of women.

Smart, James G., ed. *A Radical View: The "Agate" Dispatches of Whitelaw Reid, 1861-1865*, 2 vols. Memphis, 1978. This collection includes articles that the Radical-Republican Civil War correspondent wrote for the *Cincinnati Gazette*.

Starr, Louis M. *Bohemian Brigade: Civil War Newspapermen in Action*. New York, 1954. Starr provides an entertaining story of how colorful reporters from the North, especially New York City, contributed to the development of journalism through their reporting of the Civil War.

Venet, Wendy Hamand. *Neither Ballots nor Bullets: Women Abolitionists and the Civil War*. Charlottesville, Va., 1991. This important account highlights women abolitionists who continued their work on newspapers and magazines during the Civil War.

Weisberger, Bernard A. *Reporters for the Union*. Boston, 1953. During the Civil War, the status of reporters advanced from that of inferior newspaper staff members to that of prominent public figures and professional journalists.

ARTICLES

Abbott, Richard H. "Civil War Origins of the Southern Republican Press." *Civil War History* 43 (March 1997): 38-58. Union military support in the occupied South encouraged papers supporting the Union cause and the Republican party, serving as the foundation for that party's press in the region.

Beasley, Maurine. "Pens and Petticoats: Early Women Washington Correspondents." *Journalism History* 1 (1974): 112-5, 136. "[W]omen journalists established national reputations.... Their careers illustrated that the Civil War social climate permitted women a foothold in the masculine field of Washington reporting in spite of cultural conflicts between their roles as women and as journalists."

Bird, Stephen V. "Heralding Economic and Political Independence: Danville Virginia's Newspaper Editors Adopt James Gordon Bennett's Penny Press Model during the Civil War." *American Journalism* 20 (2003): 55-82. This study illustrates how New York models of reporting and writing affected one smaller newspaper in the South.

Bulla, David W. "Abraham Lincoln and Press Suppression Reconsidered." *American Journalism* 26:4 (2009): 11-33. During the Civil War, the federal government shut down more than 300 newspapers, mostly Democratic ones, but midway through the war Lincoln began to decide that newspaper suppression was not a good policy.

Cappon, Lester J. "The Yankee Press in Virginia, 1861-1865." *William and Mary Quarterly* 15 (January 1935): 81-8. Union troops published as many as a dozen newspapers in occupied Virginia territory. "Most of these crudely printed sheets served as a means of relaxation for the soldier ... [but to] the civilian they were a source of irritation."

Cronin, Mary M. "'War is Thundering at Our Very Gates': Texas Newspapers During the Civil War." *Journalism History* 34:1 (2008): 23-33. Despite Texas' "geographic distance from most of the battles, its editors and publishers endured the same economic and news gathering that other southern editors faced...."

___. "Fiend, Coward, Monster, or King: Southern Press Views on Abraham Lincoln." *American Journalism* 26:4 (2009): 35-61. At first noncommittal in their view of Lincoln, once the Civil War began, southern newspapers painted a critical picture of him.

Endres, Kathleen L. "The Women's Press in the Civil War: A Portrait of Patriotism, Propaganda, and Prodding." *Civil War History* 30 (March 1984): 31-53. Most women's publications during the Civil War period can be classified as either "reform" or "mainstream." Although the two types had various differences, editors agreed "that the women's press had a responsibility to build up the spirits of their readers."

Goldsmith, Adolph O. "Reporting the Civil War: Union Army Press Relations." *Journalism Quarterly* 33 (1956): 478-87. "Restrictions on handling of war news ... were extremely loose as a general rule, but unnecessarily tight in specific instances. The haphazardness of controls resulted in more damage to the war effort than if there had been no controls at all."

Guback, Thomas H. "General Sherman's War on the Press." *Journalism Quarterly* 36 (1959): 171-6. "Most generals had trouble with the press, but Sherman "was plagued mercilessly by the press during the entire war." He "hated" the press because he felt it treated him unfairly.

Hughes, Thomas Andrew. "The Civil War Press: Promoter of Unity or Neutral Reporter?" *American Journalism* 6 (1989): 181-201. This historiographical essay analyzes the various perspectives historians have used in explaining the press.

Jensen, Oliver. "War Correspondent: 1864. The Sketchbooks of James E. Taylor." *American Heritage* 31 (August/September 1980): 48-64. Taylor, an artist, covered the Civil War for *Frank Leslie's Illustrated Newspaper*, providing the combination of words and pictures that readers craved about the battlefront.

Kielbowicz, Richard B. "The Telegraph, Censorship and Politics at the Outset of the Civil War." *Civil War History* 40 (June 1994): 95-119. The telegraph made censorship necessary and feasible.

Logue, Cal M., Eugene F. Miller, and Christopher J. Schroll. "The Press Under Pressure: How Georgia's Newspapers Responded to Civil War Constraints." *American Journalism* 15 (Winter 1998): 13-34. Georgia newspapers faced three wartime problems — problems maintaining profitability, problems of newsgathering and reporting because of disrupted communication channels, and problems with censorship.

Malone, Henry Thompson. "The Charleston *Daily Courier*: Standard Bearer of the Confederacy." *Journalism Quarterly* 29 (1952): 307-15. The *Courier* remained a consistent and enthusiastic supporter of Jefferson Davis and of the Confederacy throughout the Civil War.

Marten, James. "For the Good, the True and the Beautiful: Northern Children's Magazines and the Civil War." *Civil War History* 41 (March 1995): 57-75. Children's magazines in the North encouraged readers to get involved with the war effort by inspiring them with tales of bravery and patriotism and explaining the history and causes of the war.

Mindich, David T. Z. "Edwin M. Stanton, The Inverted Pyramid, and Information Control." *Journalism Monographs* 140 (August 1993). Among the earliest examples of the "inverted pyramid" structure of news stories were the news releases written by Stanton, Lincoln's Secretary of War.

Nye, Russel B. "Freedom of the Press and the Antislavery Controversy." *Journalism Quarterly* 22 (1945): 1-11. Southern states abridged freedom with the argument that freedom did not allow the distribution of obnoxious doctrines. Northern legislatures refused to abridge press freedom, and abolitionists quickly recognized the relationship between their cause and constitutional liberty.

Park, David. "Picturing the War: Visual Genres in Civil War News," *Communication Review* 3 (1999): 287-321. This study discusses the interconnection between illustration and photography during the Civil War.

Randall, James G. "The Newspaper Problem in its Bearing upon Military Secrecy During the Civil War." *American Historical Review* 23 (January 1918): 303-23. Northern newspapers "undoubtedly did the national cause serious injury ... [but] actual governmental interference with the freedom of the press was comparatively slight."

Rhodes, Sonny. "Opposite Extremes: How Two Editors Portrayed a Civil War Atrocity." *American Journalism* 22 (2005): 27-45. Two Arkansas newspapers — one pro-Confederate and the other pro-Union — provided vastly different accounts of the Battle of Poison Spring in Arkansas.

Risley, Ford. "Peter W. Alexander: Confederate Chronicler and Conscience." *American Journalism* 15 (Winter 1998): 35-50. Alexander was one of the few southern journalists providing consistent, reliable reporting throughout the war and helped define the professional role of correspondents covering subsequent wars.

___. "The President's Editor: John W. Forney of the Press and Morning Chronicle." *American Journalism* 26:4 (2009): 63-85. Forney, publisher of the *Philadelphia Press* and *Washington Morning Chronicle*, was a strong supporter of Lincoln and turned his papers into virtual political organs for him.

Sears, Stephen W. "The First News Blackout." *American Heritage* (June-July 1985): 24-31. The compromises during the Civil War conflict between a free press and the need for military security "may not have provided all the answers, but they had raised all the modern questions."

Skidmore, Joe. "The Copperhead Press and Civil War." *Journalism Quarterly* 16 (1939): 345-55. The Copperhead press in the North was "vigorous and fearless in the face of official suppressions and unofficial mobbings and lootings."

Smith, Jeffery A. "Lincoln's Other War: Public Opinion, Press Issues, and Personal Pleas." *American Journalism* 26:4 (2009): 87-117. Federal suppression of press freedom during the Civil War frequently was unnecessarily harsh, and Lincoln sometimes relented in the face of criticism over the suppression.

Tenney, Craig. "To Suppress or Not to Suppress: Abraham Lincoln and the Chicago *Times*." *Civil War History* 27 (September 1981): 248-59. Even though Lincoln rescinded Gen. Ambrose E. Burnside's order to suppress the *Times*, he did so out of political motives rather than for concern for First Amendment principles.

Thorp, Robert K. "The Copperhead Days of Dennis Mahony." *Journalism Quarterly* 43 (1966): 680-6, 696. "A Democratic Iowa editor,... Mahony was a persistent critic of Abraham Lincoln and the Union War effort. But his Copperhead stand was in reality a conservative's attempt to hold back change."

Tucher, Andie. "Reporting for Duty: The Bohemian Brigade, the Civil War, and the Social Construction of the Reporter." *Book History* 9 (2006): 131-57. During the Civil War, "journalists were beginning to think of and present themselves as professionals and to write about their job of reporting."

Van Tuyll, Debra. "Essential Labor." *Journalism History* 31 (2005): 75-87. The author provides a "demographic analysis of a handful of Confederate printers and examines the nature of their work, both at home and in the military."

Wilson, Quintus C. "The Confederate Press Association: A Pioneer News Agency." *Journalism Quarterly* 26 (1949): 160-6. One of the major problems the CPA faced was military censorship.

10

The Frontier Press
1800 – 1900

Frontier editors at their hand-operated presses exerted an influence beyond the dusty towns in which they published. Working within a national tradition that had promoted western expansion and development, the press played a significant role in the settlement of the American West. Colorful editors and their Wild West news stories are part of frontier lore.

After the American Revolution, as white settlers moved west across the continent, agricultural development of the land from a wilderness to an agrarian garden was romanticized as basic to the creation of a new nation. In the late eighteenth century, Thomas Jefferson said the nation's moral future depended upon its farmers and the countryside. "Those who labor in the earth are the chosen people of God," he wrote. Farmers and the land would bear many fruits for the new nation while "the mobs of great cities add just so much to the support of pure government, as sores do the strength of the human body." In his first inaugural address in 1801, President Jefferson applied his view to westward expansion, saying the continent had "room enough for our descendants to the hundredth and thousandth generation."[1] He implemented his vision with the purchase of the Louisiana Territory.

Those who moved west craved news of the world they had left behind. They often congregated at the stage depots and railroad stations, not only to see who was arriving and departing, but also to be the first to get a copy of a big-city newspaper. Saloon keepers subscribed to urban newspapers as a means of enticing patrons. Some towns, taking a page from the past, called meetings at which people could pay a small admission to hear the news read. Competing newspapers in small towns worked out novel ways to get their exchanges ahead of the competition, thereby making the local paper appealing to those who didn't get the papers from New York, Atlanta, Chicago, Denver, or San Francisco. In these ways, newspapers served as a link between urban and rural life.

Newspapers promoted expansion. The most basic assumption of frontier promotion in eastern newspapers was that white set-

tlers had a right to the wilderness. Early British colonists, in particular, considered themselves "civilized" and, therefore, more qualified to manage the land than the "savages" who occupied the continent. Contrasts in dress, religion, and social habits were seen as evidence of white superiority. A more destructive weaponry gave further evidence of a more advanced, superior culture. Even natural disasters or plagues that affected the Native Americans often became evidence of God's displeasure with them and support for white control.

MANIFEST DESTINY

Expansionism became an issue for the Federalist press attacking Jefferson. In 1803, William Coleman, editor of the *New York Evening Post*, worried about an increased French presence on the continent. Claiming Jefferson was Napoleon's dupe, he maintained that the "destiny of North America" belonged to the United States, not France. "The country is ours," he wrote; "ours is the right to the rivers and to all the sources of future opulence, power and happiness, which lie scattered at our feet; and we shall be the scorn and derision of the world if we suffer them to be wrested from us by the intrigues of France."[2] While the Federalists were ready to go to war with France over continental control, Jefferson defused the issue by purchasing the Louisiana Territory from France in 1803. Despite his major expansionist move, Jefferson believed the nation would not need the western land for generations. His agrarian society would end at the Mississippi River, leaving the Far West as a large Indian reservation until the vacant land east of the river was filled.

John Louis O'Sullivan, editor of the *United States Magazine and Democratic Review*, gave life to the concept of continental expansion with the phrase "manifest destiny," coined when Texas was annexed in 1845. The "reception of Texas into the Union," he wrote, defeated all attempts by past rivals Spain, England, and France, who operated "in a spirit of hostile interference against us, for the avowed object of thwarting our policy and hampering our

---

[1]Thomas Jefferson's *Notes on the State of Virginia* and "Inaugural Address, 1801" are found in a number of places, among them Adrienne Koch and William Peden, eds., *The Life and Selected Writings of Thomas Jefferson* (New York, 1944), 280-1 and 323.

[2]*New York Evening Post,* 28 January 1803.

Manifest Destiny
When John O'Sullivan editorialized in 1845 that America's "manifest destiny" was to spread from the Atlantic to the Pacific, the phrase galvanized Americans' vision of what the country was intended to be. That year, Florida and Texas were granted statehood, and President James K. Polk rode a wave of enthusiastic expansionism aimed at incorporating California and the Oregon territory into the Union. Buoyed by newspaper support for such aims, he added more territory to the United States than had any president since Jefferson. O'Sullivan's phrase has remained a driving force for the idea that the United States' natural boundaries should be the two oceans on its east and west coasts.

power, limiting our greatness and checking the fulfillment of our manifest destiny to overspread the continent allotted by Providence for the free development of our yearly multiplying millions." California, O'Sullivan predicted, would "fall away" from Mexico and join the United States. The hand of "Providence" would then join with technology — railroad and telegraph — to unite the nation. The arguments for the railroad were so convincing, O'Sullivan wrote, "that the day cannot be distant which shall witness the conveyance of the representatives from Oregon and California to Washington within less time than a few years ago was devoted to a similar journey by those from Ohio: while the magnetic telegraph will enable the editors of the 'San Francisco Union,' the 'Astoria Evening Post,' or the 'Nootka Morning News' to set up in type the first half of the President's Inaugural, before the echoes of the latter half shall have died away beneath the lofty porch of the Capitol, as spoken from his lips."[3]

The sensational penny papers provided jingoistic editorials advocating annexation of Texas, war with Mexico, and the acqui-

[3]*United States Magazine and Democratic Review* 17: 85 (July and August 1845).

sition of Oregon from Britain in the 1840s. The partisan Democratic press was the most outspoken in favor of expansion. Many frontier papers spoke even more vociferously than those in the East. "Nothing would please the people of the entire West half so well as a war with England," proclaimed the *State Register* in frontier Illinois. British leaders had said enough about the Oregon issue, the paper continued, to justify retribution. "We are all for War! War!"[4] Later while the nation was at war with Mexico, the same newspaper advocated acquisition of the entire Mexican nation to turn a war of self-defense into a "war of philanthropy and benevolence" to free an oppressed people.[5]

War broke out in May 1846 — six months after the annexation of Texas — over whether the Rio Grande was the Texas-Mexico border. Mexico should indemnify the United States for its war expenses, said the *Cincinnati Enquirer*, or else "we are willing to extend the 'area of freedom' by accepting a portion of her territory most contiguous to our own, and important to our commercial, mercantile and industrial interests."[6] When the Treaty of Guadalupe Hidalgo ended the war in 1848, the United States got more than a third of Mexico's territory.

By the time of the Mexican War, simple printing presses were common in frontier settlements. Although presses with revolving cylinders allowed urban eastern papers to turn out 2,000 impressions per hour in the 1830s, their $20,000 to $25,000 price tag assured that they would not be used in small towns. Frontier editors used smaller, hand-operated presses. One of the most common presses, the Washington hand press patented by Samuel Rust of New York in 1821, rode on many covered wagons to frontier outposts where editors, setting type one letter at a time, placed their handiwork into an iron form on the flat bed of the press. The printer then inked the type and placed a sheet of paper over it. By turning a hand crank, the printer rolled the bed along a track, stopping it beneath the platen, which then was lowered to press the paper against the page of type. The bed was then returned along the track and the sheet of newsprint removed. The printer could make 250 impressions per hour of two pages at a time. To print the back two pages, the printer removed the type, set the other two pages, and repeated the process on the back of the original sheet. Rust's press won the West primarily because of innovations, including hollow legs, which made the bulky machine somewhat lighter to transport than its cast-iron competitors.

Soldiers frequently established newspapers when they were stationed in one place for any length of time. The *Corpus Christi Gazette*, started by an itinerant Texas printer in 1846, was the first of a series of newspapers to spring up around American camps in Texas. The United States Army established the first English-language newspaper in the Territory of New Mexico, with soldiers serving as printers. Before the invasion by white Americans, three Spanish-language newspapers appeared in Santa Fe during the 1830s and 1840s. The Army's *Santa Fe Republican* proclaimed its

[4]*State Register* (Illinois), 9 May 1845.
[5]Ibid., 12 November 1847.
[6]*Cincinnati Enquirer*, 18 August 1847.

The Press of the West
In the early 1800s, iron presses replaced the wooden design that had been used since Gutenberg's time. They were heavy, though, and not easy to move to frontier communities. Because its cast-iron legs were hollow, the Washington hand press was lighter to transport by wagon than its competitors were. Durable and inexpensive, it became the press favored by frontier editors. It consisted of a flat bed, a platen (the flat surface that applied pressure to the paper to press it against the type on the bed), and a lever to move the platen up and down. It could produce about 250 sheets printed on one side per hour, with two pressmen working it — inking type, positioning paper, and cranking the screwbar.

purpose as the spread of reliable news from the States and information about the army to both the American and Mexican populations.

NEWSPAPERS IN THE SOUTHWEST

The Mexican War added a huge territory to the United States. The Southwest — comprising the future states of Texas, New Mexico, Arizona, Nevada, and California — continued to be inhabited by former Mexican citizens, and Spanish-language newspapers increased in numbers. In a dynamic situation created when two cultures meet, newspapers reflected intense feelings and changes. The U.S. government and newly arrived Anglo-Americans set out to Americanize the region. New settlers expected that they should prosper from the region's resources. Mexican-American editors were divided about how they should respond. Some believed they should adapt to the culture of their new nation, while others argued that they should retain their own heritage. Some encouraged assimilation into the dominant Anglo system, while others resisted.

By this time, Spanish printing had a long history on the continent. The first press in the Americas was established in 1535 in Mexico City. The first Spanish periodical, *Mercurio Volante*, was founded in 1693, just three years after Boston's *Publick Occurrences*. The first Spanish-language newspaper in United States territory — *El Misisipi* in New Orleans — was not started until 1808. However, the number of papers in the Southwest increased rapidly. The first Texas paper, *La Gaceta*, began in 1813 but lasted only a few issues. The end of the Mexican War gave a strong boost to newspapers, and the Southwest saw more than 130 founded in the next half-century. Local, state, and national governments subsidized many of them.

Like their English counterparts, Spanish-language papers boosted their communities, promoted political parties, provided news, and advocated the causes and interests of their readers. Although some editors resented the American influence on their communities and culture, a large number of papers advocated Anglo-American views. Many had been started as Spanish-language sections in bilingual American newspapers, following the lead of the *Santa Fe Republican*, the first New Mexico paper to print some of its pages in English and some in Spanish.

Spanish-speaking Anglo-Americans wrote for the bilingual papers intended for Mexican-American readers, and papers employed only a small number of workers of Spanish descent, mainly to translate. Well-educated and prosperous Mexican Americans owned most Spanish-language papers. They tended to accept American values and fit more comfortably into the American system than did their more numerous lower-class countrymen.

Still, the newspapers tended to reflect the interests and lifestyles of their Mexican-American readers and to promote cultural unity. They helped maintain a sense of identity and community among readers by reporting community events, supporting efforts to solve local problems, and emphasizing the importance of retaining close links with their Mexican-American heritage. Some editors worried about the assimilation of Mexican Americans into the dominant Anglo-American culture. Others feared that the children and grandchildren of former Mexican citizens were losing the ability to speak Spanish. While these tendencies worried some editors, others believed the best future for Mexican Americans lay in adapting to their new nation.

In the cultural debate, a notable participant was Francisco Ramirez, who in 1855, at the age of seventeen, founded Los Angeles' *El Clamore Publico* (*Public Outcry*). At first moderate in tone, he changed the tenor of his weekly after Anglo-American mobs lynched several Mexican Americans. He then argued that Anglo-Americans were barbaric and inhumane and that the American system subjugated and oppressed Mexican Americans. He concluded that the best course for Mexican Americans was to emigrate to Mexico. Despite the fact that *El Clamor Publico* received extensive support from government printing, it suffered financial difficulties. Ramirez shut it down in 1859, and no other editor stepped forward to fill the activist role he had played.

NEWSPAPERS AND INDIAN-WHITE CONFLICT

The doctrine of manifest destiny assumed an empty wilderness awaiting Anglo-American civilization. Public law and national sentiment, said the *New York Morning News* in 1845, called for the immigrants from Europe and their offspring to own the continent. "We are contiguous to a vast portion of the globe, untrodden save by the savage and the beast, and we are conscious of our power to render it tributary to man." Little regard, thus, was given the original inhabitants. "We take from no man," the *Morning News* said; "the reverse rather — we give to man. This national policy, necessity or destiny, we know to be just and beneficent, and we can, therefore, afford to scorn the invective and imputations of rival nations."[7]

In the early nineteenth century, leaders of the so-called Five Civilized Tribes began adopting some of the white man's ways. Sequoya, a Cherokee, recognized the power of written language. In 1809 he began creating symbols for more than 2,000 Cherokee words, but he soon abandoned that system for a simple 86-character language. In 1828 the Cherokee Nation established the *Cherokee Phoenix*, the first Indian newspaper, in New Echota, the Cherokee capital near what is now Calhoun, Georgia. It was written partly in English and partly in Sequoya's Cherokee. Elias Boudinot, a college-educated Cherokee school teacher, was among its founders. A missionary and clerk of the Cherokee National Council, he hoped the paper would improve both the living conditions and the image of American Indians. The idea of improving a people's image through a newspaper had become a common premise of frontier journalism.

In 1829, however, the Georgia legislature stripped Cherokees of their legal rights. From that point on, they had no standing in Georgia courts. "Full license to our oppressors, and every avenue of justice closed against us," the *Phoenix* said in an editorial. "Yes, this is the bitter cup prepared for us by a republican and religious government — we shall drink it to the very dregs."[8] A year later it reported on harassment, arrest, and threats of physical harm to its staff members. When it protested the postmaster's sale of liquor to Indians, he retaliated by cutting off its mail. The *Phoenix* was left without its source of supplies and exchange papers.[9]

The Cherokees fought to maintain a free press, but Boudinot slowly came to agree with a growing minority of Cherokees that forced removal from their lands was inevitable. Principal Chief John Ross told him not to publicize dissension within the Cherokee National Council. Instead, he was to present a united front of Cherokee resistance against white encroachment. Boudinot, however, joined the "treaty faction" seeking accommodation with whites.

In a published letter of resignation in 1832, he revealed his painful decision that he could not manage the paper without a free discussion of issues so important to his readers. "I should think it

Elias Boudinot and the *Cherokee Phoenix*
Born Buck Watie, Elias Boudinot attended a missionary school and adopted the name of a white hero of the American Revolution. In 1828 he founded the *Cherokee Phoenix*, in part to help Christianize fellow Cherokees and, in part, to promote the idea of a separate Cherokee nation. He hoped that this, the first newspaper published by American Indians, would help improve their image and conditions. He faced threats from white neighbors who wanted Cherokee land and tribal leaders who resisted removal from Georgia and Tennessee. In 1839, after his nation was removed to Indian Territory in Oklahoma, members of an opposing faction murdered him.

my duty to tell them the whole truth," he said. "I cannot tell them that we shall be reinstated in our rights when I have no such hope." Ross appointed his brother-in-law Elijah Hicks editor, but Hicks lacked his predecessor's rhetorical power. Meanwhile, pressure from the outside continued. The paper became erratic in publication, and in 1834 it was suspended. Hicks' parting editorial asked readers not to give up the fight. "Although our enemies are numerous we are still in the land of the living," he wrote, "and the JUDGE of all the earth will impart the means for the salvation of our suffering Nation."[10]

Not all settlers pressed for the Indians' removal. Two Alabama newspapers printed an article lamenting the theft and destruction of Indian land and property. The article said such was the work of individuals who took "mean advantage of these who were unprotected and defenseless. Such villainy may go unpunished in this world, but the day of retribution will most certainly come."

In 1838, federal troops rounded up Cherokee men, women, and children and forced them to march to Indian Territory, which is now Oklahoma. One of every four died on this "Trail of Tears."

[7]*New York Morning News*, 13 October 1845.
[8]*Cherokee Phoenix*, 29 May 1830.
[9]Ibid., 11 July 1831; 19 August 1831.

[10]Ibid., 11 August 1832; 31 May 1834.

For signing the treaty, Boudinot and two other leaders of the treaty faction were killed by Cherokees sympathetic to Chief Ross. Tribal leaders granted amnesty to the killers.

Although the Cherokee nation was unable to start another newspaper for nine years, Samuel Worcester, who had been jailed in Georgia for his support of the Indians, helped establish printing in Indian Territory with the *Cherokee Almanac*, which was published more or less annually beginning in 1835.

The second American Indian newspaper, the *Siwinowe Kesibwi* (*Shawnee Sun*), began in 1835 under the editorship of Johnston Lykins and with the assistance of the Reverend Jotham Meeker, a missionary who took a printing press with him to the large Baptist mission in Kansas. The press at Shawnee Mission published part of the newspaper in the Shawnee language using the English alphabet. Meeker also translated religious messages and songs and published Indian material in their native language. The paper, a monthly or semimonthly, was published until 1839. Resuming publication in 1841, it ran for three more years. The first press in the area that is now Kansas, it was put out of business temporarily by the removal of the Shawnees south into Oklahoma. This was the last in a long line of moves for the Shawnees, with whom the British had first negotiated in the woodlands of Kentucky in 1774.

NEWSPAPERS AND FRONTIER CITIES

The westward surge of white Americans had roots stretching back into colonial times. Indeed, their determination to move west from the original thirteen colonies became so troublesome to the British Crown that it imposed a Proclamation Line in 1763 prohibiting settlers from crossing the Appalachian Mountains. Although the Indians did more than the British to enforce the line, colonists blamed the King for their frontier troubles. By freeing the colonists from British control, the American Revolution opened western lands to migration. Settlements followed scientific and military expeditions into the newly opened regions. Newspapers followed settlement and, in turn, encouraged additional settlement. Along with improved roads and postal services, newspapers linked remote towns to the older regions. Towns and their newspapers grew as commerce increased.

Western migration is reflected in the dates the first newspapers appeared in each state along the Ohio River. John Bradford founded the first Kentucky newspaper, the *Kentucke Gazette*, in 1787, thirteen months after the *Pittsburgh Gazette*. In 1793, Cincinnati had its first newspaper, the *Centinel of the North-Western Territory*, edited by William Maxwell.

Most editors had learned the printing trade at newspapers farther east. Elihu Stout, who began as a printer on the *Kentucke Gazette*, founded the *Indiana Gazette* in 1804 at Vincennes. After a year and a half of weekly publication, fire destroyed his printing plant and office. Obtaining a new press and supplies from Kentucky, he began the *Western Sun* in 1807. Irishman Joseph Charless, who learned the printing trade in Philadelphia, published the first *Missouri Gazette* at St. Louis in 1808. Subscriptions were payable in

Growth and Prosperity

By 1835, when the *Scioto* (Ohio) *Gazette* was founded, settlement was spreading rapidly along the Ohio River. This particular issue of the *Gazette* carried an article titled "Commerce of the Mississippi Valley" that painted a vivid picture of the region's economic growth.

flour, corn, beef, or pork. The following year Charless changed the name of the paper to *Louisiana Gazette* in recognition of the entire territory, but he returned to the original title three years later upon the organization of Missouri as a separate territory and the creation of Louisiana as a state. Illinois was detached from Indiana in 1809, and five years later the *Illinois Herald* began publishing at Kaskaskia. Its proprietor was Matthew Duncan, who had owned a small Kentucky publication called *Farmer's Friend*. Like many frontier editors, he would become a prominent figure in state politics.

Editors frequently had an interest in expansion and town development. Joseph Charless of St. Louis and John Bradford of Lexington, Kentucky, like many other editors, were members of their towns' governing councils. Most editors, however, were of lower social levels than the merchants who ran the towns. Still, if they had less income, they often had as much prestige. Although usually separated by background and training from the merchants, editors helped unify the budding frontier cities.

The number of papers grew faster than the successful towns. The *Missouri Republican* in St. Louis noted in 1829 that newspapers promised to be "thick as blackberries in the spring" on the frontier.[11] Many towns soon had two weeklies. By 1830, Cincinnati had

[11]*Missouri Republican* (St. Louis), 17 February 1829.

Settling the Frontier

Editors on the American frontier took on two preeminent issues as settlement moved westward. One was the constant conflict with the native inhabitants, and the other the promotion of their towns. Founded in 1793 as the first newspaper in Cincinnati, the *Centinel of the North-Western Territory* typified the approach of early papers. It devoted much of its space to the Indian wars in the territory. The lead article in the above issue detailed the bounties to be paid to settlers for each Indian they could kill. In 1813 the *Western Intelligencer* of Worthington, Ohio, carried a front-page story about "The Savage Tomahawk," which it described as an "agonizing weapon of murderous destruction." The conflicts between settlers and Indians continued until most of the native tribes were finally subdued in the late 1800s. In attempting to encourage town growth, newspapers in frontier communities usually pointed with pride to local progress. The first issue of the *Milwaukee Sentinel* (1837) declared that "the records of past ages may be searched in vain, for evidence of a community with so magical a growth as that witnessed in the new and flourishing Territory of Wisconsin."

seven weeklies and two dailies. The number of papers, of course, indicated growth in the number of towns and cities. Urbanization had begun to infect Jefferson's agrarian utopia.

Because a newspaper's survival depended upon the growth and prosperity of the town in which its subscribers and advertisers lived, editors became town boosters. They depended on exaggeration to attract new settlers and on optimism to assure stability of their towns. Of course, many towns and their papers died, and many successful ones rode through several boom-and-bust cycles related to unpredictable economic growth. Despite the odds, town-promotion rhetoric revealed incredible optimism — at least in print. Towns placed essays and advertisements in neighboring towns and eastern cities to extol their potential. Typical was the promotion of Town of America at the junction of the Ohio and Mississippi rivers, whose proprietors said no other point on the continent "has ever presented a fairer prospect of a greater inland commercial city."[12]

This first generation of town boosters spawned another western tradition: the spoof of boosterism. In 1819, the *Augusta* (Ga.) *Chronicle* ran a widely reprinted advertisement from "Andrew Air Castle, Theory M'Vision, and L. Moonlight Jr., & Co.," who were described as proprietors of the City of Skunksburgh. After a folksy description of the town and its location as the middle ground between all major North American cities, the "proprietors" conclud-

ed with its potential: "A line of Velocipede stages will be immediately established from Skunksburgh straight through the O-ke-fin-o-cau Swamp, to the southernmost point of the Florida peninsula; and, as soon as a canal shall be cut through the rocky mountains, there will be direct communication with the Columbia river, and thence to the Pacific Ocean. Then opens a theatre of trade bounded only by the Universe!"[13]

Editors gave hope and encouragement to struggling pioneers. They also sought to alleviate hardship by promoting civic development and reform. As the consciences of their communities, they editorialized about the health hazards of urban living. The *Pittsburgh Gazette* in 1802 attributed an increase in disease to a sudden increase in population combined with a stench in the air from "filthy gutters, putrid vegetables and matter, the stench from the foul slaughter houses, the exhalations from ponds of stagnant water."[14] Editors advocated improved sewage disposal and regulation of privies. They supported such reforms as abolition of debtors' prison, humane treatment of the insane, free education for the children of working people, and the establishment of Bible and missionary societies. Many sought to improve the level of local culture, through the literary quality of their own columns and reviews of local entertainment and cultural events. Newspaper publishers also printed books, operated bookstores, encouraged local philosophical and literary societies, and sponsored

[12]Quoted in Richard C. Wade, *The Urban Frontier: Pioneer Life in Early Pittsburgh, Cincinnati, Lexington, Louisville, and St. Louis* (Chicago, 1950), 31.

[13]Reprinted in *Cincinnati Liberty Hall*, 1 October 1819.
[14]*Pittsburgh Gazette*, 23 July 1802.

private circulating libraries. Thus newspapers served as both boosters and reformers.

Advertising columns often reflected frontier social life more accurately than the news columns. Newspapers in backwoods communities frequently carried ads for the sale of slaves or indentured servants and for the return of runaways. An early ad in the *Pittsburgh Gazette* was typical: "To be sold. A Negro Wench. She is an excellent cook and can do any kind of work in doors or out of doors. She has been registered in Westmoreland County. Produce will be taken or cattle of any kind."[15] An improving economy was reflected in the fabrics that local stores advertised. A boarding and day school for young ladies advertised that it taught how to read, how to lace, and how to knit and do other crafts. Other ads mentioned a willingness to accept payment in kind, such as firewood, pelts, or farm produce, in exchange for service or merchandise. Editors frequently took such payment for advertisements or subscriptions.

Newspapers took differing attitudes toward local news. In small towns, word of mouth spread news faster than the printed word. But editors still used editorials, essays, and letters for local reports. Some believed their very survival depended upon local news to build a sense of community. They wrote about local people, but they continued to report much of their news by reprinting official documents, such as speeches and texts of legislative proceedings. Such reprints often filled entire pages, especially in papers with contracts to do government printing. Some editors relied entirely on "exchange" newspapers farther east and even apologized when the mail failed to bring enough news. Although such news was weeks or months old, it was new to the frontier. Many long, anonymous essays carried such pseudonyms as "Subscriber," "Farmer," and "Cato." Subjects varied, covering such topics as political reform, education, weather, women, laughter, and gallantry. Backwoods philosophy and poetry added local color, and frontier papers often carried fiercely partisan political articles.

Westward migration nudged newspapers closer to the modern concept of news. In the late 1700s, frontier news traveled faster and was covered more thoroughly in personal letters and by word of mouth than in newspapers. Many early frontier publishers may not have viewed local news coverage as an important function of newspapers. Nevertheless, when the new nation began to create its own cultural identity in the early nineteenth century, editors reflected the change by including more domestic as opposed to foreign news. Exchange papers, including special-interest publications, supplied easily reprintable material for the West while colorful western stories found their way into the eastern press. Later, the telegraph offered timely news, and more towns could publish daily newspapers.

Town promoters often pointed to the growth of newspapers along with churches and schools as an outward sign of culture. Even though citizens bragged about their papers, the early publications seldom did well financially, even with dramatic growth.

The *Liberty Hall*, founded in Cincinnati in 1804 with 150 subscribers, published 2,000 copies weekly by 1813. Pittsburgh's *Mercury* had 1,400 subscribers by the end of its first year. The number of papers per city varied. The original paper might squeak by without opposition. More likely, however, an opposition political party would set up a competing newspaper. The party in power could award local printing contracts to its own paper.

Other factions and interests, such as religious denominations and abolitionists, also established papers. Mining journals appeared in the West. Specialized farm publications sprouted across the continent. Although New York City became the center of black journalism, some freedmen communities on the frontier published papers. A black political convention in Ohio voted to publish *The Voice of the Oppressed*, edited by William H. Day and Charles H. Langston. African Americans published at least four periodicals in New Orleans before the Civil War. By the end of the war, three black newspapers in California provided a strong voice for civil rights.[16]

Ethnic communities, such as the Irish and Germans, founded newspapers to provide news from the old country, help preserve cultural identities, and promote common interests. Foreign-language papers could be found in urban centers as well as isolated ethnic communities. French, Chinese, German, Spanish, Jewish, and Italian groups launched thirty-six newspapers in San Francisco in the 1850s. Germans started more than a hundred newspapers in California during the following century. Like other western papers, many ethnic ones were short-lived. Some thrived, however. Czech immigrants settling on the Great Plains in the 1880s turned publishing into a big business. Edward Rosewater, a Czech Jew in Omaha, founded the first Czech-language newspaper in Nebraska, taking advantage of the Union Pacific Railroad's settlement-promotion advertising. After six years, Jan Rosicky bought the paper and began a Czech-language chain of fourteen newspapers and specialized journals. Other ethnic newspapers worked to hasten assimilation into American life. Along these lines, missionaries started Chinese-language papers to convert immigrants to Christianity. For similar reasons, missionaries printed the earliest Hawaiian newspapers in the native language of the islands.[17]

Politicians occasionally founded newspapers with high hopes before an election only to close them if the party suffered a defeat. While death awaited some partisan newspapers after an election, government printing contracts could go to the victors. Town, county, and state governments designated official printers to handle official business, such as the printing of laws, notices of public auctions, legislative proceedings, and registration of land sales and cattle brands. In an era in which type was set one letter at a time, a contract to publish government proceedings could save time by allowing the editor to set type once for both the newspa-

[15]Ibid., 23 May 1787.

[16]William Loren Katz, *The Black West*, 3d ed. (Seattle, 1987), 44, 128; and Lauren Kessler, *The Dissident Press* (Newbury Park, Calif., 1984), 26-34.

[17]See Edward C. Kemble, *A History of California Newspapers, 1846-1848* (Los Gatos, Calif., 1962); T.L. Broadbent, "The German-Language Press in California," *Journal of the West* 10 (1971): 637-61; Emerson Daggett, supervisor, *History of Foreign Journalism in San Francisco* (San Francisco, 1939); and Paul Alfred Pratte, "Ke Alaka'i: The Role of the Honolulu *Star Bulletin* in the Hawaiian Statehood Movement," Ph.D. dissertation, University of Hawaii, 1976.

Thomas Hart Benton and Cheap Land
Along with Horace Greeley of the *New York Tribune*, Thomas Hart Benton of Missouri was one of the nation's strongest advocates of westward expansion. A United States senator, he also was co-editor of the *St. Louis Enquirer*. Born in 1782 in North Carolina, he moved to Tennessee after becoming a lawyer and then in 1815 to St. Louis. After election to the U.S. Senate in 1820, he promoted westward expansion through such policies as lowering the price of land from $1.25 to 25¢ an acre.

per and a government publication. A speech could fill an entire newspaper page.

At election time, some political debates became desperate fights for survival. Political discussion on the frontier, one historian noted in a monumental understatement, "has never been characterized by an excess of deference to an opponent's opinions, or by over-indulgence as to his personal shortcomings."[18] Political fights in newspaper columns could turn into personal abuse. Yet many editors helped neighbors, even political rivals, when their newsprint ran out or their shops burned down.

Every frontier editor faced the prospect of physical violence. William Gilpin's vitriolic attacks in the *Missouri Argus* increased the threatening mail to his boss, proprietor Andrew Jackson Davis. Despite protests, Davis kept Gilpin as editor. One opponent, holding Davis rather than Gilpin responsible, beat him over the head with an iron cane. Davis died after surgery. Gilpin lived on, eventually to become the first governor of the Territory of Colorado in 1861. Another Missouri editor, Joseph Charless, was attacked by a long-time political opponent who carried a pistol and spit in the

editor's face. The politician retreated when Charless retaliated with stones. Charless and rival editor Isaac N. Henry, a co-editor with Thomas Hart Benton (a future U.S. senator) of the *St. Louis Enquirer*, engaged in an extended editorial argument and court battle over a street fight between Henry and Charless. Charless' articles about the case led to a $20 fine for contempt of court. Refusing to pay the fine, Charless went to jail. On another occasion, he was shot at as he walked in his garden.

RELIGIOUS NEWSPAPERS

Churches founded many newspapers in the uphill battle of taking civilization, not only to the frontier "savages," but also to the many pioneers in need of redemption. Religious papers grew rapidly in the Old Northwest through the 1840s and 1850s. By the middle of the nineteenth century, most Christian denominations had at least one journal. Religious journals contained serious discussions of theology, morality, history, science, and literature. News of local congregations and such special-interest topics as farm and household management worked their way into religious papers. Generally, they were of better quality in terms of paper, printing, editing, and style than their secular counterparts.

Religious editors typically were not trained as printers and often were clergymen poorly prepared for managing a newspaper. One moral dilemma they faced was the selection of advertising. While some ruled out the quack patent medicines widely advertised at the time, others permitted the ads in the belief that, since business was not a religious concern, the advertising sections should not be subjected to religious scrutiny. The placement of advertising, however, did separate secular from religious papers. Secular papers often placed it on the front page; religious papers seldom did.

Religious editors had much to say about the morality of their countrymen. Protestant editors advised against smoking, drinking, and attending the theatre and horse races. Catholic and Jewish publications generally ignored and occasionally ridiculed such Protestant taboos. The politics of the religious press varied as much as the politics of religious leaders today. Publications advocated such reforms as improved living conditions and education. Catholic and Protestant papers differed on the war with Mexico; Catholics did not share the euphoria of white Protestant expansion into the Southwest controlled by Catholicized Indians and Spaniards. Many papers shared the nation's assumption of its "manifest destiny" to conquer the North American continent, redeeming the land from a "degenerate and less energetic race"; but some worried about the "idol of Manifest Destiny" taking control of the national temper. Some religious papers worried about living conditions among the Native Americans, and many of them took the lead in the crusade to end slavery.

The most controversial of the special-interest papers were those founded in the crusade against slavery. The frontiers of Tennessee and Kentucky hosted early abolitionist papers. Four anti-slavery papers established before 1826 were in slave states west of the Al-

[18]Reuben Gold Thwaites, "The Ohio Valley Press before the War of 1812-15," *Proceedings of the American Antiquarian Society* 19 (April 1909): 321.

legheny Mountains. Abolitionist papers generally were sponsored by religious groups or anti-slavery societies. They reprinted laws, arguments, opinions, essays, speeches, statistics, congressional proceedings, colonization efforts, and notices of books and pamphlets on abolition. Editors risked their lives and property in their pursuit of social reform. One abolitionist editor, Elijah Lovejoy, became a martyr when a mob killed him in Alton, Illinois, in 1837.

AGRICULTURAL JOURNALISM

A major impetus for special-interest frontier papers came from New England and New York State with the creation of agricultural journalism. The nation's pioneer national farm journal was the *American Farmer*, created in 1819 in Baltimore by John Stuart Skinner. He had a farm background and experience as a postmaster. "The great aim, and the chief pride, of the *American Farmer*," he announced in his first issue, "will be, to collect information from every source, on every branch of husbandry, thus to enable the reader to study the various systems which experience has proved to be the best, under given circumstances."[19] Under the flag on page one, a line in all capital letters read: "Rural economy, internal improvements, news, prices current." Skinner's example was followed by the *Genesee Farmer*, founded in 1831 by Luther Tucker, who published it along with his *Rochester Daily Advertiser*, and *The Cultivator*, founded in 1834 by Jesse Buel, editor of the *Albany Argus* and state printer for New York. In 1840 the *Genesee Farmer* and the *Cultivator* merged, and in 1853 the combined paper became the *Country Gentleman*. When the *American Farmer* suspended publication in 1834, at least fifteen publications with the same purpose survived it.

From these beginnings, agricultural journalism spread westward across the continent and encouraged more specialized publications. More than 400 farm papers were begun in the thirty years after 1829. Most lasted fewer than three years. Tucker was among the founders of the *Horticulturist*, one of the first specialized agricultural publications. Newspapers devoted exclusively to dairy farming were founded in Ohio and New York in 1859. Many general farm newspapers began specialized sections, including ladies' departments. The *Rural American* opened a matrimonial bureau as a reader service.

Agricultural papers zealously picked up on the Jeffersonian agrarian ideal. They reprinted speeches, poems, and editorials depicting the "happy plodding farmer" who lived a contented, chaste, and independent life. One such poem was "The Farmer's Song" from *Yankee Farmer* in 1835:

> I envy not the mighty king
> Upon the splendid throne —
> Nor crave his glittering diadem,
> Nor wish his power mine own,
> For though his power and wealth be great,
> And round him thousands bow

John Stuart Skinner, Farm Publishing Pioneer
Skinner founded the first national farm journal, the *American Farmer*, to provide useful information and to promote effective farming methods.

> In reverence — in my low estate
> More solid peace I know.[20]

Similar was "The Farmer's Life" from *Southern Cultivator* in 1843:

> I love the farmer's quiet life —
> His peaceful home, devoid of strife,
> With gay contentment bless'd.
> I love the virtues of his heart,
> Which peace, and joy, and love impart
> Around his tranquil rest.[21]

Poems and essays extolled the virtues of farm life and praised the pleasures of God's creation. They idealized nature, farming, and the work ethic. Besides soothing a sense of rural inferiority, such romanticism had a serious purpose: keeping people on the farm. Eastern cities and western gold fields tempted young men to leave the farms, particularly in New England, where the soils were losing productivity. The farm, said the *New Genesee Farmer*, provided stability: "The young of both sexes foolishly give up such a birthright, for a bare-foot existence in the western wilderness — amid privation, and toil, and sickness — where pork is the greatest lux-

[19]*American Farmer* (Baltimore), 2 April 1819.
[20]*Yankee Farmer*, 20 July 1835, 120.
[21]*Southern Cultivator*, 11 October 1843, 168.

HEAD OF BARON OF OXFORD.—Drawn from Life by Edwin Forbes for the American Agriculturist.

Agricultural Journalism

Specialized publications developed in the first half of the nineteenth century to serve farming interests. Like the *American Agriculturist*, founded in 1842, they both provided useful information and extolled the virtues of farm life.

ury, and a log-house raising the most exciting recreation."[22] Cities, meanwhile, were pictured as dens of iniquity, seats of corruption, and places filled with sin and sorrow. "The farm," said the *Indiana Farmer*, "is the natural home of man. Placed in any other condition he naturally degenerates, both physically and morally, and soon acquires an inferior type."[23]

Agricultural journalists took the lead in the "worn-out soil" issue in New England and New York, the state with the most farm papers. Frequently published by agricultural societies, the papers popularized such notions as fertilizing with manure and using scientific innovations in agriculture. They promoted agricultural fairs at which farmers showed their crops and judged the results of one another's harvests. They promoted tours of farms, essay contests, and agricultural societies. They tested new machinery and promoted such new devices as the steel plow, seed drill, corn planter, cultivator, thresher, mower, and reaper before 1860. Occasionally, they editorialized on such issues as women's rights, temperance, and, gradually, abolition as well as various tilling techniques and breeds of cattle. They encouraged farmers to ex-

change seeds and conduct experiments. In all of these activities, newspaper pages were opened to the exchange of ideas.

The farm papers and agricultural societies forged a strong interest group to lobby for agricultural education and a federal agriculture department. The harvest of their editorial seeds came in 1862 when President Lincoln signed into law bills creating the Department of Agriculture and agricultural colleges to be financed by grants of land from the public domain in the West. Within weeks, he also signed the Homestead Act and authorization for a transcontinental railroad. These bills passed Congress only after southern states had withdrawn from the Union. The South had opposed most of them to prevent expansion of northern influence into the territories.

"Go West"

At the same time, economic depravity in the cities forced people to look for dreams in a new land. *New York Tribune* publisher Horace Greeley was among the most visible promoters of western settlement as a "safety valve" to release unemployed urban dwellers from the pressure cooker of the inner city. During the Panic of 1837, he wrote, paupers arrived in New York City at the rate of 1,000 per day. Stop immigration from Europe, he said; encourage emigration to the frontier. His often quoted advice "Go West, young man, and grow up with the Country" dates from 1837, four years before he founded the *Tribune*. Every laborer could find opportunity in the limitless frontier. "If he go prepared to throw off his coat, fare rudely, work heartily, sleep soundly, and rise reasonably," Greeley wrote, "he will likely thrive there."[24] Unceasingly, he promoted the Homestead Bill, agricultural societies, landgrant colleges, the transcontinental railroad, and other reform measures to promote western expansion and settlement. When the Homestead Act made 160 acres of the great American West available to each settler, Greeley could hardly contain his excitement. "Young men! Poor men! Widows! resolve to have a home of your own! If you are able to buy and pay for one in the East, very well; if not, make one in the broad and fertile West!"[25] Unfortunately, Greeley's safety valve failed to account for the fact that poor innercity immigrants could not afford the trip west. So he continued to lobby for inexpensive transportation and free homesteads. And his weekly edition of the *Tribune* provided encouragement and practical tips for farmers — some of whom were ill-prepared for the hardships of western farming. Nevertheless, the weekly *Tribune* ranked with the Bible as one of the most read publications in the Midwest.

The important characteristics of the newspaper editor seen later in the Wild West originated in the frontier between the Appalachian Mountains and the Mississippi River. Frontier editors east of the Mississippi before the Civil War trained apprentices who moved farther west. Editors learned to live on a shoestring, con-

[22]*New Genesee Farmer*, January 1847, 17.
[23]*Indiana Farmer*, June 1858, 65.

[24]*New Yorker*, 22 April 1837. Greeley attributed the quotation, "Go West, young man," to Indiana editor John Soule of the *Terre Haute Express*.
[25]*New York Daily Tribune*, 6 June 1862.

California News
Artist William Sidney Mount, who sought a popular audience, completed this "California News" painting in 1850. "Paint pictures," he advised, "that will take with the public — never paint for the few, but the many." The many followed the California Gold Rush of 1849, which attracted settlers, speculators, and interest to the West more effectively than any previous promotional campaigns. President Polk stimulated interest by lending credibility to exaggerated reports of the promise of gold. Newspapers promoted gold fields in Nevada and Colorado to attract settlers when the Civil War broke out in the East. Caravans of settlers and adventurers transformed the prairie within a few decades after the California Gold Rush. Many of California's early editors were drawn there, along with other miners, by the lure of gold. Most newspapers had short lives, and few editors prospered.

tend with unreliable mail and transportation, promote their hometowns, batter political opponents, face violence, and, through exchange papers, cooperate with their counterparts in other cities. These "exchanges" provided a ready source of copy for editors usually too harried to cover their own towns thoroughly. Despite hardships, some editors developed a rugged independence.

Regardless of their locale, editors faced hard times and isolation. First, they had to transport heavy presses in horse- or oxen-drawn wagons on rough roads over difficult terrain. Once the presses were in place, they depended upon an unreliable transportation system for paper, ink, and replacement type. They relied upon the same transportation system and the unpredictable postal service to distribute their papers.

Subscribers and advertisers also experienced the hard times of isolation. They, in turn, passed hardships on to the newspapers. Editors often lectured advertisers and subscribers on their responsibility to pay bills, although they often carried unpaying clients and accepted goods and services in lieu of money.

Although some editors were well educated, they were primarily printers. Knowledge of the mechanical printing process was a basic job requirement. Editors had to be resourceful in repairing their own equipment and substituting available materials. Their survival often depended upon the quality of their printing, and many editors operated job printing shops to supplement their income or to keep the papers going in difficult times. Editors also worked outside the newspapers. Most were printers who did job printing on the side, but many were also teachers, lawyers, or postmasters.

The discovery of gold in California, along with what a historian called "one of the most effective promotional campaigns in history," stimulated a massive rush of people to the West Coast. "The

accounts of the abundance of gold in that territory," President James K. Polk said in December 1848, "are of such an extraordinary character as would scarcely command belief were they not corroborated by the authentic reports of officers in the public service." Skeptics who had refused to believe newspaper accounts took the president's word seriously. Two days after his message, the Philadelphia mint assayed a 230-ounce sample conveyed in a tea caddy, confirming the reports of gold. Newspapers abandoned all caution. "The Eldorado of the old Spaniards is discovered at last," one proclaimed. "We are on the brink of the Age of Gold," reported another. "The coming of the Messiah or the dawn of the Millennium," said another, "would not have excited anything like the interest" that the tea caddy generated.[26] The combination of national idealism and potential material rewards injected the nation with gold fever, drawing hordes of Americans westward.

NATIVE AMERICANS IN THE PRESS

The period between the Civil War and the end of the nineteenth century saw the most violent of the conflicts on the frontier and provided the backdrop against which the national legend and lore of the West were created. Images in the press often fit preconceived notions and political bias as much as real frontier conditions. Editors' views on frontier issues, such as Indian policies and railroad development, became complicated by the popularization of stereotypes of such characters as mountain men, gunfighters, soldiers, and Indians. People such as Buffalo Bill Cody, Wild Bill Hickock, Marthy "Calamity Jane" Cannary, Gen. George Custer,

[26]Quotations are from Ray Allen Billington, "Words that Won the West 1830-1850," address before the Public Relations Society of America, 18 November 1963, San Francisco, Calif. Published as a booklet by the Foundation for Public Relations Research, New York.

Uncle Horace Greeley

Horace Greeley, America's leading advocate of westward migration, had followers throughout the country. Beginning in the 1830s, he had constantly urged young men and families to move west, where opportunities awaited. "If you have no family or friends to aid you," he declared in the editorial "To Aspiring Young Men" in 1853, "and no prospect opened to you, turn your face to the Great West, and there build up a home and fortune." The great westward migration of the population, which Greeley helped to encourage, was one of the most momentous events in American history. This illustration, from *Scribner's Monthly* magazine in 1883, accompanied an article by William Dean Howells. Reflecting on his life on a country newspaper, Howells wrote that rural readers opened the weekly edition of Greeley's *New York Tribune* expectantly. "Well," they would say, "let's see what old Horace says this week."

and Wyatt Earp fulfilled expectations of eastern writers. Journalists saw familiar Civil War military leaders — Custer, William Sherman, Phil Sheridan, and Winfield Hancock, among others — transferred to the plains wars against the Native Americans.

Most eastern papers grew impatient with the military's failure to solve the Indian situation, but two — the *Chicago Times* and the *New York Herald* — reported regularly on the major campaigns between 1867 and 1881. Covering frontier violence required commitment by the paper and the special correspondent. "If he [the journalist] goes out on such business," John F. Finerty of the *Times* wrote, "he must go prepared to ride his forty or fifty miles a day, go sometimes on half rations, sleep on the ground with small covering, roast, sweat, freeze, and make the acquaintance of such vermin or reptiles as may flourish in the vicinity of his couch; and, finally, be ready to fight Sitting Bull or Satan when the trouble begins, for God and the United States hate non-combatants."[27] Correspondent Mark Kellogg, of the *Bismarck Tribune* and *New York Herald*, died with Custer and five companies of the Seventh Cavalry at the Little Bighorn in 1876.

For coverage of the frontier, most eastern papers depended on local papers from which they lifted stories and on volunteer correspondents, such as local writers, editors, or soldiers. Many of these special correspondents had stronger powers of imagination than observation, and much reporting was subjective. Stories of Indian warfare provided dramatic examples of distortion. Eastern editors sought sensational stories for a public used to reports from Civil War battlefields. Western writers wanted enough alarming news to pressure the federal government to send more troops. Reports by wire were received in the East before the mails could arrive, and they appeared in print complete with illustrations from wood engravings. The illustrated newspapers, which frequently based their pictures on descriptions from the field, provided some of the most sensational accounts of Indian battles.

Newspapers occasionally fell victim to faked stories. In 1867, Greeley's *Tribune* reported a massacre of eighty people at Fort Buford at the mouth of the Yellowstone on the Upper Missouri River. The story said soldiers held off 2,000 to 3,000 Indians before being overwhelmed. A colonel was said to have shot his wife to save her from a fate worse than death. Four days after this sensational story, the *Tribune* reported that General Sherman could not confirm the story. A month later, it reported the story as "a base fabrication." The two major illustrated newspapers, however, reported the "massacre" complete with the colonel's killing of his wife and neglected to mention that the story had been exposed as a fraud.[28]

As the frontier moved west, the natives who had been pushed ahead of settlers were squeezed with no place left to go. For a time, Indian Territory was set aside for them. When Indians were no longer in their backyard, eastern newspapers became more liberal toward them. At the same time, western editors became more violent in their rhetoric. Characteristically throwing subtlety to the wind, the *Arizona Miner* vowed that the territory was worth fighting for and that the government should not protect "the murderous savages who now bar the door to prosperity in Arizona."[29]

Exaggeration and racial hatred colored many stories. The three English-language papers in Arizona Territory in 1871 contributed to the special fear of Apaches and the defeat of the plan for reservations that, in the local view, threatened white opportunity for private ownership of the land. The *Arizonian* suggested a policy toward the Indians "to receive them when they apply for peace, and have them grouped together and slaughtered as though they were as many nests of rattlesnakes." It recommended "first class apartments in a Lunatic Asylum" for advocates of reservations.[30] Such overblown rhetoric did not prevent some eastern papers

[27]John Finerty, *War-Path and Bivouac or The Conquest of the Sioux* (1890; reprint, Norman, Okla., 1962), 80-1.

[28]Elmo Scott Watson, "The Indian Wars and the Press, 1866-1867," *Journalism Quarterly* 17 (1940): 301-12.

[29]*Arizona Miner*, 16 April 1870.

[30]*Arizonian*, 28 January 1871.

Gold in the Black Hills
When gold was discovered in 1874 in the Dakotas, reporters were on the scene — the only instance in American history when journalists witnessed the discovery of a new gold field. Their reporting helped fan the flames of the subsequent gold rush. Mining camps sprang up from the flood of prospectors. Most miners were disappointed. Numerous printing establishments and newspapers, however, followed closely afterward. Editors' boisterous approach to running their newspapers made them resemble the conditions in the mining towns, sometimes crude and rowdy. The *Black Hills Champion* (whose office is pictured here) began publication in 1877 in Deadwood City and seemed to fit its surroundings.

from depending on local weeklies and small dailies as sources for news stories. The widely reprinted *Arizona Citizen* account of the 1871 Camp Grant massacre in which Tucson residents attacked an Indian camp, killing around 110 Indians and capturing twenty-eight, mostly women and children, began: "The suffering and exasperated people have commenced the work of retaliation on the Indians. Their patience has been remarkable."[31] Some editors encouraged the massacre if they did not participate in it. They could have reported the plans, widely known in Tucson, of organizers plotting the 55-mile march to attack the village. On the other hand, many newspapers, particularly those in the East, condemned the attack as an unprovoked slaughter.

Generally, frontier editors regarded Native Americans as inferior beings or even subhuman. Many called for extermination. "A dead Indian can always be counted as reliably good," said an Albuquerque newspaper.[32] A Las Vegas, New Mexico, paper said the residents of a nearby town had subscribed $2,000 for the payment of $100 for every Indian killed and brought in. "There is a royalty for wolf scalps and why not for Indian scalps?" it asked.[33]

Many editors fought the eastern image of Indians that, they said, romanticized them. A Santa Fe weekly suggested that the Indians be relocated to New England, where philanthropists could become educated as to the "true character" of these people whose natural inclination was toward hunting, stealing, murdering, and scalping.[34] Mark Twain, a product of the frontier press, satirized the Indians and philanthropists when he suggested that washing and learning would be more successful than a massacre in eliminating the Indians: "Soap and education are not as sudden as a massacre, but they are more deadly in the long run; because a half-massacred Indian may recover, but if you educate him and wash him, it is bound to finish him some time or other. It undermines

his constitution; it strikes at the foundation of his being."[35]

Some editors supported Native Americans, but they often did not understand them. Many sympathetic whites expected natives to get an education in Protestant schools and adopt "civilized" lifestyles. Some encouraged Indians to learn English and remain on clearly defined reservations much smaller than their original territories.

Newspapers sprouted on reservations, where tribal councils sponsored many of them. In 1844, the Rev. Samuel A. Worcester and printer John F. Wheeler, Boudinot's friends who had gone to jail for working on the *Phoenix*, helped editor William P. Ross, the chief's nephew, start the *Cherokee Advocate* in Indian Territory. In 1876 the Creek Nation started the *Indian Journal*, which continues today as a small weekly.

No single event united the moderate and the extremist, the eastern and the western press, as strongly as the Battle of the Little Bighorn in which Custer led five companies of Seventh Cavalry troopers to their deaths in an attack on a Sioux and Cheyenne village in Montana Territory in 1876. The news startled a nation celebrating its centennial with little thought of Indian wars on the remaining frontier. The sense of frustration felt by nearly all the newspapers was perhaps summed up best by the *New York Herald*, which called for "one grand, consummate campaign" to settle the Indian question. "Let us," it editorialized, "treat the Indian either as an enemy or as a friend — either as a savage or a human being. Let us exterminate or capture him." The number of Indians in North America, the *Herald* said, was less than the population of Brooklyn. Yet the Indians demanded more space than the German Empire. "If the Indian will not submit to civilization, let us cage him as we would a tiger or wolf."[36]

News accounts referred to Indians as animals, savages, demons, devils, and vampires. "The only proper monument to Cus-

[31]See William B. Blankenburg, "The Role of the Press in an Indian Massacre, 1871," *Journalism Quarterly* 45 (1968): 61-70.
[32]*Daily Citizen*, 25 June 1890.
[33]*Daily Optic*, 4 February 1881.
[34]*Weekly New Mexican*, 11 November 1879.

[35]Mark Twain, "The Facts Concerning the Recent Resignation," in Arthur P. Dudden, ed., *The Assault of Laughter: A Treasury of American Political Humor* (South Brunswick, N.J., 1962), 204-5.
[36]*New York Herald*, 9 July 1876.

The Last Plains Indian War

The Sioux War of 1876 was the last major attempt of the Plains Indians to resist intrusions by the white population onto native lands. In 1876 General George Custer led an expedition to force Sioux, Cheyenne, and others to move to reservations. As he prepared to attack a village on the Little Bighorn River in Montana, Crazy Horse's force of 2,000 warriors surrounded and wiped out Custer's 265 troops. The battle gained popularity in the press as the "Custer massacre" and "Custer's Last Stand" and intensified demands that the Indians be subdued once and for all. Some newspapers called for the extinction of the entire Sioux nation. Others, though, reasoned that the blame for the "Indian problem" lay with whites' and the government's mistreatment of Indian tribes. Had the treatment been better, *Harper's* declared in the article accompanying the illustration here, the nation would not "have been compelled to lament the death of the gallant Custer and his brave comrades, or to contemplate the extermination of the Western tribes as the only means of protecting the settlers in the far West."

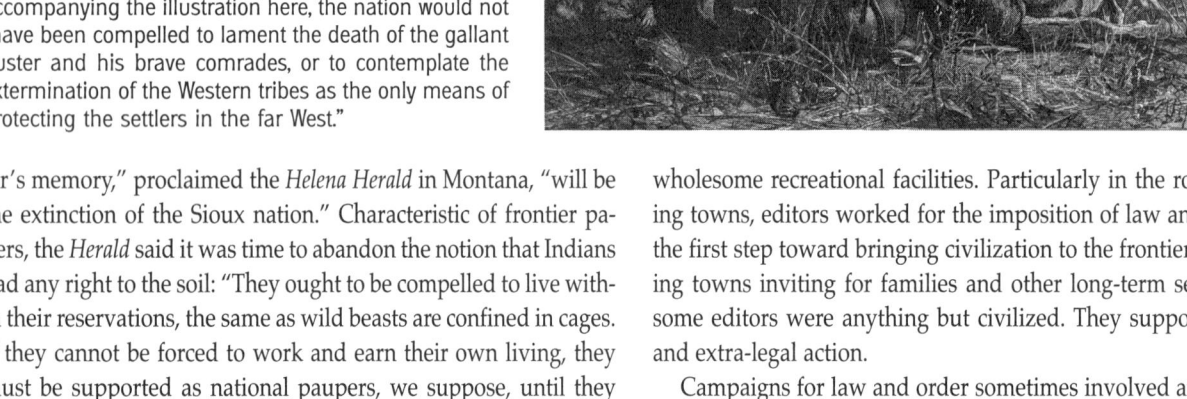

ter's memory," proclaimed the *Helena Herald* in Montana, "will be the extinction of the Sioux nation." Characteristic of frontier papers, the *Herald* said it was time to abandon the notion that Indians had any right to the soil: "They ought to be compelled to live within their reservations, the same as wild beasts are confined in cages. If they cannot be forced to work and earn their own living, they must be supported as national paupers, we suppose, until they naturally die out."[37] Even the *Indian Journal* agreed that the Sioux must be punished and driven to a reservation, but it reminded those calling for extermination that white cruelties, including the slaying of men, women, and children, had been as severe as any the Indians had committed.[38]

Coverage of the Little Bighorn battle demonstrated the strength of the idea of manifest destiny. Democratic and southern papers were not as nostalgic in their lamentations of Custer, a Union Civil War hero, and many newspapers opened their columns to opposing viewpoints. The battle and the resultant press and congressional debates rallied public opinion behind the final campaign to subdue the remaining free Indians on the Northern plains.

COWBOYS, LAW, AND ORDER

Frontier editors shared one basic dilemma. Should they boost their town and overlook its shortcomings? Or should they report the seamy side and possibly undermine the town by scaring families away? One way or another, each editor had to find a way through this tricky problem. Before becoming concerned about long-term settlements, editors paid little attention to crime. Six lynchings had occurred near an early newspaper office in Albuquerque, but the editor did not consider them newsworthy enough to report. In the end, most editors devised methods of advocating community reform without calling unnecessary attention to problems. Many advocated public education, promoted churches, and called for

wholesome recreational facilities. Particularly in the rowdy mining towns, editors worked for the imposition of law and order as the first step toward bringing civilization to the frontier and making towns inviting for families and other long-term settlers. But some editors were anything but civilized. They supported mobs and extra-legal action.

Campaigns for law and order sometimes involved anonymous committees of local citizens operating outside the law to rid the community of undesirables. Many editors backed these "vigilantes." "The hempen rope," *New York Herald* reporter Henry M. Stanley wrote from Colorado, "proved to be a necessary auxiliary to justice."[39] Montana's first newspaper, the *Montana Post* of Virginia City, romanticized the vigilantes who had lynched a corrupt sheriff and his gang of outlaws. The editor, Thomas J. Dimsdale, wrote a series in 1865 on the vigilantes later published as the first book printed in the territory. "Reason and civilization then drove brute force from Montana,"[40] he wrote, apparently missing the irony of using extra-legal force to bring conformity to the law. This impromptu system of justice purged the community of corruption and demonstrated that outlaws could not dominate respectable citizens.

As they sought to attract families to their towns, editors stressed the need for a legal system. The *Post* reported on and opposed two riots, reckless horseback riding in the streets, public dueling, and the carrying of firearms. The *Miner's Register* in Central City, Colorado, threatened to help enforce the law by printing the names of people who persisted in wild riding through the streets. Editors often balanced calls for law and order with comments about the increasing number of families peaceably making their homes within the town.[41]

Some editors — particularly in towns dependent upon the cat-

[37]*Helena Herald*, 13 and 27 July 1876.
[38]*Indian Journal*, 10 August 1876.

[39]Henry M. Stanley, *My Early Travels and Adventures in America* (1895; reprint, Lincoln, Neb., 1982), 173.
[40]Thomas J. Dimsdale, *The Vigilantes of Montana* (1866; reprint, Norman, Okla., 1972), 205.
[41]*Central City* (Colo.) *Daily Miners' Register*, 29 September 1866; *St. Paul* (Minn.) *Pioneer*, 14 January 1851.

Editors and Vigilantes
Most editors in the American West advocated law and order as a means of building their communities and aiding economic progress. Yet, in an effort to rid their areas of lawbreakers, many resorted to supporting the extra-legal, vigilante justice of the West. In this 1874 illustration from *Harper's Weekly*, a New York publication, vigilantes guard three horse thieves while waiting for a telegraph pole to be rigged up as a gallows. Some editors believed lynchings were the only effective means of bringing law to the lawless frontier.

tle trade and mining — resisted reformers. Saloons, gambling, prostitution, and a tolerance of violence often helped local business. The relationship between the editor and the saloons became complex. The editor wanted to put a good face on town news, while the saloon, often a source of conflict, attracted business to the town. The major saloons were dependable advertisers. In fact, some critics said frontier papers contained too many liquor ads. A gift of liquor from the local saloon could purchase a favorable mention in the press. Some editors even solicited such donations in their columns, mentioning the gifts when the editors reviewed the product. Although temperance advocates frequently wrote letters and occasionally became editors, miners and cowboys generally showed little interest in receiving temperance lectures through the press.

Editors in railhead towns at the end of the Texas-to-Kansas cattle drives ignored the indiscretions of visiting trail hands who spent their wages at local recreational centers. A series of cattle towns built in the 1870s in southern Kansas competed to attract the cattle drives. Town delegations occasionally met the drovers on the trail to persuade them to come to their town instead of others. Editors depended upon the cattle trade because their towns did.

Not everyone, though, favored the drovers' annual visits. Besides bringing bored and lonely cowboys who made trouble, the cattle drives posed other problems. The large herds trampled farmers' crops and sometimes brought infectious livestock diseases and parasites to the growing local ranches. Town politicians and their newspapers feuded over quarantine statutes and other laws restricting the movement of cattle. Without herd laws, the farmers, not the cattlemen, were responsible for keeping the cattle out of the fields. Editors and politicians who at first sided with drovers eventually came to look at the future differently as rail-

heads moved west and waves of immigrants settled in the surrounding countryside. Cattle drives had provided quick prosperity, but the long-term future depended on homesteaders and ranchers.

The battle between the future and the past reached its most dramatic climax in Tombstone, Arizona. Governor John Gosper described the situation as a "rivalry between the civil authorities." The sheriff, a Democrat, was on one side; and Republican Marshal Virgil Earp with two of his brothers, deputies Wyatt and Morgan Earp, were on the other. "I found," Gosper said, "two daily newspapers published in the city taking sides with the deputy marshal and the sheriff, respectively, each paper backing its civil clique and berating the other."[42] The Earps sided unofficially with town leaders in a vigilante group. They were opposed by the cowboys, who had the support of the sheriff despite their record of crimes. The town's Republican leaders considered the cowboys gangsters who threatened progress toward peaceful settlement. The cowboys fought to protect a way of life that did not have room for fences, homesteaders, and railroads. A showdown came mid-afternoon October 26, 1881, in one of the most celebrated street fights in American history near a place called the O.K. Corral. After an exchange of about thirty shots, Tom and Frank McLaury were dead; Billy Clanton, another cowboy, lay mortally wounded; and "Doc" Holliday and Morgan and Virgil Earp were injured.

Characteristically mixing news and editorial comment, the first paragraph of the *Tombstone Epitaph*'s story began by saying the previous day's shooting broke the town's peace long maintained by Marshal Virgil Earp and that "all good citizens" supported the Earps' effort to rid the country of outlaws: "If the present lesson is not sufficient to teach the cow-boy element that they cannot come

[42]Gosper to U.S. State Department, 30 September 1881, quoted in *Tombstone Epitaph*, 9 December 1881.

John Clum and the *Tombstone Epitaph*

Although Tombstone, Arizona, was best known as the site of the gunfight at the O. K. Corral, it was also important because of nearby mining interests. The first issue of its most famous newspaper, the *Epitaph*, demonstrated the high degree of local interest with a story about plans for a new mining operation that filled all but the left-hand column of page one. John Clum (inset), who had resigned as an Indian agent after Washington superiors ignored his protests about treatment of the Apaches, founded the *Epitaph* in 1880. He soon became Tombstone's mayor and postmaster. As an editor, he became an unabashed advocate of Republican U. S. deputy marshal Wyatt Earp against his Democratic rivals who controlled the county government. As mayor, he appointed Earp's brother Virgil as police chief and brother Morgan as a special officer under him. In daily and weekly editions, the Republican *Epitaph* and the Democratic *Nugget* fought over everything from county printing contracts to the proper approach to law and order in violent local feuds. Clum's support of the Earps became the basis for the later versions of the 1881 gunfight at the O. K. Corral. He sold the *Epitaph* to his rivals in 1882.

into the streets of Tombstone, in broad daylight, armed with six-shooters and Henry rifles to hunt down their victims, then the citizens will most assuredly take such steps to preserve the peace as will be forever a bar to further raids."[43] The Earps and the *Epitaph* clearly represented the townspeople. John. P. Clum, the mayor and postmaster, founded the paper, and it was he who appointed Virgil Earp town marshal. Although his tenure lasted only two years, he was a reputable *Epitaph* editor who went on to a career in the

U. S. postal service and on the lecture circuit. He believed that "every tombstone needs an epitaph" and that the name alone would assure his newspaper a place in history.

Conflict among a town's editors often had an economic as well as political basis. In Butte, Montana, newspapers played a key role in the fights among the copper barons for control over state politics and what boosters called "the richest hill on earth." Both sides poured money into a newspaper war, including bribes of editors and outright purchases of opposing papers. The outside press looked upon the whole affair with revulsion. "They are all liars," said the *Yellowstone Journal* in rural Miles City.[44] The Amalgamated Copper Company finally emerged from the fight with control of politics and with more than half the state's newspaper circulation. By the 1920s, it owned eight of the state's nine largest dailies.

The war of Butte's copper kings symbolized a change in the mining frontier. Gold and silver had created wealth for individual miners, but copper required complex processing and large corporate investments. Journalism changed with the mining industry. Papers consolidated and, in some places, came under the control of corporate interests that used them as political parties had in the past.

Such changes in newspapers revealed that journalism had moved into its modern era. In journalism as in other professions, corporate ownership and professional associations replaced the influence of the cantankerous individual.

THE CHARACTER OF EDITORS

Although newspapers promoted westward expansion and economic development, historians disagree over the extent of their influence. The disagreement illustrates the classic debate about the mass media and society: Do the media shape society, or vice versa? "Just as the six gun, the windmill and barbed wire were regarded as the principal tools in the conquest of the Great Plains, so the frontier newspaper may be regarded as another important instrument in the civilizing of the West," wrote historian Oliver Knight.[45] Newspapers were catalysts for social change. Yet, as historian William H. Lyon wrote, the pioneer editor put out the same monotonous paper year after year. "Society forced changes upon him; he did not change society," Lyon observed. "He stood among the colorful men striving for recognition and influence in frontier society; but changing conditions of journalism, his own individualistic personality, his itinerary, and his lax business methods deprived him of the stature he sought."[46] Even though editors were an independent lot, Lyon contended, they became too dependent upon patronage, advertisers, and subscribers to exercise much independence.

Yet editors were motivated by a belief that their papers raised the community's educational level and helped maintain a democ-

[43]*Miners' Register* (Central City, Colorado), 27 October 1881. The most relevant *Epitaph* stories are in Douglas D. Martin, *Tombstone's Epitaph* (Albuquerque, 1951), 176-203.

[44]*Yellowstone Journal*, 8 February 1900.

[45]Oliver Knight, "The Frontier Newspaper as a Catalyst in Social Change," *Pacific Northwest Quarterly* 58: 2 (1967): 74-81.

[46]William H. Lyon, *The Pioneer Editor in Missouri 1808-1860* (Columbia, 1965), 35-7 and 164-5.

ratic government. The frontier editor in the Trans-Mississippi West, Knight said, promoted social change through regular and frequent publication, dissemination of timely information, and advocacy of controversy. Through this process, the newspaper helped transform a "chance grouping of individuals" from diverse backgrounds into a community. It promoted schools and other institutions familiar in the metropolis, and it provided a link between the small, isolated town and the outside world. Thomas Heuterman, biographer of printer Legh Freeman, took a cautious look at the editor's influence. "While literary features served an entertainment function," he noted, "frontier newspapers by their mere existence are said to have raised the educational level of society, civilized the West, and been an agent of literacy. Frontiersmen were avid readers, but whether racist editorials or land promotion schemes achieved such enlightenment is questionable."[47]

Frontier editors defy generalization. They lived in different times and places over a century and across the continent. While involved in land-speculation and town-promotion schemes, Freeman tried to live the stereotypical life of a frontier scout. At times, his wife and family ran the paper while he traveled and sent home columns. This wanderlust was illustrated when he operated his "press on wheels," the *Frontier Index* newspaper that moved from town to town just ahead of the Union Pacific Railroad westward across Nebraska, Colorado, Wyoming, Utah, and Montana. He tried to stay ahead of advancing civilization.

Edtiors were committed to freedom of the press; and, despite the fact that one can find many examples of vituperation, for the most part newspapers didn't engage in violent rhetoric. Often, though, attacks did get personal. Editors frequently responded to criticism with comments about their opponent's drinking habits or sex life. The *Arizona Sentinel* called the editor of the *Arizona Miner* a cuss, a dirty nincompoop, a drunk, and a miserable liar and referred to the paper as "his dirty abortion."[48] The *Miner's* editor responded by claiming that the *Sentinel's* editor had been everything but independent: "Had you changed your shirts as often as you have changed masters, there would be one sand-bar less in the Colorado river."[49] The most vitriolic language was reserved for corrupt politicians, especially from the opposing party. James Goodhue, editor of the *Minnesota Pioneer*, characterized the U.S. marshal for the territory as "utterly destitute of moral principle, manly bearing or even physical courage."[50] Of course, each editor noted that the opponent was not worthy of the attention he was receiving.

Editors needed the support of their communities, and even though they made personal sacrifices for their papers, they seldom began without support. Historians have uncovered a rich variety of motives and financial arrangements for newspapers. Besides town boosters and partisan politicians, other groups founded

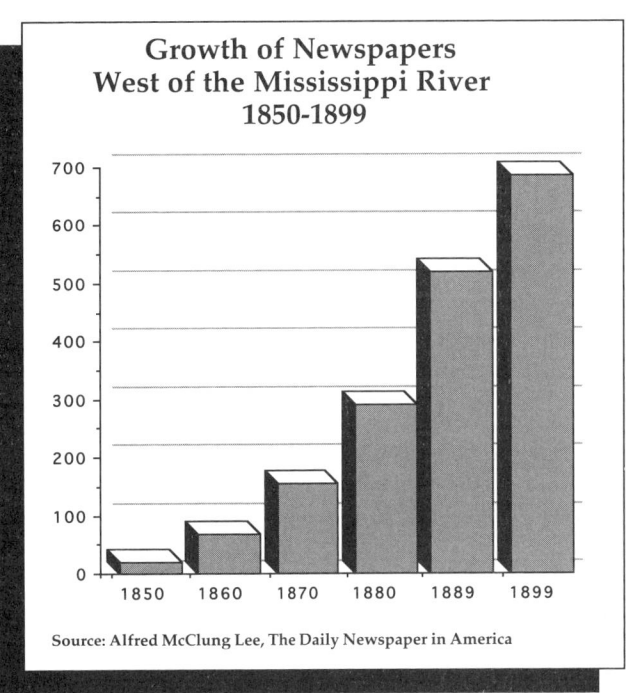

Growth of Newspapers West of the Mississippi River 1850-1899

Source: Alfred McClung Lee, The Daily Newspaper in America

newspapers to support causes like temperance, women's suffrage, abolitionism, churches, and medical groups. Editors often looked for the towns most likely to provide sustained growth for their papers. Some cooperated with newspapers in nearby towns for financial assistance.

More than one editor surely stifled his views rather than vent his true feelings about his paper's patrons. The primary audience might be the exchange papers in the East, where, editors hoped, columns would be reprinted extolling the virtues of the frontier. Minnesota winters, for example, actually looked good in booster columns. "In fact," wrote the *Minnesota Pioneer's* Goodhue, "we have no wind; so that we actually suffer less in the coldest weather than they do in the cutting winds of Illinois, at a much milder temperature."[51] Boomtown newspapers extolled their communities' peaceful future, even as on Saturday nights drunken cowboys loped their horses through the streets, yelling and shooting their guns into the air. Editors in homesteader towns dreamed in print of the day when miraculous dry farming techniques would transform barren plains into a blooming paradise.

THE EDITOR AS CELEBRITY

Some editors became local celebrities. They were important because their patrons believed the press to be necessary to the region, the party, or the cause. They were well known because of the attention they called to themselves with their language and their antics. In Denver, the site of a bitter newspaper feud, New York reporter Henry M. Stanley said the reputation of "these plain-speaking journalists" has "positively frightened me" from visiting them. After a time in the West, however, he began to admire the competition, politics, and eccentricities of the editors and their

[47]Thomas H. Heuterman, *Movable Type: Biography of Legh R. Freeman* (Ames, Iowa, 1979), 50-1 and 143-4.

[48]*Arizona Sentinel*, 7 November 1874.

[49]*Arizona Miner*, 5 January 1875.

[50]Quoted in Daniel S. B. Johnston, "Minnesota Journalism in the Territorial Period," *Minnesota Historical Society Collections* 10:1 (1905): 251.

[51]*Pioneer*, 19 December 1849.

Women of the West

Virginia Lady Remakes Herself into a Bold Frontier Editor

Some women were as involved in efforts to start frontier newspapers as their husbands and town developers were. Typical of these women was Ada Miller Freeman. Moving from town to town with her husband – proprietor of a newspaper known as the "press on wheels" – she died violently, a way that was not uncommon on the frontier. But even at the time of her death – from a falling shotgun – she was trying to do what she had done throughout her married life: provide stability for a growing family.

She was married in 1869 in Virginia to Legh Freeman, a dashing, tall-tale telling newspaper publisher who for some time had been operating various publishing ventures and writing her letters from the western frontier. Within ten years they had four children and she had remade herself into a newspaper woman. Legh Freeman worked at a variety of occupations, including frontier scout. While he traveled and sent home pieces about his adventures, Ada and the family ran the paper.

Although the couple was making its home in inhospitable territory, her work received compliments. She herself wrote of her efforts with these words:

"Be it recorded as part of the history of Utah, that a Virginia Born and Bred lady, came into Utah unacquainted with a single soul, and, within a period of six weeks, organized, established, and conducted the Ogden 'Freeman,' took charge of two infant sons, and gave birth to a third, and in that time was never censured because her endeavors to assist her husband did not accord with notions."

During her last of many household moves – this one from Utah to Montana – a shotgun fell from the wagon and discharged a load of birdshot into her hip. According to her son, she died with a great deal of pain.

Her husband remarried another would-be newspaper woman and yet another when the second one died.

Like Ada Freemen, women played a prominent role in frontier journalism, although their lives were not often as dramatic as pictured by the *National Police Gazette* in 1882 (above). Women began a number of the early prohibition and suffrage newspapers in the West. Town promotion, frontier fantasies, and real-estate deals occupied the time of Ada Freeman's husband, itinerant newspaperman Legh Freeman (left). They published several papers, but he usually moved by the time railroads and civilization reached the towns he promoted. Another Montana editor noted that all the towns in which Freeman published had died but that his *Frontier Index* always managed to start anew in another place.

environment. "I had heard that the editors were savage fellows," he wrote, "ever ready with the pistol and bowie-knife to fight anybody who differed with them; but such stories are pure slanders I think, and the next time I visit Colorado territory I shall try to see more of them."[52]

Some editors would not bend from their beliefs. One of them was Jane Grey Swisshelm. She could not be purchased or intimidated. She was not more accurate in her reporting or less caustic in her comments than her male counterparts. She fought hard for the abolition of slavery and for stronger retribution against the Indians after the Dakota War of 1862. The first part of her newspaper career was spent in Pennsylvania and Washington, D. C. After the failure of her marriage, she fought for women's legal rights to prevent her husband from taking her property. Leaving behind an unpleasant family situation, she fled in 1858 with her six-year-old daughter to St. Cloud, Minnesota.

St. Cloud's newspaper had failed, and a local Democrat with an idle press on his hands asked her to edit a newspaper. To her declaration that she was an abolitionist who could not edit a paper without full control over the columns, he replied that "all Democrats recognized a lady's right to talk any kind of politics she had a mind to." And talk she did. She approached St. Cloud's most influential politician, Sylvanus B. Lowry, seeking his backing for her fledgling paper. He agreed to help if she would support the re-election of President James Buchanan. Outraged at the suggestion, she began attacking Lowry, who she said enticed newcomers to become Buchanan Democrats through control of political appointments and removals. The newcomers' "knees," she wrote, "double up and their backbones double down like the fibers of a green cabbage blade held over the escape pipe of a steam engine."[53] In response, Lowry's lawyer made a speech on the subject of women, whom he categorized as coquettes, flirts, old maids, and advocates of women's rights who write for newspapers. Swisshelm responded with an insulting description of a woman who resembled the lawyer's wife.

Within a week, the office of Swisshelm's paper, the *Visiter*, was broken into, the press destroyed, and the type scattered in the streets and thrown into the Mississippi River. A note from the committee of vigilance warned her not to repeat her offense. The citizens of St. Cloud, the note said, "have decided that it [the *Visiter*] is fit only for the inmates of brothels, and you seem to have had some experience of the tastes of such persons." Nothing could have more outraged the strictly Protestant Swisshelm.

With financial help from embarrassed moderate St. Cloud residents and support from papers across the state and nation, she rebuilt the newspaper. She got so much mileage out of the attack that Lowry pleaded for an agreement from Swisshelm's backers that the *Visiter* would no longer mention the incident. "The men pledged their honor that the *Visiter* should not 'discuss the subject,'" Swisshelm responded. "We pledged our honor that the paper we edit will discuss any subject we have a mind." Changing

Jane Grey Swisshelm and the *Visiter*
Despite her journalistic intemperance, Jane Grey Swisshelm had many accomplishments during her newspaper career. She used her newspaper, the *St. Cloud* (Minn.) *Visiter*, to champion abolition, Republicanism, and women's rights.

the paper's name to the *St. Cloud Democrat* to avoid promises made on behalf of the *Visiter*, she continued to write about Lowry and the mob's attack.

In many ways, Swisshelm broke new ground for women, even though she often disagreed with suffrage leaders. As a correspondent for Horace Greeley's *New York Tribune*, she had been the first female reporter ever admitted into the press gallery of the U.S. Senate. When she founded her first newspaper, the *Pittsburgh Visiter*, she created an environment in which a man and woman could work together in the same print shop without arousing gossip around town. She opened the shades and lighted the normally dark shop so that people could observe her and the shop's owner working together. Otherwise, such an arrangement could have produced a scandal. More than thirty years later, two young women in South Dakota worked together as typesetters so that one wasn't working alone with a man. One of the women, Alice Bower, learned typesetting at the age of 15. After she married Joseph Gossage in 1882, they ran the *Black Hills Journal* in Rapid City for more than forty years.

After the Dakota War of 1862 in Minnesota, Swisshelm became relentless in her desire for retribution, even extermination, of the Dakota tribe; and she left Minnesota for an appointment in the

[52]Stanley, *My Early Travels*, 176-7.
[53]*St. Cloud Visiter*, 4 March 1858.

War Department, where she eventually provoked President Andrew Johnson's administration into firing her.

Editors left their mark on the frontier. The adventurous editor "did not pass away with the frontier," historian Thomas Heuterman wrote; "a legacy of tall tales, boosterism, and even racism seems to make inaccurate the statement that the frontier press bequeathed nothing that the West of the immediately succeeding era wanted to keep."[54]

MARK TWAIN

The most lasting legacy came from a journalist who was a poor reporter and, except in the absence of his boss, not an editor. Fortunately, editor Joe Goodman of the *Territorial Enterprise* in Virginia City, Nevada, enjoyed some articles he received signed "Josh." Publication of the articles mocking a local judge encouraged the anonymous writer, Samuel Clemens, to become a staff writer for the paper. He was a former riverboat pilot who was failing as a miner. The *Enterprise* was a rare frontier newspaper in that its staff, which included five full-time printers, was large enough to allow the reporters to be full-time writers, and Goodman was liberal enough to publish good writing regardless of its accuracy.

On assignment to Carson City, where he was supposed to stay one day but enjoyed the festivities so much he stayed a week, Clemens sent back a series of typically exaggerated reports, one of which he signed "Mark Twain." The *nom de plume* was from a river term indicating water two fathoms deep. His account of the Washoe delegation to the legislature, headed "The Grand Bull Drivers' Convention," included a description of one man dancing around in his red night clothes and another similarly attired trying to convince him he was a humbug. "A suspicion crossed my mind that they were partially intoxicated," Twain wrote, "but I could not be sure about it on account of everything appearing to turn around so."[55]

Twain's stories were so widely reprinted in the exchange papers that he told his mother that people knew him wherever he went. "I am proud to say," he added, "I am the most conceited ass in the Territory." Many of his colleagues agreed.[56]

Twain's talent for satire owed a debt to both the wild Nevada boomtown and the American tradition of tall tales. His cynicism received plenty of reinforcement from the environment, reflected in this "Stock Broker's Prayer":

Our father Mammon who art in the Comstock, bully is thy name; let thy dividends come, and stocks go up, in California as in Washoe. Give this day our daily commissioners, forgive us our swindles, as we hope to get even on those who have swindled us. "Lead" us not into temptation or promising wildcat; deliver us from law-suit; for thine is the main Comstock, the black sulphurets and the wire-silver and from wall-rock to wall-

Roughing It

Samuel Clemens dabbled at silver mining in Nevada until Virginia City's *Territorial Enterprise* offered him $25 a week to write full-time. At the *Enterprise* he took on the pen name "Mark Twain." He later wrote about his Nevada experiences in the book *Roughing It*. This illustration of Twain at his desk in the *Enterprise* office appeared in the book.

rock, you bet![57]

Twain lifted his expository method from a tradition of American humor. Humorists of the Old Southwest had spun tales for which the setting just as easily could have been Twain's Nevada. In Virginia City, he got to know several colleagues, including William Wright (pen name Dan De Quille). De Quille was well known locally and influenced Twain's professional development. Twain probably also listened to and told tall tales around campfires and at social gatherings.

Like other western journalists, Twain owed a debt to his predecessors in the Ohio Valley, where many newspapermen adopted pen names for the purpose of writing satire. Charles Farrar Browne, who as city editor of the *Cleveland Plain Dealer* created the character Artemus Ward, was well known before Twain began writing for the *Enterprise*. An avid reader of Ward, Twain borrowed ideas, phrasing, and tangled syntax from the Ohio writer. When Browne visited Virginia City, Twain made the most of the

[54]Heuterman, *Movable Type*, 145.

[55]Quoted in Louis L. Snyder and Richard B. Morris, eds., *Treasury of Great Reporting*, 2nd ed., (New York, 1962), 162.

[56]Forest Hill, Nev., *Placer Weekly Courier*, 17 January 1863; reprinted in ibid., 159-62.

[57]Reprinted in Edgar Marquess Branch, *The Literary Apprenticeship of Mark Twain* (Urbana, 1950), 61.

occasion, spending a good deal of time discussing technique with him. Browne advised Twain on his writing and offered him a letter that helped him publish a humorous piece in New York in 1864. For his part, Twain never acknowledged his debt to Browne.

A humorist who followed Twain in popularity by writing books, touring the lecture circuit, and writing widely reprinted columns was Edgar Wilson (Bill) Nye, who edited newspapers in Laramie, Wyoming. One of his suggestions for reform on the frontier was the creation of a School of Journalism. Questioning the idea that it was possible to train someone in journalism — a profession requiring the same information possessed by the Almighty and a willingness to work for less — he outlined a proposed course of study. Two years were necessary for meditation and prayer to compensate for the profanity resulting from years of spelling "God" with a lower case "g," five years to grasp the "mirth-provoking orthography" of English, three years of athletics to build up physical strength, ten years to learn typography and type setting, five years of proofreading and learning to correct proofs by marking "on the margin like a Chinese map of the Gunnison country," at least fifteen years to understand American politics and the civil service and to learn the relative importance of political parties, five years in medicine to learn how "to bind up contusions, apply arnica, court plaster or bandages, plug up bullet holes, and prospect through the human system for buck shot," ten years to study law to understand the difference between "a writ of mandamus and other styles of profanity," ten years of theology, and ten years of practical knowledge in areas ranging from cutting wood to winning the affections of the opposite sex. "At the age of 95," Nye concluded, "the student will have lost that wild, reckless and impulsive style so common among younger and less experienced journalists." At that point, the student's pressing question would be whether to invest in government bonds or real estate in a growing town.

In a satire on sentimentality in writing about children, Nye observed that "statistics show that the ratio of good boys who die, compared to bad ones, is simply appalling." Printing presses attacked the surviving boys: "Most job presses feel gloomy and unhappy until they have eaten the fingers off two or three boys. Then they go on with their work cheerfully and even hilariously."[58] Despite its popularity with nineteenth-century readers, Nye's humor was not as lasting as Twain's.

THE CHANGING FRONTIER

Mass production contributed to a growing uniformity of small-town newspapers even before the Linotype machine came into use in 1886. Syndication services supplied "readyprint" — pages already printed on one side — to local printers who then printed local news and ads on the back of the pages. The same syndicates also supplied "boilerplate" containing preset stories, illustrations, or pages. These services provided editors with prepared material, leaving a small space for type that was set locally. Readyprint sub-

Artemus Ward
Charles Farrar Browne, later taking on the pen name of the humorist "Artemus Ward," established his early following as a writer of brief, fanciful "locals" for the *Cleveland Plain Dealer*. He soon gained a popular following because of his comic ability, and from his local stage he expanded to a national audience and became a writer and speaker of wide fame. This caricature from *Vanity Fair* magazine in 1862 showed him as a popular public speaker.

stantially reduced the need for local typesetting, thereby allowing editors to establish newspapers on a short-term basis, such as the length of an election campaign, without investing much time in the print shop. To further simplify typesetting, many legal notices such as those claiming cattle brands or homesteads were required to run for several consecutive weeks. Once a printer had a number of the notices set in type, he was left with only a column or so to fill and could devote the rest of his time to commercial printing or, wrote one historian, "to the comforts of the saloon across the street."[59]

The syndicated services allowed publishers to create small newspaper chains in which several towns could have virtually the same paper with only minor changes. Obviously, the content of newspapers dependent upon syndicated readyprint or boilerplate lacked immediate news value. Sentimental poetry, historical pieces, fiction, and biographies of celebrities were common. Readyprints also carried ads, a service that allowed the syndicate

[58]T. A. Larsen, ed., *Bill Nye's Western Humor* (Lincoln, Neb., 1968), 50-3, 63.

[59]John Cameron Sim, *The Grass Roots Press: America's Community Newspapers* (Ames, Iowa, 1969), 42-6.

The Frontier Standardized

By the late 1800s, "frontier" newspapers had become standardized. Rather than being the romantic, adventurous enterprises that some of the earlier papers may have been, by the 1890s they had become typical small businesses. After Oklahoma territory was opened for settlement, many printers started papers as offshoots of their shops. Their offices, like this one of the *Minco Minstrel*, had poor lighting and heating, with equipment and supplies cluttering their limited work space. It and many other small papers relied extensively on boilerplate and readyprint for content, making them indistinguishable from one another except for their names and a few local items.

houses to supply the pages to the local printer with little expense compared to the cost of printing local news.

The economic structure of frontier papers reflected the changing business climate at the end of the 1800s. The earliest printers in the Ohio Valley had learned the printing trade as apprentices in the shops of other printers, probably farther east. Occasionally, they borrowed money from their master to help with the costs of starting a business. Even in colonial times, Benjamin Franklin held an interest in a number of the papers he helped young printers establish, but chain ownership was more a mark of the twentieth than the eighteenth century. Financial records of few papers are available, but there are indications of inter-newspaper relationships on the frontier. As early as the 1860s about one-fourth of Wisconsin papers were operated as parts of chains or other financial arrangements involving more than one paper.

As the nineteenth century drew to a close, small-town papers began showing the conformity of industrialism evident in their urban counterparts. Many publishers showed little resemblance to the early printers who took pride in their printing craft and their bombastic political essays. Still, some courageous small-town editors continued to throw caution to the wind in attacking local corruption or waging a fight over the county printing contract.

RECOMMENDED READINGS

BOOKS

Barnard, Sandy. *I Go With Custer: The Life and Death of Reporter Mark Kellogg.* Bismarck, N. D., 1996. The product of years of painstaking detective work, this book brings together more information about Kellogg than has ever been assembled before. At the same time, it reveals the difficulties of making a living as a journalist in the West.

Beebe, Lucius. *Comstock Commotion: The Story of the Territorial Enterprise.* Stanford, Calif., 1954. The *Territorial Enterprise* of Virginia City, Nev., in the 1860s-1870s was "the pattern and archetype of all western newspapers in pioneer times.... [It had] gunfighting editors, celebrated news beats, authority and power in affairs of state, and its hilarious and uninhibited way of life." The paper was prosperous and boisterous.

Bennion, Sherilyn Cox. *Equal to the Occasion: Women Editors of the Nineteenth-Century West.* Reno, Nev., 1990. This survey examines the lives and works of thirty-five female editors of newspapers and other western periodicals.

Cloud, Barbara. *The Business of Newspapers on the Western Frontier.* Reno, Nev., 1992. Business and economic dimensions were important to small-town frontier newspapers published in the late nineteenth century.

---. *The Coming of the Frontier Press: How the West Was Really Won.* Evanston, Ill., 2008. Editors wanted to "obliterate" the frontier. "From the day he, or sometimes she, opened an office in a mining camp or rural town, the primary goal was to bring civilization to the community."

Coward, John M., and W. Joseph Campbell, editors, *The Indian Wars and The Spanish American War,* Vol. 4 of the Greenwood Library of American War Reporting, David A. Copeland, ed. Westport, Conn., 2005. The rich section of news articles begins in 1835 with the second Seminole war in Florida and runs through the January 1891 aftermath of Wounded Knee in South Dakota.

—. *The Newspaper Indian: Native American Identity in the Press, 1820-1890.* Champaign, Ill., 1999. Newspaper reporting helped shape popular opinion of American Indians in the nineteenth century.

Dary, David. *Red Blood and Black Ink: Journalism in the Old West.* New York: Knopf, 1998. This anecdotal overview of western journalism is rich in detail and quotations from colorful editors.

Demaree, Albert Lowther. *The American Agricultural Press 1819-1860.* New York, 1941. This is the best book on the early history of agricultural journalism.

Dwyer, Richard A., and Richard E. Lingenfelter. *Lying on the Eastern Slope: James Townsend's Comic Journalism on the Mining Frontier.* Miami, Fla., 1984. Editors in the Sierra Nevada, as exemplified by the roving editor "Lying Jim" Townsend, fabricated much of the content in their newspapers, including wild tales, details of mining prosperity, comic episodes, etc., mostly in good humor in the nature of Mark Twain.

Dykstra, Robert R. *The Cattle Towns.* Lincoln, Neb., 1968. Dykstra examines newspapers, including boosterism and competition, within the social framework of Kansas cattle centers.

Fatout, Paul. *Mark Twain in Virginia City.* Bloomington, Ind., 1964. This biography follows the famous writer through his formative years as a frontier journalist.

Hage, George S. *Newspapers on the Minnesota Frontier 1849-1860.* St. Paul, Minn., 1967. This entertaining look at the earliest Minnesota newspapers includes the antics of their editors.

Halaas, David Fridtjof. *Boom Town Newspapers: Journalism on the Rocky Mountain Mining Frontier, 1859-1881.* Albuquerque, N.M., 1981. This account provides an overview of newspapers in the mining towns in Arizona, New Mexico, Colorado, Wyoming, and Montana.

Hamilton, Milton W. *The Country Printer: New York State, 1785-1830.* New York, 1936. This sympathetic study covers such topics as problems of publishing, apprenticeships, freedom of the press, ethics, financing, partisanship, shortage of capital, meager public support, the inadequacy of printers' education, newspaper content (including inadequate news), the fierce independence of pioneer printers, and finally the encroachment of city papers.

Heuterman, Thomas H. *Movable Type: Biography of Legh R. Freeman*. Ames, Iowa, 1979. Freeman, the colorful editor of the "press on wheels," had many adventures and speculations.

Hoffert, Sylvia D. *Jane Grey Swisshelm: An Unconventional Life: 1815-1884*. Chapel Hill, N.C., 2004. This brief biography of the colorful editor emphasizes her work for abolition of slavery, women's rights, and her disenchantment with Native Americans.

Karolevitz, Robert F. *Newspapering in the Old West: A Pictorial History of Journalism and Printing on the Frontier*. Seattle, 1965. Frontier journalism — as portrayed in this anecdotal, illustrated treatment of newspapers from 1840 to the latter part of the 1800s — was rough and tumble; and newspapermen were individualists, not fitting any common characteristics or stereotype.

Knight, Oliver. *Following the Indian Wars*. Norman, Okla., 1960. Knight provides a solid account of correspondents and press coverage of the plains wars from 1866 to 1891.

Lyon, William H. *The Pioneer Editor in Missouri 1808-1860*. Columbia, Mo., 1965. Lyon's work is one of the best accounts of frontier editors and their place in frontier life and journalism.

---, ed. *Journalism in the West*. Manhattan, Kan., 1980. This book reprints a special issue of *Journal of the West* on the press and adds three essays.

Martin, Douglas D. *Tombstone's Epitaph: The History of a Frontier Town as Chronicled in Its Newspaper*. Norman, 1958; reprint ed., 1997. Heavy on excerpts from newspaper articles, this book focuses mostly on the politics and feuds involving the Earp brothers and editor John Clum's role in them.

Murphy, James E., and Sharon M. Murphy. *Let My People Know: American Indian Journalism*. Norman, Okla., 1981. The authors provide a brief overview of American Indian media and treatment of Indians in white newspapers.

Myers, John Myers. *Print in a Wild Land*. Garden City, N.Y., 1967. Myers provides a sweeping look at western editors, their problems, and adventures.

Norton, Wesley. *Religious Newspapers in the Old Northwest to 1861: A History, Bibliography, and Record of Opinion*. Athens, Ohio, 1977. Frontier religious newspapers contributed to reform.

Reilly, Hugh J. *The Frontier Newspapers and the Coverage of the Plains Indian Wars*. Santa Barbara, Calif., 2010. This study analyzes the coverage that nearby newspapers gave to "eight watershed events in Native American history from 1862 to 1891."

Sibley, Marilyn McAdams. *Lone Stars and State Gazettes: Texas Newspapers before the Civil War*. College Station, Tex., 1983. The main purpose of most newspapers was to support or oppose politicians, political causes, or religious ideas. When financial support ended, most papers ceased publication.

Stillson, Richard T. *Spreading the Word: A History of Information in the California Gold Rush*. Lincoln, Neb., 2006. Easterners read newspapers, guidebooks, maps, memoirs, and personal letters from travelers to determine how to seek gold in California. Stillson looks at how people acquired and used information in making the trip.

Stratton, Porter A. *The Territorial Press of New Mexico 1834-1860*. Albuquerque, 1969. The author tells a readable, comprehensive history of New Mexico's frontier press and its role in major political and social debates.

Wheeler, Keith. *The Chroniclers*. Alexandria, Va., 1976. This colorful picture book in the Time-Life Old West series considers writers, editors, photographers, and painters in the Far West.

ARTICLES

Collins, Ross F. "Cattle Barons and Ink Slingers: How Cow Country Journalists Created A Great American Myth." *American Journalism* 24 (2007): 7-29. The press originated the "Old West myth of 'cattle barons' versus 'nesters.'"

—. "Cattlemen and Cow Town Editors: The *Bad Lands Cow Boy* of Dakota Territory." *North Dakota History* 57:2 (2000): 26-38. While some newspapers added "livestock reporters" or other cattle industry-boosting positions to their mastheads, the editor in Medora went further by naming his paper to help boost the "cow boy" image.

Cronin, Mary M. "Mixing Protest and Accommodation: The Response of Oklahoma's Black Town Newspaper Editors to Race Relations." *American Journalism* 19 (2002): 45-64. African-American editors in Oklahoma used a variety of strategies to overcome racial marginalization.

Dyer, Carolyn Stewart. "Political Patronage of the Wisconsin Press, 1849-1860: New Perspectives on the Economics of Patronage." *Journalism Monographs* 109 (1989). Patronage was a major source of income for frontier editors, and thus partisans used it to influence them.

Ellison, Rhoda Coleman. "Newspaper Publishing in Frontier Alabama." *Journalism Quarterly* 23 (1946): 289-301. The author gives an overview of printers and their environment in the early southeast.

Endres, Fred F. "'We Want Money and Must Have It': Profile of an Ohio Weekly." *Journalism History* 7 (1980): 68-71. Financial problems were severe for the frontier newspaper.

Endres, Kathleen. "Jane Grey Swisshelm: 19th Century Journalist and Feminist." *Journalism History* 2 (1975): 128-32. A reporter for the *New York Tribune* in the 1850s, Swisshelm advocated equal treatment of women. She took strong stands on several public issues.

Fisher, Paul. "A Forgotten Gentry of the Fourth Estate." *Journalism Quarterly* 33 (1956): 167-74. Tramp printers "played a vital role in the expansion of newspapers after the Civil War, until modern efficiency spelled [their] doom."

Gower, Calvin W. "Kansas 'Border Town' Newspapers and the Pike's Peak Gold Rush." *Journalism Quarterly* 44 (1967): 281-8. Historians have unjustly criticized newspapers for inciting gold fever by publishing exaggerated, reckless, and false claims.

Gutierrez, Felix. "Spanish-Language Media in America: Background, Resources, History." *Journalism History: Spanish Language Media Issue* 4: 2 (1977): 34-41 and 65-7. Gutierrez's article is most useful as a general history. This special issue of *Journalism History* also includes seven articles on the history of the Spanish-language media in the United States.

Hall, Mark W. "1831-49: The Pioneer Period for Newspapers in California." *Journalism Quarterly* 49 (1972): 648-55. California's first two newspapers, produced very crudely during the American army's occupation during the Mexican War, were similar to eastern papers of the colonial period. They were begun as a means of a printer's supplementing his meager income and carried little local news, relying primarily on news clipped from other papers. Most were vitriolic.

Hirsh, Jeffrey L. "Tocqueville and the Frontier Press." *Journalism Quarterly* 51 (1974): 116-9. Between 1835 and 1840s, in the papers of Ann Arbor, Mich., "[p]olitical struggles, violent and seemingly tasteless personal attacks, and promotion of schemes they considered beneficial to the people, were all prominent."

Housman, Robert L. "The End of Frontier Journalism in Montana." *Journalism Quarterly* 12 (1935): 133-45. Frontier journalism was a mirror of the political, social, and economic frontier. Editors brought with them the "tradition of personal journalism characteristic of the general newspaper work of the period."

Huckins, Kyle. "Religion and Western Newspapers," 134-48 in Wm. David Sloan, ed., *Media and Religion in American History*. Northport, Ala.: 2000. After the Civil War, newspapers in the American Southwest mocked traditional Christianity. In later years, they became strong supporters of spirituality and the organized church.

Huntzicker, William E. "Media," 501-05 in David Wishart, ed., *Encyclopedia of the Great Plains*. Lincoln, Neb., 2004. This section introduction offers an overview of the mass media of the Great Plains and individual entries that bring the topics to the end of the twentieth century.

Jones, Douglas C. "Teresa Dean: Lady Correspondent Among the Sioux Indians." *Journalism Quarterly* 49 (1972): 656-62. While writing about Indians for Chicago newspapers, before she had met any, Dean deplored "the state of Sioux existence, brought on, she indicated, primarily through a native laziness and indolence." After getting to know the Sioux, however, she blamed the American government's Indian affairs policies for the problems.

Jordan, Philip D. "The Portrait of a Pioneer Printer." *Journal of the Illinois State Historical Society* 23 (April 1930): 175-82. James G. Edwards, a printer in Illinois in the 1830s, was a "typical frontier newspaperman who set his type by hand, pulled the galley proofs, ran off the edition, delivered it, and then attempted to collect from his subscribers."

Journalism History, Special Frontier Issue, edited by Thomas H. Heuterman and Jerilyn S. McIntyre, 7 (Summer 1980). This issue includes essays on economics, census data, women and their relationship to frontier newspapers, and letters and handwritten newspapers.

Katz, William A. "The Western Printer and His Publications, 1850-90." *Journalism Quarterly* 44 (1967): 708-14. Publications in Washington territory indicate "a level of banality matched only by lack of individuality." Most were printed as official government records and laws and minutes of meetings.

Kerstetter, Todd. "'Mobocratic Feeling': Religious Outsiders, the Popular Press, and the American West." *American Journalism* 20:1 (2003): 57-72. Traditionally, press coverage of religions outside the mainstream has been negative.

Kindig, Everett W. "'I am in purgatory now': Journalist Hooper Warren Survives the Illinois Frontier." *Illinois Historical Journal* 79 (Autumn 1986): 185-96. Hooper, the editor of one of Illinois' earliest newspapers, faced trials and tribulations.

Lent, John A. "The Press on Wheels: A History of *The Frontier Index*." *Journal of the West* 10 (1971): 662-99. "[I]t was newspapers such as the *Index* and newspapermen such as [brothers Legh and Fred Freeman, publishers of the *Index*] who had a big hand in promoting, developing, and, in the *Index*'s unique situation, laying out Western cities and towns. They truly opened up the West as much as did the buffalo hunter, Indian fighter or railroader."

Lomicky, Carol S. "Frontier Feminism and the *Woman's Tribune*: The Journalism of Clara Bewick Colby." *Journalism History* 28:3 (2002): 102-11. Colby's newspaper promoted women's rights first in Nebraska and later when it moved to Oregon and then to Washington, D.C.

Lorenz, Larry. "Harrison Reed: An Editor's Trials on the Wisconsin Frontier," *Journalism Quarterly* 53 (1976): 417-22, 462. Frontier editors, as exemplified by Reed, succeeded or failed depending on their ability to deal with financial, social, and, above all, political pressures.

—. "'Out of Sorts and Out of Cash': Problems of Publishing in Wisconsin Territory, 1833-1848." *Journalism History* 3 (1976): 34-9, 63. Editors managed to establish newspapers on the Wisconsin frontier despite a host of problems, including primitive mail service, difficulties with obtaining needed supplies, and subscribers and advertisers who would not pay their bills.

Luebke, Barbara F. "Elias Boudinot, Indian Editor: Editorial Columns from the *Cherokee Phoenix*." *Journalism History* 6 (1979): 48-51. Boudinot edited the first American Indian newspaper, the *Cherokee Phoenix*, for four-and-one-half years. It became increasingly politicized.

Martin, Asa Earl. "Pioneer Anti-Slavery Press." *Mississippi Valley Historical Review* 2 (March 1916): 509-28. Several early abolitionist newspapers were published in the frontiers of slave and border states.

McIntyre, Jerilyn. "Communication on a Western Frontier — Some Questions About Context." *Journalism History* 3 (1976): 53-5, 63. In the 1850s in California and Oregon, the conditions of the frontier exercised a major influence on the methods of communication.

Nelson, Jack A. "The Comic Frontier." *Media History Digest* 6, 1 (1986): 46-9. "Those enduring the isolation [of the western frontier] often had little enough to laugh about, and most editors ... saw it as part of their function to offer a laugh now and then."

Nichols, Roger L. "Printers' Ink and Red Skins: Western Newspapermen and the Indians." *Kansas Quarterly* 3 (Fall 1971): 82-8. In recommending how to deal with Indians, journalists "viewed aborigines through glasses tinted by attitudes of racial or cultural superiority."

Quebral, Nora C. "Wilmer Atkinson and the Early *Farm Journal*." *Journalism Quarterly* 47 (1970): 65-70, 80. The *Farm Journal*, an agricultural magazine, succeeded because it "met the current need of a specific class of readers for a low-priced source of information tailored to their frame of interest."

Raitz, Karl B., and Stanley D. Brunn. "Geographic Patterns in the Historical Development of Farm Publications." *Journalism History* 6 (1979): 14-5, 31-2. "The earliest journals printed little more than general information on plant and animal husbandry, but as agricultural science developed and specialized farming regions evolved, the farm magazine gradually became less descriptive and more analytic and demonstrative of scientific farming techniques."

Reed, V. Delbert. "A Last Hurrah for the Frontier Press." *American Journalism* 6 (1989): 65-84. Newspapers in Wallace, Idaho, in the 1890s exhibited the diverse characteristics of frontier journalism.

Riley, Sam G. "The *Cherokee Phoenix*: The Short, Unhappy Life of the First American Indian Newspaper." *Journalism Quarterly* 53 (1976): 666-71. The *Phoenix* lasted only six-years, done in in part by the Georgia legislature.

Robbins, William G. "Some Perspectives on Law and Order in Frontier Newspapers." *Journal of the West* 17 (January 1978): 53-61. Like other Oregonians between 1850 and 1890, editors advocated law and order "in the name of community building and economic progress."

Rutenbeck, Jeffrey B. "The Rhetoric of Independence and Boosterism in Late Nineteenth-Century California Journalism." *American Journalism* 13:4 (1996): 456-74. Boosterism provided editors enough income to allow increasing numbers of them to be independent from political patronage.

Sloan, Wm. David. "The Frontier Press, 1800-1900: Personal Journalism or Paltry Business?" 104-22, in *Perspectives on Mass Communication History* (Hillsdale, N.J., 1991). This historiographical essay analyzes the approaches that historians have taken. The treatment of the frontier press has gone from laudatory to condemnatory.

Thwaites, Reuben Gold. "The Ohio Valley Press before the War of 1812-15." *Proceedings of the American Antiquarian Society* 19 (April 1909): 309-68. This article provides a lengthy overview of the history of the first newspapers in each territory of the region.

Watson, Elmo S. "The Indian Wars and the Press, 1866-1867." *Journalism Quarterly* 17 (1940): 301-10. "Depending mainly upon volunteer correspondents more gifted in imaginative writing than in accurate reporting, [eastern newspapers] spread before their readers the kind of highly colored accounts of Indian raids and 'massacres' that the most sensational yellow journals of a later period might have envied."

Williams, Nudie. "The Black Press in Oklahoma: The Formative Years, 1889-1907." *Chronicles of Oklahoma* 61 (1983): 308-19. "[W]hile ... black newspapers defended blacks almost to the point of losing objectivity, most were true newspapers in every respect...."

Wrone, David R. "John Sterling Harper, Founder of 160 Papers." *Journalism Quarterly* 45 (1968): 538-41. "'The Father of Western Journalism' ... [who] founded more newspapers than any other man ... followed a pattern.... He would found a newspaper in a promising community, it would fail or he would sell out at a good offer, and he then would ... start anew."

11

The Press and Industrial America
1865 - 1883

The Civil War was a watershed in American journalism, although the participants did not recognize it as such until a decade or so had passed. The world had changed. The country was politically united. People began to speak of the United States in the singular rather than the plural: "The United States *is*" rather than "The United States *are*" as they had done before the war. Historian Shelby Foote said the war "made us an 'is.'"[1] The Civil War had been fought over that issue. So the shift in public consciousness was not surprising.

On the other hand, the country still was riven with sectionalism. The South was prostrate from the war, which had been fought largely in the South and had bled the region of men and capital. Major cities in the Carolinas, Georgia, and Virginia were in ruins. The South's economy, relying on cotton and tobacco and having only a small industrial base, was a shambles. The slaves, freed by the war, were adjusting to the new realities, to paid jobs, ownership of stores and businesses, and political activism. Southern resistance to black enfranchisement exacerbated the situation, giving northern Radical Republicans reason to institute military reconstruction in the South in 1867.

A CHANGING NATION

The West was changing as well. What then was called *The West* extended as far as the Missouri River but centered in Illinois, Indiana, Michigan, and Ohio, states that were on their way to great wealth through agriculture, abundant natural resources such as coal, iron and wood, and manufacturing based on them.

Immigration into the United States had slowed during the Civil War, except for young men who came to fight. Now that flow began afresh. In addition to foreign immigration, Americans emigrated from the East into the exploding cities of what would become the Middle West. Political power followed their settlement. Political power, particularly given the disenfranchisement of the South under Radical Republicans, was related to population,

[1]Interview with Shelby Foote in Geoffrey C. Ward, *The Civil War, An Illustrated History* (New York, 1990), 273.

wealth, and communications. The House of Representatives had 237 members before Lincoln's inauguration. In his first administration, the 37th Congress had only 178 members as a result of southern secession. The South had only spasmodic representation in the years after the war until the 43rd Congress in 1873-1875 — during Grant's second administration — when the House had grown to 300 members, a result of southern reenfranchisement, black enfranchisement, and new states and territories in the West.

In the Far West, the enormous territory west of the Missouri River, cities and towns sprang into life, like desert flowers in the spring. Like those flowers, many lasted no longer than the first heat of summer; but most were quite sturdy, and the settlement of the West occurred rapidly. Indian Territory began to disappear, and new territories were created out of existing territories. Colorado, in what had once been the distant West, gained statehood in 1876, the centennial of the nation. The frontier had not yet closed officially, but signs of its closing were everywhere. Most of the remaining free Indian tribes were relocated to reservations. The long white-topped wagon trains, which had wound their way across the rugged plains, deserts, and mountains like a dirty white ribbon, began to be replaced with ribbons of iron that invariably altered the character as well as the face of the land. With the completion of the transcontinental railroad in 1869, passenger trains carried settlers west, especially to San Francisco and points along the way. Freight trains carried the region's bounty east: wheat from Minnesota and Kansas, fruit from California, and beef on the hoof from Texas and Oklahoma (shipped via rail from Kansas). By the 1880s, processed meats would be shipped east in refrigerated railway cars from the slaughterhouses of Chicago.

The changing landscape of the country was but a reflection of fundamental changes taking place in the issues that concerned Americans. Slavery was dead. The debate over it had convulsed political parties for decades and had spawned multiple newspapers to keep the issue fresh in the minds of the people. The issue disappeared, supplanted by women's rights and political parity for freed blacks in the South. Reconstruction dominated Congressional politics for a decade. It was a mixture of revenge, concern

A PHILOSOPHER IN ECSTASY.

Horace Greeley, Candidate
When Democrats nominated editor Horace Greeley as their presidential candidate in 1872, opponents immediately began to ridicule his eccentricity. They claimed he was naive and a dupe of professional politicians. Comparatively gentle was this Currier & Ives engraving lampooning his glee at getting the nomination.

for blacks, and greed. Education received increasing attention, in both the North and the South. Change was slow in coming, however, and changes wrought by education would have an impact on the press long after the period we are examining. For instance, the literacy rate of all whites ten years and older was 88.5% in 1870, but only 20.1% for blacks. A decade later the figures had not changed dramatically. Native whites had a literacy rate of 92.3%; foreign born, of 88%. Blacks had reached 30%.[2] The residual effects of slavery, and its prohibition against teaching blacks to read, would continue for several generations. The issue of hard money versus soft currency galvanized parties, as did immigration, tariff, and national sovereignty. The world was turned upside down — and everything affecting society affected the press.

Editors and publishers were as confused about the issues and the direction in which the country should go as were politicians, businessmen, laborers, and farmers. Newspapers wallowed in the social, economic, and political changes and became increasingly outmoded. Journalists not only did not know what direction to head, but newspaper owners were inadequate for the boiling environment. Some continued in the old ways and eventually sank, swamped by popular sentiment and political change. Others adapted by emphasizing vigorous newsgathering and increased advertising, thereby keeping themselves afloat for years. Still others recognized that these social and economic times were different. To survive and prosper, they experimented to see what methods would work. Prospering took seers and risk takers and a lot of good luck, but the successful newspapers trimmed their political sails, strengthened their financial base through advertising, and changed their news to ride through the swirling, changing times.

A New Generation of New York Editors

The northern states and their commercial centers dominated economic and political life after the Civil War, and no city was more important than New York. Its newspapers reflected its own mercantile power as well as the political power of the state. Papers known for their thorough news coverage during the war now retained their prominence, although most still were closely allied with political parties and politicians.

The seeds of independence from party and politician had been planted during the war as the exciting news attracted readers to metropolitan dailies. But for seeds to grow and produce they need water and fertilizer and protection from weeds. Advertising would enable the newspapers to grow and produce; the careful weeding of the news would attract readers for advertisers. The growth would not occur overnight, but the papers that grew independent of party would become the healthiest ones.

The old guard editors in New York City, as elsewhere around the urban centers of America, began to disappear from the stage through death and retirement. Henry J. Raymond of the *New York Times* died in 1869; William Cullen Bryant retired from the *Evening Post* in 1870 to translate Homer; James Gordon Bennett of the *Herald* died in June 1872; Horace Greeley of the *Tribune* died later that year following a grueling and acrimonious run for the United States presidency. They were giants of the personal journalism that had marked American newspapers.

Soon after they passed from the scene, a whole new generation of editors stepped into the void. The most prominent were E. L. Godkin at the *Nation* and later the *Evening Post*, Charles Dana at the *Sun*, and James Gordon Bennett Jr. at the *Herald*.

While politics and industrialization influenced these new editors, tradition also had a major impact. The penny press, which had wrought a revolution in its own time, had contributed practices that metropolitan editors widely adopted. New editors refined those practices. To some extent, the metropolitan press after the war was a sophisticated version of the penny press. While it made use of the inventions of technology and industry, it still

[2]*Historical Statistics of the United States, Colonial Times to 1970*, Part 1. Bureau of the Census (Washington, D.C., September 1975), Table H, 664-8.

A New Generation of Editors
With the passing from the scene of such notables as Horace Greeley, James Gordon Bennett, Henry Raymond, and William Cullen Bryant, many observers thought the "golden age of journalism" had passed. The post-Civil War decades, however, saw the emergence of a new generation of outstanding editors. Among them were such figures as Charles Dana of the *New York Sun*, Murat Halstead of the *Cincinnati Commercial*, Joseph Medill of the *Chicago Daily Tribune*, James Gordon Bennett Jr. of the *New York Herald*, and Henry Watterson of the *Louisville Courier-Journal*.

emphasized entertainment and news with mass appeal. Even though news filled the majority of space, many editors continued to express strong opinions and to give their papers a distinctive personality. As some newspapers were taking on certain characteristics of big business, the leading ones still were those that readers identified with particular editors.

The pre-eminent model of that personal style was Charles Dana of the *New York Sun*. He bought the *Sun* in 1868 and gained prominence by his writing style and his concept of news. Under stiff competition from James Gordon Bennett's *Herald*, the *Sun* had lost the circulation lead in the 1850s. It languished at a circulation of 43,000 until Dana bought it. In 1876 it reached 131,000, a remarkable circulation increase in just eight years. The popularity resulted from Dana's commitment to sparkling writing and interesting news, a goal he stated in the very first issue: "[The *Sun*] will study condensation, clearness, point, and will endeavor to present its daily photograph of the whole world's doings in the most luminous and lively manner."[3] He looked for bright young writers, many of them college graduates, and provided them with adequate salaries, training, assurance of tenure, and freedom to write as they chose — as long as the writing was interesting. The *Sun's* writing style was especially evident on the editorial page, the part of the paper into which Dana put most of his effort and the work of his most talented staff members. It became famous for its "casual essays" on everyday life. Perhaps the most famous editorial ever to appear in a newspaper was the *Sun's* "Is There a Santa Claus?" in which Francis Church gave the answer, "Yes, Virginia, there is...."[4] Although not written until shortly after Dana's death, it typified his approach in its style and subject matter.

In its news coverage, the *Sun*, like its chief competitor, the *Her-*

ald, emphasized murder, scandal, and gossip. Dana, though, particularly stressed stories of human interest about events with little significance but considerable emotional impact and stories of the unusual. The classic summary of that approach was the definition of news that Dana's city editor, John Bogart, gave a young reporter: "When a dog bites a man, that is not news, because it happens so often. But when a man bites a dog, that is news."[5] Dana responded to charges of sensationalism in a manner that well illustrated his theory of news coverage. "The first thing which an editor must look for," he said, "is news..., and by news I mean everything that occurs, everything which is of human interest.... I have always felt that whatever divine Providence permitted to occur I was not too proud to report."[6]

Despite his writing genius, Dana did not accomplish all that he might have. Increasingly cynical, he was flippant, almost perverse, in his editorial opinion, and as a result never achieved much editorial influence. In the 1880 presidential campaign, for example, the *Sun* endorsed Democrat Winfield Scott Hancock as "a good man, weighing 250 pounds."[7] Dana's favorite editorial technique was the derisive, clever epithet, such as his continual reference to President Rutherford B. Hayes as "his fraudulency Mr. Hayes," an approach that made for interesting, colorful reading but that made it difficult for readers to know when Dana was serious or jesting. In spite of such fatuousness, contemporaries considered Dana to be the leading editor of the post-war period, and they referred to the *Sun* as "the newspaperman's newspaper."

Dana's closest competitor as the period's outstanding journalist was E. L. Godkin, editor of both the *Nation* (1865-1899) and the *New York Evening Post* (1881-1899). He was the opposite of Dana:

[3]*New York Sun*, 27 January 1868.
[4]*New York Sun*, 21 September 1897.

[5]Quoted in Frank M. O'Brien, *The Story of "The Sun"* (New York, 1918), 241.
[6]Quoted in ibid.
[7]*New York Sun*, 19 October 1880.

Giants of Personal Journalism: Dana, Godkin, and Bennett

In the post-Civil War era, three newspaper owner-editors maintained the American tradition of great individuals in journalism. Charles Dana, E. L. Godkin, and James Gordon Bennett Jr. left lasting marks on the field. Upon hearing of Dana's purchase of the *New York Sun* in 1868, the paper's founder, Benjamin Day, declared that the new editor-in-chief would "make a newspaper of it." With the help of the profession's brightest writers, Dana made an international name for himself, his staff, and his newspaper. He proclaimed that a newspaper's duty is to give readers good writing. "The invariable law of the newspaper," he declared, "is to be interesting." As editor of the opinion journal *The Nation*, Godkin was America's leading thinker on the public issues of the last quarter of the nineteenth century. For many social problems, he blamed "newspapers and other cheap periodicals ... [which] have diffused through the community a kind of smattering of all sorts of knowledge, a taste for reading and for 'art' — that is, a desire to see and own pictures — which ... pass with a large body of slenderly equipped persons as 'culture.'" The son of the *New York Herald's* founder, James Gordon Bennett Jr. brought to the newspaper a similar instinct for news and sensationalism that his father had possessed. Despite his lavish expenditures on himself from the *Herald's* income, the paper was able to remain a circulation leader throughout the last decades of the 1800s.

deadly serious about his editorial views. After Bryant retired as editor of the *Post*, his son-in-law, Parke Godwin, served as editor until 1878, when he sold the paper to Henry Villard. In 1881 Villard made Godkin a co-editor and in 1883 the sole editor. Neither the *Nation* nor the *Evening Post* could compete with the *Sun* for news coverage or popularity; nor did Godkin wish them to. He was not interested in the news departments of his papers and concentrated instead on the editorial pages. Because of his intellect and forceful writing style, he was the foremost leader of public opinion in his day. The philosopher William James wrote of him: "To my generation, his was certainly the towering influence in all thought concerning public affairs, and indirectly his influence has assuredly been more pervasive than that of any other writer of the generation, for he influenced other writers who never quoted him, and determined the whole current of discussion."[8] During his editorship of the *Nation* and the *Evening Post*, Godkin never had more than 35,000 subscribers, but they included leaders of public opinion such as clergymen, lawyers, and college professors, who helped disseminate his views to large audiences.

From an upper-middle-class background, Godkin had little sympathy for the masses in America's growing cities. Yet he was the nation's most effective advocate of many reforms. He preferred to look beneath the surface of issues to find underlying principles, thus bringing an insight that few people could match and offering penetrating analyses of public questions in a clear,

forceful writing style. While his writing could be light and witty, it also could be sharp and cutting. The story was told of an old woman in upstate New York who was asked if she was afraid living alone in the country. No, she replied, for every evening the carrier threw her copy of the *Evening Post* onto her porch, and "it just lay there and growled all night."

The other major figure in New York journalism was James Gordon Bennett Jr., heir to his father's newspaper, the *New York Herald*, as well as to his father's taste for sensational news. In 1872 he inherited a fortune valued at more than $2 million and a newspaper with an international reputation. Spoiled from childhood by his doting parents, he was raised on wealth. During his fifty-year ownership of the *Herald*, he withdrew an estimated $30 million for his personal fancies. In 1877 his engagement to a New York City socialite was broken off after the inebriated Bennett urinated in the fireplace at a social gathering. After his fiancee's brother horsewhipped him, the embarrassed Bennett fled to France. From there, he served as absentee owner and editorial director of the *Herald* for the remainder of his life.

Despite his egotism and other faults, Bennett recognized that it was news that had made the *Herald* successful. During the 1870s it remained the nation's leading paper in the amount, speed, and thoroughness of its coverage. Like his father, Bennett sensed what people wanted. Two of the most famous episodes in American news resulted from the *Herald's* initiative. The paper financed Henry Stanley's successful search for the physician and missionary David Livingstone; and it perpetrated the "wild animal hoax,"

[8]Quoted in Edwin Lawrence Godkin, *Life and Letters of Edwin Lawrence Godkin*, Vol. 1, Rollo Ogdin, ed. (London, 1907), 221.

The Wild Animal Hoax

AWFUL CALAMITY.

The Wild Animals Broken Loose from Central Park.
TERRIBLE SCENES OF MUTILATION.
A Shocking Sabbath Carnival of Death.

On Monday morning, November 9, 1874, the *New York Herald* reported to shocked readers that the animals housed in Central Park Zoo were prowling the city's streets, mauling and devouring citizens. The vivid full-page article described a "bloody and fearful carnival."

The great escape began when a zoo keeper teased a rhinoceros. Enraged, the rhino burst out of its cage and "plunged blindly" into other cages, setting the most dangerous animals free.

The rampaging rhino trampled a zoo attendant, attacked a group of young girls, "gored a horse" on 19th Street, and continued to terrorize the public until falling into a sewer.

Other animals followed the shrieking and scurrying crowds into the streets. A leopard killed a child and mutilated several women. A lion horrified a church congregation, killing an elderly woman. A tiger pounced onto a ferryboat docked at 29th Street, causing the horses and carriages to plunge into the water, "dragging their human loads with them."

Three regiments of the National Guard, the police, and the mayor were unable to restrain the animals. General Chester A. Arthur prepared a crusade against the beasts. Governor John A. Dix shot a tiger on Madison Avenue. Whitelaw Reid, of the *Times*, and Charles Dana, of the *Sun*, were said to have already donated $50 each for the victims.

At least 200 men, women, and children were reported as dead or maimed, and the article listed more than twenty by name.

Twelve of the "wild, carnivorous beasts" were "still at large" the next morning. A proclamation from the mayor urged citizens to stay inside their homes.

Readers panicked. Rushing home from work, men armed themselves and stalked the streets, hoping to kill the animals. Parents pulled their children out of school.

Most were so excited that they did not read the article through to the end. Had they done so, they would have learned that it was nothing more than a prank. "Of course," readers would have found out, "the entire story given above is a pure fabrication. Not one word of it is true.... It is a huge hoax ... a wild romance...."

The cartoonist Thomas Nast lampooned the *New York Herald* and its owner, James Gordon Bennett Jr., for months after the wild animal hoax. In the cartoon above, he criticized Democratic papers as wild animals escaping from a zoo. In the cartoon on the left, he satirized Bennett as a promoter of inane causes. *Harper's Weekly* published cartoons about the hoax for more than a year.

Thomas Connery, the *Herald's* editor, came up with the idea, and reporter Joseph I. C. Clarke crafted the gruesome account.

The public was upset at the stunt. Critics charged the *Herald* with being irresponsible and malicious.

A brief explanation in the *Herald* the next day rationalized that the intent was to highlight safety issues at the zoo. Yet the reason was not good enough to console angered members of the press.

The *New York Tribune* urged the arrest of the *Herald* reporters. The *Times* denounced the "heartless newspaper hoax." The *Sun* condemned it as "unfeeling, cruel, heartless" and labeled it "a mere piece of stupidity." The papers claimed that the hoax not only damaged the integrity of the *Herald* but also detracted from journalism as a whole.

Today, the "wild animal hoax" is known as one of the most outrageous – and interesting – a newspaper ever perpetrated.

which terrified New York City residents with reports of animals escaped from the zoo roaming the streets. The paper always had emphasized human interest and sensational subjects. Its approach was exemplified by the observation of one of its editors that "a dogfight in New York is more newsworthy than a revolution in China." The *Herald* maintained its circulation until the 1880s, when Joseph Pulitzer arrived in New York City. Still, in 1890, it and Bennett's two other newspapers, the *New York Telegram* and the *Paris Herald*, the paper's international edition, were making a combined annual profit of $1 million. The *Herald*, however, gradually was sinking. Bennett died in 1918, and the *Herald* merged with the *Tribune* in 1924.

Some of the new editors after the Civil War, such as Dana and Godkin, continued to imprint a highly personal character on their papers and to consider editorial opinion the most important function of the press. Others, however, followed the path laid down by the senior Bennett in the 1830s and began putting more effort into producing news than presenting views. A number of circumstances encouraged this shift in the role of newspapers. For one thing, the modern daily paper was rapidly becoming a huge, heavily capitalized industrial plant. No longer would an editor-owner, with a modest political subsidy and a printing business on the side, be able to finance a mass daily in which to press his party's opinions. The need for abundant capital would split the functions of ownership and management, forcing editors from the 1870s on to serve increasingly as hired help.

AN INDEPENDENT PRESS

The metropolitan press was first to undergo a metamorphosis from political partisanship to political independence, but there were rough times as the great newspapers in New York, Boston, and Philadelphia worked out their reason for being. The shifting social, economic, and political structures of the country required changes, but change required effort and involved risk. Not everyone saw clearly the signs. A few who did pushed and cajoled their reluctant comrades.

One of those reformers was David Croly, managing editor of the *New York World*. During his tenure a contemporary claimed the *World* could have been a model for city newspapers because its news dealt with the important issues of the day and included something of interest to the genteel as well as the proletariat. Croly argued for impartial news, "given regardless of parties or persons, and without the slightest tinge of personal or partisan bias." He believed the public's views had changed, which "compelled the leading papers to refrain from printing distorted news, so that now the reports of meetings and the statements of political opponents are, in the main, correctly stated." Nevertheless, three years after the war, only the *New York Herald* practiced what Croly preached. To his mind, it was the outstanding paper in the country. It would hold that position until someone else equaled "it in enterprise and independence, and surpass[ed] it in earnestness,

ability, dignity, and moral purpose."[9]

Political independence meant editors were free to criticize their own parties' political leadership and policies when those leaders and policies were incorrect or corrupt. Some made a distinction, however, between parties and politicians. Whitelaw Reid's *New York Tribune* outlined the distinction in 1876 in response to a critical letter from a reader. Using a metaphor in which the Republican Party was a ship, the editor wrote: "We have scraped the barnacles from the bottom of the hull, but we have not sought to blow up, or burn, or scuttle the ship. In 1874, when a piratical gang [unscrupulous supporters of President Grant] gained possession of the decks and drove the regular ship's company into the hold, we joined the enemy's boats and attacked, not the ship, but those who had seized control of her and cast her adrift.... The pennant of Grantism has been torn down and the Old Republican colors are today flying at the masthead."[10] Even political newspapers could criticize the Party when pirates had gained control of the ship.

Despite the growing party independence, daily newspapers did not adopt a standardized, non-partisan approach. Independence did not mean "neutrality." Nearly everybody agreed on that, but the country's urban centers contained a considerable mix of newspapers that defied neat classification. In Chicago, for instance, the two leading newspapers were the *Times* of Wilbur F. Storey and the *Tribune*, after 1874 under Joseph Medill's editorial control. Both editors actively covered city news, generally avoided shaping news to conform to politics, and took editorial positions independent of their respective parties, but they nevertheless expressed strong views on opposite sides of political questions. There were many other well-known such papers in large cities.

Some independent editors had even recanted of their heresy. Murat Halstead, editor and proprietor of the *Cincinnati Commercial*, late in his career recounted his personal odyssey:

One who gave a good many years to independent journalism — preached it, and strove to practice it — held that the position of the journalist was outside and above parties — that the greater the men of the party the greater the necessity for hostile watchfulness, and for holding them in restraint by healthful severities; that the more certain the party was good, the clearer the duty to inform it of its faults — one with such an experience may speak of this theory [of independence] with freedom. The difficulty is that professional and dominating independence inclines to the habit of fault-finding, and leaves the fault-finder hanging rather to the fringes, or wandering on the edges of affairs, than taking them by the handle or the helm and guiding the course of events. It is the better way to go with parties, to be devoted to them, on the inside of them, to make the best of them, stick to them, maintaining their discipline, asserting the principles that they represent.... If the party will go unteachably, irreclaimably wrong, get out of it and try another.[11]

[9]D. G. Croly, "What a Newspaper Should Be," *Putnam's*, N.S., 1 (March 1868): 330, 331.
[10]"Neutrality in Politics," *New York Daily Tribune*, 4 November 1876, 6.
[11]"Maxims of the Press," *New York Tribune*, 24 January 1889, 7.

Stanley Finds Livingstone

To increase circulation and advertising, newspapers began to rely on "big news" and "stunts." The most successful in the 1870s was Bennett's *New York Herald*. The biggest stunt was reporter Henry Morton Stanley's search for the "missing" missionary doctor David Livingstone in southern Africa. Stanley's final story in his account ended with the famous words, "Dr. Livingstone, I presume?"

Epic Adventure Ends with History's Most Famous Greeting

The *New York Herald's* publisher gave correspondent Henry Morton Stanley a two-word assignment in October 1869: "Find Livingstone." The veteran reporter barely survived the search.

British missionary and medical doctor David Livingstone had disappeared four years earlier in East Africa's equatorial jungles. Known for his good works and books about the largely unexplored African continent, Livingstone was a Victorian Era celebrity. But rumors now circulated among the enclaves of Europeans on the African coast that cannibals had killed him. Finding Livingstone, dead or alive, would help the *Herald* maintain the preeminence earned by its Civil War coverage, reasoned publisher James Gordon Bennett, Jr.

He ordered the *Herald's* star reporter to work his way to Africa. Late in 1869, Stanley covered the Suez Canal opening and spent 1870 filing stories from the Middle East and North Africa. Starting from the

island of Zanzibar early in 1871, he sailed to the southeast African coast and began his trek toward Livingstone's last known camp more than 600 miles inland on Lake Tanganyika. During his 236-day journey, he contracted malaria and lost forty pounds. He also participated in a war between Arab traders and Africans that delayed his expedition for months.

But two years and twenty-four days after receiving his assignment, Stanley finally reached the object of his search and asked the question that would link him forever with one of the great scoops of journalism: "Doctor Livingstone, I presume?"

Stanley spent four months with the doctor before returning to Zanzibar. Livingstone died a year after they parted, and Stanley served as one of his pallbearers during a Westminster Abbey funeral. He returned to Africa to take up Livingstone's exploration work.

He conducted other African expeditions, but his relationship with Bennett soured. The publisher often noted that Stanley might have found Livingstone, but Bennett paid for the trip.

New Leaders for a New Era
Taking over the *New York Tribune* from Horace Greeley, Whitelaw Reid (left) eschewed Greeley's advocacy of popular causes and turned the paper into a voice for the "respectable" class. He argued that newspapers should be independent of politicians but not of parties. Reflecting journalism's move toward political independence, Murat Halstead (center) of the *Cincinnati Commercial* had taken that approach during much of his career. In later years, however, he recanted. "Dominating independence," he declared, "inclines to the habit of fault-finding," leaving journalists on the fringe of the political system. As a correspondent for the *Chicago Press and Tribune* before the Civil War, Horace White (right) formed a close, friendly relationship with Abraham Lincoln, a fellow opponent of slavery and leader in the new Republican Party. During Reconstruction, he was prominent as the reform-minded, liberal Republican editor of the *Tribune*.

Despite Halstead's forceful views on partisanship, most independents felt otherwise, and they offered many reasons of their views: politicians were not to be trusted, for they reneged on promises of postmaster positions or government printing when they got into office; readers no longer were interested in so much political coverage and comment; and more readers were attracted to the independent press, which was an inducement to advertisers.[12]

In 1881 a southern writer offered a stronger view: Partisan editors were fools. A newspaper that is "An 'organ' [for a political party] makes only such music as its master may order; ... the editor supplies the place of the monkey in picking up the coppers." The only safety for an editor was to be "right and independent."[13] This expression came late in our period, for the southern press was slow to embrace political independence. In the convention minutes of Mississippi publishers from 1866 to 1884, it was mentioned only twice. It was not a popular topic in the South.[14]

Few people in the pre-Civil War era had expected the press to be independent; and the widespread criticism of political or class influence on the news after the war[15] indicated that editors and publishers were adopting different news values. Several reasons accounted for the changes. One was the new generation of journalists coming on the scene. Their views of politics and government, as well as of journalism's role in portraying them, had been shaped in the crucible of the Civil War. They could never be the same as the generation whose "righteousness" had brought about the war. This rejection played an important role in shaping news values for the next several decades.

Equally important were three concurrent changes occurring in journalism that fostered the independence movement: Editors increasingly questioned the value of editorials as compared to news in shaping public opinion and attracting readers; stock ownership became the mode for financing newspapers; and advertising grew increasingly important as a means of support and profit.

As for the first change, astute observers, including many in journalism itself, recognized that news shaped public opinion more than editorials. A hundred years later journalism scholars would call this "agenda setting." Several arguments were advanced in the 1870s and '80s to support this view. Many readers took the paper for the news rather than opinion and tended to neglect the editorial page.[16] One experienced writer claimed, "Edi-

[12]Eugene H. Munday, "Sunday Dispatch," *The Proof-Sheet* 4 (November 1870): 42, noted that the owners of the *Philadelphia Sunday Mercury* became disenchanted because the Democratic party leadership did not reciprocate the support from the paper; so the publishers charged cash for all political ads and made themselves independent of the party's managers. The views of readers were discussed by H. P. Hall, "Independent Journalism" (speech given in Minneapolis, 3 February 1874), appendix to *Eighth Annual Session of the Minnesota Editorial Association*; reprinted in *Proceedings of the Minnesota Editors and Publishers Association, 1871-1874* (St. Paul, 1874); and Howard Owen, "Advertising Rates and Agencies" (speech, 1874), *Transactions of the Maine Editor and Publishers Association, From 1870 to 1874, Inclusive* (Wiscasset, Me., 1874), 25. Owen was publisher of the *Kennebec Journal* of Augusta, Maine.

[13]Hugh Wilson's speech reported in *Seventh Annual Meeting of the South Carolina State Press Association* (Greenville, S.C., May 4, 1881), 23, 24.

[14]*Proceedings of the Mississippi Press Association from May 1866 to May 1884* (Jackson, Miss., 1885). Only George W. Harper, "The Country Press," June 1879, 147, and R. Walpole, president of the Mississippi Press Association in 1882 and publisher of the *Yazoo City Herald*, 205, mentioned the idea. It should be noted that the southern press was in large measure a country press, and the country press generally was slower to espouse "independence" than its big-city contemporaries.

[15]M. J. Savage, "A Profane View of the Sanctum," *North American Review* 141 (August 1885): 49; "Wendell Phillips on the Press," *New York Tribune*, 5 December 1879): 2; George William Curtis, *Ars Recte Vivandi* (New York, 1898), 99; Anonymous, "The Newspaper," *Printers' Circular* 13:3 (May 1878): 55, reprinted from the *San Francisco Argonaut*, and Anonymous, "The Adulteration of News," *The Nation*, 12 August 1880, 107.

[16]Editorial, "News Versus Editorials," *Printers' Circular* 10:10 (December 1875): 266.

torials are read and forgotten. Facts remain and are remembered. It is the news column, not the editorial page, which forms public opinion. In the long run, men do their own thinking [based] on the facts which are stored in their memory...."[17] The influence of the editorial had long since waned, according to these critics. It was the events — and the reporting of them — that shaped opinion.[18]

Other writers thought the editorial still affected public opinion, but only when editors recognized public concerns. It was, they argued, the public that influenced the press, and successful editors molded that ill-formed opinion, but not if they fought it. Cincinnati's Murat Halstead, basing his conclusion on long experience, wrote, "The press does not form, it reflects public opinion. It does not make, it partakes of the character of the people."[19] Couple these concepts with the view that newspapers should present news the "public most desires to read,"[20] as Charles Dana argued, and one can see why the press had to adopt different news values.

The reasons for starting newspapers also changed. That newspapers were established to make money had always been true — but publishers and editors talked so much about politics and the public-opinion role of the press that people forgot its money-making purpose. Contemporary commentators did not forget. Time and again they noted that this aspect of journalism had come to dominate journalism. Charles Dudley Warner, an editor who with Mark Twain in 1873 wrote *The Gilded Age* — a name that stuck to the period — said of the press: "The newspaper is a private enterprise. Its object is to make money for its owner. Whatever motive may be given out for starting a newspaper, expectation of profit by it is the *real one*, whether the newspaper is religious, political, scientific, or literary."[21]

To attain this objective — to make money — publishers and editors increasingly sold stock to raise capital. Selling stock ultimately would cause most editors to lose financial control of their papers, but not during our era. Where the editor did not maintain control, the manager might use his authority over the budget to maximize profits. Dividends became more important than politics. When Horace White gained editorial control of the *Chicago Tribune* following the war, he redirected the paper's policies toward liberal rather than radical Republicanism. The change may have cost the paper circulation, but since expenses were kept low and advertising made the paper profitable, no stockholder criticized White's redirection of the editorial page. When the paper lost money following the Panic of 1873, however, the business manager and chief stockholder asked Joseph Medill to become editor.[22]

The means of earning profit also changed. Advertising became more important than political and government subsidies for metropolitan newspapers and even surpassed circulation income. By 1879 nearly 54% of all newspaper income was derived from advertising. This figure included daily newspapers with weekly editions.[23] Metropolitan dailies probably had a much higher percentage of income from advertising. The daily edition of the *New York World*, for instance, earned 47% of its income from advertising in 1866, the first full year of peace. The next year that figure reached 50%. Only once in the next nine years did it drop below 50%, and that was because 1868 was a year filled with important news, including the impeachment of President Andrew Johnson and the election campaign of Gen. Ulysses S. Grant on a Radical Republican platform.[24] That year newsstand sales of the *World* jumped 43%, while advertising increased less than 1%. In 1873 the paper earned 61% of its income from advertising. The *World* was weak compared with such New York newspapers as the *Herald* and *Tribune*, leading one to think that the strong papers earned a higher percentage of income from advertising than the census figures reveal. The Panic of 1873 was devastating to the *World*. Advertising dropped in 1874 and did not recover to pre-1873 levels until after Joseph Pulitzer bought the paper in 1883.[25]

The importance of advertising support was not lost on other editors and publishers. To sell more advertising, publishers responded to the new realities of the marketplace. They justified their conversion by arguing that advertising freed editor and publisher alike from political partisanship.

CHANGING STRATEGIES IN ADVERTISING

Just as journalism was responding to changes in society, so too were advertisers and agents. America's increased manufacturing capacity, a result of the Civil War, produced a surplus capacity in some goods. The difficulty lay in distributing and selling those goods since wholesalers or "jobbers," as they were called, determined what goods would be produced and distributed. Manufacturers submitted bids to supply wholesalers with the finished product. Since products did not have brand names, wholesalers were interested in them only as generic goods, and the lowest bid got the order.

A few manufacturers, however, did not pursue this practice. The patent medicine industry already had shown manufacturers there was a way for them to gain control of their products, if they were willing to take a risk. Patent medicines had brand names,

[17]An Old Journalist, "Power-Centres," *Lippincott's* 27 (February 1881): 179.

[18]David Croly claimed that public opinion is "created or moulded by public events,...the fluctuations of commerce, ... changes in population, the rise, progress, and decay of religious and industrial organizations, ... the conflict of races." Croly, "What a Newspaper Should Be," 333.

[19]"Maxims of the Press," *New York Tribune*, 24 January 1889.

[20]Quoted in Frederic Hudson, *Journalism in the United States, From 1690 to 1872* (New York, 1873), 680. Hudson reprints the article "The Newspaper Press" from the *New York Tribune* of 1850. Dana expressed this view *before* the Civil War.

[21]Charles Dudley Warner, *The American Newspaper* (Boston, 1881), 5. Originally read before the Social Science Association, Saratoga Springs, N.Y., 8 September 1881. (Italics added.)

[22]Lloyd Wendt, *Chicago Tribune. The Rise of a Great American Newspaper* (Chicago, 1979), 243-7.

[23]S. N. D. North, "The Newspaper Press of the United States," *International Review* 12 (1882): 200. An analysis of the census figures shows that 49.17% of newspaper income was from advertising, but North used a figure of 53.79% in the *International Review* article. The reason for the discrepancy is unclear. Weeklies by themselves got only 38.95% from advertising. S. N. D. North, *History and Present Condition of the Newspaper and Periodical Press of the United States, With a Catallogue of the Publications of the Census Year* (Washington, D.C., 1884), Table IV, 179. This was a special report of the Census.

[24]*New York World* account book, Manton Marble Papers, Vol. 42, Folio #9346, Library of Congress. The accounts run from 1863 to 1875.

[25]Calculations from a memo in *New York World* Papers, Box 1882-1885 Nov. The memo is in the January 1883 folder and summarizes advertising income for 1878-1882. It does not provide circulation income.

thus allowing producers to advertise them directly to the ultimate buyer, the consumer. The consumer, in turn, spurred by advertising and the "efficacy" of the medicine, asked the retailer for the medicine by name. The retailer then ordered that product from his supplier, usually a wholesaler or the manufacturer himself. Patent medicines were ideal for marketing because they were distinctive and cheap to produce and had a large profit margin, thus enabling producers to advertise extensively to build a market.

In the post-Civil War era, other manufacturers began to think of their products as distinctive, too, and to affix a brand name that they then could advertise. Thus the growth of brand names, coupled with new products coming on the market in the next several decades, provided the rationale for extensive advertising in newspapers and on fence posts and the sides of barns.

Another distinctive change was occurring simultaneously in retailing. One-product stores, such as women's clothing, hardware, or silverware, were too small to advertise extensively in the metropolitan papers. Most served a small area rather than the entire city. That situation changed, however, with the advent of the department store, in which numerous specialty shops became departments within a large store. A. T. Stewart in New York City opened the first such store in the United States in 1853. Macy's started in New York a decade later, as did Wanamaker in Philadelphia. All were fixed-price stores — that is, customers could not dicker, and clerks could not reduce the price. The stores emphasized extensive advertising in newspapers. Wanamaker hired an advertising writer to prepare his.

This revolution in retailing affected the newspaper in ways in addition to advertising. It stimulated the development of evening editions, which were targeted to women in the home, and spurred the spread of the Sunday newspaper, which carried news directly to the home to reach women and children.

These changes stimulated the growth of advertising. Despite the Panic of 1873, which depressed the economy for five years, total advertising grew from $40 million in 1867 to $175 million in 1880. Publishers eagerly tapped into this burgeoning market.[26]

Advertising flowed increasingly into newspaper coffers, freeing editors from financial pressures to serve political parties and politicians. The freedom, however, was not absolute, nor was it without its own cost. Publishers and editors soon found that advertisers were little better than politicians when it came to demands. At editorial convention after editorial convention, in the East, South, and West, editors condemned advertising agents because of their constant demands for discounts and preferred placement of ads, the use of reading notices,[27] and refusal to pay bills if

Rowland Macy
Macy went broke four times, but he was one of the handful of entrepreneurs who revolutionized retailing with the department store. One of the most important advances that the stores made was to advertise extensively in newspapers.

the advertiser failed.[28] These demands were irritating, but they dealt with business issues. More important was the impact the increased advertising had on the news product.

ADVERTISING'S INFLUENCE ON THE PRESS

Editors expressed concern about advertisers who acted as if their dollars gave them the right to influence the newspaper's editorial positions, or news itself, especially if the news was about their store, product, or family. Yet, advertising's *indirect* and *unintended* influences on the business offices and news values were more important. These latter influences were seldom noted publicly during the era. Only in retrospect can we determine their importance.

Believing they had a legitimate right to the editorial or news columns of papers that carried their advertising, many advertisers threatened boycotts of newspapers because of editorial positions on candidates, critical news coverage, or increases in advertising rates. Every element of the paper ultimately was influenced. Most boycotts were undertaken by local rather than national advertisers; and few, it is fair to say, were a response to political positions. After all, until newspapers truly became independent of party, advertisers expected them to take political stances. Few general advertisers felt so strongly about a paper's politics that they would

---

[26]These are total advertising figures from various government sources. Newspaper and periodical advertising was always less than this. In 1867 it was about $10 million, and in 1880 nearly $40 million.

[27]Reading notices were of two kinds, but both were written by the advertiser and appeared in the news columns disguised as news stories: 1) Reading notices were published "free" as a bonus to advertisers who had purchased "display" ads, or 2) space for reading notices was purchased along with the display ads and alternated publication dates. Patent medicine proprietors were particularly prone to reader ads, frequently using their entire space in such copy. In every case, the reader notice was set in the same type as the news columns and appeared in those columns.

[28]Several agents did pay their bills, even if the advertiser failed. Both Rowell and Ayer were noted for this practice.

club together with competitors to boycott a paper. Still, if they got excited enough, some would apply pressure. During the nation-wide strike of railroads in 1877, for instance, local merchants, most of them advertisers of the *Chicago Daily News*, claimed the paper was "inflaming" public opinion against the railroads. They asked the paper to stop publishing the news. Melville E. Stone, editor, and Victor Lawson, publisher, refused their request.[29]

Advertiser pressure on editors and publishers would increase in the years ahead, spurred in part by national efforts of patent medicine manufacturers. Such overt pressure would become an oft-told tale in journalism, and it would influence newspaper content. Because it is the most obvious kind of pressure, it has been criticized through the years. In the total scheme of journalism, however, such pressure has been minimal.

Other changes, however, did greatly affect the press. Earlier business managers had accepted advertising as it came to them. The growth in advertising, however, caused business managers to hire advertising managers. Along with the traditional job of preparing ads for display in the newspapers, they were expected to solicit advertising as well. Soon, they hired more men — women were not employed in the job — to sell advertising space to retailers, manufacturers, and advertising agents. As newspapers courted more advertising, they made themselves vulnerable to advertiser demands.[30]

Most of these demands were legitimate. Wanting to know what they were getting for their money, advertisers asked newspapers to provide circulation figures. When that finally occurred, advertisers then pressed for *accurate* as well as *meaningful* figures. For decades, papers had refused to provide circulation figures. Since they were not actively seeking advertising, they could be cavalier. Solicitors, though, found that selling space required circulation figures. So they importuned newspaper management to publicize circulation figures to advertisers.[31] Publishers and business managers began doing so. Unfortunately, they exaggerated their figures in order to beat competing papers in the chase for advertising. Inflated figures were a widespread problem. Francis Wayland Ayer, a leading advertising agent, spoke of it in 1876, after claiming that advertisers had as much right to know the correct circulation as a merchant buying a barrel of flour had the right to know the correct weight of its contents. Ayer divided publishers into four classes:

1. Those who willingly state their circulation and do it correctly, affording facilities for proof of their statements if desired.
2. Those who decline to give figures, on the ground that if they give them at all they will do so honestly, but as their neighbors are given to falsifying, such a statement would be unjust to themselves.

SMITH BROTHERS

TRADE · MARK

Product Brand Names
In the post-Civil War era, some manufacturers began to think of their products as distinctive and to use brand names that they could advertise. Two of the earliest brand-name logos were Smith Brothers cough drops and Levi Strauss pants.

3. Those who are always willing to give the desired information, but invariably add very largely to the actual figures, and when requested to furnish proof have no recourse but to decline.
4. Those who falsely report their circulation, and for proof try to palm off spurious affidavits or some similar device.[32]

Still, many publishers did offer accurate circulation figures and fixed ad rates that crafty advertising agents could not whittle down. It is not surprising that these new publishers, coming on the scene in the 1870s, were the leaders in the new journalism that began to dominate the press in the 1880s. The leaders were in the West, but New York, Boston, and Philadelphia each had honest publishers willing to stand on their circulation and rates.

Another influence of advertising was in shaping newspaper content. Newspapers relied upon "big news" to increase sales. "Big news" was defined as news that attracted readers of all class-

[29]Charles H. Dennis, *Victor Lawson. His Time and His Work* (Chicago, 1935), 41-4.
[30]See Ted Curtis Smythe, "The Advertisers' War to Verify Newspaper Circulation," *Journalism History* 3 (1986): 167-80, which summarizes the development of advertising departments in newspapers and offers conclusions about their influence on management and advertising practices.
[31]Don C. Seitz, *Training for the Newspaper Trade* (Philadelphia, 1916), 98-9. ·
[32]"Newspaper Circulation," *N. W. Ayer & Son's Advertisers Guide* 1 (September 1876): 51.

Success in the Midwest

After the Civil War, Chicago increased its importance as a center for vibrant journalism. With the *Chicago Daily News*, whose first issue was published December 23, 1875, Victor Lawson (inset) and Melville Stone built a highly successful newspaper based on fairness in reporting and on political and commercial independence. In beginning the paper, 27-year-old Stone (far right) said that the first duty of a newspaper was simply "to print news." The *Daily News* would be engaged in "something else than a mere business enterprise in which we would seek to provide anything and everything the public might crave." He was one of the editors responsible for the idea of the press' political independence.

es — political campaigns, disasters, crime, and so forth. Really "BIG news" attracted even more readers. It included such items as hotly contested presidential elections, marathon walking matches, and bicycling events.[33] Major news events, however, did not occur regularly; so circulation would fluctuate dramatically. On some days there was little news of significance or interest, resulting in declines in circulation. These fluctuations could occur because many large dailies relied on street sales rather than subscriptions. From the advertiser's standpoint, such fluctuations amounted to poor business.[34] An ad placed in a paper on the day of a major news event earned far more readership than was paid for, but some days — and one never knew when they would occur — a dearth of news earned less readership. The editor and publisher sought ways of eliminating these "dips" by raising circulation to a straight line, punctuated only by the "bumps" resulting from major news events. Subscriptions would have accomplished the goal, but major newspapers never relied entirely on subscriptions.

Instead, they reduced the dips by increasing "small news," news attractive only to a small audience, but for which that audience would return day after day. It required departmentalization — putting news into columns devoted to sports, society, labor, business, law, and other areas. The list expanded as editors found readers attracted to the news and advertisers attracted to those publications that carried departmentalized news. Specialized news quickly expanded from a column to several columns and then, as papers increased in size, to a full page.

Advertising spurred the development of this form of news.

"[A]s a rule," one successful publisher said, "a newspaper can secure more satisfactory growth out of specialties than by the extravagant exploitation of general news. In a competitive field a newspaper either succeeds or fails according to its features and individuality."[35]

NEW PUBLISHERS AND EDITORS

Not every publisher and editor understood these changes or wanted to participate in them. The old ways were comfortable and familiar. The new ways required hard work and great risk. Several publishers and editors stood out for their leadership in the new, independent journalism based upon legitimate business practices that attracted advertising and generated profit. Those publishers were largely in the West and in two major eastern cities, Boston and Philadelphia. New York had no one who grasped the new way of journalism, not even James Gordon Bennett Jr. or Charles Dana. They had led the way in New York City, but now even they were to lag behind the kind of journalism that the newcomers personified.

The new publishers and editors understood the role not only of the news and editorial side of the paper but also the business side. One of the members of this breed was 27-year-old Charles H. Taylor. He was hired as editor of the year-old *Boston Globe* in 1873, a few months after the first department store opened in Boston and one month before the great Panic of 1873. Knowing nothing about managing a newspaper, he threw himself into resurrecting a badly run paper, what one wag called a "weekly paper published every day."[36] A Republican paper, it was losing $60,000 annually

[33]"News and Newspaper Circulation," *New York Sun*, 21 May 1882, 4. Until 1882 the largest circulation the *Sun* had ever attained followed the presidential election of 1876 between Tilden and Hayes. Sales reached 222,390. Presidential election reports normally increased circulation 73 per cent, indicating that some political news was of interest to some people.

[34]Circulation income also fluctuated, making it important to level out the dips in order to keep circulation income at a steady level and to reduce the number of copies returned to the publisher by newsstand dealers.

[35]Jason Rogers, *Newspaper Building. Applications of Efficiency to Editing, to Mechanical Production, to Circulation and Advertising* (New York, 1918), 252.

[36]Quoted in James Morgan, *Charles H. Taylor. Builder of the Boston Globe* (N.P. [Boston], 1923), 49.

and would continue to lose money until Taylor gained control in 1878 and had total freedom to revamp it. He had started a Sunday paper in 1877, which became a huge success, and twice cut the price of the daily, finally arriving at two cents in 1878. He launched an evening edition that same year. Although he changed the political support of the paper to the Democrats, he gave fair and accurate treatment to Republican views. He added news for women, forcing men to take the paper home where it was more valuable to the advertiser, especially the department store. He added sports, reporting important sporting events on the front page — which appalled old-time journalists but attracted new readers. Within a year the paper broke even. The second year, it made a profit, and Taylor became one of the notable leaders of the new journalism.

Another leader was Victor F. Lawson. He bought controlling interest in the penny evening *Chicago Daily News* in July 1876, several months after his high school friend Melville E. Stone had established the paper and four months before his twenty-sixth birthday. With Stone continuing as editor, Lawson's business and journalistic skills turned the paper around, making it financially successful. Together they carved out of Chicago's highly competitive environment a new kind of journalism based on fairness in reporting, and political and commercial independence in the editorial columns.

From the first, Lawson demanded accuracy in circulation figures, based upon actual sales instead of print runs, and asked low — but fixed — prices for advertising based on circulation. He began publicizing average weekly circulation when, within a year of the paper's founding, it climbed above 10,000. He would not lie about circulation, but when December figures did not appear in the paper — and November's average remained — one knew the circulation had fallen. In 1878 Lawson bought the assets of the bankrupt *Post and Mail* for its evening Associated Press franchise. In 1881 he began the six-day *Morning News*, later renamed the *Record,* a reversal of the usual practice in which morning papers started evening editions. Also unlike most new journalism publishers, he would not offer a Sunday newspaper, despite its certainty of money making, because of his religious beliefs.

Melville Stone, meanwhile, was exploring local news and exploiting it for readership. During the Hayes-Tilden presidential campaign of 1876, the *Daily News* supported neither party editorially and did not comment on the candidates, yet it provided full coverage of campaign events and the contested results. Although sympathetic toward labor, both Stone and Lawson believed in an evenhanded approach to the news, thus providing a new kind of journalism in Chicago.

In St. Louis, a rapidly growing city just behind Chicago in the West, two men led the way toward the new journalism. The first was Joseph B. McCullagh, who, at the age of thirty-one, became editor of the *Morning Globe* in 1872. With wide experience as a war correspondent and editor in Cincinnati and Chicago, he brought a fresh style to St. Louis journalism. He demanded that the news be accurate and free of political taint, and he vigorously sought news in all corners of the city. In 1874 he bought a morning Associated

St. Louis Post-Dispatch

Even though Joseph Pulitzer is best known for his news and circulation successes, page one of the first issue of the *St. Louis Post-Dispatch* under his ownership clearly demonstrates the emphasis he placed on advertisements, which filled four of the page's seven columns.

Press franchise, which forced the competitive *Democrat* to agree to a consolidation, creating the *Globe-Democrat,* a paper that would dominate St. Louis journalism for years. McCullagh started special columns of religious news and daily railroad reports, for the city was finally becoming a railway hub.

A competitor, Joseph Pulitzer, soon joined the newspaper wars. The 31-year-old Pulitzer successfully bid for the bankrupt *Evening Dispatch* in 1878. His prize was the paper's evening Associated Press franchise, because the paper's assets were nearly worthless. John Dillon of the *Evening Post* quickly met with Pulitzer. The *Post* was one of two evening papers recently to start in St. Louis. A merger of the *Post* and *Dispatch* resulted from the meeting. Both Pulitzer and Dillon already had established their political independence although neither was politically neutral. Pulitzer was the driving force in the newsgathering and business side of the paper. It was not in his nature to share control, and within a year he bought out Dillon.

Pulitzer developed a vigorous newsgathering and exploitative journalism, adopted the "known circulation" policy, and followed a vigorous solicitation policy for advertising by building "Wants" through free insertions until the "object of the wants" had been attained. The morning *Globe-Democrat* carried far more columns than the *Post-Dispatch*, but Pulitzer built a steady income and readership, especially notable for an evening paper in St. Louis.[37]

The next year Pulitzer brought in John Cockerill as managing editor. Cockerill installed a more vigorous news style, one more sensational and active even than Pulitzer's. The 35-year-old Cockerill had wide experience in western journalism, but when he killed a local attorney in 1882 readers turned from the paper. Although he was acquitted in a grand jury hearing, the *Post-Dispatch's* circulation dropped drastically, and Cockerill resigned early in 1883. He soon joined Pulitzer as managing editor of the *New York World*, which Pulitzer had just bought.

WEST COAST JOURNALISM

Pacific Coast journalism, like the region itself, was relatively undeveloped. Yet the journalism in two cities drew attention from around the country. The cities were San Francisco, where Michel H. and Charles de Young had founded the *San Francisco Chronicle*, and Portland, where Harvey W. Scott was editor and part-owner of the *Oregonian*.

The de Young brothers founded the weekly *Dramatic Chronicle* on a borrowed $20. Three and a half years later, in 1868, after they had had a successful run covering the stage, they converted their publication into the *San Francisco Chronicle*, publishing it morning and evening, in addition to a weekly edition. They modeled it after Bennett's *New York Herald*. Soon, through aggressive reporting and editorial leadership, it became the dominant paper in Northern California. It won the fight for a new state constitution, despite an array of well-heeled opponents, and boosted its circulation dramatically.

Michel de Young claimed the paper was not sensational, but he spoke those words after William Randolph Hearst, the guru of garish journalism, had entered and left San Francisco. He may have been comparing the *Chronicle* with the sensationalism of Hearst's *Examiner*. The *Chronicle* was at least very aggressive.[38]

Scott became an editor for the *Portland Oregonian* in 1865 after graduating from Pacific University. He was known for his fluency in English, thoughtful analysis of events, and lack of invective. He gave direction to the development of Portland and Oregon over forty years, and political leaders and newspaper publishers throughout the rest of the country carefully followed his editorial comments. His prestige arose from a combination of wide reading, mature and critical thinking, and a clear, powerful writing style.

His views were especially respected in the field of religion. Reverent but tolerant, he applied an inquisitive mind to examining the nature of religion and its role in the life of humankind. Although a member of the Congregational Church, he did not adhere closely to a particular dogma. Instead, he reasoned that a belief in a Supreme Being was one of the deepest, most universal human characteristics.[39]

Publishers in many other cities — Philadelphia, Detroit, Cleveland, Cincinnati, and Kansas City — were designing newspapers adapted to 1880s and '90s America. Their journalism varied, but they shared several characteristics. Independent of political parties, they emphasized news and conducted vigorous newsgathering. Their newspapers were low priced, designed to reach the largest audience. Most of their papers also were of the new generation of evening journals. No less important, they relied upon advertising to support the news, practiced business openness by providing accurate circulation based on the sale of papers, and adhered to their advertising rate cards. These papers generally campaigned against corruption in government, both local and national. There was a lot of campaigning to do.

THE TWEED RING AND URBAN CORRUPTION

The Tweed Ring in New York City marked, at the same time, both one of the low points and one of the high points in American journalism, although historians have seldom emphasized the press' role in allowing the gang of Tammany Hall politicians to steal millions and millions of dollars from taxpayers. An exception was the *New York Times*, which risked all in attacking the Ring.

Upon Henry Raymond's death in 1869, George Jones became publisher of the *Times*. He previously had handled its business affairs. He decided to attack the Ring's rapacious ways. He launched the campaign in September 1870, with Louis J. Jennings, an Englishman, writing the editorials, and John Foord, a recently immigrated Scot, the news stories. When documents detailing the Ring's financial malfeasance were given to the *Times*, the Ring's fate was sealed. Democratic Tammany Hall no longer could accuse the Republican *Times* of acting only out of partisanship.[40]

Along with the *Times*, *Harper's Weekly* also helped bring down the Tweed Ring. Thomas Nast, the political cartoonist on the illustrated magazine, pilloried the ringleader, the rotund William Marcy Tweed, and his gang week after week. Tweed retaliated by removing Harper's Brothers textbooks from the public schools. Although the company suffered a severe financial loss, it did not back down. Nast drew a cartoon showing Tweed ripping Harper's books from the hands of school children.

[37]This sketch is based on Julian Rammelkamp, *Pulitzer's Post-Dispatch 1878-1883* (Princeton, N.J., 1967). Memoranda in the Pulitzer Papers suggest that Pulitzer believed want ads stimulated circulation. They also provided *steady* income.

[38]Addison Archer, *American Journalism. From the Practical Side* (New York, 1897), 319-22. Archer published an extensive interview with de Young.

[39]For an evaluation of Scott's abilities, see Wm. David Sloan, Cheryl S. Wray, and C. Joanne Sloan, *Great Editorials*, 2nd ed. (Northport, Ala., 1997), 108-10, and George S. Turnbull, *History of Oregon Newspapers* (Portland, Ore., 1936), 118-21.

[40]Meyer Berger, *The Story of the New York Times* (New York, 1951), 35-53, gives a well written account of the *Times'* role in bringing the Tweed Ring to justice. He is too kind on the other publishers, although he acknowledges they knew — or should have known — of the graft at City Hall. Other useful discussions about the *Times'* performance can be found in Thomas C. Leonard, *The Power of the Press. The Birth of American Political Reporting* (New York, 1986), chapter 4; and Sloan, Wray, and Sloan, *Great Editorials*, 110-13.

"Let Us Prey"
The *New York Times'* efforts to topple the Tweed Ring were joined by the cartoonist Thomas Nast of *Harper's Weekly.* One of his contributions was this cartoon, which painted Boss Tweed and his cohorts as vultures preying on the city.

Among the other New York newspapers, however, only the *Herald* supported the campaign against the ring. Where were the others? Why did the vigorous New York press not attack the wholesale thievery practiced by Tweed and his gang? The answer lay in the counting house — the business office of the press. The ring bought off the newspapers through lucrative advertising contracts with the city, which Tweed's cohorts administered. An investigation after the gang's fall revealed that eighty-nine papers had received patronage. Twenty-seven died when the patronage spigot was turned off. All "...with possibly three exceptions, were solely dependent upon this kind of advertising for support."[41] The magnitude of the thievery can be found in the comptroller's report. Joseph Howard, who owned the *New York Star*, received $218,477 from 1867-1871, and he claimed an additional $23,233. The *Daily News* received $431,623 during the same period. Tweed's *Transcript* received $783,498! A critic of New York's papers wrote:

In those halcyon days of roguery people used to glance in their morning paper over a mayor's message of six or eight columns, innocently supposing it part of the news of the day, while book-keepers were at the same moment charging it to the city as an advertisement at a dollar a line. Petty evening papers received a thousand dollars a month; and after the newspapers had been bought and silenced at this rate for five years, and the Ring had no longer control of the treasury, the unsettled "claims" of the various counting-rooms amounted to more than two millions of dollars. The writers for the press got little of this. *They* were put off with a ridiculous gratuity of two hundred dollars a year, voted by the aldermen to the reporters who omitted twice a week to tell the public what the aldermen had done.[42]

One printer set city reports in type, ran off thousands and thousands of copies, and sold them in bulk to publishers to be run in their own papers. Those publishers charged the city as though they had set the reports themselves.[43] The wholesale bleeding of the city's finances was possible only because the press, including the quality newspapers, was bought off.

Corruption was widespread in other cities and in the national government. Most papers were only tangentially involved in reporting it. They might respond if the corrupters were of a different political party, but most papers were not yet willing to take on any person and any party.[44] A survey of 130 cities in 1877 found that their collective debt, at $644.4 million, was nearly three times larger than it had been a decade earlier. That figure probably was on the low side since it relied on self-reports from city comptrollers. New York's comptroller, for instance, claimed debt at $91.4 million while a city report to the State Senate revealed debt at $149.3 million, 63% higher. The enormous funds needed for rapidly growing cities were simply too tempting for many "public servants" to overlook. Newspapers, in a few cases, reported the skullduggery, but the press generally was not alert to the corruption.

DIFFERENTIATING THE NEWS

The journalism that developed in the post-war period required vigorous, enterprising young journalists actively pursuing the news. When the *Chicago Daily News* was established in 1875, the existing Chicago papers sold for five cents a copy and were, a *Daily News* editor claimed, "eight vast pages of long, closely printed columns." Ads crowded the front pages. "Space was devoted to the printing of railroad time tables," a later Chicago editor explained, "in return for which much transportation was obtainable on request." The news was "actual or so called, all of it diluted to a painful degree, ... reprinted matter swept up from every-

[41]In *Clippings About Journalism*, Vol. 2, Library of Congress. The clipping, from an unknown newspaper, is of an article reprinted from *Harper's Weekly.*

[42]James Parton, "Falsehood in the Daily Press," *Harper's New Monthly Magazine* 49 (July 1874): 274.

[43]*Clippings About Journalism*, Vol. 2, in the Library of Congress, contains numerous newspaper clippings that dealt with the Ring's handling of newspaper advertising. See especially "A Great Leak Stopped," "The 'Subsidized Press,'" and "Subsidies to the New York Press."

[44]An exception was the Whiskey Ring fraud in which liquor taxes were diverted from the U. S. Treasury during Grant's administration. It was uncovered by a *St. Louis Globe-Democrat* reporter. Grant was Republican, as was the paper.

where."[45] The "big news" was that which all newspapers tended to get, and at about the same time.

If a major story occurred, the newsgathering agencies — the New York Associated Press, the Western Associated Press, or the numerous regional agencies — covered it, and no newspaper receiving the service had an advantage over competitors receiving the same service. The key phrase is "receiving the same service," for the news agencies allowed those newspapers that first subscribed to the service to monopolize the news. Newspapers were bought for no reason other than to gain access to their Associated Press franchise, as happened in St. Louis with the *Globe-Democrat* and the *Post-Dispatch* and in Chicago with the *Daily News.*

News brokering became very competitive. The Western Associated Press had begun as a subsidiary to the New York Associated Press. A contract in 1867 provided for news from the NYAP to be shared with the WAP, but also restricted the WAP from supplying other state or regional news agencies that might start up in the future. Despite the contract, the WAP set up subsidiary agencies in the West, a move vigorously contested by the NYAP. Control, nevertheless, largely remained in the hands of the NYAP for a multitude of reasons, not the least of which was the agreement the two groups had made in 1867. By 1882, however, the WAP had grown so powerful that it was able to persuade the NYAP to merge into one association with two divisions. Control still remained in New York — not a completely satisfactory arrangement for western newspapers — but at least it was diffused. In any case, this powerful new entity was able to provide large quantities of news to subscribers and to cut off overlapping services into the same states.

This growth and conflict resulted in distribution of national and international news cheaply and quickly to a large portion of daily papers. In 1880, one-third of all dailies took the Associated Press news report.[46] A weak competitive news service provided many of the non-AP papers with most of the major national news. As a result, competing dailies contained the same "big news" stories, although some always were at a competitive disadvantage.

For those who did share this news "budget," how then could an editor gain a news advantage over competitors? The answer was through local and specialized news and special columns. In 1874, when Joseph Medill again took over editorial control of the *Chicago Tribune*, he promoted departmentalization of specialized news: foreign, city, financial and commercial, books, religion, sports, women, and others. These changes had a positive effect on circulation. Charles Taylor did much the same thing on the *Boston Globe* but added serials and short stories, a column on housekeeping, and humor. This specialized news — "small news" — was treated differently from "big news" in that it tended to be more accurate and timely.[47]

To gather this news required reporters, lots of them. Editors

Charles H. Taylor

Few editors grasped the emerging mode of journalism in the 1870s as did Charles H. Taylor of the *Boston Globe*. He emphasized independent journalism, new types of specialized news content (known as "small news"), and sound business practices to attract advertising. Losing $60,000 annually when Taylor took control, the *Globe* began making a profit in his second year at the helm.

cast around for "knights of the pen" only to find there were not enough experienced men or women to meet their needs. The old route through the backshop as an apprentice did not provide enough people. Editors hired willy-nilly, hoping to find jewels by throwing young men and women unprepared into the workplace.[48]

Working conditions varied from city to city. New York, which had a surfeit of applicants, developed a system not widely used outside the city until the 1880s. Reporters would be "hired" as space men. This meant they would sit and wait for the city editor to assign them to a story. If they were given a lead to pursue and they found publishable stories, they were paid by the number of column inches their stories filled. Those inches were totaled at the end of the week; and, depending upon the paper, the reporters were paid from $6 a column to $8. If they were not able to get a story, they were paid up to 50¢ an hour for the time they spent gathering the information (provided they had not taken too long on the story). If they were not assigned a story, they sat all day long and received nothing. It was a vicious system, but the aggres-

[45]Charles H. Dennis, "Lawson and Stone Hailed as Pioneers," *Editor & Publisher* (21 July 1934; Golden Jubilee Number): Sec. 2, 52.

[46]Richard A. Schwarzlose, *The Nation's Newsbrokers. The Rush to Institution from 1865 to 1920.* Vol. 2. (Evanston, Ill., 1990), Table I, 248.

[47]Editorial, "Journalism and Jealousy," *New York Tribune*, 1 December 1879, 4.

[48]When Charles A. Dana took over the *New York Sun*, he quickly increased its circulation. George P. Rowell, a close observer of the paper, attributed the increase in part to the paper's improved news coverage, made possible because Dana picked good reporters, not relatives of proprietors. George P. Rowell, *Men Who Advertise* (New York, 1870), 124.

sive newsgatherers with the willingness to stick it out eventually would win a place on the paper. Many talented reporters with experience in less competitive markets faded into other jobs.[49]

One of the effects of the space system was to cause reporters to pad their stories. The problem was obvious even in 1871. "Men do not drink wine," one critic complained, "but 'indulge in a little stimulating fluid.'" Many writers buried the news under a pile of verbiage. One story began: "As the gray beams of morn began to pencil the eastern sky with the advancing light of day...." The writer finally got around to telling the reader a neighbor's hen-house had been robbed at dawn.[50] Editors fought such flowery and exaggerated writing, but reporters were desperate for column inches.

Even though reporters were not paid well, the large numbers of them needed to cover city news ate up the editorial budget. In an effort to make his reporters more efficient, Charles Taylor of the *Boston Globe* put his *regular* reporters on salary, but he found they would not produce enough copy. When they were put on space, however, some produced so much copy they earned $240 a month, a princely sum for a reporter. Taylor solved the dilemma by putting reporters on a regular, but small salary, with a quota for the amount of news required and a bonus based on one-third of all space over the salary.[51]

Such conditions led George William Curtis of *Harper's Monthly* to assert that journalism was not a profession because there was no course of study required, no examination to test what one knew, and no certification by degree. "It is a pursuit rather than a profession," he concluded.[52]

Reporters were one cog in an industrialized press — a business requiring capital to start, investment in machinery, and large staffs and expenses. Because of the financial considerations, the larger papers, like their industrial counterparts, needed to economize. It was as important for the solicitor to get the ad into the newspaper as for the reporter to get the news in, and both had to meet deadlines. The key was to operate efficiently in gathering and writing news and in selling space and writing advertisements. As a means of efficiency, both advertising manager and editor sought to systematize office routine.

The people who rose to the top of these new industrial organizations usually had come up through other newspapers, but not always as reporters. By 1875 it no longer was true, if it ever had been, that metropolitan editors arose from the rural areas, coming out of the small towns to make a career and name for themselves. A few prominent editors had indeed come from rural communities, but by 1875 the top editors of the largest newspapers were like other industrial executives: 64% of the editors versus 67% of the industrialists had fathers with business, professional, or pub-

Increases in Dailies and Circulation, 1850-1880		
	Dailies	Circulation
1850	254	758,454
1860	387	1,478,435
1870	574	2,601,547
1880	971	3,566,395

Source: North, Newspaper and Periodical Press, 187.

lic-official backgrounds. Thirty-seven per cent of the editors had started work at age fifteen or younger, reflecting the long apprenticeship many underwent in the backshop of the newspaper. But they did not stop there. Forty per cent had college degrees, while only 2% of the American population had graduated from high school. These editors did not reflect American society. Perhaps of equal importance, nearly 63% held a controlling interest in their papers. Another 14% held part ownership. The editor was a member of the elite in education, background, and, often, because of ownership, in income.[53]

Although newspapers were starting to adopt standardized practices, that fact should not lead one to think that they were all dull. The *New York Times* and *Chicago Times*, for example, began experimenting with bold, catchy headlines. The New York paper showed the brazen insensitivity of the new style when it proclaimed in 42-point bold capitals, "EXIT GREELEY," after the Democratic nominee had just been crushed, both politically and emotionally, by his wife's death and his defeat in the 1872 presidential election. In the 1870s the Chicago paper won the prize for callousness with headlines like "Jerked to Jesus," over the story of a Bible-quoting prisoner hanged at a public execution; "Brooklyn Bake," on the story of 350 patrons trapped by a fire in a Brooklyn theater; and "Hell's Halo," over the story of a massacre during an Indian uprising. By the 1880s, smaller papers were getting into the act, and an Arkansas paper headlined a story about the lynching of some African Americans with "Chocolate Drops." Alliteration, puns, doggerel, and even acrostics appeared in newspaper heads, often depicting tragedy or disaster in ways tasteless or crass, but nevertheless engaging.

The use of action pictures also invaded the mainstream press from the illustrated news weeklies (*Harper's* and *Leslie's*) that had reached full flower during the Civil War. Their success spawned a more frivolous pictorial something like the tabloids that accost shoppers in supermarket lines today. In the 1880s the *National Police Gazette* led the pack, printed on pink paper with an action picture covering most of page one. Its circulation exceeded 100,000. It did not pretend to be a general news medium, but the effectiveness of its illustrations was not lost on innovative publish-

[49]North, *History and Present Condition*, 83. For a fuller discussion of working conditions and their effect upon the news, see Ted Curtis Smythe, "The Reporter, 1880-1900: Working Conditions and Their Influence on the News," *Journalism History* 7 (1980): 1-10.

[50]Jaimes Parting, "Grasping After Sublimity," *Advertiser's Gazette* 5 (October 1871): 79. It was probably a pseudonym. The article appeared first in the *Utica* (N. Y.) *Daily Observer*.

[51]Minutes of the Ninth American Newspaper Publishers Association Convention (1895), 54-5. Taylor was recounting an earlier period.

[52]George William Curtis, *Ars Recte Vivendi* (New York, 1898), 120. This essay appeared originally in *Harper's Monthly* (October 1882).

[53]Jack R. Hart, "Horatio Alger in the Newsroom: Social Origins of American Editors," *Journalism Quarterly* 53 (1976): 14-20. Hart dispels the myth of most metropolitan editors starting from humble backgrounds.

The First Vote
Following the end of the Civil War, one of the nation's major issues was the role of African Americans in the political process. Congress passed various reconstruction acts governing the South, including attempts to assure that the states did not discriminate against African Americans. This 1867 illustration in *Harper's Weekly*, titled "The First Vote," showed a freed slave and other African Americans voting in 1867. The artist was Alfred R. Waud, who had done illustrations for *Harper's* during the war. The rights of African Americans got some attention from mainstream newspapers, but hardly any of them hired African Americans to work on their news staffs.

ers of mainstream newspapers, who began to incorporate action pictures into their publications.

AFRICAN AMERICANS IN JOURNALISM

Black Americans who wanted to work on newspapers had but three options: they could write for a black newspaper, which was issued weekly; work in the backshop of a white-owned paper as a compositor or printer; or start their own newspaper.

Certainly the most famous black journalist during the post-Civil War era was Frederick Douglass. He had made a name for himself during the antebellum period as both a public speaker and newspaper editor. Having discontinued his *Frederick Douglass' Pa-*

per during the war because of financial difficulties, he did not again contribute regularly to a newspaper until 1870, when the *New Era* was started to help former slaves adapt to their new status. When the paper fell on hard times, Douglass bought a half-interest, became editor, and then renamed the paper *The New National Era*.

It continued to struggle until he closed it in 1875 and left journalism for good. The abolitionist fervor of some white supporters in the antebellum period dissipated after the war. As a result, financial support faded quickly, and advertising and subscription income was inadequate to keep the paper going. Douglass continued to make speeches; and he fought vigorously for passage of the Fourteenth Amendment to the U.S. Constitution, which guaranteed equal protection of the laws for everyone under United States jurisdiction. He was named Marshal of the District of Columbia, giving him status as well as power to employ blacks.

African-American journalism following the Civil War was precarious and generally unrewarding. In the census of 1880, there were an estimated thirty-one black newspapers, all weekly, but they died almost as rapidly as they were started.

WOMEN IN JOURNALISM

Reporting and editing were largely male domains after the Civil War. The few female reporters generally covered meetings, weddings, and social events. There were few exceptions. The 1870 census listed only thirty-five women as journalists, 0.6% of the total number. By 1880 that figure had climbed to 288, but it still represented only 2% out of 12,308 journalists.[54]

A notable exception to those who wrote on women's topics was the handful of women who covered Washington, D.C., but even they were confined largely to background or social items. They seldom covered hard news. Mary Clemmer Ames filed a "Women's Letter From Washington" for the *New York Independent* beginning in 1866 and continued it for twenty years. Yet, though eligible to apply for the Reporters' Galleries in the Capitol building, she never did, instead reporting on Congress from the Ladies' Gallery.

Emily Briggs, under the pen name "Olivia," during the Civil War began writing on Washington government and society for the *Philadelphia Press*. She continued to write five or six letters a week after the war. Senate Historian Donald Ritchie called Briggs "one of the first women correspondents to use the telegraph for 'spot news,' a sudden flash of important and late-breaking information. Yet, since telegraphing 'cost a fortune,' she generally corresponded by letter, writing long and detailed accounts of the people and events she observed from the reporters' galleries or at an evening social gathering." Her most important talent, Ritchie noted, "lay in her colorful descriptions, her keen eye for social and fashion trends, and her witty style of writing."[55]

In the late 1870s, twenty women were accredited to the House

[54]Maurine H. Beasley and Kathryn T. Theus, *The New Majority* (New York, 1988), 7.

[55]Donald A. Ritchie, *Press Gallery* (Cambridge, Mass., 1991), 150. Ritchie devoted an entire chapter to women correspondents, most of it covering the period of this chapter.

and Senate press galleries. The Standing Committee of Correspondents, however, issued a new rule that required that members represent daily newspapers *and* use the telegraph to file copy. The rule was aimed at keeping lobbyists and other non-journalists out of the galleries; but, since most women worked for weeklies and the few who represented dailies wrote stories that were sent by mail, no woman qualified for the galleries in 1880.

TECHNOLOGY AND THE PRESS

Other changes were altering the character of newspapers. The number of papers increased dramatically, and circulation increased even faster than the population. One factor in the circulation growth was a number of technical advances enabling publishers to reduce prices, print news closer to its time of occurrence, and distribute rapidly to the suburbs or even to other states.

Newsprint costs were substantial and fluctuated over time. The high costs were particularly troublesome for papers that tried to maintain cheap prices in order to reach a popular audience. A change in the papermaking process, however, offered a solution. In Germany during the 1840s, wood pulp was used to make newsprint. That process moved to the United States in the 1860s, and the first American newspaper to convert was the *New Yorker Staats-Zeitung*. This conversion began January 1, 1868, although the paper did not switch entirely to wood pulp until 1870. For a decade or two, rag content was mixed with wood pulp to produce newsprint. As a result, the price of newsprint at first stabilized and then began a steady decline as woodpulp replaced the rags. It quickly fell from $344 a ton in 1866 to $246 in 1870. Yet, the New York Public Library found that only five of fifteen newspapers in its files converted to wood entirely in the 1870s. Nevertheless, after the price dropped further to $138 in 1880, six more converted. The price continued to decline dramatically, so that by 1890, after manufacturers introduced chemicals to process the wood pulp,

the 1880 price had been cut in half. It would be cut in half again by 1900.[56] Newspapers that stayed with rag paper or some mixture of rag and pulp faced a cost disadvantage.

Technical improvements in production also reduced costs while increasing speeds. All news and advertising copy was set by hand rather than by machine. The type was then fixed on rotary power presses, inked, and pressed against sheets of newsprint. For a newspaper to increase production by adding presses meant that duplicate pages had to be set, requiring a duplicate set of compositors and thus doubling labor costs.

A solution offered itself, however, in the stereotyping process that had been developed in the 1850s. In stereotyping, moulds were made by pounding papier-mâché into the flat pages of type. Metal plates of the pages then were cast by pouring molten lead into the moulds. In 1861 stereotyping was adapted to the large printing presses that urban papers used when the R. Hoe company designed a rotary press that used a curved *matrix* (the metal page of type). Costs dropped because a newspaper did not need to buy a second set of type or hire a second set of compositors. The process provided an additional bonus by saving wear on type, which no longer had to be used to print thousands of copies day after day. At first, stereotyping slowed production, taking forty-three minutes to cast two plates in 1856, although a publisher could add as many presses as needed to speed production, since several plates could be made from the same matrix. Faster processes of making molds also were tried. By 1880 it had become possible to produce two plates in nine and a half minutes, with the second and succeeding plates ready in two minutes.

Coupled with these technical changes was the development of the web-perfecting press. The perfecting technique had been de-

[56]Anonymous, "When Did Newspapers Begin to Use Wood Pulp Stock?" *New York Public Library Bulletin* 33 (October 1929): 745; David C. Smith, "Wood Pulp and Newspapers, 1867-1900," *Business History Review* 38 (Autumn 1964): 335, 337; H. A. Innis, "Technology and Public Opinion in the United States," *The Canadian Journal of Economics and Political Science* 17 (February 1951): 13.

Improving Press Speeds

Rotary printing came into popular use in the nineteenth century. Paper was passed between two cylinders, one of which held the page of type and the other which served as a pressing cylinder. By mid-century, curved, stereotyped plates were attached to one cylinder to replace the more tedious, earlier method of adjusting and securing specially cast type on the cylinder. One of the greatest advances in press design was the web-perfecting press. It enabled newspapers to print thousands of copies quickly. "Perfecting" designated the process of printing on both sides of a sheet of paper at the same time. The "web" referred to the continuous roll of paper that ran through the press. The top illustration here shows the Taylor company's perfecting press from 1856, one of the earliest such presses. In 1863, William Bullock of Philadelphia patented the first automatic, reel-fed rotary press making use of stereotype plates to print both sides of the paper at once. His press was constructed for the *Philadelphia Inquirer* in 1865 and produced about 8,000 to 10,000 sheets each hour. In 1873 he died from an accident while installing one of his presses for the *Philadelphia Public Ledger*. His leg got caught in the press, and gangrene set in a few days later. He died during an operation to amputate the leg. Robert Hoe's "web printing machine" (bottom) attracted crowds of spectators at its exhibit in 1876. It could deliver 30,000 copies of an eight-page paper in the brief time of one hour. Some of the other advances in presses during the nineteenth century included use of "grippers" to hold paper in place, automatic feeding mechanisms, and presses that could print two or more colors (which led to the invention of quick-drying methods such as the use of electric heaters).

veloped before the Civil War. William M. Bullock of Philadelphia in 1863 refined it into web-perfecting, and Robert Hoe of New York City improved the process in 1871. Whereas earlier presses required workers to hand feed individual sheets, the new press fed paper automatically from a continuous roll (the "web"). The paper ran between two cylinders (stereotype plates), allowing both sides to be printed simultaneously ("perfected"). A blade automatically cut the roll of paper into individual sheets. A Hoe double web-perfecting press installed in the *Missouri Republican* in 1880 could deliver 30,000 finished eight-page papers an hour.

With such technological advances, deadlines were moved closer to the time of printing. Newspaper production had become systematic, like factory work.[57]

Distribution varied from city to city, with independent agents handling most distribution in New York City and Chicago, but in Philadelphia newspapers tended toward subscriptions and handled distribution themselves. Technology also entered the distribution field, as papers could be sent only short distances if their news was to be fresh upon arrival. Boston papers were limited to twenty miles on Sunday because the railroad operated no farther. The *Springfield* (Mass.) *Republican* had to run its own train in order

to deliver papers to Birmingham, Vermont, the longest distance of any paper in the Northeast.

New York and Philadelphia were able to distribute newspapers as far as Chicago when the Pennsylvania Railroad began operating a fast mail train in 1875. This service was arranged with the U.S. Postal Department, which also allowed the train to carry a few first-class passengers. The train, running seven days a week, originated in New York City loaded with morning newspapers and delivered them in Philadelphia the same morning. It then took on Philadelphia newspapers and reached Pittsburgh with them at 6 p.m. and Chicago the next morning.[58]

These developments supplemented earlier technological changes. The telegraph had already demonstrated its utility in reducing the time lag between an event and a report in the press. From almost the beginning of telegraphy, the press had used it extensively, not only for information from distant sources but for news transmission from reporters in the suburbs, until the spread of the telephone in the cities.

The underwater cable connecting North America with England and Europe had been laid before the Civil War, but it failed. After the Civil War, another cable was installed. The cable company then repaired the earlier cable, thus providing the United States with two links with Europe. The cable reduced by days the time for

[57]"Stereotyping the Sun," *New York Sun* 8 January 1883, 3; North, "Newspapers and Periodicals," 103; and Eugene H. Munday, "The Public Ledger (and Daily Transcript)," *The Proof-Sheet* 4 (July 1870): 1-2.

[58]"A Lightening Fast Mail and Newspaper Train," *Proof-Sheet* 10 (October 1875): 209.

Communicating across Space

After the invention of the telegraph in the 1840s, the next two major advances in communicating across space were the telephone and the transatlantic cable. In 1856 the Atlantic Telegraph Company began laying the first submarine cable from England to the United States. After two failures, the company finally succeeded in August 1858. The cable carried 730 messages its first week of operation and then went dead, a victim of the dense water pressure at the bottom of the ocean. The outbreak of the Civil War delayed its replacement. The first successful transatlantic cable was then completed in 1866. This engraving (top right) from the *Illustrated London News* of that year shows its landing in Newfoundland. The cable made the transmission of news from Europe to the United States almost instantaneous, but its high cost limited its use to only a handful of newspapers. In inventing the telephone in 1876, Alexander Graham Bell drew on principles he had learned as an instructor for the deaf. When the Emperor of Brazil held the machine in his hand at the American-centennial world's fair in Philadelphia that year, he exclaimed, "My God, it talks!" In contrast to the Atlantic cable, newspapers began using the telephone comparatively quickly. Still, after the first telephone exchange opened in New Haven, Connecticut, in 1878, journalists were slow to make use of the device. The telephone would not have much impact on newsgathering for several years, largely because the telegraph was so well established in journalism. By the 1880s, however, reporters in large cities were beginning to work as two-member teams. The "leg man" gathered the information and then phoned it to the "rewrite man" in the newspaper office.

transmitting news from Europe, yet because of the high costs only a few newspapers, in addition to the news agencies, would make consistent use of the cable. Nevertheless, the technology was in place for those newspaper entrepreneurs who would use it for competitive advantages in the future.

THE SOUTH — A DISTINCTIVE DIFFERENCE

Like the eleven states that had seceded from the Union, the press of the South also was devastated by the Civil War. It took several decades to recover. Abraham Lincoln's program of reconciliation with the South was implemented by President Andrew Johnson. This first Reconstruction Act failed. Whether Lincoln himself could have succeeded against the entrenched power of Congress is debatable. In southern states, white governments had denied political equality to blacks, and Confederate leaders had been returned to influential political positions. The Radical Republicans gained control of Congress and, reacting to political developments in the South, set new criteria for readmitting former Confederate states to the Union. All but Virginia of the eleven Confederate states fell under Radical Republican rule. All black males were enfranchised, and many whites were disenfranchised.

The southern press generally opposed Republican rule, sometimes flamboyantly and intemperately. Editors had particular rea-

sons for opposing Republican newspapers. The Republican administrations subsidized party papers through state and federal payments for printing and advertising. During the three-year administration of the "Carpetbag" governor of Georgia, party papers received $98,000 for printing his proclamations. During the five years just prior to the war, Georgia had spent only $5,000 for the same purposes. Most Republican papers had little standing in their communities, but some prospered handsomely.

The newspapers in several states still had not recovered to prewar circulation levels by 1880. This was particularly true in Louisiana, Virginia, and South Carolina. Both Louisiana and Virginia increased the number of dailies from 1860 to 1880. Louisiana went from eight to thirteen, and Virginia from fifteen to twenty, even with the loss of West Virginia as a result of the war. Daily circulation, on the other hand, declined, with Virginia dropping by 27%. Adding the minuscule daily circulation of West Virginia would have had little impact on the percentage. South Carolina was hit harder, although the decline began earlier. In 1850 the state had seven daily papers, which dropped to two in 1860 but recovered to four in 1880. The circulation of those four papers was 50% less than the seven dailies of 1850.[59] Although papers in the other secessionist states had increased and circulation had held steady or marginally improved, the press still remained weak in comparison

[59]Calculated from North, "Newspapers and Periodicals," Table XI, 187.

Southern Leaders
The leading advocate of a "New South" was Henry Grady (middle) of the *Atlanta Constitution.* He used the newspaper as a pulpit from which he promoted industrial development, with Atlanta as the center of growth. As editor of the *Courier-Journal* in Louisville, Kentucky, for half a century, Henry Watterson (right) was a leading voice of a progressive South after the Civil War. He focused most of his efforts on the editorial page and became one of the most skilled opinion writers that American journalism has produced.

to the North.

It seems strange, then, that perhaps the most representative figure in the South who would persuade his northern colleagues that a New South was arising was from South Carolina. He was Francis Warrington Dawson of the *Charleston News and Courier.* He was a leader of the editors who would become identified with the New South, who stressed crop rotation, industrialization (especially by bringing mills to the South, where the cotton was located), and small farms. Independent on some social and racial issues, he still was partisan and intensely involved politically. Equally important, he owned his newspaper, which allowed him to make it his instrument for reform not only in South Carolina but in the nation. His political interests were in tune with changes occurring on the national scene, and he was a member of the Democratic National Committee. He was on the executive committee of the Society of Political Education, a northern group promoting free trade and civil service reform. These contacts, and his views regarding the South, gave him a voice in the North even as he remained a political power in South Carolina.[60] In 1889 a Charleston doctor shot and killed Dawson when he went to the doctor's office to confront him about advances he had made to the governess for Dawson's children.

Better known than Dawson as a leader of the New South movement was Henry Grady, who in 1880 bought a quarter interest in the *Atlanta Constitution* and became its managing editor. His oration in New York City titled "The New South" brought him nationwide fame as the leading spokesman of the movement. Like other advocates of that cause, he emphasized diversified agriculture and increased manufacturing, but he also had a vision of his home city of Atlanta becoming the political center of his new South. The practical result was that he made his most intense ef-

forts promoting Atlanta rather than the entire region.[61]

The most insistent voice of the New South was "Marse Henry" Watterson. As editor of the *Louisville Courier-Journal,* he was the most widely quoted southern editor for fifty years. Active as an editor during the war years — always retreating but barely staying ahead of the advancing Union army several times — he settled down in Nashville, Tennessee, as part-owner and editor of the *Banner.* There he undertook a campaign for reconciliation, what he called "The New Departure," promoting investment by capitalists in the North and diversified farming in the South. He moved to Louisville, Kentucky, in early 1868 to become editor of the *Journal.* By the end of the year he had persuaded the publisher of the *Courier* to merge the two papers. The *Courier-Journal* resulted from the deal, and Watterson became editor and one-third owner. This gave him a base to promote his views to both the South and the North. He became active in Democratic politics at the national level beginning with the 1872 campaign. His paper succeeded, but largely on its editorial views rather than its news. That fact may well indicate the difference between southern journalism and that developing in the expanding urban centers of the North. Watterson did not agree that news shaped public opinion more than editorials, and at various times the *Courier-Journal* had more editorial page writers than reporters.[62]

Many publishers in the North and West may well have agreed with Watterson, but theirs was the journalism of the past. The social, economic, and technological changes resulting from the Civil War had set in motion a different society, one that would require different media from pre-Civil War newspapers. The editors and publishers of the emerging journalism emphasized vigorous, impartial news policies based on independent journalism. This new

[60]E. Culpepper Clark, "Francis Warrington Dawson: The New South Revisited," *American Journalism* 3 (1986): 5-23.

[61]Harold E. Davis, "Henry Grady, Master of the Atlanta Ring—1880-1886," *Georgia Historical Quarterly* 69 (1985): 1-38; and Davis, "'A Brave and Beautiful City': Henry Grady and the New South," *American Journalism* 5 (1988): 131-44.

[62]Joseph Frazier Wall, *Henry Watterson. Reconstructed Rebel* (New York, 1956). Walter N. Haldeman was majority owner and manager of the paper.

newspaper design, powered with advertising and circulation, could support a massive superstructure capable of succeeding in the new urban environment. The press would be refined and shaped during the next several decades, but the form was designed in the post-Civil War era.

RECOMMENDED READINGS

BOOKS

Abbott, Richard H. *For Free Press and Equal Rights: Republican Newspapers in the Reconstruction South*. John W. Quist, ed. Athens, Ga., 2004. Republicans used newspapers to try to build support for their party.

Armstrong, William M. *E. L. Godkin: A Biography*. Albany, N. Y., 1978. The founder of the *Nation* was one of the most politically active editors of his era.

Brasch, Walter M. *Brer Rabbit, Uncle Remus, and the 'Cornfield Journalist,' The Tale of Joel Chandler Harris*. Macon, Ga., 2000. The journalist Harris was America's second most respected popular writer, next to Mark Twain.

Brown, Joshua. *Beyond the Lines: Pictorial Reporting, Everyday Life, and the Crisis of Gilded Age America*. Berkeley, Calif, 2002. Illustrators for *Frank Leslie's Illustrated Newspaper* reflected public opinion about race, labor strife, and social morés.

Caudill, Edward. *Darwinism and the Press: The Evolution of an Idea*. Hillsdale, N. J., 1989. Newspaper and magazine treatment of Darwinism demonstrated the media's inherent difficulty in covering ideas.

Clark, E. Culpepper. *Francis Warrington Dawson and the Politics of Restoration: South Carolina, 1874-1889*. Tuscaloosa, Ala., 1980. This political biography of the *Charleston News and Courier* editor focuses on his state, regional, and national influence.

Clayton, Charles G. *Little Mack: Joseph B. McCullagh of the St. Louis Globe-Democrat*. Carbondale, Ill., 1969. McCullagh successfully combined the news emphasis of Bennett with the editorial ability of Greeley.

Davis, Harold E. *Henry Grady's New South: Atlanta, a Brave and Beautiful City*. Tuscaloosa, Ala., 1990. Grady's efforts for a "New South" had as their primary goal the political and economic condition of Atlanta rather than of the South as a whole.

Desmond, Robert W. *The Information Process: World News Reporting to the Twentieth Century*. Ames, Iowa, 1978. This survey history of world news reporting covers *Acta Diurna* in 131 B.C. to the end of the nineteenth century, along with the social, political, economic, and technological background. Most of the book covers British and American correspondents, agencies, and technology in the last half of the nineteenth century.

Dicken-Garcia, Hazel. *Journalistic Standards in Nineteenth-Century America*. Madison, Wis., 1989. In the latter part of the century, as newspapers became more complicated and less understood by the public, criticism increased.

Dickerson, Donna L. *The Reconstruction Era: Primary Documents on Events from 1865 to 1877*. Westport, Conn., 2003. This volume in the "Debating Historical Issues in the Media of the Time" contains original newspaper and magazine articles, editorials, and essays published during the Gilded Age.

Evensen, Bruce J. *God's Man for the Gilded Age: D.L. Moody and the Rise of Modern Mass Evangelism*. New York, 2003. Press coverage was an important aspect of the evangelistic success of revivalist Moody.

Frisken, Amanda. *Victoria Woodhull's Sexual Revolution: Political Theater and the Popular Press in Nineteenth-Century America*. Philadelphia, 2004. Before marrying a British banker, the beautiful "bad girl" publisher of the *Woodhull & Clafin's Weekly* used celebrity and notoriety to reveal social hypocrisy as well as to promulgate unwelcome ideas, like sexual equality.

Jepson, Thomas C. *My Sisters Telegraphic: Women in the Telegraph Office, 1846-1950*. Athens, Ohio, 2000. Women held many of the jobs in telegraph offices.

Lancaster, Paul. *Gentleman of the Press*. Syracuse, N. Y., 1991. This biography of Julian Ralph of the *New York Sun* provides insight into the nature of reporting on America's urban newspapers after the Civil War.

Marcosson, Isaac. *Marse Henry: A Biography of Henry Watterson*. New York, 1951. In this detailed chronological biography of the Louisville editor and noted editorial writer. Watterson is a colorful "personal" editor.

Margolies, Daniel S. *Henry Watterson and the New South: The Politics of Empire, Free Trade, and Globalization*. Lexington, Ky., 2006. Watterson, the Louisville editor, played important roles in the New South movement, American expansion and imperialism, the Democratic Party, and journalism.

Morphet, David. *Louis Jennings MP: Editor of the New York Times and Tory Democrat*. London, 2001. Jennings was the London-born editor of the *New York Times* who led its campaign that helped topple Tammany Hall's "Boss" Tweed.

Nevins, Allen. *The Evening Post, a Century of Journalism*. New York, 1922. This gracefully written newspaper history devotes much attention to the wider social and historical context of the 1860s and '70s.

O'Connor, Richard. *The Scandalous Mr. Bennett*. New York: Doubleday, 1962. O'Connor's account is a popularized, colorful biography of James Gordon Bennett Jr., owner of the *New York Herald*.

Ogden, Rollo, ed. *Life and Letters of Edwin Lawrence Godkin*, 2 vols. New York, 1907. The intelligent, scholarly Godkin loved justice and honesty and wrote with acumen and forceful expression.

Paine, Albert Bigelow. *Thomas Nast, His Period and His Pictures*. New York, 1904. Nast was the "father of American caricature." He believed his primary goal should be the moral and political advancement of America.

Rosewater, Victor. *History of Cooperative News-Gathering in the United States*. New York, 1930. This is the standard work on the history of the Associated Press and other newsgathering organizations.

Smythe, Ted Curtis. *The Gilded Age Press, 1865-1900*. Westport, Conn., 2003. This well-researched overview is the essential work for understanding American journalism in the late nineteenth century. Among the changes were increasing political independence and a growing emphasis on news.

Steele, Janet E. *The Sun Shines For All: Journalism and Ideology in the Life of Charles A. Dana*. Syracuse, N.Y., 1993. Steele provides an intellectual biography of the editor of the *New York Sun* from 1868 until the 1890s.

Stone, Candace. *Dana and the Sun*. New York, 1938. This readable biography emphasizes Dana's editorial comment and his role in public affairs.

Summers, Mark Wahlgren. *The Press Gang: Newspapers and Politics, 1865-1878*. Chapel Hill, N.C., 1994. Summers describes the interconnection of politicians and newspapers after the Civil War.

Thompson, Julius Eric. *The Black Press in Mississippi: 1865-1985*. Gainesville, Fla., 1993. Black newspapers in Mississippi were hampered by financial problems and repression from whites.

Thompson, Robert L. *Wiring a Continent: The History of the Telegraph Industry in the United States, 1832-1866*. Princeton, N. J., 1947. This is the best account of the rise of the Western Union monopoly.

ARTICLES

Bjerga, Alan. "The Trials of Faith: Discussion of Religion and the Beecher Adultery Scandal, 1870-1880." *American Journalism* 18 (2001): 73-94. Extensive coverage of the Rev. Henry Ward Beecher's fall from grace changed public perception of the role of religion in American culture.

Caudill, Edward. "E.L. Godkin and His (Special and Influential) View of 19th Century Journalism." *Journalism Quarterly* 69 (1992): 1039-49. Godkin held a multi-dimensional attitude toward journalism, which he saw as a haven for both reformers and money-grubbers.

Cronin, Mary M. "The Liberty To Argue Freely: Nineteenth-Century Obscenity Prosecutions and the Emergence of Modern Libertarian Free Speech Discourse." *Journalism & Communication Monographs* 8:3 (2006): 163-219. The Comstock Act of 1873 banned mailing what crusader Anthony Comstock considered "obscene materials," and four opponents of the law were convicted between 1876 and 1890 for violating it and for supporting changes.

Dickerson, Donna L. "From Suspension to Subvention: The Southern Press During Reconstruction, 1863-1870." *American Journalism* (1991): 230-45. Dickerson outlines the methods of control over editors and newspapers after the Civil War.

Fedler, Fred. "Mrs. O'Leary's Cow and Other Newspaper Tales About the Chicago Fire of 1871." *American Journalism* 3 (1986): 24-38. Fanciful, erroneous reports were picked up and reprinted by other newspapers.

Goble, Corban. "Mark Twain's Nemesis: The Paige Compositor." *Printing History*

18:2 (1999): 2-16. Twain made a disastrous financial investment in James Paige's efforts to perfect a typesetting machine.

Hart, Jack R. "Horatio Alger in the Newsroom: Social Origins of American Editors." *Journalism Quarterly* 53 (1976): 14-20. Editors of the largest newspapers during 1875-1900 were comparable in origin to executives in other major industries; they were from the business class, forming a socio-economic elite.

Hume, Janice, with Amber Roessner. "Surviving Sherman's March: Press, Public Memory, and Georgia's Salvation Mythology," *Journalism and Mass Communication Quarterly* 86:1 (2009): 119-37. In the decades after the Civil War, the sacred myth of "The Lost Cause" extolled the virtues of the brave whose clever hospitality, innate charm, and beautiful homes empowered them to outwit the invading Union Army.

Hyde, Jana. "The Industrial Press, 1865-1883: Professional Journalism or Pawn of Urbanism?" 186-98 in Wm. David Sloan, *Perspectives on Mass Communication History* (Hillsdale, N. J., 1991). This historiographical essay analyzes the approaches that historians have taken to explaining the press of the period.

Johansen, Peter. "For Better, Higher, and Nobler Things: Massey's Pioneering Employee Publication." *Journalism History* 27 (2001): 94-100. Massey's was the first American publication intended solely for a company's employees.

Knights, Peter R. "'Competition' in the U.S. Daily Newspaper Industry, 1865-68." *Journalism Quarterly* 45 (1968): 473-80. The trend toward independence was well under way in the years after the war.

—. "The Press Association War of 1866-1867." *Journalism Monographs* 16 (1967). The author provides a detailed history of squabbles between the Associated Press and the Western Associated Press, and the role of Western Union.

Kolchin, Peter. "The Business Press and Re-construction, 1865-1868." *Journal of Southern History* (1967): 183-96. The business press favored moderate measures rather than the Radical Republican platform during Reconstruction.

Makemson, Harlen. "A Dude and Pharisee," *Journalism History* 29:4 (2004) 179-89. When *Harper's Weekly* editor George William Curtis attacked Republican candidates during the presidential-election campaign of 1884, pro-GOP cartoonists and editors pounced on him. Many cartoons illuminated the cultural war of moral codes.

Murray, Randall L. "Edwin Lawrence Godkin: Unbending Editor in Times of Change." *Journalism History* 1 (1974): 77-81, 89. The thinking man's editor, Godkin provided a voice of authority, though he never reached the mass reader.

Nord, David Paul. "The Business Values of American Newspapers: The 19th Century Watershed in Chicago." *Journalism Quarterly* 61 (1984): 265-73. Chicago papers shared a commitment to the "public interest" despite the differences in their nominal allegiances to various ideologies.

Reel, Guy. "Richard Fox, John L. Sullivan, and the Rise of Modern American Prize Fighting." *Journalism History* 27:2 (2001): 73-85. Richard Kyle Fox, editor and publisher of the *National Police Gazette*, helped create modern boxing by publicizing the exploits of boxing champion John L. Sullivan.

Rutenbeck, Jeffrey. "The Rhetoric of Independence and Boosterism in Late Nineteenth-Century California Journalism." *American Journalism* 13 (1996): 456-74. As journalism moved from being partisan to being independent, boosterism (promoting the region) was a stepping stone.

Spencer, David R. "Bringing Down Giants: Thomas Nast, John Wilson Bengough and the Maturing of Political Cartooning." *American Journalism* 15:3 (1998): 61-88. Nast and Bengough helped to expose corrupt political figures.

Thorn, William J. "Hudson's History of Journalism Criticized by His Contemporaries." *Journalism Quarterly* 57 (1980): 96-106. Journalists considered the newspaper's role in promoting democracy more important than its function of providing news.

Tucher, Andie. "In Search of Jenkins: Taste, Style and Credibility in the Gilded Age." *Journalism History* 27 (2001): 50-55. One reporter's purple prose, emphasis on sensationalism, and prying techniques inspired the term "Jenkins" for irresponsible, inflated copy.

Wallace, Aurora. "A Height Deemed Appalling: Nineteenth-Century New York Newspaper Buildings." *Journalism History* 31:4 (2006): 178-89. The *New York Tribune, Times,* and *World* used architecture as a means to forge their corporate identities, distinguish themselves from one another, and symbolize their own successes.

Wallach, Glen. "'A Depraved Taste for Publicity': The Press and Private Life in the Gilded Age." *American Studies* 39:1 (1998): 31-57. Press coverage of the Tilton-Beecher adultery scandal made private affairs public news.

Whisnant, David E. "Selling the Gospel News, or: The Strange Career of Jimmy Brown the Newsboy." *Journal of Social History* 5 (1972): 269-309. The newsboy became a figure in American mythology and social life.

12

The Age of New Journalism
1883 - 1900

The late nineteenth century was a decisive period for the American press, a time that in many important respects marked the emergence of the modern newspaper. In 1883 the young St. Louis publisher Joseph Pulitzer went to New York to take over the *World*, rightly convinced that the greatest opportunity for a hardworking and talented journalist was to be found in America's fast-growing metropolis. He updated and improved the formula that some publishers had used for reaching the masses and soon was hailed as the creator of a "new journalism." He quickly built the largest circulation and the tallest building in New York, helped journalism reach new heights, and applied formulas that became staples of later newspapers. In appearance, in content, and in organizational structure, salient features of today's newspapers were becoming evident by the end of the century. Important rival media also emerged, including motion pictures, wireless telegraphy (the forerunner of radio), and widely circulating magazines.

The changes and innovations did not come easily or without controversy. The closing years of the nineteenth century were a lusty and exuberant time, marked in journalism by excesses as well as accomplishments. It was the time of the flaring of yellow journalism, a complex and much maligned genre that left both enduring influences and undying myths.

Yellow journalism was a substitute term for — some might say a corruption of — the New Journalism phenomenon. The idiom "new journalism" originated in Britain in the mid-1880s,[1] crossed the Atlantic, and came to be associated with the aggressive, flamboyant New York City newspapers of Pulitzer and William Randolph Hearst in the 1890s. Pulitzer and Hearst were two towering figures of American journalism, and their rivalry and techniques attracted much attention and prompted enduring controversy.

Although New Journalism defied easy definition, it was most often associated with a bold, energetic approach to news. Typographic innovations — including lavish use of illustrations — represented one of its signature elements. So, too, did stunts, in which reporters figured as the central characters in their stories. Nellie Bly's race around the globe for Pulitzer's *New York World* in 1889-1890 is the best-known stunt in American journalism. Another component of New Journalism was a willingness to spend money to obtain the news, a tendency best exemplified in Hearst and his *New York Journal*. "Many journalists conceive great undertakings, but refrain from executing them on account of the expense," a Boston newspaper editor wrote in 1897. "The 'new journalist' is not troubled with hesitation on that score.... [H]e does not stop to count the cost."[2]

Not all newspapers were inclined to adopt or invest in the techniques associated with Pulitzer and Hearst. After all, they were expensive. Nevertheless, the rise of New Journalism reflected broader changes that were buffeting American society. "New" was the defining theme of the times and found expression in many contexts, as suggested by "New Woman," "New Politics," "New Drama," and *Art Nouveau*. "Not to be 'new' is, in these days, to be nothing," a British journalist and literary critic wrote.[3] The recognition was widespread that the country was on the cusp of rapid, perhaps even disruptive change. America's demographic profile had, for example, begun to swing from predominantly rural to urban. The United States first projected its military power beyond the Western Hemisphere in a sustained manner, in the Spanish-American War of 1898. That brief war — in which the press took conspicuous and controversial roles — thrust the United States onto the world stage.

Whether they were exponents of New Journalism or not, journalists were keenly aware of the sweeping changes taking place. As the venerable *New York Sun* observed in a 50-year retrospective article, "the New York newspaper of 1847 was for facilities very, very far behind those of 1897. It lacked the cables and the perfection of domestic telegraph systems. Reporting had not then become a fixed profession. The interview was not yet invented. Public men had not been trained to take newspapers into their confi-

---

[1]Joel H. Wiener, "How New Was the New Journalism?" in Joel Wiener, ed., *Papers for the Millions: The New Journalism in Britain, 1850s to 1914* (New York, 1988), 47.

[2]John H. Holmes, "The New Journalism and the Old," *Munsey's Magazine* (April 1897), 78.
[3]Henry D. Traill, *The New Fiction and Other Essays on Literary Subjects* (1897; reprint ed., Port Washington, N.Y., 1970), 1.

dence, for they prided themselves on reticence and were fond of surrounding themselves with an atmosphere of mystery."[4] Newspapers of the late nineteenth century experimented in, and adopted, new equipment and technologies (such as high-speed presses, Linotypes, typewriters, and telephones) and new techniques (such as bylines to identify the authors of news reports). Above all, newspapers engaged in fierce competition. Editors routinely exchanged brickbats and insults in print, and it was not unheard of for rival editors to sue or to assault each other physically.[5] These tendencies were lamented by trade journals, which felt the abuse and invective reflected poorly on American journalism. "It is a great mistake," *Fourth Estate* chided editors and publishers, "for a newspaper to use its columns to abuse a contemporary.... It is not only a waste of space, but it is in poor taste to force upon the public the particulars of some petty quarrel in which it has no interest. Yet such cases are of frequent occurrence."[6]

The temptation to disparage and ridicule rivals sprang from several sources, including the overt political partisanship that characterized many newspapers. The balanced presentation of political news was still years away. As *Fourth Estate* observed: "An impartial newspaper is always appreciated wherever it circulates.... But a newspaper without politics or [one] that does not appeal to the political leanings of one party or another has always an uphill fight for success."

Another source of the hostility among journalists was unease about the direction the field was taking. The many developments and innovations — and the rise of New Journalism, in particular — were unsettling and contributed to irritation and antagonism among competing editors. For example, Pulitzer and the irascible Charles Dana of the *New York Sun* traded insults in print for years, beginning in the 1880s, when the *World* overtook the *Sun* in circulation and importance. Their hostility turned especially ugly when Dana launched vicious, anti-Semitic attacks on Pulitzer, who, in reply, called Dana a "mendacious blackguard" capable of "any amount of distortion of facts."[7]

While not always so nasty or vindictive, newspaper competition exploded during the closing years of the century. The number of daily newspapers more than doubled, growing from 971 in 1880 to 2,226 in 1900. (See Figure 1.) The growth of weekly and monthly publications was likewise impressive. The number of weeklies expanded by 50% and monthlies by 56% from 1880 to 1900. The total number of newspapers and other periodicals swelled from 11,314 in 1800 to 18,226 in 1900.[8] Another revealing way of measuring the intensity of the competition may be found on a library shelf offering a complete set of the *American Newspaper Annual* (now called the *Gale Directory of Publications*) published each year since 1880. Volume I is no larger than a good-sized novel, but later

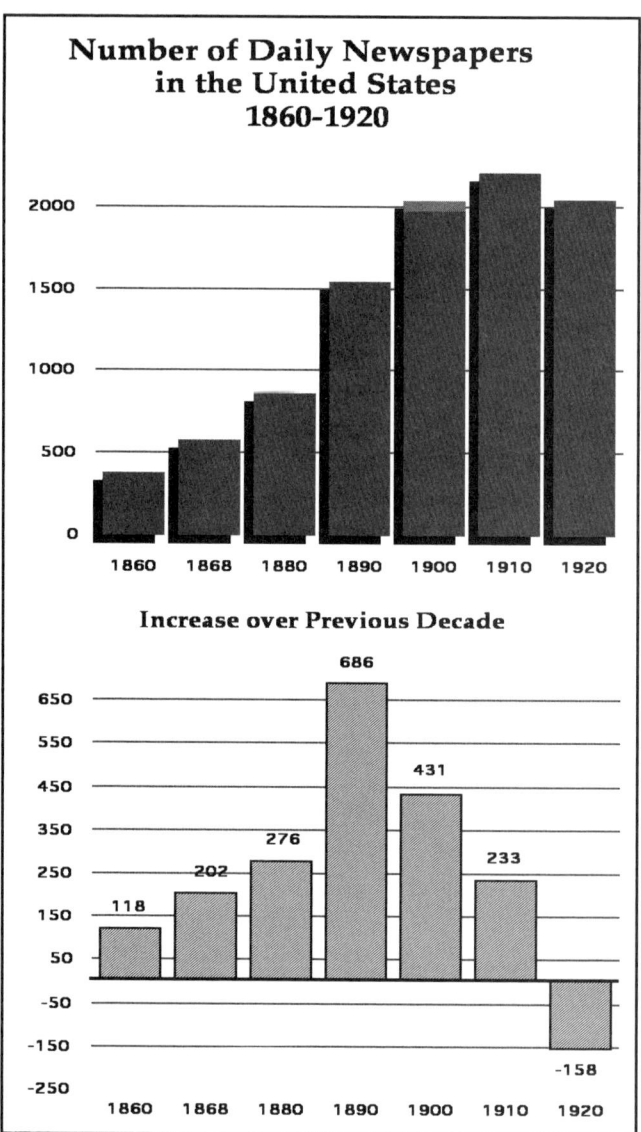

FIGURE 1

ones grow fatter and fatter, three inches thick by the late 1880s and so fat by the 1890s that the binding strained to contain the 2,000 or so pages required to list the nation's periodicals. The books begin to thin down around the time of World War I.

The greatest increases in the number of dailies came during the decades of the 1880s and 1890s. The number of weeklies was increasing at a similar pace, going up by about 4,000 in the 1880s (including semi-weeklies and tri-weeklies, too) and about 3,500 in the 1890s to reach 16,000-plus in 1899.

The urbanization of the U.S. population helped account for the surge in newspaper numbers. In 1860, only about a fifth of Americans lived in urban places (population of 8,000 or more), but a growing tide of immigrants swelled the cities so that a third of the population was urban by the 1890s. Daily circulation totals came to about half the total urban population — one paid daily newspaper for every two city residents. That was more than one copy per household, a higher saturation than one finds today in an age when so many city dwellers have turned to television or the

---

[4] "The Newspapers of 1847," *New York Sun*, 4 April 1897, sect. 2, p. 6.

[5] See, for example, "Ohio Editors at War," *Fourth Estate*, 10 June 1897, 3. The article reported the arrest of the editor of the *West Jefferson* (Ohio) *Home News* on a criminal libel charge brought by the editor of the *London* (Ohio) *Republican*.

[6] "Note and Comment," *Fourth Estate*, 31 May 1894, 4.

[7] Quoted in Denis Brian, *Pulitzer: A Life* (New York, 2001), 128.

[8] Data are from Table 15, *Census Reports, Volume IX, Twelfth Census of the United States, Taken in the Year 1900* (Washington, 1902), 1046.

Yes, Virginia

Answer to 8-Year-Old Brings Editorial Writer Lasting Fame

Francis Pharcellus Church made his journalistic reputation by telling a very public lie to a little girl.

Church is the author of America's most famous editorial – "Is There a Santa Claus?" – an homage to Santa and the very idea of Christmas. It first appeared in the *New York Sun* on Tuesday, September 21, 1897. Virginia O'Hanlon, age 8, had written to the *Sun* at the urging of her father, Philip, a police physician and New York City deputy coroner. She asked whether Santa Claus was real. This is what she wrote, perhaps with a little help:

"DEAR EDITOR: I am 8 years old.

"Some of my little friends say there is no Santa Claus.

"Papa says, 'If you see it in THE SUN, it's so.'

"Please tell me the truth; is there a Santa Claus?

"VIRGINIA O'HANLON
"115 WEST NINETY-FIFTH STREET."

Church's reply in the *Sun* tapped into deeply held notions about childhood dreams, the value of belief, and the essence of what Christmas should mean. "What Church did was sustain a child's hope while giving her a statement of ideals that are worthwhile for the adult," wrote journalism historian Wm. David Sloan in *Masthead* magazine. "He did not simply continue a myth. He gave a reason for believing."

A veteran Civil War correspondent and publisher before he joined the *Sun*, Church was not wildly enthusiastic about the assignment, recalled his editor, Edward P. Mitchell. "At first he bristled and pooh-poohed the subject," wrote Mitchell in his memoir, "but took the letter and turned with an air of resignation to his desk."

The image of Santa (above) had been created by the cartoonist Thomas Nast and was the one of popular imagination in the late 1800s. When Virginia O'Hanlon (top right) asked the *New York Sun* "is there a Santa Claus?" Francis Church (bottom right) gave her the most famous answer of all time: "Yes, Virginia, there is." As an adult, Virginia taught in New York City schools and received a doctoral degree from Fordham University. Throughout her life, she continued to receive letters about the editorial, which she said influenced her entire life in a positive manner.

Church then banged out a 500-word editorial on deadline that speaks to the power of the printed word and resonates still. It is reprinted in newspapers every year at Christmas because it reminds us about the importance of shared values and perhaps tells a larger truth than the facts of Santa's existence.

"Virginia, your little friends are wrong," wrote Church in his unsigned piece. "They have been affected by the skepticism of a skeptical age. They do not believe except they see. They think that nothing can be which is not comprehensible by their little minds. All minds, Virginia, whether they be men's or children's, are little. In this great

universe of ours man is a mere insect, an ant, in his intellect, as compared with the boundless world about him, as measured by the intelligence capable of grasping the whole of truth and knowledge.

"Yes, Virginia, there is a Santa Claus...."

There is more to the editorial, of course, which ran for nine consecutive years in the *Sun* without revealing the identity of the man who wrote it, as per newspaper policy. When he died in 1906, Church's *Sun* obituary noted – finally – that he was the author of "Yes, Virginia," earning him a coveted place in journalism history and an enduring byline in American culture.

1880s Tabloids
The *National Police Gazette*, by emphasizing illustrations and sensational stories, led the pack of tabloid newspapers in the late 1800s. Its circulation exceeded 100,000, allowing it to promote itself as "the leading illustrated sporting journal in America." It was printed on pink paper.

Internet for their news.

Other factors encouraged newspaper growth, notably the increase in literacy. Adult literacy rates rose from 80% in 1870 to 89% in 1900, while the percentage of children attending public schools rose from 57% to 72%. Moreover, newspaper prices generally declined from the end of the Civil War to 1900, and dailies that sold for a penny became common again. Americans became less provincial as transportation and communication improved. In short, the United States was building a sizable, literate urban middle class. It was only natural that newspapers would grow along with such a potential market. They soon became one of the country's largest manufacturing industries.

Inevitably, critics worried that newspapers were becoming too powerful, and the extent to which newspapers shaped and influenced public opinion stirred debate. What can be called the "powerful effects" school of thinking argued that newspapers generally exerted strong influences, sometimes to negative ends. "They 'cre-

ate' great men out of next to nothing," asserted one writer in 1899, "and destroy the reputations of men truly fit for leadership."[9]

The "limited effects" school was more nuanced, more empirical, and more inclined to recognize the increasing literacy of American society. "The common people, if we may be allowed to use that expression," the trade journal *Fourth Estate* said in 1900, "are better read and better educated than they were in the sixties and seventies. They now have ideas of their own on public topics ... and they do not wish to be told by anybody how to think and what to do."[10]

This clash between the "powerful effects" and "limited effects" schools framed what has become an ongoing dispute about whether the sensationalized contents of Pulitzer's and Hearst's newspapers created such a frenzy that they pushed the country into war with Spain in 1898. Most historians nowadays dismiss the notion that they had such a powerful influence on foreign policy. But the debate still simmers, and with it the enduring question of whether the media exert powerful or limited influences.

JOSEPH PULITZER AND THE "NEW JOURNALISM" PHENOMENON

The most prominent figures in journalism were often larger-than-life characters whose contributions to the field are intensely debated more than 100 years later. It would be a mistake, though, to consider them facsimiles of one another. Pulitzer, Hearst, and other leading journalists of the time were often headstrong individuals with their own decided views and theories about the best direction newspapers should take.

An icon of the age was Pulitzer. He acquired the *New York World* in 1883, after having run the *St. Louis Post-Dispatch* since 1878. His approach to newspapers, known as "New Journalism," gave a name to the era. When in 1934 the trade journal *Editor and Publisher* celebrated its first fifty years with a poll asking editors to name the greatest American journalist, Pulitzer got the most votes, more than two decades after his death. To get a better feel for his popularity, we need first to examine what New Journalism was.

At its core was an increased emphasis on news. The traditional urban journalism of the nineteenth century was that of thoughtful, patrician editors clipping articles from exchanges and writing editorial essays. The new method was to scour the city for the latest events of interest and to write them up in a brazen style appropriate to the leather-lunged boys who sold newspaper excitement on busy street corners.

Gossip, titillation, shouting newsboys, scoops, the 24-hour news cycle — these are the legacies of James Gordon Bennett, and many of the roots of the 1880s New Journalism are certainly to be found in his *New York Herald*. But the New Journalism drew on

[9]V.S. Yarros, "The Press and Public Opinion," *American Journal of Sociology* 5 (November 1899): 372.

[10]"The Influence of the Editorial Column," *Fourth Estate*, 27 January 1900, 6. The editorial also suggested that readers sought brevity in newspaper reports, stating: "The paragraph is read, while the long editorial is skipped by the average citizen for the reason that he has no time to wade through it. Brief discussions of live topics are what the people want, and it is a waste of effort to give them anything else."

other innovations not usually found in Bennett's bag of tricks, such as big-letter headlines, action pictures, and popular crusades.

Pulitzer is a major and yet ironic figure in American journalism. His name is associated with the profession's most coveted awards, the Pulitzer Prizes, which have been awarded annually since 1917. He endowed the prizes, along with the Graduate School of Journalism at Columbia University, early in the twentieth century. Doing so helped associate his name and career with excellence in journalism. His reputation also was burnished by a succession of admiring biographers who emphasized his successes while downplaying his harsh temper and his angry confrontations with subordinates.

Although Pulitzer's name is routinely linked to innovation in journalism, his correspondence shows that late in his career he was far more preoccupied with the business side than the newsgathering side of the *World*. By then, he was almost blind and ran the newspaper as an absentee publisher, directing it from a distance by cabling an unrelenting stream of instructions, advice, and reprimands to his top managers.

A gangling Hungarian immigrant, Pulitzer had forced his way into the American middle class with energy and cleverness. Coming to America in 1864 to join the Union Army, he began an association with Carl Schurz, then commander of a cavalry regiment and later editor of a German-language newspaper in St. Louis. He hired Pulitzer as a reporter in 1868, despite a total lack of experience. Pulitzer showed an aptitude for politics and was elected to the Missouri legislature when he was but twenty-two. A liberal within the Republican Party, he soon grew impatient (a lifelong trait) and left both legislature and party at the end of his term.

He scraped together enough money to combine two struggling English-language newspapers into the *Post-Dispatch* and announced, "The Post and Dispatch will serve no party but the people ... will oppose all frauds and shams wherever and whatever they are; will advocate principles and ideas rather than prejudices and partisanship."[11] Claims to nonpartisanship were not uncommon in the 1880s, and in reality Pulitzer's *Post-Dispatch* was a supporter of the Democratic party. In any case, Pulitzer faced strong and entrenched competition in St. Louis, where the *Republican* and the morning *Globe-Democrat* were like Goliaths towering over the new David.

Pulitzer soon launched a series of crusades against corruption and complacency, establishing himself not just as a printer of news but as a non-partisan social critic. He published a list of owners of houses of prostitution, interviewed a prominent local heiress who had eloped, and charged a singer with drunkenness on the night of her performance. It was not the kind of news St. Louis could ignore. With Pulitzer, the news had taken on a new dimension.

It should be noted that the journalistic crusade had been around for years before it became associated with New Journalism. One of the earliest crusades was the 1858 "swill milk" campaign, in which Frank Leslie filled his *Illustrated Newspaper*, week after week, with drawings of diseased and dying cows propped up so they could

Joseph Pulitzer
When Pulitzer bought the *New York World* in 1883, it was losing $40,000 a year. Within four months, he doubled its circulation to 40,000. In 1892, when he established the *Evening World*, the two papers' combined circulation of 374,000 surpassed that of any other two newspapers in the United States.

provide tainted milk to New York's babies. In 1871, the *New York Times* had published lengthy series on the corrupt Tweed ring in New York and on insurance company misdeeds. *Harper's Weekly* was known for its protracted battle with New York's Tammany Hall. But Pulitzer proved particularly successful in captivating public attention with crusades.

Within two years, the upstart *Post-Dispatch* had sales as large as the *Republic*'s, and the next year it absorbed the failing *St. Louis Star*. Profits were running $40,000 to $85,000 per year. But Pulitzer was working at such a pace that he suffered worsening health problems. When he went east in 1883, it was to seek rest and recuperation. He was headed to Europe when he learned the *New York World* was for sale. He bought the paper (at the asking price of $346,000) from Jay Gould, an unscrupulous stock manipulator. In doing so, Pulitzer assumed responsibilities that would make him famous and wealthy but leave him broken in health.

The *World* under Gould's ownership had been losing money and was hardly noted for prestige. But it had an Associated Press franchise and gave Pulitzer entry into America's largest, most robust newspaper market. The city had twenty-six English-language

Nellie Bly

Stunt Reporter Was the Central Character in Her Own Stories

Nellie Bly (1865-1922) achieved fame as a newspaper reporter at a time when fewer than 5% of full-time journalists were women. She was able to do that through a combination of daring, self-promotion, and a talent for recognizing what the highly competitive newspapers of the late 1800s wanted.

Born Elizabeth Cochrane, she entered newspaper work at the *Pittsburgh Dispatch* in 1885 armed with a high school education, an attitude, and the need to support herself. Within two years she secured a job at the sensational *New York World* by getting herself committed to a lunatic asylum and then reporting her story in lurid detail. Her most renowned stunt was her 1889 trip around the world in seventy-two days – in a quest to beat the fictional Phileas Fogg's eighty-day feat – but she also wrote about social issues, including labor strikes, the living conditions of workers, gambling, and prostitution.

She married in 1895 and temporarily left newspaper work, but by 1913 she was widowed and in debt. She used her newspaper connections to win a position at the *New York Evening Journal*, where she was soon publishing front-page bylines and her own column. She worked as a war correspondent in Austria from 1914-1918 and following World War I returned to the United States to cover the plight of orphans.

Readers and sources alike found Bly a warm and sympathetic champion of those about whom she wrote. In addition to this characteristic, part of her success was due to her highly personal and somewhat breathless style of writing and her direct appeal to readers' emotions.

But above all, no matter what story she was covering, she always made herself a central character in the drama. She never let her readers forget for a moment that it was Nellie Bly who was telling them the story.

Nellie Bly's attempt to go around the world in a shorter time than had the fictional Phileas Fogg in Jules Verne's *Around the World in Eighty Days* made her internationally known. She left Hoboken, New Jersey, on November 14, 1889, carrying only what she was able to pack in her handbag, and her checkered coat became famous. She completed the journey of 24,899 miles in just seventy-two days, six hours, eleven minutes, and fourteen seconds, arriving in Hoboken on January 25, 1890. The *New York World* published the cartoon at the bottom on the day of her return, showing her with other famous travelers from history. Along with her news stories in the *World*, she published her account in a popular book (below).

dailies (eleven of them business papers).[12] Under Pulitzer, the *World* became dominant.

The announcement of the *World*'s new editorial and news policies was similar to Pulitzer's opening lines in St. Louis five years earlier. He promised more news, brighter news, news for everybody. "There is room in the great and growing city for a journal that is not only cheap but bright," he declared, "not only bright but large, not only large but truly democratic."[13] He did not take long to begin fulfilling that pledge. The Brooklyn Bridge was just about to be opened, and Pulitzer surprised readers with an unusual three-column illustration on page one. To Pulitzer, "bright" meant well illustrated, among other things, and the use of pictures was an important contribution to New Journalism.

Pulitzer wanted to create a newspaper for the underdog, and underdogs were plentiful in immigrant-filled New York. He avoided news or features that seemed to put down the foreign-born and would not permit ethnic dialect writing even though it was one of the most popular forms of cheap literature. His crusading zeal immediately became evident with his campaign to raise $200,000 for a base for the Statue of Liberty, a gift from the people of France. Bringing in nickels, dimes, and pennies from countless poor immigrants, he succeeded not only in building circulation, but also in giving the masses a sense of ownership of an important civic monument. The Statue was unveiled in October 1886. The campaign typified the *World*'s crusading spirit. The paper took stands popular with the poor, advocating federal income taxes, inheritance taxes, civil reforms, and relentless prosecution of corruption among the privileged. It was a remarkable turnabout for the *World*, which just a few years earlier Gould had used to help manipulate stocks and monopolize telegraph services and railroads.

Pulitzer also cultivated stunt journalism — another characteristic feature of New Journalism. In 1887 he hired Elizabeth Cochrane ("Nellie Bly") to feign insanity and investigate conditions at the infamous Blackwell Island asylum. She found poor sanitation, unhealthy food, and abuse of patients. Her stories resulted in an official investigation and improvements. She later gained international fame for her feat of traveling around the world in seventy-two days to break the record of eighty days set by Jules Verne's fictional character Phileas Fogg.

In his attacks on corruption, Pulitzer showed that he was obsessed with that most readable of subjects, prostitution. His critics differ as to whether the elimination of vice and corruption was his primary goal, or the extra newspaper sales that titillating headlines created. In any event, he seemed to understand his market thoroughly. In serving that market, he grew rich; and the *World* became New York's largest newspaper, passing the threshold of 200,000 copies in just two years.[14]

He set the trade journals to buzzing in admiration, not for his innovation so much as for the remarkable success he was having

in building profits. The *World* became the trendsetter, the paper others imitated. In 1884, for example, the *World* put in its own photoengraving plant, the first newspaper in the city to do so. Within ten years every major daily in the country had one.[15]

The *World*'s growth was no doubt aided by its being a Democratic newspaper and a vigorous supporter of Grover Cleveland's successful candidacy for president in 1884. Some biographers say Pulitzer's *World* was vital to Cleveland's narrow victory.[16] Also that year, Pulitzer ran for and won a seat in the U.S. Congress as a Democrat.

But his infirmities — a nervous condition and near blindness — and his harsh ways with his managers began to take their toll. He clashed with his long-term associate, John Cockerill, who sought a greater financial stake in, and more credit for, the *World*'s successes. Pulitzer would not accede to Cockerill's demands. Their feud became disruptive, and Pulitzer ordered Cockerill to return to St. Louis to resume charge of the *Post-Dispatch*. Cockerill refused and resigned in 1891. Pulitzer then initiated a system by which he would run the *World* from afar, even when traveling abroad, by cabling instructions to his subordinates. Pulitzer, who rarely entered the *World* offices after 1890, frequently would summon editors and top managers to his retreats in Maine or Georgia. In 1892, he installed a triumvirate to run the *World*, a creaky and unsound arrangement that encouraged internal rivalries and tensions.

The *World* was still the largest newspaper in New York, but it was an increasingly dysfunctional place to work. By 1895, it was an inviting target for a young, rich, and aggressive newcomer, William Randolph Hearst. His arrival was a seismic event in New York City journalism. He inaugurated a period of intense competition in which his *New York Journal* overwhelmed the *World* and became America's ascendant and most controversial newspaper.

WILLIAM RANDOLPH HEARST

Despite his failings in sustaining the *World*'s primacy, Pulitzer is generally regarded as a venerable figure in journalism. Hearst, on the other hand, is typically depicted as deceitful and manipulative. Neither caricature is quite accurate, even though both have proven to be enduring. Suffice it to say that both men were controversial and exerted important influences on journalism.

The techniques of Pulitzer — the stunts, the crusades, the appeals to mass audiences — were well known to Hearst by the time he acquired the *New York Journal*. During an abbreviated academic career at Harvard — he dropped out in 1886 — he began reading the *World* and later adapted some of its techniques in running the *San Francisco Examiner*.

His father, George Hearst, who struck it rich prospecting for gold and silver, had acquired the money-losing newspaper in 1880 and turned it into a vehicle for boosting candidates of the Democratic party. He became a U.S. Senator in 1887, the year William Randolph took over the *Examiner*, which he touted as the "Mon-

[12]*American Newspaper Catalogue* (Cincinnati, 1885).
[13]Quoted in Brian, *Pulitzer*, 65.
[14]*American Newspaper Annual* (Philadelphia, 1886).

[15]*Fourth Estate*, 5 April 1894), 8.
[16]See Brian, *Pulitzer*, 79-96; also, W.A. Swanberg, *Pulitzer* (New York, 1967), 86-94.

William Randolph Hearst
Hearst, ever seeking popularity, aspired to be United States President. After being elected to the U.S. House of Representatives in 1902, he lost the Democratic nomination for president in 1904, lost his bid to be New York City mayor in 1905, lost a race for New York governor in 1906, lost another bid for New York City mayor in 1909, and lost a race for lieutenant governor in 1910. With that — and after having spent $2 million in his campaigns — he quit running.

arch of the Dailies." Although "Willy" did not then use the term "new," he practiced a robust journalism in San Francisco. He made lavish use of illustrations, conducted crusades that resembled the *World*'s, and spent money lavishly. He reshaped the *Examiner*'s front page and brought "excess and excitement" to the paper. He claimed the *Examiner* offered "the most elaborate local news, the freshest social news, the latest and most original sensations."[17] By 1890, he had the newspaper in the black. Soon, he was scouting for other challenges in journalism, a quest that brought him and his techniques to New York in 1895. He acquired the money-losing, down-scale *New York Journal* for $180,000 — far less than Pulitzer had paid for the *World* twelve years earlier.

What followed was one of the most compelling episodes in American journalism. Hearst's father had died in 1891, and with access to a family fortune of $7.5 million that his widowed mother controlled, Hearst possessed the financial means to create competition on his own terms. He hired many of the *World*'s best staffers, which not only bolstered the standing of the *Journal* but dealt a blow to Pulitzer. After hiring some of the staff of the *Sunday World* — including Richard Outcault, the artist who had been

[17]*San Francisco Examiner*, 12 March 1887.

drawing the popular comic strip "The Yellow Kid" — Hearst continued to raid the *World* staff. Reporters soon found themselves in a seller's market, each awaiting the legendary card in the mailbox reading, "Mr. Hearst would be pleased to have you call." In 1897 one of Pulitzer's top editors, Arthur Brisbane, went over, and the *World* was clearly hurting.

Brisbane's hiring turned out to be fortuitous for Hearst. The young editor had served as reporter and foreign correspondent for the *New York Sun* and joined the *World* in 1890. Like other editors, he had clashed with Pulitzer. He took over the editorship of Hearst's fledgling afternoon paper, the *Evening Journal*, with few regrets. He did negotiate an unusual contract. He asked that his base weekly salary be no more than the $200 he was paid at the *World* — but also asked Hearst to boost his salary by $1 for every 1,000 copies he added to the *Evening Journal*'s circulation. Hearst agreed. Brisbane had built the *Evening World* circulation to 325,000. Now, in 1897, he was essentially starting over at the *Evening Journal* with 40,000.

Under Brisbane, the *Evening Journal* outdid even the flagship morning *Journal* in rowdy content, screaming headlines, and vivid illustrations. It was, in some respects, a forerunner to today's tabloids. In any case, circulation grew rapidly, and Brisbane was on his way to becoming rich. He eventually earned $260,000 a year and for decades was the highest paid journalist in America.

The *Journal* was strikingly aggressive, soon topping even the *World* in activism and stunts. Hearst took to calling his methods the "journalism of action," which he said represented "the final state in the evolution of the modern newspaper."[18] While that statement was certainly hyperbole, the "journalism of action" produced no more stunning result than the rescue in October 1897 of Evangelina Cosío Cisneros, a 19-year-old Cuban political prisoner jailed in Havana. It was one of the most extraordinary, if unlawful, episodes in American journalism, and it came against the backdrop of Cuba's rebellion against Spanish rule — the struggle that gave rise to the Spanish-American War in 1898.

The *Journal* seized upon Cisneros' imprisonment as emblematic of Spain's mistreatment of Cuban women. She had been jailed for more than a year on murky charges of conspiring against Spanish rule.[19] The *Journal* mounted a petition drive during the summer of 1897 intended to force Spain to release her. It collected thousands of signatures, but the effort failed. Hearst then ordered Karl Decker, a correspondent in the *Journal*'s Washington bureau, to Havana to plot Cisneros' escape. With the help of shadowy collaborators and U.S. diplomatic personnel, Decker succeeded in breaking her from jail.[20] She was hidden at a private home in Havana for two days and then, dressed as a boy, was smuggled aboard a passenger steamer bound for New York. She arrived in October to a de-

[18]"The Journalism that Does Things," *New York Journal*, 13 October 1897, 6.
[19]The Spanish accused Cisneros of conspiring to kill a senior military officer. The *Journal* claimed she was defending herself from the Spanish officer's unwelcome sexual advances. The *New York Times* suggested that it was possible both versions "were quite true so far as they went," an entirely plausible interpretation. See "Personal," *New York Times*, 28 August 1897, 4.
[20]For a fuller account of the escape, see W. Joseph Campbell, "Not A Hoax: New Evidence in the *New York Journal*'s Rescue of Evangelina Cisneros," *American Journalism* 19:4 (2002): 67-94.

Arthur Brisbane
In many respects the man responsible for the mass popularity of both Hearst's and Pulitzer's newspapers, Arthur Brisbane was also one of the most popular editorial writers of all time. He wrote a daily column that ran in all the Hearst papers. When he died in 1936, a fellow journalist pronounced, "The death removes one of the most gifted and contradictory personalities in American journalism."

lirious public welcome that Hearst had organized. Tens of thousands of people turned out for what the *Journal* called "the greatest gathering New York has seen since the close of the war" in 1865.[21]

Some newspapers deplored the recklessness and lawlessness of the rescue. The *Chicago Times-Herald* called it "jail-breaking journalism,"[22] and the *New York Times* warned of repercussions in U.S. foreign policy (although there were none). But other papers applauded the *Journal's* activism. "Few novels have a more stirring theme," the *Pittsburgh Post* said of the rescue, "and no newspaper enterprise has equaled this feat."[23] *Fourth Estate* praised the *Journal* for its "international triumph."[24] The *Journal* characterized the rescue as "the greatest journalistic coup of this age"[25] and declared:

> Action — that is the distinguishing mark of the new journalism. It represents the final state in the evolution of the modern newspaper. The newspapers of a century ago printed essays; those of

thirty years ago — the "New journals" of their day — told the news and some of them made great efforts to get it first. The new journal of to-day prints the news, too, but it does more. It does not wait for things to turn up. It turns them up.[26]

However interpreted, the Cisneros rescue underscored how dramatically Pulitzer had lost the initiative to Hearst. Even Pulitzer acknowledged as much in December 1897, when he called the *Journal* "a wonderfully able & attractive and popular paper, perhaps the ablest in the one vital sense, of managing to be talked about; of attracting attention; of constantly furnishing something which will compel people wherever they meet, whether in the drawing room, or in the poor house, elevated car or dinner table, to talk about something in that paper. That is the sort of brains the World needs."[27]

But the *Journal's* enviable status as America's most "attractive and popular paper" was not to endure. By the end of 1897, it was already facing an emerging challenge from an unlikely upstart — the *New York Times* under its new owner, Adolph Ochs.

ADOLPH OCHS

When Ochs became its publisher and principal owner in August 1896, the *Times* was a moribund newspaper — a gray, conservative sheet that sold only a few thousand copies a day. Ochs had scraped together $75,000 to finance the purchase of the *Times* at auction — a scenario that scarcely suggested a long or promising future for a newspaper that had been founded in 1851. The *Times* certainly lacked the resources to compete with the *Journal*, the *World*, and the *Herald*, then the largest-circulation dailies in New York City. It relied heavily on the Associated Press for its news, while its enterprising and free-spending rivals sent correspondents across the country and beyond in search of news.

But the *Times* was on its way to prominence. It soon established itself as the cleanest alternative to the New Journalism of Hearst and Pulitzer. It represented everything that New Journalism was not. While not staid or somber, it still did not emphasize bold headlines, dramatic layouts, color comics, or front page illustrations. It tried to be authoritative.

In its editorials, the *Times* emerged as a moral counterweight to the sensation-driven *Journal* and *World* by challenging their ethics, judgment, and decency. It adopted an assertive if smug motto — "All the News That's Fit to Print" — that was an unequivocal rejoinder to the flamboyance and excesses of New Journalism. The motto was first used as a marketing device, appearing in a small advertisement in *Fourth Estate* in October 1896.[28] In February 1897, "All the News That's Fit to Print" was moved to a permanent spot at the top left corner of the paper's front page.

[21]"The People's Welcome to Evangelina Cisneros," *New York Journal*, 18 October 1897.

[22]"Jail-Breaking Journalism," *Chicago Times-Herald*, 12 October 1897, 6.

[23]Quoted in "Señorita Cisneros and the 'New Journalism,'" *Literary Digest* 15:27 (30 October 1897): 786.

[24]"New York Newspaper's International Triumph," *Fourth Estate*, 21 October 1897, 6.

[25]Charles Duval [Karl Decker], "Evangelina Cisneros Rescued by the Journal," *New York Journal*, 10 October 1897.

[26]"The Journalism that Does Things," *New York Journal*, 13 October 1897.

[27]Joseph Pulitzer, letter to Don C. Seitz, December 23, 1897, Pulitzer papers, Library of Congress, Manuscript Division, Washington, D.C.

[28]See "Advertising Medium," *Fourth Estate*, 15 October 1896, 9.

The Aggressive *New York Journal*
William Randolph Hearst hoped to appeal to the masses by using strong graphics in the *New York Journal* and by supporting the populism of Democrat William Jennings Bryan. The column to the left of this page-one cartoon by Homer Davenport recounts Bryan's recent successes in the 1896 presidential campaign.

The decisive move in the *Times'* emergence in New York came in October 1898, when Ochs abruptly lowered the price from 3¢ to a penny. Ironically, this pivotal decision was inspired not by a flash of insight or genius. Rather, it was intended to thwart the disclosure of a disgruntled former bookkeeper who had been telling advertisers that Ochs had inflated the *Times'* circulation figures. After threatening a lawsuit in a failed attempt to silence the bookkeeper, Ochs dropped the newspaper's price.[29]

The price cut thus was a desperate bid to attract readers and was widely dismissed as foolish and untenable. The *Times* insisted that many New Yorkers read the *Journal* and *World* principally because "of their price and not on account of their character or quality…. We believe that these thousands would like to buy and read a newspaper of the character and quality of The Times in preference to … the papers they have been reading. The number of persons in the city, young and old, who are educated, intelligent, refined and who by reason of their education, refinement, and intelligence would prefer to read a newspaper not given over to vulgarity and madhouse methods, must be very great."[30]

Within a few weeks, circulation had climbed to 60,000. Within three years, it had quadrupled, to 102,000. By 1908, it had climbed to 172,000.[31] Undeniably, the price cut in 1898 was crucial to the *Times'* emergence as one of the country's best daily newspapers. Years later, its in-house publication characterized the move as the "turning point in modern Times history."[32]

A year after the price cut, *Fourth Estate* said the *Times'* successful move demonstrated "that the people want and will support a clean, enterprising, high-grade newspaper that is sold for one cent and contains 'all the news that's fit to print.' Not only the Times, but decent journalism throughout the world, is encouraged … by this demonstration that sensationalism is not the only salable thing among newspaper products."[33]

Another trade journal, *The Newspapermaker*, added:

The success of The New York Times has astonished and pleased those publishers who feared the "yellow peril".… The answer is found in "All the news that's fit to print." It has modestly attempted to reflect, not to make public opinion. It has aimed to be a complete daily newspaper, edited for the self-respecting man, his wife, son and daughter. It does not print pictures, neither does it indulge in freak typography. It has avoided sensationalism and fakes of every description. It has not attempted to do stunts in the name of public service. It has cultivated impartiality and independence.[34]

That approach would prove enormously successful. Under Ochs and his descendants — who to this day control the paper — the *Times* became the country's most authoritative daily. That accomplishment seems astonishing, given the humble origins of Ochs, the oldest of six children and son of a poor businessman.

He began delivering newspapers in Knoxville, Tennessee, when he was nine years old. At fourteen he became a printer's devil at the local *Chronicle*. In 1877, he and a partner went to Chattanooga to start the *Dispatch*, but it could not pay its bills and lasted only a few months. Ochs was nineteen, and he did not have money enough to get back to Knoxville. Showing dogged persistence that he would call upon often, he published Chattanooga's first city directory and paid off his newspaper's debts. In 1878, he bought the near bankrupt *Chattanooga Daily Times*, and a local banker cosigned a note for the $250 down payment. Because he was not yet twenty-one, Ochs had to have his father travel from Knoxville to make the transaction legal.

Ochs at first was hard-pressed to build circulation above the 250 subscribers the *Daily Times* had when he bought it. But he had declared: "We shall give the people a chance to support that which they have been asking for — a newspaper primarily devoted to the material, education and moral growth of our progressive city and its surrounding territory."[35] Within a few years, the paper (re-

[29]For a discussion about Ochs' motive in cutting the newspaper's price, see Susan E. Tifft and Alex S. Jones, *The Trust: The Private and Powerful Family Behind the New York Times* (Boston, 1999), 53-6.
[30]"The New York Times: One Cent!" *New York Times*, 10 October 1898, 6.
[31]"The Times Ten Years At One Cent," *New York Times*, 10 October 1908, 6.
[32]Untitled article, *Times Talk* 5:1 (August-September 1951): 13.
[33]"A Newspaper May Be Good and Cheap," *Fourth Estate*, 21 December 1899, 6.
[34]*The Newspapermaker*, 21 February 1901.
[35]Quoted by Ruth Sulzberger Holmberg, "Adolph S. Ochs — A Granddaughter's Per-

Ochs and the *Times*

Pulitzer's *World* and Hearst's *Journal*, riding so high in the 1890s, ultimately lost out to Adolph Ochs (right, inset) at the rejuvenated *New York Times*. Losing $1,000 a day when Ochs took it over in 1896, the *Times* began turning a profit within a year or so. Even though it occupied impressive offices (center building in the drawing at left), at the time that Ochs assumed its management, it had fallen on hard times. Ochs established new policies for its approaches to both news and business, and it eventually became a model for modern newspapers. Reacting against the sensationalism of the *World* and *Journal*, Ochs emphasized even-handedness and completeness. This issue (right) of the *Times*, published the day after the *Maine* battleship blew up, treated the story with no excitement, in contrast to the screaming front pages of the *Journal* and *World*.

named the *Chattanooga Times*) turned a modest profit, and Ochs became its sole owner.

He was inevitably drawn to New York, visiting the city to attend professional conventions and to secure financing for his paper. In early 1896, he entered negotiations to acquire the declining *New York Mercury*. The talks collapsed when it became clear the paper's wire service franchise would not convey to the new owner. Although disappointing, failure to buy the *Mercury* whetted Ochs' ambition to own a New York newspaper. In March 1896, a few days after his thirty-eighth birthday, he received word that the *New York Times* was on the market. Five months and many grueling hours of negotiation later, he had become its publisher.

OTHER NEWSPAPER LEADERS

While Pulitzer, Hearst, and Ochs were setting trends in New York, others were making their marks elsewhere. Although New York exerted great pull on ambitious journalists, editors could achieve notable success in smaller cities. *Fourth Estate* lent encouragement to pursuing success in the hinterland, stating: "Instructive to the men insisting upon flocking to New York City to display their abilities … is the fact that most of those who have prospered on the metropolitan press direct their highest ambitions to ownership or editorship of an out-of-town paper, where the man is recognized as a man and not a machine."[36] The West — then considered the Midwest and beyond — took on fresh significance in journalism.

The Scripps family had been involved in western papers since the 1850s; and the first Scripps-founded paper was an important one, the *Detroit News*, established in 1873. The family started other papers in Cleveland, St. Louis, and Cincinnati; and soon Edward W. Scripps emerged as the energetic driving force of the family. By the mid-1890s, with five papers already Scripps-owned, he and his

business manager formed the Scripps-McRae League. Other chains had existed technically — newspapers in separate cities owned by the same person, as with Pulitzer and Hearst — but Scripps was first to give his energies to the group, rather than to a single paper. He was generally successful, prompting one enthusiastic historian to call him the Benjamin Franklin of his day.[37] Such comparisons, however, exaggerate the importance of the Scripps papers, which were usually penny afternoon dailies in mid-sized cities. But Scripps was the father of the modern media chain, and it is fitting that the Scripps name lives on in modern newspaper, broadcasting, and cable companies.

Other western and southern publishers built both financial strength and journalistic tradition in one location. Among the best known was William Rockhill Nelson of the *Kansas City Star*. With a background in law and business, he arrived in Kansas City in 1880 when the fast-growing town was in its adolescence. He launched the *Star* at 2¢ a copy, 10¢ a week, when competitors were selling for 5¢ a copy. It grew with the city, reaching 10,000 circulation in 1883, 25,000 in 1886, and 31,000 in 1889.

Nelson was heavy-set and walked with a waddle. A bodyguard was often at his side. He seldom spoke in public. He apparently had no desire to become a figure of national importance, but he fully intended to be a guiding force in his city — and he succeeded. His weapons did not include charm, charisma, or enchanting pen. Instead he used a cunning business sense. He concentrated on building a sound base of local retail advertising, and his paper was comparatively immune to the vagaries of national advertisers such as patent medicine producers and booksellers, who were much more likely to pull their ads during hard economic times. He recognized the potential of a city's trade area, and in 1890 he marketed a weekly edition of his paper at the unheard-of price of 25¢ a year, capturing Kansas farmers by the thousands and widening the *Star*'s geographic reach, to the discomfort of publishers in

spective," address to Chattanooga Rotary Club, 1976.
[36]"Not Room Enough For All," *Fourth Estate*, 10 June 1897, 6.

[37]See J.M. Lee, *History of American Journalism*, rev. ed. (Garden City, N.Y., 1923), 417.

Leaders of the Midwest
Even as Pulitzer and Hearst were recreating newspapers in New York City, publishers in the Midwest were making names for themselves not only in their own region but across the nation. After Joseph Medill (left) bought part ownership of the *Chicago Tribune* in 1855, he turned it into the leading Republican newspaper in Chicago and one of the most important in the nation. After the Great Chicago Fire of 1871, he was elected mayor of the city. In operating his newspaper chain, E. W. Scripps (middle) believed in singleness of control, independence from banks and advertisers, and publishing papers for the underdog. He involved his sons in the business by starting them at the top. Even though he ran his newspapers from his central office, he treated his managers well by sharing profits with them. He was particularly interested in local political reform, but he also gave a great deal of attention to the business soundness of his papers and their profitability. With the *Kansas City Star*, William Rockhill Nelson (right) eschewed the garish sensationalism of Hearst and Pulitzer. By emphasizing solid news, civic improvement, and a strong business base, he built a potent and profitable newspaper in the Midwest.

Lawrence, Leavenworth, and Topeka.

With only one year of journalistic experience at the *Fort Wayne Sentinel* (as co-owner), Nelson seldom wrote, but always supervised. He was a tough businessman, paying employees only as much as he had to, but he campaigned relentlessly for the betterment of Kansas City and showed no fear of any politician. He was not above expediency and was known to make payoffs to city commissioners to get ordinances passed that he thought would be good for the city. He died in 1915, having won a measure of the national recognition that he did not covet.

THE PROVINCIAL PRESS

Most journalists toiled in the hinterlands, in relative obscurity. The work of a country editor was demanding; and local expectations were many, as the *Beaver* (Pa.) *Argus* observed in 1894:

There is no man who does more for the community in which he lives than the editor of the country newspaper. Toiling ceaselessly from one year's end to another, often with insufficient help and unable to secure assistance, he manages to issue regularly his weekly paper, filled with the news of his county and the world. No business enterprise is started in his county that he is not expected to "give a little boost." No entertainment is projected by the church that he is not called upon to give it a

"free puff." If a leading citizen dies his columns are thrown open for liberal obituaries, while births and weddings are noticed, usually at considerable length.... If there is a railroad to be built, a new court house is wanted, or any improvement contemplated, the columns of his paper must be used to boom it. In a thousand ways he helps his county, and every issue of his paper is worth a great deal to the people of his community.[38]

Although the country press was venerated, its practices could be suspect and unprofessional. Some newspapers were subsidized by special interests such as prohibitionists, free-silver advocates, or populists. A larger number were propped up by a system of syndicates that enabled rural villages to have newspapers on the thinnest of shoestrings. The system worked this way: A syndicate (sometimes called a co-op or a newspaper union) would set up in a state's centrally located city, such as Des Moines or Nashville or Denver. Its purpose was to provide pre-printed sheets of newsprint to small-town editors. These sheets were called readyprint and could be furnished with two or three pre-printed pages.

A local printer could fill half of the unprinted front page with a house ad (mostly white space) and the paper's nameplate, and all that remained was to fill a few columns with local gossip or bits of local news. All he needed was a few dollars' worth of type and an old hand-press — and then he could print a hundred or so copies,

[38]Quoted in "The Country Editor," *Fourth Estate*, 5 July 1894, 4.

sell a few dozen subscriptions, and eke out a living. The public often thought little of such papers, and sometimes with good reason — as when Minnesota farmers read in their paper instructions on safely boarding a cable-car, and southern Californians read advice on teaching cows to drink from frozen ponds.

Less objectionable standardized content was columnar plate material. Syndicates shipped stereotype plates of news and features by train daily or weekly, and local editors could make decisions on how much of it to use. The material — called boilerplate — could include some breaking news, such as reports from the state legislature. In some ways the plate houses resembled wire services. However, they could furnish material, as they advertised, with "politics to suit." Then, they slanted the news Republican or Democratic to accord with a printer's views.

In the 1890s more than half the country's weeklies were using readyprint, and a leading plate house said it was supplying its material to 8,000 journals. The plate matter sold for $1.20 to $2 a page, and the readyprint was furnished free. It did not cost much to get into the country newspaper business, and doubtless many people entered it who had little business being there.

THE CHANGING STRUCTURE OF THE NEWSPAPER INDUSTRY

While powerful publishers and editors shaped journalism of the late nineteenth century, other, more anonymous forces were also causing dramatic changes. Newspapers were becoming big businesses, as suggested by extensive capital investment in buildings and equipment — notably high-speed presses and batteries of Linotype machines. The growing capitalization of large dailies "is turning journalism upside down," the magazine writer Lincoln Steffens observed in 1897. "Newspaper men see the drift of their profession into commercial hands." And *Fourth Estate* noted: "The daily newspaper has taken on an entirely new aspect in the last quarter of a century, in the ground it covers and in the machinery for its production and distribution."[39]

Technology and innovation were driving forces in reshaping the news business. By the late nineteenth century, presses were being built to run at speeds unimaginable at the start of the century. The *St. Louis Republic*, begun in 1806 on a wooden handpress of the type that was standard in colonial times, in 1890 was installing a Hoe press that would produce 72,000 copies (printed on both sides) and needed ten pressmen to operate it. It printed on both sides of a continuous roll (web) and used stereotype plates. By the 1890s the Hoe factory was turning out huge presses — superior to any others in the world — for newspaper work. For the next sixty years there would be no basic changes in the design.

Hoe and Co. also developed the technology that could fold newspapers as they came off the press. Folding machines had been around for awhile, but none could keep up with the speed of the rotary presses. The unfortunate juveniles who picked up met-

39J. Lincoln Steffens, "The Business of a Newspaper," *Scribner's* 22:4 (October 1897): 448; "Severe Criticism," *Fourth Estate* (22 August 1895): 5.

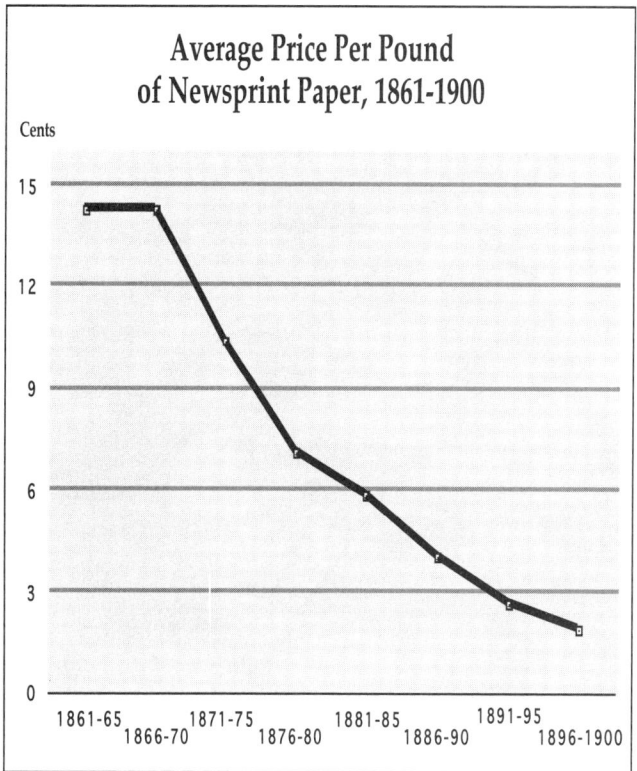

Average Price Per Pound of Newsprint Paper, 1861-1900

Papermaking advanced rapidly after 1860, and it usually is not given proper recognition by historians searching for the causes of the nineteenth-century newspaper boom. When Pulitzer published a 200-page issue of the *World* in 1893, his achievement created great excitement in the newspaper world, but the papermakers deserved much of the credit. One reason was that paper prices fell to unprecedented lows, and publishers less talented than Pulitzer could publish large issues if paper could be bought at 2¢ a pound.

ropolitan dailies for street sales had to struggle with cumbersome stacks of huge unfolded sheets thrown over their shoulders. In the days of the penny press, the *Sun* and *Herald* emerged as sheets about 15 x 20 inches, to be folded once. After that, the size of newspapers had grown through enlargement of the pages. The standard number of pages remained at four. Some of the "blanket sheet" papers opened out to prodigious widths. The *Free Press* at Burlington, Vermont, measured fifty-two inches across.

In 1883 Hoe added triangular forming bars to the press. The fast moving web of paper passed over a V-shaped plate with curved edges. The edges of the web turned downward, and the middle of the web passed over the point of the "V," forming a continuous crease or fold the full length of the web. It only remained for a revolving blade to cut the folded papers, and a conveyor belt could carry completed four-page newspapers just as fast as the press could print them. Larger papers could be produced just as fast, by running two or more webs over the plate so that multiple sheets would be folded inside one another.

Other developments in press technology permitted the use of spot color, which in turn helped make possible the Sunday comics. Among the first newspaper to publish color comics was Pulitzer's *World*. It was home to the best known early comic, which featured

The Linotype
Ottmar Mergenthaler, the inventor of the Linotype machine, gave an early demonstration to Whitelaw Reid, editor of the *New York Tribune*. It was Reid who originated the name "Linotype." The machine dominated newspaper typesetting for almost a century.

a wise-cracking urchin who appeared in Richard Outcault's "Hogan's Alley." The character was quickly dubbed "The Yellow Kid," and the strip became commonly known by that name. When Hearst lured Outcault to the *Journal* in October 1896, the *World* began a replacement comic that featured "The Yellow Kid." The rival "yellow kids" indirectly inspired the phrase "yellow journalism," which, as we shall see, first appeared in print in the *New York Press* in the winter of 1897.

Typesetting machines were badly needed, and it appeared for awhile that printing press technology was going to pull away and leave behind the technology of typesetting. The newest presses had made it possible for one pressman to produce 400 times as many sheets in 1890 as in 1800, but there had been no increase in typesetting speed. Typesetters still were setting all the type laboriously by hand, one letter at a time. In 1890 the *Chicago Herald* boasted of a new "Hall of Compositors," an area of 7,000 square feet containing work spaces for 150 men to set type. Each man had his own cabinet of type, and "large wicker baskets and brown rubber spittoons are plentifully provided throughout the floor, and every compositor is provided with an oak stool by the management."[40] No matter how luxurious these working conditions may seem, the fact remains that each man was setting type the same labor-intensive way it had been done since Gutenberg.

The breakthrough originally was made by an immigrant German watchmaker, Ottmar Mergenthaler, whose Linotype machine

went on sale in 1890. In seven years, 4,150 Linotypes were in use at 600 locations in North America. The *New York Herald* had the world's largest battery of Linotypes, with fifty-two machines. The *World* had fifty-one.[41]

Mergenthaler had been working to develop the Linotype since 1876 and was about to give up when Whitelaw Reid, publisher of the *New York Tribune*, persuaded a group of publishers to back Mergenthaler's work. A foe of the printers' unions, Reid wanted the machine to make his paper less vulnerable to strikes. The machine was keyboard-operated and set hot metal type one line at a time. It was introduced at the *Tribune* in 1886 and, after some modifications, put on the market. The larger newspapers snapped it up, and 90% of the big dailies had Linotypes by 1897. The Linotype offered dramatic economies, as one machine could do the work of five human typesetters.

Photoengraving was introduced in the 1880s, and the use of pictures began to increase rapidly — although the process could use only line drawings. In 1880, Stephen H. Horgan, an employee at the *New York Graphic*, had produced an experimental photograph in the newspaper using the halftone process. Perfected in the 1890s, the process permitted photographs to be reproduced on newspaper presses running at full speed. Illustrated newspapers had been around since before the Civil War, but they had relied on the tedious handwork of skilled woodcarvers or electrotypers, and only the high-circulation papers could afford them. By the 1880s, line drawings were being photographed onto the surface of zinc plates for acid etching. This mechanical process not only made illustration cheaper, it shortened deadline time so that last night's fire could be portrayed pictorially in the morning paper. Horgan's process gave printing the halftone screen — essentially the method used to print photographs today.

Other printing technologies were important advances when introduced. Some of these have become obscured by time: the standardization of the point system (in 1886) used to measure type; the use of electricity to drive printing presses; mechanical tension controls to replace the erratic hand-braking of webs of paper; and modular designs for stacking or lining up press units much as they are still arranged in pressrooms today.

Newsgathering technologies were particularly important, although the economies they produced were sometimes harder to measure. James Gordon Bennett may have introduced the beat system in days long past; but it would not reach perfection until reporters could cover the city on bicycles, in streetcars, or by telephones, could write their stories on typewriters with the aid of electric lights, and could benefit from reduced telegraphy and cable toll charges (lowered by Western Union's loss of monopoly status) and from the widespread use of railroad passes.

Invention and innovation were the watchwords, and the newspaper industry was ready to employ any innovation that promised to speed production or save money. Consider, for example, the use of pneumatic transmission. When city transportation proved too slow for Chicago's energetic journalists, a cooperative

[40]"A Few Words About the Chicago Herald," *Inland Printer* 9 (January 1892): 329-44.

[41]See "The Linotype," *Fourth Estate*, 29 July 1897, 2.

The Newspaper Halftone
The *New York Graphic*, founded in 1873 to make fullest possible use of photography, experimented with several processes before its photo-mechanical manager, Stephen Horgan, produced this halftone in 1880. He copied the original photograph — a picture of New York's Shanty Town — through a fine screen, producing an engraving that could give the illusion of continuous tones of gray even though it was printed with black ink. Essentially the same technique is employed in printing of pictures today.

called City News Bureau of Chicago built a tube system in 1892 to serve the city's thirteen newspapers. Canisters were propelled through three-inch brass tubes by steam jets delivering a pressure of 125 pounds per square inch. The fifteen-mile underground system served the Board of Trade and other non-newspaper customers as well. It was not exactly perfect. The steam kept the tube so damp that dispatches sometimes arrived as wet as if they had been submerged. The tubes had to be dug up, removed, and put into tunnels, so that stuck canisters could be freed more easily. Vacuum pumps had to be purchased to replace the steam pumps. But it was a new technology, and the drive to speed up publication of news was so strong that journalists were ready to try just about anything.

The stunning developments in newspaper technology signaled the demise of what was called "personal journalism" — a cerebral, reflective approach in which the editor's opinions and personality defined the newspaper and its connections with readers. "The day of the editor is not gone," *Fourth Estate* insisted in 1897. "His training and intimate acquaintance with men and affairs make him an authority on many subjects. His power as an educator and instructor is not gone. He is still a leader among men."[42] But the inspirational leadership of "personal journalism" was fading, inevitably giving way to more sophisticated, if impersonal, techniques of business management. These techniques meant increased authority for publishers and managers on the business side of newspapers.

Organizational structure came to be emphasized, a trend that characterized much of American business. Some competitors merged and formed monopolies (i.e., exclusive control of a particular market) or oligopolies (i.e., control of a market by a few sellers) and tried to raise prices. More often, businesses with common interests simply formed trade associations. One of today's most powerful media associations, the Newspaper Association of America, was founded in 1887 as the American Newspaper Publishers' Association. Its first national meeting began by dealing with the problem of unethical and unscrupulous advertising agents. Within a decade, agents had established their own group,

the American Advertising Agents Association, partly to deal with unscrupulous publishers. A primary need for the ANPA came from what publishers felt was the ineffectiveness of the previous National Editorial Association and the older state press associations. With their new, more modern structure, newspapers needed a new group aimed at meeting publishers' needs. Publishers and editors now had separate organizations. The functional distinction was clear: an editor's role was to fill half the paper with news and commentary. The position of advertising manager became common, with responsibilities for the other half of newspaper content. The publisher's job was to oversee both and to be sure the newspaper made money.

Revenues increasingly came from advertising. In 1879, newspapers and periodicals had received 56% of their revenues from circulation and 44% from advertising. By 1889 the split was about 50-50, and by 1899 the ratio was 45.5% from circulation and 54.5% from advertising. Department store advertising had become particularly important — and conspicuous. A new breed of professional advertising men became evident. The advertising agents of the 1880s were primarily brokers, shopping for the newspaper that would give the lowest rate. The ad men and women of the 1890s were often professional artists and copy writers providing creative services for clients. They also began to study demographics and found that large numbers of women were reading newspapers and shopping accordingly.

In short, the business of newspapering changed dramatically during the late nineteenth century. The old-time paper, driven by the personality and opinions of a dynamic editor, was receding in importance; and the roles of publisher, business manager, advertising manager, and circulation manager were assuming importance, establishing a structure familiar to this day.

YELLOW JOURNALISM

As the 1890s wore on, the term "new journalism" began to give way to a more evocative and sneering expression — one that is still in wide use. That term was "yellow journalism," and it first appeared in print in early 1897, in the *New York Press*. The *Press*

[42]"Editorials and Their Value," *Fourth Estate*, 9 September 1897, 4.

was edited by Ervin Wardman, a fastidious Harvard graduate uncomfortable with the searching reporting and aggressive self-promotion of the *World* and *Journal*. He began experimenting in print with phrases more denunciatory than "new journalism." The new journalism, he wrote in January 1897, "continues to think up a varied assortment of new lies." Later in the month, he asked in a single-line editorial comment: "Why not call it nude journalism?" It clearly was a play on "new journalism" and meant to suggest the absence of "even the veneer of decency."

Before long, Wardman seized upon the phrase "yellow-kid journalism," inspired by comic characters appearing in both the *World* and *Journal*. He soon shortened the phrase to "yellow journalism," and the *Press* invoked the epithet repeatedly in editorial columns. The idiom caught on quickly. By the end of March 1897, references to yellow journalism had appeared in newspapers as dispersed as Richmond, Chicago, and San Francisco. Even Hearst's *Journal* came to embrace the term.

While "yellow journalism" was born and lives on as a disparaging epithet, its practices represented an intensification or elaboration of those associated with New Journalism. The salient features of yellow journalism were said to have spread "like a prairie fire,"[43] taking hold to varying degrees in several cities, including Boston, Chicago, Denver, San Francisco, and St. Louis.

It was a highly idiosyncratic genre. Not every example of yellow journalism was a facsimile of Hearst's aggressive *Journal*. The *Denver Post* and *San Francisco Examiner* were, for example, noticeably less inclined to indulge in self-promotion than either the *Journal* or the *World*. The *Boston Post* opened its flamboyant front pages to display advertising, a practice not uncommon in Boston. The *Journal* was more inclined to use banner headlines than the *World*.

Such differences notwithstanding, those papers classified as "yellow journals" were, at a minimum, typographically assertive in their use of headlines and illustrations. They certainly *looked* different from their gray, conservative counterparts, and their use of design elements was much more imaginative. They were, moreover, inclined to campaign vigorously against powerful interests and municipal abuses, ostensibly on behalf of "the people." And they usually were not shy in doing so.

It its most developed form, yellow journalism was characterized by the following features:

• frequent use of multicolumn headlines that sometimes stretched across the front page

• generous and imaginative use of illustrations, including photographs and other graphic representations such as locator maps

• bold and experimental layouts, including those in which one report and illustration would dominate the front page, with such layouts sometimes enhanced by the use of color

• a penchant for self-promotion, to call attention in headlines to the paper's accomplishments

• an activist ethos, as suggested by the self-congratulatory campaigns, or crusades, against business trusts and municipal cor-

ruption

• a tendency to rely on anonymous sources, particularly in stories from leading reporters.

Hearst's *Journal* was easily the most aggressive, flamboyant, and controversial exemplar of yellow journalism. In reading issues of the *Journal* of the late 1890s, it is impossible to remain unimpressed by its zest and its enterprise. Its successes in obtaining confidential reports and documents were frequent and notable. They included publishing in 1896 the text of an ill-fated arbitration treaty between the United States and Britain; disclosing in 1898 the contents of an indiscreet but exceedingly revealing private letter written by Spain's chief diplomat in the United States, in which he disparaged the U.S. president; and divulging in 1899 the text of the peace treaty that ended the war between the United States and Spain.[44] Contemporaries were known to congratulate the *Journal* for its "extraordinary" enterprise.[45]

The *Journalist* trade publication attempted in 1897 to grasp the appeal of yellow journalism and concluded:

> It is not the … impertinent intrusions into privacy, the reckless printing of alleged news that is not news that makes sensational journalism popular with the majority of its supporters. It is the freshest news brightly presented, the sham sharply punctured and, above all, the feeling, justified or not, that behind and through the paper beats a warm, generous human heart alive to the troubles and miseries of humanity and anxious to alleviate them.[46]

Interviewed for a book published in 1897, Hearst's business manager, T.T. Williams, argued that yellow journalism was distinctive mainly in its typography. He declared:

> Sensationalism is largely a matter of type — of head lines, display, illustrations. The most eminently respectable newspapers in this country at times print matter that the so-called sensational newspaper would never dare to print – but the so-called respectable newspaper escapes uncriticized because it does not look sensational.[47]

As critics often noted, the yellow press did indulge in oddities and contrivance, which encouraged the view that it was eager "to sport with the facts."[48] While strange and improbable stories — such as "Is the Sun Preparing to Give Birth to a New World?"[49] —

---

[43]Will Irwin, "The American Newspaper: The Spread and Decline of Yellow Journalism," reprinted in Will Irwin, *The American Newspaper* (Ames, Iowa, 1969).

[44]"Full Text of the Venezuelan Treaty: Final Draft of the Arbitration Now Published for the First Time," *New York Journal*, 6 December 1896, 1; "The Worst Insult to the United States in Its History," *New York Journal*, 9 February 1898, 1; and "First Publication of Paris Protocols and Peace Treaty: The Journal Makes Public the Private Documents Recording the Proceedings of the Peace Commission," *New York Journal*, 1 January 1899, 25.

[45]See, for example, "Extraordinary Example," *Fourth Estate*, 24 November 1898, 4; and "Enterprise Tells: The New York Journal's Notable Achievements," *Fourth Estate*, 27 October 1900, 3.

[46]"What We Want," *Journalist*, 1 May 1897, 12.

[47]Quoted in Charles Austin Bates, ed., *American Journalism* (New York, 1897), 314.

[48]Sydney Brooks, "The American Yellow Press," *Fortnightly Review* 96 (December 1911): 1128.

[49]"Is the Sun Preparing to Give Birth to a New World?" *New York Journal*, 12 September 1897, 20-1.

The *Journal's* Stars

Hearst's *New York Journal* gave star billing to two eminent journalists it hired to cover the Cuban rebellion against Spain in 1896. The artist Frederic Remington (left) illustrated the fighting, and Richard Harding Davis reported on it. The assignment produced what is perhaps the best-known legend in American journalism — Hearst's purported vow to "furnish the war" with Spain.

were usually confined to Sunday supplements, they certainly were blighting counterfeits. And they inspired one critic to liken yellow journalism to a "contest of madmen for the primacy of the sewer."[50]

Critics also engaged in more direct and hostile assaults. Wardman's *Press* and Dana's *New York Sun* lent editorial support to a brief but intense campaign in New York in 1897 to ban the *Journal* and *World* from public libraries, reading rooms, and social clubs. Although initially successful, the campaign soon collapsed — in no small part because the yellow press was livelier and more irresistible than its conservative counterparts, including the *Press* and the *Sun*. The *World* taunted those and other rival papers as "the derelicts of journalism"[51]; and the *Journal* sneered, "The new journalism does things; the old journalism stands around and objects."[52]

Not only was the *Journal* a target of dismissive, conservative rivals, it also was at the center of the most enduring and powerful legends associated with yellow journalism. Perhaps the best-known was an infamous vow attributed to Hearst in the prelude

to the Spanish-American War in 1898.

THE SPANISH-AMERICAN WAR

The war with Spain was the upshot of the devastating rebellion in Cuba against Spanish colonial rule. The rebellion began in 1895, and Spain responded by sending an army of 200,000 soldiers to Cuba. Their commander was Captain General Valeriano Weyler y Nicolau, who insisted that "war should be answered with war." The most severe and controversial of his tactics were his reconcentration orders, which forced Cuba's rural population into urban camps in an attempt to deny the insurgents support from the countryside. Tens of thousands of noncombatants were crowded into the camps, where many of them died from disease and malnutrition. Americans were appalled, and newspapers took frequent notice. The humanitarian disaster caused by the reconcentration policies may have been more persuasive than any other factor in the U.S. decision to intervene militarily in Cuba.

In December 1896, Hearst sent Richard Harding Davis and Frederic Remington, the famous artist of the American West, to Cuba to spend a month with the rebels. By then, Davis had already become a swashbuckling hero. He was a doer, a romantic who managed to live the life of high adventure many Americans dreamed of but never came close to experiencing. He was vain and indisputably handsome, with perfectly sculpted features. A popular nickname for him was "Gibson Boy," because his flawless looks seemed ideally paired with the Gibson Girls so popular in 1890s illustrations. He appeared for his first reporting job dressed like an English dandy and soon was fired for sitting down to type still wearing his yellow kid gloves. But he did not repeat the mistake, and on a later assignment in Texas he did not hesitate to leap onto a horse to join in pursuit of a Mexican bandit, riding across thirty miles of scorching, dusty prairie.

Davis went to New York and the *Evening Sun,* where he served one of the country's most talented editors, Arthur Brisbane; but he found a daily newspaper's routine confining and accepted an editorship at *Harper's Weekly.* Gradually his career evolved toward freelance writing, and he did news work for both magazines and newspapers. He also wrote fiction, some of it autobiographical, drawing from a wide variety of experience. His best known work of fiction was *Soldiers of Fortune,* which was published in 1897 and described the exploits of an American adventurer-explorer in Latin America. His reporting assignments included the coronation of Czar Nicholas II, Queen Victoria's Diamond Jubilee, and many other events abroad, including the opening battles of World War I. An impressive and talented figure, he was welcomed into many places correspondents dream of entering — the courts of royalty and the dens of bandits and adventurers.

On assignment to Cuba, Davis and Remington arrived in Havanna in January 1897 but never reached the insurgents' camps. Remington left for home after a week. Davis stayed a month. In any event, their assignment to Cuba gave rise to what is perhaps the most famous anecdote in American journalism history.

---

[50]Brooks, "The American Yellow Press," 1131.

[51]"The Derelicts of Journalism," *New York World,* 28 March 1897, 10-11.

[52]Quoted in "The New Replies to the Old," *Fourth Estate,* 31 December 1896, 9.

Richard Harding Davis
One of the best writers ever in American journalism, Richard Harding Davis was a reporter for such newspapers as Charles Dana's *New York Sun* and William Randolph Hearst's *New York Journal.* He gained immense popularity not only for his newspaper writing, plays, and novels but for his athletic good looks.

Legend has it that Remington, seeking to cut short the assignment, cabled Hearst, saying: "Everything is quiet. There will be no war. I wish to return." Hearst is said to have sent a cable in reply, stating: "Please remain. You furnish the pictures, and I'll furnish the war."[53] The purported exchange has endured not only as evidence of Hearst's reckless arrogance but of the potentially malign effects of the news media. The exchange, however, almost certainly never took place.[54]

The yellow press is at the heart of an even larger, more powerful legend — that its overheated coverage of the Cuban insurrection forced the United States into war with Spain. The American

people supposedly were "whipped to a white heat" by over-the-top reporting, claimed one historian, for example. They were so motivated that they were "determined to have their war to free Cuba — and they got it."[55] Policymakers and Congress could do little more than to give in to the demands for war, demands that were especially insistent following the destruction of the U.S. battleship *Maine* in Havana harbor in February 1898.

It is a neat and tidy explanation, blaming a wayward press for a war that otherwise would not have been fought. But the evidence is extensive that the yellow press was not solely to blame for propelling the United States into the war. That evidence includes the following points:

• As important and devastating as the Cuban insurrection was, it was not an unending preoccupation in the yellow press. There was no steady drumbeat of coverage calling for the United States to enter the war. In fact, Cuba fell off the *Journal*'s front page for noticeable stretches during the months before the *Maine's* destruction.

• The *Journal* did not incessantly call for the United States to go to war with Spain. Its abiding call was, instead, *independence* for Cuba. The *Journal,* moreover, on several occasions in 1897 mistakenly predicted the imminent success of the Cuban insurgency.

• There is little evidence that newspapers beyond New York City, especially those in rural America, were at all influenced by the content of the yellow journals, including their exaggerated coverage holding Spanish authorities accountable for the sinking of the *Maine.* Instead, several studies have found that the U.S. hinterland press was inclined to condemn the yellow journals for their aggressive and questionable reports about the *Maine.*

• If the yellow press did foment the war, then researchers should be able to find some reference to that influence in the personal papers and the reminiscences of policymakers. But neither the diary entries of policymakers nor the contemporaneous private exchanges of U.S. diplomats indicate that the yellow newspapers exerted any influence. When the yellow press was discussed within the administration of President William McKinley, it was dismissed as a nuisance. It was regarded neither as a source of insight into popular thinking nor as a useful guide in pursuing delicate and ultimately futile negotiations with Spain about Cuba.[56]

The forces that culminated in the conflict were diplomatic in nature and far greater than the power of the yellow press to direct or notably influence. Essentially, the Cuban insurgents would settle for nothing short of independence, which Spain — mostly for reasons of domestic stability — would not grant. The United States, meanwhile, was unwilling to tolerate the mounting humanitarian disaster and economic disruption created by Spain's attempts to quell the rebellion. Hearst's and Pulitzer's papers certainly reported on, but did not create, the conditions in Cuba that led to war.

So what, then, accounts for the enduring tendency to blame the

[53]James Creelman, *On the Great Highway: The Wanderings and Adventures of a Special Correspondent* (Boston, 1901), 177-8.

[54]Reasons for doubting the anecdote are many. Hearst later denied having sent such a message; and Remington, apparently, never discussed it. The anecdote's sole original source, James Creelman, was in Europe at the time the Remington-Hearst exchange would have taken place, and he never explained how he learned about it. In addition, the passages "there will be no war" and "I'll furnish the war" are simply at odds with the rebellion then raging in Cuba. The insurrection and its privations were the very reasons Hearst sent Remington and Davis to Cuba: They went to cover a low-intensity war. It is highly unlikely, moreover, that such an exchange would have cleared Spanish censors in Havana. So strict were the censors that dispatches by U.S. correspondents covering the insurrection were often taken by passenger steamer to Florida and transmitted from there. For a detailed debunking of the purported Remington-Hearst exchange, see W. Joseph Campbell, *Yellow Journalism: Puncturing the Myths, Defining the Legacies* (Westport, Conn., 2001), 71-95.

[55]Thomas A. Bailey, *A Diplomatic History of the American People,* 8th ed. (New York, 1969), 463-4.

[56]See Campbell, *Yellow Journalism,* 98-9.

The Battleship *Maine*
The *New York Journal's* and *World's* reporting of the destruction of the American warship *Maine* in Havana harbor in February 1898 pointedly accused Spain of complicity. Many historians believe that the explosion really was caused by either gunpowder in the *Maine's* magazine or coal dust in its furnace room. A total of 266 sailors died from the explosion. Both the *World* and the *Journal* were quick to blame Spanish sabotage. "Remember the Maine" became the battle cry in America's war against Spain.

yellow press for inciting the war? At least two factors appear to be at work. One is that blaming the *Journal* and *World* for the war is a ready means to excoriate yellow journalism, a convenient way to summarize its excesses and define its supposed malevolence. More broadly, blaming the yellow press for bringing on the Spanish-American War is a way of highlighting the presumed perils of an unrestrained press.

The other factor is that the *Journal* was, in a sense, hoisted with its own petard. The *Journal* did suggest it was responsible for causing the war: It *did* place on its front page for three days in May 1898 the epigram, "How Do You Like the Journal's War?"[57] But in so asserting, it probably was mocking the claims of rival newspapers, particularly the *New York Evening Post*, which had accused the yellow press of "fomenting" the war.[58] The timing and context of the *Journal's* report is significant.

The *Evening Post's* "fomenting" editorial was published April 30, 1898. The next day, American naval vessels engaged and destroyed a Spanish squadron in Manila Bay, in the first major U.S. engagement of the war. The first sketchy reports of the stunning victory appeared in American newspapers on May 2. On its editorial page that day, the *Journal* published the portion of the *Evening Post's* editorial accusing the yellow press of "fomenting" the war. The *Journal* mocked that assertion in a headline spread across its editorial page. It read: "Some People Say the Journal Brought on This War. How Do You Like It as Far as It's Gone[?]."[59]

That headline and the epigram on the *Journal's* front page a few days later — "How Do You Like the Journal's War?" — probably were intended as taunting retorts to the *Evening Post* and, as such, were in keeping with the brickbats openly and routinely ex-

changed among newspapers. But they were not serious claims of responsibility for bringing on the conflict.

The war lasted 114 days — from April 24 to August 12 — during which time the U.S. military waged a successful, two-theater campaign, destroying Spanish naval squadrons in Manila Bay and in eastern Cuba and forcing the surrender of one of Spain's armies in Cuba. Even though the war was swift and decisive, American correspondents filled prominent and controversial roles in covering it. "Never, before or after, were correspondents so conspicuous for audacity and daring — and interference in matters not their business," one historian has written.[60] At one time or another, reporters took up weapons and joined American troops firing on Spanish forces in Cuba, collected and passed along information to U.S. naval commanders about Spanish defenses near Havana, and claimed to have captured entire towns during the American military invasion of Puerto Rico at the end of the war.

The war's most astonishing press-military encounter came during the formal surrender of Spanish forces at Santiago de Cuba in July. Santiago, the island's second-largest city, had been the focal point of most of the fighting in the Caribbean theater. After battles on the heights near the city and after a sweeping American naval victory off Santiago, the Spanish forces gave up. The centerpiece of the surrender ceremony was raising the American flag above the Governor's Palace, the seat of Spanish authority in the city.

As the ceremony began, the *World's* senior war correspondent, Sylvester Scovel, clambered to the palace rooftop, apparently intent on positioning himself near the flagpole, so that he would appear in photographs of the flag-raising. American officers spotted him and ordered him down. A few moments later, Scovel approached the American military commander, Major General Will-

[57]The epigram appeared on the front page, on either side of the newspaper's nameplate. See *New York Journal*, 8, 9, and 10 May 1898. As John D. Stevens perceptively noted: "Because it fit the picture of Hearst as an evil genius, [the epigram] is about the only Hearst boast that historians ever believed." See Stevens, *Sensationalism and the New York Press* (New York, 1991), 97.

[58]"The New Political Force," *New York Evening Post*, 30 April 1898, 4.

[59]"Some People Say the Journal Brought On This War. How Do You Like It as Far as It's Gone[?]," *New York Journal*, 2 May 1898, 10.

[60]Charles H. Brown, *The Correspondents' War: Journalists in the Spanish-American War* (New York, 1967), vii.

iam Rufus Shafter. They exchanged heated words; and Shafter slapped Scovel, who swung wildly at Shafter. Although accounts differ, Scovel probably landed his blow. In any case, he was arrested and deported, his career as a war correspondent at an end.

The episode was an acute embarrassment to the *World*, which in the early phases of the war had offered outstanding coverage. Scovel, notably, had filed exceptionally detailed reports about the destruction of the *Maine*. The *World* scored the news beat of the war in publishing the first detailed report of Commodore George Dewey's stunning naval victory at Manila Bay on May 1. The scoop was attributable to the savvy of Edward Harden, a correspondent the *World* had engaged just before the war. He and two other journalists accompanied Dewey and his squadron in steaming from Hong Kong to the Spanish-ruled Philippines soon after war was declared in April. Dewey engaged and destroyed a decrepit Spanish fleet in Manila Bay, but only fragmentary reports were transmitted before the cable link to the rest of the world was cut.

A few days after the battle, Dewey sent a vessel back to Hong Kong to telegraph his official report to Washington. Harden and his two rivals — John T. McCutcheon, an artist for the *Chicago Record*, and Joseph L. Stickney of the *New York Herald* — went along, eyeing one another nervously throughout the two-day voyage. In Hong Kong, Harden filed a 50-word summary of the battle at "urgent" rates — or almost $10 a word — and then a longer dispatch at less expensive rates. His clever move meant that his summary dispatch superseded all other cable traffic — and it arrived in New York hours ahead of McCutcheon's and Stickney's accounts. Even Dewey's message arrived after Harden's summary.

It was a stunning scoop. The *World*, indulging in customary self-promotion, called it the news beat of the century. McCutcheon later said Harden beat him because "inexperience in handling cable material had put me at a disadvantage. I didn't know about 'Urgent!' dispatches!"[61]

But it was Richard Harding Davis who emerged from the war as America's best known war correspondent. His dispatches for the *New York Herald* and longer articles for *Scribner's Magazine* helped ensure his reputation — and that of Theodore Roosevelt, the irrepressible second-in-command of a dismounted volunteer cavalry unit known as the Rough Riders. In an account in *Scribner's* about the battle on the heights above Santiago in July, Davis wrote that the image of Roosevelt, "mounted high on horseback, and charging the rifle pits at a gallop and quite alone[,] made you feel that you would like to cheer. He wore on his sombrero a blue polka-dot handkerchief … which, as he advanced, floated straight behind his head, like a guidon."[62] Davis' articles in *Scribner's* were so rich and detailed, one critic wrote, that he deserved "a reputation as one of the most vivid and picturesque of living writers" who worked in English.[63]

Davis certainly had a memorable war. During the first encounter between American and Spanish troops near Santiago, he grabbed a carbine and began firing — wildly — at the Spanish. He accompanied U.S. troops in their invasion of Puerto Rico and years later claimed that the inhabitants of Coamo in south-central Puerto Rico surrendered their town to him.[64]

Davis credited Stephen Crane, the famed novelist and a rival correspondent, with the "capture" of Juana Diaz, another town in south-central Puerto Rico. Crane approached it before dawn one morning in early August, nonchalantly "smoking a cigarette," Davis wrote. "His khaki suit, slouched hat, and leggings were all that was needed to drive the first man he saw, or rather, the man who saw him first, back upon the town in disorderly retreat." The mayor was awakened and surrendered the town to "the American conqueror.… Crane told me that no General in the moment of victory had ever acted in a more generous manner. He shot no one against a wall, looted no churches, levied no 'forced loans.'"[65]

At least three female correspondents wrote about the war. The most visible and enterprising was Anna Northend Benjamin, who reported for *Leslie's Magazine* and showed impressive resourcefulness in reaching Cuba. She was barred from troop transports leaving Florida for the war zone — so she talked her way onboard a coal-carrying schooner headed for eastern Cuba. She wrote a dispatch from Guantanamo Bay and then took a steamer for Santiago de Cuba. She was among the first American correspondents to reach the city after the Spanish surrender.

Inevitably perhaps, Hearst took a conspicuous role in the climactic naval battle of the war, in which U.S. vessels destroyed a Spanish squadron off Santiago de Cuba. Hearst had arrived in the Caribbean about a week before, traveling in luxury aboard a converted fruit steamer, the *Sylvia*. During the naval battle, the *Sylvia* moved close to the action as the Spanish warships — which were trying to run a blockade — were destroyed, one by one. After the battle, Hearst brought twenty-nine Spanish sailors on board the *Sylvia* as prisoners.

Even by Hearst's free-spending standards, the war was exceptionally costly to cover. *Fourth Estate* estimated that the *Journal* spent $50,000 a week[66] — the equivalent nowadays of roughly $1.5 million — on cable tolls, reporters' salaries, and dispatch boars that ferried correspondents' reports from Cuba to Jamaica or Haiti for transmission to the United States. The additional war-related expenses for the *World* were estimated at $30,000 a week.[67] The *Herald*, the *Sun*, and the Associated Press are estimated to have spent about $250,000 each. Meanwhile, advertising revenues fell off dramatically. *Fourth Estate* noted as the war unfolded: "It is mainly upon the advertising that the publishers must rely for their profit. In these times of war, however, the volume of advertising is contracted to a marked degree. Many liberal advertisers have either stopped advertising altogether or have cut down their expenditures 50 or 60 per cent."[68]

[61]John T. McCutcheon, *Drawn From Memory* (Indianapolis, 1950), 114.
[62]Richard Harding Davis, "The Battle of San Juan," *Scribner's Magazine* 24:4 (October 1898): 402.
[63]Quoted in "Newspaper Men in the War," *Literary Digest*, 15 October 1898, 457.
[64]Richard Harding Davis, *The Notes of a War Correspondent* (New York, 1910).
[65]Richard Harding Davis, "How Stephen Crane Took Juana Dias," in R. W. Stallman and E.R. Hagemann, eds., *The War Dispatches of Stephen Crane* (New York, 1964), 197-8.
[66]"The Year's Record," *Fourth Estate*, 12 January 1899, 2.
[67]"War Reporting," *Fourth Estate*, 28 April 1898, 1.
[68]"War and Newspapers," *Fourth Estate*, 5 May 1898, 6.

Immigrants and the Press
With a flood of immigrants entering the United States, foreign-language newspapers helped prepare the newly arrived for assimilation and citizenship. This cartoon from *Leslie's Weekly* in 1888 illustrated the attitudes between old Americans and the newcomers. Many immigrants preferred to retain their native language rather than learn English, and numerous foreign-language newspapers were started to appeal to them.

A few years after the war, the *Journal* scoffed at claims that it fomented the conflict as a cynical attempt to build circulation and boost profits. On its best day the *Journal* printed 1,068,000 copies. Brisbane later said 200,000 more could have been sold. "Would you like to know what effect the war had on the money-making feature of this particular newspaper?" the *Journal* asked rhetorically. "The wholesale price of paper was greatly increased. Advertising diminished, expenses increased enormously." It added that its total expenses related to covering the conflict exceeded $750,000 — the equivalent today of more than $20 million.[69]

Yellow journalism reached its zenith during or soon after the war. Inevitably, the energy and flamboyance of the genre proved difficult to sustain. The fading of yellow journalism was attributable to a convergence of multiple forces. Conservative competitors began to incorporate features of the genre, notably in somewhat

[69]"Just One Small Fact," *New York Journal*, 21 January 1902, 14.

more vivid page layouts. Muckraking magazines such as *McClure's* became journalism's most prominent crusaders, exposing municipal corruption and corporate greed and misconduct. Pulitzer grew increasingly feeble, and Hearst broadened his interests to state and national politics and ran unsuccessfully for president in 1904.

ALTERNATIVE NEWSPAPERS

While the yellow press and thousands of other newspapers were operating in the mainstream of American journalism, many demographic groups were living at the margins of society. A number of publications tried to appeal to them.

In this period of heavy immigration — with approximately 9 million people moving to the United States between 1880 and 1900 — foreign-language newspapers filled important functions in readying the recently arrived for assimilation and citizenship. The German-language papers were the most numerous, with the 1880 census showing 641 papers with an aggregate circulation of about 2.5 million. Eighty of them were dailies.

Native Americans, especially in Indian Territory (now part of Oklahoma), needed their own papers to help preserve their culture and provide forums for discussion of the difficult issues they faced. The Cherokee Nation led the way, using the alphabet that Sequoya had invented, and by 1891 had its own newspaper, the *Daily News*.

Anarchists founded their own newspapers. *Liberty* (1881-1908) was edited by *Boston Globe* writer Benjamin Tucker, who advocated freedom and laissez-faire capitalism. But his energy was also needed to combat the more militant anarchist following of Johann Most and his German-language *Freiheit* ("Freedom"). Along with the anarchist newspapers *Truth* and *Alarm*, *Freiheit* ran inflammatory articles on how to make bombs. One masthead read, "Truth is five cents a copy and dynamite forty cents a pound."

Newspapers advocated many other interests. Numerous papers served the labor movement. One of them, the *Standard* (1887-1891), gained national attention as the voice of its editor, political economist Henry George of single-tax fame. Another hundred or so papers, scattered around the country, were devoted to the causes of temperance and prohibition. Populist papers numbered around 1,000 at their peak in the early 1890s.

Without doubt, however, the group in greatest need for a voice was African Americans. Six-and-a-half-million strong, they saw their recently won freedom taken away bit by bit under the sharecropper system and forced labor laws in the South, followed by new Jim Crow laws that the U.S. Supreme Court affirmed in 1896 in *Plessy v. Ferguson*. Despite the hardship of targeting a newspaper to such an economically bereft market, many black editors emerged to serve it.

In the four decades following the Civil War, 1,200 black newspapers were started, mostly in the South. John P. Mitchell established the *Richmond Planet* as the largest circulation weekly in Virginia with 13,000 subscribers. One of the first African Americans

Ida B. Wells

Ida B. Wells decided that by using the press she could expose the horrors, immorality, and illegality of the lynching of black men. In 1892 she wrote an exposé that ran in the *New York Age*. It was republished as a pamphlet titled *Southern Horrors: Lynch Law in All Its Phases*. Based on articles that ran in the white press and interviews, Wells' work was a damning indictment of the inequality that African Americans faced. In 1895 she published another pamphlet, *The Red Record*, based in part on photographs, illustrations, and statistics on lynchings that ran in the *Chicago Tribune*. In 1899 she did another book, *Lynch Law in Georgia*, based on material from the *Atlanta Journal* and *Atlanta Constitution*. Lynchings did not stop because of the work of Wells and other crusaders, but they did decrease dramatically after the 1890s. Forty states from 1890 through 1930 passed codes to deal with lynchings and race riots. One of the people who deserved much of the credit was Wells.

African-American Editor Fights Lynchings and Discrimination

Many women throughout history have contributed to the betterment of society with determination that defied the odds. But none faced more difficult challenges than Ida B. Wells, a tenacious crusader who would not back down in the fight for what she saw as righteous causes.

An African American born into slavery in Mississippi in 1862, Wells lived during a time when being a woman meant not having the right to vote and not expecting to have a career. And even though slavery was abolished while she was a young girl, discrimination and violence made that newfound freedom seem hollow.

She attended Shaw University (now Rust College) in Mississippi and taught school in Memphis, Tenn. She was known for having strong political views, and she had the fortitude to express them. Nearly three-quarters of a century before Rosa Parks became famous for refusing to give up her seat on a bus to a white passenger, Wells took a similar stand on a train in 1884.

A conductor told Wells to give up her seat and to move to a crowded and segregated smoking car. She refused and was physically removed from the train. But she was not content to let the incident go at that, and she wrote about it in a newspaper article. She also filed a lawsuit against the train company and won her case, although the Tennessee Supreme Court overturned the lower court ruling.

Violence against African Americans was not unusual, and the lynching of three friends in 1892 presented perhaps her greatest test of courage. Wells, then the editor and co-owner of the *Memphis Free Speech* newspaper, was outraged. She used her editorials to encourage black residents to leave the city in protest. While she was on a trip to New York, a mob ransacked the newspaper office, which was housed in a black church, and vowed to kill her. She relocated to Chicago.

Wells never wavered, however, in her activist approach to social ills. She worked for women's suffrage and participated in a march in Washington in 1913 to demand the right to vote. She collaborated with Jane Addams to fight segregated schools in Chicago. She also helped to establish the Negro Women's Club movement, spoke out for the rights of African-American soldiers in World War I, and was at the founding meeting of the National Association for the Advancement of Colored People.

An eloquent speaker, she traveled across the country and even to England, where she spoke out against lynching and the segregation of African Americans. She also produced pamphlets that documented episodes of hatred and violence directed by white citizens against African Americans.

Wells married Ferdinand Barnett, the founder of a black newspaper in Chicago, in 1895, and they had four children. Before her death in 1931 at age 68, she wrote an autobiography with the fitting title *Crusade for Justice*.

to work as a journalist on a metropolitan daily was T. Thomas Fortune, who began writing for the *New York Sun* in 1887. He was born a slave but early became interested in newspapers, working on black-owned weeklies in both the South and the North after the Civil War. He gained journalistic experience after buying the *Globe* in New York (1879-1884) with a colleague. They kept it going by working as compositors on another paper.[70] He reached his peak influence at the *New York Age*, which he edited from 1889 until 1907. He was African Americans' leading voice in the denunciation of lynching, disenfranchisement, and Jim Crow laws.

Ida B. Wells emerged as the leading black female editor, using the *Memphis Free Speech* to condemn the lynchings that were frequent in the heart of the South. A former slave and teacher who turned editor in Memphis, Tennessee, she understood the plight of African Americans. Having been thrown from a train for refusing to move from a car carrying whites and removed as a teacher in Shelby County, Tennessee, she began work in 1889 as editor and co-owner of the *Free Speech*. Its other co-owner was Rev. R. Nightingale, the pastor of Beale Street Baptist Church. He encouraged his congregation to subscribe to the paper, thus allowing Wells to take up journalism full-time. A contemporary biographer wrote that she was "the 'Princess of the Press,' and she has well earned the title. No writer, the male fraternity not excepted, has been more extensively quoted; none have struck harder blows at the wrongs and weakness of the race." Threatened with violence, Wells moved to New York City to write for Fortune's *Age* and then to Chicago, where she earned fame as an organizer and lecturer, both here and abroad.

COMPETITION FROM OTHER MEDIA

Historians of media economics have found much evidence to support what has been called the Principle of Relative Constancy. It holds that a fairly constant proportion of personal income will be spent on media, and if a new mass medium enters the picture, its share of revenue comes at the expense of reduced shares for existing media.[71] Data to support this proposition (also called the Scripps Hypothesis) are derived mainly from the twentieth century, because records on consumer spending before 1900 are almost non-existent. But it is clear that in the 1880s and 1890s other media began to challenge newspapers' dominance.

Books, of course, had been around longer than newspapers. However, mass production and cheap transportation began to deliver them to the marketplace in unprecedented numbers. Not only did public school attendance increase, but sales of textbooks went up even faster as pupils bought their own readers and spellers. The popular McGuffey textbooks were selling more than 2 million copies a year. In popular literature, the increase in sales was even more dramatic. The most widely published author was Horatio Alger, whose first novel appeared in 1867 and who wrote

T. Thomas Fortune
Born into slavery in Florida, T. Thomas Fortune was emancipated in 1863, when he was six years old. After working on Florida newspapers and studying journalism at Howard College, he worked on the *People's Advocate* in Washington, D.C. Moving to New York City in 1881, he worked as a printer and then became co-owner and editor of the *Globe*. He changed its name to the *New York Freeman* and then *to* the *New York Age* in 1887. Under Fortune's direction, it became the leading African-American newspaper of its era. It was at the forefront in the fight against discrimination and lynchings. He is often credited with coining the term "Afro-American" and was instrumental in founding the National Afro-American League, a forerunner of today's NAACP.

about 100 more before he died in 1899. Sales of his books are estimated at about 250 million. It was the era of the dime novel, and hundreds of writers (few of whom took their craft as seriously as Alger, a former minister) produced hackneyed plots and well-worn characterizations to meet the demand for cheap literature.

A third market appeared, as paperback collections, or "libraries," came into vogue. The growing middle class wanted an inexpensive introduction to serious literature, and the classics and best sellers were increasingly sold in groups. By 1887, twenty-six libraries were on the market, offering selections that ranged from cheap romances to the classics. A forerunner of the book club, Funk and Wagnalls had a subscription list of 16,000 who had signed up at $4 a year to receive a book every two weeks. Serious readers could fill a bookshelf with the same few dollars they might otherwise spend for the canned contents of a readyprint newspaper. No doubt many of them did.

[70]Clint C. Wilson II, *Black Journalists in Paradox* (New York, 1991), 38-41.
[71]See Maxwell E. McCombs, "Mass Media in the Marketplace," *Journalism Monographs* 24 (1972), and Benjamin M. Compaine, *Who Owns the Media?* (White Plains, N.Y., 1979).

Dime Novels

Cheap Fiction Brings Western Adventure into America's Parlors

Termed the "first profitable mass literature in the United States," the dime novel from 1860 to about 1920 played much the same role television does today. The favored form of entertainment read by nearly everyone, including adolescents and the working class, the inexpensive books sold millions of copies, often in long-running series.

Like television, dime novels both reflected and helped shape society. Also, like television, they were blamed for crime and other societal ills. Clergy and other critics proclaimed dime novels immoral, an ironic charge since publishers went out of their way to edit sex and rough language from their manuscripts.

Because the nation was enamored by the frontier after the Civil War, and because the frontier offered unlimited opportunity for tales of derring-do, it was natural for the Western adventure story to be the first, most successful dime novel genre, supplemented later by detective and self-improvement books. Historical figures like Buffalo Bill, Calamity Jane, and Kit Carson took on heroic proportions and mixed with fictional characters created by Edward Ellis, Ned Buntline, Edward Wheeler, Prentiss Ingraham, and other writers.

Dime novelists were competent, though perhaps second-rank, authors who were unceremoniously dubbed hacks because of their commercialism. They cranked out prodigious amounts of copy using pen and ink and, later, typewriters. Ingraham produced more than 600 novels, once, it is claimed, writing a 35,000-word book in twenty-four hours. Authors generally received $75 to $300 per manuscript. The most important publisher was the House of Beadle and Adams in New York, which originated dime novels by publishing Ann S. Stephens' *Malaeska: the Indian Wife of the White Hunter* in 1860. Beadle and Adams alone published more than 7,500 novels.

Dime novels succumbed in the 1920s to changing times, postal regulations, pulp fiction magazines, and movies.

Beadle & Co. inaugurated dime novels with the 1860 work by Ann Sophia Stephens' (bottom left) *Malaeska; the Indian Wife of the White Hunter* under the slogan "Books for the Millions!" Because of the book's popularity, Beadle reissued the novel with the illustrated cover above. It promoted its line of dime novels as "the choicest works of the most popular authors." Among the most popular of the dime novelists was Ned Buntline (bottom right), who played to the hilt the public image of a western adventurer.

Magazines were expanding their markets. Many trimmed their prices in the 1890s, putting monthlies like *Munsey's* and *McClure's* within the purchasing power of almost everyone. Frank Munsey lowered his price from 20¢ to 10¢ a copy and quintupled circulation from 40,000 to 200,000 in the mid-1890s. That surge represented a new kind of competition for newspapers.

The cinema, an entirely new form of mass media, began to reach large audiences by the mid-1890s. Thomas Edison (who received a patent for his Kinetoscope in 1897) and other inventors developed a way of projecting moving pictures onto screens — and audiences responded enthusiastically and in numbers. The "wonderful moving pictures"[72] were shown where space allowed — in storefronts, vaudeville houses, libraries, department stores, and recital halls. The films usually were no longer than a minute, and their topics represented slices of daily life. For example, the subjects of a succession of Biograph exhibitions in Washington, D.C., in early 1897 included "a superb view of the Allegheny Mountains, with the Pennsylvania Limited winding its way around the curves at full speed and size; bathing in the surf at Atlantic City; callisthenic drills of United States soldiers, boys building snow men, and others."[73] President-elect McKinley strolling the lawns of his home in Ohio was the subject of a popular "view," as motion picture segments were then called. His presidential inauguration in March 1897 was the first in American history captured on film.

Footage of the Spanish-American War — some of it authentic, some of it faked — lent a story-telling dimension to the emergent cinema. Hearst was particularly cognizant of the potential of this new medium, and his *Journal* collaborated with the leading rival companies — Edison and Biograph — in securing moving images of the destruction of the *Maine* and of the war's Caribbean campaign. The association with Edison was especially important to Hearst, one of his biographers has written, because it linked him with Edison, "the most important name in moving pictures and brought the paper free advertising in every vaudeville hall where the *Edison-Journal* films were shown."[74]

The phonograph was yet another new technology. Its inventor, Edison, had been pushing it for more than a decade as a means of dictation, but in the early 1890s he began to market it as an entertainment medium. When Emile Berliner introduced the disc to replace Edison's cylinder, mass production became practical. Berliner called it the Gramophone, and by 1896 the disc was being called a phonograph "record." In 1897 Edison designed a machine for the mass market, priced at about $20. The most common use of the phonograph, though, was in arcades where machines would play a record for a nickel.

Other mass communication technologies began to appear. Although they provided no serious immediate competition for newspapers, they offered signs of rivalries to come. One already on the market was the stereograph, a device with a separate lens for each eye to look at dual photographs, giving a 3-D effect. These stereopticon slides were printed in large numbers, using the new halftone process, and found their way into many thousands of living rooms.

An even more important breakthrough came in 1898, when young Guglielmo Marconi loaded his equipment onto a steamer and set out to cover the Kingstown Regatta — by sending wireless messages ashore for the *Dublin Daily Express* in Ireland. The news of the race made it to the streets before any of the ships returned to port, and the feat earned Marconi an invitation to cross the Atlantic and provide similar coverage of the America's Cup race for the *New York Herald*. He did so, successfully, in October 1899 — the first commercial use of wireless telegraphy to transmit news in America. "With these two yachting events at the close of the nineteenth century," one broadcast historian has written, "news and radio were joined. Broadcast journalism, in dots and dashes, was born."[75] Meanwhile, Paul Nipkow's scanning disc, a forerunner of television, had been patented in Germany.

In 1898, the Danish engineer Valdemar Poulsen patented a radical new device that he called a "telegraphone." He theorized that if sound could be converted to magnetic impulses in some electrically charged carrier, such as a wire, then the impulses could be converted back to sound, and after use the magnetic field could be erased and the carrier used to record over and over again. It was demonstrated successfully at the 1900 Paris Exposition, where it created a sensation, although witnesses could hardly know that it would take decades before the principle could be successfully applied and disseminated into the average middle-class home. More than half a century later, Poulsen's invention — magnetic recording — reached full development in the audio tape.

But marvelous innovations and inventions did not completely dim the appeal of the newspaper. Max O'Rell, a popular French author and journalist, wrote in the *North American Review* in 1890: "Speak of electric light, of phonographs and gramophones, if you like; speak of those thousand and one inventions which have come out of the American brain; but if you wish to mention the greatest and most wonderful achievement of American activity, do not hesitate to give the palm to American journalism: it is simply the *ne plus ultra.*"

HOW YELLOW JOURNALISM LIVES ON

The journalism of the late nineteenth century lives on in many ways. For example, the decidedly American idiom of "yellow journalism" has found recent expression in an astonishing variety of international settings. "Yellow journalism" has been associated with bribe-taking by journalists in Thailand and with "rumor-mongering factories" in Pakistan. It has been blamed for "creating chaos, despondency, and lies" in Kenya. A large number of complaints filed every year with the press commission in India are about "yellow journalism."[76] Letter-writers to contemporary American newspapers are quite fond of the term "yellow journal-

---

[72]"Cinematographic at Willard Hall," *Washington Post*, 14 January 1897, 7.
[73]"Biograph Views in National Colors," *Washington Post*, 26 February 1897, 7.
[74]David Nasaw, *The Chief: The Life of William Randolph Hearst* (Boston, 2000), 133.

[75]Edward Bliss Jr., *Now the News: The Story of Broadcast Journalism* (New York, 1991), 2.
[76]See Campbell, *Yellow Journalism*, 175-6.

From Golden to Yellow Journalism

As Pulitzer and Hearst tried to outdo one another in sensational techniques, some publications and many members of the public reacted negatively. This cartoon — which appeared in 1897, even before the height of yellow journalism — caricatured Pulitzer and Hearst as being swept away by their own excesses.

ism," invoking it to assail bias, distortion, sensationalism, and other failings of the news media.

But "yellow journalism" resonates in ways more systemic and integral than the offhand dismissals of irritated letter-writers. The legacies of yellow journalism are complex and multifaceted. Pieces of its DNA can be identified in the practice and theory of at least two strains of activist-oriented, contemporary journalism.

An intriguing parallel to yellow journalism as it was practiced more than a century ago can be found in London's often outlandish, over-the-top tabloid press. The unabashed self-promotion of London tabloids — such as that of the *Sun* and *News of the World* — reflects an important defining feature of yellow journalism.

The genetic material of yellow journalism also can be detected in the "public" or "civic" journalism movement that emerged in

the United States late in the twentieth century. Public journalism regarded the press as a force for reinvigorating participatory democracy. The problem-solving component central to public journalism is reminiscent of the activist ethos of the yellow press. The *New York World* and the *New York Journal* styled themselves as the public's agents in attacking the abuses of big business and corrupt government. In some respects, yellow journalism was a self-promoting precursor of public journalism.

Such parallels are more than merely curious or coincidental. Indeed, they suggest a little recognized interconnectedness in journalistic practice and style over time. The parallels serve as well to demonstrate that the more contemporary variations of journalism are not altogether new but, in reality, spring from important antecedents.

RECOMMENDED READINGS

BOOKS

Alexander, Ann F. *Race Man: The Rise and Fall of the "Fighting Editor," John Mitchell, Jr.* Charlottesville, Va., 2002. As editor of the *Richmond Planet*, Mitchell campaigned vigorously against lynching and other abuses and mistreatment that African Americans suffered.

Baker, Nicholson and Margaret Brentano. *The World on Sunday: Graphic Art in Joseph Pulitzer's Newspaper (1898-1911)*. New York, 2005. This volume reprints 128 color pages from the *New York World's* Sunday issues. Pulitzer had bought a color press for the *World* and began using color in the newspaper just as his eyesight began to fail.

Baldasty, Gerald J. *The Commercialization of News in the Nineteenth Century*. Madison, Wis., 1992. During the 1800s, newspapers were transformed from a political to a commercial base, with the change becoming virtually complete in the last two decades.

---. *Scripps and the Business of Newspapers*. Urbana, Ill., 1999. "Edward Willis Scripps revolutionized the newspaper industry by applying modern business practices to his chain of more than forty newspapers and creating a telegraphic news service and an illustrated news features syndicate."

Blackbeard, Bill. *R.F. Outcault's the Yellow Kid*. Northampton, Mass., 1995. This account traces the development of the Yellow Kid and reproduces 250 of Outcault's comics with commentary on their meaning.

Brian, Denis. *Pulitzer: A Life*. New York, 2001. Brian's is an admiring biography of Joseph Pulitzer.

Brown, Charles H. *The Correspondents' War*. New York, 1967. Brown approaches the Spanish-American War as convenient for reporters to cover and describes reporters as a self-important bunch.

Campbell, W. Joseph. *The Year That Defined American Journalism: 1897 and a Clash of Paradigms*. New York: Routledge, 2006. The year 1897, marked by numerous importants events, was arguably the most important in American journalism history.

---. *Yellow Journalism: Puncturing the Myths, Defining the Legacies*. Westport, Conn., 2001. Campbell debunks prominent myths of the yellow press and explores the genre's lasting contributions to the profession.

Carlson, Oliver. *Brisbane: A Candid Biography*. New York, 1937. Arthur Brisbane, Hearst's top editor, preferred the esteem of businessmen and material success to social and journalistic ideals.

Churchill, Allen. *Park Row*. New York, 1958. This entertaining, popular history covers the colorful era of New York City journalism from the 1880s to the 1930s.

Dillon, Michael. *The Life and Times of Edward H. Butler, Founder of the Buffalo News (1840-1914): A Crusading Journalist Navigates the Gilded Age*. Lewiston, N.Y., 2003. Butler was "emblematic of the late 19th-century new journalists who built the modern press by wrenching civic discourse from its narrow partisan roots and carving out vital new cultural, social, economic and political roles for newspapers."

Dreiser, Theodore. *Newspaper Days*, T.D. Nostwich, editor. Philadelphia, 1991. This reprinted and expanded version of the American novelist's recollections, first published in 1922, covers his newspaper reporting days in the 1890s.

Frasca, Ralph. *The Rise and Fall of the Saturday Globe*. Cranbury, N.J., 1992. The *Globe* was the first national weekly newspaper, published from 1881 to 1924.

Harp, Dustin. *Desperately Seeking Women Readers: U.S. Newspapers and the Construction of a Female Readership*. Lanham, Md., 2007. Starting in 1890, when they designed separate pages for female readers, American newspapers created an image of women as people who were interested in news that was different from that which interested men.

Johns, George S. *Joseph Pulitzer: His Early Life in St. Louis and His Founding and Conduct of the Post-Dispatch up to 1883*. St. Louis, 1932. At the *Post-Dispatch*, Pulitzer developed a new form of journalism, combining the news techniques of Bennett with the enlightened editorial approach of Greeley.

Johnson, Gerald. *An Honorable Titan*. New York, 1946. Adolph Ochs' belief in traditional American values accounted for his success with the *New York Times*.

Johnson, Icie F. *William Rockhill Nelson and the Kansas City Star*. Kansas City, Mo., 1935. Nelson devoted himself and his paper to the improvement of Kansas City, and he was the premier reason for the town's progress from a small pioneer outpost to a metropolis.

Juergens, George. *Joseph Pulitzer and the New York World*. Princeton, N.J., 1966. The *World* was the originator of the modern newspaper, with its approach to illustrations, appearance, sports, women's news, concern for the underprivileged, and other features.

Kilmer, Paulette D. *The Fear of Sinking: The American Success Story in the Gilded Age*. Knoxville, Tenn., 1996. Some new ideas on the Horatio Alger "myth" help to relate this popular cultural theme to the media of the time.

King, Homer W. *Pulitzer's Prize Editor: A Biography of John A. Cockerill, 1845-1896*. Durham, N.C., 1965. King argues that Cockerill, as the managing editor of the *New York World*, was the true originator of New Journalism.

Kobre, Sidney. *The Yellow Press and Gilded Age Journalism*. Tallahassee, 1964. American journalism changed from one of personal journalism to an industry marked by mechanization, urbanization, centralization, and standardization.

Kroeger, Brooke. *Nellie Bly: Daredevil, Reporter, Feminist*. New York, 1994. Bly was a daring reporter.

Lubow, Arthur. *The Reporter Who Would Be King: A Biography of Richard Harding Davis*. New York, 1992. The dashing journalist became widely known in the 1890s for his reporting and fiction.

Lutes, Jean Marie. *Front-Page Girls: Women Journalists in American Culture and Fiction, 1880-1930*. Ithaca, N.Y., 2006. Female journalists were seen in stereotypical manner as emotional rather than rational and empathetic rather than objective.

Marzolf, Marion Tuttle. *Civilizing Voices: American Press Criticism, 1880-1950*. New York, 1991. As New Journalism changed the nature of American newspapers, critics raised "the issues of moral purpose and democratic idealism to counter the strong forces of commercialization and impersonality."

Milton, Joyce. *The Yellow Kids: Foreign Correspondents in the Heyday of Yellow Journalism*. New York, 1989. The highly competitive reporters for Pulitzer's *World* and Hearst's *Journal* were both dashing and devious.

Morris, James McGrath. *Pulitzer: A Life in Politics, Print, and Power*. New York, 2010. Pulitzer made the *New York World* the most widely read American newspaper of all time and ushered in the modern era of mass communication.

——. *The Rose Man of Sing Sing: A True Tale of Life, Murder, and Redemption in the Age of Yellow Journalism*. New York, 2003. "As city editor of Pulitzer's *New York Evening World*, Charles E. Chapin was the model of the take-no-prisoners newsroom tyrant: he drove reporters relentlessly — and kept his paper in the center ring of the circus of big-city journalism."

Morris, Roy, Jr. *Ambrose Bierce: Alone in Bad Company*. New York, 1995. Bierce's acidic view is explained by events in his life, particularly his Civil War experiences.

Nasaw, David. *The Chief: The Life of William Randolph Hearst*. Boston, 2000. This biography taps newly available resources and offers a balanced portrait of yellow journalism's foremost practitioner.

Procter, Ben. *William Randolph Hearst: The Early Years, 1863-1910*. New York, 1998. This biography gives a fast-paced study of the emergence of Hearst in journal-

ism and national politics.

Raskin, Jonah, ed. *The Radical Jack London: Writings on War and Revolution*. Berkeley, Calif., 2008. London was a great literary journalist and novelist, as well as a leading socialist. This anthology includes twenty-eight selections from his wide range of writing.

Robertson, Michael. *Stephen Crane, Journalism and the Making of Modern American Literature*. New York, 1997. "Crane was one of the first in an extraordinary succession of major American writers, from the 1890s to the present, who began their careers as newspaper reporters."

Roggenkamp, Karen. *Narrating the News: New Journalism and Literary Genre in Late Nineteenth-Century American Newspapers and Fiction*. Kent, Ohio, 2005. The *New York Sun*, *World*, and *Journal* "developed a novel way of narrating the news that came to be known as 'new journalism' — an innovative, commercialized, sensationalistic, and above all dramatic style of reportage."

Schlesinger, Carl, ed. *The Biography of Ottmar Mergenthaler, Inventor of the Linotype*. New Castle, Del., 1989. This book is a reprint of Mergenthaler's autobiography, along with an 1889 article describing the first Linotype installation and the severe conditions under which the operators worked.

Spencer, David R. *The Yellow Journalism: The Press and America's Emergence as a World Power*. Evanston, Ill., 2007. The author traces the roots of sensationalism to the John Peter Zenger trial of 1735 and calls Hearst a shameless copycat of Joseph Pulitzer.

Swanberg, W. A. *Citizen Hearst*. New York, 1961. The best known of the biographies of Hearst, this study paints him as a newspaper owner and politician driven by a desire to have things his way.

Taft, Robert. *Photography and the American Scene, A Social History, 1839-1889*. New York, 1938. Photojournalism brought a new dimension of journalistic impact on American society.

Thompson, Mildred I. *Ida B. Wells-Barnett: An Exploratory Study of an American Black Woman, 1893-1930*. Carlson, 1990. Thompson examines journalist Wells-Barnett as a writer and reformer within the social context of her work.

Wiener, Joel, ed. *Papers for the Millions: The New Journalism in Britain, 1850s to 1914*. New York, 1988. This edited volume examines New Journalism in its native land.

Wilkerson, Marcus. *Public Opinion and the Spanish-American War: A Study of War Propaganda*. Baton Rouge, La., 1932. This is one of the earliest studies examining the influence of the press on the Spanish-American War.

ARTICLES

Adams, Edward E., and Baldasty, Gerald J. "Syndicated Service Dependence and a Lack of Commitment to Localism: Scripps Newspapers and Market Subordination." *Journalism & Mass Communication Quarterly* 78:3 (2001): 519-32. "[T]he Scripps chain's heavy dependence on syndicated material and lack of commitment to local issues contributed to its subordinated market position."

Baldasty, Gerald J. "The Economics of Working-Class Journalism: The E.W. Scripps Newspaper Chain 1878-1908." *Journalism History* 25:1 (1999): 3-12. The Scripps chain "avoided aggressive competition with other newspapers by marketing papers to working-class readers and minimizing competition in advertising and distribution."

Bekken, Jon. "'The Most Vindictive and Most Vengeful Power': Labor Confronts the Chicago Newspaper Trust." *Journalism History* 18 (Spring-Summer 1992): 11-17. The Daily Newspaper Association of Chicago, founded in 1884, included most of the major English-language daily newspapers, which collaborated on editorial policy and labor matters.

Berg, Meredith, and David Berg. "The Rhetoric of War Preparation: The New York Press in 1898." *Journalism Quarterly* 45 (1968): 653-60. The New York press helped prepare the public for the Spanish-American War because there was "a powerful linkage between the press and the people."

Bjork, Ulf Jonas. "'Scrupulous Integrity and Moderation': The First International Organization for Journalists and the Promotion of Professional Behaviour, 1894-1914." *American Journalism* 22 (2005): 95-112. The International Congress of the Press tried to promote professional behavior among its members.

Bradley, Patricia. "Joseph Pulitzer as an American Hegelian." *American Journalism* 10:3-4 (1993): 70-82. The titan's intellectual associations explain how his idealist

New Journalism could coexist with sensational journalism.

Burt, Elizabeth V. "A Bid for Legitimacy: The Women's Press Club Movement, 1881-1900." *Journalism History* 23:2 (1997): 72-84. The woman's press club movement helped female journalists gain credibility.

Colbert, Ann. "Philanthropy in the Newsroom: Women's Editions of Newspapers, 1894-1896." *Journalism History* 22 (1996): 91-9. The 1890s phenomenon — turning over editions of newspapers to be run by women for a day — showed what opportunities and limitations women faced.

Connery, Thomas. "Julian Ralph: Forgotten Master of Descriptive Detail." *American Journalism* 2 (1985): 165-73. The *New York Journal* reporter, though not as well known as some other journalists, was an accomplished writer.

Cronin, Mary M. "Mixing Protest and Accommodation: The Response of Oklahoma's Black Town Newspaper Editors to Race Relations, 1891-1918." *American Journalism* 19:2 (2002): 45-64. Most of Oklahoma's African-American frontier newspaper editors opposed Jim Crow legislation, black disfranchisement, and debt peonage.

Dillon, Michael. "'Satanic Journalism and its Fate': The Scripps Chain Strikes Out in Buffalo." *American Journalism* 20:2 (2003): 57-82. Buffalo, N.Y., experienced a bitter newspaper feud in the early 1880s.

Domke, David. "The Black Press in the 'Nadir' of African Americans." *Journalism History* 20 (1994): 131-8. Black newspapers covered Supreme Court decisions in the 1880s and 1890s that upheld discrimination against blacks.

——. "The press, race relations, and social change." *Journal of Communication* 51:2 (2006): 317-44. The mainstream press "encouraged racial values and attitudes that were simultaneously being institutionalized in several cultural arenas by social Darwinism, Booker T. Washington's accommodationism, and legalized segregation."

Fedler, Fred. "Insiders' Stories: Coping with Newsroom Stress, An Historical Perspective." *American Journalism* 21:3 (2004): 77-106. Journalists in the late 1800s and early 1900s suffered from much stress; but, unlike today, they received no help trying to overcome it.

Ferré, John P. "The Dubious Heritage of Media Ethics: Cause-and-Effect Criticism in the 1890s." *American Journalism* 5 (1988): 191-203. Ferré provides a useful discussion about the interpretation of media influences.

Gates, Sharon Joyce, and Catherine C. Mitchell. "Adolph Ochs: Learning What's Fit To Print." *American Journalism* 8 (1991): 228-9. Ochs developed his principles about news early in his journalism career.

Gleason, Timothy W. "The Libel Climate of the Late Nineteenth Century: A Survey of Libel Litigation, 1884-1899." *Journalism Quarterly* 70 (Winter 1993): 893-906. Gleason compares libel suits filed by public officials and public figures in the late nineteenth century.

Gottlieb, Agnes Hooper. "Networking in the Nineteenth Century: The Founding of the Woman's Press Club of New York City." *Journalism History* 21:4 (1995): 155-62. Jane Cunningham Croly ("Jenny June") opened the first women's club in the United States of America.

Hamilton, John Maxwell, Renita Coleman, Bettye Grable, and Jaci Cole. "An Enabling Environment: A Reconsideration of the Press and the Spanish-American War." *Journalism Studies* 7:1 (2006): 78-93. Agenda-setting research reconstructs historical public opinion to challenge historians' views of the media's influence on the Spanish-American War.

Henry, Susan. "Reporting 'Deeply and At First Hand': Helen Campbell in the 19th-Century Slums." *Journalism History* 11 (1984): 18-25. Depth reporting on urban problems was a feature of New Journalism, and in this case it illustrated the problems that female reporters encountered.

Howard-Pitney, David. "Calvin Chase's *Washington Bee* and Black Middle-Class Ideology, 1882-1900." *Journalism Quarterly* 63 (1986): 89-97. The *Bee's* black editor "was neither exclusively accommodationist nor protest-oriented, but a pragmatic blend of the two."

Hyde, Jana. "New Journalism, 1883-1900: Social Reform or Professional Progress?" 199-212 in Wm. David Sloan, *Perspectives on Mass Communication History* (Hillsdale, N.J., 1991). This historiographical essay analyzes the approaches that historians have taken to explaining the press of the period.

Kilmer, Paulette D. "Flying Around the World in 1889-In Search of the Archetypal Wanderer." *American Journalism* 16:2 (1999): 63-84. The American public was fascinated with world travel, as demonstrated by the interest in the 1889 competitive race between journalists Nellie Bly of the *New York World* and Elizabeth Bisland of *Cosmopolitan* magazine.

Lorenz, Larry. "The Whitechapel Club: Defining Chicago's Journalists in the 19th Century." *American Journalism* 15:1 (1998): 83-102. In this bohemian club, journalists created an image of the hard-drinking, wise-cracking, cynical reporter that lasted well into the twentieth century.

Mander, Mary S. "Pen and Sword: Problems of Reporting the Spanish-American War." *Journalism History* 9 (1982): 2-9, 28. Motivated by a sense of personal responsibility, correspondents performed well despite many difficulties.

Ponder, Stephen E. "Conservation, Community Economics, and Newspapering: The Seattle Press and the Forest Reserves Controversy of 1897." *American Journalism* 3 (1986): 50-60. The *Seattle Post-Intelligencer's* changing stands on creation of a new national forest indicated that daily newspapers were "subject to ... complex influences on local editorial policy...."

Reel, Guy. "This Wicked World: Masculinities and the Portrayals of Sex, Crime, and Sports in the *National Police Gazette*, 1879-1906." *American Journalism* 22:1 (2005): 61-94. The author explores the illustrations in the New York-based *National Police Gazette*, traces their evolution, and analyzes how the newspaper responded to the changes and challenges posed to modern manhood in the face of societal changes.

Simpson, Roger. "Seattle Newsboys: How Hustler Democracy Lost to the Power of Property." *Journalism History* 18 (1992): 18-25. After its establishment in 1892, the Seattle Newsboys Union tried to protect newsboys, but it failed to last long.

Smythe, Ted Curtis. "The Reporter, 1880-1900. Working Conditions and Their Influence on News." *Journalism History* 7 (1980) 1-10. Economic conditions such as low salaries resulted in poor reporting and sensationalism.

Steele, Janet E. "The 19th Century *World* Versus the *Sun*: Promoting Consumption (Rather than the Working Man)." *Journalism Quarterly* 67 (1990): 592-600. Dana and Pulitzer reflected the transformation from old to new journalism, with Pulitzer ushering in a new consumer culture among the working classes.

Stevens, Summer E., and Owen V. Johnson. "From Black Politics to Black Community: Harry C. Smith and the Cleveland *Gazette*." *Journalism Quarterly* 67 (1990): 1090-102. Smith used the *Gazette* "to serve as a forum for political debate and to promote the development of a black identity and community."

Sumpter, Randall S. "Sensation and the Century: How Four New York Dailies Covered the End of the Nineteenth Century." *American Journalism* 18 (Summer 2001): 81-100. This study "[e]xamines the nature of newspaper sensationalism at the beginning of the 1900's, comparing contemporary definitions with the actual coverage practiced by New York City journals."

Sweeney, Michael S. "The Desire for the Sensational: Coxey's Army and the Argus-eyed Demons of Hell." *Journalism History* 23:3 (1997): 114-25. "A mass march of unemployed people to Washington, D.C., in 1894 generated an enormous amount of newspaper coverage."

Welter, Mark M. "The 1895-98 Cuban Crisis in Minnesota Newspapers: Testing the 'Yellow Journalism' Theory." *Journalism Quarterly* 47 (1970): 719-24. The author challenges the notion that the Cuban coverage of the yellow press was widely influential.

White, Lisa A. "The Curve Lynchings: Violence, Politics, Economics, and Race Rhetoric in 1890s Memphis." *Tennessee Historical Quarterly* 64:1 (2005): 44-61. This study contrasts the anti-lynching campaign of black journalist Ida B. Wells with the white supremacist rhetoric of editor Edward Carmack after the 1892 lynching of three well-respected African-American businessmen.

Winfield, Betty Houchin, and Janice Hume. "The American Hero and the Evolution of the Human Interest Story." *American Journalism* 15 (1998): 79-99. The rise of the human interest story gave readers heroes they could relate to just as Horatio Alger did in fiction.

13

American Magazines
1740 - 1900

American magazines grew from tentative eighteenth-century beginnings as a "cottage industry" serving a small, elite audience, to the brink of becoming a national industry by the end of the nineteenth century. Editors and publishers developed their product in reaction to wars, social changes, and economic developments that transformed the American nation itself from a child to an adolescent.

The American magazine had its roots in the periodical tradition of the British Isles — a tradition that had begun with a learned journal[1] and had progressed through a variety of other forms. Other periodicals of the 1600s mixed news and low humor to amuse the not-so-learned and usually identified themselves by the title "Mercurius": *Mercurius Fumigosus*, for example. More dignified periodicals such as the *Athenian Mercury* entertained by answering readers' questions. The earliest English periodical to give readers a taste of fiction and verse was *The Gentleman's Journal* (1692); and Daniel Defoe's *Weekly Review* (1704) included some essays, thus presaging the essay papers that would soon follow.

Influencing the style of popular writing for many decades to come was Irish-born Richard Steele's *Tatler* of 1709, a thrice-weekly essay paper that was closed after a year and replaced with the *Spectator*, edited daily by Steele and his even more talented partner, Joseph Addison. In these two periodicals and their legion of imitators, writers commented in a witty, urbane, entertaining way on the vices, virtues, and conventions of the day.

The earliest English periodical to call itself by the name "magazine" was *The Gentleman's Magazine* of 1731, which left the reporting of the news to the newspapers and instead emphasized elegant writing, amusement, and instruction via miscellaneous content that included the literary, political, biographical, and critical. The designation "magazine" caught on rapidly. The English word "magazine" derived from the French *magazin*, which in turn came from the Arabic *makhzan*, meaning "storehouse."

By 1740 the American colonies' great innovator, Benjamin Franklin, had resolved that the time was ripe for an indigenous monthly magazine modeled roughly after the British miscellanies being read by a select colonial audience. The busy Franklin engaged John Webbe, who earlier had contributed to Franklin's newspaper, the *Pennsylvania Gazette*, to handle the project as editor. In an apparent bid for better pay, Webbe revealed the plan to Franklin's rival printer, Andrew Bradford, who gave Webbe a sweeter deal and succeeded in bringing out his *American Magazine* just three days before the February 1741 appearance of Franklin's *General Magazine and Historical Chronicle*. Both magazines were indifferently received. Bradford's lasted for only three monthly issues, Franklin's for six.

More American magazines soon appeared. In 1743 two were introduced in Boston. The first printed a mere three issues; but the second, lawyer Jeremiah Gridley's *American Magazine and Historical Chronicle*, managed to publish for three years. New York City was home to the next magazine, a four-page political essay paper of Whig leanings. Similarly political was *The American Magazine and Monthly Chronicle*, founded in 1757 and continued for a year in Philadelphia by another of the Bradfords, William III. It was a pro-British, anti-French periodical published in the midst of the French and Indian War (1754-1763) and also entertained with *Tatler*- and *Spectator*-inspired essays of manners, most notably the "Timothy Timbertoe" series.

Yet another interesting though short-lived colonial title was the *Royal American Magazine*, which Isaiah Thomas founded in Boston prior to the Battle of Lexington. It appeared in 1774 and '75. Despite the word "Royal" in its title, it was sympathetic to the Patriot cause and is noteworthy not only for its solid articles on serious topics and its Paul Revere cartoon engravings, but for its entertaining copy and for having introduced song lyrics and scores to the American magazine market.

A final magazine founded prior to the Revolution was Philadelphia's *Pennsylvania Magazine* (1775-1776), edited by Robert Aitken, who, on Ben Franklin's recommendation, hired Thomas Paine, later to become known as a propagandist pamphleteer in both the

[1]The earliest known periodical in Europe was the *Mercurius Gallobelgicus* ("Franco-Belgian Mercury") from 1595. In March 1665 in England Henry Oldenburg founded the *Acta Philosophica Societates Anglia*, later re-titled the *Philosophical Transactions of the Royal Society*, a learned periodical of scientific bent that was modeled after Paris' *Journal des Savans*, founded slightly earlier in January 1665.

America's Magazine Pioneers

Magazines have enjoyed a long, rich history in America. Several early ones stood out in their attempts to bring a new form of periodical material to the reading public. Andrew Bradford, publisher of the *American Mercury* newspaper in Philadelphia, announced his intentions of offering America its first magazine in October of 1740. The announcement sparked a controversy between Bradford and Benjamin Franklin, who also planned to begin a magazine. The argument played out in the pages of the *Mercury* and Franklin's newspaper, the *Pennsylvania Gazette*, for longer than either magazine actually lasted. Once Bradford's *American Magazine, or a Monthly View of the Political State of the British Colonies*, actually appeared in February 1741, it lasted only three months. Bradford abandoned the venture without explanation. Coinciding with the American colonies' revolution against Great Britain, the *United States Magazine* began publishing in Philadelphia in 1778 despite the chaotic social and political conditions that threatened to douse its fire from the start. Its publisher, lawyer and writer Hugh Henry Breckenridge, attempted to use the Revolution as a selling point, filling the pages with essays and literature of a patriotic nature. When the magazine folded after a year, he blamed its failure on the disinterest of the colonists in the welfare of America. In the years immediately following the Revolution, five Philadelphians joined together in a publishing venture in the 1780s. Their combination of talents spelled immediate success. Writer Mathew Carey, engraver John Trenchard, printer Charles Cist, bookseller William Spotswood, and T. Seddon introduced *The Columbian Magazine* in the wake of the American Revolution. The partnership began to disintegrate after three months of publication, when Carey defected to publish his own magazine. However, the *Columbian* endured in its original form for four years, after which it published primarily as a history of the Revolution.

American and French revolutions. The only magazine to be introduced during the war years was Newark's *United States Magazine* (1779), edited by H.H. Breckenridge.

OBSTACLES AND SUCCESSES

In the mid to late 1700s most Americans were still too busy seeing to their basic needs to devote much time to reading. Even if time were not a problem, most were unable to afford the cost of a magazine subscription.[2] On the supply end, few colonial writers were adept at providing good magazine copy. As a result, many magazines were filled largely with "selected" material taken, usually without either payment or permission, from books, newspapers, and other magazines, frequently those of English origin.

[2]See David Paul Nord, "A Republican Literature: A Study of Magazine Reading and Readers in Late Eighteenth-Century New York," *American Quarterly* 40 (March 1988): 42-64. In this study of *The New York Magazine* of 1790, the writer concludes that magazine reading in that period might have been "more broadly democratic than has usually been supposed."

Editors and publishers also faced challenging distribution problems: few and poor roads, uncertain mails, and unfavorable postal rates. The postal act of 1792 gave magazines no break at all from the ordinary letter rate; and though the act of 1794 allowed them a lower rate, postmasters were given the right to refuse the mails to magazines if carriers could not conveniently handle the extra load. With a small population spread thinly over an enormous geographic area, getting magazines to distant subscribers was difficult. Collecting from them was often even more challenging. Also, presses, type, paper, and ink had to be imported at no small cost at a time when magazines contained scant advertising.

Even so, a desire for cultural independence from England, oddly coupled with the hope of emulating the success of the leading English periodicals, led a number of Americans to found magazines between the end of the Revolution and the start of the new century. Noteworthy were Noah Webster's *American Magazine* (1787) of New York, the graphically impressive *Columbian Maga-*

zine (1786-1792), and its co-founder Mathew Carey's next venture, the *American Museum* (1787-1792) of Philadelphia. Also published in Philadelphia was Joseph Dennie's *Port Folio*, a Federalist organ and the first U.S. magazine to achieve substantial national circulation. Virginia's first magazine, the *National Magazine* (1799-1800) of Richmond, was in the opposite political camp: Anti-Federalist. The favorite target of its outspoken editor, James Lyon, was Alexander Hamilton, whom Lyon called "the most dangerous man in the Union."[3]

The foremost publishing centers were Philadelphia, Boston, and New York. Unless one includes the *North-Carolina Magazine, or Useful Intelligencer* (1764-1765), which was part magazine, part newspaper, the earliest magazine south of Philadelphia was the *Free Universal Magazine* (1793) of Baltimore, a city that thereafter made impressive strides in publishing and produced five more titles before the new century. The only other southern city to gain any real importance in 1700s publishing was Charleston, South Carolina, where three magazines were published before 1800.

Magazines Gain Ground

In the early 1800s, editors began to find original copy easier to obtain. Original stories and other contributions were frequently identified as such under their headlines, yet most items were run without credit to the author or were signed only with initials, a pen name, or a line such as "by the author of...." This preference for anonymity can be attributed in part to the Puritan belief that art and literature should be their own reward; partly to the notion that writing for the public was not an altogether respectable occupation for the genteel; and partly to the selfish, if often necessary assertion by the editors/publishers that if writers remained unknown to the reading public, they would not be able to command much pay for their writing. Also, publishers sometimes declared that by running unsigned copy, the work of new, unknown writers would be on a more even footing with that of famous contributors. In case after case, however, giving bylines actually would have been an embarrassment to the editor, who frequently had to write most of an issue's original copy himself.

Although most early magazines can be described as "miscellanies," they usually had a generous measure of political content, entirely natural in such politically charged times. Later, especially after the War of 1812, "literary miscellanies," magazines whose editors wished to popularize native American literature, emerged. Also in the decade from 1810 to 1820 appeared "special miscellanies,"[4] magazines that directed their general content at identifiable groups: members of specific organizations, women interested in fashion, persons who still had a keen interest in our nation's English heritage, and the like.

Magazines were largely elitist — published by and for the "aristocracy" and a small but growing middle class. Subscribers

First Southern Magazine
Although the *North-Carolina Magazine* had some of the characteristics of a newspaper, it sometimes is considered the first magazine published south of Philadelphia. Founded in 1764, it lasted only one year. The first true southern magazine was the *Free Universal Magazine* of Baltimore, founded in 1793.

could be more accurately viewed as supporters than customers, and writers were usually educated business and professional people or clergy who wrote for pleasure, not for profit. A feeling of *noblesse oblige* pervaded much of the copy. The writers' polished, genteel prose and verse, replete with classical allusions, often reflected on the civic virtue of the higher orders of society.

On the whole, copy was far less frivolous and much less commercial than its present-day equivalent. It usually employed the essay style that Addison and Steele had popularized. It was not until the 1840s, the era of Jacksonian democracy, that elitism's hold began to relax substantially. Fiction occupied little space in these magazines, although there was plenty of poetry, both reprinted and original. By today's standards, some of the most memorable verse was satirical; some of the worst, sentimental.

In the early part of the century, magazines increased in number, emphasized fiction, and, except for the verse they carried, paid increased attention to Americanizing their content. In 1800 only a dozen American magazines were being published. Yet in the two

---

[3]See Sam G. Riley, *Magazines of the American South* (Westport, Conn., 1986), 136. This quotation appeared in the *National Magazine's* first issue (p. 91).

[4]Neal L. Edgar, *A History and Bibliography of American Magazines, 1810-1820* (Metuchen, N.J., 1975), 20.

Sports Pioneer
Among the many magazines published in Baltimore in the early 1800s was the ground-breaking sports periodical *American Turf Register*. It was founded in 1830 and published for fifteen years. Its purpose was to provide amusement as a diversion from "studious and...grave" inquiries.

decades that followed, the total increased to well over 100. Fiction increased in popularity, and homegrown verse took a back seat to the work of British poets, especially Sir Walter Scott and Lord Byron. On balance, though, the early nineteenth century exhibited a strong nationalistic expression.

Increasing the quantity and quality of the nation's literary output was hampered by the overriding importance of commerce and politics to most educated citizens and by the almost complete absence of full-time, professional writers. In various cities, small literary societies lent support to the efforts of the magazines. Prominent among them were Boston's Anthology Club, New York's Friendly Club, Baltimore's Delphian Club, and Philadelphia's Tuesday Club. Despite these efforts, most prose remained ponderous and the verse less than memorable. Articles continued to be run unsigned, but a few periodicals began to pay contributors. In this period of highly personalized publishing, when the same person sometimes held the titles of editor and publisher and profits were small, editors often worked without pay.

An interesting assortment of individuals were involved in magazine work. Novelist Charles Brockden Brown, for example, attempted to further American letters through his editorial work with four short-lived literary magazines. The flowery writer Stephen Carpenter edited an ambitious "journal of record" for both political history and literature in Charleston. Washington Irving of "Rip Van Winkle" and "Ichabod Crane" fame co-edited a satirical New York periodical titled *Salmagundi* (after a kind of hash) and then became editor of the *Analectic Magazine* (1813-1820) in Philadelphia, a year of which convinced him that the life of a magazine editor was not for him.

Magazines were largely limited to local circulation, if not always to local outlook. As a consequence, circulations remained small. Boston's population growth and importance as a magazine center fell behind the pace set by Philadelphia and New York. Philadelphia had begun the 1800s as the nation's leader so far as magazines were concerned, but New York's impressive growth in population and commerce gradually helped it overtake its rival city.

Baltimore remained a lively magazine center in the early 1800s, with such long-lasting titles as Hezekiah Niles' prototype news magazine *Niles' Weekly Register* (1811-1849) plus postmaster John S. Skinner's early agricultural magazine *The American Farmer* (1819-1897) and his ground-breaking sports periodical *The American Turf Register and Sporting Magazine* (1830-1844).

RENEWED GROWTH AND DEVELOPMENT

The antebellum period brought unprecedented magazine growth. The total number of magazines in 1860 was 600.[5] Of the general monthlies, *Graham's Magazine* (1840-1858) of Philadelphia and Lewis Gaylord Clark's *Knickerbocker Magazine* (1833-1865) of New York City stood out.

Sara Josepha Hale's *Ladies' Magazine* (1828-1836) of Boston was the first successful American women's magazine, but it was the next such periodical she edited, Louis A. Godey's *Godey's Lady's Book* of Philadelphia, that really epitomized the genre. Running a combination of prose and verse by the best writers, alongside more average fare, and hand-colored fashion plates, by 1850 *Godey's* reached the largest circulation attained by any American magazine to that time — roughly 40,000.

Along with her magazine editing, Hale worked on a variety of other endeavors. She wrote the verse "Mary Had a Little Lamb"; introduced the term "lingerie" to describe undergarments; oversaw the fund-raising for the Bunker Hill Monument commemorating the Revolutionary War battle; helped with the preservation of Mount Vernon, George Washington's home; and founded the Ladies' Medical Missionary Society, whose purpose was to give women the right to serve as medical missionaries in other lands. She also was the person primarily responsible for getting Thanksgiving declared a national holiday. Beginning in the 1820s, she lobbied five U. S. presidents for creation of the holiday, finally suc-

[5]Frank Luther Mott, *A History of American Magazines, 1741-1850* (Cambridge, Mass., 1930), 321.

Magazines for Women

Women's Magazine Founder (left)
Sara Josepha Hale started the first successful American women's magazine in 1828. Published in Boston, it was the *Ladies' Magazine* and lasted until 1836. Although it was short-lived, hundreds of later publishers took up the idea of aiming periodicals at a female audience.

Amelia Bloomer (right)
The editor and publisher of America's first women's suffrage magazine, the *Lily*, Amelia Bloomer scandalized popular opinion when, in 1853, she appeared in trousers to deliver a speech criticizing the requirement that women cover their legs. Her fashion design took on the name "bloomers."

ceeding in convincing Abraham Lincoln when she had reached the age of seventy-five.

Imitators of *Godey's Lady's Book* were many, but the best was *Peterson's Magazine* (1842-1898), also of Philadelphia, edited by the prolific sentimentalist Ann Sophia Stephens, best remembered as the author of the first Beadle Dime Novel, a profitable series of low-priced popular novels heavy on adventure, sentimentality, and moralism.

Unlike today's magazines, which often are geared to practical concerns, most periodicals of the 1820s-1850s mainly provided popular literature — reading for the sake of reading. The *Saturday Evening Post* (1821-1969) was one of the many literary weeklies that became popular. Similar in content, but distinct in appearance were *Brother Jonathan* (1839-1845) and *New World* (1840-1845), both of New York, which used enormous page sizes to provide heavy doses of popular fiction, including whole novels.

Taking their cue from earlier English periodicals, a few U. S. publishers contributed to the cause of popular education. More serious or scholarly readers could opt for another magazine genre copied from British predecessors: the sober, often ponderous quarterly review. Among the most noteworthy were the Harvard-connected *North American Review* (1815-1914) and, in the South, Hugh Swinton Legare's *Southern Review* (1828-1832) and Daniel Whitaker's *Southern Quarterly Review* (1842-1857), both of Charleston. In addition, another serious periodical, the *Dial* (1840-1844), allowed New England's Margaret Fuller and Ralph Waldo Emerson to show literary America a different kind of quarterly: a journal that combined opinion and *belles-lettres* and that became the forum for American transcendentalism.

Other serious-minded Americans were moved more by social than by literary motives. As the debate over slavery intensified, numerous periodicals were founded as forums for addressing this crucial issue. The most important was the *Genius of Universal Emancipation*, founded by the Quaker Benjamin Lundy, who underwent extreme difficulties to continue publishing and speaking

out against what he decried as the nation's greatest evil. The nation's earliest woman suffrage periodical (and also an advocate of temperance) was the *Lily* (1849-1856), edited and published by Amelia Bloomer, for whom the then scandalous garment known as "bloomers" was named. Bloomers were pantaloons, or women's "trowsers," which the *Lily's* editor wore and defended as more sensible than the ordinary women's fashions of the day.

MAGAZINES AT MID-CENTURY

Mid-century found America's cities jockeying to secure, maintain, or improve their positions as influential magazine centers. By 1850 New York's population was vastly larger than that of any other city, and its lead in publishing was greater than ever. By 1860 about one-third of all circulation was accounted for by the titles published in New York City. Its outstanding new entry in 1850 was *Harper's New Monthly* (1850-current).[6] It was well illustrated and fat in number of pages per issue. It and the dignified *Atlantic Monthly* positively influenced the standard of popular reading.

Thanks, however, to the efforts of such major Massachusetts literary figures as Henry Wadsworth Longfellow, James Russell Lowell, Ralph Waldo Emerson, Henry David Thoreau, Nathaniel Hawthorne, and Oliver Wendell Holmes, Boston's influence in periodical literature had outstripped that of Philadelphia. The Midwest and the West Coast also were adding new magazines.

In the South, Charleston's William Gilmore Simms was the dominant figure, editing several literary magazines. The most acclaimed magazine in all the pre-Civil War South, though, was Richmond's *Southern Literary Messenger* (1834-1864). Providing the region a widely noticed cultural forum, it was edited for about a year by the brilliant but troubled Edgar Allan Poe. The South's dominant magazine of general commerce was *DeBow's Review* (1846-1880) in New Orleans. Because the South had no really large

[6]"New" was dropped in 1900 and "Monthly" in 1939 when the title was altered to *Harper's Magazine*. Since 1976, the title has been simply *Harper's*.

Nineteenth-Century Leader
Founded in 1850 by Fletcher Harper (inset, left), *Harper's New Monthly Magazine* became the leading American periodical of the nineteenth century. By publishing the writings of some of the nation's outstanding literary figures, it not only influenced popular reading but helped make New York City the center of magazine publishing in the United States. Within a short time after its founding, it had taken on a stronger graphic appearance (illustrated by its December issue from 1857 in the middle) than it had when it had begun publication only five years earlier. During the Civil War, its leadership in illustrations was enhanced by the work of the cartoonist Thomas Nast and the artist Winslow Homer. The latter's drawings were especially effective in documenting soldiers' daily routine, especially camp life and leisure time.

cities, magazines were overwhelmingly regional in appeal.

With added attention being given New World literary efforts, this mid-century period was marked by intensified rivalry between American and English writers. Much space was occupied in U. S. magazines by replies to the charges leveled at American cultural life by European authors Charles Dickens, Harriet Martineau, Frances Trollope, and Frederick Marryat. All the same, this animosity did not prevent the continuing practice of pirating British writers. In return, British periodicals did their share of stealing the work of the best American writers.

One reason for American magazines' use of pirated material was economic. Another was that quality American fiction was still sparse. Despite the fine work of Poe, Washington Irving, and Hawthorne, the short story was not yet a well defined literary genre; and much short fiction by Americans, especially in the women's magazines, was sentimental and moralistic. That situation, though, was to improve, due in part to the increasing professionalism of magazine publishing. The 1840s marked the emergence of a few individuals designated "magazinists," men and women who made their living by writing for, and sometimes editing, magazines. Nathaniel Parker Willis was perhaps the first, followed by Poe, Park Benjamin, Simms, Lydia Sigourney, Ann Stephens, and others. By 1850 the popular magazines, especially women's magazines and the literary weeklies, had begun giving bylines, and a few leaders had started to pay at least their better-known contributors.

By 1850 a far greater variety of periodical reading was available to the public. The magazine business had not yet become "the magazine industry." With the advent of better and more regular payment to writers, though, a new class of magazine specialists was able to emerge, promoting stronger editorial standards and encouraging the development of American authorship.

The next half-century was one of tremendous upheaval in

American life: first the Civil War, then enormous changes as the nation urbanized and industrialized. Magazines duly reflected all these developments. As the nation moved toward war, the number of political periodicals grew, roughly doubling during the 1850s. The vast majority of magazines were still either regional or local in circulation. Only a handful of general and women's magazines and a few journals of law, medicine, and religion had national circulations of any size. Even most magazines having "U. S.," "American," or "National" in their titles were unable to gain much circulation outside their own locales; and when war came, this localism intensified.

Of considerable importance were the large-format, abundantly illustrated weeklies, led by *Gleason's Pictorial Drawing-Room Companion* (1851-1859); *Frank Leslie's Illustrated Newspaper* (1855-1891), which actually was more of a magazine than a newspaper; and *Harper's Weekly* (1857-1916). They offered large wood engravings, light literature, and news. They also provided another instance of U. S. magazines following the lead of Great Britain, where engravers, many of whom had their start at the *Illustrated London News*, had recognized the commercial potential of lavish pictorial content and had founded their own illustrated magazines. These British publications pioneered the use of steam-driven multiple-cylinder stereotype printing in the mass-production of large, low-cost pictures. Illustration was done by both wood and metal engraving. A number of illustrated British magazines became enormously popular. By 1855, when English-born Frank Leslie launched his first U. S. title, they had reached circulations over 200,000, and then eventually became the first magazines to gain circulations of 1,000,000 or more.[7] Leslie's real name was Henry Carter. He initially used "Frank Leslie" to hide his identity be-

---

[7]See Patricia J. Anderson, "A Revolution in Popular Art: Pictorial Magazines and the Making of a Mass Culture in England, 1832-1860," *Journal of Newspaper and Periodical History* 6 (1990): 16-25.

Edgar Allan Poe
One of the most important American fiction writers of the nineteenth century, Edgar Allan Poe helped to popularize American short stories through his magazine writing in the 1840s and 1850s. This portrait of him appeared on the cover of the March 1853 issue of *The National Magazine*.

cause his father disapproved of his interest in drawing. He retained the name, however, after becoming the wealthy publisher of a whole stable of magazines that bore the Leslie name. Curiously, following his death, his widow, Miriam, had her own name legally changed — to Frank Leslie.

Mass culture took a giant step in the 1840s and '50s, inasmuch as the illustrated weeklies were the first magazines to reach a truly mass audience. The visual images they presented so affordably — of great leaders, faraway places, art works, exotic animal life, noteworthy architecture, and so on — appealed to all segments of society and did not demand formal education to be enjoyed. They became a readily accessible window on the world, especially for those whose horizons had previously been much closer.

Other content was changing. A popular weekly in the 1850s was *Saturday Press* (1858-1866), the magazine in which humorists Mark Twain and Josh Billings first reached a large, wide audience. The staid quarterly reviews had lost some of their former importance. Some had broadened their traditional content and had taken on the look of the more dignified general monthlies. Correspondingly, some general magazines began to run book reviews.

A variety of magazines on special topics proliferated. The largest genre in number of titles was the religious periodical — quarterlies, monthlies, and weeklies published all over the nation

by a wide array of faiths. The next most active category was the agricultural periodical, a prominent example of which was *Country Gentleman* (1853-1955). As the Midwest and West became more developed agriculturally, the number of their farm periodicals increased accordingly. Although their great growth period had not yet begun, specialized business periodicals proliferated.

MAGAZINES AND THE CIVIL WAR

In the prewar years, most northern religious periodicals spoke out against slavery, while their opposite numbers, and many other more general magazines in the South, sought to rationalize their region's "peculiar institution." One of the leading antislavery magazines was William Lloyd Garrison's *Liberator* (1831-1865). A terrific outpouring of magazine comment on both sides of the conflict followed publication of the era's best-selling book, *Uncle Tom's Cabin* (1852), which already had appeared serially in the Washington, D.C., magazine *National Era*. In addition to abolition, temperance was a leading cause, supported by various issue-specific periodicals.

Before the Civil War most magazine writing was still being done by "ladies and gentlemen" as a leisure pursuit rather than in expectation of payment, but some of the larger or better magazines were paying a few dollars a page. Advertising did not yet provide much of a magazine's income, and sales were mostly by subscription. The typical monthly of the 1850s sold for three dollars yearly, most weeklies for two dollars.

Whereas intensified demand for war news kept newspaper subscriptions from declining during the war, magazines — especially those few that previously had enjoyed substantial national circulation, such as *Harper's* and *Godey's* — suffered major losses. In the North the financial panic of 1857, followed by the war, which cut off southern subscriptions, caused a decline in the number of magazines. In the South, shortages of paper, ink, and printing equipment that had formerly been brought in from the North, high postal rates, a labor shortage, and, finally, the arrival of hostile troops caused most magazines either to discontinue publication until war's end or to fold permanently. On the other hand, a surprising number of new magazines were founded in the South during the conflict.

In the North the illustrated weeklies provided good war coverage, giving the region's newspapers stiff competition. In addition, several military periodicals were published. A handful of periodicals took a dim view of the North's role in the war.

England had long served as the model for American magazines. At mid-century American readers were still bound to the "Mother Country" by the enormous popularity of English writers, especially Charles Dickens for fiction, Thomas Carlyle for nonfiction, and William Wordsworth and Alfred Lord Tennyson for verse. Some French and German writers — such as Dumas and Goethe — also were popular. By the 1870s, some American magazines were finding readers on the English side of the Atlantic. *Scribner's*, *Century*, and *Harper's Monthly* were selling well in Bri-

VOL. V.   NOVEMBER, 1864.   NO. 11.

Illustrating the Civil War
Magazine illustration continued to increase lavishly even during the Civil War. Much magazine content, however, naturally focused on the war. *The Child at Home*, a specialty magazine produced by the American Tract Society, a Christian missions organization, illustrated both trends. The lead story in this 1864 issue was titled "'Thanksgiving' in the Hospital," with the accompanying illustration showing a woman and a girl visiting the wounded.

tain, their popularity due in large part to their lavish illustration.

Content continued to change. Novels were popular and ran serially in magazines. Some periodicals encouraged domestic novelists, while others took advantage of the absence of international copyright law and mainly used English material without permission or payment. Much fiction and most verse were sugary and sentimental. History and biography were more in demand, probably due to the politically charged times, and travel articles appeared everywhere.

Humor had become a staple. Especially popular were the dialect humorists Artemus Ward (whose real name was Charles Browne), Petroleum Vesuvius Nasby (David Locke), Bill Arp, and Mr. Dooley (Finley Peter Dunne). Ward edited the humorous *Vanity Fair* (1859-1863). *Southern Punch*, (1863-1865) surprisingly commenced publication in Richmond, Virginia, after Lee's defeat at Gettysburg and quickly attained a sizable circulation.

Many specialized periodicals were published. Prize fighting and horse racing were the sports that got the most attention, al-

though sports and games were not yet as popular as they would later become in America. Spiritualism was a craze that resulted in magazines of its own. Secret societies such as the Freemasons and Odd Fellows were also popular and had their own periodicals.

POST-WAR GROWTH

The years following the Civil War saw dramatic growth in magazine publishing. In 1865 there were 700 magazines and, in dramatic contrast, 3,300 in 1885.[8] Even in the Reconstruction South magazine activity was considerable. Magazines began going after subscribers more aggressively, boosting circulation by using premiums such as books and pictures to reward new or renewed subscriptions. Ebenezer Butterick's *Dileneator, A Monthly Magazine Illustrating European and American Fashion*, for example, used dress patterns as premiums and boosted circulation to an impressive 200,000 by 1888. Circulation growth in general was given a major boost by the Second Class Postage Act of 1879, which allowed magazines a more favorable postal rate.

There were other changes as well. During the lean economic years 1873 to 1878, advertising became more important. *Scribner's Monthly* (1870-1881) and *Galaxy* (1866-1878) took the lead in attracting advertisers by touting their large circulations.

Also changing was the style of writing. It lightened and became less didactic. Most articles were run signed instead of anonymous, as the manners of the prewar years began to fade. Even so, many of the era's most popular "magazinists," such as Eugene Benson, Junius Browne, Frederick Perkins, Titas Coan, and David Wasson, have been all but forgotten. The quality of literary magazines ranged from the high-toned, non-illustrated *Atlantic* to many of more humble quality.

Regional interests continued to be important. In the South the most active cities were Atlanta, Baltimore, Louisville, Richmond, and New Orleans. Atlanta's *Sunny South* (1875-1907) and Louisville's *Home and Farm* (1876-1918) were the leaders in a region where a circulation of 100,000 was considered enormous. New Orleans was remarkable for the number of French-language periodicals — roughly forty — published there during the 1800s. Reconstruction was a common topic in northern magazines, and some southern writers found ready markets in the North for their work.

The many religious newsapers that had become popular in the 1820s began reducing coverage of secular news in the 1870s, probably due to the growth of city dailies better equipped to handle hard news. Overall, however, the number of religious publications, of which magazines made up the majority, doubled between the Civil War's end and 1885.

Magazines for women increased in number also. Most major magazines came out against female suffrage, despite the fact that far more women than men were subscribers. Consequently, small journals sprang up all over the country to speak for women's rights: not just the legendary *Revolution* (1868-1879) that Susan B.

[8]Frank Luther Mott, *A History of American Magazines* (Cambridge, Mass., 1938), 3:5.

Petroleum V. Nasby
Humorists writing in dialect were especially popular during the Civil War era. Among the most successful was David Ross Locke, who wrote under the pen name "Petroleum Vesuvius Nasby." Locke began the satirical Nasby character in 1860 for the *Toledo* (Ohio) *Blade* and used him to criticize slavery, southerners, secessionists, Democrats, and alcohol. In the debate over Reconstruction following the war, he at first sided with the moderate approach of President Andrew Johnson. Later, however, he became an outspoken radical who advocated punishment of the former Confederate states.

Anthony and Elizabeth Cady Stanton conducted in New York, but many others in a variety of locations. The most outspoken was *Woodhull and Claflin's Weekly* (1870-1876). Not all women joined the movement, though, as was evidenced by the antisuffrage *True Woman* (1870-1873). At the same time, fashion magazines became more popular than ever. *Harper's Bazar* (1867-current) took the lead. Two especially successful home magazines were *Woman's Home Journal* (1878-1909) and Cyrus Curtis' *Ladies' Home Journal* (1883-current), with which editor Edward Bok introduced to the women's market the concept of service journalism. *Ladies' Home Journal* was the first American magazine to reach 1,000,000 subscribers (in 1903).

The growth of specialized or "class" periodicals was enormous following the Civil War. Many new journals appeared in all the sciences; and as the nation industrialized, innumerable engineering, manufacturing, and mechanical periodicals were established. Literature in a real sense was being elbowed aside by science and a consuming interest in commerce and industrial progress. Professional journals, especially in medicine, also enjoyed considerable growth, and education journals published by teachers' organizations or by state government agencies were plentiful. "Booster magazines" began to appear and extolled the virtues of their regions to attract economic development. Also, the number of agricultural journals roughly tripled between 1870 and 1885. To further the farmers' interests, thousands of local granges were formed, and many of them published their own periodicals.

Interest in sports broadened, and each sport had its own magazines, with hunting, fishing, and boating particularly popular. The earliest bicycling periodical was published in New York City in 1869, but cycling suffered a decline in popularity until the solid rubber tire was introduced in the early 1870s. Then *American Bicycling Journal* (1877-1879) and several similar periodicals capitalized on the revived craze. Of the spectator sports, horse racing remained preeminent and was represented by several specialized periodicals. Second in popularity was baseball, the first periodical

for which was *Ball Player's Chronicle* (1867) of New York.

More than any other nation, America published magazines for young readers. About half were Sunday school or other denomination-affiliated periodicals, although they did not match the overall circulation of the secular juveniles. An older juvenile magazine was *Merry's Museum* (1841-1872), edited for a time by Louisa May Alcott, author of *Little Women*. New titles sprang up. The best one was the lavishly illustrated *St. Nicholas* (1873-1943), ably edited by Mary Mapes Dodge, author of *Hans Brinker, or the Silver Skates*. Contributors to *St. Nicholas* included Mark Twain, Rudyard Kipling, and Theodore Roosevelt.

A new process of electrotyping made wood a practical medium for long pressruns, and wood engraving began to replace steel and copper in the late 1850s and early '60s. Especially known for their wood-engraved illustrations were *Appleton's Journal* (1869-1881) of New York, *Scribner's Monthly*, *St. Nicholas*, and the pictorially splendid, large-format *Harper's Weekly*. A steam-powered lithographic press developed in France reached the United States in the 1860s, and illustration in American magazines increased so greatly that some critics began to worry that pictorial content had encroached too far on space that written copy might otherwise have occupied.

A variety of genres of writing, particularly fiction, increased in popularity. The serial novel became more important, thanks in large part to the popularity of foreign novelists. The 1870s and '80s were a time of growing importance for the short story, although most short fiction continued to be blighted by what *Harper's New Monthly* editor Henry Mills Alden characterized as the precious, the mock-heroic, and the morbid. Similarly dreadful was much of the poetry, although Walt Whitman, Sidney Lanier, and Lowell provided quality verse for various magazines. After fiction, travel writing was next in popularity with readers, who reportedly wanted fewer pretty descriptions, less sentiment, more historical treatment, and more attention to morés. Travel writing had to become more practical because more Americans had begun to travel

Mary Booth

Harper's Bazar Editor Succeeds Through Intuition and Taste

Give the reader what she wants. That was the philosophy of *Harper's Bazar's* founding editor, Mary L. Booth. "An editor's first qualifications," she explained, are sagacity to discover what the public wants, and knowledge of how to supply the demand."

And Booth, a luminary among nineteenth-century magazine editors, had both.

Her magazine was a sort of *Harper's Weekly* for women. Owned by Harper & Brothers, *Harper's Bazar* debuted with Booth at the helm on November 2, 1867. From an upstart fashion magazine, she built a journal known more for its literary leanings than its fashion prowess. Thomas Nast and other leading artists and novelists such as William Dean Howells found a forum in it.

Booth herself scoffed at critics who dismissed her magazine as a fashion folio. "It seems to me," she asserted, "that a journal which numbers among its constant contributors the best writers of light literature, both of Europe and America, which treats, in the course of each volume, of almost every subject that would be likely to interest the family circle, and which contains some of the finest art illustrations published in any newspaper in the country, can hardly be ranked by any one as a mere journal of fashion."

Booth used her magazine forum to encourage women to achieve beyond their domestic sphere. By her very presence at the head of a respected, high-circulation magazine, she became a celebrity and role model for other women of her era.

She believed women like herself were "eminently" qualified for journalistic work because "[t]heir acute and subtle intuition, and habits of keen observation, readiness of thought, and refined taste, fit them to succeed both as contributors and editors."

Booth herself had lots of that intuition. She led the highly successful, mass circulation, national weekly from its first issue until her death in 1889.

In the popular trend toward fashion magazines in the post-war period, *Harper's Bazar* took the lead. Fletcher Harper started it in 1867 as a sister publication of the esteemed general-interest periodical *Harper's Weekly*. He modeled it after a women's publication he had seen in Berlin, Germany. Mary Booth served as editor from its first issue until her death in 1889. Under her editorship, the magazine included dressmaking patterns, news on current styles, and the latest fashions from New York and Europe. It also contained stories and drawings similar to those in *Harper's Weekly*, even occasionally borrowing its famous cartoonist, Thomas Nast. *Harper's Bazaar*, the spelling of its name changed, still publishes today.

abroad. Supplying the South's need for historical accounts of former glories and the Lost Cause were several magazines designed specifically for that purpose, such as North Carolina's *Our Living and Our Dead* (1873-1876).

Among humor magazines, the preeminent one was *Puck* (1877-1918), edited for many years by the gifted parodist H.C. Bunner. In the 1880s came two outstanding competitors, *Judge* (1881-1939) and *Life* (1883-1936). Particularly popular in the latter were its splendid drawings by Charles Dana Gibson, creator of the "Gibson man" and "Gibson girl." *Texas Siftings* (1881-1897) began in Austin and later was also published in New York, providing a sort of humor bridge between East and West. Similarly, Opie Read's *Arkansas Traveler* (1882-1916) was in Little Rock before it offended too many locals and had to "travel" to Chicago.

Once again politics began to be discussed in more of the general magazines. The old prewar partisanship was breaking down, and most of the magazines that ran political material were not tied to a particular party. A thoughtful new journal of opinion was E.L. Godkin's *Nation* (1865-current). It developed an avid nationwide following among the educated and professional classes. Labor unions organized and became politically active, and by 1885 around 400 labor periodicals were being published, most of them local in scope.

As cities grew, so did their social problems — awful living conditions for the poor, prostitution, violent crime, corrupt government — but Victorian manners were still too reticent for most magazines and newspapers to risk offending readers with frank attention to these problems. In the celebrated fight against New York City's Tweed Ring, the only magazine to commit itself fully was *Harper's Weekly*. Still, the progress of science and technology, plus the democratization of politics, made more intense by great waves of immigration, eventually served to weaken the hold of traditional values on the American mind, causing a great deal of interest in changing manners and morés. Many travel articles, for instance, were in reality comparative glimpses at how other peoples lived.

TOWARD CENTURY'S END

In the late 1880s and the 1890s some of the larger national magazines reduced their prices and thus set the stage for the era of low-priced, giant-circulation monthlies and weeklies of the early 1900s. The prices of the most popular magazines generally were in the range of 20¢ to 35¢, but *Munsey's* (1889-1929), *Peterson's*, and *Godey's* went to 10¢ in the 1890s. *Collier's* began as *Once a Week* in 1888, gaining a large circulation at 7¢ a copy. *Ladies' Home Journal* likewise built an enormous circulation at 5¢ a copy, and the low-priced *McClure's* (1893-1933) reached a circulation upward of 350,000 by 1900 by emphasizing biographies and stories of success. These price cuts were made possible in part by cheaper paper, lower printing costs, and halftone photoengraving, which by the early 1890s was on its way to replacing the far more costly wood and metal engraving processes.

ON THE ROAD TO LAKE GEORGE. BY WINSLOW HOMER

Growth of Illustration
With the steam-powered lithographic press available beginning in the 1860s, magazine illustrations increased so greatly that some critics began to worry that pictures were encroaching on the space available for text. One of the most visual magazines was *Appleton's Journal*.

The popular magazines were not sensational in content, but they were heavily illustrated compared to earlier decades. Subject matter had gained in variety, and articles on the problems of the day had become more common. Fiction was de-emphasized in favor of history, politics, and economics. Even *Atlantic Monthly* became less literary and followed the trend.

Magazine growth was furthered by still other influences. Mail rates were reduced in 1885, and in 1897 rural free delivery was inaugurated. Advertising headed up sharply the last decade of the century, and full-page ads became fairly common. Single-copy sales increased, as well.

By 1890 magazines were able to recruit editing and writing talent from a substantial pool of persons who had worked for other magazines. Prior to that time most staffing had come from newspapers or from contributors who had little or no full-time magazine experience. It became common for writers to prepare copy first for magazine publication, and then collect it and try to have it published in book form. Even the best writers were happy to use

Circulation Leader

Founded in 1883, *Ladies' Home Journal* became an enormous success by providing useful information to homemakers at a low price. Selling for 5¢, it achieved one of the nation's largest circulations in the 1890s, and in the early 1900s it became the first American magazine to reach a circulation of 1,000,000. Founded by Cyrus Curtis, it provided the cornerstone for the Curtis Publishing Company, one of the most successful magazine publishers of the twentieth century, and remains today one of the nation's leading periodicals.

magazine publication as a means of pre-promoting their books.

Illustrated weeklies were losing ground, although the finest of them, *Harper's Weekly*, still enjoyed a solid position, as did *Frank Leslie's Illustrated Weekly* (renamed *Leslie's Weekly* in 1895).

Local and regional magazines became much more popular. One type of local periodical was the city weekly, which offered a mix of politics, commentary on the entertainment scene, humor, society chit-chat, and light literary fare. Most large cities had at least one such periodical. Austin, Texas, had the humorous *Rolling Stone* (1894-1895), owned and edited by William Sydney Porter, later to find lasting fame as O. Henry, America's premier short-story writer. Regional magazines were published in most parts of the country, from Florida to the Rocky Mountains to the Pacific Northwest. Students of magazine history should resist the temptation to think of city and regional magazines as inventions of the 1960s

and '70s, a more recent major growth period for this genre.

Sports got heavy attention, both from general and specialized periodicals. Two of the period's most resilient titles were *Sports Afield* (1887-current) and *Field and Stream* (1896-current).

In the more literary magazines, the short story finally had become an important staple, and by the late 1890s writers were supplying what came to be called the "short short story." The major literary debate was over the merits of realistic as opposed to romantic fiction. *Harper's* and *Dial* spoke for realism, but most magazines that aimed at a mass circulation and had to please popular taste retained their faith in romanticism. By the end of the decade poetry was receiving far less space than it had previously.

General magazines developed a more practical bent, decreasing their emphasis on literature, history, and travel in favor of politics, the economy, and social problems. Thus the content of magazines and newspapers became more similar. Much attention was directed at monopolies and trusts, imperialism, protective tariffs, and socialism as magazines tried to deal with the ramifications of the nation's growing wealth and influence. Speaking out on issues important to black women in America was *Woman's Era* (1894-1898), published in Boston and edited by Josephine St. Pierre Ruffin. By this time, in fact, quite a number of magazines by and for African Americans were in publication, although they still suffered the difficulties in attracting good contributors and willing advertisers that had troubled mainstream publishers in the early 1800s. Religious or other organizations supported many of them, but the first black magazine in the South did not appear until 1890.

Poised on the brink of a new century, the American magazine had changed a great deal. It was becoming a part of a large industry led by national magazines of enormous circulation, and it informed, as opposed to entertained, more than it had done in the mid 1800s. A far greater range of practical specialized periodicals had come into being, and even the general-content magazines were placing more emphasis on providing useful factual matter to readers. Historian Agnes Repplier once described nineteenth-century magazines as characterized by propriety-bound patronization — editors seeming to say to their readers: "We will help you. We will uplift and improve you."[9] By century's end the tone was less gentle and polite, more frankly journalistic. Less literary in purpose than before, the American magazine was nevertheless stronger and soon would be ready to enter a period in which magazines shined in investigative reporting.

RECOMMENDED READINGS

BOOKS

Aronson, Amy Beth. *Taking Liberties: Early American Women's Magazines and Their Readers.* Greenwood, Conn., 2002. Women's magazines in the eighteenth and nineteenth centuries encouraged readers to take a greater role in public affairs.

Ballou, Ellen B. *The Building of the House.* Boston, 1970. This book is a history of the influential *Atlantic Monthly.*

Brown, Joshua. *Beyond the Lines: Pictorial Reporting, Everyday Life, and the Crisis of Gilded Age America.* Berkeley, Calif., 2002. The author takes a close look at how

[9]Agnes Repplier, "American Magazines," *Yale Review* 16 (1926-27): 261-74.

The Writing Life

Amelie Rives published short stories and poetry in magazines.

Brander Matthews regularly contributed to major national magazines.

Frank Stockton wrote the short story "The Lady or the Tiger?"

Sarah Orne Jewett specialized in "local color" articles about rural life.

Lafcadio Hearn became a popular short story writer in Japan.

Thomas Janvier was known for essays and commentaries.

Some notable magazinists of the 1880s

Freelance 'Magazinists' Begin To Make a Living

The names Mark Twain and Rudyard Kipling may be familiar to you, but what about Amelia Barr, Frank Stockton, and Lafcadio Hearn? Whether common or unfamiliar, the names have something striking in common – they were all well-known (and well-paid) freelance writers for magazines between 1880 and 1900.

Whereas most writers for magazines before this era were either staff writers or established writers in other fields (such as Mark Twain, who was already famous for his extremely popular novels and short stories), this time period brought about one of the most important changes in magazine history. It marked the beginning of the "magazinist," a term used to designate a freelance magazine writer.

Amelia Barr was one such writer. Her life and career illustrate what it meant to be a freelance writer in the late nineteenth century. A widow who moved to New York in 1886 with her three children and just $5, she wrote often for such national magazines as *Harper's*, *The Ledger*, and *Lippincott's*. In a day when women rarely supported their households financially, she made excellent money writing articles, short fiction, and essays. In her autobiography, *All the Days of My Life*, she revealed that she began making money writing in the mid-1880s and supported her family "comfortably and never wanted for a thing."

Numerous other writers made their living by freelancing for magazines. Frank Stockton was a popular and well-paid writer of short fiction and popular culture. Lafcadio Hearn wrote regional pieces full of local color. Sarah Orne Jewett regularly wrote rural short stories for *Harper's* and *The Atlantic Monthly*. Kate Chopin freelanced for various magazines before she won adulation for her feminist novel *The Awakening*.

The time was ripe for such prolific professionals, for magazines had risen in popularity and were in need of writers. From 1865 to 1885 the number of magazines had jumped from just 700 to 3,300. The price of magazines had also decreased dramatically (from 20¢ or 30¢ a copy in 1880 to 5¢ or 10¢ at the end of the century), making them more accessible to the public. The subject matter of magazine content also changed, going from highbrow fiction and commentary to a more popular format of travel articles, short stories, health, sports, science, and fashion.

The popularity, accessibility, style, and volume of magazines made it necessary for editors to obtain writing from more sources – thus the increase in professional magazinists, a truly new genre of writers.

Gleason's, Frank Leslie's, Harper's Weekly, and Collier's Weekly made use of new technology that allowed more and better illustration in magazines.

Cane, Aleta Feinsod, and Susan Alves, eds. 'The Only Efficient Instrument': American Women Writers & the Periodical, 1837-1916. Iowa City, Iowa Press, 2001. Women writers used the magazine as an instrument for general public education.

Chielens, Edward E., ed. American Literary Magazines: The Eighteenth and Nineteenth Centuries. New York, 1986. A general essay covers the years 1774-1900 and sketches of ninety-two titles.

Edgar, Neal L. A History and Bibliography of American Magazines, 1810-1820. Metuchen, NJ, 1975. The author provides a well written commentary on the general magazine history of this period, followed by thumbnail descriptions of 223 individual periodicals.

Entrikin, Isabelle Webb. Sarah Josepha Hale and Godey's Lady's Book. Lancaster, Pa., 1946. Hale, who made many contributions to magazine editing, was concerned about improving social and cultural conditions.

Fackler, Mark P., and Charles H. Lippy, eds. Popular Religious Magazines of the United States. Westport, Conn., 1995. This collection profiles 100 of the more important magazines in this genre, past and present.

Foletta, Marshall. Coming to Terms with Democracy: Federalist Intellectuals and the Shaping of an American Culture. Charlottesville, Va., 2001. Founders of the North American Review were the second-generation Federalists who paved the way for the American Renaissance by helping American readers break free from imported standards.

John, Arthur. The Best Years of the Century: Richard Watson Gilder, Scribner's Monthly, and Century Magazine, 1870-1909. Urbana, Ill., 1981. This important American magazine was founded as Scribner's Monthly and in 1881 became The Century Illustrated Monthly Magazine.

Luxon, Norval Neil. Niles' Weekly Register: News Magazine of the Nineteenth Century. Baton Rouge, 1947. Until 1832, the Register took strong editorial positions in favor of a protective tariff, aid to western development, Clay's American System, etc.

Mott, Frank Luther. A History of American Magazines. Cambridge, 1930, 1938, 1957. Volume I of this encyclopedic five-volume work covers 1741-1850; Vol. II, 1850-1865; Vol. III, 1865-1885; and Vol. IV, 1885-1905.

Okker, Patricia. Social Stories: The Magazine Novel in Nineteenth-Century America. Charlottesville, Va., 2003. The author provides copious detail about a sample of the novels serialized in American magazines during the 1800s.

Price, Kenneth M., and Susan Belasco Smith, eds. Periodical Literature in Nineteenth-Century America. Charlottesville, Va., 1995. This collection includes excellent essays on a variety of magazine topics.

Richardson, Lyon F. A History of Early American Magazines, 1741-89. New York, 1931. Magazines, although they lasted for only short periods, were important as forums for the expression of opinion and for discussion.

Riley, Sam G. Magazines of the American South. Westport, Conn., 1986. The author includes descriptive sketches of eighty-nine southern magazines.

–, ed. American Magazine Journalists. Vols. 73 (1741-1850) and 79 (1850-1900) of Dictionary of Literary Biography. Detroit, 1988, 1989. The author provides biographical essays on most of the important magazine editors/publishers.

Sampson, Robert D. John L. O'Sullivan and His Times. Kent, Ohio, 2003. Under O'Sullivan's editorship, the U.S. Magazine and Democratic Review endorsed Jacksonian principles.

Schneirov, Matthew. The Dream of a New Social Order: Popular Magazines in America, 1893-1914. New York, 1994. This is a useful study of magazines at the turn of the century.

Tebbel, John, and Mary Ellen Zuckerman. The Magazine in America, 1740-1990. New York, 1991. The authors provide a general history of periodical publishing.

Wells, Daniel A., comp. The Literary Index to American Magazines, 1850-1900. Westport, Conn., 1996. This reference works is an excellent source for the literary content of magazines.

Zuckerman, Mary Ellen. A History of Popular Women's Magazines in the United States, 1792-1995. Westport, Conn., 1998. Women's magazines played an important role in the lives of readers, while culture and economics were especially important in the lives of the magazines themselves.

ARTICLES

Cronin, Mary M. "Brother's Keeper: The Reform Journalism of The New England Magazine," Journalism History (1996) 22:1:15-23 "Under the direction of Edward Everett Hale and Edwin Doak Mead between 1889 and 1901, the 'New England Magazine' became a premier secular reform journal that promoted government action and philanthropy to end working-class poverty.'

Garcia, Hazel. "Of Punctilios Among the Fair Sex: Colonial American Magazines, 1741-1776." Journalism History 3 (1976): 48-52, 63. Men wrote most of the magazine material about women and dealt with love and marriage, but that written by women showed them asserting themselves.

Kitch, Carolyn. "Changing Theoretical Perspectives on Women's Media Images: The Emergence of Patterns in a New Area of Historical Scholarship." Journalism & Mass Communication Quarterly 74 (Autumn 1997): 477-89. The author surveys the historical research on images of women as portrayed in magazines and other media.

Kuhn, Martin. "Drawing Civil War Soldiers: Volunteers and the Draft in Harper's Weekly and Frank Leslie's Illustrated Newspaper, 1861-1864. Journalism History 32 (2006): 96-105. The differences in their editorial positions — with Harper's supporting the draft and Leslie's opposing it — influenced how the two magazines covered the draft riots of 1863.

Landers, James. "Island Empire: Discourse on U.S. Imperialism in Century, Cosmopolitan, McClure's – 1893-1900." American Journalism 23:1 (2006): 95-124. In the years surrounding the Spanish-American War, these leading magazines provided forums for complex debates that shaped public opinion and national policy on U.S. territorial expansion.

Lilly, Thomas. "The National Archive: Harper's New Monthly Magazine and the Civic Responsibilities of a Commercial Literary Periodical, 1850-1853." American Periodicals 15 (Autumn 2005): 142-62. Harper's was one of the most influential magazines of the 1800s, an age when more Americans were inclined to read for pleasure.

Lueck, Therese L. "Women's Moral Reform Periodicals of the 19th Century: A Cultural Feminist Analysis of The Advocate." American Journalism 16 (Summer 1999): 37-52. Operated entirely by and for women, The Advocate crusaded against prostitution and sexual assault.

Mader, Rodney. "Politics and Pedagogy in the American Magazine, 1757-58." American Periodicals 16 (Spring 2006): 3-22. American Magazine, an important early magazine, hoped to educate, not merely entertain, especially in political affairs.

Marvin, Thomas F. "'These Days of Double Dealing': Edgar Allan Poe and the Business of Magazine Publishing." American Periodicals 11 (2001): 81-94. Poe worked in the magazine business and also satirized it.

Phegley, Jennifer. "Literary Piracy, Nationalism, and Women Readers in Harper's New Monthly Magazine, 1850-1855." American Periodicals 14 (Spring 2004): 63-90. In the mid-1800s, literary piracy was easy to do without punishment.

Prettyman, Gib. "Harper's Weekly and the Spectacle of Industrialization." American Periodicals 11 (2001): 24-48. The content of the influential magazine revealed the conflicting aspects of a newly industrialized, commercialized America.

Riley, Sam G. "Exotic Americana: The French-Language Magazines of Nineteenth Century New Orleans." Journal of Magazine and New Media Research 2 (Fall 1999). New Orleans was home to at least forty-two French-language magazines in the 1800s.

Roggenkamp, Karen. "Dignified Sensationalism: Cosmopolitan, Elizabeth Bisland, and Trips Around the World. American Periodicals 17 (Spring 2007): 26-40. A magazine, Cosmopolitan, tried to compete with a newspaper, the New York World, in stunt journalism. Bisland's account of her round-the-world travels was serialized in Cosmopolitan in 1890.

Scholnick, Robert J. "Scribner's Monthly and the 'Pictorial Representation of Life and Truth' in Post-Civil War America." American Periodicals 1 (Fall 1991). Scribner's transformed the American magazine by applying photographic processes to wood engraving a decade before the introduction of halftones.

Taketani, Etsuko. "The North American Review, 1815-1835: The Invention of the American Past." American Periodicals 5 (1995): 111-27. The magazine played an important role in the creation of a national identity.

14

The Development of Advertising

1700 – 1900

When volcanic ash was removed from Pompeii, which was destroyed by an eruption of Mt. Vesuvius in 79 A.D., a sign was found carrying the name of a candidate for political office. It was typical of the advertisements of early merchants and promoters. They were used to direct prospective customers to a shop or to identify it. Like the barber's red, white, and blue pole of modern times, the signs often were symbolic.

Along with signs, early advertising also took the form of criers and trademarks. Signboards were posted in some ancient cities, and criers told the public about merchants' wares. As products moved beyond local consumption and were marketed in nearby towns, trademarks were used to assure the purchaser of a particular level of quality. Advertising remained in a primitive state for most of human history — until the development of movable type in the 1450s made possible the mass production of publications.

EARLY AMERICAN ADVERTISING

Although criers and hawkers were popular in England, they were not in the American colonies. The earliest commercial advertising in America appeared in pamphlet and signboard forms. Pamphlets explained in-depth what was available. Signboards usually contained only symbols and business addresses. Various symbols were used, for example, for tobacco shops — from the black boy and the Indian to the Smoking Dutchman. Signs for taverns were the most visible. Although signs were popular throughout the colonies, the most colorful appeared in large towns, such as Philadelphia and Baltimore.

Newspaper advertisements appeared less than a century after the founding of the first settlement in New England at Plymouth, but the printing press had been in the colonies for sixty-six years before it was used to print an advertisement in a newspaper. Boston had several presses, while Philadelphia and New York had at least one each. These presses printed the *Bible*, the *Freeman's Oath*, tracts, almanacs, and other books. The colonies' first newspaper, Boston's *Publick Occurrences Both Forreign and Domestick*, carried no advertising in its sole issue in 1690.

The earliest newspaper ads, which were published in the *Boston News-Letter* in 1704, resembled today's classified or want ads. When John Campbell, the postmaster in Boston, began the *News-Letter*, space was at a premium in its two pages, and he limited advertising to a maximum space of twenty lines. The third *News-Letter*, dated May 1-8, 1704, contained the first paid ads. The cost per line was about 1 1/2 cents. Although there were three ads, together they occupied only four inches of space in one column. They consisted of several lines of small type with no display elements. The only typography that separated them from the news was the word "advertisements." Two advertised rewards for the capture of thieves. The third was the first real estate ad to appear in an American newspaper. It read:

> At Oysterbay, on *Long Island* in the Province of *N. York*, There is a very good Fulling-Mill, to be Let or Sold, as also a Plantation, having on it a large new Brick house, and another good house by it for a Kitchen & work house, with a Barn, Stable &c. a young Orchard, and 20 acres clear Land. The Mill is to be Let with or without the Plantation: Enquire of Mr. *William Bradford* Printer in *N. York*, and know further.[1]

As Campbell's *News-Letter* continued, other kinds of advertising appeared. Runaway servants, slaves for sale, and merchandise for sale were the most commonly advertised items. Advertising remained meager, however. Even after three years, five inches devoted to advertising was rare. Some issues were devoid of any advertising whatsoever.

Colonial advertising received its greatest boost when Benjamin Franklin, while still in his early twenties, purchased the *Pennsylvania Gazette* in 1729. He turned his inventive and creative mind to upgrading its finances, and it soon grew crowded with ads. He brought his genius as a writer to bear on the advertising as well as the editorial content. He was the first advertising copywriter worthy of the name in American history. In fact, his contributions to advertising are so important that the American Advertising Fed-

[1]*Boston News-Letter*, 1-8 May 1704.

Benjamin Franklin's *Gazette*

After purchasing the *Pennsylvania Gazette* in 1729, Benjamin Franklin turned his creative mind to advertising, and the newspaper soon was crowded with ads. It was one of early America's most prosperous newspapers.

eration selected him as one of the first members of its Hall of Fame.

Franklin increased the number of pages in his paper from two to four so he could handle more ads and news stories. He separated each ad with white space. He used at least a 14-point heading for each one. Later, he incorporated small stock cuts or illustrations. Realizing that illustrations could enhance an ad, he used half-column and column cuts made especially for certain advertisers. A cut of a clock face, for example, was used to identify a watchmaker's ad. Readers could recognize what was being sold merely by glancing at the illustration. Another innovation he used was rules to separate ads. Retailers who had stayed away from advertising in newspapers realized they could increase sales by advertising in Franklin's. As a result, he had to enlarge his newspaper again. Instead of two short columns, he put in three deep columns, which made the newspaper about the size of a modern tabloid. He sometimes ran full pages — including page one —

filled with ads. He advertised numerous products and services, including glasses, wine, cheese, chocolate, mathematical instruments, codfish, tea, coffee, and stoves. No other colonial printer did more for advertising.

Although John Peter Zenger is best known for the fact that his trial in 1735 enlarged freedom of the press, he also helped advance advertising. His *New York Weekly Journal* normally contained eight to ten ads, while most other papers usually contained two or three. He used column rules to separate ads, and he did not restrict advertising to a particular amount of space. He ran one ad that was more than a half-page deep. Like Franklin, Zenger realized the importance of illustrations and used various cuts to improve the appearance of ads. He charged three shillings (equivalent to about $10 today) for the first insertion and one shilling for each insertion thereafter. He apparently reasoned that advertisers would advertise more often if they received a discount.

Another innovator in advertising was James Parker, who founded the *New York Weekly Post-Boy* in 1742. Ads in the paper occupied as much as six columns, or half of the space. They were for real estate, slaves, runaway apprentices, books, wines, medicines, and lotteries. Their captions were capitalized in 10-point and sometimes 14- or 18-point type. By 1760, type sizes and typefaces varied within most ads, with captions at least eighteen points. Display ads sometimes filled entire columns. The *Post-Boy* became so successful that ads filled three of the four pages. The October 30, 1760, issue's entire front page was covered with ads, one of the first times that had occurred in a colonial paper.

As the American Revolution approached, however, events began to hurt advertising. The British Parliament taxed ads with the Stamp Act of 1765, which the colonists aggressively opposed. In 1765, primarily because of a shortage of paper in the colonies caused by the Stamp Act, Benjamin Franklin cut display advertising from the *Pennsylvania Gazette*. Instead of large type and illustrations, he filled advertising columns with small type and thumbnail art.

When the Revolution started, George Washington used posters, an advertising medium, to recruit soldiers. Conditions worsened in the colonies during the war, and many newspapers died. One paper, though — the *Pennsylvania Packet and the General Advertiser*, founded in 1771 by John Dunlap — illustrated how advertising could help sell newspapers. It is obvious that Dunlap learned from Franklin. He realized the importance of how an ad looked. As a result, the *Packet's* ads were easier to read and attracted reader interest. The newspaper featured commercial news, too, rather than political stories. Commercial news attracted merchants. Thus Dunlap was able to attract those who needed to advertise. He revived the illustration and created special cuts for certain advertisers. Within two years, the newspaper was so successful that he had to enlarge its size and increase its columns. Advertising accounted for two-thirds of the paper's content. In 1784, the newspaper, which had started as a weekly, became the second daily to be published in America. The reason was not because of readers' hunger for news. Rather, Dunlap received so much advertising

Advertising Design

During the American Revolution, John Dunlap's *Pennsylvania Packet* succeeded in part because Dunlap recognized the importance of how an advertisement looked. He frequently used woodcut illustrations to enliven ads.

that he found it necessary to increase the frequency of publication.

Another daily appeared a year later. Published in New York by Francis Childs, the *New York Daily Advertiser* contributed to advertising by running captions in type as big as 36-point. Usually one word, the captions were bold to capture attention.

By the early 1800s, the number of newspapers published in the United States had grown to more than 300. Despite the fact that advertising volume was increasing, few papers depended on ad revenue. Most were operated for political purposes and were supported by private contributions or subscriptions. Most publishers were satisfied with their advertising. Few worried about how ads appeared. Thus, advertising remained constant in appearance for many years. In most cases, no more than one cut illustrated each ad. The copy was dull and usually small in size.

Yet, advertising remained popular with businesses. The reason was simple: cities were growing. Consequently, proprietors realized that prospective customers were increasing in number every day; thus, they had to be informed. Otherwise, advertising, if it had depended on the creativity of publishers, might have failed.

ADVERTISING IN THE PENNY PRESS

When Benjamin Day began the *New York Sun* in 1833, he not only revolutionized journalism but newspaper advertising as well. By the second year, the *Sun* was selling 20,000 copies, more than twice the number of any other newspaper in the United States. The large circulation made it a popular medium for advertisers.

Advertising in the *Sun* cost $30 (equivalent to about $780 today) a year for a "square" of ten lines a day — equal to 1¢ a line (equivalent to about 26¢ today). Day wrote most of the copy, which, in most cases, consisted of ten or fewer lines. The ads were similar to those in other newspapers, except for their size. Day realized the importance of the want ad, which advertisers in London had used. He solicited these small ads from businesses and readers and placed them under the heading "Wants." Each, two or three lines in length, cost 50¢. Day also published ads for theaters and museums as well as marriage and death notices.

As the number of ads increased, Day had to increase the *Sun's* page dimensions. By 1836 the size was 12 x 19. Advertising accounted for thirteen columns a day. In 1839, two years after Day sold the *Sun* to Moses Beach for $40,000, ads accounted for seventeen columns in the 24-column newspaper.

Penny journalism grew as the result of the *Sun's* success. In New York alone, thirty-five penny papers were started between 1834 and 1839. Not all survived. In 1835, though, James Gordon Bennett founded the *New York Herald*, which, like the *Sun*, presented news of every type. Eventually, the *Herald* surpassed the *Sun* in circulation. Like the *Sun* and the *New York Daily Advertiser*, the *Herald* catered to merchants and manufacturers by the kind of news stories it printed. Ad rates applied to a "square" of space — from 50¢ a day to $30 a year.

Most newspapers followed standard practices in regard to advertising. Ads were separated by lines but contained no bold-face headings. Most ads carried little, if any, illustrations although a few papers in Boston and Philadelphia were exceptions to the rule. Most ads were similar to want ads. They contained small first-line headlines, small amounts of copy, and thumbnail cuts of houses, hats, ships, and other illustrations that identified a certain kind of business.

Bennett was more creative than his rivals in dealing with advertisers. In 1836, his *Herald* published a two-column ad for the American Museum that contained a two-column illustration. For several years after that, the *Herald* and other New York newspapers published two-column ads, some with illustrations. However, in the late 1840s, advertisers who placed small ads every day complained so much about the few advertisers who placed large display ads occasionally that the *Herald* finally banned all display. As a consequence, the *Herald's* advertising columns looked the same, and advertising — at least in the *Herald* and other New York newspapers — seemed to regress.

The Industrial Revolution that reshaped the United States in the nineteenth century produced dramatic changes in advertising. Before the 1830s, the United States had few industries. Newspaper ads frequently were intended as much for personal as for business purposes. Agriculture provided unprocessed food; and individuals, a slow craft system, and foreign sources supplied clothing, furniture, and other hard goods. Power came from animals and water. The Industrial Revolution brought steam power and machines that could be connected to it to produce more goods — merchandise in search of a market. Advertising helped supply the market. With the spread of railroads and other forms of transportation and new manufacturing plants, newspaper advertising became important to these industries as well as to new small businesses. These forms of transportation also helped newspapers increase their circulations, thus encouraging a growth in advertising volume.

In addition, there was an influx of immigrants from Europe. Those who could read English read newspapers and magazines to learn about their new home and to obtain employment. While most immigrants moved into cities and became a part of urban society, others migrated west. Territorial expansion was rapid, and advertisers realized new markets.

In the 1850s, Robert Bonner, who had worked as a compositor on the *Hartford* (Conn.) *Courant*, purchased the *Merchants' Ledger*, a business sheet, and changed the name to the *New York Ledger*. He at first accepted no advertising. However, he made advertising history by publishing stories that appealed to women, which resulted in women becoming more interested in reading stories in newspapers and in ads directed to women. He serviced advertising in another way, too, when he advertised his publication in other newspapers. He broke the barriers against display and soon made publishers of penny papers realize they had made a mistake, monetarily speaking, by restricting the format that they allowed advertisers to use. He experimented with copy and typography, which caused other publishers to do the same. His *New York Ledger*, which sold for 4¢, soon had a circulation of 400,000.

Bonner's ads in other newspapers were similar to those by auctioneers in London, who split their messages into separate announcements and ran ads of equal length down a column. Each ad began with the same two lines in capital letters. Like the auctioneers in London, Bonner wrote his ad in the want-ad style, repeated it ninety-three times, and filled a column in the *New York Herald* in this manner:

> ORION, THE GOLD BEATER is the title of Cobb's sensation story in the *New York Ledger*.
> ORION, THE GOLD BEATER is the title of Cobb's sensation story in the *New York Ledger*.
> ORION, THE GOLD BEATER is the title of Cobb's sensation story in the *New York Ledger*.

It was difficult for any reader to miss Bonner's ad.

Bonner soon went to two columns with reiteration, then to a full page. Some of his ads included the following line printed more than 600 times: "Don't go home to-night without the *New York Ledger*." He was the first advertiser to spend $27,000 a week. Only the patent medicine advertisers spent as much in a single year. His methods had an immediate effect on advertising. Although most newspapers did not publish large bold display ads until the late 1800s, most experimented with type faces and sizes.

Robert Bonner

In the 1850s, Robert Bonner (inset) established a number of firsts in advertising. One of his accomplishments was to begin publishing stories in the *New York Ledger* that appealed to women, thereby creating a market for advertising of products of particular interest to them. When James Gordon Bennett banned display advertising from the *New York Herald*, Bonner got around the prohibition by printing small lines and repeating them endlessly, sometimes filling an entire page with the same message. These two columns in 1859 urged readers to buy Bonner's own *New York Ledger*. The reason for Bennett's ban was that he did not want small advertisers' messages to be lost among large ones.

In New York, after the Civil War, two large department stores — Macy's and Lord & Taylor — broke away from agate and column rules and moved to two-column ads. Lord & Taylor's ads contained announcements of specific products or groups of products. Its logo was usually the largest type — 30-point. The size was increased to 36-point in the 1870s. Lord & Taylor also broke up copy so that ads for three or four products could be printed one under the other in one column. Thus, readers saw its logo more than once. Other advertisers, such as John Wanamaker in Philadelphia, copied this style.

Not every merchant, however, wanted to advertise, as Daniel Frohman, a young advertising solicitor, realized. In 1869, in a brochure titled *Hints to Advertisers*, he discussed the average merchant's attitude:

The man who doesn't believe in advertising is constantly doing what he deprecates. He hangs costs outside of the door, or puts dry goods in his window — that's advertising. He sends out drummers through the country, or puts his name on his wagon — that's advertising. He labels the articles of his manufacture — that's advertising. If he has lost his cow, he puts a written notice at the post office, or tells his sister-in-law about it — that's advertising. He has his name put up in gilt letters over his door — what is that but advertising?... A man can't do business without advertising; and the question is whether to call to his aid the engine of the world — the printing press ... or to go back to the days when newspapers, telegraphs and railroads were unknown.[2]

Frohman also noted that newspaper reporters as well as novelists were writing advertising copy and that there were two schools of writing. One school produced flowery language. The second produced ad copy that was interspersed with news copy. Patent medicine advertisers employed the second form, particularly when they advertised in rural newspapers. Some advertisers also used jingles and teaser copy to arouse readers' curiosity.

MAGAZINE ADVERTISING

The first ad to appear in an American magazine was a reading notice about a ferry. Dated May 10, 1741, it ran under the heading "Advertisement" in Benjamin Franklin's *General Magazine*.

Magazines, however, survived only briefly in the 1700s. Most merchants refused to place ads in them. No merchant wished to advertise in a magazine that had financial problems, and without advertising most magazines had financial problems. Would-be advertisers wondered: Would the printer be paid? Would the merchant's ad appear? Or would the magazine die as a result of too few readers or too few advertisers?

In the 1800s, in order to attract advertisers, magazine publishers allowed ads to appear on the covers. Special sections of four to eight pages catering to advertisers were common. They allowed numerous businesses to advertise products and services in copy-filled blocks. Display was seldom used.

Many publishers refused to carry advertising because they believed it was demeaning and lowered their magazines' value. The only advertising appearing on the pages of *Harper's Weekly* was for the publishers' forthcoming books.

In the mid-1800s, however, several of the most popular magazines began running advertising for the first time. The *Atlantic Monthly* had fourteen pages of advertising in its December 1865 issue. Women's periodicals such as *Godey's Lady's Book*, *Peterson's*, and *Ladies' Wreath* carried advertising for numerous products and services — from musical instruments, sewing machines, and sil-

Leading the Way in Advertising Design
Beginning in the 1850s, dry-goods stores became the leaders in bigger ads and bolder designs. This ad for ready-made clothes and a variety of other items appeared in 1855 in Milledgeville, Illinois. It was a circular printed on one side. Soon, department stores would begin to use similar designs in newspaper ads.

verware to schools. The ads contained copy and some illustrations. *Frank Leslie's Illustrated Newspaper*, a weekly periodical, published a full-page ad of Mason & Hamlin musical instruments on October 20, 1860. The ad contained eleven illustrations, which was unusual. Most ads contained one or two.

Many magazines depended on patent medicine advertising. Typical was the following ad in an 1862 issue of *Vanity Fair*:

To Soldiers, Sailors, and the Public
THE PREVAILING DIFFICULTY
a general lassitude seizes the frame,
which often resembles the torpor preceding death....
Now whether this be in
THE NORTH OR THE SOUTH
the remedy is the same.
Take at once six or eight of Brandreth's Pills....[3]

As a result of such advertising, journalists criticized the industry. One of them, Frank Leslie, wrote:

The art of advertising is one of the arts most studied by our lit-

---

[2]Quoted in Frank Presbrey, *The History and Development of Advertising* (Garden City, N.Y., 1929), 255-6.

[3]*Vanity Fair*, 2 August 1862.

Frank Leslie's Illustrated Ads
Magazine advertising in the mid-1800s began to carry illustrations of products. In the October 20, 1860, issue of *Frank Leslie's Illustrated Newspaper* appeared this full-page ad for Mason & Hamlin musical instruments.

erary vendors of fancy soaps, philanthropic corn doctors, humanitarian pill-makers, and all the industrious professions which have an intense feeling for one's pockets. Every trick that can be resorted to for the purpose of inducing one to read an advertisement is practiced, and, it must be confessed, very often with complete success....[4]

Such tricks were used primarily because newspapers refused to accept display ads. Magazines, however, preferred full-, half-, or quarter-page display ads from large advertisers. Profits, after all, were greater from these than from the small copy-filled ads.

After the Civil War, advertising in magazines became popular. Circulations increased as more Americans learned to read. *Scribner's*, which enjoyed a large circulation, was one of the first magazines to attract numerous advertisers. Its December 1880 issue contained forty-nine pages of advertising. *Galaxy* was the first high-class magazine to run a variety of miscellaneous ads in color.

[4]*Frank Leslie's Illustrated Newspaper*, 3 October 1857.

From 1868 to 1870, it used colored inserts — one of the main reasons it had at least twenty-four pages of advertising a month.

Magazine advertising increased until 1873. In that year, businesses saw profits decrease because of a depressed economy and, consequently, for the next several years withheld advertisements. Magazine publishers tempted advertisers with various offers. Many of their offers, however, went unnoticed; and their magazines died.

Ads contained brief but bold captions, bold logos, copy in various sizes and typefaces, and one or more illustrations, depending on the sizes of the ads.

Advertising rates in the late 1800s reflected circulations. In 1865, the *Saturday Evening Post*, which had a circulation of 20,000, charged 30¢ an agate line. In 1885, it charged 25¢ an agate line; yet it had a circulation of 40,000. The explanation for the apparent paradox is that as circulations increased, the cost of advertising decreased. This was the case for such periodicals as the *Spirit of the Times*, *Harper's Monthly*, *Century Magazine*, *Ladies' Home Journal*, and *Godey's Lady's Book*.

By the beginning of the 1890s, new industries had been founded, and old industries had grown. Businesses realized that magazines were reaching more consumers, especially in December, and consequently placed more advertising. Rates in some magazines were expensive. *Harper's* charged $250 for a full-page ad, while the *Ladies' Home Journal* charged more than $2,000 (equivalent to about $48,000 today). As the century ended, magazines accounted for about one-fourth of the dollars businesses spent on advertising. One reason for this growth was national advertising by manufacturers such as W. L. Douglas, Lydia Pinkham, and Royal Baking Powder. Among the firms with large advertising expenditures were clothing manufacturers such as Warner's Celebrated Coraline Corsets, Plymouth Rock $3 Pants, and Cluett Shirts and Collars. Agencies for many of these firms used pictures in ads to illustrate the benefits of the product.

Other big advertisers included manufacturers of pianos and other instruments, housewares, appliances, bicycles, cameras, breakfast foods, phonographs, soaps, safety razors, and medicine, to name a few. Some companies became famous as a result of their advertising. Consumers remembered Pears' after reading its slogan: "Good morning, have you used Pears' Soap?" Procter & Gamble's Ivory Soap was remembered, too, because it was "99 44/100 per cent pure."

Although many magazines advertised practically anything and everything in the late 1800s, some publishers protected readers by not running fraudulent ads. Fake remedies were especially troublesome. However, even the most reputable magazines ignored other complaints, including those about the use of pictures of women to sell corsets and underwear, which was considered taboo.

HOW P. T. BARNUM CHANGED ADVERTISING

Phineas Taylor Barnum learned to advertise early in life. Before he was twenty he created ads for lottery tickets. They consisted of

"Have You Used Pears' Soap?"
Through effective advertising, Pears' became the most popular body soap of the last half of the nineteenth century. Its slogan "Have you used Pears' soap?" became famous, and the texts of its ads reinforced the idea that Pears' enjoyed immense popularity. The caption for this 1886 ad read, "PEARS' SOAP — The Great English Complexion Soap — is sold throughout the United States and in all other parts of the World, and its praises are heard and echoed everywhere."

handbills, circulars, gold signs, and colored posters. When he was twenty-one, he edited and published *The Herald of Freedom* at Danbury, Connecticut, and claimed that a church deacon had "been guilty of taking usury of an orphan boy." Barnum was jailed for libel — and, in true promotional style, he used the occasion to his advantage. When released, he rode in a parade, preceded by a brass band and forty horsemen and followed by carriages filled with friends and supporters. Of course, the press gave much attention to the event.

Three years later he and his wife moved to New York, where he learned about Joice Heth, an African American who, supposedly, had been the slave of George Washington's father. She was, she said, 161 years of age. Barnum purchased her for $1,000. Through handbills, posters, and newspaper ads, the public learned that she

was the first to clothe young George. Within the first week of her appearance Barnum earned a profit. After New York, he took Heth to other cities.

To sell Heth's appearances he placed informative ads in newspapers and mailed anonymous letters to editors denouncing her credibility. Income increased until her death a few months later. Barnum claimed that he learned only after her death that she had been about eighty years old. He, like the public, had been deceived.

In 1841 — after several years of earning a meager living and supporting a family of four through such jobs as writing ads for the Bowery Amphitheater for $4 a week — Barnum acquired Sudder's American Museum. Filled with natural and unnatural curiosities, it brought Barnum fame and fortune. He entertained the public with educated dogs, industrious fleas, jugglers, ventriloquists, giants, dwarfs, mechanical figures, and American Indians. He knew how to advertise the museum. He placed newspaper ads to announce acts. Sometimes the ads had qualities of incantations, as illustrated by the following one:

VISION OF THE HOURIS
VISION OF THE HOURIS
VISION OF THE HOURIS
A Tableau of 850 Men
Women and Children
CLAD IN SUITS OF SILVER ARMOUR
CLAD IN SUITS OF SILVER ARMOUR
CLAD IN SUITS OF SILVER ARMOUR[5]

Other advertising appeared in various forms. A brass band, which could be heard for several blocks, played on the museum's balcony. Barnum placed gas lights, which had the effect of modern electronic spectaculars, on top of the museum, where they illuminated lower Broadway. He had large paintings of rare animals made in panels and placed on the outside of the museum. Banners announcing a rare find were strung across streets. He also used handbills, as well as the reliable news-column, which he had perfected. "I thoroughly understood the art of advertising," he later wrote, "not merely by means of printers' ink, which I have always used freely, and to which I confess myself so much indebted for my success, but by turning every possible circumstance to my account. It was my monomania to make the Museum the town wonder and town talk. I often seized upon an opportunity by instinct, even before I had a very definite conception as to how it should be used, and it seemed, somehow, to mature itself and serve my purpose."[6]

When ordinary forms of advertising failed, Barnum improvised. For instance, he instructed a man to place bricks on the corners of several streets and then to carry at least one brick to each corner and exchange it for the other. The man was not to comment to anyone. On the hour, he was to go to the museum, present a

[5]In E.S. Turner, *The Shocking History of Advertising* (New York, 1953), 130.
[6]P.T. Barnum, *Barnum's Own Story: The Autobiography of P.T. Barnum* (New York, 1961), 102.

Barnum's Jumbo
One of P. T. Barnum's great promotional gimmicks was an elephant he claimed to be the largest in the world and which he named "Jumbo." This cartoon by Thomas Nast, titled "Mutual Admiration," has Barnum telling Jumbo, "You are a HUMBUG after my own heart. You have even beat me in advertising."

ticket, and then enter. Within the first hour, approximately 500 bystanders stood and watched, trying to solve the mystery. When the man went to the museum, the crowd followed and purchased tickets, hoping to learn the answer inside. Barnum's walking advertisement attracted so many people that after a few days the police asked Barnum to withdraw the man from the street. Newspapers played up the event for several weeks.

Another example of improvisation was his invention of "Dr. Griffin" and his preserved mermaid. "Dr. Griffin" was actually Levi Lyman, an associate of Barnum. To promote the mermaid, Barnum placed stories in numerous newspapers. They said Dr. Griffin had purchased the mermaid in China for the Lyceum of Natural History in London but would be exhibiting it at Concert Hall for one week. A week later Barnum announced that he had secured the rare specimen for the American Museum. When the museum displayed the mermaid, the exhibition was a huge success.

Barnum also put on baby shows, baby contests, and beauty contests to arouse the public's curiosity. He was probably the first in the United States to use these shows and contests to attract attention. He was responsible for implementing the first successful advertising campaigns primarily because he realized that they increased sales.

"TOM THUMB"

Charles Stratton, a midget, was born in Connecticut. When he was five, his parents signed an agreement with Barnum that allowed him to exploit the child. Of course, the parents could accompany their son and would get paid.

In order to sell "Tom Thumb," Barnum had him tour the United States. He advertised Tom's age as eleven instead of five and his place of birth as England instead of Connecticut. He had Tom introduced to prominent families, which was mentioned in ads. He printed biographies as well as lithographs and distributed them wherever Tom toured. Newspaper editors published stories about Tom, which sparked additional interest. When he appeared at the American Museum, most of the public had read about him and desired to see him. Barnum introduced him as "General Tom Thumb freshly arrived from England," and the crowds laughed. In the thirteen months he was at the American Museum, almost 100,000 persons paid to see him.

Barnum applied reverse psychology in his advertising. Before Tom appeared anywhere, Barnum had an announcement posted. He directed the public not to get excited but to keep quiet. He perfected such techniques during a tour of Europe that lasted three years. In England and on the Continent, Barnum and the General entertained royalty, including Queen Victoria. Dressed like Napoleon, Tom made an unforgettable impression on the noble class. He and Barnum were invited to palaces, estates, and chateaus. Of course, news stories featured these exploits because readers wanted to learn about society's elite. In Paris the General was so popular that a cafe was named "Tom Ponce." Artists begged him to sit for them. Composers wrote songs about him. Shop windows had statuettes of him. After Paris, he and Barnum toured southern France, Spain, Belgium, and other countries. He was greeted with the same enthusiasm wherever he toured. During the three years in Europe, approximately 5,000,000 people paid to see him. The tour's profits were more than $1,000,000. Tom's share was half. He and Barnum remained friends for life.

JENNY LIND

Jenny Lind, the "Swedish Nightingale," was the most famous performer in Europe in the 1800s. Barnum offered her $1,000 per concert, plus expenses, for touring America. She accepted with stipulations. Barnum had to assure her that he would pay for her conductor, composer, and pianist, as well as a sixty-member orchestra. He also had to deposit in a London bank $187,500 before she left Europe.

When Barnum realized that most Americans had never heard of Jenny Lind, he used press releases to publicize her. He then distributed an authorized biographical pamphlet and photograph that informed readers of her inimitable talent.

Before Lind left for the United States, she gave, at Barnum's request, two concerts in Liverpool. Both sold out. A London critic wrote a review praising her performances. Barnum was able to get the review published in newspapers throughout America before she arrived.

When Lind's ship docked in New York harbor on Sunday, September 1, 1850, Barnum, accompanied by a reporter from the *New*

Barnum's Stars

During his day, Tom Thumb was the most popular star in the world. England's Queen Victoria invited him and P. T. Barnum to visit her palace, and she took him by the hand and showed him around her art gallery. He told her, in his high treble voice, that the gallery was "first rate," one of his favorite expressions. He sang and danced for members of the royal court for an hour, at the end of which Victoria invited him to return at a time when the Prince of Wales might meet him. Jenny Lind, already a famous European soprano nicknamed the "Swedish Nightingale," was contracted by Barnum in 1850 to tour the United States. He — like most Americans — had never heard her sing, but he believed he could promote her well enough to take a chance. The tour saw concert halls packed at every engagement.

York Tribune, and about 40,000 persons greeted her. The crowd followed her and her entourage as they traveled in Barnum's carriage to the Irving House Hotel.

Barnum then promoted the Great Jenny Lind Opening Concert Ticket Auction. He persuaded his friend John Genin to be the first person in America to purchase a ticket to hear Lind sing. He then visited Dr. Brandreth, who was known for his patent medicines, and persuaded him to buy the first ticket at auction. Barnum assured him that it would be an excellent opportunity to advertise his medicines. Several thousand attended the auction to bid against one another, including Genin's bookkeeper and Dr. Brandreth's cashier. The publicity was so encouraging that Barnum repeated the auction in several cities.

The tour covered fifteen cities in the United States and Havana, Cuba. Reviews of Lind's performances were filled with superlatives. Some critics claimed she was the greatest singer they had heard. Barnum was ecstatic. Lind gave ninety-five concerts.

In June 1851, however, she informed Barnum she was ending the tour. She tried to go it alone but was unsuccessful. Organizing the advertising was too much for her. In May 1852, she performed her last American concert where she had performed her first, except this time the Castle Garden was half empty.

The campaign for Jenny Lind was characteristic of Barnum's brilliance. Because of his imagination and energy, he influenced these advertising techniques: (1) keeping one's name or business before the public; (2) using unique or original devices to produce conversation as well as attention; (3) taking advantage of every opportunity to bring about editorial comment or news; and, of course, (4) providing more real value than one's competition. Like advertisers today, Barnum advertised primarily to generate interest and consequently income.

THE BIRTH OF THE ADVERTISING AGENCY

The advertising agency in America developed in the 1800s, in a time of quacks and promotional geniuses like P. T. Barnum. Before the country's first major multi-service agency, N. W. Ayer & Son, was founded in Philadelphia in 1868, ad agencies had passed through four stages.[7] The earliest agencies represented newspaper publishers, serving mostly as wholesalers of newspaper space. Orlando Bourne was acting as an agent as early as 1828. The pioneers, however, were Volney B. Palmer, who by 1846 had offices in Boston, New York, Baltimore, and Philadelphia, and John L. Hooper, who worked in New York. Whereas most agencies worked for one or a few newspapers, Palmer and Hooper represented several. In addition, they promoted advertising as an integral part of marketing and produced as well as delivered ads to publishers. Palmer was particularly active in those techniques.

The second stage in the development of agencies occurred in the 1850s when agents became independent. Space-jobbing, as this stage was called, became popular as agents realized they could earn more by selling space to advertisers. When advertisers wanted space, the agents would buy it for them in newspapers. This stage caused many agents to question their role. After all, they did not work for publishers, and they did not work for advertisers. Yet, they referred to themselves as agents.

The third stage developed out of the second when George P. Rowell purchased large amounts of space in newspapers and then resold it in small amounts to advertisers. This stage, which has been called space-wholesaling, began in 1865.

The fourth stage was based on Rowell's idea and appeared in the late 1860s. Marked by the advertising concession agency, this stage began when Carlton & Smith (later the J. Walter Thompson

---

[7]For a detailed discussion of these stages, see Ralph M. Hower, *The History of an Advertising Agency* (Cambridge, Mass., 1949), 13-9.

Promoting Modern Conveniences

By the mid-1800s, industrialization was transforming American life. The factory system made mass production possible, and it produced manufactured items cheaply and in great numbers. In many ways, production methods in the United States surpassed in quality and efficiency those in Great Britain, giving rise to the term "the American system of manufacture." Items for home use, "modern conveniences," became readily available and increasingly popular. Singer sewing machines, for example, were introduced in 1850; and within a decade 100,000 were being produced annually. With so many manufactured items available for purchase, a primary challenge was how to market them. Advertising was seen as an integral part of the process. Magazine advertising, like this ad for a new washing machine with two cylinders, emphasized explanatory text and frequently included illustrations.

Company) purchased most — if not all — of the advertising space in certain publications for a specified period of time. Consequently, the agency — not the publisher — was responsible for securing advertisers for the entire publication. This practice actually closed the gap between agent and publisher, but the agent worked as an independent middleman nonetheless.

VOLNEY B. PALMER

Volney Palmer, who had worked in real estate, started advertising his business in 1842 in *M'Elroy's Philadelphia Directory*. One of his early ads read:

V.B. Palmer's
REAL ESTATE AND COAL OFFICE
No. 104 South Third Street (a few doors below the Exchange) Philadelphia
Agency for the Purchase and Sale of Houses and Lots, Farms, Farming, Timber and Coal Lands, Bonds and Mortgages, Ground Rents, Anthracite Coal, &c. ADVERTISEMENTS and Subscriptions received from some of the best and most widely circulated newspapers in Pennsylvania and New Jersey, and in many of the principal cities and towns throughout the United States, for which he has the agency, affording an excellent opportunity for Merchants, Mechanics, Professional Men, Hotel and Boarding House Keepers, Railroad, Insurance and Transportation Companies, and the enterprising portion of the community generally, to publish extensively abroad their respective pursuits — to learn the terms of subscription and advertising, and accomplish their object here without the trouble of perplexing and fruitless inquiries, the expense and labor of letter writing; the risk of making enclosures of money &c, &c.[8]

Palmer remained in real estate for the next several years, even though his advertising interests were fruitful. In 1849 he used "Advertising Agency" in an ad for the first time. Advertisers would have him place their ads in selected newspapers. After assuring that an ad had been printed, he then billed the advertiser and paid the publisher. He claimed to be the sole representative of 1,300 newspapers, thus allowing merchants to be selective about where they advertised. He also created speculative presentations for prospective advertisers.

Of course, advertisers had to pay the total cost for Palmer's services, not just the space rates for each newspaper selected. Palmer also received a 25% commission from the publisher. The 25% rate remained standard among agents into the 1860s. The commission system is still used today, except agencies normally receive 15%, not 25%. Increasing competition among agents, however, allowed advertisers, who frequently ran three or more campaigns a year, to seek the lowest bid on each campaign. Some agents responded by haranguing publishers for lower and lower space rates and cheating on the number of times an ad was published or on the number of newspapers in which it was run.

Palmer provided a number of other services. According to his *Almanac* of 1850,

- he is Agent for the best papers of every section of the whole country.
- he is empowered by the proprietors to make contracts and give receipts.
- his long experience and practical knowledge qualify him to give valuable information....
- a selection can be made suitably adapted to the various pursuits of advertisers.
- a complete system of advertising can be adapted upon either a large or small scale.
- the papers are on file at the Agency, where advertisers can

[8]*M'Elroy's Philadelphia Directory* (1842), 1.

examine them, see the terms, and obtain all requisite information to enable them to advertise judiciously, effectively and safely.[9]

The list of services made it clear that Palmer's agency did more for advertisers than most other agencies.

Both publishers and advertisers were delighted to use his agency. He promoted his services by using endorsements from publishers. By the mid-1850s, with numerous clients considering him a godsend, his agency grew. He opened offices in four major cities. He maintained the office in Philadelphia and hired others to manage the other three. He visited the other offices at various times throughout each year.

In the late 1850s, John E. Joy, W. W. Sharpe, and J. E. Coe became partners. When Palmer retired, in either 1862 or 1863, Joy and Coe operated the Philadelphia and New York offices. Sharpe eventually purchased the latter office. S. R. Niles controlled the Boston office.

Palmer died in 1864 at the age of sixty-five. Perhaps no other agent did more for advertising. Not only did he help advertisers, but he also helped newspaper publishers. Indeed, he sold the idea of advertising to advertisers and consequently made hundreds of proprietors realize how important a role advertising played in a capitalistic society.

GEORGE P. ROWELL

George P. Rowell and his partner Horace Dodd founded an advertising agency in Boston in 1865. Like Palmer, they made up a list of newspapers for advertisers to consider. Unlike Palmer, they persuaded some publishers to give them an additional discount based on continued patronage. They received an additional 3% if they paid in cash within thirty days. They did not have to pay more than 25% of the card (that is, the advertised) rate for most of the newspapers they handled. Rowell was responsible for the cash discount in addition to the commission.

He was also responsible for buying space in bulk and selling it to advertisers. He used the system first with newspapers in New England, and then he instituted it in other regions when the George P. Rowell & Co. agency opened its headquarters in New York in 1867. His early success was based on his novel "select list" of newspapers, most of them weeklies, in which he would guarantee the publisher a column of advertising in each issue for an entire year. To get this guarantee, publishers gave Rowell such discounts on the regular rates that he could sell a one-inch ad four times in 100 papers for $100 and still clear 25% to 40% or more. Rowell was not the first to offer select lists, but he was the first to require that advertisers take the entire list. The select list required that he take a risk: he had to fill those yawning columns of space with ads or suffer financial loss — but the profits made the risk worthwhile.[10]

George P. Rowell
Although Rowell is best remembered as founder of the first trade journal of advertising, *Printer's Ink*, he also brought legitimacy, stability, and other needed improvements to the advertising agency system. After starting his own agency in 1865, he established the practice of guaranteeing newspapers payments for ads himself (rather than waiting until his own clients paid him). He also began the practice of buying space annually rather than on an ad hoc basis. In 1869 he produced *Rowell's American Newspaper Directory*, the first complete list of newspapers throughout the country and their circulation figures.

Rowell tried to assure that circulation figures that publishers claimed were accurate. As he candidly pointed out in an agency flier,

In fixing the value of advertising space in any particular journal, the first question to be considered is the number of copies issued; next the character or quality of the circulation. A well-printed paper is worth more than one badly printed; an influential journal carries more weight than one without reputation.

[9]V.B. Palmer's *Business-Men's Almanac* (New York, 1850).

[10]George P. Rowell, *Forty Years an Advertising Agent, 1865-1905* (New York, 1906). Rowell

had some flexibility. He guaranteed to send a group of ads every month and always provide at least one-quarter of a column and never more than two columns without the publisher's consent. See "The List System," *American Newspaper Reporter* 7 (3 March 1873): 173-92. This is an advertisement for the list system, including sample contracts and advertisements. The *Reporter* was Rowell's house organ.

ASKING.

"He stole from my bodice a rose,
My cheek was it's color the while;
But, ah! the sly rogue! He well knows,
Had he asked it, I must have said no."

"Yes, I remember that occasion. I was young then. I am not old now. I had not a pain nor an ache. My blood was pure and my cheeks showed its crimson. I was happy and healthy. But now, woe is me! I do not see a well day. I have these distressing dragging-down pains, this constant weakness, and I feel all the time worn and weary."

For all such sufferers, Dr. Pierce's Favorite Prescription is a panacea of inestimable value.

As an invigorating tonic, it imparts strength to the whole system. For over-worked, "worn-out," debilitated teachers, milliners, dressmakers, seamstresses, "shop-girls," housekeepers, nursing mothers, and feeble women generally, Dr.

Pierce's Favorite Prescription is the greatest earthly boon, being unequaled as an appetizing cordial and restorative tonic. Contains no alcohol to inebriate; no syrup or sugar to derange digestion; a legitimate *medicine*, not a beverage.

As a soothing and strengthening nervine, "Favorite Prescription" is unequaled, and is invaluable in allaying and subduing nervous excitability, exhaustion, prostration, hysteria, spasms and other distressing nervous symptoms, commonly attendant upon functional and organic diseases. It induces refreshing sleep, and relieves mental anxiety and despondency.

WORLD'S DISPENSARY MEDICAL ASSOCIATION, No. 663 Main Street, Buffalo, N. Y

DR. PIERCE'S PELLETS.

Purely Vegetable and Perfectly Harmless.

Unequaled as a Liver Pill. Smallest, Cheapest, Easiest to Take. One Tiny, Sugar-coated Pellet a Dose. Cure Sick Headache, Bilious Headache, Constipation, Indigestion, Bilious Attacks, and all derangements of the stomach and bowels. 25 cents by druggists.

"He Stole from My Bodice a Rose"
Magazine circulations increased so substantially in the latter decades of the 1800s that publications such as *Godey's Lady's Book* became important vehicles for advertising. Many ads, such as this one for a patent medicine, combined interesting text with appealing illustrations intended to grab readers' attention.

So also a paper which habitually charges high prices for its advertising thereby makes its columns exclusive, and will have fewer, and as a rule, a better class of advertisements, and is worth something more on that account. The value of all these considerations is recognized, but exactly *how* much each one is to be considered becomes a question of judgment.[11]

Rowell realized that if his agency could supply advertisers with accurate information about newspapers and their readers, then advertisers would know how much to pay for space.

In 1869, as a service to all who were interested in advertising, his agency published the first issue of *Rowell's American Newspaper Directory*, which listed circulations of more than 5,000 publications in the United States and more than 300 in Canada. Although Rowell had tried to eliminate the so-called private list — a list containing inflated circulation figures the publisher created — other agents criticized him for making available at a nominal cost more information than they offered. Publishers criticized him for printing conservative circulation figures. They accepted advertising from his agency nonetheless. As a result of his publication, publishers eventually changed their circulation claims to reflect accurate figures.

Rowell was responsible for the *American Newspaper Reporter*, a house organ published for the purpose of informing advertisers and publishers about advertising and how to do it. In the November 20, 1871, issue, he wrote about "The Principles of Advertising":

Honesty is by all odds the very strongest point which can be crowded into an advertisement. Come right down with the facts, boldly, firmly, unflinchingly. Say directly what it is, what it has done, what it will do.... Do not claim too much, but what you do claim must be claimed without the smallest shadow of weakness.... Say flatly "the best," or say nothing. Do not refer to rivals. Ignore every person, place or thing except yourself, your address and your article.... Be serious and dignified, but active and lively. Leave wit, however good it may be, entirely aside.[12]

Rowell realized that advertising copy, which suffered from too many words and overstatement, needed improving. He also realized that every ad — even small ones — had to attract attention.

His house organ became *Printers' Ink* in 1888. By then it had become famous as an instrument in improving advertising. Rowell retired in 1905.

N. W. AYER & SON

Francis Wayland Ayer, who was born in 1848, was influenced by the changes occurring in agencies and by his father, Nathan Wheeler Ayer. A graduate of Brown University, N.W. Ayer named his son after Dr. Francis Wayland, one of Brown's presidents. N.W. Ayer, a devout Baptist, practiced law for several years in Massachusetts, taught in Massachusetts and New York, and then purchased a seminary in Philadelphia in 1867. He was not successful financially, earning only a modest living until he suffered from ill health.

Francis Wayland Ayer learned from his parents, particularly his father, the basic principles that helped him throughout his life. He knew what responsibility, integrity, and honesty meant. When he was fourteen, he taught in a country school in New York State. A year later he was offered a position in a village school. For the next several years, one promotion followed another. He desired to go to college, however, and in 1867 attended the University of Rochester. Within a year he had spent his savings. His father, who was barely earning an income, was unable to help. F. W. Ayer left the university in search of a job. The publisher of the *National Baptist*, a weekly religious newspaper, hired him to solicit ads. Ayer earned $1,200 in commissions in less than a year. His employer

[11]Quoted in Presbrey, *The History and Development of Advertising*, 269.

[12]*American Newspaper Reporter*, 30 November 1871.

Francis W. Ayer
In 1869, at the age of twenty, Ayer began his advertising agency with about $250 borrowed from his father. Believing that combining his name with his father's would add a sense of stability to the agency, he thus came up with the name "N. W. Ayer & Son." His father, a devout Baptist and owner of a seminary, had taught him responsibility, integrity, and honesty. Applying these principles to the advertising business, Francis Ayer made his agency the largest in the nation by the late 1880s.

offered him $2,000 a year to stay with the firm. Ayer refused the opportunity, certain he could earn more on his own. He persuaded his father to work with him, and on April 1, 1869, he opened his agency, N. W. Ayer & Son. The agency bore the name of his father for several reasons. He not only admired his father, but he also preferred using the combined name of father and son. It sounded more impressive than one name alone, he thought, and his father already had agreed to join him.

The Ayer agency began with eleven religious newspapers. Like other agents of his day, Ayer solicited ads from merchants and then placed them in the publications listed with his agency. He also purchased the total advertising space in certain publications and then resold it in parcels to advertisers. Thus he acted as a manager of advertising departments of some publications. He also placed ads in publications that were not on his list. With those, he estimated how much the space would cost and then quoted a price to advertisers that was slightly higher than his estimated cost. He earned income the best way he knew: by selling and bargaining. There was little time for experimenting, especially during the

agency's formative years. By the end of its first year, the agency represented several newspapers in addition to the original eleven. Growth continued, and in 1870 Ayer had to move to a larger office and hire his first employee, George O. Wallace, who was responsible for the bookkeeping.

Within two years, the agency had to move again. It was handling more than 300 publications located in twenty-seven of the thirty-seven states that made up the nation. In addition, it placed ads for clients in other publications through other agents.

In 1873, N. W. Ayer died. Since Francis' mother did not have the experience or the interest to be a partner, he purchased his father's share of the business from her. The same year, as a result of growth, he asked Wallace to become a partner, and Wallace accepted one-fourth interest in the firm.

Throughout the 1870s, the Ayer agency grew. In 1875, Ayer created a printing department so the agency could produce most ads in-house. Thus, by the following year, his agency could place ads in any newspaper published in the United States or Canada. This ability gave it an advantage since most other agencies hired independent printers to produce their ads.

In 1877, Ayer purchased Coe, Wetherill & Co., another agency in Philadelphia. Coe, Wetherill & Co. had succeeded Joy, Coe & Co., which had acquired Volney Palmer's agency. Ayer's agency, like Rowell's, also published its own directory, *Ayer & Son's Manual for Advertisers*, to promote its list of publications and later *The Advertiser's Guide*, a quarterly magazine filled with informative features and promotional pieces on advertising.

Following the lead of other agencies, Ayer placed ads for patent medicine, such as "Compound Oxygen," "Kennedy's Ivory Tooth Cement," "Rock & Rye," and "Dr. Case's Liver Remedy and Blood Purifier." Of course, Ayer represented other firms, too, including John Wanamaker, Montgomery Ward, Whitman's Chocolates, Blackwell's Durham smoking tobacco, and Singer sewing machines. He also represented manufacturers of farm machinery as well as educational institutions such as Harvard College.

It was during this time that Ayer analyzed Rowell's methods of handling publishers and clients and realized that Rowell had put himself in the middle. That is, although he was supposedly representing the advertiser, the publisher was paying him. How could an agent serve both? Ayer wondered. He decided to represent the advertiser. Unlike Rowell, he would tell an advertiser how much space cost. Furthermore, he would inform an advertiser what the agency received for its services. Instead of being merely a space-seller like other agencies, Ayer's agency would become a space-buyer and therefore be paid by the client. Ayer believed this plan was fair to the client and actually superior to Rowell's plan.

He persuaded a longtime client to allow his agency to handle all of the client's advertising for an entire year. They agreed upon a 10% commission (a figure Ayer soon regretted and changed to 15% with other advertisers) with Ayer to charge the advertiser only what he himself was charged by publishers. This gave the advertiser the benefit of all discounts Ayer arranged. Ayer also chose the best newspapers in which to place the ads. Under the bid sys-

Sex in Advertising

Early Marketers Titillate with Glimpses of Knees and Necks

Most of us are familiar with the erotic images in contemporary advertising. Marketers such as Victoria's Secret, Abercrombie & Fitch, and Calvin Klein leave little to the imagination when they promote their products with provocatively posed – and barely clothed – supermodels. However, scintillating images are not new. They have been used to sell products and services since at least the 1840s – and perhaps even since the beginning of advertising itself.

Sexual content in mainstream media prior to 1900 pales, however, compared to what we see now. Almost without exception, early images featured females. Viewers were treated to glimpses of the nap of a woman's neck, her come-hither gaze, her hemline raised to her knee, or her low-cut bodice. Images of couples – typically, tuxedoed men enraptured by attractive women – appeared occasionally. Far from putting audiences to sleep, these peek-a-boo images evoked responses similar to today's prurient images. Not surprisingly, sex was used for the same purposes as today – to attract attention to the ad, to associate sexual meaning with the brand, and to offer sex-related brand promises as reasons for buying the product. "Use our product," they implied, "and others will find you attractive."

Many images appeared in ads for soft drinks, bottled water, tonics, and lotions. Other dicey images appeared in ads for undergarments such as corsets and hosiery. Advertisers in 1897, for example, debated whether models in corsets should be shown covered or uncovered. A similar controversy raged ninety years later when in 1987 a woman – as opposed to a mannequin – clad only in a Playtex bra from the waist up aired for the first time in a television commercial. Critics asked the same question as early ad professionals,

"Why show skin when you can show how the bra enhances a woman's *clothed* figure?"

Even more graphic depictions of women were found in tobacco and beer ads targeted to men. In the 1880s, for in-

Advertisers in the 1800s began using suggestive images to try to help sell products. Sex appeal in their ads usually relied on women with low-cut bodices or raised skirt hems. In 1871 Pearl tobacco used the image on the left for its posters. Like many other women in ads of the era, the model for the artwork posed in a style reminiscent of classical art. As illustrated by the 1898 ad above, some corset manufacturers believed the best way to promote their product was to show it on a woman's body rather than underneath her clothes. This ad ran in a women's fashion magazine.

stance, Duke Cigarettes enclosed in its packs small cards showing scantily clad "women of the stage," which encouraged purchasers to keep buying to complete the whole set – similar to today's baseball cards. Large full-color posters of topless women could be found in many saloons and taverns. Posters with names such as "Betrothed" and "La Debutante" appeared in a series of displays for Portner Ale of Alexandria, Virginia. "Compliments of" was printed on one image, suggesting that brewers supplied the posters free-of-charge to drinking establishments much like today's brewers supply bars and clubs with images of bikini-clad women. Unlike present times, however, only male consumers saw yesterday's posters.

tem, in contrast, each agent strived to use the cheapest papers rather than the best ones. If Ayer felt a publisher's space rates were too high, he had the right to change newspapers during a campaign. This prerogative kept the list "open," thus giving the practice the name "The Open Contract." This new way of doing business forced the agent to work for the advertiser. If the advertiser succeeded, he rewarded the agent by renewing the contract. The Ayer open-contract-plus-commission plan was initiated in 1875. Through trial and error, Ayer learned how to earn a profit from his commission system.

That was not as difficult as persuading advertisers to look at advertising from a different perspective. Indeed, the advertiser had to trust Ayer and vice versa. Ayer would buy space at the lowest possible cost for the advertiser. The advertiser would have access to Ayer's lists of rates. Thus the advertiser could determine the cost of advertising space in a specific publication and consequently the commission to the agency.

This system allowed Ayer to buy space wisely as well as consider the advertiser's needs. The system, although sound, was not adopted by every agency, but it forced every agency to recognize that advertisers had interests that needed servicing and, to a certain extent, protecting.

In 1879, the Ayer agency started another service when it conducted a market survey of the nation to entice the Nichols-Shepard Company, which manufactured threshing machines, to advertise. The survey examined the production of grains by counties and states. The agency also included an in-depth advertising plan in its proposal to Nichols-Shepard. The resulting campaign was the first based on a market survey. Nichols-Shepard hired Ayer as a result of the survey, and Ayer realized that surveys could be performed for other advertisers.

In 1880, the agency focused on writing advertising copy in addition to printing ads. It explained to prospective clients:

> The Composition, Illustration and Display of Newspaper Advertisements has so long been a study with us that we have become admittedly expert in preparing the best possible effects.
>
> Having at command the services of an Artist, a Wood Engraver, and a number of Printers who have been for years engaged almost exclusively in this work under our direction, we possess entirely unequaled facilities for serving those who desire to entrust their business to our care.[13]

During the same year, the agency issued the *American Newspaper Annual*, which listed every newspaper and magazine published in the United States and Canada. It later became the *N.W. Ayer & Son's Directory of Newspapers and Periodicals*, which is still published as the *Gale Directory of Publications and Broadcast Media*. Revenue came from advertising that newspapers placed in it.

In the late 1880s Ayer began to refuse advertising that would discredit the agency or would disappoint the advertiser. In 1887 he presented his agency's philosophy in a circular:

[13]Folder advertisement for N.W. Ayer & Son (April 1880).

GUITAR-BANJO-N MANDOLIN - VIOLIN

Self-Taught, without Notes, by Figure Music. Send stamp for Big Illustrated Catalogue of Self-Instructors and Instruments. We ship the first Instrument in each locality at a big discount, simply to advertise our goods and establish a trade. Address E. C. HOWE, 429 Bay State Building, CHICAGO.

When Writing Mention Chicago Sat. Blade.

WETO GRAPH

The Great Secret Writing System

FOR LOVERS AND OTHERS.

Every lover and everyone who writes letters should have a Weto Graph. It is a system of secret sign writing for correspondence, etc. If you have a Weto Graph you can preserve recipes, secret memorandum, addresses, or information you do not want anyone to find out. You can write to your friends on a postal and no one can find out what you have written. Lots of fun to have a Weto Graph. Don't miss it. Send 10 cents and we will send the Weto Graph by mail, with full instructions. Address, PENN PUBLISHING CO., PARNASSUS, PA.

When Writing Mention Chicago Sat. Blade.

AGENTS WANTED

$8 TO $10 PER DAY at Fairs with FUTURESCOPE. Jonas N. Bell & Co., 586 W. Lake St., Chicago

When Writing Mention Chicago Sat. Blade.

GIRLS earn a handsome ring or camera selling our toothpowder. We trust you. N. IMPORTING CO., Box 204, Detroit, Mich

When Writing Mention Chicago Sat. Blade.

Newspaper Advertising, 1899

As the recession of the 1890s ended, advertising increased, and newspapers again experienced the prosperity that came with it. Typical advertising columns, as exemplified by this 1899 one from the *Chicago Blade*, retained some of the characteristics that earlier newspapers had exhibited; but a stronger emphasis on graphics was evident.

We do not wish any advertising which cannot reasonably be expected *to pay the advertiser*.

We do not wish any advertiser to deal with us unless it is to *his interest to do so*.

We always say just what we believe, even though we have to advise a man not to spend any money in newspaper advertising.

We aim to give as conscientious consideration to little as to larger matters. Small orders entrusted to us receive just as careful attention as the largest ones get.

We thoroughly believe in newspaper advertising, and that there is more value in it than most people think. We therefore contend that the subject deserves an intelligent and unprejudiced con-

Uneeda

The National Biscuit Company (today's Nabisco) in 1899 was the first to mass market a packaged food item, its Uneeda Biscuit. To promote sales, it contracted with the Ayer advertising agency. The campaign that Ayer developed emphasized Uneeda's "sanitary packaging," which preserved the product's taste and was safer than the unhealthy practice of store customers scooping crackers out of open barrels. The campaign, which continued into the early 1900s, was the first to spend $1 million. The two ads above were from 1899 (left) and 1923, respectively.

sideration, to which should be applied as good business sense as any other matter of business commands.

We are not anxious for any order with which there does not come the reasonable expectation, *first*, that the advertising will pay our customer; and *again*, that we can so handle the business as to convince him that his interests will be best served by entrusting to us all his future advertising orders.[14]

Most of the advertising the agency handled in the 1880s came from small businesses such as retail stores and from schools and colleges. With time, however, it added many large accounts, such as Hires' root beer, J. I. Case threshing machines, Procter & Gamble soaps, the N. K. Fairbanks soap company, and Mellin's Baby Food. From 1894 to 1898, the recession affected some clients, and they reduced their ad budgets. When these businesses expanded in the late 1890s, so did Ayer. It started to handle advertising for Standard Oil and several of its subsidiaries. In 1899 it handled the major campaign that introduced the "Uneeda Biscuit," the first such product to be mass marketed in individual airtight packages. The campaign, which was for the National Biscuit Company and was the largest up to that time, included newspaper, magazine, and outdoor ads. The campaign was an overwhelming success. Consumers began asking for the product by name.

Ayer realized that advertising specific brands was just as important as advertising new products. He made sure that businesses were aware of this principle. When in 1900 he conducted a massive campaign for his agency, he advertised in trade journals and other periodicals, informing businesses that the agency put this principle to practice.

The business that Ayer received from respectable clients made

up for the loss he incurred when he stopped handling accounts for questionable products. In 1896 his agency dropped beer advertising. Three years later it halted whiskey advertising, and in the early 1900s it stopped patent medicine advertising.

By 1900 Ayer saw his agency, which was based on the principles his father had taught him and on innovative ideas, grow into the largest in the nation, with more than 160 employees.

PATENT MEDICINE ADVERTISING

Before 1900, several kinds of questionable advertising appeared in newspapers and magazines. The two worst offenders were patent medicine advertising and abortion advertising.

Colonial Americans depended on homemade remedies to cure illnesses. Usually, the formulas were passed from one generation to the next. Colonists who lived in towns could visit physicians who would charge them for their herbal remedies. However, many colonists could not afford physicians. As an alternative they could purchase patent medicines which, in most cases, caused drunkenness and nothing else.

Patent medicine advertising appeared in newspapers during the 1700s and 1800s partly because it paid the bills. Many newspapers would have died after a few issues had it not been for such advertising.

A number of advances in medicine were made during the colonial period. The most dramatic was the use of inoculation against smallpox. After the Rev. Cotton Mather had advocated the practice, Boston newspapers initiated a heated debate in the 1720s. Despite the vituperative attacks in the *New-England Courant*, inoculation eventually gained general acceptance. In newspaper ads, however, makers of patent medicines continued to make exhorbitant claims. Their products could cure, they said, not only minor ailments such as common colds but also noxious ones, including smallpox. Most of the ads were straightforward. Soon, creativity replaced the straightforward style in copy. The following ad for Dr. Bateman's Pectoral Drops was typical. It appeared in the *Pennsylvania Gazette* on July 1, 1736:

Dr. Bateman's PECTORAL DROPS, which are given with such great Success in all Fluxes, Spitting of Blood, Consumptions, Small Pox, Measles, Colds, Coughs, and Pains in the Limbs or Joints; they cure Agues, and the most violent Fever in the World, if taken in Time, and give present Ease in the most racking Torment of the Gout; the same in all sorts of Pains (be they ever so violent) they give Ease in a few Minutes after taken; they ease After-Pains, prevent Miscarriages, and are wonderful in the Stone and Gravel in the Kidneys, Bladder and Ureters; bringing away Slime, Gravel, and oftentimes Stones of a great bigness, and are the best of Medicines for all Stoppages or Pains in the Stomach, Shortness of Breath, and Straitness of the Breast, re-enkindling the almost extinguish'd natural Heat in diseas'd Bodies, by which Means they restore the languishing to perfect Health: Their manner of working is by moderate Sweat and

---

[14]"Our Creed." Folder advertisement for N.W. Ayer & Son (1887).

Lydia Pinkham

On this page are some of the ads for Lydia Pinkham's Vegetable Compound — although the banner spanning the Brooklyn Bridge (top) was only imagined. The portrait of Mrs. Pinkham showing her in robust condition (bottom left), above the slogan "Yours for Health," was used even after her death.

Vegetable Compound Brings Its Creator Fortune and Fame

America's first successful businesswoman and perhaps first millionairess, Lydia E. Pinkham was one of the most widely known women of the nineteenth century. A devotee of natural foods, a worker for temperance, abolition, and woman's rights, she was, like many women, disenchanted with orthodox medicine that prescribed dangerous cathartic drugs and bleeding for most female ailments.

She concocted root and herb-based home remedies laced with a 20% alcohol preservative and at first gave away gallons to friends and neighbors. The dire financial straits inflicted on the nation by the Panic of 1873, however, forced her to begin selling her brew as "Lydia Pinkham's Vegetable Compound."

Sales soared after Dan Pinkham, her husband, placed a $60 ad in the *Boston Herald*. The Pinkhams built a factory in Lynn, Massachusetts. They trumpeted the Compound's effectiveness for male as well as female ailments from kidney disease to uterine prolapse, and they got rich off the patent medicine.

Key elements in the ad campaign were the trademark countenance of the attractive 55-year-old grandmother, her advice service, and testimonial letters. Her *Guide for Women* was reprinted over the years in millions of copies. Originally a four-page folder describing in plain language women's physiology and its many potential disorders, by 1901 the booklet had sixty-two pages and was printed in five languages, with her image and her motto on the cover: "Yours for Health, Lydia E. Pinkham."

She died in 1883, but her Compound lived on, with users unaware of her death. In 1902 a muckraker tried exposing her in the *Ladies' Home Journal* by juxtaposing current letters, signed with her name, with a photograph of her tombstone. After a brief setback, the Compound doubled its sales within ten years and reached its all-time high in 1929. The company sold out to Cooper labs in 1968, sixty-two years after passage of the Pure Food and Drug Act.

HOW A LIFE
WAS SAVED.

——

THE LIFE OF

Chas. S. Prentice

SAVED
BY THE USE OF

WARNER'S
SAFE
KIDNEY and LIVER
CURE.

——

The following letter proves that BRIGHT'S DISEASE, in its worst form, IS CURABLE:

TOLEDO, O., Sept. 25, 1879.

Messrs. H. H. WARNER & Co., Rochester, N. Y.— Gentlemen: Having escaped death from Bright's disease by the use of your Remedy, I feel it a duty not only to acknowledge my gratitude to you personally, but also to bring my case before the public, and have those who are suffering similarly to judge whether a medicine not prepared by the "regulars" will cure this frightful malady or not.

In the summer of 1872 I was first taken ill with symptoms which, I was informed, were those of Bright's disease. I went to Marquette, Mich., and

Patent Medicine Advertising, Late 1800s

Urine. For Children's Distempers, no Medicine yet discover'd can compare with it: For it cures the Gripes in their Stomach and Bowels, by expelling Wind upwards and downwards. It causes weak and forward Children to take their natural Rest. It is taken with great Success in the Rickets, and, in a Word, it hath restored Hundreds of poor Infants to their strength and liveliness, that have been reduced to meer Skeletons.

Sold by *Miles Strickland* in *Market-Street, Philadelphia,* price 3 s. a Bottle, with Directions.

This remedy, according to the advertising, cured more than thirty illnesses, diseases, or abnormalities. Only three shillings (equivalent to about $10 today) a bottle, the product sold well throughout the century. Other imported patent medicines were also advertised throughout the colonies; and most, like Dr. Bateman's Pectoral Drops, offered relief from practically any illness or disease.

Some advertisers pointed out that royalty sanctioned their concoctions. In a 1770 issue of the *Boston Chronicle,* the London Book-Store of Boston advertised the "Essence of Pepper-Mint, by his Majesty's Royal Letters Patent."[15] The product sold for one shilling four pence. In return, the consumer received "speedy relief" from colic, gout, and other illnesses.

During and after the Revolutionary War, ads for imported medicines were curtailed. Yet Americans realized that the need for medicines was great. Consequently, they started producing medicines domestically. Lists of medicines sold at apothecaries were advertised weekly in newspapers. Physicians also served as dentists, veterinarians, druggists, and barbers and often advertised their services and cure-all potions.

As newspapers increased in size and in number of pages, they carried more medicine advertising. In the 1800s, patent medicine advertising occupied most of the space in numerous newspapers. Products such as Dr. Ryan's Incomparable Worm-Destroying Sugar-Plums, Turlington's Balsam of Life, Godfrey's Cordial, Steer's Genuine Opodeldor, Stoughton's Bitters or Elixir, Antipertussis, Lockyer's Pills, James' Fever Powder, Dalbey's Carminative, and Anderson's Pills, just to name a few, were advertised from New England to Florida. Their sellers seemed to imply that certain names and labels could ward off illnesses even if the product could not.

Mineral waters, such as Dr. Willard's Mineral Water, Ballston or Congress Mineral Water, and Godwin's Celebrated German Water, were advertised like patent medicines: the copy was filled with outrageous claims. In an 1803 ad in the *New York Herald,* Dr. Willard claimed that the water from his mineral spring in Connecticut could cure such maladies as "Erisipelas, Salt Rheum, Leprous Affections, and indeed almost every cutaneous complaint," including cancer, gout, paralytic disorders, and other diseases.[16]

In the 1830s and 1840s, some patent medicines romanticized the American Indian through illustration, name, and advertising copy. Ads for Dr. Freeman's Indian Specific pointed out that the product

[15]*Boston Chronicle,* 19 February 1770.
[16]*New York Herald,* 15 June 1803.

was made from herbs that Indians used to cure consumption. Wright's Indian Vegetable Pills, which sold exceptionally well in the 1840s, were advertised as "THE ORIGINAL AND ONLY GENUINE INDIAN MEDICINE."[17]

Makers of patent medicines soon realized that it was more profitable to manufacture and advertise several remedies for a variety of illnesses than to produce one remedy and advertise it as a cure-all. Dr. Bardwell had Aromatic Lozenges of Steel, Re-Animating Solar Tincture or Pabulum of Life, Genuine Ague and Fever Drops, and Annodyne Essence — all for different illnesses.

Some companies manufactured gadgets that were to be worn as a cure. Supposedly using electricity, the devices were said to restore the nervous system as well as cure all kinds of disease. Of course, they could cure nothing. Yet, like ads for patent medicines, ads for these contraptions were filled with testimonies, superlatives, and claims of being "genuine," "original," or "nature's own."

By the end of the 1800s, the nation's households were filled with patent medicines and devices. The products did not die until the early 1900s, when newspapers began receiving an adequate amount of advertising from other manufacturers and businesses. By then, muckraking journalists had begun discrediting the patent medicine industry and consequently encouraged lawmakers to enact legislation that would eliminate or at least restrict the cure-alls. As a result of the efforts of advertising professionals and the muckrakers, the Associated Advertising Clubs of America embarked on a "Truth-in-Advertising" crusade in 1911, which led to the establishment of today's better business bureaus. The federal government also joined the effort to clean up advertising. In 1914, Congress established the Federal Trade Commission (FTC), which exercises a measure of control over all advertising. Court decisions and later congressional additions gradually have enhanced the power of the FTC.

ABORTION ADVERTISING

In the early 1800s, advertising for abortifacients and abortion appeared, although the word "abortion" was not used. Most of the ads for "female monthly regulating pills," for example, contained such words as "suppression," "irregularity," or "stoppage" in reference to menses.

Ads for "Madame Restell" (Anna Lohman), the most notorious of the abortionists, which appeared in newspapers in New York City, were carefully worded to guard against prosecution. Abortion was illegal. Thus, she was committed to secrecy for her clients, as the following ad indicated:

MADAME RESTELL, FEMALE PHYSICIAN, residence 148 Greenwich Street, where she can be consulted with the strictest confidence on complaints incident to the female frame.[18]

NATIONAL POLICE GAZETTE.

Vol. 2, No. 27—$2 A YEAR.   NEW-YORK, SATURDAY, MARCH 13, 1847.   FOUR CENTS A NUMBER.

THE FEMALE ABORTIONIST.

"Madame Restell"
Anna Lohman became notorious for performing abortions under the name "Madame Restell." She built her trade through advertising that thinly veiled her practice, and police finally arrested her.

In another ad, she hinted that pregnancy, if not desired, should not be tolerated. "Irregularity and suppression," the ad claimed, caused "violent and convulsive headaches, derangement of the stomach, gnawing in the side, burning in the chest, disturbed and feverish sleep, frightful dream, languor, debility, weakness, a most distressing lethargy." The ad claimed that some pregnant women suffered from depression and, as a result, contemplated suicide. The reader was reassured: "These dreadful and alarming symptoms and all others arising from female irregularity or suppression are removed in a few days by Mme. Restell."[19]

Madame Restell advertised her products and services from 1839 to 1846 in the *New York Herald* and the *New York Sun*. Some newspapers, such as Horace Greeley's *New York Tribune*, refused to run her ads. Nonetheless, her business prospered. She opened offices in Boston and Philadelphia and sold abortifacients through seven franchises in three cities.

Another advertiser, Catherine Costello, copied Madame Restell. Identifying herself as a "female physician," she advertised pills, her services, and a place to recover. In the early 1840s she and Madame Restell engaged in an advertising war. They called one another's pills counterfeit, and the two battled for three years. Both were criticized in print. The *National Police Gazette* publicized the trial of Costello's husband, Charles Mason, who sold the

[17]Quoted in Cedric Larson, "Patent-Medicine Advertising and the Early American Press," *Journalism Quarterly* 19 (December 1937): 338.
[18]*New York Herald*, 15 July 1841.

[19]*New York Sun*, 27 September 1840.

corpse of one of his wife's patients. This series ended Costello's career, as prospective patients grew concerned. The magazine then attacked Madame Restell. In 1847 she was arrested for conducting an abortion and was found guilty. She served a one-year sentence, but upon her release she resumed advertising her services. In 1878, she was arrested a second time and committed suicide the evening before her trial was to begin.

By this time, some newspapers refused abortion ads. Eventually, most — if not all — did so, much to the delight of the public, who for years had cried for political pressure or police action to close or prosecute abortionists.

There were other efforts as well to clean up advertising. People associated with the business began taking note of the negative impact on legitimate advertising produced by false and misleading ads. They talked of collective action against such advertising and the advertisers who ran it. The result was the earliest advertising clubs, the first of which may have been one founded in Denver in 1891. Regional advertising organizations with similar interests followed.

RECOMMENDED READINGS

BOOKS

Advertising: Today, Yesterday, Tomorrow — Printer's Ink. New York, 1963. This compilation contains articles on the most influential shakers in advertising as well as the growth of advertising in the various media.

Applegate, Edd. *Personalities and Products: A Historical Perspective on Advertising in America.* Westport, Conn., 1998. The author examines advertising in colonial America as well as certain advertisers from the 1800s and 1900s.

Goodrum, Charles, and Helen Dalrymple. *Advertising in America: The First 200 Years.* New York, 1990. This history of the major changes in American advertising since its beginning is illustrated with numerous advertisements.

Harris, Neil. *Humbug: The Art of P. T. Barnum.* Chicago, 1973. Barnum used advertising and publicity techniques and capitalized on Jacksonian democracy and cultural trends to become the most famous showman of his time.

How It Was In Advertising: 1776-1976. Chicago, 1976. This study, which is compiled by the editors of *Advertising Age*, highlights some of the most important advertisers and agencies.

Hower, Ralph M. *The History of an Advertising Agency: N.W. Ayer & Sons at Work 1869-1939.* Cambridge, Mass., 1939. Francis Wayand Ayer typified the nineteenth-century success story: beginning with no money, he worked hard and used good judgment to build an enterprise.

Laird, Pamela Walker. *Advertising Progress: American Business and the Rise of Consumer Marketing.* Baltimore, 2001. From its earliest days, advertising had a major impact on both society and business.

Pincas, Stephanie, and Marc Loiseau. *A History of Advertising.* Los Angeles, Calif., 2008. This account covers advertising from the earliest days to present.

Presbrey, Frank. *The History and Development of Advertising.* Garden City, N.Y., 1929. Presbrey's account is an in-depth history of advertising filled with illustrations.

Rowell, George. *Forty Years as an Advertising Agent.* New York, 1906. This is Rowell's autobiography.

Sutphen, Dick. *The Mad Old Ads.* New York, 1966. The author examines advertising in the latter half of the nineteenth century.

Turner, E.S. *The Shocking History of Advertising!* New York, 1953. This account is a critical history.

Wood, James Playsted. *The Story of Advertising.* New York, 1958. Wood's account, although brief, is one of the standard histories of advertising in America.

Young, James Harvey. *The Toadstool Millionaires.* Princeton, 1961. Young gives an account of the "patent medicine era."

ARTICLES

Endres, Kathleen L. "Strictly Confidential: Birth Control Advertising in a 19th-Century City." *Journalism Quarterly* 63 (1986): 748-51. Birth-control advertisers used carefully worded classifieds in Cleveland newspapers.

Holland, Donald R. "Volney B. Palmer (1799-1864): The Nation's First Advertising Agency Man." *Journalism Monographs* (1976). Holland provides a straightforward biography of the pioneer advertising agent.

Larson, Cedric. "Patent Medicine Advertising and the Early American Press." *Journalism Quarterly* 14 (1937): 333-41. Widespread advertising campaigns made patent medicine a highly complex industry. Colonists had simple faith in the claims of advertisers.

Lawson, Linda. "Advertisements Masquerading as News in Turn-of-the-Century American Periodicals." *American Journalism* 10 (1988): 81-96. Reading notices permeated publications in the second half of the nineteenth century. These notices were ads that appeared in news and editorial columns.

Olasky, Marvin. "Advertising Abortion During the 1830s and 1840s: Madame Restell Builds a Business." *Journalism History* 13 (1986): 49-55. Some advertising in the penny press, as Restell's ads demonstrated, was motivated by the desire for profit, not by morals. The advertising influenced some newspapers not to criticize abortion editorially.

Schafer, Judith Kelleher. "New Orleans Slavery in 1850 as Seen in Advertisements." *Journal of Southern History* 47 (February 1981): 33-55. An analysis of ads indicates "a booming slave trade in which the equivalent of one in five of the bondsmen in New Orleans were sold annually."

Shaw, Steven J. "Colonial Newspaper Advertising: A Step Toward Freedom of the Press." *Business History Review* 33 (Autumn 1959): 409-20. Advertising revenues helped free newspaper publishers from political subsidies and/or political parties.

Smythe, Ted Curtis. "The Advertisers' War to Verify Newspaper Circulation, 1870-1914." *American Journalism* 3 (1986): 167-80. Advertisers and agencies "worked together to force publishers to provide circulation figures, then to provide *accurate* and *meaningful* circulation figures." Their efforts culminated in the founding of the Audit Bureau of Circulations in 1914.

15

The Emergence of Modern Media
1900 - 1945

Major changes in the media in the United States occurred between 1900 and 1945. At the beginning, the printing press dominated. By the end, the electronic media were challenging print. The period started with an emphasis on written words as the primary means of imparting knowledge. When it was over, visual images and words spoken over the airwaves had become major contenders for public attention.

Unknown in 1900, the term "mass media" entered the language in the 1920s, denoting a new world of communication to the masses transmitted, or mediated, through technological means. When commercial television burst on the scene after World War II, the population was prepared to welcome it. But print still held its own. Newspapers had learned to incorporate visual elements and remained powerful forces for interpreting the world.

The first decades of the twentieth century saw tremendous change in the United States amid tumultuous social upheaval. The nation confronted the shock of World War I, the frenzy of the Roaring '20s, the poverty of the Great Depression, and the horror of World War II. It grappled with the problems of increased industrialization counterbalanced by labor organization and governmental efforts to ensure benefits for the majority of citizens. Increasingly, the mass media served as the glue that held together most of society. They created a consumer culture based on mass marketing, advertising, news, and entertainment.

Newspapers, which depended on advertising for more than half their revenue, laid claim to a unique status in the nation's economic and political structure. The industry professed a philosophy of journalism that rested on a concept of public good. That philosophy included support for democratic institutions based on the First Amendment guarantee of freedom of the press, a claim of adherence to truth and objectivity as primary journalistic values, and service to the public as its champion and watchdog on government.

Translation of this ideology into the news product varied. Newspapers differed in appearance, content, political loyalties and control, ties to advertisers, editorial opinions, appeals to readers, and class, racial, and ethnic orientation. Although the number of foreign-language newspapers declined after World War I, the African-American press grew, fought for civil rights, and emphasized religious, social, and civic activities in the black community.

Some publishers attracted millions of readers by employing formulas that stressed pictures and simply written stories. Improved photographic and reproduction equipment produced new kinds of newspapers and magazines that emphasized images over words. Tabloid newspapers (half the size of regular newspapers) sprang up after World War I. Relying on photography, they targeted an audience of relatively low reading skills.

Using automated transmission equipment, the Associated Press and other wire services created uniform news products that went to small towns as well as big cities and served to standardize the formats of news articles. Teletype machines (that combined the telegraph and typewriter to print out news stories), teletypesetting equipment, and phototransmission devices as well as national radio networks were set up by 1926 and sent news across the country with breathtaking speed.

As the media searched for subjects to catch the attention of their vast, variegated audience, the new fields of advertising and public relations moved into professional image-making. The "celebrity" was born, personified by entertainers and even Prohibition-era gangsters — individuals heralded not because of their heroic deeds but simply for being well-known. Celebrities and professional models endorsed products and became part of the national media scene, appealing, in particular, to women, who were identified as key consumers.

Formal study of mass communications as a discipline began. It was initially pegged to efforts to learn more about propaganda, which had been used as a psychological weapon in World War I. New methods in social science research led to the use of polls and surveys to measure public opinion. Both government and private industry set up public relations arms, often called information offices, in attempts to build goodwill with the public.

The growth of the film industry added another dimension to mass communications. Silent motion pictures, followed by talking pictures in the 1920s, dimmed the line between news and enter-

Old Newspapers and New Challenges

In 1900, newspapers were the unchallenged means for providing information. Founded in 1801, the *New York Evening Post* of the 1920s typified the old-style newspapers that provided a variety of news and thorough coverage. The newspaper industry, however, had grown so large that it was slow to meet new conditions; and many of the old newspapers such as the *Post* faltered against the competition. To revive it, later owners redesigned it as the sensational tabloid *New York Post.*

tainment. Newsreels purported to show actual news events but depended heavily on reenactments. They became staples at theaters. Movies helped prepare the public for the advent of television after World War II.

As the twentieth century dawned, however, it was hard to conceive of any medium other than newspapers dominating the news scene. This chapter tells how newspapers reacted to the changes and redefined their place in mass communications.

THE NEWSPAPER AS KING

In the early years of the twentieth century, the number of newspapers stood at a record high. In 1910, there were 2,200 English-language daily newspapers of general circulation and about 14,000 weekly newspapers. Cities commonly had numerous competing papers, with afternoon papers purchased by workers on their way home. In New York City alone, considered the model for metropolitan journalism during most of the twentieth century, there were twenty-nine daily newspapers in 1899.

Daily circulation far outstripped increases in population.

Representing about a three-fold increase, the population of the United States grew from 23.2 million in 1850 to 75.9 million by 1900. But the circulation of newspapers increased by twenty-fold, from about 758,000 in 1850 to 15.1 million by 1900.

By the turn of the century, big-city newspaper owners had discovered the something-for-everyone formula of news, sports, entertainment, and advertising that still characterizes the daily press today. With the advent of cheap newsprint in the nineteenth century, Anthony Smith, a scholar of technology, has noted, "it became apparent that great fortunes could be made by turning the medium into a universal one, rather than restricting it to ... special groups."[1] In the last few years of the nineteenth century, most newspapers changed from organs of editors' personal opinions to impersonal vehicles for the luring of mass audiences so advertisers could gain entry into large numbers of households.

To improve news gathering and transmission, papers in the early 1900s used a wide variety of inventions. They included electric lighting (which facilitated the operation of newspaper plants around the clock), colored ink, high-speed presses, Linotypes, mechanical folders, the halftone process for printing photographs, the wireless telegraph, long-distance telephone, and radiophone service. Metropolitan papers with different sections for men and women put out as many as ten editions per day, feeding readers' appetites for the latest happenings. Children yelled out the headlines on crowded streets, selling papers for a penny or two. Newspapers rushed into print with "extras," unscheduled editions that offered the latest news developments.

Yet competition from an array of new media soon caused retrenchment and consolidation in the newspaper business. More papers would come under chain ownership. Media barons would transform local, family-owned papers into complex corporate structures at the same time the industry shrank. By 1946, the number of daily papers would decline to 1,763.[2]

TABLOIDS AND JAZZ JOURNALISM

In the 1920s the success of the tabloids helped divide newspapers into two broad categories. The first, often associated with Adolph Ochs, who bought majority ownership of the *New York Times* in 1896, presented information in a staid, middle-of-the road fashion that became the quality standard for journalism. Newspapers that followed this course prided themselves on recording official events, used a factual format in the news columns, and frequently developed close ties with the governing elite, who became sources of information.

The second, highlighted by the tabloids, updated the late nineteenth-century innovation of "yellow journalism" promoted by Joseph Pulitzer and archrival William Randolph Hearst. The tabloids enlivened the earlier sensationalism of blaring headlines,

---

[1] Anthony Smith, *Goodbye Gutenberg: The Newspaper Revolution of the 1980s* (New York, 1980), 13-4.

[2] The drop continued as population growth outpaced newspaper circulation and a drastic reduction occurred in the number of competing papers. The trend has continued up to the present.

Pig Woman Testifies

Of the varied murder trials the tabloids played up, hardly any was more sensational than that of Mrs. Frances Hall for the murder of her husband and his mistress, Mrs. James Mills. The key witness was Jane Easton, who said she saw the murders take place in a field and said three men and two women were shouting and arguing. One of them was later identified as Mrs. Hall, and she was charged along with her two brothers and a cousin with murder. Fattening and selling pigs was Easton's main source of income, leading newspapers to dub her "the pig woman." Stricken with cancer, she had to be carried into court on a bed. Reporters ringed the courtroom and filed stories for newspapers around the nation.

garish comic strips, and tear-jerking feature stories with bold new elements: eye-catching, sometimes faked, photography and a condensed, colorful style of news writing. In one instance, the effort to stage an "execution" for a photograph for the *New York Graphic* almost resulted in the hanging of a staff member. Reporters, previously the romantic figures of newsgathering, now shared top billing with photographers, since advances in photography led newspapers to depend more heavily on pictures.

The two contrasting models were keyed to class divisions within the reading audience. The emphasis on story-telling and unusual events in the sensational newspapers were geared toward newly literate and newly urban individuals. The more respectable papers spoke in rational, reasonable tones and were aimed at a middle and upper-class audience.

The tabloid newspaper had originated in England, and Joseph Medill Patterson brought it to the United States. The grandson of Joseph Medill, founder of the *Chicago Tribune*, Patterson launched the *New York Daily News* in 1919, billing it as an "illustrated" newspaper. It was subsidized by the *Tribune*, which Patterson's cousin, the autocratic Col. Robert R. McCormick, ran.

The tabloid captured buyers with an emotional mix of sex and crime news pushed by coupons and promotional schemes. Its size made it convenient to read on crowded subways and buses. Apparently finding an audience that did not read other papers, the *Daily News* hit the million mark in circulation in 1925. Within a decade of its founding, it had imitators in New York and other major cities from Washington to Los Angeles.

Tabloids personified the "jazz journalism" of the Roaring '20s when Prohibition outlawed alcoholic drinks. Photographers carrying bulky cameras roamed the streets, looking to record scenes in an era of bootleggers, speakeasies, love nests, movie stars, bathing beauties, and the foibles of the rich and famous. Pictures splashed across the entire front page became the story. Brief captions, which intellectuals sneered at as "picture-writing," explained the illustrations. Relating to readers who increasingly sought entertainment from newer media — motion pictures and radio — the tabloids furnished terse, melodramatic accounts of crimes and scandals and sometimes resorted to falsification.

The most famous tabloid photograph ran in the *Daily News* in 1928. To take it, Tom Howard sneaked into Sing Sing prison with a concealed camera strapped to his left leg and photographed convicted murderer Ruth Snyder literally frying to death in the electric chair. Following a much publicized trial, she and her lover, a corset salesman, had been convicted for the murder of her husband. The huge headline above the picture screamed "DEAD!" Although a "storm of protest was aroused," as one writer of the day put it, "the *News* could afford disapproval of an action which sold an estimated 500,000 extra copies of the paper."[3]

With the advent of the Depression, the excesses of jazz journalism died out. The nation turned its attention to serious economic problems, overturning Prohibition and looking to the federal government for new programs to aid citizens. Some tabloids failed, but the *Daily News* continued to enthrall a working-class audience with its snappy combination of pictures and words.

Efforts to aim a New York tabloid at affluent readers failed. In 1940 Ralph Ingersoll, formerly publisher of *Time* magazine, and associates started *PM* (for Picture Magazine) to reach an audience that supported liberal causes. It accepted no paid advertisements but, recognizing the news value of advertising, gave readers synopses of ads in other papers. With an editorial policy that stressed social justice and consumer rights, it became a journal of interpretation. Unable to attract a sufficient audience, it died after eight years in spite of a heavy infusion of funds from Marshall Field III, the wealthy grandson of a Chicago department store owner.

Although lamenting the excesses of the tabloids, which critics called gutter journalism, contemporary observers praised the metropolitan newspaper as a manifestation of progress. Willard Bleyer, an early journalism educator, blamed sensationalism on the audience. It resulted from immigration, he said, since it "flourished in larger cities where the number of half-assimilated foreigners was the greatest."[4] He believed newspapers functioned as vehicles of democracy and thus had to perform responsibly.

Others saw newspapers more negatively, accusing the press of cowardly caving in to advertising pressures. In a scathing attack in

[3]Simon M. Bessie, *Jazz Journalism: The Story of the Tabloid Newspapers* (New York, 1938), 117.
[4]Willard G. Bleyer, *Main Currents in the History of American Journalism* (Boston, 1927), 390.

Public Enemies

In 1930s Crime Wave, News Media Make Murderers into Stars

John Dillinger, Bonnie Parker and Clyde Barrow, Baby Face Nelson, Machine Gun Kelly, Pretty Boy Floyd, and Ma Barker were outlaws who became household names because of extensive press coverage in the early 1930s. Print and radio competed fiercely in a race for the largest audience, and one of the most popular topics was crime news. It dominated the media during the short, but intense period of 1931 to 1935.

Particularly in the Midwest, high profile criminals made headlines almost every day. Radio gained an advantage with timely interviews of witnesses, prison guards, and police. Print reporters filed stories of bank robberies and witnesses who were forced to lie on the floor while the public enemies threw cash into bags. If bank clerks or customers did not obey orders, they could get a pistol-whipping or a bullet. Wire service reporters interviewed witnesses to shootouts. Bystanders snapped photographs and sold them to the press. Newsreels presented the gunmen's exploits as exciting adventures.

Crime coverage thus brought about the rise of the celebrity gangster. No one fit the mold better than Dillinger. He started out as a small-time crook, but after serving eight years in prison, he gained fame for bold bank robberies and blasting out of police traps. He became a star in the press, and he was acutely aware of the media frenzy he could create. He stayed in the public eye by seizing opportunities to make news. He posed for photographs with politicians when he was about to stand trial. He broke out of a jail with a wooden gun. Following his escape, he robbed two more banks and sent a picture of him holding the fake gun to an Indianapolis newspaper.

As Dillinger became the number one

During their short criminal careers, some outlaws became stars in the media. Newspapers ran poetry that Bonnie Parker wrote, stories featured Baby Face Nelson as a loving son, and news photographs showed John Dillinger posing with his arms around his captors. Nearly all of the big-name criminals, though, came to the same end. When lawmen finally killed them, their deaths made big news, but they also ended the field day that newspapers had had.

public enemy, J. Edgar Hoover, the head of the young Federal Bureau of Investigation, along with the "government men," whom journalists nicknamed "g-men," joined local law enforcement in the hunt for Dillinger. On July 22, 1934, g-men and police followed a tip and killed him outside Chicago's Biograph Theatre, where he had attended a gangster film starring Clark Gable. In his Indiana hometown, nearly 10,000 people viewed his body – more than the town's population.

The crime spree that had made such exciting news was quickly coming to an end. Only eight months before Dillinger's death, Machine Gun Kelly had been arrested and convicted of kidnapping. He spent the remaining years of his life in prison, dying of a heart attack in 1954. Of the notorious Midwest criminals of the 1930s, his death was the only one that

didn't make big news. On May 23, 1934, two months before the law got Dillinger, Bonnie and Clyde were killed in a police ambush in Louisiana. On October 24, FBI agents and local police officers shot and killed Pretty Boy Floyd as he tried to escape through an Ohio cornfield. On November 27, Baby Face Nelson was killed in a gun battle with FBI agents in a small town in Illinois. On January 16, 1935, g-men killed Ma Barker in Florida. Most members of her gang had been killed during 1934.

For a year and a half, the big-name Midwest criminals had murdered numerous people and committed an untold number of robberies. For victims and law enforcement, the crime wave had been a period of anguish and violence. For the media, it had been a headlines heyday.

1919, Upton Sinclair, the muckraking novelist, compared journalists to patrons of prostitutes. In a tongue-lashing to reporters, he wrote, "[it is] you who take the fair body of truth and sell it in the market-place, who betray the virgin hopes of mankind into the loathsome brothel of Big Business."[5]

NEWSPAPER CONSOLIDATION

For all of their collective popularity, individual daily newspapers confronted a saturated marketplace. A case in point was Pulitzer's *New York World*, the largest newspaper in the United States in 1897, with combined morning and evening circulations of one million copies. In 1931, twenty years after Pulitzer's death, his family faced huge operating losses and sold the newspaper, which had abandoned its sensationalism to become a liberal voice. It consolidated with Roy Howard's *Telegraph*. The end came after the *World* found itself squeezed between two types of competitors: the "establishment" press, symbolized by the *New York Times* and the newly created *Herald Tribune*, itself the merged descendant of James Gordon Bennett's *New York Herald* and Horace Greeley's *Tribune*, on the one hand; and the *Daily News* and its imitators, on the other. By 1940 New York was down to eight daily newspapers, equally divided between morning and afternoon publications.

Mergers became common in the World War I era and thereafter, as newspapers faced many of the same financial pressures as other industries. Whether the product was steel, shoes, or whiskey, businesses sought to consolidate in the name of increased efficiency and greater market shares. Efforts to restrain competition resulted in trusts and monopolies that muckraking journalists exposed and that the Federal Trade Commission Act of 1914 and earlier legislation had made illegal.

Consolidations made economic sense in the newspaper field. It was cheaper for advertisers to buy space in one paper with wide circulation than in two with overlapping circulations. Combinations of morning and afternoon papers allowed for efficient, round-the-clock utilization of plant facilities. To critics, however, mergers led to further standardization of the newspaper and a decrease in opportunities to express conflicting viewpoints.

Chain ownership — or "group" ownership, as the newspaper industry prefers to call it today — played an important role in consolidations. While only one-tenth of all newspapers at the turn of the century were group owned (meaning that one individual or company owned newspapers in two or more cities), by 1945 the proportion had increased to two-fifths. (By century's end, it stood at four-fifths.[6])

Among those most active in this phenomena were Hearst and E. W. Scripps, a self-proclaimed "damned old crank," who championed the cause of labor. Hearst, the prototype for "Citizen Kane" in the Orson Welles movie of that name, assembled a complex media empire of newspapers, magazines, feature syndicates, wire

RUTH SNYDER'S DEATH PICTURED!—This is perhaps the most remarkable exclusive picture in the history of criminology. It shows the actual scene in the Sing Sing death house as the lethal current surged through Ruth Snyder's body at 11:06 last night. Her helmeted head is stiffened in death, her face masked and an electrode strapped to her bare right leg. The autopsy table on which her body was removed is beside her. Judd Gray, mumbling a prayer, followed her down the narrow corridor at 11:11. "Father, forgive them, for they don't know what they are doing!" were Ruth's last words. The picture is the first Sing Sing execution picture and the first of a woman's electrocution.—*Story p. 2; other pics. p. 24 and last page.*

Tabloid Journalism

Like other tabloid newspapers of the 1920s, the *New York Daily News* brought new approaches to design and illustration. The *Daily News'* boldest play was this page-one photograph of the execution of the convicted murderer Ruth Snyder.

services, and motion picture interests. His newspaper chain, which backed nationalistic policies and engaged in hunts for Communists, reached its peak in 1935 with twenty-six dailies. Two years later his empire had collapsed, in part because of the Depression, but also because of his personal extravagance, symbolized by the exotic art treasures and lavish entertainment that characterized life at his palatial California estate, San Simeon.

By loaning money to bright young men who ran his enterprises, Scripps established tightly edited, low-cost afternoon papers aimed at working people in smaller cities. Although he lived in style on a 2,100-acre ranch, Miramar, near San Diego, he insisted that his papers editorialize in favor of labor and of the poor against the rich. Over the years, his holdings grew to include the Scripps-McRae and Scripps Howard newspaper chains, United Press, feature syndicates, and other companies. After mergers and restructuring, by 1940 nineteen papers survived out of a total of fifty-two once associated with Scripps.

It was Frank Munsey, a businessman dubbed the Grand High Executioner of newspapers, who occupied a special and unrevered place in the annals of consolidation. His efforts to build a

[5]Upton Sinclair, *The Brass Check* (Pasadena, Calif., 1919), 436.
[6]Erwin K. Thomas and Brown H. Carpenter, *Handbook on Mass Media in the United States: The Industry and Its Audiences* (Westport, Conn., 1994), 94.

Scripps Newspapers

Ohio Publisher Provides Model for Modern Chains

During the first half of the twentieth century, E.W. Scripps controlled the largest newspaper chain in America in number of newspaper properties owned. It is difficult to provide an exact number because he opened and closed papers almost every year while purchasing and merging others. By 1930, the chain numbered twenty-three papers. It also owned the syndicated wire service United Press, the feature service Newspaper Enterprise Association, the Scripps Editorial Service, and the Scripps Science Service.

From his flagship paper in Cleveland to his retirement project in San Diego, Scripps' papers crisscrossed the country. They could be found in major cities such as Washington, D.C., and New York and small cities such as Terre Haute and Evansville, Ind.

Ohio, though, was his stronghold. After working for his half-brother James Scripps on the staff of the *Detroit News*, E.W. founded the *Cleveland Press* in 1878. After his success there, he purchased the *Cincinnati Post*. Years later Scripps papers were published in Columbus, Toledo, Akron, and Youngstown.

Scripps utilized the corporation for expansion. In that, his organization would serve as a pioneering model for the modern newspaper chain corporation. He created smaller newspaper corporations in cities by putting up seed money and providing stock to the editor and business manager as incentives. The salaries were low, but potential was great. The remaining stock he took for himself, family members, and close associates. The syndicated services supported the startups with content.

Other chains were forming but were small when compared with Scripps in number of properties. William Randolph Hearst had a few newspapers in major cities, which gave him an edge over Scripps in total circulation, but did not come close to the number of papers. Gannett had six newspapers, with four of them in New York. Paul Block formed another more significant chain. By 1927 he had eleven newspapers, but by the end of the Depression he was down to three.

E. W. Scripps got his start in newspaper ownership when in 1873 he began working as an office boy at his brother's newspaper, the *Detroit News*. Using loans from his half-brothers, he then founded the *Penny Press* in Cleveland in 1878, when he was twenty-four years old. Then, with financial help from his sister, he soon started or acquired twenty-five additional papers. He then loaned money to promising young publishers to start papers under an agreement that gave him majority ownership. He thus built one of the largest newspaper chains in history.

Scripps didn't own just one chain of newspapers – he owned several. By the early 1900s, he was a majority owner of Scripps McRae with newspapers concentrated in the Midwest. Scripps West Coast papers concentrated in Pacific coast states, and the Harper Group of Scripps was located primarily in Texas and Oklahoma. He was also a minor owner in Clover Leaf Newspapers started by his nephew, and he held stock in his half-brother's company, Scripps-Booth Newspapers in Michigan. A split with his son, James, in 1920, created a new company, The Scripps League of Newspapers. Scripps then consolidated the remaining properties where he held a majority of interest into a new holding company, Scripps Howard.

chain by purchasing newspapers in New York, Washington, Boston, Baltimore, and Philadelphia ended with the death of most of them. His attitude toward newspapers as mere business entities brought a stinging attack from William Allen White of Emporia, Kansas, the best known small town editor of his day. In the *Emporia Gazette* White wrote a widely reprinted obituary of Munsey. It declared, "Frank Munsey contributed to the journalism of his day the great talent of a meatpacker, the morals of a money-changer and the manners of an undertaker. He and his kind have about succeeded in transforming a once-noble profession into an eight percent security. May he rest in trust."[7]

Although the newspaper industry underwent the same tendency toward oligopoly (control of the market by a few sellers) as other industries, individual papers were viewed as local, not national, enterprises. They were rarely candidates for antitrust action by the federal government in its efforts to break up monopolies. Wire services were a different matter. The Associated Press, a co-operative owned by member papers, kept out new members until 1945 when the U. S. Supreme Court ruled that it was illegally restraining trade.[8]

The decision favored the *Chicago Sun*, a liberal newspaper established by Marshall Field III, the department store magnate who also backed *PM*, in opposition to McCormick's *Tribune*. The *Tribune* had blocked the *Sun*'s attempt to have access to AP service. Before the court ruling, papers with AP memberships could — and did — refuse to let competing publications gain membership. Consequently, publishers had been forced either to buy weak papers with existing AP memberships or to subscribe to competing, but less complete, private wire services like United Press.

WOMEN IN JOURNALISM

Although important, wire services did not replace local news staffs. With printing presses rolling out thousands of copies several times a day, the news became a hot commodity endlessly pursued by zealous reporters and photographers. Newspaper offices — dirty, noisy, and cluttered — acquired a romantic image in a culture that pictured reporters and photographers as daring bohemians with front-row seats for human dramas. In reality, journalism represented an insecure, underpaid, male-oriented occupation.

Women who managed to break free of gender roles had to display spectacular talents and ingenuity. In the first history of women journalists written in 1936, Ishbel Ross, a veteran of New York journalism, described scores of women who followed in the footsteps of "Nellie Bly" (Elizabeth Cochrane). Her race around the world for Pulitzer's *World* in 1889 had made her famous as a "stunt girl," but by the early 1920s she was eking out a living writing a column on abused and missing children for Hearst's *Journal*. Her fame had long since gone. Yet, while Pulitzer had once capitalized on her adventurous spirit to attract readers, most editors

Frank Munsey
Munsey was notorious for merging and killing newspapers. He believed that they should use the same economic principles that other businesses used. Multiple competitors, he believed, did not make for efficiency; and he set out to reduce the number of newspapers in New York City. He began by buying the *Sun* in 1916, and then in 1920 he bought the *Herald* and combined the two papers. By the time he finished his mergers, he had combined five New York newspapers into a single publication.

continued to assign women to limited roles.

With the advent of the tabloids, "stunt girls" came back into vogue. Since the tabloids "had to astonish, bemuse, dazzle or horrify the reader," Ross wrote, "editors did handsprings to startle the town.... A group of clever girls adopted the new technique with success."[9] In pursuit of material that would shock and excite, tabloid women reporters purloined photographs, tracked down gangsters, and charmed murderers into giving them exclusive interviews.

A few women, such as Lorena Hickok of the Associated Press, gained recognition as reporters and attained what Ross called the coveted designation of "front page girl." These women displayed almost superhuman effort to convince male editors they could perform as well as, or better than, their male counterparts on all assignments. An example was Hickok's attempt to produce a scoop while covering the 1932 kidnapping of the infant son of aviator Charles A. Lindbergh. This was a story so big it pushed the Depression off the front page as readers followed every detail of the crime, the discovery of the baby's body, and the trial and execution of the murderer, Bruno Hauptmann.

A top political writer, Hickok was determined to go to the kid-

[7]*Emporia Gazette*, 23 December 1925.
[8]*Associated Press v. United States*, 326 U.S. I (1945).

[9]Ishbel Ross, *Ladies of the Press* (New York, 1936), 262.

Changing of the Guard
James Gordon Bennett Jr. (left), whose father had entered the newspaper business in the early 1800s, epitomized the traditions that were giving way in the early 1900s. His *New York Herald* was faltering, and numbers of women were beginning to enter what had once been a virtual male domain. One of the most popular was Elizabeth Meriwether Gilmer (right), who, under the pen name "Dorothy Dix," for more than half a century worked as a reporter, a "sob sister," and a syndicated advice columnist. She was one of the most widely read newspaper writers of the twentieth century, advising women that the means to happiness in the face of difficulties was a determination to be content.

napping scene in Hopewell, New Jersey. After a fruitless search for clues to find the baby herself, she crawled on her hands and knees up a snow-covered mountain at 2 a.m., peering in the windows of Lindbergh's isolated home to check out a vague rumor that the infant might have been returned. All she received for her exertion was flu due to exposure. Her editors were annoyed — not at her ethics but at her failure to produce a story.

Relatively few women journalists could ever hope for front page bylines. In most cases the women's and society pages provided their only viable opportunities for newspaper careers. The product of the late nineteenth century, the women's pages drew a large audience for department store advertising. Their success was an important factor in the expansion of daily newspaper readership, which doubled between 1892 and 1914.

Despite their role in the newspaper organization, the women's pages were barely tolerated by male journalists. Segregated from the main city room in areas given such names as the "hen coop," women's page staff members received even poorer pay than their male counterparts. Often male editors limited the women's pages to a trite formula of fashion, beauty hints, and domestic chitchat. Nevertheless, coverage of women's organizations and community interests made these sections a limited means for women to communicate among themselves. To some degree women's pages showcased women of achievement, although most of the women pictured there were portrayed as wives of prominent men.

One woman journalist who built an extraordinary career appealed to millions of readers, chiefly women. Elizabeth M. Gilmer, who wrote as "Dorothy Dix" from 1895 until 1949, achieved fame, first as a "sob sister," who wrote highly emotional feature stories for Hearst newspapers, and then as a syndicated advice columnist, whose counsel on personal relationships was avidly sought by her devoted followers. In an era when newspapers used narrative stories more than today, "sob sisters" emoted in lurid

human interest accounts that built circulation. As a reporter, Gilmer specialized in covering trials of women charged with murder and befriended the accused, picturing them as victimized by males. Conventional in her views on women's behavior, in her advice columns she urged women to seek inner happiness as a way of overcoming their misfortunes.

Mary Baker Eddy, founder of the Christian Science Church, established a daily newspaper, the *Christian Science Monitor*, in 1908, not as a religious organ, but as a protest against sensationalism in news coverage. It featured high-quality foreign and cultural news and downplayed news of crimes and tragedies. In the World War I era it had a circulation of 120,000 and was distributed more widely over the United States than any other daily newspaper.

Coverage of the campaign for women's right to vote, which ended with the adoption of the Nineteenth Amendment to the U.S. Constitution in 1920, enhanced the visibility of women's issues and women reporters. It brought together women who worked on newspapers and women who sought publicity for the suffrage cause. In Washington, D.C., for example, women journalists and women publicists (an early term used for public relations practitioners) joined forces in 1919 to form their own organization, the Women's National Press Club. It served as an outlet for the professional development of women, who were denied admission to the male-only National Press Club until 1971. The New York Newspaper Women's Club, still in existence today, was founded in 1922 after women reporters who had covered the suffrage campaign together found they missed the camaraderie of frequent gatherings.

Other women edited and published suffragist newspapers. Alice Stone Blackwell, the daughter of Lucy Stone and Henry Blackwell — both of whom were dedicated to the cause of women's rights — edited the *Woman's Journal*, the leading women's-rights newspaper, for thirty-five years after her graduation from Boston

Lindbergh Kidnapping

These front pages from New York City, Los Angeles, and Columbus, Georgia, illustrate how Charles Lindbergh's Atlantic flight and the kidnapping of his child filled the news media.

'The Greatest Story Since the Resurrection'

In 1927, 25-year-old Charles Lindbergh accomplished the first nonstop solo flight across the Atlantic Ocean and became one of the most admired people in the world. His fame brought him great fortune and also great misfortune.

On March 1, 1932, his 19-month-old son, Charles Jr., was kidnapped from the Lindbergh home in New Jersey. A ransom note was found on the nursery window sill, and a ladder was left against the outside wall of the house.

Although the Lindberghs paid a ransom and were given the baby's pajamas as evidence that he was alive, the child was not returned. A truck driver found his body in woods near the house two months later.

The abduction of "The Little Eagle," as the media affectionately dubbed the baby, captivated public attention; and newspapers and newsreels avidly reported every detail of the crime and its aftermath. News photographers even managed to photograph the baby's body in the morgue.

For two and a half years, investigators struggled to solve the case. Finally, in September 1934, some of the marked ransom bills began showing up, and police traced them to an illegal German immigrant, Bruno Richard Hauptmann. Police found some of the marked money in his garage, and experts later said his handwriting matched that on the ransom note. More than 700 reporters and photographers descended on Flemington, New Jersey, in January 1935 for the final chapter of what many called "the crime of the century" – the trial of Hauptmann. Author H. L. Mencken called the trial "the greatest story since the Resurrection." Emotions were so high that several journalists openly expressed their opinion that Hauptmann was guilty.

After Hauptmann was convicted and sentenced to death, the Lindbergh family moved to England to escape publicity.

Sob Sisters

Female Reporters Get Tagged for Sappy Copy

Heartbreaking, tear-jerking stories of sex, murder, and abuse, all written from the feminine perspective. These were the hallmarks of sob stories, and the women who wrote them were known as sob sisters.

A male reporter coined the pejorative to describe the four female reporters hired to provide a feminine account of the 1907-08 trial of millionaire Harry Kendall Thaw. He was accused of shooting to death his wife's former lover in New York's Madison Square Garden rooftop restaurant.

Thaw's murder of world-famous architect Stanford White shocked and titillated New Yorkers, who couldn't get enough of the story. Editors responded by arranging to have Winifred Black Bonfils ("Annie Laurie"), Elizabeth Meriwether Gilmer ("Dorothy Dix"), Ada Patterson, and Nixola Greeley-Smith, granddaughter of Penny Press editor Horace Greeley, seated at their own private table at the front of the courtroom to produce daily doses of emotion-laden copy designed to wring tears from even the hardest New Yorker's eyes.

Journalist Irvin S. Cobb insultingly described the four women as "sob sisters" because of their soppy, sappy copy, and the sobriquet stuck.

The explosive growth in the 1880s of evening papers and the increase of Sunday editions helped editors recognize that women were an important component of newspaper circulation. That trend – followed by the Yellow Journalism of the 1890s and combined with the stunt journalism initiated by Joseph Pulitzer's Elizabeth Cochrane ("Nellie Bly") and her countless copycat reporters – gave rise to the perfect environment for the sob sisters. Add to that mix the 1900s' muckraking reform journalism, which focused on exposing the excesses of big businesses and the corruption of political leaders, and the increase of women in the workplace due

Winifred Bonfils, writing under the byline "Annie Laurie," was one of the most notable of the sob sisters. Along with several others, she helped make the Thaw-White murder a national sensation. She loved newspaper work and once said, "I'd rather smell the printer's ink and hear the presses go around than go to any grand opera in the world." She became so well known that her funeral was a major event.

to industrialization and immigration, and the result was a growth of women's pages and in particular a surge in news stories that provided a woman's point of view.

Bonfils, Gilmer, Patterson, and later Adela Rogers St. John and others focused their reporting skills on providing sensationalized coverage of murder trials and the legal affairs of the rich and famous. They went under cover to expose the mistreatment of women and the poor.

Annie Laurie, one of the original sob sisters, worked for William Randolph Hearst's media syndicate for more than fifty years and was the only woman in "W.R.'s" inner circle of friends. Aside from her coverage of the Thaw case, she was famous for pretending to faint on a San Francisco street in a test of the city's emergency medical services. After being taken to the hospital in a hearse, she posed as a patient at San Francisco Receiving Hospital to report on the emergency room

treatment she received. Her story of being ignored by police on the street after she fainted and the "thrashing" she endured at the hospital as treatment led California's governor to inspect the hospital. As a result, numerous hospital employees were fired, and an ambulance service was initiated.

Pen names – such as Bonfils' "Annie Laurie" – were a common custom for female journalists in the late 1800s and early 1900s because for a woman to work as a newspaper reporter was considered unsavory and disreputable.

The term "sob sister" had come into common use by 1910. By then, it was being used to denote any female journalist who wrote excessively emotional human interest stories. The derogatory nickname was later applied to all female journalists and even to female fiction authors whose writing was judged as unduly emotional and artificial.

The Metropolitan Daily
In the first half of the twentieth century, newspapers continued on the growth spiral that had begun in the 1830s. Along with circulation increases, they expanded their staffs in all departments of their operations. Simply taking care of sending copies to subscribers and newsstands required a major operation, as illustrated in this drawing from the early 1900s. On average, major dailies employed approximately sixty workers in their mail rooms.

University in 1881. Rheta Childe Dorr, a journalist who exposed injustices against working women and was a World War I war correspondent, became the first editor of the *Suffragist*, the publication of the militant wing of the suffrage movement, in 1914.

Another veteran of the movement, Clara Bewick Colby, started her newspaper, *The Woman's Tribune*, in Nebraska in 1883. Four years later, she shifted it to Washington, D.C., where she published it until 1904. That year she moved the paper to Portland, Oregon, where it continued until 1909, although the emphasis remained on national, not local, suffrage news.

In spite of the presence of a limited number of capable women on daily papers, editors assumed that most women were unfit to be general assignment reporters and did not belong in city rooms. One reporting textbook in the 1930s stated bluntly, "The general tempo — with the deadline-fighting element always present — is such to bar many women because of nervous temperament."[10]

The rakish, smoke-filled atmosphere within big city newspaper offices was dramatized by Ben Hecht and Charles MacArthur, former reporters, in their 1928 play, *The Front Page*. The drama, which revolved around a love-hate relationship between two males — a cynical reporter and a manipulative city editor — presented a fantasized notion of journalism as a disreputable, but enthralling, occupation for men only. It was made into a movie that has been remade three times and become an icon of newspaper lore. In the 1940 version — titled *His Girl Friday* — the reporter is a woman, a theatrical touch that highlights the eventual acceptance of women on newspaper staffs. Women, however, remained marginal figures in the newspaper world until passage of civil rights legislation in 1964 that outlawed discrimination in employment on grounds of sex as well as race.

SMALL-TOWN JOURNALISM

In small towns and rural areas, the journalistic pace was far slower than the frenzied race to meet deadlines that marked the newsrooms of metropolitan dailies. Still, the work was just as hard and the hours just as long, or longer, as in the big cities for even less monetary reward. Country weeklies, which remained an important element in journalism during the first decades of the century, required skill and devotion from their owners, who sometimes were the only staff members. With 51% of the population of the United States still classified as rural before World War I, small newspapers played vital roles in their communities, serving as boosters and bulletin boards as well as political voices.

The preeminent exemplar of a weekly journalist was William Allen White of the *Emporia* (Kan.) *Gazette*. He purchased the languishing newspaper in 1895 and moved back to the small town where he had been born in 1868. Then he quickly gained national fame with a single editorial in 1896. He wrote it in answer to a group of Populist farmers who cornered him on a street on a Saturday morning when they had come into town to do their weekly shopping. They challenged him to defend his conservative opinions, demanding that he explain his argument that the Populist political movement was harming Kansas. Befuddled and angered, he could not give them a coherent answer. He rushed back to his office and, employing bold sarcasm, wrote out his answer, an editorial titled "What's the Matter with Kansas?"[11] He and his wife then left on their summer vacation. Unbeknown to White, Republican newspapers around the country reprinted the editorial, and he returned to his office two weeks later to find himself famous. In later years, his political views moderated, while his writing style improved. He won the 1923 Pulitzer Prize for an editorial dealing with press freedom, but his most enduring editorial was a masterpiece on the death of his 17-year-old daughter in 1921. Among all

---

[10]Philip W. Porter and Norval N. Luxon, *The Reporter and the News* (New York, 1935), 8.   [11]*Emporia Gazette*, 15 August 1896.

William Allen White

Small-Town Editor
Wins Huge Following

They called him the "Sage of Emporia," and it's easy to see why.

Newspaper editor William Allen White earned two Pulitzer Prizes and ten honorary college degrees, including one from Harvard. Middle-class Americans adored him. He was their unofficial spokesman.

But, incredibly, White never worked for big city newspapers on the east or west coasts, where most famous journalists have built their reputations. Instead, he spent almost his entire career with the *Emporia Gazette*, a small daily that served a city of 10,000 in rural Kansas. He was a country editor.

White was born in 1868 and after college worked three years as an editorial writer for the *Kansas City Star*. In 1895, he purchased the *Gazette* for $3,000 and began writing editorials on a wide range of local and national topics.

A year later he attracted national attention with a stinging attack on William Jennings Bryan, Populists, and Democrats titled "What's the Matter with Kansas?" The editorial pointed out that Kansas was running behind other states in terms of revenues and population. White blamed the Populists and their ideas.

"What's the matter with Kansas?" he asked satirically. "Nothing under the shining sun. She is losing wealth, population, and standing. She has got her statesmen, and the money power is afraid of her. Kansas is all right. She has started in to raise hell, as Mrs. [Mary Elizabeth] Lease [a Populist campaign speaker] advised, and she seems to have an overproduction. But that doesn't matter. Kansas never did believe in diversified crops."

White opposed corruption and predatory business. After his early anti-Populist years, he became a leader of the Progressive movement and opposed the railroads, which were overcharging farmers for shipping their crops. In 1912, he helped Teddy Roosevelt form the Progressive (Bull-

From his office at the *Emporia Gazette*, William Allen White wrote editorials that gained national attention, and he carried on a correspondence with leaders around the nation.

Moose) Party, which opposed Republican president William Howard Taft.

White's editorials idealized small town life and the importance of "community" and morality. They often contained humor and a commonsense approach to understanding problems. When a publisher who built his reputation on buying and closing down newspapers died, White wrote: "Frank A. Munsey contributed to the journalism of his day the talent of the meatpacker, the morals of the money changer and the manners of the undertaker.... May he rest in trust." When his 17-year-old daughter died in a horse-riding accident in

1921, he wrote a stirring tribute about her joyous approach to life. He directed many of his writings to the modern middle class, whose sense of community was being threatened by the transition from an agricultural nation to an industrial one.

In 1923, he won a Pulitzer for an editorial about freedom of speech that criticized the Kansas governor's order that businesses could not display placards supporting striking railroad workers.

By the time White died in 1944, his reputation was worldwide. His autobiography was published posthumously. In 1947, it won a Pulitzer Prize.

editorials ever published in American newspapers, it comes closest to being a genuine classic of literature.[12]

Country weeklies often were family businesses, involving husbands, wives, and children, with some women as adept as men in setting type and performing backshop mechanical chores. To cite one example, in Oklahoma Territory Elva Ferguson founded the *Watonga Republican* in 1892 with her husband, Thompson, who became territorial governor. Also a powerful figure in politics, she carried on the newspaper following her husband's death in 1921 until she sold it in 1930.

PROFESSIONALIZATION

Before World War I, journalism, in line with other technically oriented occupations like accounting, business, public management, and engineering, moved toward attaining professional status. Universities established journalism schools, enabling graduates to move into the field without long apprenticeships as "cub" reporters. Countering the perception of newspaper work as an unconventional, if not shady, occupation, both formal training programs and newly organized professional associations called on journalists to act as responsible public advocates.

The first four-year school of journalism, which emphasized practical experience on its own newspaper, opened in 1908 at the University of Missouri. From the beginning, the idea of college preparation met hostility from some editors and publishers who ridiculed academic instruction, foreshadowing a debate that goes on today. Summing up criticism of the need for college education, the *Moberly* (Mo.) *Democrat* sniffed at the Missouri school: "So long as men can embark in the newspaper business without education, character, brains or money, there is very little inducement to take higher courses in journalism."[13]

Frequently located in the Middle West, where public universities had a tradition of assisting farmers and businesses, the early journalism schools were backed by state press associations. Their members wanted to elevate the status of newspapers as well as have a supply of trained employees. As contrasted with the Missouri model, some schools followed the pattern set up at the University of Wisconsin, which stressed social science research along with skills training.

Journalism schools were part of a broader movement to professionalize the editorial side of newspaper work by establishing standards of conduct. Organized in 1922, the American Society of Newspaper Editors (ASNE) one year later adopted its "Canons of Journalism," an ethical code with high-minded phraseology that contrasted sharply with prevalent tabloid practices. "Journalism... demands of its practitioners the widest range of intelligence, of knowledge, and of experience, as well as natural and trained powers of observation and reasoning," the code said. "To its opportunities as a chronicler are indissolubly linked its obligations as

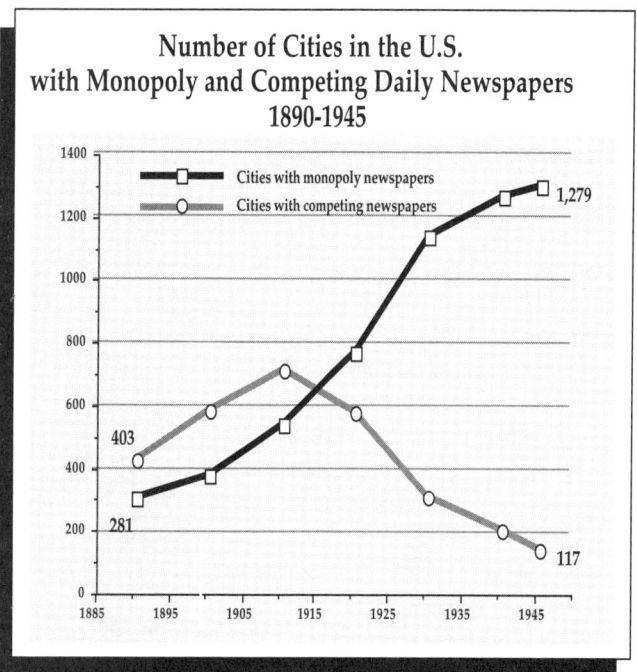

Number of Cities in the U.S. with Monopoly and Competing Daily Newspapers 1890-1945

teacher and interpreter."[14]

The code's weakness was illustrated the following year. An attempt was made to censure and possibly expel Frederick G. Bonfils, co-publisher of the flamboyant *Denver Post*, which printed giant headlines in red ink and was run from an office with red walls known as the "Bucket of Blood." At issue was an accusation that Bonfils had accepted a payoff to withhold news of the Teapot Dome oil scandals. ASNE members disagreed on the interpretation of the code, and Bonfils was allowed to resign.

One institutionalization of the concept of journalism as a public trust was the Pulitzer Prizes, journalism's most coveted professional awards. First given in 1917, they were endowed with funds Joseph Pulitzer left to Columbia University, where he helped establish a school of journalism that started in 1912.

In setting up the prizes that recognized work in literature, drama, and music as well as journalism, Pulitzer described a vision of newspapers as progressive social forces untainted by selfish, commercial considerations. He specified three different types of annual prizes in journalism: One for "the most disinterested and meritorious public service rendered by any American newspaper during the preceding year"; the second for the best editorial, "the test of excellence being clearness of style, moral purpose, sound reasoning, and power to influence public opinion in the right direction"; the third for reporting based on "strict accuracy, terseness, the accomplishment of some public good commanding public attention and respect."[15] Over the years the prizes have been expanded to include additional categories — such as foreign correspondence, photography, feature writing, and criticism.

In 1937 Anne O'Hare McCormick of the *New York Times* became

[12]"Mary White," *Emporia Gazette*, 17 May 1921. For this and other editorials, see Wm. David Sloan, Cheryl S. Wray, and C. Joanne Sloan, *Great Editorials*, 2nd ed. (Northport, Ala., 1997).

[13]Quoted in Robert F. Karolevitz, *From Quill to Computer: The Story of America's Community Newspapers* (National Newspaper Foundation, 1985), 117.

[14]Quoted in John L. Hulteng, *The Messenger's Motives: Ethical Problems of the News Media* (Englewood Cliffs, N.J., 1976), 18-20.

[15]Quoted in John Hohenberg, *The Pulitzer Prizes: A History of the Awards in Books, Drama, Music, and Journalism Based on the Private Files Over Six Decades* (New York, 1974), 20.

Weekly Newspapers

Despite Canned Copy, Influential Editors Serve Small Towns

At the start of the twentieth century, weekly newspapers relied heavily on syndicate services for much of their content. "Ready-print," "canned copy," or "boilerplate," as the syndicate material was called, had many users, but it also had its critics.

A small but vocal group of weekly publishers resisted the use of the material. They believed newspapers should be publishing local material rather than a hodge-podge of general-interest items.

One of the most outspoken leaders among the "all-home-print" editors was William Allen White of the *Emporia* (Kan.) *Gazette*. He earned a national reputation for his well-crafted editorials on local, state, and national issues. Other publishers joined him to encourage small-town editors to incorporate more local news and features so that their publications reflected their distinctive communities.

White's strategy of emphasizing local news paid off in local subscriptions and advertising revenue increases for his newspaper. Readers across the nation also admired his editorial opinions as examples of common sense and honesty originating from small-town America. Weekly editors from around the country exchanged newspapers with him and reprinted his editorials. His writings became so well known that the *Gazette* attracted subscribers nationwide, especially from the nation's capital. Despite his growing celebrity – and continual pleas from the nation's leading newspapers and magazines for him to join their staffs – he remained in Emporia to do the work he loved most, publishing a community newspaper.

Despite White's successes, a vast majority of weeklies filled space with material from syndicate services. The most influential of the syndicates was the Western Newspaper Union. Established in Des Moines, Iowa, in 1880, the WNU had more

The use of syndicate services allowed publishers to put out weekly newspapers at lower costs. One result, though, was that many papers carried much material that was unrelated to their reading audience. Some of them also seemed the same. That sameness can be seen in the two newspapers shown here. The one on the left is a 1903 issue of the *Chipley Banner* in Florida, and on the right is a 1918 issue of the *Jasper News* in Missouri. Many weeklies were dependent on the syndicate services. When the *Holt* (Mich.) *Weekly News*, which had begun publication in 1914, ceased operation in 1952, it announced that it was closing because the Western Newspaper Union had discontinued its ready-print service.

subscribers and geographic spread than any other weekly news service.

Wright A. "Pat" Patterson, the Missouri-born son of a Methodist minister, joined WNU in 1906 as news editor and remained as its editor-in-chief until 1940. He had started work with the Kellogg syndicate service as a 19-year-old. By the 1920s, he was one of the country's most influential journalists – although few readers knew his name. The important role he played was reflected in a feature article about him in the October 1927 issue of *The American Magazine*. The headline read: "Patterson Helps to Edit Twelve Thousand Newspapers." The list of newspapers that subscribed to WNU material included most weeklies in the nation, and their readership covered half of the nation's population.

The article began with an account of a meeting between President Theodore Roosevelt and Patterson, who was requesting that the administration treat the coun-

try press and metropolitan press equally when releasing important information. Roosevelt was unaware of the number of newspapers that Patterson represented. Veteran newspaperman Edward B. Clark, who was in the room, asked Roosevelt, "I wonder if you know exactly who this is you are talking to?" When Roosevelt replied, "Yes," Clark responded, "Do you realize that Patterson helps to edit twelve thousand newspapers; that the biggest paper in the country has nowhere near so many readers as he has?" With renewed interest, Roosevelt asked for another meeting with Patterson to learn about the syndicate's operation.

When Patterson died in 1954, few knew of his enormous contributions to the country press, but small-town editors throughout the country knew him to be the man behind numerous stories and advice-filled columns for more than sixty years.

the first woman journalist to receive a Pulitzer for foreign correspondence. She was one of the first journalists to interview the leaders of the totalitarian regimes in Europe that led to World War II. She began sending columns to the *Times* from Europe while accompanying her husband on business trips. In spite of the high quality of her work, she referred to herself as a "stepchild" in the *Times'* family and was not allowed to become the first woman on the newspaper's editorial board until 1936, after the death of publisher Adolph Ochs. Like many publishers of his day, he did not think women belonged in newspaper offices.

McCormick was not the only woman to achieve distinction as a foreign correspondent. In 1924 Dorothy Thompson became the first American woman to head a European news bureau when she was made chief of the Berlin office of the *Philadelphia Public Ledger* and the *New York Evening Post*. She decided to pursue foreign correspondence to escape being limited to writing about women's groups in the United States. In 1936 she signed a contract with the *New York Herald Tribune* for a syndicated column of European political analysis that reached an audience of 8 million at its peak. Another influential woman foreign correspondent during the 1930s was Sigrid Schultz of the *Chicago Tribune*.

OBJECTIVITY

The concept of "the public" as a force that could be influenced to the good by responsible journalism fit well with the pragmatic views of a society that had an optimistic faith in democracy. To some philosophers the reportorial search for facts became a search for truth that could be laid out before a reasoning audience. In the early 1900s, explains one historian, "objectivity was an ideal to which the press aspired. It represented not only the journalists' desire to present the truth in as accurate and unbiased a manner as possible, but also an attempt to recover their status as independent gatherers of news," which "had been tarnished by the sensationalism of yellow journalism at the turn of the century."[16]

Not all theorists saw the gathering of factual information as likely to provide enlightenment. The increasing complexity of a society torn apart by modern war spread disillusionment with the idea of purported facts speaking for themselves. To some it seemed almost impossible to obtain true facts in a world where citizens were subjected to downright lies by devious sources.

In 1920, Walter Lippmann, an intellectual who became the last editor of the *New York World*, reacted to the propaganda that had characterized World War I. "[W]here all news comes at secondhand," he wrote, "where all the testimony is uncertain, men cease to respond to truths, and respond simply to opinions. The environment in which they act is not the realities themselves, but the pseudo-environment of reports, rumors and guesses."[17] He called for the professionalization of journalism and urged that reporters

Famous and Infamous
Journalism in the 1920s had many highs and lows. Illustrating the good and the bad were Dorothy Thompson and Frederick Bonfils. The first American woman to head a European news bureau, Thompson covered Germany from 1924 until expelled in 1934. She was one of the first foreign correspondents to recognize the dangers of Nazism. Bonfils, on the other hand, made his first money in gambling. With partner Harry Tammen, a hotel bartender, he bought the tottering *Denver Post* in the 1890s. They turned it into a sensational paper and claimed to be crusaders for the welfare of working people. Unscrupulous, though, they used threats to extort money from opponents and used the *Post* for their own power and advantage.

be trained to be as objective as possible. Lippmann later achieved fame for his syndicated column of political commentary that alternated with Dorothy Thompson's column in the *New York Herald Tribune*.

The ideal of objectivity led journalists to subscribe to techniques of reporting that now are standard. These included attributing information to official sources, trying to balance coverage by giving both sides of issues, and attempting to offer some context for news events. The objective reporter no longer presented facts in isolation but strived to paint a broader picture.

Many reporters themselves realized that objectivity might be an unattainable quest, particularly since some editors and publishers wanted news slanted to suit their own preferences. In a study of Washington correspondents in the 1930s, a researcher found forty-two reporters who agreed that "it is almost impossible to be objective." But another twenty-four disagreed with the statement.[18]

Lippmann was a leading thinker in the new area of public opinion. In his influential book *Public Opinion*, first published in 1922, he outlined the concept of the "public" as an emotional, rather than a logical, entity. He contended that each individual thinks in terms of stereotypical pictures carried in the mind rather than in realistic terms. He wrote that the press is too weak an institution "to supply spontaneously the truth which democrats hoped was inborn."[19] To Lippmann, news was a limited commodity, and the public's ability to absorb facts and act on them for its own good a questionable concept.

[16]Barbara M. Kelly, "Objectivity and the Trappings of Professionalism, 1900-1950," Chapter 11 in *Fair & Balanced: A History of Journalistic Objectivity*, Steven R. Knowlton and Karen L. Freeman, eds. (Northport, Ala., 2005), 150.
[17]Walter Lippmann, "The Basic Problem of Democracy: What Modern Liberty Means," *Atlantic Monthly* 124 (November 1919): 624.

[18]Leo C. Rosten, *The Washington Correspondents* (New York, 1937), 351.
[19]Walter Lippmann, *Public Opinion* (New York, 1922), 273.

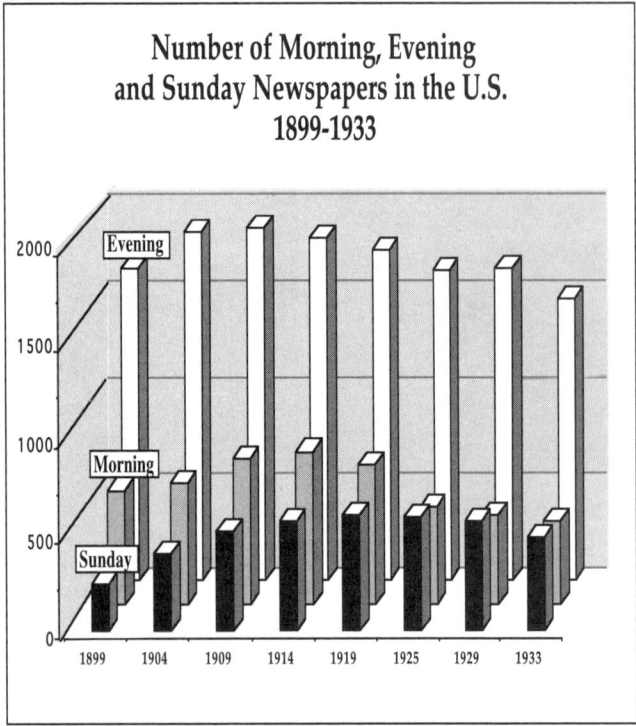

Number of Morning, Evening and Sunday Newspapers in the U.S. 1899-1933

lic opinion polling as a result of measuring reader interest in newspaper content. Starting in the 1930s, advertisers and political candidates used his polling to assess public reaction to their campaigns. Newspapers covered his findings as news, informing readers which candidates were leading in the polls. Another pioneer researcher, Harold Lasswell, a political scientist, developed a technique called "content analysis" to study communication messages. He classified their components into different categories for statistical measurement. As the leading member of a Rockefeller Foundation seminar on communication in 1939-40, he originated a five-question model for communication study that dominated the field for many years: "Who says what to whom in what channel with what effect?"

The ideas of Lasswell and others influenced the government, as well as the news media, during World War II when social scientists were involved in efforts to enhance support for the war effort. Convinced that the war involved a battle for the minds of individual citizens, Lasswell headed a project in Washington to analyze media content for propaganda from both allies and enemies and to advise officials on the best way for the United States to carry out its own propaganda/information program. His staff worked with various agencies concerned with mobilization, including the Office of War Information, which employed journalists and PR professionals to prepare and coordinate news releases. Newspapers, which supported the war overwhelmingly, made extensive use of the material.

THE NEWSPAPER AS MINORITY VOICE

Among specialized publications, the ethnic press played an important role in preparing immigrants to support the American system and to play an active role as citizens in their new country. Its number peaked in 1914 when about 1,300 journals, including 140 dailies, were being published in thirty-six languages. About 40% were printed in German, a percentage that declined rapidly after the United States entered World War I against Germany.

The ethnic press waxed and waned in response to succeeding waves of immigration. From 1884 to 1920, some 3,444 newspapers were begun, while 3,186 ceased publication, although some merged into stronger publications. By 1948 only 973 foreign-language newspapers remained.

The ethnic press was the subject of one of the most influential academic writings on the newspaper. Robert E. Park, a former reporter in Minneapolis and an important figure in the "Chicago School" of sociology, which pioneered in applied social research at the University of Chicago, published *The Immigrant Press and Its Control* in 1922. It was written in response to concerns about whether the foreign-language press had been loyal to the United States during World War I.

Along with the philosopher John Dewey, also a key intellectual at the University of Chicago, Park saw the newspaper as a unifying element in society. He considered it a means of restoring personal communication between individuals lost in the anonymity

PUBLIC RELATIONS

The idea of the public as a somewhat inert mass subject to persuasion lay behind the emerging profession of public relations. Notable for its mid-nineteenth century roots in the ballyhoo of press agents who promoted circuses and theatrical events, the field of publicity broadened into public relations as politicians and representatives of big business employed publicists to present them to the public in a favorable light. John D. Rockefeller Jr., criticized for strike-breaking and other "robber baron" activities, hired Ivy Lee, one of the first PR practitioners, to improve his personal image in 1914.

Other PR pioneers included Edward L. Bernays and his wife, Doris E. Fleischman. The nephew of Sigmund Freud, Bernays approached public relations from an intellectual, rather than a business management, viewpoint. Writing the initial theory in the field, he believed that the public could be manipulated positively for its own good.

Some journalists saw public relations as a threat to their professional autonomy. PR practitioners, many of whom were former reporters, furnished stories to newspapers on behalf of clients. Although journalists made use of this material, questions arose as to what degree the practice of accepting PR "handouts" compromised the ideal of objectivity. Journalists maintained they were advocates of the public interest and therefore purer than PR practitioners who represented specific clients. The latter, on the other hand, resented being seen as inferior to journalists.

In both academic and commercial realms, a new science of mass communications research emerged. George Gallup, a journalism teacher at Iowa State University, originated scientific pub-

SPECIAL

Extra **Chicago Defender** Extra

SUNDAY, NOVEMBER 14, 1915

Booker T. Washington

DEAD!

1:23 Sunday Morning at Tuskegee

Full Particulars in Saturday's Paper

The *Chicago Defender*
Founded by Robert S. Abbott in 1905, the *Chicago Defender* built its huge success by using a formula emphasizing sensational news geared to racial issues. Abbott's news sense was demonstrated with its special issue upon the death of Booker T. Washington in 1915. The most popular African American of his time, Washington emphasized moderation in race relations. By the time of this issue, the *Defender's* circulation had reached 230,000.

of big-city life. In his book he concluded that most publications in foreign languages helped immigrants adjust to the United States and did not emphasize loyalty to their native countries.

In the case of the Spanish-language press of the Southwest, one authority estimated that 248 newspapers were begun between 1900 and 1958.[20] They served an audience of Chicanos (American citizens of Mexican background) that increased markedly from 1910 to 1920 in response to economic dislocation created by the Mexican Revolution. Editors took diverse positions toward the revolution and whether the United States should intervene, but the press helped maintain a sense of cultural identity among Chicanos and encouraged sympathy for the Mexican people.

Large numbers of African-American newspapers were started in the late nineteenth and early twentieth centuries. Between 1865 and 1950, around 2,700 began. Of those, only 175 remained in existence by the middle of the twentieth century. The average life span was nine years. Many of the papers faced difficulty in establishing an advertising base, while others received political subsidies that did not last beyond a particular political campaign. These subsi-

dies came from Republican interests, since until the Depression African Americans remained loyal to the party of Lincoln, whom they credited with freeing them from slavery during the Civil War.

The newspapers articulated the aspirations of an oppressed population. Although local papers often were in no economic position to challenge the white power structure, weekly papers with multiple editions and national circulations highlighted racial inequities. Their influence can be judged, in part, from the campaigns waged against them. According to a contemporary observer, in Somerville, Tennessee, in 1919, an order was issued that no "colored newspapers" could be circulated in the town and that the "darkey" population had to read a local white paper edited by a Confederate veteran.[21]

National newspapers, particularly the *Chicago Defender*, played a major role in promoting the "Great Migration." This was a movement of African-American agricultural workers from the South to the North in the World War I era and thereafter to seek better opportunities. Other leading newspapers included the Baltimore-based *Afro-American*, the *Pittsburgh Courier*, whose editor, Robert Lee Vann, championed social justice under law, and the *Norfolk Journal and Guide*.

Founded by Robert S. Abbott in 1905, the *Defender* developed an attention-getting formula for sensationalized news geared to racial issues. By 1915 its circulation had reached 230,000. Its call to African Americans in the South to leave the cotton fields and head North so threatened the existing order that in some areas it was banned from regular channels of distribution. Instead, African-American railroad porters handed it out surreptitiously. Other black papers adopted the *Defender* formula to try to meet the needs of an audience largely cut off from the mainstream press.

As black and white communities became increasingly separate worlds in the first decades of the twentieth century, African-American newspapers served as a platform for action to secure civil rights. At the end of the nineteenth century, T. Thomas Fortune, the editor of the *New York Age*, stood out as an opponent of disenfranchisement, unequal school funding, and other injustices. His influence, however, waned after he became closely allied with Booker T. Washington, who advocated that African Americans seek vocational training and accommodate themselves to segregation, at least in the South. Washington was instrumental in obtaining subsidies for some African-American newspapers.

To counter the ideas of Washington, in 1901 William Monroe Trotter, an African American who was a Phi Beta Kappa graduate of Harvard University, founded the *Boston Guardian*, which published until his death in 1934. He was an initial backer of W. E. B. DuBois, a professor who emerged as the most articulate and important of the anti-Washington forces. With a doctorate from Harvard University, DuBois was a significant figure in African-American history. He also served as director of publications for the National Association for the Advancement of Colored People and founded its official journal, the *Crisis*, in 1910.

Since most mainstream newspapers refused to hire minorities

[20]Cited in Felix Gutierrez, "Spanish-Language Media in America: Background, Resources, History," *Journalism History* 4 (Summer 1977): 34.

[21]Frederick G. Detweiler, *The Negro Press in the United States* (Chicago, 1922), 1.

DAYTON CRIES FOR LIGHT AS SCIENCE PLEA RINGS

THE PREACHER

Scopes Defender Drives Out Effect of Bryan's Wrathful Tirade and "Sells" Modernism to Tennesseeans

WAVES OF APPLAUSE DRAWN BY ADDRESS

Stern Fundamentalists Join in Ringing Ovation for Man Who Would Open New Book of Revelations

Dayton, Tenn., July 16.—"Shall the parents have a right to say that no teacher paid by their money shall rob their children of faith in God and send them back to their homes, skeptical, infidels, agnostics, or atheists?"

Thus William Jennings Bryan set forth the case for the prosecution in the Scopes trial today.

"Close no doors of knowledge from them. Let science and theology both be loved, but let them not be confused."

Thus Dudley Field Malone put the case for enlightenment.

BY PHILIP KINSLEY

(Special to The Times-Picayune)

Dayton, Tenn., July 16.—Dayton began to read a new Book of Revelations today.

If God spoke, at this climax of the Scopes trial, on this day of days in Tennessee, it was in a strange tongue, in favor of science, rather than through the lips of William Jennings Bryan.

When William Jennings Bryan yesterday trumpeted his challenge to science in the Dayton courtroom his mein was far from that of Sunday when he occupied the pulpit in a Dayton church. Photo shows the shirt-sleeved Commoner in the pulpit at the beginning of his sermon.

The Monkey Trial

One of the big news events of the 1920s was the so-called "monkey trial." When the Tennessee teacher John T. Scopes challenged the state law prohibiting the teaching of the theory of evolution, his 1925 trial became a national media event. More than 100 journalists descended on the small town of Dayton. Most portrayed the local residents as yokels and religious zealots. Much of their reporting reflected the prejudice of the journalists, treating Scopes' lawyer, Clarence Darrow, heroically and the state's attorney, William Jennings Bryan, as a man of small intellect. The *New Orleans Times Picayune* contrived the "photograph" accompanying the story above by superimposing the shot of Bryan on a scene of a church.

and covered racial news mainly as reports on crimes, the black press provided a crucial journalistic service for its readers. Most cities with sizeable African-American populations sustained black newspapers that protested against discrimination as well as offered social and cultural news missing from white publications.

The activism of the black press led the *Kansas City Call* in 1939 to back efforts by Lucile Bluford, its managing editor, to gain admission to the University of Missouri's school of journalism. Although she had an undergraduate degree in journalism from the University of Kansas, Missouri turned down her application to its master's program on grounds of race. Unlike Kansas, the state of Missouri was legally segregated. Bluford brought suit in state court, but her plea was rejected, highlighting the lack of educational opportunities for African Americans to study journalism before segregation was outlawed in 1954. (In 1989 Bluford, then editor and publisher of the *Call*, received an honorary doctorate in humanities degree from the University of Missouri in recognition of her outstanding political writing.)

NEWSPAPERS AND RADIO

The devastating Great Depression, which hit the United States with the collapse of the stock market in 1929, brought additional changes to newspapers. Even during the economic boom of the 1920s, newspapers ran into unexpected competition from a new medium: radio. First thought a mere toy, radio soon became a potent instrument of mass communication. With the advent of widespread commercial broadcasting in the 1920s, the public discovered that it could get news and entertainment with far greater immediacy and impact via the airwaves than on the printed page.

The period between World War I and World War II had many memorable voices and strong personalities able to project well with a microphone — President Franklin Roosevelt, who led the news agenda from his inauguration in 1933 until his death in 1945; Adolf Hitler, who screamed his totalitarian message to fanatic Nazi followers; Benito Mussolini, who roused his Fascist following in Italy; and Winston Churchill, England's prime minister, who rallied his countrymen to fight against the Axis war machine. Listeners were enthralled as they gathered around their radios to hear world leaders speak, find out election results, and receive actual coverage of events such as the Scopes "monkey" trial in Tennessee over the teaching of evolution in public schools.

Publishers found it hard to adjust to the new reality of broadcasting. When the Depression hit in 1929, radio continued to flourish, but newspapers did not. Radio attracted the mass audience that once had belonged to newspapers. A total of 584 daily newspapers stopped publication from 1931 to 1945, although the number was offset somewhat by 386 dailies that began publication.

Advertising plummeted, forcing newspapers to cut salaries and production costs. In 1929 newspapers received 54% of all national advertising in mass media, magazines 42%, and radio only 4%; but by 1939 the percentage had fallen to 38% for newspapers and 35% for magazines but had risen to 27% for radio. While newspapers continued to lead in local advertising, here too radio threatened them.

Newspapers reacted by attempting to cut off radio access to news. In the early days of radio, stations often were owned by papers, which expanded into broadcasting as a way of enhancing local prestige. When it became apparent that radio was endangering newspaper profitability, however, publishers attempted to re-establish their monopoly over news transmission. In 1933 the American Newspaper Publishers Association brought pressure on the Associated Press and private wire services not to furnish news to radio stations except for brief bulletins that would encourage newspaper readership.

The effort proved futile. Radio networks struck back initially by setting up their own news operations. This costly undertaking ended in 1934 when the leading press associations agreed to set up a Press-Radio Bureau to furnish two brief news broadcasts daily to the networks. Nevertheless, news agencies not bound by the bureau agreement soon sprang up and supplied reports directly to broadcasters. By 1935 the bureau experiment had ended, and radio had emerged as the victor in the press-radio war. Not until 1940, however, did the Associated Press start a service aimed at radio clients. By then newspapers were running radio columns and giving news of programs and personalities, among whom were network commentators with their personal views on the news.

When World War II broke out in Europe in 1939, radio brought the sounds of actual warfare into Americans' living rooms. News of the Japanese bombing of Pearl Harbor on December 7, 1941, precipitating the entry of the United States into the war, reached Americans via radio hours before they read about it in their papers. Print journalists realized that they could not compete with radio for timeliness, but they could, and did, offer far more details and background reports.

Total newspaper circulation increased, although it failed to keep pace with population growth. Radio news limited the need for newspaper extras. Nevertheless, they continued to be published during the war. Motion pictures as well as radio and new types of magazines cut into the potential newspaper audience. From a high of 1.36 copies per day per household in 1910, newspaper circulation fell to 1.18 by 1940. This figure, still quite impressive, showed an industry that remained profitable.

NEWSREELS

Newsreels, ten-minute productions that showed news events before feature films in theaters, drew attentive audiences from 1911 until their demise in 1967. They provided a dramatic mixture of actual news pictures, staged reenactment, sports, war coverage, and human interest material. In part because early equipment was hard to transport, newsreel companies had a history of faking prize fights and other events. Parades were popular features since cumbersome cameras, which had to be fixed in place, could record news subjects as they passed by.

One enterprising newsreel company signed a contract in 1914 with Pancho Villa, a Mexican revolutionary, for exclusive coverage of his battles during the Mexican Revolution. The company paid him $25,000 and 50% of the royalties from the newsreel. In exchange, he delayed raids until cameramen arrived and scheduled them during daylight hours. Whether the footage that resulted was authentic or faked is unclear, but audiences flocked to see it.

As camera equipment became more portable, newsreels showed footage of spectacular news events — among them: Charles Lindbergh's takeoff for his historic solo flight across the Atlantic from New York to Paris in 1927, the explosion of the German zeppelin *Hindenburg* in 1937, and scenes of World War II, many of which the U. S. military supplied. Leading movie companies and publishers, including Hearst and Henry Luce of the *Time-Life* media empire, entered the newsreel business.

In 1935 Luce started *The March of Time*, a twenty-minute series that lasted sixteen years. Seen by some 25 million moviegoers monthly in more than 9,000 theaters, these programs used a documentary format — one based on real people and events — to ex-

The *Hindenburg*
Of the many world news events of the 1930s, few were bigger than the crash of the German zeppelin *Hindenburg* on her maiden voyage to the United States in 1937. Radio and newspaper reporters, along with newspaper and newsreel photographers, were all on hand to record her arrival in Lakehurst, New Jersey. The corps of journalists quickly spread the news of the crash to readers, listeners, and viewers across the nation.

plore social issues, although they employed dramatizations that merged fact and fiction. *The March of Time* emphasized interpretation and touched on political issues, making it different from conventional newsreels that sought to avoid controversy. The series ran in newsreel form, on the radio, and later on television.

Whether or not the newsreels were credible, millions watched them as quasi-journalistic sources of news, even though they emphasized show-business values. Starting in 1929, movie theaters that screened newsreels exclusively were opened in New York and other cities. The *All-American News*, a newsreel for African Americans, was shown regularly in most of the nation's 450 black motion picture theaters in the World War II period. Newsreels finally died as television's popularity increased.

NEW MAGAZINES

New types of magazines that presented news as well as views also challenged the newspaper. In 1923 Luce and a Yale classmate, Briton Hadden, started *Time*, the first weekly newsmagazine. Responding to the pressures of urban life, *Time* promised to save

Heywood Broun and Organized Labor
The leader of the American Newspaper Guild, Broun was a hero of liberals in the 1920s and 1930s. Along with efforts to unionize working journalists, he wrote a syndicated column in which he vehemently condemned what he considered to be injustice. His writing often was bitter, but acquaintances said that he was friendly and kind, and many held him in deep affection. In the efforts to unionize newspapers, organizers were hampered by isolated instances of violence. A member of a union (unconnected with the Newspaper Guild) in the American Federation of Labor confessed to having thrown the bomb that killed twenty employees at the non-union *Los Angeles Times* in 1910. AFL membership declined nationwide for the next several years.

time for the "busy man" by organizing the news into separate categories — national, foreign, business, education, art, and other areas. Not pretending to be objective, it offered opinions intermingled with facts in a somewhat flippant style.

Luce, who took charge after Hadden died, recognized the public's appetite for the visual. In 1936 he inaugurated *Life*, a weekly picture magazine designed to appeal to a nation increasingly interested in buying cameras for home use. It set standards for both photography and layout. In an era before color photographs became commonplace, *Life* featured striking photographic essays in black and white. Readers soon demanded five to six million copies a week, far more than could be produced. Crowds almost came to blows in the street to get copies. Clearly, the public wanted a photographic report on the world, just as it wanted a photographic record of personal life. Other picture magazines, particularly *Look*, began publication in clear imitation of *Life*.

Photographers, not reporters, were the stars at *Life* and its imitators. Among them was Margaret Bourke-White, whose spectacular pictures brought her international fame. Chosen to shoot the first cover for *Life*, Bourke-White, a pioneer in industrial photography, pictured a dam in Montana built as part of a Depression work relief project — a symbol of the nation's belief in technology to solve problems.

Although not able to provide slick paper reproduction of photographs, newspapers adjusted to their new competitors. They made more attempts to departmentalize their contents, with front-page news summaries becoming regular features during the 1930s. They used more bylines and allowed reporters more latitude to express themselves, even though most news continued to be written impersonally in line with the ideal of objectivity.

THE NEWSPAPER AND THE FEDERAL GOVERNMENT

Franklin Roosevelt was elected President of the United States four times — in the Depression years of 1932 and 1936 and in the World War II years of 1940 and 1944 — in spite of opposition from a majority of newspaper publishers. As a group, the publishers, who tended to be conservative Republicans, like other business people, feared the social and economic consequences of Roosevelt's Democratic New Deal. Roosevelt himself spoke out against "press lords" like Hearst (after Hearst, an initial backer, broke with the administration in 1935) and Robert McCormick, contending that 85% of the nation's papers editorially were against the New Deal.

While Roosevelt exaggerated the extent of the enmity, it was formidable. According to surveys, about 40% of dailies supported his first election in 1932 and 36% backed his re-election in 1936, while only 22% endorsed his election to an unprecedented third term in 1940 and to a fourth term in 1944. The fact that he won overwhelmingly served as proof that newspaper endorsements meant relatively little in presidential elections. Nonetheless, newspapers were potent forces in the entire political process.

Roosevelt showed himself to be a master at political communication in spite of hostility from publishers. Aided by his press secretary, Stephen T. Early, he cultivated the Washington press corps more than his predecessors had done. Inspiring confidence with his melodious voice, he also took his case for economic recovery directly to the American people in a series of twenty-eight radio "fireside chats." These presented his programs in terms that the public could understand.

Roosevelt took steps personally to make front-page news that was favorable to his administration. During his presidency he held a total of 998 press conferences, an average of eighty-three per year, a figure far higher than that of his successors. Displaying his warm and magnetic personality, he provided an endless source of stories for reporters. In return, they valued his friendship and admired his leadership. His popularity with the White House press corps, many members of which he knew by name, was illustrated in his relations with still and newsreel photographers. Although Roosevelt, as a result of infantile paralysis, was unable to walk without assistance, photographers acceded to a "gentleman's agreement" not to snap pictures of him in a wheelchair.

Publishers took particular exception to New Deal legislation that had an impact on their own businesses. Roosevelt's National Recovery Act of 1933, which set up codes of fair practices for industries, was outlawed by the U. S. Supreme Court in 1935, but it promoted the organization of labor and led to the founding of the American Newspaper Guild. The guild was the first union of newspaper personnel not involved in mechanical operations like printing, which long had been unionized and paid better than editorial work.

Led by Heywood Broun, a syndicated columnist, the guild fought for contracts that raised pay and provided job security, sick leave, and other benefits. Based on a standard forty-hour work week, the contracts helped improve the atmosphere of newspaper city rooms, described by novelists as refuges for aged alcoholics worn out by years of long hours and low pay. Higher pay led to the employment of better educated individuals.

Faced with resistance from Hearst and other publishers, guild units went on strike against some twenty newspapers in the 1930s. The Supreme Court in 1937 upheld the right of reporters and other personnel to join the guild when it ruled against the Associated Press for discharging an employee engaged in union activity. The AP argued that the formation of unions in editorial offices was contrary to the constitutional guarantee of freedom of the press. In its ruling, the high court made a distinction between newspapers as a business, subject to general laws governing all businesses, and newspapers as an instrument of free expression operating under the First Amendment.

Six years earlier the Supreme Court had ruled by a 5-4 decision that a Minnesota statute, known as the "Gag Law," which outlawed malicious and scandalous publications by court injunction, violated the freedom of the press clause. The case, *Near v. Minnesota*, involved a disreputable newspaper, the *Saturday Press*, that had attacked public officials. The majority of the justices held that a court injunction represented prior restraint on publication and was illegal under the U. S. Constitution, no matter how unsavory the newspaper might be.

As the Roosevelt administration put through a complicated legislative agenda to deal with the Depression and World War II, newspapers, influenced in part by the popularity of news magazine analysis and radio commentators, turned to interpretative reporting to explain involved economic, political, and social questions. Interpretative reporting offered an approach to news, often provided by syndicates, that stressed interconnections between facts and permitted specialists in areas such as science, economics, and labor to share their expertise with readers. It bore relatively little relationship to the slap-dash race for scoops that remained part of journalistic lore.

Background material for interpretative reports came from government public information offices, which Roosevelt saw as important facets of New Deal activities. To argue the case for relief programs, the administration tried to document the extent of poverty. In part this was because newspapers did not cover the De-

The Roosevelts

Upon Franklin Roosevelt's election as President in 1932, both he and his wife, Eleanor, became accomplished at working with the media. He initiated regular meetings with journalists and appealed effectively to the public through his radio "fireside chats." Mrs. Roosevelt wrote a syndicated newspaper column, "My Day," held press conferences, and made frequent radio broadcasts. She became one of the best known radio personalities in the country during and after the twelve years she was in the White House, from 1933 to 1945.

pression in great detail, hoping for a return of consumer confidence to boost economic conditions. Roosevelt's Farm Security Administration sent out teams of photographers, including Dorothea Lange, Walker Evans, and other well-known professionals, who captured on film the plight of rural Americans affected by drought and dust storms. The same agency also commissioned notable documentary films.

Some Washington correspondents became syndicated political columnists called "pundits," who pontificated on national and international issues. Representing opposite extremes were the somber Walter Lippmann, known as the dean of the pundits, and Drew Pearson, who gave a behind-the-scenes view of Washington political shenanigans. Syndicates also sold comic strips, features, and gossip columns. One of the most popular columnists was Walter Winchell, a Broadway "insider" who offered intimate gossip about show business personalities for both newspapers and radio.

One syndicated columnist occupied a class by herself. First Lady Eleanor Roosevelt wrote a column, "My Day," that ran from 1936 until her death in 1962. It gave an informal, diary-like account of the people she met and the places she went. Like her husband, Eleanor Roosevelt held press conferences, scheduling some 348 during her twelve years in the White House. She also gave sponsored radio broadcasts.

The First Lady limited her press conferences to women reporters only, attempting to help them hold jobs during the Depression by giving them news that, as she expressed it, "the women reporters might write up better than the men."[22] In initiating the press conferences just after her husband's inauguration in 1933, she received guidance from Lorena Hickok, an intimate friend. Hickok left the Associated Press to become an undercover reporter for the Roosevelt administration, touring the country to write confidential reports on relief efforts. In 1934 she accompanied the First Lady and a small group of women reporters on a fact-finding mission to Puerto Rico and the Virgin Islands.

At the time of Franklin Roosevelt's death in 1945, shortly after the start of his fourth term, newspapers retained their status as mass vehicles of news and entertainment. Yet the Roosevelt years had seen enormous changes in the mass media — changes that Franklin and Eleanor Roosevelt had recognized and in which they personally had participated. Newspapers still provided news and advertising oriented to local communities and not available from other sources.

But the public had been primed for change. Fascinated with radio, motion pictures, and still photography, it stood ready for the advent of network television, which World War II delayed. Newspapers had yet to meet their most formidable challenger.

RECOMMENDED READINGS

BOOKS

Abramson, Phyllis Leslie. *Sob Sister Journalism*. Westport, Conn., 1990. The newspaper "sob sister" became prominent during the Thaw murder trial of 1907.

Alexander, Ann Field. *Race Man: The Rise and Fall of the "Fighting Editor" John Mitchell Jr.* Charlottesville, Va., 2002. The editor and publisher of the *Richmond Planet* was a staunch advocate of African Americans' rights who became conservative over time.

Associated Press Reporters. *Breaking News: How the Associated Press Has Covered War, Peace, and Everything Else.* New York, 2007. This collection of accounts tells how AP reporters got many of history's most memorable stories.

Beasley, Maurine H. *Eleanor Roosevelt and the Media: A Public Quest for Self-Fulfillment.* Urbana, Ill., 1987. Eleanor Roosevelt became the most notable woman in American public life by skillful use of the media.

Boylan, James. *Pulitzer's School: Columbia University's School of Journalism, 1903-2003.* New York, 2003. Controversies have marked journalism education since its founding.

Britt, George. *Forty Years, Forty Millions: The Career of Frank A. Munsey.* New York, 1935. Munsey made journalism into a business with a primary concern for money.

Burt, Elizabeth V., ed. *Women's Press Organizations, 1881-1999.* Westport, Conn., 2000. The author provides information on the formation of women's press groups and shows their relationship to changing times.

Cairns, Kathleen A. *Front-Page Women Journalists, 1920-1950.* Lincoln, Neb., 2003. Some female reporters covered major news topics, not just material for the women's pages.

Carlebach, Michael L. *American Photojournalism Comes of Age.* Washington, D.C.,

1997. This history of photojournalism as a profession, covering 1880 through the 1930s, focuses on the news photographer as a witness to history.

Carroll, Brian. *When to Stop the Cheering: The Black Press, the Black Community and the Integration of Professional Baseball.* New York, 2007. The black press over time changed from a booster of Negro league baseball to an objective reporter.

Cochran, Negley. *E.W. Scripps.* New York, 1933. Scripps, the founder of the Scripps Howard chain, was a true public servant.

Cohen, Jeremy. *Congress Shall Make No Law: Oliver Wendell Holmes, The First Amendment, and Judicial Decision Making.* Ames, Iowa, 1989. The noted Supreme Court justice was more concerned with jurisprudence than with free expression.

Cohen, Lester. *The New York Graphic: The World's Zaniest Newspaper.* Philadelphia, 1964. In the 1920s journalism was livelier and more fun than it became shortly afterwards. The *Graphic* was one of the most colorful tabloids of the period.

Covert, Catherine L., and John D. Stevens, eds. *Mass Media Between the Wars: Perceptions of Cultural Tension, 1918-1941.* Syracuse, N.Y., 1984. Essays examine the growth of mass communications and their impact on American society.

Czitrom, Daniel J. *Media and the American Mind: From Morse to McLuhan.* Chapel Hill, N.C., 1982. This survey provides an intellectual history of modern communication rooted in social context.

Emery, Edwin. *History of the American Newspaper Publishers Association.* Minneapolis, 1950. This history explains the newspaper industry from the publishers' viewpoint, including its position on governmental and labor issues.

Fitzpatrick, Vincent. *Gerald W. Johnson: From Southern Liberal to National Conscience.* Baton Rouge, La., 2002. The *Baltimore Sun* editorial writer and essayist loved the South but opposed prejudice and ignorance.

Fowler, Gene. *Timber Line.* New York, 1933. This is a highly entertaining, readable account of Bonfils, Tammen, and the *Denver Post*.

Goldberg, Vicki. *Margaret Bourke-White: A Biography.* Reading, Mass., 1987. Bourke-White's career was important in the evolution of photojournalism.

Good, Howard. *Acquainted with the Night: The Image of Journalists in American Fiction, 1890-1930.* Metuchen, N. J., 1986. The author provides a synopsis of fictional treatment of reporters in relation to social changes.

Griffith, Sally Foreman. *The Autobiography of William Allen White*, 2nd ed., Revised and Abridged. Lawrence, Kan., 1990. This shortened version of White's *Autobiography*, published in 1946 and now one of the classics of American literature, is more accessible to the modern reader.

—. *Home Town News: William Allen White and the Emporia Gazette.* New York, 1989. This biography of the prominent Kansas editor especially emphasizes his political dimension.

Harris Jr., Roy J. *Pulitzer's Gold: Behind the Prize for Public Service Journalism.* Columbia and London: University of Missouri Press, 2007. This book provides accounts behind several of the stories that won the Pulitzer Prize in the public-service category from 1918 to 2007.

Hohenberg, John. *The Pulitzer Prize Story.* New York, 1959. The author, the secretary of the Pulitzer Prizes, tells their history and reprints examples of prize-winning work.

Keever, Beverly Ann Deepe, Carolyn Martindale, and Mary Ann Weston. *U.S. News Coverage of Racial Minorities: A Sourcebook, 1934-1996.* Westport, Conn., 1997. This collection of essays draws together scholarly work assessing news coverage of Americans of African, Native, Asian, Hispanic, and Pacific Islander origin in the mainstream U. S. media.

Knight, Oliver, ed. *I Protest: Selected Disquisitions of E. W. Scripps.* Madison, Wis., 1966. This collection contains a biographical introduction and key documents from Scripps' papers that present his thinking on journalism, politics, and related subjects.

Knowlton, Steven R., and Karen L. Freeman, eds. *Fair & Balanced: A History of Journalistic Objectivity.* Northport, Ala., 2005. Objectivity has been "one of the most troubling yet most fascinating concepts in journalism." Sixteen authors provide accounts of how it was approached from colonial times to the present.

Kobre, Sidney. *Modern American Journalism.* Tallahassee, Fla., 1959. This survey history details the growth of newspapers by region in the first half of the century.

Leidholt, Alexander S. *Editor for Justice: The Life of Louis I. Jaffé.* Baton Rouge, La., 2002. The *Norfolk Virginian-Pilot* editor fought racism.

Marzolf, Marion T. *Up From the Footnote: A History of Woman Journalists.* New York, Hastings House, 1977. Women attempted to be accepted as professional equals

[22]Eleanor Roosevelt, *This I Remember* (New York, 1949), 102.

with men in the field of journalism.

McPhaul, John J. *Deadlines and Monkeyshines: The Fabled World of Chicago Journalism.* Westport, Conn., 1962; rev. ed., 1973. The history of journalism in Chicago had many storied newspapers, editors, and reporters.

Meyer, Karl E., ed. *Pundits, Poets, and Wits: An Omnibus of American Newspaper Columns.* New York, 1990. This anthology contains newspaper columns from colonial times to the present.

Pfaff, Daniel W. *Joseph Pulitzer II and the Post-Dispatch.* University Park, Pa., 1991. This biography of the elder Pulitzer's middle son reveals how the liberal *St. Louis Post-Dispatch* handled major crucial issues from World War I through the 1950s.

Ponder, Stephen. *Managing the Press: Origins of the Media Presidency, 1897-1933.* New York, 1999. U. S. presidents before Franklin Roosevelt set the stage for contemporary news-management practices by the White House.

Procter, Ben. *William Randolph Hearst: The Later Years, 1911-1951.* New York, 2007. Hearst was determined to get his way in public affairs and used his newspapers to succeed.

Rogers, Everett M. *A History of Communication Study: A Biographical Approach.* New York, 1994. The author recounts the establishment of communication study as a formal discipline through biographies of leading communications scholars.

Seldes, George. *Lords of the Press.* New York, 1938. The author was one of the most visible liberal critics of the press during his time. In this critique, he argues that big newspapers were controlled in most instances by wealthy money-makers who were conservative and failed to ensure fair news treatment for labor and for social and economic reforms.

Sloan, Wm. David, and Cheryl S. Wray. *Masterpieces of Reporting.* Northport, Ala., 1998. This anthology of outstanding examples of news writing includes many from the first half of the twentieth century.

Sloan, Wm. David, Julie Hedgepeth, Patricia Place and Kevin Stoker. *The Great Reporters: An Anthology of News Writing at Its Best.* Northport, Ala., 1992. This collection includes biographies of and famous news stories by well-known reporters from World War I through the 1940s.

Sloan, Wm. David, and Laird B. Anderson, eds. *Pulitzer Prize Editorials, 1917-2003,* 3d. Ames, Iowa, 2003. This anthology includes one Pulitzer Prize editorial from each year.

Sloan, Wm. David, Valerie McCrary, and Johanna Cleary, eds. *The Best of Pulitzer Prize News Writing.* Columbus, Oh., 1986. This anthology includes eighty-two Pulitzer-Prize-winning news stories selected for the quality of their writing.

Smith, Wilda M., and Eleanor A. Bogart. *The Wars of Peggy Hull: The Life and Times of a War Correspondent.* El Paso, Tex., 1991. Hull was a pioneer woman foreign correspondent in the early twentieth century.

Snyder, Louis L., and Richard B. Morris, eds. *A Treasury of Great Reporting,* 2nd ed. New York, 1962. Of the many anthologies of news reporting, this is one of the best. Including articles from the Zenger trial in 1735 to the early 1960s, it is particularly strong on articles from the 1920s to 1940s.

Startt, James D. *Woodrow Wilson and the Press: Prelude to the Presidency.* New York, 2004. Wilson's career illustrates the relationship of political figures to the modern mass media system.

Stevens, John D. *Sensationalism and the New York Press.* New York, 1991. From the penny-press era to the present, New York City readers have been particularly interested in tabloid journalism.

Stoltzfus, Duane C. S. *Freedom from Advertising: E. W. Scripps's Chicago Experiment.* Champaign, Ill., 2007. Scripps' attempt to publish the *Day Book,* a newspaper without advertising, failed within five years because it never got enough subscriptions to sustain it.

Stott, William. *Documentary Expression and Thirties America.* New York, 1973. Social conditions were documented in spite of opposition from interests that preferred not to make a record of the Depression.

Suggs, Henry Lewis. *P. B. Young, Newspaperman.* Charlottesville, Va., 1988. Young, publisher of the *Norfolk Journal and Guide* from 1910 to 1954, was sometimes called "Dean of the Negro Press." A founder of the NAACP, he nevertheless was cautious and favored black accomodationism.

Swanson, Walter S. J. *The Thin Gold Watch, A Personal History of the Newspaper Copleys.* New York, 1964. Ira Copley was one of the first 20th-century businessmen to recognize that the newspaper was a business that could make a profit.

Teel, Leonard Ray. *The Public Press, 1900-1945.* Westport, Conn., 2006. Faced with a variety of challenges, the press moved "toward a vision of professionalism and public responsibility." This book is the best general history of journalism during the period.

Trimble, Vance H. *The Astonishing Mr. Scripps: The Turbulent Life of America's Penny Press Lord.* Ames, Iowa, 1992. The author provides a comprehensive biography of the penny press baron of the late nineteenth and early twentieth centuries.

Underwood, Agness. *Newspaperwoman.* New York, 1949. Underwood's autobiography details her career from her early days as a telephone operator at the *Los Angeles Record* to becoming a reporter for the *Herald-Express* and eventually becoming its first female city editor.

Villard, Oswald Garrison. *The Disappearing Daily: Chapters in American Newspaper Evolution.* New York, 1944. The author offers a liberal criticism that too many newspapers had given up crusading in the interests of the public, growing concerned instead with "crass materialism."

Williamson, Samuel T. *Imprint of a Publisher: The Story of Frank Gannett and His Newspapers.* New York, 1948. In a great success story, Gannett was a poor boy who went from rags to riches through buying and merging newspapers.

Winfield, Betty Houchin. *FDR and the News Media.* Urbana, Ill., 1990. Franklin D. Roosevelt tried to manage the news during critical periods in American history.

ARTICLES

Althaus, Scott. "The Forgotten Role of the Global Newsreel Industry in the Long Transition from Text to Television." *International Journal of Press/Politics* 15 (March 2010): 193-218. Newsreels were the first step from a text-based information culture to the visual-based information culture that arose in the post-war years.

Asher, Brad. "The Professional Vision: Conflicts Over Journalism Education, 1900-1950." *American Journalism* 11 (1994): 304-20. Journalism schools were part of a trend toward professionalization, but newspapers did not embrace the concept.

Beasley, Maurine H. "Lorena A. Hickok: Journalism Influence on Eleanor Roosevelt." *Journalism Quarterly* 57 (1980): 281-6. Hickok, who first covered Mrs. Roosevelt for the Associated Press, was important in advising her on press relations.

Bekken, Jon. "The Chicago Newspaper Scene: An Ecological Perspective." *Journalism & Mass Communication Quarterly* 74 (1997): 490-500. A variety of specialized and foreign-language newspapers coexisted with the English-language dailies in Chicago from 1880 to 1930.

Bennion, Sherilyn Cox. "Reform Agitation in the American Periodical Press, 1920-29." *Journalism Quarterly* 48 (1971): 692-9, 713. Mass magazines of the 1920s were reluctant to bring up subjects related to social reforms because their readers were not interested in such topics.

Brazil, John R. "Murder Trials, Murder and Twenties America." *American Quarterly* 33, 2 (1981): 163-84. Tabloids competed for public attention with cheap literature and movies.

Christians, Clifford G. "Fifty Years of Scholarship in Media Ethics." *Journal of Communication* 27 (Autumn 1977): 19-29. Definitions of ethics changed from the 1920s to the 1930s.

Del Castillo, Richard Griswold. "The Mexican Revolution and the Spanish-Language Press in the Borderlands," *Journalism History* 4 (Summer 1977): 42-7. Mexican-American editors helped promote an emerging sense of nationalism in Mexico.

Digby-Junger, Richard. "The Guardian, Crisis, Messenger, and Negro World: The Early- 20th-Century Black Radical Press." *Howard Journal of Communications* 9:3 (1998): 263-82. The three black newspapers advocated change in the political and social systems.

Gottlieb, Agnes Hooper. "Grit Your Teeth, Then Learn To Swear: Women in Journalistic Careers, 1850-1926." *American Journalism* 18 (2001): 53-72. Female journalists faced various obstacles in the newspaper field.

Harrison, Stanley L. "'The Wayward Press' Revisited: The Contributions of Robert Benchley." *Journalism History* 19 (1993): 19-25. From 1927 to 1939, Benchley used his "Wayward Press" column in the *New Yorker* to uphold high standards.

Johnson, Thomas J., and Wayne Wanta, with John T. Bird and Cindy Lee. "Exploring FDR's Relationship with the Press." *Political Communication* 12 (1995):

157-72. Roosevelt used the press for agenda setting.

Kaszuba, Dave. "Bringing Women to the Sports Pages: Margaret Goss and the 1920s." *American Journalism* 23:2 (2006):13-44. Margaret Goss, the first female American sportswriter, covered women's sports at the *New York Herald Tribune* in 1924 and 1925.

Kaul, Arthur J., and Joseph P. McKerns. "The Dialectic Ecology of the Newspaper." *Critical Studies in Mass Communication* 2 (1985): 217-33. The newspaper industry became an oligopoly.

Lewis, Norman P. "From Cheesecake to Chief: Newspaper Editors' Slow Acceptance of Women." *American Journalism* 25:2 (2008): 33-56. For much of the period from 1925 to 1988, male newspaper editors "saw women as sexual objects and housewives whose fragile and emotional natures left them ... unsuited for newsroom roles beyond the women's sections." Editors were more sexist than the general population was.

Mangun, Kimberley. "The (Oregon) *Advocate*: Boosting the Race and Portland, Too." *American Journalism* 23 (2006): 7-34. The black press in the Pacific Northwest did an important job of keeping its readership informed in the early 1900s and of helping build a sense of community.

Mirando, Joe. "Lessons on Ethics in News Reporting Textbooks, 1867-1997." *Journal of Mass Media Ethics* 13 (1998): 26-39. Textbooks on reporting and news writing devoted little attention to matters of ethics and often overlooked important moral and intellectual questions.

Olasky, Marvin N. "Journalists and the Great Monkey Trial." 217-29 in Wm. David Sloan, ed., *Media and Religion in American History*. Northport, Ala., 2000. Reporters covering the Scopes trial considered themselves open-minded, but they were opposed to fundamental Christianity and thus interpreted the trial and its participants to fit their prejudices, giving biased and inaccurate accounts.

Perry, Earnest. "We Want In: The African American Press's Negotiation for a White House Correspondent." *American Journalism* 20:3 (2003): 31-47. African American journalists worked to cover the White House. The issue took greater importance during WWII as the government sought the support of African American newspapers for the war effort.

Ponder, Stephen. "That Delightful Relationship: Presidents and White House Correspondents in the 1920s." *American Journalism* 14 (1997): 164-81. Management of the press by executive officials became institutionalized during the decade.

Rivas-Rodriguez, Maggie. "Ignacio E. Lozano: The Mexican Exile Publisher Who Conquered San Antonio and Los Angeles." *American Journalism* 21:1 (2004): 75-90. Lozano began the first successful large Latino newspapers in San Antonio and Los Angeles.

Ross, Felicia G. Jones, and Joseph P. McKerns. "Depression in 'The Promised Land': The *Chicago Defender* Discourages Migration, 1929-1940." *American Journalism* 21:1 (2004): 55-74. When job opportunities declined during the Great Depression, the *Defender* discouraged southern blacks from moving north.

Schiller, Dan. "An Historical Approach to Objectivity and Professionalism in American News Reporting." *Journal of Communication* 29 (Autumn 1979): 46-57. By the turn of the century, objectivity was increasingly threatened, becoming "professionalized" and incorporated into ethical codes in hopes of preserving it.

Sloan, Wm. David. "Historians and the American Press, 1900-1945: Working Profession or Big Business?" *American Journalism* 3 (1986): 154-66. This essay examines how historians have explained the press of the period.

Smethers, J. Steven. "Pounding Brass for the Associated Press: Delivering News by Telegraph in a Pre-Teletype Era." *American Journalism* 19:2 (2002): 13-30. The AP employed 1,500 telegraphers to send stories to member newspapers.

Smith, Carol, and Carolyn Stewart Dyer. "Taking Stock, Placing Orders: A Historiographical Essay on the Business History of the Newspaper." *Journalism Monographs* 132 (1992). The authors examine how historians have treated newspaper economics and business practices.

Smith, Reed W. "Southern Journalists and Lynching: The Statesboro Case Study." *Journalism & Communication Monographs* 7:2 (2005). The author uses the case of the 1904 Statesboro, Georgia, white mob murder of two black men, Paul Reed and Will Cato, to examine how journalism influenced lynching.

Stevens, John D. "The Black Press Looks at 1920's Journalism." *Journalism History* 7 (1980): 109-13. The black press "had always been a 'fighting press,' and while it did not abandon that opinion-leader role, it turned more and more to news as its staple" in the 1920s. Black newspapers became "viable businesses."

Strother, T. Ella. "The Black Image in the Chicago 'Defender,' 1905-1975." *Journalism History* 4 (Winter 1977-78): 137-41, 156. The *Defender* presented a positive black image throughout the newspaper although it headlined anti-social behavior to sell newspapers.

Sullins, William S., and Paul Parsons. "Roscoe Dunjee: Crusading Editor of Oklahoma's 'Black Dispatch,' 1915-1955." *Journalism Quarterly* 69 (1992): 204-13. The weekly newspaper editor was a crusading civil rights activist who urged peaceful change.

Teel, Leonard Ray. "W. A. Scott and the *Atlanta World*." *American Journalism* 6 (1989): 158-78. The success of the *World*, the first African-American daily newspaper in the United States, was the result of the owner's business sense.

Tripp, Bernell. "The Black Media, 1865-Present: Liberal Crusaders or Defenders of Tradition?" in Wm. David Sloan, ed., *Perspectives on Mass Communication History* (Hillsdale, N.J., 1991), 172-83. This historiographical chapter examines the various ways historians have explained the black press.

Weigle, Clifford F. "The Young Scripps Editor: Keystone of E.W.'s 'System.'" *Journalism Quarterly* 41 (1964): 360-6. Scripps got promising young men to start new papers by directing them to a city, advancing them capital, and then leaving them alone and allowing them to buy a share of the paper. Many were so inspired by these principles that they worked tirelessly on starvation budgets.

16

The Media and Reform

1900 – 1917

By 1900, the United States had become an industrial nation. Its *laissez faire* approach to the economy had allowed aggressive entrepreneurs to gain not only great financial power, but influence on the government also. From local town halls to the halls of Congress, they seemed to have many officials in their pockets, and they were allowed to operate with little oversight. At the same time, reformers were at work on behalf of social and legal changes. The role that journalists and magazine writers came to play in the movement for reform set the tone for much of the mass media in the first several years of the twentieth century.

The media have long been a valuable resource for reformers. The same is just as true, too, of those interested in forestalling reform. They exerted a great deal of influence, both direct and indirect, over newspapers and magazines. This paradoxical relationship between the press and reform can be seen in the Progressive era of American history, roughly the period from the inauguration of Theodore Roosevelt as president in 1901 until the United States entered World War I in 1917. "The fundamental critical achievement of American Progressivism was the business of exposure," historian Richard Hofstadter has written, "and journalism was the chief occupational source of its creative writers. It is hardly an exaggeration to say that the Progressive mind was characteristically a journalistic mind, and that its characteristic contribution was that of the socially responsible reporter-reformer."[1]

One brand of journalism these reporter-reformers practiced earned the title "muckraking." Expressing his displeasure with the 1906 magazine series "The Treason of the Senate," President Roosevelt compared the over-zealous reporters to the man with the muckrake in John Bunyan's *Pilgrim's Progress*. In remarks before a club of Washington, D.C., journalists, Roosevelt said the man could "look no way but downward, with muckrake in his hands; ... was offered a celestial crown for his muckrake, but ... would neither look up nor regard the crown he was offered, but continued to rake to himself the filth of the floor."[2] Roosevelt's la-

bel stuck. Indeed, some journalists wore it as a badge of honor.

Muckrakers, although the most visible reform journalists, were hardly alone in their efforts. Socialist and labor groups sponsored newspapers that explored the harmful effects of the new economic order, the feminist press criticized unjust social arrangements, and some civic improvement associations found newspapers ready allies for their municipal reforms. Still, muckraking marked a new departure in reform journalism. For the most part, muckraking exposés appeared in national consumer magazines. Hence, they were aimed at the middle class and could tackle a wide range of topics. Typically, muckraking journalists and magazines claimed independence from interest groups, although many worked loosely with insurgent Republicans and reform-minded Democrats. The better articles marshaled details unearthed in thorough investigations. Significantly, the exposés derived their power from well-selected facts, not the forceful polemics characteristic of earlier journalistic essays. For a relatively short period at the beginning of the century, then, reform journalism in mainstream magazines flourished as never before or since.

The concerted journalistic effort during the Progressive era was a by-product of developments in the mass media, particularly the magazine industry. The ultimate question, perhaps, is whether the press succeeded in promoting worthwhile reforms.

THE PROGRESSIVE MOVEMENT

Although Roosevelt's ascension to the presidency often is cited as marking the beginning of the Progressive era, another event of symbolic importance occurred at about the same time. In April 1901, United States Steel became the first American firm incorporated with more than $1 billion in capital stock. The event had been preceded by several decades of growth of giant industries. The power associated with such economic concentration was, in the eyes of the Progressives, wielded without concern for the public good. Government regulation of the industrial behemoths was virtually unknown, although Populists in the West and South had

[1]Richard Hofstadter, *The Age of Reform: From Bryan to F.D.R.* (New York, Vintage Edition, 1955), 186.

[2]Theodore Roosevelt, speech, April 14, 1906. The complete text of the speech may be found on the "American Rhetoric: Top 100 Speeches" website at http://www.americanrhetoric.com/speeches/teddyrooseveltmuckrake.htm.

been fighting the railroads, banks, and grain companies for decades. The Progressive movement picked up elements of the Populist agenda but tended to concentrate more on problems connected with urban America.

The specific goals varied among the individuals and groups that assembled under the banner of Progressivism, but a few reforms were shared by most. Curbing the excesses of big business, principally through government regulation, was high on the agenda. Progressives worried about business corrupting the political process. Thus, they sought to reduce the political influence of special interests by making government more responsive to the electorate. Ameliorating social problems associated with industrial, urban America occupied the attention of many. Of interest to fewer Progressives but still noteworthy were concerns about racial discrimination.

Despite the generally liberal nature of the Progressive movement, it did embody conservative elements. For example, some historians have argued that the reform the Progressives wrought enhanced the competitive edge of big business, for federal regulations tended to eliminate competition in some industries and gave remaining firms greater control of markets. Other historians accurately point out that all but a few Progressives, far from being wild-eyed radicals, subscribed to basic American values — responsible corporate capitalism, traditional morals, individualism, representative democracy, and social order. Their acceptance of the basic structure of the American political and economic system limited the extent and nature of change that they envisioned — but it also made them more effective. Rarely did they advocate sweeping structural changes in the system. Had they done so, even if they had wished, radical proposals would have caused more harm than good, most historians have concluded.[3]

FORERUNNERS OF MUCKRAKING

Reformers had used the press as an instrument of change long before the advent of the Progressive movement. Abolitionists launched an antislavery pamphlet campaign in the 1830s that provoked a violent backlash. Later in the century, women suffragists, temperance groups, and other reform movements sponsored publications to promote their causes and to communicate with like-minded citizens throughout the country. But these efforts to communicate messages of reform suffered one major handicap — for the most part they were read by the already converted and failed to reach large, mass audiences.

An important precursor of muckraking was the reform press of agrarian activists in the 1880s and 1890s. Populists and the Farmers' Alliance waged much of their battle against railroads, banks, and food processors on the pages of their newspapers. Many pro-

moted alternative economic structures such as agricultural cooperatives. In 1891, the editors formed the National Reform Press Association, which eventually attracted more than 1,000 members. Although most of these papers were small weeklies, at least one claimed a circulation approaching 100,000.

At the same time, urban citizens' groups were forging loose alliances with sympathetic city newspapers. These reformers understood the new environment of large cities with their mass-circulation papers. The press was the best means to communicate with disparate groups in urban areas that now were too large and socially complex for personal contacts to suffice. In a sense, mass communication took the place, at least in part, of communication through city-wide political machines. For example, the *Chicago Daily News* and *Chicago Tribune* helped put problems of transportation, utilities, and pollution on the political agenda. But elsewhere (St. Louis, for instance) most of the press was indifferent or opposed to reform.[4]

Much of what the reporter-reformers did in the early twentieth century built on venerable traditions in American journalism. Police courts and tenement life had regularly furnished stories since the 1830s. Occasionally reporters had entered prisons, asylums, and other institutions to describe conditions. Such excursions seemed to be motivated as much by a desire to titillate readers with sensational details as to expose inhumane conditions. The sins of big corporations had been chronicled, too, long before the Progressive movement. Charles F. Adams, Jr., had exposed some of the machinations of the Erie Railroad and associated financiers as early as 1868. W. T. Stead cleverly titled his 1894 study of Chicago's seamy underbelly *If Christ Came to Chicago*. And in the same year Henry Demarest Lloyd published *Wealth Against Commonwealth*, a weighty book that anticipated much of the later muckraking. Although newspaper reporting was not part of concerted campaigns to reform urban life, the better writers captured the plight of the disadvantaged in big, impersonal cities. There were also precedents for editorial leadership on behalf of city improvement. Joseph Pulitzer campaigned in his *New York World* to abate the sufferings of the poor, while in Kansas City William Rockhill Nelson and his *Star* promoted plans to beautify the city.

Some historians have pointed to B.O. Flowers' *Arena* as a prototype for later muckraking magazines. In 1895 it had begun publishing articles focusing on conditions in need of reform. Harry Vrooman's "Crime and the Enforcement of the Law," for example, dealt with the issue of how big business helped corrupt municipal government. Early *Arena* articles, however, tended to be more like sermons than investigative reports, as the later muckraking articles would be. By the end of the nineteenth century, though, *Arena* — along with magazines such as *McClure's*, *Cosmopolitan*, and *Century* — was frequently running articles dealing with social conditions in need of solutions.

The nineteenth-century reform tradition culminated in the work of Jacob Riis, one of the first important photojournalists and

---

[3]See Gabriel Kolko, *The Triumph of Conservatism* (New York, 1963), 1-9, for the argument that the Progressive movement had more conservative consequences than most historians imagined. Hofstadter, *The Age of Reform*, 196, notes that the Progressives were hardly revolutionaries. For an incisive analysis of historians' discussions of muckraking, see Wm. David Sloan, "The Muckrakers, 1901-1917: Defenders of Conservatism or Liberal Reformers?" in *Perspectives on Mass Communication History* (Hillsdale, N.J., 1991), 271-82.

[4]David P. Nord, *Newspapers and New Politics: Midwestern Municipal Reform, 1890-1900* (Ann Arbor, Mich., 1981).

Jacob Riis, Photojournalist Reformer
In the 1880s and 1890s, reporter Jacob Riis began photographing the squalid conditions in which many poor New Yorkers lived. The subjects of this photograph were three "Street Arabs," homeless boys living in the Mulberry Bend district. Riis' work led to the renovation of the district, one of the worst in New York City. His reform efforts also foreshadowed the work of the muckrakers in the twentieth century.

a reporter who influenced muckrakers of the Progressive era. Born in Denmark in 1849, he immigrated to the United States in 1870 and held a number of odd jobs before becoming a reporter. He covered the police for the *New York Tribune* and thus saw firsthand the consequences of life in the city's poorer neighborhoods. Even though many of his stories dealt with people who had run afoul of the law, he tried to affirm the humanity of his subjects and assure his middle-class readers that the newly arrived immigrants wanted the same kind of life they enjoyed. He then expanded his purview to include the city's health department. He began accompanying inspectors as they made nightly rounds of overcrowded flop houses, but his newspaper stories, Riis felt, made no impression. It then occurred to him to take photographs at night using dangerous flash techniques. In his autobiography, *The Making of an American*, he described how he and the inspectors would enter a room crowded with sleepers, ignite the flash powder to take the picture, and trigger a panic. Twice his flash set fire to houses and once to himself. Many of his photographs were collected as engraved drawings in the book *How the Other Half Lives* (1890), and his work led to the renovation of one of the worst areas, Mulberry Bend. Like many of the reporter-reformers who followed, Riis combined his observational powers with literary techniques. He even wrote short stories that were little more than thinly disguised versions of his newspaper reports.

In fact, the move toward realism in literature left its mark on muckraking. Literary realism in the United States started with the works of Mark Twain, Stephen Crane, and William Dean Howells. In 1894 Crane had published an article about the conditions in coal mines in *McClure's* magazine that had several of the hallmarks of later muckraking. Realism's most extreme adherents were such writers as Jack London and Theodore Dreiser. All these men had worked on newspapers; and, in varying degrees, what they had seen as reporters shaped their outlook on life. Dreiser is a good example. Having spent his boyhood mostly in small Indiana towns and in the medium-sized city of Terre Haute, he first experienced the world as a newspaperman in Chicago. He covered both the inner-city poor and industrialists, two extremes of

American society. The contrasts troubled him and influenced the tone of his novels. Characters in such works as *Sister Carrie* (1900) were buffeted by social and economic forces over which they had no control. Frank Norris' *The Octopus* (1901) made a fictional indictment of predatory railroads akin to later factual stories. Many muckrakers, aspiring novelists themselves, were influenced by this major current in American literature.

MUCKRAKING MOVES TO MAGAZINES

Muckraking was a distinctly twentieth-century phenomenon in at least one respect: it was closely associated with the rise of nationally circulated, inexpensive magazines that reached millions of readers. National magazines were ideally suited to the purposes of muckrakers. They permitted a more developed and coherent presentation of complex facts than was possible in daily newspapers. Much muckraking endeavored to show broad patterns that transcended any one city or state. Thus, national magazines were the logical medium. Other stories dealt with national institutions — Congress and big business were two favorites — and needed to be placed before a national audience. Extensive research often was needed to document charges, and daily newspapers lacked the resources to allow reporters to undertake such digging. Finally, local scandals could be broken by national publications, whereas community interests might pressure newspapers to remain silent.

Muckraking can be viewed at least in part as a by-product of structural changes in the magazine industry. Until the late nineteenth century, most magazines were very expensive or specialized. A few religious magazines attained huge circulations but were limited in scope. The more eclectic magazines, on the other hand, set subscription rates so high that they restricted readership. Changes began in the late 1800s. Underlying the emergence of general-audience magazines — the first true national media of mass communication in the United States — were basic changes in the nation's economy.

Manufacturing was becoming the economy's driving engine, and the hallmark of manufacturing was the cheap production of

**Ida Tarbell Exposes
Standard Oil**

Ida Tarbell made her reputation with magazine biographies of Napoleon and Abraham Lincoln. Her exposé on the Standard Oil Company began as a biography of its head, John D. Rockefeller. More than four years of research and writing went into the articles. Tarbell used old law suits, reports of congressional investigations, and other public documents as well as a few confidential sources to ground her story. *McClure's* printed the first of the series' eighteen parts in November 1902, helping *McClure's* assume the leadership role in exposure journalism. The series was so popular that it initiated the flood of muckraking articles that filled American magazines over the next decade.

goods for mass consumption. Accompanying this change was the growth of a national distribution network, based largely on railroads. The retail sector of the economy shifted, too, from exclusively local, independently owned outlets to national chains and department stores. Together, these developments brought about the mass marketing of goods, which depended on advertising for the large volume of sales needed to sustain huge capital investments. Beginning chiefly in the 1890s, advertisers sought national markets, and inexpensive general-circulation magazines provided the best vehicle. Ironically, this economic transformation produced both the social problems that the muckrakers critiqued as well as the means the reporter-reformers used to investigate them. In a further irony, exposés often appeared alongside advertisements for products created by the very system they were attacking.

While economic changes provided the stimulus for large-circulation magazines, technological improvements made their publication feasible. In the 1880s and '90s, magazines began adopting the rotary presses that had revolutionized newspaper publishing. Switching from flatbed to rotary presses increased the potential output of some magazines tenfold. Also important to attracting larger audiences was the artwork that magazines could offer. The old methods of reproducing drawings, especially in color, were time-consuming and expensive. Sketches had to be engraved by hand. To add color, *Godey's Lady's Book* hired 150 women to tint illustrations. But by 1893, rotary presses could handle multicolor reproductions. The introduction of more sophisticated and expensive technology provided another impetus for publishers to seek massive audiences. Huge capital investments were needed to equip printing plants, and the costs could best be recouped through large circulations.

In addition to improved technology, delivery systems — both public and private — extended the market of periodicals.

Congress, through the Post Office Act of 1879, bestowed the fullest mailing privilege on magazines — the low rates long enjoyed by newspapers. The American News Company virtually monopolized the distribution of non-local newspapers and magazines carried outside the mails. It served the thousands of newsstands that increasingly carried magazines as the century drew to a close.

McClure's and Ida Tarbell

On this foundation of printing technology, economic supports, and delivery systems, a few enterprising publishers began issuing magazines, usually priced at 10¢, for larger audiences that could never afford the more typical 25¢ or 30¢ subscriptions. Some of the new publishers, such as Frank Munsey, simply applied principles of mass production and distribution to magazines in order to make a profit. Others, though partly impelled by the profit motive, also hoped to reach an untapped class of readers with interesting fare. S. S. McClure was one, and through the magazine bearing his name he provided a forum for many muckraking journalists.

A native of Ireland who had emigrated to Indiana as a boy, McClure ran a newspaper feature syndicate with his partner John S. Phillips for eight years. In 1893 they launched *McClure's Magazine* as an outlet for feature material they already owned. They initially invested $7,300. From the first number, the magazine made liberal use of illustrations and sold for 15¢ a copy. Unfortunately, it appeared just as a general financial decline started. Circulation hovered between 30,000 and 40,000, and *McClure's* stayed alive only through the loans of friends, contributors, and advertisers.

The magazine found its formula for success with the publication of "Napoleon," a well-illustrated feature by Ida M. Tarbell, who became one of the most important muckrakers. This biography boosted *McClure's* circulation and was followed by a series on the "Early Life of Lincoln" in 1895. With circulation rising, *McClure's* lowered its price to 10¢, joining the two other major illustrated ten-cent monthlies, *Munsey's* and *Cosmopolitan*. *Munsey's* sold more copies; but *McClure's* attracted more advertising. By 1896, it claimed to carry more pages of advertising than any other magazine in history.

McClure's most noteworthy contribution began in 1902, when it carried the first major magazine pieces identified as muckraking journalism. The January 1903 issue recognized that something unusual was happening. A prefatory piece editorialized:

> We did not plan it so; it is a coincidence that this number contains three arraignments of American character such as should make every one of us stop and think. "The Shame of Minneapolis," the current chapter of the history of Standard Oil by Miss Tarbell, Mr. Ray Stannard Baker's "The Right to Work" — they might all have been called "The American Contempt of Law." Capitalists, Workingmen, Politicians, Citizens — all breaking the law or letting it be broken. Who is there left to uphold it?... There is no one left — none but all of us.[5]

The three articles in the issue outlined concerns that were central to the Progressive reformers, and the closing injunction — that all citizens should become involved — was the movement's rallying cry.

Tarbell was the first to begin working on muckraking articles for *McClure's*, though hers were not the first to be published. Building on her earlier successes, the sketches of Napoleon and Lincoln, she persuaded her editors to let her undertake another biography of sorts — a serialized history of John D. Rockefeller's Standard Oil Company. Her series capitalized on two interests of American readers: the infatuation with the rags-to-riches stories of millionaires and the growing unease over the increasing power of trusts and combinations in big business. Tarbell's father had been an independent oil producer who suffered from the business practices of Standard Oil.

A painstaking researcher, Tarbell spent more than four years gathering information and writing her stories on Standard Oil. Fortunately, the magazine allowed her the time and the resources — nearly $50,000 — to pursue the story. She worked like a historian, poring over the evidence, mostly public documents available to anyone with the patience to sift through them. Old lawsuits and the reports of congressional investigations furnished many of the details. She made only sparing use of information from confidential sources, unlike some investigative reporters today. In an eighteen-part series, she detailed the illegal or at least underhanded practices that Standard Oil used to drive competitors out of business. Shedding light on some of the ignoble journalism of the day, she found that Standard Oil's public relations agency had contracted with at least 110 Ohio newspapers to run editorials and "news" favorable to the company.[6]

What did her history-exposé accomplish? It prompted government investigations of Standard Oil, leading to the 1911 U. S. Supreme Court ruling that dissolved the giant corporation into smaller companies. When government investigators retraced the ground that Tarbell had covered, they verified most of her important allegations. Rockefeller responded to Tarbell's and others' characterizations of him by employing public relations counsels to restore his reputation. Tarbell's labors yielded rewards for her employer, too. *McClure's* circulation climbed, a result, at least in part, of "The History of Standard Oil."

LINCOLN STEFFENS AND "THE SHAME OF THE CITIES"

While Tarbell was readying her work for publication, a colleague at *McClure's*, Lincoln Steffens, published "Tweed Days in St. Louis" in October 1902. This first installment in what became "The Shame of the Cities" series was hardly distingushed, especially in comparison to Tarbell's work. But Tarbell credited it with being the "first muckraking article."[7] Whether it was is open to debate, and arguments over historical "firsts" are usually unproductive. Without a doubt, the series was one of the most important contributions to muckraking journalism, and in many ways Steffens epitomized the reporter-reformer of the Progressive era. Because he left a detailed and engaging *Autobiography* (1931) — one of the best written by any American — it is possible to trace his method of investigation and reflections on his own work.

Born in 1866 in San Francisco, Steffens enjoyed the amenities of an upper-middle-class life. He majored in history at the University of California-Berkeley (after failing the admissions test on his first try) and then began graduate studies in Germany. In 1892, following three years of study and travel in Europe, he went to New York, where, using his father's connections, he landed a reporting job on the *Evening Post*. He encountered some of the leading Wall Street figures of the day and began honing his interviewing skills. He also covered the police beat and became acquainted with New York's reformers, including Theodore Roosevelt. Although working on the *Evening Post* exposed him to a world he never had experienced, he chafed under the heavy-handed editing of E. L. Godkin.

Steffens left the *Post* in 1897 to become editor of the *New York Commercial Advertiser*, a position he hoped would permit him greater latitude. He assembled a group of talented writers, not reporters, as he fondly recalled, and freed them to capture the life of the city in their graceful prose. Many of them went on to distinguished literary careers. During Steffens' tenure on the *Commercial Advertiser*, a friend he had met while studying in Germany left him an inheritance that, through careful investment, Steffens used as the basis for the financial security and editorial independence he enjoyed the rest of his life.

He left the *Commercial Advertiser* in 1901 to devote himself to writing fiction, his first love. His wife already had published a

[5]Samuel McClure, Editorial, *McClure's Magazine*, January 1903.
[6]Ida M. Tarbell, *All In The Day's Work: An Autobiography* (New York, 1939), 202-53.
[7]Ibid., 59.

Lincoln Steffens and Cities' Shame
Corruption in the governments of some of America's cities in the early 1900s surpassed that of New York City's earlier Tammany Hall. Following Lincoln Steffens' exposé of Minneapolis in *McClure's Magazine* in 1903, the mayor resigned, and many officials were prosecuted. Steffens continued his series in St. Louis again, then Pittsburgh, Philadelphia, Chicago, and New York. He began his research by looking for any patterns or discrepancies in the structure of the city's politics. With this information he was able to evaluate the state of the city's government. His goal in his exposés was to reform modern urban life on the ideals of Christianity. "I have been contending all my life," he wrote at the end of his autobiography, "and always with God."

novel, but that attainment eluded him. So he joined *McClure's Magazine* as managing editor. Restless with life in the office, he traveled in pursuit of stories. He noticed that newspapers sometimes focused on corruption in their communities; but, with a glut of other news, accounts in the papers often failed to make an impression with readers. He reasoned that similar stories developed comprehensively in a monthly magazine might prove to be a more powerful stimulus for change. His chance to test the idea came while he was in St. Louis, where a courageous district attorney was trying to prosecute corrupt city officials. Steffens commissioned a local writer, Claude Wetmore, to prepare an article for *McClure's*. Wetmore, however, feared local pressures if he published all the facts he uncovered; so Steffens added his own name to the byline to diffuse responsibility. Wetmore's trepidation probably explains why reporters sometimes shied away from exposing corruption in local papers where outside pressure could more readily be exerted on them.

Steffens' second installment, "The Shame of Minneapolis," appeared in the January 1903 *McClure's*, an issue that attracted so much attention that it sold out. "The Shame of Minneapolis" was also the first muckraking article that Steffens researched himself, exercising the interviewing skills he had cultivated as a newspaper reporter. He went to Minneapolis when the broad outlines of corruption were already well known. He talked to reporters for the local papers who often knew much more than they put in print. Typically, he would also draw out the grafters themselves, sometimes playing the role of a knowledgeable police reporter, other times ingenuously marveling at the criminals' accomplishments. Whatever guise he adopted, he refrained from treating his subjects in a condescending manner, and he never passed judgment or moralized in their presence. In short, he developed a rapport with his subjects.[8]

The corruption revolved around Minneapolis Mayor Albert Alonzo Ames. He had served three terms as mayor in the 1880s, both as a Republican and as a Democrat. He was, by some accounts, the most popular man in the city. After winning the election again in 1900, he and his cohorts set about creating a system of graft eclipsing that of his previous administrations. On inaugural day, he appointed his brother chief of police and dismissed 107 of the 225 policemen. As mayor-elect, Ames had been screening replacements, personally interviewing all the finalists. With hand-picked officers in all key police department posts, he and his lieutenants devised various schemes to gather graft. Criminals were invited to Minneapolis to work under the auspices of the police. Saloons, brothels, and gambling houses flourished by paying for police protection. The police even guarded burglars as they worked, and they dissuaded victims of rigged gambling games from filing complaints.

Two Minneapolis newspapers, the *Journal* and the *Times*, had opposed Ames' election. The *Tribune*, a recipient of city printing contracts, was a quasi-official organ of the administration. As crime mounted, the *Journal* and *Times* intimated that the police were involved, but such stories appeared too infrequently for the average reader to sense the extent of the graft. An aggressive grand jury eventually uncovered the corruption. Empaneled in April 1902, the grand jury decided to work with the assistant prosecutor to tackle the Ames gang. The chief prosecutor was afraid, and prominent citizens urged the jurors to drop the investigation. As the grand jury heard testimony, stories began appearing in the *Journal* and *Times* linking the mayor to police graft. The pro-administration *Tribune* rallied to Ames' defense until a ledger was produced that showed his share of the take. Even the *Tribune* then had to concede that "there is a state of affairs in the municipal gov-

[8]This discussion of "The Shame of Minneapolis" is based on Richard B. Kielbowicz, "The Limits of the Press as an Agent of Reform: Minneapolis, 1900-1905," *Journalism Quarterly* 59 (1982): 21-7 and 170.

ernment of Minneapolis that discounts anything Tammany Hall ever dreamed of."[9]

The Ames administration crumbled. Detectives and police captains were convicted or fled the city, and Ames resigned. The president of the city council assumed duties as mayor and began enforcing ordinances against prostitution and gambling. But the tangible results of the grand jury's digging and the newspaper's coverage were limited. Existing laws were better enforced, but ineffectual statutes were not rewritten. Despite massive publicity linking Ames to the graft — some of which he admitted in court — four juries failed to convict him, probably because of his popularity. Vested interests that profited from the Ames regime, including church-going landlords who collected rent from brothels, resisted reforms. The possibility of alternative government structures — for example, a city manager form — was never raised in the columns of the city's papers. Driving the guilty from office, a comparatively modest change, was the principal improvement.

Steffens did not unearth the story. His contribution was to synthesize the uneven newspaper coverage, add details from interviews with several of the principal figures, and elevate the story to a national arena. Publication of the story in *McClure's* came at a critical moment. Interest in the scandal had waned in Minneapolis by late 1902, and Ames quietly left town after resigning as mayor. The Minneapolis papers lost interest. But publication of "The Shame of Minneapolis" in a national magazine spurred the local press and the authorities to seek Ames' return for prosecution.

Steffens went on to muckrake other cities — St. Louis again, then Pittsburgh, Philadelphia, Chicago, and New York. He dismissed claims that he was a scientist, but his method combined the techniques of journalism with those of social science. He examined the structure of city politics, looking for patterns as well as unique features, and thus was able to generalize about the state of city governance. The shame of the cities, he concluded, was the shamelessness of citizens. In most cities he visited, he found that "corruption was not merely political; it was financial, commercial, social...."[10] Respectable business owners colluded with politicians to secure privileges from government. Such corruption was hardly a secret in most places. Indeed, leading citizens often were involved.

Finally dissatisfied with what he considered superficial reforms of the Progressive movement, Steffens turned to more radical solutions. Intrigued by the Russian communists' claims of social and economic justice, he traveled to the Soviet Union in 1917 and 1919 to observe their programs firsthand. He was impressed with long-range Soviet planning and the translation of theories into practice. When asked of his reaction, his well-rehearsed answer was "I have seen the future, and it works." Such a candid endorsement of the repressive Soviet system earned him many enemies. Toward the end of his life, he spoke less enthusiastically of it.

AMERICA UNDER THE MUCKRAKE

About 2,000 muckraking articles appeared in the first decade and a half of the twentieth century, but some stand out. One of the most sensational efforts was "The Treason of the Senate." Sitting in the Senate press gallery one day, Charles Edward Russell noticed that many of the men on the floor below were little more than "butlers for industrialists and financiers." He proposed a series of articles on the subject for *Cosmopolitan*, just purchased by William Randolph Hearst. Another project, however, sidetracked Russell; and Hearst assigned the story to David Graham Phillips, a noted political journalist and novelist. A historian did much of the research, though Phillips wrote the stories. The series opened with a salvo: "The treason of the Senate! Treason is a strong word, but not too strong, rather too weak, to characterize the situation in which the Senate is the eager, resourceful, indefatigable agent of interests as hostile to the American people as any invading army could be...."[11] Phillips named senators who consistently voted on behalf of certain interests. Heavily promoted by Hearst, the series triggered a strong reaction, including Roosevelt's famous "The Man With the Muck-rake" speech. Historians have credited Phillips' stories with unseating some of the senators.[12]

Even churches came under the muckrake. Among the most biting investigations was Charles Edward Russell's "The Tenements of Trinity Church," published by *Everybody's* in 1908. The story turned on a bitter irony: Trinity Church raised money for its charities from rents it collected on some of the worst tenements in New York. According to Russell, the tenements were firetraps, lacked sanitary facilities, and bred diseases, particularly tuberculosis. Trinity fought back by criticizing Russell and *Everybody's* for their sensationalism, and much of the public seemed to agree. A few years later, though, Trinity quietly tore down about four blocks of its most miserable buildings. Russell went on to expose the abuses of the convict labor system in Georgia.

Even more restrained magazines such as *Ladies' Home Journal* entered the fray, at least on some topics. The *Journal* spearheaded the war against patent medicines, which, at the turn of the century, had sales of about $100 million a year. Magazines had a self-interest in the sales, for patent-medicine producers were among the biggest advertisers. Some of the big sellers were Lydia Pinkham's Vegetable Compound, Dr. Williams' Vegetable Jaundice Bitters, and Colden's Liquid Beef Tonic. Ads claimed that these nostrums cured everything from cancer to catarrh to piles to eczema. The formulas were worse than ineffective; they were dangerous. Most contained alcohol, and some used narcotics. In 1892, long before most other publications exhibited any interest in reform, *Ladies' Home Journal* announced that it would no longer accept ads for these spurious remedies. Its editor, Edward Bok, stepped up the campaign in 1904, encouraging boycotts of periodicals that still

[11]David Graham Phillips, "The Treason of the Senate," *Cosmopolitan* 40 (March 1906), 488.

[12]Two anthologies of the best muckraking journalism are Harvey Swados, ed., *Years of Conscience: The Muckrakers* (New York, 1962), and Arthur Weinberg and Lila Weinberg, eds., *The Muckrakers* (New York, 1961). The articles discussed in this section can be found in these collections.

[9]*Minneapolis Tribune*, 1 June 1902.

[10]Lincoln Steffens, *The Shame of the Cities* (New York, 1904), 14.

Teddy and the Muckrakers

President Roosevelt Wants Journalists To 'Let in Light and Air,' Not 'Sewer Gas'

Theodore Roosevelt was mad. An article in *Cosmopolitan Magazine*, under the title "The Treason of the Senate," had attacked Senator Chauncey Depew. Roosevelt liked "poor old Depew." A man of reform, the president nevertheless sensed that the exposé of one of the Senate's most venerable members – even though he was receiving $20,000 annually from an insurance company – went too far and could disrupt social order. He vented his rage in a dinner address at the Gridiron Club, an association of old-timer journalists, by comparing the crusading journalists in 1906 to "the man with the muckrake." He took the metaphor from John Bunyan's *Pilgrim's Progress*.

Ray Stannard Baker, a "muckraker," reminded Roosevelt that the president himself had contributed to the "letting in of light and air" by exposing "rascals." Roosevelt replied: "I want to 'let in light and air,' but I do not want to let in sewer gas."

Despite muckrakers' arguments, Roosevelt's talk to the Gridiron Club had been well received, and he decided to go further with his idea. On April 14, 1906, on the occasion of the laying of the cornerstone of the United States House of Representatives office building, he made muckrakers the main topic. With teeth gleaming beneath his dark, bristling mustache, the stocky and energetic president thundered: "The man who never does anything else, who never thinks or speaks or writes save of his feats with the muckrake, speedily becomes, not a help to society, not an incitement to good, but one of the most potent forces of evil."

Lincoln Steffens, Roosevelt's close friend, told him, "Well, Mr. President, you have put an end to all these journalistic investigations that have made you." Roosevelt replied that he had no such design and that he hadn't intended to include Steffens in his criticism.

To Roosevelt's embarrassment, the applause for his speech came from newspapers he branded as "organs of the criminal rich." And the reporter-reformers took pride in the term Roosevelt had coined, which has lived ever since in the language of American politics.

After David Graham Phillips' series "The Treason of the Senate" began appearing in *Cosmopolitan Magazine* and exposing that body's corruption, one reader wrote to the magazine: "Glory Hallelujah! You have found a David who is able and willing to attack this Goliath of a Senate." One of the targets was Senator Chauncey Depew. This photograph of him (top right) ran in the magazine above the caption "Here is the archetypal face of the sleek, self-satisfied American opportunist in politics and plunder." President Theodore Roosevelt (bottom right) thought the article had gone too far and gave his famous "muck-rake" speech in response. Phillips (seen here in the bottom left photograph, which accompanied his article in the magazine) was aloof and goal-oriented. One friend said that he had a "secretiveness, especially about his own affairs, purposes, and hopes.... He intended to get all he could out of newspaper work ... as a training in the study of men and social conditions.... [H]e would then make a big name for himself as a writer of books." In 1911 he was shot and killed by a manic depressive who thought one of Phillips' novels was about the man's family.

carried ads.

Muckraking journalism was not confined to magazines, as Upton Sinclair proved. His book *The Jungle* possibly touched more Americans than any other exposé of the period. Sinclair was born into a poor family, though some of his relatives enjoyed an upper-class lifestyle. Living and attending college in New York City, he witnessed the effects of urbanization and industrialization on those around him. His early novels were undistinguished, but about 1902 he was exposed to the writings of a Grinnell College professor who argued that socialism was the natural culmination of Christianity. Nearly all Sinclair's subsequent works bore the marks of his socialist ideology. In 1904 he began writing a series of articles on an unsuccessful strike in the Chicago meat-packing industry for the *Appeal to Reason*, a Kansas-based socialist magazine. He decided to expand these articles into a novel about wage slavery.[13]

Although he planned to write a work of fiction, Sinclair researched the topic much as a journalist would today. In Chicago he interviewed laborers, social workers, lawyers, doctors, saloon-keepers, and others. He visited the homes of workers and toured the meat-packing plants both as an official visitor and, disguised, as a worker. The result was *The Jungle*. Shocked by the book's descriptive realism, five publishing houses rejected the manuscript. Doubleday, Page & Co. then expressed interest and commissioned a report by a Chicago journalist to verify Sinclair's allegations. The journalist, it turned out, was a publicity agent for the stockyards; and he advised against publication. But Sinclair persisted and was able to persuade the publisher to send its own investigator, whose report substantiated Sinclair's claims. Doubleday published *The Jungle* in 1906.

Sinclair wrote to dramatize the plight of exploited laborers. His unstated goal was to generate support for the socialist movement, but his descriptions of the packinghouse conditions were so vivid that they overshadowed the workers' problems. "I aimed at the public's heart and by accident I hit it in the stomach," he said of the reaction to his book.[14] The novel focused on the life of Jurgis Rudkus, a Lithuanian peasant lured to Chicago by the promises of high wages in the packinghouses. He slowly succumbed to the inhumane conditions of the packing plant. He was injured, members of his family contracted horrible diseases, and the women turned to prostitution. He almost gave up all hope until he heard the promises of socialism. Although the characters were fictional, the situations and conditions were real. Sinclair reported that diseased carcasses were sold as prime meat, that rats and rat feces were ground up with the meats, and that inspectors routinely accepted bribes. But his most stunning scene underscored the callous disregard for human life: workers fell into open vats "and when they were fished out, there was never enough of them left to be worth exhibiting. Sometimes they would be overlooked for days, till all but the bones of them had gone out to the world as Anderson's Pure Leaf Lard!"

[13] Leon Harris, *Upton Sinclair: American Rebel* (New York, 1975).
[14] Upton Sinclair, "What Life Means to Me," *Cosmopolitan* (October 1906), 594.

"The Great American Fraud"
Although some publishers may have been in the muckraking business because it increased circulation, a few magazines gambled their best interests by attacking industry. Patent-medicine producers, one of the biggest advertisers, promoted products that were not only ineffective but sometimes deadly. This million-dollar industry advertised products that producers claimed could cure everything from cancer to warts. Most of the products, however, contained mainly alcohol; and many added narcotics. *Ladies' Home Journal* was one of the first magazines to refuse to print ads for these "medicines." In 1904 it also encouraged readers to boycott periodicals that still carried the ads. The following year, *Collier's* published Samuel Hopkins Adams' exposé, "The Great American Fraud." This cartoon, one in a series, illustrated the exposé. The article outlined the dangers of the alcohol and laudanum (an opium solution) in the formula and cited a coroner's report on a Cincinnati child who died from the opium in a bottle of Doctor Bull's Cough Syrup.

Virtually all aspects of American society fell under the muckrake sometime between 1902 and 1912. The range of inquiry is suggested by the following articles, some of the most distinguished writings of the period. Unchecked businesses were scrutinized in much the same way that Tarbell had studied Standard Oil: Charles Edward Russell told "The True Story of the Great Vanderbilt Fortune" (*Hampton's*, 1909); and Louis D. Brandeis, in "The Great Life Insurance Wrong," explained how the interests of the insured were ignored (*The Independent*, 1906). Racial problems received serious attention in print for the first time since the Civil War: Ray Stannard Baker wrote of "The Clash of the Races in a Southern City" (*American Magazine*, 1907), while William English

Scrutinizing the Press

Although journalists are quick to examine other institutions, they rarely have
brought the same energy to scrutinizing
themselves or the institution of the
press. The first systematic attempt to critique journalism was that by Will Irwin, a
veteran reporter, in the 1911 series "The
American Newspaper" in *Collier's* magazine. "I had no precedents to go by," he
wrote later of his landmark series. "Journalism was still finding itself." Irwin applied his reporting, interviewing, and investigative skills during visits to publishers, editors, and reporters across the
country. He concluded that the power of
the press resided in its news columns,
rather than its editorials, because of the
power of what, a half century later, would
be defined as agenda setting. Irwin's
series remains a model work even today.

Walling noted the terrible irony of white mobs killing blacks in
Springfield, Illinois, Abraham Lincoln's home ("The Race War in
the North," *The Independent*, 1908). The special problems of working women and children were ably detailed by Rheta Childe Dorr
in her book *What Eight Million Women Want* (1910) and by Robert
Hunter in "The Children Who Toil" (*World's Work*, 1905). Confidence in the quality of justice was shattered by such articles as C.
P. Connolly's "Big Business and the Bench" (*Everybody's*, 1912).[15]

MUCKRAKING THE PRESS

One important American institution, the press, escaped incisive
examination until muckraking's declining years. One historian
has speculated that interest in the press was piqued when the
muckraking magazines were being purchased and forced out of
business by some of the very companies they had criticized.[16]

Before muckraking's heyday, criticism of the press was mainly
episodic or internal and hence limited in its effect. News coverage,
for instance, of major events such as the Spanish-American War
provoked cries of sensationalism and jingoism but then ebbed as
the story receded from front pages. When journalists talked
among themselves at conferences or on the pages of trade journals,
they also raised some ethical concerns. This self-examination,
however, typically focused on a limited range of business concerns
— exaggerated circulation claims, advertisements disguised as
news stories, and the like.

It remained for Will Irwin to undertake a systematic study of
the press. He examined it in a fifteen-part series on "The American
Newspaper" for *Collier's* that began in January 1911. Since little
had been written on the press, Irwin obtained most of his information in remarkably candid interviews with reporters and edi-

tors. Before the first word was set in type, Irwin was offered a
bribe and William Randolph Hearst threatened to sue for libel. He
carried out the threat, but his $500,000 suit was dropped before
reaching court. Irwin was not intimidated. He showed that the
Hearst newspapers ran news stories and editorials favorable to
those who purchased advertising. A $1,000 theater advertisement,
for instance, bought an editorial lauding a play. In such cities as
Pittsburgh and Cincinnati, Irwin revealed, the papers excluded
news about citizens' reform efforts, a problem that Lincoln Steffens had encountered before.[17]

One news organization, the Associated Press, was the object of
several critics. In the most extreme view, the AP was a monopoly
that suppressed news unfavorable to capitalistic institutions. Irwin, writing in *Harper's Weekly* on March 28, 1914, had a more
moderate view. He did express concern that a few of the older,
more conservative newspapers exerted disproportionate influence
in conducting the affairs of the AP, a cooperative. AP bylaws made
it virtually impossible for a new, perhaps more liberal publisher to
receive a franchise in a community with an established member.
Irwin discounted the claim that the AP conspired with banks, utilities, industries, and others to keep unfavorable news off the wires.
He did believe, however, that the association (and many newspapers) tended to hire reporters and editors who were generally conservative in outlook. The most vitriolic attack on the AP and the
American press, Upton Sinclair's *The Brass Check* (1920), came after
the muckraking movement had waned. Much of the evidence for
his attack, however, was drawn from the period, when the practices of big business made it particularly susceptible to criticism.

Muckraking generally, and the exposés of corrupt press practices in particular, prompted some institutional self-reflection.
While Irwin, Sinclair, and others pointed to the press' shortcomings, the general thrust of the muckrakers underscored journal-

[15]See the anthologies by Swados, *Years of Conscience*, and Weinberg and Weinberg, *The Muckrakers*, for these articles.

[16] C.C. Regier, *The Era of the Muckrakers* (Chapel Hill, N.C., 1932), 165.

[17]See Will Irwin, *The Making of a Reporter* (New York, 1942), 164-9.

Writers for Social Justice
Scores of writers practiced muckraking at the beginning of the twentieth century, but the works of a handful of them stood out — and they were motivated by a sense of the need to restore justice to America's social system. Among the most important were (left to right) Frank Norris, Upton Sinclair, and Ray Stannard Baker. Norris' powerful indictment of slum life in San Francisco became the novel *McTeague* in 1899. It was to have been followed by a trilogy of novels excoriating the transportation trusts and corrupt exchanges trading in wheat. Norris died, however, a year after the first of the trilogy, *The Octopus*, was published in 1901, exposing unethical practices among railroads. He was only thirty-one years old. The author of the best-selling muckraking novel about the meat-packing industry, *The Jungle*, Sinclair saw himself as a critic of a "materially prosperous but spiritually starving" generation. Baker, best known for his work "Railroads on Trial" and his investigation of southern race relations, was a Wisconsin-born Presbyterian who decried "a lack of moral vision" in American public life. The effort to achieve "social justice," he was convinced, required a journalism of "righteous indignation."

ism's power to affect public opinion and people's lives — for better or for worse. Cultivating journalistic professionalism was one way to channel this power and prevent its abuse. Universities launched the first formal degree programs in journalism, students organized Sigma Delta Chi (now known as the Society of Professional Journalists) at DePauw University, and some state press associations began adopting codes of ethics — all as muckraking peaked. Also, in keeping with Progressives' faith that experts could remedy social problems, more idealistic measures were proposed to improve the press. The most notable, though unsuccessful, were the licensing of journalists to improve the quality of reporters, accuracy bureaus to judge the truthfulness of news accounts, and even adless or endowed publications that could report without having to favor commercial interests.[18]

THE DECLINE OF MUCKRAKING

The heyday of muckraking journalism was relatively brief. It peaked about 1906 and started its decline within two years. The movement enjoyed a brief resurgence during the 1912 presidential campaign when Roosevelt ran as the Progressive party candidate, but it ebbed until it all but disappeared at the outbreak of World War I. Several reasons have been advanced to explain its demise: vested interests killed the reform-minded magazines; the public

[18]For a fuller discussion of such efforts, see Marion T. Marzolf, *Civilizing Voices: American Press Criticism, 1880-1950* (New York, 1991), 34-75.

grew tired of a continuous stream of exposés; the best reporter-reformers moved on to other endeavors; muckraking journalists lost their base of support as the Progressive impulse in the nation declined; and, in the most optimistic view, the jounalistic investigations had prompted reforms and thereby diminished the need for further muckraking. Some combination of these reasons probably best explains the decline of muckraking.

Most interesting is the claim that some of the companies that had suffered at the hands of the muckrakers drove the offending magazines out of business. There is evidence for this allegation, but it has to be weighed carefully with the knowledge that its source was often the frustrated muckrakers themselves. *Hampton's Magazine* may have suffered such a fate. The owner, Benjamin Hampton, had boosted circulation to 440,000 in 1910 when his was possibly the most aggressive muckraking magazine. As part of a series on the great railroads, Charles Edward Russell did a story on the New York, New Haven, and Hartford line. The story charged that the company secretly had been able to monopolize just about all public transportation in New England, steamship as well as railroad traffic. Before the story was printed, Hampton later wrote, an agent of the railroad visited him and threatened reprisals unless he pulled the articles. He refused, and the December 1910 issue carried "The Surrender of New England."

Hampton claimed that spies the railroad planted in his office stole a list of the magazine's stockholders and then bombarded them with notes undermining confidence in the publisher's ability to run the publication. When Hampton sought a loan to tide the magazine over a slow summer, bankers refused to provide funds despite the firm's substantial collateral. Hampton was forced to sell. The new owners, he claimed, drained the magazine's assets and were guilty of criminal mismanagement, but he was unable to prove his case in court. Other accounts place more of the blame on Hampton's poor management. For whatever reason, the magazine folded in 1912.[19]

Similar pressures were claimed to have been exerted on other magazines. Shortly after *Success* assailed the powerful speaker of the U.S. House of Representatives, Joseph Cannon, advertising dwindled, paper suppliers started demanding cash, and banks refused loans. The magazine, which had been worth about $400,000, was sold for $2,250. At about the same time, *Twentieth Century* was sold when its muckraking editor failed to secure credit. Another journal that ran occasional muckraking pieces, *Human Life*, changed ownership in 1911 while running a serialized novel that dealt with New York City's chief of police. The new owners suspended the series. Even the pathbreaking *McClure's* ended up as the property of West Virginia Pulp and Paper Co. S.S. McClure blamed his own mismanagement, but Upton Sinclair and others seized on the sale as another example of a muckraking magazine that succumbed to special interests.

Some muckrakers believed that their distribution channels were threatened, too. They accused the American News Company, which distributed magazines to newsstands, of choking *The Arena*. And when President William Howard Taft and his postmaster general proposed raising magazine postage rates in 1909, some muckraking journals interpreted it as an assault on them.

Even if big business had killed some magazines, it is doubtful that such interests, no matter how powerful, were ultimately responsible for the death of muckraking. Part of the explanation lies in the nature of the magazine business itself. Once a few magazines such as *McClure's* demonstrated the popular appeal of muckraking, imitators entered the field. *Success*, for example, originally had thrived by featuring stories about successful people. Converting to a muckraking formula — with stories critical of successful businesses — the magazine may have alienated its original readership. At some point, there were just too many muckraking magazines vying for a limited audience. Since they depended on mass circulations, splintering the readership might have been a fatal mistake. In addition, not all publishers combined imaginative editorial leadership with the business acumen needed to survive.

Muckraking, moreover, suffered from its own excesses and an evaporating political base. Roosevelt's 1906 speech lashing the muckrakers had signaled growing doubts about their motives and goals. When muckraking journals began attacking such institu-

Margaret Sanger, Reproductive Rebel
Feminist publications had begun in the nineteenth century and were especially active in the early twentieth. One of the most notable was *The Woman Rebel*, edited by Margaret Sanger. She used it as a platform for asserting women's reproductive rights. Police arrested her, but her supporters remained faithful. This photograph was made after her arraignment in January 1917.

tions as the church, some readers felt they had gone too far. By the close of the decade, critics were complaining that many so-called muckrakers were little more than shrill and careless imitators of Steffens, Tarbell, and Russell.

Support eroded further when Roosevelt fragmented the Progressive movement with his third-party bid for the presidency in 1912. Some supporters gravitated to his Progressive party while others backed Democrat Woodrow Wilson. The Progressive party's agenda shifted from an emphasis on domestic reforms to a preoccupation with preparing for impending war. Once America entered World War I in 1917, a frenzy of idealism and patriotism preempted debates about social reforms.

Muckraking journalism did not disappear with the advent of World War I — it entered a different phase. In its heyday, muckraking articles were appearing in major magazines with a combined circulation of about 3 million. By the outbreak of war, most muckraking articles had disappeared from mass-circulation magazines, but stories were reappearing in different forums. Opinion magazines such as *The Nation* filled part of the void, though they reached a much smaller audience. Books became the most important outlet for muckraking. Upton Sinclair and others sustained the muckraking tradition by publishing their exposés between hard covers, and some of them sold well.

The small radical press, especially socialist and feminist publi-

---

[19]Regier, *The Era of the Muckrakers*, 175-6, and Louis Filler, *The Muckrakers: Crusaders for American Liberalism*, rev. ed. (Chicago, 1968), 366-8, tend to accept Hampton's claims that the railroad killed the magazine. A contrasting opinion can be found in Frank Luther Mott, *A History of American Magazines*, 5 vols. (Cambridge, Mass., 1930-1968), 5:150-1. Mott seems to believe that Hampton's careless business practices were responsible. The best treatment of this topic is Michael D. Marcaccio, "Did a Business Conspiracy End Muckraking? A Re-examination," *The Historian* 47 (1984): 58-71.

cations, proved particularly durable. They had preceded muckraking, thrived with less public attention during its heyday, and survived after the major popular magazines had lost interest in reform journalism. In 1912, about 1,000 socialists held public offices in the United States, and allied publications often boosted their candidacies. The Industrial Workers of the World had at least seventy newspapers. The *Daily Milwaukee Leader* claimed a circulation of 31,000. *The Masses*, edited by Max Eastman, published muckraking articles and radical views on politics, sex, and art from 1911 until postal authorities revoked its mailing privileges and its editors were indicted under the Espionage Act in 1917.

A healthy mix of periodicals that dealt with issues of interest to women coexisted with the muckraking magazines. Some lobbied almost exclusively for the right of women to vote. Others had a much broader reform agenda and worked to improve the social and economic lot of women. Margaret Sanger used her publication, *The Woman Rebel*, to press for women's access to birth control despite actions by federal authorities. These and similar organs of dissident groups formed an important reservoir of activist journalism in the United States.

In terms of circulation, however, mainstream women's magazines eclipsed the feminist press. At the outset of the Progressive era, the *Ladies' Home Journal* reached a circulation of 1 million, the first American magazine to pass that milepost. It and kindred magazines succeeded by appealing to traditional interests and developing a formula that defined women's roles largely in terms of consumption. Yet, that idea was not necessarily antithetical to the feminist publications, for the popular magazines conveyed a sense that consumption could partly liberate women from drudgery. Some of the mainstream magazines embraced Progressive reforms such as limits on patent medicines. And even when they resisted reforms, their female readers might disagree. For instance, Edward W. Bok, who replaced Louise Curtis as editor of the *Journal*, opposed women's suffrage although a poll of readers revealed that they supported it.[20]

Many mainstream newspapers also advocated various reforms. The conservative *New York Evening Post*, for example, through the work of its women's page editor, Rheta Childe Dorr, helped lead efforts to improve the lot of working women. She focused on hard conditions, long hours, and low pay, arguing that women should receive treatment in the workplace equal to that given men.

THE ACCOMPLISHMENTS OF MUCKRAKING

Histories of the Progressive period offer differing assessments of the impact of the press on reform. Carl N. Degler sees the muckrakers' most enduring contribution as throwing "a flood of light upon the social results of the factory and the city." Investigations by the press altered middle-class attitudes by introducing "principles of political realism," according to Vernon L. Parrington. Other

Reform's Decline and Accomplishments
A number of factors led to the end of muckraking. Many of the causes that the reformers had advocated, such as women's right to vote, were accomplished; and they entered the mainstream of American thinking and found their way into a variety of publications. This cover of a 1920 issue of *Leslie's Illustrated Weekly Newspaper* illustrated a woman voting for the first time. The Nineteenth Amendment, guaranteeing women's suffrage, had been approved in August of that year.

historians — C.C. Regier, Louis Filler, and Fred Cook, for example — assert that the press had a more profound and tangible impact. They argue that muckraking aroused public opinion and compelled substantial legislative reforms. Richard Hofstadter takes the more cautious view that legislative reforms short of "structural alterations in the American social and economic system" resulted from journalistic investigations. The muckraking journalists themselves expressed opinions that covered a similar gamut.[21]

Muckrakers have been credited, at least in part, with producing an impressive array of legislative reforms. Passage of the Pure Food and Drug Act followed publication of *The Jungle* and, some said, marked the culmination of the long war against patent medicines. A few states adopted an eight-hour work day for women, and more passed child-labor laws. More than half the states had workers' compensation laws by the end of the muckraking period. Prison reforms were enacted, too. Journalistic efforts also helped

[20]For an elaboration of this idea, see Helen Damon-Moore, *Magazines for the Millions: Gender and Commerce in the Ladies' Home Journal and the Saturday Evening Post, 1880-1910* (Albany, N.Y., 1994).

[21]Carl N. Degler, *Out of Our Past* (New York, 1955), 364; Vernon Parrington, *Main Currents in American Thought: Beginnings of Critical Realism in America* (New York, 1930), 407; Filler, *The Muckrakers*, 379-94; Regier, *The Era of the Muckrakers*, 197 and 210; Fred Cook, *The Muckrakers* (Garden City, N.Y., 1972); Hofstadter, *The Age of Reform*, 197.

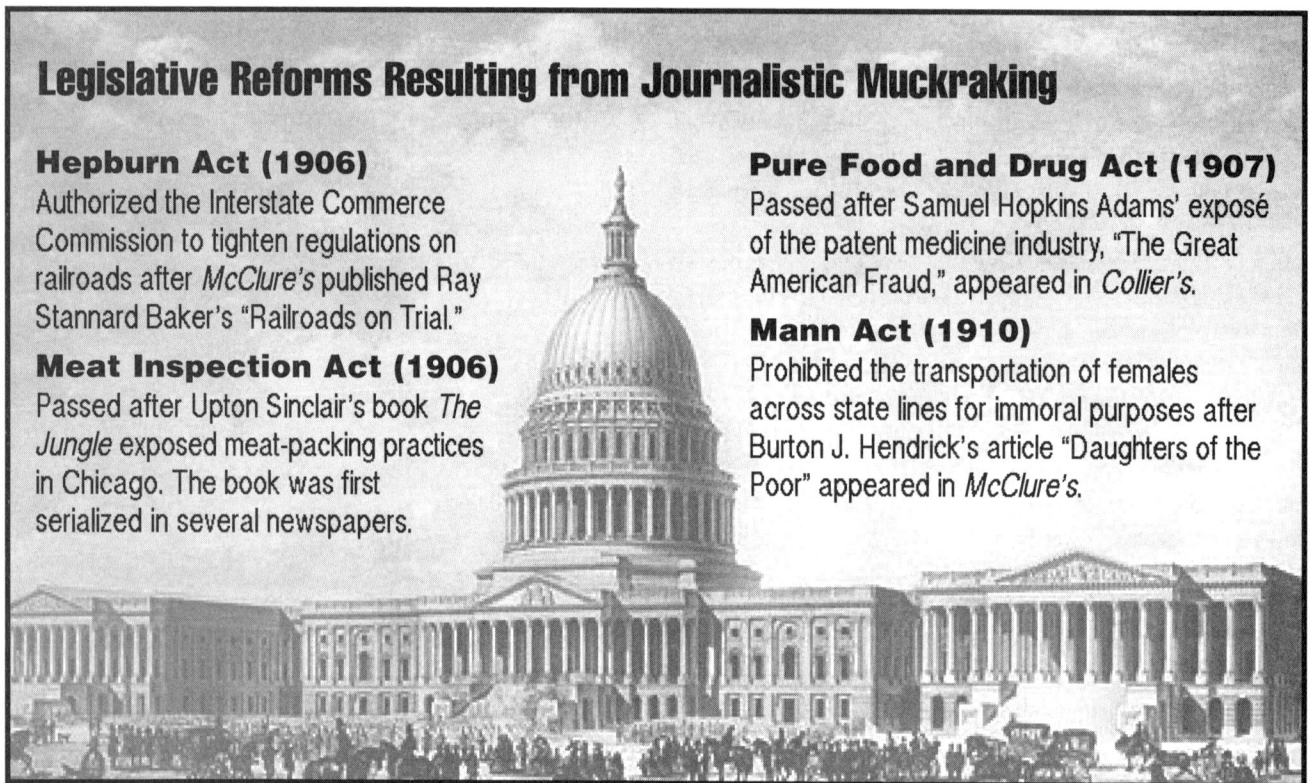

Legislative Reforms Resulting from Journalistic Muckraking

Hepburn Act (1906)
Authorized the Interstate Commerce Commission to tighten regulations on railroads after *McClure's* published Ray Stannard Baker's "Railroads on Trial."

Meat Inspection Act (1906)
Passed after Upton Sinclair's book *The Jungle* exposed meat-packing practices in Chicago. The book was first serialized in several newspapers.

Pure Food and Drug Act (1907)
Passed after Samuel Hopkins Adams' exposé of the patent medicine industry, "The Great American Fraud," appeared in *Collier's*.

Mann Act (1910)
Prohibited the transportation of females across state lines for immoral purposes after Burton J. Hendrick's article "Daughters of the Poor" appeared in *McClure's*.

make government more responsive to the people. A constitutional amendment providing for the popular election of U. S. senators was the most notable accomplishment along these lines. Reforms at the state level included the adoption of the referendum, recall, and initiative. Exposés preceded and perhaps propelled the legal actions that broke up Standard Oil and the huge tobacco companies. Charles Edward Russell's study of the Southern Pacific Railroad helped break its stranglehold on California politics, and Trinity Church cleared some of its tenements after he focused attention on its hypocrisy.[22]

To be sure, these reforms were realized. But what was the role of the press? In many of the reforms, the press functioned chiefly as an auxiliary to larger forces. Grand claims, for example, have been made for the effects of Sinclair's *The Jungle*. That the Meat Inspection Act and the Pure Food and Drug Act were passed after the publication of the book is undeniable. Often overlooked, however, are the other influences that contributed to this important legislation. Earlier exposures had alerted the public to the problem of adulterated meats. In fact, some of the moguls of the meatpacking industry already had been indicted. President Roosevelt, sensitive to the issue ever since his troops had eaten tainted meat in Cuba during the Spanish-American War, introduced legislation. Publication of *The Jungle* kept public pressure on Congress but probably was not a sufficient stimulus for change.

Typical, too, was the experience of Steffens as he investigated "The Shame of the Cities." He never uncovered municipal corruption himself. Instead, he wrote about others' discoveries in an engaging fashion for a national magazine. In just about all cases, a local reform group or an agency of government had initiated the investigations. As Will Irwin explained, the press generally waited until an incident or problem came "before court or commission, thus becoming news in the conventional sense."[23] Along with government agencies, reform groups often raised the issues that muckrakers explored.

The ultimate barrier blocking some reforms was the public itself. The press could and did direct the public's attention to problems, a power that communication researchers today label the agenda-setting influence. Doubtless, muckraking increased the public's awareness of social problems associated with modern, industrial America. Attitudes, however, were not so easily altered. Although historians lack sophisticated methods to detect shifts in past public opinion, evidence suggests that in some matters muckraking indeed touched public attitudes. This power was probably most important on issues that could be dramatized graphically and affected readers directly. But where readers' interest in an issue was remote, and where the audience was predisposed to disagree with the findings of an exposé, muckraking probably was less effective in changing attitudes.

Reforms more tangible than shifts in public opinion — removing corrupt officials from office, enforcing existing laws, and rewriting statutes — followed some muckraking efforts, but journalists usually contributed ammunition to a campaign that other reformers had initiated. The most fundamental reforms — structural changes in the political, economic, and social system — were the

[22]Filler, *The Muckrakers*, Regier, *The Era of the Muckrakers*, make the grandest claims for the effects of muckraking. For a thorough assessment of *The Jungle*'s impact on pure food laws, see James W. Davidson and Mark H. Lytle, *After the Fact: The Art of Historical Detection* (New York, 1982), 232-62.

[23]Will Irwin, *The American Newspaper* (1911; reprint, Ames, Iowa, 1969), 35.

hardest to realize. The most noteworthy changes occurred in the political system, with a number of reforms that increased the direct participation of people in government. All but a few of the muckrakers were more interested in fine-tuning the system than overthrowing it. Thus, they rarely advocated radical changes, which irritated some in the socialist movement.[24]

Nevertheless, most historians give the muckrakers much credit for, if nothing else, creating an atmosphere that encouraged reform. Through their exposés, they legitimized those who worked to better the lives of women, children, and workers. Edward Markham's remarkable articles on child labor for *Cosmopolitan* in 1906, for example, pulled back the curtain of tenements that hid the sordid reality of 2 million children, some as young as five, laboring in factories, mills, and mines. His articles helped change people's attitudes about child labor, raising support for those who crusaded for child labor laws. Muckraking awakened a slumbering nation and in the process saved American democracy from Big Business and Big Industry that knew no limits to their greed.[25]

For journalism, the enduring legacy of the muckraking period was not so much that the press worked on behalf of reform. More important, it taught reporters the power — and limitations — of facts. A bit naively, some journalists embarked on their muckraking careers believing that reforms flowed naturally from stories laying a problem before a rational public. Facts, indeed, had power, but by themselves they accomplished little. Interestingly, the growing realization that facts were weapons contributed to the rise of modern public relations. It was more than coincidental that the first American public relations firm had as clients some companies that were targets of the exposés.[26] The muckrakers also discovered the value of gathering and reporting facts in a systematic manner. In a sense, they anticipated the social science techniques reporters use today. Journalists can look to this period with pride, but that pride should be tempered with the knowledge that certain elements of the press played a less than noble role during the Progressive era.

RECOMMENDED READINGS

BOOKS

Applegate, Edd. *Journalistic Advocates and Muckrakers: Three Centuries of Crusading Writers.* Jefferson, N.C., 1997. The 101 biographies shed light on crusading and muckraking journalism.

Baker, Ray Stannard. *American Chronicle: The Autobiography of Ray Stannard Baker.* New York, 1945. Baker traces his years with the *McClure's* group and after.

Burt, Elizabeth V. *The Progressive Era: Primary Documents on Events from 1890 to 1914.* Westport, Conn., 2004. This collection includes newspaper articles from the period.

Chalmers, David M. *The Social and Political Ideas of the Muckrakers.* New York, 1964. The author provides a good, quick overview of the ideology underlying the

works of leading muckrakers.

Chamberlain, John. *Farewell to Reform.* New York, 1932. Chamberlain, a Marxist, was critical of Progressivism because of its superficial approach to solving deep-seated problems, when radical solutions were needed. Muckrakers accomplished many reforms, but they were powerless to solve the underlying problems of the system.

Cook, Fred J. *The Muckrakers.* Garden City, N.Y., 1972. The author provides a readable overview of the leading writers.

Crunden, Robert M. *Ministers of Reform: The Progressive Achievement in American Civilization, 1889-1920.* New York, 1982. The author sees muckrakers as key players in building public support for Progressive reform.

Filler, Louis. *The Muckrakers: Crusaders for American Liberalism.* Chicago: Gateway edition, 1968. Filler has spent much of his scholarly career studying muckraking and Progressivism; this is the best of the traditional approaches.

Fitzpatrick, Ellen F., ed. *Muckraking: Three Landmark Articles.* Boston, 1994. Fitzpatrick includes the texts of three articles from the January 1903 issue of *McClure's* that inaugurated muckraking. Her introduction has an insightful section on how the three reporters investigated their subjects.

Gallagher, Aileen. *The Muckrakers: American Journalism During the Age of Reform.* New York, 2006. The goal of the progressive movement and the muckrakers was to reform America's new industrial society.

Harris, Leon. *Upton Sinclair: American Rebel.* New York, 1975. Harris' is the best biography of Sinclair.

Harrison, John M., and Harry H. Stein, eds. *Muckraking: Past, Present and Future.* University Park, Pa., 1973. This collection has essays on specialized themes.

Hofstadter, Richard. *The Age of Reform: From Bryan to F.D.R.* New York, 1955. Muckrakers were more interested in their own social situation than in true reform.

Hudson, Robert V. *The Writing Game: A Biography of Will Irwin.* Ames, Iowa, 1982. Irwin, a noted critic of the press, was a versatile writer with a deep concern for public issues.

Kaplan, Justin. *Lincoln Steffens: A Biography.* New York, 1974. Kaplan's is the best biography of the leading muckraker.

Kochersberger, Robert C., ed. *More Than a Muckraker: Ida Tarbell's Lifetime in Journalism.* Knoxville: University of Tennessee Press, 1996. This collection of Tarbell's writing demonstrates that she contributed greatly to the origins of modern journalism.

Lawson, Linda. *Truth in Publishing: Federal Regulation of the Press's Business Practices.* Carbondale, Ill., 1993. Federal regulation of newspapers' business practices in the Progressive era culminated in the Newspaper Publicity Act of 1912, which used second-class mailing privileges as the basis for some government regulation of the press.

Lyon, Peter. *Success Story: The Life and Times of S.S. McClure.* New York, 1963. The *McClure's* group influenced the age of reform.

Mattson, Kevin. *Upton Sinclair and the Other American Century.* Hoboken, N.J., 2006. Sinclair, although sometimes acting as little more than as a propagandist for the left, was a principled social reformer. He was particularly concerned about the conditions of the poor and powerless.

McClure, S.S. *My Autobiography.* New York, 1914. McClure provides an inside look at the birth of American mass magazines and muckraking.

Miraldi, Robert, ed. *The Muckrakers: Evangelical Crusaders.* Westport, Conn., 2000. This collection of essays examines the muckrakers' roots, impact, and motivations.

———. *Muckraking and Objectivity: Journalism's Colliding Traditions.* Westport, Conn., 1990. Journalism moved away from the activist approach of the muckrakers to an objective, neutral stance of later journalists.

———. *The Pen Is Mightier Than the Sword: The Muckraking Life of Charles Edward Russell.* New York, 2003. Russell was one of the most important muckrakers.

Regier, C. C. *The Era of the Muckrakers.* Chapel Hill, N.C., 1932. The muckrakers exposed many social, economic, and political evils. Muckraking was "the inevitable result of decades of indifference to the illegalities and immoralities attendant upon the industrial development of America."

Serrin, Judith and Williams, eds. *Muckraking! The Journalism That Changed America.* New York, 2002. This collection of original muckraking articles includes commentary on each one.

Steffens, Lincoln. *Autobiography.* New York, 1931. Perhaps the most engaging auto-

---

[24]A number of historians from the "consensus" school have argued that the real strength of the muckrakers lay in the fact that they did not propose radical changes but worked within the democratic system fundamental to the strength of the United States.

[25]For an elaboration of this argument, see Arthur M. Schlesinger, *Political and Social History of the United States, 1829-1925* (New York, 1925), 441-2.

[26]See Scott M. Cutlip, "The Nation's First Public Relations Firm," *Journalism Quarterly* 43 (1966): 269-80.

biography of an American journalist, this work is full of useful information, too.

Steinberg, Salme H. *Reformer in the Marketplace: Edward W. Bok and the Ladies' Home Journal*. Baton Rouge, 1979. Even fairly traditional magazines engaged in some muckraking.

Swados, Harvey. *Years of Conscience: The Muckrakers*. Cleveland, 1962. This is one of the better anthologies of muckraking journalism.

Tarbell, Ida. *All in a Day's Work*. New York, 1939. One of the earliest and best of the muckrakers tells of her life and work.

Tichi, Cecelia. *Exposés and Excess: Muckraking in America 1900-2000*. Philadelphia, 2004. This study, dealing mainly with books and with muckraking as narrative literature, compares muckraking from the early twentieth century with that toward the end of the century.

Tomkins, Mary E. *Ida M. Tarbell*. New York, 1974. Tarbell was primarily a defender of traditional, Puritan New England values. Thus her Standard-Oil exposé attacked Rockefeller because of his lack of concern for morality and his ruthless methods.

Underwood, Doug. *From Yahweh to Yahoo! The Religious Roots of the Secular Press*. Urbana, Ill., 2002. Many of the basic principles of American journalism can be traced to religious ideals. The muckrakers particularly relied on them.

Ware, Louise. *Jacob A. Riis. Police Reporter, Reformer, Useful Citizen*. New York, 1938. Riis helped reform housing conditions because he believed that such conditions as those found in the slums were the true cause of people's troubles and wrongdoing.

Weinberg, Arthur, and Lila Weinberg, eds. *The Muckrakers*. New York, 1961. This anthology features useful background and many interviews with the muckrakers.

Wilson, Harold. *McClure's Magazine and the Muckrakers*. Princeton, 1970. Wilson provides a good account of the leading muckraking magazine.

—. *Progressivism and Muckraking*. New York, 1976. This critical bibliography covers muckraking throughout American history.

ARTICLES

Buddenbaum, Judith M. "The Religious Roots of Sigma Delta Chi." 206-16 in Wm. David Sloan, ed., *Media and Religion in American History*. Northport, Ala., 2000. The students at DePauw University who founded SDX (now the Society of Professional Journalists) based their journalistic values on the Methodist religion.

Burt, Elizabeth. "Conflict of Interests: Covering Reform in the Wisconsin Press, 1910-1920." *Journalism History* 26:3 (2000): 95-107. The author examines how newspapers in one state covered reform issues.

Cassedy, James H. "Muckraking and Medicine, Samuel Hopkins Adams." *American Quarterly* 16 (1964): 85-99. Adams progressed from a muckraker exposing problems in medicine to a medical writer. Although not an expert on medicine, he did help educate the public and bring about reform.

Chalmers, David. "The Muckrakers and the Growth of Corporate Power." *American Journal of Economics and Sociology* 18 (1959): 295-311. Muckrakers opposed big business.

Clark, John G. "Reform Currents in Polite Monthly Magazines, 1880-1900." *Mid-America* 47 (1965): 3-23. The muckraking magazines did not represent a radical departure.

Cobb-Reiley, Linda. "Not an Empty Box With Beautiful Words On It: The First Amendment in Progressive Era Scholarship." *Journalism Quarterly* (1992): 37-47. The Progressive era produced influential interpretations of the constitutional guarantees of free speech and press.

Endres, Kathleen L. "Women and the 'Larger Household': The 'Big Six' and Muckraking." *American Journalism* 14:3-4 (1997): 262-82. Women's magazines published muckraking on issues of concern to women and sometimes formed societies to push for reform.

Evensen, Bruce. "The Evangelical Origins of Muckraking." 186-205 in Wm. David Sloan, ed., *Media and Religion in American History*. Northport, Ala.: 2000. The muckrakers' primary motivation was religious.

Fee, Frank E. Jr. "Reconnecting With the Body Politic: Toward Disconnecting Muckrakers and Public Journalists." *American Journalism* 22 (2005): 77-102. Muckrakers

began an aggressive journalism that had some similarities to more recent public journalism.

Feldstein, Mark. "A Muckraking Model: Investigative Reporting Cycles in American History." *Harvard International Journal of Press and Politics* 11:2 (2006): 105-20. Throughout history, muckraking has ebbed and flowed, flourishing when there was a high level of supply (new technology and media competition) and of demand (social, economic, and political upheaval).

Grenier, Judson A. "Muckraking and Muckrakers: An Historical Definition." *Journalism Quarterly* 37 (1960): 552-8. The author tries to define muckraking and what it meant to different individuals.

Hays, Samuel P. "The Politics of Reform in Municipal Government in the Progressive Era," *Pacific Northwest Quarterly* 55 (1964): 157-69. This case study probes the role of muckrakers in achieving municipal reform.

Marcaccio, Michael D. "Did a Business Conspiracy End Muckraking? A Reexamination," *The Historian* 47 (1984): 58-71. The author provides a balanced analysis of the reasons for the decline of muckraking.

Marmarelli, Ron. "William Hard as Progressive Journalist." *American Journalism* 3 (1986): 142-53. Hard was the typical muckraker: "a champion of order and efficiency, and of social justice and social control."

McCormick, Richard L. "The Discovery That Business Corrupts: A Reappraisal of the Origins of Progressivism," *American Historical Review* 86 (1981): 247-74. Progressive reform stalled because the muckrakers prematurely encouraged control over the trusts that did not go far enough.

Poitras, Marc, and Daniel Sutter. "Advertiser Pressure and Control of the News: The Decline of Muckraking Revisited." *Journal of Economic Behavior & Organization* 72:3 (2009): 944-58. There is no evidence that advertiser boycotts contributed to the decline of muckraking.

Reynolds, Robert D. "The 1906 Campaign to Sway Muckraking Periodicals." *Journalism Quarterly* 56 (1979): 513-20, 589. Some magazines were more interested in economic survival than journalistic integrity.

Rodgers, Ronald R. "The Press, Pulpit and Public Opinion: The Clergy's Conferral of Power and the Concomitant Call for a Journalism of Advocacy in an Age of Reform." *Journal of Media and Religion* 9:1 (2010): 1-18. The clergy conferred "its role of agent of education and moral uplift to the press as the moral agent of change in an age of reform and demographic upheaval."

Schultz, Stanley K. "The Morality of Politics: The Muckrakers' Vision of Democracy," *Journal of American History* 52 (1965): 527-47. Schultz probes the view of democracy that led to muckraker agitation for a re-moralized America.

Semonche, John. "The American Magazine of 1906-1915: Principle vs. Profit." *Journalism Quarterly* 40 (1963): 36-44. There was tension between idealism and the need for a realistic business sense at one of the leading muckraking magazines.

Shultz, Stanley Key. "The Morality of Politics: The Muckrakers' Vision of Democracy." *Journal of American History* 52 (1965): 527-47. The author analyzes the political objectives of the muckrakers.

Sloan, Wm. David. "The Muckrakers, 1901-1917: Defenders of Conservatism or Liberal Reformers?" 271-82 in *Perspectives on Mass Communication History* (Hillsdale, N.J., 1991). This historiographical essay analyzes the approaches that historians have taken to explaining the muckraking period.

Stein, Harry H. "Lincoln Steffens: Interviewer." *Journalism Quarterly* 46 (1969): 735-6. Steffens used interviewing techniques that made him successful in eliciting incriminating information.

Thelen, David P. "Social Tensions and the Origins of Progressivism," *Journal of American History* 56 (1970): 323-41. The author provides an excellent summary of the social context within which muckrakers agitated for the creation of a civil society.

Thornton, Brian. "Muckraking Journalists and Their Readers: Perceptions of Professionalism." *Journalism History* 21 (1995): 29-41. The author examines what readers and editors said about muckraking and journalistic ethics.

Uselding, Paul, ed. "In Dispraise of Muckrakers: United States Occupational Mortality, 1890-1910," 334-71 in *Research in Economic History I*. Greenwich, Conn., 1976. In their attacks on industry for its danger to mortality, muckrakers exaggerated or misread the statistics.

17

The Media and National Crises

1917 - 1945

The United States faced grave challenges between 1917 and 1945. The challenges included two world wars and a devastating economic depression that altered the very nature of the American government and its relationship to citizens. The media played a crucial role in the progression of these crises because of the media's status as important social, political, and economic institutions. Citizens turned to radio, newspapers, and, increasingly, newsreels for vital information about the domestic and international events that were transforming the world. The media's involvement in the crises that shaped the period began on the eve of this country's entrance into World War I.

REPORTING BEFORE AMERICA'S ENTRY

Frankly, the Austro-Hungarian leadership was not especially saddened by the assassination of Franz Ferdinand, heir to their country's throne. He was unpopular with many officials and not particularly well-liked within the Imperial family. In fact, his murder on June 28, 1914, provided an opportunity to settle a few pesky matters that had been points of contention in the Balkans for some time. The opportunity, though, presented some difficulties, but no one — and that included the American journalists covering central Europe in the summer of 1914 — foresaw that those difficulties would morph into the "war to end all wars," World War I.

Concerns over the balance of power in Europe and long-standing enmities that resulted from earlier European wars were at the heart of the conflict. Franz Ferdinand was assassinated by Gavrilo Princip, a member of a secret Serbian nationalist group, and Austria-Hungary saw that fact as a justification for provoking a limited war with its rival and enemy, Serbia. Its intention was complicated, however, by a series of alliance treaties among the various European nations. Russia was allied with Serbia, and Austria with Germany. Russia could not allow Serbia to be destroyed, and Germany could not allow Austria-Hungary to fall. When Russia and Germany entered the fray, other treaties were invoked; and before long, what Austria had intended to be a convenient little war to regain some of its power and prestige had turned into a global war

involving not only Germany and Russia but also France, England, India, South Africa, New Zealand, Australia, and Canada, soon to be followed by Japan and Turkey and then the United States.

American newspaper correspondents in Europe had trouble at first convincing their editors that anything significant was happening. Austria took three weeks to decide on how to respond to the assassination, and Germany pretended to have no interest in the unfolding events. Kaiser Wilhelm II, for example, conveniently contracted lumbago to avoid attending Franz Ferdinand's state funeral. His backache was not so bad, however, as to force him to cancel a cruise through the Norwegian fjords.

Editors sitting in their offices in the States were more interested in the story of a conflict closer to home: the Mexican civil war. The United States was deeply involved in it. In 1914, American troops occupied Vera Cruz, and two years later Gen. John J. "Black Jack" Pershing would pursue Pancho Villa's rebel army across northern Mexico in retaliation for a raid into New Mexico. He was not successful in his efforts to capture Villa. However, he had little time to dwell on his failure, for upon America's entry into World War I in 1917 he would be tapped to lead the American Expeditionary Forces to Europe. American journalists had been on the scene for three years by the time the Expeditionary Forces arrived.

Thus, even before the United States got involved, Americans got a comprehensive picture of the early stages of the Great War. During the war's first three years, America remained neutral. England, however, was the only country with more correspondents covering the war than the United States. Representing a neutral country, American correspondents were able to report from either side. A few were already in Europe as events heated up in the summer of 1914. The *New York Times*, for example, had reporters Wythe Williams and Walter Duranty already stationed in Paris. Duranty, who was British by birth, would win a Pulitzer Prize for his favorable treatment of Russia and its 1917 revolution. His biased coverage, however, including intentional falsification of what was happening in Russia, led to his being branded one of the greatest scoundrels of the twentieth-century press. In the early 2000s, there was a move to rescind his Pulitzer, but the committee

German Propaganda Loses to Action

The German government and several German-language newspapers in the United States carried on an intense campaign to keep America from entering World War I and continued the efforts once America was involved. This article (left) from the *Saturday Evening Post* in 1918 warned about the German methods and the dangers. Despite the efforts to influence American opinion through propaganda, German actions eventually swayed Americans to favor joining the war in Europe against Germany. The Germans' sinking of the British liner *Lusitania* in May 1915 provided a major turning point in American and press sentiment. Although the *Los Angeles Times'* news treatment of the event (center) was straightforward, many newspapers published editorials attacking Germany for its submarine warfare. When American agents intercepted the note that German Foreign Secretary Zimmermann had sent to Mexico, newspapers across the United States published the story (right). Offering Mexico the American Southwest if it would join the Central Powers, the note galvanized American opposition to Germany.

ultimately decided not to take that step. After America entered the war, those correspondents already in Europe were soon joined by droves of reporters, including Richard Harding Davis, whom H. L. Mencken had referred to as "the hero of our dreams."[1] Davis was America's best known war reporter. He had gained his fame during the Boer War in South Africa and during the Spanish-American War for coverage of Teddy Roosevelt's Rough Riders in Cuba. When he arrived in Europe, he was reporting for clients of the Wheeler syndicate and was paid an enormous salary for the time: $600 a week. He also made $1,000 per story for *Scribner's* magazine. Immediately upon the start of World War I, he made headlines with his account of the German army's invasion of Belgium.

In the early days of the war, the belligerent nations tried to control what information was disseminated about the conflict. Both the Allies and the Central Powers vied for supremacy in the propaganda war to gain American sympathy. Britain, in an attempt to win the battle for American support, cut the transatlantic cables between Germany and the United States in August 1914. That meant the only cables available for transmission of news about the war were ones passing through England. The situation allowed England to censor all information. German propagandists tried to create sympathy for German *kultur*, but they failed to be persuasive.

Despite their neutrality, American correspondents were not entirely free agents. Early in the conflict, France, England, and Germany all tried to control what reporters wrote by a variety of

means, including jailing uncooperative journalists on espionage charges. Later, France and England both turned to a less drastic measure. They required that reporters be properly credentialed, and both were stingy in handing out credentials. The military tightly controlled access to the battlefield. For the most part, field correspondents were limited to writing features about events on the front. What information was divulged about important battles came via official communiqués from the military. This procedure led to the rise in importance of the newsroom military analyst back home who combed through the official dispatches and tried to discern what was actually happening at the fronts.

Many battlefield reporters, though, were untroubled by the military restrictions on their movements and illegally went to the front without credentials. When Davis did that, he and several other reporters were captured and placed on a prisoner train headed for Germany. The other passengers were French and English soldiers whom the Germans had captured as prisoners of war. Eventually released, Davis wrote several dramatic stories that exposed German war crimes he had witnessed while on the prison train, including a firsthand account of the burning of Louvain, Belgium.[2]

Non-credentialed correspondents were stuck in positions far behind the lines. They gathered news as best they could, though they were never able to get much of it past censors. Even when news did get out, it often had to be slanted to put a better spin on dreadful battlefield losses and Allied retreats. Wilbur Forrest, who

[1]Quoted in John Hohenberg, *Foreign Correspondence: The Great Reporters and their Times* (Syracuse, N. Y., 1995), 90.

[2]Richard Harding Davis, *With the Allies* (New York, 1914).

covered the war for United Press, claimed that censors forced reporters to describe heavy defeats as "strategic withdrawals" or as taking up new positions in accordance with a plan. He argued, though, that such an approach was the right thing to do because of the magnitude of the global struggle, one that required the press not to be neutral. Frederick Palmer later declared that his role as a World War I correspondent sometimes cast him as a "public liar" for the purpose of maintaining strong public support for the war and for the Army at home.

Initially, the only American to have official press credentials from the British was Palmer, a correspondent for *Collier's* magazine and a veteran war reporter who also worked for all the American wire services and newspapers. He, along with all the other correspondents whom the British later credentialed, had to accept certain restrictions. They were not allowed to go anywhere without military press officers. They were restricted on what they were allowed to write about, but they were rarely censored because they knew too well what lines they could and could not cross.

Censorship was sometimes lifted when there was news the Allies wanted out or when there was some other military advantage to be gained. For example, when a German submarine sank the passenger liner *Lusitania* off the Irish coast in May 1915, Wilbur Forrest alone was allowed to send some 7,000 words about the attack and the more than 1,000 people who died. Reporters who covered the air campaigns had great liberty to tell the stories of the fabulous dogfights over Germany and France. They depicted the pilots as knights of the air and romanticized them almost beyond recognition.

AMERICA'S ENTRY INTO WORLD WAR I

The reasons for American entrance into the war have been a topic of ongoing dispute among historians. The most prominent themes are the following: (1) a German-dominated Europe would imperil American security, (2) American economic ties to the Allies were so important that intervention to preserve them was necessary, (3) President Woodrow Wilson and his advisors risked serious encounter with Germany in order to defend law, morality, national prestige, and Americans' traditional beliefs in neutral rights, and (4) Germany's resorting to submarine warfare against neutral ships in European war zones represented an intolerable infringement on American rights. Accompanying these major issues, a number of diplomatic exchanges and declarations usually are cited as well as some specific events, such as the sinking of the *Lusitania* on May 7, 1915, which resulted in the loss of 1,198 lives, including those of 128 Americans. Finally, the theme of pro-Allies American public opinion runs throughout interpretations of U.S. intervention in the war.

The most prominent editor arguing for intervention was Henry Watterson of the *Louisville Courier-Journal*. He had been a reporter during the American Civil War. His grand writing style had already made him known nationally in the late 1800s, but his popu-

The Adventurers
World War I's two most adventurous reporters were Richard Harding Davis (left) and Floyd Gibbons (right). Davis seemed destined to be a writer from the very start. He was born in 1864 to a novelist mother and a newspaper editor father. He never had any notion of doing anything but writing and being a traveling adventurer. He gained great fame covering the Spanish-American War and, by the time World War I started, was the world's most famous reporter. His eyewitness account of the Germans burning Louvain, Belgium, in 1914 helped sway American opinion against Germany. Gibbons gained fame with his eyewitness account of a German submarine's sinking of the British cruise liner *Laconia* in 1917. Newspapers around the world reprinted the story. Always wanting to be in the middle of the action, in 1918 he advanced with a group of American Marines across a wheat field toward German lines at Belleau Woods. A sniper with a machine gun opened fire, hitting Gibbons three times. One of the bullets went through his helmet and knocked out his eye. "I caught [the eye] in my hands as I fell," he recalled. He became easily recognizable for the rest of his career by the eyepatch that he wore.

larity never was higher than when he took up the trumpet to call for war against Germany after it attacked Belgium and France in 1914. He had coined many political phrases earlier in his career, but he was never more pleased than with the sulfurous imprecation he hurled against Germany at that time: "To hell with the Hohenzollerns and the Hapsburgs." It became a battlecry for those who wanted the United States to take up arms, and Watterson made it a standing part of the *Courier-Journal's* nameplate. When Congress finally declared war in 1917, he wrote two rousing editorials — "Vae Victis" and "War Has Its Compensations" — for which he won the Pulitzer Prize.

When Wilson asked Congress to declare war on Germany on April 2, 1917, he had the majority of public and press opinion behind him. The American people had been jarred out of their neutrality by Germany's announcement at the end of January that it would launch unrestricted submarine warfare against neutral ships entering European war zones. One reporter, Floyd Gibbons of the *Chicago Tribune*, was determined to find out about the torpedoing of American ships firsthand. When he was assigned to combat reporting in Europe in February 1917, he booked passage on a ship he was guessing German submarines would torpedo. When he boarded the ship, he was equipped with a special life

War Correspondence
American war correspondents provided much on-the-scene reportage of World War I. One of the leading correspondents was Irvin S. Cobb of the *Saturday Evening Post*. This story in March 1918 recounted a submarine attack on a ship crossing the Atlantic.

preserver, brandy, fresh water, and flashlights. As he expected, a German sub attacked. Thirteen of the 289 passengers and crewmen were lost. Gibbons' story about the sinking ran on February 26, the same day President Wilson claimed in Congress that Germany had not yet committed any overt act of war with a submarine.

Then on March 1, news of the Zimmermann Telegram flashed across the country. The note stated that if Germany and the United States went to war, Mexico should be invited to ally with Germany. In return, Mexico would receive New Mexico, Arizona, and Texas, pending the victory of the Central Powers. The German Minister in Mexico also was to ask President Carranza to invite Japan, one of the Allies, to join the compact. Intercepted in transit to the German embassy in Mexico, the message was released and published. Secretary of State Robert Lansing leaked the telegram to the Associated Press. It was one of the great news breaks of the century, and it electrified the American people and press. Zimmermann admitted the telegram was authentic but claimed his instructions were to have been followed only if America declared war on Germany.

On March 18, German submarines sank three American merchant ships without warning, with the loss of many lives. Wilson saw no alternative but to ask Congress to recognize that a state of

war existed with Germany. Although some Americans opposed entrance into the war, most accepted it, and most newspapers endorsed it overwhelmingly. America entered the war on April 6, 1917.

COVERING THE GREAT WAR

When General Pershing, the commander of the American Expeditionary Forces (AEF), landed in Liverpool, England, British censors refused to let correspondents mention where he had arrived. Floyd Gibbons' cable, which censors approved, cleverly got around the restriction. It read: "Pershing landed at British port today and was greeted by Lord Mayor of Liverpool."[3] Pershing's approach to controlling the press was to have as few reporters with him as possible, to make it difficult to become an accredited journalist, and to have the best man he could find take charge of censorship. He decided to allow no more than twelve reporters to accompany his forces. This limit, though, was soon raised. By the time the war ended, sixty American correspondents had been accredited to cover the AEF.

Acquiring credentials to cover Pershing's army was not easy. Reporters had to file a $2,000 bond and make a deposit of $1,000 for their food and shelter. They also had to do the following:

1. Appear before the Secretary of War or his designate;
2. Swear to report the truth, but not anything that would aid the enemy;
3. Hand write an autobiography, including an account of the correspondent's work, experience, character and health; what he planned to do in Europe; and where he was going;
4. Agree to wear a green armband with a big red "C" on it;
5. Pay an additional $500 fee if he were bringing an assistant along.

To handle censorship activities, Pershing hired Frederick Palmer as his Chief Press Officer at a salary of $175 a month. As a correspondent for the *New York Herald*, Palmer was making $40,000 a year. He had been a journalist for nearly thirty years, beginning his career at age fifteen by writing for the *Jamestown* (N. Y.) *Morning Post*. He was one of the most experienced war correspondents of his time, having covered the Greek-Turkish war, the Spanish-American War, the Philippine insurrection, the Boxer Rebellion, the Russo-Japanese war, and the Mexican border war.

Palmer became an enthusiastic censor. All correspondents, by Pershing's order, had to be in uniform. By Palmer's order, they were herded together and not allowed to go off on their own. Their copy all had to be cleared, and the censor's office was zealous in accomplishing its mission. Because of Palmer's tight censorship, it was the British news agency Reuters that carried the first news of the landing of the AEF in France. Palmer had decided American reporters could not send any stories about the landing until the last ship had arrived, and he refused to rescind that order even when the British papers published the news. When Daniel Dillon, an International News Service correspondent, tried

[3]Quoted in Wm. David Sloan, et al, *The Great Reporters* (Northport, Ala., 1992), 99.

Frederick Palmer

An experienced newspaperman and war correspondent, Frederick Palmer (shown in the portrait above when he was in college) served as Chief Press Officer of the American Expeditionary Forces in Europe. He had to organize his own department and formulate censorship regulations that had to conform in general to those of the other Allies. According to correspondents, he distributed too little information and exercised too much censorship.

to send his expense account report to his employer, it was censored because it included a $250 bill for entertaining Pershing. The press office did not want anyone to know that the general had been spending time with reporters. As a result of the enthusiasm of his assistants, Palmer became particularly unpopular among reporters.

The censorship efforts were not without justification, for there were excesses in the reporting about the war. Competition among reporters, most often the basis of excess, was fierce. Exuberance and competition combined to get two reporters thrown into a military jail in the fall of 1917. While Palmer was shepherding correspondents to the front that October, so they could witness the first American gun crew in action, a battery of American artillery passed them. One of Palmer's group recognized American correspondents Floyd Gibbons and Raymond Carrol with the artillery. The two were placed under arrest for forty-eight hours. They were allowed to send in their stories only after other journalists had done so. By the end of 1917, Palmer was glad to return to the United States. In early 1918, his replacement, Gerald Morgan, liberalized censorship and restrictions on reporters.

Reporting the war required resources and resourcefulness. To stay ahead of rivals, reporters had to use the fastest cable services possible. That required sending telegrams at the "double urgent" rate of 75¢ per word. Doing so allowed newspapers to publish battlefield news on the day it occurred.

Among the most widely read and flamboyant war correspondents were Gibbons and Irvin S. Cobb of the *Saturday Evening Post.* Some — such as Heywood Broun, Westbrook Pegler, and George Seldes — would become well known in later years as polemical journalists.

Women correspondents were also active. The Newspaper Enterprise Association's Peggy Hull, the first woman correspondent to receive accreditation from the War Department, not only reported news from Europe but went to Siberia with the American expedition to Vladivostok at the end of the war. The best-known woman correspondent was Rheta Childe Dorr. She managed to accompany the Russian women's Battalion of Death to the front. The *New York Mail* carried her dispatches on the front page, and she later reproduced them in an engaging book, *Inside the Russian Revolution.*

Newreels, which offered a new opportunity in war coverage, saw restricted use. Since first appearing in this country in 1911, they had grown rapidly as a popular news medium. But once the war began, all the belligerents limited civilian cameramen both at the front and at home. After the United States entered the war, the U.S. Army Signal Corps produced most of the newsreel footage that American audiences saw. The film was carefully edited to serve military and national war goals.

War conditions also influenced how the press at home treated the war. The Committee on Public Information (CPI) coordinated the media war effort. Established by executive order on April 14, 1917, just eight days after the declaration of war, the CPI included the secretaries of state, war, and navy. George Creel, a newspaper editor, writer, and devotee of President Wilson, headed it. It was divided into a Foreign Section that dealt with propaganda for use abroad and a Domestic Section that dealt with mobilizing opinion on the home front. Many intellectuals and journalists, including a number of ex-muckrakers, served the Committee.

Among its many domestic and foreign propaganda activities, the CPI informed and influenced the press by publishing America's first daily government-produced newspaper, the *Official Bulletin,* which reached a peak circulation of 118,000. The CPI also published press releases and news digests for urban and rural papers. One of its projects, the Official Film News, created bi-weekly programming that movie theaters showed.[4]

[4]For the activities of the CPI see George Creel (Chairman), *Complete Report of the Chairman of the Committee on Public Information* (Washington, D.C., 1920); James R. Mock and Cedric Larson, *Words That Won The War: The Story of the Committee on Public Information* (Princeton, N. J., 1939); Stephen Vaughn, *Holding Fast the Inner Lines: Democracy, Nationalism and the Committee on Public Information* (Chapel Hill, N. C., 1980). For his own lively defense of the CPI see George Creel, *Rebel At Large: Recollections of Fifty Crowded Years* (New York, 1947). For examples of the CPI's activity abroad, see James D. Startt, "American Propaganda in Britain During World War I," *Prologue: Quarterly of the National Archives* 28 (1996): 17-33; Startt, "American Film Propaganda in Revolutionary Russia," *Prologue* 30 (1998): 167-79; and Gregg Wolper, "Wilsonian Public Diplomacy: The Committee on Public Information in Spain," *Diplomatic History* 17 (1993): 17-34.

George Creel and the CPI
Headed by newspaper editor George Creel (left), the Committee on Public Information was appointed by President Woodrow Wilson to prepare propaganda for use abroad and to help mobilize public opinion at home. Although receiving some criticism, it provided informative and usually accurate material to newspapers across the country. It produced much material aimed at aiding the war effort. One of its first concerns was preventing loose talk from providing useful information to German secret agents. This poster of Uncle Sam (right) presented the message effectively with one word: "Shhhh!"

Creel and the CPI were roundly criticized for their propaganda efforts. Creel himself, though, saw his work as contributing to the preservation of freedom of expression, and he argued against enforced press censorship during the war. Instead, he advocated a voluntary press agreement that asked editors to act as their own censors. To help editors with this task, the CPI issued guidelines in May 1917 on what kinds of information should be kept secret.

While the press operated with considerable freedom domestically, laws were passed making it illegal to criticize the government. The Sedition Act of 1918 specifically curtailed freedom of expression and of the press. Further, control of America's telegraph lines was given to President Wilson. He created a Censorship Board to deal with telegraph issues. Creel, who served on that board, helped block some of the more "dangerous" materials and periodicals from leaving the United States.

PRESS SUPPORT OF THE WAR

World War I was a conflict of unprecedented proportion, a total war. For good or ill, it affected all institutions in the participating countries and beyond. When a democracy enters a major war, the public must be mobilized, not only for manpower and resources but also for support. The press was no exception. One effect of the war was that journalists became, willingly or otherwise, part of the effort to manage public opinion. The liberal Woodrow Wilson and the liberal George Creel ended up with what one historian called "perhaps the most gigantic propaganda campaign in all American history."[5] The press was instrumental in helping mobilize the American population to support the war effort.

The large scale of the war created a need for loyalty. Most of the

[5]Selig Adler, *The Isolationist Impulse: Its Twentieth Century Reaction* (New York, 1961), 37.

press supported the war effort and cooperated with the CPI, although some, such as the Hearst papers and the *Washington Post*, sometimes were at odds with the government. As a rule, the press printed all the news the government allowed and spared no expense in gathering it. The war was an absorbing and commanding event that deserved and received ongoing publicity.

American opinion quickly accepted the need to mobilize public support for the war effort. Strong currents of nativism and antiradicalism ran amid the swelling tide of support for the war. If the public came to accept the war in terms of right and wrong, as a struggle of democracy against autocracy, it should be remembered that, in some respects, the press prepared the way for such thinking. In the first decade of the century, the exposé and "advocacy journalism" of the muckrakers made a deep impression on American thought. Some of the same traits that had characterized muckraking appeared in exaggerated form in war propaganda. American opinion grew intolerant of criticism and impatient with suspected cases of disloyalty. Responsibility for this attitude rested, in part, with government officials and with the CPI. It also rested on the shoulders of journalists who allowed the war spirit to influence their work.

Once America entered the war, a wave of superpatriotism spread across the country. Two months after the United States' entry, *The Literary Digest* invited readers to clip and send to that journal any editorial that seemed "seditious or treasonable." The Espionage Act empowered the postmaster general to exclude from the mails newspapers and periodicals containing treasonable or seditious material. The Post Office Department threatened to deny mailing privileges to more than seventy-five publications and actually did to a handful. Even the prestigious liberal journal *The Nation* was denied use of the mails until President Wilson intervened to have the ban lifted after four days.

Radical and Socialist papers, most of which resisted the nation's war efforts, and German-language papers were hardest hit. The well-known radical periodical *The Masses*, as well as several Socialist papers such as the *New York Evening Call* and *Milwaukee Leader*, lost mailing privileges. German-language papers, most of which had supported Germany before the war but for the most part were loyal to America once it entered the war, suffered from a number of pressures. Many other papers criticized them. The *Topeka Capital*, for example, demanded the suppression of all German-language papers. In October 1917, President Wilson signed a law requiring German-language papers to supply English translations of all articles relating to the American government and to the war. Translation was a costly operation that many papers could not afford. Most simply ceased publication.

Various forms of pressure impaired those remaining in business. In some cases, advertisers refused to place ads, and government officials broke into the offices of some radical and Socialist publications in search of subversive material and arrested a few editors. One historian wrote that "in other instances, trainmen threw off bundles of German-language newspapers at wrong stations; Boy Scouts burned stolen bundles; and teachers discouraged their pupils from delivering 'disloyal' newspapers."[6]

Most black newspapers also supported the nation's war aims.[7] Between the 1880s and the opening of World War I, hundreds of black newspapers had been founded. Many failed to survive for long; but at least 173, and perhaps as many as 288, existed in 1914. Among them were some that became venerable publications such as the *Baltimore Afro-American*, the *Indianapolis Recorder*, and the *Pittsburgh Courier*. A few black journalists wondered if the problems of their race were receiving the attention they deserved. Editors such as Robert S. Abbott of the *Chicago Defender*, William M. Trotter of the *Boston Guardian*, and W. E. B. DuBois, editor of the NAACP'S monthly journal *The Crisis*, were among the militants who became angry with the conciliatory philosophies of leaders like Booker T. Washington.

Wilson's relations with black leaders became strained during his first administration because of the segregation and discrimination practiced in government departments and agencies. Wilson himself was a segregationist. America's entry into the war made matters worse. Although about 200,000 black Americans served in France, only 42,000 were combat troops — and they had to fight to gain a place on the front lines. A tide of black protest arose. Some black editors questioned Wilsonian idealism. DuBois, the editor of *The Crisis*, complained, "Poland? The President loves it. His interest in everything that concerns it is very deep.... But twelve million American Negroes? Silence! Distance from Washington certainly lends enchantment to Democracy."[8] A. Philip Randolph's socialist magazine *The Messenger* announced that rather than make the

W. E. B. DuBois
The founder and editor of *The Crisis*, the monthly journal of the National Association for the Advancement of Colored People, W. E. B. DuBois provided militant leadership for African Americans on issues of racial equality during World War I. He argued that President Wilson was more concerned about conditions in Europe than about the plight of black Americans.

world safe for democracy it "would rather make Georgia safe for the Negro."[9]

Given the force of the black press protest, it was uncertain how far its critique of the government would go. In June 1918, however, Creel organized a meeting of thirty-one leading black editors in Washington. They adopted and published a petition strongly urging black Americans to "make every sacrifice to win the war."[10] Then, in July 1918, DuBois, whose popularity among blacks was second only to that of Booker T. Washington, wrote a much-heralded editorial titled "Close Ranks" characterizing the war against German power as "the crisis of the world." He urged black Americans, as the war entered its final four months, not to hesitate. "Let us," he said, "while the war lasts, forget our special grievances and close our ranks shoulder to shoulder with our white fellow citizens.... We make no ordinary sacrifice, but we make it gladly ... with our eyes lifted to the hills."[11]

The war stimulated black hopes for better treatment at home. As it went on, faith in democracy increased across the Western world, and black Americans shared in the expectation of its great-

[6]Frederick C. Luebke, *Bonds of Loyalty: German-Americans and World War I* (DeKalb, Ill., 1974), 243.

[7]See Lester Jones, "The Editorial Policy of Negro Newspapers of 1917-1918 as Compared with That of 1941-1942," *Journal of Negro History* 29 (January 1944): 24-31.

[8]*The Crisis*, March 1918, 216.

[9]Quoted in Robert H. Brisbane, *The Black Vanguard: Origins of the Negro Social Revolution 1900-1960* (Valley Forge, 1970), 58.

[10]*Afro-American* (Baltimore), 5 July 1918, 1.

[11]*The Crisis*, July 1918, 110.

er implementation. Rarely had our government placed such emphasis on democracy, and never had it publicized American idealism to the extent that it did in the final years of the war.

THE UNSETTLED AFTERMATH OF WAR

As the end of the war approached, censorship was tighter than before. Anticipation of the Armistice signing was great. It was so great, in fact, that when an apparently authentic telegraph announcing the end of the war came to the headquarters of the U.S. naval forces in France, the commanding admiral released the information to the local newspaper and to Roy W. Howard, president of UP, who happened to be at the headquarters. Howard sent the scoop home only to discover later that the telegraph had been a hoax. The real Armistice was signed five days later, on November 11, 1918.

Following the Armistice, the press and the nation engaged in a year-long debate over the negotiation and ratification of a peace settlement. During the summer and fall of 1919, Wilson needed all the support he could muster. Many elements in the American press opposed him. The papers owned by two "press lords" — as their liberal critics called them — Frank A. Munsey and William Randolph Hearst, denounced the settlement. Some of the leading liberal journals such as *The Nation* and *The New Republic* also opposed the treaty, believing that Wilson had compromised liberal principles at the conference table. The Irish-American and the German-American press attacked the treaty. Across the country many newspapers, particularly in the Northeast and Midwest, opposed it on a number of grounds. Many partisan newspapers were virulent in their attacks on Wilson and the treaty.[12] Nevertheless, journalists played an important role in the negotiation of the Paris Peace treaty not only by covering the talks but also by acting as informal diplomats. This involvement led to extensive discussions on the proper role of the press in diplomatic affairs.[13]

The debate over the treaty occurred against the backdrop of widespread domestic disturbances: a wave of strikes across the land, some of the worst race riots in American history, and the nation's first Red Scare. Newspaper response to the crises was far from constructive. The press resorted to sensational reports and scare headlines, thus increasing public alarm. It showed an inclination to support the anti-radical persuasion then sweeping the country.[14] Perhaps the *New York World's* Frank Cobb was correct when he reflected at the end of 1919 that the nation's newspapers "were not prepared for the waves of discontent and unrest that spread over the country. They were not prepared for the social ferment that followed the war. They were not prepared for the indus-

War's Aftermath
Americans and their Allies were jubilant over Germany's surrender to end World War I. The exhilaration that the *Citizen* of Columbus, Ohio, displayed typified the reaction.

trial upheavals that came."[15]

There was, however, a limit beyond which the press in general refused to go. In time, a number of newspapers feared that mob rule was becoming a national menace as a result of the race riots and lynchings. They demanded that the "supremacy of law" be reasserted over "jungle rule" and that some permanent remedy to the fundamental causes of the trouble be found. Early in 1920 the New York State Legislature denied five elected Socialist members their seats in the assembly. That action may have marked the beginning of the end of the public excitement, for many newspapers condemned it. The conservative *Chicago Tribune* commented that it was "an unusual piece of small-bore politics."

THE PRESS AND MODERN REVOLUTIONS

The media helped shape public thought about foreign affairs even more than domestic affairs. At the beginning of the interwar years, two modern revolutionary movements established themselves in two major Western countries — Russia and Italy. Now that the United States had become a world power, it was imperative that the public be informed about these movements, since from the start they challenged the international order. The press, however,

[12]For press opinion regarding the ratification of the treaty, see James D. Startt, "American Editorial Opinion of Woodrow Wilson and the Main Problems of Peacemaking in 1919" (Ph.D. diss., University of Maryland, 1965).

[13]Joseph R. Hayden, *Negotiating the Press: American Journalism and Diplomacy, 1918-1919* (Baton Rouge, La., 2010).

[14]Robert K. Murray, *Red Scare: A Study in National Hysteria, 1919* (Minneapolis, 1955), 178. Also, numerous examples of anti-radicalism and anti-labor press opinion can be found in the many *Literary Digest* articles published on the subject in 1919.

[15]Frank I. Cobb, "The Press and Public Opinion," *The New Republic*, 31 December 1919, 147.

was far from exhaustive in its handling of these revolutions.

Even as Russia participated in World War I as an ally of England and France, internal disturbances were simmering. Military failure and economic collapse triggered a full-fledged revolution in March 1917, followed seven months later by the Bolshevik Revolution. American correspondents were on hand to cover the story. The most famous was John Reed, who was buried at his death in 1920 in the Kremlin wall in Moscow, along with other "heroes of the revolution." He was from a well-to-do family from Portland, Oregon, and a graduate of Harvard University. He covered the Russian Revolution not as a correspondent but as a partisan. He became a trusted observer of the Bolsheviks and was witness to much of the revolution planning that was going on in October 1917. As a mouthpiece for the revolutionists, he was almost the only foreign correspondent who could work without restriction during the revolution. Other American reporters were beaten by soldiers, shot or jailed, and threatened with execution.

Following the Bolshevik revolution, Russia signed a peace treaty with Germany and withdrew from World War I. The new government was more repressive than the czarist government had been and inaugurated one of the most brutal regimes in history. It instituted greater controls on journalism, including strict censorship and falsification of news when necessary. An instance of "necessary" fabrication occurred when the czar and his entire family were executed in 1918. *Izvestia*, the official state newspaper, reported that the czar had been shot but that his wife and heir had been sent to safety. It was several months before UP correspondent Carl W. Ackerman reached Ekaterinburg, where the executions had occurred, and found out the truth. Once the Bolsheviks took power, they imposed a harsh regime of repression on the populace, executing 20 million or more people for political reasons over the next few decades. The conditions went virtually unreported, though, primarily because of the severe restrictions that the Soviet government placed on press coverage.

Between 1922, when he came to power, and 1933, Benito Mussolini, Italy's Fascist dictator, got more attention in the American press than any other world leader. He was anything but passive in creating a positive image for himself. American journalists of all persuasions traveled to Italy to interview him, and he welcomed them. *Il Duce* impressed most of them. There was, to be certain, some press criticism of and apprehension about his use of force and about the brutal aspects of his regime. Nevertheless, until the start of Hitler's regime in 1933 and the Italian-Ethiopian War of 1935-1936, Mussolini's popular appeal survived. He enjoyed an image as a man who had saved Italy, as someone who had answered the communist challenge, as a self-made, courageous, and practical man who accomplished things. The fact that some American correspondents complained about his censorship and control of the press did not seem to tarnish his image. Will Rogers called him a "Regular Guy"; Irvin S. Cobb said he was "one of the most human human beings" he ever saw; Ida Tarbell called him a "despot with a dimple."

Despite some shortsightedness, the American press deserves a

The American Press' Supporters of Revolution
A leftist American journalist who gained notoriety for his support of the Bolshevik Revolution, John Reed (left) gave an insider's view of the revolution in his book *Ten Days That Shook the World*. The Bolsheviks buried him as one of the heroes of their cause in 1920. The 1981 movie *Reds*, starring Warren Beatty, provided a sympathetic account of Reed's work for the Bolsheviks and the hardships he suffered and acquainted a new generation with him. A reporter for the *New York Times*, Walter Duranty (right) gained prominence covering World War I and became one of the most respected foreign correspondents of his time. Sympathetic to the Russian Revolution and the Marxist regime that it placed in power, however, after the war he misrepresented Soviet conditions to readers by ignoring serious economic and social problems and by downplaying Joseph Stalin's ruthlessness. With time, his bias and fraud became apparent; and critics gave him the nickname "Stalin's Apologist," a title later used by his biographer.

good deal of credit for the effort it made to cover the world in the 1920s. Europe, of course, was a center of news, and a number of old internationally minded papers expanded their services there. Some newcomers such as the *Baltimore Sun* also entered the field. In Asia, Japan became the center of operation for a small group of correspondents serving the major news agencies and some of the major dailies such as the *Chicago Daily News*, the *Chicago Tribune*, the *Christian Science Monitor*, the *New York Herald Tribune*, and the *New York Times*. Conditions were more difficult in China, but a few American correspondents survived handicaps of distance and poor communications to report on the new republic of Dr. Sun Yat-sen and, after him, Chiang Kai-shek. Reuters, the British news agency, covered India extensively; and in 1930 the Associated Press opened its own bureau in Calcutta. Moreover, a handful of special correspondents visited Asia from time to time for American publications.

The events of the 1930s forced the public to become more involved in debating international affairs. As the controversies of that intensely political decade ensued, the media occupied a powerful position in shaping and supporting the various arguments. Japan's invasion of Manchuria in 1931, the advent of Adolf Hitler in 1933 and Nazi Germany's subsequent persecutions at home and expansion abroad, the Italian invasion of Ethiopia in 1935, and, with these events, the collapse of collective security, all combined to create a dangerous international atmosphere.

The Ne

VOL. LXXIII....No. 24,105.   •••   NEW YC

LENIN DIES OF CEREBRAL HEMORRHAGE; MOSCOW THRONGS OVERCOME WITH GRIEF; TROTSKY DEPARTS ILL, RADEK IN DISFAVOR

Captain

SOVIET CONGRESS IN TEARS

Mass Hysteria Only Averted by a Leader's Brusque Intervention.

BODY WILL LIE IN STATE

Is to Be Taken to Moscow Today From Village Where Premier Passed Away.

KREMLIN WALL HIS TOMB

Washington Expects No Immediate Change in the Policy of the Russian Government.

By WALTER DURANTY.

NIKOLAI LENIN (VLADIMIR ILYITCH ULIANOV), A sketch made from life for THE NEW YORK TIMES by Oscar Cesare in Moscow, November, 1922, and autographed by Lenin.

EXPERTS PROPOSE GERMAN GOLD BANK

It Would Be Absolutely Inde-

BRITAIN ACCEPTS THE LIQUOR TREATY

Document Is Approved by All of

DECLARE FORCED PART OF

DENIES HE

Lenin's Death and a New U.S.S.R.

By the time Nikolai Lenin died in 1924, the American press had developed news bureaus around the world. Newspapers had followed Lenin's seizure of power during World War I when Germany had helped him return to Russia to topple its liberal provisional government. Upon his death, the western press focused on the struggle for power among his followers and was particularly interested in the direction that the Soviet Union would take in international affairs.

There was more response to Joseph Stalin's diplomatic moves. In 1934 the Soviet Union joined the League of Nations and a year later signed mutual assistance pacts with France and Czechoslovakia. These moves met strong and varied press reaction. Liberal journals of opinion, long sympathetic to the Soviets, applauded them. Conservative journals generally perceived ideological expansion as the prime goal of Soviet policy.

THE GREAT DEPRESSION

Seldom in history can one find two more crowded decades than those that fell between the two world wars. Movements grew across the world that would challenge the long-standing international order. In the West, the period began with widespread cultural disenchantment, the result of the experience of World War I and of long-growing strains and doubts regarding modern life. Communism, fascism, and nazism all developed and spread during these years. Midway through the period there occurred one of

the most agonizing episodes known in American life, the Great Depression. The 1920s and 1930s were also important years in the life of the press. More than ever it became an integral part of the nation's life, playing an essential role in the great domestic and international challenges.

The greatest challenge to domestic stability was the Great Depression. It was, in fact, the severest domestic test the country had faced since the Civil War. It was preceded by a number of economic tremors such as the languishing state of American agriculture, wild investment in the stock market starting in 1927, the unnerving stock market crash of 1929, the failure of banks, the disruption of world trade and the world monetary system, and a decline of investment. Once it struck, it occasioned widespread anguish and frustration. The economic collapse of the early 1930s is hard to imagine today. A few statistics provide a rough picture. By 1932 the country's industrial production was down by half, its foreign trade had declined 70%, and unemployment soared to about 12 million. The national gdp in 1932 was $59 billion (down from $104 billion in 1929), and per capita income declined from $750 in 1929 to $495 in 1932. Salaries decreased by about 40%; manufacturing wages by about 60%. Banks closed by the thousands. The Depression lingered on in some form until 1940, but the worst of it hit in 1932.

The press did not foresee this unprecedented tragedy. By the same token, economists of the day did no better in predicting the Depression. Still, George Seldes, a liberal critic of the press, a few years later charged: "It is held by many people that the failure of our newspapers to inform us honestly and accurately about the economic situation from 1927 to 1929, and the wish-fulfillment policy from 1929 on, constituted its [the press'] greatest failure in modern times."[16] In the 1920s the press had tended to stress sensational "big stories" and give the trivial equal coverage with the significant. Its emphasis on prosperity and its praise of Wall Street may have created a false sense of confidence among readers. Most journalists didn't have either the inclination or the ability to take a longer and deeper view of major economic issues. The press may have spent too much time and energy on a dramatic, sensational, and episodic type of journalism and too little on the comprehensive and orderly presentation of news.

As an agent for stimulating public debate and participating in the shaping of a public agenda, the press floundered at the beginning of the Depression. One study of front-page news stories of newspapers with major circulations indicates that there was no significant increase in stories about economic matters before the crash of 1929 or during the early years of the Depression. An increase only occurred in 1931. Economic stories reached their peak of 26% in 1935. Moreover, the number of stories that linked economic matters to political action was much fewer than those that merely described economic events and conditions. The author of the study concluded by underscoring "how little economic cover-

[16]George Seldes, *Freedom of the Press* (Garden City, N.Y., 1937). See also Margaret A. Blanchard, "Press Criticism and National Reform Movements: The Progressive Era and the New Deal," *Journalism History* 5 (1978): 36.

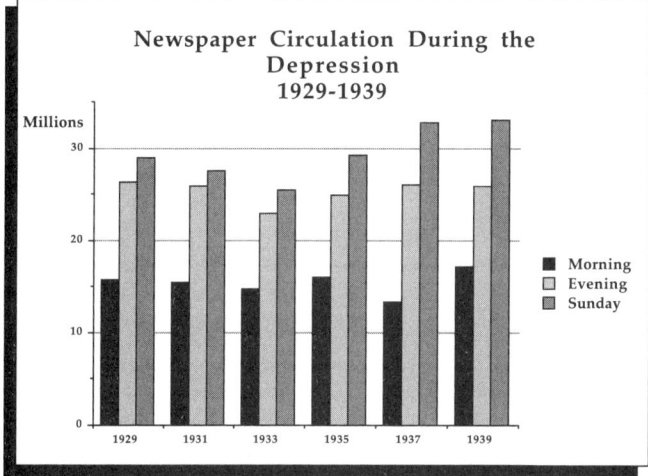

The Press and the Great Depression
On Monday, October 28, 1929, prices on the stock market began to tumble. The next day, panic selling began, and the market lost much of its value. Although many economists and officials argued that the downturn was temporary, nearly every American daily newspaper, like the *New York American*, gave prominent display to the crash. In the economic depression that ran throughout the following decade, newspapers suffered along with other businesses. Their circulation, as indicated in the chart above, stagnated and remained almost level for the next ten years.

age the early years of America's greatest depression received and how reluctant the press was to politicize economic issues and bring new, unorthodox solutions into the political arena."[17]

Some critics charged that anti-labor prejudices prevailed in the press and that the press was more interested in saving the nation's business than in reporting what had happened. William Allen White, the Republican editor of the *Emporia* (Kan.) *Gazette* and an astute observer of journalism, commented that the press was more concerned with the state of American business than with how individuals were faring. In 1932 he wrote to Kent Cooper of the Associated Press: "It is so easy for a reporter, a copy-reader, the city editor, and the staff of our prosperous papers to take the Country

Club attitude, the boss's slant, toward those who for one reason or another are whacking the established order."[18]

There are, however, several mitigating factors to consider. First, it is easier to recognize the Great Depression in retrospect than it was to perceive it in its early years. The stock market crash of 1929 had not directly affected the majority of Americans. Most people had not invested in the market. No one knew in 1930 that the Depression had begun. There was, moreover, a natural tendency to believe that recovery would come. As the Depression deepened and spread, there may have been a natural impulse among journalists not to be alarmists and to attempt to act as a restraint on public emotions. Without excusing the press response, it might be admitted that the Depression was a soul-searching and baffling experience. It confused many Americans and, no doubt, many journalists, too.

THE PRESS AND THE NEW DEAL

With the election of Franklin Roosevelt in 1932, the country and the press entered one of their most exciting times. His recovery program, the New Deal, became a center of public debate for the remainder of the decade. Against the backdrop of totalitarianism abroad, the New Deal offered hope and action. Roosevelt's buoyant leadership and experiments with economic policy inspired the majority of Americans with feelings of a democratic resurgence. To others, he appeared as a charlatan, even a dictator. Critics viewed his New Deal as a program for an unwanted revolution. The press displayed a vigor regarding public affairs that it had not demonstrated for years.

That vigor was many-sided. For years the news media had been expanding their role in the political culture, and by the time of Roosevelt's presidency they reached into American life in an unprecedented manner. Before World War I, news film had gained considerable prominence, and during the war it played a significant role in covering the conflict. With the addition of sound in 1927, the newsreel entered a golden age that lasted until the 1950s. There may have been some truth in actor Oscar Levant's remark that a newsreel was "a series of catastrophes, ended by a fashion show," but the American people welcomed newsreels. By the 1930s they had become an accepted and popular news medium.

Roosevelt's buoyant personality and confident approach to the nation in distress made him a natural subject for the newsreel camera. When Americans by the millions went to the "movies" during the New Deal years, they saw the President and watched and listened as he popularized his administration's programs and achievements. Aside from their attraction to news showing dramatic, sensational, and even tragic events, newsreel editors appreciated the positive news that Roosevelt was able to supply. Since newsreels were shown along with feature films in practically every theater, they afforded FDR an ideal communications opportunity, and he was able to take advantage of it.

[17]Richard L. Rubin, *Press, Party, and Presidency* (New York, 1981), 124.

[18]William Allen White to Kent Cooper, 29 August 1932, in Walter Johnson, ed., *Selected Letters of William Allen White 1899-1943* (New York, 1947), 326.

The radio was another new medium with a huge political potential. Since its first scheduled broadcast in the United States in 1920, its popularity had grown enormously. Roosevelt and his administration recognized its publicity value and, from his first days in office, sought to maximize it as a political instrument. His Fireside Chats, beginning the month he took office, became legendary as a means of connecting him and the people in an intimate way. In these and his longer broadcasts, Roosevelt, working with a team of speech writers and mobilizing his superb rhetorical skills, was able to reach a vast audience. The networks also extended public speaking privileges to Mrs. Roosevelt and to members of the president's cabinet. Beyond that, the networks produced numerous informational programs, and while claiming to be politically neutral, they carried "administration information" as a public service. By 1941 radio had become the most significant source of public information, and Roosevelt was masterful in using it.

Meanwhile the print media were busy extending political journalism. New periodicals, many designed for specialized audiences, appeared. Some were immensely popular. News magazines such as *Time*, founded in 1923, and *Newsweek*, founded in 1933, enjoyed large circulations. No media development vitalized American political life more than the advent of public affairs syndicated columnists. Hundreds of newspapers subscribed to popular columns such as Walter Lippmann's "Today and Tomorrow," begun in 1929, and Raymond Clapper's "Watching the World Go By," begun in 1936.

A great deal has been written about Roosevelt and the press. At his first press conference, he exhilarated the correspondents. After the disappointing relations the Washington press corps had had with his predecessors, it is no wonder that journalists were impressed by Roosevelt's jaunty personality and his efforts from the start to establish rapport with them. He told the reporters that they would no longer have to submit written questions in advance and that he would attempt to handle questions in a spontaneous manner. There would be, of course, ground rules regarding which of his comments could be published and which would be intended as "background information" and as confidential "off the record" remarks. The old rule of "no direct quotes without authorization" would be retained.

The first press conference typified many of his early meetings with the correspondents, and it has become something of a legend. It ended with the reporters spontaneously applauding the President. As the years went on, however, some correspondents began to complain about his using his wit to evade questions and, particularly after 1935, about his limiting of news by labeling many remarks as "off the record." It is clear, however, that Roosevelt had the correspondents' support during the crucial early years of the New Deal.

He found it more difficult to accept certain members of the press. Some mass-circulation columnists such as Frank Kent, Westbrook Pegler, David Lawrence, Mark Sullivan, and Walter Lippmann opposed Roosevelt and the New Deal. Others such as Walter Winchell, Drew Pearson, and Robert S. Allen generally sup-

"ANYBODY ELSE?"

The New Dealers and the Press

Even the considerable press opposition to Franklin Roosevelt and his New Deal could not overcome his immense popularity. In his campaign for reelection in 1936, he challenged his critics directly and won the biggest electoral victory since 1820. He remained perturbed by the large percentage of newspapers that opposed him and his policies. He was not, however, without defenders. Among his New Dealers, his Secretary of the Interior, Harold Ickes, was the most pugnacious in dealing with opposition newspapers. As a result, he became the subject of frequent editorial cartoons. This one shows him fighting all types of enemies, including the press, fascism, academics, and the Ku Klux Klan. Having punched out those four, the cartoon caption has him asking, "Anybody else?"

ported him. Roosevelt, however, had little respect for most columnists and could even be contemptuous of them. He was antagonistic also toward publishers as a group although he enjoyed friendly relations with a number of individual publishers and editors. On behalf of the American Newspaper Publishers Association, William Allen White told the President at one point: "Most of us have agreed with most things that you have tried to do. If some of us have disagreed with a few of the things, it was in sorrow, not in anger, and it hurt us much more than it did you."[19]

Such a conciliatory gesture, however, does not alter the well-publicized hostility that Roosevelt had for the press in general. He repeatedly said that 85% of the nation's press opposed him. That was an erroneous appraisal of the strength of his opposition, and one investigation shows that he had reason to know it was exaggerated.[20] The idea of a largely hostile press, however, no doubt

[19]Quoted in Graham J. White, *FDR and the Press* (Chicago, 1979), 121.
[20]Ibid., 69-71.

added a degree of public sympathy to his support.

Although it did not reach the degree he claimed, Roosevelt and his New Deal did attract press hostility. Conservative papers thought his program too liberal while liberal journals thought it too conservative and weak on principles. The general pattern of press treatment of the New Deal was strong support at first followed in ensuing years by a more critical tone. Sometimes, as the criticism mounted, it became bitter, but at other times it was temperate. Even the President's most extreme opponents in the press — William Randolph Hearst and the *Chicago Tribune's* Colonel Robert McCormick — supported the New Deal at first. McCormick broke with Roosevelt rather quickly, as a result of spending policies and his conviction that the New Deal was a threat to press freedom. Hearst's departure was slower. By 1935, however, he decided he could not endure what he thought were socialistic, even communistic, tendencies in the New Deal.

Roosevelt's administration was not defenseless. It gave criticism as well as received. The President himself was harsh toward individual journalists and papers. So were other New Dealers. The head of the National Recovery Administration, Hugh Johnson, not the most temperate of men, lashed out at an article in the *Washington Post* in this manner: "With little less than libel, a trifle more than backstairs gossip, this writer in whose veins there must flow something more than a trace of redent [sic] blood, exalts some who are weak and throws mud at some who are strong, for no other apparent reason than to provide salable copy." Then he called the *Post* a "dying newspaper."[21] The most famous New Dealer critique of the press was that of Harold Ickes, the Secretary of the Interior, who, in his *America's House of Lords*, made a trenchant attack on the press as a business. Such criticism provides evidence of the stormy involvement the press had in the public debate after 1932.

There was another important factor in Roosevelt's relations with the press: his expertise at organizing publicity. The New Deal's publicity organization was big.[22] Many of the newly created government agencies had their own publicity bureaus. Stephen Early, Roosevelt's press secretary, was in charge of publicity for the President. Modeling his work on George Creel's CPI organization of World War I days, he created an effective and centralized information distribution center.

The press benefited from that organization and its mountain of news releases, but it also discovered that it faced a new vigorous competitor in its efforts to influence public opinion. Lorena Hickok, one of the first female reporters for the Associated Press, gave up her job in 1933 to gather information for the Federal Emergency Relief Administration. As a chief investigator for the FERA, she traveled the nation on fact-finding tours to observe relief programs and reported directly to the FERA's chief, Harry Hopkins, and to Eleanor Roosevelt, whose friend and confidante she was. Some of her reports formed the basis for newspaper articles, while

[21]Quoted in an untitled address by Eugene Meyer, 5 March 1935, Box 85, Eugene Meyer Papers, Manuscript Division, Library of Congress, Washington, D.C., p. 5.
[22]Betty Houchin Winfield, "The New Deal Publicity Operation: Foundation for the Modern Presidency," *Journalism Quarterly* 61 (1984): 40-8.

PIECE PEACE?

Isolationism
In the 1930s American and press sentiment opposed involvement in European affairs. When Adolf Hitler demanded that Czechoslovakia cede part of its territory to Germany during the "Munich Crisis," American newspapers, like this cartoon from the *Boston Post*, generally criticized Hitler without urging that the United States take any action to stop him.

others resulted directly in government efforts to solve problems.

THE PRESS AND INTERNATIONAL AGGRESSION

Events elsewhere between 1931 and 1936 also attracted widespread attention in the press. Hitler's coming to power in 1933 and the Nazi reconstruction of Germany that followed caused a great deal of uneasiness. The Italian invasion of Ethiopia in 1935 shattered Mussolini's favorable image in the press. Italy became an aggressor nation. When Japan invaded Manchuria in 1931, the American press was at first divided. Among other things, the invasion was a violation of the Nine Power Pact that both the United States and Japan signed in 1922. To some papers, as well as to some diplomats, it still seemed possible at that point to construct a case for Japan. As the crisis continued, however, press opinion gravitated around hostility to Japan coupled with the hope that a settlement could be reached without hostilities between the United States and Japan. The idea was widespread that the United States had no interest in the Far East that justified a confrontation. Some papers did support sanctions against Japan, but the press in general felt relieved when they were not employed.

Before long, though, events did threaten to draw the United States into intervention, even war, as aggression continued in Europe and Asia. Germany's reoccupation of the Rhineland in 1936, its incorporation of Austria in 1938, and its destruction of Czechoslovakia jarred American opinion. Meanwhile, in 1937 the Sino-Japanese War began. When World War II started in Europe, with Hitler's invasion of Poland on September 1, 1939, the United States was pushed to the brink of decision. After the fall of France in the spring of 1940, whether the United States should supply Britain became an acute question. If Germany won, what would be the nature of the Nazi menace to the Western World, and to the Western Hemisphere in particular? Seldom has popular clamor over American policy been as severe as it was between 1936 and 1941. It is difficult to quarrel with the judgment that "never before in their history had Americans been so well informed about events abroad and never before had they followed them so closely."[23]

With international problems increasing, however, American isolationist sentiment also increased. After World War I and the frustrations of peacemaking of 1919, American opinion turned away from the international idealism that had characterized its brief departure from the isolationist impulse, and became disillusioned about participating in the international controversies of Europe and Asia. Rejecting the League of Nations, the American people felt secure in their geographical position, buffered on east and west by oceans separating them from foreign turmoil.

As the events of the 1930s unfolded in Europe and Asia, an abhorrence of war grew in America. Coupled with this was the idea that with its depression-shattered economy, the country needed to direct its energies toward curing domestic problems. Moreover, as fear of involvement in another war emerged, revisionist writing about World War I reached its highmark. The revisionists argued that the United States should have stayed out of World War I and, indeed, that the British and munitions manufacturers had manipulated our intervention to serve their own self interests.

The currents of isolationist sentiment were broad and deep. The press vitalized all shades of opinion. Its pronouncements ranged from ill-informed chauvinism in some editorials to fair-minded critiques. Both conservative and liberal papers endorsed isolationism, as did old progressive organs. Papers opposed to Roosevelt's New Deal policies tended to be isolationist. So did many that agreed with those policies. In 1938 the journalist Elmer Davis, an internationalist, commented: "Twenty years ago we went on a crusade which would have made sense if we had got what we wanted; but we failed to find the Holy Grail, and the experience ought to have cured us of our inclination to go grailing."[24] Isolationism was truly heterogeneous; and the majority of Americans, for one reason or another, believed in it.

The isolationists' persuasion, however, was not complete.

[23]William L. Langer and S. Everett Gleason, *The Challenge to Isolation 1937-1940* (New York, 1952), 11.

[24]Quoted in Allan M. Winkler, *The Politics of Propaganda: The Office of War Information 1942-1945* (New Haven, 1978), 33.

America First

American opposition to involvement in the problems of the rest of the world took a number of media forms in the 1930s. One was music, with the song "America First" proclaiming that Americans should place the welfare of their own country ahead of international troubles that the other countries caused themselves.

When Roosevelt suggested in a 1937 speech that aggressor powers be "quarantined," his idea received strong press support. Among the major papers siding with him were the *New York Times, Washington Post, Washington Evening Star, Cleveland Plain Dealer, Chicago Daily News, Portland Morning Oregonian,* and *New Orleans Times-Picayune.*

Nevertheless, Roosevelt retreated from putting his words into action. American opinion on isolation was not as settled as it might seem. *The Nation* and *The New Republic* were shocked by the Allied capitulation at Munich in 1938, by the Nazi-Soviet Pact of the following year, and by the Nazi blitzkrieg of Denmark, Norway, and the Low Countries in the spring of 1940. Slowly these stalwarts of liberal opinion relinquished their resistance to intervention. Even the *Saturday Evening Post,* the voice of middle-class America and an outspoken isolationist magazine, became interventionist in 1941.

Organizations formed to advocate both sides of the controversy. One was the Committee to Defend America by Aiding the Allies, a group that had William Allen White as one of its organizers and leaders. He was one of the most respected figures in the country, and he explained his purpose in a radio interview:

Two views are honestly held up by intelligent people. One group contends that by isolating ourselves we can let the Allies fall and Hitler rise and then retire behind our own barriers.... The other group believes that isolation is impossible. The Nazis have overrun Czechoslovakia by force, Poland by force, Norway by force, Denmark by force, Holland by force, and are now by force overrunning France and will conquer England by force if they can. We are next.... It makes no difference whether it is a war with guns or an economic war, or a social upheaval which will menace our way of life.[25]

That idea was gaining in the public mind.

Why the weakening of the isolationist impulse? Perhaps isolationism floundered as a result of the mass media's publicizing the war in Europe after 1939. After the war began, the British government engaged in no propaganda activities in the United States as it had in 1914. It simply gave out "information on demand." But a strong, latent pro-English sentiment existed in this country, and it surfaced as news of the Battle of Britain filled the press. "This ... is London," Edward R. Murrow's dramatic opening of each of his broadcasts from the British capital while the Germans were bombing it, conveyed the reality of the Blitz to millions of Americans and created sympathy for the beleaguered British. Murrow put together a team of correspondents for CBS, and they became the first broadcast "news stars" to achieve that status not as commentators but as on-the-air reporters.[26] Meanwhile, popular radio commentators such as H. V. Kaltenborn and Raymond Swing favored intervention. No doubt these things impressed American opinion. The Germans, moreover, had operated an active propaganda organization in the United States since 1933. It tried to foster isolationism and even worked to defeat Roosevelt for re-election in 1940. In the end, such activity probably damaged the isolationist cause, for most of the Americans who had little desire to intervene had even less respect for Nazism. They were recognizing the dangers the Axis powers posed.

Gradually events exposed the fallacies of the isolationist position. But that persuasion remained alive in some quarters of the press. It could erupt and strike sharply at the various measures that Roosevelt took in 1940 and 1941 to aid the countries fighting Germany. The hard-core anti-Roosevelt isolationist newspapers refused to budge from their contention that he was leading the country into war. Just three days before Pearl Harbor, in fact, the *Chicago Tribune*, in an effort to discredit the administration, splashed a story across its front page announcing that Roosevelt had war plans. A strategic plan the War Department drew up to be used in case the United States should declare war on Germany had been leaked to the *Tribune*, and the paper made full use of it. That such a document existed was not surprising, but its publication during times so critical for the world shows the degree to

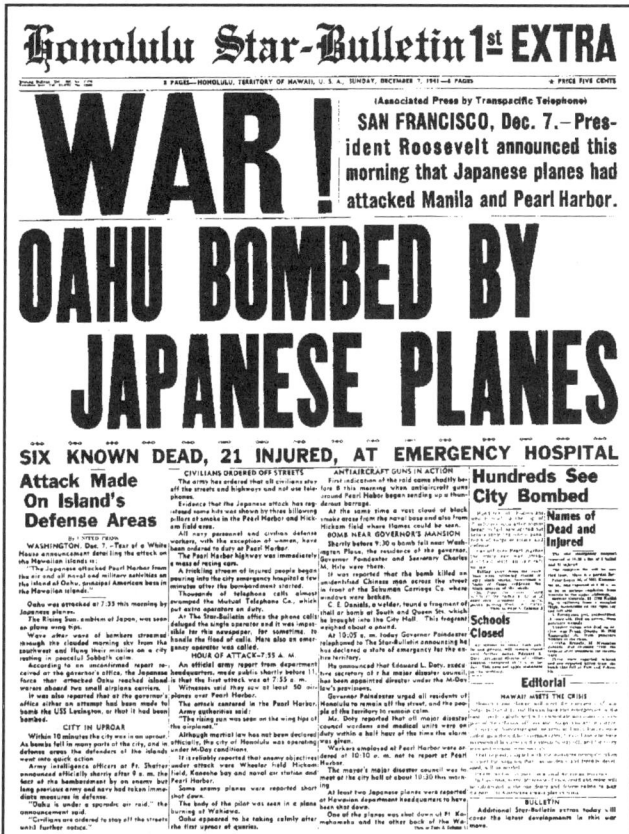

Pearl Harbor

When Japanese planes bombed the American naval base at Pearl Harbor on December 7, 1941, the act immediately brought the United States into World War II as a combatant. The report reproduced above was from the same day in the *Star-Bulletin* of Honolulu, the site of the bombing.

which the isolationist press would go in making its case. In the end, dramatic events abroad overtook the isolationist cause and revealed the weaknesses of its premises. The attack on Pearl Harbor removed most of the remaining doubt.

WORLD WAR II

During the first two years of the war, the United States remained, for the most part, neutral, at least in official policy. Through the Lend-Lease program, though, America provided war materiel to England, the Soviet Union, and China to support their war efforts against the Axis. Then on December 7, 1941, Germany's ally, Japan, put a definitive end to American neutrality with its attack on Pearl Harbor.

The attack caught not only the military by surprise, but journalists as well. One reporter assumed the noise from the attack was a practice exercise the American military was conducting and went out for a swim, only to find out when he returned that he had missed the story. Other reporters were more astute. A United Press reporter, whose apartment had a view of Pearl Harbor, immediately recognized the enemy airplanes. He put a long-distance call through to his San Francisco office and left his wife to handle the

[25]"Radio Interview with W. A. White," n.d., William Allen White Papers, Series D, Box 13, Manuscript Division, Library of Congress, Washington, D.C., pp. 1-2.

[26]The team Murrow assembled included Mary Marvin Breckinridge, Cecil Brown, Winston Burdett, Charles Collingwood, William Downs, Thomas Grandin, Richard C. Hottelet, Larry Le Sueur, Eric Sevareid, William L. Shirer, and Howard K. Smith.

call once the operator had completed it. As a result, the first eye-witness account of the bombing of Pearl Harbor that the UP carried was actually phoned in by a reporter's wife.

With the Japanese attack on Pearl Harbor, the debate ended over the position the United States should take regarding the war. When Americans heard over their radios that Japan had attacked the "Gibraltar of the Pacific," they reacted much as they did a half-century later when on 9/11 terrorists crashed airplanes into the World Trade Center. On December 8, Congress declared war on Japan. Three days later, Germany and Italy honored their Tripartite Pact with Japan and declared war on the United States. The United States reciprocated with a declaration of war against the Axis powers on the same day.

America had entered a war of unprecedented magnitude and faced one of the most severe crises in its history. It confronted a staggering combined menace, for by late 1941 Hitler had overrun Europe. His armies were poised to strike at the Middle East. Where they would move after that no one could say — perhaps eastward to join forces with Japan, which was already in China and had begun to overrun Southeast Asia.

Unlike what had happened in World War I, the United States had been attacked, and Americans were saying that this was "our war." Pearl Harbor united the country. "We must from now on think not only in terms of total war, but also in terms of a world-wide area of conflict," editorialized the liberal *The New Republic*. On the other end of the political spectrum, William Randolph Hearst wrote in his newspaper column: "Well, fellow Americans, we are in the war and we have got to win it."[27]

The war, however, was not to be won entirely on distant shores. Most Americans applauded the war aims, but questions were raised in some corners. Before Pearl Harbor, the *Pittsburgh Courier* and the *Chicago Defender*, both African-American papers, questioned the nature of the war then underway. Was it a white man's war for the preservation of the status quo? For black Americans to receive the human freedoms that all Americans believed were theirs, the status quo would have to be changed. After Pearl Harbor, the NAACP's *Crisis*, edited since 1934 by Roy Wilkins, a forceful advocate of civil rights, announced, "Now is the time *not* to be silent." The *Pittsburgh Courier* agreed and advanced the "Double V" slogan for "victory over our enemies at home and victory over our enemies on the battlefields abroad."[28] Discrimination in the armed services and in war industries as well as the racial segregation practiced across the country seemed intolerable to many black editors. In retrospect, their exertions helped to establish the groundwork for the civil rights movement of the 1950s and 1960s; but at the time the issue of discrimination was a matter of serious concern for the Roosevelt administration, which moved only hesitantly toward redressing black grievances.

Black citizens appear to have supported both the militancy of their press and the nation's war effort. When the armed forces moved toward greater racial equality in 1944 and sent more black units into combat, black correspondents accompanied them and reported on their accomplishments. "No previous venture in public relations," surmises the historian John Morton Blum, "had the impact on blacks of the reports of the war correspondents of Afro-American newspapers."[29] As important as the correspondents' work was to the black community, it also can be seen as a part of the larger and unprecedented news coverage of the war.

Radio also was able to make a unique contribution to the coverage. Listening to the news had become a national habit, and the American public could hear about the war on its 56 million radio sets. As entire families gathered to hear the evening news broadcasts, radio reporters took on an important role in bringing the realities of the war home to American living rooms. The most influential one was Edward R. Murrow of CBS. His nightly broadcasts from London, always beginning with a grave, "This ... is London," grimly, yet vividly, described the destruction that German bombing was causing to the British capital. Some evenings, the sound of bombs exploding would punctuate his broadcasts. The war brought radio commentators and their listeners into the most intimate relationship they had ever experienced. Walter Winchell's rapid fire opening, "Good evening, Mr. and Mrs. North America and all the ships at sea. Let's go to press," echoed in millions of homes. There was a reassuring quality in Lowell Thomas' melodious sign off, "So long until tomorrow." The commentators, with their individual rhetorical styles, were national figures and a vital part of the nation at war.

Americans also were able to watch war news. In some respects, the newsreel reached its peak during the war as it responded to the public's great demand for war news. As in World War I, the work of both civilian and military cameramen again was censored because of the conditions that a great war imposed. Yet the newsreels gave the public an unparalleled graphic picture of the many sides of modern war, with films ranging from portrayals of national strength and unity to scenes of actual battle and appalling discoveries the Allies made upon entering the Nazi death camps at Buchenwald and Dachau.

Reporting on World War II marked a major change in war coverage. The colorful and romantic foreign correspondents of World War I were replaced in World War II by more professional, dispassionate, and, in many cases, college-educated journalists. These new reporters, both men and women, faced a staggering job of covering a truly global conflict. Because of their greater access to the front lines, the dangers increased significantly over those that World War I correspondents had faced. Yet they managed to cover the war, for the most part, accurately and with integrity. Government interference with reporting was less than it had been in World War I. There were no total news blackouts and no long periods when the public did not know what was happening, as there had been in the World War I and previous wars.[30] Another differ-

[27]"Our War," *The New Republic*, 15 December 1941, 812; and W. A. Swanberg, *Citizen Hearst* (New York, 1961), 499.

[28]Quoted in John Morton Blum, *V Was for Victory: Politics and American Culture during World War II* (New York, 1976), 208.

[29]Ibid., 209.

[30]Joseph J. Matthews, *Reporting the Wars* (Minneapolis, 1957), 176.

Ernie Pyle

WWII Reporter Told the Story of G.I. Joe

Few journalists enjoy Ernie Pyle's enduring popularity.

Born in 1900 near Dana, Indiana, the skinny farm boy studied economics at Indiana University but discovered an affinity for journalism. He joined the Scripps-Howard newspaper chain and in the 1930s crisscrossed America in search of feature stories. After World War II began, he volunteered to be a civilian combat reporter. When Americans fought in Africa, Europe, and the Pacific, Pyle went with them. His syndicated column covered the war the same way troops fought it: one small piece at a time. Soldiers loved how he captured life in the military. Civilians appreciated columns about hometown heroes as well as his keen eye for detail.

While many journalists wrote about strategy and tactics, Pyle preferred spending time with ordinary soldiers before retreating to his typewriter. "Ernie Pyle left for OP-3," a combat journal of the 36th Division recorded in 1943. An "OP" – observation post – was as near to the enemy as one could get. That particular trip to the Italian front resulted in a celebrated column in which Pyle described soldiers saying goodbye to their dead captain. Pyle asked a few questions, but mostly he watched as one by one they took the captain's hand, straightened his uniform, or softly swore and moved on.

In another famous dispatch, Pyle strolled along a French beach shortly after D-day. He described bodies in the surf, burned vehicles, and a litter of personal items including a tennis racket and a pocket Bible. "I walked around what seemed to be a couple of pieces of driftwood sticking out of the sand," he wrote. "But they weren't driftwood. They were a soldier's two feet. He was completely covered except for his feet; the toes of his GI shoes pointed toward the land he had come so far to see, and which he saw so

briefly."

Analysts of America's 2003 war in Iraq lionized Pyle as "the original embedded reporter." That was both blessing and curse. Pyle won a Pulitzer Prize, and his best-selling books remain popular. However, he repeatedly suffered depression from exposure to combat.

While covering what he said would be his final campaign, Pyle died April 18, 1945, on Ie Shima from a Japanese sniper's bullet. American soldiers retrieved his body and erected a crude sign. It said, "At This Spot, the 77th Infantry Division Lost a Buddy."

Ernie Pyle wrote about the common soldier for audiences back home, hungry for news of their loved ones, and he told the truth about the horrors of war. One reason for his success was that he got to know soldiers personally (as illustrated in the top photograph of him sharing cigarettes with infantrymen). He gained immense popularity with readers on the homefront. Collections of his columns sold well as books, two of which — *Here Is Your War* and *Brave Men* — were made into the realistic movie *The Story of G.I. Joe*, starring Robert Mitchum (middle in the photograph above) as an officer based on Captain Henry Waskow and Burgess Meredith (right) as Pyle. General Dwight Eisenhower said it was "the greatest war picture I've ever seen!" Soon after the movie was made, Pyle was killed by a hidden Japanese machine-gunner.

ence in the coverage of World War II was that news consumers got information much more rapidly than in the past due to advancing technology, though a good deal of the news that was published was human interest rather than hard news.

More than 1,600 American journalists covered the war in Europe, Africa, and Asia, and most of them wore officers' uniforms. The uniform was an indication of the position of reporters as a sort of quasi-soldier, a position that brought both perks and difficulties since it implied that correspondents had a duty not to question military practices and policies.[31] Of those 1,600, thirty-seven would die doing their jobs, and another 112 would be wounded.

Most correspondents had to deal with censorship and the hardships of war. Reporters covering Germany in the early days of the war had particular problems that arose from covering a dictatorship determined to build a good image in the neutral United States. Reporters who refused to toe the Nazi line faced expulsion. Throughout the rest of Europe, Asia, and Africa, reporters risked arrest or execution as spies if their reports deviated from approved limits that local governments imposed, and many were forced to flee in the wake of advancing armies that preferred their activities not be reported in the press.

Yet for all that was new in reporting the war, much of the old remained, including two common problems for war correspondents: censorship and difficulties with transportation. Censorship in the wake of the German invasion of France in May 1940 left many reporters with little to write about beyond the domestic lives of French women whose men had all gone to the war. The bombing of Louvain resulted in a trail of refugees said to be 200 miles long. Taylor Henry of the Associated Press and P. J. Philip of the *New York Times* hired bicycles to try to get through the mob headed toward relative safety in Belgium. Reporters covering the German side, though, got transportation to the front, courtesy of the Nazis, who wanted to ensure that the West knew what was happening.[32]

Reporters in Japan and other Asian locations had a horrendous time after Pearl Harbor. Otto Tolischus of the *New York Times* was one of the first journalists to be captured in Tokyo. He was imprisoned and questioned endlessly. In Saigon, Vietnam, seven reporters were taken into "protective" custody. Others evaded capture by pretending to be drunk or employing other clever means.

With a total war being waged on several fronts, the press had to split its resources to keep Americans informed about what was happening in both Europe and the Pacific. The big story in the Pacific centered on the Philippines, where the Japanese had Gen. Douglas MacArthur's troops penned in on the Bataan Peninsula and Corregidor. The few reporters left in the Philippines went to heroic lengths to tell the stories of the men fighting there. After the fall of Bataan and Corregidor, the story of the Coral Sea victory in 1942, covered by lone *Chicago Tribune* correspondent Stanley

Johnston, was at least temporary relief for Americans.

Just over a month later, though, Johnston and his paper were accused of publishing information about Japanese strength at Midway that could have let the enemy know U. S. cryptographers had broken their code. The *Tribune* carried Johnston's story on the front page of June 7, 1942, reporting the American naval victory at Midway. The headline read "Navy had Word of Jap Plan to Strike at Sea." Authorities believed this statement revealed to the enemy that the Navy had broken the Japanese code, which had been one of the reasons for the American success. Consequently, the government charged the *Tribune* with violating the Espionage Act as well as the Censorship Code.[33] A federal grand jury investigated but did not return an indictment, and no evidence was presented to indicate the Japanese realized that their code had been broken.

After the fall of Bataan and Corregidor, the fighting in the Pacific became even bloodier and more desperate. Correspondents who covered the campaign to retake the Pacific Islands faced graver dangers than before. Many were injured or captured and tortured, and several did not return from their assignments. Jack Singer of the INS and Byron Darnton of the *New York Times* both were killed in Japanese attacks. In Europe, INS reporter Larry Meier was killed covering his first big battle, Dieppe, in August 1942. The UP's Leo Disher managed to swim ashore when the ship he was on sank off the Algerian coast. He survived the twenty-six bullet wounds he received in the action.

One reason correspondents suffered more in World War II than in World War I was that they were more likely to be at the front with the troops or on other dangerous expeditions. Ernie Pyle, the best-known and loved correspondent of the war, lived at the front with the infantry first in Tunisia and then in Europe.[34] Walter Cronkite, then of United Press but who would become America's most popular television journalist in the latter part of the twentieth century, accompanied American pilots on bombing raids over Germany. He survived, but Robert P. Post of the *New York Times* was killed on a similar ride.

Pyle was among the twenty-eight journalists chosen to accompany the Allies as they prepared for one of the most significant campaigns of the war: the 1944 invasion of France. Office of War Information chief Elmer Davis proclaimed the invasion was the best covered military operation in all of history. Cronkite and others flew in with bomber units, and at least one enterprising reporter, Leonard Mosley of the *London Daily Telegraph*, jumped with a paratrooper unit. Reporters for CBS, the United Press, and several other news outlets raced ahead of the Allied forces, without permission, so they could be on hand in Paris to witness its liberation.

The ugliest aspect of the war dealt with the Nazi persecution of the Jews and the implementation of Hitler's "final solution" for them. The Nazis executed 6 million European Jews. The media

[31]Nathan Lande, *Dispatches from the Front: News Accounts of America's Wars from 1776-1991* (New York,, 1995), 216; Loren B. Thompson, "The Media Versus the Military: A Brief History of War Coverage in the United States," in Thompson, ed., *Defense Beat: The Dilemma of Defense Coverage* (New York, 1991), 30.

[32]Hohenberg, *Foreign Correspondence*, 201.

[33]The illegality of willful publication in wartime of information about national defense useful to the enemy was implicit in the Espionage Act of 1917. Still in effect, that Act had been amended in 1940 to increase penalties for peacetime violation. The government believed that the *Tribune* also had violated the Voluntary Censorship Code.

[34]James Tobin, *Ernie Pyle's War: America's Witness to World War II* (New York, 1997), 242.

War Propaganda

Axis Propaganda Fights the Enemy with Racism and Black Ink

The war of words and images became one of the most important struggles of World War II. Axis nations used the news and entertainment media – and even the arts – to build national unity among their own people, to try to bolster or gain support from other nations, and to try to discourage their enemies.

Germany's effort, led by Josef Goebbels, was the most comprehensive. He believed propaganda should be omnipresent. Long before the war began, the press, films, radio, literature, theater, and art promoted Hitler, the Nazi Party, and such ideas as "one people, one nation, one leader," and "the Jews are our misfortune."

Unlike the Nazis, the Fascists did not attempt to make party views a new national religion. Propaganda aimed at Italians focused on religion, national pride, and family values. Later, however, Italians were fed increasingly racist depictions of the enemy, similar to much German and Japanese propaganda. Like the Nazis, the Fascists believed in early indoctrination. Even comic strips in youth newspapers promoted Fascist military values.

The Japanese embraced what they termed "thought war" later than did most Western nations, but they also had a propaganda system firmly in place by the mid-1930s. Many of the themes and much of the style came from German propaganda, with the two nations even co-producing two films.

Propagandists used "leaflet bombings" and radio to try to demoralize enemy soldiers. Radio stations, which could be used to broadcast propaganda, became key prizes for advancing armies. A common theme was the suspicion of what lonely wives and girlfriends of "naive" soldiers might be doing at home. Americans Iva Toguri and Mildred Gillars – termed "Tokyo Rose" and "Axis Sally" – both were sentenced to prison after the war for their radio propaganda work in Japan and Germany.

The Nazi party in Germany had used propaganda beginning in the 1920s to advance its ideas, including German racial superiority. Its most vicious campaign was against the Jewish population of Europe. The most infamous example of the campaign was *The Eternal Jew,* a film and exhibit that presented Jews as subhuman. Despite such material, journalists of the Allied nations found it difficult to believe later that the Nazis were carrying out the systematic extermination of Jews, as they were indeed doing. Nazi propaganda like the cartoon at left provided clear evidence to many black Americans that, even though problems existed in the United States, German ideas of racial superiority made it imperative that they support the war effort against the Axis. In the cartoon, one black G.I. declares, "We are fighting for culture, Jimmy." The other replies, "Yes, but what is culture?"

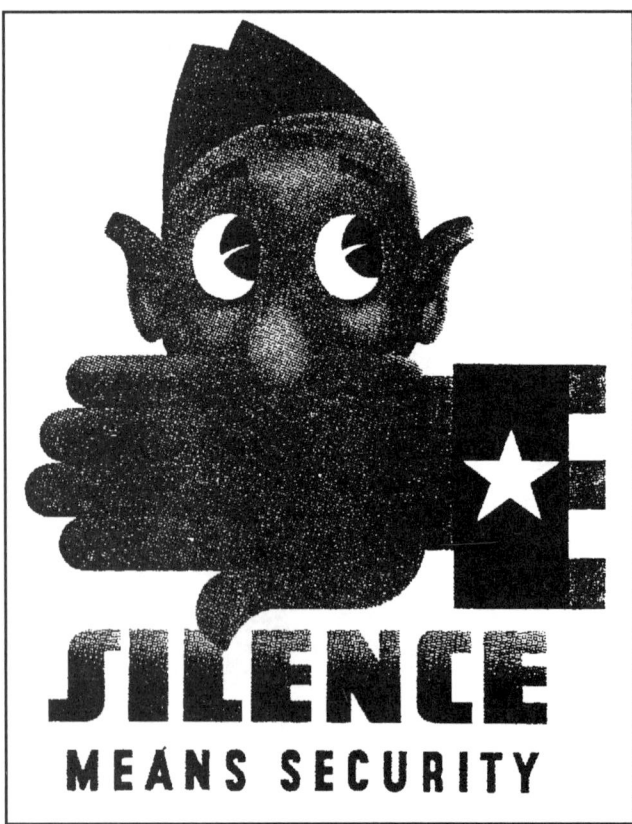

"Silence"
The Office of War Information, headed by veteran journalist Elmer Davis, was responsible for propaganda abroad and information distributed domestically. One of its continuing campaigns, of which the poster reproduced above was a part, was to warn Americans not to talk carelessly about details that enemy agents might pick up, thus endangering the war effort.

published news of the persecution beginning in the 1930s and during the war made known the horrors of the extermination to the limits that information was available — although it was impossible to comprehend the full meaning of "extermination." Such news made the front pages but did not hold them for long. As the war in Europe was racing to its end in April 1945, reporters accompanying Allied forces on their invasion of Germany were appalled by the horrors of the concentration camps. A few stories that had appeared about the camps during the war had not gotten the attention of the battle reports themselves. Once the American Army entered Germany, correspondents such as Murrow and Gene Currivan of the *New York Times* gave much attention to the Nazis' death camps.

The reporting of the end of the war in Europe was controversial because one correspondent was accused of breaking the embargo on the news. The Germans surrendered on May 7, 1945, in Rheims, France. Several reporters had been summoned the day before to Rheims for what they were promised would be an important briefing. They were told to embargo the story until 3 p.m. on May 8. Edward Kennedy, the chief AP correspondent assigned to Eisenhower's headquarters, protested the embargo and filed his story anyway. The AP flashed his story almost as soon as it arrived,

leading fifty-three correspondents in Paris to protest that they had been double-crossed. Newspapers in the United States denounced Kennedy, though many used his story anyway, and the AP fired him.

Japan continued to fight even after its European allies had surrendered. Only after atomic bombs destroyed two of their cities were the Japanese prepared to throw down their arms. The story of the end of the war in the Pacific, therefore, was inextricably tied up with the story of a new technology of mass destruction.

It was a story that would be told by a 57-year-old *New York Times* science writer, Bill Laurence. Even before the United States entered World War II, he was writing about experiments with atom splitting. Not only did he write about the new developments in physics for the *Times*, but he also did some freelance writing. On September 7, 1940, the *Saturday Evening Post* published one of his articles about the tremendous release of energy that occurred when a uranium atom was split. Two years later, the FBI ordered the *Post* to remove that issue from circulation and to report immediately anyone who sought a copy of it. In the spring of 1945, the military recruited Laurence to write a top-secret history of the development of the bomb. Despite his work for the government, Laurence was not on the flight of the *Enola Gay*, the plane that dropped the first atomic bomb on Hiroshima. Journalists had to piece together the story from government announcements and Japanese radio reports. However, Laurence was the first American reporter to witness the effects of an atomic bomb firsthand. He flew on one of the bombers accompanying the *Great Artiste* in its flight to Nagasaki,[35] and he won a Pulitzer Prize for his story and for the preliminary work he had done for the government. Japan announced its surrender the day after the attack on Nagasaki and agreed to an unconditional surrender less than a week later.

THE GOVERNMENT AND INFORMATION

As was the case in World War I, censorship existed during World War II. It began before the United States entered the war, with the belligerent nations subjecting correspondents to various regulations. Compared to most of the other nations involved in the war, American censorship was loose. After the United States entered the war and as conditions grew perilous, the government asked the press to apply its own "voluntary censorship." In some cases the press heeded that appeal. In others, it did not. In Hawaii, the press regularly reported the movements of the American fleet despite the request by Secretary of the Navy Frank Knox that such information be withheld from publication. Immediately after the attack on Pearl Harbor, the Army and Navy imposed military censorship.

To deal with the home front, President Roosevelt created the Office of Censorship on December 18, 1941. He appointed as its head Byron Price, formerly executive news editor of the Associated Press. Price established a Code of Wartime Practices for news-

[35]William L. Laurence, "Reporter Saw Atomic Bomb Dropped on Nagasaki," *New York Times,* 9 September 1945.

The Big News
The events of World War II resulted in some of the biggest news coverage in history, as illustrated by these two front pages from the last year of the war in Europe. With almost 2,000 American news personnel covering the war around the globe, readers were kept well informed of events as they happened daily. One of the biggest stories was the Allied invasion of Europe, D-Day, on June 6, 1944. In the days following the invasion, newspapers provided detailed accounts of the advance of the armies into France. The story reproduced here (left) is from the June 14 issue of the *New York Sun*. With the front page of this special edition (right), the *Los Angeles Times* of May 7, 1945, captured the overwhelming excitement over the defeat of Germany. Many newspapers throughout the country published the news in similar page designs.

papers and radio stations and urged a system of "voluntary censorship." His office's policies were far less restrictive than the direct military censorship. The press cooperated, but there were a few exceptions.

To oversee government information, Roosevelt in 1942 consolidated the several publicity agencies then in existence into the Office of War Information, headed by veteran reporter and news commentator Elmer Davis. The OWI's job was to oversee foreign propaganda (except for Latin America); supervise government war information programs on the radio, motion picture, and other mass media; and serve as a liaison between the press and the government. The OWI functioned somewhat differently from the Committee for Public Information in World War I. The CPI had controlled most government information programs. In World War II, however, many different government departments had information functions.[36] The OWI was the agency in charge of coordinating what war news should be released and what should not. The appropriate department rather than a central agency then disseminated the news.

This method was only partially successful. Davis and those who worked with him, including the poet Archibald MacLeish, favored openness and the dissemination of news and information to the public. The office not only dealt with the news media, but the entertainment media as well. MacLeish, for example, developed a "strategy of truth" that formed the basis of government regulations for the film industry.[37] Key military departments, including War and Navy, claimed control of information in their possession. When Roosevelt was called on to resolve these disputes, he typically would defer to the military. Eventually, the

press began to criticize the tight controls on information, particularly those of the Army and Navy. Roosevelt himself was also criticized for placing restrictions on the press once the war began and for giving increasingly useless press conferences. Old antagonisms continued and grew between the President and the press.

THE MEDIA'S WORLD WAR II PERFORMANCE

The American media covered World War II more thoroughly and better than any war in history. However, the role of the media went beyond reporting. The media also played an important role in defining the issues and in shaping public opinion about them. Some recent historians have criticized journalists about the stands they took on issues. One criticism, for example, is that they treated America's actions differently than the actions of enemy countries. In the 1930s, for example, journalists had professed shock about the bombing of civilians in Spain and China. Critical historians have argued that once the United States entered World War II, though, the distinction between proper and reprehensible acts of war diminished. There was little press criticism but widespread endorsement of dropping the atomic bombs on Japan.

Of course, the performance of the press must be considered in light of the huge scope of World War II. It is no exaggeration to say that the future of the world was at stake, and the aims of the Axis nations were dramatically different from those of the Allies. It is not difficult to understand journalists' support of Western democracy in a war for survival against Axis totalitarianism. Furthermore, the performance of the American press must be considered in light of the utter subservience of the Axis press to its national war aims. The American press may have lent its support to the nation's war effort, but it did not do so blindly or become simply an organ of the government, as occurred in the Axis countries. Germany's Nazi regime, for example, made all the media of that country an arm of its war machine. Films and the press glorified

[36]"Role of Information in World War II," an address by Elmer H. Davis, 16 November 1951, Box 4, Elmer H. Davis Papers, Manuscript Division, Library of Congress, Washington, D.C., pp. 9 and 21.

[37]Ramon Girona, "From the 'Strategy of Truth' to the 'Weapon of Truth': The Government Information Manual for the Motion Picture Industry, 1942," *Public Relations Review* 36 (September 2010): 306-09.

Germany's aggressive military actions and became a powerful tool of its racist policies toward Jews and other ethnic groups.

The American press remained, overall, both lively and critical. Its primary contribution was the reporting of the largest war in history. Yet, its performance was not evenly excellent. Some critics claim that war coverage was less than accurate, and these criticisms have some validity. In the midst of heated, sustained battles, not even commanding generals always know exactly what has happened or what the acquisition or loss of a certain front really means for the war effort. The very nature of war means that journalists, like generals, are often working without complete information. War correspondents, because of access restrictions and other limitations on information-gathering, did not always have the full story at the time they filed their stories.

Other historians have criticized the press for not taking stronger stances against the erosion of civil liberties during the war. A particular hot-button issue has been press support for the internment of Japanese-Americans in California. The powerful Hearst papers of California have been singled out for special criticism because they led the campaign to intern Japanese-Americans. Although the critics make strong points, their arguments must be considered in context. When a democratic country is at war, the press not only must inform citizens about the war effort but also must report on the policies and politics of how the war is being planned and conducted. Government policy-making is often controversial even during peaceful times. It is much more so during war. The heat and threat caused by a large war result in actions that gain acceptance but that would be considered more dispassionately during tranquil times.

Total wars, like World War II, are often good for news media, for they create demand for information; but they also bring problems with access, information flow, and government restrictions. Considered in that light, press errors during momentous national and international crises may not be easily excusable, but they become more understandable.

RECOMMENDED READINGS

BOOKS

Bassow, Whitman. *The Moscow Correspondents: Reporting on Russia from the Revolution to Glasnost*. New York, 1988. Foreign correspondents' unfamiliarity with Russia, its language, and culture — combined with Soviet restrictions — led to distorted reporting.

Best, Gary Dean. *The Critical Press and the New Deal: The Press versus Presidential Power, 1933-1938*. Westport, Conn., 1993. Press opposition to New Deal policies provided a check against expanding government power.

Carlisle, Rodney P. *Hearst and the New Deal: The Progressive as Reactionary*. New York, 1979. Hearst's position on foreign and domestic policies during the Roosevelt era became increasingly anti-liberalism.

Cornebise, Alfred E. *The Stars and Stripes: Doughboy Journalism in World War I*. Westport, Conn., 1981. The military newspaper covered the war from the common soldier's perspective, rather than that of the brass; it was a true newspaper rather than a public relations organ, subject to little interference from military authorities.

Covert, Catherine L., and John D. Stevens, eds. *Mass Media Between the Wars:*

Perceptions of Cultural Tension, 1918-1941. Syracuse, N.Y., 1984. This collection of fourteen essays by various authors deals primarily with the relationship between the media and American culture.

Culbert, David Holbrook. *News for Everyman: Radio and Foreign Affairs in Thirties America*. Westport, Conn., 1976. Commentators' broadcasts changed public opinion on American involvement in World War II from isolationist to interventionist, thus greatly influencing the foreign affairs process.

Desmond, Robert W. *Crisis and Conflict: World News Reporting Between Two Wars 1920-1940*. Iowa City, 1982. This history of news is an indispensable account of international journalism and world crisis.

Doenecke, Justus D. *When the Wicked Rise: American Opinion-Makers and the Manchurian Crisis of 1931-1933*. Cranbury, N.J., 1984. During the Manchurian crisis, the press played an important role as an articulator of opinion.

Finkle, Lee. *Forum for Protest: The Black Press During World War II*. Cranbury, N.J., 1975. Black editors were more conservative than their readers. While they favored elimination of discrimination, they believed a world crisis was no time to demand a complete change in racial practices.

Hayden, Joseph R. *Negotiating the Press: American Journalism and Diplomacy, 1918-1919*. Baton Rouge, La., 2010. Journalists influenced the Paris Peace talks at the end of World War I, even participating as informal diplomats and evoking new discussions of the role of the press.

Hohenberg, John. *Foreign Correspondence: The Great Reporters and Their Times*. New York, 1964. This account is one of the standard works on the topic.

Horton, Gerd. *Radio Goes to War: The Cultural Politics of Propaganda during World War II*. Berkeley, Calif., 2003. Radio was important in promoting consensus in civic and cultural life in the United States.

Hosley, David H. *As Good as Any: Foreign Correspondence on American Radio, 1930-1940*. Westport, Conn., 1984. American correspondents performed well in covering the events leading to and including the early years of World War II despite the fact that they were working under technical constraints.

Hynes, Samuel, ed. *Reporting World War II: American Journalism 1938-1946*. New York, 2001. This anthology contains articles by more than fifty journalists.

Jordan, William G. *Black Newspapers and America's War for Democracy, 1914-1920*. Chapel Hill, N.C., 2001. Editors encouraged support of the war effort despite discrimination against African Americans.

Juergens, George. *News from the White House: The Presidential Relationship in the Progressive Era*. Chicago, 1981. Presidents and reporters needed each other but also at times antagonized each other.

Karetzky, Joanne L. *The Mustering of Support for World War I by the Ladies Home Journal*. Lewiston, Me., 1997. This women's magazine helped gain support for America's war effort in the first global conflict.

Knightley, Philip. *The First Casualty*. New York, 1975 (3d ed., London, 2004). Although ideologically biased, this is the best known of the critiques of the failures of war reporters.

Koppes, Clayton R., and Gregory D. Black. *Hollywood Goes to War: How Politics, Profits, and Propaganda Shaped World War II Movies*. Berkeley, Calif., 1990. The movie industry and the federal government used films to further the Allied effort.

Leff, Laurel. *Buried by the Times: The Holocaust and America's Most Important Newspaper*. New York, 2005. The *New York Times* downplayed information about the Holocaust.

Levin, Linda L. *The Making of FDR: The Story of Stephen T. Early, American's First Modern Press Secretary*. Amherst, N.Y., 2008. Early was one of Roosevelt's most trusted advisors.

Liebovich, Louis W. *Bylines in Despair: Herbert Hoover, The Great Depression, and the U.S. News Media*. Westport, Conn., 1994. Herbert Hoover's favoritism and stubborn, self-righteous personality ultimately undermined his relationship with the press.

Lipstadt, Deborah. *Beyond Belief: The American Press and the Coming of the Holocaust 1933-1945*. New York, 1986. Although newspapers and magazines carried many stories about the Nazi extermination of the Jews, they did not recognize it as a central part of the Nazi program.

Lowitt, Richard, and Maurine Beasley. *One Third of a Nation: Lorena Hickok Reports on the Great Depression*. Urbana-Champaign, Ill., 1983. Hickok was the Associated Press' highest paid female correspondent before she went to work for the

Federal Emergency Relief Administration, for which she reported on what she observed about the effect of the Great Depression on ordinary Americans.

Manz, William H. *Civil Liberties in Wartime: Legislative Histories of the Espionage Act of 1917 and the Sedition Act of 1918.* Buffalo, N.Y., 2007 This collection of documents contains such items as congressional debates and hearings about the bills, amnesty hearings for those convicted under the laws, and a report on prosecutions.

Mock, James R. *Censorship, 1917.* Princeton, N. J., 1941. Although there were some excesses, World War I censorship generally was done acceptably. The danger was the threat to American democratic government resulting from carrying over into peacetime the repressive measures used during the war.

Reporting World War II, 2 vols. New York: 1995. This anthology of American reportage during the war covers the years from 1938 to 1946 and is based on a variety of print journalism sources and radio transcripts.

Ross, Robert W. *So It Was True: The American Protestant Press and the Nazi Persecution of the Jews.* Minneapolis, 1980. The Protestant press reported the news of the Holocaust, although often in disbelief.

Seib, Philip M. *Broadcasts from the Blitz: How Edward R. Murrow Helped Lead America into War.* Washington, D.C., 2006. Murrow's broadcasts from London influenced America's decision to enter World War II.

Short, K.R.M., ed. *Film and Radio Propaganda in World War II.* Knoxville, Tenn., 1983. Governments used movies and radio on a massive scale. Essays by various authors examine the use of propaganda by the Allies, Germany, Italy, and Japan.

Shulman, Holly Cowan. *The Voice of America: Propaganda and Democracy, 1941-1945.* Madison, Wisc., 1990. The Voice of America advanced American views in World War II.

Simmons, Charles A. *The African American Press: A History of News Coverage During National Crises..., 1827-1965.* Jefferson, N.C., 1998. Four black newspapers took distinctive approaches to covering incidents of national importance, including the Civil War, World War I, and World War II.

Soley, Lawrence C. *Radio Warfare: OSS and CIA Subversive Propaganda.* Westport, Conn., 1989. Political, military, and communication strategies shaped the use of radio during World War II.

Steele, Richard W. *Propaganda in an Open Society: The Roosevelt Administration and the Media, 1933-1941.* Westport, Conn., 1985. Presidential-press relations included broadcast, film, and the print media.

Sterne, Joseph H. *Combat Correspondents: The Baltimore Sun in World War II.* Baltimore, 2009. *Baltimore Sun* correspondents covered World War II on both the European and Pacific fronts.

Sweeney, Michael S. *From the Front: The Story of War.* Washington, D.C., 2003. This illustrated history tells the story of war reporting from the Crimea to the 1990s.

---. *Secrets of Victory: The Office of Censorship and the American Press and Radio in World War II.* Chapel Hill, N. C., 2001. The news media abided by a voluntary domestic censorship code during the war.

Taylor, S.J. *Stalin's Apologist, Walter Duranty: The New York Times' Man in Moscow.* New York, 1990. Reporter Duranty, although respected in the journalism profession, downplayed Soviet problems and Stalin's ruthlessness in doing away with his opponents.

Vaughn, Stephen. *Holding Fast the Inner Lines: Democracy, Nationalism and the Committee on Public Information.* Chapel Hill, N.C., 1980. The CPI was a nationalizing agent in a democratic society.

Voss, Frederick. *Reporting the War: Journalistic Coverage of World War II.* Washington, D.C., 1994. Journalists helped readers and listeners make sense of World War II.

Wade, Betsy. *Forward Positions: The War Correspondence of Homer Bigart.* Fayetteville, Ark., 1992. This collection includes the news stories written by the famous reporter for the *New York Times* and *New York Herald-Tribune*.

Wagner, Lilya. *Women War Correspondents of World War II.* Westport, Conn., 1989. This collection of biographies brings attention to journalists who often have been overlooked.

Washburn, Patrick S. *A Question of Sedition: The Federal Government's Investigation of the Black Press During World War II.* New York, 1986. The federal government tried to silence the black press during World War II, claiming its demands for civil rights undermined the war effort.

Winfield, Betty Houchin. *FDR and the News Media.* New York, 1994. Roosevelt gradually became more secretive with the press during his presidency.

Winkler, Allan M. *The Politics of Propaganda: The Office of War Information 1942-1945.* New Haven, Conn., 1978. The OWI reflected American policy and values.

Zacher, Dale E. *The Scripps Newspapers Go to War, 1914-18.* Champaign, Ill., 2008. Newspapers in the Scripps chain supported President Woodrow Wilson and the war effort.

ARTICLES

Allen, Chris W. "Reporting World War II for the Local Audience: Jack Shelly's Experience as a Local Radio Reporter in the European Theatre." *American Journalism* 17 (2000): 35-52. WHO radio correspondent Jack Shelley used a variety of reporting styles in covering local soldiers serving in Europe.

Bishop, Robert L., and LeMar S. MacKay. "Mysterious Silence, Lyrical Scream: Government Information in World War II." *Journalism Monographs* 19 (1971). This study outlines the "main problems encountered in setting up U.S. information agencies for World War II."

Bowles, Dorothy. "Newspaper Support for Free Expression in Times of Alarm, 1920 and 1940." *Journalism Quarterly* 54 (1977): 271-9. Large-city newspapers supported free expression.

Broussard, Jinx Coleman, and John Maxwell Hamilton. "Covering a Two-Front War: Three African-American Correspondents During World War II." *American Journalism* 22 (2005): 33-54. Three journalists who reported on World War II for the *Norfolk Journal and Guide* provided richly nuanced coverage that not only gave information about the war but also addressed African Americans' domestic struggle for equal rights.

Costrell, Edwin. "Newspapers' Attitudes Toward War in Maine 1914-17." *Journalism Quarterly* 16 (1939): 334-44. American attitudes toward participation in World War I as reflected by six Maine newspapers refute the notion that U.S. leaders got America into war contrary to popular desire.

"Editorial Cartoons in Wartime." *American Journalism* 21:2 (2004). This special issue of the history journal contains these articles: Lucy Shelton Caswell, "Drawing Swords: War in American Editorial Cartoons"; David R. Spencer, "Visions of Violence: A Cartoon Study of America and War"; and Harry Amana, "The Art of Propaganda: Charles Alston's World War II Editorial Cartoons for the Office of War Information and the Black Press."

Elmore, Cindy. "Stars and Stripes." *Media History* 16 (August 2010): 301-17. When the American military's newspaper, *Stars and Stripes*, was established, it was given editorial freedom, but that freedom has been dependent upon the support of military commanders and strong editors and publishers who would defend that independence.

Friedman, Barbara. "'The Soldier Speaks": Yank Coverage of Women and Wartime Work." *American Journalism* 22:2 (2005): 63-82. *Yank, the Army Weekly* was subtler than other publications in its assumption that women would give up paid work after the war but still contributed to the larger propaganda effort pressuring women to do so.

Haarsager, Sandra. "Choosing Silence: A Case of Reverse Agenda Setting in Depression Era News Coverage." *Journal of Mass Media Ethics* 6 (1991): 35-47. Seattle newspapers behaved unethically when they intentionally downplayed news about unemployment and bank failures during the Great Depression.

Kornweibel, Theodore, Jr. "'The Most Dangerous of All Negro Journals': Federal Efforts to Suppress the *Chicago Defender* During World War I." *American Journalism* 11 (1994): 154-68. The government targeted the *Defender* for its legitimate criticisms of lynching and other injustices against blacks.

Larson, Cedric. "Censorship of Army News During the World War, 1917-1918." *Journalism Quarterly* 17 (1940): 313-23. The censorship operations of the Military Intelligence Section were necessary for control of information.

Mander, Mary S. "American Correspondents During World War II: Common Sense as a View of the World." *American Journalism* 1,1 (1983): 17-30. The "hallmark" of World War II reporters was *common sense*. "Gone were the days of the flamboyant romantic of the nineteenth century; in his place stood the down-to earth, realistic reporter of modern times."

"Media and World War II, The," special issue of *American Journalism* 12:3 (1995). Along with the articles, especially useful are five historiographical essays: Maurine Beasley, "Women and Journalism in World War II: Discrimination and Progress"; Louise Benjamin, "World War II American Radio Is More Than Murrow"; Margaret A. Blanchard, "Freedom of the Press in World War II"; Patrick S. Washburn, "The Black Press: Homefront Clout Hits a Peak in World War II"; and Betty Houchin Winfield and Janice Hume, "Shhh, Do Tell! World War II and Press-Government Scholarship."

Mizuno, Takeya. "The Federal Government's Decisions in Suppressing the Japanese Language Press." *Journalism History* 33 (2007): 14-23. Civilian and military authorities disagreed over how far to go in suppressing the Japanese-language press early in World War II; and, although suppression was not complete, by May 1942 most had ceased publication.

Moffett, Albert E. "Hometown Radio in 1942: The Role of Local Stations During the First Year of Total War." *American Journalism* 3 (1986): 87-98. Local radio stations helped "create a national consensus on the World War II home front."

Perry, Ernest L. "It's Time to Force A Change." *Journalism History* 28 (2002): 85-95. The African-American press used the dual victory campaign to link the desire to continue fighting for equal rights during World War II with the patriotic impulse to give full support to the war effort.

Ponder, Stephen. "Presidential Publicity and Executive Power: Woodrow Wilson and the Centralizing of Governmental Information." *American Journalism* 11 (1994): 257-69. Wilson tried to centralize the release of government information in the White House to better manage the news.

Pratte, Alf. "The Honolulu *Star-Bulletin* and the 'Day of Infamy.'" *American Journalism* 5 (1988): 5-13. The work of the *Star-Bulletin* on the day the Japanese bombed Pearl Harbor "provides one of the more dramatic illustrations in American history of the press' performance in a major, fast-breaking crisis."

Ross, Felecia Jones. "The Cleveland *Call and Post* and the New Deal: A Change in African-American Thought." *Journalism History* 19 (1993): 87-92. The African-American newspaper rejected New Deal reforms in favor of economic self-help as espoused by the Republican opposition.

Sloan, Wm. David. "The Media in Trying Times: Propagandists, Patriots, or Professionals?" 283-99, in *Perspectives on Mass Communication History*. Hillsdale, N.J., 1991. This historiographical essay analyzes the approaches that historians have taken to explaining the press during this period.

Socolow, Michael J. "'News is a Weapon': Domestic Radio Propaganda and Broadcast Journalism in America, 1939-1944." *American Journalism* 24 (2007): 109-31. "The Roosevelt administration elected not to operate a domestic network for propaganda purposes because the commercial networks effectively performed that function."

Somers, Paul P., Jr. "'Right in the Führer's Face': American Editorial Cartoons of the World War II Period." *American Journalism* 13 (1996): 333-53. Cartoonists completely supported the war effort.

Stevens, John D. "From the Back of the Foxhole: Black Correspondents in World War II." *Journalism Monographs* 27 (1973). Black reporters did an admirable job despite the problems they faced because of their race.

Sweeney, Michael S. "Censorship Missionaries of World War II." *Journalism History* 27 (2001): 4-14. To encourage compliance with voluntary self-censorship guidelines during World War II, the U.S. Office of Censorship recruited journalists to be informal representatives to local news media, especially newspapers.

—. "Harvey O'Higgins and 'The Daily German Lie." *American Journalism* 23 (2006): 9-28. "The Daily German Lie," a series of press releases written by the associate chairman of the Committee on Public Information during World War I for newspapers and magazines, attempted "to kill destructive rumors and shape public opinion."

Theoharis, Athan. "The FBI, the Roosevelt Administration, and the 'Subversive' Press." *Journalism History* 19 (1993): 3-10. At the behest of the Roosevelt Administration, the FBI investigated isolationist reporters and newspapers.

Yang, Mei-Ling. "Creating the Kitchen Patriot: Media Promotion of Food Rationing and Nutrition Campaigns on the American Home Front During World War II." *American Journalism* 22 (2005): 55-75. Working cooperatively with advertising and propaganda campaigns, newspaper women's pages were instrumental in leading readers to make changes in food preparation and consumption necessitated by government-sponsored food rationing programs in World War II.

18

Radio Comes of Age

1900 - 1945

The history of broadcasting is a story of electronic information services — journalism and entertainment. It is the story of a revolutionary technology — from wire to wireless and back to wire. It is the story of the role of technology in the evolution of the information age, prophetically described by Senator Clarence C. Dill as the "whispering gallery of the skies."[1]

Radio had its roots in the late 1800s with the development of electronic telegraphy. The telegraph was the first rapid information medium. It enhanced the ability of the printing press by overcoming the obstacle of time. Whereas printing was hampered by the requirement that it be carried physically from place to place, the telegraph allowed information to be transmitted instantaneously by wire.

PIONEERS OF ELECTRONIC TECHNOLOGY

Michael Faraday and Samuel F. B. Morse were the names associated with the development of telegraphy. Faraday's discovery of electromagnetic induction led to Morse's development of the telegraph and experimentation in distance communication. Morse acquired the patent and sent the first official message May 24, 1844. Dictated by Annie Ellsworth to Morse, the message asked, "What hath God wrought?"

Following the invention of telegraphy, several people made individual contributions that combined to produce wireless telegraph transmission. Two Americans who did early work were William Henry Ward of Auburn, New York, and a dentist of Washington, D.C., Mahlon Loomis. Both received patents for an aerial conduction telegraph. Ward began his work before the Civil War, with a long series of experiments. The telegraphic tower he patented in 1872, he said, would permit the crossing of oceans without cable. Loomis, too, began his work before the Civil War. He conducted trial runs in the Blue Ridge and Catoctin Mountain ranges of Virginia and Maryland and secured some support in Congress. When the panic of 1873 struck, however, funds for experimentation dried up.

The early era in radio history was a complex period of experimentation, litigation, and financial turmoil for the many inventors who had vision but who often missed out on the rewards of success. James Clerk Maxwell (1831-1879), a Scottish physicist, theorized about electromagnetic energy in 1864. His theories ignited the interest of a German physicist, Heinrich Hertz (1857-1894), who was able to demonstrate the projection of the magnetic field into the air. The name "Hertz" (Hz) has been carried forward today as a credit to his contribution to broadcast technology.[2]

A recluse named Nathan B. Stubblefield has been credited by many as the "inventor of radio." Beginning about 1890 he broadcast speech and music around Murray, Kentucky. He did not use the Hertzian, electromagnetic wave radio we know today but an induction system. It worked without wires and covered five or six miles. He first demonstrated his wireless telephone publicly in 1892, but it was sixteen years before he patented the system. One of the great mysteries for historians is why he waited so long.

To bring his invention to the attention of the public, he staged a giant, open demonstration on January 1, 1902. Guglielmo Marconi had just demonstrated telegraphy across the Atlantic, and Stubblefield compared his own achievement to that of Marconi:

I have solved the problem of telephoning without wires through the earth just as Signor Marconi has of sending signals through space. But, I can also telephone without wires through space as well as through the earth, because my medium is everywhere.[3]

After a report of the demonstration appeared in the *St. Louis Post-Dispatch*, it created a great deal of national interest, and Stubblefield became widely known among experimenters and scientists.[4]

A short time later, Stubblefield became the first person to conduct a marine broadcast. It occurred at a public demonstration in

---

[1]C.C. Dill, "Traffic Cop For The Air," *American Review of Reviews* 75 (February 1927): 191.

[2]Electromagnetic radiation is known as "Hertzian waves," and a "hertz" is a unit of frequency equal to one cycle per second.

[3]*St. Louis Post-Dispatch*, 10 January 1902.

[4]Waldon Fawcett, "The Latest Advance in Wireless Telephony," *Scientific American*, 24 May 1902, 363.

Radio Pioneers
Among the individuals who were conducting experiments with radio in the early 1900s, Guglielmo Marconi (left) received the most attention. His most publicized experiment was the simultaneous transmission and reception of a transatlantic signal in 1901. He soon began transmitting for official agencies, and in 1907 his company began sending transatlantic wireless messages for the public. After working for Thomas Edison's company, Reginald Fessenden (center) started his own company and patented numerous inventions in telephony and telegraphy. In 1906 he broadcast words and music over radio waves from a ship off the Atlantic coast. However, historians recently have begun to question whether he actually conducted such broadcasts as early as he claimed, December 21. There is, though, little doubt that he was the first to transmit both words and music. Lee De Forest (right) called himself the "father of radio" for his development of the Audion tube in 1906. It was an electronic amplifying vacuum tube and was a key to industrial advances. De Forest sold his original ownership of technology to the American Telephone and Telegraph Company. The Audion tube remained standard in radio sets until transistors replaced it in the 1950s.

Washington, D.C., on March 20, 1902, from the deck of the steamship *Bartholdi* off the Virginia bank of the Potomac River where he sent wireless messages to receivers on the shore.[5]

Two years later, Stubblefield told a reporter for the *Washington Post*, "Eventually [radio] will be used for the general transmission of news of every description."[6] Most others at the time seem to have thought about wireless as point-to-point communication and not as broadcasting. Stubblefield's statement predated by more than a decade the oft-quoted 1916 memorandum of David Sarnoff, later to be president of RCA, who urged his firm to manufacture a "radio music box" for home use that might also pick up the news. After perfecting his device, Stubblefield was granted a patent in 1908.

Despite Stubblefield's early discoveries, Guglielmo Marconi (1874-1937) was the best known experimenter. He was, however, more than an inventor; he was an entrepreneur. He foresaw the commercial value of his inventions and patented each experimental development. As his work progressed rapidly, he established the British Marconi Corporation, the Canadian Marconi Corporation, and the American Marconi Corporation.

In 1901, Marconi conducted his most publicized experiment. He succeeded in sending a wireless signal from Cornwall, England, to St. Johns, Newfoundland, Canada. Soon after, he began es-

tablishing coastal radio stations meant to replace the aging transatlantic telegraph cables. The purposes of the stations were to provide ship-to-shore communication and issue warnings of storms and dangerous ice flows — and to make profits.

While Marconi was sending wireless Morse code signals, Reginald A. Fessenden succeeded in adding voice communication to a transmission. That demonstration sent wireless from one point to many points and occurred a few days before Christmas 1906 — December 21, to be exact. Writing about it years later, he told a vice president of Westinghouse that the broadcast occurred on Christmas Eve and added he conducted a similar broadcast on New Year's Eve.[7] These two broadcasts entered the history books without question until, on the 100th anniversary of the experiments, two historians published an article questioning the Christmas Eve legend. As it turns out, there was no independent evidence of the broadcasts in ships' logs, records of other avid amateur radio operators, or contemporary newspaper and magazine articles.[8] In all likelihood, the legendary broadcasts did not take place. However, the December 21 transmission did show Fessenden could transmit both voice and music — a feat for which he should be recognized. As his experiments illustrate, radio at that point was a laboratory

[5]*Washington Times*, 21 March 1902.
[6]*Washington Post*, 10 August 1904.

[7]For a description of the experiment, see Reginald A. Fessenden to S.M. Kinterner, 29 January 1932, Clark Manuscript Collection, Smithsonian Institution, Division of Electricity and Nuclear Energy.
[8]Donna Halper and Christopher Sterling, "Fessenden's Christmas Eve Broadcast: Reconsidering an Historic Event," *Antique Wireless Association Review* 19 (2006): 119-38.

toy that was becoming increasingly important as a means of point-to-point informational maritime and ship-to-shore communication. It was a wireless telephone of sorts.

Lee De Forest called himself the "father of radio" for developing the Audion tube in 1906, but he did not fully understand how it worked. This vacuum tube was a keystone to industrial development. Today's chip technology traces its history to this invention: the chip was preceded by the transistor, a series of vacuum tubes, and the Audion tube. In his most famous experiments, De Forest transmitted speech via radio in laboratory tests conducted in New York and Europe. His most publicized test was one from the Eiffel Tower, with reception reported as far away as 500 miles. Like many of his predecessors, De Forest was an inventor and not an entrepreneur. He formed his own company, but lawsuits with Fessenden and his own financial problems plagued his career. Eventually, he sold his interests to the American Telephone and Telegraph Company (AT&T).

At the beginning of the twentieth century, major corporate players began taking an interest in radio. The General Electric Company developed the alternator to assist Fessenden in his voice experiments. AT&T, which had acquired De Forest's Audion tube, and the Marconi companies were growing rapidly.

THE TITANIC DISASTER AND THE 1912 RADIO ACT

The event that catapulted radio technology into national prominence was the sinking of the *S.S. Titanic* in April 1912 after it collided with an iceberg. The ship *Carpathia* was also at sea, about fifty-eight miles from the *Titanic*. When its wireless operator received the *Titanic's* emergency transmission, the *Carpathia* began steaming to the scene of the disaster. By the time it reached the site, however, the *Titanic* already had sunk. With no rescue ship at hand, 1,513 passengers lost their lives. The disaster created national headlines, at the same time focusing attention on a new technology. The press coverage did more to increase public awareness of wireless communication than any historic experiment had done. The disaster brought attention to the role that radio could play in ship safety on the high seas and to the need for laws governing emergency transmissions.

The Radio Act of 1912 passed in part because of the *Titanic* disaster. America's isolationist tendencies previously had kept it from joining the first world radio conferences to control broadcasting at Berlin in 1903 and London in 1906. But Congress did pass the Wireless Ship Act of 1910 requiring ocean vessels to have both licensed equipment and operators. That act, the precursor of the Radio Act, was simple legislation — less than a page long — acknowledging the potential of radio as a ship-to-shore and ship-to-ship communications tool. The Radio Act of 1912 placed the Secretary of Commerce in charge of licensing radio stations and assigning operational wave lengths. It gave priority to distress signals and established the SOS standards. It also mandated the use of "special call letters" and gave priority to shipping over commercial experimentation.

The *Titanic* Disaster
When the liner *Titanic* struck an iceberg and sank on April 15, 1912, the disaster alerted the public to the possible uses of wireless transmission in emergencies. Much of the story in the *New York Times'* right-hand column about the disaster dealt with the role that wireless played.

The 1912 act had a maritime focus, but with more regulatory discretion than its 1910 predecessor. The new law was the first comprehensive governmental action dealing with radio, and it lasted fifteen years. However, while it recognized the maritime possibilities of the developing technology, it did not envision the regulatory standards necessary for the events and technology that would occur as soon as radio made the transformation from a maritime device to a medium of general public importance.

WORLD WAR I AND THE PATENT POOLS

Radio did not develop by unanimous consent but through an evolutionary process that reflected the social, political, and technological environment of the time and that witnessed a variety of social, corporate, and individual conflicts. The issues included monopoly, censorship, news and educational programming, advertiser support, and regulation. The resolution of each conflict contributed to the structure of the broadcasting system.

As World War I approached, radio's usefulness shifted from general maritime shipping to defense and the Navy. When the United States entered the war on April 6, 1917, the government ordered all wireless stations closed and on April 7 placed them under the administrative control of the Navy. The government then combined the patent resources of the heretofore competitive experimenters toward a common wartime goal. The individual and corporate rivalries that had previously existed were forced into cooperation. Patents were brought together to facilitate the war effort. The practical result was that previously competitive patent ideas were pooled, thus laying the groundwork for the rapid commercial development that followed the war. The patent pools quickly moved electronic telecommunications from a period of experimentation and maritime communication into an era of commercial broadcasting in the 1920s.

At the conclusion of World War I, the pool was dissolved, and the patents were returned to their owners. The date July 11, 1919, when the Navy returned the patents to private enterprise, marked the beginning of renewed competition and growth on a new corporate scale. First, at the urging of the Navy and U. S. government, Marconi's patents were sold to General Electric. The government did not want a foreign power operating a monopoly — American Marconi — in the United States. General Electric formed a new company, Radio Corporation of America (RCA), to control Marconi's patents and assets. Second, the release of the patent pool meant that the growing corporations had access to almost 2,000 patents. In heated competition, they battled for exclusive and competitive rights to the integral parts of the radio system. The results of the competition left AT&T in control of the manufacture and sale of transmitters, while General Electric and Westinghouse manufactured receiving sets and RCA operated as a sales agent collecting royalties for the use of its patents in manufacturing. The patent pools and the intense rivalries marked the beginning of an age of corporate monopoly in broadcasting within an extremely competitive atmosphere and with a government that would grow suspect of the radio monopoly.[9]

RADIO'S GROWING POPULARITY

While some called radio a fad, its popularity soon reached into all the nation. The number of stations was only about thirty in 1921, but the total had soared to 600 by 1923. At first, all the receiving sets were handmade at home. When Westinghouse began marketing its model number one in 1920 with the building of radio station KDKA, the total number of sets in 1923 climbed to 600,000.

With the growth in radio's popularity, major corporations became a part of the radio landscape, and each pioneered practices to give it a competitive edge. KDKA, Pittsburgh, the Westinghouse station, was one of the first stations, if not the first, to carry regularly scheduled programs. At first, such programming lasted only one hour each night. KDKA earned its place in history with a broadcast on November 2, election night, 1920. It obtained voting results through an agreement with the *Pittsburgh Post* newspaper and then reported them in what KDKA claimed was "the world's

The Magnavox Reproducer and the Magnavox Power Amplifier

Radio's Popularity

As the popularity of radio surged in the early 1920s, a number of companies worked feverishly to capture the market for receiving sets. General Electric, RCA, De Forest, AT&T, and others developed new equipment and innovations and advertised them extensively. In 1923 Magnavox was selling items to boost the sound from "feeble" receivers. The Latin name "Magnavox" means "great voice."

first scheduled broadcast." KDKA was eager to know if anyone was listening and asked, "Will anyone hearing this broadcast please communicate with us, as we are anxious to know how far the broadcast is reaching and how it is being received?"[10]

The broadcast was, indeed, the first scheduled one in the United States, but other stations throughout the world had conducted similar experiments. CFCF, Montreal, Canada, a station that Marconi owned, had broadcast a scheduled experimental program a few months earlier. Its program, which aired May 20, 1920, was aimed at Canadian radio hobbyists and the mariners whose ships were anchored in the St. Lawrence River. Eager, like KDKA, to know if it had an audience, CFCF advertised the broadcast and even prearranged for an audience of Canadian dignitaries.[11]

Such experimentation helped to refine programming and to publicize a growing new telecommunications service. Popular enthusiasm for radio grew rapidly during the 1920s as did the number of radio stations. The traveling Chautauquas around the country offered dazzling displays of radio, importing distant signals for an audience who had never before witnessed such a marvel. Along with the station program experiments and the Chautauqua publicity, significant advances were made in technology, and industry-wide operational patterns began to develop. WEAF's engineers contributed to the development of the control board, an important tool in programming that is still used today.

With increased popularity, the industry grew. In 1925, the Department of Commerce issued more than 1,400 station authorizations.[12] In 1930 the number of receiving sets stood at 14,000,000. Some were in automobiles; and while the classic custom cars such as Packard and Pierce Arrow had them earlier, the assembly-line 1930 Model A Ford could be had with radio. The 1940 census showed 44,000,000 radios around America. In 1945, there were radio sets in 33,000,000 homes, with many having more than one.

RADIO AND ADVERTISING

While several stations experimented with selling or bartering time, radio station WEAF in New York City set a precedent when its advertising practices created a stir. Licensed to operate a "toll" station in 1922, it made commercial airtime available to businesses. On August 28, it broadcast its first income-producing program: a ten-minute message from the Queensboro Corporation to sell apartments in suburban Jackson Heights. The sponsor paid $50.

The WEAF experiment created profound and, at times, heated debate. Some people considered advertising outrageous. Secretary Herbert Hoover felt that "the quickest way to kill broadcasting would be to use it for direct advertising."[13] Congressman Emanuel

Celler of New York denounced the "pabulum and disguised advertising...." He felt that too many stations would be given over to deceptive marketing practices. Criticizing radio station advertising from the floor of the House of Representatives, Celler satirized the approach: "This is station KOKO broadcasting lectures from the sanitarium on Pink Pills for Pale People."[14]

Despite the opposition, advertising seemed a viable means of financing the new industry. The concept that advertisers could operate a station, or talk about their products on a station, was attractive for many manufacturers and station operators. Programs such as the American Tobacco Company's *Lucky Strike* soon went on the air. During the 1920s no station was well financed by advertising revenue, but advertising provided an allure to investors. Thus, the first WEAF "toll" broadcast gave the fledgling broadcast industry an impetus — a dollars and cents reason to improve. For the listening public, advertising provided a popular system of financing radio, for hardly anyone wanted a tax on receiving sets.

At first no government knew how to finance a broadcast system. The British opted for a system that gave exclusive control to a government corporation funded by a license fee on receiving sets. The BBC developed programs based on the idea of elevating the general public's taste. Many other countries owned the systems outright, but the British attempted to insulate broadcasting from political interference through an independent corporation.

In the United States similar arguments arose, but a privately owned commercial system was chosen. In the beginning it was felt if one wanted to advertise he would have to build his own station. Thus Westinghouse built KDKA and other stations to help sell its radio receivers on the sensible theory that one could not sell a radio set if there were nothing to listen to. Rudy's Department store built a station in Paducah, Kentucky; and the American Telephone & Telegraph Company built WEAF in New York. The Bell System, which owned telephone lines needed for radio station interconnection, believed it was the only firm that legally could sell time over its lines for advertising. When an intense legal contest arose over Bell's monopolistic theory, Bell decided to duck the fight and sold its radio interests to RCA for $1 million. Others quickly followed the lead of WEAF in broadcasting advertising, and the present commercial system was soon established for American radio.

Soon advertising agencies were buying air time on individual stations and the networks just as they did from newspapers and magazines. Stations began to hire time salesmen. The station representative firm then was organized, selling time to agencies and advertisers for a group of stations. The rise of networks saw advertising grow by leaps and bounds.

The prices for network advertising were high, but the broadcasts seemed to be worth the cost. By 1930 the average family kept its radio on 3.9 hours per day. The 1940 figures showed that 86% of all families listened more than five hours per day — something like a total of 122,000,000 hours every day in all homes across the

[10]For a description of KDKA, see Westinghouse Radio Stations, Inc., Histories of KDKA, Shortwaves, WBZ, KYW, Frequency Modulation, and KEX. Unpublished manuscript (n.d.) "History of KDKA," 10, in Lawrence W. Lichty and Malachi C. Topping, *American Broadcasting: A Source Book on the History of Radio and Television* (New York, 1975), 102-10.

[11]Donald G. Godfrey, "Canadian Marconi: CFCF, The Forgotten First," *Canadian Journal of Communication* 8:4 (1982): 56-69.

[12]*Broadcasting Yearbook, 1939* (Washington), 11.

[13]Herbert Hoover, *Third National Radio Conference, Proceedings and Recommendations for Radio Regulation, October 6-10, 1924* (Washington, D.C., 1924), 4.

[14]*Congressional Record, 1926*, 67:5:5488.

nation. The Hooper Ratings (of Claude E. Hooper) were giving advertisers the figures on all the major programs. By World War II, with the resultant newsprint and other shortages, radio was one of the few places advertisers could turn to promote their wares and services.

PIONEERS OF NETWORK BROADCASTING

With the increasing popularity of radio, the industry began to look for ways to manage the growth. One of the innovations was the network system. WEAF — which had broadcast the first commercial — also was first to provide network broadcasting. AT&T, which owned WEAF, already had telephone lines reaching all over the country. Linking chains of stations together for purposes of programming became a logical extension of that technological opportunity. It would give AT&T the competitive edge. AT&T's first network experiment, in 1923, linked two stations together, WEAF in New York and WNAC in Boston.[15] In October 1924, a network broadcast featuring a speech by President Calvin Coolidge was sent to twenty-two stations coast-to-coast.

By the end of the following year, AT&T had a permanent network linking twenty-six stations. A pattern had been established, in which early experimental stations evolved into "key stations" owned and operated (0&0) by a network corporation. The network was organized around the key stations and strong affiliate contracts.

At the same time that AT&T was making its debut into toll and network broadcasting, its chief competitor, RCA, began network experimentation with stations WJZ and WGY. The former was the RCA-owned station in New York City, and WGY, the General Electric station in Schenectady, New York. Since AT&T claimed the exclusive right to sell broadcast time and thus prevented competitors from using its telephone lines, RCA contracted the lines of Western Union. Thus, its network did not grow as rapidly.

By 1926 RCA and General Electric had entered into ultra-secret talks with AT&T to set up a national network broadcast system. The negotiations resulted in AT&T's abrupt halt in its involvement in broadcasting as well as in the sale of its radio assets to RCA. The resulting networks would pay AT&T for the interconnections needed for network program distribution. The combination of its own existing operation, plus the newly acquired WEAF-AT&T operation, placed RCA in the dominant position. Nineteen permanent stations were on the RCA network in 1926, and in 1928 RCA established its first permanent national network. The former WEAF-AT&T operation became known as the NBC Red Network, and RCA's WJZ-based network was known as the NBC Blue. Since the Red network had the pick of programming and most of the advertising revenue, it assumed the lead position.

The pioneer who developed NBC was David Sarnoff. Kenneth Bilby, Sarnoff's biographer, wrote that Sarnoff, more than any other industry leader of the time, not only had a vision but "the

implacable determination to fulfill it." Implementing his (and others') vision of a "radio music box" transformed the industry and the listening public. His leadership created one of the largest networks in broadcast history, and he became one of the giants of industrial history.

The inaugural broadcast by NBC, the first network, was aired from 8 p.m. until midnight (Eastern time) on November 15, 1926, from the grand ballroom of the Waldorf-Astoria. Dr. Walter Damrosch conducted the New York Symphony Orchestra. The broadcast featured a comedy team, two singers, an oratorio group, actor-comedian Will Rogers, both a grand and a light opera company, a brass band, and four dance bands. The cost was $50,000, a high price at the time; and yet the prices for network programming continued to rise as they have ever since. When Dodge introduced its new Victory Six automobile with the *Dodge Victory Hour* in 1928, it had to pay NBC $67,000 for time and talent, including Will Rogers, Paul Whiteman, and Al Jolson, among several others.

CBS had it roots in the activities of George A. Coates. He was a promoter who had taken up radio's cause in its battle with the American Society of Composers, Authors and Publishers (ASCAP) over music rights. During the mid-1920s, ASCAP — which saw radio as a new profit opportunity for its artists — demanded higher royalty fees for music played on the air. The struggling new radio industry argued that the rates were too high and unfair. Coates and the National Association of Broadcasters (NAB), which was organized to help the broadcasters win their battle with ASCAP, worked with Arthur Judson, the business manager of the Philadelphia Orchestra. They formed the United Independent Broadcasters, Inc. (UIB). Their plan was to provide network programming for affiliated stations, purchase time from them, and sell advertising on the programming. UIB programming debuted in 1927, but UIB's financing was weak. It was not long before it needed additional backing.

UIB and Columbia Phonograph Corporation joined forces in 1927. Columbia's motivation was to sell records. It was afraid that RCA, which was talking about a merger with the Victor Talking Machine Company, would dominate the record industry. So Columbia merged with UIB and established a sixteen-station lineup. The agreement gave UIB a temporary financial boost and a name change — the Columbia Phonograph Broadcasting System (CPBS-UIB). Advertisers, however, still did not flock to CPBS-UIB. In contrast, RCA was growing rapidly. When it appeared that the RCA/Victor merger would not occur, Columbia Phonograph decided to sell its interest in the CPBS-UIB network.

William S. Paley, the young vice-president of the Congress Cigar Company of Philadelphia, and his father then purchased UIB. Shortly thereafter, the network began showing a profit. Paley retained the name Columbia and purchased as its first key station WABC, New York (now WCBS). A decade later, the Columbia Broadcasting System (CBS) purchased the American Record Corporation, which included the Columbia Phonograph label.

There were a number of attempts at other radio network operations, including the Quality Network, the Amalgamated Broad-

[15]*Report on Chain Broadcasting*, Federal Communications Commission, Order 37, Docket 5060 (May, 1941): 5-20.

It Bridges the Vastness of Space

SINCE Marconi first successfully spanned the Atlantic Ocean, with the wireless telegraph, radio has ever been outstanding as an invention of unlimited importance to humanity.

In 1909 the broadcasting of that now famous distress call, CQD, from the sinking passenger liner, S. S. Republic, established in the eyes of the entire world the tremendous importance of radio on the high seas.

A Specially In 1912, when that gigantic liner, *Designed Tube for* the S. S. Titanic, struck an iceberg far *Every Radio Use* from shore, in the north Atlantic, with thousands of passengers aboard, it was the SOS call of her wireless that brought rescue ships from all parts of the ocean. Here again radio demonstrated to the world its great service in the saving of human life.

During the war communication controlled the destinies of armies. Here radio played an exclusive part in the establishing of communication between ships at sea, from ship to shore, and from aeroplane to ground, where the use of wires was impossible.

In recent years the development of the vacuum tube has not only improved radio for the purpose of marine, commercial and military communications, but through radio telephony and public broadcasting, has established a new and even greater service to humanity.

Cunningham Vacuum Tubes are the product of years of research and experimental work by the Engineers of that great scientific organization, the Research Laboratory of the General Electric Company.

Cunningham Tubes are standard for all makes of receiving sets. Each of the numerous types have been designed to operate with maximum efficiency in one or more of the various applications of vacuum tubes to the radio art.

Cunningham Radio Tubes
C-301A—6 Volts ¼ amp.
Amplifier $6.50
C-299—3 Volts .06 amp.
Dry Battery Det. & Amp. 6.50
C-300—6 Volts Gas Content Detector . . . 5.00
C-11—1.1 Volts .25 amp.
Dry Battery Det.& Amp.
Special Base . . . 6.50
C-12—Similar to C-11 with standard base . . 6.50

Patent Notice: *Cunningham tubes are covered by patents dated 11-7-05, 1-15-07, 2-18-08, and others issued and pending. Licensed for amateur, experimental and entertainment use in radio communication. Any other use will be an infringement.*

E. T. Cunningham Inc.

Home Office:
248 First Street **154 West Lake St.** **30 Church Street**
San Francisco, Cal. **Chicago, Ill.** **New York City, N. Y.**

"Unlimited Importance to Humanity"
In the mid-1920s, with radio's popularity increasing rapidly, companies expanded by developing networks of stations and manufacturing equipment. This ad for a new vacuum tube from General Electric, one of the early station owners, noted the popularity and value of radio by listing historic achievements ranging from Marconi's transatlantic transmission to the role radio had played in the *Titanic* disaster and World War I.

casting System, and numerous regional networks. However, following NBC and CBS the most significant network was the Mutual Broadcasting System. It was different from both NBC and CBS. Begun in 1934, it was not developed from a key station but as a cooperative among WXYZ Detroit, WLW Cincinnati, WGN Chicago, and WOR New York. In fact, it had no studios or central ownership. Its popularity was built around one strong program, the *Lone Ranger*. It then added such features as *The Green Hornet* and Gabriel Heatter as a leading newsman, and it always aired the World Series. As Mutual grew, it promoted itself as "the largest network in the world." The claim was true: it did have a larger number of affiliate stations. However, they were mostly smaller and rural operations. Mutual was never able to attract the powerful stations that were already firmly tied to NBC and CBS.

A federal government rule forcing divestiture upon individuals and companies that owned more than one station or network in the same service made NBC sell its Blue Network in 1943 to Edward J. Noble, whose millions had come from selling Lifesavers, "The Candy Mint With the Hole." He renamed the organization the American Broadcasting Company.

By 1945 network revenues were up to about $130 million, with one client alone, Procter & Gamble, spending $11 million for advertising time. The 900 stations employed about 25,000 full-time workers at an average weekly wage of $60.52.

THE REGULATORY DEBATES, 1922-1934

As more and more stations took to the airwaves, they began to interfere with each other, ruining the use of the resource for both broadcaster and listener. People both inside and outside the industry quickly recognized the need for government oversight and regulation to bring order and usefulness to broadcasting. The Radio Act of 1927 established the fundamental principles of broadcast regulation and, as revised by the Communication Act of 1934, continues today as the legal foundation of the industry.

The legislative history of the 1927 Radio Act began within the Hoover Radio Conferences. Secretary of Commerce Herbert Hoover was in charge of regulating radio. The 1912 Radio Act had placed the responsibilities upon his office. As the industry began to grow in the early 1920s, it became apparent that new legislation would soon be needed. In order to draft a proposal, Hoover organized a series of conferences in 1922, 1923, 1924, and 1925.[16] They included representatives of industry and government, and they grew in number and intensity as radio grew in popularity.

Each year, different bills were formulated and, under the direction of Wallace H. White, a Maine Republican, submitted to a disinterested Congress. Few on Capitol Hill understood the legislation, and radio was simply not yet an issue for most congressmen. White, however, persevered. As a member and later chair of the Merchant Marine and Fisheries Committee, he played a key role in generating and drafting several legislative proposals, including

[16]Edward F. Sarno, Jr., "The National Radio Conferences," *Journal of Broadcasting* 13 (1969): 189-202.

one of the first radio bills in 1923. After it failed, White, an outspoken advocate of the public's right in broadcasting, continued to hammer away at drafting legislation from several subsequent proposals until 1927.

The legal catalyst that led to the law finally adopted was a breakdown of the Radio Act of 1912. It had placed the Secretary of Commerce in charge of assigning wavelengths and issuing licenses. However, as radio grew from a maritime instrument into one of general public interest, the law proved inadequate. The legislative crisis came to a head when, in 1926, the Zenith Radio Corporation challenged the powers of the Secretary and the courts ruled in favor of Zenith. The ruling threatened chaos, as it left the Secretary with no discretionary regulatory power. He was in a position of merely granting licenses upon request. Since he had no regulatory control, stations could change power and use "other wavelengths at will," declared Attorney General William J. Donovan. He told Hoover that "if the present situation requires control, I can only suggest that it be sought in new legislation, carefully adapted to meet the needs of the present and the future."[17]

The potential crisis finally caught the attention of Congress, but its members disagreed on what approach to take.[18] Senator Cole Blease (D-S.C.) wanted censorship provisions to prevent the discussion of evolution on radio. Senator William E. Borah (R-Idaho) wanted stronger monopoly restraints against what he saw as the growing power of the RCA monopoly.[19] At that point, Clarence C. Dill played a key role in drafting legislation and getting it passed. Compared to White, Dill was a latecomer to radio legislation, but his influence was important. He modified White's proposals by adding a commission to replace White's recommendation that the Secretary of Commerce have control over broadcasting. He then fought forcefully for passage of the amended bill. It was not until February 1927, however, that "Congress woke up," Secretary Hoover said, "and finally passed the law which we recommended and which establishes the public ownership and regulation of the wavelength channels."[20]

A clause in the law that states that broadcasting must operate in the "public interest, convenience and necessity" remains the governing principle of electronic media regulation. It has been interpreted within the following seven basic principles:[21]

(1) Radio waves belong to the people.

(2) Broadcasting is a unique service.

(3) Service must be equally distributed.

(4) Not everyone is eligible to use a channel.

(5) Broadcasting is a form of expression protected by the First Amendment.

[17]Quoted in Marvin R. Bensman, "The Zenith-WJAZ Case and the Chaos of 1926-27," *Journal of Broadcasting* 14 (1970): 423-40.

[18]Donald G. Godfrey, "The 1927 Radio Act: People and Politics," *Journalism History* 4 (1977): 74-8.

[19]*Congressional Record, 1926*, 67:11:12615. See also Donald G. Godfrey and Val E. Limburg, "The Rogue Elephant of Radio Legislation: Senator William E. Borah," *Journalism Quarterly* 67 (1990): 214-24.

[20]Herbert Hoover, "The Reminiscences of Herbert Clark Hoover," Oral History Project, Columbia University Oral Research Office, 142.

[21]Sydney W. Head, *Broadcasting in America*, 2nd ed. (New York, 1972), 160-1.

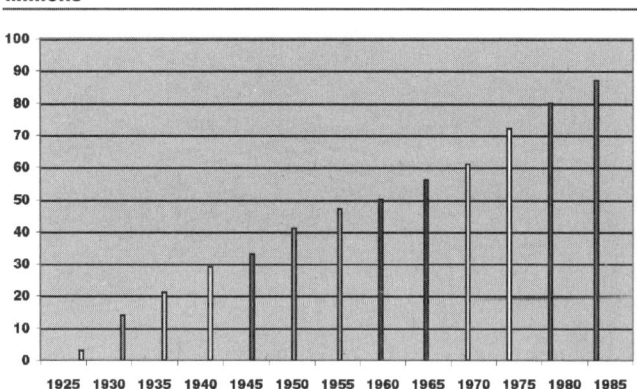

Number of Households with Radios in the United States 1925-1985

Millions

Per Cent of Penetration of Radios in U. S. Households

As the number of radios increased in the 1920s, calls for regulation grew louder.

(6) The government has discretionary regulatory powers.

(7) Government's powers are not absolute.

The 1927 Radio Act established the Federal Radio Commission as the regulatory agency over broadcasting. Among the first things the commission did was to revoke all licenses. The revocation forced the stations to reapply and gave the Commission time to consider the administrative law that would govern broadcasting. This body of law became an elaborate set of "Rules and Regulations" and a code of "Standards of Good Engineering Practices," which have been expanded, contracted, and amended in many different forms. These rules and regulations remain in a state of continual evolution, but they embody a strong directive force behind the electronic media's development.

There was considerable debate about radio in the hectic years of change after 1927. The networks were still growing, the educational nonprofit broadcasters were being shunted aside by commercial interests, and new technology and regulatory standards were still developing. As conditions changed, it became clear that the Radio Act could not adequately cover them, and new legislation was proposed. When President Franklin Roosevelt asked for an expansion of the Federal Radio Commission in 1934, however, he felt the old Radio Act could scarcely be improved.

The resulting Communications Act of 1934 may have seemed to have changed little in the regulations. It brought forward the same fundamental principles from the Radio Act, and some have said that it was one of the least significant pieces of Roosevelt legislation. However, it was not a carbon copy of the Radio Act.

The new law enlarged the commission from five to seven members and changed its name to the Federal Communications Commission. It included a larger role for the commission, extending its control over wire and wireless communication — television, telephone, telegraph, undersea cables, and all radiated and "wired communications" — both interstate and foreign.

MUSIC: CLASSICAL TO COUNTRY

At first, networks and local stations offered only irregular programming. When radio was new, programming did not have to be good or interesting. Just the fact that one heard something — anything — was a wonder that could hold attention for hours on end. Regular scheduling evolved with the stations' technological ability and with audience demand.

Programming was mostly music, most of which was classical.[22] As early as 1910 Enrico Caruso was heard over Lee De Forest's station in New York. Frank Conrad of Westinghouse with his 8XK — later to be KDKA — began to play phonograph records over the airways in 1919 for the entertainment of his fellow amateurs.

Most music, however, consisted of live performances. Musicians were more than willing to perform on radio in hopes of increasing their own popularity. At first, they were afraid of radio as a competitor of their recordings. Later they realized that they could receive fees for broadcasting and promote the sales of their records at the same time.

The networks had their own orchestras and designed programs for studio performance. The studios were large and draped with curtains, and performers dressed in formal attire for a show's performance even though they would not be seen. All broadcasts were live and were scheduled during the evening.

The audience for this new medium was a receptive one; and as the audience grew, so did the demand for more information and entertainment. Stations responded by increasing their offerings. In Detroit, WWJ of the *News*, another claimant to be America's oldest radio station, picked up a full dance orchestra in September 1920. One of the most popular violinists in America was Fritz Kreisler. He performed over KDKA Pittsburgh in January of 1922. Judith Carey Waller, first station manager of WMAQ in Chicago, presented as its first program a performance by opera star Sophie Braslau the following month. The telephone company station WEAF in New York (now WNBC) pulled a *coup* on January 1, 1925, when it presented a concert by noted Irish tenor John Mc-

Music Brought "to You in Person"
Music, ranging from country to classical, has been a staple of commercial radio since its beginning. In 1932, Philco advertised its receivers as having the capacity to make listeners feel as if they were in a concert hall with Leopold Stokowski conducting the orchestra.

Cormick and Metropolitan Opera star Lucrezia Bori. That same year WEAF sold a regular Sunday series featuring stars of the opera and the concert stage. When NBC began operations in 1926, concert music was often on the schedule.[23] In 1927, when CBS began competing with NBC, it ran an original opera by Deems Taylor, *The King's Henchman*. The poet Edna St. Vincent Millay helped on the lyrics. In 1930 CBS began airing the Sunday afternoon concerts of the New York Philharmonic Symphony Orchestra.

Radio began to make talent famous, too. On WDAF in Kansas City, a group called the Nighthawks starring Leo Fitzpatrick as the "Merry Old Chief" kept Americans up half the night. There was also the Coon-Sanders band from the Plantation Grill of the Muehlebach Hotel. The band would play fifteen minutes and rest ten. Desperate to fill the breaks with something on these remote broadcasts, announcers read telegrams and told jokes that proved almost as popular as the music.[24]

[22]In February 1925, music accounted for 71.5% of the programming time. Other programming proportions were as follows: 0.1% drama; 11.5% information-oriented — education, market reports, politics, news, and sports; 6.8% children's and women's entertainment; and 10.1% religion, health, and miscellaneous. See John W. Spaulding, "1928: Radio Becomes A Mass Advertising Medium," *Journal of Broadcasting* 8 (1963-64): 31-44.

[23]Analysis of NBC "Fiftieth Anniversary of NBC Radio," by Ray Mofield, aired on NBC network November 1976; copies in Library of Congress and various other libraries.

[24]William Paley, from the CBS Taped Radio Show "Fiftieth Anniversary of CBS Radio," aired September 1977; copies in Library of Congress, Washington, D.C., and various other libraries.

Rockwell Kent, with the Eskimos in Greenland,

...hears the tango played in distant Argentina

MODEL M-86—Typical of the many new G-E All-wave models in this smartly styled console. Priced at $119.50. Other long- and short-wave sets as low as $39.95.

GENERAL ⊕ ELECTRIC RADIO

BORN OF THE PIONEERING ACHIEVEMENTS OF THE FAMOUS "HOUSE OF MAGIC"

Programs from Around the World
Like other manufacturers, General Electric tried to sell radio receivers by emphasizing the programming available to listeners. This 1934 ad mentioned several varieties of music, news, celebrity gossip, messages from police and ham operators, and network programs.

Radio tried to please the taste of every type of listener. Country music was one of the early favorites, with the first of the big national barn dances arriving on WLS Saturday night, April 19, 1924. Sears executives (the call letters stood for World's Largest Store) exploded when they heard "Turkey in the Straw" on the air, but 400 telephone calls and a bushel of mail showed that their customers loved it. George D. Hay, "the Solemn Old Judge," was the announcer. The biggest star of the early years was Bradley Kincaid of Kentucky. He moved to WLW in 1931 and stayed there through its day as a half-million watt station. He drew more than 20,000 people to one performance. Hay moved on to WSM in Nashville in 1925 to begin an even more popular barn dance called the *Grand Ole Opry*. John Lair began the *Renfro Valley Barn Dance* in Kentucky over WHAS Louisville a little later. All these became so popular they made the national networks for at least a half hour per week. Chicago and Nashville fed theirs to NBC while Louisville's was programmed through CBS.

Popular music provided many hours of programming in the early years. In CBS's battle to catch the older NBC, William Paley began running dance bands every night. Three pick-ups were used each evening beginning at 11:30 p.m. (Eastern time). New York and Chicago hotels were the favorites for such bands as Paul Whiteman's. In later years, there were Glenn Miller, Tommy and Jimmy Dorsey, and Kay Kaiser. Many other sites made the list, too, including the Roosevelt Hotel in New Orleans fed by WWL and the Peabody in Memphis fed by Hoyt Wooten's WREC. Local stations, of course, did the same, broadcasting local orchestra performances from nightclubs and hotels.

DRAMA AND COMEDY BY RADIO

It took radio some time to realize that the world's greatest stage is the human mind. As the early radio historian E. P. J. Shurick said, "In imagination colors are more brilliant, the pageantry more spectacular, and the action more robust."[25]

General Electric at WGY led the way in drama. It aired the stage play *The Wolf* by Eugene Walter in 1922. WGY was so encouraged with the broadcast's popularity that it began a regular weekly feature and broadcast more than 200 Broadway favorites. Some became motion pictures. Far from hurting attendance, they whetted the appetite of the audience.

In 1923, KDKA Pittsburgh broadcast *Friend Mary* from the Broadway stage as its first dramatic production. WJZ New York, the old Westinghouse station that became the key of NBC's Blue Network (now WABC-770), did Shakespeare's *Romeo and Juliet* from the Henry Miller Theater in the same year. A month later it broadcast *As You Like It* from the 44th Street Theatre. The trend continued, and one of the top-rated shows by the end of World War II was the *Lux Radio Theatre* in which noted movie director Cecil B. De Mille put on radio play versions of his own and other famous movies.

The adventure serial drama that was broadcast five days a week in the early evening began just a bit later. It was patterned after the continued story approach used in magazines or the *Perils of Pauline* type of movie. The first was *Sam 'n' Henry* on WGN. It moved in 1928 to NBC's WMAQ-670 as *Amos 'n' Andy*. It may have been the most popular show of all time. In some areas even theaters stopped their movies while Freeman Fisher Gosden and Charles J. Correll worked their magic as Amos Jones and Andy Brown, along with the Kingfish and other characters. From Peoria, Illinois, Marion and Jim Jordan went to Chicago's WENR to start a once-a-week smash hit called *Fibber McGee and Molly*. It led the ratings for a number of years; and Johnson's Wax, its sponsor, led the sales parade.

These programs gave rise to another kind of daily drama that would attack the problems of the housewife at home. WGN aired the first of these, *Painted Dreams*, in 1930. Soon there were more; and as large audiences were delivered at low cost, the giant soap firms of Procter & Gamble, Colgate-Palmolive-Peet, and Lever Brothers bought up these dramas. They became known as "soap operas." *Ma Perkins* ran for thirty-three years on CBS. There were also *Road of Life*, *Big Sister*, *The Second Mrs. Burton*, and *Our Gal*

[25]Text of Queensboro Corporation spot on Hawthorne Courts in Ray Mofield tape collection (Murray State University; Murray, Kentucky) from Rick Sklar, ABC, New York.

Radio Soap Operas

Virginia Payne was only 23 years old when she began the radio role of the matronly Ma Perkins. When the program's cast made public appearances, an older actor would substitute for Payne so that the audience would continue to have the illusion of "Ma" being a middle-aged widow.

Guiding Light, the longest running program in broadcast history, was the creation of Irna Phillips. After giving birth to a still-born baby, she found comfort in radio church services and wanted to create radio drama that provided spiritual support.

"Washboard Weepers" Appeal to Loyal Listeners and Soap Manufacturers

In 1933 an advertising agency trying to boost sales of Procter and Gamble's laundry detergent brand Oxydol tested the idea of sponsoring a daily radio program. The program was to run weekdays in 15-minute installments during an afternoon time slot.

It was tested on a local Cincinnati station, WLW, beginning on August 14, and the impact on sales of the soap was so great that P&G moved the program to Chicago. On December 4 the program went nationwide on the NBC radio network.

The program, *Ma Perkins*, lasted on NBC until 1949 and remained on the air with a variety of other networks until the end of daily radio soap operas in 1960.

Though not the first soap opera, *Ma Perkins* is considered the "mother of all soap operas" because it exemplified the genre in many ways. It had an open-ended storyline with a central cast of characters and was broadcast weekday mornings and afternoons. Its sole sponsor for 23 of its 27-year run was a laundry detergent.

The term "soap opera" came about in the late 1930s when journalists were looking for a colorful name for the dramatic serials that were dominating daytime radio. Publications such as *Newsweek* began using terms like "washboard weeper" and then "soap opera."

The reasons for the terms were simple. The five leading sponsors for the serials were soap companies Procter and Gamble, Lever Brothers, Colgate Palmolive-Peet, Babbitt, and Manhattan Soap. P&G was by far the largest. By 1937 it was spending $4.5 million a year on radio advertising, with 90% of that on daytime serials. At its peak it was sponsoring more than a dozen quarter-hour serials on a variety of networks.

The soap operas proved to be a very effective sales tool for the companies sponsoring them. Listeners, mostly homebound housewives, developed a fierce loyalty to the serials. Shows moved slowly, allowing listeners to develop an attachment with the characters and making it easy to follow story lines if an episode or two was missed. Characters often remained on the shows for years. Virginia Payne played Ma Perkins for 27 years and all 7,065 episodes of the program. She had been only 23 when she began the role.

In developing the connection with the characters, listeners also developed a connection with the products that sponsored them. One survey at the height of the soaps found that 61% of women said they bought items advertised on their favorite soaps.

By 1960 television had cut deeply into radio dramas and soap operas. CBS was the only network still broadcasting daily soap operas, and in the summer of 1960 it announced that on November 25 all serials would end. On that day the serials still on the air broadcast their last episodes – but, in keeping with the "open-end" format, there were no conclusions to the storylines.

One story that did continue was *Guiding Light*. Started in 1937, it was cancelled briefly in early 1942. However, more than 75,000 letters from irate fans helped bring it back. With one short hiatus in 1946 it remained on the radio until 1956. In 1952 CBS brought it to television, where it lasted until 2009, at 71 years the longest run by any broadcast program in history.

War of the Worlds

Martians Strike Terror in the Hearts of Earthlings

There are still people who remember the panic that began shortly after 8 p.m. eastern time on October 30, 1938. Hundreds evacuated their homes. Frightened citizens jammed east coast roads and telephone lines trying to warn friends and relatives. Hundreds contacted police, hospitals, newspapers, and radio stations asking how to protect themselves from an unidentified poisonous gas. Some went to church to pray. Some were treated for shock and hysteria. Families huddled on street corners waiting for what they thought would surely be the end of the world.

During Orson Welles' Halloween national broadcast of "War of the Worlds," dance music was interspersed with realistic sounding news bulletins. The adaptation of H. G. Wells' novel created frightening realism and convinced millions of listeners from San Francisco to Boston and from Canada to New Orleans that there had been a Martian invasion and widespread death and destruction.

Listeners believed what they heard because they trusted radio's ability to deliver important information. News bulletins often interrupted programs to report unsettling European developments. Many listeners of Welles' program missed or ignored announcements at the beginning, end, and during the broadcast that emphasized its fictional nature.

Some were indignant when they learned about this Halloween hoax. One New Yorker called it "the most asinine stunt I ever heard of." Another denounced it as a disgrace and an outrage.

In the wake of the controversial broadcast, CBS decided not to use simulated news broadcast techniques "when the circumstances of the broadcast could cause immediate alarm to numbers of listeners." Expressing profound regret and bewilderment that his dramatic efforts caused such consternation, Welles apologized, "I don't think we will choose anything like this again."

This single broadcast remains a prime example of the power of broadcasting to dramatically influence attitudes and beliefs.

Orson Welles did not foresee the panic he would cause with his Halloween night broadcast of H. G. Wells' novel *The War of the Worlds* in 1938. It caused more panic than any other fictional program has ever done. The top picture shows Welles (arms raised) and the members of his Mercury Theater group rehearsing the production. With the fame he gained from the program, he got a chance to direct and star in his first movie, *Citizen Kane*. Critics generally consider it the greatest movie ever made.

Here's how the *Philadelphia Inquirer* reported on Welles' "War of the Worlds" the day after the broadcast.

Mars Invasion Terrorizes Listeners

Terror struck at the hearts of hundreds of thousands of persons in the length and breadth of the United States last night as crisp words of what they believed to be a news broadcast leaped from their radio sets — telling of catastrophe from the skies visited on this country.

Out of the heavens, they learned, objects at first believed to be meteors crashed down near Trenton, killing many.

Then out of the "meteors" came monsters, spreading destruction with torch and poison gas.

It was all just a radio dramatization, but the result, in all actuality, was nation-wide hysteria.

In Philadelphia, women and children ran from their homes screaming. In Newark, N.J., ambulances rushed to one neighborhood to protect residents against a gas attack. In the deep South men and women knelt in groups in the streets and prayed for deliverance.

In reality there was no danger. The broadcast was merely a Halloween program in which Orson Welles, actor-director of the Mercury Theatre on the Air, related, as though he were one of the few human survivors of the catastrophe, an adaptation of H.G. Wells' "The War of the Worlds."

In that piece of fiction men from Mars, in meteor-like space ships, come to make conquest of Earth. The circumstances of the story were unbelievable enough, but the manner of its presentation was apparently convincing to hundreds of thousands of persons....

The realism of the broadcast, especially for those who had tuned in after it had started, brought effects which none — not the directors of the Federal Radio Theatre Project, which sponsored it, nor the Columbia Broadcasting Co., which carried it over a coast-to-coast chain of 151 stations ... — could foresee....

Sunday.

The power of radio drama was demonstrated in World War II by Kate Smith's successful sale of millions of dollars in War Bonds on her radio programs. It may be, however, that the single most potent story was Orson Welles' Halloween program on CBS in 1938. The October 30 airing of the *Mercury Theatre* is well remembered today, a prime example of the power of broadcasting. The dramatization of H. G. Wells' *War of the Worlds* terrified listeners in the New York-New Jersey area where the story was set. Using the CBS news roundup device of calling in live reports — featuring "news bulletins" that sounded like real announcers reporting news of an invasion from Mars — Welles created such realism that the audience panicked. Many listeners called their local police and left their homes thinking a real attack was taking place. The resulting FCC investigation brought CBS and the other networks to the realization that they would have to be more cautious when playing with radio's dynamite.

SPORTS COVERAGE

The 1920s have been called the Golden Era of Sports. Those were the days of Jim Thorpe, Red Grange, Babe Ruth, Jack Dempsey, and the reporting giants such as Grantland Rice who wrote about them. Some feeble efforts were made to air sports in radio's amateur days such as the 1912 University of Minnesota experiment to use a spark gap transmitter to relay telegraph signals of a football game. A university station, WTAW, in College Station, Texas, did the first football broadcast: the Texas A&M Aggie game with the University of Texas on Thanksgiving Day, 1920. But as was often the case, the pioneer among commercial stations was KDKA Pittsburgh. The first play-by-play of a baseball game originated at Pittsburgh's Forbes Field in 1921 as the Pirates took on the Philadelphia Phillies. Almost a year earlier WWJ in Detroit had run the World Series scores as they came into the *Detroit News* office. Later in 1921 KDKA did its first football play-by-play, and the first ever by a commercial broadcaster, as West Virginia played the University of Pittsburgh Panthers. Another first effort by KDKA was its broadcast of the first Davis Cup tennis matches in 1921.

Boxing was big in the 1920s. The first blow-by-blow description was on KDKA in 1921 in the Johnny Ray versus Johnny Dundee match. Later that year, the listening audience broke all previous records when KDKA took its remote mike ringside in Hoboken, New Jersey, via a feed from WJY. The attraction was Jack Dempsey against Georges Carpentier.

The first play-by-play World Series came also in 1921. It was an all-New York Series. With a direct line from Pittsburgh, Grantland Rice called the action for KDKA. The Giants of John McGraw took the series that year over the Yankees and repeated the feat in 1922. WJZ took over the World Series play-by-play for 1923. There was a new announcer, Graham McNamee, but the faces on the field were once again the Giants and Yankees, and this time the Bronx Bombers prevailed. When the Yanks came back for the 1926 World Series, McNamee was still around for WJZ, which came up with

Network Programming
National radio networks in the 1940s were as competitive as the television networks are today. In 1946 ABC used this ad to promote its most popular programs and performers — singer Bing Crosby, *Theatre Guild on the Air*, the gossip reporter Walter Winchell, the Metropolitan Opera, and *Cavalcade of Sports*.

another first: a nation-wide network broadcast.

Other sports also made it to the airwaves. For Memorial Day 1924, WGN Chicago took its microphones to Indianapolis Speedway for the 500-mile classic and saw the average speed pass ninety-nine miles per hour. That fall, WGN seemed to be everywhere, doing football from every campus of the Big Ten Conference and also Nebraska, Pennsylvania, and Southern California. When 1925 rolled around, WGN headed for Louisville on the first Saturday in May to air the first and most famous of the Triple Crown thoroughbred races, the Kentucky Derby. That "handy guy named Sande" was aboard Flying Ebony in the Run for the Roses. Earl Sande was one of the few jockeys to win the Derby three times. WMAQ Chicago aired every home baseball game of the Chicago Cubs from Wrigley Field in 1924. The networks organized sports divisions in 1927. Ted Husing called everything for CBS, including the Kentucky Derby and tennis, though by the 1940s Clem McCarthy did the big horse races, and Red Barber got the nod in baseball. The first live basketball game appears to have been on KGEZ in Kalispell, Montana, at a local high school in 1927. Other sports were added rapidly, and this period of sports broadcasting culminated with the first international coverage of the Olympic games from Berlin in 1936.

PUBLIC SERVICE

From the beginning of commercial broadcasting, public service has been a significant part of its work. The earliest radio stations broadcast crime news and police descriptions of suspected criminals. They helped build community and youth centers. Over the years they have aired public service commercials for a variety of organizations such as the National Safety Council, the U. S. Treasury, the Red Cross, and the Girl Scouts, as well as local fire and police departments. Broadcasters provide such services on both a planned and unplanned basis, and the information can be particularly effective and helpful during natural disasters.

Relief for disasters often was spontaneous as radio presented the need and listeners responded. The most destructive tornado in American history hit Murphysboro, Illinois, in 1925. As WLS Chicago presented the news, a telephone caller asked the question, "Will you accept $5 for the relief of storm sufferers?" George Hay began to plead with the audience to donate. After an all-night run, the station had collected $11,000. Within a week, donations reached $50,000.

Since radio's advent, listeners have depended upon it for the latest weather forecasts. Such has been true everywhere, but especially in farming regions and in the hurricane belt around the Gulf of Mexico. One example was the great hurricane that struck Miami in 1935. The area depended upon WIOD, which went to a half-hourly storm information schedule. Another major hurricane hit New England in 1938, and once more WTIC Hartford gave its microphones to civil defense and governmental authorities. Floods, too, have given radio stations an opportunity for public service. One of the most devastating of all time hit the Ohio Valley in January and February 1937. From Pittsburgh to Cairo, Illinois, WHAS Louisville fed a network of stations that spread information throughout the valley and saved countless lives and brought relief to millions. The stations included WFBM Indianapolis, WEAP Lexington, and two 50,000-watt giants, WSM in Nashville and WCKY in Covington-Cincinnati. Later, much of the information was fed to CBS and NBC, the Canadian Broadcasting Corporation, and even the BBC. The WHAS service continued without interruption from 6 a.m. Sunday, January 24, until 2:30 a.m. Monday, February 1, when the water had begun to recede. Similar activities on a smaller scale were carried on from Paducah's pioneer WPAD. When chased from its transmitter site, the station continued from the home of owner Pierce Lackey. That station gained fame during the Depression years by giving three hours' broadcast time daily during the two weeks before Christmas for Paducah Police Chief William E. Bryant to ask for money to help the city's poor.

Radio has led the way in fighting disease also. One of the first campaigns to gain attention was the March of Dimes organized in the 1930s under the aegis of President Franklin Roosevelt to fight infantile paralysis. Radio provided extensive assistance, and funds thus collected paid for the discovery of both the Salk and Sabin

Front Seats in the theatre of the world

A FASCINATING place, the theatre of the world! Its program for one short week includes addresses by the President of the United States, four great concerts by the New York Philharmonic Orchestra, a Sunday morning full musical church service with a sermon by one of the nation's greatest preachers, the ringside report, blow by blow, of a heavyweight boxing championship, and a bewildering array of music, educational talks, and last-minute news reports from all over the country.

Something over ten million people go to this theatre by radio every week—but they don't all sit in the front seats!

Up in the gallery sit the newcomers in radio, getting enough with their simple sets to make them wish for more. Nearer yet to the great stage sit the owners of more powerful receivers—and in the front seats, getting every word of the great national performance, clearly, distinctly, without the blur of a word or a note—sit the satisfied owners of De Forest Radiophones.

The proved supremacy of De Forest Radiophones is a natural thing. Remember that Dr. De Forest discovered the vacuum tube, without which there would be no present-day radio receiving or broadcasting. Every tube set made, no matter by what maker, rests on De Forest's discovery. Remember that De Forest did the first broadcasting in the world. Twenty-three years ago De Forest was the pioneer in radio—and De Forest is the pioneer in radio today.

The three-tube D-7-A Reflex Radiophone at $125.00 has external batteries; the four-tube D-10 Reflex Radiophone at $150.00 has a drawer of its cabinet for dry cells. Both operate long distances on indoor loop, with wet or dry cells, with headphones or loud speaker. (Prices plus approximately 6% for territories west of the Rockies.)

After you get through experimenting you will come to De Forest, so you might as well get the facts now.

FREE RADIO CATALOGS
for the asking, with prices and full details of De Forest sets, tubes, and parts. Drop us a postcard:

De Forest Radio Tel. & Tel. Co.
DEPT. L3, JERSEY CITY, N. J.

If located west of Pennsylvania address

De Forest Radio Tel. & Tel. Co.
Western Sales Division
Dept. L3, 5680—12th St., Detroit, Mich.

Dr. Lee De Forest, discoverer of the 3-electrode vacuum tube, which makes all present-day radio possible. Below is the De Forest D-10 Reflex Radiophone.

Spectators on the World
With its invention, radio brought events from around the world into listeners' homes. This 1923 ad for the De Forest company's Reflex Radiophone tried to lure buyers with the excitement and entertainment it made possible – a presidential speech, orchestral concerts, church services, a heavyweight boxing match, and news reports from around the world. The genius of Lee De Forest, the "pioneer in radio," provided another selling point for buyers interested in true quality.

vaccines that have virtually eliminated the disease.

All these historic events were unusual in size and scope, but radio has also brought listeners many smaller items that add to the quality of life. Time and weather are two examples. The first Naval Observatory Time signals were aired in 1922 by WJZ New York, which also started daily weather forecasts on the same day. The year 1922 was a prolific one for WJZ. It also saw the introduction of health talks by a physician, financial news from Wall Street, and a weekly children's story hour. The practice of hiring a meteorologist, almost universal among today's television stations, was begun by Boston's WEEI in 1925 with E. B. Rideout. The practice of providing regular series for minorities was begun in 1944. Titled *New World A-Coming*, the series was broadcast on WMCA New York.

THE RADIO IN POLITICS

Those who wrote the Radio Act of 1927 and the Communications Act of 1934 made provisions for political broadcasting. Today broadcasters must make some time available to legally qualified candidates for public office, must treat all for the same office alike, must charge rates comparable to those offered to business, and must give the "lowest unit charge" within forty-five days of a primary or sixty days before a general or special election. Modern commercial political broadcasting began with the 1920 coverage of the Harding-Cox presidential election. The 1924 election saw the candidates campaign by radio and included the first coverage of a national convention, although that was not the first campaign of any kind that radio covered. KDKA got that credit, broadcasting the messages of William A. McGee, Republican candidate for mayor of Pittsburgh. Warren G. Harding was the first U. S. president to address the nation by radio. In 1923 he spoke in St. Louis over KSD on America's participation in the World Court. The broadcast was fed to only one other station, WEAF New York, but was heard over most of the eastern United States since every other station in the nation signed off for the period, allowing WEAF's signal to be received.

The 1924 conventions proved to be quite a sensation for a number of reasons. For one, they marked the first time a presidential convention was broadcast. Since no national network then existed, a special network of sixteen stations in twelve cities was set up to cover the Republican convention from Cleveland. Reception was good, and listeners could hear President Calvin Coolidge win the nomination. Graham McNamee put in three days of practice but may not have been prepared for the Democrats, who began their convention nearly two weeks later from New York's Madison Square Garden. The badly divided Democrats went on for sixteen days before settling on darkhorse John W. Davis. During the campaign, the candidates gave several radio speeches. By 1924 there were nearly three million receivers in the country, up from only 400,000 in 1920. Twenty stations broadcast Coolidge's inaugural address.

By 1932 the conventions of the two major parties had become giant media events aimed at the nation more than the people in the arena. Franklin Roosevelt, elected in 1932, was a master at using radio. In his famous "Fireside Chats," he explained to vast audiences the nature of the bank moratorium, farm relief, and the many alphabet agencies developed by his New Deal to solve the problems of the Depression. By 1945 local radio was covering the campaigns of virtually every governor, mayor, and county judge.

THE RADIO IN RURAL LIFE

In 1921 Pittsburgh's KDKA aired the first daily program of farm market reports and in 1923 hired the first full-time farm director. He was Frank E. Mullen, born in Kansas, reared in South Dakota, and recently graduated with a degree in agriculture from Iowa State College at Ames.

For rural America, radio proved to be a unifying force. It reached the farm as nothing had done before. Market news was the life of the farm economic picture. Some stations were started for the sole purpose of disseminating grain and livestock prices. Grain dealer James Bush built WDZ in Tuscola, Illinois, in 1921 so he could report prices to elevator operators and not have to make telephone calls.

In the fall of 1928 *Prairie Farmer* magazine bought WLS from Sears. Louisville native Burridge D. Butler, the new owner, pledged to make WLS a voice of agriculture. He announced to listeners:

> I am fired with the deep responsibility which rests upon me as I sit here and think of you millions of farm families sitting about your living rooms, listening to this inaugural program. Every day you will be there listening and every night. To give you help in your business by sending you over the air prompt and accurate markets, to help in your production by giving you the best and latest in farm practices, to brighten the home with appropriate musical and educational programs for the mornings and afternoons, to be with you in the evening with restful, inspirational and educational music and talks — to do this every day of the year — and all of the years to come wherein I am given the privilege of serving — to do this I pledge to you my utmost endeavor.[26]

Butler was as good as his word and ran a farm station until it was sold to ABC. The station brought speakers to farm day programs, worked for June Dairy Month with the National Dairy Council, started Peach Week in cooperation with the Illinois Fruit Growers Exchange, and promoted many other efforts.

NBC's *National Farm and Home Hour* on the Blue Network from Chicago brought farmers information and entertainment until well after World War II. Gardening for farm or city was the topic of CBS's *The Garden Gate*, Saturday mornings with Sam Caldwell, "the Old Dirt Dobber." Some stations built model farms and held

---

[26]Quoted in James F. Evans, *Prairie Farmer and WLS: The Burridge D. Butler Years* (Urbana, Ill., 1969), 177.

demonstrations of the latest methods of farming. One was WLW in Cincinnati. From its 137-acre farm near Mason, Ohio, the farm director began daily remote broadcasts in 1941.

The farm director became a famous person within his coverage area, and many of the big farm stations broadcast on 50,000-watt clear channels. Following in the footsteps of Frank Mullen came other pioneers such as George C. Biggar, the first farm director at WLS. While Everett Mitchell was not a farm director, one could scarcely mention farm programming without listing him, announcer for the *National Farm and Home Hour* for most of the years 1928-1960 on NBC. His opening, "It's a beautiful day in Chicago," will forever be remembered by those who lived during the period. One of the best loved programs in the South was WSB's *The Dixie Farm & Home Hour* with Bynum Prance as farm director. In the big midwest farm state of Iowa, there were many farm directors, and most came earlier than the one at WHO Des Moines. But when the station put Herb Plambeck on the air in 1936, he quickly became the most noted because of WHO's 50,000-watt clear channel.

EDUCATION ON THE AIRWAVES

Radio has performed an educational function for every part of the population. Its universal tutoring has softened regional dialects, and eventually they may disappear. Commercial stations have reduced the amount of their education programming since World War II with the success of the drive to set aside reserved educational channels in both FM and television and with the passage of the Education Broadcasting Act of 1965.[27]

Though there were no reserved frequencies for education on the AM band, there were, from the first, licensees who voluntarily refrained from using their channels for commercial purposes. Probably the earliest was WHA at the University of Wisconsin, which began in 1919 while it still had the experimental call of 9XM. The following year, the University of Minnesota offered foreign-language classes over 9XI. Other efforts of the same type occurred in Iowa and at the University of Illinois, where all three of the WILL stations (AM-FM and TV) were educational. Some colleges built profit-making stations that have virtually supported the schools, thus making them educational in another sense. Among them is WWL, Loyola University of the South, dating from 1922.

At least two of the national radio networks programmed lessons to be used in the classrooms of the country. The *Music Appreciation Hour* with Dr. Walter Damrosch played for years on the NBC network as a supplement to classroom instruction. It began in 1928. Two years later CBS began an even more ambitious project, covering all topics and disciplines usually taught in secondary schools. The *American School of the Air* was to be used as a substantial aid to classroom instruction. The network prepared elaborate instructional manuals, and the local CBS affiliates gave them to the schools within their coverage area. Beginning in 1941

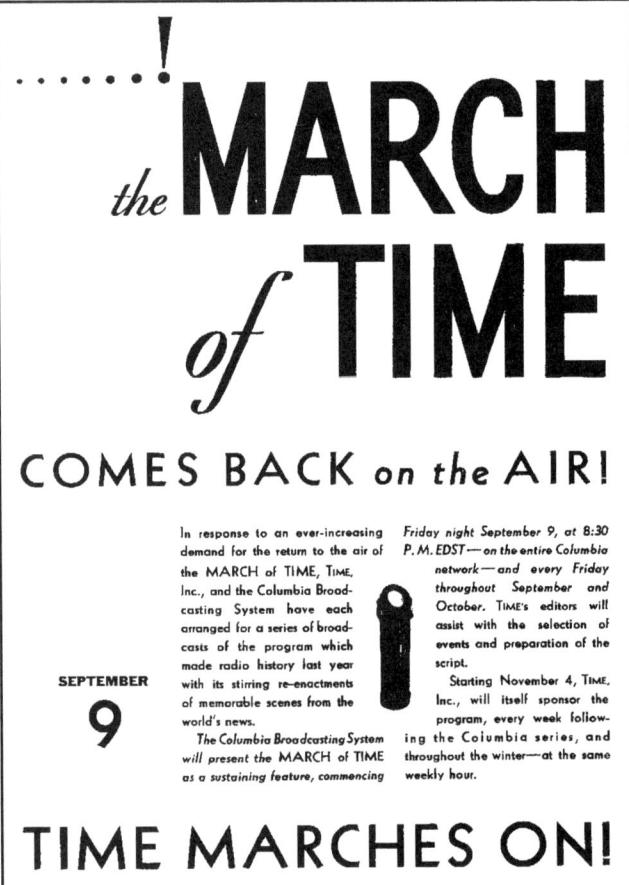

The March of Time
Roy Larsen originated the "newscast" in 1928 with weekly 10-minute radio summaries of items taken from *Time* magazine. This 1932 ad announced that after a one-year hiatus from broadcasting, *The March of Time* would resume with "newsacting" vignettes of dramatic events performed by professional actors.

WBKN, Youngstown, Ohio, ran *The Student Congress of the Air*, which taught parliamentary procedure and debating ability. WLS in Chicago began national school band contests in 1928, and educational groups have continued them. In 1931 the *University of Chicago Round Table*, intended to stimulate thinking on questions of national importance, began airing on WMAQ. Two years later the Chicago station began feeding the show to the NBC network.

RELIGION AND RADIO

In religious broadcasting, KDKA in Pittsburgh once again was the pioneer. The decision to broadcast Sunday church services was made early in KDKA's first broadcast year. In 1921 it put on the air the full service of the Calvary Episcopal Church in Pittsburgh. Much planning had gone into the project. A special amplifier was built, and microphones were set up to pick up the entire service from the ringing of the chimes in the belfry at the beginning to the organ postlude at the end. Other microphones were installed to broadcast the choir, congregational singing, certain responses by the congregation, and the sermon. Reaction by the broadcast's

[27] S. E. Frost, Jr., *Education's Own Stations: The History of Broadcast Licenses Issued to Educational Institutions* (Chicago, 1937); and *Broadcasting Yearbook* (Washington, 1984).

audience was enormous, and the program continued. Other stations around the nation inaugurated similar programs.

A standard observation has been that radio gave preachers a larger daily audience for the "Good News" than the Apostle Paul spoke to during his entire ministry. The networks provided a pulpit for speakers from almost all religious persuasions on such programs as *The Church of the Air*. Few broadcasters wanted to alienate any segment of their audience. So programming usually was from a Judeo-Christian viewpoint, but even Buddhists and Hindus found time on some stations. Some religious denominations established their own programs. Beginning July 15, 1929, KSL in Salt Lake City fed the Mormon Tabernacle Choir's program *Music and the Spoken Word* to the CBS Network. Today, the program promotes itself as the longest-running radio fare in the United States. Beginning in 1938, KOA Denver has fed the Easter Sunrise Service from the *Garden of the Gods* to the NBC Network. From the early days there were also stations that devoted themselves largely to religious programming, one of which was WMBI in Chicago. It was operated then, as it still is, by the Moody Bible Institute and began broadcasting in 1926. A month later, it introduced what is believed to be the first children's Bible program, *The Know Your Bible Club*.

Early radio stations and networks generally carried religious programming on a "sustaining" basis — that is, at no cost and without commercials. Conditions for religious broadcasting, however, were not always accommodating. Evangelist Aimee Semple McPherson, for example, challenged Herbert Hoover's authority to regulate the frequency of her station. She reasoned that she had the right to fit into God's wavelength and ordered Hoover to leave her station alone. Unfavorable regulation affecting religious broadcasting was not always overt, but owners of religious stations generally did not receive the best spectrum space. In 1940 the National Religious Broadcasters association was organized to lobby Washington for more favorable treatment.

Television has decreased the emphasis on religious radio, but the format still remains popular today. The only radio formats listing more stations than "religious" are country and adult contemporary.

RADIO AND SPECIAL NEWS EVENTS

In today's world of communication satellites, radio listeners and television viewers are all familiar with the special events crews who allow Americans to be present at every major newsmaking happening.

Early radio was the father of on-the-scene news programming. One of the leaders was WGN Chicago. As the home of Clarence Darrow and the birthplace of William Jennings Bryan, Illinois had a special interest in the so-called Tennessee Monkey Trial. Thus, in 1925 at a cost of $1,000 per day for long-distance loops, WGN broadcast the entire trial of J.T. Scopes, who had taught evolution in his high school biology class in Dayton, Tennessee. That same year WHAS in Louisville touched American hearts with Skeet Mil-

ler's broadcasts from Horse Cave, Kentucky, where Floyd Collins was trapped in Crystal Cave. The jockey-sized reporter even took a microphone underground for a macabre interview with the dying Collins. Broadcasting of funeral services for presidents began in 1923 when WRC Washingon transmitted the memorial for Warren G. Harding, who died in office. Less than a year later a three-station network aired the funeral of former president Woodrow Wilson, fed by WEAF.

Other special-event shows from outside the studios were often stunts, but the public soon became aware that there were places radio had difficulty going. In 1924 WID Philadelphia broadcast from the bottom of the sea. In 1922 the wedding of Bertha Ann McMunn and George A. Carver was broadcast from Motor Square Garden by KDKA; in 1923 the Al Barnes Circus was broadcast by WFAA in Dallas; that same year KSD St. Louis broadcast from a dirigible in flight; on Easter Sunday, 1924, the Easter Egg Treasure Hunt was staged and broadcast by WCAU Philadelphia. Other such events included Big Ben from London striking midnight over WJZ New York and WRC Washington in 1925; the Liberty Bell from Philadelphia over WCAU on July 4, 1926; the first 24-hour station, KGFJ Los Angeles in 1928; and King Edward VIII's abdication of the British throne for "the woman I love," American divorcee Wallis Warfield Simpson (which was the world-wide broadcast reaching the largest audience of all time) in 1936.

Often the programs were live, but even those recorded for the purpose of later broadcast were soon on the air ahead of the print media reaching the streets. Moreover, radio attracted listeners by giving them the sense of having been at the event in person. A few newspapers saw the wave of the future and realized their readers would continue to use both print and broadcast. The *Pittsburgh Post* began to do what almost every paper does today — print the schedules of broadcast stations. It broke new ground in 1921 with the KDKA schedule. It was well into the era of television, however, before all newspapers were printing program schedules.

One unusual piece of news programming grew out of the mind of Roy Larsen, originally circulation manager and then general manager of *Time* magazine. It finally became known as *The March of Time* and eventually moved to the motion picture theaters of the nation. In 1924 Larsen first broadcast a 15-minute quiz show called *Pop Question*. It lasted one year. He waited until 1928 to try again with a series of 10-minute news summaries from *Time* magazine featuring what he called a "hair-raising" story. The program aired on thirty-three major stations in the United States. Larsen originated the term "newscasting" for the programming technique. Later, the program incorporated "newsacting" vignettes with professionals dramatizing events for which the program had no recordings of voices. The program was expanded to fifteen minutes and given to any station that would air it along with its built-in promotions for *Time*. More than 100 stations carried it with some regularity.

But Larsen was still unhappy. Lowell Thomas for *Literary Digest* was on NBC. Larsen wanted to top Thomas; and Henry Luce, *Time*'s publisher, promised the money. From the Broadway pro-

The Fireside Chats
Elected in 1932, President Franklin Roosevelt gave the first of his many "fireside chats" just eight days after his inauguration. Delivered in a friendly, informal manner, the radio addresses did much to show average citizens in the midst of the Great Depression that Roosevelt was interested in them and their problems. Each address began with the salutation "My friends" and was aimed at building confidence in the capacity of the country to solve the grave problems confronting it.

duction of Earl Carroll's *Vanities*, Larsen took Harold Arlen's song "The March of Time" as not only the program title but also the logo music. Ted Husing became the "Voice of Time" followed by Harry Von Zell and, later, Westbrook Van Voorhis. CBS broadcast the first show on March 6, 1931. Agnes Moorehead, Art Carney, Arlene Francis, and Orson Welles were among the noted actors on the program. It became such a hit that it was expanded to thirty minutes and ran, off and on, until 1945 with such commercial sponsors as Servell Electrolux, Remington Rand, and Wrigley's gum. A film verson began in 1935 and ran in theaters until 1951.

THE GREAT DEPRESSION

When the stock market crashed in October 1929, the Roaring '20s ended. The Great Depression that followed was of global proportions and set an emotional tone that was in complete contrast to the optimism of the 1920s. It demanded a New Deal, the name that President Franklin Roosevelt gave to his domestic program.

Even during the harsh conditions of the Depression, radio grew in popularity. It had, as a result, a profound effect on the lives of Americans. Historians often equate this period with radio's "golden age." One of the reasons radio was so popular was precisely because of the social context the Depression provided. People were careful with what money they had, and now instead of going out for entertainment they sat before the large console of a radio receiver. Programming matured; and network patterns, advertising practices, and news operations changed.

In the politically charged climate of the Depression, radio was not only the most popular source of entertainment, but also an important platform for the discussion of ideological issues. Some politicians developed styles well attuned to the new medium. President Roosevelt epitomized those who successfully made the transformation.

In the 1930s, radio programming grew in popularity. Of the total programming, 64.1% was music (with 23.5% dance music and 4.5% phonographs); 13.3% women's, children's, and feature entertainment; 12.1% information, education, news, and politics; and 6.5% drama. Programs such as *Suspense, Amos 'n' Andy, The Shadow, Little Orphan Annie, One Man's Family, The March of Time,* and *The Lone Ranger* propelled radio's popularity. In 1938, the number of network quarter-hours of programming in a typical week were of the following types: music variety, 52; concert music, 48; vaudeville and comedy, 36; general and talk variety, 30; thrillers, 23; news, 23; and light dramas, 17.

RADIO NEWS

The development of radio news was one of the important outcomes of the Depression and the oncoming World War II. During the 1930s, and particularly as the war approached, radio news and news gathering practices took on many characteristics that continue today. *Fortune* magazine noted that "The nation's favorite recreation was listening to radio ... [and] newscasts ranked third among favorite radio programs." An article in *Scribner's* magazine underscored the impact of the dramatic character of Edward R. Murrow and the importance of radio news. It noted the advantages that Murrow's radio programs had over "the greatest American newspaper."[28] According to William S. Paley of CBS, "Radio news grew up with World War II."[29]

News programming as we know it today did not exist during the 1920s and early '30s. It resembled programming that today would be public affairs or special-event coverage. Radio carried speeches, the fireside chats of President Roosevelt, political debates, religious sermons, and celebrations of all sorts. "News staffs" were comprised of a few people at the networks and even fewer, if any, at the local stations. Some newspapers owned radio stations, and some of the broadcast news consisted of a staff member simply reading stories from the paper. At the *Milwaukee Journal*, for example, reporters sometimes were pressed into service as news readers even as they pooh-poohed radio news as a superficial upstart.

The network news staffs were there to support commentators and included engineers and producers who arranged for the broadcast of public events. Lowell Thomas had become the first commentator at CBS in 1930. Before the decade was over, CBS had hired the first news director, Paul White. He put together a team of reporters to get the news at the scene of happenings and a commentator back at the studio to tell what it meant. The dean of commentators was Hans von Kaltenborn, an editor of the *Brooklyn Eagle* who began broadcasting in 1922, joined CBS in 1930, and com-

[28]Robert J. Landry, "Edward R. Murrow," *Scribner's* 104 (December 1938): 7-11.
[29]William S. Paley, Foreword to *History in Sound,* by Milo Ryan (Seattle, 1963), 5.

Edward R. Murrow

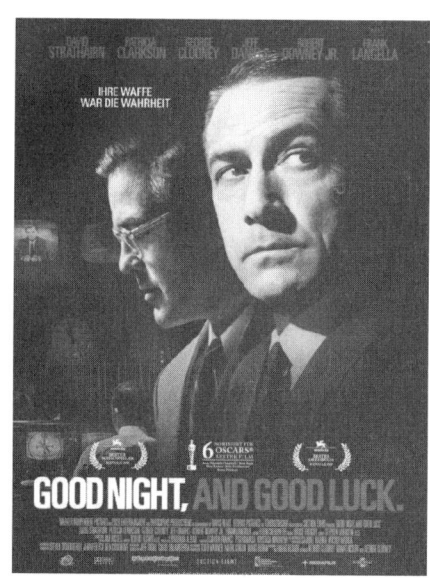

With his ability to connect with the audience, Edward R. Murrow became one of the best known and most honored journalists of all time. During his lifetime, he was featured in many magazines, numerous biographies and programs have been produced about him, and in 2005 his confrontation with Senator Joseph McCarthy was the subject of the movie *Good Night, and Good Luck*. Since 1971, the Radio & Television News Directors Association has honored "outstanding achievements in electronic journalism with the Edward R. Murrow Awards." The RTNDA chose Murrow's name for the awards because his "pursuit of excellence in journalism embodies the spirit of the awards.... Murrow Award recipients demonstrate the excellence that Edward R. Murrow made a standard for the electronic news profession."

Master Communicator Left a Model for Broadcast Journalism

Edward R. Murrow invented broadcast journalism. That is our lore. Does that honor only come from the warm glow Murrow enthusiasts feel when they consider their hero? And if the attribution is accurate, then what, exactly, did Murrow actually *do*?

The simple answer is that he brought "humanness" to broadcasting. He was the first to consistently communicate *with* the audience, not *at* them. When he first sat in front of a radio microphone on March 13, 1938, he had never taken a journalism class. His diploma from Washington State University was in Speech.

During his academic years, he mastered how people hear things and how they think. He knew how good speakers craft messages of precision and clarity.

With an uncanny perceptiveness Murrow found meaning in the events around him. As a master communicator, he then shared that meaning with his audience, one person at a time. Millions of Ameri-

cans heard his words. Yet each could feel that Murrow was speaking directly to him or her. Prior to Murrow, on-air voices were more akin to performances, resembling game show hosts or DJs. The prevailing style prior to Murrow was mannered and distant, dissociated from the audience.

Murrow's studies included Socrates and his philosophy of powerful communication. In *Phaedrus*, Socrates declares that messages must be true to the "soul" of the communicator and conveyed so the words are "graven in the soul of the hearer." Anything less is dishonorable and a disgrace.

Murrow wanted to *ex*-press rather than *im*-press. His messages were personal, with real meaning for him and for his "hearer." For example, he saw the Nazis' expansion as a threat the sleeping world needed to know about. So he stepped up to the microphone only to satisfy his sense of duty to the world, not with any pretense of a new career in journalism.

People were so moved by Murrow's

communication, though, that other reporters began imitating him. Newspapermen who would not have stooped to give their stories on the air before were now falling over each other to get on the radio.

Great inventions seem so natural once we get used to them that we don't remember they were once revolutionary. If they resonate with us and satisfy a deep need, we soon accept them and the novelty disappears. Murrow's new broadcasting style was no exception.

Invention is also a matter of the right person in the right place at the right time. Murrow, the mindful observer of human affairs and master communicator, was just that person.

He was simply striving to enlighten his audience. Soon, though, the power of his communication was such that people called what he was naturally doing "broadcast journalism." The name stuck, and we're still trying to live up to the Murrow standard today.

My adventure with the invisible

by Lowell Thomas, *World Traveler—Radio Commentator*

MACHINES chattered around me, a bewildering complexity of mechanism endowed with superhuman faculties of precision. They had cost millions of dollars—years of thought and research. As I stood on the fifth floor of the Gillette factory in Boston I reflected: "Imagine this prodigious assembling of technological perfection, just to make a blade."

My guide corrected me, saying: "That isn't what we are turning out here. We are all collaborating here to produce a perfect edge. And that, actually and positively, is a thing that you *cannot see.*"

I was to learn he was right. My guide took me upstairs and introduced me to a technician who presided over an amazing instrument. The pet gadget of the blond young modern Merlin from M. I. T. is a "sharpness comparer." Within its mysterious interior an adaptation of the weird usefulness of the photo-electric eye detects to an uncanny degree of accuracy whether that precious edge comes up to Gillette standards of sharpness.

There I realized that what my guide had told me was true. The perfect edge is perfectly invisible. It can be measured only with light-waves!

In my wanderings around the globe this is just about the most astounding spectacle I have observed in modern industry. I mean all this mighty, elaborately mechanized organization engaged in producing the unseeable.

Electric furnaces in which coils of steel are hardened and tempered, furnaces that look like long, miniature tunnels. Inside they are 1500 degrees hot, outside they are so cool you can rest your hands upon them. Diamonds from the fields of Kimberley or Brazil that play their part in the testing machines. Microscopes with a 3000-power magnifying capacity. Cathode ray oscillographs that far outstrip man's poor faculties of perception or accuracy.

And all for what? To turn out something too fine for the human eye to perceive—to produce a shaving edge of incomparable keenness. The doctors of physics, the draughtsmen in the designing room, the toolmakers in the machine shop are constantly experimenting, to produce an even sharper, smoother-shaving edge—and it's difficult for me to imagine that today's Gillette blade could be improved upon. I know—I've tried them all—in all parts of the world.

So in view of what I've seen and experienced, I can't imagine how any shaver could select a blade other than Gillette.

Here are the facts about razor blades. Why let anyone deprive you of shaving comfort by selling you a substitute! Ask for Gillette Blades and be sure to get them.

GILLETTE SAFETY RAZOR COMPANY, BOSTON, MASS.

Celebrity Commentators
In the 1930s, radio commentators became some of the most popular figures in America. Faithful listeners thought of them as family friends. In this 1936 ad, the Gillette Safety Razor Company relied on the popularity of Lowell Thomas, radio's first commentator, to convince men to buy its product by telling of his tour of a razor blade factory.

pleted his career at NBC. Other popular commentators included Boake Carter, Dorothy Thompson, Elmer Davis, Fulton Lewis, Edward R. Murrow, Father Charles Coughlin, and Walter Winchell.

The numbers of commentators rose steadily during radio's golden years (from about 1929 to about 1948). In 1931 there were

six network commentators. By 1947 there were more than 600 national and local commentators. The best known, such as Thomas and Kaltenborn, whose voices and views entered countless American homes regularly, became national personalities. They were, indeed, one of the most colorful groups of journalists in history. They enlivened, enlarged, and personalized the public debate of the 1930s and 1940s as they made radio a major force in the political perceptions of millions of listeners.

The newspaper industry recognized the potential impact of radio news in the early 1930s. Radio held the advantage over the print media of being able to distribute news instantly to its audience. Threatened by radio's potential, newspapers tried to limit the growth of radio news, contriving rules that forbade the Associated Press to sell news to radio stations. The corporate competition between newspaper and network owners soon led to the "Press-Radio War." Although called a war, it was really a short-lived conflict created by business rivalry. In 1933, the rivalry heated to such a degree that newspapers began to pressure the news information services (Associated Press and United Press International) into withdrawing their services from radio stations. A few newspapers even refused to publish radio program schedules.

At a meeting called to resolve the conflict, broadcasters and newspaper owners reached a compromise (known as the "Biltmore Agreement" after the New York City hotel where the meeting was held). Newspapers would publish radio schedules, CBS and NBC would eliminate their news services, stations would limit the amount of news they broadcast, and a Press Radio Bureau would be established to provide stations with news and information. For awhile, the Bureau supplied two five-minute news summaries per day, but they could not be broadcast before 9:30 a.m. or after 9:00 p.m. The arrangement seemingly limited radio news. However, since the networks' emphasis was on "commentary" rather than "news," the commentary staffs continued to grow slowly; and producers continued arranging speeches, sporting events, and, according to Murrow, "the Vatican Choir at Easter time."[30] William L. Shirer, in his *Twentieth Century Journey: The Nightmare Years, 1930-1940*, said he and Murrow were in Europe busy "putting kids' choirs on the air for ... Columbia's American School of the Air" even as war clouds darkened.

In December 1938, the Biltmore Agreement fell apart, and the Press Radio Bureau ceased to serve the networks. Even after accepting the agreement, both NBC and CBS had continued to develop their commentary and public affairs program schedules, even to the point of issuing guidelines for the growing staffs who, according to broadcaster Paul White, were to "elucidate and illuminate the news of common knowledge and to point out the facts on both sides."[31] This approach provided the structure that eventually led to today's radio newsroom. The networks were ready to make the transition from commentary to news.

The commentators became news reporters and personalities

[30]Edward R. Murrow, "We Take You Back," CBS Radio News Documentary, March 13, 1958. CBS-KIRO Milo Ryan Phonoarchives, National Archives, Washington, D.C., Tape 4065.

[31]Paul W. White, "Covering A War for Radio," *Annals of the American Academy of Political and Social Science* (January 1941): 83. See also Paul W. White, *News On The Air* (New York, 1947), 199.

WHAT WILL HAPPEN TODAY?

Events move so swiftly that he is a bold man who will hazard a guess. What will the day bring forth? Who can say? Only of one thing can we be certain: that whatever happens and in whichever corner of the world it takes place, you will hear about it immediately on all-wave radio. From Rome, Paris or Moscow comes the news. From America comes informed, uncensored comment on that news. And with a 1940 Philips, you get it all. Today you can listen to history being made. See your dealer. Learn all about the new Philips sets.

Philips 1940 Range consists of 4 table models, a console and a radiogram, ranging in price from £9.5.0 to £26.10.0. These are mains models. For listeners without mains supply, there are two new battery receivers at £7.10.0 and £9.5.0, and a portable at £9.15.0.

MODEL 735. 5-valve all-wave superhet receiver with extended short-waveband down to 13 m. **£14.10.0**
H.P. terms available.

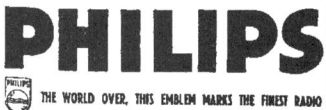

THE WORLD OVER, THIS EMBLEM MARKS THE FINEST RADIO

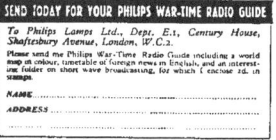

SEND TODAY FOR YOUR PHILIPS WAR-TIME RADIO GUIDE

To Philips Lamps Ltd., Dept. E.1, Century House, Shaftesbury Avenue, London, W.C.2.
Please send me Philips War-Time Radio Guide including a world map in colour, timetable of foreign news in English, and an interesting folder on short wave broadcasting, for which I enclose 2d. in stamps.

NAME ....
ADDRESS ....

"This Is London"

With the German Luftwaffe bombing Great Britain in 1940, American journalist Edward R. Murrow provided eyewitness accounts, making famous his nightly introduction, "This is London." Britain's Philips radio company prompted countrymen to buy receivers to get the immediate news of World War II, including "informed, uncensored" comment from American newsmen such as Murrow.

presenting commentary and eyewitness accounts. Beginning with the Czechoslovakian crisis and the Austrian *Anschluss* of 1938 culminating in the Munich meeting between Hitler and Britain's Neville Chamberlain, networks began a rapid expansion of facilities and personnel. As World War II spread in Europe, the commentators' names became household words; and the network commentary staffs grew into webs of news-gathering bureaus that covered the globe. Following the lead of CBS, all four national radio networks were systematically gathering news for broadcast by the beginning of World War II.

With a new shortwave transmitter, CBS developed the "world news roundup," with correspondents reporting live from the scene of action.[32] Edward R. Murrow was sent to London. From

there he began to put together a team later known as the "Murrow Boys" to get the news from all of Europe. They included, among others, William L. Shirer in Berlin, who later wrote the well-known standard account of Hitler's Germany, *The Rise and Fall of the Third Reich*. During World War II, radio delivered timely news to Americans at home. Murrow became noted for his "This is London" sign-on with the sound of exploding bombs as background. Speaking in honor of Murrow and his works covering the German bombing of Great Britain, historian and poet laureate Archibald MacLeish reflected the feelings of Murrow's contemporaries. Of Murrow, he said, "[Y]ou have accomplished one of the great miracles of the world.... You have burned the city of London in our homes and we felt the flames that burned it."[33]

By the end of the war, the Hooper Ratings showed half the people in the nation received most of their news from radio. When the Japanese surrender was signed in September 1945 aboard the battleship *Missouri*, the world's people heard it all on radio. They had been there. The event even gave rise to a popular news feature on CBS called *You Are There*, re-creating the signing of the Magna Carta, the Battle of Gettysburg, and other historic events.

A number of local stations had made news a part of their standard budget. WPAD Paducah was one of many with one local reporter. WJNT in Jamestown, New York, employed three. WMAZ in Macon, Georgia, hired five full-time; and WHO Des Moines was spending more than $100,000 a year on news. Its news staff totaled twelve persons, the most up to that time.

FM RADIO'S PIONEER: EDWIN H. ARMSTRONG

In the late 1920s there were two technical innovations still ahead that would revolutionize the new medium. The developments were frequency modulated (FM) radio and "visual radio" (television). The two inventors responsible for these developments were Edwin Howard Armstrong and Philo Taylor Farnsworth. They were the last of their kind — the individual inventor working independently from corporations.

Armstrong was the father of FM broadcasting. His biographer, Lawrence Lessing, called him "a young man of the twenties." With the "sensitivity of his romantic generation," he "shared the great creativity of the era and [had] more than a touch of its madness."[34] Early in his career, he and Lee De Forest, who had been working on similar experiments, wound up in a bitter patent suit. Armstrong's primary work revolved around the elimination of the "static" that interfered with the transmission of the AM (amplitude modulation) radio signal. He conducted his experimentation during the late 1920s and early 1930s. Since he was well-to-do, he funded most of his own work and walked among affluent friends and associates. He was a close friend of David Sarnoff, whose children called Armstrong "the coffee man" because he was always dropping by the Sarnoff home to discuss his experiments over a

---

[32]Donald G. Godfrey, "CBS World News Roundup: Setting the Stage for the Next Half Century," *American Journalism* 7 (1991): 164-72.

[33]Archibald MacLeish, *"In Honor of a Man and an Idea..." Three Talks On Freedom* (New York: Columbia Broadcast System, 2 December 1941): 5-7.
[34]Lawrence Lessing, *Man of High Fidelity: Edwin Howard Armstrong* (New York, 1969), 169-70.

Edwin H. Armstrong
The inventor of FM radio, Edwin Armstrong began to be depressed from his legal battles over ownership of his invention. In 1954, despondent over his inability to reconcile with his estranged wife, he committed suicide by jumping from his thirteenth-floor apartment.

cup of morning coffee.

His demonstrations of FM radio were impressive. There was no static in his signal. His most noted public broadcast came in 1935 as a part of a research presentation to an engineering conference in New York. The demonstration was to illustrate and climax his report. As it turned out, it produced moments of surprise even for Armstrong. He had arranged the exhibition with the technical assistance of his friend Randy Runyon. At the point in the report at which the broadcast was to have occurred, a colleague stepped to the podium and whispered to Armstrong, "Keep talking; Runyon has just burned out [the] generator." Armstrong continued reading from his paper until he received the "all clear" signal from Runyon. Then, a glass of water was poured before the microphone — and it really sounded like water being poured — paper was crumpled and torn, Sousa marches were played, and local talent performed from Runyon's living room. The music sounded more alive and crisp than music that had ever been broadcast. Armstrong appeared to have the answer to radio static, the problem on which engineers had been struggling for years.

Armstrong was dedicated to his system. To him, his new FM signal was more than an answer to the static problem of AM. It

was a system that would replace AM. Still, some saw it as merely an innovation that would improve the existing signals. Sarnoff and RCA viewed FM as an opportunity within the development of television, with which they were beginning to experiment. However, it soon became apparent that those with a financial investment in AM were not willing to consider anything new, and another confrontation began.

The conflict prompted legal delays in the allocation of frequency space for FM. Armstrong's personal relationship with Sarnoff became strained and finally broke. Armstrong, however, never gave up. He spent most of his family's fortune defending his FM system as a revolutionary technology that would make AM obsolete. According to Kenneth Bilby, Sarnoff's biographer, the embittered Armstrong "lacked the Sarnoff stomach for a prolonged battle" with the large growing corporate broadcast industry.[35] FM would be delayed three decades before it would achieve the inventor's vision.

PHILO FARNSWORTH AND VISUAL RADIO

The story of the technological development of television has striking parallels to that of FM. Television too had a dominant and independently spirited inventor who was pitted against a major corporation. This time, the inventor was Philo Farnsworth, who battled with the giant RCA and David Sarnoff.

"Visual radio," as television was first called, had two primary pioneers, Farnsworth and Vladimir K. Zworykin. The latter was a Russian immigrant to the United States who worked for Westinghouse as a member of its research staff. Westinghouse's primary interest, however, was radio. So at first Zworykin worked on his own until his experiments attracted the attention of Sarnoff. He asked Zworykin what it would cost to develop television. Zworykin put the price tag at $100,000. Sarnoff thought it a good investment and hired Zworykin to undertake the job of pioneering television for RCA. Zworykin's estimate would grow significantly over the years as RCA took the lead in the development of television into the 1940s.

The young Farnsworth was the leading competitive and independent inventor of television.[36] He was raised on family farms in Utah and Idaho, but from his youth he took a much greater interest in science than farming. Even his job on the farm was taking care of the family's source of electricity, the Delco generator. While still fifteen years old and attending high school in Rigby, Idaho, he sketched on the classroom blackboard his theory for the development of television. His high school teacher, Justin Tolman, recalled that drawing years later and served as an important witness in the patent suits between Farnsworth and RCA, which had been completely caught off guard by Farnsworth's work.

[35]Kenneth Bilby, *The General: David Sarnoff and the Rise of the Communications Industry* (New York, 1986).

[36]For details on Farnsworth's career, see Stephen F. Hofer, "Philo Farnsworth: Television's Pioneer," *Journal of Broadcasting* 23 (1979): 153; T. Ropp, "Philo Farnsworth: Forgotten Father of Television," *Media History Digest* 5:2 (1985): 42-58; and Elma "Pem" Farnsworth, *Distant Vision* (Salt Lake City, 1989).

Philo Farnsworth
Unlike most other inventors, Philo Farnsworth was successful in his legal battles with RCA and David Sarnoff over ownership of his television patents. However, others tried to claim that they — rather than Farnsworth — were the real inventors of television. After his death, his widow, who described how as a teenager Farnsworth had conceived of the technological principle behind television while working in the field on his family farm, continued the fight for her husband to be rightfully recognized.

Like Armstrong before him, Farnsworth the independent inventor ended up in court battling the corporate giant. Elma Farnsworth (Philo's wife, who worked with him in the laboratory) described the confrontation as a "David and Goliath" fight. Farnsworth finally won the court battle, and RCA was forced to come to an agreement with him for use of his patents.

While he won in court, Farnsworth, like Armstrong, did not have the "Sarnoff stomach" for a prolonged war. His health proved a detriment, and after a series of frustrating setbacks and personal tragedies he tired of his television research and its resulting conflict. His work moved from television to nuclear fusion.

While best known for his work in television, Farnsworth also was a leader in radio science and manufacturing. The radio work in his laboratories, though, was primarily in short-wave and audio experimentation to accompany his work in television. In 1938 his company, the Farnsworth Television and Radio Corporation, purchased the famous Capehart Company, known for the superior quality of its radio receivers and for its phonographs and juke-boxes. In 1945 Farnsworth purchased WGL-AM, thus becoming a broadcaster as well as an inventor.

RADIO COMES OF AGE

Since its inception, radio and electronic media technology have been in a state of continual evolution. In the late 1800s, wireless telegraphy replaced wire. By the 1920s, maritime-oriented wireless was replaced by commercial AM radio. In the 1950s, radio was stunted in its growth by television. Today the quality of FM has created an audience shift away from the AM signal. The evolution continues: color replaced black and white television; the chip has replaced the tube. At first, broadcasting replaced the telegraphic and coaxial cable, but cable now has re-evolved in a new distribution form and eroded the power of the traditional networks. The Internet is the newest form for providing radio services. Using real-time audio from stations and other providers, it extends the service of the broadcaster and expands the opportunities for traditional broadcasting. Today, the audience has greater program selection opportunities, satellite has replaced cable delivery, microwave and satellite have combined to decentralize network news — shifting emphasis to the local stations. The marketplace has made people rethink regulation, and technology is still developing. Who knows what technology will do to the future of the electronic medium?

As with technology, the ideological issues of history bear a striking resemblance to the issues of today. Conflicts over monopoly, network control, news and educational programming, censorship and free speech, the law, and spectrum space are still with us. The platforms surrounding these issues are almost the same. Only the players and the size of the stakes have changed.

RECOMMENDED READINGS

BOOKS

Abramson, Albert. *Zworykin: Pioneer of Television*. Chicago, 1995. This biography reconstructs the inventor's life from his early years in Russia, through his career with RCA, and to his death in 1982.

Archer, Gleason L. *History of Radio to 1926*. New York, 1938. This detailed but ideological history of early radio is written mostly from the files of RCA and NBC. Its emphasis is on economics and organization.

Baker, John C. *Farm Broadcasting: The First Sixty Years*. Ames, Iowa, 1981. This definitive work has all you ever wanted to know about farm broadcasters.

Balk, Alfred. *The Rise of Radio, from Marconi through the Golden Age*. Jefferson, N.C., 2006. This survey history analyzes radio in relation to its social, political, and cultural setting and covers a wide range of topics, such as programming and the roles of women and African Americans.

Barnouw, Erik. *A Tower in Babel: A History of Broadcasting in the United States to 1933*. New York, 1966. This is the first of a three-volume work that comprises a detailed history of the electronic media. Volume II, *The Golden Web*, covers 1933 to 1953.

Benjamin, Louise M. *Freedom of the Air and the Public Interest: First Amendment Rights in Broadcasting to 1935*. Carbondale, Ill., 2001. By the time the Communications Act of 1934 became law, the parameters for freedom of expression and the public interest and their relationship to broadcasting had been firmly established. They developed through interwoven concerns over censorship, speakers' rights to access to the medium, broadcasters' rights, and listeners' rights.

Benjamin, Louise M. *The NBC Advisory Council and Radio Program Development, 1926-1945*. Carbondale, Ill., 2009. Influential council members influenced radio program development, especially cultural and education programs and programs aimed at rural audiences.

Chase, Francis, Jr. *Sound and Fury*. New York, 1942. This is an "informal history" of the growth of radio in the U. S., told in terms of people and anecdotes: Marconi, DeForest, Sarnoff, early history, the chaos of the early 1920s, the development of networks, FTC, technology, entertainers, etc. This is not a book intended for the serious historian.

Cloud, Stanley, and Lynne Olson. *The Murrow Boys: Pioneers on the Frontline of Broadcast Journalism*. New York, 1996. This book is a vivid and personalized account of the development of broadcast reporting during World War II.

Collins, Philip. *Radio: The Golden Age*. New York, 1988. The author gives special attention to radio's cultural setting during this fascinating period.

Cox, Jim. *The Great Radio Sitcoms*. Jefferson, N.C., 2007. This book examines twenty popular radio sitcoms that aired between the mid-1920s and early 1950s.

---. *Music Radio: The Great Performers and Programs of the 1920s through Early 1960s*. Jefferson, N.C., 2005. This book reviews a broad range of musical programming, including jazz, country, classical, gospel, pop, big band, western, and semi-classical forms.

Craig, Steve. *Out of the Dark: A History of Radio and Rural America*. Tuscaloosa, Ala., 2009. This study of radio's role in rural life from the 1920s through the 1950s includes diffusion of radio receivers in various geographic regions, listening patterns of rural families, and programs designed to appeal to rural listeners.

Davidson, Randall. *9XM Talking: WHA Radio and the Wisconsin Idea*. Madison, Wis., 2006. WHA was one of the earliest stations in the United States.

Donahue, Hugh Carter. *The Battle To Control Broadcast News: Who Owns the First Amendment?* New York, 1989. This survey history covers broadcast regulation since the 1920s, with an emphasis on the concepts of equal time and fairness.

Douglas, Alan. *Radio Manufactures of the 1920s*, vols. 1-3. New York, 1991. This illustrated work provides an excellent reference on manufacturing and corporations.

Douglas, George H. *The Early Days of Radio Broadcasting*. New York, 1987. The author provdies technical details not found in every other book of this type.

Edelman, Murray. *The Licensing of Radio Services in the United States, 1927 to 1947*. Urbana, Ill, 1950. The author analyzes the policies and actions of the regulatory agencies in licensing radio services.

Everson, George. *The Story of Television: The Life of Philo T. Farnsworth*. New York, 1949. The author worked with and financed Farnsworth's earliest experiments.

Fang, Irving. *Those Radio Commentators*. Ames, Iowa, 1977. The author examines fifteen commentators and the influence they had on America from 1929 to 1948.

Fielding, Raymond. *The March of Time, 1935-1951*. New York, 1978. The author provides an account of the radio beginnings of the news documentary as well as an important movie newsreel.

Fones-Wolf, Elizabeth A. *Waves of Opposition: Labor and the Struggle for Democratic Radio*. Urbana, Ill., 2006. Battles over radio helped spark the massive upsurge of organized labor during the Depression.

Godfrey, Donald. *Philo T. Farnsworth: The Father of Television*. Salt Lake City, Utah, 2001. This scholarly biography presents the story of Farnsworth's life and analyzes his contributions to television's development.

---. *Reruns on File: A Guide to Media Archives*. Hillsdale, N.J., 1992. This reference work lists media archives state by state.

Godfrey, Donald G., and Frederic A. Leigh. *Historical Dictionary of American Radio*. Westport, Conn., 1998. This reference work provides an alphabetical listing of topics and terms, with entries covering almost every subject related to radio.

Hall, Randal L. *Lum and Abner: Rural America and the Golden Age of Radio*. Lexington, Ky., 2007. The popular radio series was a reflection of rural America.

Halper, Donna L. *Invisible Stars: A Social History of Women in American Broadcasting*. New York, 2001. Women were important in early radio.

Hand, Richard J. *Terror on the Air! Horror Radio in America, 1931-1952*. Jefferson, N.C., 2006. This account analyzes six programs in the horror genre.

Havighurst, Craig. *Air Castle of the South: WSM and the Making of Music City*. Urbana, Ill., 2007. WSM was important in helping Nashville, Tennessee, to become a major center for country music.

Hilliard, Robert L., and Michael C. Keith. *The Broadcast Century: A Biography of American Broadcasting*. Boston, 1992. The authors provide an overview of broadcasting history.

Hilmes, Michele. *Radio Voices: American Broadcasting, 1922-1954*. Minneapolis, 1997.

This social/cultural history during its golden era has a special emphasis on race, ethnicity, and gender.

Inglis, Andrew. *Behind the Tube: A History of Broadcasting Technology and Business*. Boston, 1990. This survey begins with the origins of the electronic theory and works its way to current developments.

Keith, Michael, and Mary Ann Watson, eds. *Norman Corwin's One World Flight: The Lost Journal of Radio's Greatest Writer*. New York, 2009. The personal journal of one of radio's greatest writers gives today's reader a reflection on the study of international affairs that is still relevant.

Koch, Howard. *The Panic Broadcast: Portrait of an Event*. Boston, 1970. The Halloween broadcast in 1938 by boy wonder Orson Welles terrified America and sparked an FCC investigation.

LaFollette, Marcel Chotkowski. *Science on the Air: Popularizers and Personalities on Radio and Early Television*. Chicago, 2008. The increasing number of broadcasters in the early years of radio led to a growing demand for entertainment programming, leading in turn to a decrease in the demand for scientific programs.

Lenthall, Bruce. *Radio's America: The Great Depression and the Rise of Modern Mass Culture*. Chicago, 2007. Radio in the 1930s was a product of mass culture and mass consumption.

Lewis, Tom. *Empire of the Air: The Men Who Made Radio*. New York, 1991. The inventors of radio clashed with the corporations that came to control it.

Lichty, Lawrence W., and Malachi C. Topping. *American Broadcasting: A Source Book on the History of Radio and Television*. New York, 1975. This book covers broadcasting's pre-history to the 1970s, bringing most of the documents, facts, and figures together in one place.

Lyons, Eugene. *David Sarnoff: A Biography*. New York, 1966. Sarnoff played a leading role in the major developments in wireless communications and broadcasting.

MacDonald, J. Fred. *Don't Touch That Dial: Radio Programming in American Life From 1920 to 1960*. Chicago, 1979. Radio in the "Golden Age" reflected a "commerical democracy and the character of the people who made it work."

Maltin, Leonard. *The Great American Broadcast: A Celebration of America's Golden Age*. New York, 1997. Based on oral history interviews, this book is a lively account of radio until the mid-1950s.

McChesney, Robert W. *Telecommunications, Mass Media, and Democracy, 1928-1935*. New York, 1993. Commercial radio's development was heavily influenced by commercial interests that outlobbied reformist opponents.

McLeod, Elizabeth. *The Original Amos 'n' Andy: Freeman Gosden, Charles Correll, and the 1928-1943 Radio Serial*. Jefferson, N.C., 2005. This book reexamines the *Amos 'n' Andy* radio program to provide fresh insights and, in part, to refute the usual condemnations of the show.

McMahon, Robert Sears. *Federal Regulation of the Radio and Television Broadcast Industry in the United States, 1927-1959*. New York, 1979. The FCC failed to become an effective guardian of the public's interest, as it was charged to do, in its first twenty-five years.

Paper, Lewis J. *Empire: William S. Paley and the Making of CBS*. New York, 1987. While Paley has told his own story, Paper captures some insights that reveal Paley's flaws as well as his greatness.

Ray, William B. *FCC: The Ups and Downs of Radio-TV Regulation*. Ames, Iowa, 1990. Since the FCC was established by the Communications Act of 1934, it has been flawed by political favoritism.

Robinson, Thomas Porter. *Radio Networks and the Federal Government*. New York, 1943. This history of the legal relationship of the government and broadcasting puts particular emphasis on network broadcasting.

Rosen, Philip. *The Modern Stentors: Radio Broadcasting and the Federal Government, 1920-1934*. Westport, Conn., 1980. This legislative history focuses on the developing years of broadcasting, especially the formulation of radio regulation and the growth of radio as a business.

Schubert, Paul. *The Electric Word: The Rise of Radio*. New York, 1928. This early history surveys American governmental and technical developments and the importance of economic factors before 1928.

Silvia, Tony. *Baseball over the Air: The National Pastime on the Radio and in the Imagination*. Jefferson, N.C., 2007. This narrative, focusing on radio's imaginative power, integrates radio and baseball historically, sociologically, and culturally.

Slotten, Hugh R. *Radio's Hidden Voice: The Origins of Public Broadcasting in the United*

States. Urbana, Ill., 2009. From the pre-war wireless period through the height of the network era in the 1930s-40s, university stations dealt with such matters as programming practices and regulatory issues.

Smith, Ralph Lewis. *A Study of Professional Criticism of Broadcasting in the United States 1920-1955*. New York, 1979. This study of the ideas and perspectives of selected broadcasting critics includes the background and nature of criticism, program genres, advertising, and the effects of criticisms.

Smulyan, Susan. *Selling Radio: The Commercialization of American Broadcasting, 1920-1934*. Washington, D.C., 1994. This book critiques the development of American commercial broadcasting in its early years.

Sterling, Christopher, ed. *The Museum of Broadcast Communications Encyclopedia of Radio*. New York, 2004. This reference includes more than 600 articles covering topics from radio's invention to radio on the Internet.

Sterling, Christopher, and John Michael Kittross. *Stay Tuned: A History of American Broadcasting*, 3d ed. Belmont, Calif., 2002. This narrative history emphasizes the basic events and developments since 1920.

Sterling, Christopher, and Michael C. Keith. *Sounds of Change: A History of FM Broadcasting in America*. Chapel Hill, N.C., 2008. This survey work provides a decades-long history of FM radio.

Thomas, Lowell. *Good Evening, Everybody*. New York, 1976. This light, entertaining autobiography details Thomas' adventures covering news around the world.

Udelson, Joseph. *The Great Television Race: A History of the American Television Industry, 1925-1941*. Tuscaloosa, Ala., 1982. This study focuses on the history of television technology: survey of research, experiments, and telecasting prior to 1941, when commercial television was authorized.

Will, Thomas E. *Telecommunications Structure and Management in the Executive Branch of Government, 1900-1970*. Boulder, Colo, 1978. The U. S. government played an important role in the formulation of broadcast regulation.

ARTICLES

Arceneaux, Noah. "A Sales Floor in the Sky: Philadelphia Department Stores and the Radio Boom of the 1920s." *Journal of Broadcasting and Electronic Media* 53 (2009): 76-89. Commercialization of the radio industry was not a dramatic paradigm shift in the late 1920s as much as a continuation and professionalization of ongoing practices.

Baudino, Joseph E., and John M. Kittross. "Broadcasting Oldest Stations: An Examination of Four Claimants." *Journal of Broadcasting* 21 (1977): 61-83. Which station is the oldest in the United States? The authors award the crown of first commercial license in continuous operation to KDKA.

Benjamin, Louise. "In Search of the Sarnoff 'Radio Music Box' Memo." *Journal of Broadcasting and Electronic Media* 37 (1993): 325-35. The author provides a concise account of the story of David Sarnoff and the development of radio.

—. "Regulating the Government's Airwaves: Creation of the Interdepartmental Radio Advisory Committee (IRAC)." *Journal of Broadcasting and Electronic Media* 51 (2007): 498-515. The struggles among government and non-government radio entities in the 1920s led to the formation of the agency responsible for regulating the government's spectrum allocation.

—. "Working It Out Together: Radio Policy from Hoover to the Radio Act of 1927." *Journal of Broadcasting and Electronic Media* 42 (1998): 221-36. This article traces the development of radio policy and lawmaking from their inception through the Radio Act of 1927.

Bensman, Marvin. "The Zenith WJAZ Case and the Chaos of 1926-7." *Journal of Broadcasting* (1970): 423-37. The author covers historical developments surrounding the period of chaos.

Bohn, Thomas W. "Broadcasting National Election Returns: 1916-1948." *Journal of Broadcasting* 12 (1968): 267-86. The author gives an overview from Charles Evans Hughes' surprise to the similar defeat of Tom Dewey.

Chester, Giraud. "The Press Radio War: 1933-1935." *Public Opinion Quarterly* (1949): 252-64. The fight developed when radio began to compete with newspapers.

Clark, David G. "H.V. Kaltenborn and His Sponsors: Controversial Broadcasting and the Sponsor's Role." *Journal of Broadcasting* 12 (1968): 309-21. Kaltenborn's experiences indicate that commitment to principle by the sponsor appears to be the determining factor in whether a company will sponsor a controversial program in the face of critics and opponents and the resulting economic pressure.

Cleary, Johanna. "'Genêt' on the Air: Janet Flanner's Wartime Broadcasts." *Journalism History* 35:1 (2009): 34-41. Journalist Janet Flanner recorded a "series of radio commentaries in 1945-46 from the hotspots of Europe in the critical months surrounding the end of World War II.... [H]er foray into radio was an important indicator of the growing significance of this medium."

Cranston, Pat. "Political Convention Broadcasts: Their History and Influence." *Journalism Quarterly* 37 (1960): 186-94. The electronic media have helped shape the way in which convention sessions are conducted and have influenced the behavior of delegates.

Crawford, Amy Graban. "A Universal Speaking Service: The Role of Westinghouse Electric and Manufacturing Company in the Development of National Network Broadcasting, 1922-1926," *Journal of Broadcasting and Electronic Media* 51 (2007): 516-29. Westinghouse executive H.P. Davis and the Radio Group designed and implemented a national radio network.

Ehrlich, Matthew C. "Radio Prototype: Edward R. Murrow and Fred Friendly's Hear it Now." *Journal of Broadcasting and Electronic Media* 51 (2007): 438-56. *Hear It Now* provided a capstone to Murrow's career in his preferred medium of radio while building the foundation for his and Friendly's work in television news.

Garvey, Daniel E. "Secretary Hoover and the Quest for Broadcast Regulation." *Journalism History* 3 (1976): 66-70, 85. Herbert Hoover, as U. S. Secretary of Commerce, 1921-1928, "was a staunch and unceasing advocate of strong federal regulation of broadcasting."

Hammargren, Russell J. "The Origin of Press-Radio Conflict." *Journalism Quarterly* 13 (1936): 91-93. The war between press and radio began "with the formation of chain broadcasting, competition for the national advertising dollar, and sharp focusing of national attention upon the Dodge advertising program of 1928 and the national election of the same year."

Howard, Herbert H. "Broadcast Station Group Ownership: A 20th Century Phenomenon." *Journalism History* 2 (1975): 68-71, 83. Multi-station ownership began in the 1920s, shortly after radio moved from amateur status to commercial.

Lewis, Tom. "'A Godlike Presence': The Impact of Radio on the 1920s and 1930s." *OAH Magazine of History* (Spring 1992): 26-33. The author discusses the meaning radio had to American culture, religion, and politics during its first years.

Lott, George E., Jr. "The Press-Radio War of the 1930s." *Journal of Broadcasting* 14 (1970): 275-86. Newspapers tried to keep news off the air.

McChesney, Robert. "Media and Democracy: The Emergence of Commercial Broadcasting in the United States, 1927-1935." *OAH Magazine of History* (Spring 1992): 34-40. Political and economic forces shaped broadcasting in its early years.

Michael, Rudolph D. "History and Criticism of Press-Radio Relationships." *Journalism Quarterly* 15 (1938): 178-184, 220. The author provides a narrative history of newspaper attitudes toward radio from 1922 to 1938, including competition, use of news, AP regulations, newspaper ownership of stations, etc.

Orbison, Charley. "'Fighting Bob' Shuler: Early Radio Crusader." *Journal of Broadcasting* 21 (1977): 459-72. In the 1920s, California minister Bob Shuler "considered it his responsibility to expose sin and corruption in the wicked city of Los Angeles." He used his broadcasts to do so, and the FCC revoked his radio license.

Pusateri, C. Joseph. "FDR, Huey Long and the Politics of Radio." *Journal of Broadcasting* 21 (1977): 85-95. Politics played an important role in the case of the Federal Radio Commission's 1934 decision allocating a highly desirable channel to one of two competing Louisiana radio stations, thus showing that the FRC was susceptible to political pressure.

Rose, Ernest D. "How the U. S. Heard About Pearl Harbor." *Journal of Broadcasting* 5 (1961): 285-98. Americans heard on radio that they were at war. Although imperfect, the reports helped shape the nation's attitude and world events.

Smith, F. Leslie. "Education for Broadcasting: 1929-1963." *Journal of Broadcasting* 8 (1964): 383-98. The growth of education has coincided with the growth of broadcasting as a profession.

Smith, R. Franklin. "'Oldest Station in the Nation'?" *Journal of Broadcasting* 4 (1959-1960): 40-55. This study proposes criteria by which to judge claims that particular radio stations are the oldest or were the first, attempting to formulate a workable definition of the term "broadcasting station." WHA, which sometimes has been cited as the first, was not the first.

Smith, Robert. "The Origins of Radio Network News Commentary." *Journal of*

Broadcasting 9 (1965): 113-22. News commentary began in the 1930s, not during World War II as most historians have argued, from social and political developments of the 1930s.

Spaulding, John W. "1928: Radio Becomes a Mass Advertising Medium." *Journal of Broadcasting* 8 (1963-1964): 31-44. In the late 1920s broadcast facilities, audiences, programs, and station owner attitudes were right for the national advertiser to enter radio sponsorship in a serious way. Radio took advantage of the conditions in 1928 and developed into an advertising-supported medium.

Tenney, Craig. "The 1943 Debate on Opinionated Broadcast News." *Journalism History* 7 (1980): 11-15. The evolution of broadcast news philosophy began with the CBS news rule that stories carry no personal opinions or editorial comment.

Udelson, Joseph. *The Great Television Race: A History of the American Television Industry, 1925-1941*. Tuscaloosa, Ala., 1982. This history of television technology surveys research, experiments, and telecasting prior to 1941, when commercial television was authorized.

Vos, Tim. "A Cultural Explanation for Early Broadcast Policy: Professionalism, Voluntarism, and U.S. Broadcast Networks." *Journal of Broadcasting & Electronic Media* 54 (2010): 179-93. Professionalism and voluntarism helped lead to a policy that favored broadcast networks in the 1920s.

Weeks, Lewis E. "The Radio Election of 1924." *Journal of Broadcasting* 8 (1964): 233-43. Radio "grew up" during the 1924 campaign. The campaign introduced new techniques in political campaigning and served as a proving ground for nationwide broadcasting.

Wesolowski, James Walter. "Before Canon 35: WGN Broadcasts the Monkey Trial." *Journalism History* 2 (1975): 76-79, 86. Radio coverage had an impact on the Scopes trial. Since this was the first time radio had covered a trial, participants and officials had no precedents by which to determine their practices.

Wik, Reynold. "The Radio in Rural America During the 1920s." *Agricultural History* 55 (October 1981): 339-50. "The radio was of profound importance for [rural] American people because it opened their ears to the sounds of the world and provided a medium which became an instrument for social change."

Williams, Robert. "The Politics of American Broadcasting: Public Purposes and Private Interests." *Journal of American Studies* 10 (1976): 329-40. Since regulation began in the 1920s, broadcasters have been "pretty much free to pursue their private interests without fear of government controls."

19

The Entertainment Media

1900 – Present

The mass media provide more than just essential news and information. As early as the mid-1700s, newspaper publishers recognized that entertainment was an important selling point. By the mid-1880s, Sunday editions included feature stories, columns, and comic drawings.

The entertainment media have now expanded from print to sophisticated interactive forms, and Americans' use of them continues to rise steadily. The hours each one spends with cable and satellite television, home video, video games, and the Internet averages almost five months annually. Consumer spending on media rose by 60% between 2000 and 2010, to approximately $1,000 annually per person. Some media — including broadcast television, newspapers, and books — are predicted to lose some of their share of consumers' time, but no one is predicting the demise of any of these media.[1]

With the introduction of each new medium came dire predictions that an existing medium would disappear: the phonograph would hurt live performances, radio would kill the phonograph and the newspaper, television would damage radio and comic books, VCRs would close movie theaters, cable TV would put broadcasters out of business. In reality, shrewd businesspeople in each threatened field adapted to the changes — although some reluctantly — and succeeded in preserving their medium. That process continues today. Americans have more entertainment choices than ever before, and the traditional media have found new ways to attract users.

All entertainment media are finding ways to use the Internet. Based upon traditional media (including publishing, motion picture, and broadcasting models), the Internet is growing into its own unique form. The traditional media are using this growth not only to jump into the interactive arena but also to mold the Internet into forms that complement older forms of entertainment. Although today much attention is focused on the Internet and new technology as sources of entertainment, they are simply two forms built on a long tradition of entertainment in mass communication.

[1]U.S. Bureau of the Census, *Statistical Abstract of the U.S.: 2007*, 127th ed. (Washington, D.C., 2007), 709.

COMIC BOOKS

Comic books, like most media, grew and changed over time, combining old and new ideas until the comic book we recognize finally emerged in the 1920s. Cartoons appeared sporadically in newspapers as early as the 1750s. In the late 1860s, papers began publishing cartoons regularly. The first comic strip, however, did not appear until 1896. It was not a true strip, but instead was a single panel full of action. Richard F. Outcault's "The Yellow Kid" depicted the adventures of a youth from the tenements of New York. He got his name from the yellow clothes he wore. The cartoon was first published in Joseph Pulitzer's *New York Sunday World*. When a competing paper, William Randolph Hearst's *New York Sunday Journal*, hired Outcault away, George B. Luks drew the panel for the *World*, and New York City enjoyed two Sunday versions of "The Yellow Kid." The cartoon inspired the term "yellow press," which critics applied to the sensational newspapers of the day.

Seeking to capitalize on the popularity of cartoons and comic strips, publishers released a number of books featuring collections of comics. The modern comic book format did not appear, however, until the late 1920s. Even then, most of the booklets were just reprints of comic strips. Finally, in 1935, a comic book with original material appeared on the newsstands. Titled *New Fun Comics*, it was published by Major Malcolm Wheeler-Nicholson and sold for a dime.

Nicholson may have been a creative talent, but he was not a good businessman. His mistakes allowed pulp fiction publisher Harry Donenfeld to take over his operation. Donenfeld eventually established DC Comics, one of the most successful comic book companies. In June 1938, with world war threatening to involve the United States, DC's Superman made his first appearance, to a rather lackluster response. The Superman story was one of several action-packed tales in a new comic book titled *Action Comics*, but the superhero's picture was not even on the cover. The first three issues sold moderately well, but then the fourth issue unexpectedly sold out. When Donenfeld learned that Superman was the draw, he had the superhero plastered on the cover of the fol-

The Yellow Kid
Created in the 1890s for Joseph Pulitzer's *New York World*, Richard Outcault's "The Yellow Kid" holds the distinction of being the first newspaper comic strip. To critics, the toothless, virtually witless boy seemed to epitomize New York's sensational press, and they began referring to its techniques as "yellow journalism."

lowing issues. Sales of *Action Comics* soon reached 900,000 copies a month. Superman was such a success that DC gave him his own book in 1939, although Superman stories continued in *Action Comics*. By 1940, sales reached 1,250,000 copies a month.

With Superman's success, other now familiar superheroes followed: Batman in 1939, Captain Marvel in 1940, Captain America in 1941, and, later, Spiderman and the Incredible Hulk in 1962. The superheroes seemed to reflect the mood of the day, and comic book plots often mirrored the concerns of readers. This was most apparent during World War II, when superheroes defended the American way of life by dispatching spies, Nazi troops, and saboteurs. Even before the United States entered the war, patriotic comic book artists joined the fray. Many stories featured superheroes attired in red, white, and blue, and addressed the fears of spies, invasions, and sabotage. The Sub-Mariner and the Wizard attacked German sailors; Yank and Doodle, "America's Fighting Twins," beat up Nazi villains; and Captain America, the superpatriot, battled spies. In 1941 alone, three female patriotic characters debuted: Miss America, Miss Victory, and Pat Patriot. One series, *Military Comics*, devoted its pages entirely to adventure tales of the Army and Navy.

After the war, with enemies not as well defined, superheroes lost much of their appeal. They either disappeared or had to look for new jobs. Batman fought organized crime, and Superman rescued innocent victims of crime and natural disasters. The Korean

War encouraged more combat comic books in the early 1950s. The national hysteria surrounding communism provided fodder for characters like Yellow Claw, a Communist Chinese villain. In an unusual twist, however, the hero of the series was also Chinese. Comic book publishers also turned to a variety of subjects to boost sales.

CHANGING COMIC BOOK CHARACTERS

Not all superheroes were male, though female characters rarely appeared in the original comic books of the 1930s. A few exceptions — Sandra of the Secret Service, Dale Daring, and Sheena, Queen of the Jungle — appeared in the late 1930s. As early as 1942, Wonder Woman showed she could be just as much the hero as Superman or Batman. When Marvel Comics introduced female comic book characters in 1943, it discovered almost by accident that teenage girls could be comic book fans. Soon, characters designed to appeal to girls populated the newsstand shelves: Miss America, a female version of Captain America; Patsy Walker, a teenager whose antics and adventures eventually led her to assume the mantle of Miss America; Millie the Model; Nellie the Nurse; the Blonde Phantom, a masked crime fighter with moviestar glamour; and Mary Marvel, Captain Marvel's little sister.

Glamour girls, looking every bit the pinup, became popular comic book subjects in the 1940s. These dimwitted, sexy girls did not fight crime but did presage another trend in comics: romance. The late 1940s and early '50s were rife with comics such as *Secret Romances*, *Young Love*, and *Sweethearts* — subjects sparked by pulp magazines like *True Confessions*. By the end of 1949, romance comics outsold every other genre.

Other popular comic book lines emerged around 1950. Horror comics became especially popular. With titles like *Adventures into the Unknown*, *Eerie*, and *Tales from the Crypt*, the stories echoed the trend toward science fiction and horror at the movies. The glut of cowboy programs on television fueled a similar interest in comic books with western themes.

Alongside the western and horror stories and the crime-fighting superheroes, silly and humorous comic books filled the newsstand shelves. Familiar faces like Mickey Mouse, Donald Duck, and Woody Woodpecker shared shelf space with lesser-knowns such as Rufus Lion and Ziggy Pig. Most of the animal humor portrayed slapstick comedy, but *Mad*'s satire and Archie and Jughead's teen humor offered slightly more sophisticated fare.

The 1950s, however, saw growing criticism of comic book content, especially crime and horror. Literary critics, psychologists, and the mass media combined forces to condemn comic books, claiming they contributed to juvenile delinquency. To the alarm of children everywhere, teachers, civic, and religious leaders encouraged the burning of comic books. One photograph taken at the time showed a smug adult tending the fire, while obviously dismayed boys looked on. The misgivings of parents and civic leaders led, in 1954, to the establishment of the Comics Code Authority, which awarded its stamp of approval to comic books that cut

Romance for Young Girls
Shortly after World War II, in 1947, the team of Joe Simon and Jack Kirby created *Young Romance*. It introduced the romance genre to comic book publishing. Its main audience was teenage girls, who became comic book readers by the millions.

out the crime, horror, sex, and gore. A combination of factors, including competition from television and a miniature golf craze, led to a significant decline in comic book sales between 1952 and 1956, prompting some to observe that the Golden Age of comics was over.

Criticized in the 1960s for emphasis on whites and males, Marvel Comics tried to reflect more egalitarian views by including women and minority characters. The superhero Black Panther, who emerged as a character in a story in 1966, eventually claimed his own series in 1973. *Luke Cage, Hero for Hire* was the first series to be named after a black character. Cage, who debuted in 1972, eventually became Power Man and lasted until 1986. *Master of Kung Fu*, in 1974, introduced an Asian hero. A 1972 series featuring a Native American hero, *Red Wolf*, survived for only nine issues.

Few female characters lasted long. When the women's movement intensified in the 1970s, Marvel tried several female characters. Most of them failed, but Spider-Woman and She-Hulk, both spin-offs of male superheroes, became relatively successful. In spite of the success of a few strong female characters, however, most of the women in comic books have been helpless, scantily

dressed, and in bondage. Comic book covers have often used voluptuous, practically naked women to attract male buyers. The tactic is similar to that used by beer ads on television.

Since the beginning of comic books, so-called "underground comics" have tackled subjects that mainstream comics would only skirt around. No subject was taboo for the authors. Highly charged political satire, explicit sex and violence, depictions of bodily functions, and drug use characterized underground comics. Despite several pornography suits in the 1970s, underground comics flourished. They did not account for a large part of comic book sales, but they did stretch the limit of what the "straight" comics considered acceptable.

The comics industry went through a boom-and-bust phase in the 1990s, with the number of comics stores more than doubling and then shrinking back to pre-boom levels. The Internet affected the industry in numerous ways, including sales channels and distribution methods. Consumers could use any search engine and find thousands of websites where they could purchase comics and comics paraphernalia. Comics became common on auction sites. Some of the larger publishers offered web-only versions of their comic books.

After struggling early in the Internet age, comics industry has thrived. In 2010, two early comic books sold at auction for $1 million or more. That same year, the movie *The Dark Knight*, based on Batman, had earned more than $1 billion worldwide and was listed in the top ten movies of all time.[2] Superman, Men in Black, Dick Tracy, the Rocketeer, the Crow, and X-Men also inspired movies. Television networks aired series based on Superman, Batman, Wonder Woman, Spiderman, and the Incredible Hulk. Action figures and other toys earned many more millions of dollars. Marvel Comics, which owns Spider-Man, the Incredible Hulk, and X-Men, expanded beyond toys, t-shirts, and video games to party goods, housewares, wireless entertainment, and personal care items.

THE RECORDING INDUSTRY

When Thomas Edison invented the phonograph in 1877, he had no idea how important his little machine would be to music. He believed it would be most useful to business people, who could record letters on the wax cylinders. The device could protect private information from nosy stenographers.[3] In fact, the generic term for the phonograph, "talking machine," reflects its early use. Edison did not focus on its musical potential until the early 1890s.

Emile Berliner in 1887 made some changes and improvements to Edison's phonograph. The result was the Gramophone, which played flat discs instead of the cylinders Edison used. Berliner also developed a method for duplicating records in 1893. Until then, every record sold was a first-generation recording taken directly from the performance. To make multiple copies of the same musi-

[2]http://www.imdb.com/boxoffice/alltimegross?region=world-wide. Accessed 28 August 2010.
[3]Thomas A. Edison, "The Phonograph and Its Future," *North American Review* (May-June, 1878): 531-2.

Emile Berliner
The inventor of the gramophone, Berliner emigrated from Germany to the United States in 1870 when he was 19 years old, during the Franco-Prussian War. During the American centennial celebrations of 1876, he saw a demonstration of Alexander Graham Bell's new telephone, and it fascinated him. He thought, though, that its transmitter was too weak, and — although he had no technical training — he set about to devise a better one. Bell's company was so impressed that it purchased the patent and hired Berliner as a researcher. He later set up on his own as an inventor and came up with the gramophone, which allowed for recording and reproducing sound through the use of record discs.

cal number, engineers surrounded the performers with several recording phonographs, started them at the same time, and recorded the performance on all machines simultaneously. After the song ended, the engineers replaced the recorded discs or cylinders with uncut ones, and the performance was repeated, ad nauseam, until they made enough copies to fill the order.

By 1900, record manufacturers had developed a relatively sophisticated method of duplicating recordings, especially for the Gramophone disc. Technicians placed a highly polished zinc disc, coated with a thin layer of fat, on a turntable. A sound made through the horn of the recording device vibrated a diaphragm, which in turn vibrated a stylus. The stylus traced a spiral groove through the layer of fat as the turntable revolved, leaving a thin, spiral line of exposed zinc. When the artist and the engineer were satisfied with the results of a take, technicians immersed the disc

in acid for about ten minutes. The acid ate at the exposed zinc, leaving a narrow groove that, when played back, reproduced the original sound fairly accurately. From this master disc, engineers then made copies to be sold. A typical record could hold about two minutes of music.

Up until the time musical recordings became available to the public, most popular music gained exposure through sheet music. Since most middle and upper-class homes had pianos, the market for sheet music was large. Publishers devised many creative ways to bring songs to the attention of the public in order to sell sheet music. Song pluggers, employed by publishing houses, helped popularize the songs. Some pluggers played songs from flatbed trucks in downtown areas; others played songs on department store pianos; still more convinced popular vaudeville players to use their songs on-stage. Perhaps the most inventive method of plugging involved prepared pictorial representations of the songs on slides projected onto movie theater screens. The slides also contained the song lyrics so the audience could sing along. The sheet music business was cut down in its prime, though, by improved recordings. Why should someone go to the trouble to buy sheet music and spend hours learning it when all one had to do was play the song on the Victrola? Sheet music sales declined in the 1910s, but music publishers did not mind since record sales were soaring.

Around 1922, when radio broadcasters began airing popular music, publishing houses howled. Although the broadcasters were able to give a new song phenomenal exposure, the life of that song was shortened from several months or years to only a few weeks. Since broadcasters played popular new songs several times a day, the public tired of them quickly, often before they bought the sheet music or recording. Music publishers, as a result, made less money on each new song and needed a constant supply of fresh tunes.

Early recordings consisted mainly of vocal selections and brass bands. Instrumental solos were also common. The first musical recording was a cornet solo of "Yankee Doodle" performed in 1878 in a demonstration of the phonograph in New York City.[4] Recording companies chose music with care, to de-emphasize the limitations of the phonograph's recording capabilities. The voice, with its limited frequency range, and the flashy brass band with its ensemble sound were practical choices. Brass bands were so popular, in fact, that they accounted for one-third of the selections offered in the Gramophone Company's catalogs before 1914.

Popular music made up most of the choices in the record catalogs partly because the subtle nuances of most classical compositions would be lost in the crude method used for recording. Compared to today's high-tech studios, early acoustic recording methods were primitive. Some studios were merely sheds or rented hotel rooms, containing a piano or small orchestra crammed together on a high platform. The recording phonograph sat high and

[4]Fred W. Gaisberg, *The Music Goes Round* (New York, 1942), 83; Robert Dearling and Cecilia Dearling, *The Guinness Book of Recorded Sound*, with Brian Rust (Middlesex, England, 1984), 21, 30.

Music Recording, 1900
In the early days of music recording, the artists were required to sing into horns attached to the recording device. For quiet passages, they had to lean closer to the horn. The engineer sometimes would try to help the singer remember to move by pushing him forward or back. If singers forgot to change their distance, their voice could be inaudible on the record. Some instrumental musicians constructed chairs with wheels on them so they could easily move back and forth. Recording sessions could be very trying for pampered opera stars. One prima donna said that recording was "the hardest kind of work" and that she would have preferred "two arduous stage rehearsals to one recording séance."

had a small horn into which the artists sang or played. In order to be heard, singers stood and sang into the horn. For quieter passages, they had to lean toward the horn so the machine could pick up the words. When the artists increased volume, they would have to pull away so the sound would not be distorted. Madame Oberon, a Wagnerian soprano, had to stand ten feet away from the recording horn because her high notes knocked the recording needle off the master disc. Often, the artist would forget to move back and forth. Since it was the engineer's responsibility to ensure the recording was made, he frequently had to pull and push the performer back and forth to get the best results. This frequently created an antipathy between artist and engineer.[5]

Another reason popular tunes made up the bulk of the catalogs was that, for many years, prominent opera stars refused to make recordings. The quality of the recordings was not good enough. Operatic singers jealously guarded their reputations, believing the phonograph could not display their voices to best advantage. Also, they were accustomed to luxury and adoration from fans. The recording sessions could be long and arduous. The unfamiliar surroundings of the recording studio were distracting. Singing into a horn was, to say the least, unfulfilling.

As the mechanics of recording improved sound quality, singers became less reluctant. The most important figure in improving the mechanics was Eldridge Johnson, a New Jersey craftsman and model-maker. He designed a spring motor to replace Berliner's hand-wound apparatus, and the company gave him a contract to produce 200 such motors. He made other improvements to the machine: a mechanism to ensure constant turntable speed, an enhanced sound box, and an improved record using shellac instead of hard rubber. He continually improved Berliner's machine, ultimately salvaged Berliner's Gramophone Company, and reorganized it into the Victor Talking Machine Company. Then, in 1902, operating under the names Victor Talking Machines and Victor

Records, he recorded the great tenor Enrico Caruso in Milan, Italy. Soon, other opera stars followed Caruso into the recording business — thus giving birth to popular recorded music.

Caruso's success sparked an interest in classical music for many people previously unexposed to it. Instead of paying high ticket prices to see an orchestra or opera performance, people could buy an inexpensive record and listen to a piece over and over again.

THE FAD TURNS MAINSTREAM

At first, the public looked on the phonograph as a novelty or fad. When inventors made improvements in the performance and sound of the machine, however, people took notice and phonograph sales jumped. By 1922, over 6 million families owned phonographs. Record sales jumped, too. Record companies had made 2.7 million cylinders and discs in 1899. That number rose to over 27 million in 1914 and to nearly 107 million by 1919. Consumers bought an average of thirty-five records for every phonograph.[6]

When radio broadcasting became wildly popular in the early 1920s, many record companies blamed it for a decline in sales. That is partly true, but radio eventually helped popularize records. Many phonograph manufacturers merged with radio manufacturers to create combination units that contained both a radio and a phonograph. The union seems natural today, but during the 1920s and '30s, the two industries were bitter enemies.

Ironically, radio technology contributed to a significant improvement in phonograph technology: electrical recording and playback. The Victor Talking Machine Company introduced the first electrical phonograph in 1925. Using microphones, vacuum tubes, and loudspeakers — all radio technologies — the electrical impulses translated into a "much warmer and more natural" sound, replacing the old morning-glory-shaped sound horn on the phonograph.[7]

[5]Gaisberg, *The Music Goes Round*, 38, 40; "How it Feels to Sing for the Phonograph," *Literary Digest*, 10 May 1924, 28-9; Joe Higgins, interview by Columbia University Oral History Office, November 1959, transcript, Columbia University Oral History Collection, New York City, 1935; Arthur Judson, interview, in John Harvith and Susan Edwards Harvith, eds. *Edison, Musicians, and the Phonograph: A Century in Retrospect*, Contributions to the Study of Music and Dance Series, number 11 (Westport, Conn., 1987), 89.

[6]"Phonograph Sales Show Big Growth," *New York Times*, 22 January 1922, sec. II, 13; "Phonograph Rivals Motor Car's Vogue," *New York Times*, 12 March 1922, sec. II, 10.
[7]Milton Gabler, interview by Columbia University Oral History Office, November 1959, transcript, Columbia University Oral History Collection, New York City, p. 1879.

Enrico Caruso, Superstar
In 1902, Victor Records recorded the great tenor Enrico Caruso in Milan, Italy. Because of his immense popularity as a classic opera performer, he suddenly made recorded music seem respectable to other opera stars. Soon, many of them followed him into the recording business — thus giving birth to popular recorded music. Caruso's recordings sparked a new interest in classical music and made it available to members of the public who could not afford opera tickets.

Artistically, the 1930s and '40s were tremendous years for the recording industry. The Big Band sounds of Glenn Miller and Benny Goodman livened the air with dance music. The crooning style of singing ushered in an era of such stars as Bing Crosby and Rudy Vallee. In 1932, the first disc jockey program hit the airwaves in Los Angeles. Radio stations had been using records for programming since the experimental days, but records were used mostly as filler and were considered inferior to live programming. Los Angeles station KFWB is widely considered to be the first station to program a disc jockey show. Al Jarvis' *Make Believe Ballroom* succeeded, in part, because of the way he highlighted the records. Using his listeners' imaginations, Jarvis created the illusion of a ballroom full of dancers. In this fictitious ballroom, the greatest bands and singers of the day played especially for the listening audience.

Jarvis introduced the musicians, pretending to talk to them in between numbers, much like an emcee.[8] The innovative program made an impression on Martin Block, a young announcer who, in 1935, copied the idea for independent station WNEW in New York City. Block later became the highest paid disc jockey in the country, earning as much as $750,000 per year in the late 1940s. By 1955, radio stations across the country played more than 300,000 records a day.[9]

The recording industry did not entirely ignore black performers and listeners, although until the 1950s, record companies promoted "race music" separately from music directed toward whites. "Race music" was a generic term for almost any black-oriented popular music until the terms "blues" and "rhythm and blues" came into vogue in the 1950s to distinguish it from jazz. Many radio stations would not play race music even after it became popular, because the lyrics often were sexually suggestive. White artists recorded cleaned-up versions of popular race records, and often the cover versions outsold the originals. Motown music, a descendant of rhythm and blues, finally brought black artists into the mainstream in the mid- to late-1950s. The Miracles, the Supremes, and the Marvelettes, among others, combined influences from blues, gospel, pop, and jazz to create a recognizable sound that appealed to a wide audience, both black and white. By the mid-1960s, Motown Records was selling more 45 r.p.m. records than any other record company.

In 1958 the Recording Industry Association of America (RIAA) began auditing and certifying record sales. At that time, an album needed $1 million in manufacturer's sales to be considered "gold." Since 1975, though, albums have had to sell a half million copies worth at least $1 million. Singles (records having only one song on each side) must sell 1 million copies. Perry Como received the first certified gold record in 1958 for his single "Catch a Falling Star." The RIAA's program for platinum certification for albums began in 1976, doubling the requirements for gold certification. The Eagles' *Their Greatest Hits* received the first platinum award in 1976. In 1999 the RIAA introduced the Diamond Awards for albums or singles selling 10 million or more copies. Recognizing the increasing sales of music in digital formats, in 2004 the RIAA added a Digital Sales award. In 2006 it added a Digital Ringtone Award to include songs sold for cell phone ringtones. *Billboard*, the industry's leading publication, includes digital and mobile charts, alongside the traditional singles and album charts. There is no organization that counts global music sales, but Bing Crosby's 1942 recording of "White Christmas" is thought to be the best-selling single of all time, with more than 50 million copies sold.[10] Michael Jackson's *Thriller* is considered the biggest selling album of all time, with sales estimated to be more than 110 million copies.

[8]"Radio Showmanship," *Variety*, 14 August 1935, 46.

[9]Paul Ackerman, "300,000 Spins a Day Throw Music Industry Into Whirl," *Billboard*, 12 November 1955, 1.

[10]Roy J. Harris, jr. "The Best-Selling Record of All," *Wall Street Journal*, 11 December 2009, W15.

Big Bands and Soloist Stars

In the 1930s and 1940s, "big band" music became the rage. Then individual singers who had started out with bands went out on their own as soloists. They became the big music stars of the 1940s. Along with such band leaders as Glenn Miller, Tommy Dorsey, and Artie Shaw, Benny Goodman (left) pioneered a new music style of "swing." In contrast to the leisurely orchestral dance music so prominent in the early 1930s, swing was a lively music based on New Orleans jazz, and it attracted a young following. Among the big band musicians, Goodman, shown here on a poster for a 1935 concert in Pittsburgh and sporting his trademark white pocket handkerchief, is credited with starting the swing craze. America's most popular recording star by 1940 was Bing Crosby. He had debuted with Paul Whiteman's big band in 1926 and often is credited with creating the "crooning" style of singing. It was a soft, sentimental sound as contrasted with the powerful technique of earlier singers such as Al Jolson. Advances in microphone technology made crooning possible for recorded music. In 1931, at the age of 28, Crosby began a successful solo career. His song "White Christmas," which Irving Berlin wrote for the 1942 movie *Holiday Inn* (middle picture), has sold perhaps 50 million copies. Because the recording was released before the RIAA certified sales, the number of sales cannot be verified. Worldwide, versions of the song by various performers have sold at least 170 million copies, more than any other song in history. Among the other solo stars to start with big bands, Frank Sinatra eventually became the most successful. He began with the Harry James band in 1939 and then signed with Tommy Dorsey in 1940. By the following year, he topped popularity polls. His solo recordings became so successful that in 1942 James Stein, founder of the record company MCA, bought his contract from Dorsey for $75,000.

RECORDING TECHNOLOGY

The introduction of stereo recording and playback in the mid-1950s helped fuel another era of prosperity for the record industry. Prior to stereo, all recordings were monaural, which meant that the sound was recorded on only one channel and sounded like one was listening with only one ear. Stereo recording uses two channels and is the equivalent of listening with two ears. In a stereo recording of an orchestra, for instance, the violins sitting on the left side of the stage will sound as if they are playing out of the left speaker.

Magnetic tape, brought to the United States after World War II, made multitrack recordings possible. Today, multitrack recording is the standard. Multitrack recording allows an artist to record one instrument or voice at a time on separate tracks. All of the tracks are combined, or mixed down, into two tracks for stereo effect. Multitrack recording is ideal for classical music since the recording engineer can record solos on separate tracks from the whole orchestra and emphasize those solos in the mix-down. Multitrack recording makes it possible for musicians to play more than one instrument on the same song. A six-piece band may actually use

only one performer. Todd Rundgren, Paul McCartney, Stevie Wonder, and Prince, to name just a few, have all done this routinely.

The compact disc, introduced in 1983, was the next important development in recording technology. The CD is significant because it reproduces sound digitally. The disc itself contains strings of microscopic pits that represent the music. A tiny, low-intensity laser beam reads the patterns of pits and translates the data into music. A phonograph needle can wear out the grooves on a record, but a laser does not wear down the data on a CD. Another attractive feature is the fact that the discs are harder to damage than traditional vinyl records or cassette tapes. Originally priced at over $1,000, the first CD players were targeted primarily at audiophiles — those consumers who put a premium on exceptional playback and spent thousands of dollars on stereo systems. Early CDs cost around $25 each, but falling prices made the technology the medium of choice. Now, the CD has lost ground to digital downloads; and in 2009, manufacturers shipped 52% fewer than they had in 2000.

New digital formats continued to emerge, but some did not gain much popularity. The Digital Audio Tape (DAT) and the MiniDisc (MD) were never widely accepted; but digital audio

Elvis Presley

Fans of Elvis Presley can argue persuasively that he is the biggest entertainment star ever. After making his first million-selling record, "Heartbreak Hotel," in January 1956, he recorded more than sixty other songs that sold a million or more copies and had twenty that made it to number one on the national music charts. In two consecutive years — 1956 and 1957 — he had the top records of the year: "Don't Be Cruel/Hound Dog" and "All Shook Up." Altogether, his records sold more than 350 million copies. He starred in more than thirty movies, and his soundtrack album to *Blue Hawaii* in 1961 remained at number one for twenty weeks. A later rock star, Bruce Springsteen, said of him, "There have been a lot of tough guys. There have been pretenders. There have been contenders. But there is only one King." The three photographs here show him at different stages in his career: upon his return to performing following service in the U.S. Army (top, with entertainers Joey Bishop, Frank Sinatra, Nancy Sinatra, and Sammy Davis Jr.), early in his career (middle), and later (bottom) when he made a singing comeback with a glitzier approach.

Poor Mississippi Boy Becomes Superstar

One of the defining elements of the 1950s was the emergence of rock 'n' roll and Elvis Presley, who became known as the King of rock 'n' roll and, later, simply as the King.

From humble beginnings as the son of a Mississippi sharecropper, Elvis became a superstar through his music, movies, and television appearances. He signed with Sun Records in Memphis, Tennessee, in 1954 and a year later contracted with RCA Victor to record some of his biggest hits, "Heartbreak Hotel," "Don't Be Cruel," "Blue Suede Shoes," and "(You Ain't Nothin' But a) Hound Dog."

In 1958, at the height of his initial popularity, he was inducted into the Army and showed that even he, like all young American men, was subject to the demands of the Cold War.

Elvis starred in more than thirty movies, among them *Love Me Tender, King Creole,* and *Blue Hawaii.* Most of the movies were merely vehicles to showcase his singing, and it was his musical appeal that kept him among the world's favorite performers.

After a period of relative lackluster success in the early 1960s, Elvis launched a comeback through a series of highly popular concerts and television specials in 1968. His "Aloha from Hawaii" television special in 1973 was broadcast via satellite to half a billion people in forty countries.

On August 16, 1977, Presley died of an apparent heart attack, complicated by an increasing dependence upon prescription drugs and an indulgent lifestyle. He was buried at Graceland, his stately southern mansion in Memphis; and thousands of fans visit there every year to pay their respects. His legacy lives on as his music, movies, and the industry he left behind bring in millions of dollars from those who still regard him as the King.

files, such as MP3 files, continue to grow in use. In recent years, technology allowed users to convert music tracks into MP3 format or download MP3 files from the Internet onto their computers or portable MP3 players.

The music industry struggled with copyright issues surrounding these digital files. In 2001, Napster.com, a website with technology allowing users to store digital music files, lost a long battle with the recording industry over Napster's infringement of artists' copyright. The file-sharing feature made it possible for users to trade music files, getting, in effect, free music without compensating the artists.

When the RIAA began filing lawsuits against file-sharing pirates — mostly college students — illegal downloading began to slow. The creation of legal fee-based sites such as iTunes and mp3.com helped, too. Within two years of their founding, it was estimated that more than 10 million Americans legally downloaded music from such sites. The International Federation of the Phonograph Industry reported that, in 2008, users legally downloaded more than 1.4 billion songs. Apple's iTunes store has sold more than 10 billion songs since its inception in 2001. In the United States in 2009, digital sales made up about 40% of revenues.[11]

CRITICISM OF POPULAR MUSIC

The music industry has been subjected to continuous criticism. In the 1920s, social critics censured popular music recordings, believing they lowered the tastes of the common person. Later, popular music, especially rock 'n' roll, faced criticism from those afraid that it would atrophy the brain, cause delinquency, or incite crime. Rock 'n' roll and its descendants have come under especially harsh criticism for language and music video content. The criticism of pop music is akin to the criticism comic books experienced in the 1940s and '50s. Not all of the music came under attack, just that with violent or sexual content.

In the 1980s, the Parents' Music Resource Center (PMRC) persuaded the recording industry to label albums that contained explicit lyrics. There was no legal reason a minor could not purchase an album, but the PMRC wanted parents to know which albums were "anti-social," giving parents the opportunity to make decisions about the music their children bought.

Labeling records became common in the late 1980s, but the criticism did not stop. Rap artist Ice-T's song "Cop Killer" created such an uproar that his company pulled the album off the shelves and re-released it without the offending song. Gangsta rap came under fire for the violent content of lyrics. Some crimes have been linked to the music of gangsta rappers.

While the process of recording music has not changed significantly since the late 1960s, the recording industry has. In the late 1980s and early 1990s, the industry made a move toward consolidation of the larger companies. In contrast, some smaller independent record labels suddenly experienced tremendous success

when their artists became stars. DGC, which released the multi-platinum album *Nevermind* by the group Nirvana, grew exponentially as the band and its album climbed the charts. Another small label, Epitaph, also had significant growth when one of its artists, Offspring, released an album that quickly became popular. The success of Offspring's album, *Smash*, is even more remarkable when one realizes that Epitaph, unlike many small labels, did not have a contract with a major record company to distribute albums to record stores.

Some artists have used the Internet to their advantage. The band Radiohead initially released the album *In Rainbows* online, allowing fans to pay only what they wanted. In addition to web sites, most artists use social media like Twitter, Facebook, and My-Space to promote tours and sell music. This method of distribution allowed artists to bypass the record companies and go straight to the public. The band Cinderella even auditioned new drummers through the Internet. Applicants downloaded a thirty-second music track, added their own drum track to it, and then uploaded it back to the group.[12]

The recording industry learned early on that it must adapt to new competition. Today, new technologies allow for experimentation with sounds, recording media, and distribution. Some of the larger companies are merging and creating entertainment monoliths. At the same time, the system is fragmenting, allowing unknown bands and labels to get their music to their audiences. But the industry is slowly changing. Digital sales grew 940% between 2004 and 2009 and now account for $4.2 billion worldwide. However, overall sales have fallen by 30% during the same time frame.[13]

THE FILM INDUSTRY

Although Thomas Edison usually gets the credit for inventing the movie camera, his work was based on experiments by others. Eadweard Muybridge started the process around 1874 with his sequential photographs of a running horse. To catch the horse in motion, he ran several wires across a racetrack to still cameras. As the horse ran past each camera, it tripped the wires, causing the camera to take a still picture. The result was a series of still pictures, which Muybridge then placed on a disc that was rotated in front of a projector to create images of the horse running. Muybridge's results inspired Edison to experiment with motion photography.

In 1891, Edison received patents for the Kinetograph, or movie camera, and the Kinetoscope, a machine that allowed the viewer to look through a peep-hole at the moving film. Since the Kinetograph weighed about a ton and could not be moved easily, Edison's films were made in a studio that moved to catch the sunlight. The subjects were shot in full sun against a black backdrop. The public responded enthusiastically to the earliest films, of ani-

---

[11] International Federation of the Phonographic Industry, *IFPI Digital Music Report* 2010, p. 10 and http://www.apple.com. Accessed 22 August 2010.

[12] James Daly, "Totally Wired," *Rolling Stone*, 1 December 1994, 40.
[13] International Federation of the Phonographic Industry, *IFPI Digital Music Report* 2010, pp. 6-7.

The Nickelodeon
The first filmed moving images, which were the brainchild of Thomas Edison, were shown at penny arcades. Edison was succeeding financially with his first movie machine, the Kinetoscope, a coin-operated "peep-show" cabinet that contained a continuous loop of short film. He thus showed little interest in developing a projection system for his films. Other producers, however, looked for ways to exhibit their films. At first they showed them on sheets hung up in small rooms and in tents. With the growing popularity of moving films, they moved into structures with the express purpose of showing movies. The early theaters were known as "nickelodeons" (picture at left), where audiences paid a nickel to see a short silent film on a small screen with a pianist providing musical accompaniment. When not showing films, the nickelodeons offered live stage performances.

mals and humans performing tricks. But Edison moved on to other projects. As with his phonograph, he left the motion picture to others to develop its commercial potential.

A pair of French brothers, Auguste and Louis Lumiere, developed a portable camera and projector combined in one unit. They presented their first films to audiences in the basement of a Paris cafe in 1895. The films were not staged like Edison's Kinetoscope films. The Lumieres simply set up a camera and filmed events taking place in front of them. *Workers Leaving the Lumiere Factory*, *Boat Leaving the Harbor*, and *Fish Market at Marseilles* were typical examples of their slice-of-life films. The subject matter may not have been especially interesting, but audiences enjoyed the novelty of seeing events recorded and shown *moving*.

Film screenings moved from cafe basements to vaudeville theaters, opera houses, and music halls. Proprietors showed the short films in addition to the regular stage program as fillers or curiosities. Soon, these venues were devoting one or two evenings a week exclusively to films. Other entrepreneurs presented films in "black tops" — tents that had the top dyed black to block out daylight. Around the turn of the century the first movie theaters opened. They were usually screened-off sections at the back of an arcade; but as films proved popular with the public, movie houses devoted entirely to showing films sprang up around the country. Most shows cost only a nickel. The term *nickelodeon* came from combining "nickel" and "odeon," the French word for "theater." Although "nickelodeon" later referred to coin-operated musical instruments or phonographs, it originally meant simply "Five-cent Theater." Nickelodeons were often regular buildings with a fancy facade added to attract attention. Around 1912, the nickelodeon era began to die out as theater owners began building movie palaces — large, ornate buildings specifically for showing movies. They often cost hundreds of thousands of dollars to build. Their primary purpose was to show movies; but most had traditional stages, orchestra pits, fly lofts, and dressing rooms for live stage performances so the theater owners could offer a variety of entertainment.

Early films had no sound. Producers designed them so that the action on the screen told most of the story. If the action got a little complicated, plot cards edited into the film advanced the story line. A pianist or organist usually accompanied films with a musical score that fit the mood of the action on the screen.

Silent films were more sophisticated than most people realize. In fact, most basic film techniques were developed during the silent era: editing, close-ups, multiple exposures, slow- and fast-motion shots, and moving cameras. Improvements on these building blocks continued as technology improved. Filmmakers produced silent films in all genres, including drama, science fiction, documentary, comedy, western, and action.

It was during the silent era that movie stars originated. Mary Pickford, Charlie Chaplin, and Douglas Fairbanks all began their careers in the legitimate theater but gravitated toward Hollywood. Many actors could not make the transition from stage to screen, but those who did found more fame and fortune in Hollywood than was ever possible in the theater.

The United States government made good use of that star power during World War I to help sell Liberty Loans to the public. Pickford, Chaplin, and Fairbanks all helped the war effort by making personal appearances and filming short "trailers," or short films shown along with feature films, exhorting movie-goers to participate in the Liberty Loans program.

Woodrow Wilson, seeking a public relations outlet for war messages, set up the Committee on Public Information (CPI) to take charge of disseminating war films produced by the Signal Corps. George Creel, chairman of the committee, was a sort of press agent for the war effort. As such, he had to invent a method of reaching movie-going audiences with official government war messages. Prior to the CPI's founding, the Red Cross had distributed the Signal Corps' war films rather haphazardly through its fundraising meetings. Creel realized that, in order to make an impact, government films had to be distributed like commercial motion pictures: through movie theaters. He established the Division of Films in order to do just that. Unfortunately, the film industry was exceed-

Movie Milestones
Along with director D. W. Griffith's *Birth of a Nation*, made in 1915, two early motion pictures stand out as landmarks. Produced by Edison's Kinetoscope process, *The Great Train Robbery*, made in 1903, was the first film to together a series of scenes in one coherent narrative. Edison produced this ad to sell the film to exhibitors. *The Jazz Singer*, which was made in 1927, was the first full-length film with synchronized sound. Contrasted with the silent movies, it was a "talkie." Many producers considered sound a passing fad, but by 1929 silents had virtually disappeared.

ingly fragmented, and it was impossible to get complete dissemination of the films through established channels of distribution. The government had the same distribution problems any commercial film producer had getting the final product to the public. As a result, the Division of Films produced only four war films, but each did achieve fairly wide circulation.

The war in Europe had a favorable effect for American filmmakers. Prior to the war, London was the center of the world film trade. The war changed that dramatically as American producers capitalized on Europe's misfortune. Hollywood has been the world film leader ever since.

THE TALKIES ARRIVE

The introduction of sound to motion pictures was a tortuous process. Edison synchronized phonographs with films as early as 1894, but his attempts were not commercially successful. Other experimenters followed, including radio pioneer Lee De Forest. It was not until 1924 that Western Electric, the same company that invented electrical recording, developed the Vitaphone, a system similar to Edison's. It allowed a musical score to be recorded and synchronized with the film. In 1926, Warner Brothers released the first sound picture, *Don Juan*, starring John Barrymore and Mary Astor. *Don Juan* received a favorable response from the $10-a-seat premiere audience. Nevertheless, most major studios were wary of sound pictures. The earliest Vitaphone pictures did not synchronize voices with the films; but in 1927 *The Jazz Singer*, starring Al Jolson, did just that. Box office records tumbled as enthusiastic crowds filled theaters to see the newest wonder of the world. *The Jazz Singer* ushered in a new era of filmmaking, requiring new studios, new theater equipment, and new acting techniques. Not all actors made the transition from silents to talkies. Some did not have the voices to fit their images; others simply could not act.

Despite the thrill of the talkies, the Great Depression hurt the movie industry. Competition from radio, which entertained for free, kept audiences home from theaters. By 1932, attendance had dropped by 30% from the beginning of the Depression in 1929. Many small studios were unable to survive, but others emerged relatively unscathed. While we may think of the movies made in the 1930s as great classic films, many were produced inexpensively on assembly-line schedules. There were exceptions, of course. Busby Berkley's intricately choreographed extravaganzas, such as *Gold Diggers of 1935* and *Varsity Show*, used scores of dancers and hundreds of costumes and cost around $10,000 for each minute on the screen. By the end of the 1930s, most studios were regaining strength and were capable of supportng the U.S. war effort.

When World War II threatened to involve the United States, the movie industry, along with most other industries, swung into wartime production. Much like the comic book industry, Hollywood demonstrated its patriotism by distributing anti-Nazi films. The U.S. government, through the Office of War Information (OWI), assisted filmmakers in producing war films. Chief of Staff Gen. George C. Marshall recruited celebrated director Frank Capra to produce *Why We Fight*, a series of seven films, to indoctrinate recruits about the threat from the Axis nations. The government encouraged Hollywood to use its resources to keep up morale, instill a sense of duty, and combat Axis propaganda. Many movie stars enlisted in the armed services or volunteered to entertain troops, setting an example for their fans to follow. Even with shortages of materials needed to make movies, including raw film, the studios churned out almost as many new features during the war as they had during peacetime.

World War II benefited the movie industry in two main ways. First, wartime jobs put an end to the Depression. Many people who had been out of work were now employed and had money to spend. Theaters sold between 85 and 100 million tickets per week. The second thing the war did for Hollywood was to put a temporary stop to television development. America needed all of its re-

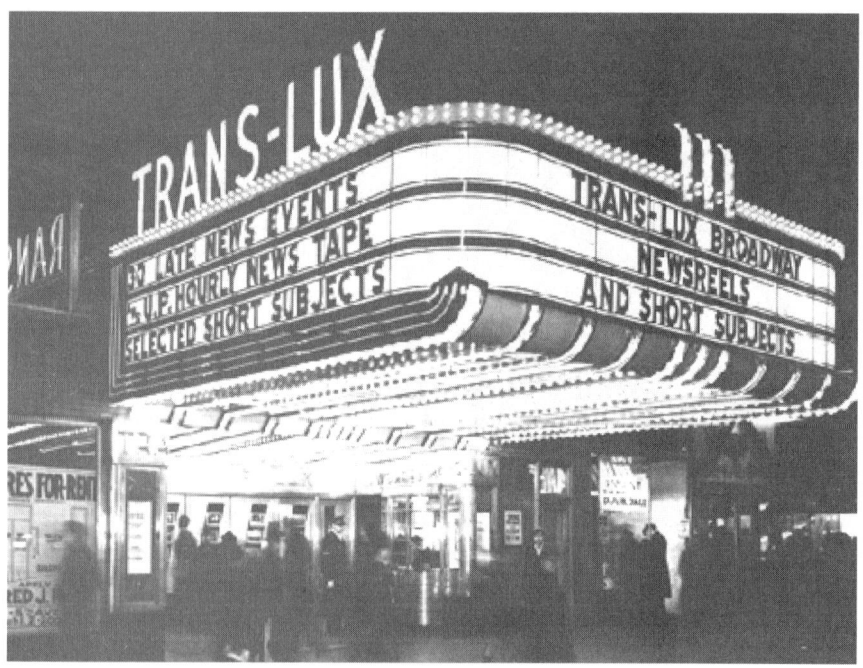

sources for the war effort, which meant that unnecessary research and manufacturing slowed to a halt. The Federal Communications Commission stopped issuing licenses for experimental television stations (although existing stations could still broadcast), and television manufacturers converted their plants to war production.

COMPETITION FOR MOVIES

The movie industry suffered, though, when the war ended. TV stations multiplied quickly, and consumers snatched up the primitive TV sets at a rate of 200,000 per month in 1948. Movies also felt the effects of the return to one-income families as servicemen returned home to their old jobs and women returned to duty as housewives. New entertainment fads, like miniature golf and bowling, took time and money away from the movies. By 1956, weekly movie attendance had fallen to fewer than 47 million.

While Hollywood was down economically, it also suffered a blow to its reputation. After the war, U.S.-Soviet relations deteriorated, and anti-Communist passions and fears rose, leading Congress to convene several hearings investigating the Communist influence in the movie industry. The hearings led to blacklists, jail sentences, and suicides for some members of the Hollywood community. Those on the blacklist could not find employment in Hollywood under their own names for a long time, if ever again. Studio executives fired employees who would not cooperate in the hearings, feeling they had to do something to calm public fears that the studios were infested with Communists. Some uncooperative witnesses were charged with contempt of Congress and sentenced to jail. Hollywood's reputation has never fully recovered from the damage done by this "Red Scare."

Ever since a scantily dressed (for 1895) woman undulated across a Kinetoscope lens, the content of some films has raised public ire. *Dolorita in the Passion Dance* was banned in Atlantic City

in 1895, but her legacy continues. The film industry was unable (or unwilling) to abide by a voluntary production code until the mid-1930s, when the Catholic Church's Legion of Decency began its campaigns against objectionable movies. Producers, hesitant to antagonize the meager audiences of the Depression era, began following a strict production code.

If the code were not enough to curb objectionable material, filmmakers were often in awe of local and state censorship boards, which held enough influence to ban certain movies. The First Amendment did not apply to movies until 1952, when the U.S. Supreme Court decision in *Burstyn v Wilson* revoked the power of a municipality to license movies for local showing. Several Supreme Court decisions favoring Hollywood, as well as an increasing disregard for the Legion of Decency, mitigated the Legion's influence in the 1950s. The movie industry reached a sort of compromise with its critics by implementing a rating system in 1968. The original system had four categories, but over time, it was expanded and refined. Today, "G" movies are for audiences of all ages; a "PG" rating alerts parents to potentially mature situations; "PG-13" means no one under thirteen will be admitted without a parent; "R" movies are restricted to viewers over age seventeen, unless accompanied by a parent; and "NC-17" movies will not allow anyone under seventeen to enter. Although American society has grown more permissive, blood and nudity still provoke criticism.

WOMEN AND MINORITIES IN THE MOVIE INDUSTRY

Although often overlooked, women have played an important role in the movie industry. We are all familiar with the seductive screen enchantress, the shy ingenue, and the strong-willed rebel who gives in to her man in the end. Hackneyed screen roles such as these made up the typical view of women in film. In reality, however, women were a power behind the camera in the medi-

Alice Guy
Perhaps the first director of narrative films was Alice Guy. Working as a secretary for a filmmaker in France, she wrote and filmed her first production in 1896. Over her career, she produced nearly 300 films.

um's earliest years. As a matter of fact, some historians argue that the first director of narrative films was a woman. In 1896, Alice Guy (later Alice Guy Blaché), a secretary for a photographer and early filmmaker, wrote a short play called *La Fee Aux Choux* (The Cabbage Fairy) and filmed it. She soon was making films full-time. In her lifetime, she produced nearly 300 films in every genre, including the 1912 science fiction film *In the Year 2000*.

Blaché had plenty of company: more women had decision-making power before 1920 than at any other point in film history. We tend to remember the actresses whose faces are so familiar. Often ignored is the fact that many of these famous actresses owned their own production companies and directed some of their own films. Besides acting awards, 100 or so women have won Academy Awards for their work behind the camera.

Film histories have also given little attention to minority contributions. For many years, most minority roles were stereotyped: Blacks as maids, Hispanics and Native Americans as the bad guys in westerns, Asians as enemies in war films. Some notable minorities, though, have made names for themselves. Paul Robeson, a talented singer and actor on stage and in film, played a variety of roles, including the stereotypical black male. He was recognized as a brilliant actor, but his accomplishments were overshadowed

by his political stance against lynching and in favor of friendship with Russia following World War II. No longer able to earn a living in America, he eventually emigrated to England. After several years, he returned to America in poor health and lived the rest of his life in seclusion.

Puerto Rican-born Rita Moreno won an Oscar for her role as the feisty Anita in *West Side Story*. She fought most of her life to overcome type-casting in American films as "the Spanish spitfire." She had to move to Broadway to be cast for her talent and not her ethnic heritage. In the 1990s, though, she was producing films and making decisions about what would appear on screen.

TECHNOLOGICAL COMPETITION

In 1975, the motion picture environment began to change, forcing production companies to adjust to a powerful new technology. That year, Sony introduced its $1,300 Betamax videocassette recorder. It did not take long for people to realize that the VCR was an ideal companion to movie theaters. Only three years after the VCR hit the market, the video rental industry was born. Business was slow at first; but as VCRs became cheaper and the number of homes owning VCRs rapidly increased, video stores seemed to spring up on every corner. When movie production companies realized how profitable the video rental business had become, they tried to collect a portion of the rental fees. But the courts ruled that, under the First-Sale Doctrine, the purchaser is buying the right to resell a tape or to rent it out. When a studio sells a cassette, it loses the right to any further profits. The purchaser does not, however, gain the right to copy the movie. The copyright owner holds that right. Once introduced, DVD's quickly replaced videocassettes. Studios now make more money from sales of DVD's than from theater showings. The DVD is usually released even before pay-cable channels get the movie. Some movies never even make it to the theater — they go straight to video.

Home video had a great impact on movie entertainment. In 2006, 93 million American households had VCRs and 95 million had DVD players. The amount of money — along with the number of hours — that Americans spend on home video now surpasses the amount they spend on movies in theaters.

Even with so much money going to home video, the movie industry continued to thrive. Domestic box office receipts reached $10.6 billion in 2009, and worldwide receipts that year hit an all-time high of $29.9 billion. The Internet offered another challenge, but the motion picture industry did not wait for it to gain the upper hand. Independent producers and large studios alike experimented with distributing movies over the Internet. iTunes in 2010 had more than 5,000 movie titles available for purchase or rental.

THE RADIO INDUSTRY

When a young Italian named Guglielmo Marconi developed wireless telegraphy in 1895, he was far from creating radio broadcasting as we know it. His intention was to improve on the tradition-

First Scheduled Radio Broadcast
KDKA, Pittsburgh, earned its place in history with a broadcast on November 2, election night, 1920. It obtained voting results from the *Pittsburgh Post* and then reported them in what KDKA claimed was "the world's first scheduled broadcast." KDKA was eager to know if people were listening and asked, "Will anyone hearing this broadcast please communicate with us, as we are anxious to know how far the broadcast is reaching and how it is being received." KDKA's purpose with the broadcast was to stimulate consumer interest in purchasing radio receivers that its parent company, Westinghouse, manufactured.

al wired telegraph. The "wireless," as it was known, was simply a method for sending Morse code through the air. It proved to be a useful technology for ships and trains that could not use stationary telegraph lines.

The fact that Marconi invented radio telegraphy from materials available to anyone spurred a widespread amateur interest in tinkering with wireless technology. Men and boys built their own transmitting and receiving sets and spent evenings tapping out Morse code or straining to hear messages from faraway stations. Maritime wireless communication before and during World War I demonstrated the usefulness of the technology; and experimentation among amateurs expanded to experimentation among such larger institutions as the military, AT&T, Westinghouse, and General Electric.

Experiments in sending voices and music over the air began as early as 1903. Listeners expecting to hear Morse code were often astounded to hear voices. Reginald Fessenden startled wireless operators on ships in the Atlantic with a 1906 Christmas Eve broadcast of music and a reading from the biblical book of Luke telling of the birth of Jesus. Around 1909, Charles D. Herrold set up an experimental station in San Jose, California. He and his wife, Sybil, began broadcasting programs every Wednesday night. Most nights he played phonograph records, but sometimes a singer would perform. When their first child was born, his wife held the baby up to the microphone so listeners could hear it crying.

Although many experimental stations were broadcasting before 1920, KDKA of Pittsburgh usually takes the honors of being the first to broadcast regular programming. It began its history by airing the returns for the 1920 presidential election between Warren G. Harding and James M. Cox. KDKA's importance lies in the fact that it was established not as an experimental station, but one with a commercial purpose: to stimulate sales of radio receivers in the Pittsburgh area. The Westinghouse Corporation, which owned the station, manufactured receiving sets.

Most early station owners viewed radio broadcasting as an indirect way to sell merchandise. "Toll broadcasting," or paid advertising, did not exist until 1922. The earliest stations did not air commercial ads, but their owners considered the stations selling

tools. Some had an immediate benefit from owning stations: a station owned by a department store provided customers with a reason to buy a radio set; likewise, a station owned by a radio equipment manufacturer gave people a need to buy vacuum tubes and other parts. Some station owners had no other relationship with the radio industry. Automobile dealers and newspapers, for instance, reasoned that having their names mentioned on a regular basis during their stations' broadcasting provided a kind of advertising. Colleges and universities also obtained licenses for stations to provide educational programs and fodder for research for their engineering and budding broadcasting departments.

MILLIONS OF RADIO LISTENERS

Americans' fascination with radio grew with such incredible speed that, in 1922, the Bureau of Standards estimated the radio audience at nearly 1 million people. By September of 1924, that audience had grown to around 5 million. A broadcasting industry publication estimated the 1926 audience to be nearly 20 million, and 26 million the following year. By the 1930 census, more than 12 million American families, or 40%, had radios in their homes. Three years later, that number rose to 16.8 million families. With an average family size of about four people, that meant radio had a potential audience of nearly 61 million people after less than thirteen years of existence. Radio sets appeared in even the poorest homes. In 1933, 36% of families with annual incomes under $1,000 owned sets.[14]

The earliest programs consisted mostly of phonograph records, player piano rolls, lectures on various subjects, and a musician or two. AT&T's New York radio station WBAY (later WEAF) included phonograph records in its first day of programming on July 25, 1922. The programmer alternated records with songs played on a piano. Mixing records and piano music worked very well for these

[14]"Radio Air Police," *New York Times*, 2 April 1922, sec. VII, 2; "Varied News and Comment on Radio," *New York Times*, 21 September 1924, sec. VIII, 14; "Radio Audience Totals 20,000,000," *New York Times*, 3 January 1926, sec. VIII, 13; "Nation-wide Survey Reveals 6,500,000 Sets in Use," *New York Times*, 9 January 1927, sec. VIII, 11; U.S. Department of Commerce, Bureau of the Census, *15th Census of the United States: 1930, Population, Volume VI, Families* (Washington, D.C., 1933), 33; U.S. Department of Commerce, Bureau of the Census, *Vertical Study of Radio Ownership* (New York, 1933), 16, 50-1.

Radio Listening, 1920s

With improvements in technology, radio's popularity increased tremendously in the 1920s. The earliest receivers had used leaky batteries for power and headsets for listening. By 1923 (left) radio sets had been redesigned so that they fit into house decor and had replaced headsets with speakers. In its October 1923 issue *Radio Broadcast* magazine exulted, "Suppose you had a compact little ... instrument which you plugged into any one of your electric light sockets and received ... the latest world and local news, music of all kinds, play-by-play (or blow-by-blow) reports of the big sporting events, extension courses in whatever might interest you, information regarding where to shop for everything ... with a minimum of interference, three hundred and sixty-five days in the year...." The RCA Radiola from 1926 (right) operated on house electrical current and included a loudspeaker.

pioneers—until the next day, that is, when the Victrola was out of order. From 7:30 to 8:00 in the evening, programmers alternated records and player piano rolls. From 8:00 to 10:30, however, programming was all live.[15]

Because early radio sets had earphones for the operator, most of the audience was made up of the men and boys who were experimenting with the technology. In the early 1920s, the listeners were not so much interested in program content as they were in tuning in distant stations. Any programming would do. But after the novelty wore off, programming became more important. In the mid-1920s, loudspeakers were developed and added to radio sets, negating the need for earphones. Programs then became available to the entire family. Listeners did not want programs of phonograph records and piano rolls. Many listeners could play their own phonographs for that matter. They wanted more sophisticated programming — live programming.

Live programming was the mainstay of radio in the 1930s. Broadcasting phonograph records was considered inferior to broadcasting live performers. Local performers filled the airwaves with music from pianos, organs, guitars, and all types of ensembles. Most stations, however, did not have enough local talent to fill the broadcasting day; so many joined a network to take advantage of quality live programming.

RADIO NETWORKS

RCA established the first national network in 1926, the National Broadcasting Company (NBC). Stations across the country, linked by telephone lines, could now deliver the same programming

from New York. NBC was actually made up of two separate networks: the Red and the Blue. The two had separate affiliates and programming. In 1927, CBS debuted as the Columbia Phonograph Broadcasting System, with programming similar to NBC. The Mutual Broadcasting System, never able to compete successfully with NBC and CBS, began broadcasting in 1934. In 1943, NBC sold one of its two networks to the Lifesavers candy tycoon, Edward Noble, who renamed it the American Broadcasting Company (ABC).

The networks, all headquartered in New York City, had access to the big-name talent — talent the smaller local stations could not afford. A network affiliate, however, could provide listeners with quality live entertainment. Famous musicians, comedians, and actors reached audiences across the country with programs like *Amos 'n Andy*, *Buck Rogers in the Year 2433*, and *Easy Aces*.

Families gathered around the radio and visualized the action of the programs in their minds. Network orchestras, often with famous conductors, provided live performances of classical works for millions of listeners. Although phonograph records had spread interest in orchestral and opera compositions, they could not touch the sheer numbers radio broadcasting reached with classical music. The free entertainment on the radio often took the place of going to movie theaters or buying new phonograph records.

Radio programs were divided into two main categories: sponsored and sustaining. An advertiser paid to sponsor a particular program, and the station promoted the advertiser's name with the show. Pepsodent sponsored *Amos 'n Andy*, Kellogg's sponsored *Buck Rogers*, and Lavoris sponsored *Easy Aces*. Texaco's sponsorship of the Metropolitan Opera's performances was the longest-running on radio. From 1930 to 2004, the oil company participated in bringing classical works such as *Tosca*, *La Traviata*, and *The Bartered Bride* to millions of opera fans. Sustaining programs, on the other hand, had no advertising. They filled in gaps between spon-

[15]WBAY, Master Programs and Final Program Records for 25 July 1922, 26 July 1922, and 3 August 1922, unpaged, item 1290, NBC Collection, Broadcasting and Recorded Sound Division, Library of Congress, Washington, D.C.

Live, with Sound
In the earliest years of commercial radio broadcasting, all programming was done live. Dance music, including jazz and country 'n' western, was a staple. The *Grand Ole Opry* barn dance proved especially popular. Other types of programs, such as comedies and children's bedtime stories, were read on air. When NBC debuted in 1926 as the first national radio network, it, too, did its programming live. The ensemble of eleven actors pictured here not only read their lines but also provided sound effects.

sored shows. Although networks aired sustaining programs, they were much more common on local stations during non-network hours or on independent (unaffiliated) stations.

RECORDED PROGRAMMING

Despite the emphasis on live entertainment, broadcasters continued to use recorded programming. In the 1930s, though, it became more sophisticated. Programs similar to network programs were recorded on 16-inch discs, called electrical transcriptions (ETs). The ETs were high-quality recordings that usually needed special phonographs to play them. Researchers reported that most people could not tell the difference between a live program and an electrical transcription. Some broadcasters implied that the recorded programs were live, prompting accusations of fraud; so the Federal Radio Commission required all recorded material to be announced as such. Some stations used regular phonograph records unapologetically, building such programs around them as disc jockey Al Jarvis' *Make Believe Ballroom*.

Broadcasters learned early on to program for audiences that would be listening at certain times of the day. In the mornings, when most women were home, soap operas and other programs geared toward women filled the airwaves. In the afternoons, children home from school could hear programs like *Little Orphan Annie* and *Skippy*. At night, the programs drew audiences of all ages, when practically everyone was likely to be home. Some stations even experimented with a story time in the late evenings, when children were going to bed.

Radio's Golden Age continued through World War II until television became popular. Television had been introduced in 1939 but did not get far before the country turned its research and manufacturing efforts to the war. Its growth was effectively halted until 1945. After the war, however, a prosperous country was ready for television. Consumers were buying sets at the rate of 200,000 per month in 1948. Applications for television licenses poured in on the FCC, overwhelming the agency and prompting a freeze on application grants from 1948 to 1952. Although New York City and Los Angeles each had seven TV stations, most cities had only one.

Some major regional cities did not have any stations at all. Some historians have implied that radio's Golden Age ended the minute the war ended and television began ascending. Because of the freeze on licenses for TV stations, and because many cities were without TV service, however, the radio networks continued to operate, although their primary interests and efforts swung toward TV. Major radio artists defected to TV, and radio lost much of its Golden Age talent.

The freeze on TV applications may have saved radio from complete destruction by giving radio executives time to see what was coming. Many predicted that within a few years, radio would no longer exist. But radio, like film and comic books, adapted to its changing environment. One change was a greater use of recorded programming. Technical improvements in sound recording had muted many arguments against recorded programming, and broadcasters learned to use recordings to attract listeners.

THE DISC JOCKEY

Perhaps the biggest boost to recorded programming was the disc jockey. DJ programs were easy and inexpensive to produce. Many record companies sent records to DJs for free. Other records were fairly inexpensive to buy. Instead of paying for unionized musicians, actors, scriptwriters, and large studios, broadcasters began paying DJs to spin free records. Sponsoring a DJ program cost much less than sponsoring a live music program or a dramatic program. Broadcasters gained an unexpected bonus when DJs and disc jockey programs proved to be popular. Martin Block, of New York's WNEW, was the most popular DJ of the 1940s. *The New Yorker* magazine reported that his broadcast spiel about an icebox sent over 100 people out in a blizzard to buy one; and after only a month on the air with Block, a bakery's sales increased by 432,000 doughnuts per week.[16] With results like that, broadcasters, advertisers, and listeners were happy.

The DJ proved to be the savior for radio stations when network program fare diminished and audiences moved to television. DJ programs gained in popularity all over the country, becoming the

16"Profiles: Socko!" *New Yorker,* 29 July 1944, 27.

Alan Freed

One of the disk jockeys who helped to popularize rock 'n' roll in the 1950s was Alan Freed. He coined the term "rock 'n' roll" in 1951 from the song "My Baby Rocks Me With a Steady Roll." Along with his radio program, he hosted live concerts with many of the performers of the era. In 1960, however, he suspended his work during the federal investigations of the payola scandals.

predominant form of programming in the 1950s. Some disc jockeys and record companies, however, abused the power of the DJ. Companies often paid influential DJs to promote their records, hoping to boost sales. Drugs, trips, prostitutes, and other favors were also common. In 1959, "payola" scandals shook the industry, revealing fraud that had been going on for years. One song promoter said that payola had been around since the late 1930s.[17] It is nearly impossible to estimate the impact payola had on the popularity of certain songs. Many songs that climbed to the top of the charts might have made it without any help from the bribes. On the other hand, some hits may have had only marginal success without the exposure payola ensured. The scandal prompted regulations making payola illegal, although it is widely believed to abound today.

Another factor that helped radio survive after television was the introduction of FM in 1941. Previously, all stations had been on the AM band. Wondrous as radio was, irritating static and unearthly howls often detracted from the programming. FM, however, utilized a different method for transmission. Although its range was shorter than AM's, it was virtually static-free. World War II

did not hamper FM as much as it did the other media. In fact, FM got a chance to prove itself. Although its commercial development was arrested, the military used its technology for tanks, jeeps, and other vehicles. After the war, however, FM struggled for acceptance. RCA attempted to kill FM in favor of television. One FCC decision moved FM's frequency allocation to higher frequencies, making the earliest FM receivers obsolete. Another FCC decision allowed simulcasting of FM programming on AM stations, effectively eliminating the need for listeners to buy a new FM radio since they could listen on their existing AM sets. It was not until the 1960s that FM began to recover from its numerous setbacks. By programming disc jockey shows much like AM radio did, FM attracted listeners with its superior fidelity. Classical music lovers benefited greatly from FM since the transmissions could more accurately reproduce subtle changes in tone and dynamics. By 2007, 65% of U.S. radio stations were FM.[18]

MINORITIES AND WOMEN IN RADIO

Minorities played important roles in radio, especially during the post-War struggle between radio and television. Other than celebrities like Jimmie Lunceford, Nat King Cole, and Dolores Williams, though, minorities did not find employment easily in broadcasting. Not until after World War II did blacks begin to make headway. Of the 3,000 DJs on the air in 1947, only sixteen were black. In the 1950s, black musicians could get their records played on the air, but usually they were played by white DJs. Rhythm and blues (R&B) music traditionally had a black audience; but when white DJs in southern California began playing R&B records, their white listeners began buying them. One DJ who owned an R&B record shop in Hollywood saw his clientele go from almost 100% black to about 40% white. The record distributors in the area credited the increase in non-black buyers of black music to exposure of R&B records on several DJ shows. In the 1950s, when DJs and talk-show hosts were still primarily white, fewer than 4% of radio stations and formats were geared toward black audiences. In large cities, one could find radio stations that programmed blocks of ethnic music, such as Asian, Greek, and Arabic, or whose formats were entirely geared toward a specific ethnic group.[19]

Women have had more success than minorities in the radio industry. In 1909, Charles Herrold's wife, Sybil, experimented with broadcasting alongside her husband. Broadcasters realized early on that daytime listeners were mostly women working around the house, and they geared programming to that audience. Female radio personalities provided gardening, cooking, and child raising tips; many music programs featured female musicians; soap operas involved the emotions of women listeners; and female characters populated prime time network programs. Female DJs appeared almost as early as male DJs and, in some cities, were very popular. More often than not, though, their programs were

[17]Juggy Gayles, quoted in Holly George-Warren, "Leader of the Old School," *Rolling Stone*, 24 March 1994, 14.

[18]http://www.fcc.gov. Accessed 28 September 2007.

[19]Lex Gillespie, "Early-day Black DJs Were Rare," *Colorado Springs Gazette Telegraph*, 25 February 1995, E1; "White Fans Hyping R&B Platter Sales," *Billboard*, 31 May 1952, 20.

relegated to late-night or the wee hours of the morning. Women also worked in broadcast stations, not always in positions of management, but some reached the upper echelons and held such positions as National Advertising Sales Manager or Assistant Programming Director. Women did not begin to populate station management until the 1970s; and although their ranks continue to swell, they are still in the minority. The FCC has considered women a minority and included them in minority-preference programs, helping more of them to purchase and program their own stations.

Most stations in recent years followed a music format. In 2010, Arbitron, the primary radio ratings company, listed more than sixty formats, including Country, Talk/Personality, Urban Contemporary, Gospel, and Tejano. Of these formats, forty-seven have a share of 2% or more of the listening audience. The most popular is News/Talk/Info, followed closely by Country.[20]

Radio made significant strides in competing with other media by focusing on its sound quality in the late 1980s and early 1990s. For years, some cable and satellite systems have offered subscription audio services to customers. In early 1995, however, the FCC allocated frequency space for digital satellite transmission of audio signals directly to consumer receivers. As of 2010, more than 19 million Americans subscribed to satellite radio. Terrestrial broadcasters, however, had their own plan for transmitting digital signals. Most radio stations began Internet sites allowing users to listen at their computers. Other Internet sites started subscription-based music services. About 2,000 radio stations are broadcasting in high definition, with many broadcasting multiple channels of programming.

THE TELEVISION INDUSTRY

Television often seems to have sprung suddenly onto the scene as soon as World War II ended. It is true that TV's popularity grew quickly, but that could not have happened without a long history of research behind it. As early as 1919, researchers were experimenting with television. Vladimir Zworykin, a Russian immigrant, demonstrated his television prototype to his employers at Westinghouse in 1923. AT&T, also researching television, gave public demonstrations in 1927. Ernst F.W. Alexanderson, head of General Electric's television experiments, began testing from an experimental station in Schenectady, New York, in 1928.

In 1939 television was ready for the world — appropriately, at the World's Fair in New York. RCA head David Sarnoff had no doubts about the importance of television. "It is with a feeling of humbleness," he said prophetically at the dedication of the RCA exhibit, "that I come to this moment of announcing the birth in this country of a new art so important ... that it is bound to affect all society."[21] President Franklin Roosevelt helped Sarnoff unveil television before the public on April 30. Sets available to consumers cost

FAR-OFF SPEAKERS SEEN AS WELL AS HEARD HERE IN A TEST OF TELEVISION

LIKE A PHOTO COME TO LIFE

Hoover's Face Plainly Imaged as He Speaks in Washington.

THE FIRST TIME IN HISTORY

Pictures Are Flashed by Wire and Radio Synchronizing With Speaker's Voice.

COMMERCIAL USE IN DOUBT

Mr A. T. & T. Head Sees a New Step in Conquest of Nature After Years of Research.

"Like a Photo Come to Life"
Bell Laboratories of AT&T demonstrated a system for transmitting images in 1927. President Herbert Hoover made a speech in Washington, D.C., that was sent 200 miles to an audience in New York City. The system transmitted pictures by wire at the rate of eighteen images per second. In reporting on the demonstration, the *New York Times*' front-page story declared that television had "annihilated" the distance between the speaker and the audience. "It was," the reporter said, "as if a photograph had suddenly come to life and begun to talk, smile, nod its head and look this way and that." Despite television's promise, development was put on hold until after World War II, thus allowing radio time to adjust to its new competitor.

between $199 and $600. By 1940, twenty-three TV stations across the country were broadcasting.

World War II halted progress in TV's expansion and technical improvements. As with other industries, all efforts were turned toward the war. But when the war ended, the TV boom was on. In 1946, manufacturers produced 6,000 sets. In an incredible feat of peacetime manufacturing conversion, 1947 saw a jump in TV set manufactures to 179,000 and in 1948 to 975,000. Despite an FCC freeze on new station licenses in 1948, manufacturers made 3 million sets in 1949. By 1960, 87% of American homes had at least one set. In 2007, 98.2% of households owned sets.

THE ORIGINS OF PAY TELEVISION

Although the FCC's license freeze in 1948 locked many communities out of television service, some communities got around that

---

[20]Radio Station Formats," www.arbitron.com. Accessed 10 August 2010.
[21]David Sarnoff, address at New York World's Fair, Flushing Meadows, April 20, 1939. Reprinted in *Looking Ahead: The Papers of David Sarnoff* (New York, 1968), 100.

problem by erecting community antennas (CATV), the ancestor of cable television. A powerful antenna on a tower or hill near the town picked up signals from the nearest stations. For a one-time fee, residents' TV sets were hooked up to the antenna. Subscribers paid a monthly fee for the service. Broadcasters initially welcomed the CATV systems because CATV extended their service areas, allowing them to charge more for ads. By 1952, when the FCC lifted the television application freeze, seventy CATV systems served 14,000 subscribers. Beginning in the 1960s, microwave transmission allowed some CATV systems to receive more distant stations. Now, superstations, such as WOR in New York and WGN in Chicago, are common on cable systems across the country.

Until 1975, cable TV's main purpose was delivering more and better reception of existing broadcast stations. That year, however, subscription movie service Home Box Office (HBO) began broadcasting via satellite to cable systems around the United States. Local cable systems installed $100,000 satellite receiving dishes, three meters in diameter, that picked up signals beamed down from satellites orbiting 22,300 miles above the equator. The cable system then distributed the satellite's signal into subscribers' homes.

What seemed like a revolution in 1975 is commonplace today. Most cable networks are delivered to local cable systems by satellite. Other cable channels may be delivered by microwave signals, a ground-based transmission system. Today there are about 1,200 cable systems in the United States. Although that number has shrunk from a high of more than 11,000, cable industry revenues continue to increase due to rising rates, more advertiser-supported channels, and additional services such as pay-per-view, satellite music channels, broadband Internet services, and phone.[22]

With the introduction of non-broadcast programming, cable TV became a competitor with traditional broadcasters. To make room for the ever growing cable networks, some systems dropped local broadcasters. Tensions between the two groups grew, prompting passage of the Cable Communication Act of 1993. Part of that law required cable companies to compensate local broadcasters for the right to carry their signals. Most broadcasters did not receive a cash payment from the cable companies, but received trade-offs in advertising and promotions. As part of the negotiations, some broadcasters even established their own local cable channels.

COMPETITION FOR CABLE

Alternative systems for program delivery became available in recent years. Wireless cable, which sounds like a contradiction in terms, allowed subscribers to receive many of the same cable channels offered by a traditional cable company. The signal is delivered to the subscriber's home by microwave transmission and is received by a special antenna placed on the roof of the house. Wireless is frequently offered in areas that already have a wired cable system.

C-band satellite service has been available to consumers since 1975, when HBO began its satellite broadcasting. A three-foot Tele-

22"Industry Statistics," www.ncta.com. Accessed 20 August 2010.

Television, 1939
In 1939, RCA exhibited its first commercial television set at the World's Fair in New York. The screen on this model, an RCA Victor, measured 7 1/2 by 5 1/2 inches.

vision Receive Only (TVRO) dish can pick up signals sent from many satellites orbiting the earth. Most satellite signals are scrambled, requiring consumers to subscribe to a particular channel, or a package of channels, to get an unscrambled signal. Direct Broadcast Service (DBS) allows subscribers to receive many more channels than wireless cable. The Ku-band signal is received on a satellite dish about the size of a large pizza. In 2009, more than 32 million U.S. households subscribed to satellite services, giving cable some competition.

In the mid-1980s, broadcasters began to look toward the next big development for the television industry: High Definition Television. HDTV systems provide dramatically better picture quality on a rectangular screen shaped like a movie screen. Japan introduced its analog (non-digital) HDTV system in the mid-1980s. In the early 1990s, American broadcasters began testing digital delivery of HDTV signals; and in 2009, all U.S. television stations began broadcasting exclusively with a digital signal, freeing the analog channels for other communication uses.

Television, like movies, comic books, and music, has come under its share of criticism for program content. In 2007, a study by the media watchdog group Parents Television Council found that sexual content, violence, and offensive language appeared every

3.5 minutes during the evening family viewing time.[23] The sex and violence on TV have been blamed for all sorts of social ills from teenage pregnancy to violent crime to illegal drug use. Although the preponderance of research has shown a link between television and behavior, there has been disagreement about how guilty TV is as a cause of the problems.

Early TV programming took most of its inspiration from radio. Many stars simply adapted their radio shows to television's visual demands. Classical music programs beamed orchestral and operatic performances live to millions of people, much as radio networks had done previously. With television, though, opera fans could see the elaborate sets and costumes and the action on stage. Many Americans now round out July 4th celebrations with stirring performances of the National Symphony or the Boston Pops on television. By the 1970s, many TV shows relied primarily on visual aspects to attract viewers. Action programs like *Starsky and Hutch* and comedies like *Laugh-In* relied on visual excitement and visual gags for their success. In the 1980s, with the introduction of the cable channel Music Television (MTV), the audio components of programs regained some importance. *Miami Vice* and *Moonlighting*, for instance, relied heavily on music to establish the mood of certain scenes and to affect viewers' emotions. MTV also influenced the filming and editing of TV programs and commercials. Frame composition, rapid cuts between shots, computer graphics and animation, and unorthodox camera angles once found only in music videos became common in commercials and prime-time fare.

Minorities experienced the same barriers in television as in other entertainment media. Most had stereotypical, subservient roles until 1968, when Diahann Carroll starred in her own show, *Julia*. Julia, the main character, was a nurse but lived like a movie star. Although Carroll's role was an atypical portrayal of black life in the '60s, later programs such as *Good Times, The Jeffersons*, and *Cosby* tried to depict black families as more true-to-life. Other minorities have had the same sort of treatment, but have had less exposure. Racial minorities also were underrepresented in TV commercials, making up only around 5% of characters in the early 1990s, although they were portrayed negatively less frequently than white characters were.[24] In recent years, early stereotypes had been reversed so that white male characters were most frequently portrayed in a derogatory manner in commercials.

Women's roles in television paralleled those of radio. Female-oriented programs and soap operas usually featured female personalities. Women in station management had a harder time than in radio, but more were successful in reaching decision-making positions. No woman delivered any network's evening news until 1967, and it wasn't until 2006 that a woman became the sole anchor of a weeknight network news program. TV fictional roles for women were less numerous than roles for males. Female roles por-

Diahann Carroll

Diahann Carroll, star in her own show, *Julia*, starting in 1968, broke television's color barrier. The show, though, was designed to be palatable to largely white audiences. Julia, the main character, was a nurse to a physician played by Lloyd Nolan. The two are shown here in the first publicity photograph for the show.

trayed most working women in less powerful jobs, although the number of working female characters increased over the last twenty years. Despite the progress in women's roles, stereotyping was common. Women in MTV commercials, for instance, appeared less often than men and usually were beautiful, with fit bodies and skimpy clothing.[25]

VIDEO GAMES

Americans used their TV sets for more than passive viewing. Video games have been enormously successful. Children and adults have spent countless hours pressing buttons and moving joysticks. Invented in 1966, the first video game consisted simply of two spots that chased each other around the television screen. Nevertheless, the technology had become sophisticated enough to market by 1972.

Odyssey, made by Magnavox, offered consumers twelve different games including Table Tennis, Haunted House, Ski, and Football, all for about $100. An additional set of shooting games was available for another $39.95. To play the games, the user inserted the correct circuit card into the game console and attached a plas-

[23]"The Alarming Family Hour: No Place for Children," September 2007, www.parentstv.org. Accessed 1 October 2007.

[24]Nancy Signorielli, Douglas McLeod, and Elaine Healy, "Gender Stereotypes in MTV Commercials: The Beat Goes On," *Journal of Broadcasting and Electronic Media* (Winter 1994): 91-101.

[25]David Vest, "Prime Time Pilots: A Content Analysis of Changes in Gender Representation," *Journal of Broadcasting and Electronic Media* (Spring 1992): 25-43; David Atkin, "The Evolution of Television Series Addressing Single Women, 1966-1990," *Journal of Broadcasting and Electronic Media* (Fall 1991): 517-23; Signorielli, et al., ibid.

tic overlay to the television screen to provide the correct background: a green table and net for Table Tennis, a dilapidated house for Haunted House, a map of ski courses for Ski, and a green field with yard lines for Football. The game could not keep score, but Odyssey did provide a cardboard scorecard with the set.

Pong was the first successful video game. It began as an arcade game and then moved into the home in 1975. Pong was an electronic version of table tennis. It needed no plastic overlays to produce the effect of the paddles and net, and it kept score automatically.

With the development of microprocessors, video games became much more complex. The video games of today use cartridges and CD-ROMs to store the game information or are played online. Hand-held video games are popular and almost as sophisticated, as are smartphone-based games.

As the popularity of video games grew, so did societal concerns over the effects the games had on children. Describing the games as "electronic drugs," some people believed they were addictive. Since most of the games involved destroying an enemy, many adults worried that children were learning antisocial behaviors. School officials took steps to prevent students from skipping school to spend time in the arcades. Recently, game developers have been creating active games and fitness programs. By remaining creative, games have survived and prospered. In fact, video games are one of the fastest growing media, behind only the Internet and home video. In 2009, the industry raked in $20 billion in U.S. sales alone.[26]

FACING THE INTERNET

All of the entertainment media had to adapt to a changing and competitive media environment. Remarkably, all of them continued to thrive, but only if they evolved into more sophisticated forms than those in which they originated. Each medium competed in an increasingly crowded arena for a share of consumers' entertainment budgets. Some media enjoyed increasing popularity, while others struggled to keep up with changes.

The Internet offers opportunities and challenges to the entertainment media, and these industries must be adaptable and tuned in to what consumers want. Of all the entertainment media, the music industry has been the most resistant to change ever since the days of the phonograph. But all of the media are still searching for ways to remain viable as the online environment continues to shift. With the growing popularity of mobile and social media applications, the media must once again find relevance and profitability in unfamiliar territory.

Finally, even as Americans' total hours spent with entertainment media have been rising, some media have lost a share of their time and are expected to continue to lose. While TV viewing has increased, most of the increase has gone to subscription cable and satellite systems and not to traditional broadcasters. Time spent with the Internet has increased dramatically, while newspapers, books, and magazines have decreased steadily.

The biggest beneficiary of consumers' changing entertainment use has been mobile and Internet services as TV shows, radio programming, music, movies and video games are delivered online.[27]

The Internet's impact is not likely, however, to bring an end to any of the entertainment media. Just as, in the past, each medium weathered the introduction of new forms of entertainment, other media are expected to adapt to the new environment, changing to make the Internet a beneficial partner rather than a destructive foe.

RECOMMENDED READINGS

BOOKS

Ackler, Ally. *Reel Women: Pioneers of the Cinema, 1896 to the Present.* New York, 1995. Many women occupied decision-making positions as producers, directors, and writers.

Andrew, J. Dudley. *The Major Film Theories: An Introduction.* London, 1976. The author traces film history and development through a study of major theories.

Andrews, Bart, and Ahrgus Juilliard. *Holy Mackerel!: The Amos 'n' Andy Story.* New York, 1986. The authors explore the racial stereotypes presented on radio, television, and film, and attempt to explain why this type of program was so popular.

Behlmar, Rudy, ed. *Memo from Darryl Zanuck.* New York, 1993. Selected correspondence of the filmmaker provides an interesting view into the golden age of film.

Blue, Howard. *Words at War: World War II Era Radio Drama and the Postwar Broadcasting Industry Blacklist.* Lanham, Md., 2002. Radio provided propaganda and boosted morale during World War II. After the war, a blacklist of suspected Communisits destroyed many careers.

Bowers, Q. David. *Nickelodeon Theatres and Their Music.* Vestal, N. Y., 1986. This account of the evolution of music in early movie theaters includes hundreds of photographs from the author's collection.

Daniels, Les. *Marvel: Five Fabulous Decades of the World's Greatest Comics.* New York, 1991. The author provides a behind-the-scenes look at one of the most successful comic book companies in America.

Denisoff, R. Serge. *Solid Gold: The Popular Record Industry.* New Brunswick, N. J., 1975. This account of the development of the American record industry gives particular emphasis to the rock and roll era.

Dickerson, James. *Women on Top: the Quiet Revolution that's Rocking the American Music Industry.* New York, 1998. Females have had a growing influence in American popular music.

Douglas, Susan J. *Listening in: Radio and the American Imagination.* New York, 1999. Radio created various audiences during its long history.

Estren, Mark James. *A History of Underground Comics.* Berkeley, Calif., 1974. This history of non-traditional comic books includes many illustrations.

Fornatale, Peter, and Joshua E. Mills. *Radio in the Television Age.* Woodstock, N.Y., 1980. Radio evolved from its Golden Age before World War II to the formula-format stage it assumed after television arrived.

Gelatt, Ronald. *The Fabulous Phonograph, 1877-1977.* 2d rev. ed. New York, 1977. The author gives an account of the phonograph's history from Edison's first tinkerings through technical and musical developments in the 1970s.

Goulart, Ron. *Over 50 Years of American Comic Books.* Lincolnwood, Ill., 1991. This chronological and topical study of the evolution of comic books includes beautifully reproduced examples of comic book art.

Hilmes, Michele. *Hollywood and Broadcasting: From Radio to Cable.* Urbana, Ill., 1990. The author examines the relationship of film and broadcasting from the days of network radio to the present.

Huebner, Andrew J. *The Warrior Image: Soldiers in American Culture From the Second*

---

[26]"2009 U.S. Video Game Industry And PC Game Software Retail Sales Reach $20.2 Billion." www.npd.com. Accessed 25 August 2010.

[27]"Media Usage and Consumer Spending: 2004 to 2012." www.census.gov. Accessed 24 July 2010.

World War to the Vietnam Era. Chapel Hill, N.C., 2008. In media portrayals, the warrior image "reflected how Americans came to terms with the meaning of war and the conduct of its soldiers."

Jones, Gerard, and Will Jacobs. *The Comic Book Heroes*. Rocklin, Calif., 1997. The authors recount the last forty years of comic book history.

Lardner, James. *Fast Forward: Hollywood, the Japanese, and the Onslaught of the VCR*. New York, 1987. The author examines the effects of the VCR on the American film industry.

Long, Louis S. *The Development of the Television Network Oligopoly*. New York, 1979. In the development of the broadcasting networks, a small number of companies amassed power.

Mott, Robert L. *Radio Live! Television Live! Those Golden Days When Horses were Coconuts*. Jefferson, N.C., 2000. A former sound-effects creator shares personal reminiscences of live broadcasting.

Ramsaye, Terry. *A Million and One Nights: A History of the Motion Picture*. New York, 1926. In arguably the first film history, the author gives an rreverent, slightly disorganized account that is entertaining nonetheless.

Sanjek, Russell. *From Print to Plastic: Publishing and Promoting America's Popular Music, 1900-1980*. Brooklyn, N. Y., 1983. The author offers a critical study of the business practices of the recording industry throughout its history.

Smulyan, Susan. *Selling Radio: the Commercialization of American Broadcasting, 1920-1934*. Washington, D.C., 1994. Advertising shaped the content of programming.

Stanley, Robert H. *The Celluloid Empire: A History of the American Movie Industry*. New York, 1978. This account of Hollywood's birth and growth gives particular emphasis to the studios involved.

Toll, Robert C. *The Entertainment Machine: American Show Business in the Twentieth Century*. New York, 1982. Technology had a major impact on entertainment.

Wertheim, Arthur Frank. *Radio Comedy*. New York, 1979. The author examines the influences on early radio comedies.

Wilder, Alec. *American Popular Song: The Great Innovators, 1900-1950*. New York, 1972. Black music, especially ragtime, influenced American popular music in the twentieth century.

ARTICLES

Austin, Mary. "Petrillo's War." *Journal of Popular Culture* 12 (Summer 1978): 11-8. The American Federation of Musicians instituted a successful ban on recording.

Benjamin, Louise M. "In Search of the Sarnoff 'Radio Music Box' Memo." *Journal of Broadcasting and Electronic Media* 37 (1993): 325-35. The author examines the validity of the memo in establishing David Sarnoff's reputation as a visionary of broadcasting.

Christie, Thomas B., and Andrew M. Clark. "Framing Two Enemies in Mass Media: A Content Analysis of U.S. Government Influence in American Film during World War II." *American Journalism* 25:1 (2008): 55-72. The Office of War Information (OWI) recognized the power of using movies for propaganda and set suggested guidelines for depicting the enemy, usually as deceitful, lying, and cruel.

Fellow, Anthony R. "American Film, 1890-present." Chapter 15 in Wm. David Sloan, *The Age of Mass Communication*, 2nd ed. Northport, Ala., 2008. Since the early 1900s, "the American film industry has evolved into a powerful communications entity that has shaped, and sometimes changed, the nation's perception and understanding of politics and society."

Hiatt, Brian. "How iTunes conquered the music biz." *Rolling Stone*, September 20, 2007: 15-16. iTunes rose rapidly as the world's biggest seller of digital downloads.

Hiatt, Brian, and Evan Serpick. "The Record Industry's Slow Fade." *Rolling Stone*, June 28, 2007: 13-14. The record industry was slow to respond to changing consumer needs and technology.

Holmes, Marian Smith. "Who Could Resist the Kind of Music They Made at Hitsville?" *Smithsonian*, October 1994, 82-95. The author provides a brief explanation of the reasons for success at Motown Records.

Hugunin, Marc. "ASCAP, BMI and the Democratization of American Popular Music." *Popular Music and Society* 7 (1979): 8-17. The author describes the formation and competition in the music licensing business.

Hyde, Jana. "The Recording Industry, 1890-present." Chapter 16 in Wm. David Sloan, *The Age of Mass Communication*, 2nd ed. Northport, Ala., 2008. "[T]he invention of recorded sound changed our entertainment, business, and personal worlds."

Lent, John A. "Cartoons and Comics, 1750-present." Chapter 14 in Wm. David Sloan, *The Age of Mass Communication*, 2nd ed. Northport, Ala., 2008. The author provides a readable survey of the history of editorial cartoons, comic strips, and comic books in the United States.

MacDonald, J. Fred. "Black Perimeters — Paul Robeson, Nat King Cole and the Role of Blacks in American TV." *Journal of Popular Film and Television* 7 (1979): 246-64. The author describes the state of black employment during television's early years.

MacDonald, J. Fred. "Government Propaganda in Commercial Radio: The Case of Treasury Star Parade, 1942-1943." *Journal of Popular Culture* 12 (1979): 285-304. The author argues that government-sponsored programming helped convince Americans to support the United States' participation in World War II.

Schultz, Quintin J. "Evangelical Radio and the Rise of the Electronic Church, 1921-1948." *Journal of Broadcasting and Electronic Media* 32 (1986): 289-306. Religious broadcasting encountered barriers from the FCC and the networks.

20

The Age of Mass Magazines
1900 - Present

As the twentieth century dawned, it was evident that those mass magazines that previously had dominated the American scene were faltering. The high-minded approach that had brought them huge circulations — "leisurely in habit, literary in tone, retrospective rather than timely, and friendly to the interests of the upper classes"[1] — belonged to an era that was ending. The new popular magazines were reflecting instead the hectic pace of a mechanized and urban nation, emphasizing timely information rather than literary fare, and appealing to the tastes of the masses, not the upper classes.

The genteel tradition of literature, represented by and nurtured carefully through magazines such as *Century*, *Harper's Monthly*, *Scribner's*, and *Atlantic Monthly*, had given way to newer, more popular publications. New political forces emanating from the masses — instead of being dictated by the upper classes — were gaining momentum. Class distinctions based on dress, speech, and manners were disappearing. Nationwide industries and the mass-marketing of products were promising a revolution in advertising; and new technologies had removed formidable economic barriers that previously limited entry into magazine publishing.

THE APPEARANCE OF MASS MAGAZINES

The end of the genteel era began in 1893 when an onslaught of inexpensive, lively magazines attracted a huge audience of previously untapped readers. *McClure's*, *Munsey's*, and *Cosmopolitan* were the first to challenge successfully the traditional leaders. The most influential was *McClure's*, named for its owner-founder, Samuel S. McClure. He began issuing his magazine in 1893 at 15¢ a copy, less than half the price of the leading magazines. By 1900 the circulation of this lively, readable publication with articles pertinent to everyday life had reached 365,000. *Munsey's*, which had been founded in 1889, lowered its newsstand price to 10¢ in 1893 and, with content that was less distinguished than that of *McClure's*, achieved a circulation of 70,000 by 1900. John Brisben

Walker's *Cosmopolitan*, in existence since 1886, reduced its price from 25¢ a copy to 15¢ in 1893.

In 1896, C.C. Buell, assistant editor of the greatest of the older magazines, *The Century*, counted thirty-five cheap new magazines at a newsstand. He told his editor, Richard Watson Gilder, that in the next few years two or three additional ones a week would be appearing. "I believe," he naively predicted to Gilder, "that the very multiplicity of them is going to reawaken the people to a sense of the value of the serious, 'high-priced' magazines."[2] Buell was wrong. Just three years later *The Century's* associate editor, Robert Underwood Johnson, desperately proposed new measures to counter the "emergency" and "possible debacle" that appeared imminent for the once-powerful magazine.[3] He suggested ways to reduce costs and proposed that some bold new editorial project be initiated to restore lagging staff morale.

At *Harper's Monthly* the situation seemed even more critical. The New York magazine and its parent firm, Harper & Bros., had slid into bankruptcy. The great financier J. Pierpont Morgan, holder of the note that Harper & Bros. had been unable to pay, turned over the company to — of all people — the newcomer S.S. McClure, thinking he could provide the magic needed to restore its vigor. In Boston the *Atlantic Monthly* had started losing money in 1894, a trend that continued into the twentieth century.[4]

What had brought about this dramatic decline for established magazines and the emergence of new ones? One of the primary reasons was technological. The established magazines had seemed impregnable for decades because wood engravings, essential to their popularity, were so costly that they discouraged new competitors. The development of photoengraving changed the situation, for large illustrations now could be made at little cost.[5] Other important factors were at work, especially advertisers' search for a national audience. Advertisers would flock to the magazine that

[1]Frank Luther Mott, *A History of American Magazines, 1885-1905* (Cambridge, Mass., 1957), 2.

[2]C.C. Buell to Richard Watson Gilder, 25 March 1896, Box 2, Richard Watson Gilder Papers, New York Public Library, New York, N.Y.

[3]Robert Underwood Johnson to Richard Watson Gilder, 30 August 1899, Richard Watson Gilder Letters, Century Collection, New York Public Library, New York, N.Y.

[4]Eugene Exman, *The House of Harper: One Hundred and Fifty Years of Publishing* (New York, 1967), 180-1; Ellen B. Ballou, *The Building of the House* (Boston, 1970), 452 and 463.

[5]S.S. McClure, *My Autobiography* (New York, 1914), 207.

the awe of the wicked, and the sympathy of the saints in Paradise, and the service of the mighty angels of God. On Him also would rest, the true aureole for His head, the Spirit of God and the love of His Heavenly Father.

With the supreme good taste of Holy Scripture it is simply written, that the Child increased in stature and in wisdom, and in favor with God and man. It is enough that Jesus lived His first thirty years at home in Nazareth, since home gathers into it the five factors which influence nature when it is plastic and give it a permanent shape. The first is that word which is of one blood with home, since none can think of home without at the same time saying mother. In the Bible, which is the standard record of human life, the mother has prepared the servants of God from

whose face is the mirror of Heaven. The wise men open their coffers, and lay their treasures at the feet of the Child, the shepherds do homage with adoring faces, while some gentle animals in the background represent the lower creation at this shrine of holiness. Here indeed is a narrow space, but it is full of Heaven; here is lowliness, but no indignity; here is weakness, but also reverence.

With the after-look the disciples of Jesus may prefer to see the inner glory of His Nativity rather than its outer circumstances; but no one would desire that these should have been different. He was to show unto His time and all ages that the greatest force in life is not position nor wealth, but character, and that character is independent of all circumstances, so that goodness, cradled and reared in poverty, without advantages and without favor, persecuted and slain, is yet the most beautiful and triumphant power on earth. Before this infant, so inhospitably received of the world, lay the cruelty of Herod, and the narrow lot of Nazareth, and the homeless mission of Galilee, and the contempt of the great, and the shame of the Cross. But that would be only the appearance of things, not the heart. Around Him also would gather the loyalty of faithful disciples, and the love of women, and the praises of little children, and the gratitude of the poor, and the reverence of holy souls, and

Moses to Samuel, from David to the Baptist, but among all women and mothers surely the most blessed is Mary. Christians may not all unite in paying almost divine honors to the Virgin, or in believing that she is a mediator with her Son, but surely in every reverent mind she must have a solitary

McClure's, 1900
At the start of the twentieth century, *McClure's* was one of America's most popular magazines. Using well-illustrated biographies, it had a circulation of 350,000. Its lead feature in the January 1900 issue was a story on the life of Christ.

could deliver a huge circulation. Magazines could attract huge circulations with cheap prices and popular content, and increased advertising revenues would more than cover the losses incurred by pricing a magazine at less than cost.

The new magazines also reflected a change in editorial philosophy. Nineteenth-century editors typically had sat back and selected the best of whatever manuscripts happened to arrive in the office. *The Century*, without aggressively soliciting manuscripts, received 5,000 in 1882 and about 10,000 a year by 1890.[6] Practically the only solicitation of manuscripts occurred when editors arranged with leading authors to publish their novels.[7]

By 1900 *McClure's*, with a circulation of 350,000, had become the leading magazine in the nation. Its articles explored the wonders as well as the problems of contemporary society. It boasted a staff

of excellent writers, the quality of which probably has not been equalled to this day. The staff included, among others, Lincoln Steffens, Ida Tarbell, Ray Stannard Baker, and Viola Roseboro. They wrote about politics, railroads, business, or anything that the editors conceived might appeal to large numbers of readers. Especially popular were profiles of individuals. The long essays that had been the backbone of the nineteenth-century magazine were gone. "The wise editors won't have them any more, because the people won't read them and won't even take magazines that get the reputation of harboring them," observed the writer David Graham Phillips in 1903. Why? Because the "present generation," he offered, was impatient with anything that was not important to the concerns of "here and now."[8] McClure decided that readers wanted "success" stories, and from 1895 to 1901 nearly 65% of the magazine's non-fiction content was "success oriented."[9] On the eve of the great muckraking era that was to be introduced in 1903 by *McClure's* and that magazine's famous staff, Phillips declared that the "real secret" of the revolution was not the reduction in magazine prices but the addition of more meaningful content. The new magazine was written "for the people," and it was a reflection of the "atmosphere of our time."[10]

Two of the four great quality magazines of the nineteenth century succumbed to slow, painful deaths because they failed to adjust. *Century* and *Scribner's* disappeared entirely, while *Harper's* and *Atlantic Monthly* survived — barely — with a small, dedicated audience. They were to develop in the twentieth century a reputation for quality journalism rather than for fiction, and no longer would they be dominant publications.

Ironically, those magazines that so abruptly signaled the new age would not continue as the leading magazines of the next era. Their life spans were meteoric — brilliant but short. Among the things they accomplished was to break the dominating hold of the eastern literary establishment. No longer would the few editors of marked similarities and tastes be the arbiters of magazine journalism — and indeed of American culture as well. McClure and Frank Munsey were brash Midwesterners; Walker of *Cosmopolitan* an automobile manufacturer; Walter Hines Page a Southerner; and Edward Bok, a Dutch emigrant. They were "go-getters," involved in things more tangible than literary products. They employed, as the journalist Phillips said, an "almost uncanny energy, a kind of hop-skip-and-jump imagination and mode of action."[11]

One of these new editors, Page, foreshadowed in his publishing career what would be one of the dominant successes of the twentieth century: the news magazine. A North Carolinian, he brought to both the *Forum* and *Atlantic Monthly* a new approach in editing: he determined himself what their content would be rather than merely printing what his contributors happened to offer. His emphasis always was on the present and the future, not the past. Literary criticism he regarded as mere "talkee-talkee," and he down-

[6]Arthur John, *The Best Years of the Century, 1879-1909* (Urbana, Ill., 1981), 146.
[7]Some notable exceptions should be mentioned, particularly *The Century's* great series on the Civil War and the Old South, both of which brought much acclaim.

[8]David Graham Phillips, "Great Magazines and their Editors," *Success*, May 1903.
[9]Fred J. Endres, "The Pre-Muckraking Days of *McClure's Magazine*, 1893-1901," *Journalism Quarterly* 55 (Spring 1978): 154.
[10]Phillips, "Great Magazines and Their Editors."
[11]Ibid.

THE WORLD'S WORK

VOLUME I   NOVEMBER 1900   NUMBER I

The March of Events

THE concrete results of American character and enterprise during the uninterrupted period since the civil war now appear in such variety and volume as to indicate the rich meaning of life under democratic conditions; for they denote a shifting of the working centre of the world.

The United States is become the richest of all countries. We sell fuel as well as food to Europe, and the rapid increase of our manufactures for export was never matched. We have developed the skilled workman whose earnings are larger and whose product is cheaper than any of his competitor's, because he is a better master of himself and of the machinery that he uses. Our commercial supremacy is inevitable, and European governments are already our debtors for cash as well as for manhood suffrage.

We have constructed industrial and commercial machinery, too, of a scope and of a precision of action that were hitherto unknown. All wise plans for the future must rest on the changes wrought by modern machinery, the organization of industry, and the freedom of the individual; for the perfection of method and of mechanism has done more than to spread well-being among the masses and to enrich and dignify labor: it has changed social ideals and intellectual points of view. It is, in fact, changing the character of men. As soon as material prosperity is won they care less for it; what they enjoy is the work of winning it. The higher organization of industry has for half a century engaged the kind of minds that once founded colonies, built cathedrals, led armies, and practised statecraft; and, to an increasing number, work has become less and less a means of bread-winning and more and more a form of noble exercise. The artist always took joy in his work: it is the glory of our time that the man of affairs can find a similar pleasure in his achievements.

It is with the activities of the newly organized world, its problems and even its romance, that this magazine will earnestly concern itself, trying to convey the cheerful spirit of men who do things.

AT THE CENTURY'S END

AND "THE WORLD'S WORK" begins its career at a fortunate time: for whatever may be thought of the nineteenth century when it can be seen in the perspective of universal history, to men who have caught the spirit of its closing years, it seems the best time to live that has so far come. It is unlike all former periods in this, that it has seen the simultaneous extension of democracy and the rise of science. These have put life on a new plane, and made a new adjustment of man to man and of man to the universe.

An incalculable advantage that we have over men of any other century is the widening of individual opportunity. It has been the century of the abolition of slavery throughout

3

A New Magazine Formula

Eschewing the artwork and fiction that were the staples of most popular magazines, Walter Hines Page's *World's Work* emphasized serious material on timely topics. It presaged the formula that later would make *Time* magazine successful.

played it to a secondary role.[12] In 1900, thinking that he must be owner and publisher if he were truly to establish the ideal contemporary magazine, Page founded the monthly *World's Work*. Its purpose was to describe the nation's progress in the primary aspects of life: education, agriculture, industry, social life, and politics. The concept was novel. The *Chicago Evening Post* observed, "To have literary style injected into articles on American exports, cotton and cotton goods, life and fire insurance, country banks, wholesale and retail dry goods, will be cheerful and inspiring."[13]

The magazine's first issue had a press run of 35,000 copies. In 1909 its circulation peaked at about 125,000. This success was achieved in a manner that contrasted with the formula of *McClure's*, *Munsey's*, and the newly prospering *Saturday Evening Post*, for *World's Work* contained no fiction, not much artwork, a serious tone, and a price of 25¢ per copy. It anticipated what would become one of the outstanding success stories in the years ahead: *Time* magazine. Each issue opened with a section titled "The March of Events" which dealt with a timely subject such as politics, business, or agriculture. Next came between twelve and twenty articles on other topics. By eliminating all fiction, Page boldly

rejected the most popular magazine feature of the time. Yet another distinctive feature of the magazine was its exclusive use of photographs for illustrations, eschewing wood engravings. These photographs were spread throughout the pages of the magazine. Page established in *World's Work* a *news* magazine, and to this endeavor he dedicated himself until 1913 when President Woodrow Wilson appointed him ambassador to Britain.[14]

CURTIS' PUBLISHING SUCCESS

While interesting because of its trailblazing format and the formula it provided for *Time* and *Newsweek*, *World's Work* did not otherwise leave its mark on the industry. What was to become the most enduring publishing success of the first half of the twentieth century was a weekly magazine that appealed particularly to the nation's growing middle class, the *Saturday Evening Post*.

Its success initially was tied to that of the *Ladies' Home Journal*, developed by Cyrus H.K. Curtis and his wife, Louisa Knapp, who laughed at his efforts in covering women's news for a publication called *The Tribune and the Farmer*. She took over the job herself, and the column grew to a page, then a supplement, and then, in 1883, a distinct magazine, the *Ladies' Home Journal*. Curtis was publisher; and his wife, identified by her maiden name, was founding editor. With her editorial formula, circulation soared. Edward Bok took over the editorship from Knapp in December 1890. Shortly thereafter, Curtis formed the Curtis Publishing Company. By the late nineteenth century *Ladies' Home Journal* had achieved the greatest circulation of any magazine, 900,000. In 1904 it became the first magazine ever to reach the magical figure of 1 million readers, and by 1912 its circulation was approaching 2 million. Bok boldly carried readers to new areas of interest, including crusades for sex education, which included using the word "syphilis" for the first time in any American popular magazine.

The early enthusiastic reception of *Ladies' Home Journal* led Curtis to believe that a similar feat could be achieved with a men's magazine. Thus in 1897 he paid $1,000 for a struggling, unillustrated sixteen-page weekly that was being edited on a part-time basis by a Philadelphia reporter for $10 a week. Its circulation of 1,800 had been dwindling rapidly. The energetic temporary editor Curtis hired from the *Boston Post*, George Horace Lorimer, managed to stay on the job until 1937, creating one of the nation's greatest publishing successes. The original idea for Lorimer's *Saturday Evening Post* and one that provided its motivating force for many years was to romanticize the accomplishments of American business in a way that was neither intellectual nor sensational. The contents of the *Post* of 1895 were described as "action stories, romances, stories of business; the life stories of successful men of action; articles on economic and political subjects so dramatized that they were at once informing and entertaining; comment on current events; and a modicum of the serious and sentimental

[12]Burton J. Hendrick, *The Life and Letters of Walter H. Page*, I (Garden City, N.Y., 1922), 48-63 passim; Ballou, *The Building of the House*, 454-5.

[13]*Chicago Evening Post*, 29 September 1900, clipping in Walter Hines Page Papers, Houghton Library, Harvard University, Cambridge, Mass.

[14]John Milton Cooper, Jr., *Walter Hines Page: The Southerner as American, 1855-1918* (Chapel Hill, 1977), 162-205 passim.

poetry countenanced by the businessmen of the period."[15] It was a publication that appealed to what was becoming the dominant force in American society — the middle class. It eschewed radicalism and the bizarre, and it championed middle-class virtues. It printed inspirational biographies, factual reports, and fiction.

The competition in the weekly field was formidable. *Harper's Illustrated Weekly*, *Frank Leslie's Illustrated Newspaper*, and *Collier's* were dominant. Lorimer was undaunted by the old leaders and the additional competition of the popular new monthlies, and he solicited fiction from the nation's best authors. In the first four years of the rejuvenated *Post's* existence, the magazine published such noted writers as Stephen Crane, Bret Harte, Richard Harding Davis, Emerson Hough, Owen Wister, and William Allen White. Lorimer also persuaded the nation's outstanding public figures to write about contemporary events — men such as Senator Albert J. Beveridge and Speakers of the House Thomas B. Reed and Champ Clark. He promised that the *Post* would become the largest weekly magazine in the world. It reached a circulation of 1 million in 1908 and surpassed *Ladies' Home Journal*. By 1937, when Lorimer retired, circulation was 3 million. In 1968 its circulation would reach 6.8 million.

Advertising revenue climbed as well, reaching $360,000 annually by 1902 and $28 million in 1922. Indeed, it has been said with much justification that the advertising industry and *Saturday Evening Post* and *Ladies' Home Journal* grew and prospered together. One of the chief reasons for the *Post's* advertising growth was the automobile industry's adoption of the *Post* as its favorite advertising medium. By 1914 more than forty manufacturers of automobiles and automotive accessories were advertising in it. Tobacco and liquor advertising were notably missing from the *Post*. It did not accept them until 1930 and 1960, respectively.

Ladies' Home Journal's success was by no means diminished by that of the *Post*. In a 1908 edition, which marked the publication's twenty-fifth anniversary, Edward Bok boasted that his was the first magazine of large circulation to sell at 10¢ an issue, the first to

introduce the idea of monthly cover changes, the first to refuse to accept questionable advertising, and the first to create personal columns between editor and reader. Another innovation was yet to occur: the magazine would be the first to introduce color printing in its pages.

Curtis Publishing Company's domination of the magazine industry, led by these two giants, seemed complete during the first third of the century. During the peak years between 1918 and 1929, 48¢ of every advertising dollar spent in American magazines went to either the *Post*, the *Journal*, or a third Curtis publication, *Country Gentleman*. The *Post's* high mark occurred in 1929 when a single issue contained 272 pages and weighed almost two pounds. Lorimer, in a 1927 editorial, commented that the *Post's* readers were the "most intelligent and progressive audience in America — the backbone of the community's buying power." They were, he averred, the kind of people "who support the nation's industries rather than its nightclubs."[16] Among the most notable and popular features of the magazine were the regular covers by artist Norman Rockwell depicting middle-class life.

The *Post's* success emanated from the American heartland, and that success was to continue through the greater part of the twentieth century. When, however, the nation became more urbanized and more sophisticated in its tastes, and when the magazine industry seemed to shift in focus in the 1960s, the *Post* formula would fail to accommodate the new conditions.

Of an entirely different nature was *The New Republic*, a magazine of current affairs founded by Herbert Croly in 1913 as an outgrowth of the Progressive era. Its early staff included a brilliant young journalist named Walter Lippmann, whose recent and thoughtful book, *A Preface to Politics*, called for regulation of monopolies and an expanded role for the federal government. *The New Republic* would maintain a high level of political, cultural, and literary commentary through the present time. Its circulation remained modest, as did that of similar publications such as *The Nation* and *The Progressive*; but its influence was formidable.

[15]See Walter D. Fuller, *The Life and Times of Cyrus H.K. Curtis* (New York, 1948), 17.

[16]Quoted in Joseph C. Goulden, *The Curtis Caper* (New York, 1965), 32.

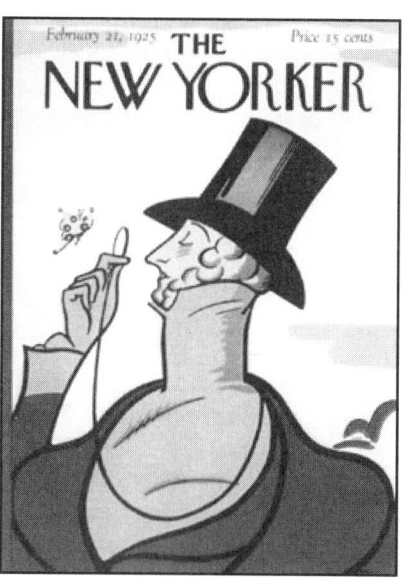

New Approaches

Going against the approaches that made entertaining and inspiring magazines such as the
Saturday Evening Post hugely popular, Herbert
Croly's *The New Republic* emphasized serious,
liberal discussion of political issues and current
affairs. It had a comparatively small circulation,
but its readership consisted of members of influential groups such as college professors. Another magazine with a small circulation but a
mass influence was *The New Yorker.* Once every
year since its inception, it has run the cover
shown here. "Eustace Tilly," the fictitious character depicted, seemed to symbolize the sophisticated, literate tone that Harold Ross had envisioned for the magazine when he started it in
1925. He was not trying to appeal to the mass
audiences, as other magazines such as the *Saturday Evening Post* were doing.

While these publications were imbued with the liberals' optimistic view of the possibilities of perfection for the human race, a
magazine that emerged in the 1920s with commentary on current
affairs took a far more skeptical viewpoint. This publication, the
American Mercury, was the product of the iconoclastic and irascible H. L. Mencken of Baltimore. First appearing in 1924, the
American Mercury gleefully identified and poked holes in the rosy
optimism of the 1920s. Nothing in American life seemed to escape
Mencken's caustic attention. The magazine, clad in a bright green
cover, attracted widespread popularity, especially among the
nation's college youth. As the boom of the 1920s faded into the
stark Depression days of the 1930s, however, the magazine's
attraction dimmed and Mencken's cynical views lost popularity.

NEW SUCCESSES IN MAGAZINE PUBLICATION

Three magazines founded in the 1920s seemed to match perfectly
the faster pace of the Roaring Twenties. They continue to find
favor with the reading public even today. *Time, Reader's Digest*, and
New Yorker were not at all alike. Yet, each found a ready audience.
While *The New Yorker's* audience was small and literate, those of
Time and *Reader's Digest* came from middle America. *Reader's Digest* became for a time the magazine with the greatest circulation
in the world. *Time*, the brainchild of two Yale graduates, spawned
the nation's most prominent and visible publishing empire. These
three magazines survived beyond an age characterized by the
demise of the mass-circulation, general-interest publication as represented by *Saturday Evening Post* and *Life*.

They were founded during a decade that was unusually important in American life. Radio became in the 1920s a central factor in
the daily life of almost every American. Literature blossomed in
the post-war years. So, too, did the magazine industry flourish
with the advent of these new magazines.

The New Yorker made little attempt to attract a mass circulation
— yet it had a formidable influence. Appealing to a highly literate
audience, it endured with hardly any changes in its physical ap-

pearance while mass magazines were dying during a struggle for
circulation and advertising in the 1960s.

The New Yorker was founded in 1925 by Harold Ross, a Colorado native, World War I veteran, and ex-newspaperman. Like the
editors of *Time* and *Reader's Digest*, he settled in New York City
after the war to establish his publication. Estimating start-up costs
at $50,000, he obtained half the amount from Raoul Fleischman, an
investor who also provided an office for the publication. Ross,
who was to edit *The New Yorker* and to set its unique tone for the
rest of his life, intended for it to reflect metropolitan life and to
keep up with the affairs of the day in a gay and satirical vein not
aimed at "the little old lady in Dubuque." This he did through
sophisticated fiction and humor, in-depth profiles of prominent
personalities, a gossipy and literate "Talk of the Town" column,
lengthy "letters" from around the world, and wry cartoons. The
magazine was slow to take hold. Its readership, never approaching the numbers of *Time* or *Reader's Digest* or *Saturday Evening Post*,
reflected an audience that was upperclass, highly educated, literate, and sophisticated. It developed such writers as E.B. White and
James Thurber, and it changed forever the nature of magazine humor.

The founding of *Reader's Digest* and its success represented a
publishing miracle, giving hope to all aspiring publishers who
have an idea but no money. DeWitt Wallace, a Minnesota-born college dropout, discovered the principle upon which the magazine
would be based when he was working in St. Paul as a writer of
sales promotion letters for a textbook publishing firm. In his reading he noticed an abundance of excellent pamphlets from the Department of Agriculture and state agricultural stations. It occurred
to him that the best of these should be digested and reprinted in a
single booklet. This he did in 1916, and he sold 100,000 copies of
the 120-page booklet, *Getting the Most Out of Farming*, to banks for
distribution to their customers. The same thing could be done,
perhaps with equal success, he reasoned, by digesting the best
magazine articles into a single publication. These thoughts were
interrupted by World War I. Serving in the U.S. Army in Europe,

The Reader's Digest

"An article a day" from leading magazines —each article of enduring value and interest, in condensed, permanent booklet form.

Vol. 5   OCTOBER 1926   Serial No. 54

Gleams of Mark Twain Humor

Anecdotes Reflecting the Whimsical Quality of the Humorist

Excerpts from The Mentor

EVEN as a child Mark Twain gave glimpses of the first outcroppings of the original genius that would one day amaze and entertain the nations. At bedtime he would sit up in bed and tell astonishing tales of the day's adventures, tales that caused his listeners to wonder why the lightning was restrained so long. Friends of his mother asked her if she believed anything the child said.

"Oh, yes," she replied, "I know his average. I discount him 90 per cent. The rest is pure gold. Sammy is a well of truth, but you can't bring it all up in one bucket."

One Sunday morning, during his early married life in Buffalo, Mark Twain noticed smoke pouring from the upper window of the house across the street. The owner and his wife, comparatively newcomers, were seated upon the veranda, unaware of impending danger. Clemens stepped briskly across the street and bowing with leisurely politeness, said: "My name is Clemens; we ought to have called on you before, and I beg your pardon for intruding now in this informal way, but your house is on fire."

The Clemens home at Hartford was next door to that of Harriet Beecher Stowe, and Mark Twain the author of Uncle Tom's Cabin were the best of neighbors. Mrs. Stowe was leaving for Florida one morning, and Clemens ran over early to say good-by. On his return Mrs. Clemens regarded him disapprovingly: "Why Youth," she said, "you haven't on any collar and tie."

He said nothing, but went up to his room, did up these items in a neat package, and sent it to Mrs. Stowe by a servant, with a line: "Herewith receive a call from the rest of me."

Mark Twain was often subjected to the importunities of young and aspiring authors who sought his advice and, in some cases, asked him to read their manuscripts. One of these had accompanied his request with an inquiry as to the right diet for an author, asking Mark Twain if it was true, as Professor Agassiz had said, that fish was good brain food. Mark Twain replied as follows "Yes, Agassiz does recommend authors to eat fish, because the phosphorous in it makes brain. So far you are correct. But I cannot help

The Reader's Digest   **321**

Reader's Digest

From its founding in 1922, *Reader's Digest* used the same formula for decades. Its editors found interesting stories in other publications and condensed them into brief articles for easy reading. It remains successful even today. In 2009, it was maintaining a U.S. circulation of 6 million.

Wallace suffered shrapnel wounds, and as he recovered in the hospital the idea forcefully recurred to him as he thumbed through magazine after magazine. As he lay in bed he began to practice tightening up articles, editing out words, phrases, sentences, and whole paragraphs without damaging the articles, often even enhancing them. Returning to St. Paul, he prepared a sample copy of a new publication he called "The Readers Digest." Publisher after publisher refused to sponsor his proposal, and Wallace finally accepted a position in the publicity department of Westinghouse Electric Co. in Pittsburgh.

When a brief recession hit the nation, Westinghouse found Wallace expendable and fired him. He decided he must take his fate into his own hands. He began promoting his magazine project by mail, moved to New York City, rented a storeroom under a Greenwich Village speakeasy as headquarters, borrowed $5,000 from family and friends, and — on the eve of this risky project — married his longtime sweetheart, Lila, who would become a partner in the venture. When the couple returned from their honeymoon, they found in their mailbox enough subscriptions to pay the print-

ing bill for the first issue of *Reader's Digest*, dated February 1922. It contained "thirty-one articles of enduring value and interest, in condensed and compact form." In the Wallaces' early days as publishers, so short of funds were they that they copied the articles by hand from publications in the New York Public Library.

The formula that Wallace envisioned for the fast-paced life that followed World War I was inherently correct for a nation that, according to the 1920 census, for the first time was predominately urban. The reading public was ready for brevity, and a magazine that condensed the best from other magazines had distinct appeal. Before 1922 ended, *Reader's Digest* could boast of a circulation of 7,000 — not spectacular but certainly satisfactory — and the Wallaces found better facilities in Pleasantville, New York. Actually, the headquarters was no more than a pony shed and garage located on an estate, but here they remained for three years, living above the garage and working in the former pony stalls. In 1925, with circulation reaching 20,000, the Wallaces bought land adjoining their pony stall office, built a home on it, and moved the magazine office into the new ground-floor study.

There was nothing meteoric about the growth of *Reader's Digest*. It was slow but certain. Still, by 1929 circulation had reached 109,000. Wallace introduced the publication on the nation's newsstands rather than relying strictly on subscriptions. He also began signing contracts with certain magazines to ensure his exclusive right to reprint articles.

Despite its reprint policy, *Reader's Digest* developed an editorial formula of its own. In the early years the Wallaces sought to get into every issue something from a long list of categories: science, medicine, education, government, the art of living, international relations, biography, movies, sports, travel, humor, essays, labor, business, nature, and agriculture. In 1933 *Reader's Digest* began to produce its own articles as well. Gradually there emerged a penchant for articles that emphasized the successes of people who worked hard and earned rewards as a result. During the 1940s the magazine began to assume a conservative political stance, lamenting excessive government regulation and championing free enterprise.

The magazine's continuing prosperity was evidenced in 1938 by construction of a four-story building on an eighty-acre site in Pleasantville. In the same year a British edition was published in London. Two years later South American editions were introduced in Spanish and Portuguese. Soon, *Reader's Digest* became the most widely read magazine in South America. Not until the 1950s did the magazine open its pages to advertisers, and in 1950 the firm began a lucrative side-adventure: Reader's Digest Condensed Books. By 1990 *Reader's Digest* enjoyed a world-wide circulation of more than 28 million and a readership within the United States of more than 16 million. Until the newcomer *TV Guide* surpassed it in the early 1970s, it had been the circulation leader for many years. It then regained that position when *TV Guide's* circulation dropped; and in 2009 its circulation was behind only *AARP The Magazine*, *AARP Bulletin*, and *Better Homes and Gardens*. As usual, such success as *Reader's Digest* experienced bred imitation. *Pageant, Coronet, Fleet's Review,* and *Quick* were among those to challenge, but none achieved lasting success.

TIME MAGAZINE

It was this twentieth-century idea of brevity that prompted two idealistic graduates of Yale University, Henry Luce and Briton Hadden, to found *Time* magazine. Their venture started modestly enough but went on to become the most prominent publishing company in the nation, Time Inc., under whose aegis would appear *Fortune, Life, Sports Illustrated, People, Money,* a book series, and for a number of years a radio news show and movie newsreel.

Of the two founders, Luce is the one with whom the company is identified in the modern public's mind, for Hadden died in 1929, six years after the magazine was founded. The child of Presbyterian missionaries, Luce was reared in China. He developed intensely patriotic notions about his native America. Upon coming to the United States to attend the exclusive Hotchkiss School in Connecticut, he met and formed a friendly rivalry with the editor of the school newspaper, Hadden. The two went on to Yale. Although World War I interrupted their undergraduate careers, both graduated in 1920. Luce was named "most brilliant," and Hadden "most likely to succeed." After brief careers as reporters, they rejoined one another as newsmen on the *Baltimore News,* where in their off hours they prepared a prospectus for a new magazine they had envisioned since their days at Yale.

They observed that although daily journalism was more highly developed in the United States than in any other nation of the world, its citizens were for the most part poorly informed. Why? "Because no publication has adapted itself to the time which busy men are able to spend on simply keeping informed," they argued. Their working title, "Facts," soon was changed to *Time.* It would be a publication created on a "new principle of complete organization" with materials appearing in a brief, organized manner under fixed department headings: foreign news, sports, and so forth.

Resigning from their positions in Baltimore, they moved to New York City to raise the $100,000 they believed would be necessary to begin the publication. They reasoned naively that ten rich Yale men should be willing to contribute $10,000 each. After raising $86,000 from seventy-two investors, they had exhausted their list of potential backers and decided to move ahead. In a promotional campaign, they offered three free issues before an individual had to decide whether to subscribe for a year at $15. Some 25,000 readers accepted the offer.

On March 3, 1923, the first issue of *Time, the Weekly News-Magazine,* appeared. It was divided into twenty-two departments. Since it had no reporters, the staff lifted the news almost entirely from the *New York Times.* Hadden and Luce each preferred to be editor, but the publication needed a business manager as well. They flipped a coin. Hadden won. The agreement was that they would alternate positions each year, but three years passed before Luce could untangle himself from business affairs to permit him to take his turn as editor.

Time, **Master of Brevity**
Henry Luce and Briton Hadden began *Time* magazine from the belief that Americans in 1923 were so busy that they had little time to read. They reduced each week's news into twenty-two departments in a magazine that that could be read in less than an hour. Its name, however, came not from the idea of saving time but from Luce, on his subway trip home at night, seeing advertisements containing slogans such as "time to retire" and "time for a change."

It was under Hadden's editorship that the peculiar writing known as "Time style" evolved. "Backward ran sentences until reeled the mind," wrote Wolcott Gibbs in a famous parody of *Time* that appeared in *The New Yorker.*[17] The magazine developed other stylistic mannerisms: "cinemactor" for movie star, "socialite" for one involved in high society, "great and good friend" for mistress, and such sentences as, "As it must to all men, death came last week to...." People in *Time* never "said" anything. They snapped, gruffed, croaked, chuckled, gushed, or sneered. Neither did they "walk." They strode, stalked, bounced, leaped, or shot ahead.

The magazine departed from the standard of journalistic objectivity. There was no editorial page because editorial opinions were inserted in the articles. *Time* did express, however, an interest in achieving fairness in its coverage.

As the magazine prospered, Hadden and Luce grew apart. Hadden was flamboyant; Luce, serious. In his will, Hadden sought to exclude Luce from gaining his share of the company, but Luce managed to do so anyway; and in the many decades that followed Hadden's death, Time Inc. and Henry Luce were nearly in-

---

[17] Quoted in James Thurber, *The Years with Ross* (Boston, 1957), 217.

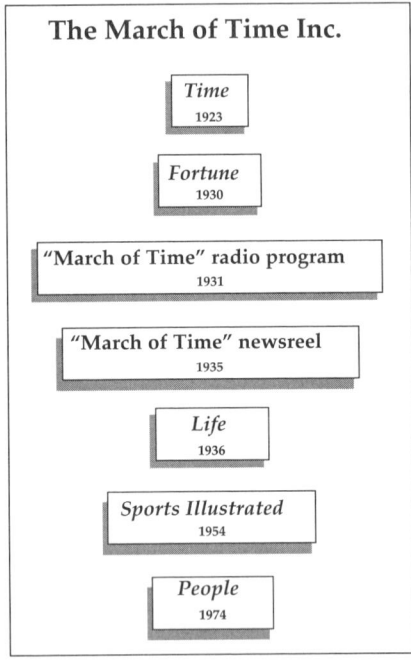

The March of Time Inc.

Time
1923

Fortune
1930

"March of Time" radio program
1931

"March of Time" newsreel
1935

Life
1936

Sports Illustrated
1954

People
1974

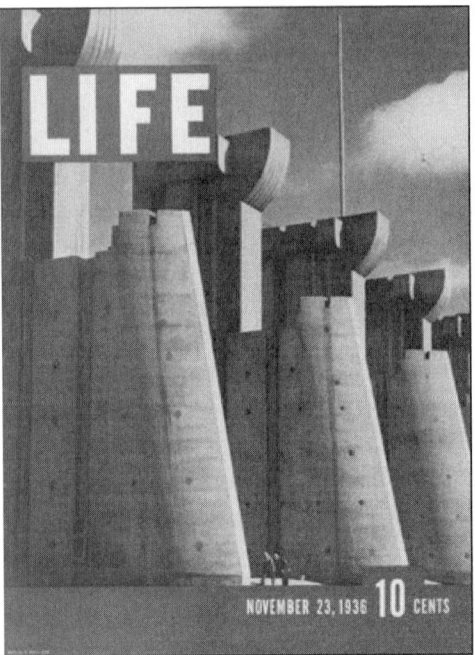

LIFE

NOVEMBER 23, 1936 10 CENTS

Picture of Success
Time Inc. created a group of magazines whose success was virtually unmatched. Beginning with *Time* in 1923, it published several of the most popular magazines in the twentieth century. For years, its most popular periodical was *Life*, the pioneer among picture magazines. Filled with photographs and photo stories, it was an instant success when Time Inc. introduced it in 1936. Over the years it published some of the best photojournalism ever produced and included work by the most notable American photographers. The merger of Time Inc., Warner Communications, and America Online in 2001 created the world's largest media conglomerate. After separating from AOL shortly after the merger, Time Warner remained America's largest media corporation.

separable in the public mind.

Luce's success with *Time* led into other ventures. *Fortune*, a monthly designed to give business a publication, was started in 1930 at an inauspicious time — the beginning of the Great Depression — and sold for the startlingly high price of $1 an issue. It did more than survive the hard times; it prospered. Other ventures followed, including a radio news show and the movie newsreel, "The March of Time."

LIFE MAGAZINE

Introduced in 1935, "The March of Time" indicated Luce's growing interest in pictorial journalism; and in early 1936 he announced his intention to begin a new pictorial magazine. After months of planning and in-fighting among the staff, the first issue of the weekly picture magazine, *Life*, appeared in November of 1936, bearing on its cover Margaret Bourke-White's black-and-white photograph of Fort Peck Dam in Montana.

The magazine was an instant success. The entire press run of 466,000 sold out. The same thing happened in the following few weeks, and circulation surpassed 500,000. Just how extensive could the market be? Time Inc. executives got an idea from sales in Worcester, Massachusetts. On the first day of publication 475 copies sold out in a few hours. With the December 4 issue the decision was made to flood the city's newsstands with 2,000 copies. These were purchased just as quickly as the 475 copies. In the weeks that followed, shipments were raised to 3,000, then 4,000, and then 9,000. After the latter figure was reached, a Worcester distributor telegraphed: "Send 12,000 next week." The result was yet another sell-out. It was concluded that the potential national demand was between five and six million copies a week. The projection proved to be accurate.

Life's impact on Time Inc. was substantial. In 1939 the maga-

zine's annual revenues were just under $30 million. Its before-tax profit was nearly $4 million. In 1941 the figures had climbed to $45 million in revenue with before-tax profits of $8.1 million. The average net paid circulation had reached 3,290,480, second to the *Saturday Evening Post's* 3,386,950. *Life* also was second to the *Post* in dollar volume of advertising. Its revenues surpassed those of its older brother, *Time*, and its circulation was about four times as great.

Life photographers achieved national fame. They included Bourke-White, Alfred Eisenstaedt, W. Eugene Smith, Robert Capa, Carl Mydans, David Douglas Duncan, and Gordon Parks. Their candid photographs were made possible through *Life's* adoption of the 35mm camera, so much more portable and discreet than the old 4 x 5 press camera.

Time Inc. began to acquire an international flavor as *Time, Life,* and *Fortune* attracted subscribers and developed newsstand sales all over the world. Before World War II, a weekly excerpt from *Time* was translated into Spanish and distributed to a number of Latin American newspapers. It was followed by a special edition of *Time* printed on lightweight paper and delivered by air to South America.

Time Inc. was not the only publishing company in the mid-1930s to see promise in a magazine based on photojournalism. At the same time *Life* was being envisioned, John and Gardner Cowles, the brothers who published the *Des Moines Register and Tribune,* were planning their own picture magazine, *Look*. There were no secrets about the separate ambitions, for the Cowles brothers were friends and stockholders of Time Inc. They accordingly shared with Luce the dummy copy of their magazine and even offered Time Inc. a 20% interest in the venture. Time Inc., after careful consideration, accepted the offer, purchasing 45,000 shares. It was acknowledged that *Look* might be even more successful than *Life* because of *Look's* far more modest scale of opera-

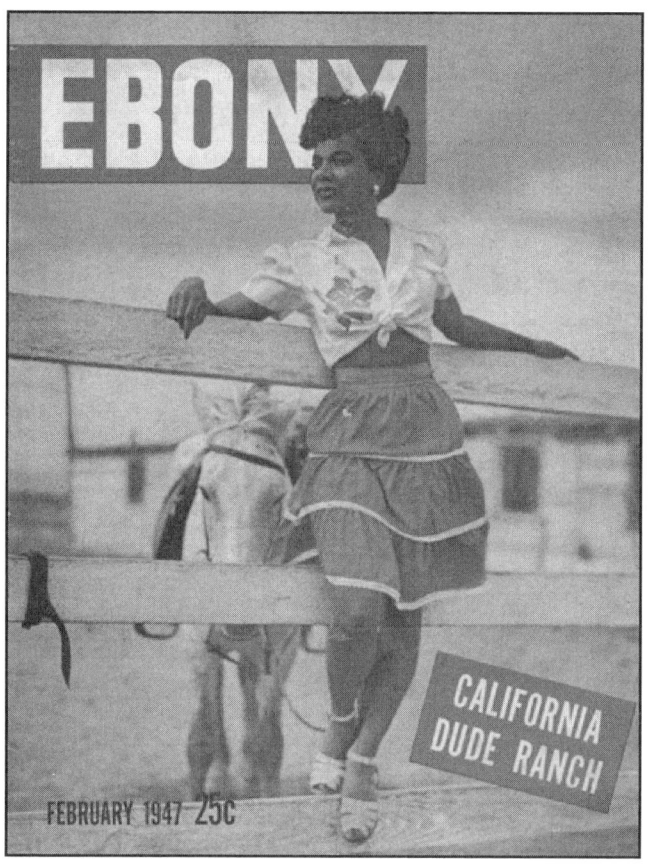

Ebony
In 1945 John H. Johnson took the graphic approaches used by *Life* magazine and adapted them to *Ebony*, a publication for African Americans. Celebrating their achievements, *Ebony* helped Johnson become America's leading black magazine publisher.

tions. After both *Life* and *Look* were in operation, the Cowles brothers requested that Time Inc. resell its shares in the company. The transaction was made in 1937, and Time Inc. earned a nifty profit of $675,000.

In 1942 an entrepreneur named John H. Johnson, noting the success of magazines with broad appeal, decided that a market existed for a national publication directed toward African-American readers. He raised a little money by mortgaging his mother's furniture and used it to start *Negro Digest*, patterned after *Reader's Digest*. Three years later he founded *Ebony*, a publication for African Americans that was reminiscent of *Life*, although its goal was to emphasize the positive aspects of African-American life. Johnson went on to become the nation's most prominent black publisher, with additional magazines such as *Jet* and *Ebony Jr*. Other black-oriented publications emerged in and survived through the latter twentieth century.[18]

Johnson's daughter, Linda Johnson Rice, received her master's degree in management from Northwestern University and then became president and chief operating officer of Johnson Publishing Co. In that position, she continued the global expansion of the

company. By 2004, *Ebony* and *Jet* combined reached half the black households in the United States. Worth $350 million and employing about 2,000, Johnson was the largest black-owned publishing firm in the world.

COMPETITION AT THE TOP

There seemed to be plenty of room following World War II for all these magazines. Curtis Publishing Company alone printed more than 25 million copies of its magazines each month. Its annual consumption of ink — more than 10 million pounds — was said to be enough to paint an area of 500 square miles. Despite *Life's* remarkable reception and a circulation of 5.2 million, which was just ahead of the *Saturday Evening Post's*, advertisers continued to view the *Post* as the more reliable vehicle; and it regularly contained more advertising.

Life's rates, however, were higher than those of the *Post* because of its larger circulation, and the company initiated a campaign to persuade advertisers that their money was better spent in *Life*. Red labels and posters began to appear in shop windows and retail counters proclaiming, "As advertised in Life." Efforts simultaneously were made to boost the circulation to 6 million while the price per issue was increased to 15¢. The increase suggested in a subtle way that *Life* was worth 5¢ more than the *Post*, which sold for a dime.

The *Post* was prepared for the challenge. The era of World War II and afterwards has been called the *Post's* "Silver Age." Editor Ben Hibbs, a Kansan, addressed the conservative American heartland in the magazine's pages. The editors of the other Curtis publications, *Jack and Jill*, *Ladies' Home Journal*, and *Country Gentleman*, also had been born and bred in the Middle West; and their publications reflected that. Hibbs engineered a series of biographical and autobiographical articles on such American heroes as Dwight Eisenhower, Casey Stengel, and Douglas MacArthur. In a series of "I Call On" articles in the 1950s, senior editor Pete Martin engaged in chatty, intimate interviews with such celebrities as Bing Crosby, Clark Gable, Grace Kelly, and Marilyn Monroe. When entertainer Arthur Godfrey's story appeared in the magazine with his portrait on the cover, the magazine sold 2 million copies on the newsstands alone.

As the historian James Playsted Wood wrote, "There is only one comfortable place for a mass magazine to be — first."[19] Advertising salesmen for the *Post* were unaccustomed to the secondary role in which they found themselves as *Life* pushed ahead in circulation, and an energetic marketing campaign answered *Life's* challenge. According to the *Post's* promotions, people loved and trusted the magazine; more *Post* readers owned their homes; more held executive positions; and so on.

The year 1953 saw the *Post's* circulation go above 5.5 million and ad sales reach almost $81 million. But 1954 saw a puzzling development: a loss in ad revenue of almost $2 million. Why? Not for a lack of faithful readers, for there were nearly 6 million of them,

[18]Armistead S. Pride and Clint C. Wilson II, "Magazines, Radio, and Television," in *A History of the Black Press* (Washington, D.C., 1997), 249-53; and Roland E. Wolseley, *The Black Press, U.S.A.*, 2nd ed. (Ames, Iowa, 1990), 86-9.

[19]James Playsted Wood, *The Curtis Magazines* (New York, 1971), 194.

Guideposts Magazine

Founder's Positive Attitude Helps *Guideposts* Overcome

Two years after *Guideposts* was founded in 1945, a fire destroyed its borrowed offices and subscriber list. The situation looked grim for the financially strapped magazine. But *Guideposts* was founded by the Rev. Dr. Norman Vincent Peale, a minister who preached that positive thinking would overcome obstacles.

Lowell Thomas reported the magazine's struggle on his popular radio show, generating an influx of new subscribers.

But *Guideposts*' struggles were not over. Peale, who had been a newspaper reporter before entering the ministry, knew how to write. But he knew little about the publishing business other than his vision of a magazine that emphasized true inspirational stories. The first design was an unstapled set of four leaflets that flew apart so that the message would spread farther. It didn't. A year after the fire, *Guideposts* couldn't even pay for a typewriter.

Peale recalled that the turning point came when a friend chastised the *Guideposts* staffers that they were focusing on problems rather than visualizing success.

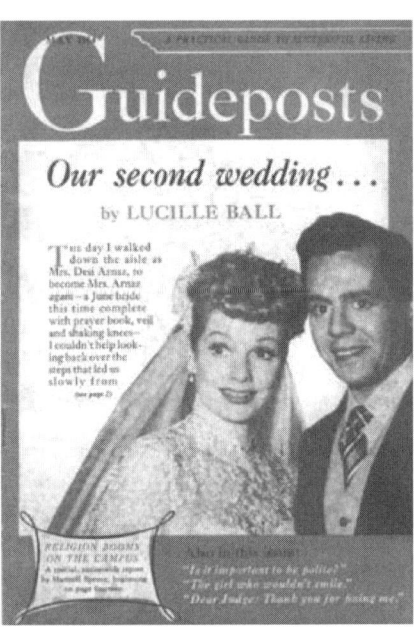

Left: Norman Vincent Peale; Above: A 1960 Issue of *Guideposts*

The staff rededicated itself and gradually got out of debt.

The experience strengthened Peale's optimistic philosophy, which he explained in *The Power of Positive Thinking*, a book that stayed on the best-seller lists for 186 weeks after its 1952 publication. Its popularity helped *Guideposts* go from 200,000 subscribers in 1951 to 500,000 in 1953.

Guideposts' formula of real-life stories about people who, as one writer described

it, have "walked up to adversity and kicked it," still resonates with readers, many of whom ask the staff to pray for them.

Peale died in 1993 at the age of 95. But his followers can still hear him preach on *Guideposts*' website and read his optimistic philosophy in the magazine's print edition, which has about 3.3 million subscribers, making it one of the top twenty American magazines.

---

but because advertisers were beginning to lose faith in the *Post* and its middle-America predelictions. Madison Avenue was East Coast, and advertising account executives tended to prefer *Life* as an advertising vehicle. *Life* was jazzier. It had less type and more pictures. More people saw a single issue of *Life* than saw the *Post*. In fact, *Life* produced figures indicating that its readers were better educated and more affluent than the *Post*'s and that they tended to be community leaders. The *Post*'s circulation was not declining, for it passed the 6 million mark in 1959. Still, net earnings of $2.8 million that year for Curtis Publishing Company were down from the previous year by about $3.5 million.

MAGAZINES IN THE AGE OF TELEVISION

Besides the growing competition within the mass magazine field, ominous new competition for the advertising dollar had risen

from another source: television. It reached audiences in gigantic numbers beyond the range of any magazine. If mass magazines thought they could attract millions of readers by appealing to mass taste, they were hopelessly outmatched by television's ability to do the same. Advertisers readily responded. Between 1952 and 1956, television ad revenue tripled from $454,000 to $1.2 million. TV had little effect on the public's appetite for general magazines, but its effect on advertising was devastating. Indeed, while magazine circulation continued to grow in the 1950s, the Golden Age of Television was capturing the imagination of millions more Americans who retired each evening after dinner to their comfortable chairs before the TV set.

That problems lay ahead for all mass magazines was clearly suggested in December 1956 with the sudden demise of *Collier's*, a publication that had been in existence for sixty-eight years as a general-interest fortnightly. Its publisher, Crowell Publishing Co.,

Death from Television

With the growing popularity of television in the 1950s, the magazine industry suffered several high-profile casualties. *Woman's Home Companion*, *American Magazine*, *Collier's*, *Coronet*, *Saturday Evening Post*, *Look*, and *Life* — with combined circulations that once reached 37 million — all died between 1956 and 1972. *Life* and *Saturday Evening Post* later re-emerged as monthlies and restructured shadows of their former selves. What the failed magazines had in common was, for the most part, that they were all aimed at a "general" audience of all ages, races, and genders. TV appealed to the same broad audience. So it and the general magazines were competing against one another for the same advertising dollars. Few, if any, of them were suffering dramatic circulation losses at the time of their demise. What they were suffering was the loss of advertisers of everyday household products who found they could better promote their wares on television. TV provided not only larger audiences, but sound and pictures to describe the products. The 1950s marked the beginning of the most profound adaptation the magazine industry was to make in the twentieth century. As magazines realized that they could no longer compete with TV for ad dollars for a broad audience, magazine content became increasingly specialized. New magazines identified audience niches with special interests and found advertisers who wanted to reach that audience.

Major Magazines That Failed in the Twentieth Century

These were mostly "general interest" magazines. Eight failures came during the Depression years of 1929-1932, and seven more during the rise of television between 1956 and 1972.

Title of magazine	Year Began	Year Ended	Total Lifespan	Highest Circulation
The Merchant's Ledger	1847	1902	55	400,000
Arena	1889	1909	20	n.a.
Lippincott's Magazine	1866	1916	49	n.a.
Leslie's Weekly	1855	1922	67	379,000
Independent	1848	1928	80	n.a.
The Dial	1880	1929	49	n.a.
Everybody's Magazine	1899	1929	30	735,000
Munsey's Weekly	1889	1929	40	700,000
McClure's	1881	1929	48	563,000
Century Illustrated Monthly	1881	1930	49	200,000
Smart Set	1890	1930	40	250,000
World's Work	1900	1932	32	100,000
Outlook	1867	1932	65	125,000
Review of Reviews	1891	1937	46	250,000
Delineator	1873	1937	64	500,000
Literary Digest	1890	1938	48	1.5 million
Scribner's Magazine	1887	1939	52	200,000
North American Review	1815	1940	125	76,000
Forum	1887	1940	53	30,000
Littell's Living Age	1844	1941	97	n.a.
Woman's Home Companion	1897	1956	59	4.4 million
American Magazine	1876	1957	80	2.6 million
Collier's	1888	1956	68	4.1 million
Coronet	1936	1961	36	3.1 million
Saturday Evening Post	1821	1969	148	6.9 million
Look	1937	1971	34	7.7 million
Life	1936	1972	36	8.5 million
American Mercury	1924	1980	54	84,000

announced at the same time that *Woman's Home Companion*, with an 83-year history, also was suspended. The two magazines, boasting combined circulations of 8.3 million, had lost $7.5 million between them for the year, threatening the very existence of the parent company.

Look, eager to catch up with *Life* and *Saturday Evening Post* in the circulation war, snatched up *Collier's* subscribers, bringing its list to 4.2 million. Determined to stay in the race, *Look* began promoting itself as the magazine that "likes people ... what they do, what they feel, what they want, what they think." As a *Look* memorandum to an advertising agency elaborated, "*Life* — in spite of all efforts at informality — remains the lofty pundit, superior, condescending, jesting, ponderous with moral instruction for the lesser masses. Standing shoulder to shoulder with man, *Look* asks questions. *Life* is impersonal; *Look* is personal. *Life* likes theories, causes, paradoxes, heroes and vast movements in time and space; *Look* likes people." Such an approach, Henry Luce felt, was "a sure-fire American line."[20] He observed that it likely had been inspired by his own personal reputation for being aloof, cold, and inhuman. So

long as *Life* demonstrated a capacity for humanness, though, it would be fine, he believed.

Along with television and intensified competition, rising costs for production and distribution were threatening mass magazines. By 1969, despite the 40¢ cover price for *Life*, special subscription rates brought the average price per issue down to 12¢. Yet the cost to edit, print, and distribute was 41¢ per issue. The difference of 29¢ had to be made up by advertisers. At the beginning of 1970, ad revenues for *Life* were just 27¢ per copy, meaning that each copy sold brought the company a 2¢ loss. Thus, at a time when circulations for magazines such as *Life*, *Look*, and *Post* were higher than ever in their history, at a time when the magazines' acceptance by the public was enthusiastic, these magazines were approaching economic disaster and the end to a long era in publishing. Advertisers who wished to address a mass audience had a better vehicle in television. They were becoming more and more reluctant to pay the high ad rates that mass magazines were compelled to ask in order to sustain themselves.

The *Post*, in desperation, initiated a series of changes, some of which were revolutionary and none of which worked. It took on as an editorial philosophy "sophisticated muckraking," a stance

[20]Quoted in Robert T. Elson, *Time Inc.: The Intimate History of a Publishing Enterprise, 1923-1941* (New York, 1968), 426-7.

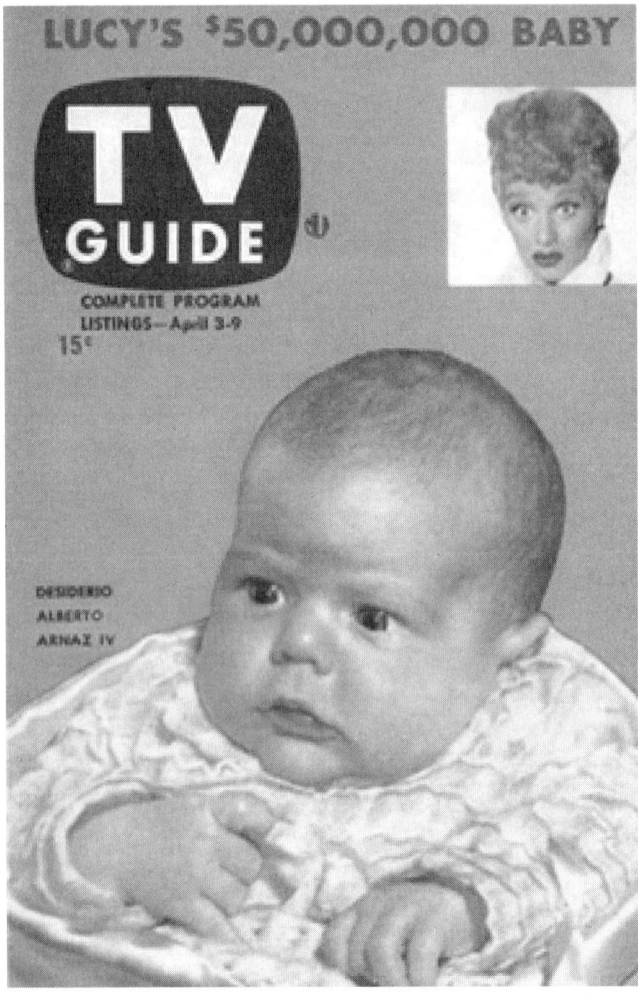

Made by Television
The success of *TV Guide*, which consistently had the highest revenue of any magazine, coincided with the rise of television in American life. The cover of its inaugural issue in 1953 carried a picture of Lucille Ball and her newborn son. *TV Guide* contained television listings until 2005. Now it carries general interest articles on television and entertainment, including profiles of celebrities.

that offended old readers and won few new ones. It decided to reduce circulation by an arbitrary formula so that it could claim to deliver to advertisers an elite audience representing the more affluent counties in the nation. To achieve this end, it eliminated 3.8 million of its 6.8 million subscribers. Among the victims, because of accounting errors, were the *Post's* former editor, Ben Hibbs; Arkansas Governor Winthrop Rockefeller; and the magazine's own president, Martin Ackerman. As 1969 arrived, the *Post* found itself losing some $400,000 a month, an untenable situation. Later that year the inevitable occurred: the magazine folded. Several years later it re-emerged as a quarterly under new ownership, and while the product was designed to resemble the *Post* of pre-World War II days, it was a drastically different publication.

Meanwhile, *Life* and *Look* were struggling with the same economic forces. *Look* was next to fail, and *Life* saw its gross ad revenue drop from $170 million in 1966 to $91 million in 1971. Costs continued to rise, including the price paid for printing paper and

a new U. S. Postal Service rate that sought an end to the long-time indirect subsidies for magazine mailing costs.

Life's last regular issue was published December 29, 1972. As was true for the *Saturday Evening Post*, however, *Life* did not disappear forever, for Time Inc. issued occasional special issues at a price of $1.50 to $2 each. In 1978 it re-introduced *Life* as a regular monthly "specialized" magazine. The magazine was suspended again, however, in 2000, when Time Inc. announced that it would return to publishing only special issues. A thin but glossy *Life* magazine reappeared as a weekly newspaper supplement in 2004 and ran for 125 issues in 103 newspapers. It found stiff competition, though, with Advance Magazine Group's well established *Parade* and Gannett's *USA Weekend*. As another run of *Life* came to an end with the April 20, 2007, issue of the newspaper insert, managing editor Bill Shapiro promised that *Life* would "continue to publish beautiful books that celebrate great lives and commemorate historic events." He also noted in that last edition that the staff would be "supercharging" its web site, which would catalogue the photographic archives of the magazine's 2,306 issues and include seventy years of unpublished photographs.

A New Magazine Age

As *Post, Look,* and *Life* struggled with the new economic forces, other magazines were emerging that seemed to recognize and take advantage of a new age in publishing. These were the specialized magazines, aimed at readers with specific interests that could not be satisfied by a general publication or by television and its quest for mass audiences.

Of course, there always had been specialized magazines, but they had existed in the shadow of the mass magazines. Now emerged special-interest magazines that achieved mass-circulation status. The categories were many, ranging from men's magazines such as *Esquire* and *Playboy*; sports magazines such as *Sports Illustrated* and *Outdoor Life*; business magazines such as *Business Week* and *Forbes*; women's magazines as varied as *Redbook, Ms.,* and *Mademoiselle*; music publications such as the highly successful *Rolling Stone*; travel magazines such as *Travel and Leisure*; and popular science magazines as varied as the venerable *Scientific American* and *Popular Science*.

Sports Illustrated, founded by Time Inc. in 1954, capitalized on the nation's continuing interest in sports that had been evident in sport magazines as early as the first half of the nineteenth century. Despite its acceptance by some 350,000 charter subscribers and excellent newsstand sales, it brought Time Inc. losses of $6 million in 1954. Not until ten years had passed did it achieve its first profitable year. By 1972, however, it not only enjoyed a circulation of 2.2 million but stood second only to *Time* as a profit-maker for the corporation.

Two years later, in 1974, Time Inc. launched yet another periodical, *People Weekly*, which highlighted personal aspects of interesting and important people. *People's* brief, conversational articles, usually about celebrities, accompanied by candid photographs,

Targeted Audiences

As magazines appeared to face extinction in the face of competition from television, magazines taking new approaches achieved a large degree of vitality and prosperity. A variety of factors accounted for their success, but the most effective device that publishers used to succeed was to target their magazines at specific audiences with special interests. One of the most successful of the new magazines was *Sports Illustrated*. Aimed at America's sports enthusiasts, it lost $6 million in its first year. It was ten years before the magazine became a financial success, but it eventually became one of Time Inc.'s most profitable publications. By riding the crest of America's aging population, *Modern Maturity* became the magazine with the nation's largest circulation. Founded in 1958, it came as a free benefit to members of the American Association of Retired Persons. As suggested by *Sports Illustrated* and *Modern Maturity*, magazines were created to appeal to virtually every interest of potential reading markets. *Self Employed* was one of the many magazines that targeted owners of small businesses and home-based businesses that proliferated in the 1990s. Scores of other magazines attempted to take advantage of Americans' growing interest in financial success. Even special areas of interest were subdivided into smaller segments. Illustrative of that approach were magazines in the field of religion, a market that today has scores of magazines. That market is further broken into such areas as denominations, with a number of magazines — such as the Baptist *Home Life* — appealing to different audiences in each denomination.

found a ready audience. After just five years of publication it reached a circulation of 2.3 million, and by the time of its tenth anniversary it had become Time Inc.'s most profitable publication.

A few years earlier, as *Saturday Evening Post* and *Life* had been battling for supremacy during the great circulation wars of the 1950s, another publication devoted to analysis and commentary on current events that was to make a significant contribution to political thought made a quiet debut. This was the *National Review*, first appearing in November 1955 and offering readers a decidedly conservative outlook with wit and sparkle. From the beginning, it was identified with its founding editor, William F. Buckley Jr., who gained the appellation of the "patron saint of conservatism." The *National Review* provided an ideological home for the nation's leading intellectual and political conservatives, nearly all of whom wrote on occasion for the magazine. On its pages were developed the conservative ideology for the nation that reached a pinnacle when Ronald Reagan was elected president in 1980. The magazine, in typical lighthearted fashion, proclaimed that for the first time it had become "an establishment organ" and that it no longer could indulge in levity. "Connoisseurs of human [foibles] will have to get their yuks elsewhere," it declared. "We have a nation to run."[21] Buckley stepped down as editor-in-chief in 1990, and in 2004 he divested his controlling shares of the magazine.

By 1970 the "hot magazines" were those such as *TV Guide*, *Playboy*, *Car Craft*, *Southern Living*, *New York*, *Cosmopolitan*, and many other smaller publications that appealed to readers with such diverse interests as skeet shooting, yachting, knitting, photography, drag racing, and gourmet dining. Some 750 magazines for the general consumer were being issued, up 10% from 1965. *TV Guide* sought to escape the economic dilemma that sank *Life* and *Post* by offering regional editions, and in 1970 it had eighty-one different editions. *Time*, *Newsweek*, and other magazines with hefty circulations also offered regional editions that had identical editorial content but permitted advertisers to buy space only for a particular geographical area. In 1963 *Time* was the first magazine to offer a "demographic" edition — a special edition that went only to college students. This was followed by special editions for doctors and educators.[22]

This trend toward "targeting" special audiences continued to grow. By 1990 the number of magazines issuing special geographic or demographic editions had passed 200.[23] As the decade of the 1980s yielded to the '90s, a targeted publication, *Modern Maturity*, a slick bi-monthly issued by the American Association of Retired Persons (now known as AARP), surprisingly stood alongside two other magazines, *Reader's Digest* and *TV Guide*, as having the highest circulations in the nation. With a distribution of nearly 20 million copies, *Modern Maturity* reflected changing demographics in which an increasing proportion of the nation's population was more than fifty years of age. As AARP grew, so did the magazine's circulation, for all members of the organization received a subscription as a benefit. *TV Guide* was selling approximately 17 million copies a week. The familiar *Reader's Digest*, once the circula-

[21]Quoted in Alan Nourie and Barbara Nourie, eds., *American Mass-Market Magazines* (New York, 1990), 18.

[22]"The Hot Magazines Aim at Special Targets," *Business Week*, 2 May 1970, 64-74.
[23]John Tebbel and Mary Ellen Zuckerman, *The Magazine in America* (New York, 1991), 263-4.

Magazine Numbers and Circulation, 1950-1995

Year	Number of titles	Consumer titles	Business titles	Publishing groups	Per-issue circulation in millions	Adult pop. in millions	Circ. per adult
1950	6,960		1,772	249	146	105	1.40
1960	8,422		2,310	260	188	115	1.62
1970	9,573	874	2,376	303	245	134	1.83
1980	10,236	1,200	2,305	406	275	160	1.71
1990	11,092	1,978	2,784	563	369	186	1.98
1995	10,387	2,454	3,098	583	363	193	1.87

Magazine Growth

These tables chronicle the growth in consumer and business magazines from 1940 until the end of the twentieth century. They also indicate that the number of magazines the average adult reads in any given month increased from 1.4 in 1950 to around 1.9 in the 1990s. Competition and a recession starting in 2008 led to a decline in numbers. In 2009 approximately 17,000 magazines were being published, down from about 18,000 in 2005. Magazines searched for ways to survive and prosper. Some converted to online-only publication. Those aiming at specialized interests continued to find a market. According to the American Society of Magazine Editors, in 2009 the categories with the most magazines were Regional Interest (1,126 publications), Medicine (1,119), Ethnic (952), Religion & Theological (772), Travel (735), Business & Industry (626), College Alumni (532), Automotive (492), Health & Fitness (488), College Student Press (435), and Music & Music Trades (400).

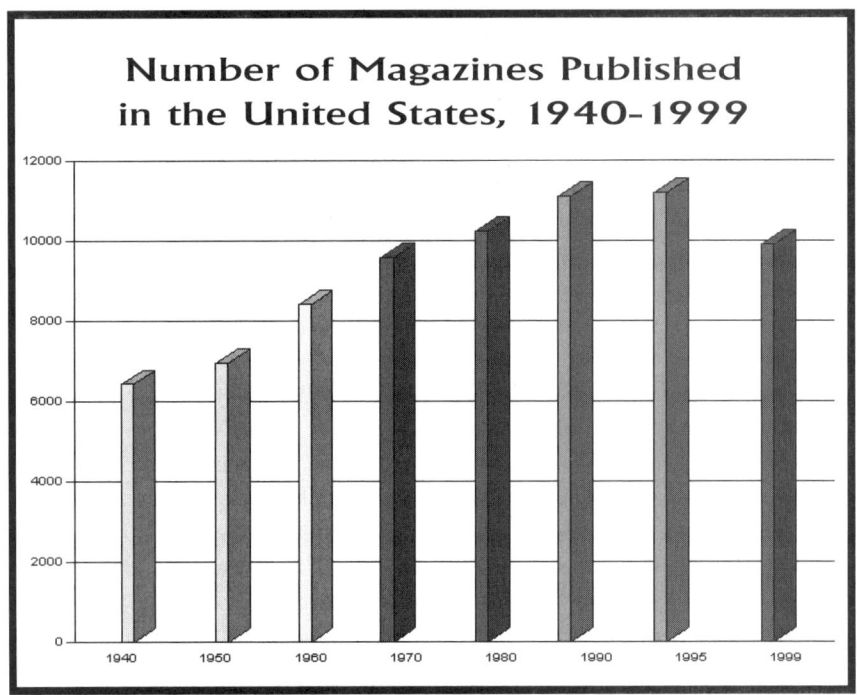

tion leader, continued to be popular with a monthly circulation of more than 16 million.

Despite a downturn in the nation's economy that brought declining ad revenues in the late 1980s, optimism was undaunted. Between 1985 and 1989 a total of 1,238 new magazines were started. Startups in the 1990s continued to appeal to an increasingly diverse audience and a wider variety of popular interests. In 1991 some 35% of those new magazines still were in existence, and this was a higher survival rate than that of the first half of the 1980s.

The mass magazine landscape is shifting. In addition to its print tradition, the magazine today maintains an online presence in order to pursue interactive dialogue with readers, engage new subscribers, and share content, from advice to recipes. *Better Homes and Gardens* has overtaken *Reader's Digest* in circulation; but with a change in its organization and its magazine name, *AARP The Magazine* outpaced them both to become, in 2005, the best-selling magazine in the United States. In that same year, *People* topped the advertising revenue charts with its $1.38 billion. Although

People has lost advertising since that time, it is still the leader. *TV Guide* has seen a dramatic drop in circulation — down to 2 million in 2009, when it ranked thirtieth in the United States.

Recent changes in mass magazines resemble the transformation in the early twentieth century from the elite publications of the nineteenth. As with the advent of photoengraving, today's technological innovation of the Internet has heightened competition among new and traditional media for audiences and advertising dollars. It also has hastened the repositioning of traditional media and the demise of start-ups as well as standard-bearers. However, some magazines that folded, such as *Cosmo Girl*, have started Internet editions.

Recognizing the importance of magazines in the cultural dialogue, some experts have noted that they will not die out but will need to adapt to a "permanently altered marketplace."[24] Distinctions between media are blurring as newspapers adopt the tradi-

[24] Cathie Black, "Despite Recent Events, the American Magazine Is Not an Endangered Species," *Advertising Age*, 23 February 2009.

tional magazine format and as Internet-only magazines have come of age. A leading magazine publisher, Condé Nast Publications, has become an innovator in Internet marketing by selling articles and issues that readers can download to mobile devices.

Even as magazines have faced challenges in recent years, they continue to be a fascinating, essential part of the increasingly complex communication industry.

RECOMMENDED READINGS

For related books and articles, some of which include the twentieth century, see the list of "Recommended Readings" for Chapter 13 "American Magazines 1740-1900."

BOOKS

Abrahamson, David. *Magazine-Made America: The Cultural Transformation of the Postwar Periodicals.* Cresskill, N.J.: Hampton Press, 1996. General-interest magazines both reflected and reinforced social values.

Ballou, Ellen B. *The Building of the House.* Boston, 1970. This thorough history of the *Atlantic Monthly* covers not only the editorial aspects of the company but also its business side.

Bass, Thomas A. *The Spy Who Loved Us: The Vietnam War and Pham Xuan An's Dangerous Game.* New York, 2009. Pham Xuan An worked as chief correspondent for *Time* magazine whom fellow journalists held in high regard, even as he won sixteen medals while serving as a spy for North Vietnam and providing it with strategic military information.

Baughman, James L. *Henry R. Luce and the Rise of the American News Media.* Twayne's Twentieth-Century American Biography Series. Boston, 1987. The author stresses Luce as a journalist rather than a publisher and analyzes his journalistic style.

Brinkley, Alan. *The Publisher: Henry Luce and His American Century.* New York, 2010. This biography provides a portrait of Luce's business ventures and private life.

Doss, Erika, ed. *Looking at Life Magazine.* Washington, D.C., 2001. This collection of *Life* magazine photographs shows how they captured some of the crucial events in American history.

Elson, Robert T. *Time Inc.: The Intimate History of a Publishing Enterprise, 1923-1941.* New York, 1968; and vol. 2, *The World of Time Inc.: The Intimate History of a Publishing Enterprise, 1941-1960.* New York, 1973. These two books provide not only an intimate history of Time Inc. and its leading figures, but also insight into the magazine publishing industry as well.

Endres, Kathleen, and Therese L. Lueck, eds. *Women's Periodicals in the United States: Consumer Magazines.* Westport, Conn., 1995. The authors provide a useful reference source on an important sector of the magazine business.

Farrell, Amy Erdman. *Yours in Sisterhood: Ms. Magazine and the Promise of Popular Feminism.* Chapel Hill, N.C., 1998. *Ms.*, a mass-market women's magazine, had an explicitly feminist agenda.

Goulden, Joseph C. *The Curtis Caper.* New York, 1965. The author examines the demise of the *Saturday Evening Post* after so many years of success.

Greenwald, Marilyn. *Cleveland Amory: Media Curmudgeon and Animal Rights Crusader.* Hanover, N.H., 2009. This biography of the critic Amory includes workings of the magazine industry and its personalities.

Heidenry, John. *Theirs Was the Kingdom: Lila and DeWitt Wallace and the Story of the Reader's Digest.* New York, 1993. This work is a critical examination of the magazine and its founders and editors.

Kitch, Carolyn. *Pages from the Past: History & Memory in American Magazines.* Chapel Hill, N.C., 2005. Magazines have played an important role in popular understanding of history.

Kornweibel, Theodore, Jr. *No Crystal Stair: Black Life and the Messenger, 1917-1928.* Westport, Conn., 1975. The *Messenger* was founded as a socialist organ; but once it became clear that the Socialist Party offered no promise for blacks, its publisher moved the magazine to a pro-business position and toward the center of

American mainstream politics.

Kunkel, Thomas. *Genius in Disguise: Harold Ross of The New Yorker.* New York, 1995. This work is a significant biography of the founder of *The New Yorker*.

Lyon, Peter. *Success Story: The Life and Times of S. S. McClure.* New York, 1963. McClure "revolutionized American journalism," editing "the best general magazine ever published anywhere." His exposure of political corruption, monopoly trusts, unscrupulous meat packers, etc., had a tremendous influence on legislation. He channeled creative writing into a more meaningful field.

Mott, Frank Luther. *A History of American Magazines, Sketches of 21 Magazines, 1905-1930.* Cambridge, Mass., 1968. This invaluable resource, the culmination of Mott's classic five-volume study of American magazines, includes information about the magazines.

Nourie, Alan, and Barbara Nourie, eds. *American Mass-Market Magazines.* New York, 1990. This essential reference for the student of magazines contains brief histories with bibliographies of 106 of the most significant mass magazines of the late nineteenth and the twentieth centuries.

Payne, Darwin. *The Man of Only Yesterday: Frederick Lewis Allen.* New York, 1975. The author provides an interesting look at the editorial workings of *Harper's*, *Atlantic Monthly*, and *The Century*.

Peterson, Theodore. *Magazines in the Twentieth Century.* Urbana, Ill., 1964. This account continues where Mott left off concerning modern magazines.

Sheed, Wilfrid. *Clare Booth Luce.* New York, 1982. The managing editor of *Vanity Fair* and originator of the concept for *Life* also wrote short stories, satire, and plays. She was a member of Congress, and in the 1950s she was U.S. ambassador to Italy.

Swanberg, W. A. *Luce and His Empire.* New York, 1972. This ia a readable and thorough account of the co-founder of *Time*.

Tebbel, John W. *George Horace Lorimer and The Saturday Evening Post.* Garden City, N.Y., 1948. This uncritical narrative of Lorimer and the *Post* covers the years before the *Post* headed toward its demise.

Thurber, James. *The Years With Ross.* Boston, 1957. This satisfying study of the demanding founder and editor of the *New Yorker* also provides an intimate portrait of the magazine.

Wainwright, Loudon. *The Great American Magazine: An Inside History of Life.* New York, 1986. The author of this fascinating anecdotal portrayal of *Life* worked there during its heydey.

Walker, Nancy A. *Shaping Our Mothers' World: American Women's Magazines.* Jackson, Miss., 2000. Magazines presented women both in traditional roles and as complicated humans.

Wood, James Playsted. *Lasting Interest: The Story of the Reader's Digest.* Garden City, N.Y., 1958. The author provides a friendly profile of the magazine and its rise from its origin as an idea.

ARTICLES

Anderson, Fenwick. "Inadequate to Prevent the Present: *The American Mercury* at 50." *Journalism Quarterly* 51 (1974): 297-302, 382. Founded by H.L. Mencken and George Jean Nathan in 1924 to ridicule the attitudes and values of the middle class, the magazine was sold a number of times to publishers who tried to make it succeed financially. By the 1950s it had become conservative.

Bennion, Sherilyn Cox. "Reform Agitation in the American Periodical Press, 1920-29." *Journalism Quarterly* 48 (1971): 692-9, 713. The mass magazines of the 1920s did not talk about reform because their readers did not want to hear about reform. Changes in society had occurred since before World War I, and magazines simply reflected the interests of the public; they were reflectors rather than molders of opinion.

Bissonette, Devan. "Between Silence and Self-Interest: *Time, Life,* and the Unsilent Generation's Coming-of-Age." *Journalism History* 35:2 (2009): 62-71. By the late 1950s, *Time* and *Life* magazines "began to examine youth culture, providing ample space for the coming unsilent generation to address, and at times contest, dominant cultural values."

Bullock, Penelope L. "Profile of a Periodical: The 'Voice of the Negro.'" *Atlanta Historical Bulletin* 21 (Spring 1977): 95-114. The establishment of the *Voice of the Negro* in 1904 "marked the substantive beginnings of the commercially published magazine in Atlanta." It reflected black life and provided a black interpretation of events, but it ceased publication after only two years.

Forde, Kathy Roberts. "Libel, Freedom of the Press, and the *New Yorker.*" *American Journalism* 23 (2006): 61-91. The *New Yorker* magazine "created editorial and legal procedures and strategies to combat libel complaints," since libel threats influenced its editorial "decision-making and processes, content, and use of human and financial resources."

Fowler, Gilbert L., Jr., and Edward J. Smith. "The Status of Magazine Group Ownership." *Journalism Quarterly* 56 (1979): 572-6. This brief study shows how magazine groups owned a large number of the nation's magazines.

Haygood, Daniel Marshall. "Henry Luce's Anti-Communist Legacy: An Analysis of U.S. News Magazines' Coverage of China's Cultural Revolution." *Journalism History* 35:2 (2009): 98-105. When Luce stepped down as chairman of Time Inc., his "anti-Communist legacy, and remaining influence as owner and 'editorial chairman,' did not have a ... lasting ... effect on the output of *Time.*"

Hirsch, Paul M. "An Analysis of *Ebony*: The Magazine and Its Readers." *Journalism Quarterly* 45 (1968): 261-70, 292. The author explains the magazine's appeal to a broad group of black readers.

Hoopes, Roy. "Birth of a Great Magazine." *American History Illustrated* 20, 5 (1986): 34-41. *Life* pioneered a new form of journalism and became "one of the great American magazines of the twentieth century."

"Hot Magazines Aim at Special Targets, The." *Business Week*, 2 May 1970, 64-74. This contemporary account examines the rise of special-interest magazines.

Hynes, Terry. "Magazine Portrayal of Women, 1911-1930." *Journalism Monographs* 72 (1981). Popular magazines did not portray liberated women as typical.

Johnson, Charles S. "The Rise of the Negro Magazine." *Journal of Negro History* 13 (January 1928): 7-21. Since the early 1800s the problems facing black magazines have been "in essence the same.... Increasing literacy, economic improvement, and the shifting facets of such general social questions as temperance, religion and morals, have determined largely the changes."

Julian, Bea. "Mass Magazines, 1900-Present: Serious Journalism or Mass Entertainment?" 259-70, in Wm. David Sloan, *Perspectives on Mass Communication History* (Hillsdale, N.J., 1991). This historiographical essay analyzes the approaches that historians have taken to explaining magazines during this period.

Mott, Frank Luther. "The Magazine Called 'Success.'" *Journalism Quarterly* 34 (1957): 46-50. "The signficance of the magazine *Success* [1897-1911] lies mainly in its embodiment of the cult of success that was so prominent an element of the national spirit at the beginning of the twentieth century, but it was also important as a popular general magazine and as a participant in the last phase of the muckraking movement."

Root, Christine V., and Robert Root. "Magazines in the United States: Dying or Thriving?" *Journalism Quarterly* 41 (1964): 15-22. The authors describe the transition of magazines between 1938 and 1963 into specialized publications.

Smith, Reed. "*Sports Illustrated's* African American Athlete Series as Socially Responsible Journalism." *American Journalism* 23:2 (2006): 45-68. Through a 1968 investigative series, *Sports Illustrated* was the first to take issue with discrimination in professional sports. The series was instrumental in raising public awareness as well as the level of social responsibility in sport reportage.

Stinson, Robert. "McClure's Road to *McClure's*: How Revolutionary Were 1890s Magazines?" *Journalism Quarterly* 47 (1970): 256-62. In founding *McClure's* magazine in 1893, S.S. McClure took what he considered to be a popular formula for magazines and aimed it at a mass audience through a low price.

Ward, Douglas B. "From Barbarian Farmers to Yeoman Consumers: Curtis Publishing Company and the Search for Rural America, 1910–1930." *American Journal* 22 (2005): 47-67. Curtis Publishing Company "saw the farm market as crucial to creating a truly national marketplace as a consumer economy in the United States began to expand rapidly."

Webb, Sheila. "The Tale of Advancement: *Life* Magazine's Construction of the Modern American Success Story." *Journalism History* 32:1 (2006): 2-12. In the late 1930s and the 1940s, *Life* magazine's success narratives injected essential creativity, individuality, and optimism into the construction of the modern American story of success.

21

Modern Advertising
1900 – Present

Advertising has experienced dramatic change since 1900, and the change has expressed itself in virtually every dimension of the business. The advertising industry actively participated in the often chaotic and frenetic events of the period. An integral part of the American business system, advertising was buffeted by forces both inside and outside the industry. It survived internal strife as its practitioners sought the most effective means of appealing to consumers. Detractors used the very methods and messages the industry created to question its value to society.

In 1900 advertisers spent $450 million to promote products in newspapers and magazines. Today, expenditures are in the hundreds of billions. The number of ad messages has expanded by a similar magnitude. Media that did not exist a century ago have exerted a profound influence on advertising and on society as well. Due, in part, to the proliferation of media and an abundance of goods with little differentiation, advertising's role in the marketing of products and services has become increasingly important.

Much of the change that occurred in advertising grew out of the nature of American society and the transformations that occurred in it — growth of and changes in population, development of new technologies, and the general affluence since the end of World War II. Advertising participated actively in this dynamic period. Early on, it helped bring an awareness of the fruits of industry into the home. It told consumers about automobiles, personal products, packaged goods, food, tobacco, candy, alcohol, and television and other appliances. It introduced figures who became national celebrities: Bob Hope, Jack Benny, Amos and Andy, and others. It created easily identifiable characters that gave products personalities with whom consumers could identify. Speedy Alka-Seltzer, the Jolly Green Giant, Aunt Jemima, and Elsie the Cow became as familiar as best friends. As society became more service oriented, advertising was pressed into the cause. In time, it was harnessed to political machinery as never before to help elect candidates to office. In recent years, the Internet has helped to revolutionize advertising.

What, then, is modern advertising? It is a process producing persuasive messages that sponsors pay media to carry. The pro-cess is complex — and face-to-face, digital, and special-event advertising make it even more complicated.

Modern advertising began simply enough a century and a half ago, with ad agencies serving as middlemen between marketers and the media. Ads were produced and placed in the media (primarily newspapers and magazines) that reached the greatest number of people. As society grew more complex and media rates increased, the advertising industry sought ways to maximize revenues by identifying and reaching specific groups of people. Some of the history of modern advertising relates to the development of the advertising process. That history is itself complex.

One reason is that advertising is not monolithic. The most visible segment of the industry produces advertisements seen nationwide on television and in magazines. The bulk of this work is done by large advertising agencies in the major business centers of the world. Most advertising, however, appears locally and comes from small local and regional agencies or from advertisers. In addition, the media themselves produce many of the advertising messages they carry. Moreover, advertising employs all the media to carry advertisements, thus further dividing the industry along message delivery lines. Some ads promote the sale of products and services. Some deal with political issues and candidates. Others seek to rent apartments or to find lost pets.

Partly because of its complexity, advertising did not respond effectively to several issues that troubled the industry year after year. As advertising's influence and visibility expanded, the industry and its critics tried to answer one basic question: what was the role of advertising in society? Was advertising a messenger? Did it exist to sell? Was it a service for consumers?

This basic inquiry touches on the three dimensions of advertising: economic, communicative, and societal. The advertising industry dealt continually with these dimensions, and they will appear repeatedly as we move through our story.

Economic. What was the role of advertising in marketing? Did it sell? Did it rigidify demand for specific products? If so, it was, as economists tended to claim, monopolistic. Or did it produce demand that resulted in economies of scale and reduced the prices of

Magazine Advertising, 1900
Magazine advertising at the beginning of the twentieth century typically included an illustration and display type, with the remaining space filled with informative copy. About one-half of all ads included a mail-in form.

products? If it did, then it had a competitive effect. The economic issue was of greatest interest to economists and marketing people.

Another element of the economic dimension was the financial support that advertising provided mass media. Print media typically derived up to about two-thirds of their revenue from advertisers. Broadcast media depended even more on advertising. Because advertisers provided the principal support for the American media system, however, a perennial issue was whether they deserved influence in the editorial process.

Communicative. Although advertising messages changed over the years, the basic question remained the same: should advertisements be hard-sell or soft-sell? Both views had their articulate and energetic advocates, and they often clashed. Before the twentieth century, little disagreement existed. Most advertisements were informational: For the most part they called attention to the availability of a product, perhaps providing some reasons for purchasing it. During the early years of the twentieth century the concept of advertising-as-salesman emerged, producing messages that sounded much like sales pitches, in contrast to the earlier infor-

mational advertisements. During the 1910s and 1920s, soft-sell approaches appeared, especially image building.

Societal. This dimension of advertising involved legal and ethical issues. Did advertising make people buy things they did not want and could not afford? Did it serve or manipulate people? Did advertising frame society's values, or did it reflect independently established conventions?

ALBERT LASKER AND THE BEGINNINGS OF MODERN ADVERTISING

The roots of modern advertising are normally associated with the early twentieth century in the United States. The nation was a confident youngster flooded with immigrants. Manufacturing and other activities attracted large numbers of people to mostly eastern cities. Literacy and educational levels were climbing. Newspapers with sensational content in large cities gained unprecedented circulations. Magazines also experienced extraordinary growth. Both media offered opportunities for manufacturers to reach large markets.

Typical magazine advertisements reflected the times. One for Baker's Chocolate, for example, showed factory scenes in the corners of the ad. A large picture of a maid carrying what appeared to be hot chocolate was situated in the middle of the ad. Large headline type provided the name of the advertiser, Walter Baker & Co., and one of its products, Breakfast Cocoa, above and below the maid. The remaining space was occupied by copy, which said, in part, of the company's chocolate: "The pure product of selected cocoa beans, to which nothing is added, and from which nothing is taken away. Celebrated for more than a century as a delicious, nutritious and flesh-forming beverage. Best plain chocolate in the market for cooking purposes."[1]

About half of the magazine ads during the first decade of the century sought a response by mail from consumers, and about a fifth of all ads were for food and drink products. During the following decade, food accounted for slightly less than a third of all ads.

From the standpoint of the message, advertising lacked a sense of direction. It was largely passive. Albert Lasker, a partner in one of the nation's largest advertising agencies, found himself puzzling over the role of advertising and the effects that role had on the advertisement itself.

In the first few years of the twentieth century, Lasker rose rapidly to the top of Lord & Thomas, one of three major agencies in the nation, although its billings in 1898 were less than a million dollars. Others were N.W. Ayer & Son and J. Walter Thompson. In his early twenties, Lasker was to become one of the dominant and most influential figures in American advertising, playing a major role in its development.

Lasker was born in 1880 and grew up in Galveston, Texas, where his father, Morris, was a prosperous businessman and a

[1]Reprinted in Susan Strasser, *Satisfaction Guaranteed: The Making of the American Mass Market* (New York, 1989), 114.

Albert Lasker
One of the dominant figures in advertising history, Albert Lasker was instrumental in determining the approaches that ads should take. He asked one question about the effectiveness of an ad: "Will it move the goods profitably?" Arguably a genius with an insatiable curiosity, he never stopped asking questions. His most notable one was the famous, essential inquiry, "What is advertising?" John E. Kennedy gave him the even more famous answer: "Salesmanship in print."

towering figure in young Albert's life. By the time he was 12 years old, Albert had started a weekly newspaper that he published for a year. In high school, he involved himself in a busy array of activities, at the same time writing for the local daily newspaper and working for his father. High energy characterized him as a young man. Throughout his life, this quality proved helpful to him, but he also had several breakdowns.

He was also resourceful. While writing for the Galveston daily newspaper as a teenager, he wrangled an interview with a visiting celebrity by posing as a Western Union messenger boy. No other local reporter talked to the visitor. As a young man of eighteen ready to embark on his career, Lasker seemed determined to become a newspaperman, but his father's stern resolve forced him to reconsider. Morris Lasker thought that journalists drank too much, and he extracted from his son a promise that he would take another job for a brief period. The elder Lasker prevailed upon Lord & Thomas to repay a favor and hire his son as an office boy.

In 1898, Albert made the two-day train trip from Galveston to Chicago. He planned to be away only a few months but stayed with Lord & Thomas until, as sole owner, he closed it on December 31, 1942. His starting salary was $10 a week, and his duties involved the usual grubby responsibilities assigned to office boys. He might have made good on his plans to leave Chicago shortly after arrival, but a large gambling debt incurred during his first weeks on the job forced him to borrow from one of the agency's owners and thus remain long enough to repay the loan.

In order to increase his salary and reimburse the lender more quickly, Lasker began focusing his talents on his job. His performance led rapidly to responsibilities as a full-time salesman at a salary ten times the one at which he began and then quickly to twenty times his starting salary. The retirement of one of the firm's founders in 1903 gave him an opportunity to purchase a partnership. As a partner, he got a salary increase to $52,000 a year. In time, the death of the other founder made him the sole owner. During his forty-four years with Lord & Thomas, he earned about $45 million.

"SALESMANSHIP IN PRINT"

Lasker as partner became responsible for writing ads at the agency, and he became increasingly troubled by the question, "What is advertising?" He sought the advice of the best people in the business, but none satisfied him. One day a copywriter from another city came to Lord & Thomas and offered an answer.

Advertising is "salesmanship in print," John E. Kennedy told Lasker. Kennedy then gave him lessons about making this definition work. Readers of ads must be given reasons why they should purchase the product. Thus, an ad must sound much like the presentation a salesperson makes to prospects. It must answer questions a customer may have. Therefore, it must contain long copy that is positive and persuasive.

This concept, sometimes called the "reason why" approach, would guide Lasker throughout his professional career. He argued heatedly against ads that strayed away from this hard-sell approach. This copy philosophy accounted for most of the approximately $750 million in billings that Lord & Thomas placed during its seventy years of life.

Kennedy had learned the idea of advertising-as-salesman earlier in his career from others who had developed it. Lasker polished the concept and brought attention to it. He trained copywriters — his own and those of other agencies — in this approach. Lord & Thomas printed and distributed thousands of copies of a booklet that touted the idea.

Kennedy, who had drifted from job to job before his meeting with Lasker, joined Lord & Thomas as a copywriter. He worked slowly and ponderously and remained with the agency only about two years. His replacement was Claude C. Hopkins, who shared Kennedy's copy philosophy, but whose work habits were vastly different. He toiled long hours every day, including weekends, and wrote prolifically and rapidly.

Salesmanship in Print
Albert Lasker and John E. Kennedy believed advertisements must act much like the presentation that a salesperson for a product would make in person. They therefore advocated long copy that was positive and persuasive, as in this automobile ad.

His views of advertising were embodied in *Scientific Advertising*, a 1923 volume that supported its title: "The time has come when advertising has in some hands reached the status of a science. It is based on fixed principles and is reasonably exact." And elsewhere in the book: "Advertising is multiplied salesmanship. It may appeal to thousands while the salesman talks to one."[2]

Hopkins proved to be well ahead of his time by employing a technique in his ad copy of emphasizing something unusual and memorable about a product. In one ad, written before he joined Lord & Thomas, he stressed the purity of Schlitz beer because the brewery steam-cleaned its bottles. All breweries, of course, did the same thing, but Hopkins preempted the idea and offered it as an argument for drinking Schlitz. In another ad, written at Lord & Thomas, he said that Quaker's puffed wheat and rice were "shot from guns." This technique of emphasizing something noteworthy about the product was popularized later by Rosser Reeves, president and chairman at the Ted Bates agency, who developed it as a "unique selling proposition," or USP. Hopkins also popular-

ized the use of coupons in ads that people could use to obtain a free sample of a product.

THE RESORS AND PSYCHOLOGY IN ADVERTISING

As Lasker, Kennedy, and Hopkins were emphasizing hard-sell copy, competing agencies were developing other approaches. During the latter part of the nineteenth century, a literary quality had found its way into copy, replacing much of the straightforward listings and descriptions that had been used in American advertising for most of its first two centuries. Some people in the field rejected the literary approach. Arguing that art did not sell, they opened the way for the "salesmanship-in-print" philosophy that Kennedy espoused and Lasker promoted vigorously. Soon, others began to find great power in advertising copy that suggested rather than insisted and operated at the consumer's subconscious rather than at the conscious level. Walter Dill Scott's seminal book, *The Psychology of Advertising* (1908), supported this new view of copy.

Among the leaders of this psychological approach were the J. Walter Thompson agency and its dynamic leader, Stanley Resor. Founded under a different name toward the end of the Civil War, JWT handled mostly religious advertising until James Walter Thompson purchased it for $1,300 in 1878 and moved forcefully into the burgeoning field of magazine advertising. Thirty years later, he had tired and had lost touch, and the agency had declined. In 1908, Resor joined the agency as manager of the Cincinnati office. Four years later he was in New York as vice-president and general manager. In 1916, a group under Resor bought J. Walter Thompson for $500,000, and Resor became president. The agency was billing about $3 million a year.

Resor's vision of an advertising agency greatly broadened its role. Instead of only buying space and providing copy for advertisements, Resor saw the agency as an integral part of an advertiser's selling program. Moreover, he employed research and the social sciences, especially psychology, to help advertisers in their sales efforts.

Resor was not a copywriter and therefore relied on Helen Lansdowne to develop the actual ads. With one interruption, the two had been together since Resor's days as manager of the Cincinnati office of JWT. In 1917, they married and continued to run the company. While Lansdowne did not totally reject the reason-why approach to copy, her messages tended toward the emotional. For Woodbury's Soap she developed a sensual advertisement with the theme line, "For the skin you love to touch."

Another example of the type of ad that was challenging the popular reason-why approach was developed in 1915 for Cadillac. Titled "The Penalty of Leadership," it promoted pride in the status of Cadillac. The name of the automobile appeared only once in the ad, and the message never mentioned that the product being advertised was an automobile. In a distinguished looking layout employing a conservative type face and considerable white space, the ad delivered the key message that leaders drive Cadillacs. The ad,

---

[2]Claude C. Hopkins, *My Life in Advertising & Scientific Advertising* (Lincolnwood, Ill., 1986), 213 and 221. Two books are contained in this edition. *Scientific Advertising* was originally published in 1923, and *My Life in Advertising* in 1927.

Live Your Romances!
Keep That Schoolgirl Complexion!

The Slogan That Sold Soap
Employing Stanley Resor and Helen Lansdowne's device of appealing to the emotions and the subconscious, Palmolive soap experienced substantial increases in sales in the 1920s using the slogan "Keep That Schoolgirl Complexion."

which is reproduced on page 418, read:

The leader is assailed because he is a leader, and the effort to equal him is merely added proof of that leadership. Failing to equal or to excel, the follower seeks to depreciate and to destroy — but only confirms once more the superiority of that which he strives to supplant.

TRUTH-IN-ADVERTISING AND OTHER REFORMS

While the debate about how to write copy continued within advertising circles, an external storm was nearing a climax. It had been developing for many years.

A steady river of advertising messages during the nineteenth century promoting patent medicines and all manner of quackery had created a basic doubt about the honesty and trustworthiness of advertising. Concerned about the future of their livelihood, people in the business began considering options for dealing with false and misleading advertising. By the 1890s they were beginning to organize local advertising clubs: Denver in 1892, Chicago in 1894, New York City in 1896, Seattle in 1902, and Cincinnati and Spokane in 1903. A truth-in-advertising movement appeared with-

in the business to enforce local standards on advertisers.

The problem, however, extended beyond municipal borders. In response, regional organizations emerged, in part to face the issue of false and misleading advertising. In 1904 the West Coast Advertising Men's Association was established, and two years later the Associated Advertising Clubs of America originated from a meeting in St. Louis.

While undertaking other projects — the west coast group, for example, helped to tell the world that San Francisco after its 1906 earthquake was now an excellent place to live — advertising organizations continued to press their commitment to truth in advertising. A vigilance committee of the San Francisco ad club told members in 1915 that it intended to take "definite action [against] those using illegitimate methods of advertising.... [The committee] is completely organized, it has been assured of the cooperation of Judges, the District Attorney and the Police Department, and its own members are capable and ready to act as special prosecutors in any case undertaken...."[3]

Members of the renamed Pacific Coast Advertising Men's Association pushed legislation in western states to regulate advertising. In the East, the Associated Advertising Clubs of America organized a national vigilance committee at its 1911 convention, launching a national truth-in-advertising movement and, in the process, the predecessor of the Better Business Bureaus. Numerous other ad clubs also formed local vigilance committees.

In 1911, *Printer's Ink* magazine, an advertising trade publication, offered its model statute for control of false and deceptive advertising. The proposed legislation declared that "Any person, firm, corporation, or association who, with intent to sell or in any way dispose of merchandise, securities, service, or anything ..., makes, publishes, disseminates, circulates, or places before the public, in this state, in a newspaper or other publication ... or in any other way, an advertisement ... which ... contains any assertion, representation or statement of fact which is untrue, deceptive, or misleading, shall be guilty of a misdemeanor."[4] Most states adopted the statute in some form.

At the same time that the advertising industry was running its own programs to control abuses, outside parties began pressing their case. Progressive reformers, with the muckrakers in the lead, wanted to cleanse society. Big business and advertising attracted their attention — patent medicine advertising in particular. The Progressives achieved most of their objectives. Along with other reforms, they played a role in the passage of legislation that created the Federal Trade Commission (1914), which gradually assumed significant control over advertising. In addition, a 1912 law required that all editorial material for which newspapers and magazines were paid be labeled as advertising.

Also helping to improve advertising was the formation of the American Association of Advertising Agencies in 1917 during a meeting of 150 agency presidents. Of the 1,400 agencies in exis-

---

[3]Quoted in Bruce Roche, "AAF ROOTS: A History of the American Advertising Federation," *(E)xchange* (February 1983): 3.
[4]Quoted in H.J. Kenner, *The Fight for Truth in Advertising* (New York, 1936), 27-8.

Cadillac Pride
Developed in 1915, "The Penalty of Leadership" advertisement was designed to promote pride in ownership of the Cadillac automobile. The conservative design of the ad was intended to reflect the status of Cadillac.

tence, only N. W. Ayer & Son of the larger ones did not affiliate. The largest agency in number of clients, Ayer had 391, followed by Lord & Thomas with 139 and J. Walter Thompson with 119.

ADVERTISING DURING WAR AND GOOD TIMES

As the Progressives and forces within the advertising industry were achieving some victories, the attention of the nation was drawn increasingly to Europe, where a war of unprecedented magnitude raged. After resisting involvement for three years, the United States finally entered World War I in 1917. Albert Lasker's response was indicative of how the war engaged advertising. He served briefly in the administration of President Woodrow Wilson. The secretary of agriculture, for whom Lasker worked as an assistant, used Lasker's familiarity with the marketing of foods to assist with programs designed to encourage home canning.

Lasker symbolized the public-spirited response to the war effort by many in advertising and by the industry itself. Shortly after President Wilson, by executive order, established the Committee on Public Information in April 1917, representatives of the advertising industry contacted its chairman, journalist George Creel, and offered assistance.[5] Wilson authorized the formation of an ad-

vertising division within the CPI. By this act, Creel said later, "every advertising man in the United States was enrolled in America's second line, and from the very moment of their enrollment, we could feel the quickening of effort, the intensification of endeavor."[6]

The advertising division harnessed the efforts of media, advertisers, agencies, ad clubs, and other components of the industry to the execution of numerous campaigns. For example, it developed a communication plan by which 13 million American men between the ages of 18 and 45 were told that they must register for possible military service. Creel estimated after the war that the value of the advertising division's work approximated $5 million, including contributions of space by media and the time and talent that advertising professionals donated. Creel's figure also included ad space that private business purchased and gave the government.

While some businesses directly supported the war effort, others chose to reduce or eliminate advertising because they lacked raw materials to produce goods or because their entire output was going to the government. Still others continued regular advertising schedules. In their messages, they sometimes promoted products as usual, but they also used them to tell the public of the advertisers' contributions to the military effort, to promote worthy war-related projects — such as the sale of Liberty Bonds to help finance the war — and to remind people that a company's products would be available again after the cessation of fighting.

When the war ended in 1918, the nation entered a decade of prosperity. Although the agricultural sector lagged behind, a general affluence permeated society. The return of consumer goods and the ability to purchase them produced good times for business and for advertising.

Advertising was maturing by the 1920s. Of all ads in print media, 40% were full page, and about three out of four focused on product benefits rather than features. Psychology was replacing "salesmanship in print." Personal care products replaced food as the largest category being advertised. Sexiness was the dominant theme in magazine ads, appearing in one out of four.

The appearance of another advertising medium, radio, added to the mix. Radio was the first totally new advertising medium since newspapers. The first commercial station went on the air in 1920, and the number of profit-making stations mushroomed. Initially, though, the use of ads on radio encountered resistance. Newspapers saw a threat to their income, and many leaders within radio itself did not favor commercial messages, fearing an intrusion on the service-oriented nature of the medium. In spite of this opposition, some stations saw an opportunity to make money — lots of money — and began offering time to advertisers.

Early radio advertising time was purchased in longer blocks than today's 30- or 60-second announcements. In 1922, New York

---

[5]Fleming Newbold, chairman of the Bureau of Advertising of the American Newspaper

Publishers Association, to George Creel, Nov. 23, 1917; Creel to Newbold, Dec. 1, 1917; Alan C. Reiley, president of the Association of National Advertisers, to Creel, Nov. 21, 1917; and Creel to Reiley, Dec. 1, 1917. This correspondence is in the CPI Records, F.G. 63/CPI 1-A1, box 6, folder 149, National Archives, Washington, D.C.

[6]George Creel, *How We Advertised America* (New York, 1920), 158.

City radio station WEAF sold several ads for $50 to $100 each. The messages were woven into scripts about apartments the advertiser was offering for sale. By the end of the 1920s, ad messages were no longer enclosed in essays but rather were direct statements designed to encourage listeners to buy the sponsor's product. The amount of money spent on radio advertising grew rapidly. From nothing in 1920, advertisers invested $4 million in network advertising alone in 1927 and $10.5 million in 1928.

After Lasker initially resisted radio — a belief likely linked to his preference for long copy, which people could not understand easily by ear — he began to realize the new medium's advertising potential. During 1927 and 1928, Lord & Thomas spent almost as much money with the National Broadcasting Company as did all other agencies combined. It put *Amos 'n' Andy* on network radio for Pepsodent toothpaste. The show became a sensation, and sales of the toothpaste increased dramatically.

Much of the programming on radio was developed for advertisers. One of the earliest "soap operas" (so called because soap manufacturers sponsored the first programs), *The Story of Mary Marlin*, went on the air for Kleenex. Another, *Just Plain Bill*, was done for Kolynos toothpaste. Comedians such as Bob Hope and Jack Benny, Bing Crosby and other singers, and radio drama were used to reach audiences — audiences whose members were responsive to the new medium. The system worked well for advertisers and also for radio. In a capitalist economy during a decade oriented to business, the emergence of advertising as radio's financial base was probably inevitable.

At the same time that radio was growing as an advertising medium, the reason-why, salesmanship-in-print approach to copy was in decline. One reason, of course, was that print was no longer the only advertising medium. Another grew from the affluence of the 1920s. Still another related to Albert Lasker's temporary absence from the advertising scene.

As World War I was nearing an end, former President Theodore Roosevelt enticed Lasker into serving as the communications chief of the Republican National Committee. The party was out of power and needed campaign funds for both the 1918 congressional elections and the 1920 presidential election. Lasker's job was to handle the promotional aspects of the drive. He devoted three years to that and other political efforts, all within the Republican party, and another two years to a governmental post as chairman of the United States Shipping Board.

In 1923, after a five-year absence, Lasker returned to Lord & Thomas. He was not pleased with what he found. The other two of the big three agencies — N. W. Ayer & Son and J. Walter Thompson — had pulled even with or slightly ahead of Lord & Thomas in billings. Just as bad, Lord & Thomas had begun to stray from the gospel of reason-why copy. Lasker applied his energy with renewed dedication to correct these deficiencies.

He was now fighting more, though, than a philosophical war. The times had changed. Consumers had more options for purchases, including many luxuries. Moreover, the affluence of the 1920s was changing the way people viewed the world and the way they responded to persuasive messages. Intangibles became as important as the physical characteristics of a product. Advertisers carried the psychological appeals in a Woodbury's Soap message ("for the skin you love to touch") and the "pride" element in Cadillac leadership yet another step. They began talking about what the consumer became by using a product.

This change provided the introduction of the image-building copy appeal, which sought to establish an atmosphere about a product. No ad caught the spirit of this new appeal more than one developed by a former copywriter at Lord & Thomas who had gone into the automobile business. Ned Jordan fashioned a message that created a tight relationship between the spirit of the times and his automobile. The ad was published in 1923 in the *Saturday Evening Post*. Beneath a stylized drawing of a roadster and a horse being driven at punishing speed by a cowboy and a young woman, respectively, the copy began: "Somewhere west of Laramie there's a bronco-busting, steer-roping girl who knows what I'm talking about."[7] The words painted a sensuous canvas in

[7]*Saturday Evening Post*, 23 June 1923, 129.

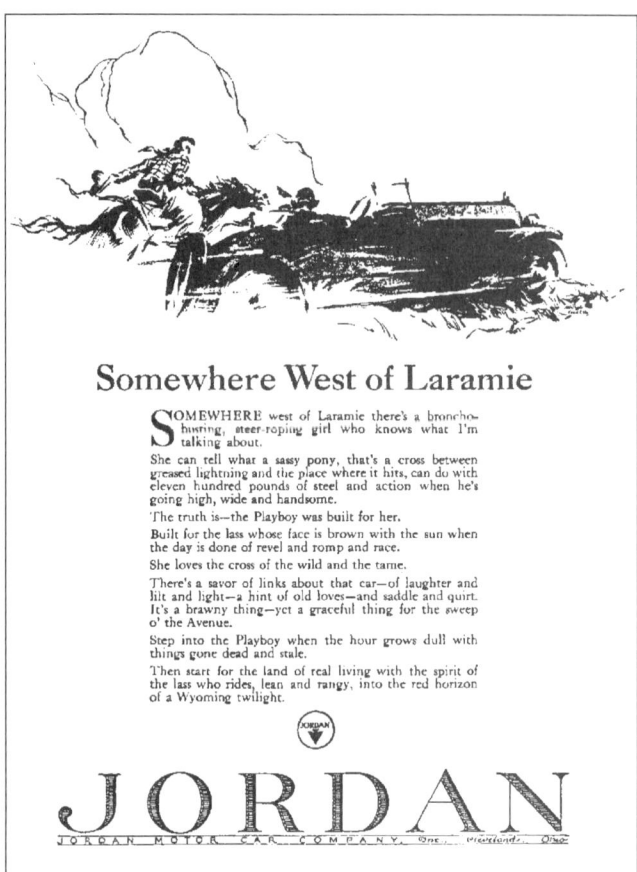

"Somewhere West of Laramie"
This 1923 ad for Jordan automobiles is one of the best examples of the image-building approach to advertising. Rather than listing the tangible, mechanical qualities of the cars, it presented an image of the lifestyle that one could obtain through ownership of them.

the mind. They told not of pistons and rings or even of styling or leadership, but of an ambiance. The ad implied that the purchaser would buy not just an automobile but a lifestyle.

Traditional reason-why copy, on the other hand, sounded dull in comparison. Another car ad, for example, explained:

In the construction of Dodge Brothers Motor Car, every consideration has been given to the owner's safety. This is particularly evident in the brakes, which, with their 14-inch drums and 2 1/4 inch lining, are appreciably larger than the average. The extra surface thus provided develops friction when the brake bands contract over the drums — and it is this friction which stops the car....[8]

Social psychologist Roger Brown provided, in the 1960s, a rationale for the power of image-building ads. "When people," he explained, "are living well above the subsistence level — when food, drink, transportation, and shelter are all adequate — they begin to be interested in buying expressive symbols. A desirable symbol is any product that will suggest that its owner is the kind

of person he wants to be — rich, virile, devil-may-care, thoughtful, youthful, cultivated, or what-you-will."[9] Some advertising professionals in the 1920s seem to have learned that lesson forty years before Brown wrote it.

Prosperity and social status dominated the themes in national ads of the 1920s. Automobiles were placed in settings such as the golf course and resorts. Maids were shown in ads for common products such as soaps and polishing wax. Ads for products such as underarm deodorant, coffee, and linoleum suggested that the advertised item would add to the social prestige of its purchaser.[10]

Historian Roland Marchand, in his book *Advertising the American Dream: Making Way for Modernity* (1985), concluded that 1920s advertising introduced people into a modern consumer culture. The images the ads created, he argued, were more associated with the ideal society that the agency copywriters envisioned than with reality. His contention conflicts with the general notion among historians that ads reflect the values and conventions of their time.

There were other dimensions to advertising in the 1920s. The first Burma-Shave roadside signs offering brief commercial homilies were posted in 1925:

HE HAD THE RING /
HE HAD THE FLAT /
BUT SHE FELT HIS CHIN /
AND THAT WAS THAT /
BURMA-SHAVE

The last year for the signs was 1963.

During the '20s, advertising helped market an army of new products that grew out of technological advances; and the general affluence of the nation permitted a great many people to purchase them: automobiles, radio sets, and refrigerators, among other electrical appliances. In addition to conveniences, such items became status symbols.

At the same time, ads began offering solutions to hygienic problems such as bad breath, body odor, and athlete's foot. Some people found distasteful this intrusion into individual privacy and public discussion of these private matters.

The negative approach that ads took to these personal problems also found its way into the volatile cigarette competition that characterized the 1920s. Three major tobacco companies — American, Liggett & Myers, and Reynolds — were fighting for control of the cigarette market. American Tobacco's George Washington Hill and Albert Lasker developed a campaign to encourage women to "Reach for a Lucky instead of a sweet," a reference to Lucky Strike cigarettes. This approach solved two concerns of the decade: women smoking and obesity. The two men saw that if they could overcome society's taboo against women smoking, they potentially could double cigarette sales. To do that, they raised the specter of fatness produced by eating too many candies

[8]Reprinted in Frank Rowsome, Jr., *They Laughed When I Sat Down* (New York, 1959), 122.

[9]Roger Brown, *Social Psychology* (New York, 1965), 567.
[10]Tammie Byrd-Howard, "Advertising in the *Ladies' Home Journal* from 1923-1945," unpublished masters thesis (University of Alabama, 1991).

Helps you men look your best

How a certain ingredient in Williams' actually benefits the skin

MEN used to think that all a shaving soap could do was to give a good heavy lather. But the makers of Williams' were not content with a shaving soap that merely did that. They knew the troubles men have with sensitive skins. They knew they could help those men—all men—by giving them a soap which is beneficial to the skin also.

What one ingredient does

There is in Williams' a certain ingredient which is distinctly helpful to the skin, leaving it supple, soft and pliant after every shave. You can feel the smoothness of this ingredient by simply rubbing a bit of Williams' Shaving Cream between your fingers.

Williams' lather containing this ingredient is heavier, thicker, more profuse than you are accustomed to. It acts as a cushion for the edge of your blade, keeping the skin resilient and making the whole shave a delightful one.

Soothing after-effect

After the shave, this same ingredient has a pronounced soothing effect on the skin. You are pleasantly aware of this effect because of the feeling of utter comfort and relief that comes at the end of every Williams' shave. Use Williams' regularly and see how helpful to your face it is.

Trial Tube Free

On request, we will send you a "Get Acquainted" tube which contains enough Williams' Shaving Cream to let you test it fully. Mail coupon below.

For men who prefer the Stick, Williams' Holder Top Stick gives you the genuine Williams' in stick form.

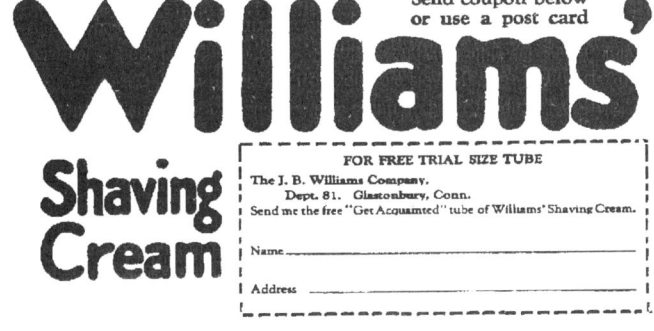

Send coupon below or use a post card

Williams'

Shaving Cream

FOR FREE TRIAL SIZE TUBE
The J. B. Williams Company.
Dept. 81. Glastonbury, Conn.
Send me the free "Get Acquainted" tube of Williams' Shaving Cream.

Name _____

Address _____

Advertising Prosperity

Reflecting the prosperity of the 1920s, advertising appealed to consumers' desires for social status. Many ads, such as this one for a men's shaving cream, were set in posh locations and included characters of obvious social standing. Ads even for everyday products such as hosiery and canned foods often included maids and butlers or incorporated exotic locales. Although not all Americans lived in such conditions, the ads appealed to their interest in having a high material standard of living.

and connected cigarette smoking with beauty.

ADVERTISING DURING HARD TIMES

The wide-open '20s, good times, and affluence ended with the closing months of 1929. An abrupt crash in the stock market spread into a deep economic depression that lasted for more than ten years. Business, the darling of the 1920s, suffered severe losses during the 1930s. Banks closed — more than 2,000 in 1931 — and bankruptcy was common. Industrial stocks fell in 1933 to a fifth of their 1929 value. Agriculture had not shared the prosperity of the 1920s with the rest of the nation, and it experienced even more hardship during the Great Depression. About a quarter of the work force was unemployed. For those who did work, salaries fell. Welfare assistance was severely limited, compared to the needs of the destitute. Soup kitchens, with their free meals, attracted long lines.

Advertising suffered the same fate as the rest of the economy. Nationally, ad expenditures had risen from $1.9 billion in 1919 to $2.9 billion a decade later. In 1933, however, at the deepest point of the Depression, advertisers spent only about half of their 1929 expenditures. For most of the 1930s, spending remained at less than $2 billion per year.

Critics attacked business in their search for a culprit, and advertising — one of the most visible components of business — did not escape. Earlier detractors, such as the muckrakers, had directed their fire largely at the content of ads. Now the critics turned on the institution itself, raising the issue of whether advertising was necessary in a supposedly rational society. Researchers probed into consumer motivation and found that purchasing decisions often had emotional rather than rational bases.

Society's indictment of business produced massive regulation in the 1930s. Advertising did not escape. Congress passed laws tightening controls over advertising. It greatly strengthened the power of the Federal Trade Commission, which had been established in 1914, to regulate advertising. In 1934 it established the Federal Communication Commission and gave it some indirect authority over advertising. The Treasury Department was given power over advertising and other practices of the liquor, wine, and beer industries.

Society's displeasure with business and advertising also was expressed through an active consumer movement, which led to the formation in 1936 of the Consumers Union, a nonprofit organization. It sought to provide consumers information on products and services by distributing information through a monthly publication, *Consumer Reports*, which carried no advertising. Consumers Union quickly acquired 37,000 members and still exists today, testing and reporting on products and on questionable advertising and marketing practices.

An earlier organization, Consumer Research, was founded in 1927. After the Depression began, its membership doubled. CR's 1933 book *1,000,000 Guinea Pigs*, which reported on misleading advertising in the drug and cosmetics industry, was a best seller.

Depression Advertising
The hard economic times of the Great Depression of the 1930s saw advertising shift away from the emphasis on prosperity that had characterized the 1920s. In its place appeared the theme of thrift. Gone were the exotic and elegant locales, and replacing them were commonplace situations, such as the modest kitchen in this ad, which was presented as affordable rather than elegant.

Scrutinized from the outside, advertisers also adapted to the realities of the Depression. Their ads reflected the severe conditions. Fear appeals and testimonials gained widespread use. An increased use of comic strip ads demonstrated that advertisers were working harder to deliver their messages to consumers. The use of black-and-white photography increased dramatically. Layouts became bolder and plainer, and hard-sell appeals more common.

In magazines such as *Ladies' Home Journal*, themes of economy and thrift, not surprisingly, were popular. Basic products such as household cleaners and toothpaste were more prone to use these themes. Woodbury's Soap, for example, changed from its 1920s approach that socially prominent women use its product to one emphasizing that Woodbury's lower price did not mean lower quality. Similarly, a soup company that had advertised its product as part of a meal during the 1920s now offered its soup as a meal by itself.

Although most advertisers were not moved by altruistic motives, they assisted the national morale during the Depression by sponsoring entertaining radio programs that helped people forget the misery they saw around them daily. These included daytime soap operas such as *Ma Perkins* and *Our Gal Sunday* sponsored by advertisers that used hard-sell commercials. Night-time radio ads were likely to be somewhat more sophisticated.

ADVERTISING AND WORLD WAR II

At the end of the 1930s, economic conditions — though not appreciably better than at the beginning of the Depression — had at least stabilized. The nation appeared to face a prolonged future of economic downturn. Events abroad, however, would radically change that prospect. Throughout the decade, the nation, wrestling with economic woes, had fearfully watched small wars and preparation for a larger conflict occurring in Europe, Africa, and Asia. Then, as the United States was trying to avoid involvement, war hit the nation in December 1941. Business, which so lately had been reviled, was called to deliver the hardware necessary for the war effort. The nation went back to work. As employment rose, people again had money to spend. But on what? The entire output of some industries went to the military. Civilian goods were in short supply, with many rationed.

Learning from earlier marketers who stopped advertising under similar conditions and subsequently went out of business, many advertisers during World War II continued to tell the public about their products, advising people that the merchandise would be available again after the war. Governmental policy, which discouraged excess profits, also helped promote this practice. Products that were available, of course, were advertised.

Large national advertisers tied into the war effort in some way by encouraging the purchase of war bonds or by promoting a patriotic effort, often related to a company's business. Pabst Brewing Co., for example, toasted the enemy's navy. "Bottoms up," it said in an ad, with intended double meaning. A hat company cautioned against spreading rumors with an ad that said, "Keep it under your STETSON."

The formal contribution of the ad industry to the war effort came through the War Advertising Council. Volunteers from ad agencies, media, and business joined to produce and distribute ad campaigns supporting many aspects of the national effort to win the war. Similar to the Creel Committee during World War I, except that they functioned outside of government, advertising volunteers in the 1940s did campaigns for, among others, the Red Cross and war bonds. They also recruited women through ads for a variety of civilian and military jobs and encouraged people to grow some of their own food by planting Victory Gardens. The Council also served as a means for the radio industry to handle the inordinate number of requests it received from governmental agencies and other organizations to promote a variety of worthwhile projects associated with the war effort.

Altogether, the council produced 150 campaigns. Representatives of ad agencies and advertisers designed the campaigns, and media contributed hundreds of millions of dollars in space and time to carry the messages. In terms of the dollar value of in-kind contributions to its efforts, the council was infinitely more suc-

World War II Advertising

As it had done in the First World War, the advertising industry during World War II lent its aid to the American military effort. The War Advertising Council led the work. Many of the ads it produced, such as this one (left), were part of the national effort to raise money for the war through the sale of war bonds to the public. With many soldiers away during World War II, advertisers frequently used war themes and aimed their messages at women on the homefront. This ad for Listerine (middle) as an antiseptic and mouthwash included a serviceman in uniform and encouraged women to keep up their morale and health.

cessful than its World War I counterpart, so successful in fact that its work was converted to peacetime. The organization dropped "War" from its title and became simply the Advertising Council.

In its many years of peacetime service, the council has planned and executed numerous public service campaigns. Best known of its efforts probably is the one for the prevention of forest fires, which still features Smokey the Bear. Other campaigns were developed for Keep America Beautiful (with the slogan "Every Litter Bit Hurts"), the USO, the United Community Funds, and Better Schools. The council estimated that about $4 billion in media time and space and in agency commissions had been contributed during its first twenty-five years.

Magazine ad content in the 1940s showed continued emotional elements, with patriotism, courage, and sacrifice replacing fear. Ads were art heavy. As might be expected, war themes became popular. In *Ladies' Home Journal*, these themes found expression within a woman's context. Readers were urged to remain beautiful for the men in uniform. Other ads told women how they could assist with the war effort at home by preparing healthy meals and not wasting food.

The first full year of American involvement in the war was also the year that Albert Lasker, now in his 70s, decided to retire from advertising. By his own admission, he was tired. It may have been that advertising no longer represented a challenge to him. He was a Renaissance man, and his intellect demanded more than advertising could deliver in the 1940s. Moreover, the structure of business was changing, with advertising responsibilities moving down the corporate ladder. The change required him to work with the marketing department at corporations rather than with top-level management. He did not like the change because he considered the people at the highest echelon of a business his professional equals. One notable exception was the Lucky Strike account at American Tobacco Co., where Lord & Thomas continued to work with the mercurial George Washington Hill, president of the corporation.

So Lasker decided in the waning months of 1942 that he would close Lord & Thomas. He turned to the managers of the agency's three major offices — Los Angeles, Chicago, and New York — and offered to sell them the agency, which he insisted be renamed. They accepted, and the new agency came into existence on January 1, 1943. It was called Foote, Cone & Belding.

TELEVISION AND GOOD TIMES II

Experimental television broadcasting in the United States goes as far back as the 1920s. The first commercial may have been telecast as early as 1940. However, as TV was being developed, World War II interrupted. Rather than expand this new communication technology, scientists focused on the war.

When the end of the war in 1945 brought to a close a four-year shortage of consumer goods, the maturing of television was several years away; but long-awaited products such as automobiles and appliances became available quickly. At first, manufacturers could not meet consumer demand, and waiting lists were common. Advertising was not needed. As supply began to match demand shortly after the war, however, ads became necessary again in the competition for consumer business.

Radio, outdoor, and print media did most of the work during the last half of the 1940s, since television remained undeveloped. Starting in the late '40s, TV began its rapid ascent to become central to advertising. In 1950, advertisers spent $10 million on small screen commercial messages. In 2010, television, which passed newspapers in total ad expenditures in the 1990s, attracted about $64 billion.

The 1950s saw the solution of technical problems, the development of color TV, and an explosion in the number of local stations. The new medium had caught up with the good times of the postwar era, and it grew and prospered along with the economy.

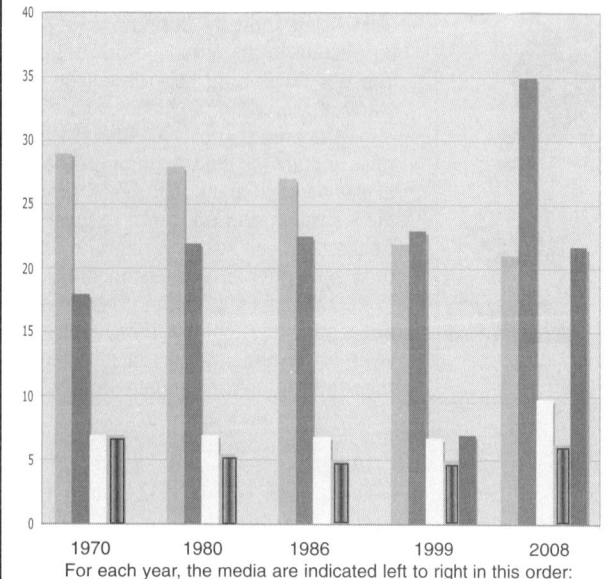

Percentage of Advertising Expenditures on Various Media 1970-2008

$ amounts are in billions

1970   1980   1986   1999   2008

For each year, the media are indicated left to right in this order: Newspapers, Television, Radio, Magazines, Internet (Internet for 1999 and 2008 only)

tisers to begin relying almost totally on 30- and 60-second spots.

ISSUES IN A NEW ADVERTISING AGE

Through print as well as broadcast media, the advocates of hard-sell and soft-sell continued their debate, both with some success. In a healthy economy, ads focused on benefits. During economic downfalls, they focused on features. During the 1950s, the over-whelming emphasis was on the benefits of products. Those favoring a highly creative message clearly won the battle in the 1960s. Led by Doyle Dane Bernbach, they created messages that got attention — with icons such as the Marlboro Man, the Jolly Green Giant, and the man with the black eye patch in the Hathaway shirt. During the 1960s, in print ads there was also heavy use of photographs and a continuing growth in the size of ads. A downturn in the economy during the 1970s returned hard-sell copy to the fore. That decade was also marked by an increase in couponing and in direct marketing. In the affluent 1980s, more creative messages again replaced hard-sell. Thus the conflict over copy philosophy continued.

The issue of advertising's role in society entered another dimension in the 1950s as political advertising and television were linked. Early on, critics charged that TV emphasized style over content, citing the Eisenhower commercials during the 1952 presidential campaign. One of the most controversial TV political commercials, broadcast by the Democratic Party during the 1964 presidential campaign, showed a little girl picking the petals from a flower while a voice intoned a countdown. Then came an atomic explosion and a message implying that the Republican candidate, Barry Goldwater, might lead the nation into a nuclear holocaust. During the 1968 election, advertising — especially through TV — stood accused by at least one critic of having "sold" Richard Nixon to the electorate.[11] In recent years, negative political commercials and print ads have become increasingly common and have attracted criticism.

Controversy has accompanied TV almost since the first commercial. People have called TV ads manipulative, annoying, boring, in poor taste, misleading, false, too loud, and too hard-sell. No doubt, examples could be found that justify each of these complaints. Nevertheless, such ads were generally effective; and the tactics continued. Along with crude commercials, though, entertaining and meaningful ones have also run. One of the best was a commercial that Coca-Cola used during the Christmas season showing young men and women of many races singing together on a mountain top.

The charge that TV commercials are manipulative — the same argument that has been leveled at all advertising — has been the most difficult to refute. They use sound, pictures, motion, immediacy, and emotion to carry the commercial message, and they *are* designed to be persuasive. Critics of TV advertising for children have been especially outspoken and have won concessions from advertisers, especially during Saturday-morning programming.

Paradoxically, the rise of this gargantuan mass medium occurred at a time when other media were facing decline. As television prospered, radio networks virtually disappeared, and radio splintered into thousands of local units and, as specialized programming for specific markets appeared, into yet smaller units. Traditional mass magazines began disappearing: *Life, Look,* and *Saturday Evening Post,* for example. In their place appeared an army of smaller publications designed for audiences with specialized interests. These new media would produce significant changes in message content. Readers of specialized magazines might, for example, be less prone to respond to image and more likely to read lengthy copy.

But this problem lay largely in the future, and the interest of advertising professionals in the 1950s and 1960s focused strongly on television. Arthur Godfrey emerged as TV's first advertising star. Art Linkletter also became highly visible. Both had popular programs. Cartoons were a popular format for commercials in TV's early years. Speedy Alka-Seltzer began a long run in 1952. Ten years later, Volkswagen and its agency — Doyle Dane Bernbach — started its ribbing of American automobiles with a commercial likening its van to a box. That was about the time that Pepsi-Cola began its battle with Coca-Cola. Coke responded to Pepsi's campaign with the slogan "Things go better with Coke."

Following the radio tradition, during television's first twenty years, sponsors owned most shows. By the early 1970s, however, the high cost of sponsorship and other problems associated with ownership — notably involving quiz shows — prompted adver-

[11]Joe McGinniss, *The Selling of the President 1968* (New York, 1969).

Advertising Icons

Below are *Advertising Age's* "Top 10 Ad Icons of the 20th Century." Can you name them?

Ad Characters Sell Product Brands, Become Part of American Culture

Advertising, in the first half of the 20th century, developed a strong product focus in an attempt to separate brands from nearly identical competitors. Ad campaigns were built around secret ingredients, new and improved formulas, and product features most often described using "-er" words such as bigger, brighter, and better.

Market segmentation gave advertisers and their agencies a new framework within which to address the changing audience of the late 1950s. Ad campaigns emphasized consumer benefits rather than product features alone. The newest and potentially most powerful audience delivery channel, television, offered advertisers the ability to use both sight and sound.

These combined market and media forces paved the way for greater use of advertising icons: characters who not only personify their brand but who, their creators hope, will become popular culture symbols representing the values of entire age groups. These characters are unique, as they were created for the sole purpose of selling products, meaning that they did not exist prior to their appearance in advertising. They have been used to communicate brand benefits to consumers and to establish associations in consumers' minds between the brand and qualities that consumers find desirable.

Television advertising brought many famous advertising icons to life and gave them staying power for decades – but others got their start much earlier. Aunt Jemima has one of the oldest icon pedigrees, dating back to the early 1890s when she first appeared on boxes of pancake mix. The Michelin Man was first rendered by an artist in 1898. Betty Crocker hosted the first radio cooking show in 1924. Elsie the Cow was first featured in a cartoon series for Borden in 1936.

The Green Giant was not so jolly when he first appeared in 1928 wearing a bearskin and a scowl. He was given a makeover by a young advertising copywriter named Leo Burnett, who went on to secure an important place in advertising icon history. His agency, Leo Burnett Worldwide, founded in 1935 in Chicago, created some of the most famous icons, including Tony the Tiger, Charlie the Tuna, the Pillsbury Doughboy, Morris the Cat, and the Marlboro Man. Burnett once said, "None of us can underestimate the glacier-like power of friendly familiarity."

In 1999, *Advertising Age* selected the Top 10 Ad Icons of the 20th Century based on their effectiveness, longevity, recognizability, and cultural impact. The list (in order) includes The Marlboro Man, Ronald McDonald, The Green Giant, Betty Crocker, The Energizer Bunny, The Pillsbury Doughboy, Aunt Jemima, The Michelin Man, Tony the Tiger, and Elsie the Cow. In 2010, the Advertising Icon Museum in Kansas City opened to provide an interpretation of their importance to our culture.

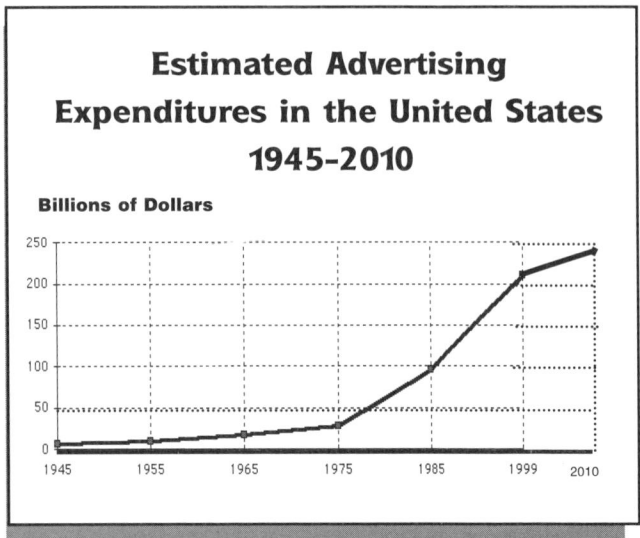

Estimated Advertising Expenditures in the United States 1945–2010

Billions of Dollars

Most visible of the critics charging manipulation were Vance Packard and Wilson Bryan Key. Their arguments were similar. In his 1957 book, *The Hidden Persuaders*, Packard claimed that advertisers used symbols in their messages to reach consumers' subconscious and stimulate the real reasons behind purchases. Key found all manner of sexual symbolism in ads, which he explored in *Subliminal Seduction*, first published in 1973. He said that advertisers embedded these symbols in their messages, and the symbols tapped into the powerful sex drive to obtain a response to the messages. Serious research has had difficulty finding support for Key's argument.

In response to some concerns of society, in 1971 the American Advertising Federation, the American Association of Advertising Agencies, the Association of National Advertisers, and the Council of Better Business Bureaus joined in forming the National Advertising Review Board. The NARB has proven effective at its task of policing national advertising and has spawned a number of local review boards.

As the federal government relaxed regulatory controls of advertising after 1980, state attorneys general moved more aggressively against national advertisers, with mixed results. In contrast, the courts have found in recent years that commercial speech — including advertising — enjoys limited First Amendment protection, although decisions have tended to hold advertisers to higher standards than are applied to non-commercial speech.

WOMEN AND MINORITIES

The advertising industry has not always encouraged the employment and promotion of women and minorities. During the early 1900s, advertising was a white male-dominated field. Accurate figures are difficult to obtain, but it is clear that the number of females employed in agencies did steadily increase after 1910 although it remained small. During the 1920s and 1930s, men outnumbered women by a ratio of ten to one. Women — with a few exceptions — were limited to secretarial and clerical responsibilities.

Despite their small numbers, women made an impact. They worked as copywriters at some of the largest agencies. Helen Lansdowne Resor of JWT and Dorothy Dignam of N. W. Ayer became famous for copywriting. Many female writers developed copy for products such as cosmetics, soaps, fashion, and housewares aimed at the female market. Women also worked as account executives and space buyers and headed research departments. For many years, though, they were excluded from ad clubs and other associations, which men headed. In response, women created their own clubs during the the 1930s for networking, camaraderie, and support.

After World War II, the number of women working in agencies grew substantially, and their ability to attain upper-management positions increased. Some — such as Jane Trahey, a well-known copywriter — opened their own agencies. Mary Wells was the first woman to rise to the status of principal at a major agency. One of the world's highest paid female executives, she worked as a copywriter for two agencies recognized for developing innovative ads, McCann-Erickson and Doyle Dane Bernbach. She created the "I Love New York" campaign and came up with the concept of painting Braniff jets outlandish colors in the late 1970s. She opened her own agency, Wells Rich Greene, in 1966 with Stew Greene and Dick Rich.

Although women entered the industry in small numbers in the early 1900s, African Americans and members of other ethnic groups did not. Advertisers did not recognize African Americans as potential consumers until the 1940s. Few worked in advertising until the 1960s. It was not uncommon, however, for advertisers to use them as trademarks to promote products. The R. T. Davis Mill and Manufacturing Company introduced "Aunt Jemima," a black maid, to sell its pancake flour in the 1890s. *Advertising Age* ranked Aunt Jemima as one of the twentieth century's top-ten advertising icons. In 1925 Emery Mapes, one of the owners of the Diamond Milling Company, decided to use "Rastus," with the face and smile of a black waiter he had met in Chicago, for the company's Cream of Wheat boxes. The Aunt Jemima and Rastus trademarks continue to adorn the packaging today.

Advertising's general neglect of ethnic groups as consumers, however, created opportunities for enterprising African Americans with products to market and promote. Former laundress and domestic C. J. Walker became the first black female millionaire by advertising and selling her hair straightener to African-American women in the early 1900s. In addition to ads in black newspapers, she trained agents to sell the product door-to-door and sold it in beauty salons. By 1911 her company grossed more than $100,000 annually. When she died in 1919, she left an estate worth more than $1 million.

Her success demonstrated that African Americans made up a lucrative consumer market. Advertisers, however, for the most part turned a blind eye until the civil rights movement made them impossible to ignore. Critics accused the ad industry of reinforcing racist and stereotypical images, and a 1964 article in the publica-

Subliminal Advertising

The Un-hidden persuaders

If you draw your conclusions from the self-styled experts in the field these days, advertising and selling are pretty sneaky stuff.

To hear these boys talk, you'd think advertising was one part psychiatry to two parts brainwashing, with a couple dashes of henbane and dragonwort thrown in.

We happen to think that most people buy things because they need, want, and can use them.

And that these people, regardless of their libidos or ids, like the kind of advertising that shows arresting pictures of these products and delivers fresh, truthful, interesting words about them.

Thank heavens, that's the kind of advertising our clients seem to like, too.

JAY THORPE 24 west 57

THE HIDDEN PERSUADERS
perfumes that gratify a lady and her "id" . . . motive enough for choosing her gift from the Jay Thorpe collection of internationally acclaimed fragrances.

RAPHAEL'S RÉPLIQUE
the perfume men love—on women—made, bottled and sealed in France . . . perfume, 10.00 to 50.00 . . . ¼ oz. purse atomizer, 5.00 . . . eau de toilette, 4.50 to 13.50 . . . bath oil, 3.00 and 5.00

'Hidden Persuaders' Help Sell Popcorn and Soda Pop

Beginning with early publishers adding woodblock illustrations to attract attention and create a favorable environment for their advertising messages, marketers have searched for more and more subtle ways to influence buyer behavior. Straightforward selling gave way to a gradual blending with other, less direct techniques, employing humor, positive associations, and other devices.

Then, as the practice of advertising began to mature approaching the middle of the twentieth century, innovative practitioners sought ways to utilize tools of the young science of psychology. The ultimate in advertising subtlety was to be subliminal advertising, a technique designed to present a message that could influence buying behavior at an unconscious level. That goal was accomplished, at least in theory, by presenting stimuli that were either so fast, so faint, or so small that a person received them below his threshold of conscious awareness and processed them with his subconscious mind.

The first publicized use of subliminal advertising was in 1956, when a theater in Fort Lee, New Jersey, flashed the words "popcorn" and "drink Coca-Cola" on the screen so quickly during the showing of a film that audience members were unaware it was happening. Concession sales of both popcorn and Coke, reports said, were overwhelming.

Public concern at the thought of being secretly manipulated by this type of advertising was fueled in large part by Vance Packard, who in 1957 in his popular book *The Hidden Persuaders* warned that consumers were becoming the unknowing victims of marketing "tricks" like subliminal advertising.

The federal government, as well as broadcast and movie industry groups, were quick to respond, pledging that no such psychological manipulation would be allowed. Today the controversy continues, with print ads most often accused of hiding messages within their artwork.

Advertisers responded in different ways to Vance Packard's claims of subliminal messages hidden in ads. One leading agency ran a house ad (top left) debunking the claim and declaring that effective advertising appealed directly to people's real needs. Other advertisers used the concept of sexual subliminal appeal to market their products, as the Jay Thorpe company did (top right) by calling its perfume "the hidden persuaders." Seagram's distillery used the idea of subliminal persuasion humorously in its ad (middle). The picture of the two glasses ran under the caption "Refreshing Seagram's Gin Has Hidden Pleasure. Welcome into the Fold." The ad then instructed the reader to fold the picture so that the two glasses overlapped. The resulting image (bottom) revealed a man and a woman, in a style reminiscent of the 1800s, in a swing.

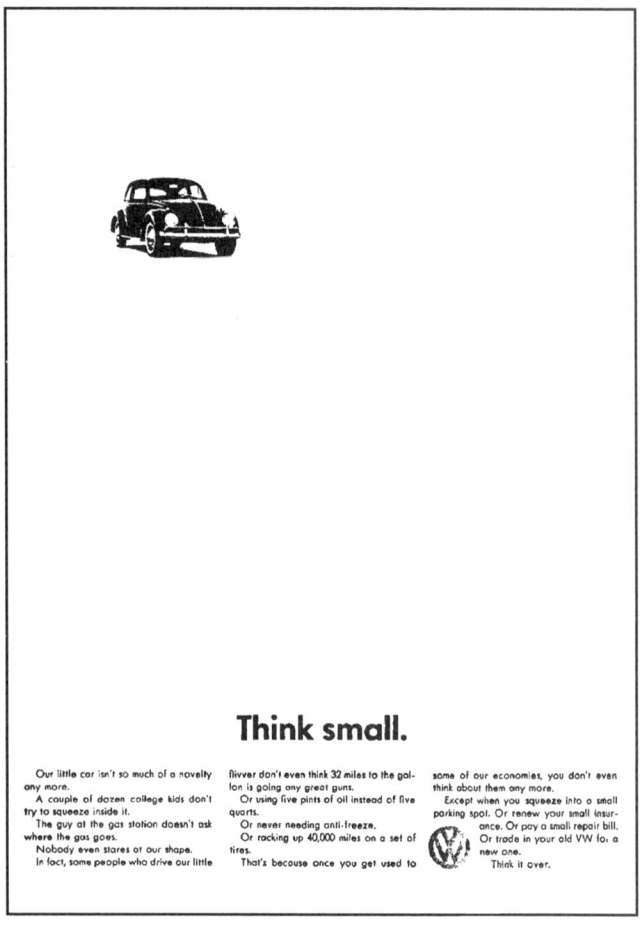

Think small.

Our little car isn't so much of a novelty any more.

A couple of dozen college kids don't try to squeeze inside it.

The guy at the gas station doesn't ask where the gas goes.

Nobody even stares at our shape.

In fact, some people who drive our little flivver don't even think 32 miles to the gallon is going any great guns.

Or using five pints of oil instead of five quarts.

Or never needing anti-freeze.

Or racking up 40,000 miles on a set of tires.

That's because once you get used to some of our economies, you don't even think about them any more.

Except when you squeeze into a small parking spot. Or renew your small insurance. Or pay a small repair bill.

Or trade in your old VW for a new one.

Think it over.

Advertising Bugs
The Doyle Dane Bernbach agency created a new wave in advertising with television and print ads for the Volkswagen Beetle in 1960. Its witty approach was picked up by other advertisers, such as the Avis automobile-rental company, whose slogan became "We Try Harder," referring to its market position behind the Hertz company.

tion *Variety* criticized agencies for not keeping up with social changes. However, the Civil Rights Act of 1964, educational opportunities, rising incomes, and other factors encouraged businesses to see minorities as a large potential market.

African Americans also began to work in most agencies. Douglass Alligood joined Batten, Barton, Durstine & Osborn (BBDO) in 1962 as an account executive, working on campaigns for Dodge cars and trucks, Pepsi-Cola, and Ford's Autolite division. Tom Sims began his career at Elmer Roper & Associates, moved to BBDO, and in 1967 became vice-president of McCann-Erickson. William Sharp served as advertising manager of Coca-Cola and held the highest office in the American Advertising Federation, one of the industry's major professional groups.

As employment opportunities in large agencies increased, several African Americans turned their experience into opportunities for self-employment. Vince Cullers founded Vince Cullers Advertising, one of the first black-owned agencies, in 1956. Tom Burrell began his career in the mailroom of Wade Advertising in Detroit. After working twelve years as a copywriter and copy supervisor at Leo Burnett and Needham Harper Speers, he teamed with Ed

McBain of Vince Cullers Advertising and opened Burrell McBain in Chicago in 1971. The agency's name was changed to Burrell Communications in 1992. It specialized in advertising targeted to African Americans for clients such as McDonald's, Coca-Cola, Procter & Gamble, and Stroh Brewery. Although many considered the agency an expert in minority marketing, Burrell's goal was to compete in the general market. Today, its billings are equal to those of many large national agencies.

OGILVY AND BERNBACH

Of the many women and men who have worked in advertising since World War II, two deserve special attention: David Ogilvy and William Bernbach. Perhaps the most visible advertising person in the United States in recent years was Ogilvy, a principal in the Ogilvy & Mather advertising agency and the author of a popular 1963 book titled *Confessions of an Advertising Man* that spelled out his advertising philosophy. Ogilvy also obtained considerable attention as one of the more creative people in a business noted for its creativity. A native of England, he came to the United States to study advertising, which fascinated him. He acknowledged the influence in his professional career of both the hard-sell and soft-sell philosophies. In 1951 he developed the idea for the man with the black eye patch wearing a Hathaway shirt in settings that identified him as a person of class.

William Bernbach perhaps more than any other person in advertising nurtured and symbolized the creative hurricane of the 1960s. Under him, the agency created some of the most memorable ad campaigns of that era, indeed, of the entire twentieth century. He maintained that the power of advertising messages lay in their difference from the ordinary. Disdainful of scientific research, he felt that individuals possessing inspiration could best establish that difference. He joined with others in establishing Doyle Dane Bernbach in 1949.

The other partners took care of new accounts, management, and financial matters. Bernbach became the creative soul of the shop. He hired people capable of imaginative work, encouraged them, offered ideas, critiqued their work in a positive way, and let them create. The most memorable work of the agency was done to introduce and sell to American consumers a humble little automobile called the Volkswagen (German for "people's car"). While domestic automobiles were being advertised with an emphasis on size, power, and prestige, the VW campaign advised people to "Think small."

RECENT TRENDS IN ADVERTISING

Several recent trends in advertising merit attention. The most historical of them is simply the growth in the number of advertisements and corresponding growth in the problem of obtaining attention for any one ad. That problem has led to a number of strategies in advertisers' attempts to reach the audience.

As the number of ads increased, so did agency size. Shortly af-

Top Advertising Slogans of the Twentieth Century

1. A diamond is forever — *DeBeers, 1948*
2. Just do it — *Nike, 1988*
3. The pause that refreshes — *Coca-Cola, 1929*
4. Tastes great, less filling — *Miller Lite, 1974*
5. Melt in your mouth, not in your hand
   — *M&M candies, 1954*
6. We try harder — *Avis, 1963*
7. Good to the last drop — *Maxwell House, 1907*
8. Breakfast of champions — *Wheaties, 1933*
9. Does she . . . or doesn't she? — *Clairol, 1956*
10. When it rains it pours — *Morton Salt, 1911*
11. We bring good things to life
    — *General Electric, 1979*
12. Where's the beef? — *Wendy's, 1984*
13. Think different — *Apple, 1997*
14. Let your fingers do the walking
    — *Yellow Pages, 1961*
15. Look, Ma, no cavities!
    — *Crest toothpaste, 1958*
16. Loose lips sink ships — *public service, 1942*
17. It takes a lickin', but it keeps on tickin'
    — *Timex, 1956*
18. When you care enough to send the very best
    — *Hallmark Cards, 1944*
19. Don't leave home without it
    — *American Express, 1975*
20. You're in good hands with Allstate
    — *Allstate insurance, 1950*

This ranking is a consensus of several polls that have been taken of advertising professionals.

ter World War II, the globalization of American advertising began. Large agencies in the United States now have offices throughout the world, giving this nation a commercial influence worldwide.

Another trend, which has diminished in recent years, is the increase in the size of ad agencies through mergers and holding companies. The question that observers of the advertising scene have raised is whether good creative work can be done in large agencies. Ad agencies have been expanding their services or merging with public relations agencies, reflecting a proliferation of the strategy known as "integrated marketing communications." In response, critics raise questions about disclosure and accuse corporations of paying — either directly or indirectly — for events and news coverage that appear to originate from outside sources or to be spontaneous. Although such criticism is supported with numerous examples, most organizations willingly disclose sponsorship of special and media events that promote products.

Another frequent criticism has dealt with the issue of stereotyping based on race and gender. In the last several years, stereotyping changed. The ad industry for many years had portrayed minorities and women in inferior roles: African Americans, for example, as servants or likable mammies and women as housewives who could not solve simple household problems without advice from a male figure speaking for the advertiser. By the 1990s, though, the ad industry had become much more sensitive to treating women and minorities positively and made a determined attempt not to represent them unfavorably. However, since advertising frequently relies on recognizable images, stereotyping remained a common approach, and new images appeared. The result was that a new stereotype — which some observers call the "dumb white guy" — took the place of the former gender and racial ones. "The majority of commercials that depict both white and black male characters," according to a study published in 2004, "show the black character in a superior position." The study found that women and men appeared about an equal number of times in prime-time commercials and that, "although many commercials still portray males and females in traditional gender family roles, when commercials portray both male and female characters in professional settings, the female frequently occupies a superior position."[12]

Perhaps the most profound trend affecting advertising is the narrowing of target markets. Until the 1960s, almost all ads were addressed to large, heterogeneous markets reachable through traditional mass media. In time, targets narrowed to loosely bound groups and mini-groups suitable for specialized publications, cable TV, and the Internet. The splintering of markets into increasingly smaller and smaller components – triggered initially by the transformation of media into vehicles to reach specialized markets and more recently enhanced by computers and the Internet – has arrived at a point where individuals are identifiable and reachable.

Consequently, messages today are often designed for target markets that are quiet homogeneous and extremely narrow. These markets lend themselves best to direct marketing techniques, introducing – as a side issue – some concerns about the privacy of individuals. This trend, sometimes called "narrow casting," has been encouraged by the Internet and the variety of advertising formats that it provides.

The concept of product placement is not new, dating back to the early days of entertainment radio; but advertisers have increasingly used product placement in entertainment forums, both online and in television and film. One of the most famous product placements appeared in the 1982 movie *E.T. the Extra-Terrestrial*, which drastically increased sales of Reese's Pieces candy. Along with such traditional product placement, the Internet created opportunities for placing products in virtual communities, such as

SecondLife, and computer games.

In the 1990s, the Internet dramatically altered the advertising landscape. Since then, expanding technologies have made online advertising an essential component of almost every major advertising campaign and have provided a forum for small organizations to reach a large audience with minimal costs.

Early Internet advertising focused on targeted email campaigns, pop-up or pop-under and banner advertisements, and organizational web sites. Such controlled ads shared many characteristics with traditional print and broadcast ads. But as digital technology developed, more and more formats appeared, and multi-media components grew increasingly impressive.

With the advent of these new technologies, advertisers quickly embraced search engine optimization, which improved their chances of appearing at the top of a search list. In the early 2000s, Google, the most widely used search engine, capitalized on the ubiquitous nature of Internet searches and launched an innovative format that consisted of low-profile text ads related to search terms and placed alongside search results. After a slow start, the format now generates significant client results as well as the majority of Google's revenue.

Along with creating new revenue sources, online advertising has greatly reduced one of the newspaper industry's most profitable resources — the classifieds. Sites such as Craiglist.org and monster.com offer space for low-cost or free classifieds along with options for searches, photo placements, and email communication. Most large newspapers have attempted to duplicate the format but, thus far, have not attracted broad national audiences.

In recent years, interactive Web 2.0 technologies have given advertisers an opportunity to establish an ongoing dialogue with audiences. Customers provide real-time feedback on blogs and social networking sites such as Facebook, Twitter, and YouTube while advertisers have the ability to respond immediately. Many advertisers also place more traditional ads on these same sites where they can direct their messages to a highly defined target audience.

Social networking has also changed the face of political advertising and how candidates communicate with voters. Several recent presidential candidates launched effective social media campaigns and even made breaking announcements via YouTube. The 2008 Obama campaign stands out as a case study in effectiveness and fund raising. Along with more than 3 million Facebook connections, the campaign's custom social network attracted more than 1 million members who contributed unprecedented amounts of money and helped win the election.

In many ways, social media have enabled candidates to bypass traditional media and control messages. Organizational editors rather than news editors address YouTube announcements and blog posts. So candidates have both audience dialogue and message control without an editorial filter and without paying high prices for advertising space. For example, rather than filtering election night family photos through the national or local news, the Obama campaign posted behind-the-scenes images on its own Flickr site (a photo sharing web site).

Almost all of these online platforms are available via widely used smart phones (mobile phones combined with a handheld computer), making online advertising even more viable.

Because of the growing popularity of the sites and because the sites provide access to attractive and defined demographics, advertisers have been spending more and more in these venues. Estimated 2009 expenditures were more than $24 billion.

Advertising has matured since the beginning of the twentieth century. It has changed drastically, and that change continues. Thanks to ongoing advances in Internet communication, the number of advertising formats has been continually increasing. Nonetheless, traditional print, radio, and television advertising remains as an essential component of most national ad campaigns. Although the future probably will hold a multitude of advances, the approaches likely will still contain old-fashioned or "traditional media" advertising methods. Outlets are expanding, but the expansion still encompasses traditional formats. There remains a convergence of the old and new rather than a replacement of the old with new.

The new approaches may appear to be taking us away from what we have known in the past as advertising, but the future of commercial messages by whatever name seems as tantalizing in prospect as the history of advertising in retrospect.

RECOMMENDED READINGS

BOOKS

Atwan, Robert, Donald McQuade, and John W. Wright. *Edsels, Luckies, and Frigidaires: Advertising the American Way*. New York, 1979. This collection of print ads covers the twentieth century premised on the thesis that advertisements reflect society.

Barnouw, Eric. *The Sponsor: Notes on a Modern Potentate*. Oxford, 1978. The author examines the rise and role of sponsors of broadcast programs.

Cleary, David Powers. *Great American Brands: The Successful Formulas That Made Them Famous*. New York, 1981. The author discusses the history of more than thirty companies and the products they manufactured.

Cone, Fairfax M. *With All Its Faults*. Boston, 1969. One of the successors to Albert Lasker provides a "candid account of forty years in advertising."

Creel, George. *How We Advertised America*. New York, 1920. The director of the Committee on Public Information, often called the Creel Committee, gives an account of its work during World War I.

Diamond, Edwin, and Stephen Bates. *The Spot: The Rise of Political Advertising on Television*. Cambridge, 1984. This study of political advertising from 1952 to 1980 includes a discussion of styles and effects.

Dotz, Warren, and Masud Husain. *Meet Mr. Product: The Art of the Advertising Character*. San Francisco, 2003. This gallery of more than 500 characters includes a brief text describing their origin and development.

Ewen, Stuart. *Captains of Consciousness: Advertising and the Social Roots of the Consumer Culture*. New York, 1977; 2001. According to this leftist critique, capitalists used advertising to expand consumption and control the marketplace after 1900.

Foster, G. Allen. *Advertising: Ancient Market Place to Television*. New York: Criterion Books, 1967. This book provides a good general survey.

Fowles, Jib. *Advertising and Popular Culture* (Feminist Perspective on Communication). Thousand Oaks, Calif., 1996. Modern advertising both influences and is influenced by popular culture.

Fox, Stephen. *The Mirror Makers*. New York, 1984. This history of twentieth-century advertising emphasizes the most influential people in the business.

Gunther, John. *Taken at the Flood*. New York, 1961. A journalist who also was a friend of the advertising agent Albert Lasker tells his story.

Hall Jamieson, Kathleen. *Packaging the Presidency: A History and Criticism of Presidential Campaign Advertising*, 3rd ed. New York, 1996. The author examines the development of presidential campaigning from early political songs and slogans through newsprint, radio, and television.

Hopkins, Claude C. *My Life in Advertising* and *Scientific Advertising*. Chicago, 1986. The creative copywriter provides two volumes of personal recollections.

Johnson, Patricia. *Real Fantasies: Edward Steichen's Advertising Photography*. Berkeley, Calif., 1997. The author presents the commercial photography of Steichen as a case study in the development of consumer culture based on images of romance and desirable lifestyle in the 1920s and 1930s.

Jones, Howard A. *50 Years Behind the Scenes in Advertising*. Philadelphia, 1975. Written by an advertising man, this book focuses on Albert Lasker and Will Grant.

Kenner, H. J. *The Fight for Truth in Advertising*. New York, 1936. The general manager of the Better Business Bureau of New York City tells its story.

Kern-Foxworth, Marilyn. *Aunt Jemima, Uncle Ben, and Rastus: Blacks in Advertising, Yesterday, Today, and Tomorrow*. Westport. Conn., 1994. The author includes many examples and often disturbing truths.

Lasker, Albert. *The Lasker Story: As He Told It*. Lincolnwood, Ill., 1987. This book reprints the text of a six-hour lecture in 1925 that Lasker gave to his staff about his life and principles.

Lears, Jackson. *Fables of Abundance: A Cultural History of Advertising in America*. New York, 1994. Sometimes the book's emphasis is more on culture than advertising, but it is useful for its study of the cultural setting of advertising.

Lykins, Daniel L. *From War to Total Diplomacy: The Advertising Council and the Construction of the Cold War Consensus*. Westport, Conn., 2003. The Ad Council helped promote American values during a critical period.

Marchand, Roland. *Advertising the American Dream: Making Way for Modernity 1920-1940*. Berkeley, Calif., 1985. The author argues that advertising distorts reality, employing evidence from two contrasting decades.

Marin, Allan, ed. *50 Years of Advertising as Seen Through the Eyes of Advertising Age 1930-1980*. Chicago, 1980. This collection of ads and articles is organized by decade, with a nice overview of the decades.

McGinniss, Joe. *The Selling of the President 1968*. New York, 1969. The author indicts political advertising on television.

Morello, John A. *Selling the President, 1920: Albert D. Lasker, Advertising, and the Election of Warren G. Harding*. Greenwood, Conn., 2001. Lasker used advertising and public relations to shape the 1920 presidential campaign.

Ogilvy, David. *Confessions of an Advertising Man*. New York, 1963. Ogilvy, one of the most creative men on the recent advertising scene, tells his advertising philosophy.

Pope, Daniel. *The Making of Modern Advertising*. New York, 1983. This account of the development of national advertising looks at it from a business perspective.

Reichert, Tom. *The Erotic History of Advertising*. Amherst, N.Y., 2003. Marketers have used sex appeal in advertising as a major theme since the 1800s.

Rowsome, Frank Jr. *They Laughed When I Sat Down*. New York, 1959. This informal history of advertising through World War II is especially helpful for its reproductions of early advertisements.

Schudson, Michael. *Advertising, The Uneasy Persuasion: Its Dubious Impact on American Society*. New York, 1986. Advertising lacks the importance assigned to it by critics and advocates.

Seldin, Joseph. *The Golden Fleece: Selling the Good Life to Americans*. New York, 1963. The author examines American advertising since World War II.

Sivulka, Juliann. *Soap, Sex, and Cigarettes: A Cultural History of American Advertising*. Belmont, Calif., 1998. This is one of several recent books exhibiting historians' concerns for the relationship of advertising to culture.

---. *Stronger than Dirt: A Cultural History of Advertising: Personal Hygiene in America, 1875-1940*. New York, 2001. Advertising influenced the notion of personal hygiene and encouraged vast changes in cultural attitudes toward cleanliness.

Smulyan, Susan. *Selling Radio: The Commercialization of American Broadcasting, 1920-1934*. Washington, D.C., 1994. The author explains how advertising gradually came to be accepted as the appropriate method of supporting radio.

Tungate, Mark. *Adland: A Global History of Advertising*. London, 2007. The author traces the history of advertising from the Industrial Revolution to the present and examines the relationship between advertising and economy.

Watkins, Julian L. *The 100 Greatest Advertisements: Who Wrote Them and What They Did*. New York, 1949. The author includes background information about each advertisement.

ARTICLES

"Advertising Century, The." *Advertising Age* 70:13 (1999). This special issue commemorates the top campaigns, ads, and people who shaped the industry.

Avery, Donald R. "Advertising, 1900-Present: Capitalist Tool or Economic Necessity?" Chap. 17 in Wm. David Sloan, *Perspectives on Mass Communication History* (Hillsdale, N.J., 1991). This historiographical essay analyzes the approaches that historians have taken to explaining advertising.

Bowers, Thomas A. "The Bankhead Bill: How a Threatened Press Subsidy Was Defeated." *Journalism Quarterly* 53 (1976): 21-7. The proposed legislation would have subsidized World War I newspapers through War Bond ads.

"Centennial of the J. Walter Thompson Company: Commemorating 100 Years of American Advertising, The." *Advertising Age*, 35 (December 7, 1964): Sec. 2. This special section is keyed but not limited to JWT; includes history, biography, and media.

Cochrane, Robert H. "Beginning of motion picture press agenting." *Film History* 19:3 (2007): 330-32. Innovative motion picture advertising challenged the industry standard.

Donohue, Julie. "A History of Drug Advertising: The Evolving Roles of Consumers and Consumer Protection." *Milbank Quarterly* 84:4 (2006): 659-699. The author discusses the history of direct-to-consumer pharmaceutical advertising and its regulations in the context of securing rights for medical patients and consumers.

Griese, Noel L. "Rosser Reeves and the 1952 Eisenhower Spot TV Blitz." *Journal of Advertising* 4 (1975): 34-8. Television commercials were not a factor in the Eisenhower victory.

Hulser, Kathleen. "Larger than Life: Billboards and Signs in the 20th-Century Landscape." *Ephemera News* 15:4 (Summer 1997): 1, 16-19. Billboards and oher forms of outdoor advertising used bold, simple illustrations to appeal to consumers.

Kreshel, Peggy J. "The 'Culture' of J. Walter Thompson, 1915-1925." *Public Relations Review* 16:3 (Fall 1990): 80-9. Stanley B. Resor tried to interject "science" into advertising and to elevate the pervasive perception of advertising from a trade to a profession.

Lathan, James. "Technology and 'Reel Patriotism' in American Film Advertising of the World War I Era." *Film & History* 36:1 (2006): 36-43. World War I advertisements for war-related films served as persuasive tools to promote American patriotism.

Lovett, Laura. "The Popeye Principle: Selling Child Health in the First Nutrition Crisis." *Journal of Health Politics* 30:5 (2005): 803-38. The cartoon character Popeye the Sailor was used to promote nutrition during the 1920s.

Maddox, Lynda M., and Eric J. Zanot. "The Image of the Advertising Practitioner as Presented in the Mass Media, 1900-1972." *American Journalism* 2 (1985): 117-29. As the emphasis on consumerism increased, the image of advertising professionals as presented in books, popular magazines, and professional journals declined. The professional was often depicted in stereotypical terms as a huckster.

McClure, Leslie. "An Analysis of Advertising Volume in World War I." *Journalism Quarterly* 19 (1942): 262-7. World War I influenced the volume of newspaper and magazine advertising, but it did not halt the trend toward more use of advertising by American business.

Miracle, Gordon E. "A Historical Analysis to Explain the Evolution of Advertising Agency Services." *Journal of Advertising* 6 (1977): 24-8 and 10. This account of the evolution of advertising agency services identifies major factors explaining the evolution.

Mullen, James J. "Newspaper Advertising in the Johnson-Goldwater Campaign." *Journalism Quarterly* 45 (1968): 219-25. During the 1964 presidential election, both parties sought to "peak" (in number, size, and cost of advertisements; appeals used; and campaign expenditures) just before the election.

Nichols, John E. "Publishers and Drug Advertising: 1933-38." *Journalism Quarterly* 49 (1972): 144-7. "[W]hen publishers were faced with a major loss in advertising revenue that would come if Congress approved a bill strengthening the Pure

Food and Drug Act of 1906, they fought the bill with inaccurate and distorted reporting, lobbying and testimony before Congress."

Norris, Vincent P. "Advertising History — According to the Textbooks." *Journal of Advertising* 9 (1980): 3-11. Advertising textbooks provided a badly distorted history of advertising.

Parmelee, Stephen. "Remembrance of Films Past: Film Posters on Film." *Historical Journal of Film, Radio, & Television* 29:2 (2009): 181-95. This article documents the development of advertising posters in the film industry.

Peiss, Kathy. "'Vital Industry' and Women's Ventures: Conceptualizing Gender in Twentieth Century Business History." *Business History Review* (1998): 219-41. The author explores the role of women in advertising and marketing.

Pinzon, Charles, and Bruce Swain. "The Kid in Upper 4." *Journalism History* 28:3 (2002): 112. Nelson Metcalf, Jr., built public support for World War II with public affairs advertising.

Pollay, Richard W. "The Subsidizing Sizzle: A Descriptive History of Print Advertising, 1900-1980." *Journal of Marketing* 49 (1985): 24-37. The author analyzes the content of magazine advertisements for the first eight decades of the twentieth century.

Pope, Daniel. "Advertising as a Consumer Issue: An Historical View." *Journal of Social Issues* 47:1 (1991): 41-56. The author discusses the Federal Trade Commission and consumer movements since the early twentieth century.

Reynolds, Robert D., Jr. "The 1906 Campaign to Sway Muckraking Periodicals." *Journalism Quarterly* 56 (1979): 513-20 and 589. Businesses placed "editorial" advertisements in an attempt to blunt muckraking attacks.

Sullivan, Paul W. "G. D. Crain Jr. and the Founding of *Advertising Age*." *Journalism History* 1 (1974): 94-5. Crain, a consumer advocate, referred to *Advertising Age* as "a real newspaper" based on hard news, investigative reporting, and informative columns. This favorable biography covers 1930 to World War II.

Taylor, James D. "Elliott White Springs — Maverick Ad Leader." *Journal of Advertising* 11 (1982): 40-6. The president of Springs Mills developed a twelve-year campaign of controversial advertisements.

22

Public Relations
1900 - Present

In December 1842, master showman Phineas T. Barnum signed a contract with the parents of Charles S. Stratton. For $7 a week, plus travel and board, Stratton was indentured to Barnum, and his parents, Sherwood and Cynthia, were bound to the contract for two years. In return, Barnum made young Charles one of the most famous people of his generation — a child most people knew as General Tom Thumb.

Tom Thumb was a midget, who at five years old stood just over two feet tall and weighed fifteen pounds. Barnum bought ponies and tiny carriages for him, dressed him in miniature costumes, added a few years to his age, and taught him to dance and sing. The "General" appeared at Barnum's American Museum in New York City, toured the United States, and even traveled to England, bringing in hundreds of dollars a day in box office receipts. Barnum raised his allowance to $25 a week.

Although many such promoters existed, P.T. Barnum was in a class by himself. He used advertising and publicity techniques to draw tremendous crowds to see Tom Thumb and many other attractions, such as the American Museum, his circus, or the singer Jenny Lind. To promote Tom Thumb, for example, in addition to paying for advertising, Barnum commissioned biographies, circulated lithograph pictures of the boy, and stirred interest among newspaper editors, who wrote stories that in turn stirred the interest of many readers. The showman consequently became a very rich man.

Barnum had an unusual flair for publicity, but his efforts to influence public opinion were not unique. While he sold tickets to exhibits, abolitionists advocated the end of slavery, the religious sought conversion of the lost, and corporations experimented with imaginative product promotions. People have long conducted organized campaigns to persuade the public to buy, vote, think, or act a certain way.

But nineteenth-century industrialization brought a major change. For the first time, "public relations" became not just an activity but a full-time occupation. Industrialization brought about a host of social and economic changes, creating pressures that led business, government, and organizations to try new strategies to

deal with the changing environment. Among other things, they added PR practitioners to their staffs or hired outside counsel. The field grew from a handful of practitioners at the turn of the twentieth century until, in 2000, nearly 200,000 Americans described themselves to the U. S. Department of Labor as "public relations specialists" or "public relations managers."

Public relations counselors often say that their role is to present clients' views on an issue before the bar of public opinion or in the marketplace of ideas. They assert that every individual or organization has a right to speak before the public, whether to sell circus tickets or peddle a political candidate. However, the history of public relations reveals that, while it can and often does make positive contributions, PR has not invariably been a democratic force. As ideas about how best to persuade people changed, practitioners sometimes, but not always, used their knowledge for the public good.

THE RISE OF BIG BUSINESS

Throughout the nineteenth century the United States lagged behind Great Britain in industrial production, but the tremendous boom of railroad building after the Civil War signaled a major change. The railroads spurred steel and machine manufacturing, adding to the already rapid growth in textiles and other industries. The 1900 census showed for the first time that more Americans were employed in industry than in agriculture.

The railroads changed commerce. They were the nation's first big businesses, and, to make their work more efficient, they developed managerial hierarchies to administer the day-to-day operations of thousands of employees working in widely dispersed locations. They also made it possible for other companies, and farmers, to transport their goods quickly, over long distances, and at relatively inexpensive rates. Instead of small, family-owned businesses that relied on individual artisans, the new corporate bureaucracies increasingly relied on machines to manufacture goods and paid wages to workers simply to run them.

Industrialization changed much more than simply the organi-

Making Human Junk
Although industrialization provided products that people enjoyed, it also brought with it such problems as child labor, unsafe working conditions, and long hours. Some social activists, such as the photographer Lewis Hine, attacked the problems through campaigns to create public awareness and action. One of his main efforts was against child labor, of which this photograph of a young girl in a cotton factory was a part. He claimed that industry was treating children as "human junk." In the face of such public criticism, many companies began their own public relations efforts to put their practices in a good light.

zation of work. With it came a loss in the close connection between owners or managers and their employees and customers. No longer did they know one another by name. Although it gave many people products that they enjoyed, industrialization also brought with it child labor, low-quality products, unsafe working conditions, and working-class slums in cities where corporations located their factories.

During the Progressive era of the early 1900s, social reformers, journalists, and politicians all responded to the negative byproducts of industrialization, often urging political action to curb industry's excesses. A group of muckraking journalists exposed both political evils of the new big cities and abuses by the corporations. Reformers tried to change everything from labor laws to the electoral process, and people began to demand that the federal government regulate industry. While links between the public and the private sectors had always existed, Americans generally believed business should function independently. The bigness of business changed this assumption, as companies and industries held increasing power over the consumers who grew to depend on them.

The story of the railroads provides a good example. Although railroads drastically improved the nation's transportation system, they also angered many citizens. Railroads had monopolies in some areas, and companies often made agreements among themselves to fix prices. They could charge almost any amount, for people had few viable transportation alternatives. In 1887 Congress created the Interstate Commerce Commission, charging it to regulate the railroad industry. One of its first rules required all railroads to publish their rates and to abide by the published prices.

Railroads were not the only problems, and Congress dealt with other companies, too. "Trusts," giant corporations that controlled entire industries, formed in the oil, sugar, steel, and tobacco industries, among others. In response Congress passed the Sherman Antitrust Act in 1890, making it possible for the courts to break up, or "bust," the trusts.

In other words, pressures from reformers, journalists, and the government combined, creating an environment that seemed increasingly anti-business. In response, business leaders developed new managerial strategies in a whole range of areas. Much like mass production created the necessity that fostered innovation in advertising, big business created new sets of problems that managers tried to solve by adding public relations to their arsenals. To mollify public opinion, focus journalists on the more positive aspects of industrialization, and decrease political threats to corporate independence, managers turned to PR. Not surprisingly, railroads — the first big businesses — were among the first corporations to experiment with press agentry and public relations. The first agency, the Publicity Bureau, formed in Boston in 1900. A belief that public opinion should rule and the availability of urban newspapers and national circulation magazines that could reach large audiences created a climate in which PR appeared to be a good solution to many business problems.

IVY LEE AND THE ORIGINS OF PR

Ivy Lee's career demonstrates how public relations could be used to respond to employee, media, and public opposition. Often called the "father of public relations," Lee was the son of a Georgia minister and was educated at Emory and Princeton universities. He joined with George F. Parker to form the first PR counseling agency, although that term had not yet been coined, in 1904. They issued a "Declaration of Principles" outlining Parker & Lee's policies for the press, because many reporters and editors objected to corporate demands for "free advertising," as some journalists called publicity. "In brief, our plan is, frankly and openly, on behalf of business concerns and public institutions," they wrote, "to supply to the press and public of the United States prompt and accurate information concerning subjects which it is of value and interest to the public to know about." They also vowed not to hide

Ivy Lee, Father of Public Relations
Ivy Lee originated modern public relations in the early 1900s with a philosophy that emphasized openness in dealing with the press. He did not always adhere to his philosophy, but his efforts created a new profession from what had been mere press agentry.

their sponsorship of work and explained that they would not pay for placement of their stories, as many press agents did.[1] The partnership split in 1913, when Parker went to work for the Episcopal Church. One of Lee's greatest challenges occurred when he accepted a new account, the Colorado Fuel and Iron Company.

Colorado Fuel and Iron's principal stockholder, John D. Rockefeller, Jr., retained Lee because mine workers had gone on strike in the coal fields of southern Colorado in September 1913. The company paid the state militia to subdue the strikers, who were living in tents because their families had been evicted from company housing. On August 20, 1914, a gun battle broke out, and three strikers and one member of the militia were killed. Even worse, eleven women and children were found suffocated in an earthen storage pit, where they had hidden to escape a fire that swept through the tent city. Ten days of rioting followed the "Ludlow Massacre," and more than fifty people died.

Rockefeller hired Lee at $1,000 a month to help resolve the crisis. Lee later said that he had insisted on a policy of "absolute frankness," although for some six months he did not tell the press

that Rockefeller had hired him. He issued bulletins "containing the facts of the situation" to prominent individuals and to newspapers — forerunners of today's news release — which were later found to contain inaccuracies.[2] He had violated some of his own guidelines for corporate publicity, and muckraker Upton Sinclair thought his behavior was so atrocious that he gave him the nickname "Poison Ivy," which followed Lee for the rest of his life.

Lee cannot be entirely faulted, however, for the problems. Mine owners and managers had provided the factual errors that appeared in the bulletins; and when Lee found out about them, he immediately issued corrections. He also repeatedly advised the Rockefellers and the mining company that they should be open and honest, but they did not always accept his advice. Finally, after the stike ended, he insisted that the company create procedures to address workers' grievances, thus revealing his good intentions.

Corporations such as Colorado Fuel and Iron were by no means the only organizations seeking counsel from PR practitioners. Many groups came to believe that in the new industrial society, public relations could help to solve problems by reaching large numbers of people with messages, whether requests for funds or votes or simply information about an organization. In fact, two of Ivy Lee's fellow pioneers in counseling, both of whom also founded agencies in the early years of the twentieth century, worked initially on non-corporate accounts. Hamilton Wright promoted the U.S.-occupied Philippines from his San Francisco office, which opened in 1908. In New York City the Trinity Church, under attack in the press because it owned a number of ramshackle tenement buildings, retained Pendleton Dudley, who had opened an agency in 1909. Additionally, Edward Bernays, who in 1921 created the term "counsel on public relations," started his career as a publicist for theater, ballet, and opera stars in 1913.

GOVERNMENT, EDUCATION, AND PR

Partly because of the changes brought about by industrialization, the federal government and the electoral process changed, and bureaucracy grew in the public sector just as it did in the private. Progressive reform in many cases led to the creation of new regulatory bodies like the Food and Drug Administration, thereby increasing the number of people working for the federal government. Big government, like big business, soon set up a better public information apparatus. Gifford Pinchot, who headed the U. S. Forest Service, created the first officially designated "press bureau" in the Executive Branch in 1905. He promoted one of President Theodore Roosevelt's pet projects — a campaign for government conservation of natural resources. A Congressional report from 1912 suggests that press bureaus (under a variety of names) existed in the Bureaus of Biology, Census, Education, Public Roads, and Soils, in addition to the Post Office, the State Department, and other agencies.

Politicians, especially U.S. presidents, similarly began to desig-

[1]Sherman Morse, "An Awakening on Wall Street," *American Magazine* 62 (September 1906), 460.

[2]Henry F. Pringle, "His Master's Voice," *American Mercury* 9 (October 1926), 150.

Gifford Pinchot
Appointed head of the U.S. Forest Service, Gifford Pinchot created the federal government's first "press bureau" in 1905. He used it to promote the conservation of the nation's natural resources, developing today's system of national forests.

nate individuals to handle PR-related activities. Some historians believe that the first PR counselor was Amos Kendall, who during the 1820s and 1830s had served in essence as a press secretary and campaign manager for President Andrew Jackson. Presidential publicity did not become common, however, until the turn of the century. In the 1890s one of President William McKinley's secretaries conducted a nightly press briefing. Theodore Roosevelt worked still more closely with the press, even allowing reporters to interview him during his morning shave. He made presidential messages available to correspondents ahead of time so that they could telegraph their stories to their newspapers. Articles about his speeches appeared on the street almost as he spoke. Although he and many of the presidents who followed did not allow direct attribution of their statements in the press, his practices had created the foundation for a more open discussion of public issues.

Members of Congress were slower to begin experimenting with PR. Representative Frank O'Hair, a Democrat from Illinois, hired Associated Press reporter Lambert St. Clair to be his press secretary in 1912. Six years later California Senator Hiram Johnson hired a San Francisco reporter, Franc Havenner, to handle his publicity and correspondence. The Progressive campaign for the Seventeenth Amendment, the direct election of senators, ratified in 1913, made senators more accountable to public opinion and may

have contributed to their interest in PR.

Another area of growth for PR was higher education. After the Civil War, greater competition for enrollment and the growth of the mass media gave rise to a need for recruitment and for better communication within the expanding universities. Much as a hierarchy had grown in big business, university administrations began to expand. Unlike the corporate model, though, universities did not rely on outside counsel but turned quickly to "in-house" public relations. The University of Michigan's office opened in 1897, and by 1937 there would be more than 200 such offices in higher education. These departments were often innovative in their attempts to attract students and raise funds. For instance, the Hampton Normal and Agricultural Institute, a historically black college in Virginia, produced its own promotional films in the 1910s because some mainstream media would not distribute its persuasive messages.

Despite the rapid proliferation of PR specialists in every area of American life, counseling remained a field closed to many people. Like the clients who retained them, counselors were as a rule white men. Women were excluded in part because industrialization contributed to a major shift in perceptions about the appropriate role of women in the workplace. When the U. S. economy was based on agriculture, both men and women of all races worked to keep their families going. But feminist scholars have shown that, during the nineteenth century, changes in the organization of work led many, especially among the white middle class, to believe that men should hold jobs and that women, particularly married women, should work only inside the home. Women and people of color were sometimes able to secure jobs in advertising by arguing that they were best able to create ads that appealed to other women and people of color. But because PR practitioners had to work closely with company presidents, journalists, and politicians, who were almost always white men, that argument rarely won PR jobs for women or minorities. There were exceptions. In 1920, for instance, Pendleton Dudley hired a woman to work with female audiences. The field of paid counseling remained, however, the domain of white men for many years.

PRESS AGENTRY, PUBLICITY, AND PR

During the first decades of the twentieth century, PR activities were usually limited to press agentry. A press agent's only goal was to secure favorable mentions of his employer in newspapers and magazines. For instance, churches promoted special attractions such as giving a Bible at a Sunday service to the father and son who looked most alike. This competition could be publicized twice: newspapers might announce the contest ahead of time and then mention it again when the winners had been selected. Many press agents were former — or current — reporters who understood what newspapers wanted, and they used their knowledge to obtain good coverage.

PR counseling was different from simple press agentry in that counselors, in addition to seeking positive press coverage, also ex-

Teddy Roosevelt Meets the Press
Theodore Roosevelt was one of the earliest American presidents to court the press. He believed the presidency should be a powerful office and that he should use the press to help him obtain his political goals. "In our country," he declared, " I am inclined to think that almost, if not quite, the most important profession is that of the newspaper man...." He allowed reporters to interview him during his morning shave, and he provided the texts of his messages to them before he gave speeches. A group of reporters and cartoonists loyal to him gave him favorable treatment. He was then able to use the press to fight his opponents. This photograph of him talking with reporters was made shortly after President William McKinley, his predecessor, was assassinated.

pected their clients to modify their behavior to match public expectations. "Publicity is a one-way street," one PR pioneer later explained; "public relations, a two-way street."[3] In the case of churches, ministers made their sermons more topical (related to current events, for example, by including references to popular books and plays) in an attempt to attract more attention in the press and among newspaper readers who might then choose to attend. In other words, some churches became more responsive to what members or potential members found interesting or important, rather than simply publicizing their usual activities.

Ivy Lee insisted that all PR counseling, which he simply called publicity, must take on this dual role of informing the public and of advising the client about how to align activities with public interests. "The great publicity man," he said, "is the man who advises his client as to what policy he shall pursue, which, if pursued, would create favorable publicity," and, once the policy is set, publicizes it.[4]

During the early years of the twentieth century, most people seemed to assume that publicity techniques were effective. Many believed in the power of the press. The muckrakers, for example, thought that to solve major social issues, they needed only to expose a problem — graphically and with supporting evidence — to the public, who would then take action. Ivy Lee believed people were influenced by a combination of fact and feeling. The people, he said, "are not moved by mind, they are moved by sentiment."[5] Skillfully prepared publicity or news stories, he believed, could influence public opinion and spur action.

During this formative period, PR counselors first began to develop the picture of themselves as advocates for their clients before the bar of public opinion. They argued that public opinion was the final arbiter. "I believe in telling your story to the public," Lee said. "If you go direct [sic] to the people and get the people to agree with you, you can be sure that ultimately legislatures, commissions, and everybody else must surely give way in your

favor."[6] This notion corresponds precisely with the American ideal of free speech. As Justice Oliver Wendell Holmes described the marketplace of ideas, many Americans hold that "the best test of truth is the power of the thought to get itself accepted in the competition of the market...."[7] PR practitioners presented their clients' views to the public, believing that individuals would decide for themselves what to think.

Ray Stannard Baker pointed out a major flaw in the "bar of public opinion" explanation of the role of public relations. A muckraker, he criticized railroad publicity campaigns, asking, "[A]gainst such an organization as [the railroads], supplied with unlimited money, representing a private interest which wishes to defeat the public will, to break the law, to enjoy the fruits of unrestrained power, what chance to be heard have those who believe the present conditions are wrong?"[8] Not all people benefited from public relations representation, and those who *could* organize and pay for PR expertise apparently had an advantage over others.

Thus, societal changes brought about by the new industrial age gave rise to the counselor, a new development in public relations. Counselors devoted their careers to promoting the interests of a number of clients and, in their best moments, worked to assure that public interest was served as well as client interest. A new era in opinion management had begun.

THE CREEL COMMITTEE

World War I was in many ways a crucial moment in the history of public relations, not because of innovations in technique or practice, but because of the lessons American propagandists took away from their experiences. The government had, of course, waged small campaigns for opinion before, especially in times of war. But the unprecedented scale of operations and the apparent success of campaigns led many Americans, including PR specialists, to be-

[3]Edward R. Bernays, *Public Relations* (Norman, Okla., 1952), 5.
[4]Ivy Lee, *Publicity: Some of the Things It Is and Is Not* (New York, 1925), 41.
[5]Ibid., 47.

[6]Ibid., 60.
[7]*Abrams v. U.S.* (1919), 250 U. S. 616.
[8]Ray Stannard Baker, "Railroads on Trial; How Railroads Make Public Opinion," *McClure's Magazine* 26 (March 1906), 538.

Public Relations and the Great War
To promote the American effort during World War I, the federal Committee on Public Information produced an abundance of material for activities ranging from industrial productivity to public morale. Its campaign to raise revenues to help finance the war, of which this poster (left) was a part, was one of its most successful, raising more than $13 billion. The "Creel Committee" employed a group of speakers known as "Four Minute Men" to spread the war message. They made prepared presentations to various gatherings, such as movie audiences, on "subjects of national importance." The illustration on the right is the front page of one of the program's bulletins.

lieve that the seemingly irrational public could be easily swayed.

President Woodrow Wilson created the Committee on Public Information (CPI) in April 1917 to censor war information and to coordinate communications from the federal government about American war efforts. The creation of the CPI was not earth-shattering in significance. It was merely an extension of Wilson's ongoing efforts to centralize the flow of information from the executive branch through the White House. He selected George Creel, a muckraking journalist, to chair the committee. Creel believed he could win public support simply by laying out facts, and he disseminated information about Wilson's strategy for the United States to "make the world safe for democracy."

Although the committee was called "Public Information," its work was actually propaganda rather than public information or public relations. The Creel Committee did not practice two-way communication as Ivy Lee described. In no instance did it seek to influence government policy. Instead, it only sought to inform and persuade people to subscribe to the Wilson administration's view of American participation in the war.

With a multi-million dollar budget, the CPI recruited actors, advertisers, artists, educators, journalists, poets, and photographers to spread through every available medium messages explaining U. S. goals and achievements. It wrote short speeches for 75,000 volunteer "four-minute men," who repeated the lectures at movie theaters and other public gatherings across the nation. Special branches of the CPI created brochures, posters, radio programs, films, and handouts for journalists — in English and other languages — in the United States. Others prepared materials for international audiences, both ally and enemy. They planned loyalty demonstrations and other special events to rally public support.

Several factors influenced CPI success. First, because of its budget, the committee was able to saturate the media with a flood of official information. One clipping bureau located 15,000 CPI-related newspaper stories in eighteen months. Segmentation was a second important element. The committee subdivided the general public into groups, like women or immigrant groups, and target-ed each group through different media, such as magazines or the foreign-language press. Finally, the CPI based its work largely on "facts" rather than shrill emotional appeals. The News Division, Creel explained, presented "facts without the slightest trace of color or bias, either in the selection of the news or in the manner in which it was presented."[9] This did not mean that its work failed to stir emotions, only that it was not so obviously propagandistic that people dismissed it.

One of the most significant effects of the committee was that many of its staff concluded that the public *could* be influenced by media messages. Although the CPI presented what it saw as "the facts," public emotions flared in unexpected ways. For instance, the committee did not as a rule try to stir sentiment against Americans of German descent, but it did sometimes go overboard. A popular poster, called "Spies and Lies," asked citizens to report suspicious activities to the Justice Department. In the wartime atmosphere it is not surprising that some citizens began to harass German-Americans, questioning their loyalty. This extreme response convinced many people that the public was easily influenced — that publicity could herd the crowd. CPI executive Carl Byoir said that the lesson he learned from his World War I experience was that "publicity was a great dynamic force; that if you had the truth, if you had a cause that was right, and could get the facts of that truth or cause over to 130 million people, nobody could hurt you."[10] Creel was so impressed with his committee's work that he subtitled his book about the CPI "The First Telling of the Amazing Story of the Committee on Public Information that Carried the Gospel of Americanism to Every Corner of the Globe." Many Americans believed that propaganda had been an important element in the struggle. Although subsequent research on mass communication would dispute propaganda's power, some citizens said that words won the war.

[9]George Creel, *How We Advertised America* (New York, 1920), 72-3.
[10]Carl Byoir, speech before National Advertising Executive Association, New York City, 7 June 1943.

COUNSELING IN THE 1920s

Taking these lessons and modeling themselves perhaps after their colleagues in advertising, World War I publicists and their associates made significant strides toward institutionalizing the PR agency during the 1920s. As the communication center of the United States, New York City became the most favored location for PR firms, which consisted of a principal or partnership, plus other executives and clerical workers. A number of young men who would later found influential agencies got important experience during the war. Edward Bernays worked in CPI's Latin American section, and John Price Jones promoted the purchase of Liberty Loans, which eventually provided more than $13 billion to finance U. S. participation in the war. Arthur Page, William Baldwin, and Carl Byoir all worked at the CPI, with Byoir serving as Associate Chairman, and Baldwin and Byoir later established their own New York agencies. Among the many other agencies founded after the war were two of lasting significance: Carlton Ketchum formed an agency in Pittsburgh in 1919; and in Cleveland in 1927 John W. Hill opened a shop that would later become Hill and Knowlton, the largest agency in the world.

Public relations continued its crucial role in employee relations, especially in stopping the organization of labor unions, during the 1920s. John Price Jones found his agency's first client in a group of coal operators who wanted to thwart the growth of the United Mine Workers in West Virginia in 1919. Jones' duties were limited; he mainly provided information on supporters of the UMW campaign. Ivy Lee had a much greater role in trying to suppress the nearly 400,000 striking West Virginians. He entered the fray in 1921 after the "Battle of Blair Mountain," a bloody labor skirmish in Logan County, where as many as seventy men were killed. Lee's strategy included publication of *The Miner's Lamp*, a weekly bulletin much like the one published in Ludlow during the Colorado coal strike, and *Coal Facts*, lengthier background memoranda that provided details about positions the mine operators took. The owners, a group that included the Rockefellers, did halt the workers' attempts to unionize.

Arthur Page's consumer relations practices at American Telephone and Telegraph (AT&T) stood in sharp contrast to the reactive approaches of Lee and Jones. As AT&T's vice president of public relations, Page practiced the "two-way street" model of PR: not only did he work to build public acceptance of the company, but he also kept management aware of public opinion. The Bell System sought details on customers' desires about every aspect of service, down to the placement of memo pads in public telephone booths. Most importantly, the company listened and responded to consumers' wishes. Page insisted that all employees be well-informed, so that they could be both courteous and able to respond to customers' questions about the company or its services. In other words, he believed that all Bell System employees were part of the PR department. Managers wanted to build a good relationship with consumers partly, of course, because they wanted to turn a profit — but they also worried that some people might want to

Arthur Wilson Page
At American Telephone and Telegraph in the late 1920s, Arthur Page developed the "two-way street" approach to public relations. Along with promoting his company to the public, he attempted to keep AT&T alert to the public's concerns.

make the company a public utility rather than a private company. AT&T assumed that if consumers were satisfied with their service, they would be content with the status quo. The company therefore tried to keep consumers happy by proactively seeking audience input into company policy.

Between these two extreme proactive and reactive uses of corporate PR lay the most common use: product publicity. Many companies simply wanted to use PR techniques to sell more products. Instead of paying for advertising, companies chose to publicize their products in more innovative, and less expensive, ways. Edward Bernays, together with his wife and partner, Doris Fleischman, became especially astute at using the special event to draw attention to their clients' products. Because of a promotion for Ivory, millions of children learned to carve soap — Ivory soap — sculptures in school contests. The Bernays agency attracted attention in the editorial columns rather than in the advertising portions of newspapers by giving awards, announcing the results of scientific surveys, throwing parties, offering symposiums, and holding banquets for such accounts as United Fruit, American Motors, and General Motors. They made news happen.

Government officials also continued to use public relations to advance their goals. The U. S. Secretary of Commerce, Herbert

Hoover, conducted several campaigns during the 1920s, including one to improve housing. The Commerce Department's Building and Housing Division, formed in 1921 and chaired by Harvard professor John M. Gries, was the driving force behind the program, although other government offices such as the Departments of Labor, the Interior, and Agriculture also participated. Gries recruited national associations such as the Chamber of Commerce to help reduce housing shortages caused by the suspension of home building during World War I. Hoover joined with the editor of a women's magazine to form a volunteer organization, "Better Homes in America," which was funded by private sources but cooperated fully with the Department of Commerce's campaign. In fact, all "Better Homes" publicity was cleared through Hoover's office. The organization recruited volunteers and sent field agents to visit women's clubs and educational leaders to encourage them to help publicize and end the housing shortage. Hundreds of thousands of homes were built during the 1920s, perhaps in part because of Hoover's program. With that experience in public relations, Hoover, when he became President, created the White House Press Secretary's office in 1929.

After World War I many social reform organizations used PR tactics to campaign for their causes. The passage of two Constitutional amendments verified their success. After many decades of campaigning, in 1919 advocates of temperance finally achieved Prohibition (the Eighteenth Amendment), and in 1920 suffragists obtained women's right to vote (the Nineteenth Amendment). These changes in the nation's fundamental law showed that citizens could form organizations and successfully crusade for changes in government and society.

PR could also be applied to less democratic causes. In Atlanta, the Southern Publicity Association, a small agency run by partners Elizabeth Tyler and Edward Young Clarke, helped to revive the Ku Klux Klan, which had been founded after the Civil War but was disbanded in 1871 by an act of Congress, the Act to Enforce the Fourteenth Amendment. In 1915, William Simmons, whose father had been a member of the original Klan, reformulated the Knights of the Ku Klux Klan as a "bottle club," with an elaborate ritual and rules. (Georgia was a "dry" state, and private bottle clubs were the only places where liquor could be served legally.) With the advent of Prohibition, Simmons' club was going bankrupt. So he brought in Tyler and Clarke to reinvigorate the organization. Using the fundraising techniques they had developed for World War I clients such as the Salvation Army and the Red Cross, Tyler and Clarke created a national plan for organizing Klans all over the United States. In addition to spreading anti-Catholic, anti-Jewish, and anti-black messages, these Klans actively sought to keep black citizens from voting by marching in parades, burning crosses, and even attacking black sections of some towns.

PUBLIC RELATIONS AND PSYCHOLOGY

Despite such abuses, public relations flourished during the 1920s, in great part because of a growing fascination with the human

mind. Books such as Walter Lippmann's *Public Opinion* and Gustave Le Bon's *The Crowd: A Study of the Public Mind* captivated the public. Viennese psychoanalyst Sigmund Freud — whose work his nephew, Edward Bernays, avidly promoted in the United States — had tremendous influence. His work suggested that people were driven by irrational desires, which tied directly into Bernays' opinions about the success of the Creel Committee in World War I. Not only did Bernays arrange for translation and sale of Freud's book, *Introductory Lectures in Psychoanalysis*, in the United States, but he also began to apply psychology to PR work.

One example of Bernays' use of psychology in public relations occurred during a cigarette promotion during the 1920s. His client, American Tobacco, believed that women liked to smoke but that they chose not to do so in public because of social taboos. Bernays consulted a psychologist, who suggested that women might identify cigarette smoking with the battle for sexual equality. Bernays then had his secretary telegraph thirty New York debutantes with the message, "In the interests of equality of the sexes and to fight another sex taboo I and other young women will light another torch of freedom by smoking cigarettes while strolling on Fifth Avenue Easter Sunday."[11] Ten women smoking cigarettes marched in the Easter Parade, and their story became big news. Although American Tobacco's premiere cigarettes, Lucky Strikes, were never mentioned, Bernays had managed to make the papers with an angle carefully calculated to appeal to the target audience.

Psychology gave public relations access to a scientific literature that had the potential to make PR a profession rather than an art. Public relations had never been considered an honorable occupation. Many people associated it with "Poison Ivy" Lee's inaccurate press handouts at Ludlow or the manipulative activities of Barnum or the railroad press agents. Bernays fought for acceptance of PR by distinguishing what he did from mere publicity. He taught the first class specifically called PR (at New York University in 1923) and wrote books about its role in society (beginning with the first book published on PR, *Crystallizing Public Opinion*, also in 1923). He insisted that a counselor's work "is comparable to that of any special counsel in the highly organized society of today, the lawyer, the engineer, the accountant."[12]

Bernays was also among the first to define his role specifically as "a special pleader before the court of public opinion." He said counselors owed high ethical standards to the client, the public, the news media, and themselves.[13] To live up to these standards, counselors had to refuse to represent clients who were "unsocial or otherwise harmful" and had to make certain their clients' policies conformed to public interest.[14] This strategy left it to the individual counselor to determine what the public interest was.

[11]Edward L. Bernays, *Biography of an Idea: Memoirs of Public Relations Counsel Edward L. Bernays* (New York, 1965), 387.

[12]"Counsel on Public Relations—A Definition," advertisement in *Editor & Publisher*, 29 January 1927.

[13]Ibid.

[14]Edward L. Bernays, *Crystallizing Public Opinion* (New York, 1923), 87.

"Light a Lucky and you'll never miss sweets that make you fat" *Constance Talmadge*

Constance Talmadge, Charming Motion Picture Star

INSTEAD of eating between meals...instead of fattening sweets...beautiful women keep youthful slenderness these days by smoking Luckies. The smartest and loveliest women of the modern stage take this means of keeping slender...when others nibble fattening sweets, they light a Lucky!

Lucky Strike is a delightful blend of the world's finest tobaccos. These tobaccos are toasted—a costly extra process which develops and improves the flavor. That's why Luckies are a delightful alternative for fattening sweets. That's why there's real health in Lucky Strike. That's why folks say: "It's good to smoke Luckies."

For years this has been no secret to those men who keep fit and trim. They know that Luckies steady their nerves and do not harm their physical condition. They know that Lucky Strike is the favorite cigarette of many prominent athletes, who must keep in good shape. They respect the opinions of 20,679 physicians who maintain that Luckies are less irritating to the throat than other cigarettes.

A reasonable proportion of sugar in the diet is recommended, but the authorities are overwhelming that too many fattening sweets are harmful and that too many such are eaten by the American people. So, for moderation's sake we say:—

"REACH FOR A LUCKY INSTEAD OF A SWEET."

"It's toasted"
No Throat Irritation-No Cough.

Constance Talmadge, Charming Motion Picture Star

LUCKY STRIKE "IT'S TOASTED" CIGARETTES

Reach for a Lucky instead of a sweet.

Making Smokers of Women
Under the guidance of public relations counsel Edward Bernays, American Tobacco encouraged women in the 1920s to smoke cigarettes in public by equating smoking with social equality and with glamour. The campaign began with debutantes smoking while walking in New York City's 1923 Easter Parade. National advertising related smoking to feminine beauty, including a campaign in the early 1930s that encouraged women to smoke instead of eat sweets in order to keep down their weight. The ad above was part of that campign.

THE GREAT DEPRESSION AND THE RISE OF BIG GOVERNMENT

The Great Depression brought wholesale changes to the economy and consequently to the federal government, resulting in expansion of the role and occupation of public relations. The Depression left industry at a loss — no economic problem of its magnitude and duration had taken place in the industrial age. The crisis gave the government license to take over more and more of the decisions that management traditionally made. Business leaders worried about the future of the free enterprise system. Would Americans turn to radical solutions, like the Russian people had during the Revolution of 1917? Not surprisingly, PR activities increased in both the public and the private sectors as government and industry leaders reacted to the Depression.

President Franklin Roosevelt and Congress responded to the Depression with, among other things, new laws that controlled

prices and made it easier for labor unions to form. To explain and to sell new laws and regulations to the American people, the Roosevelt administration greatly expanded PR in the government agencies, although no one called it "public relations." Government PR employees worked under such titles as "specialist in information," "director of publicity," "special correspondent," "copy writer," and "editor." At least three separate agencies were responsible for public information, in addition to the information officers in nearly every other agency. Roosevelt also spoke directly to the people through his radio "fireside chats." Some critics denounced his administration for its extensive PR apparatus. "Reams and reams of statements are issued daily by the 'information' chiefs of the various government departments," one critic wrote in 1935. Despite the fact that he could find little hard evidence of a change in the economy, the author said, "hardly a day passes when some department does not issue a statement to the effect that business is 'picking up.'"[15]

Both government intervention and organized labor were anathema to most business executives, who believed that only management and owners should make business decisions. One commentator in 1935 described an audience of manufacturers as "mad — mad at Washington — and keyed, emotionally, to snort defiance at the Administration...."[16] Arguing that Roosevelt's solutions to the Depression were little different from socialism, they turned to public relations to sell "the American way": free enterprise. Their campaigns explained that the people had benefited greatly from private industry and that therefore a separation between government and industry should be maintained. The National Association of Manufacturers (NAM), a conglomeration of many smaller groups such as the Chamber of Commerce, conducted a campaign that utilized every medium, ranging from motion pictures and film strips, print and outdoor advertising, and direct mail to a speakers' bureau and a radio program. Business executives, including PR practitioners, denounced the government, especially Roosevelt, and labor unions whenever the opportunity arose.

PR counseling also moved into political campaign management. The first agency dedicated to political PR was founded by a husband-and-wife team, Clem Whitaker and Leone Baxter, in California in 1933. Campaigns, Inc.'s first major battle sought the 1934 reelection of California Governor Frank Merriam. His opponent was Upton Sinclair, a socialist best known for his exposé of the meat-packing industry, *The Jungle*. Whitaker and Baxter did not think Merriam had been a good governor. So, rather than seeking reelection on his record, they maligned Sinclair. For example, they developed a series of cartoons that ran in dozens of California newspapers that condemned the "blot of Sinclairism." Each cartoon showed a traditional American scene with a giant blob of ink dashed over it, accompanied by a denigrating quote from Sinclair's writings, including dialogue spoken by his fictional characters. One cartoon showed a picture of a Madonna and child accompanied by a quote that called religion "a mighty fortress of

[15]George Michael, *Handout* (New York, 1935), 11.
[16]Arthur H. Little, "Industry Writes Its Story," *Printers' Ink* 173 (December 19, 1935), 10.

FDR Masters PR

Perhaps no American president was more effective in working with the press than was Franklin Roosevelt. Ivy Lee, the founder of modern public relations, had helped him establish good relations with the press. During the Great Depression, his administration set up numerous government PR offices. FDR used PR, including radio and film, to gain public support for his policies aimed at combating economic problems and the international aggression of the Axis powers in the 1930s. He himself enjoyed the company of supportive reporters and held small press conferences in his White House office, such as the one in this photograph.

graft." Merriam, who had not been particularly popular, won the election.

Other Depression-era campaigns were more constructive. Carl Byoir, formerly George Creel's top CPI lieutenant, together with one of his oil industry clients, Henry L. Doherty, helped to build the National Foundation for Infantile Paralysis. Byoir, whose agency promoted the interests of Chrysler, B.F. Goodrich, and other corporate giants, organized a series of local "birthday balls" held on President Roosevelt's birthday (because FDR was one of the disease's most famous victims, having contracted polio at the age of thirty-nine). Despite the challenge posed by the Depression economy, Byoir raised more than $1 million for polio research in 1934 alone, spending money out of his own pocket to start the program. The program benefited both Byoir's client, who was associated with a good cause, and polio research.

The Depression had a mixed effect on public relations as an industry. New York counsel William Henry Baldwin III found that business at his agency fell about 10% during the economic downturn. Cleveland executive John W. Hill, however, gained so much business that he decided to take on a partner, Donald Knowlton, and open a New York branch office. Trade associations became prime accounts because the National Industrial Recovery Act required companies to work together to write codes to regulate their own industries, giving them an important role in Roosevelt's plan to respond to the Depression.

Three important refinements in the practice of PR counseling occurred during the Depression. First, some counselors began to participate in the formation of a client's policies, so they could advise management about how an organization's plans might affect or be affected by its relationships with key audiences. Two highly respected counselors, Earl Newsom, of Earl Newsom and Associates, and John W. Hill, of Hill and Knowlton, insisted that they work closely with the top management of client organizations. Although Ivy Lee had long recommended this arrangement, it had not been a regular policy for client-agency relationships for Lee or

anyone else. Hill attended virtually every board meeting of the American Iron and Steel Institute for about forty years. Newsom developed close associations with such executives as Frank Stanton, president of the CBS television network, and Henry Ford II. Hill felt so strongly about policy-making that in 1938 he invited a select group of elite counselors (a group nicknamed "The Wisemen") to dinner, and they agreed to participate in monthly dinners and discussions about issues related to counseling.

This period also saw the beginnings of an important trend, the establishment of PR departments within organizations. United States Steel created its own PR department in 1936, for example, and Standard Oil of New Jersey (later renamed Enco and then Exxon) followed suit in 1942. For the most part, however, outside consulting continued to dominate. Major League Baseball, for example, hired Steve Hannagan & Associates to promote its centennial anniversary in 1939.

A third development involved codification of the process of creating a PR program. Bernays developed a set of "four steps essential to formulate a program" of public relations in 1935. In an article titled "Molding Public Opinion," he wrote that the PR counselor must formulate objectives "in the public interest," analyze public attitudes, study that analysis and make the program or policy "part and parcel of the thinking and action of the leaders in the industry," and use the media to carry the policy.[17] Although many objected to the notion that Bernays could "mold" public opinion, these steps are still important in PR counseling.

Despite such changes, practitioners continued to suggest that the role of PR was to represent clients' opinions before the bar of public opinion. "For fair judgment," counselor John Price Jones wrote in 1939, "conflicting ideas must be brought into the open for free discussion.... Eventually public opinion will be so crystallized that through action of a majority of the people, new and higher standards will be established in legislation, in public morals and

[17]Edward L. Bernays, "Molding Public Opinion," *Annals of the American Academy of Political and Social Science* 179 (May 1935): 85-7.

economic methods." He also noted that not every idea got a fair hearing. To assure a workable marketplace of ideas, he said, "[t]he nature and meaning of conflicting ideas must be presented adequately, at the bar of public opinion."[18]

WORLD WAR II:
BIG GOVERNMENT GETS BIGGER

As in World War I, federal PR activities during World War II concentrated in the executive branch, but they were markedly different from those of the Creel Committee. In 1942 the Office of War Information (OWI) replaced the three government information agencies Roosevelt had previously created. His team disagreed on the role the OWI should take. Some wanted a centralized office, like the Creel Committee, that would provide not only information but morale-building activities; but Stephen Early, a former journalist and the President's closest communications adviser, opposed a new CPI. Thus, although the new agency was huge, with more than 9,000 employees worldwide, news formed the backbone of the OWI's programs at home and abroad. Respected radio commentator Elmer Davis headed the new agency.

OWI executives believed that years of European propaganda efforts had deafened people to emotional appeals and that honest news stories therefore would be more effective. They relied on radio news, especially in Europe, in addition to newspaper and magazine stories and leaflets to reach audiences. "Before OWI, reporters might obtain from different agencies, on the same day, three or four different versions to the same story — each of them partial, and at least to that extent inaccurate," Elmer Davis reported to the President. "We sometimes made them wait a day, but what we gave them was coherent and correct."[19] The agency spent more than $130 million in its overseas, domestic, and administrative branches to keep people informed.

Although the OWI is usually remembered for its earnest news presentation, it also disseminated propaganda through films, magazines, and other entertainment media. It influenced movie content both by censoring and by offering advice on what should appear. Among other things, executives wanted the Hollywood studios to prepare citizens for the deaths of American soldiers. So the movie *Tender Comrade*, for example, showed scenes of a mother telling her baby that his father "went out and died so you could have a better break when you grow up." The OWI's Magazine Bureau similarly encouraged publishers to include war messages in their periodicals. One of its more famous campaigns, the Womanpower project, provided pictures and reports about women, symbolized by "Rosie the Riveter," who entered the labor force to take the places of men who had gone to war. The campaign also suggested plots for fictional stories about such women.

Unlike the Creel Committee, the OWI did not spawn a large number of new practitioners or agencies. In fact, two of the most

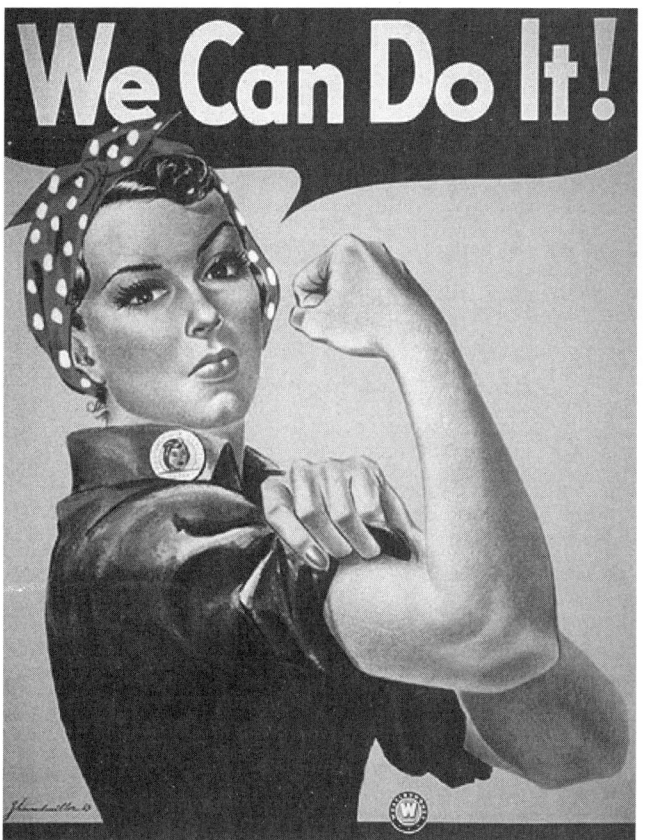

Women at War
With many men serving in the military during World War II, women had to take up factory production jobs. Both the government and private industry produced many campaigns to encourage the effort. The government's most famous campaign was "Rosie the Riveter." Production companies, though, emphasized the expectation that the factory work that women were doing would make it possible for them to quit their jobs when the war was over and return to caring for their homes and staying with their children.

important postwar counselors, Farley Manning of Manning, Selvage & Lee and Harold Burson of Burson-Marsteller, worked for the military — which mobilized as many as 100,000 public information officers during the war — not the OWI. Nor did PR practitioners leave their wartime positions with the belief that opinion management was simple or easy.

Unlike the First World War, World War II experiences with propaganda indicated that the effects of mass-mediated messages were limited. Theories about persuasion changed during World War II, in large part because of an influential communication experiment conducted on U. S. soldiers. General George C. Marshall recruited Frank Capra, who had directed popular movies such as *Mr. Smith Goes to Washington*, to make a series of documentary films, titled *Why We Fight*, that explained the reasons and principles behind the U. S. role in the war. Capra produced seven fifty-minute films, such as *Prelude to War* and *The Battle of Britain*, that became part of the Army's training program for recruits. A team of social scientists from Yale conducted surveys of trainees before and after they watched the films, and compared the results to those of control groups that had not seen the movies. The scholars

[18]John Price Jones and David McLaren Church, *At the Bar of Public Opinion: A Brief for Public Relations* (New York, 1939), 5-6.
[19]Elmer Davis, "Report to the President," *Journalism Monographs* 7 (August 1968).

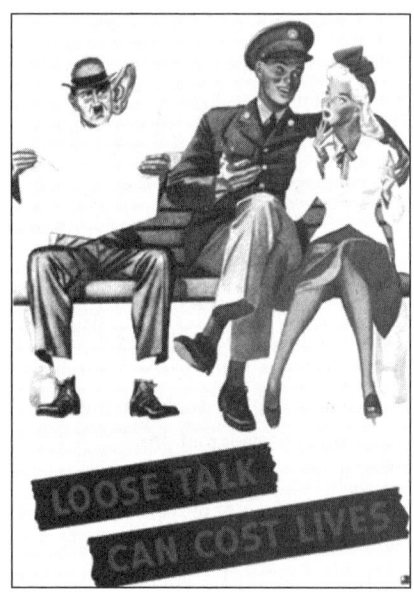

Supporting the War at Home
During World War II, the federal government employed a variety of media to promote the Allied effort among the American citizenry. Movies and films were important, but traditional methods such as posters continued to be used also. The posters pictured here illustrate some of the areas at which the promotional efforts were aimed. The poster on the left encouraged Americans to invest in war bonds by poking fun at Adolf Hitler, Hermann Göring (German air force commander), and Joseph Goebbels (propaganda minister). With the need for military personnel, numerous efforts were made for recruiting personnel into the armed forces, as illustrated by the middle poster. Both civilians and servicemen also were alerted to the need for vigilance in security and discouraged from discussing topics that might seem innocent but could be of use to the enemy (poster on right).

concluded that, although viewing the films did help soldiers to learn facts and in some cases change attitudes, they were not effective at strengthening the overall motivation or morale of the viewers. In short, these social scientists argued, mass communication effects were not powerful but instead were quite limited.

EXPANSION IN CORPORATE PR

Despite the growing belief among scholars of public opinion that people were not easily persuaded by mass communication, the post-World War II era was one of unprecedented expansion in public relations. As before the war, PR was important in every sector: corporate, government, and non-profit. In 1950 there were 19,000 "public relations specialists," according to the U. S. Department of Labor. A decade later there were 31,000. The field grew in size, scope, and professionalism, but in fundamental ways PR counseling remained the same.

The postwar growth occurred for several reasons. Industrial relations were particularly important. Several waves of strikes after the war cost industry in lost production and in consumer dissatisfaction. Additionally, one survey indicated that in 1948 nearly half the public demanded government regulation of big business, often arguing that prices were too high. Many business managers, including PR counselors, believed that people felt this way only because they did not understand the contributions big business had made to the American standard of living. Therefore, they insisted that corporate advertising and PR should do more than just promote products: they should also promote capitalism. Among

business priorities after the war, one survey revealed, were "indicating the company's contribution to the general welfare, building confidence in the company's product, and promoting a belief in the free enterprise system."[20] Those ideas opened the door for increased PR budgets, invigorating the field.

Over the years, corporations gradually de-emphasized the idea of selling "free enterprise," but they continued to use PR activities to manage government regulation of business. One of the best-known examples involved a bitter fight between truckers in Pennsylvania and the Eastern Railroads. During the early 1950s the Pennsylvania Motor Truck Association lobbied the state legislature to increase truck weight limitations so that trucks could carry heavier loads on the state's highways. The Eastern Railroads Presidents Conference worried about the truckers' growing power. Fearing that larger loads would take away business from the railroads, it hired Carl Byoir and Associates to implement a campaign opposing the truckers.

Byoir's campaign had an important unintended effect: the legal controversy it created resulted in a Supreme Court opinion that gave First Amendment protection to PR activities. Byoir ran an advertising campaign, commissioned free-lance writers to prepare magazine articles, sought radio airtime on the controversy, and recruited support from other organizations by suggesting that heavier loads were dangerous and would ruin the state's roads. When the truckers obtained a copy of Byoir's file on the railroad campaign, they charged the Railroad Presidents and Byoir with

[20]"Industry's Public Relations Job," *Business Record* 2 (March 1945), 75.

violating the antitrust laws by engaging in a conspiracy to eliminate competition. In particular they questioned Byoir's use of the "third party technique," when the agency formed seemingly independent citizens' groups specifically to support the client's position. Litigation on the case continued all the way to the U. S. Supreme Court, which ruled in 1961 that attempts to influence the passage or enforcement of laws did not violate the Sherman Act, even when the petitioner's motive was to seek legislation that would damage a competitor.[21]

Public relations also maintained its important role in product publicity. New York counsel Benjamin Sonnenberg, for example, promoted several large department store chains such as Bergdorf-Goodman and Federated Department Stores, which operated Bloomingdale's, Filene's of Boston, and other prominent shops. In addition to holding fashion shows and pitching feature stories to the press, he put live models pretending to be mannequins in store windows to capture public attention. To celebrate Bergdorf-Goodman's fiftieth anniversary, in 1951, he planned a dinner and dance at the famed Plaza Hotel in New York City. As many as 800 people attended, paying $50 each.

Another area of growth occurred due to the acceleration of the trend of establishing in-house PR departments. In the decade following the war, such corporations as Ford, Allis-Chalmers, the Pennsylvania Railroad, Socony-Vacuum, Gulf Oil, Chrysler, and Northwestern Mutual Life Insurance created their own PR departments. In later years non-profit and government organizations, ranging from hospitals and voluntary organizations to public utilities, also increasingly established internal counsel.

In-house public relations did not grow at the expense of outside counsel. In 1960 *Printers' Ink* reported that New York City alone was home to 704 PR agencies. They ranged from giants like Hill and Knowlton and Byoir "to the one-man operation whose apartment is his office."[22] Along with H&K, which both PR executives and newspaper editors ranked as the best firm, other top agencies included Ivy Lee and T. J. Ross, Selvage and Lee (later Manning, Selvage & Lee), Dudley-Anderson-Yutzy, and Ruder and Finn.

Perhaps the most important development of the postwar era was the creation of the modern PR agency. During the first part of the twentieth century, PR firms were identified with the individuals who founded them. When George Parker left Parker & Lee, for example, the agency simply dissolved. The modern agency was more than a consultancy built around an individual. Carl Byoir and Associates and Hill and Knowlton had large staffs — each with more than 200 employees — with many executives who shared the responsibility of counseling clients, and both continued to operate for many years after the principals retired. An agency did not have to be large to be modern. Earl Newsom's firm, for example, had five partners and, at its peak, only twenty-three employees. But it represented such prestigious clients as Campbell's Soup, CBS Television, Eli Lilly, Ford, General Motors, Internation-

al Paper, Merrill Lynch, the New York Stock Exchange, and Trans-World Airlines, and continued to do so long after Newsom retired.

INTERNATIONAL PUBLIC RELATIONS

Still more growth lay overseas. After World War II many American businesses began to invest in other nations — direct foreign investment tripled in the decade immediately following the war — and to market their products to a war-torn world. Hill and Knowlton, which had become the leading U. S. agency, recognized that American business was moving overseas; and it was the first PR firm to establish successful offices in foreign countries. It fashioned a network of associated PR firms in Europe by affiliating with leading practitioners in England, France, the Netherlands, and Belgium, beginning in 1954. H&K paid each affiliate a $500 retainer. In return, the affiliates promised to work with H&K exclusively, and to handle any PR activities H&K clients might require in Europe on a per-job basis. The agency also opened an international office in Geneva, headed by Loet Velmans, a Dutch citizen who had trained in H&K's New York office, and a subsidiary in Australia.

The American practice of PR counseling did not transfer easily to other nations. One German industrialist, for example, could not see a need for PR activities at all. He explained to Hill and Knowlton representatives that prices were fixed by the German cartels, so that product promotion was not necessary; that industries had significant influence over legislation affecting them; and that German public opinion already favored industry. U. S. PR counselors thus first had to sell public relations in general and then sell their own services in particular. For some years H&K found it easier to obtain U. S. clients who were working in other nations (multinational corporations like California Texas Oil and American Cyanamid) than to find foreign employers.

One agency, Barnet & Reef, specialized in international PR during the 1960s. By the end of 1958, the year it was founded, its international client list included Dow Chemical and American Machine and Foundry. Within a few years it added such powerhouse clients as Goodyear, Philip Morris, United Fruit, and John Deere. At its peak Barnet & Reef associates worked in forty-eight nations, although its New York headquarters had only fifteen employees.

THE PROFESSIONALIZATION OF PUBLIC RELATIONS

The postwar era also saw a drive to improve the professionalism of public relations. In 1948 two organizations (the National Association of Accredited Publicity Directors and the American Council on Public Relations) combined to form a national professional organization, the Public Relations Society of America. The PRSA developed a system of accreditation, which involved a practitioner's taking an examination to demonstrate expertise in public relations and pledging to uphold the Society's Code of Standards, which was adopted in 1954. Herbert Muschel created a special PR wire service, the *PR NewsWire*, that same year. New journals, in-

[21]*Eastern Railroad Presidents Conference v. Noerr Motor Freight, Inc.*, 365 U.S. 127 (1961).

[22]"Public Relations: A Communication System Ripens," *Printers' Ink* 273 (25 November 1960), 66.

Three Mile Island

Nuclear Disaster Brings 'Crisis Management' to PR

Although it could be argued that professional crisis communication efforts began with Ivy Lee's PR efforts in response to the "Ludlow Massacre" in 1914, it took the Three Mile Island nuclear incident in 1979 to illustrate how important the practice would become.

The "disaster" galvanized public imagination. Media coverage gripped the nation, overwhelming the staff at the plant and at the Nuclear Regulatory Commission, which couldn't reach plant operators, who described the situation as "total chaos." The problem at the Pennsylvania nuclear project was real – a coolant leak led to a partial meltdown of the reactor core and the release of some radioactivity into the environment.

Responses included a governor-ordered evacuation of young children and pregnant women and media images of a

landscape decimated by a "China syndrome" melt-down that would destroy everything within sight. Those fears gained currency with the release just prior to the incident of the action thriller movie *The China Syndrome*, which had plot lines eerily similar to the actual event, including a stuck valve that misled plant operators, wildly conflicting information about what actually was going on inside the reactor, and allegations of a cover-up of the facts.

Despite assurances that everything at Three Mile Island was under control, un-

expected radiation releases and the completely unpredicted emergence of a potentially explosive hydrogen gas "bubble" inside the reactor vessel emphasized that a real crisis did exist and damaged the prevailing beliefs that "experts" could effectively manage such complex events.

The event was an economic disaster for the nuclear industry. Afterward, sixty nuclear projects were abandoned, and anti-nuclear forces gained increased credibility in the debate over U. S. energy policy.

But, largely as a result of this incident, numerous states passed "right-to-know" legislation, and crisis management became a staple in PR curricula and in organizational planning around the world. The importance of quick on-site response, rigorous fact-finding, controlling lines of communication, and empowering responsible spokespersons all emerged from the miasma of garbled communications and mixed messages so prevalent during the twelve days of the Three Mile Island event.

---

cluding *PR News* (1944), *Public Relations Journal* (1945), and *PR Reporter* (1958), also testified to the growing interest in improving the practice and reputation of public relations.

Professionalization also included a push for better education. Immediately after World War II, only about two dozen U. S. universities offered instruction in public relations. By 2007 that number had grown to more than 700, including many that offered graduate degrees. Educators recommended greater attention to interpersonal communication than Lee, Bernays, and other pioneer counselors had considered. One study of political decision-making suggested that persuasion was actually a two-step process. *The People's Choice*, published in 1948, analyzed the behavior of voters in Erie County, Ohio. The investigators found that some individuals were opinion leaders who paid close attention to political messages and who shared what they had learned with others. It seemed that ideas flowed from radio or print to the opinion leaders and from them to less active members of the population.

PR practitioners quickly adopted the notion of targeting opinion leaders for their messages, with the assumption that certain individuals would use their personal influence to sway others. Paul Lazarsfeld, who led *The People's Choice* research team, suggested that the study's results "have a meaning for the changing

of minds in commercial advertising campaigns as well as in a political campaign."[23] For this reason PR practitioners began to send materials, such as brochures and newsletters, directly to opinion leaders such as clergy or teachers, instead of trying to place articles in any newspaper or magazine that would print them. They also planned grassroots campaigns by providing information and materials to the leaders of local organizations, such as farm or women's groups, that could be used at small group meetings.

The American Medical Association's campaign to halt President Truman's plan for compulsory medical insurance in the late 1940s and early 1950s was an example of a campaign that utilized the "two-step flow" approach. The association retained California's Whitaker and Baxter, who spent over $4.5 million in three and a half years. The PR agents prodded doctors to support voluntary group insurance plans and then promoted that position with the slogan "The Voluntary Way Is the American Way." It paid for billboards and posters of the famous painting "The Doctor," by Sir Luke Fildes, which showed a "bearded, frock-coated physician" turning "a compassionate glance on his small patient," a sick

[23]Paul F. Lazarsfeld, "Who Influences Whom—It's the Same for Politics and Advertising," *Printers' Ink* 21 (8 June 1945), 32.

Presidential PR

Television changed the nature of presidential relations with the press and public. National commercial television had begun during the presidency of Harry Truman, but it was during the presidency of Dwight Eisenhower (left) that it became a national force. Through his press secretary, James Hagerty, he experimented with televised "fireside chats" and then with edited television news conferences. TV's need for compelling visuals and drama made the president's image and public speaking ability increasingly important. One might say that image over substance became the norm. Political public relations responded by providing opportunities for coverage that gave TV reporters ample time to prepare for evening network newscasts. Unlike other presidential administrations that tried to control the flow of important information from the White House, the Richard Nixon administration (1969-1974) attempted to set the news agenda. Because Nixon (right) had an intense distrust of the news media, he created the White House Office of Communications to manage media relations and shield him from the press.

child, and the words "Keep Politics Out of This Picture."[24] Whitaker and Baxter mobilized doctors by providing speeches, resolutions, and press releases to the many state and county medical societies across the country. The materials could be modified to fit the local situation and then used to help publicize the doctors' fight against what they called "socialized medicine" at the local level. They distributed over 54 million pieces of literature in 1949 alone.

Not all practitioners, however, adopted the new approach. Hollywood publicists, for example, continued to utilize some of the tactics of the old railroad press agents. Rogers and Cowan, based in Los Angeles, went to any length to publicize the actors they represented — Joan Crawford, Frank Sinatra, Marlene Dietrich, Jane Wyman, Dean Martin, and Bette Davis, to name a few. The agency told a series of extravagant lies to get Rita Hayworth on the cover of *Look* magazine in a photo that made her famous. The only purpose of such campaigns was to obtain positive press coverage for clients.

GROWTH IN POLITICAL PR

Public relations also continued to grow in importance in the political arena. The 1952 Democratic and Republican presidential nominating conventions were the first to be televised coast-to-coast, and elected officials began to rely more heavily on TV to reach their constituents. President Dwight Eisenhower's press secretary, James Hagerty, and his staff had constant access to the chief executive, meaning that they could provide counsel much like Hill or Newsom did for their corporate accounts. The Eisenhower administration experimented with televised "fireside chats" and then with specially edited television news conferences. Presidents Kennedy and Johnson then began the practice of allowing live

broadcast of their news conferences.

Some scholars argue that the increasingly active role of PR in political policymaking has been a detriment to the democratic process. The increasing importance of TV and of "image" rather than substance has made PR a more dominant force in politics. Yet PR is not part of classical democratic theory, which posited the press as an intelligence service for the people. The complexity of both government and society means that reporters can no longer keep up, and they must depend on PR practitioners to help.

Because of these factors, the White House PR apparatus continued to expand until 1969, when President Richard Nixon created the White House Office of Communication. This office functioned in addition to the White House Press Office headed by the press secretary, Ronald Ziegler. The Office of Communication's four staff members, directed by a former journalist, Herbert Klein, coordinated the flow of information from the entire Executive Branch. Klein reported to H. R. Haldeman, the White House Chief of Staff, who had been an advertising executive at J. Walter Thompson.

Nixon used the Office as a political tool to influence — not just inform — the public; and when the administration's lies to the public and to Congress were exposed in the Watergate scandal, the entire White House PR operation was discredited. But the Office survived. Presidents Ford and Carter attempted to rebuild a good relationship with journalists and the public by being open about their decisions and activities. By the Clinton era, White House staff involved in PR activities numbered in the hundreds.

PUBLIC RELATIONS TODAY

By 2008 the Bureau of Labor Statistics counted more than 275,000 PR specialists in the United States, and the Bureau predicts that employment will continue to increase faster than the average for

[24] "The Doctors Gird for Battle," *Newsweek* 33 (20 June 1949), 50.

Reagan, "The Great Communicator"
The media's role in influencing public opinion has required modern American presidents to devote considerable attention to public relations. One of the most effective was Ronald Reagan. Even though journalists generally were hostile toward him, he managed to appeal directly to the public through such activities as well-planned news conferences.

all occupations. Far more significant was the increasing diversity of people in PR. At the turn of the twentieth century, there were apparently no full-time, paid PR counselors who were women. In 1968 about one-quarter of PR specialists were female, and in 2000 about 70% were.

Women's entry into the field was not easy, but the outstanding work of a few pioneers paved the way for others after World War II. The career of Jane Stewart provides an example. After graduating from Ohio Wesleyen in 1939, she found a job as secretary to the president of Hill and Knowlton. Recognizing her skills, including leadership and a talent for writing, John Mapes recruited her when he left H&K to form a survey research company, Group Attitudes Development Corporation. A few years later, Hill and Knowlton bought Group Attitudes, making it a subsidiary of H&K, where it had its own clients in addition to doing work for H&K clients when needed. Stewart was entirely responsible for running the subsidiary when she was named president in 1961, and she did the job with great success. A few other women became executives during the 1960s, and in 1970 Marion Pinsdorf became the first woman vice-president on H&K's general account staff. In 2000, women headed about one-third of the top PR agencies.

Minority participation in public relations remained smaller, but it too grew. By 2009 more than 12% of PR practitioners were minorities. D. Parke Gibson, an African American who opened a New York City agency during the 1960s, is one person who found it difficult to move into the mainstream of PR practice. African Americans constituted a multi-million dollar market and could not be ignored. Practitioners were therefore able to find work targeting other people of the same minority group. But many minority practitioners could find work only in minority-owned organizations, and, as Gibson discovered, minority-owned agencies had difficulty obtaining accounts other than those targeting minority audiences exclusively.

Because minorities were marginalized by society, they used PR techniques to forward the cause of civil rights during the 1950s and 1960s. The Southern Christian Leadership Conference, headed by Martin Luther King, Jr., did not retain external counsel, but

it did practice public relations. PR figured in many of the SCLC's activities, including alliance building, political advocacy, consumer boycotts, and grassroots communication. In addition, the Student Nonviolent Coordinating Committee conducted citizenship and political education campaigns designed to recruit volunteers, increase voter registration, and train citizens about nonviolent methods to solve social problems. Its PR activities contributed to the eradication of both segregation and African-American disenfranchisement.

Mass communication research after World War II continued to undermine the idea that people are uniformly or directly affected by media messages, but it also indicated that effects do exist. Scholars argued that variables such as education, media use, and individual needs for information contribute to how much any individual pays attention to or is affected by messages.

PR practitioners responded by developing methods of targeting audiences through messages tailored to meet individual needs and through media such as direct mail and the Internet. New social media tools like weblogs and wikis, which allow multiple Internet users to generate content, have the potential to allow practitioners to collaborate with key publics in decision-making and the distribution of information.

One final significant trend in PR counseling was the development of the mega-agency. A series of mergers of PR firms with advertising and lobbying firms created a small number of huge, full-service agencies. Hill and Knowlton, for example, joined the J.W.T. Group, which included the advertising agency J. Walter Thompson, in 1980. Over the next several years H&K purchased ten PR and lobbying firms, including its long-time rival, Byoir. In 1987 a British firm, the W.P.P. Group, executed a hostile takeover of J.W.T.

Public relations has changed dramatically since 1900 — the number of practitioners expanded geometrically, persuasion theory became increasingly sophisticated, and the practice of public relations modified in response — but at least one thing has remained constant throughout the history of PR counseling. In 1971 pioneer Bernays claimed that "this profession makes it possible for minority ideas to be more readily accepted by the majority"; but

Press Secretaries

As the federal government and the Executive Branch grew in size, the position of White House Press Secretary was created in 1929 during the Hoover presidency. Its function was to serve as a liaison between the president and the news media, in an effort to keep the press and the public informed. Ultimately, its function has been to create a positive image of the president and his decisions. Since press secretaries work closely with journalists, presidents usually have chosen former journalists to fill the position. Shown above in 2006, with President George W. Bush, are six press secretaries who had served since 1975. They are (from left to right) Joe Lockhart (who served under Bill Clinton), Dee Dee Myers, the first female press secretary (Clinton), Marlin Fitzwater (Reagan and Bush I), Tony Snow (Bush II), Ron Nessen (Ford), and James Brady (Reagan). Brady, whose wife stands behind him in this photograph, was shot in the head and permanently paralyzed when a would-be assassin attacked President Ronald Reagan in 1981. In 2000 the press briefing room in the White House was renamed in his honor. Dana Perino (top right) served as Bush's press secretary in his final year in office, and Robert Gibbs (bottom right) served as Barack Obama's press secretary during his first two years in the presidency. Gibbs was unusual in not having any journalism experience.

he also admitted that "regrettably, public relations, like other professions, can be abused and used for anti-social purposes."[25] The discrepancy between the ideal model of two-way communication for social good and the reality of PR practice had not altered since Bernays first wrote about it fifty years earlier. Although there exist plenty of examples of PR activities that have benefited the democratic process, PR techniques and counseling have also made negative contributions.

RECOMMENDED READINGS

BOOKS

Allen, Craig. *Eisenhower and the Mass Media: Peace, Prosperity, and Prime-Time TV.* Chapel Hill, N.C., 1993. Eisenhower used the new medium of television as a regular part of his administration's public relations practices.

Cutlip, Scott M. *The Unseen Power: Public Relations, A History.* Hillsdale, N.J., 1994. Public relations has been a dominant, if unrecognized, force in twentieth-century U. S. history.

Ewen, Stuart. *PR! A Social History of Spin.* New York, 1996. The meanings of public, public opinion, and persuasion and the ways these ideas were applied to visual and verbal propaganda changed dramatically during the twentieth century.

Hiebert, Ray Eldon. *Courtier to the Crowd: The Story of Ivy Lee and the Development of*

Public Relations. Ames, Iowa, 1966. Lee's career is best seen as a part of the democratic crisis that resulted when the mass — mass culture, mass production, mass communication — replaced pluralism. Lee developed techniques that allowed groups to express themselves, thus maintaining pluralism.

Honey, Maureen. *Creating Rosie the Riveter: Class, Gender, and Propaganda during World War II.* Amherst, Mass., 1984. The U. S. government's strategy to recruit women for war work was carefully constructed so that women's participation did not threaten traditional gender roles.

Juergens, George. *News from the White House: The Presidential-Press Relationship in the Progressive Era.* Chicago, 1981. The flow of power from Congress to the White House during the Progressive era created both the modern Presidency and the modern Washington press corps. Presidents and reporters needed each other, but also at times antagonized each other.

Maltese, John Anthony. *Spin Control: The White House Office of Communications and the Management of Presidential News.* Chapel Hill, N.C., 1992. When Nixon created the Office of Communications, he lifted presidential public relations to a new — although not better — level, creating a precedent with which presidents since have had to contend.

Marchand, Roland. *Creating the Corporate Soul: The Rise of Public Relations and Corporate Imagery in American Big Business.* Berkeley, Calif., 1999. The author highlights the rise of corporate PR and advertising from 1920 to 1945.

Miller, Karen. *The Voice of Business.* Chapel Hill, N.C., 1999. The author examines the founding and operation of Hill and Knowlton.

Murphree, Vanessa. *The Selling of Civil Rights: The Student Nonviolent Coordinating Committee and the Use of Public Relations.* New York, 2006. Students used both traditional and innovative PR tactics to transform attitudes, traditions, and laws relating to civil rights.

Olasky, Marvin. *Corporate Public Relations: A New Historical Perspective.* Hillsdale, N.J., 1987. Business and public relations executives did not use PR to stop gov-

[25]Edward L. Bernays, "Emergence of the Public Relations Counsel: Principles and Recollections," *Business History Review* 45 (Autumn 1971): 297, 299.

ernment intervention in business. Instead, they "worked diligently to kill free enterprise" by promoting an alliance between government and business.

Raucher, Alan R. *Public Relations and Business, 1900-1929.* Baltimore, 1968. The rise of corporate public relations was related to both the internal and the external problems of corporations, but the policy of adopting public relations techniques was initiated primarily as a political device.

Tedlow, Richard S. *Keeping the Corporate Image: Public Relations and Business, 1900-1950.* Greenwich, Conn., 1979. Public relations was a product of "a general movement to increase efficiency" and the need to respond to "journalistic criticism which was reaching a wider audience than ever before." Business leaders wanted to control the news that corporations could not help generating.

Tye, Larry. *The Father of Spin: Edward L. Bernays and the Birth of Public Relations.* New York, 1998. Bernays manipulated symbols to persuade people on his clients' behalf, and he took part in many of the pivotal moments in twentieth-century American history.

ARTICLES

Anderson, William B. "Crafting the National Pastime's Image: The History of Major League Baseball Public Relations." *Journalism and Communication Monographs* 5 (2003). MLB's history as a large business enterprise reveals much about the changing role of public relations in sports and society.

Bernays, Edward L. "Emergence of the Public Relations Counsel: Principles and Recollections." *Business History Review* 45 (Autumn 1971): 296-316. Bernays describes key clients and campaigns in his career as counsel on public relations.

Cutlip, Scott M. "Public Relations in Government." *Public Relations Review* 2 (Summer 1976): 5-28. Government public relations "is a weapon of power," but the history of public information operations shows that journalists need assistance to cover the government adequately.

Endres, Fred F. "Public Relations in the Jackson White House." *Public Relations Review* 2 (Fall 1976): 5-12. Amos Kendall, who managed President Jackson's campaigns and press relations, should be considered the first public relations counselor.

Ferré, John P. "Protestant Press Relations in the United States, 1900-1930." *Church History* 62 (December 1993): 514-27. Many churches conducted public relations activities, and clergy considered publicity an effective way to increase attendance and contributions.

———. "Protestant Press Relations, 1930-1970." Ch. 17 in Wm. David Sloan, ed., *Media and Religion in American History,* 261-74. Northport, Ala., 2000. As society became secularized, church leaders "were preoccupied with reaching the American public through the most effective means they knew — the secular media," recognizing that the Protestant press had a limited reach.

Fleener, Nickieann. "'The Creation of a Right Public Spirit': The Hampton Institute's Pioneering Use of Sponsored Films, 1913-1917." *American Journalism* 21 (2004): 93-113. Sponsored films played an important role in this historically black college's early PR efforts.

Girona, Ramon. "From the 'Strategy of Truth' to the 'Weapon of Truth': The Government Information Manual for the Motion Picture Industry, 1942." *Public Relations Review* 36 (September 2010): 306-09. Government guidelines developed for the film industry during World War II were based on a "strategy of truth" and constituted an example of the ethical use of propaganda techniques.

Gower, Karla. "US Corporate Public Relations in the Progressive Era." *Journal of Communication Management* 13 (2008): 305-18. Publicity, press agentry, and public relations have had different meanings at different times. These terms originated during the Progressive era.

Gower, Karla K., and Margot Opdycke Lamme. "Public Relations on Trial: 'The Railroad-Truckers Brawl.'" *Journalism History* 29 (2003): 12-20. Vicious debate between the railroads and the trucking industry led to the Supreme Court's legal recognition of the practice of public relations.

Hallahan, Kirk. "Ivy Lee and the Rockefellers' Response to the 1913-1914 Colorado Coal Strike." *Journal of Public Relations Research* 14 (2002): 265-315. Lee's cam-

paign was a milestone in PR history because of controversial informational bulletins and government relations work.

Henry, Susan. "There is Nothing in This Profession ... that a Woman Cannot Do: Doris E. Fleischman and the Beginnings of Public Relations." *American Journalism* 16 (1999): 85-111. Fleischman worked mainly anonymously with her husband, Edward Bernays, as they established public relations as a profession.

Horsley, J. Suzanne. "Women's Contributions to American Public Relations, 1940-1970." *Journal of Communication Management* 13 (2008): 100-15. Women played important roles in public relations during the middle of the twentieth century.

Kitch, Carolyn. "'A Genuine, Vivid Personality': Newspaper Coverage and Construction of a 'Real' Advertising Celebrity in a Pioneering Publicity Campaign." *Journalism History* 31 (2005): 122-37. A railroad advertising and publicity campaign from 1901 to 1917 featured the adventures of an illustrated woman named Phoebe Snow. Fans thought she was real, in part because newspaper reporters rode the trains and interviewed the model used to create Phoebe — raising questions on how this intersection of journalism, advertising, and publicity might blur the definition of news.

Lamme, Margot Opdycke. "Outside the Prickly Nest: Revisiting Doris Fleischman." *American Journalism* 24 (2007): 85-107. Fleischman believed she was "as much of a public relations pioneer as [Edward] Bernays was, without, perhaps, his drive for self-promotion."

Lamme, Margot Opdycke, and Karen Miller Russell. "Removing the Spin: Toward a New Theory of Public Relations History." *Journalism and Communication Monographs* 11 (2010): 281-362. Prior to 1900 the field of public relations was vibrant and innovative long before corporations institutionalized its practices.

Lucarelli, Susan. "The Newspaper Industry's Campaign Against Spacegrabbers, 1917-1921." *Journalism Quarterly* 70 (1993): 883-92. After World War I, the newspaper industry campaigned against press agents, accusing them of trying to get free space. The hostility between the two factions continues today.

Martinelli, Diana Knott, and Shannon A. Bowen. "The Public Relations Work of Journalism Trailblazer and First Lady Confidante Lorena Hickok, 1937-45." *Journalism History* 35:3 (2009): 131-40. Hickok held a PR position in Franklin Roosevelt's administration.

Miller, Karen S. "Woman, Man, Lady, Horse: Jane Stewart, Public Relations Executive." *Public Relations Review* 23 (1997): 249-69. Stewart was one of the first women to take on the counseling role at a major agency.

Murphree, Vanessa. "Public Relations, 1900-1950: Tool for Profit or for Social Reform?" Chap. 16 in Wm. David Sloan, *Perspectives on Mass Communication History.* Hillsdale, N.J., 1991. This historiographical essay analyzes the approaches that historians have taken to explaining public relations.

Olasky, Marvin. "Retrospective: Bernays' Doctrine of Public Opinion." *Public Relations Review* 10 (Fall 1984): 3-12. Bernays "stuck to his belief that the job of the public relations counsel was to produce socially useful propaganda."

"Persuasive Communication." *American Journalism* 21:4 (2004). This special issue of the history journal contains these articles: Stacey Cone, "Democratic Morality and the Freedom Academy Debate: A Conflict About Institutionalizing Propaganda in America, 1954-1968"; Robert L. Kerr, "Creating the Corporate Citizen: Mobil Oil's Editorial-Advocacy Campaign in The New York Times to Advance the Right and Practice of Corporate Political Speech, 1970-1980"; Margot Opdycke Lamme, "Tapping into War: Leveraging World War I in the Drive for a Dry Nation"; and Nickieann Fleener, "'The Creation of a Right Public Spirit': The Hampton Institute's Pioneering Use of Sponsored Films, 1912-1917."

Ponder, Stephen. "Presidential Publicity and Executive Power: Woodrow Wilson and the Centralizing of Government Information." *American Journalism* 11 (1994): 257-69. Many government agencies had press bureaus in the early twentieth century, and Wilson took steps to consolidate the flow of information from the executive branch.

Raucher, Alan R. "Public Relations in Business: A Business of Public Relations." *Public Relations Review* 16 (Fall 1990): 19-26. Public relations "emerged and grew as an institutional response to the distinctive features of a democratic America."

23

The Media in Transition

1945 - 1974

The phenomenon of television swept through America in the decades after World War II, asserting itself as the premier mass medium, modifying most other media, and changing the way people lived their lives. It introduced a new kind of journalism best defined by the title of an early TV magazine program, *See It Now*.

The other media reacted and tried to meet the new competitor. Newspapers, the media with the longest tradition, attempted to hold on to their practices more than the other media did, but even they ultimately found that they had to change also. The story of the mass media in America following World War II is, then, in many ways the story of television.

THE TELEVISION PHENOMENON

The first public demonstration of television took place on September 7, 1927, from the laboratory of Philo Farnsworth in San Francisco. The experiment, which consisted of the transmission of a photograph, might have been demonstrated months earlier; but investors wanted to wait until a photo could be used, thinking it more impressive than the triangles and dollar signs that had been used in earlier private demonstrations.

Farnsworth's television system had gone unnoticed by the corporate giant RCA (the Radio Corporation of America) until the 1930s, when Farnsworth and RCA became fierce competitors. RCA had tried to purchase Farnsworth's patents, but he did not want to sell, since he had royalty payments in mind. RCA, however, did not want to pay royalties, insisting instead on an outright purchase of the patent rights.

Despite the setbacks and corporate battles that engaged his attention, today hundreds of patents are filed under the name of Farnsworth, "the father of television." He was the last of the independent inventors, a scientist rather than an entrepreneur.

The development of television moved slowly throughout the 1930s as the Federal Communications Commission proceeded cautiously in determining technical and regulatory standards. Not only was there fierce competition between television's develop-

ment engineers, but several proposals were placed before the FCC to consider, including one from CBS for color TV. The FCC did not act on television until 1941, and then World War II interrupted progress on its development. It was not until after the war that TV was widely introduced. In 1946 there were six stations in the United States. By 1970 there were 900.

What was the distinctive nature of television? Through sophisticated electronic technology, it combined spoken sound and natural sound, writing, and pictures. It did all these things at once in a continually changing effusion of stimuli that could be transmitted instantaneously over a wide area. Audiences did not simply see and hear television — they experienced it. At every given moment of every day, by the early 1950s millions were experiencing television. Thus, it was an incredibly rich medium for broadcasters. In the 1940s and until the invention of VCR's and DVD recorders, television was rigidly chronological in nature. It operated on a schedule. One either saw a program when it was broadcast or never, or at least not until it was rerun.

At first people were transfixed by the miracle of television. They would look with wonder at the lines and numerals of the test pattern on a tiny seven-inch set. Stores put sets in their windows, and crowds gathered outside to watch. A home with a TV set attracted the neighbors, much as a literate person with a newspaper and a good reading voice attracted illiterate listeners in the early days of newspapers. Soon the illiterate in those days learned to read. Soon, in the days of television, every home had a set (more than 95% by 1970). By the early 1950s urban apartment roofs had sprouted TV antennas and looked as if they had contracted a metallic fungus. Rickety sharecropper cabins in the rural South seemed to be supported by a TV antenna pole on one side and a pre-war used car on the other.

Early TV content was influenced by radio and the movie industry. Radio was an electronic medium under the supervision of the FCC. It was primarily an entertainment industry with news and cultural events as ancillary content. Advertising revenue financed it, with sponsoring businesses often producing their own content and networks distributing it. Radio developed a full array of con-

The Visual Entertainer
Even before commercial television went on the air, its primary appeal was conceived to be entertainment rather than news and information. This 1944 ad told consumers that with television the most popular radio programs "could all become real visual experiences ... experiences for you to watch as well as hear."

tent: news, drama, comedy, music, lectures — using sound alone. Early television developed from this heritage.

From Hollywood motion pictures, television inherited all the techniques needed to add visual stimuli to the sound. At first, TV programming was live. A drama had to be performed on a set in front of a camera, with commercials performed live at the appropriate moment. If something went wrong, everyone watching knew it. For example, John Cameron Swayze was a radio journalist who became the pitch man on Timex watch commercials. After putting a watch through a terrible ordeal, he would hold it up to the camera and exult, "It takes a licking and keeps on ticking!" Once, though, a Timex was lashed to an outboard motor propeller and thrashed about in a barrel of water. When the propeller emerged from the water, the Timex had disappeared, leaving Swayze speechless.

Early programming (such as Milton Berle's *Texaco Star Theater*, the first popular comedy) was not recorded. Lucille Ball's *I Love Lucy* show was one of the first to be filmed at the same time it was broadcast, and it still is in reruns.

TV's popularity spurred technological change. Early developments that modified the content of television included the film chain and the use of 16mm film. The film chain is a device that points a TV camera at a movie projector and at a slide projector, gathers images from them, and transmits the images to the TV. No longer was live programming the only possibility. The 16mm format rapidly replaced 35mm, which was the motion picture industry standard. The smaller format was popular as an educational audio/visual tool. It was less bulky, less expensive, and easier to handle. Very soon most stations were doing their own 16mm processing and editing. By the mid-1960s, videotape was replacing film.

In the 1950s, cities were linked, eventually coast to coast, by coaxial cable and later by microwave transmission, allowing instantaneous network broadcasting. In small towns individual receivers were linked by coaxial cable to a tall community antenna tower that could bring in signals from a city at some distance. This technology was the beginning of cable TV. By 1970, 80% of local stations had a network affiliation, and 2,800 community antenna systems (the largest with 50,000 subscribers) were serving 6,000,000 households in 5,300 communities.

Miniaturization of electronics and the development of sophisticated rockets had allowed satellites to orbit the earth and bounce back TV signals over large areas. The first trans-Atlantic live satellite transmission occurred in 1962 between Andover, Maine, and locations in Cornwall, England, and Britanny, France. RCA launched the first satellite specifically designed for television in 1975.

Two of the radio networks, CBS and NBC, and a manufacturer of TV sets, Dumont, organized the first TV networks in the 1940s. Soon Dumont went out of business, and ABC joined the list. The FCC at first authorized twelve VHF channels, later adding two dozen UHF channels. The VHF channels had wider range and better quality, and the network stations dominated them. The networks of stations provided a superb national advertising medium. Universities and other public entities established educational stations that were prohibited from carrying advertising. Governmental and public subsidies sustained them, and in the late 1960s PBS was established as a network of public stations.

Following the experience of radio, success of a TV program or series was based on the number of sets tuned in. A successful program or a popular national issue, event, or personality on one network led the other networks to duplicate or match what their competitors were doing. The measure of success was not of the quality or importance of what was communicated, but rather how well the communication appealed to the popular appetite.

The dominance of the three commercial networks and the great popularity of television allowed the medium to set a national agenda of what the public experienced. Sports blossomed, particularly the national professional sports of baseball, football, and later basketball. People talked about "America's team" instead of their own high school team. The TV commercial emerged as a creative kind of communication in which imagery, dialogue, music, and sound were distilled into an intense instantaneous experience. One of the results was to change the nature of political campaigning from long messages, such as speeches, to short commercials or

News of Television

With the advent of commercial TV, *Variety* added it to the topics that the weekly entertainment publication covered. The 1952 page-one story "B'casters Chart Industry Future" examined the proposed lifting of a freeze on television channel allocations and the consequent millions of dollars in profits that the channels would make for those receiving one.

news clips. The mass communication philosopher Marshall McLuhan defined what television was achieving with the term "global village."

EARLY TELEVISION NEWS

TV news had its beginnings at the local level based on radio news practices. Announcers read items gleaned from the wire services, from local newspapers, or from original reporting. They brought news sources into their studios and interviewed them. They pointed their cameras at still news photographs. Soon, however, TV reporters were taking advantage of 16mm motion picture film. TV news was starting to take advantage of its capacity to improve on the things that radio and newspapers did. It was combining sound with moving pictures. Local stations also began to follow the lead of the new network news programs, and by 1950 newscasters anchored the programs at more than 60% of local stations.

Edward R. Murrow was the most distinguished early TV journalist. His background was radio. He had broadcast for CBS from London and even from a British bomber over Berlin in the early days of World War II. The print journalists, such as Walter Cronkite, whom he recruited for CBS during the war, were the nucleus of CBS news for its first decades. Murrow pioneered the TV documentary, looking at the darker side of American life in such offerings as *Harvest of Shame*, reporting the abysmal conditions of migrant workers. His *See It Now* offerings of "Christmas in Korea" (1953) and "Annie Lee Moss Before the McCarthy Committee" (1954) are classics in early in-depth TV reporting. On a lighter note, his *Person to Person* celebrity interviews were primarily entertainment.

CBS premiered *Douglas Edwards and the News* in 1948, and NBC followed with John Cameron Swayze's *Camel Caravan* the next year. They relied on newsreel companies such as Fox, Hearst, and MGM for film footage. Beginning in the mid-1950s, NBC started to upgrade its newsgathering operation and obtained good evening news ratings with the successful combination of Chet Huntley, reporting from New York, and David Brinkley, headquartered in Washington, D.C. Their popular closing, "Good Night, Chet ... Good Night, David ... and Good Night for NBC News," became the source of parody on entertainment shows, on a par with Walter Cronkite's "and that's the way it is ..." in the 1960s and 1970s.

The evening network news programs were limited until the 1960s to a fifteen-minute time slot, evidence of their secondary role to entertainment in television. NBC was also addressing the issues of the day on a weekly basis as early as 1947 with *Meet the Press* (which survives to this day). CBS followed suit with *Face the Nation* in 1954, and ABC initiated *Issues and Answers* six years later. Panels of journalists interviewed officials and other important news sources. The programs usually were relegated to unpopular viewing hours.

The lines between news, public affairs, and entertainment became less distinct in the 1950s with the introduction of talk and interview shows such as *Today*, which won acclaim under host Dave Garraway, and *Tonight* with Steve Allen. Along with the popular *Jack Paar Show*, these were entertainment-oriented, programmed in the early morning or late weeknights. They became serious-minded only with a visit from a political dignitary or with the intrusion of a major news event.

TELEVISION'S IMPACT ON OTHER MEDIA

As television increasingly captured the attention of the public, it had a profound effect on radio and the print media.

Television pre-empted drama and variety programming from radio. Radio networks began to specialize in news and sports, providing segments of local stations' programming. Local stations emphasized music programs presided over by disc jockeys, and in metropolitan areas stations targeted niche audiences by age group or cultural preferences.

Most of the bulging, high-circulation weekly national maga-

Quiz Show Scandals

Cerebral Celebrity Becomes a Living Symbol of Shame

On November 28, 1956, Charles Van Doren smiled into a TV camera and became a celebrity.

His popularity was not just because he came from a family of famous writers. Not just because he taught at Columbia University. Not just because of his boyish good looks, which a producer called "sexy yet wholesome."

Van Doren, who appeared that night on the quiz show *Twenty-One*, became an instant celebrity because of his mind, of all things. Audiences revered him and other contestants because of their intellectual, not (necessarily) their looks. One person gratefully called Van Doren the "antidote to Elvis."

However, in a matter of months he would become the living symbol of shame.

In the mid-1950s, more than two dozen quiz shows ruled network TV. They were challenging. "By the standards of the dumbed-down game shows of a later epoch," observes the Museum of Broadcast Communication, "the intellectual content ... was downright erudite. Almost all the questions involved some demonstration of cerebral aptitude."

The sponsor of the first show saw its sales go up 200% in two months. Such high stakes moved producers to manipulate contestants. They supplied them with questions and answers in advance and even prescribed their on-air dress and mannerisms.

When complaints started trickling out, no one wanted to believe them. But eventually, the cat got out of the bag.

A grand jury investigation, congressional hearings, and national publicity finally forced the shows, along with contestants like Van Doren, to their knees. He was convicted of lying to the grand jury but spent no time in jail. Fired from Columbia, he moved to Chicago, raised a family, and worked for *Encyclopedia Britannica* before retiring to Connecticut.

The scandals finished advertiser control over TV programming.

The first of the big-money giveaway quiz shows was *The $64,000 Question*. Its popularity was phenomenal. Virtually overnight it caught the imagination of millions of viewers and spawned a host of similar quiz shows like *The $64,000 Challenge*, *Tic Tac Dough*, and *Twenty-One*. Contestants could be elevated instantly to wealth and fame. Charles Van Doren, the big winner on *Twenty-One*, became a national celebrity — including a full feature in *Life* magazine (top left) in early 1957.

The quiz shows' wildly successful ride came to a crashing end in 1958. Questions had been raised by the middle of 1957 (as indicated by the *Look* magazine feature at

the top right) when a disgruntled contestant claimed that the programs were rigged. A subsequent congressional investigation found that program sponsors, who had acquired nearly total control over the quiz shows, had decided to feed answers to Van Doren and certain other contestants to assure that the most popular or most colorful ones would win. *Life's* feature in September 1958 (bottom) indicated the changed attitude about the quiz shows and contestants. Van Doren still declared that he knew nothing of the fixing. "I was completely fooled," he avowed. "I thought [the disgruntled contestant] was sweating as hard as I was [trying to answer questions]."

zines disappeared. Television pre-empted the national advertising that had made *Collier's, Saturday Evening Post, Look,* and *Life* extremely profitable. *Life* appeared in a new, expensive, skinny monthly reincarnation. The news weeklies, *Time, Newsweek,* and *U.S. News,* slimmed down and raised their prices to stay afloat. Magazine publishers sought out consumer niches that the networks could not serve, and the number of titles increased even as mass circulations declined.

Newspapers found TV was taking some of their advertising revenue and making substantial inroads into the time their subscribers previously had spent reading. And although they realized TV was a major competitor, newspaper editors were soon reporting copiously on it. That was what their readers wanted.

While editors soon came to realize that they could never enthrall the public the way TV could, they also realized that their print medium could inform readers in ways TV and radio could not. The newspaper was a manufactured product. Readers could pick it up when they wanted to and turn to the content on their own schedule, rather than on the schedule of the broadcast station. The entire newspaper was produced locally. So its content could be tailored to the interests of the locality. At the same time it could carry items of interest to only a few of its readers without boring those who were not interested. Words in print were permanent and not fleeting. They could be studied at leisure and saved for the future. The newspaper could publish coupons in its advertisements; and it could classify advertising in the want-ad section, allowing a potential customer to seek out the product or service desired. TV primarily entertained. Newspapers primarily informed. Thus an environment existed in which the broadcast and print media co-existed.

A COMMUNITY NEWSPAPER, 1940s

In the period between 1945 and 1974, newspaper technology was revolutionized as publishers embraced computers and new ways of getting ink on paper. In 1945, for example, a small city newspaper's technology included only one electronic device, the Associated Press teletype machine.

The newsroom of the *Evening Mirror* (circulation 6,000) in Hillsboro, Texas, right after World War II was typical of American papers. It was equipped with the AP teletypewriter that punched out state, national, foreign, sports, and feature stories at forty-five to sixty words a minute. It also had a double desk for the news editor (who edited all the copy, wrote headlines, and laid out the pages) and a reporter. Two other desks equipped with battered typewriters were occupied by the society editor (who also took classified ads and sold back issues at a counter near the door) and a reporter who also wrote sports. A closet darkroom and a Speed Graphic camera, which used 4" x 5" film, completed the news staff's equipment.

The two advertising salespeople, who shared the room next door with the bookkeeper and circulation manager, also used the camera from time to time, but most illustrations for their ads came

Percentage of American Households with Television Sets, 1950-1969

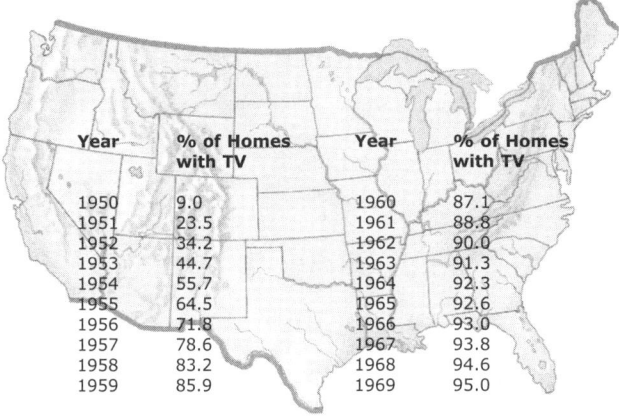

Year	% of Homes with TV	Year	% of Homes with TV
1950	9.0	1960	87.1
1951	23.5	1961	88.8
1952	34.2	1962	90.0
1953	44.7	1963	91.3
1954	55.7	1964	92.3
1955	64.5	1965	92.6
1956	71.8	1966	93.0
1957	78.6	1967	93.8
1958	83.2	1968	94.6
1959	85.9	1969	95.0

Television Explodes
Soon after the introduction of commercial TV in the late 1940s, it became the dominant medium in American homes. The chart above traces its rapid expansion.

from a mat (short for "matrix") service — line drawings and photographs that had been engraved in metal and then, through the process of stereotyping, impressed into papier-mâché, with the impression mailed to the newspaper.

The composing room, which also housed the press, was at the rear of the building. It was the busy nerve center. There printers, who were paid much more than reporters, sat tapping on the keyboards of three clattering eight-foot-high Linotype machines that shot two to four lines of metal type a minute into trays. Other printers slid galleys of type into metal frames, along with zinc engravings of pictures, and locked the hundreds of individual pieces of metal tightly into page forms. With the stereotyping process, printers made mats of entire pages. The mats then were used as molds to make heavy semi-cylindrical metal plates to put on rotary presses. Bigger papers also could afford a new device the AP called Wirephoto, an amazing machine that would transmit and receive photographs using telephone lines. The production process had been universal on small papers and large for the first half of the twentieth century. Every word typed in the newsroom had to be edited with pencil, scissors, and pastepot, re-keyboarded, and set in metal type in the composing room.

The rationale for newspaper content was as firmly established as the production method. The First Amendment to the Constitution had for more than 150 years indicated to publishers and editors that news was defined as what they and they alone decided to print. Most publishers (even if they were not owners) tried to present themselves as pillars of the community — capable of deciding on the basis of their knowledge of newspaper work and of their community what their readers wanted to read and how it should be presented.

Of reporters they asked for "objectivity" in the sense that news should be presented impersonally with the newspaper reacting to events, reporting attributable information in a straightforward style. Opinions, judgments, criticism, and advice emanating from

The Newspaper of the Early '50s
The typical newspaper front page after World War II was reserved for news of major importance. This one from the *Scranton* (Pa.) *Times*, published on October 3, 1951, carried the story of Bobby Thomson's ninth-inning home run to give the New York Giants the win in the playoff game for the National League championship. In the face of new ideas and new competition, newspapers in the era just ahead were to change their concepts of both content and design.

the newspaper office itself would appear on the editorial page as editorials, columns, or cartoons.

The front page was reserved for news of major importance, spiced with a humorous short item frequently, and on rare occasions with a longer "human interest" feature. More features and straight news filled the inside news pages. There was a society page that included women's news centering around club, home, food, clothing, and cosmetics. For men there was the sports page, and the comics page ostensibly was aimed at children. Reporters and editors always were white and almost always male, except for the society page staff and an occasional feature writer.

Newspapermen considered it a good system. The public voted daily with their nickels (or 45¢ weekly for subscriptions) as to whether the paper was doing its job. Most larger cities had competing newspapers (although increasingly only one published in the morning and one in the evening).

Although chain ownership was continuing to grow, the newspaper still was viewed as a local institution. On the editorial page below the name of the newspaper there usually appeared opposite

the title of publisher or president the name of a local family of long standing. Such was as true in small cities as in New York City (where the name was Sulzberger or Reid), or in Dallas and Houston (Dealey and Hobby), or Los Angeles and Oakland (Chandler and Knowland).

NEW TECHNOLOGY AND CHANGING NEWSPAPERS

Revolutionary change in newspaper technology most significantly began with paper tape, an inch wide. It came in rolls about a foot in diameter and was installed so that it ran through a small black box called a "perforator." An operator could tap on a keyboard, and the attached perforator would punch holes across the tape in combinations of one to six holes. These combinations represented every letter, figure, punctuation mark, and spacing combination that a Linotype machine could produce.

Small newspaper chains developed and used the system, and the wire services rapidly adopted it. When a wire service editor decided a story punched into the tape should go to a thousand newspapers across the country, he would run the tape through a black box called a "reader" that put the story on the teletypewriter circuits. In the thousand newspaper offices, perforators reproduced the tape at the same time the story was printed on the teletypewriter. If the local editor chose to use the article, he sent the tape to the composing room along with the printed version that was marked with headline and editing information. One Linotype operator could keep tapes running through the black boxes hooked to several Linotypes, greatly increasing his productivity.

By the mid-1950s the system was almost universal on non-unionized newspapers. Papers bought their own perforator keyboards and used low-salaried clerical workers to produce tapes instead of depending on expensive Linotype operators.

The system was called Teletypesetter, and it had a noteworthy impact beyond productivity on the way newspapers were produced. Teletypesetter made it easier and much less expensive to use wire service material than previously, and that created a difference between the low cost of using wire service material (precomposed) and more expensive local material (although the latter could be produced by Teletypesetter less expensively than before). By using the wire service, the publisher dramatically reduced his labor costs.

Teletypesetter created trends toward newspaper uniformity in three ways. First, it was easier and less expensive for an editor to print a wire service story written by a skilled national writer than to assign a local story to a reporter and go through all the steps of producing it.

Second, the technology of Teletypesetter hardened punctuation, capitalization, abbreviation, and usage style. The Associated Press, United Press, and International News Service agreed on a basic style in the 1950s, and their jointly prepared stylebook set the standards for style in mainstream newspapers.[1]

[1]International News Service and United Press eventually merged into United Press International.

The Newspaper Technology Revolution

In the late 1940s newspapers still were using the hand-operated Linotype machine, which had been invented in the late 1800s, for setting type. Despite the boasts of the Linotype company (left) for its new "Blue Streak" machine, the manual process was slow — and it was about to be revolutionized through the Teletypesetter system (middle). With it, newspapers would enter a new technological age. The Teletypesetter system, invented in the 1950s, sped the process of setting newspaper type and reduced labor costs by connecting a tape-perforating machine to Linotype machines. Unplanned by its inventor, however, was the standardization it helped to bring to newspaper writing, content, and design. Along with the Teletypesetter system, the other great innovations in the printing industry in the decade after World War II were photocomposition and offset printing (right). By eliminating the use of metal type, they speeded up the printing process, reduced costs, and changed much of the newspaper printing process from a heavy industry into quiet office work.

Third, the Teletypesetter system also locked newspapers into a narrow range of column widths, making one paper look like and read like all others. The tendency was alleviated greatly when computerized editing and typesetting became almost universal in the 1970s.

The other great technological innovation of the first twenty years after World War II was the adaptation of photocomposition and offset printing to newspaper production. Since Gutenburg's time, most printing had been done from raised surfaces on metal or wooden type. Photocomposition, on the other hand, produces type by photographic processes. The type then is "pasted up" on the page. Offset printing is a form of lithography, using a photographic process to produce the plate and making it easier to reproduce pictures.

COMPUTERS IN THE NEWSROOM

Computers entered newspaper offices as a means of streamlining the way the right side of a column of type is evened up (justification). Justification always has been done by varying the amount of space between words from one line to the next and, if a particularly long word came at the end of the line, by hyphenating it. Both Linotype operators and Teletypesetter operators were required to slow down at the end of each line and make sure they did not crowd the type together. In the 1960s computer salesmen con-

vinced publishers that a hyphenation dictionary and the width table for any font of type could be stored in a computer, allowing it to determine how each line of type ended. After the introduction of these first-generation newspaper computers, Teletypesetter operators' fingers could fly over the keys at an unvarying speed as they produced "idiot tape" with no line endings. The tape was fed into the computer, and it produced a second tape containing the perforator codes to justify the lines.

The next step was to combine this kind of computer with a photocomposition machine. The computer rode herd on the machinery, making sure it did all the typing and typesetting functions at a steady maximum speed as Teletypesetter tape was fed into it.

For a long time, computer operators had been using teletypewriter keyboards to give instructions to their machines, and the machines would respond with material fed out through printers. Once computer people began to use cathode ray tubes (video screens) to look into computer memories, they realized that they had a new and useful communications tool — a text-editing system. They combined the data storage and retrieval capabilities of computers with what is now known as word processing and created a "front-end system." Reporters could write on their keyboards and rewrite from the words on the cathode ray tubes. Copy editors could edit the stories on their terminals and write headlines, with the computer checking to see if the heads were too long or too short. Great savings were accomplished because there was no need for re-keyboarding at any time.

What a difference in production the video display terminals made. In classified advertising, for example, a clerk took information by phone and typed the want-ad into a VDT along with data about publication and the advertiser. The computer automatically made a credit check and did the necessary bookkeeping while the ad copy went into storage. At deadline time, all of the previous day's ads that were not to be run again were purged. Previously, all these chores had to be done separately by hand.

The entire atmosphere of newspaper plants changed. Composing rooms shrank as they lost their clatter, heat, and inky grime. They became lighted, carpeted, and populated by printers in white shirts who with knives and rulers pasted up pages at sloping tables. In newsrooms the banging of typewriters and scurrying of copy boys were gone. When the newspaper went to press, its contents existed almost identically in two forms — the pasteups in the composing room and the stories in the computer memories.

By the 1970s, heavy and repeated capital investments by newspapers had given them greater flexibility, content resources, and productivity. Yet increased competition from other media made publishers more concerned about the future of newspapers than they had been in 1945.

MCCARTHY AND OBJECTIVITY

Senator Joseph McCarthy of Wisconsin gained notoriety, much of it through televised hearings his committee conducted, in the early 1950s by making largely unsubstantiated charges about Communist subversion in the U. S. government and other institutions, including the media. The Soviet Union and China had powerful Communist governments with professed policies of international domination. United Nations forces, predominantly American and commanded by an American, were opposing the North Korean and Chinese invasion of South Korea. The charges of McCarthy and others struck a responsive chord of fear in the American public.

"McCarthyism" played a major part in bringing about a change in the way journalists perceived their role in society. The change was caused in great part by the issues and the social changes on which journalists found themselves reporting. The case of Associated Press war correspondent Edward Kennedy illustrates the relation of reporters to government at the end of World War II. Kennedy and other correspondents, although they had witnessed the signing of an armistice at Allied Headquarters, had agreed not to report the end of the war in Europe (V-E Day) in 1945 until the next morning. When at midnight Kennedy heard Radio Berlin telling the news to the defeated Germans, he decided to break the embargo and let Americans in on the facts. To stay in the good graces of the military, the AP fired him. By contrast, in the latter stages of the Vietnam War, a wire-service reporter, Seymour Hersh, frustrated not only with military and governmental information policies, but also with wire service policies, quit his job and, despite the refusal of major news media to pay attention to his story, got it

The Media and McCarthyism
Senator Joseph R. McCarthy demonstrated how an uncritical mass media could be manipulated for ideological purposes. Because the press reported only the routine, deadline news, he was able to take advantage of journalism's practices to gain wide publicity for his charges while escaping critical examination of his own behavior. He did have opponents among journalists, though. Robert Fleming, a *Milwaukee Journal* reporter, exposed as a fabrication McCarthy's claim that he had been a military hero during World War II. The exposure provided ammunition for McCarthy's foes. Despite his talent for exploiting the traditional practices of journalism, it was a CBS *See It Now* television program and live television coverage of the Army-McCarthy hearings that signalled his decline in popularity. As a result of McCarthy's dealings with the press, many journalists began to question the principle of objectivity.

published and won a Pulitzer Prize for international reporting.[2]

A change in reporting and publishing the news had taken place between the two events that had nothing to do with "marketing" the newspaper. At the beginning of the period "objectivity" was a reporter's highest ideal. As time and events moved on getting the "real" story — the story beyond the official statements and surface events — was, for many journalists, the ideal. *A Free and Responsible Press*, which the media criticized when it was released in 1947, contained ideas that newspaper reportage reflected more and more: "a truthful, comprehensive and intelligent account of the day's events in a context which gives them meaning" and the accurate portrayal of all social groups.[3]

The old concept of objectivity required reporters to lay aside most of their own wisdom when they sat down to write a story. They told what they had seen, what witnesses or spokesmen had said, and what written sources could provide for background. That was reporting, and that was what Sen. McCarthy capitalized on as he alleged the existence of substantial numbers of Communists in the State Department, elsewhere in government, and final-

---

[2]Thirty-six newspapers ran Hersh's series of stories through a syndication service, the Dispatch News Service, created solely for the series. The first article was published in, among other newspapers, the *St. Louis Post-Dispatch*, 13 November 1969.

[3]Commission on Freedom on the Press, *A Free and Responsible Press* (Chicago, 1947), 21.

**National Television
and the Emmett Till Trial**
Members of the news media from around the nation converged on the 1955 trial of two men charged in the murder of Emmett Till, a black teenager. The trial was one of the first that national television cameramen covered. Till's murder and the acquittal of the accused men provided much of the impetus for the media's coverage of the early civil rights movement.

ly in many private institutions such as newspapers that took exception to his tactics. Reporters dutifully reported his statements and speeches, which seemed to be paced so that rebuttals and denials never caught up with the on-going story.

At its 1953 meeting, the Associated Press Managing Editors Association raked coverage of McCarthy over the coals in one of its most rancorous debates. McCarthy was the subject, but "objectivity" was the issue. The *Washington Post's* J.R. Wiggins warned that "if we circulate day after day ... month after month the infamous allegations that there's treason in the White House, in the Chiefs of Staff, in the Secretary of State and in all the other departments of government, we need not be surprised if an hour comes when the American people have confidence in no one." Robert P. Early of the *Indianapolis Star* said he was "surprised that McCarthy's name came up at all. I don't think we should snipe at the way McCarthy handles his news conferences. After all, he is a United States Senator."[4]

Later, new reporters who came on the scene in the 1960s and 1970s studied a textbook, *Interpretative Reporting*, written by a crusty Northwestern University professor named Curtis MacDougall, or other texts that also questioned "pure objectivity." The debate they raised about "objectivity" and the new kind of "interpretive" reporting continues even today.

Edward R. Murrow was among the first to point out the weakness of McCarthy's allegations and his use of innuendo to damage the reputations of public officials and private citizens. In *A Report on Senator Joseph R. McCarthy*, Murrow and his associate, Fred Friendly, used film of McCarthy's speeches and interviews to demonstrate contradictions and point out that his accusations extended to highly respected publications and military heroes.

However, it was the nationally televised Army-McCarthy Senate hearings that demonstrated TV's power to present an event to the public unmediated by a journalist. The hearings pitted Army Secretary Robert Stevens, a mild-appearing executive, and his attorney, an elderly New Englander named Joseph Welch, against the heavy-jowled McCarthy and his two aides, a hulking David Schine and a glowering attorney, Roy Cohn. When McCarthy tried to link one of Welch's aides to an alleged Communist front, Welch zeroed in on the danger of character assassination that McCarthy represented before a TV audience of millions of Americans. Mc-

[4]Victor Hackler, ed., *The APME Red Book 1953* (New York, 1953), 57, 58.

Carthy steadily lost credibility thereafter, and the Senate censured him.

The Army-McCarthy hearings, like the Kefauver organized crime hearings that preceded them and the Watergate hearings that came two decades later, allowed TV cameras and microphones to bring the national public face to face with important issues and key players.

THE MEDIA AND CIVIL RIGHTS

In 1954 the Supreme Court issued a landmark decision on school desegregation, and the beginning of a story called Civil Rights shot up like a skyrocket. For the first time, African Americans and other minorities seemed to have articulate spokesmen and effective strategies for combating discrimination from the national level down to county courthouses. The activism began with the black lawyers who fought the *Brown v. Board of Education* case through to the 1954 decision and its implementation. It included Dr. Martin Luther King; college students and others who conducted sit-ins, freedom rides, and voter registration projects; a rejuvenated black press, including new national magazines; and a new crop of ambitious black political leaders and local activists.

There was strong opposition in southern states, and both sides in the conflict used all the tools of persuasion they could command. News people were challenged. Whom should they believe? Whom should they quote? What should they cover? Were events staged solely for media coverage? What was the real picture? No ultimate authority provided answers. More than ever before, journalists made up their own minds at the scene of the news.

The power of local TV news was demonstrated in 1955 by coverage of the funeral in Chicago of a black teenager, Emmett Till. His mutilated body had been discovered in the Tallahatchie River in Mississippi. Two white men had taken him from his uncle's plantation cabin at night. He allegedly had whistled at the wife of one of the abductors. His mother asked for an open-casket service. Televised pictures of the body brought thousands of mourners to the church. The story reached most of the northern industrialized centers that had large populations of blacks who had migrated from the South.

The trial of the two men, which ended in their acquittal, attracted more than 100 reporters from across the nation. Film was shot

Hazel Brannon Smith

Mississippi Editor Fights Racial Injustice Despite Threats

"Hazel Brannon Smith of the *Lexington* (Miss.) *Advertiser* was the bravest journalist I have ever known. No qualifiers. She wrote in a time and place when you could be killed for what you wrote. She wrote anyhow."

The words were those of Richard Lee, editor of the quarterly journal of the International Society of Weekly Newspaper Editors, on Smith's death in 1994. The sentiments were those of legions of colleagues, peers, and friends who had feared for her safety in the collision of civil rights and violent resistance thirty years earlier.

An Alabama native and graduate of the University of Alabama, Hazel Brannon took out a $3,000 loan in 1936 to buy a weekly paper in Mississippi. Later she acquired additional community newspapers. For twenty years, she was a successful and somewhat flamboyant country editor, known for her outspokenness, her big hats, and her white Cadillac convertible.

She returned to Lexington from an ocean cruise in 1949 with the ship's purser, Walter Smith, at her side. They married the following year.

In 1954, three events shattered the status quo and charted her editorial course forever: The Supreme Court declared segregation in public institutions, specifically schools, unconstitutional; in her home community, a law enforcement officer shot an unarmed black man; and a Citizens' Council was organized to resist, at all costs, any movement toward integration. She was asked to "cooperate" with the resisters. She refused. Thereafter, she increasingly spoke out against what she saw as rank injustice.

"Laws were made to protect the weak in our society from the strong," she wrote in a front-page editorial calling for the resignation of the officer who had shot the black man.

Hazel Brannon Smith's fight against the White Citizens' Council and its opposition to civil rights for African Americans ruined her financially. When she filed for bankruptcy in 1985, the building that housed her newspaper was crumbling. By then, though, she had developed Alzheimer's disease, and she seemed unaware of conditions around her.

Another episode involving violence against a black man and his family prompted her editorial observation that "it is not moral or just that any man should live in fear or be compelled to sleep with a loaded gun by his bedside."

"Over the next 15 years," she recalled years later, "as the Councils' influence spread to the highest offices in the state, my newspapers were boycotted, bombed and burned, a new newspaper was organized in Lexington to put me out of business, my life was threatened, and my husband lost his job as county hospital administrator – all because of pressure brought by this professional hate-peddling organization."

In 1960, Smith won the Elijah Parish Lovejoy Award for Courage in Journalism, conferred by Southern Illinois University. Four years later, she won the Pulitzer Prize for her "steadfast adherence to editorial duty."

Such plaudits failed, however, to achieve reconciliation with those elements of southern society who perceived her stance as an unrelenting assault on their culture and heritage. They burned a cross on her lawn. Advertising lineage continued to plummet. Readers disappeared. Eventually bankruptcy claimed her properties. Hazel Brannon Smith was a success as a crusading editor – and it ruined her.

in the courtroom during recesses. Interviews were conducted outside on the courthouse lawn. Interviewees sat in folding chairs in front of microphones. Movie cameras were pointed at them, and reporters behind the cameras shouted questions at them.

The Till trial was the first of the major civil rights stories that took TV reporters all across the South — to the Montgomery bus boycott, the Little Rock school desegregation crisis, the Birmingham Sunday School bombing, the sit-ins, the freedom rides, and eventually to Dr. Martin Luther King's "I Have a Dream" speech on the steps of the Lincoln Memorial. Two decades later PBS broadcast the *Eyes on the Prize* series that documented not only the civil rights movement but the new kind of TV news. Television went to crises and reported not only the official views, but the views and the pictures of ordinary people directly involved. Reporters developed a skeptical attitude toward officials that was to be a hallmark of journalism until today.

For the national press, civil rights was a story about the South that became a story about the national condition. The *New York Times'* Atlanta bureau, headed by Claude Sitton, the wire service bureaus, and a few dozen southern newspapers provided bases of operations for correspondents from many metropolitan papers who roamed the South. They and their broadcast colleagues developed into a corps of expert reporters who eventually replaced the aging World War II correspondents on all the big stories. There existed for them no clear line of what was in the national interest — as had existed for the World War II press corps. The new generation sifted through pronouncements from the highest levels right down to quotes from illiterates at the scene of the action in attempting to determine what was of real significance.

In the South some newspapers simultaneously labeled black people as too backward for desegregation and condemned them for using cunning and unfair methods. The great majority of papers deplored the threat to law and order and supported the existing pattern of segregation. A few warned readers that changes were inevitable and argued for fair play for African Americans.

Particularly in the South, the ongoing civil rights story brought out the best in many journalists. The southern editors who took stands for moderation did so in the face of staunch opposition to the civil rights struggle on the part of their white readers, the political leadership, and much of the business establishment. In Arkansas, for example, where Gov. Orval Faubus called out the National Guard to block nine black students from desegregating all-white Central High School in 1957, the state's leading daily, the *Arkansas Gazette*, stood for law and order. Editor Harry Ashmore, backed by publisher J.N. Heiskell, vehemently opposed Faubus editorially, alienating readers and resulting in significant losses in circulation and advertising. The nine students finally gained admission to Central High after President Eisenhower sent in the 101st Airborne to enforce court orders, and the *Gazette* won two Pulitzer Prizes in recognition of Ashmore's editorial leadership and the newspaper's coverage of the crisis.

Across the South, other editors exercised similar leadership. Between 1957 and 1964, southern editors dominated the Pulitzer

NUMBER OF WEEKLY NEWSPAPERS IN THE UNITED STATES, 1935–1960

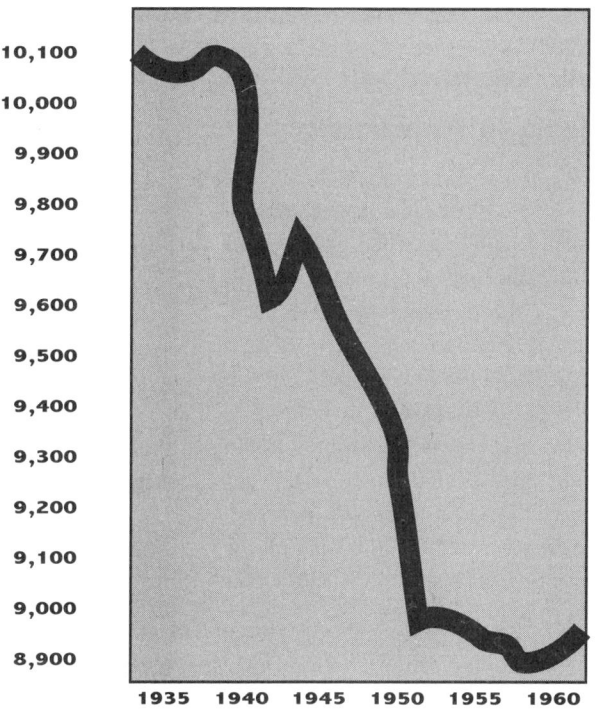

Prizes in editorial writing. The winners were Buford Boone of the *Tuscaloosa* (Ala.) *News* (1957), Ashmore (1958), Ralph McGill of the *Atlanta Constitution* (1959), Lenoir Chambers of the *Norfolk Virginian-Pilot* (1960), Ira B. Harkey, Jr., of the *Pascagoula* (Miss.) *Chronicle* (1963), and Hazel Brannon Smith of the *Lexington* (Miss.) *Advertiser* (1964). Most of them were not radical crusaders for integration. Rather, they argued for equal justice for all citizens regardless of color as their communities faced desegregation crises.[5]

Other journalists defended the racial caste system in the South. Two notable ones were Jimmy Ward of the *Jackson Daily News* in Mississippi and James Kilpatrick of the *Richmond News-Leader* in Virginia. Ward was probably the most vehement in expressing the worst of Mississippi racism in his daily newspaper column, "Covering the Crossroads." As civil rights activists increased their calls for equal justice in Mississippi in the early 1960s, he derided them as unkempt hippies and outside agitators who were needlessly stirring up trouble. His column even included racist jokes. Kilpatrick, on the other hand, was a leader of southern "massive resistance" to the Supreme Court's school desegregation orders. In the mid-1950s, he was the most prominent spokesman for "interposition," a long-discredited legal doctrine that argued that states had the constitutional right to ignore federal authority.

A spin-off from the civil rights story resulted in a 1964 Supreme Court decision that strongly affected media coverage into the fol-

---

[5]Typical of the stands they took was Hazel Brannon Smith's "Arrest of Bombing Victim is Grave Disservice," *Lexington* (Miss.) *Advertiser*, 16 May 1963, one of the editorials for which Mrs. Smith was awarded the Pulitzer Prize. Similar writings by other editors are included in W. David Sloan and Laird Anderson, *Pulitzer Prize Editorials*, 3d ed. (Ames, Iowa, 2003).

Communication Satellites

New Technology
Changes Reporting

The world entered the space age on October 4, 1957, when the Soviet Union (USSR) launched the first man-made satellite, *Sputnik*. The United States made its first successful launch in early 1958. As the USSR and the United States competed during the Cold War to establish a presence in space, the number of satellites quickly increased. For the public, the significance of these satellites was overshadowed by the race to land a man on the moon, a goal that the United States achieved in August 1969.

In 1958, though, President Dwight D. Eisenhower believed that communication satellites would have greater consequences for the world than sending a man to the moon. Certainly photo-reconnaissance from satellites played a part in ending the Cold War in addition to seriously eroding individual privacy – but satellite technology brought important changes to many other areas, including domestic and international news reporting.

Satellites made possible the global transmission of live events via television. As early as 1945, the writer Arthur C. Clarke speculated about the possibility of establishing a system of geosynchronous satellites to establish a communication network. In 1962, President John F. Kennedy signed the Communication Satellite Act that authorized the development of Intelsat, the first worldwide system for satellite communication. By 1969 the system achieved global coverage; and by the early 1970s, Intelsat provided a communication network for more than sixty countries. The first major event to be broadcast live internationally was the 1969 *Apollo* moon landing. President Richard M. Nixon's visit to Communist China in 1972 was also carried by satellite. Satellites also transmitted sports and entertainment, including the first Muhammad Ali-Joe Frazier championship boxing match in 1971.

After the Soviet Union launched *Sputnik*, it issued the postage stamp (top left) to commemorate the event. The United States followed with *Telstar*, a communication satellite launched in 1962 (bottom left). The space race culminated with *Apollo's* landing on the moon in 1969 (top), an event that had the largest television audience in history, thanks to the capacity that satellites had provided for international transmission of TV signals.

In 1973, more than one billion people watched Elvis Presley's "Aloha from Hawaii" concert.

During the 1970s the American presence in space continued to expand. By 1981, 250 U. S. television stations had the capacity to use broadcasts from satellites. The Public Broadcasting System (PBS) was an early leader in this area. So, too, was Ted Turner's Cable News Network (CNN), which in 1980 used Intelsat to establish a 24-hour news channel. During the decade that followed, other cable channels adopted satellite technology.

Improvements in satellite technology enhanced the ability of TV stations to peer into areas previously closed to the press by dictatorial governments or hazardous natural environments. In 1990 and 1991, millions of people worldwide were able to watch the Gulf War live. Even more opportunities to see events in real time presented themselves during the 1990s as communication satellites provided coverage for the rapidly expanding Internet. During the early 21st century, journalists used geographic information systems provided by satellites to prepare in-depth stories about natural disasters, population changes, and many other topics.

In 2000, Associated Press Television News and Reuters Television dominated most of the video used by broadcasters internationally. Competitors, though, soon appeared. In the Middle East, the Arab television station Al Jazeera began broadcasting in 1996 and soon became widely available in that region. After the al Qaeda terrorist attacks of September 11, 2001, it gained worldwide prominence and used satellites to transmit news that was pro-Arab and often highly critical of America and Israel.

Satellite technology influenced people's lives by both creating and helping to resolve national security problems, enhancing and complicating the conduct of American foreign policy, diminishing personal privacy, and greatly increasing the information we have about the world around us.

lowing decades. In *New York Times v. Sullivan* (a case involving an advertisement that a civil rights group placed in the *Times*) the court established the doctrine that public officials (later expanded to public figures) must prove what it called "actual malice" before successfully suing for libel.[6] The Supreme Court coined the term — which had little to do with the traditional meaning of malice as "ill will" — and defined it as a journalist's publishing false information while knowing it was false or publishing it with "reckless disregard" for its falsity. *Times v. Sullivan* provided the media with a much fuller opportunity to report and comment on public matters, creating a virtual immunity against libel suits. Later cases reduced the protection, but the decisions continued to guarantee journalists broad protection.

TELEVISION AND THE SPACE RACE

In 1957 the "beep-beep" radio signal beaming from *Sputnik I*, the first satellite launched successfully from Earth, gave American educational, scientific, military, and political institutions and the general public a rude wakeup call. The Soviet Union, considered well behind Western Europe and America scientifically, was leading what became known as the Space Race. Soon TV viewers were seeing American attempts to launch a satellite fail, then eventually succeed. They saw a Russian dog emerge from a satellite that had been brought back home, and they got to know a monkey named Ham who performed as directed in an American satellite. Yuri Gagarin became a world hero as the first human to leave Earth's atmosphere and orbit in a Russian space capsule.

When the United States began to launch two-man Gemini spacecraft, TV cameras accompanied them. Throngs in New York's Grand Central Station watched live pictures of Earth on giant screens. On July 20, 1969, a camera mounted on the lunar lander Eagle transmitted live pictures of Neil Armstrong putting a human foot on the moon for the first time.

The space race was made for TV. Public interest was combined with a government agency (NASA) eager to build public support. Journalists and experts explained with ingenious audio-visual models and graphics everything that was happening. The countdown to launch, the live pictures from space, and the moments of danger during re-entry stretched and sharpened the capabilities of television to go anywhere and show everything. The NASA program was so successful that the exploration of space soon seemed commonplace. A manned space exploit became just another item of national news.

THE MEDIA AND VIETNAM

When the next great issue, the Vietnam War, increasingly began to dominate front pages, two kinds of reporters — war correspondents and veterans of the civil rights story — packed off to Southeast Asia. Their backgrounds would influence their reporting.

Vietnam was an agrarian nation that for centuries had endured

[6]*New York Times Co. v. Sullivan*, 376 U.S. 254 (1964).

The Press and Vietnam
Most newspapers supported United States involvement in the Vietnam war in its early stages. By the late 1960s, however, opposition had grown strong. Some critics claimed that the media opposition led to biased coverage and the ultimate military defeat. Whatever a newspaper's stance on involvement, however, the war was one of the biggest stories in the post-World War II era. The attention it occupied in the press can be gleaned from this front page of the *Dubuque* (Iowa) *Telegraph-Herald* in 1970.

the domination of China, Japan, and France. When the Japanese were defeated at the end of World War II, Vietnamese forces defeated France when it attempted to renew its colonial rule. Two governments existed, a Communist regime in Hanoi and a pro-Western one in Saigon (now Ho Chi Minh City). The United States became involved in the resulting war between the two because it feared a Communist victory would lead to a "domino effect" in that region with numerous developing nations coming under Soviet and Chinese Communist domination. American participation escalated from non-combatant advisers to hundreds of thousands of troops (many of them draftees) carrying the brunt of the fighting, with the support of Air Force and Navy units operating from distant bases.

An incident described by David Halberstam illustrated the difference between the traditional and the new reporting of the Vietnam War. After graduation from Harvard in the 1950s, Halberstam went to work on a small Mississippi daily. He wrote little for the paper about the civil rights story that swirled all about but wrote a lot about it for the *Reporter* and other magazines. His views about journalism led him to question not only the local social and

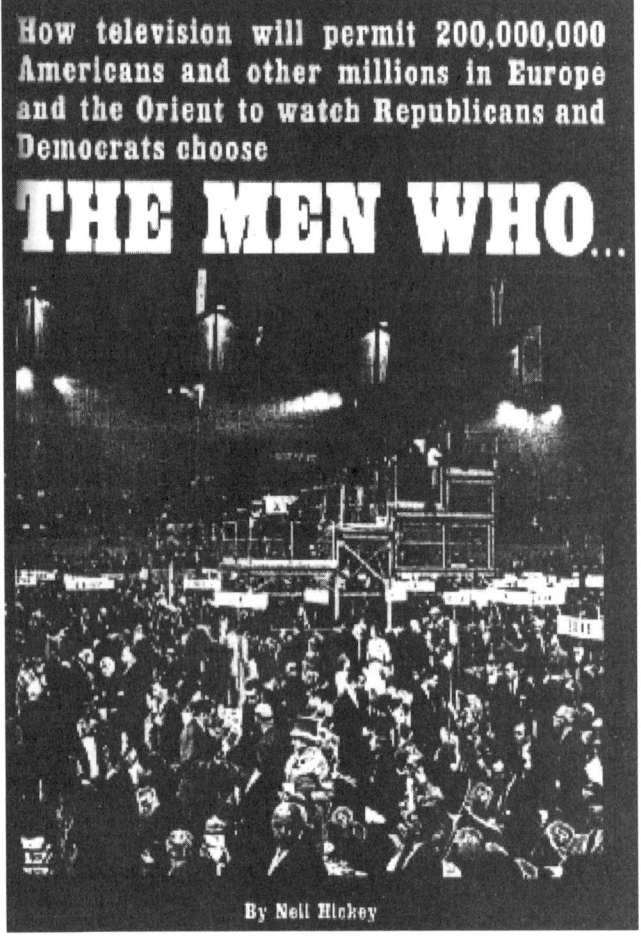

How television will permit 200,000,000 Americans and other millions in Europe and the Orient to watch Republicans and Democrats choose

THE MEN WHO...

By Neil Hickey

1968 Convention Coverage

Protest over the Vietnam War had become widespread by 1968 as the national political conventions were set to begin. The national TV networks were well prepared to cover the conventions, as this cover story in the August 8 issue of *TV Guide* demonstrated, but their biggest story became the violent demonstrations outside the Democratic convention hall in Chicago. Coverage of the rioting showed to the nation a Democratic party that appeared incapable of governing.

political establishment but also his own editor. He moved through the *Nashville Tennessean* to the *New York Times*. In Saigon he began to cover the war with the same type of skepticism toward the U. S. military and the South Vietnamese government.

He became convinced that the military had underestimated the strength and "historical dynamism" of the enemy and that the American policy of "small war, use technology to get in cheap, hope for the best" was proven wrong. He and others reported those problems, and "that made us different from war reporters in the past." He recalled a two-day tour of the Mekong Delta in 1963 (when he was twenty-eight years old) with one of his journalistic heroes — Richard Tregaskis, World War II correspondent and author of *Guadalcanal Diary*. He introduced Tregaskis to several of his valued, non-government sources and discussed the war at length. As they returned to Saigon, Tregaskis quietly told him, "If I were doing what you are doing I would be ashamed of myself."[7]

[7]Frances Ring, ed., "Excerpts from Conference Panels," *The Journalist* (University of Southern California School of Journalism, May 1983), 34.

The stony silence that followed was symptomatic of the changes underway in reporting. Halberstam won a Pulitzer Prize for his Vietnam coverage, although he was one of a number of reporters whom the military and the government accused of not knowing whose "team" they were on.

The media's reporting contributed to the disaffection of the American public toward the war in Vietnam and toward the leaders in Washington, D. C. After the Pentagon Papers were published and the My Lai massacre became public, disillusionment with the war was irreversible. The respected columnist Walter Lippmann had opposed the war very early and carried on a dove-hawk debate with Joseph Alsop on alternate days in the same spot on the editorial page of the *New York Herald Tribune*. Harrison Salisbury of the *New York Times* was criticized severely for going to North Vietnam and reporting major U. S. bombing damage to non-military targets. CBS questioned government policy as early as 1965 in *Vietnam: The Hawks and the Doves* and later in a series titled *Vietnam Perspective*. NBC presented a full year of *Vietnam Weekly Review*, and ABC addressed the Vietnam question in more than 100 half-hour documentaries. In 1966, when CBS declined to carry Senate committee hearings on involvement in Southeast Asia, Fred Friendly resigned as president of CBS News.

The news media covered the Vietnam story on three fronts: with the combatants in Vietnam, with the officials usually in Washington, D. C., and with the public that was deeply divided between those who vehemently opposed the war and those who resented what they viewed as disloyalty by the opponents.

TV reporting from the scene was dramatically different from what Americans were accustomed to. World War II newsreels had shown American troops welcomed into European cities liberated from Nazi occupation, American amphibious forces ousting the Japanese from Pacific islands they had invaded, and United Nations forces fighting alongside South Koreans defending themselves from a North Korean and Chinese invasion. From Vietnam in 1965 Americans saw U. S. Marines burning a Vietnamese village, Cam Ne, with Morley Safer of CBS providing the narration. They saw a Buddhist monk burn himself to death in Saigon in protest of the violence. They saw a South Vietnamese policeman take out his pistol and summarily execute a bound prisoner in the middle of a street, with Jack Perkins of NBC describing the scene. They saw reports of the South Vietnamese president's assassination by his own Army. They saw civilians, including a naked six-year-old girl, fleeing from American bombs. These were pictures of conflict inconsistent with what the American public felt it could support.

The news from U. S. cities and campuses was also disturbing. Thousands of young people, many politicized and energized by the civil rights movement, demonstrated against America's involvement in the war. Some became violent, burning buildings and seizing university administrative offices. Pro-war Hawks and anti-war Doves of all ages debated the war.

The domestic climax came at the 1968 Democratic National Convention in Chicago, when thousands of anti-war demonstrators took up residence in Grant Park. The demonstrations and eventual violence detracted from the convention (where reporter Dan Rather was physically assaulted on the floor) and culminated in "a police riot," in the words of the Walker Report, an official inquiry into the events. Reporters, clearly identified by press credentials, were "hit, maced or arrested" by the police without provocation, according to the report. Former CBS News chief William Small described the final hours of the convention: "It reached its climax, not in the nomination of Hubert Humphrey but in the confrontation between anti-war demonstrators and jumpy police.... The consequent loss of control and restraint by police offered a violent scene that was carried around the world."[8]

Turmoil and dissent over Vietnam drove the incumbent president, Lyndon Johnson, from office. His initial attempts to deal with the issue in a temperate, even low-key, manner on radio and TV were in stark contrast to his personal attempts to manage the news and stifle dissent later. His press aides not only hounded broadcast company executives at work but also placed personal calls to the homes of network reporters. Johnson, overwhelmingly popular in 1964, chose not to seek re-election in 1968.

The "Pentagon Papers" drove another stake into America's war effort and another wedge between the media and the government. The papers were documents that Daniel Ellsberg, a military analyst, took from Defense Department files and gave first to congressmen and then to the press. They revealed that the government had not been frank with the American people about its intentions in Vietnam. When the *New York Times* began publishing the papers, the government got a court order halting publication. The *Washington Post* and other newspapers picked up the publication, bringing further court orders. Eventually the *Times* and the *Post* won in the courts on the issue of prior restraint of publication.

Whereas the Pentagon Papers indicated deception at home, My Lai demonstrated dehumanization abroad. Using a modest foundation grant, his own money, and his knowledge of the military, reporter Seymour Hersh began from a brief Defense Department announcement about the scheduled court martial of Lt. William Calley and discovered the details of the massacre of 300 to 500 Vietnamese civilians by American soldiers in the village of My Lai. He uncovered the story by traveling across the country interviewing returned veterans who had been at the village. Hersh offered the story to leading publications and, after being rejected, placed the story in a few dozen newspapers through a small news service headquartered in Washington, D.C. Soon all the media were seeking every detail they could get. Pictures of the victims being shot and of their bodies eventually were published.

Richard Nixon, elected president in 1968 on a platform of ending the war, was dogged by Vietnam as the conflict dragged into the 1970s. CBS broadcast *The Selling of the Pentagon*, with Roger Mudd detailing government efforts to promote U. S. intervention and equally widespread efforts to deceive reporters regarding events in Vietnam. A Congressional committee investigated the matter, and an attempt to hold CBS President Dr. Frank Stanton in

[8]William Small, *To Kill A Messenger: Television News and the Real World* (New York, 1970), 204.

The Pentagon Papers
After the *New York Times*, on June 13, 1971, began printing the "Pentagon Papers," the federal government obtained an injunction to prevent further publication. In the meantime, other newspapers started publishing the classified documents. The first to do so was the *Washington Post.* On July 1 the *Times* exulted that the Supreme Court had voted to lift the injunction. The episode convinced many journalists that the government was their enemy, and the military viewed publication of the papers as another instance of reckless behavior by the press.

contempt of Congress failed in the House of Representatives by a 226-181 vote. Two military officers, Lieut. Col. Anthony Herbert and Gen. William C. Westmoreland, sued the network over postwar telecasts. Westmoreland, who commanded U. S. forces in Vietnam for a time, received an out-of-court settlement.

POLITICS AND PRESIDENTS

Politicians, including presidents, recognized that the power of television might drive them from office, but they also recognized it as a tool to put them in office and keep them there. President Franklin Roosevelt had used radio to promote his New Deal reforms to combat the Great Depression and mobilize the nation after the 1941 attack on Pearl Harbor. He used radio as his direct link to the citizenry.

Television enhanced this link between office holder or candidate and the voting public. It changed the nature of politics and particularly presidential politics. Local political bosses found their ability to deliver the vote to a candidate more difficult when voters were given the opportunity to see and hear all the candidates

Kennedy Assassination

President's Murder Revolutionizes News

John F. Kennedy had been president for a little more than 1,000 days when he was assassinated in Dallas, Texas. An unspeakable tragedy for the country, the assassination also marked a turning point in American journalism, as the country learned to rely on television for breaking news.

Kennedy traveled to Texas in November 1963 to lay the groundwork for the 1964 presidential election. By 12:30 p.m. CST on Friday, November 22, his motorcade had nearly finished wending its way through downtown Dallas and was in Dealy Plaza when gunfire rang out.

Almost immediately, Dallas radio stations reported the shooting, although it was not immediately clear whether the president had been hit. UPI's Merriman Smith reported the news from the motorcade on a press car radio phone. His first dispatch, reporting simply that three shots had been fired, moved as a bulletin on UPI's "A" wire at 12:34 p.m. Newspapers immediately began printing multiple extra editions.

But this was television's moment. From the instant Walter Cronkite interrupted a CBS soap opera at 12:40 p.m., until President Kennedy was buried at Arlington Cemetery three days later, Americans were glued to their TV sets.

Live television news coverage of such magnitude had never before been attempted, and the technology of the day was primitive. Until cameras could be warmed up, the networks' first reports were essentially radio reports, the only visual a static "bulletin" slide. Within thirty minutes, viewers could see anchors and reporters scurrying to gather facts in real time. On CBS, voices could be heard feeding Cronkite information that viewers had already heard for themselves on the air. Meanwhile at NBC, Frank McGee was reduced to repeating Robert McNeil's phone report, even after technicians had — unbeknown to

  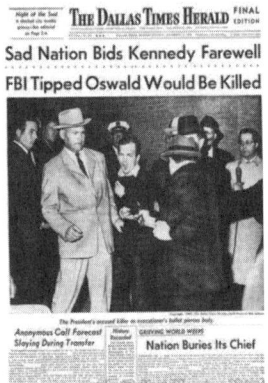

Soon after Lee Harvey Oswald shot President John Kennedy, the TV networks interrupted regular programming to report live. CBS anchor Walter Cronkite (above) annouced Kennedy's death immediately after getting the word. Many newspapers issued special "extra" editions, and they all reported on the daily events over the next several days.

McGee — finally managed to put McNeil's audio on the air. There was no live video from the scene. It would be years before Dallas businessman Abraham Zapruder's graphic home movie of Kennedy's murder would be televised.

When the AP "flash" brought confirmation of Kennedy's death, Cronkite momentarily lost his composure, regaining it after a brief pause and a clearing of his throat.

The TV networks pooled resources to stay on the air through a weekend of solemn proceedings that were abruptly interrupted on November 24 by more shocking

news from Dallas. NBC viewers watched live as Jack Ruby, a Dallas night club owner, shot dead Kennedy's accused assassin, Lee Harvey Oswald. Back in Washington, an estimated 250,000 people filed past Kennedy's coffin in the Capitol Rotunda.

By Monday, November 25, the day of Kennedy's funeral, an unprecedented 93% of American households were estimated to be watching by television. It cost the networks an estimated $40 million, but television was later lauded as a "national cathedral" where Americans could mourn together.

frequently and make their own choices. State political conventions at which delegates to national conventions were chosen gave way to presidential primaries. Soon, by the time the national convention took place, the candidate it would choose already had been determined. The convention became a pep rally for the party faithful in which the candidate was showcased to the nation.

President Harry Truman was the first to use television, broadcasting from the White House and inviting cameras into some cabinet meetings. He was the first to be televised tossing out the baseball at the start of a major league season.[9] But he did not exploit the medium as some of his successors did. Dwight Eisenhower's smile was made for TV, but his speaking style was not. He hired actor Robert Montgomery to be his television adviser. His inauguration was the first to be televised, and segments of his press conferences were released for television; but it was Richard Nixon, his 1952 running mate, who first exploited the medium to enhance his political fortunes.

When Nixon was accused of having set up a personal, political slush fund, he responded with an address televised by CBS and NBC. He disclosed details of his finances and provided a careful examination of his family history and work ethic. He noted that his wife had no furs but wore a "good Republican cloth coat" and concluded with a plea of support for Eisenhower and a staunch promise to retain a gift, a little dog named Checkers, from a Texas supporter to his daughter. The Checkers speech resulted in an outpouring of public support and Nixon's retention on the ticket.

However, it was Nixon's opponent in the 1960 campaign who emerged as the master of television. By 1960 mobile equipment allowed TV journalists to follow the candidates about. John F. Kennedy showed his willingness to chance embarrassment by allowing cameraman Robert Drew to accompany him behind the campaign scenes, and in the first of four television/radio debates, he excelled on TV although Nixon did better on radio.

Historians and critics have questioned the relevance of the debates to key issues of the day, but there is no question that they elevated the interest level of the electorate. In assessing their impact, Kurt and Gladys Lang maintained in *Politics and Television* (1968) that Kennedy's performance strengthened his support among uncertain Democrats.

Kennedy introduced the live TV news conference and was a master at the ad lib response to reporters as well as at defusing tough questions with a one-word answer. He had a cultured delivery and youthful appearance that worked to his advantage. Perhaps his most effective use of TV to inform the public and enlist its support was his open facedown of the Soviet Union over the installation of missiles in Cuba in 1962. He vowed to get rid of them and mobilized the military, all the while keeping the nation informed and working through diplomatic channels with Soviet leader Nikita Khrushchev. Perhaps the image of a resolute leader supported by Congress and the public played a role in the peaceful resolution of the crisis. Certainly television had a central role in

Six. Five. Four.

LYNDON JOHNSON (OVER):
These are the stakes.

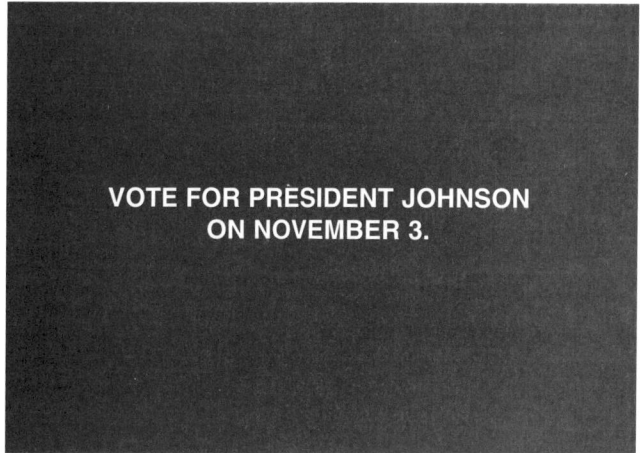

VOICE OVER: Vote for President Johnson on November third. The stakes are too high for you to stay home.

Political Advertising
Politicians began extensive use of TV commercials in the 1960s. The most infamous was this one. It implied that presidential candidate Barry Goldwater would start a nuclear war if elected.

[9] Raymond L. Carroll, "The 1948 Truman Campaign: The Threshold of the Modern Era," *Journal of Broadcasting* 24 (Spring, 1980): 175.

international relations. A criticism, described by historian Erik Barnouw, was that the public was "left with the misleading picture of a good guy/bad guy crisis.... It was oversimplification — a defect not uncommon in television messages."[10]

When Kennedy was assassinated in November 1963, television was just barely mature enough to cover the story live from Dallas. The televising of assassin Lee Harvey Oswald's murder and the Kennedy funeral could not have been broadcast live only a dozen years earlier because the technology was not available. Also, co-incidentally, CBS and NBC had expanded their evening news programs to one-half hour less than three months before the assassination. Expansion at ABC occurred later. The assassination and funeral were media events of the first order. The networks suspended regular programming for nearly three and a half days. The tragedy was an example of the communication philosopher Marshall McLuhan's global village concept, an event in which the world shared an experience via TV. Taped footage of later assassination attempts on major figures such as Pope John Paul, Presidents Ford and Reagan, and Alabama Governor George Wallace was on the air within minutes after the events occurred.

Kennedy shared a quality with Roosevelt and (at times) Truman that is vital to good television communication. He spoke to the person sitting on the other side of the TV screen without pomposity. His successor, Lyndon Johnson, though he wanted to project the image of a great commoner, never achieved informality, nor did Nixon. The Vietnam War put both Johnson and Nixon on the defensive at their press conferences, which became increasingly confrontational; and both were reduced to making speeches at military installations and a few safe campuses because of public hostility.

The Nixon administration was hostile to broadcasters, with Vice President Spiro Agnew delivering addresses in which he first described network journalists as "a tiny and closed fraternity of privileged men, elected by no one," and later attacked them as liberals who were "nattering nabobs of negativism." The deaths of four students at Kent State University at the hands of National Guardsmen during an anti-war demonstration and the trial of Lt. Calley for his part in the My Lai massacre exacerbated this hostility. Nixon called on a "silent majority" of citizens to make their views known in support of the government. His television adviser, Clay Whitehead, warned the Indianapolis chapter of the Society of Professional Journalists that broadcasters would suffer the wrath of their local communities at license renewal time if they did not adhere to a standard of balanced reporting.

THE MEDIA AND WATERGATE

Ultimately for Nixon, it was the media that brought the climax to his presidency. The courts and the newspapers first brought to the public eye the incident — known as "Watergate" — that finally resulted in the only resignation of a U. S. president. When TV joined the hunt, there was no escaping for Nixon.

[10]Erik Barnouw, *Tube of Plenty: The Evolution of American Television* (New York, 1975), 319.

The story began with a botched burglary attempt in the summer of 1972 at Democratic campaign offices in a Washington building named Watergate. Carl Bernstein and Bob Woodward, two city desk reporters for the *Washington Post*, doggedly pursued the story from the day five burglars were caught in the act until the Judiciary Committee of the House of Representatives conducted impeachment proceedings.

They traced the chain of responsibility for the burglary and the funds to pay for it through Nixon's re-election campaign organization, past the gates of the White House, and into the Oval Office itself. They scrutinized every record they could find, pounded the pavements, and telephoned day and night to discover sources and get information. They had the resources of the biggest newspaper in the nation's capital behind them, and they and their editors avoided being discredited by having two reliable sources for every fact they published. Their tenacity resulted in Nixon and his closest aides having to admit again and again that they had been less than candid with the public. The Watergate cover-up became a bigger story than the Watergate burglary.

The Woodward-Bernstein coverage led other newspapers and the wire services to increase their attention to Watergate. The *New York Times* put reporter Seymour Hersh on the story in an effort to match the *Post's* coverage. What the public read in the papers was supplemented by what it saw daily on TV, as cabinet members, campaign officials, and the president's advisers faced sharp questioning from reporters, Congress, and the courts.

Two nationally televised sets of Congressional hearings turned Watergate into a national scandal. The first was before a Congressional Committee chaired by Sen. Sam Ervin of North Carolina. The networks carried it live day after day, as the burglars admitted their crimes and officials from the White House and the Committee to Re-Elect the President testified under oath. Ultimately, the existence of audio tapes that recorded all Oval Office conversations came to light, and they demonstrated that Nixon's denials of knowledge and complicity in the break-in were false. The second round of hearings was before the House Judiciary Committee chaired by Rep. Peter Rodino. It voted before a national TV audience to recommend impeachment.

Nixon was forced to defend himself repeatedly in public addresses, and the few press conferences he held became increasingly sharp. When it became apparent in August 1974 that he would face impeachment, he resigned. By that time, a series of trials were underway that sent the burglars to prison along with presidential advisers at the highest level.

Woodward and Bernstein won the Pulitzer Prize for reporting. Perhaps a more significant measure of the impact of their story on the public was the eagerness of the two leading motion picture actors — Robert Redford and Dustin Hoffman — to play the Woodward-Bernstein roles in a film based on the reporters' book on how they covered Watergate, *All The President's Men*.

Watergate provided a model for investigative reporting, an increasingly popular term in newsrooms. Investigative reporting is characterized by the use of conventional reporting techniques,

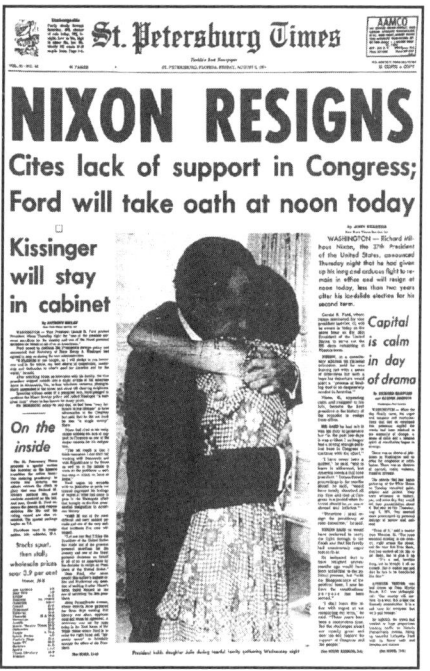

Nixon and the Media
From the beginning of Richard Nixon's presidency, many journalists believed he hated the press and posed a danger to the institution itself. When the 1972 burglary of the Democratic Party headquarters at the Watergate office building was discovered, hardly anyone paid much attention, but it became the event that tore down Nixon's presidency. *Washington Post* reporters Bob Woodward and Carl Bernstein began tracking down evidence as crime investigators would. What they found finally convinced public officials and other journalists to investigate. This 1973 issue of *Newsweek*, as the investigation heated up, declared that "journalists and politicians have many things in common, but these days their most notable shared characteristic seems to be suspicion." Nixon eventually was implicated and resigned from office in 1974, the only American president ever to do so.

but with reporters zeroing in on a subject and pursuing it relentlessly. It is one manifestation of the goal of getting to the truth behind the facts. Because the reporter stands aloof from the story, investigative reporting contrasts with another manifestation of the truth-behind-the-facts goal, the New Journalism of the 1960s and '70s.

In New Journalism, newspaper writers immersed themselves in stories, giving subjective reports. They even delved into what they thought their sources were thinking. Tom Wolfe, author of *The Kandy-Colored Tangerine Flake Streamlined Baby*, and Gay Talese, author of *The Kingdom and the Power*, became the best-known of the New Journalists. However, fiction writers such as Truman Capote, in his nonfiction novel *In Cold Blood*, and Norman Mailer, in *Armies of the Night*, did the same kind of reporting.

CONTROL AND CRITICISM

In the United States, the government has more control over radio and television than it does over newspapers, magazines, and books. When the First Amendment was ratified in 1791, it prohibited federal government control of the press. This concept represented libertarian thinking: Let all kinds of information compete in an open marketplace, and the truth will rise to the surface. The idea of social responsibility, though, was strong in the twentieth century when radio and later television were introduced. The Commission on Freedom of the Press, for example, emphasized the responsibility of the media to provide a meaningful and complete presentation of the news in its 1947 report, *A Free and Responsible Press.*

Orderly allocation of broadcast frequencies was the responsibility of the Federal Communications Commission, and it created regulations seeking to assure that broadcasting would be carried out in the public interest. One effect of this system was to make broadcasters much more sensitive than print journalists were to public and official criticism.

Several avenues existed for influencing broadcasting. The FCC could refuse to renew a station's license, as it had done in Jackson, Mississippi. In that case, station WLBT-TV had lost its license when African Americans demonstrated that its programming had failed to address the concerns of the black community. Congress could act, as in *The Selling of the Pentagon* episode in 1971. The Supreme Court could rule, as in the *Red Lion* case in 1969. In addition, advertisers could exert strong pressure by threatening to withdraw commercials.

In the early 1950s, when fear of Communist domination was at its height, government agencies and some businesses were demanding that employees sign loyalty oaths. Blacklisting, the practice of barring employment to someone with Communist ties, developed in broadcasting as well as in the motion picture industry. A byproduct of the blacklist phenomenon was a 1950 document, *Red Channels: The Communist Influence in Radio and Television*, which listed more than 100 people in broadcasting alleged to have Communist sympathies. The most prominent cases involved Jean Muir, an actress for NBC's *The Aldrich Family*, and John Henry Faulk of CBS, both of whom lost their jobs in radio. Faulk's distinction lies in his successful legal battle over more than a decade to clear his name. His 1954 autobiography, *Fear on Trial*, became the subject of a TV docudrama.

The networks were also responsive to the reports of government commissions. In the 1960s black contributions to society were brought to the forefront and represented in documentaries such as *Black History: Lost, Stolen or Strayed?* narrated by Bill Cosby. They were offered in response to the Kerner Commission's examination of TV's role in fostering prejudice by not reporting racial issues and failing to address black Americans.

Regulations regarding political campaigns influenced news and public affairs television programming. For example, Congress had to enact legislation to allow candidates Kennedy and Nixon to debate one-on-one on TV in 1960 because the Equal Time regulations in the FCC's Fairness Doctrine required broadcasters to give every candidate for an office the same access to the airways, and there were a dozen or so minor party candidates for president.

Outside the political arena, the Fairness Doctrine resulted in the Supreme Court's 1969 *Red Lion* decision, in which an author took exception to criticism a TV evangelist leveled at him. The court ruled that the station, owned by Red Lion Broadcasting, would have to allow the author time to respond.

In this era the three major networks dominated the airways. Their technical ability to gather and edit information into effective communications was recognized. Thus, when the documentary *The Selling of the Pentagon* in 1971 set off a debate over foreign policy and Defense Department self-promotion, CBS came under criticism for the way it had edited and presented its material. A Defense Department official and an Army officer claimed their comments were used out of context and distorted their intent. A complaint was filed with the FCC, and a U. S. House of Representatives subcommittee launched an investigation, subpoenaing all material used in preparing the telecast. After the network refused to provide unbroadcast videotape and film (called "outtakes"), the subcommittee's effort to cite CBS President Frank Stanton for contempt was brought before the entire House but failed.

Conservatives, liberals, and others established organizations such as Accuracy in Media (AIM) to examine and comment on media performance, particularly television. At the same time, broadcast news coverage faced its share of critics. In *News from Nowhere* (1973), Edward Epstein studied the decision-making process for network news coverage and put into perspective the idiosyncrasies of what gets covered and why. He described the logistics of putting together a news program and the priorities, including time and visual content, that frequently dictate whether a story is told. *TV Guide* columnist Edith Efron confronted the issue of liberal news bias during the 1968 election in her book *The News Twisters* (1972). It received a great deal of attention; and Efron and an associate, Clytia Chambers, went on to document a public relations campaign by CBS News against publication of *The News Twisters*, ostensibly because of her indictment of CBS's performance in the election and its decidedly liberal bias. Another popular publication addressed methods of political campaigning and reporting. In *The Boys on the Bus* (1972), Tim Crouse accused the press corps of "pack journalism" on the political trail.

NEW COMPETITION FOR NEWSPAPERS

The numbers of daily newspapers remained stable around the 1,750 level until 1980, when they slumped to 1,700. Television became a dominant medium, and the big general-interest magazines disappeared. Soon, newspapers turned to what had been the mag-

Daily Newspaper Circulation in the United States, 1940-1987

azines' staple: displays of photography and graphic art and lengthy nonfiction prose. With radio, TV, billboards, and other media from which to choose, advertisers hesitated to buy space in more than one paper in a city with competing dailies. The paper falling behind in circulation and advertising lineage therefore usually continued to lose ground as time passed, rather than regaining first place.

One time-tested way to combat rising production and distribution costs was to increase newsstand and subscription prices. But an increase also tended to hasten busy media consumers' decision to forsake their second (often an afternoon) paper in favor of television or of more time spent elsewhere. Another way to combat high overhead was to abandon subscribers outside the newspaper's trade area. The *Fort Worth Star-Telegram*, for example, which had carrier delivery routes 350 miles from its Central Texas presses in the 1940s, had retreated to its local county and surrounding environs by the late 1960s.

Three other kinds of competition appeared largely because of the new print technology. First, suburban newspapers succeeded. Some were chains surrounding a city and sometimes owned by a big downtown paper. Others, like *Newsday* of Long Island, New York, rivaled the metropolitan papers in size, coverage, and profitability. City and regional magazines sprang up. Some prospered. Some soon withered away. Most ubiquitous of the new print competitors were the shoppers, distributed free to every address in the market area. By trimming the news staff to a person who processed publicity releases and by aggressive ad sales, these "throwaways," as traditional editors called them, operated with minimal editorial costs. The established papers countered with "TMC" (total market coverage) schemes in which they distributed streamlined editions to all non-subscribers.

In cities and towns too small to support a TV station but big enough to have a substantial base of advertisers, daily and weekly papers thrived. The computerized newsroom-composing room let these "community" papers do things they had never done before. At last they were freed from expensive engraving of photographs; and the offset printing press, more efficient for small press runs than for giant runs, gave them the opportunity for printing quality as good as or better than the big-city paper had. Community papers banded together in joint printing ventures. A weekly or small daily publisher would put the page pasteups on the truck seat beside him and drive to a central printing plant (sometimes a larger morning paper that got extra revenue by using its idle press time to roll out a half dozen smaller papers). A few hours later, after calling on possible advertisers or playing a round of golf, the publisher would head home with his bundles of papers ready for distribution. Sometimes they would be mailed directly from the printing site.

The trend toward chain — or "group," the term publishers preferred — ownership of newspapers accelerated. In part, it can be explained by the fact that chain management was more attuned than individual publishers to the competitive imperatives. Another part of the explanation can be found in two quirks in tax laws. Media groups embraced the law that allowed them to avoid paying capital gains taxes by investing their profits in additional "properties." At the same time, many newspaper families were finding it difficult to deal with inheritance laws that required them to seek large amounts of credit to pay the taxes required when the newspaper passed from one generation to the next.

Corporate practices began to replace traditional community journalism practices. They included aggressive as opposed to paternalistic management practices and credibility for the newspaper as opposed to credibility for the local editor-publisher. Many a city afflicted with generations of inept or even venal local ownership found that the management sent in by a major group produced a newspaper that served both advertisers and readers far better. Others, where a community-minded publisher sold his paper to a chain, discovered that a bright young publisher (perhaps an Ivy League MBA) might be around just long enough to get some local wisdom, only to be transferred to a bigger job and replaced by another bright young man or woman. Numerous communities found the local paper was being run by mediocre management sent in by owners, such as the British newspaper tycoon Lord Thomson, who lived half a continent away or on the other side of the world.

Advertising and news departments began to use social science research soon after World War II, most notably when Rudolph Flesch's formula for the "fog index" of complicated writing came to the attention of editors. An Austrian-born readability expert, Flesch found that many ads were not only poorly written but also difficult to read. So he promoted the use of simple words and short

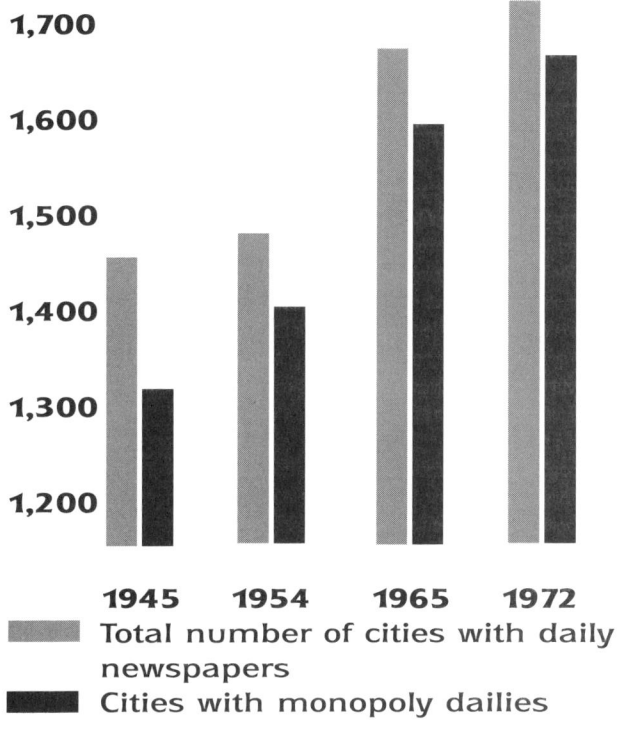

NUMBER OF U.S. CITIES WITH MONOPOLY NEWSPAPERS 1945–1975

Total number of cities with daily newspapers

Cities with monopoly dailies

sentences. Soon information on readership and on the income and spending habits of the public was a routine part of newspaper planning.

In the face of competition, the executives of newspaper groups turned, not surprisingly, to the kind of social science research other major corporations had used to increase the sales and acceptability of their products. In speeches before media groups, Robert Marbut, president of Harte-Hanks newspapers, could be heard during the early 1970s quoting the demographic statistics that researcher Daniel Yankelovich had uncovered, to the effect that more and more young people were reading newspapers less and less, that they were more interested in information about their own lives than about the world, and that papers must reach them or suffer. The newspaper had to be "marketed."[11]

The traditional society and women's pages vanished to be replaced by "lifestyle" sections. Old-line newspaper people shook their heads when "people" pictures (as opposed to "news" pictures) and fluffy features began to appear on front pages every day. Vigor and style replaced much of the stuffiness of newspapers, but traditionalists questioned whether an analysis of the world's best-fitting jogging shoe matched in news value an analysis of the world's political health.

[11]"Marketing" of the newspaper was urged by Marbut in numerous speeches and in articles in professional publications. The remarks cited here are from an address delivered at the Southwest Journalism Symposium, San Antonio, Tex., 14-16 October 1978.

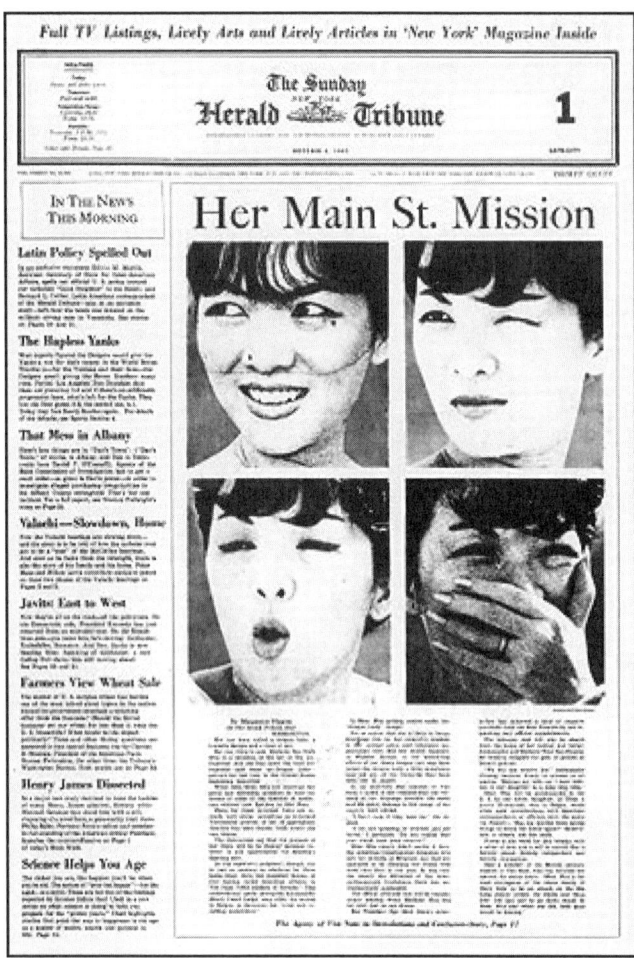

The *Trib* and a New Approach to Design

In its struggle for survival, the *New York Herald Tribune* brought in James Bellows as editor in 1962. He hired Peter Palazzo, an art director and former advertising designer. With his redesign of the Sunday edition of the *Trib*, Palazzo revolutionized newspaper design by combining it with principles of magazine design. Before him, most people who laid out newspapers were editors who had no training in graphic design. One of the best designed newspapers even before Bellows' and Palazzo's arrival, the *Trib* continued to win awards afterwards. The imaginative changes they made, however, were unsuccessful in the face of competition from the *New York Times* and the tabloid *Daily News*. The *Trib* printed its last issue in 1966.

THE TRIBUNE'S STRUGGLE

In cities where newspaper competition continued to exist, it became cut-throat. Such competition existed for the *New York Herald Tribune*. A look at its effort to survive and why it failed illuminates the concerns with which papers struggled during these decades.

In the late 1950s John Hay Whitney, a wealthy member of an old East Coast family, purchased the *Herald Tribune* from the Reid family. He hoped to reverse the 120-year-old paper's decline in advertising and circulation, to make it the voice of the moderate wing of the Republican party, and to return it to a prominent position among the city's seven daily papers.[12]

He hired as editor the typographically innovative John Denson

12*Time,* 8 September 1958, 49.

to provide a showcase for the *Trib's* stable of brilliant writers and reporters, including Walter Lippmann, Joseph Alsop, Marguerite Higgins, Robert Donovan, Art Buchwald, Walter Kerr, Judith Crist, Tom Wolfe, and Jimmy Breslin. The *Tribune's* stately vertical makeup had won many awards for typographical excellence. That look changed radically. Denson used large, terse one-line headlines spread across the page on a liberal background of white space, with stories and pictures packaged by bold borders. Promotional boxes at the top or bottom of page one touted inside content. A two-column summary of all the day's news always ran on the left side of page one to help readers crowding subways, buses, and commuter trains get the news without struggling to turn pages.

An ad agency was employed to create a new image for the *Trib*. Soon billboards and carcards were asking New Yorkers: "Who Says a Good Newspaper Has to be Dull?" Not long after, the *Tribune's* logo appeared beneath the slogan to confirm to the public which newspaper was livelier than the fat, gray *New York Times* and more serious than the flashy tabloids, the *Daily News* and the *Mirror*.

Although circulation began to rise, the paper still was losing money. In 1962 James Bellows replaced Denson not long before a labor-management dispute shut down all seven Manhattan dailies for 114 days. Bellows and his top editors used the hiatus to design an entirely new *Sunday Herald Tribune* and a new Sunday magazine supplement, *New York*. Their goal was total design; and when publication resumed, they came close to achieving it. A rule framed the front page of each section of the paper. Photographs, drawings, headlines, and type were integrated to provide the reader with logical and attractive packages of information.

New York magazine was pure lifestyle. The February 9, 1964, issue capitalized on Valentine's Day with a "Love in New York" theme. Tom Wolfe described a languorous weekend of apartment living in "A Sunday Kind of Love." Jimmy Breslin captured a raucous City Hall wedding in "When the Last of the Roths Got Married." The back of the magazine had columns in which the critics gauged the impact of romance on the cultural scene in art, dance, and the rest.

The good news about the *Trib*, though, was just a silver lining to dark clouds. Its competitors, the comprehensive *Times*, with the largest news staff of any U. S. paper, and the sensational *Daily News*, with more than twice the circulation of any other, remained fat with advertising. When the strike ended, the four morning papers doubled their newsstand prices to 10¢. Almost at once the tabloid *Mirror* went out of business, despite its half-million circulation. The *Tribune* lost circulation, as many readers who had been willing to spend a dime to buy it and one of the other papers now chose to dump the *Trib* and spend the same dime on just one paper.

In 1964 moderate Republicans (including Whitney and the *Tribune*) failed to stop the nomination of conservative Barry Goldwater for the presidency; and for the first and only time in its history, the *Tribune* supported a Democratic presidential candidate,

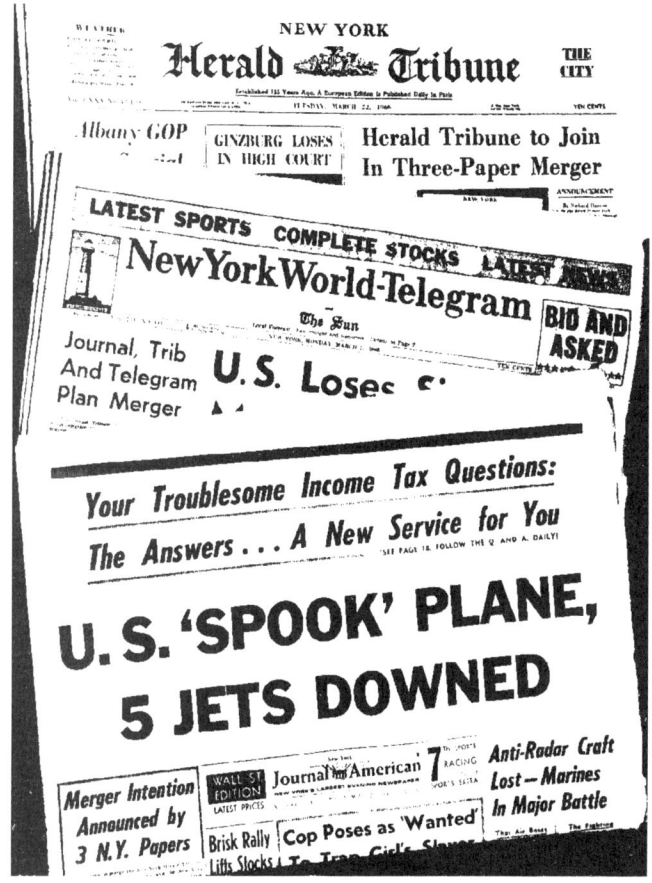

The End
When competition brought the merger in 1966 of the *New York Herald Tribune*, the *World-Telegram*, and the *Journal-American*, it marked the end of the famous newspapers founded in the 1800s by James Gordon Bennett, Horace Greeley, Joseph Pulitzer, and William Randolph Hearst. The combined *World Journal Tribune* published for less than a year before it, too, died.

Lyndon Johnson. The *Trib* had not reached its goal of Republican leadership. It was time to retrench. The last *Trib* was published in March 1966. An attempt to publish it after merging with two afternoon papers failed.[13]

The *Herald Tribune*'s experience was different in some ways from that of most newspapers of the post-1945 era: its competition was with other newspapers, not other media, and it did not have the new technology available to enhance productivity. But the things it did to make itself more appealing to readers — new design, new kinds of content, new marketing methods — were prophetic for the 1970s.

PROFESSIONALISM AND SELF-AWARENESS

Forces in addition to media competition and new technology contributed to changes in news content of papers. Professionalization of news staffs through education, introspective examination by the media, scrutiny by social scientists, the impact of powerful insti-

tutions (government and business particularly), and national and world events contributed to changes in coverage and writing.

College-educated reporters and editors came to dominate news rooms. A mid-1950s study showed that fewer than 20% of the staff members of Texas papers had been to college. An early 1970s study found the figure was approaching 90%.[14] College journalism programs burgeoned during the 1960s and '70s. Courses dealt with historical, ethical, and theoretical perspectives of the media, as well as with the practical skills needed to work for the media. Upon graduation students took their college perspectives to their jobs. They looked upon fellow students and their professors as professional partners, and they established informal nationwide networks of alumni and colleagues who shared their views.

Mass communication scholars delved into critical and scientific examination of the media. The Graduate School of Journalism at Columbia University established the *Columbia Journalism Review* in the early 1960s, the prototype and one of the few survivors of several dozen academic and professional journals dedicated to critiquing media performance. Thousands of research reports on the media went onto library shelves as masters and doctoral theses, journal articles, and books. One of the most popular and useful was Philip Meyer's *Precision Journalism*, a book that explained the techniques and limits of social science research and showed how reporters could use it as a source of newsworthy information.

Education contributed to an attitude of self-examination by the media. So did immediate past events. Since the 1940s, the press had dealt with civil rights, the resignation of a president, man's trip to the moon, and other major events. Editors no longer believed that the role of the newspaper was simply, as Wilbur Storey, editor of the *Chicago Times* in the nineteenth century, had said, to "print the news and raise hell."[15]

One journalist, Henry Luce, founder and publisher of *Time*, *Life*, and other news-oriented magazines, funded the Commission on Freedom of the Press in the late 1940s. Headed by Robert M. Hutchins, president of the University of Chicago, the Commission included in its inquiry all of the major media at that time — radio and motion pictures as well as newspapers, magazines, and books. It addressed itself to "the responsibilities of owners and managers of the press to their consciences and the common good for the formation of public opinion." Despite great technical achievements, the Commission found that, in general, the press was failing to meet the needs of society. It was disturbed by the concentration of ownership of the press and questioned if the "struggle for power and profit [had] been carried to such a point in this field that the public interest ... [had] suffered." It also concluded that the press devoted too little time and space to information and discussion about public affairs and too much to "scoops and sensations." The press was too prone to accommodate itself to the whims and pressures of the audience on the one hand and to the preferences of owners on the other, the Com-

---

[13]The story of the demise of the *WJT* is detailed in Joseph Sage, *Three to Zero: The Story of the Birth and Death of the World Journal Tribune* (New York, 1967).

[14]Alan Scott and Raymond West, "Personnel Turnover on Small Texas Dailies," *Journalism Quarterly* 32 (1955): 183-9; and Harry Marsh, "Correlates of Professionalism and News Performance Among Texas Newsmen" (Ph D. diss., University of Texas, 1974), 51.

[15] Quoted in Justin E. Walsh, *To Print the News and Raise Hell* (Chapel Hill, N.C., 1968).

mission believed.[16] Its report, *A Free and Responsible Press*, led in establishing responsibility to society, alongside freedom to publish, as a tenet of American journalism.

Codes of ethics, largely unenforceable under the First Amendment, gained renewed popularity. Joining the 1923 Canons of Journalism of the American Society of Newspaper Editors were codes by the Society of Professional Journalists-Sigma Delta Chi, the National Conference of Editorial Writers, and others.

A MEDIA WATERSHED

In the 1960s and '70s, the Vietnam issue had ousted one president, and the Watergate controversy ousted his successor. The media had focused attention on both, and in the process they had changed also. As the third quarter of the twentieth century came to a close, they seemed to have unprecedented power. TV stations and newspapers were being bought and sold at highly inflated prices. Journalism schools were experiencing record enrollments. It was a watershed for the media with new challenges ahead.

RECOMMENDED READINGS

BOOKS

Allen, Craig. *Eisenhower and the Mass Media: Peace, Prosperity, and Prime-Time TV.* Chapel Hill, N.C., 1993. Eisenhower should be considered the first TV president because he and his staff masterfully managed the new medium.

Aronson, James. *The Press and the Cold War.* Indianapolis, 1970. The press between 1945 and 1970 helped lead the United States into a dangerous political reactionarianism.

Aucoin, James L. *The Evolution of American Investigative Journalism.* Columbia, Mo., 2005. Investigative reporting took on renewed vigor starting in the 1960s and flourished because of the reporters' enthusiasm for the practice.

Avery, Robert K., and Robert Pepper. *The Politics of Interconnection: A History of Public Television at the National Level.* Washington, 1979. The authors provide an account of the internal politics of public TV from 1968 to 1976.

Barnouw, Erik. *The Image Empire.* New York, 1970. The third part of the author's trilogy on the history of broadcasting focuses on television.

Bass, Thomas A. *The Spy Who Loved Us: The Vietnam War and Pham Xuan An's Dangerous Game.* New York, 2009. Pham Xuan An worked as chief correspondent for *Time* magazine. Fellow journalists held him in high regard, even as he won sixteen medals while serving as a spy for North Vietnam and providing it with strategic military information.

Baughman, James L. *Television's Guardians: The FCC and the Politics of Programming, 1958-1967.* Knoxville, Tenn., 1985. The FCC was unsuccessful at regulating television because it could not get cooperation from either the legislative, executive, or judicial branch of the federal government.

—. *The Republic of Mass Culture: Journalism, Filmmaking, and Broadcasting in America since 1941,* 3d ed. Baltimore, 2006. By becoming the primary mass medium in the 1960s, TV altered the lives of Americans and forced newspapers, film, radio, and magazines to adapt to a rapidly changing media marketplace.

Bayley, Edwin R. *Joe McCarthy and the Press.* Madison, Wis., 1981. The anti-Communist senator battled with the press.

Bluem, A. William. *Documentary in American Television.* New York, 1965. The author provides a detailed look at documentaries containing a listing of films.

Braestrup, Peter. *Big Story: How the American Press and Television Reported and Interpreted the Crisis of Tet 1968 in Vietnam and Washington.* Boulder, Colo., 1977. In

the Tet military offensive during the Vietnam war, logistical and structural problems in press operations and the press' negative reaction to President Lyndon Johnson's tactics resulted in distorted news and interpretations and outright falsification.

Bray, Howard. *The Pillars of the Post: The Making of a News Empire in Washington.* New York, 1980. This favorable history of the *Washington Post* from Eugene Meyer's purchase of the paper in 1933 to Donald Graham's becoming chairman of the board in 1979 includes financing in the early years, Vietnam, racism on the paper's staff, and Watergate.

Brown, Lee. *The Reluctant Reformation: On Criticizing the Press in America.* New York, 1974. The author outlines the major themes, patterns, and concerns of media criticism.

Conway, Mike. *The Origins of Television News in America.* New York, 2009. This study documents the 1940s founding and early years of TV news at CBS.

Davies, David R. *The Postwar Decline of American Newspapers, 1945-1965.* Westport, Conn., 2006. In the years after World War II, the newspaper industry was slow to react to serious threats to its existence.

Davies, David R., ed. *The Press and Race: Mississippi Journalists Confront the Movement.* Jackson, Miss., 2001. Mississippi editors, ranging from segregationists to integrationists to moderates, led their communities in the turbulent 1950s and 1960s.

Felsenthal, Carol. *Power, Privilege and the Post: the Katharine Graham Story.* New York, 1993. The *Washington Post* publisher built a profitable media empire through her will and determination.

Friendly, Fred W. *Due to Circumstances Beyond Our Control.* New York, 1967. Murrow's associate gives his personal account of the early days at CBS News.

Garay, Ronald. *Gordon McLendon: The Maverick of Radio.* New York, 1992. McLendon, a radio broadcaster, was known for his innovations in programming and management in the 1950s and 1960s.

Gomery, Douglas. *A History of Broadcasting in the United States.* Malden, Mass., 2008. Radio and television were important socially, culturally, and politically.

Godfrey, Donald G. *Philo T. Farnsworth: The Father of Television.* Salt Lake City, 2001. Farnsworth played the pivotal role in the early television industry.

Greenberg, David. *Nixon's Shadow: The History of an Image.* New York, 2003. The politician's image evolved over the decades.

Halberstam, David. *The Powers That Be.* New York, 1979. This examination of the rise to power by the *Washington Post, Los Angeles Times,* CBS, and Time Inc. argues that the huge media dominated American public thought and often shaped politics and society, acquiring status and large profits for themselves.

Hammond, Charles Montgomery, Jr. *The Image Decade: Television Documentary, 1965-1975.* New York, 1981. This study considers the period since Murrow and Friendly did their work and updates Bluem's study.

Hammond, William M. *Reporting Vietnam: Media and Military at War.* Lawrence, Kan., 1998. Relations between the military and press deteriorated during the Vietnam War. However, negative media coverage did not undermine public support for the war.

Heil, Alan L., Jr. *Voice of America: A History.* New York: Columbia University Press, 2003. The official overseas broadcasting service of the United States succeeded because it emphasized news reporting rather than propaganda.

James, Doug. *Walter Cronkite: His Life and Times.* Brentwood, Tenn., 1991. The author traces the 41-year career of the veteran CBS newscaster.

Kaul, Arthur J., ed. *Dictionary of Literary Biography Vol. 185: American Literary Journalists, 1945-1995.* Detroit, 1997. This collection includes biographies of the most prominent of the literary journalists who came to the fore after World War II.

Kendrick, Alexander. *Prime Time: The Life of Edward R. Murrow.* Boston, 1969. Murrow was an outstanding broadcast journalist. He would have made the news even better had it not been for pressure from advertisers and CBS management.

Kisseloff, Jeff. *The Box: An Oral History of Television, 1920-1961.* New York, 1995. This account traces television's formative years through interviews with 500 individuals who played a role in its development.

Kluger, Richard. *The Paper.* New York, 1986. This account — which details the rise of the *New York Tribune* and the *New York Herald,* their merger, and their decline as a newspaper subsidized by two influential families — covers the same newspaper environment as Talese's *The Kingdom and the Power.*

Lashner, Marilyn A. *The Chilling Effect in TV News: Intimidation by the Nixon White*

---

[16] Quoted in Commission on Freedom of the Press, *A Free and Responsible Press,* 50-1 and 54.

House. New York, 1984. The Nixon administration used a wide range of tactics to intimidate TV journalism, diminishing its freedom and willingness to report.

Leidholdt, Alexander. *Standing Before the Shouting Mob: Lenoir Chambers and Virginia's Massive Resistance to Public-School Integration.* Tuscaloosa, Ala., 1997. One editor's leadership on school desegregation led his community through social change in relative peace.

Liebovich, Louis W. *The Press and the Modern Presidency: Myths and Mindsets from Kennedy to Election 2000.* Westport, Conn., 2000. The period saw increasing antagonism between presidents and the media.

—. *Richard Nixon, Watergate, and the Press: A Historical Retrospective.* Westport, Conn., 2003. Nixon tried to manipulate the press during Watergate.

Lindstrom, Carl E. *The Fading American Newspaper.* Garden City, N.Y., 1960. Newspapers in the 1950s failed to compete effectively with TV and became primarily business enterprises.

McKeen, William. *Outlaw Journalist: The Life and Times of Hunter S. Thompson.* New York, 2008. Thompson, "gonzo" journalist, was a writer of considerable talent, whose success came, at least in part, because he did not conform to traditional views of journalism.

Mickelson, Sig. *The Decade That Shaped Television News: CBS in the 1950s.* Westport, Conn., 1998. An insider gives his account of the rise of TV journalism in its first full decade.

Mills, Kay. *Changing Channels: The Civil Rights Case that Transformed Television.* Jackson, Miss., 2004. A legal battle forced WLBT in Jackson, Miss., to modify its racial policies.

Prochnau, William W. *Once Upon a Distant War.* New York, 1995. American correspondents who covered the Vietnam conflict from its earliest days changed from adventuresome journalists to critics of U. S. policy.

Rader, Benjamin G. *In Its Own Image: How Television Has Transformed Sports.* New York, 1984. TV has had a major impact on the nature of sports since the late 1940s.

Roberts, Gene, and Klibanoff, Hank. *The Race Beat: The Press, the Civil Rights Struggle, and the Awakening of a Nation.* New York, 2006. Press coverage of the civil rights movement beginning in the 1950s awakened Americans to the civil rights struggle and so helped to bring about racial change.

Rucker, Bryce. *The First Freedom.* Carbondale, Ill., 1968. Overwhelming economic concentration transformed the news media in the 1960s into gigantic interconnected conglomerates that approached every aspect of the news process as a business.

Schwoch, James. *Global TV: New Media and the Cold War, 1946-69.* Champaign, Ill., 2008. Both the Soviet bloc and the West used television as a propaganda tool during the Cold War.

Sims, John Cameron. *The Grass Roots Press: America's Community Newspapers.* Ames, Iowa, 1969. The author examines the state of weekly, community, and suburban newspapers, their operating conditions, their journalistic idealism, and their vigor in crusading.

Sloan, Wm. David, ed. *Makers of the Media Mind: Journalism Educators and Their Ideas.* Hillsdale, N.J., 1990. Journalism education, while continuing to teach professional newspaper skills, became increasingly theoretical.

Small, William. *To Kill A Messenger.* New York, 1970. The author provides an account of broadcast news treatment of events of the 1960s.

Smith, Anthony. *Goodbye Gutenburg: The Newspaper Revolution of the 1980s.* New York, 1980. Changing demographics and improved printing methods brought about a revolution in newspaper economics.

Sperber, Ann M. *Murrow: His Life and Times.* New York, 1986. This biography emphasizes Murrow's professional career, from the development of radio news in the 1930s to the documentaries of the 1960s.

Strout, Lawrence N. *Covering McCarthyism: How the Christian Science Monitor Handled Joseph R. McCarthy, 1950-1954.* Westport, Conn., 1999. The *Monitor* provided incisive and deliberate coverage of the Wisconsin senator.

Talese, Gay. *The Kingdom and the Power: The Story of the Men Who Influence the Institution That Influences the World — The New York Times.* New York, 1969. This insider view of *New York Times* reporters, editors, executives, and publishers focuses on the struggle among them to determine the nature of the paper and the direction it would take.

Teel, Leonard Ray. *Ralph Emerson McGill: Voice of the Southern Conscience.* Knoxville, Tenn., 2001. McGill was the most prominent moderate southern editor in the postwar years.

Tofel, Richard J. *Restless Genius: Barney Kilgore, the Wall Street Journal, and the Invention of Modern Journalism.* New York, 2009. Kilgore, who served on the *Wall Street Journal* from 1943 until 1966, led it from being a narrow financial newspaper of 30,000 circulation to a national general-interest paper with an emphasis on business and a circulation of a million.

Udell, Jon G. *Economic Trends in the Daily Newspaper Business, 1946 to 1970.* Madison, Wis., 1970. Economic trends, particularly rising costs and trends in advertising and readership, buffeted newspapers in the postwar years.

Waldron, Ann. *Hodding Carter: The Reconstruction of a Racist.* Chapel Hill, N.C., 1993. The progressive racial views of the editor of the *Delta Democrat-Times* in Greenville, Miss., made him a leader among moderate editors in the South after World War II.

Watson, Mary Ann. *The Expanding Vista: American Television in the Kennedy Years.* New York, 1990. TV was instrumental to the civil rights movement, expanding democracy, and other major facets of American society.

Weinstein, David. *The Forgotten Network: DuMont and the Birth of American Television.* Philadelphia, 2004. Founded in 1946 and ceasing operation in 1955, the DuMont network despite its short life nevertheless was important in the development of commercial television.

Wyatt, C. R. *Paper Soldiers: The American Press and the Vietnam War.* Chicago, 1995. The media did not exercise a profound impact on the war.

ARTICLES

Ashdown, Paul G. "WTVJ's Miami Crime War: A Television Crusade." *Florida Historical Quarterly* 28 (1980): 427-37. Miami TV station's 1966 campaign against Dade County crime was possibly "television's first and most significant editorial crusade."

Baird, David A. "An Emerging Emphasis on Image: Early Press Coverage of Politics and Television." *American Journalism* 20:4 (2003): 13-31. Newspaper writers believed TV's emphasis on appearance would change presidential politics.

Barrett, Edward. "Folksy TV News." *Columbia Journalism Review* (November-December, 1973): 16-20. The author gives a summary analysis of the happy news phenomenon examining the role of consultants.

Bliss, Robert M. "Development of Fair Comment as a Defense to Libel." *Journalism Quarterly* 44 (1967): 627-37. This analysis of the *New York Times v. Sullivan* case traces the historical development of the doctrine of fair comment in libel cases.

Broussard, Jinx C. "Saviors or Scalaways: The Mississippi Black Press's Contrasting Coverage of Civil Rights Workers and Freedom Summer, June-August 1964." *American Journalism* 19 (Summer 2002): 63-85. The author examines how black newspapers framed the violent events of Freedom Summer in 1964.

Conway, Mike. "Before the Bloggers: The Upstart News Technology of Television at the 1948 Political Conventions." *American Journalism* 24 (2007): 33-58. "The 1948 conventions became television's political coming out party, launching the medium as a serious journalistic platform."

Cook, David A., ed. "The Economic and Political Structure of American Television." *Quarterly Review of Film Studies* 8, 3 (1983): 1-55. This special issue of *QRFS* contains two historical articles: David A. Cook, "The Birth of the Network: How Westinghouse, GE, AT&T, and RCA Invented the Concept of Advertiser-Supported Broadcasting," pp. 3-8, providing an economic explanation of the motives of the founders of the NBC radio network; and Gary Edgerton and Cathy Pratt, "The Influence of the Paramount Decision on Network Television in America," pp. 9-24, a discussion of the 1948 antitrust decision against Paramount.

Cranston, Pat. "Political Convention Broadcasts: Their History and Influence." *Journalism Quarterly* (1960): 186-94. The author provides an overview of political convention coverage with attention to trends.

Cumming, Doug. "Building Resentment: How the Alabama Press Prepared the Ground for *New York Times v. Sullivan.*" *American Journalism* 22 (2005): 7-32. The Supreme Court case *New York Times v. Sullivan* "grew out of the civil rights turmoil in the Deep South."

Ehrlich, M. "Living with the Bomb: Fred Friendly's 'The Quick and the Dead.'" *Journalism History* 35:1 (2009): 2-11. Friendly's 1950 NBC radio series "represented a key moment in the evolution of broadcast news documentaries.... [It] bridged the news and entertainment worlds."

Fleighery, Glen. "The Warren Report's Forgotten Chapter: Press Response to Criticism of Kennedy Assassination Coverage." *American Journalism* 20 (Spring 2003): 83-101. The press reacted to the Warren Commission's call for a press code of conduct.

Garay, Ron. "Television and the 1951 Senate Crime Committee Hearings." *Journal of Broadcasting* 22 (1978): 469-90. The 1951 Kefauver Committee hearings on organized crime "captured the attention of millions, transformed obscure politicians into national figures, and promoted television during the industry's formative years."

Hensher, Alan. "No News Today: How Los Angeles Lost a Daily." *Journalism Quarterly* 47 (1970): 684-8. The death of the *Los Angeles Daily News* in 1954 resulted not so much from TV or suburban press competition but from debilitating labor union demands and lack of the immense capital required in a metropolis.

Hofstetter, Richard C. "News Bias in the 1972 Campaign: A Cross-Media Comparison." *Journalism Monographs* 58 (November 1978). Network TV, the wire services, and two newspapers gave biased coverage of the 1972 presidential campaign because of the nature of the media and their structure, rather than because of partisan bias.

Landers, James. "Specter of Stalemate: Vietnam War Perspectives in *Newsweek*, *Time*, and *U.S. News & World Report*, 1965-1968." *American Journalism* 19:3 (2002): 13-38. Negative commentary in the magazines prompted the Johnson administration to mount a campaign to persuade journalists that the war was going well.

Larson, Carl M. "The Struggle of Paddock Publications Versus Field Enterprises, Inc." *Journalism Quarterly* 48 (1971): 700-6. The success of a group of suburban Chicago papers resulted from market research, good management, and new information systems.

Logue, Cal M. "Ralph McGill: Convictions of a Southern Editor." *Journalism Quarterly* 45 (1968): 647-52. McGill, editor of the *Atlanta Constitution*, was a crusader for equal rights, justice, education, economic opportunity, and freedom for black Americans.

Long, Stewart L. "A Fourth Television Network and Diversity: Some Historical Evidence." *Journalism Quarterly* 56 (1979): 341-5. The demise of the DuMont network in the 1950s decreased the diversity of programming.

Lorenz, Lawrence. "Truman and the Broadcasters." *Journal of Broadcasting* 113 (1968-69): 17-22. The author reviews radio's role in the beginning with attention to the rise of TV in politics.

McIntyre, Jerilyn S. "The Hutchins Commission's Search for a Moral Framework." *Journalism History* (1979): 54-7 and 63. The author examines the questions confronted by the Hutchins commission on freedom of the press and ethics and how "the implementation of moral principles is shaped by practical restrictions."

Nixon, Raymond B., and Jean Ward. "Trends in Newspaper Ownership and Inter-Media Competition." *Journalism Quarterly* 38 (1961): 3-14. The newspaper industry after World War II attained the highest degree of stability in its history, and fears of a monopoly on the expression of ideas caused by the decline in newspaper competition were unfounded.

O'Brien, Michael. "Robert Fleming, Senator McCarthy and the Myth of the Marine Hero." *Journalism Quarterly* 50 (1973): 48-53. A *Milwaukee Journal* reporter debunked the myth that McCarthy was a war hero.

O'Kelly, Charlotte G. "Black Newspapers and the Black Protest Movement, 1946-1972." *Phylon* 41 (1980): 313-24. Four large black newspapers favored integration and non-violence.

Peterson, Wilbur. "Loss in Country Weekly Newspapers Heavy in 1950s." *Journalism Quarterly* 38 (1961): 15-24. The blame for the decline in the number of weekly newspapers was poor economies in small towns, increasing newspaper production costs, and the failure of papers to increase their advertising and subscription prices to keep pace with cost increases.

Schaefer, Richard J. "Reconsidering 'Harvest of Shame': The Limitations of a Broadcast Journalism Landmark." *Journalism History* 19 (1994): 121-32. The famous 1960 documentary failed to affect public policy because its moralistic presentation lessened its impact.

Sharp, Harry. "Live from Washington: The Telecasting of President Kennedy's News Conferences." *Journal of Broadcasting* 113 (1968-69): 23-32. The author provides reporters' views on advantages and disadvantages of live telecasting of presidential press conferences.

Sloan, Wm. David. "The Contemporary Press, 1945-Present: Profiteering Business or Professional Journalism?" 104-22, in *Perspectives on Mass Communication History* (Hillsdale, N.J., 1991). This historiographical essay analyzes the approaches that historians have taken.

Smith, F. Leslie. "CBS Reports: The Selling of the Pentagon." In *Mass News*, eds. David Leroy and Christopher Sterling, 200-12. Englewood Cliffs, N.J., 1973. The author provides a concise overview of the controversy with an appendix of sources and film availability.

Sterling, Christopher H. "Trends in Daily Newspaper and Broadcast Ownership, 1922-70." *Journalism Quarterly* 52 (1975): 247-56, 320. While the number of newspapers decreased, the expansion of broadcasting meant an increase in the total number of outlets and voices. However, the trend is toward increasing concentration.

Wiebe, Gerhart D. "An Historical Setting for Television Journalism." *Journal of Broadcasting* 1 (1956): 33-8. TV seems to be a means by which officials can present their ideas to the public, who have clamored to participate in making political decisions but who prefer only to be spectators.

Williams, Julian. "Broadcast Segregation: WJTV's Early Years." *American Journalism* 19:3 (2002): 87-103. The United Church of Christ challenged the license of the Jackson, Miss., station on the basis of racial bias.

Wyatt, Clarence R. "'At the Cannon's Mouth': The American Press and the Vietnam War." *Journalism History* 13 (Autumn-Winter 1986): 104-13. The press was not overly adversarial in covering the Vietnam conflict.

Yaeger, Murray R. "The Evolution of *See It Now*." *Journal of Broadcasting* 1 (1956): 337-44. This narrative of the development and history of the *See It Now* TV program includes where the idea came from, its radio background, changes, etc.

24

The News Media

1974 – 2000

I n the years immediately after Vietnam and Watergate, the power of the media seemed unprecedented. Stories having their genesis in the news media had toppled two administrations. Media properties were being sold at record prices. Enrollments at schools of journalism and mass communication broke records every year.

Money follows power; and in the next twenty-five years, media chains and entrepreneurs such as Rupert Murdoch purchased newspapers and broadcast stations large and small at prices often exceeding their expected profits.

TV journalists and newspaper reporters comprised a new national media elite. Personalities such as Barbara Walters and Walter Cronkite achieved celebrity status, as did newspaper reporters such as Bob Woodward and Carl Bernstein. Here were individuals who had seen their stories measurably influence national public opinion and, in some instances, change American policy. Journalists in newsrooms throughout the land emulated them.

Despite the triumphs, all was not bright on the media horizon. For some journalists, the quest for prestige superseded the quest for quality performance. Even as newspapers gained national recognition for their coverage of political and international events, they faced a growing economic threat from television. As TV gained prominence as a news medium, it bore the brunt of wideranging criticism from the public and from within the media's own ranks. As the news media's visibility in public affairs grew, their credibility shrank. Even as they were buoyed by professional, economic, and technological success, the media faced major difficulties in the last quarter of the twentieth century.

ADVANCES IN TELEVISION NEWS

With more attention and an infusion of new dollars, TV news made significant improvements in personnel. Some network news departments grew to a size comparable to those on the nation's leading newspapers. Reporters at both the national and local levels became more specialized, and coverage was enhanced. One station, WCCO-TV in Minneapolis, set up its own Washington,

D.C., bureau, the first local station to do so.

The great bulk of radio and TV journalists at the local level remained general assignment reporters, but in major cities specialization in such areas as consumer affairs and medical and science reporting became commonplace. Some local feature reporters began syndicating their work nationally. They included automotive specialists, food experts, pharmacists, and others. In meteorology, a province once populated by TV "weather girls," bona fide atmospheric scientists with graduate training and membership in the American Meteorological Association became the norm in most major cities and in some smaller communities, particularly those vulnerable to severe weather.

Some broadcast reporters, particularly at the network level, were recruited from the ranks of the nation's major newspapers, and specialization continued. Bill Lawrence had joined ABC in the early 1960s after serving as White House correspondent for the *New York Times* for more than twenty years. Ray Brady, a former *Wall Street Journal* staffer, became business correspondent at CBS News, and Dan Cordtz joined ABC as economics editor. Investigative reporter and columnist Jack Anderson teamed up with ABC's *Good Morning America,* and Carl Bernstein of Watergate fame and the *Washington Post* did a stint at ABC. The Watergate story also elevated two lawyers, Fred Graham and Carl Stern, to specialized positions in TV news.

There were also advances in the status of women and minorities. In 1974, ABC named Ann Compton chief White House correspondent, a TV "first." In 2001, she was the only TV reporter to accompany President George W. Bush on Airforce One in the immediate aftermath of the terrorist attacks of September 11. Lesley Stahl covered the Watergate Committee hearings for CBS, moved to the White House beat, and then joined the staff of *60 Minutes.* Catherine Mackin's appointment as NBC floor reporter made news at the political conventions even though another female, Pauline Frederick, had worked for the network as early as 1948 as a United Nations specialist. Nancy Dickerson also covered the capital for NBC. At ABC Marlene Sanders anchored an early news broadcast, produced documentaries for the innovative *Close-Up*

Marlene Sanders
Marlene Sanders was part of a growing trend of more women in journalism at the national level. She anchored an early news broadcast and in 1976 became ABC's first female news vice president.

series, and in 1976 became the first female news vice president at ABC. Barbara Walters got a million-dollar contract from ABC in 1976, setting off a public debate over the relative worth of a broadcast interviewer/reporter. Connie Chung joined NBC News from the CBS affiliate in Los Angeles, and Jane Pauley followed in Barbara Walters' shoes on NBC's *Today* after Walters' defection to ABC. Diane Sawyer won praise at *CBS Morning News*, joined the staff of *60 Minutes*, and then switched to ABC. In an unprecedented move, NBC reporter Judy Woodruff left commercial broadcasting to join PBS's news team in the early 1980s before joining CNN (and then returning to PBS). Charlayne Hunter-Gault, one of the two black students integrating the University of Georgia in the early 1960s, served as key reporter and sometimes host for the *Newshour*. In 2001 Katie Couric, a ratings winner at NBC's *Today*, signed a contract for an annual salary of $16.5 million. In 2007 she became the first sole female TV anchor on *The CBS Evening News*.

While fewer in number, minority journalists made significant strides in the 1970s and '80s. William Raspberry and Thomas Sowell, among others, worked as syndicated columnists. *Black Journal* and *Tony Brown's Journal* started on public TV. Two black males achieved celebrity status at the commercial network level as hosts of nationally televised series. Ed Bradley, a former Philadelphia school teacher, emerged at CBS News as a weekend anchor, docu-

mentary narrator, and then host of *60 Minutes*. Sportscaster Bryant Gumbel excelled as host of NBC's *Today* morning program before joining CBS briefly in 1997. ABC experimented with anchor desks for its evening newscast centered in three locales. Chicago, one of the three cities chosen for the experiment, featured minority journalist Max Robinson at the helm. But the three-anchor approach was shelved after the death of Frank Reynolds, one of the anchors. CNN's Bernard Shaw won laurels for his reporting on the first Gulf War against Iraq as a first-hand observer in 1991. After stints at several newspapers and NBC, Gwen Ifill became the host of *Washington Week*, the weekly PBS program, in 1999.

Numerous other minority journalists achieved prominent positions at the local level, and some turned down lucrative offers with national media to stay in their communities. The minority reporters who achieved high-level positions almost universally shunned the notion that they be given assignments on the basis of a tie-in with their race, as had been the practice in both print and broadcast journalism in many locales during the civil rights era.

REVOLUTIONS IN TECHNOLOGY

One of the most visible changes in mass communication was the advance in technology. In the 1970s, it had a pervasive influence in both broadcast and print media. The most far-reaching changes were those that resulted from computerization. Apple Computer Inc. introduced desktop computing with the Apple II personal computer in 1977. The company scored another breakthrough in 1984 when it introduced the user-friendly Macintosh. Because of the ease with which it could do desktop publishing, it came into widespread use among newspapers and magazines for designing pages.

IBM responded to the Apple II by introducing the 5150 Personal Computer in 1981. However, because the Macintosh used such a revolutionary operating system, IBM and other manufacturers of clone computers requested that Apple license the Macintosh software to run on their machines. When Apple refused, IBM and the others turned to Microsoft Corp. for an operating system and to Intel Corp. and other companies for microprocessors. Because of IBM's dominance, its computers and PC's from other makers took over most of the market.

Along with computers, mobile equipment came into wide use in broadcasting. The editorial uses of modern technology were supplementing important changes being made in news personnel. The history of the development of TV news has been like a game of editorial and technological leapfrog in which equipment bolstered news coverage in order to further support advances in technology.[1] This progression took a dramatic leap forward in 1974 with the introduction of highly mobile electronic news gathering (ENG) equipment, allowing for live transmission from the field using microwave technology. CBS affiliate KMOX-TV (now KMOV), St. Louis, was the first all-ENG station. ENG reporters learned a special need for sensitivity to situations and an aware-

[1]Av Westin, *Newswatch* (New York, 1982).

The Cable Landscape
Along with the home use of computers, the most visible change brought about by new communication technology was the proliferation of television offerings. Cable television had been available in the 1950s, but it was the 1980s that saw the introduction of the huge variety of programming that some people had originally envisioned. As the opportunities multiplied, however, a small number of large corporations dominated the programming landscape. MSNBC, for example, was started as a business venture co-owned by Microsoft and the NBC television network. Its activities in the 1990s included, in addition to this giant television screen in New York City's Times Square, a 24-hour-a-day television news channel, a digital satellite network, and a web news service.

ness of potential legal and ethical problems that live coverage of events presents. Because of the pitfalls associated with live ENG reporting, it often was limited even at the network level, where more of the budget traditionally went to specialized staff.

Newspapers also made technological advances in newsgathering. In addition to the traditional notebook, pencil, and camera, the newspaper journalist began carrying an audio cassette recorder and a portable computer terminal. Many reporters used data bases and computerized financial programs to track the activities of business, government, and other public institutions. Technology enhanced accuracy and efficiency in gathering the news, writing stories, and getting them to the public. In contrast, the high-technology used by TV news traditionally demanded a team, including reporter and camera operator, and equipment that was relatively cumbersome and obtrusive.

Along with changing newsgathering, technology affected newspaper production. Display ads up to four columns wide were being produced routinely on single pieces of photographic paper. They used graphic design VDTs (video display terminals) that allowed blocks of type, borders, line drawings, logos, and even screened photographs to be sized and coordinated on the screen before being produced photographically. In some plants (beginning with the Rockland-Westchester papers of New York state) all the type and pictures were laid out on a page-sized VDT and then transmitted directly to a plate maker, a process called pagination.

In another technological development, newspaper pages were scanned and committed to computer memory and then transmitted via satellite to one or more printing plants hundreds of miles distant for simultaneous publication of the same newspaper in more than one city. The *Wall Street Journal* pioneered multiple-site publication using Teletypesetter technology. Dow Jones, the parent company, correctly predicted that the growing interest in financial, investment, and business information would make the *Journal* a national financial newspaper if it could be distributed on the day of publication. Founded in 1982, Gannett's *USA Today*, a

national newspaper, utilized the same technology. In five years it became the nation's biggest newspaper in circulation totals and set the pace in use of color and graphics.

Amazingly, on smaller newspapers a new revolution in production was taking place by the end of the 1980s. The waist-high photocomposition machines that in the 1960s had made the Linotypes obsolete were themselves gathering dust in storerooms, displaced by laserprinters the size of a desktop copying machine. The new technology was appropriately named desktop publishing and combined the laserprinters, which used xerography rather than photochemicals, with generic personal computers and software capable of producing text and graphics. More than half of American newspapers were using this technology in 1987.

New technology also affected methods of delivering newspapers to readers. The newly developed interactive videotex systems used combinations of databases stored in large computers. Through ingenious linkages of satellite, microwave, and telephone lines, the databases were made available to the subscriber's home computer. By asking for categories of information (business, sports, classifieds, news, new products, etc.), the subscriber could get a broad choice from current information. If subscribers knew what they wanted, one or two key words typed into their computer could bring up the specific information.

Viewdata, based in Miami and founded by Knight-Ridder, a newspaper chain, began offering its service in the early 1980s at a monthly subscription of $12 (about one-third higher than that of a metropolitan newspaper) plus the cost of the user's computer and 90¢ an hour for phone line charges. The service was, however, unsuccessful and in 1987 was discontinued. Michael Bloomberg, though, succeeded on a grand scale with Bloomberg Financial Markets in the field of information services.

A variety of newspapers attempted more modest efforts to take advantage of the large bodies of information they acquired. The *Albuquerque Tribune* each day published a password to allow users of personal computers with modems to gain access to expanded information contained in its computers. The *Kansas City Star* launched an extensive "Startouch" program whereby readers could use their touch-tone telephones to get additional information through audio reports, to express their opinions, and even to order merchandise. Such services indicated an awareness on the part of publishers that no longer were they strictly in the business of putting ink on paper.

THE SATELLITE AGE

Multi-channel cable television (a potential of 100 or more program choices) made possible the all-news format, specialized content for various age groups and interests, and new opportunities for local programming and advertising.

Ted Turner, who bought a UHF station in Atlanta in 1970 and turned it into "superstation" WTBS-TV, based his marketing on transmission of the station signal by satellite and acceptance by cable systems nationwide. When in 1980 he launched Cable News Network (CNN), the nation's first 24-hour TV news service, he predicted news channels eventually would fulfill all the needs of newspaper readers. He hired Reese Schonfeld, founder of the Independent Television News Association, as the network's president and recruited former CBS News correspondent Daniel Schorr to serve as chief Washington correspondent.

CNN soon demonstrated the advantages of round-the-clock news broadcasting. In 1983 national attention focused on Atlanta when the accused murderer of twenty-eight black youths, Wayne Williams, went on trial. Photographers were barred from the courtroom, but reporters in an elaborate press room viewed closed-circuit TV cameras that focused only on the judge and jury. CNN, by virtue of its Atlanta base of operations, was able to provide hourly updates and won praise for its coverage.

The next year, though, CNN came under fire for coverage of two criminal trials, opening up the issue of invasion of privacy and free press/fair trial debates. Both controversies revolved around the use of cameras in the courtroom that forty-nine states allowed, with varying restrictions, in the early 1980s. The first case involved a Massachusetts rape trial in which four men were charged. Although CNN did not show the face of the victim in its extensive coverage, her name was mentioned in court while the network was on the air. As a consequence, other news organizations felt justified in providing her name, and CNN was regarded as "smut peddling" and infringing on the victim's right of privacy. In a second sensational trial in California, a 115-count indictment charged the proprietor of a nursery school and six teachers with sexual abuse of over 100 children. CNN requested permission to provide live coverage of pretrial hearings and temper its reporting while studying use of a time-delay system, to avoid the problem of exposing identity encountered in the Massachusetts case.

Cable offerings soon proliferated. A non-profit public service network, C-SPAN expanded to twenty-four hours a day in 1982. The National Broadcasting Company started CNBC, a 24-hour cable business news channel, to compete with CNN. Specialized

Number of Subscribers to Cable Television in the United States, 1952-1999

In Millions

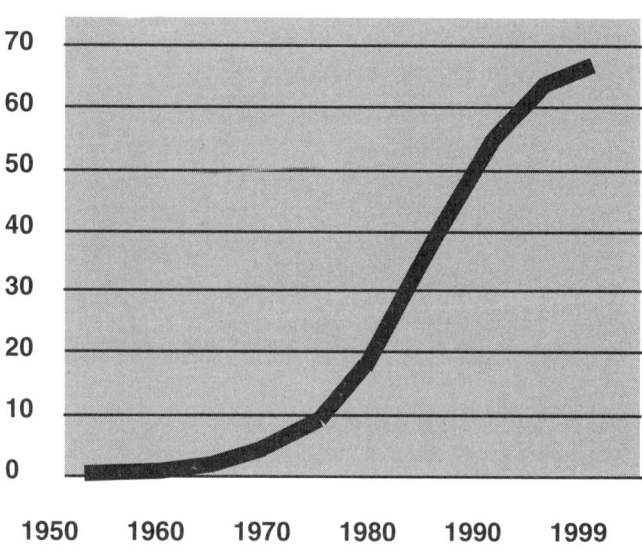

The Cable Technology Revolution

Among the many technological advances in television, one of the most important was cable. In the 1950s an enterprising person living in some remote mountains decided to improve his reception by placing an antenna atop a mountain and running a coaxial cable from the antenna to his TV set. Before long, neighbors were asking for a cable of their own run from the same antenna. Thus began community antenna television (CATV). By the 1960s CATV had become cable TV. Small local systems provided subscribers access both to signals from distant stations and to interference-free signals from local stations. Numbering only seventy systems serving some 14,000 households in 1952, by 1999 more than 10,700 systems were providing service to approximately 68 million households.

cable networks — such as the Health Network — offered viewers a steady diet of nutrition-related features. Warner Cable's Qube experiment in Columbus, Ohio, offered interactive capability (two-way television) to cable subscribers. The U. S. Chamber of Commerce gave birth to the American Business Network (BIZNET) in 1982.

The Christian Broadcasting Network (CBN) began specialized news coverage in the 1980s with an emphasis on topics of interest to evangelical Christian viewers. In addition, evangelical groups received broadcast coverage of their efforts to effect change in broadcast programming. When broadcasters came under fire by religious groups in 1982, Moral Majority leader Jerry Falwell could claim administration support since he had campaigned vigorously for Ronald Reagan's candidacy and for Reagan's stand on controversial issues such as abortion and aid to private schools. Both Reagan and his deregulation-minded FCC chairman, Mark Fowler, spoke to the National Religious Broadcasters' 1982 convention. The leader of another group, the Reverend Donald Wildmon, founder of the American Family Association, threatened broadcasters with a boycott if the content of popular TV programming were not improved. Reagan sided with the religious supporters although he steered clear of the boycott issue.

The addition of cable TV to the media complex presented challenges to the other media. Just as the introduction of radio and television had increased competition for the potential subscriber's time, additional TV channels increased the competition for the audience's time. In particular, the competition lessened the dependence of the public and of advertisers on the three major networks and their affiliated stations.

REVOLUTIONS IN TELEVISION PROGRAMMING

To their credit the TV networks went beyond technology in their efforts to improve news and public affairs programming. They produced more specialized programs and did some experimentation. Public broadcasting offered the weekly business-oriented series *Wall Street Week* beginning in 1970 and then added a *Nightly Business Report*. William F. Buckley introduced a steady diet of political views on *Firing Line*, and three weekly PBS talk shows — *Agronsky and Company, Washington Week in Review,* and the *McLaughlin Group* — all focused on Capitol Hill. In the 1970s the networks began to employ politicians to provide insight and commentary on special stories. ABC hired two famous presidential "losers," Barry Goldwater (1964) and George McGovern (1972), to provide perspective at the 1976 political conventions.

Noncommercial TV presented a weekly interview program, *The Dick Cavett Show,* which also aired briefly over ABC. Cavett had guests from politics as well as from the arts and entertainment fields. In a talk show initially syndicated from the Midwest, Phil Donahue invited audience participation in questioning guests on controversial issues. He achieved a unique distinction among TV talk-show hosts in 1984, when the FCC agreed that his show qualified as a bona fide news program, thus freeing him to invite political candidates without having to air the views of opponents. He concluded twenty-nine years on the air in 1996.

The commercial networks experimented with the formats of their evening news programs. The early ABC experiment of *World News Tonight* with anchor desks in three important locales, including London, was an important attempt to provide international perspective. In the mid-1970s, *NBC Nightly News* introduced a mini-documentary series, three or four minutes in length, titled "Segment Three." This extended-format coverage allowed the network to go into more detail on the more significant, ongoing stories. ABC News followed suit with a "Special Assignment" series with related stories on a particular issue running in sequence for as many as three or four evenings in a row. The series was a forerunner of *Nightline*.

Despite such advances, many people, including some prominent broadcasters, still considered broadcast news a headline service. Progress was acknowledged when PBS extended its *MacNeil-Lehrer Report* to one full hour in the early 1980s; but, plugged as

"no nonsense news," the program became the *NewsHour with Jim Lehrer* and was an exception to the standard news format. Even with technical imperfections and lack of manpower by comparison to the commercial networks, the *NewsHour* provided flexibility and perspective in covering stories in more depth. It also forced the commercial networks to take notice and got the attention of critics, bringing welcome relief for cutbacks in documentaries that had occurred in the 1970s.

FROM DOCUMENTARIES TO INFO-TAINMENT

The 1960s had been a growth era for TV documentaries. *CBS Reports* and ABC News *Close-Up* led the field with important treatment of political and social issues. NBC also aired more than thirty-five documentaries a year that decade. Since that time, documentary production had dwindled to the point that by 1983 the networks were providing fewer than half that number.[2] The decline resulted from the buildup of news departments, the realignment of internal resources in favor of successful magazine shows such as *60 Minutes*, and the poor ratings documentaries attracted.

It was especially difficult for public broadcasters to justify high expenditures to attract viewership without a sensational interest-grabbing component. Two PBS documentary efforts were *World* and *Frontline*. *World* included some provocative stories with veteran broadcaster Daniel Schorr serving as narrator. One topic examined was the international press. Another was America's dominance of communications technology and flow of information, preliminary to the controversial UNESCO debates along the same lines. A 1980 docudrama, *Death of a Princess*, investigated the execution of a Saudi princess for adultery and set off a dispute between Saudi Arabia and Great Britain. It also resulted in a law suit and alienated the American oil industry but, in so doing, achieved the fifth highest viewer rating in PBS history. Another PBS series aired its first episode in 1983. In it, *Frontline* alleged that National Football League games had been rigged and that the owner of one team, the Los Angeles Rams, who reportedly drowned in 1979, actually had been "more or less murdered." The veracity of the report was questioned as well as the policy of paying some key sources appearing in the program.

In spite of the flaws of some of these efforts, television can be credited with taking itself more seriously, for the most part, in the 1970s and early 1980s, risking public criticism, in both its news and entertainment, and showing a greater willingness to tackle tough issues. Of course, the public can also be credited for showing a greater appetite for these new directions. Network documentary dramas, while taking liberties with historical events, dealt with some of broadcasting's controversies and principal figures such as John Henry Faulk, Edward R. Murrow, and Joseph McCarthy. NBC's portrayal of McCarthy in the 1977 presentation of *Tail Gunner Joe* was attacked for sensationalism; and McCarthy's former colleague Roy Cohn claimed that dramatic license, caused

---

[2]Bill Carter, "Whatever Happened to TV Documentaries?" *Washington Journalism Review* (June 1983): 43-6.

by commercial pressures, destroyed the true McCarthy story. A popular 2005 movie, *Good Night, and Good Luck,* directed by George Clooney helped to clarify the conflict between McCarthy and Murrow. In 1974 *ABC Theatre* broadcast a re-creation of "The Trial of Ethel and Julius Rosenberg." The Rosenbergs were executed for espionage and conspiracy to deliver atomic secrets to the Soviet Union. Ten years later, public TV aired another docudrama in two parts, presenting the story of Whittaker Chambers and Alger Hiss — the basis for much of the anti-communist impulse of the 1950s. Other documentary dramas dealt with President Kennedy's Cuban missile crisis performance in *The Missiles of October* and with another international crisis in *Pueblo*, the story of a Navy intelligence ship that the North Koreans captured in 1968. Political overtones were felt again in 1977, when a thinly veiled mini-series on Watergate featured Jason Robards as President Richard Monckton, who bore a transparent similarity to Richard Nixon. ABC also presented *Friendly Fire*, the true story of Gene and Peg Mullen of La Porte, Iowa, whose son had been killed in Vietnam. The show was an example of popular TV making news with attention to an unpleasant reality.

Gradually the networks began to integrate actuality footage into these docudramas to add realism. In 1982, footage from an Air Florida jet crash outside Washington's National Airport was used a short time after the actual event in a drama about the disaster. The tape was available because news crews from local stations were coincidentally on hand and witnessed the chaos as the plane crashed on a bridge jammed with commuters on their way home. Another made-for-TV docudrama, *Special Bulletin*, simulated how a network might handle a nuclear incident involving terrorism; and an international sensation was created in 1983 when ABC broadcast *The Day After*, the fictionalized account of events surrounding the start of a nuclear exchange between the United States and the Soviet Union set in Kansas City, Missouri, and Lawrence, Kansas. Since the showing of the film coincided with deployment of Pershing II missiles in West Germany, some critics ascribed the motivation to the network's being either pro- or anti-nuclear freeze, while others viewed it as a comment on America's lack of preparedness. After the program aired, a public debate ensued among scientists over whether the extent of damage depicted in the film was exaggerated or moderate when compared to the potential from a real attack.

Surprisingly little public dissent was heard when public TV aired a bona fide documentary, *Vietnam: A Television History*, at about the same time in 1983. In thirteen hour-long segments the series presented what was generally considered to be a dispassionate, evenhanded chronicle of the conflict employing interviews with participants and documentary footage gathered from more than fifty film archives around the world. Lawrence Lichty, a television historian, directed research for the project that took six years and more than $4,000,000 to complete. Ken Burns became television's key documentarian, with thirteen historical efforts, during the 1980s and '90s. They included *The Civil War* (1990), *Empire of the Air: The Men Who Made Radio* (1992), *Baseball* (1994), and

Barbara Walters — Journalist, Celebrity
By the 1970s, television journalists and newspaper reporters comprised a new national media elite. Barbara Walters, for example, who joined Harry Reasoner as co-anchor of ABC's national evening news program, got a million-dollar contract in 1976. One half of the salary was for co-anchoring the news, and the other half was for other work. Reasoner himself benefited from Walters' deal. His own anchor salary of $400,000 was raised to $500,000 to equal Walters'. Her $1 million deal, though, set off a debate — among both journalists and the general public — over the worth of a broadcast interviewer/reporter and over whether news was becoming entertainment.

Lewis and Clark (1997). Later, he made *Jazz* (2001), *Mark Twain* (2002), and *The War* (2007).

Obviously, though, more news is not better news; and at times it became hard to discriminate between news and entertainment. Television discovered an industry news equivalent of *Variety* or *People* magazine in the 1980s. A syndicated series, *Entertainment Tonight*, concentrated on information about television and the movies. Used as a lead-in to local newscasts in many cities, it attracted a large viewership. The program was followed by others with descriptive titles such as *A Current Affair*, *Inside Edition*, and *Hard Copy*, raising once again the term "tabloid television." Syndicated talk shows also proved to be popular with viewers.

While good for the TV industry and profitable for local stations, these "Info-tainment" programs, in the view of many critics, contributed to stunting the medium's growth as a serious news source. The success of *60 Minutes*, ABC's *Nightline*, and *20/20*; the expansion of *MacNeil-Lehrer*; and the presentation of informational programming — although not fulfilling the expectations of the early years — helped counter this trend toward purely entertainment-oriented news.

60 *MINUTES*

Even as *60 Minutes* served up much criticism of its subjects, the show itself was not without its own critics. Until the success achieved by *60 Minutes*, however, few national news programs attracted enough of a following to make a difference. Historically, news and public affairs shows have done poorly in attracting audiences. Edward R. Murrow was apt to point out that he was enabled to do *See It Now* by virtue of the ratings success of his celebrity interview series, *Person to Person*. Although the formats of Murrow's two shows differed, together they exemplified the best of what *60 Minutes* put forth. It was not without a struggle, however, that *60 Minutes* achieved popular acceptance.

Over the years *60 Minutes*, which went on the air in 1968, sustained its share of criticism. Media critic David Shaw concluded that leading network news and public affairs shows such as *60 Minutes* were guilty of ignoring important stories in favor of "subjects with an immediate emotional impact — sex, crime, consumer rip-offs...." Pointing to the use of confrontational interview techniques, Shaw accused one of TV's best known investigative reporters, Mike Wallace, of playing a character in the "prime-time-news-as-soap-opera saga that *60 Minutes* often is."[3] The show also was accused of "checkbook journalism." It compensated Sirhan Sirhan, G. Gordon Liddy, and H. R. Haldeman for personal interviews. CBS paid former Nixon aide Haldeman $100,000 for a two-part interview. *60 Minutes* aired a talk with Nixon in 1984, in spite of the network's refusal to purchase an interview with Nixon that British expatriate broadcaster David Frost had conducted years earlier. A special network of more than 150 stations broadcast four ninety-minute segments of these extended talks. Later, CBS admitted paying $10,000 to an unnamed informant who claimed to have information regarding the disappearance of labor leader Jimmy Hoffa.

One of *60 Minutes'* most intensely contested segments, which aired in 1975, revolved around the depiction of Syrian Jews.[4] The American Jewish Congress accused the show of inaccuracy and distortion in a complaint to the National News Council.

Two decades later, *60 Minutes* made headlines when CBS management permitted broadcast of a tape of an assisted-suicide by Dr. Jack Kevorkian. The broadcast was widely criticized.[5] An earlier controversy erupted when *60 Minutes* suspended its popular commentator, forty-year-broadcast veteran Andy Rooney, for alleged racially derogatory off-air comments that an alternative

publication attributed to him. The program's ratings declined briefly until Rooney was reinstated, using the occasion to deny ever having made the remarks. In an unusual move, *60 Minutes* signed up CNN's chief international correspondent, Christiane Amanpour. She filed important stories for both CBS and CNN. Iranian by birth, she came under criticism in 2010 for pro-Islamic and anti-Israeli and anti-Christian bias.[6]

The popularity of *60 Minutes* encouraged experiments such as *48 Hours* and *60 Minutes II* at CBS. NBC tried *Weekend*, *First Tuesday*, and *Chronolog* before settling with *Dateline NBC*, first hosted by Jane Pauley and Stone Phillips. At ABC, *20/20* with Hugh Downs and Barbara Walters became a success; and the interest in news stirred by *20/20* may have been responsible for helping *Nightline*, as well as *Prime Time Live* and an expanded *20/20* with Diane Sawyer and Sam Donaldson.

DANGERS TO NEWSPAPERS

As television became the dominant medium, newspapers found that their own status and fortunes were more fragile than journalists previously had imagined. The stresses on newspapers fell under the broad heading of increased competition.

The stakes in the press business were high. The value of media properties increased. Newspapers had operating profit margins that were attractive to investing companies, and the sale prices of newspapers soared dramatically.

Alert to the economic dangers that TV posed, publishers attempted to restrict some of the competitors. They closed ranks, for example, in an effort to prevent regional telephone companies from adding information services to their traditional communication services.

Despite such efforts, newspapers faced increasing economic difficulties. All newspapers had to face dramatic increases in the costs of their basic raw materials: paper and ink. Beginning in the 1970s the cost of energy to run presses and to power delivery trucks more than doubled. Increases in labor costs also were substantial. Publishers needed the increased productivity brought about by new technology in offsetting the increased costs.

When chains and other owners found that their efforts to compete — whether with other newspapers or other types of media — were unsuccessful, they frequently sold out. The Gannett Corporation in 1977 purchased the *Oakland Tribune*, which the politically powerful Knowland family of California had long owned; but, when it failed to be profitable, Gannett decided to close it. A Gannett executive, however, Robert Maynard, joined with Oakland business leaders in 1983 and, going against the tide of chain ownership, bought it from Gannett. In 1990, with the paper again threatening to close, the Gannett Foundation (now known as the Freedom Forum) bailed it out with a multi-million dollar grant. Maynard was one of few African Americans to become publisher-owner of a mainline newspaper; but, with the paper again facing

[3]David Shaw, "The Trouble with TV Muckraking," *TV Guide*, 10 October 1981, 7. Also see "Magazines prime earners in prime time," *Broadcasting and Cable*, 9 May 1994, 40.

[4]Robert Chandler, Vice President and Director, Public Affairs Broadcasts, CBS News, letter to the author, 20 April 1978. See also "Steadfast at *60 Minutes*," *Quill* (March, 1976): 19-20; and John J. O'Conner, "How Fair is the Fairness Doctrine?" *New York Times*, 15 June 1975, 27.

[5]See Frazier Moore, "TV Gets Downright Ghastly," *Newsday*, 2 January, 1999, C3.

[6]See, for example, *MSNBC Live with Dan Abram*, 27 August 2010, which included a panel discussion critiquing a series titled "God's Warriors" that Amanpour had produced.

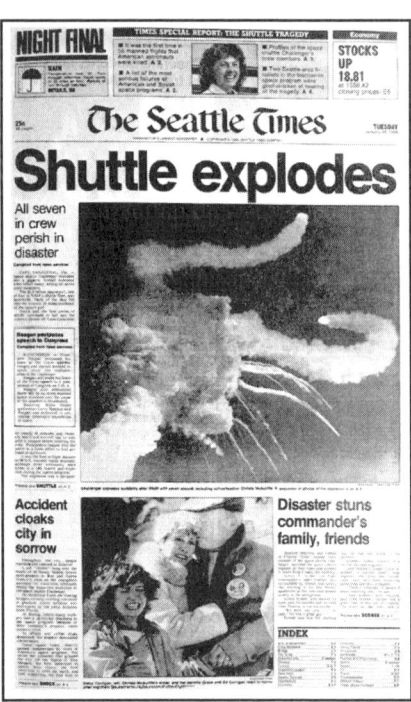

USA Today and Newspaper Design
When the Gannett Company founded *USA Today* in 1982, journalists saw the national newspaper as a visual competitor with television. With its short stories, modular format, catchy graphics, and lavish use of illustrations and color — demonstrated by its front page (left) — it soon provided a new design formula. It accelerated a move to make newspapers more eye-pleasing and reader friendly. Many newspapers, as typified by this issue of the *Seattle* (Wash.) *Times* (right), began borrowing visual elements from it. Despite *USA Today's* success and the popularity of newspapers that imitated its visual approach, critics charged that newspapers were pandering to readers and trying to outdo television at its own game.

financial problems, he sold it to the Alameda Newspaper chain in 1992.

NEW NEWSPAPER APPROACHES

Faced with competition from television, newspapers explored new techniques for making themselves more relevant to the audience. Publishers and editors looked at shrinking household penetration figures and unfavorable results of public opinion polls and began to question whether their traditional methods would provide the profits the new owners expected. For the most part newspapers maintained or enhanced their profitability into the 1980s, but stresses caused long-established metropolitan newspapers to disappear, and trends in circulation sent executives of newspaper groups to social science researchers seeking to find new ways to attract and keep readers.

First, newspapers had to face, in the 1970s, the "credibility" issue as a public reaction to the anti-establishment tone of the investigative reporters and New Journalists. Then, in the 1980s — after the arrival of *USA Today* in a rainbow of graphics — publishers, circulation managers, advertising directors, and editors created such slogans as "customer obsession" in an effort to make newspapers more appealing. In the 1990s, newspapers more and more were turning to "value added" efforts such as reader hotlines, telephone information services, shopping discount cards, and personal computer links.

Despite the problems that confronted newspapers, their advocates argued that the changes in newspapers and in the whole media situation actually worked to newspapers' advantage. The position of newspapers as the basic source of information and local advertising messages would be strengthened, reasoned newspaper executives. With dozens of TV channels from which to

choose, viewers more than before needed an up-to-date and detailed schedule of what was available on their sets, with concise descriptions of content. Newspapers provided the information in convenient formats updated daily. Editors expected reader-viewers to increase their dependence on newspapers for the service.

Newspapers, print journalists claimed, maintained superiority over other media in the quantity of important and interesting information they originated and made available to the public. Most of the news gathering still was done by newspaper reporters and made available to all the media by major and supplementary news services. In the broadcast media, news was still a mostly ancillary operation; and videotex services admitted that they were conveyors, rather than originators, of information.[7]

Newspapers continued to offer tangibility and availability. Even now, newspapers' defenders declare, the latest edition remains on the coffee table until the next day's issue supplants it. Professors tape comic strips and political cartoons to their office doors. Obtuse students can find relief from lectures in crossword puzzles. Clippings are mailed across the continent or pressed in family Bibles. No capital investment is required of the user. A coin gains access to a paper in a vending machine, and a paid subscription routinely brings one to the front door (or under the nearby rose bush). In the 1990s, the newspaper remained the traditional source of daily information for the public.

MEDIA-GOVERNMENT RELATIONS

As the news media increasingly took on characteristics of big business, they also developed as a profession. Activities oriented to professional journalism — such as college training, professional journals, and organizations of working journalists — flourished as

[7]Viewdata employed three "mini-reporters" during its first years of operation.

they never had before. These and other factors contributed to an increasing recognition of journalism — both print and broadcasting — as a well-defined field with its own training, practices, ethics, and other features denoting an occupation as a profession.

One of the manifestations of professional self-awareness by journalists in the 1970s and '80s was the First Amendment Congress movement that sought through local convocations public support and awareness on the need for an unfettered media. The Reporters Committee on Freedom of the Press reported on legal and procedural efforts to stifle the flow of public information, and the Investigative Reporters and Editors Association sought to spread the techniques of in-depth investigation of important issues by bringing successful practitioners together with other professionals and with students at conferences.

Perhaps the most marked change that the increased professionalization brought about was the media's relationship with government. Whereas in the 1940s and 1950s the media generally were supportive of government, the period after the Vietnam War saw a swing toward a neutral-to-antagonistic attitude. Many critics claimed such an attitude indicated that the media had a liberal bias — a claim borne out by surveys that showed that the majority of journalists held liberal political and social views — but it appears also that the attitude represented journalists' institutionalized, professionalized view of themselves as the "watchdogs" of government and other institutions such as business and religion. Such attitudes had grown out of the Vietnam War and the Watergate political scandal. In these episodes, the media found themselves critical of the government power structure.

Many journalists accepted media opposition to established institutions as a professional standard. Some believed that support of the underdog was a function of the media and that the proper role of the press was to serve as a watchdog or adversary of established institutions. They sometimes viewed journalism in terms of the media fighting evil in American politics and society. Their heroes were journalists crusading to correct the ills and problems of their communities and the nation; and the opposition, they believed, was composed of authorities or groups that espoused repression and injustice, the wealthy class in American society, demagogues, or government. Some journalists and publications went so far as to declare that one of the government's paramount intentions was to control information, silence the media, and deceive the public.[8]

Despite that outlook, there was considerable crossover of journalists into government employment.[9] When Richard Nixon re-signed the presidency in 1974, broadcast reporters must have mused as his successor, Gerald Ford, appointed one of their own as White House press secretary. Ron Nessen, a one-time Vietnam War correspondent for NBC, became the first network broadcast veteran to become a chief press aide.

During his short presidency (1974-1976), Ford enjoyed mostly congenial relations with the media. Journalists, however, seemed to delight in portraying him, a former football player at the University of Michigan, as clumsy. Every time he stumbled, it seemed that camera shots made network news and newspaper front pages. A similar media fascination with the superficial surfaced during the presidency of Ford's successor. One of the long-running stories about Jimmy Carter was of a "killer rabbit," as journalists dubbed it, that tried to bite the president during a fishing trip.

THE CARTER YEARS

The 1976 political campaign between Ford and Carter took place against a backdrop of unprecedented circumstances tied to the first resignation of an American president and the result that the incumbent up for election had never before been on his party's presidential ticket. Ford's use of television had been limited, of course, by his short term in office, although he did preside over the formal end of America's Vietnam involvement. Carter emerged initially as a Washington outsider intent on restoring integrity to national government. He derived advantage from a small, cohesive organization that provided continuity for his campaign and was the only primary candidate who in 1976 never changed media directors or broadcast advertising techniques. In the televised debates, he did a credible job, while Ford's confusion over the geopolitics of Europe hurt his election prospects.

After winning the election, Carter experienced a brief grace period with the press, as has been the case with most American presidents. His media specialist, Gerald Rafshoon, encouraged his participation in televised town meetings, a radio call-in show, and gala dinners with news executives to enhance his press relations and image. But the image-making strategies wore thin as the economy worsened. The perceived theatricality associated with a televised "Fireside Chat" in which Carter dressed in a cardigan sweater and sat by a fireplace in the White House addressing the energy issue probably had the effect of undermining his substantive achievements such as his efforts in international peace negotiations. Coverage of his brother Billy Carter's drinking problem detracted from his image as a national leader in the tradition of F.D.R. A variety of problems hurt Carter's presidency, but in *The Other Side of the Story* (1984), his press aide, Jody Powell, insisted that unfair press attention to specious allegations of drug use by another close aide, Hamilton Jordan, also affected his boss' public stature and chance for re-election.

Media reporting on the important issues of the day was increasingly under study during Carter's term in office and throughout the 1970s and 1980s. The Media Institute, a Washington-based

---

[8]For examples of this view, see William Rivers, *The Adversaries: Politics and the Press* (Boston, 1970), and William E. Porter, *Assault on the Media: The Nixon Years* (Ann Arbor, Mich., 1976). The latter argued, for example, that President Richard Nixon viewed the press with hostility and waged a deliberate campaign to "intimidate, harass, regulate and damage" the news media.

[9]Edward R. Murrow once headed the United States Information Agency; and John F. Kennedy's press secretary, Pierre Salinger, eventually went to work for ABC in Europe. Bill Moyers also accomplished this feat in reverse, going from a former print journalist/publisher and press secretary for President Johnson to become an influential broadcast journalist with both PBS and CBS. John Chancellor served briefly as Director of the Voice of America under Lyndon Johnson; and another of broadcasting's elder statesmen, John Scali, achieved cabinet rank as ambassador to the United Nations, a post he held for two years before returning to ABC News as a senior correspondent.

Jimmy Carter's Media Difficulties
After winning election in 1976, President Jimmy Carter experienced a brief honeymoon with journalists. As the national economy worsened and the hostage crisis in Iran dragged on, media scrutiny became harsher. Carter made a number of efforts to improve his public image with planned media appearances, but they were not effective, and his popularity slowly diminished. Although difficulties in dealing with major national problems plagued his presidency, a number of his staff members believed that much of the blame for his faltering support from the American public could be laid at the feet of the media. His press secretary, Jody Powell, published a book, *The Other Side of the Story,* criticizing the Washington press corps for its tactics after Carter lost the 1980 election to Ronald Reagan.

non-profit but corporate-sponsored research organization designed to improve business and economic reporting, gave the media a failing grade for their coverage of both the 1973-74 and 1978-79 oil crises — crises that included reports from gas lines at America's service stations.

Carter was damaged also by negative coverage of a major news item that was due, more or less, to unanticipated circumstances abroad. When about 500 Iranians seized the U. S. Embassy in Teheran in 1979, the action caught most Americans, including the news media, off guard. Taken in retaliation for cooperation of the United States with the Shah of Iran and because of the growing influence of Western culture and industrialization, it resulted in a demand that the Shah, seeking medical attention in New York, be returned to stand trial. Because of his failing health, return was impossible. The TV networks were ill-equipped to handle this kind of international story although a decade earlier ABC had concentrated a great deal of energy, manpower, and money on exhaustive coverage of the 1972 Munich Olympics. The reporting of ABC's sports team during an Arab terrorist attack on Israeli athletes had won high praise for the network, the traditional follower in news. It also brought attention to ABC sports chief Roone Arledge. He later was made head of the network's news operation, although his lack of journalism credentials became a cause of concern in some quarters. When the Iranian situation developed, Arledge requested special airtime for the story. The result was "The Iran Crisis: America Held Hostage," a series of twenty-minute updates that ran for nearly four months until ABC formally established *Nightline* as a regular part of its program schedule with more than thirty segments devoted to Iran.

For the first three and a half days of the crisis, ABC News had a virtual monopoly on coverage because one of its reporters, Bob Dyk, was able to slip into the country the day after the takeover with a cameraman at his side. Iranian TV allowed ABC to send reports via satellite using electronic newsgathering equipment. The competing networks were forced to rely on film shot by British and West German news organizations and shipped by air. This

arrangement gave ABC an edge in covering the story even if the exclusive lasted only a few days.

Later, when the United States attempted to rescue the hostages, *Nightline* provided after-the-fact coverage, including biographical information on the eight American servicemen who lost their lives on the mission. When the American hostages were finally released and Ronald Reagan was inaugurated as president, both on January 20, 1981, *Nightline,* along with the other news media, provided detailed coverage. Follow-up stories — such as treatment of the hostages by the press once they returned to the United States — helped the show and an offspring, *Viewpoint,* gain high regard as a media monitor. The continued success of the series could be attributed also to ABC's willingness to extend coverage on special occasions, the performance of the series' master interviewer, Ted Koppel, and extensive use of satellite coverage of breaking events.

REAGAN: MASTER OF THE MEDIA

Sometimes referred to in press reports as "The Great Communicator," Ronald Reagan was regarded as the most effective television president since John F. Kennedy. He held the distinction of having been an actor and host of a TV series, *General Electric Theatre.* His presidency helped usher in a new age of technology. Cable News Network provided live coverage of the major events surrounding his first inaugural — and some of the minor ones — and the inauguration was the first to be closed captioned for the hearing impaired for TV.

A study of the 1980 election found, however, that the media, especially CBS, were predominantly negative in reporting about the candidates.[10] Even before the election, Reagan was involved in a controversy when NBC News projected his win before voters in the West, Alaska, and Hawaii had gone to the polls. It was argued that Carter's early concession speech had the effect of turning

---

[10]See Michael Robinson, "Media, Rate Thyselves," *Washington Journalism Review* (December 1983): 31-3. Surprisingly, this study showed a disproportionate amount of negative reporting by the press in stories about itself.

Nightline

Ted Koppel emerged as one of television news' master interviewers during the American hostage crisis in Iran. His authoritative and engaging live broadcasts on *Nightline* helped to establish ABC-TV as a leading news organization. (Photo courtesy ABC. Copyright 1990 Capital Cities/ABC, Inc.)

away voters in those states. A later CBS News poll showed that nearly 10% of those who did not vote cited Carter's apparent loss in their decision.

Once in office, Reagan's TV performances received rave reviews. After his first televised press conference, Tom Shales declared in the *Washington Post* that "whatever else he does during his administration, at least President Reagan won't be wasting his time learning how to look good on television.... It may not be possible to look any better on television than he already does."[11]

Reagan courted reporters in a manner not unlike John F. Kennedy. When a mini-press conference was held to address a drop in unemployment in 1983, Mrs. Reagan interrupted with a birthday cake for her husband halfway into the meeting. TV cameras from all three networks caught news correspondents in a chorus of "Happy Birthday to You," Reagan's 72nd, before returning to regular programming.

Reagan had trouble with press leaks during his early administration and suffered major setbacks with the televised Congressional grilling of some of his advisors, nominees, and appointees. Media coverage tended to be negative in several areas. An independent study of network economics reporting found an anti-ad-

ministration bias at CBS. A follow-up study of CBS, NBC, and ABC reporting as the economy turned around in early 1983 discovered a sense of skepticism on the part of the news media. The study concluded that among the TV networks ABC was providing the most comprehensive view of the economy while CBS was doing the least effective job.[12]

Reagan's major media problem during his presidency was an international guns-for-money deal that was dubbed the Iran-Contra scandal. The story was broken, not in the United States, but in the Middle East by an obscure magazine. What it reported and the rest of the world's press expanded on was the sale of arms by the United States through Israel to Iran, then under a U. S. embargo, and the use of millions of dollars from the sale to finance the Contra rebels fighting the Marxist government of Nicaragua, despite a federal law prohibiting the U. S. government from financing the Contras. Iran-Contra raised questions in the minds of many liberal critics as to whether the American media were carrying out adequately their responsibility to inform the public of what official institutions were doing.

MEDIA ACCESS TO WAR

Reagan also became embroiled in the issue of press access to government information, particularly access to military operations in foreign countries — an issue largely forgotten in the United States since the Vietnam conflict.

In 1983, when American troops invaded tiny Grenada in the Caribbean, the military invited no reporters to go along, and those who appeared on the scene in the first days were not allowed to file stories. Journalists and news organizations expressed their dismay when the government restricted press coverage of military action on the island of Grenada. *NBC Nightly News* commentator John Chancellor was widely quoted for his condemnation of the action — an invitation to bureaucrats, he said, to "Do anything. No one is watching."

When journalists complained about the restrictions, public sentiment sided with the government. Journalists seemed almost as alarmed over the public's apparent unwillingness to support their demand for access as they had been over the original military restrictions. Although surveys found that opposition to the press was less pronounced than journalists might have thought,[13] Chancellor — dipping into his mailbag and recounting a dozen letters from viewers in response to his Grenada commentary — noted that most letter writers felt restrictions placed on the press were justified. He concluded with an advisory that military censorship outside the context of a declared war courts disaster in a democracy, as had been evidenced by Vietnam.[14]

In the wake of the Grenada invasion, a consortium of news

[11]Quoted in *Broadcasting*, 16 February 1981.

[12]See David Gergen, "How Television Weakens the Presidency," *Channels of Communication* 10 (March-April, 1984): 63-4; and Vernon Guidry, "How Television Covered the Recovery," *Washington Journalism Review* (July-August, 1983): 41-4.

[13]Carl Sessions Stepp, "In the Wake of Grenada," *Quill* (March 1984): 12-5.

[14]Chet Huntley Memorial Lecture, New York University, reprinted in John Chancellor, "The Media and the Invasion of Grenada: Facts and Fallacies," *Television Quarterly* 20:4 (1984): 27-33.

organizations banded together to try to negotiate an understanding for future access to combat zones. PBS's *Inside Story* presented highlights of the dispute, including the views of prominent reporters and public reaction against the journalists' position. Michael Burch, assistant secretary of defense for public affairs, pointed to the absurdity of a hypothetical military operation in which a TV news program such as *60 Minutes* is allowed access to information from American forces, and then leaves to cover the story from the other side, getting the views of opposing troops. He also noted the additional space requirements for TV equipment, the logistics of transporting technicians, and the other unique problems associated with operating TV equipment in a combat zone.[15]

To attempt to accommodate both military and press interests, the military instituted a "pool system" that reduced the number of news people allowed direct contact with the fighting. The pool was used in Panama in 1989 when the U. S. military intervened to capture President Manuel Noriega. The system required an officer to be present whenever a reporter interviewed a serviceman. Most journalists condemned what they claimed was interference with independent reporting. Military officials responded that battlefield conditions and concern for the safety of civilian reporters necessitated the precautions.

Journalists voiced similar complaints during the Persian Gulf War in 1991. Media pool operations and video press briefings by General Norman Schwarzkopf were often cited as examples of military control of outgoing information; but coverage of the conflict won both big audiences and critical acclaim for newspapers and the TV networks, especially CNN, which provided around-the-clock coverage. The pool setup resulted in much lower costs for the news organizations, although CNN still spent $18 million on its war coverage and each of the other networks invested twice as much, over $40 million apiece.[16]

A number of reporters emerged from this coverage receiving wide praise: CNN's Bernard Shaw and Peter Arnett, for example; as well as Bob McKeown of CBS News, who was among the first to enter a liberated Kuwait City just ahead of coalition troops, and NBC's Arthur Kent, whom the national press colorfully dubbed "the Scud Stud," referring to his live broadcast performance in an area under attack by Scud missiles. Arnett and Kent were treated as media celebrities upon their return stateside, and their opinions were sought on a variety of political and domestic issues.[17] NBC fired Kent in 1992, however, for refusing to report from war-torn areas in Yugoslavia. Then in 1999 CNN fired Arnett after he reported erroneously that the U.S. Air Force in 1970 had dropped nerve gas on civilians during the Vietnam War. In 2003, during the second Gulf War, he received wide criticism for appearing on Iraqi state-run television and criticizing the American effort while praising Iraqi determination. NBC fired him.

THE FIRST BUSH PRESIDENCY

Even before he became Chief Executive, the first President George Bush made broadcast performance an issue while appearing live on TV in 1988. The then Vice President confronted Dan Rather on the *CBS Evening News*, claiming his appearance was being used as an excuse to cross examine his role in the Iran-Contra scandal. "It's not fair to judge my whole career by a rehash on Iran," Bush said. "How would you [Rather] like it if I judged your career by those seven minutes when you walked off the set in New York?"[18] Bush's reference was to an incident five months earlier when Rather refused to appear on the air as a protest over a sporting event running over into the news slot. For seven minutes, the network telecast went dead. Rather responded that Bush's campaign for the presidency was much more important than Rather's gaffe. Bush's handling of this interview, along with other campaign issues — such as an advertisement that criticized his opponent, Michael Dukakis, for a Massachusetts prison furlough program that resulted in repeat offenses — provided controversy.

During the Bush presidency, the role and propriety of journalists, particularly broadcasters, performing as commentators, which had been widely accepted in an earlier era, were being questioned. Broadcasters functioning as quasi-mediators and interpreters of events arose in a variety of international contexts, including the fall of the Berlin Wall.

The importance of TV in modern world affairs seemed to have been epitomized by a joint appearance by Soviet premier Mikhail Gorbachev and Russian president Boris Yeltsin on ABC. Their appearance occurred in the wake of the disintegration of the Soviet Union and its Communist system. Admitting the failure of the system, Russian television began its newscast with: "Today, September 5, 1991, we all began living in a new country: The Soviet Union is no more."[19]

During the 1992 campaign, Vice President Dan Quayle made news when he castigated fictional TV host "Murphy Brown," played by Candice Bergen on CBS, for her decision to have an out-of-wedlock baby. The ensuing debate, in which the influence and values of Hollywood and television were often raised, became central to the campaign.

Congress was also a target of criticism. Members of the Senate Judiciary Committee were castigated, for example, for their handling of the televised confirmation hearings on the U. S. Supreme Court nomination of Judge Clarence Thomas, while the networks were praised for their decision to preempt profitable daytime programming to air the hearings. Focusing on charges of sexual harassment, the hearings had the unique distinction of outdrawing a major league championship baseball game on opening night.

[15]Lyle Denniston, "Planning for Future Grenadas," *Quill* (January 1984): 10-16.

[16]See Richard Zoglin, "Assessing the War Damage: ABC Establishes Air Supremacy," *Time*, 18 March 1991, 88-9; "CNN: Where Have All the Viewers Gone?" *Broadcasting*, 1 July 1991, 45-7.

[17]See Thomas J. Collin, "Will Success Spoil 'Bagdad Pete'?" *Washington Journalism Review* (May 1991): 18.

[18]CBS Evening News, 25 January 1988. Copies of the nine-minute exchange between Bush and Rather are available from C-SPAN, c/o Purdue University Video Archive.

[19]"Communism Failed, Soviets Agree in American TV Show," *St. Louis Post-Dispatch*, 6 September 1991, 1.

Television Criticism

As television became pervasive and demonstrated its capacity for immediacy in covering events, critics subjected it to increasing scrutiny. Among their charges was that TV journalists allowed themselves to be used irresponsibly because of their desire to get breaking news. Some of the most intense criticism of the 1980s occurred when television crews carried live a "news conference" that Islamic terrorists staged with American hostages in an attempt to influence negotiations with Israel. Most American daily newspapers carried, as the *Providence Journal* did, stories of the conference on page one.

THE MEDIA UNDER SCRUTINY

Periodically throughout history the American news media have become the subject of intense criticism. Penny and yellow journalism in the nineteenth century attracted much denunciation. Likewise, in the twentieth century muckraking and conservative newspaper ownership during the New Deal bore many attacks. Rarely, however, was the criticism more widespread than in the late twentieth century. It came not just from special-interest groups and the elite segments of society. Suspicion about the media seemed at times pervasive. Generally, the criticism revolved around the issue of media bias.

Much of the criticism was aroused by journalists who appeared to think that their role was to be critical of almost everyone else. Often journalists measured their own accomplishments in terms of their ability to expose some other person's or institution's weaknesses. The public and important institutions reacted against what seemed to be an arrogant mass media. Public opinion polls indicated low esteem for journalists and even a willingness to have government control certain press practices if abuses occurred. In the first Nixon term, Vice President Spiro Agnew had attacked the TV networks and big eastern papers as constituting an unrepresentative elite that had too much power. The criticism of the media continued to enlarge over the following years.

On the legal front, there was a slight reaction. The expansive freedom that the media earlier had enjoyed began to be restricted. The courts, led by the Supreme Court under Chief Justice Warren Burger, limited the *N.Y. Times v. Sullivan* rule by narrowing the definition of public figure[20] and public official. The right to privacy was strengthened against media intrusion by court decisions and by legislative action to protect the rights of the accused following their arrest and during court actions. On the other hand, many official acts and records previously closed to the public became available through legislation calling for open records and open meetings.

Big business, long a target of critical press investigation, began to return fire. Both the skeptical investigative reporters and the more conventional writers in the lifestyles sections were interested in business matters. The influence of major corporations on political life, waste in public contracts, the contribution of manufacturing and of manufactured products to environmental pollution, the effects of conglomerates on the companies they acquired, prices as compared to costs — all these issues made headlines. In response, many elements of the business community began to monitor media performance in such areas as energy, pollution, and consumer information, becoming sharply critical of perceived anti-business biases. In public relations campaigns, they refuted media coverage and spoke out frankly and harshly on many occasions. They were joined by women's groups, ethnic groups, religious groups, and single-issue political groups across a wide spectrum in calling for careful reporting — and even careful use of nouns, pronouns, and adjectives — when topics sensitive to them were in the news.

60 Minutes faced public humiliation in the late 1970s, when the subject of one of its investigative reports, Illinois Power, waged a public relations campaign circulating more than 1,000 copies of a videotape to community groups and stockholders pointing out *60 Minutes'* flaws in preparing a report on the company. The tape employed excerpts from the original *60 Minutes* broadcast and some outtakes not included in the story as aired.[21]

Many journalists recognized the seriousness of the credibility problem they were facing and took steps to resolve it. They began

[20]*Time, Inc.*, v. Firestone, 424 U.S. 448 (1976).

[21]See Sandy Graham, "Illinois Power Pans *60 Minutes*," *Wall Street Journal*, 27 June 1980; and Tom Dorsey, "*60 Minutes* Can Skirt the Spotlight As Well As Wield It," *Louisville Courier Journal*, 9 June 1981, C1.

publishing in the late 1960s and early '70s, often in league with college journalism departments, magazines that focused on press practices. Joining these journalism reviews as monitors of media performance were a dozen local and state press councils in which media consumers met with practitioners to air grievances and discuss current issues.

The National News Council, founded in 1974 and funded privately, accepted complaints from the public against the national news media — wire services, networks, major newspapers, and the like — studied them, and reported its findings. The Council was often called upon to render judgments on behalf of aggrieved parties who were willing to have a decision prepared by peers working on their behalf rather than taking their case to court. It ceased operation in 1984, never having gained adequate support from the news media.

Another effort to reconcile the media and the public, the institution of the ombudsman was imported from Europe by newspapers seeking new ways of being responsible.[22] Of the several dozen ombudsmen newspapers employed, most were readers' representatives, taking complaints from the public, looking into them, and reporting to executives and the staff of the newspaper and the complainant. Others independently critiqued their newspapers systematically and wrote reports, sometimes published in the paper and often highly critical of its performance.

Typifying the concern that journalists had for adherence to proper standards was the media reaction to the Janet Cooke affair in the early 1980s. That episode represented the ultimate in overreaching to achieve journalistic success. A young reporter for the *Washington Post*, Cooke wrote about an eight-year-old heroin addict named Jimmy, including direct quotes from the child and his mother and explicit descriptions of the two. Only after Cooke received a Pulitzer Prize for reporting was it discovered that there was no Jimmy and, indeed, that in applying for a job with the *Post*, Cooke had claimed an academic degree she did not have. The child who *Post* readers had been led to believe existed was, Cooke admitted, a composite created from what she had learned about addiction. The Pulitzer was withdrawn. Cooke and the *Post* parted company. An irony was that Bob Woodward was Cooke's editor.

The nation's most prominent newspaper, the *New York Times*, faced similar embarassment in 2003 when it was revealed that another young reporter, Jayson Blair, had also fabricated stories. That revelation was followed by another that Jack Kelley, a longtime foreign correspondent for *USA Today*, had fabricated sources for thirteen years. The same year, Rick Bragg, who had won the Pulitzer Prize for feature writing, resigned from the *New York Times* when he was accused of not giving credit to a stringer who had gathered facts for stories. He pointed out that using stringers without crediting them was common practice, but the controversy over the Blair and Kelley affairs had made the news media particular sensitive to any claims that might damage their credibility.

TELEVISION UNDER ATTACK

With TV news occupying so much of the public's attention and other forms of programming such as *The Day After* and *Roots*, the historic mini-series on a black family's ancestry, having such a wide social impact, television began to receive more critical attention. Publications such as *Variety*, *Broadcasting and Cable*, and *Radio-Television Age* offered mostly specialized treatment for the trade; but as TV's informational programming progressed, the print media began to take the broadcast scene more seriously. Magazines such as *Saturday Review*, *The New Yorker*, and *TV Guide* contained some serious writing about broadcasting and for many years went beyond program listings for the general reader. Newspapers progressed more slowly in their coverage, no doubt hampered by their traditional mindset toward entertainment programming and the "boob tube."

Some newspapers, however, devoted considerable coverage to television. The *New York Times* covered broadcasting for more than twenty-five years with informed critiques by Jack Gould and, since 1972, John J. O'Connor. Les Brown was added as a broadcast correspondent and later became known for his authorship of two important books about TV and editorship of *Channels of Communication* magazine. Over the years the *Times* received criticism for assignment of reporters with little or no radio or TV experience to the broadcast beat.[23] In light of the fact that some medium-sized newspapers such as the *Louisville Courier-Journal* employed former TV news directors for their broadcast beats, perhaps the criticism was justified. Most columnists who wrote about TV, however, were required, by virtue of the limited numbers of reporters on newspaper staffs, to go beyond broadcast news in their coverage; and an argument could be made that they needed to be generalists.

Some of the nation's big newspapers, including the *Los Angeles Times*, employed a team of entertainment reporters, sometimes using smaller papers as training ground for broadcast critics. For awhile, the *New York Times* employed five TV critics with a division of labor drawn between fiction and nonfiction programming, including Sally Bedell, a former *TV Guide* writer and author of *Up the Tube: Prime Time and the Silverman Years* (1981). In addition to the *New York Times* and the *Los Angeles Times*, metropolitan newspapers employed many of the nation's most respected TV critics. One of the nation's premier broadcast critics made the transition to print from National Public Radio in 1972. Tom Shales joined critics Lawrence Laurant and John Carmody at the *Washington Post* and was made chief television critic seven years later. In *On the Air* (1982), a compilation of his columns, he presented perceptive, tongue-in-cheek commentary on the major events and personalities of TV journalism of the 1970s and early '80s. In the essay "Jugular Journalism" he assessed the debate over a program produced and aired in 1980 over CBS-owned WBBM-TV in Chicago titled "Watching the Watchdog," which questioned the methods of ABC's investigative reporter Geraldo Rivera and CBS's own Mike

---

[22]An ombudsman is an official or agent who receives, investigates, and attempts to resolve complaints and problems between parties within an institution or organization.

[23]See "Television and the Times," *Broadcasting*, 7 March 1983, 86-9.

Walter Cronkite
The dean of network television news reporters and anchors, Walter Cronkite was one of many members of the CBS News team, including Eric Sevareid and Charles Kuralt, to criticize attempts to jazz-up newscasts in an effort to attract viewers. Cronkite is remembered also for his visit to Vietnam and subsequent stand against the American war effort. He also advocated the expansion of network evening news to one hour. He is shown here (third from left) in a 1981 White House photograph being toasted by President Ronald Reagan and other dignitaries upon his retirement from CBS.

Wallace. Shales also presented provocative profiles of TV journalism's other key performers, including Walter Cronkite, Dan Rather, Tom Brokaw, Ted Koppel, and Barbara Walters.

Much of the attention of critics focused on the issue of salaries. The question of excessive compensation for TV figures was raised with the publication of Barbara Matusow's *The Evening Stars: The Rise of the Network Anchors* (1983). High-paid TV journalists reacted passionately to such criticism from their newspaper counterparts. Matusow quoted CBS newsman Eric Sevareid as pointing out to publishers that "broadcast journalism is the only business in the country I can think of that has its chief competitor as its chief critic."[24] Veteran CBS producer Don Hewitt claimed professional jealousy was one motivation for the attention broadcasters' salaries received from print columnists. Another prominent broadcaster questioned the sanity of exorbitant salaries when Bill Leonard published *In the Storm of the Eye: A Lifetime at CBS* (1990), detailing Dan Rather's contract negotiations on the eve of Walter Cronkite's retirement. Cronkite aired his own views on the subject in his book *A Reporter's Life* (1996) and in a variety of speeches.

Despite such occasional attention to media practices, there were few instances in which broadcasters took a critical look at their own industry. Rarely did they examine their own network or their competition as harshly as they scrutinized outside individuals and organizations. One of the few occasions when broadcast journalists reported on their own shortcomings was during the national presidential election of 2000, when they made major mistakes in projecting results. Most reports examining the media came in special editions of ABC's *Viewpoint*, *Inside CBS News'* broadcasts from affiliate stations, CBS's *Eye on the Press*, and public TV's *Inside Story*. CBS Reports' "Inside Public Television" focused on a competitor and came under fire from many members of the media when it aired in 1976. It dealt with growing commercialization, especially the use of auctions, at the tax-supported network. The reporter on the story, Charles Kuralt, questioned the sincerity of

PBS executives in their pledge to stay out of the ratings war with commercial competitors. Rare reports by in-house critics such as Jeff Greenfield at ABC and Ron Powers at CBS examined programming, trends, policy, or political uses at their own networks.

Overall, though, journalists showed little inclination to examine the practices of the field critically. They did produce some trade journals and journalism reviews and held professional conferences at which improved practices were often the subject. Their efforts at self-criticism, however, paled in comparison with their criticism of the rest of society. In a survey of practices in 1998, Fred Bales, a journalism professor at Xavier University in New Orleans and a former journalist, concluded, "Because the mass media are obligated by tradition to print and broadcast criticism of other major American institutions — and many do so frequently and zealously — it might be assumed that they cover and criticize themselves to the same degree. Not so.... As Maxwell King, former executive editor of the *Philadelphia Inquirer*, has said, 'We have been much better at self-righteousness than self-criticism.'"[25]

HAPPY NEWS

In 1974, Eric Sevareid, in his analysis section for the *CBS Evening News with Walter Cronkite*, questioned his broadcast brethren for jazzing up reality in their nightly newscasts: "In city after city, the news is delivered by newsmen turned actors, very bad actors. They grin, they laugh, they chuckle or moan the news....They kid each other or applaud each other. And any day now, one of them will sing the news while doing a buck-and-wing stark naked."[26] Sevareid's satire was consistent with other serious criticism concerning the emergence at the local level of "happy news" or "eyewitness" formats. In an effort to attain higher ratings, many broadcasters followed the advice of consultants, placing more emphasis on shorter and more entertaining stories and appearance than on

[24]Quoted in Barbara Matusow, "Intrigue at NBC," *Washington Journalism Review* (July-August, 1983): 83.

[25]Fred Bales, "Can the Media Criticize Themselves?" chapter 24 in Wm. David Sloan and Emily Erickson Hoff, eds., *Contemporary Media Issues* (Northport, Ala., 1998), 393.
[26]See *CBS Evening News with Walter Cronkite*, CBS News, 22 April 1974.

substance in story selection. When the actor who played Bozo the Clown on Chicago's WGN-TV died in 2001, Dan Rather, the CBS national news anchor, commented, "Rest assured; there'll never be a shortage of Bozos on television."

One of Sevareid's colleagues at CBS News, Charles Kuralt, well known for a decade of "On the Road" reports and host of *CBS Sunday Morning*, told the Radio-Television News Directors' Association that his lasting impression of local TV news was of the anchorman's hair. In *The Newscasters: The News Business as Show Business* (1978), Ron Powers made a persuasive case that beginning in the late 1960s and early 1970s broadcast managers sacrificed good news judgment and turned some of their decision-making authority over to "news doctors," consultants who depended on marketing strategy to win an audience.

Philadelphia's KYW-TV and its former news chief, Al Primo, frequently were identified with the trend starting in the 1970s of letting reporters tell their own story in their own way, rather than relying on the old style news anchor approach. Broadcast historian Edward W. Barrett profiled the consultants and found an increased emphasis on show-business techniques.[27]

A decade later, the show business elements of TV news were spotlighted by a law suit brought by Christine Craft, a former anchorwoman for KMBC-TV, Kansas City, Missouri. She sued Metromedia, the station's owner, for $1.2 million, charging sex discrimination, unequal pay, and fraud. *Craft vs. Metromedia* raised issues regarding television's journalistic integrity because Craft had been asked to improve her appearance in deference to viewers.

Inevitably the "show-business" trend resulted in what CBS's *60 Minutes* referred to as "tabloid news." A graduate journalism class at the University of California, Berkeley, taped all news programs for a week at top-rated KGO-TV in San Francisco during 1974.[28] *60 Minutes* reported that more than half of all stories fell into the tabloid category consisting of "fire, sex, tear-jerkers, accidents, and exorcism." This "eyewitness news" approach included more frequent exchanges between on-air personnel. Within a decade, some critics claimed that the formation of investigative units, or "I Teams," at some stations was simply an extension of "happy talk."

In the O. J. Simpson case in 1995, which included elements of sex and murder — and which followed a trial of police brutality involving another black man, Rodney King — the nation was overwhelmed with more than 2,000 hours of live broadcast and cable coverage. The next year, similar charges of press preoccupation with tabloid aspects of the murder of a child, JonBenet Ramsey, followed the failure of authorities to discover a suspect and prosecute the case. In the aftermath of the death of the Princess of Wales, Lady Diana, in an automobile crash, photographers were accused of having contributed to her death.

NEWSPAPERS UNDER TELEVISION ATTACK

While occasionally finding their own journalistic standards challenged, broadcast journalists seldom took their print counterparts to task for sloppy reporting or lack of professionalism. Only rarely did they make press performance a part of their job.

In 1974 Harry Reasoner castigated the *New York Times* for attention it paid to the motion picture *The Exorcist*, with five stories devoted to the film. "I'm afraid," he concluded, "the good old paper is possessed. Rites of exorcism in the city room and every bureau, performed by some tough minded city editor, are indicated.... If the union would permit the rites in the composing room, it might even reduce the typographical errors in the early edition."[29] In a more serious mood, Reasoner took *Time* and *Newsweek* to task in his ABC commentary for lack of objectivity in the handling of Watergate. He condemned *Newsweek* especially for reporting on indictments before they were given to Judge John Sirica and for "spoon-feeding conclusions in the style of pejorative pamphleteering."

In another exception to the rule, Hughes Rudd examined *The Business of Newspapers* in a TV documentary, using an intense struggle for advertising dollars in Boston between the *Boston Globe* and *Boston Herald-American* as its base. The documentary included an analysis of newspaper chain ownership, which writers such as Ben Bagdikian also had criticized.

THE CLINTON PRESIDENCY

While the nation was experiencing tremendous economic prosperity and growth during Bill Clinton's presidency, the media became preoccupied with stories of sex and scandal. Bolstered by excessive coverage of the O. J. Simpson case in California and JonBenet Ramsey in Colorado, came charges of a dissolution of standards and of radical changes in news orientation. This "tabloidization," critics claimed, created a new norm for covering public affairs. Some observers argued that the media paid an inordinate amount of attention to the so-called Whitewater affair, which dated back to Clinton's term as governor of Arkansas. It involved financial dealings of his wife, Hillary, and close friends and placed them under close scrutiny. While some involved in the scandal did go to jail, the President himself was cleared. Investigations expanded from Whitewater to allegations of improper sexual conduct dating back to his years as governor and then targeted his relations with a White House intern, Monica Lewinsky. When independent counsel Kenneth Starr released his office's voluminous report on its investigations, many newspapers reprinted it in its entirety, and some cable TV networks gave the report continuous coverage. Clinton's testimony before a grand jury and Congressional hearings prior to his impeachment likewise received extensive newspaper and TV coverage, and a variety of radio and TV shows for months devoted their daily programs to the scandals

[27]Edward W. Barrett, "Folksy TV News," *Columbia Journalism Review* (November-December 1973): 16-20. See also Gabriel Pressman, "Local Newscasts—A Continuing Identity Crisis," *Television Quarterly* 11 (Summer 1974): 25; and "Local News in 31 Different Flavors," from *The Quill*, reprinted in Leonard L. Sellers and William L. Rivers, eds., *Mass Media Issues: Articles and Commentaries* (Englewood Cliffs, N.J., 1977), 76-85.

[28]*60 Minutes*, CBS, 10 March 1974. The study is reviewed in Edwin Diamond, *The Tin Kazoo: Television, Politics, and the News* (Cambridge, Mass., 1975), 65-6.

[29]*The ABC Evening News with Howard K. Smith and Harry Reasoner*, ABC News, 28 January 1974.

Clinton-Lewinsky Affair

The Tuscaloosa News

$1.50

354 • 8 Sections   SUNDAY, DECEMBER 20, 1998   Tuscaloosa/Northport and West Alabama

ARTICLE ONE	ARTICLE TWO	ARTICLE THREE	ARTICLE FOUR
APPROVED 228-206: First article of impeachment, alleging that Clinton perjured himself before a grand jury.	**REJECTED 229-205:** An article accusing Clinton of committing perjury in the Paula Jones lawsuit.	**APPROVED 221-212:** An article accusing Clinton of obstruction of justice in the Monica Lewinsky matter.	**REJECTED 285-148:** An article alleging Clinton abused the powers of his office by giving false answers to Congress.

HOUSE IMPEACHES CLINTON

■ House approves two of the four articles against Clinton ■ Livingston resigns, urges president to do the same ■ Five Republicans, five Democrats break party lines

President Clinton addresses Democratic lawmakers who joined him outside the Oval Office of the White House Saturday after the House of Representatives voted to impeach the president.

By ALISON MITCHELL
N.Y. Times News Service

WASHINGTON — William Jefferson Clinton was impeached on charges of perjury and obstruction of justice Saturday by a divided House of Representatives, which recommended virtually along party lines that the Senate remove the nation's 42nd president from office.

A few hours after the vote Clinton, surrounded by Democrats, walked onto the South Lawn of the White House, his wife, Hillary, on his arm, to pre-empt calls for his resignation.

Livingston will quit Congress, urges the president to resign

House Speaker nominee Rep. Bob Livingston, R-La., shown in this television image, speaks during the House session Saturday in Washington during his debate on the four articles of impeachment against President Clinton.

By KATHARINE Q. SEELYE
N.Y. Times News Service

WASHINGTON — Rep. Bob Livingston, who contested to his colleagues Thursday night that he had had adulterous affairs, stunned the House chamber Saturday morning by saying in the impeachment debate on President Clinton that he would not serve as speaker and would quit Congress in six months. He urged the president to follow his example and quit, too.

But at the White House, where calls for Clinton's resignation are decided as a Republican strategy, the president sent a spokesman into the driveway to urge Livingston to reconsider his resignation.

Livingston stood in the well of the House he has served for two decades and called on Clinton to resign his **Please see QUIT Page 9A**

INSIDE

■ **SURPRISE:** A close Republican were caught off guard by Bob Livingston's resignation. **7A**

■ **ANALYSIS:** What's certain now is uncertainly. **8A**

■ **CHRONOLOGY:** Key events in the investigation that led to Clinton's impeachment. **10A**

The Clinton-Lewinsky scandal and the resultant Senate impeachment trial provided one of the biggest media stories of the last half of the twentieth century. Television, magazines, and newspapers repeatedly showed photographs (top) of the president and the intern. The affair gave countless opportunities for editorial cartoonists (right). Newspapers around the country played the impeachment story with banner headlines.

Deering—*Arkansas Democrat-Gazette*

White House Sex Scandal, Exposed Online, Absorbs the Nation's News Media

What began as a second-hand report circulated by an obscure online journalist culminated in saturation coverage by major news organizations. Disclosure of President Bill Clinton's affair with a White House intern dominated the national news media in 1998 as no political scandal had before.

Matt Drudge broke the story on the Internet in January. He reported that *Newsweek* had delayed publication of a report that Clinton had a sexual relationship with Monica Lewinsky, a White House intern and staff member from 1995 to 1997. Within hours, mainstream news outlets enthusiastically pursued the story. Critics said all-news cable channels and Internet sites forced reporters to rely recklessly on rumors and anonymous sources for fresh angles.

Questioned by reporters in January, Clinton indignantly denied a sexual relationship with Lewinsky. After being called to testify before a federal grand jury in August, he gave a televised speech admitting he had lied but insisting that he broke no laws.

Independent Counsel Kenneth Starr disagreed, sending Congress a 445-page report alleging eleven impeachable acts, including perjury and obstruction of justice. The document included explicit descriptions of sexual acts committed in the White House. Editors and broadcasters were forced to reconsider their own standards for language and taste. Many newspapers and online sources published the entire report, warning readers of its content. Starr later released a videotape of Clinton's grand jury testimony. While most TV and radio news programs broadcast excerpts, cable news channels repeatedly showed the whole tape.

Some columnists and commentators called the coverage excessive. The public seemed to agree. Yet, while polls indicated that Americans thought the story was out of proportion to its importance, audience ratings remained high.

In early 1999 the U. S. Senate tried and acquitted Clinton on two articles of impeachment that the House of Representatives passed against him, one alleging that he lied under oath and the second accusing him of obstructing justice.

The Internet

Myths Surround ARPANET Origins

The Internet seemed to have emerged from nowhere in the 1990s with the development of Web browsers such as Mosaic and Netscape. But the Internet does have a history   and much written about its early history is wrong.

Many of the histories of ARPANET, the forerunner of the Internet, claim it arose out of Cold War hysteria. Historians note that President Dwight Eisenhower created the organization under which ARPANET developed, the Department of Defense's Advanced Research Projects Agency, in 1958 after the Russians had launched the satellite Sputnik. Eisenhower, though, did not envision ARPA as an arm of the military, but as an agency to conduct pure scientific research. The Cold War argument is also based on the fact that Paul Baran, who developed the idea of a decentralized communication network that provided the foundation for the Internet, brought his idea to the government in 1964 as a way for communication systems to survive a nuclear attack.

But the first leaders of ARPA, J.C.R. Licklider and his successor, Robert Taylor, were hardly Cold Warriors. Licklider quickly shifted the focus of ARPA away from defense-related communicating to time-sharing systems in which numerous researchers on separate terminals could

One of the pioneers of the Internet, J.C.R. Licklider foresaw the potential in having computers linked to one another through a network. In 1962 he was named head of a group at ARPA who had the mission of improving the U.S. military's use of computers. Because of his visionary ideas, he was sometimes called "Computing's Johnny Appleseed," planting seeds for the computer age. Despite his achievements, he was humble about them. An acquaintance said of him: "He was the most unlikely 'great man' you could ever encounter.... He was gentle, courteous, and outgoing." He died from complications from asthma in 1990 at the age of seventy-five.

use a single computer simultaneously. He formed alliances with computer scientists at major academic computer centers to form what he called an "Intergalactic Computer Network," an interactive network that would link people together by com-

puters so that researchers across the globe could share information and communicate with each other.

Taylor shared Licklider's vision. Frustrated that he had three computer terminals that operated by a different set of commands, he wanted to create a national computer network that would allow researchers to share resources quickly and easily across geographic distances. This national computer network would create a community of scientists who could share files and communicate with each other.

Licklider's and Taylor's vision culminated in the creation of ARPANET in 1969, the precursor of the Internet. ARPANET was designed to connect computers at four university sites, with the goal of connecting research centers across the country and eventually around the world. The actual work of trying to connect these four sites was done primarily by sixty-eight graduate students calling themselves the Network Working Group. Internet historians have claimed the open, non-hierarchical nature of this group, many of whose members were '60s hippies, greatly influenced the culture of the early Internet in which there was a distinct distrust of authority and a belief that information should be free and all views should be openly discussed and debated.

So ARPANET of 1969 was more a product of the hippie movement than the military establishment that spawned it in 1958.

---

and investigations and to the House proceedings and Senate trial.

Criticism of media coverage came from a variety of quarters. Former TV anchor Walter Cronkite took journalists to task for excessive use of unidentified sources and investigative leaks.[30] A number of other journalists echoed those charges. Other criticisms, however, clearly were tinged with ideology. Steve Brill, liberal publisher of *Brill's Content*, castigated journalists for what he claimed was a lack of fairness and balance, particularly targeting the use of anonymous sources and hearsay. He accused several

publications and specific journalists, including NBC correspondent David Bloom and ABC's Jackie Judd, of being virtual extensions of Starr's investigation.[31] Starr himself sharply attacked Brill's charge as bordering on libel. Conservative critics, for their part, believed that the media's attention to Clinton's problems finally brought some ideological balance to the news media; but, they argued, had it been a Republican president involved in the scandals, media treatment would have been much harsher.

Because of the controversies surrounding the Clinton presidency, they dominated media coverage, and he made a number of

[30]Joel Connelly, "Walter Cronkite Pontificates on Trends in TV News Today," *St. Louis Post-Dispatch*, 15 May 1998.

[31]*Brill's Content*, June 1998.

efforts to direct attention elsewhere. One of the most notable was a visit to China in 1998. There, he was allowed to conduct a live, uncensored 70-minute news conference broadcast across China and telecast back to the United States. Taking a generally conciliatory approach to China — whose record of human rights' abuses, critics pointed out, had been highlighted in 1989 with a crackdown on demonstrators in Tiananmen Square — Clinton predicted that democracy would eventually come to the world's most heavily populated country, aided by the fact that it was "moving into the world of cellular phones and the Internet."[32] At the same time that his broadcast in China received much play, some American journalists saw a paradox in the fact that the President had given a press conference in a foreign country while avoiding such give-and-take meetings with the American media after news of his relationship with Monica Lewinsky broke.

A Revolution in Mass Communication

Broadcasting came into its own in the final decades of the twentieth century as a fairly reliable conveyer of news and information, but also as a major moneymaker. By the latter part of the century, broadcast news and information programming — once a throwaway item at the major TV networks — had become a mainstay and a major moneymaker. *60 Minutes* was consistently rated in the top ten most watched programs, while NBC's *Meet the Press* with Tim Russert and ABC News' *This Week* frequently made news with important interviews from the nation's capital. *Nightline* also provided insight and perspective on the critical issues of the day. NBC also succeeded with its multi-part series *Dateline NBC*, which forced both ABC and CBS to rethink their once-a-week airing of *20/20* and *60 Minutes*. PBS offered an hour's worth of news daily and scored a major ratings coup with a twelve-hour documentary series, *The Civil War*, in 1990. Four years later, Ken Burns' series *Baseball* became the most watched series in PBS history. The Cable News Network performed admirably on many occasions. It started "Special Assignment," which won praise for coverage of serious stories, such as a savings and loan scandal, investigations of former Panamanian dictator Manual Noriega, coverage of the release of Nelson Mandela after twenty-seven years in South African prisons, and a Washington, D.C., summit conference in 1990 between President George Bush and Soviet President Mikhail Gorbachev.

At local stations, news was, beyond commercial time sales, the major source of employment and the peg around which the station image was formed and promoted. Technological developments had the potential to enhance local prospects for covering national and international stories. Specialized news services, such as those that Michael Bloomberg (later New York City mayor) first developed, improved financial and business reporting. Expansion of news and increased emphasis on public affairs programs offered television the opportunity to gain public confidence. By the end of

the twentieth century, electronic journalism enjoyed unprecedented opportunities to cover events as they happened and to provide unique perspectives on important issues. With the combination of broadcasting, the Internet, and new approaches in the print media, a revolution in mass communication was under way.

RECOMMENDED READINGS

BOOKS

Allen, Craig M. *News is People: The Rise of Local TV News and the Fall of News from New York*. Ames, Iowa, 2001. Local TV news appealed to ordinary local audiences.

Arnett, Peter. *Live From the Battlefield: From Vietnam to Baghdad — 35 Years in the World's War Zones*. New York, 1994. The veteran war correspondent gives his memoirs.

Bloomberg, Michael. *Bloomberg on Bloomberg*. New York, 1997. The business-information giant outlines the development of his service.

Brandt, J. Donald. *A History of Gannett, 1906-1993*. Arlington, Va., 1993. An insider gives his account of the growth of the media giant.

Brinkley, David. *A Memoir*. New York, 1995. The former NBC anchor and commentator provides his personal account of television's development.

Brokaw, Tom. *Boom! Voices of the Sixties*. New York, 2008. The anchor/managing editor of NBC Nightly News from 1983 to 2004 reflects on his Midwest roots and coverage of events from the firsthand perspective of reporting from Los Angeles and Atlanta.

Conway, Mike. *The Origins of Television News in America*. New York, 2009. Television news began in the 1940s, with CBS taking the lead at the national level.

Craft, Christine. *Too Old, Too Ugly, and Not Deferential to Men*. New York, 1988. The anchorwoman provides her personal account of her removal from airwaves and subsequent litigation.

Cronkite, Walter. *A Reporter's Life*. New York, 1996. The dean of television news tells his story.

Dawkins, Wayne. *Black Journalists: The NABJ Story*. Sicklerville, N.J., 1993. The author provides an anecdotal history of the early years of the National Association of Black Journalists.

Diamond, Edwin. *Behind the Times: Inside the New New York Times*. New York, 1994. The author profiles changes at the *New York Times* in the 1960s, 1970s, and 1980s.

Goldberg, Bernard. *Bias: A CBS Insider Exposes How the Media Distort the News*. Washington, D.C., 2002. The national news media show a liberal bias on most issues.

Hertsgaard, Mark. *On Bended Knee*. New York, 1988. The author tells the story of "coordinated" news activity in the Reagan White House.

Hewitt, Don. *Tell Me a Story: Fifty Years and 60 Minutes in Television*. New York, 2001. The founder and executive producer of *60 Minutes* gives his memoirs.

Matusow, Barbara. *The Evening Stars: The Rise of the Network News Anchors*. Boston, 1983. The selection of anchors was based too much on appeal rather than journalistic ability.

McPherson, James Brian. *Journalism at the End of the American Century, 1965-Present*. Westport, Conn., 2006. This survey covers the 1960s to the end of the 1990s. During that time, the American news media dealt with major movements and events such as Vietnam, civil rights, the women's movement, and Watergate. Ultimately, the public lost faith in the news media, and the media themselves tended toward an emphasis on entertainment values, corporate ownership, and profit.

Morgan, Arlene Notoro, et. al., eds. *The Authentic Voice: The Best Reporting on Race and Ethnicity*. New York, 2006. This anthology includes news stories honored as the Columbia University Graduate School of Journalism.

Morton, Paula E. *Tabloid Valley: Supermarket News and American Culture*. Gainesville, Fla., 2009. Today's tabloid journalism can be traced to the penny press, and yellow journalism in the late 1800s contributed greatly to its emphasis on bold headlines, sensational play, and other characteristics seen in today's tabloid newspapers.

Mudd, Roger. *The Place to Be: Washington, CBS, and the Glory Days of Television News*.

---

[32] "Clinton, Leaving China, Predicts Democracy Will Come," *St. Louis Post-Dispatch*, 4 July 1998.

New York, 2008. Between 1961 and 1980, CBS's Washington bureau did some of the biggest news stories of the era.

Murray, Michael, ed. *Encyclopedia of Television News*. Phoenix, 1999. This large work includes entries on major figures and issues.

Murray, Michael, and Roy Moore, eds. *Mass Communication Education*. Ames, Iowa, 2003. Twenty-four chapters examine how mass communication and journalism have been taught recently in American universities. The book includes short biographies of nineteen professors.

O'Connor, John E., ed. *American History/American Television: Interpreting the Video Past*. New York, 1983. "[I]n a very real sense, *television is American Culture*.... At least for the vast majority of Americans — people who may never attend a play or a concert, visit a museum, or read a book — TV is all there is."

Powers, Ron. *The Newscasters: The News Business as Show Business*. New York, 1977. To get higher ratings, TV executives from the 1960s to 1977 debased local newscasts by pushing news toward show business.

Primo, Albert, T. *Eyewitness Newsman*. Philadelphia, 2008. Primo's autobiography tells of his career in television news and his pioneering role as the creator of eyewitness news.

Read, Donald. *The Power of News: The History of Reuters*. New York, 1992. This book is a detailed history of the rise of the worldwide news service, from the start of telegraphy in the 1840s to 1990.

Robertson, Nan. *The Girls in the Balcony: Women, Men and The New York Times*. New York, 1992. A reporter for the *Times*, the author provides sketches of women reporters at the *Times* through the years and gives an insider's account of gender discrimination.

Rozell, Mark J. *The Press and the Ford Presidency*. Ann Arbor, Mich., 1992. This survey of press coverage of the Ford presidency concludes that the press was unduly harsh toward Ford.

Salisbury, Harrison E. *Without Fear or Favor: The New York Times and Its Times*. New York, 1980. The *Times* became a powerful independent voice with its stands on such issues as civil rights, McCarthyism, and the Pentagon Papers.

Schonfeld, Reese. *Me and Ted Against the World: The Unauthorized Story of the Founding of CNN*. New York, 2001. Schonfeld claims to be the genius behind the creation of CNN's news operation.

Shawcross, William. *Murdoch*. New York, 1992. Rupert Murdoch built a worldwide media empire on a foundation of sensationalism.

Smoller, Frederic T. *The Six O'Clock Presidency: A Theory of Presidential Press Relations in the Age of Television*. Westport, Conn., 1990. CBS coverage of the presidency was "determined by the political, technical and commercial nature of the medium itself, producing a bias toward negative coverage."

Tifft, Susan E., and Alex S. Jones. *The Patriarch: The Rise and Fall of the Bingham Dynasty*. New York, 1991. The authors profile the Bingham family of Louisville and the dissolution of its media empire.

Trotta, Liz. *Fighting for Air: In the Trenches with Television News*. New York, 1991. The author, the first woman correspondent in Vietnam and a twenty-year network news veteran, critiques changes in TV news.

ARTICLES

Allen, Craig. "Television, 1948-Present: Entertainment or Information?" in Wm. David Sloan, ed., *Perspectives on Mass Communication History*, 334-46. Hillsdale, N.J., 1991. This historiographical essay provides a useful overview of explanations of television history.

Lowry, Dennis T. "Network TV News Framing of Good vs. Bad Economic News under Democrat and Republican Presidents: A Lexical Analysis of Political Bias." *Journalism & Mass Communication Quarterly* 85:3 (2008): 483-98. In covering Presidents Bill Clinton and George W. Bush, the mainstream TV news was more biased against Bush than Clinton.

Murray, Michael. "A Passion for Politics: A Conversation with Tom Brokaw." *American Journalism* 17 (2000): 110-17. The author interviews the NBC anchorman and author of the book *The Greatest Generation*.

----. "Network Insiders Look at CBS." *American Journalism* 5 (1988): 248-57. This review essay examines half-dozen books about CBS.

----. "Reporting History's First Draft: A Conversation with Byron Pitts." *Television Quarterly* 33 (2003): 26-33. This interview covers such matters as broadcast coverage of the terrorist attacks of September 11, 2001.

Olmsted, Kathryn. "'An American Conspiracy': The Post-Watergate Press and the CIA." *Journalism History* 19 (1993): 51-8. The press was often deferential to the executive branch in the years after the Watergate scandal.

Shmanske, Stephen. "News as a Public Good: Cooperative Ownership, Price Commitments, and the Success of the Associated Press." *Business History Review* 60 (Spring 1986): 55-80. In a free-market economy, the non-profit AP succeeded because of its cooperative ownership structure.

25

The Contemporary Media

2000 - Present

At the beginning of the twenty-first century, technology spawned by the Internet brought new problems and possibilities for mass media. Despite the fact that an ever-decreasing number of corporations controlled more of the media, in some ways it became increasingly difficult for media users to determine the sources of their information and, thus, to judge the credibility of messages. That uncertainty increased the potential value of credible mainstream news media, but the audiences for those mainstream media — and trust in them — were shrinking. After all, audiences could read or watch their news, view movies, or listen to music in more ways than ever before, without leaving their home computers or cell phones (which offered an increasing number of services). Messages could seemingly appear everywhere almost instantly. At the same time, largely because of the combined potential hazards of the information explosion and international terrorism, government officials began seeking new ways to control information. Journalists attempted to continue to cover traditional news stories in meaningful ways, while also trying to keep up with the flood of information, with changing definitions of news, and with the new ways that audiences could access their news. Today, the technological evolution of mass media continues at a breakneck pace. Young journalists and media producers who stay current with technological trends may enjoy potential advantages their predecessors never had.

THE BUSINESS OF NEWS

The trend toward media mergers and corporate growth that had begun in the early 1900s accelerated toward the end of the twentieth century, and it continued afterwards. As corporations bought up newspapers, local ownership decreased, a trend that concerned critics. Chain ownership of newspapers increased substantially. Whereas in 1960 a total of 114 chains had owned 563 dailies (32% of all dailies), by 1977 chains owned 1,061 dailies (60% of the total). According to the Project for Excellence in Journalism, in 2005 the largest twenty-one chains owned approximately 560 newspapers (40% of dailies), representing 70% of daily circulation.

A related trend was the elimination of competing newspapers in the same city. Whereas 117 cities had had competing dailies in 1945, only forty-one cities had more than one newspaper by 2004, and twelve of those had joint operating arrangements. In cities such as St. Louis, Dallas, and Little Rock, newspapers that had co-existed profitably for nearly a century were locked in a struggle for survival. Eventually, each of those three cities had only one newspaper. Overall, the numbers of daily papers remained stable around the 1,760 level until 1980, when they slumped to 1,745. By 2008 the number had declined to 1,408.

Mergers in mass communication reflected the same trend that had occurred in other businesses. In the automobile industry, for example, Chrysler had recently merged with Daimler Benz; and in petroleum, the giants Exxon and Mobil had combined. By 2000, the ten largest TV cable operators served 90% of all subscribers. In recent years, some notable mergers had occurred in the cable industry. AT&T purchased TCI and MediaOne to create AT&T Broadband, the largest cable TV operator in the nation, serving 16.5 million subscribers. Comcast, one of the largest systems, bought AT&T Broadband in 2003. Viacom, cable provider and owner of MTV, bought CBS Corp. The combined companies owned more than 40% of the nation's TV stations, exceeding the limit of 35% that the law permitted.

The year 2000 also saw the creation of one of the largest newspaper companies in the nation and the beginning of negotiations that ultimately would result in the biggest media conglomerate in the world. When the Tribune Co., parent of the *Chicago Tribune*, bought Times Mirror Co., it created America's third largest newspaper corporation. The $6.5 billion value of the combined companies was the largest newspaper transaction in history. Along with the *Tribune*, the company owned ten other newspapers with a total circulation of 3.6 million, including the *Los Angeles Times, Hartford Courant, Baltimore Sun, Orlando Sentinel*, and *Newsday* on Long Island. The circulation of the *Times* was the fourth largest in the country, behind only *USA Today*, the *Wall Street Journal*, and the *New York Times*. The only two publishers with more total newspaper circulation than the Tribune Co. were Gannett (with seventy-four dailies and 6.7 million circulation) and Knight Ridder (with thirty-one newspapers totaling 3.9 million circulation). Along with its newspapers, the enlarged Tribune Co. also owned twenty-two TV stations — including WGN in Chicago, WPIX in New York, and KTLA in Los Angeles — that reached 75% of U. S. households. Explaining the thinking behind the Tribune Co.'s purchase of Times Mirror, its chairman, John Madigan, said, "I can't predict what other people are going to do, but if other people look at the future of the business as we have, they'll see that consolidation is the future."[1] A few years later, the corporation faced bankruptcy.

Despite the size of the Tribune Co.'s purchase of Times Mirror, the merger paled in comparison to another the same year. When America Online, the Internet provider, merged with Time Warner, the new company was valued at $162 billion. AOL, the smaller partner in the deal, owned such "new media" companies as Netscape and CompuServe. Time Warner — which was the result of a merger in 1990 between Time Inc., the publisher, and Warner Bros., the entertainment company — owned *Time*, *Sports Illustrated*, *People*, other popular magazines, HBO, the Turner Broadcasting System (including TBS, Cartoon Network, TNT, and CNN), Time Warner Cable, Warner Music, and other media. The AOL-Time Warner deal was the biggest corporate merger of all time.

Competitors, such as Disney and Viacom-CBS, among others, viewed the merger as a threat. They began considering arrangements in which they could accomplish their own mergers with new media partners such as Yahoo and Microsoft. Their concern was almost entirely financial. "We have no obligation to make history," explained Disney's CEO, Michael Eisner. "We have no obligation to make art. We have no obligation to make a statement. To make money is our only obligation."

The Federal Communications Commission also was concerned that the merger would endanger competition, raise costs, and limit choices for consumers. It began hearings once AOL and Time Warner announced their merger plans. Despite assurances that competitors would not be harmed, five months later Time Warner eliminated ABC TV programs from its cable systems. The owner of ABC was Disney, Time Warner's biggest rival as a media company. At issue was how much Time Warner should have to pay Disney to carry its cable channels, including the Disney Channel, the Soap Channel, and Disney Toon. Time Warner's decision eliminated local ABC stations from cable systems serving 3.5 million homes. The FCC almost immediately ruled that Time Warner violated communications law.

At the end of 2000, almost a year after Time Warner and AOL had announced their merger plans, the Federal Trade Commission approved. It required safeguards, though, that assured that the new communications giant would not restrict consumers' access to the Internet and required concessions that would prevent it from using its size and ownership of media content to thwart competitors. "Our concern here," explained FTC Chairman Robert Pi-

Dying Newspapers and Democracy

Because of economic conditions and because readers and advertisers began to desert newspapers for the Internet, newspapers downsized or went out of business in increasing numbers after 2000. Journalists worried about the impact. "Journalists," the *American Journalism Review* declared in 2009, "have long touted the indispensable role that newspapers play in a democracy, shining a bright light on the activities of elected officials." Studies showed that, among other effects, the percentage of people voting in elections declined when local papers ceased publication.

tofsky, "was with access, that these two powerful companies would create barriers that would injure competitors...."[2]

The FCC, though, reduced ownership restrictions even further in 2003. Despite considerable opposition and a single public hearing at which most participants opposed the changes, the FCC voted to allow ownership of three television stations, eight radio stations, a cable system, and a daily newspaper within a single city and to permit a single corporation to own stations that reached 45% of Americans. At the time of the decision, Viacom and News Corp (owners of CBS and Fox) already exceeded the legal limit of 35%. After the House of Representatives voted to block the changes, President George W. Bush and Congress agreed to a cap of 39%, or about what Viacom and News Corp already had.

Media ownership changes came as audiences were leaving newspapers and network TV for other sources of news. According to Pew Research Center statistics, nearly half of Americans relied primarily on newspapers for campaign news in 1996, while another 39% relied primarily on network TV. In October 2008, while 72%

[1]Michael White, ["Deal creates third-largest U.S. newspaper company"], Associated Press, 14 March 2000.

[2]Kalpana Srinivasan, ["FTC approves merger of AOL, Time Warner"], Associated Press, 15 December 2000.

listed television as one of their top two sources of campaign news, 46% of those cited cable and only 24% traditional broadcast networks. The Internet passed newspapers in the number of those who listed it as one of their primary sources, 33% to 29%, with radio at 21%. Of course, newspapers or broadcast companies had generated much of what people were reading on the Internet.

A troubled economy, increased competition from electronic media, and declining readership brought heavy economic losses for many newspapers. The Newspaper Association of America reported that newspaper advertising revenues fell by 23% in 2007 and 2008, and then plunged another 26% in 2009. Local TV revenue fell by 24% the same year.[3] Much of the revenue loss came in classified advertising, with online sources such as Monster.com and Craigslist drawing away many of the would-be advertisers. Some notable newspapers closed their doors, including the *Rocky Mountain News* — the winner of four Pulitzers since 2000 — and the *Tucson Citizen,* the oldest newspapers in Colorado and Arizona. Newspapers such as the *Los Angeles Times* and the *Chicago Tribune* (both owned by the Tribune Company), *the Denver Post, San Jose Mercury News,* and *Salt Lake Tribune* (all owned by MediaNews), the *Minneapolis Star Tribune,* the *Philadelphia Inquirer,* and the *San Diego Union Tribune* all went through bankruptcy proceedings, sometimes falling into the hands of corporate banking entities that had little other connection to news.

Some organizations reduced the "paper" in *newspaper,* producing some web-only versions with smaller staffs. The *Seattle Post-Intelligencer* and *Kansas City Kansan* went all-electronic. The *Christian Science Monitor* offered a weekly print magazine to supplement its web content, while other newspapers offered full print versions only a few days a week. Dozens of papers dropped Monday editions, which in many cases had become embarrassingly small. Papers also shrank in another way, narrowing in width.

Buyouts and layoffs became the norm, with some 13,500 journalists losing their jobs between 2007 and 2010. One side effect was a slight decline in the percentage of minority journalists, an area in which despite its best efforts the industry has always found problematic.[4] Despite a 24-hours news cycle, the major networks employed perhaps half as many journalists as in the 1980s.[5]

Along with slashing news staffs and cutting pay and benefits for the remaining journalists, news organizations "outsourced" more printing, production, and administrative functions. Some collaborated with former competitors, such as a local newspaper and television station combining resources for a story, or relied increasingly on "citizen" media in which interested non-journalists provided text, photos, or video for stories that ranged from plane crashes to city council meetings. Some news organizations cooperated with non-profit organizations, including two founded in the 1970s, Investigative Reporters and Editors and the Center for Investigative Reporting. A newcomer, ProPublica, started in 2008

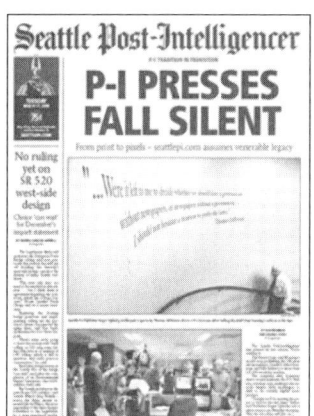

Goodbye, Newspapers
The *Rocky Mountain News* and *Seattle Post-Intelligencer* both shut down their print editions in 2009. The "Rocky" had begun publication in 1859. Its first issue is shown at top left. The *Post-Intelligencer* had begun as the *Seattle Gazette* in 1863 and, through a series of mergers, took on the *P-I* name in 1881. Shown top right is an early issue bearing that title. As the prosperity of both papers diminished after 2000, the owners tried to find buyers, but both failed. Staff members of the Denver paper attempted to continue with an online publication, but they did not find enough support for the venture. The *Post-Intelligencer*, on the other hand, converted successfully to an online-only publication.

and won a Pulitzer Prize for investigative reporting in 2010. By then it had partnered with dozens of traditional news organizations, including CNN, PBS, the *New York Times, Los Angeles Times, Washington Post,* and *Newsweek.*

Some broadcast companies benefited with the arrival of digital television and the switch to high-definition TV in 2009, as the switch opened up more channels for existing companies. A viewer might switch from one channel to another that the same company owned.

News organizations sought new forms of revenue, including ways to "monetize" the web. Some asked readers to pay for online content, at least for archived stories and photos — with limited success, since readers could easily go elsewhere for free information. Some media experts even proposed government funding of news organizations to try to keep public-affairs journalism alive. Asked about the economic future of news, leaders in print and

---

[3]Reported in "State of the News Media, 2010." Pew Project for Excellence in Journalism, http://www.stateofthemedia.org/2010/newspapers_economics.php. Accessed 23 August 2010.

[4]"Decline in newsroom jobs slows," American Society of Newspaper Editors, 11 April 2010.

[5]Reported in "State of the News Media, 2010."

broadcast media offered a common answer: "Good question."[6]

THE 2000 PRESIDENTIAL ELECTION

The 2000 presidential election between George W. Bush, Republican governor of Texas, and Democratic Vice President Al Gore embroiled the news media — both newspapers and television — in one of the biggest controversies they had faced in many years. In the election, Florida was thought to be a pivotal state. On the evening of election day, Tuesday, November 7, shortly after the polls in eastern Florida closed at 8:00 p.m. Eastern Time, the TV networks and the Associated Press — based on exit polls — declared Gore the winner.

Members of Bush's campaign staff immediately criticized the declaration because polls in the Florida Panhandle, which is in the Central Time Zone, were still open and because they believed that a premature TV announcement could discourage potential Bush voters in the Panhandle and in other states from going to the polls.

Shortly after 10:00 p.m., with Bush taking the lead, the networks retracted the Gore victory declaration and said the Florida election was too close to call.

At 2:18 a.m. Wednesday, November 8 — with Bush holding a lead of more than 50,000 votes and 98% of the votes counted — the networks declared him the winner. Many newspapers in the Eastern and Central Time Zones — which had delayed going to press as long as they could — then published their next morning's editions with front-page banner headlines declaring Bush the winner. By 3:00 a.m., however, his lead had shrunk to 1,800, and the networks retracted their declarations that he had won.

The Gore camp contested the election, and Bush was not officially acknowledged the victor until challenges had gone through both the Florida and U. S. Supreme Courts. In the many days of controversy while Gore and his supporters contested the election, CNN, Fox News, and MSNBC continued 24-hour coverage.

An independent report by three veteran journalists declared later that "[t]elevision interfered with the electoral process and the election result.... [T]hat constitutes an abuse of power, if unintentionally so, by CNN and by all the mainstream television news operations."[7] In the days following the voting, Republicans in the U. S. Congress were so concerned that they called for an investigation of election-night reporting. In February 2001, a congressional committee summoned network executives and other witnesses to hearings to try to determine what had gone wrong and how to prevent the problem from recurring. The committee replayed tapes of the network coverage. One included Dan Rather declaring that viewers could "take it to the bank" in referring to CBS's early declaration that Gore had won Florida.[8] In time, all the networks committed to changing their methods of declaring winners before the 2004 election.

[6]Based on on the author's conversations with more than twenty industry leaders in January 2009 in New York City and Washington, D.C.

[7]Associated Press, ["Report calls CNN election coverage 'debacle'"], 3 February 2001.

[8]N.Y. Times News Service, ["Panel flogs TV executives for election-night mess"], 15 February 2001.

And the Winner Is ...
In the 2000 presidential election, Florida's electoral votes turned out to be critical. When partial but nearly complete returns in the state around 2:00 a.m. the morning after the election indicated that George Bush had a large lead, it was thought that he had won the presidency. Most newspapers in the Eastern and Central time zones, which had held off printing until the results of the voting were known, then went to press declaring Bush the winner. This edition of the *Herald-Sun* in Durham, N. C., which came off the press at 3:00 a.m., was typical of newspaper reporting. Bush eventually was declared winner of the Florida election but only after days of partisan wrangling over the voting.

THE MEDIA AND THE TERRORISM WAR

Many journalists thought the 2000 election presented them the story of a lifetime. Within a year, though, they had an even bigger one.

On September 11, 2001, Islamic terrorists hijacked four American passenger jets and crashed two of them into the Twin Towers of the World Trade Center in New York City and one of them into the Pentagon in Washington, D. C. The other crashed in a field in Pennsylvania after passengers overpowered the hijackers. The attacks killed 3,000 people.

Immediately after the first jet hit the trade center, TV stations and networks showed video tape of the crash and began broadcasting live shots of the aftermath. As audiences watched the live scene, video cameras caught a second plane crashing into the other tower eighteen minutes after the first attack. Most TV networks switched from their regular programming to provide continuing news of the attacks. That was true not only of the traditional news networks, such as ABC, CBS, and NBC, but also those with specialized programs, such as ESPN, the sports network. Most of the all-news channels broadcast commercial-free. Radio stations around the country replaced regular programs by patching into the TV networks for extended coverage of the events. Afternoon newspapers quickly put together front pages devoted to the disaster. More than 170 morning newspapers, which had already published their daily editions, produced rare "extras" for distribution in the afternoon. Round-the-clock TV coverage continued for days. Explaining the decision for such coverage, NBC News president Neal Shapiro said, "This is the most important story of my lifetime. I think it's our job to stay on the air."9

In the aftermath of the attacks, the United States military went on the offensive against al Qaeda, the terrorist organization that carried them out, and against the radical government of Afghanistan that harbored it. Fox News Channel, MSNBC, and CNN, the cable news networks, focused almost exclusively on the war against terrorism in the following months. At the suggestion of the White House, six major TV news organizations agreed to abridge videotaped statements that the terrorist leader, Osama bin Laden, made that were inflammatory or might have included coded messages to terrorists around the world. It was the first time the networks had ever agreed to a joint arrangement to limit their news coverage. "This is a new situation," explained Andrew Heyward, president of CBS News, "a new war, and a new kind of enemy. Given the historic events we're enmeshed in, it's appropriate to explore new ways of fulfilling our responsibilities to the public."10

Some journalists objected to cooperating with the government to decide how to handle the news. In response to a possible White House request that newspapers not run full transcripts of tapes that al Qaeda issued, editors indicated that they would listen to requests but would make their own judgments about what should be run. "Our response would be to consider these [requests] on a case-by-case basis ...," stated Leonard Downie Jr., executive editor of the *Washington Post*. "Inflammatory propaganda is not a reason to keep things out of the paper."11 When the Knight Ridder chain learned that U. S. commandos were operating secretly in Afghanistan, it chose not to publish the story, its Washington bureau chief explained, "on the grounds that it could endanger the lives of the servicemen...."12 *USA Today*, however, published the story once it discovered it, and other newspapers and TV networks followed

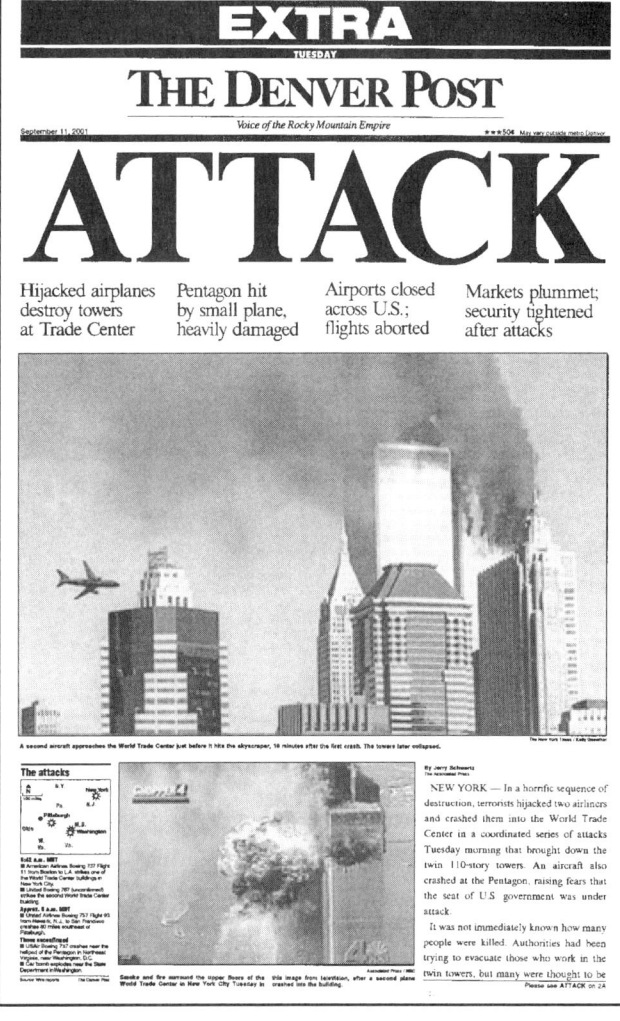

A second aircraft approaches the World Trade Center just before it hits the skyscraper, 18 minutes after the first crash. The towers later collapsed.

Reaction to Terrorism
When Islamic terrorists crashed two passenger jets into New York City's World Trade Center and another into the Pentagon on September 11, 2001, television and newspapers reacted immediately. Many papers that already had published their day's editions rushed to print "extras" in the afternoon. With television broadcasting live from the scene, some newspapers, as illustrated by the bottom photograph on the front page of the *Denver Post*, were able to get some of their shots from broadcast images.

suit. A senior editor for National Public Radio declared that he had ordered his reporters to track down the commandos, for "the game of reporting is to smoke 'em out."13 Despite such attitudes, the majority of journalists appeared to reject the idea that journalists should publicize information that might endanger Americans or act as neutrals in a war against terrorism. "I can't remember," argued Tom Brokaw, national anchor for NBC News, "when our profession in all its dimensions performed so well under such difficult circumstances. I hope this will be the beginning of another golden age of television news in which we stay on the big, important stories and the audience stays with us."14

9David Bauder, ["Television news executives face difficult decisions"], Associated Press, 14 September 2001. See also "The Story of Their Lives," *TV Guide*, 22 December 2001.

10Bill Carter and Felicity Barringer, ["TV news execs agree to limit broadcasts from bin Laden"], N. Y. Times News Service, 11 October 2001.

11["Newspapers will be asked to use restraint on al Qaeda statements"], *Boston Globe*, 11 October 2001.

12Clark Hoyt to Knight Ridder editors, quoted in Jeff Jacoby, ["Journalism's 'neutrality fetish'"], column, *Boston Globe*, 31 October 2001.

13Quoted in ibid.

14Quoted in *Today's Word on Journalism*, http://www.hardnewscafe.usu.edu, 25 October 2001.

Images of War

TV camera crews and photojournalists for newspapers and magazines followed the war in Iraq in 2003 and its aftermath and made a number of impressive shots. The two most widely reproduced were of Iraqis and American forces toppling a statue of Saddam Hussein in Baghdad in April and a "mug shot" of Hussein after his capture in early 2004. TV networks had broadcast the toppling of the statue live. For many, the photograph symbolized victory in the war, and the shot of Hussein seemed to reveal how desperate a figure he had become as he tried to elude capture after the war. Both photographs received widespread play on TV, and most American daily newspapers reproduced both of them on their front pages. It was later revealed that the toppling of the statue was largely a staged event, planned by a U.S. military officer, directly opposite the hotel where most of the international media were based. Wide-angle shots showed the presence of about 200 people, mostly journalists and U.S. troops.

The issue of the news media cooperating with the government was raised again during the U.S.-Iraqi war in 2003. During that brief war and the military operations against insurgents that continued for several years, journalists were allowed to accompany troops as "embedded reporters." That system resembled the methods of reporting used in World War II, and it offered more opportunities for on-the-scene reporting than had been allowed in such military actions as Grenada. Some journalists complained, however, that it compromised news coverage because of reporters' close proximity to and reliance on American soldiers. From the beginning of the war until the mid-2010, a total of 149 journalists — including two Americans, Michael Kelly and David Bloom — died covering hostilities, making it the deadliest war ever for news people, according to the Committee to Protect Journalists.

After the war began, critics claimed that journalists did not fully investigate some pre-war claims about the need for war. The *New York Times* acknowledged that it had relied on biased information for some erroneous reports about Iraqi weapons programs and terrorist training camps, and an editor's note admitted to "a number of instances of coverage that was not as rigorous as it should have been."[15] A few days later the *Times'* ombudsman wrote that, although one reporter's stories were the most consistently flawed, "The failure was not individual, but institutional," characterized by a "hunger for scoops," a dysfunctional editing process, and "anonymity-cloaked assertions of people with vested interests."[16]

The last American combat troops left Iraq in 2010 (while 50,000 advisors remained), but for all practical purposes the news media had pulled out some time before. Iraq had mostly disappeared from front pages, replaced first by the 2008 presidential election and then a variety of other events.

THE PRESS/GOVERNMENT CONFLICT

Along with the war in Iraq, the United States and some western allies mounted a sustained attack on terrorists in the Middle East, while adopting measures to attempt to stymie acts of terrorism domestically. The war against terrorism created conditions that raised questions about both media performance and government activities, with journalists and others debating the potential conflicts between protecting Americans from harm and preserving civil liberties.

Media organizations sometimes were frustrated when the war against terrorism prompted increased efforts by the federal government to obtain information useful in fighting terrorism while keeping secret some other types of information. The Bush administration removed substantial quantities of information from official libraries and ordered federal agencies to tighten restrictions concerning Freedom of Information Act requests. Previously declassified reports were reclassified, including some information already published in newspapers. Congress passed a bill that exempted many Pentagon files from Freedom of Information Act requests, while the PATRIOT Act and later legislation expanded officials' authority to search homes and businesses, to examine library

[15]Editor's note, *New York Times*, 26 May 2004.

[16]Daniel Okrent, "Weapons of Mass Destruction? Or Mass Distraction?" *New York Times*, 30 May 2004.

records, and to track suspicious Internet surfing and phone company records.

The most dramatic press-government showdown may have come with the case of CIA case officer Valerie Plame. *New York Times* reporter Judith Miller spent eighty-five days in jail in 2005 for refusing to tell a grand jury the name of a White House source who may have illegally identified Plame as a covert CIA employee. As details later came to light, Plame, an opponent of the war, had encouraged the CIA to dispatch her husband on a fact-finding mission in the expectation that his report would be critical. Upon completing the mission, he did, indeed, write a *New York Times* guest column criticizing the Bush administration.

Miller was released from jail only after her source, Vice Presidential Chief of Staff Lewis "Scooter" Libby, admitted giving her the information. Libby faced charges of perjury and obstruction of justice; and Watergate journalist and author Bob Woodward, *Washington Post* columnist Walter Pincus, *Time* magazine reporter Matthew Cooper, and NBC journalist Tim Russert all were called to testify at the trial. Libby claimed that he first heard about Plame from Russert, which the newsman denied, saying he had never heard of Plame until he read a piece by columnist Robert Novak. Like Miller, Cooper had been called to testify before the grand jury that brought the charges, and he also initially refused to testify. He was about to be sent to jail for contempt when his source — Presidential Deputy Chief of Staff Karl Rove — gave him permission to reveal Rove's involvement. Left unclear was the question of whether "outing" Plame was illegal, and only Libby was charged. He was convicted of perjury and obstruction. *New York Times* editors supported Miller's refusal to give up a source but criticized her close relationship with administration officials. She left the *Times* later that same year, saying she was retiring because she had "become the news."

As tensions escalated between the government and the media and between the United States and radical Islamists, concerns arose about whether some basic journalistic principles were being endangered. One of them was accuracy in reporting. Some journalists claimed that government restrictions prevented them from getting complete stories, while journalists were sometimes criticized for letting what seemed to be an anti-government bias influence their reporting. The most controversial of the latter instances was a report in *Newsweek* magazine in May 2005 that claimed that U.S. military officials had desecrated the Quran, the Islamic holy book, while interrogating Islamic prisoners. The report touched off demonstrations and rioting by Muslims around the world. After a week, *Newsweek* admitted that its report, based on an unnamed source, was erroneous and that the desecration had never occurred. By then, the riots had resulted in at least fifteen deaths.[17]

Another concern was that the conflict with radical Islam threatened tolerance for ideas even in the West. The strict notions of the radical branch of Islam, coming out of the anti-democratic culture of the Middle East, collided with the Western tradition of free expression. As the ideas of the two worlds came into daily contact,

it seemed inevitable that conflict would result. The differences in the two views — a rigid religious one versus a generally libertarian one — became clear in a controversy that started when in September 2005 a Danish newspaper, *Jyllands-Posten*, printed twelve cartoons of Muhammad, Islam's founder. A Danish author had complained that he had found it impossible to find anyone to illustrate his book about Muhammad. The paper then printed the cartoons because of concern that fear of Islamic protests and terrorism had led to self-censorship in the West.

Muslims declared the cartoons blasphemous and threatened the newspaper and some of its staff. A number of newspapers in other countries then reprinted the cartoons as a show of support for *Jyllands-Posten* and, most said, for the right to free expression. Muslims in many countries responded with protests, burned the flags of Western nations, and threatened boycotts of European businesses. Ambassadors of Islamic nations lodged formal complaints with the Danish government.

In the United States, the reaction of newspapers and television networks was mixed. A few reprinted some of the cartoons or placed them on their websites, but others declared that to do so was irresponsible and showed disrespect for the sensitivities of Muslims. The U.S. government requested that American media show restraint and not inflame Islamic opposition by publishing the cartoons.

The controversy and the caution of some news media in soft-pedaling around it struck some observers as an indication that the media were failing to fulfill their proper role. Controversial times, they argued, were not when the media should be timid. It was in such times that boldness in defending freedom of expression was most necessary. Timidity on the cartoon controversy, critics said, indicated that freedom of expression — indeed, the basic principles of Western democracy — was in danger.[18]

As president, Barack Obama loosened some secrecy restrictions implemented during the Bush administration and established a new National Declassification Center for the National Archives designed to speed the declassification of many historical documents. But journalists criticized him for refusing to release records regarding government surveillance and alleged torture of enemy combatants.[19] He also signed a bill renewing the PATRIOT Act.

The Internet also created new problems for those who would keep secrets, however, as demonstrated by the international website WikiLeaks. Started in 2006, it released in 2010 several hundred thousand American documents related to the war in Afghanistan and to diplomatic relations with various countries. Some mainstream media published the material, but others criticized the release. The U.S. government considered legal action against Australian WikiLeaks director Julian Assange, and Sweden arrested him on rape charges. Internet and credit-card providers denied services for WikiLeaks. In retaliation, supporters of WikiLeaks launched attacks against the websites of a number of government

[17]Seth Sutel, "[Newsweek Retracts Quran Abuse Story]," Associated Press, 17 May 2005.

[18]For an example of such criticism, see Paul Greenberg "[Liberty Is First Challenged on the Margins]," Tribune Media Services, 13 February 2006.

[19]Charlie Savage, "Obama Curbs Secrecy of Classified Documents," *New York Times*, 29 December 2009.

offices and businesses in an attempt to disrupt their services or shut them down.

NEW COMPETITORS AND RIVALRIES

While the news media were dealing with professional issues, the development of additional television networks such as Fox News — part of Rupert Murdoch's News Corporation — provided evidence of further growth potential for broadcast news and public affairs programming, notwithstanding the effects of corporate takeovers such as Capital Cities' acquisition of ABC and General Electric's takeover of NBC in 1985, and major management changes at CBS. Cable news became increasingly competitive — and contentious. The $500 million advertising market once dominated exclusively by CNN faced increased challenges, especially from Fox.

Corporate rivalry affected the recruitment of on-air talent in the aggressive effort to poach viewers from competitors. CNN hired Paula Zahn away from Fox News in 2002. When CNN broadcast a promo for her morning program and referred to her as "sexy," she reacted angrily at being portrayed as a sex symbol. The network recanted, but no one could be found to take credit for the gaffe. A few months later, Fox hired Greta Van Susteren, anchor of *The Point*, CNN's second highest rated program, to host the Fox program Zahn had once anchored. Fox also recruited Geraldo Rivera away from CNBC; and CNN lured the popular Keith Olbermann, former anchor for Fox Sports.

The newcomer to the competitive field of TV news, Fox, made the most impressive gains in viewership. Among cable channels, it had been quickly closing the gap between itself and CNN until the terrorist attacks of September 11, 2001; but viewers switched back to CNN for a time in the aftermath of the attacks. On the day of the attacks, CNN drew an average of 6.4 million viewers, twice as many as Fox. With time, however, Fox began to pull even with CNN and eventually passed it on a daily basis. In 2004, Fox then passed CBS in ratings for its evening news program. It also had the highest rated news talk show on cable, Bill O'Reilly's *The O'Reilly Factor*.

While cable news channels were becoming increasingly competitive, major personnel changes occurred in broadcast news, as a number of prominent figures stepped down from their lofty network positions. William F. Buckley retired from *Firing Line*, his celebrated interview program on PBS, after thirty-three years on the air. Don Hewitt, the founder and driving force behind TV's most celebrated public affairs program, *60 Minutes*, also retired. The most visible changes, however, came in the evening-news staffing. In 2004, Brian Williams became NBC anchor when Tom Brokaw retired after many years in that position, and CBS anchor Dan Rather announced at the same time that he would soon be retiring. NBC's *Today* anchor Katie Couric replaced Rather. ABC anchor Peter Jennings died in 2005, the same year that Ted Koppel left *Nightline*. Tim Russert, who had moderated NBC's *Meet the Press* for sixteen years, died in 2008, and longtime hosts Lou Dobbs and

Larry King left CNN in 2009 and 2010.

Jennings was replaced briefly by co-anchors Elizabeth Vargas and Bob Woodruff, and then *Good Morning America* host Charles Gibson became sole anchor for three years before giving way to Diane Sawyer. For the first time, women anchored two of the "big three" nightly news programs, but by then the networks had lost much of their audience to the more openly partisan personalities on cable. NBC led the three broadcast networks in the ratings for a dozen consecutive years, although its cable channel, MSNBC, trailed both Fox and CNN in the ratings. Fox and CNN had no traditional broadcast news outlets, while neither ABC nor CBS had a cable partner.

THE CREDIBILITY CRISIS

During the last few decades, the news media have suffered from declining credibility. Both critics and concerned journalists attributed the problem to public perceptions that the media were abandoning the practice of objectivity and that they were politically biased. Surveys beginning in the 1970s revealed a growing distrust of the media, and the proliferation of means of scrutinizing and criticizing the media probably contributed to the problem. Some very public controversies added ammunition for the critics.

In the late 1970s, in the aftermath of the Watergate affair, Gallup surveys found that more than half of Americans had a lot of confidence in the news media. Since that time, however, the level of trust continually declined. By the late 1990s, fewer than one-third of those surveyed said they had high confidence in newspapers, and only about one-twelfth expressed such confidence in television news. Almost 25% said they had no confidence at all in either newspaper or TV news. Even fewer believed that journalists had high standards of ethics or honesty. Gallup's director of research concluded that even though "there is a great latent distrust that Americans have for many institutions in the country, ... print and broadcast journalists and commentators have suffered a greater erosion of public confidence than have many other professions."[20] A 2009 Pew survey found that public assessment of the accuracy of news stories had fallen to its lowest level in more than two decades, while Americans' views of media bias and independence matched previous lows. Just 29% of respondents said news organizations generally got the facts straight, with 63% saying news stories were often inaccurate.[21]

Observers gave different reasons for the diminishing confidence in the media. Many journalists were prone to say that the fault lay with trendy ideas, such as a featurized approach to news writing, an emphasis on "soft" news, and the failure of journalists to be hard-hitting and aggressive. Some journalists suggested that the reason was that the public simply didn't understand that the proper function of the media in a democratic society is to be skeptical.

The most common complaint of critics, though, was quite dif-

[20]Rick Garlick, "What the Polls Show," in Bruce J. Evensen, ed., *The Responsible Reporter*, 2nd ed. (Northport, Ala., 1997), vi.
[21] "Press Accuracy Rating Hits Two Decade Low." Pew Research Center for People & the Press, 13 September 2009.

Talk Radio

Radio Personalities Gain Huge Followings, Create Controversy

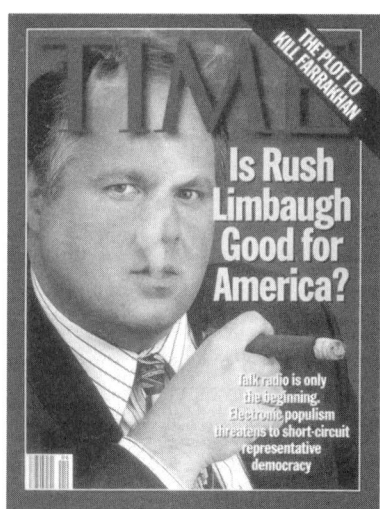

Talk radio has existed almost since the advent of broadcasting.

Some such figures as evangelists Aimee Semple McPherson and Robert Pierce "Fighting Bob" Shuler, Sr., successfully used radio to vigorously push their religious agendas in Los Angeles in the 1920s. McPherson purchased her own station in 1924 and became one of the most popular religious speakers of her time. Shuler, a Methodist minister, railed against politicians, police, Jews, and African Americans from radio station KGEF, which he ran from 1926 to 1932. In a portent of what was to come in the history of talk radio, the Federal Radio Commission revoked his broadcast license.

In the 1930s Father Charles Coughlin, a controversial Roman Catholic priest, also ran into trouble because of anti-Semitic rhetoric. He also opposed the Roosevelt administration and later rationalized Hitler and Mussolini. Even though his broadcasts may have reached 40 million listeners per week, the Vatican wanted him silenced. Then, new federal regulations, apparently devised mainly to get at him, temporarily forced him off the air. He was unable to obtain a permit to broadcast his talks live, and he had to buy airtime on individual stations for recorded talks.

Although talk radio has changed over the years, the format since the mid 1990s has been fairly standard. It includes listener call-ins (and venting) and strong rhetoric. What has not changed is that controversy and talk radio go hand in hand.

The thing that gets talk radio so much attention today is its wide reach and potential persuasiveness. Many believe it is capable of in-fluencing national opinion and politics on a grand scale. Even though talk radio comprises many genres, including sports talk and shock radio and others, its most popular genre is politics.

The combination of politics and influence worries many critics. The most popular shows are overwhelmingly conservative. Despite some modern pioneers like Howard Stern and Larry King, hosts with the most listeners, ranging to as many as 20 million per week, are conservative, with some having libertarian tendencies. Pew researchers found that among Americans who regularly listened to talk radio in 2010, 41% were Republicans and 28% were Democrats. Approximately 17% of the public listened to talk radio regularly. Air America, a network founded in 2004 to act as a "progressive alternative" to the conservative shows, collapsed into bankruptcy in January 2010.

In 2009, according to the *Los Angeles Times*, the Barack Obama administration, under siege from conservative talk show hosts, was advancing a political strategy of persuading the nation that talk show king Rush Limbaugh had hijacked the leadership of the Republican party. The effort apparently escalated into a feud between the administration and the Fox Broadcasting Network, where some of the strongest critics of the administration (such as Bill O'Reilly and Glenn Beck) hosted TV talk shows – along with their radio shows with listeners in the millions.

According to *Talkers* magazine, the top ten hosts in 2010 were (1) Rush Limbaugh (on 590 stations and more than 20 million listeners); (2) Sean Hannity (more than 14 million listeners); (3) Glenn Beck; (4) Michael Savage; (5) Laura Schlessinger; (6) Laura Ingraham; (7) David Ramsey; (8) Mark Levin; (9) Lou Dobbs; and (10) Thom Hartmann, the only self-professed progressive among the group.

Ever since commercial radio went on the air, individuals have used it to promote their causes. Some have developed huge followings — and become controversial in the process. Aimee Semple McPherson (top) was known nationwide as an evangelist before she began broadcasting in 1924. She was only the second woman to receive a permit to operate a radio station. Father Charles Coughlin (middle) began his public career as a supporter of Franklin Roosevelt and his New Deal program to solve social problems. When he turned and became a harsh critic, as well as a vocal anti-Semite, both the Vatican and the federal government took steps to try to get him off the air. In recent times, Rush Limbaugh (bottom) attracted the largest audience among radio talk show hosts. Conservative in politics, he gained huge popularity with conservatives and was a favorite target of many liberals.

ferent. It dealt with concerns that journalists themselves too frequently were biased and had substituted their own ideological views for a straight presentation of facts. Both liberal and conservative critics made such claims, but nearly every survey of public views showed that most respondents believed that the media had a liberal bias. A 1996 poll that Louis Harris and Associates conducted for the Center for Media and Public Affairs found that about three-fourths of respondents considered political news to be biased, and more than two-thirds of them thought the bias was a liberal one. More than 60% thought that news was influenced too much by the reporters' opinions.

For evidence of bias, critics frequently pointed to the voting patterns of journalists. In every presidential election since 1976, the majority of journalists voted for the Democratic candidate. In 1992, the margin was 89% for Bill Clinton and 7% for George Bush. In a 1996 survey for the American Society of Newspaper Editors, approximately 60% of journalists identified themselves as Democrats, while only 15% said they were Republicans. Before 2004, newspapers editorially had almost always endorsed the Republican candidates for president. In the 2004 election, though, a majority (56%) endorsed Democrat John Kerry over George W. Bush, who carried the popular vote by a slight majority. In 2008, an even larger number endorsed Democrat Barack Obama. Some critics, including some media professionals, complained that too many journalists were "in the tank" for Obama and that their coverage was biased. A survey by the Pew Research Center for Excellence in Journalism found that overall press coverage tended to favor Obama. On average, 36% of stories about him were positive and 29% negative, compared to 14% about John McCain that were positive and 57% negative. Among national TV outlets, the study found, MSNBC was the most slanted and favored Obama.[22]

A growing segment of the public became increasingly restless with such numbers and other concerns related to bias. Increased television outlets for expressing views — such as C-SPAN, CNN, and Fox News — fueled the fire. Internet sites and the proliferation of radio and TV programs devoted to political talk provided forums. A growing number of books dealt with the issue. The most popular was Bernard Goldberg's *Bias: A CBS Insider Exposes How the Media Distort the News*. In 2002 it reached the number-one spot on the *New York Times*' list of best sellers. A former reporter for CBS, Goldberg described a number of instances to support his charge that liberal views dominated the national news media. His main target was CBS anchor Dan Rather, who, he claimed, like the majority of national journalists tilted toward the left.

Charges of conservative bias were not as widespread, but liberalism did have a number of advocates. Their arguments consisted primarily of two points. One, which mainstream liberals some-

A Question of Bias
In the debate about media bias, National Public Radio's firing of news analyst Juan Williams in 2010 created a national controversy. In a program on Fox News, he commented that, even though he was a great defender of civil rights, "when I get on the plane ... if I see people who are in Muslim garb and I think, you know, they are identifying themselves first and foremost as Muslims, I get worried." The Council on American-Islamic Relations urged NPR to disciplne him. NPR, in firing him, said he had crossed the line from analysis into stating his own opinions. Critics claimed that the firing again demonstrated NPR's liberal bias and a media hypersensitivity not to offend Muslims.

times made, was that the media were corporately owned and thus reflected the conservative ideology of their owners. Michael Moore's 2004 political documentary film *Fahrenheit 9/11* reflected this view. The second point, which leftist critics favored, was that America is inherently a conservative society (as opposed, for example, to being socialist) and the media naturally are advocates of the society in which they operate. The most widely quoted work defending the liberal view was Eric Alterman's 2000 book, *What Liberal Media? The Truth about Bias and the News*. It argued that the charge of liberal bias was refuted by such facts as that a number of conservative journalists worked for the national media, that the media had not been uniformly hard on conservatives such as President George H. W. Bush, and that they had carried much material scoring President Clinton during the Lewinsky affair.

Some observers reasoned that what appeared to be media bias was not ideological at all but was simply the natural result of professional journalistic practices. For example, in their 2003 book *The Press Effect*, Kathleen Hall Jamieson and Paul Waldman argued

[22]Gerhard Peters, "2008 General Election Editorial Endorsements by Major Newspapers," *The American Presidency Project*, John T. Woolley and Gerhard Peters, eds. Santa Barbara: University of California, 1999-2008, at http://www.presidency.ucsb.edu/data/2008_newspaper_endorsements.php. Journalism.org, "The Color of News: How Different Media Have Covered the Election," 29 October 2008, at http://www.journalism.org/node/13436; and "Winning the Media Campaign: How the Press Reported the 2008 General Election," 22 October 2008, at http://www.journalism.org/node/13307.

that "many biases, most of them professional, not political, shape the news. Reporters have a bias toward the use of official sources, a bias toward information that can be obtained quickly, a bias toward conflict, a bias toward focusing on discreet events rather than persistent conditions, and a bias toward the simple over the complex."[23] Besides such analytical reasoning, some journalists simply declared that charges of bias were just ill-informed because journalists aren't biased. They argued that the fact that both conservatives and liberals claimed journalists were biased really indicated that journalists were impartial and that critics were simply displaying their own biases.

The extended arguments over bias indicated the difficulty of resolving the issue or even coming to a consensus that bias existed and, if it did, what the nature of the bias was. Part of the problem was that both audiences and journalists perceived bias or lack of it in terms of their own biases. For example, conservatives saw more liberal bias, liberals saw more conservative bias, and journalists were inclined to see no bias even when it was present. Generally, though, one could conclude that some journalists were not biased, some had conservative biases, a larger number had liberal biases, and some of those who were biased still did not let their personal views influence all their reporting.

Despite such defenses as Alterman and Jamieson/Waldman made against the charges of media bias, two episodes during the 2004 presidential election campaign provided ammunition for conservatives, while another did so for liberals. All three episodes involved national TV news. In one, Marc Halperin, the political director of ABC News, sent a memo telling the staff to be more critical in examining the Bush than the Kerry campaign. Both Bush and Kerry, he claimed, employed distortions, but ABC News, he declared, should not "hold both sides 'equally' accountable." He told the news staff that it had a duty to expose Bush's misstatements but that it should not be as tough on Kerry. The national newspaper columnist Paul Greenberg wrote that the startling thing about the memo was that it was so straightforward in making the case that ideology should influence news decisions. Audiences generally expect bias to influence such things as columns and TV talk shows, he wrote, but "[i]t's the pretense of objectivity at the old established networks that offends, or should. Now it lies shattered."[24]

Compared to the ABC affair, another episode involving Dan Rather at CBS whipped up a firestorm. It began when he hosted a *60 Minutes Wednesday* segment based on photocopied memos claiming that George W. Bush had performed improperly while serving in the Air National Guard in the 1970s. Immediately after the program aired, experts questioned the authenticity of the memos. It quickly was determined that *60 Minutes* rushed the program onto the air without adequately checking out the suspicious

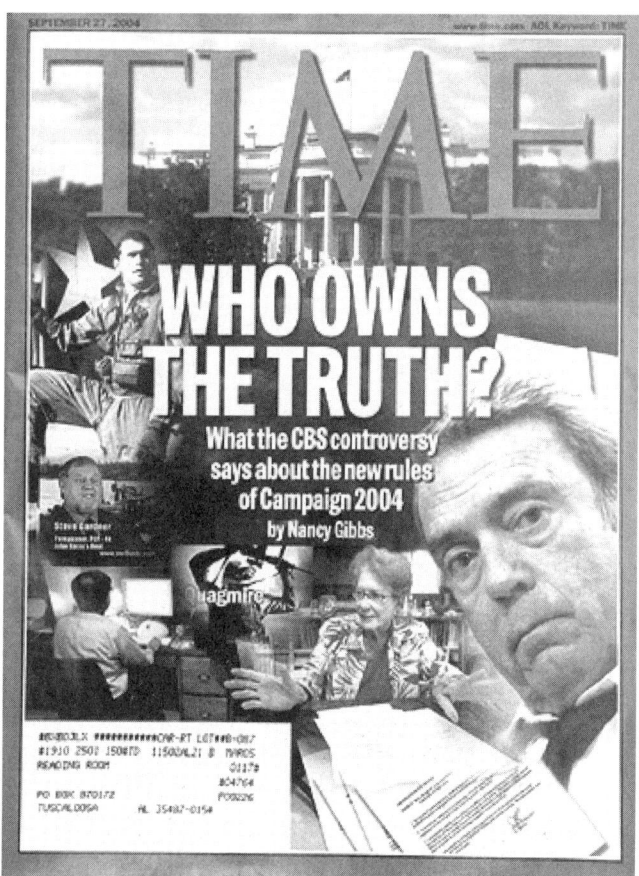

The Document Controversy

CBS News anchor Dan Rather became the subject of a national controversy in the concluding weeks of the 2004 presidential election when he narrated a *60 Minutes Wednesday* report criticizing George W. Bush. It was based on suspicious documents about Bush's service in the Air National Guard three decades earlier. Conservative critics claimed the report was motivated by political bias. Rather initially defended the report, but a CBS investigation concluded that the documents were probably forgeries and that the CBS staff committed "errors of credulity." He left CBS shortly after that, replaced by Katie Couric. In 2007 Rather sued CBS for $70 million, claiming that it had made him the "scapegoat" for the problems with the Bush story.

documents. Questions also were raised about the motives of the segment's producer, Mary Mapes; about Rather's political bias; and about contacts between Mapes and the Kerry campaign. CBS initially defended itself and issued a statement standing by the memos' authenticity. To exacerbate the problem, at the height of the controversy Rather claimed that the effort to challenge the memos was "an attack from right-wing nuts" and then hosted another program criticizing Bush. The gist of the program was that, even if the memos were fake, their accusations still were true. After several days of controversy, CBS began an investigation, determined that the memos "were likely forgeries after all," and then issued an apology for a "mistake in judgment." While critics complained that the affair demonstrated once again the liberal bias of CBS and Rather, a number of journalists were concerned that it had cast another pall over their profession. Following the election and after the storm had subsided, Rather retired as anchor of CBS

---

[23]Kathleen Hall Jamieson and Paul Waldman, *The Press Effect: Politicians, Journalists, and the Stories That Shape the Political World* (New York, 2003), 170.

[24]Paul Greenberg, ["Thanks to ABC executive, Liberal Media Bias now is in writing"], syndicated column, 22 October 2004. An ABC staff member had leaked the memo, and it appeared on a number of Internet sites and received publicity in some cable TV programs and newspapers.

Evening News but said that the controversy had nothing to do with his decision. CBS fired Mapes and asked three other employees to resign. Rather sued CBS for $70 million, claiming it had made him the scapegoat, but the suit was dismissed in 2010.

The third case involved the Sinclair Broadcast Group, which owned more TV stations than any other U.S. company. Just before the 2004 election, it announced it would require its sixty-two stations to air a prime-time documentary titled *Stolen Honor*. Produced by former journalist and Vietnam veteran Marc Sherman, the documentary criticized Kerry's antiwar activities. A political organization, "Swift Boat Veterans for Truth," heavily promoted the film and claimed in commercials that Kerry had falsified his own Vietnam record. Sinclair fired its Washington bureau chief, Jon Leiberman, after he publicly called the documentary "biased political propaganda." After protests from viewers and advertisers, Sinclair canceled the documentary and then offered a more balanced program that ran on forty stations and excerpted the documentary.[25]

Despite the fact that people of all political persuasions lamented bias in the media, new factors aggravated the situation. American politics became more polarized than they had been in generations, and some media contributed to the division — particularly radio talk, cable television, partisan books and newspaper columns, and Internet blogs. Often those segments worked together, creating an "echo chamber" in which biased or distorted information was repeated and reinforced. An error corrected in one place was unlikely to be fixed throughout the blogosphere. Fox News and MSNBC staked out the right and left ends of the political spectrum on cable, both running news during the day but usually turning prime time over to entertaining partisan "commentators": Glenn Beck, Bill O'Reilly, and Sean Hannity on Fox; Keith Olbermann, Rachel Maddow, and Chris Matthews on MSNBC. "Maybe one of the few questions left about cable news is whether a channel attempting to build its brand around neutral reporting and balanced conversation can succeed," noted a Pew Foundation report. But unlike other media, cable TV was thriving.[26]

HURRICANE KATRINA

Along with the 2000 election, the events of September 11, 2001, and the Iraq War, the most dramatic news story of recent years was Hurricane Katrina, which slammed into the Gulf Coast in August 2005. It caused levees to collapse, flooding the city of New Orleans. In the aftermath, news cameras captured images of people stranded on rooftops and freeways, and the damaged Superdome became a massive emergency shelter. Many stories criticized federal and state officials for what some journalists claimed was a slow response to the disaster, which killed more than 1,800 and caused more than $100 billion in damage. Some media coverage itself, though, was criticized. Among other lapses, there were un-

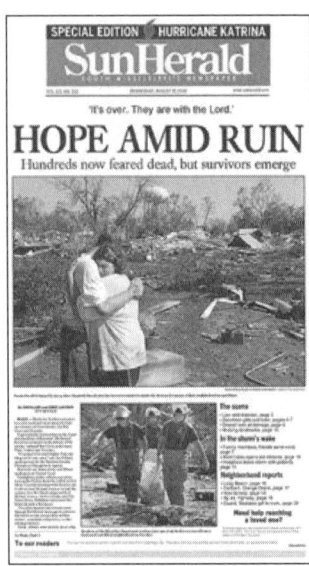

Hurricane Katrina
In the aftermath of Hurricane Katrina, which hit the Gulf Coast in 2005, the *New Orleans Times-Picayune* won a Pulitzer Prize for its coverage and shared the Prize for public service with the *Biloxi* (Miss.) *Sun Herald*. For several days, the *Picayune* was unable to print its paper and carried news on its Website.

founded stories of rapes and murders; and a study soon determined that most were untrue.[27] Some critics claimed that coverage was racially biased, and others argued that it showed partisan bias. Leaders of the relief effort attempted to block journalists from reporting on efforts to recover bodies in New Orleans, but the government reversed the ban after CNN filed a lawsuit and obtained a temporary restraining order against it.

In some cases the media themselves became conduits of information between victims and authorities. For its hurricane coverage, the *New Orleans Times-Picayune* won a Pulitzer Prize for breaking news and shared one for public service with the *Biloxi* (Miss.) *Sun Herald*. For several days the *Times-Picayune's* coverage was carried only on its website because the paper had lost its presses and was forced to evacuate its building. "The paper, which normally has a circulation of 270,000, had to report the biggest story in its history," the *New York Times* reported, "with no electricity, no phone access and no place to work."[28] The website also aided rescue operations and later helped reunite scattered residents. The paper's efforts prompted the Pulitzer Committee to open all of its categories to online entries for the first time.

DIGITAL MEDIA AND CONVERGENCE

Newspapers and broadcast stations began producing web editions shortly after the arrival of the Internet in the 1990s, although at first most papers simply dumped stories and photos from their print edition onto their website. By a decade or so later, though,

[25]"Sinclair fires reporter for criticizing anti-Kerry program." CNN.com., http://www.cnn.com/2004/ALLPOLITICS/10/19/sinclair.kerry. Accessed 24 August 2010.
[26]"State of the News Media, 2010."

[27]Sarah Rosenblatt and James Rainey, "Katrina Rumors." *Los Angeles Times.* 27 September 2005.
[28]Lisa Guernsey, "Hurricane forces New Orleans newspaper to face a daunting set of obstacles," *New York Times*, 5 September 2005.

many began including items on the web such as longer stories, extra sidebars, and more photos that did not fit into the print version. For example, before the 2006 elections, the *Washington Post* maintained a database of incumbent congressional votes, and the *Los Angeles Times* updated statewide campaign spending daily. Most also included "hyperlinks" that could take the reader to other websites, expanding the reader's knowledge of events, while "transaction technology" let the reader read a book review or article about a new product and then click on a link to a vender that sold the product. "Streaming" technology allowed the use of video on a site, so that even newspaper sites began including moving images.

The new technology concerned some media professionals who worried that readers could easily stray from the news organization's website or that readers might give up newspapers altogether. Furthermore, while the Internet allowed for longer stories and better photos, when combined with digital technology it also made ethical breaches easy to commit. Photos could be shot and placed on pages much more quickly, but they also could be modified more easily. The fact that digital cameras produced no negatives worried journalists and historians. "It literally will be possible to purge information, to alter a historic event that occurred five years ago because no original exists," noted one editor in the 1980s when digital photography was coming into use. "There's enormous potential for great wrong and great misuse."[29] Most of the intentional misuse came not from the news media, however, but from amateurs with home computers who spread hoax photos and edited videos via the Internet.

Thanks to digital technology, those amateurs began producing more of the images seen on the nightly news. Cell phone cameras, some of which shot video images, gave news organizations access to many more pictures than would have once been possible. Local TV stations regularly called for amateur footage from viewers. The Internet and cut-and-paste technology also meant that almost anyone could become a "news" provider. Some "journalists" whom mainstream news organizations never would have hired became famous for their websites or blogs (short for "web log"). As early as 1998, the *Drudge Report* broke a story that mainstream news organizations had withheld for lack of confirmation: the story of President Bill Clinton's affair with White House intern Monica Lewinsky. After the report appeared on the web, mainstream journalists felt freer to pursue the issue. Many bloggers began tracking events in the news, and some developed substantial followings. Besides the *Drudge Report*, other leading "news aggregators" — which combined news from various sources while sometimes producing their own stories — also showed obvious political leanings. Conservative sites included Instapundit, Breitbart.com, and Little Green Footballs. Those from the left included the Huffington Post, the Daily Kos, and the Daily Beast.

Newspapers hired some bloggers, and many media organizations began having reporters or editors produce their own blogs.

The *New York Times, Washington Post, Wall Street Journal, Chicago Tribune, Los Angeles Times, Miami Herald,* and *Boston Globe* all had political blogs before the 2006 election. Newspapers and broadcasters also hosted links on their own websites to other bloggers. "Rather than be afraid of it or work against it, we should be going with the flow," said one newspaper web editor. "If this is where communication in our society is going, we should try to figure out how to facilitate it."[30] Political gatherings also began granting access to bloggers. Today most newspapers have bloggers.

Video-sharing computer software allowed YouTube to become a billion-dollar company just a year after its 2005 arrival. A YouTube video featuring Virginia Senator George Allen making what some perceived to be a racist statement may have cost him his U.S. Senate seat and cost the Republicans a Senate majority in 2006. Politicians quickly learned that YouTube could also be a friend, allowing them to post their own videos to the site.

Having amateurs and committed partisans able to produce professional-looking media cheaply and easily led to complications. First, figuring out where a photo or recording originated could be difficult. Bloggers — and search engines — freely used content from other sources, often without crediting them. Material that news organizations spent time and money to produce popped up everywhere. For example, when *Sports Illustrated* broke a story about baseball star Alex Rodriguez using performance-enhancing drugs, the Huffington Post used the Associated Press' version of *SI*'s story. The Huffington Post report was "initially tops on Google, which meant that it, and not SI.com, tended to be the place readers clicking through to get the gist of the breaking scandal would land."[31]

Another problem was determining what was actually "real." Inexpensive computer software made it simple to "edit" photos, video, and sound recordings. Some were intentionally misleading, such as an edited video in which a government official seemed to make blatantly racist statements. Blogger Andrew Breitbart ran the spliced video, leading to the official's firing from her job. Even fakes created as spoofs could fool viewers. One example included a video in which Barack Obama supposedly "admitted" he was a Muslim. In a more humorous case, supporters of Osama bin Laden in Bangladesh carried posters with a photo taken from the Internet. In the picture, a *Sesame Street* Muppet peered over bin Laden's shoulder. Even without phony images, the Internet meant that even the unlikeliest of conspiracy theories could easily spread. Two of the most persistent involved "birthers," who claimed that Obama should not be president because he was Muslim or was born outside of the United States, and "truthers," who maintained that the Bush administration was somehow involved in the 9/11 attacks on the World Trade Center and the Pentagon.

In another example of an amateur driving the news, an anonymous blogger in 2005 posted information that Florida Congress-

[29]Quoted in J.D. Lasica, "Photographs that Lie," *Washington Journalism Review*, June 1989, p. 24.

[30]Dan Webster, "Blogger's Choice," *Spokane* (Wash.) *Spokesman-Review*, 10 April 2004.
[31]Alissa Quart, "Expensive Gifts: What Does Free Culture Cost?" *Columbia Journalism Review*, July/August 2009.

man Mark Foley had sent sexually suggestive e-mails to a former Congressional page. The blogger had sent the information to the *Los Angeles Times* months earlier, but it declined to investigate. Four days after the posting appeared on the Internet, however, an article about it appeared on the ABC website. A day later, confronted by ABC, Foley resigned. Bloggers also were the first to report discrepancies in Dan Rather's *60 Minutes Wednesday* report about President George W. Bush's National Guard service and Senate Majority Leader Trent Lott's 2002 use of what some viewed as racist remarks in praising former segregationist Senator Strom Thurmond. Their credibility damaged by the political fallout, both Rather and Lott ended up resigning from their positions.

The Internet and digital technology led many news organizations to a news model emphasizing what became known as "convergence." In some cases, print and broadcast media belonging to the same company combined forces, with journalists writing news for a newspaper, a nightly newscast, and a website. The web address would appear on screen during TV newscasts and on the front page of the newspaper, letting the three media reinforce one another. In some cases, separate news staffs shared information and a newsroom. Journalists for a single traditional news outlet such as a newspaper sometimes provided written stories, photos, and even video for the newspaper website. University journalism departments — most of which had become "communication" programs — turned news writing classes into "media writing" courses that involved any combination of print news, broadcast news, writing for the web, advertising, and public relations writing.

At the same time that journalists were starting to work with new kinds of media, producers of news faced more worries about lost audiences and shifting attention spans. TV used increased sound and visual elements to hold the attention and perhaps stir the emotions of viewers. A CNN viewer, for example, might be forced to try to process, simultaneously, spoken words, music, and several separate moving visuals. Networks began using video game-style graphics to "recreate" news events, such as the attack in which a roadside bomb injured ABC newsman Bob Woodruff in 2006 in Iraq. And as entertainment techniques further infected news, entertainment programming increasingly became a source of news. Many young adults began to admit getting most of their knowledge of current affairs from two "fake news" programs, *The Daily Show* and *The Colbert Report* on the Comedy Central network. Those shows became so popular that John Edwards announced his 2004 presidential bid on *The Daily Show*, after which host Jon Stewart said, "I have to warn you that we are a fake show, so you might have to do this again somewhere."[32] Even the federal government was not above using a different form of fake news. In 2005 NBC reported that the government had spent millions of dollars to produce video news releases promoting its policies. VNRs, used by businesses and government officials since the Clinton administration, were presented as news, sometimes including a fake "reporter" to present the story.

[32]Quoted in Geneva Overholser and Kathleen Hall Jamieson, eds., *The Press* (New York: Oxford University, 2005), 436.

THE 2008 CAMPAIGN AND ITS AFTERMATH

The biggest ongoing news event every four years is typically the presidential campaign, and the 2008 campaign mixed normal electoral politics with new media and, in ways never seen before, issues of race, gender, and age. The Republican nominee emerged fairly quickly: Senator and former Vietnam prisoner of war John McCain. The Democratic race lasted longer, coming down to a contest between two opponents who in previous years might never have made it that far. U.S. Senator Hillary Clinton, the wife of a former president, would have been the first woman ever to gain the nomination for a major political party. Barack Obama — whose father was black, and his mother white — was the first African-American candidate to gain the Democratic or Republican nomination.

Various political reasons contributed to Obama's victory, but also greatly important was the way the campaign waged an all-out "social media" blitz that used an interactive website, Facebook, Twitter, and YouTube videos. While many of the messages flew below the radar of traditional political journalists, they allowed Obama to communicate with voters — and to build a large donor base — using methods that, ironically, Republicans had pioneered years earlier through direct mail. Obama had less experience in governing than his opponents, but he also had less history to try to explain — and he had managed to explain much of it himself, often bypassing mainstream media, through social media and a popular autobiography. Like winners Jimmy Carter, Ronald Reagan, Bill Clinton, and George W. Bush before him, Obama was the candidate who could most legitimately run as a "Washington outsider" and about whom the Washington political press corps knew the least. He did make a "new media" misstep that emphasized the continuing power of sound bites when a Huffington Post "citizen reporter" recorded him saying that rural voters sometimes "cling to guns and religion." McCain's biggest media blunder came when he told a conservative radio host, as the economy was spiraling downward, "The fundamentals of the economy are strong." Both political opponents and the news media repeated the damaging statements throughout the campaign.

McCain and Clinton ran into problems Obama did not have. McCain was over 70 years old. After surprising most experts by picking Sarah Palin, the little-known governor of Alaska, as his running mate, he often looked old and tired on TV in comparison to her and Obama. Cable TV hosts and bloggers criticized Clinton's attire, her hair, her voice, and her emotions. Palin also faced sexism, as some critics — often while focusing cameras on her legs — called her dumb or said she should be home raising her children. She also had little experience with national media, and her few interviews did little to dispel concerns. Particularly damaging was an interview with Katie Couric in which she seemed nervous and unprepared. It did not help that Tina Fey began doing wickedly funny parodies of Palin on the TV show *Saturday Night Live* — parodies that were posted on websites and that Sunday morning news programs often repeated. After the election, Palin wrote an

Presidential Campaigning and New Media

Barack Obama made history as the first African American elected to the U.S. presidency. He made history another way, though, by being the first presidential candidate to integrate social media, websites, and other means of digital communication into his campaign. By doing that, he was able to go around the traditional news media to get out his message. He also raised a record $600 million in campaign funds and created numerous clips and messages that individual computer and smartphone users viewed millions of times. Younger voters, who tended to favor Obama over his Republican opponent, John McCain, turned out in large numbers, providing the margin of victory for Obama.

autobiography and was in great demand as a speaker, and by 2010 was generally considered a possible frontrunner for the 2012 GOP nomination.

THE MEDIA AND A COMPLICATED FUTURE

The future of the news media depends on a variety of factors. Of obvious importance will be the quality and credibility of messages they produce and the decisions that media producers make in terms of direction and focus. News and entertainment options likely will continue to expand as they have throughout most of media history, and news consumers must have help in breaking through the clutter to find the information that can help them make necessary decisions. Just as newspapers once found themselves threatened by television, now both of those media — along with traditional magazines, film, music sources, and radio — face threats created by the Internet. All of those media have been forced to adapt to the technological explosion of the so-called Information Age. To varying degrees, all have begun to do so.

The news media bear much of the burden for providing an ever-rising level of understanding of an increasingly complicated and frequently divided society. More than three centuries after the founding of America's first newspaper, informing the public remains the primary responsibility of the press — even as the term

"the press" has come to encompass news sent via airwaves and bounced off satellites. How to best inform the public prompts disagreement, even among those who produce the news. Some journalists, as indicated by the *Washington Post's* late publisher, Katharine Graham, believe the method is for "hard-nosed editors and digging reporters"[33] to continue to employ professional practices vigorously. Yet others recognize that in a world of blogs, cable TV, and convergence, even defining who or what defines a "journalist" can be increasingly difficult. The increasing complexity of media and society demonstrate the need for media literacy, including an understanding of the media's role in American history.

Others believe that the answer is to erase the professional detachment that mainstream news media have established between themselves and the rest of society, restoring some features of a more communal relationship that existed before the Vietnam War. Citizen journalists and bloggers might be seen as steps in that direction. Yet society itself has in many ways become more divided and fragmented, apparently in part because many Americans have turned away from traditional news sources. Though their roles are shifting and perhaps less clear than they have seemed at times, the American media clearly remain indispensable parts of the American democracy and its day-to-day life.

[33]Address to national convention of the Society of Professional Journalists/Sigma Delta Chi, Chicago, 1969.

RECOMMENDED READINGS

BOOKS

Anderson, Bonnie M. *News Flash: Journalism, Infotainment, and the Bottom-Line Business of Broadcast News*. San Francisco, 2004. TV news evolved into entertainment for business reasons.

Anderson, Robin. *A Century of Media, A Century of War*. New York, 2006. The media have served to publicize various wars.

Boehlert, Eric. *Bloggers on the Bus: How The Internet Changed Politics and the Press*. New York, 2009. This account covers the history of political blogging and its effects.

Clark, Jessica, and Tracy Van Slyke. *Beyond the Echo Chamber: How a Networked Progressive Media Can Reshape American Politics*. New York, 2010. As conservative voices in the media became stronger around 2000, political liberals attempted a number of efforts to start media outlets and programs.

Domke, David. *God Willing? Political Fundamentalism in the White House, the War on Terror and the Echoing Press*. London, 2004. The president set the media agenda and tone during the buildup to the war in Iraq.

Downie, Leonard Jr., and Robert G. Kaiser. *The News about the News: American Journalism in Peril*. New York, 2003. The industry has changed significantly, especially in the late twentieth and early twenty-first[t] century.

Fenton, Tom. *Bad News: The Decline of Reporting, the Business of News, and the Danger to Us All*. New York, 2005. The increasing emphasis on the bottom line had a harmful effect on journalism.

Gillmor, Dan. *We the Media: Grassroots Journalism by the People, for the People*. Cambridge, Mass., 2006. Journalists and others can use the Internet for producing news and changing the news environment.

Grabe, Maria Elizabeth, and Erik Page Bucy. *Image Bite Politics: News and the Visual Framing of Elections*. New York, 2009. This study analyzes the visual images the media used in the 1992, 1996, 2000, and 2004 presidential elections.

Kenski, Kate, Bruce W. Hardy, and Kathleen Hall Jamieson. *The Obama Victory: How Media, Money, and Message Shaped the 2008 Election*. New York, 2010. This study examines key issues, voter data, and the major presidential and vice presidential candidates themselves to explain strengths and weaknesses of each party's media messages.

McPherson, James Brian. *The Conservatism Resurgence and the Press: The Media's Role in the Rise of the Right*. Evanston, Ill., 2008. The mainstream and alternative media helped conservatives gain control of Congress and the White House.

---. *Journalism at the End of the American Century, 1965-Present*. Westport, Conn., 2006. This survey history of the news media covers the major themes and events in American journalism from 1965 through 2005.

Overholser, Geneva, and Kathleen Hall Jamieson, eds. *The Press*. New York, 2005. This sweeping work discusses the history and practices of the news media.

Sloan, Wm. David, and Jenn Mackay, eds. *Media Bias: Finding It, Fixing It*. Jefferson, N.C., 2007. On a variety of issues, critics writing from various points of view have argued that the media are biased.

Sweeney, Michael S. *The Military and the Press: An Uneasy Truce*. Evanston, Ill., 2006. The relationship between the news media and the military throughout American history has rarely been tranquil.

Viguerie, Richard A., and David Franke. *America's Right Turn: How Conservatives Used New and Alternative Media to Take Power*. Chicago, 2004. This critique focuses most heavily on Viguerie's specialty, direct mail, but also discusses talk radio and the Internet.

ARTICLES

Fahmy, Shahira and C. Zoe Smith. "Photographers Note Digital's Advantages, Disadvantages," *Newspaper Research Journal* 24 (2003): 82–96. Digital technology enhances flexibility but poses potential ethical hazards.

Hutcheson, John, David Domke, Andre Billeaudeaux, and Philip Garland. "U.S. National Identity, Political Elites, and a Patriotic Press Following September 11." *Political Communication* 21 (2004): 27–50. Echoing administration sources, following the terrorist attacks of September 11, 2001, the news media chose patriotism over serving as a watchdog on government.

Kanihan, Stacey Frank, and Kendra L. Gale. "Within 3 Hours, 97 Percent Learn About 9/11 Attacks." *Newspaper Research Journal* 24 (2003): 78–91. As illustrated by media treatment of the terrorist attacks, various media work together to reach Americans quickly in a time of crisis.

Lasorsa, Dominic. "News Media Perpetuate Few Rumors About 9/11 Crisis." *Newspaper Research Journal* 24 (2003): 10–21. Despite the scope of the news on September 11, 2001, the press committed few significant errors in coverage.

Love, Robert. "Before Jon Stewart." *Columbia Journalism Review* (March/April 2007), 33-77. The author provides a brief history of "fake news" in America.

Lowry, Dennis T. "Network TV News Framing of Good vs. Bad Economic News under Democrat and Republican Presidents: A Lexical Analysis of Political Bias." *Journalism & Mass Communication Quarterly* 85:3 (2008): 483-98. In covering Presidents Bill Clinton and George W. Bush, TV news was more biased against Bush than Clinton.

Randle, Quint, Lucinda D. Davenport, and Howard Bossen. "Newspapers Slow to Use Web Sites for 9/11 Coverage." *Newspaper Research Journal* 24 (Winter 2003): 58–71. Following the terrorist attacks, newspapers had websites but did not use them well, focusing instead on the printed product.

Shelley, Dan. "Voice of the World." *Communicator* (April 2007): 30-38. CNN's chief international correspondent, Christiane Amanpour, has reported from around the world.

Various authors. "Into the Abyss." *Columbia Journalism Review* (November/December 2006), 14-78. This "oral history" includes forty-seven journalists' recollections of scenes from the first three years of the Iraq War.

INDEX